D1605239

MARRIAGE AND FAMILY

MARRIAGE AND FAMILY

J. KENNETH DAVIDSON, SR.
UNIVERSITY OF WISCONSIN - EAU CLAIRE

NELWYN B. MOORE
SOUTHWEST TEXAS STATE UNIVERSITY

Wm. C. Brown Publishers

Book Team

Editor *Paul L. Tavenner*
Developmental Editor *Sue Pulvermacher-Alt*
Production Editor *Anne Scroggin*
Art Editor *Miriam J. Hoffman*
Permissions Editor *Karen L. Storlie*
Visuals Processor *Amy L. Saffran*
Visuals/Design Consultant *Marilyn Phelps*

Wm. C. Brown Publishers

President *G. Franklin Lewis*
Vice President, Publisher *Thomas E. Doran*
Vice President, Operations and Production *Beverly Kolz*
National Sales Manager *Virginia S. Moffat*
Group Sales Manager *John Finn*
Executive Editor *Edgar J. Laube*
Director of Marketing *Kathy Law Laube*
Marketing Manager *Pam Cooper*
Managing Editor, Production *Colleen A. Yonda*
Manager of Visuals and Design *Faye M. Schilling*
Production Editorial Manager *Julie A. Kennedy*
Production Editorial Manager *Ann Fuerste*
Publishing Services Manager *Karen J. Slaght*

WCB Group

President and Chief Executive Officer *Mark C. Falb*
Chairman of the Board *Wm. C. Brown*

Cover credit Renoir, *The Luncheon of the Boating Party* © The Phillips Collection, Washington, D.C.

Photo Research Carol Smith and Janet George

The credits section for this book begins on page 623, and is considered an extension of the copyright page.

Library of Congress Catalog Card Number: 90–83806

ISBN 0–697–05194–3

Printed in the United States of America by Wm. C. Brown Publishers, 2460 Kerper Boulevard, Dubuque, IA 52001

10 9 8 7 6 5 4 3 2 1

Dedicated to
our families of orientation and procreation
among whom we have lived much

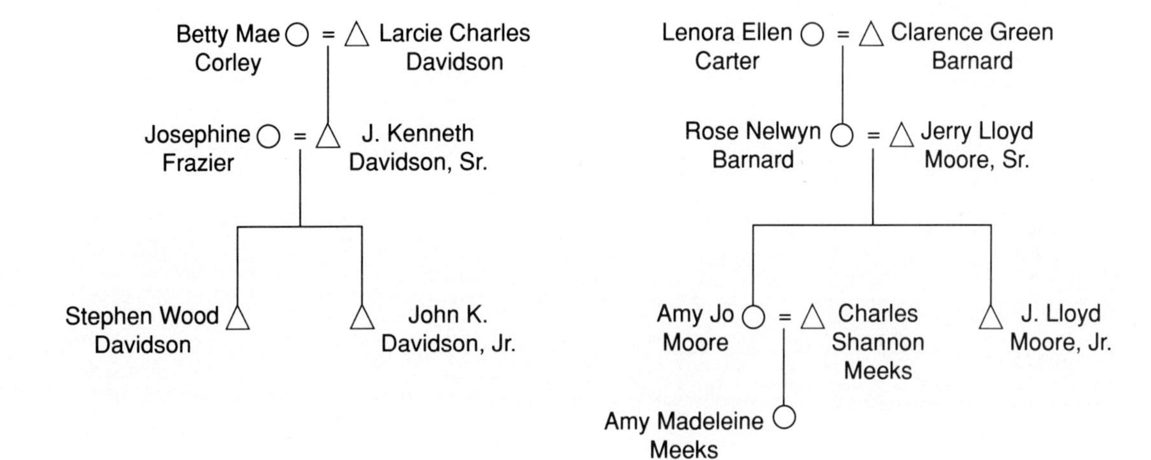

Brief Contents

CONTENTS

PART II

PERSONAL CHOICES 55

CHAPTER 3

DATING 61

CHAPTER 4

PREMARITAL SEXUALITY 87

CHAPTER 5

ALTERNATIVE LIFE-STYLES 113

PREFACE

"Tempora mutantur et nos mutantur in illis." "The times change, and we change with them." The Davidson and Moore text reflects the realities of both change and continuity in the marriage and family experience of the 1990s. The book itself, from inception to fruition, has been characterized by both of these realities. With every product there is a process story. In this case, negotiating the sometimes slippery path between a sociologist/researcher and a home economist/family therapist was not always an easy task. However, we feel the results are well worth the team efforts. Together we have interwoven the complex phenomena from a field known for its diversity of concepts, issues, and theories. The final product, a lively written, comprehensive text with a clear, strong research voice, resounds with the latest developments in the family science field.

A marriage and family course, as an integral part of a family science major, helps prepare students who as future professionals will promote the overall goal of family life education—improving the quality of individual and family life. Increasingly, marriage and family courses are also taken as electives by university students, many of whom have no professional interest in family, but all of whom will have a life-long personal investment in family. Years of teaching in the family science field has afforded us valuable insight into the needs of both majors and nonmajors in marriage and family courses.

Students need to clarify, through appropriate educational methods, their own concerns, attitudes, values, and needs related to family-life choices. To do so, they need information that addresses basic personal competencies required to succeed in marriage and family relationships. They need facts with which to understand the institutions of marriage and family including their forms, functions, and statuses. Perhaps more significantly, this information must be presented in such a manner that motivation for further learning is enhanced. This book is conceived to fill such a composite of educational needs.

Respect for the integrity of the professor and for the student is a hallmark of this text. Since our belief is that teachers bring their own personality to the process of facilitating learning and that students are both interested and capable of learning, this text is purposefully classic in format, challenging in content, and devoid of gimmicks or jargon.

The focus of this text is primarily functional, and secondarily theoretical, its parameters going beyond the boundaries of any specific theory. Throughout the text, systems theory, developmental/family life cycle theory, and exchange theory are used as underlying frameworks. The book's organization is logically developmental with a life cycle sequence of topics. The content chosen and its interpretation are based on years of professional and personal commitment to the goals of education for family life. The authors' years of university teaching in family science, service in professional family organizations, clinical practice as a marriage and family therapist (by one author), and experiential background as family members; all are a part of the design of choice. Although subjectivity necessarily influenced the choice of material, objectivity in interpretation was the aim in keeping with the overall goal of preparing students to make their own informed choices concerning marriage and family. Chapter summaries, highlighting of key concepts, and an extensive glossary should facilitate easier mastery of basic materials. The boxed inserts offer a variety of viewpoints concerning often controversial issues. Annotated suggested readings help connect the classroom to the outside world by furnishing an impetus for continued learning. Application, synthesis, or evaluation are required for answers to the Questions for Critical Reflection, expanding the major concepts of the text.

Photo essays are a distinguishing feature of this text. Appearing as part openers, color photographs pictorially portray those concepts to be explored in the chapters that follow. The use of color is an aesthetically pleasing pedagogical plus for students accustomed to all forms of media presenting "life in living color."

An indisputable strength of the book is its comprehensiveness and the in-depth coverage of a surprising array of neglected topics. For example, child rearing and family finance, so conspicuously absent in many marriage and family texts, receive more than cursory attention. Comprehensive coverage of child rearing is based on the authors' belief in the central importance of parent-child relationships. A framework for successful parenting provides a conceptual vehicle for a consideration of parenting roles and goals, principles of child development, and guidance. Date violence, date rape, spouse and child abuse, marital rape, and incest are featured as are various issues of sexuality. Discussion of dual careers, marriage, and parenthood focus on issues inherent in the majority of American homes today in which there are children and dual earners. The consideration of commuter marriages reflects attention to a little researched topic. In addition, the impact of divorce on children and parents is considered as is the difficult process of blending families. Finally, the book's research base, and the careful attention to cultural diversity and gender inclusive language are distinguishing features in which the authors take pride.

In part 1, "The Marriage and Family Experience: Balancing Change and Continuity," an overview presents the rationale for the study of marriage and family. Changing patterns of structure, function, and gender roles are introduced from an historical perspective as they are viewed throughout the book. Part 2, "Personal Choices," emphasizing the self in marriage, strikes an underlying theme that success in marriage and family is more related to "being" the right partner than "finding" the right partner. The role of love is related to the search for personal fulfillment. "Couple Challenges," presented in part 3, highlight early marital adjustment and managing marital conflict within the context of the attributes of healthy couples. In part 4, "Parenting Decisions and Beyond" addresses decisions about childbearing and child rearing, family finances, and dual-career families. Part 5, "Disruptive Change and Reaffirmation," describes unanticipated change in the lives of individuals and families resulting from divorce, widowhood, and remarriage.

Ancillaries

The ancillary materials for this text include a comprehensive *Instructor's Manual for Davidson/Moore Marriage and Family* with a *Test Item File* and a *Student Study Guide,* both prepared by Karen G. Arms, Ph.D., University of Connecticut-Stamford and Carol Akkerman Sain, Ph.D. A student reader, *Cultural Diversity in Families,* coedited by Karen G. Arms, J. Kenneth Davidson, Sr., and Nelwyn B. Moore, will facilitate student understanding of cultural differences and similarities. In addition, the *Marriage and Family Transparency Set* and videotapes, to be given to qualified adopters of the text, will offer valuable visual aids for introducing topics and focusing group discussion. Finally, a unique classroom management system, *TestPak 3.0* with *QuizPak* and *GradePak,* is offered free to adopters of this text. These teaching aids will save hours of preparation time for busy instructors.

Instructor's Manual. The comprehensive instructor's manual includes chapter learning objectives, Questions for Critical Reflection, Debating the Issues, class projects, and an annotated Audiovisual Directory of recent 16mm films and videotapes for each chapter. The test item file contains true/false questions and Concept Questions for Analysis, as well as multiple choice questions measuring three levels of knowledge: facts, concepts, and applications. Answers with page references are also provided.

Cultural Diversity in Families. A collection of particularly salient articles, this ancillary addresses marriage and family issues within those racial/ethnic groups predicted to experience burgeoning population growth by 2030: Asians, Blacks, Hispanics, and Native Americans (American Indians).

Student Study Guide. Features in the study guide facilitating student attainment of knowledge include chapter learning objectives, key terms, true/false questions with answer rationales, three conceptual levels of multiple choice questions with answer rationales, and Concept Questions for Analysis with answer rationales.

TestPak. Two easy-to-use computerized testing options are available. Option I, designed for instructors with access to an Apple II, IIC, IIGS, a MacIntosh, or an IBM PC, will print test masters via the *TestPak* program. Instructors can also construct a test for students to take on a personal computer, which automatically grades the test. Additionally, computer quizzes are available through *QuizPak* to help students prepare for their examinations. *GradePak* will compute and graph individual student and class records. Option II features a convenient call-in/mail-in/FAX service. Using the test item file that accompanies the text, instructors can select the questions to be included in their customized test, indicate them on a special order form and call, mail, or FAX their request to WCB. Within two working days, a test master, student answer sheet, and answer key will be sent via first class mail or faxed to the instructor. Details and other features of *TestPak 3.0* can be supplied by your local WCB sales representative.

Transparency Set. A set of 31 acetate transparencies provides topical teaching tools for use with an overhead projector. The majority are tables, boxes, and figures taken from the text with others drawn from supplementary sources.

Videotapes. Qualified adopters may choose from a number of videotapes covering an array of topics pertinent to the marriage and family course.

Acknowledgments

First among persons acknowledged for contributions to this book must be those thousands who shall remain nameless: students who over a combined 53 years of teaching have taught us far more valuable lessons about life and humanity than we ourselves have taught. Many of those family professionals along the way who have served as mentors may be unaware of their influence in our lives, but it is present just the same. Some are names instantly recognizable, but not all. Some are no longer with us, some are retired, while still others who have touched our lives significantly and kept us true to our purposes are today's promising young scholars. We also are deeply indebted to Gerald R. Leslie and Elizabeth M. Leslie who provided the initial opportunity and encouragement to write a text in marriage and family.

Our faith in the review process has been strengthened by the significant contributions made by our colleagues who served as reviewers: Katherine Allen, Virginia Polytechnic Institute and State University; Karen G. Arms, University of Connecticut–Stamford; Charles Britt, Auburn University; Rodney M. Cate, Washington State University; Thomas R. Holman, Brigham Young University; Richard Joliff, El Camino Community College; William F. Kenkel, University of Kentucky; Kay Murphy, Oklahoma State University; and Connie Steele, University of Tennessee. More than merely helpful advice, their wisdom has served as a catalyst, resulting in a product more fully formed and refined. Additionally, we wish to thank Amy M. Meeks, Southwest Texas State University; Katherine Shultz, San Marcos Academy; and Sue Thompson, Southwest Texas State University for their valuable suggestions in select areas of the manuscript.

The editorial and production staff at William C. Brown have labored valiantly by our sides. In particular, George Bergquist, Edgar J. Laube, Kathy Law Laube, Sue Pulvermacher-Alt, Ann Shaffer, Heidi Baughman, Miriam Hoffman, Amy Saffran, Carol Smith, and Karen Storlie deserve accolades. Especially, Production Editor Anne Scroggin's expertise has made an invaluable contribution to the finished product.

A number of research assistants helped with the project in various capacities including library research and bibliography preparation. In particular, we wish to express our appreciation to Susan L. Belau, Cynthia L. Choren, Linda J. Fankhauser, Barbara L. Finstad, Amy J. Renshaw-Neeb. Sue A. Hulberg, Jane S. Meredith, and Amy L. Smith deserve special recognition for typing the manuscript and their many other efforts beyond the call-of-duty. Finally, we wish to express our appreciation to Elizabeth C. Swift and Jennifer A. Tobiason for their contributions including tasks associated with the glossary, name index, and sources of assistance.

Without the loving support and encouragement of our families, to whom the book is dedicated, this project would not have been possible. They have contributed in myriad ways but most of all in their understanding and acceptance of our passion to complete what was an infinitely more complex, difficult, and time-consuming task than originally perceived. And, finally, they have loved us unconditionally along the way. For that, our undying love and gratitude.

J. Kenneth Davidson, Sr.
Nelwyn B. Moore

PART I

THE MARRIAGE AND FAMILY EXPERIENCE: BALANCING CHANGE AND CONTINUITY

An overview of the delicate balance between change and continuity in the marriage and family experience is presented in part 1. While families have changed throughout time, it is the unprecedented speed of change today that has resulted in inordinate discontinuity in once continuous life-styles. This speed was suggested by Margaret Mead to be of such magnitude that it is almost as if today's young were left in a strange land without forbearers. Young people growing up in earlier rural America learned about love and marriage as well as parenting from observing and interacting with their mother, father, siblings, extended family members, and a community of caring persons. Some of these lessons are not so easily learned in today's urban settings and diverse family forms, such as the single-parent family, the fastest growing segment of society. Formal instruction in marriage and family is one way that today's young persons can learn about life's most important roles and relationships. Those areas believed to be basic to such understanding are previewed in chapter 1: marriage, family and culture; self in marriage; marriage decisions; human sexuality; the family life cycle; childbearing and child rearing; and family resources.

In a world characterized by change, individuals can ill afford to simply do faster that which they have always done, lest they find themselves like Alice in Wonderland, "running in place to stand perfectly still." Instead, changing roles for women and men, as reflected in chapter 2, demand that new relationship paradigms be developed and fostered. The wine is new, so must be the wineskins. And the time has never been more ripe for change than in today's global world of cultural diversity. However, productive change depends upon a continuity made possible only through knowledge that confirms the realities of the American family, past and present. Family science theory and research offers such a knowledge base.

How will the changing cast of characters at home and in the workplace affect the continuity of the institutions of marriage and family? Will, as predicted by some, the tidal wave of change engulf the family, or will, as believed by others, diverse family forms surface stronger than ever? These and other questions can be more knowledgeably addressed after reading chapters 1 and 2.

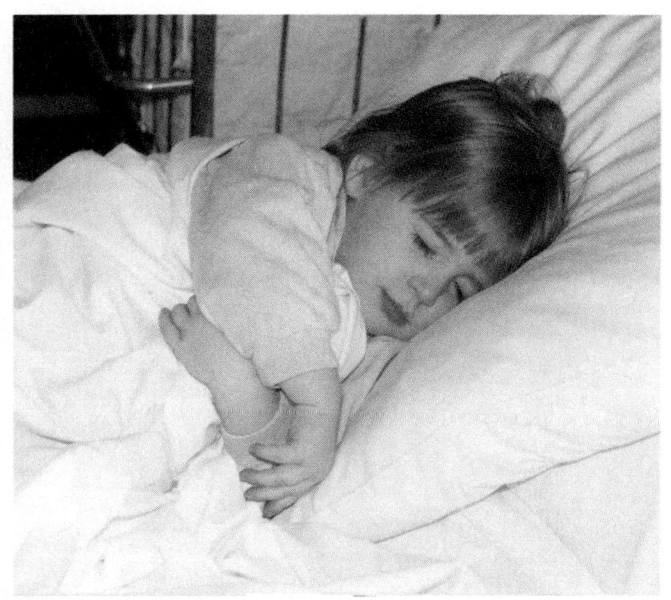

8401
WARNING
WARNING

CHAPTER 1

Marriage and Family: Continuity and Change

The crucial social unit, the family, is assembled primarily by sheer dumb luck, in most cases with little or no preparation. It harbors our most intense emotions and is expected to solve our deepest social problems.
—Margaret Duggan, 1985

OUTLINE

Exploring Knowledge about Marriage and Family

Marriage and family: two familiar words easily, but differently defined by each person who begins the study of this popular subject in the discipline of family science. By college age, all students have encountered unique life experiences that indelibly color their subjective view of the concepts, marriage and family. So, why study something so natural that virtually everyone has already experienced it at some level? Some even argue that studying courtship, mate selection, and love takes out all of the romance. However, the explosion of knowledge in the field of marriage and family over the last two decades has increasingly focused attention on the benefits of learning more about these primary relationships. One obvious benefit in exploring new knowledge in any field is that it promotes critical thinking, especially when such exploration is based on research findings that confirm reality (Wells, 1986; Adams, 1986). Studying new knowledge in marriage and family also addresses what has been determined to be priority issues for most Americans (Yankelovich, 1981). Social surveys indicate that the most important issues in America today are love and work, in that order. Employees who are increasingly refusing to work extra hours, resisting relocation, and jumping off the fast track before they reach the peak of their careers report that family life and time for personal growth are more important to them than their jobs ("Work and Family," 1983). As this generation's transformed values and expectations for personal happiness emerge, new forms of education for life are required. In the words of Winston Churchill, "We make a living by what we get, we make a life by what we give" (1989, p. 1). The study of marriage and family encompasses those areas most significant in "making a life."

At this point, a note of caution. The study of marriage and family cannot nor should not be separated from one's own experiences in family relations. In fact, firsthand exposure to the basic elements of family life is a sturdy base on which to build further knowledge. However, such familiarity can make it more difficult to consider marriage and family objectively, a fact that may not be particularly apparent until test time in college or in life! An individual's sense of **ethnocentrism** (belief in the superiority of one's own cultural group) may preclude an understanding of family systems that differ from one's own. An awareness of the origin of these feelings can prevent the negative consequences of a closed mind (Adams, 1986).

For the vast majority of people, no decision will more significantly affect their happiness in life than choices concerning marriage and family. Therefore, the decision to study this subject may well represent a turning point in the lives of college students, a time of taking charge of their own futures. In today's world of exponential change and accountability, young people especially are being challenged to invest in a futures market of successful interpersonal relationships. Such a wise investment has the potential for high yield dividends in years to come. While the process of acquiring information for the foundation of one's own family begins with life's earliest memories of the family in which one grew up and encompasses all former life experience, it does not have to stop there. Blending the latest scientific facts about the institutions of marriage and family with one's personal history increases the odds for wise decisions. Accomplishing this task requires that time and energy be invested in exploding myths and exploring facts related to myriad aspects of marriage and family. The overall goal of this book is to promote such a process.

Because of each student's unique background, there will be various personal objectives to be attained in addition to the course goals. Based on a combined total of over 50 years of teaching marriage and family in college and university settings, the authors believe that such objectives are best achieved through an awareness of a core of knowledge in the discipline of family science. The resulting insight should enable more reasoned choices and the ultimate attainment of personal and course goals. Thus, students need to explore knowledge related to the following basic areas: marriage, family, and culture; self in marriage; marriage decisions; human sexuality; family life cycles; childbearing and child rearing; and family resources. A brief introduction to each of these topics will raise questions that will be pursued more fully in the chapters to follow.

Marriage, Family, and Culture: Continuity and Change

Exploring knowledge in any discipline begins with current controversial issues, a variety of which exist in the rapidly growing field of family science. One of the major controversies of recent years is whether or not marriage and family, as we know them, will become extinct in future generations. Fueling the debate is the fact that throughout the 1970s both first marriage and remarriage rates declined, and the divorce rate more than doubled. In 1989, 1.16 million divorces were reported, a rate of 4.7 divorces per 1,000 population (National

Convention for some but invention for others. Today, weddings are as individualized as thumbprints.

Center for Health Statistics, 1990d). Further, in 1980, while only 15% of persons aged 65 to 74 reported that their first marriages had ended in divorce, almost one half of 24-year-olds had either ended their first marriage by divorce or were expected to do so before they reached age 75 (Glick, 1984b). However, there is little long-range evidence suggesting that marriage is losing its popularity. Some have suggested that indeed Americans love marriage, just not who they are married to (Sussman, 1983)! But even in the midst of continuity, change is inherent.

In today's world of kaleidoscopic change, family-related questions inevitably arise. Some pertain to demographics. For example, how will the children of baby-boomers, today's young adults ages 18–26 whose unprecedented numbers crested in 1982, impact birth, marriage, and divorce rates in the 1990s? Other questions concern family structure. Will the increased rate of divorce and numbers of babies born to and reared by single mothers further escalate the fastest growing family form in America, the single-parent family? The proportion of children born to single mothers rose from 4% in 1950 to 20% in 1986 (Johnson, 1989). Today, at least 92% of these babies are kept by their mothers, many of whom establish single-parent households (Lindsay, 1985). How will the number of cohabiting couples, which has increased more than five times from 500,000 in 1960 to over 2.5 million in 1988, affect the institution of marriage (Glick, 1989a)? Will such a rising trend continue to further change the form of families in America?

Changing social and economic agendas must also be considered. To what degree will the women's movement and changing gender identities further influence roles in spouse and parent relationships? Will external cultural variables such as economics and education be significantly related to family stability in the future? As burgeoning numbers of women and men receive college educations, how will this affect their likelihood of marrying, parenting, or divorcing? Reportedly, as the educational level of the husband increases, so does his earning potential and his ability to divide the household resources through a divorce. The rising educational level of American women also increases the likelihood of their economic independence and thus their unwillingness to remain in an unhappy marriage (Wilson & Neckerman, 1989). Further, as women's educational levels increase, so will their influx into the work force. Such past migration has led to changes in values, relationships between women and men, and housework and child-rearing patterns. Researchers have found such change not to be without inner conflict (LaFarge, 1983). In fact, employment for women is not consistently positive in terms of outcomes because it often trades one source of low control (lack of family power) for another—role overload (Rosenfield, 1989). How will the changing cast of characters at home and at work affect the continuity of family life?

Finally, questions surrounding racial and ethnic minority family issues are compounded by a lack of understanding regarding cultural diversity (Barbee, 1985). Past descriptions and analysis of minority family life have emphasized the unique and the exotic. Without depreciating these differences, an understanding of family life in America demands a sensitivity to the great variety of life-styles among all racial and ethnic groups. As Americans increasingly move toward a pluralistic society, will they be better prepared to recognize the situational determinants of differing family forms and patterns of adaptation for family life in the last decade of the 20th century (Willie, 1988)?

Life in the 1990s provokes these and many other questions for which ready-made answers are not available. However, as one's knowledge about marriage and family is expanded, increased insight may offer a sturdier base for personal decisions related to these issues.

Self in Marriage

It surprises most people that finding the right marriage partner is not the most significant variable in a successful marriage. Becoming a "good" marriage partner is. The first step in becoming a good marriage partner is to learn as much as possible about one's personhood, to clarify the vision of personal adequacy that is inevitably reflected in intimate partnerships (Marks, 1986).

Such self-evaluation is, at best, very unscientific, difficult, and complex, especially since most people see what they wish to see and believe what they wish to believe. While to fully know oneself, to understand one's desires, aspirations, strengths, and weaknesses is a continuous process, it should be well underway before a lifetime partner is chosen. Discovering a sense of who and what we are is a process in which two things must happen: the crystallization of a gender identity, one's concept of self as feminine or masculine and the maintenance of **ego boundaries,** those psychological self-boundaries that differentiate one from others (Rubin, 1983). Persons who have accomplished these developmental tasks will be better able to clarify their own needs, attitudes, and values and thus make wiser, conscious choices concerning family matters.

Although marriage is a chain of experiences within an entire life span, the study of marriage and family too often begins with the courtship process ignoring the significance of previous life stages. Courtship in our culture normally bridges that span of time from adolescence to adulthood and progresses from individualism to couple bonding. A merging of these unfolding life patterns with their preshaped tendencies propel each person to seek a partner who will continue that process in the most desired direction (Marks, 1986). Choice of a lifetime mate is usually made during what has been called the decade of decision, ages 17–27. This period is a crucial time for young people to determine not only if or who they will marry but also what profession or trade to enter and where they will live. At the same time, serious political, religious, and ideological questions are usually entertained. Understanding this process of moving from singleness to pairing in a world of consummate change may facilitate wiser decisions.

Even though marriage preparation most appropriately begins with self-assessment, learning how to objectively assess potential partners prior to marriage also increases the odds for long-term success. Those who expect to eventually marry probably possess an imaginary list of qualities to seek in a lifetime partner. However, for various reasons, despite their best efforts this list of qualities may fail the test of mate selection. One reason for this failure seems inherent in the very nature of the courting process: gamesmanship. According to the game theory of interpersonal relationships, games are basically dishonest transactions whereby participants hide their true feelings (DeVito, 1986). Everyone is familiar with the courtship game in which each of the partners presents her/his best possible image while at the same time covering up more undesirable qualities. Another easily recognized culprit clouding objectivity during courtship is the lens through which the relationship is viewed. Love may not be blind, but the usual rose-colored glasses of romance tend to distort reality and the accurate assessment of partner compatibility (Moore, 1976). A less obvious but more significant issue is the hidden agendas deep within the psyches of most persons by marriageable age. Without self-awareness, the process of mate selection is often motivated by such unmet needs, resulting in the selection of a partner who either seeks or allows a neurotic relationship to develop.

Marriage Decisions: Customs and Laws

To marry or not to marry may seem to be a rhetorical question. As social conventions are increasingly challenged, this query becomes a testament to the changing reality of marriage by choice. Whether or not to marry, whom and when to marry, and decisions about parenting—all are truly options of the 1990s. However, young people today are confronted with the frightening realization that along with fewer cultural prescriptions come greater personal responsibilities for wise choices. Whatever the answer, the decision of whether or not to marry has far reaching implications for individuals and ultimately for the institutions of marriage and family. Studies suggest that the weakening of the cultural imperative to be married and the increasing economic independence of women are the two significant factors in the decline of marriage. These variables apply to poor and nonpoor, blacks and whites alike (Cherlin, 1988).

In 1989, there were 2.40 million weddings, which translates into a rate of 9.7 marriages per 1,000 population (National Center for Health Statistics, 1990e). This figure represents the lowest annual marriage rate since 1967. There is widespread evidence that such data reflects not an aversion to marriage but that many individuals are postponing the decision to marry. The median age for first marriage for women in 1988 was 23.6 years compared to 20.3 years in 1960. For men, the figures were 25.9 years and 22.8 years, respectively (Glick, 1989a). This represents an age increase for the 13th consecutive year (National Center for Health Statistics, 1990b). Preliminary data for 1989 suggest that men are now waiting past age 26 to marry for the first time ("Americans Postpone," 1990). Available data do not permit a clear-cut conclusion regarding the question of how many individuals currently plan to never marry, but indications are that eventual marriage still remains a goal of most women and men in our society. However, the increasing delay of marriage or the **deferral syndrome** is disordering the timing of family life cycle events (Teachman, Polonko, & Scanzoni, 1987).

Human Sexuality: Gender Identity and Gender Roles

Unless one has a clear sense of gender identity and an adequate understanding of one's own and her/his partner's sexuality, difficulty is inevitable in this important aspect of intimate relationships. Before and after marriage, there are many practical issues of sexuality to be faced. Before marriage, a couple must decide the best answers for themselves concerning responsible, healthy expression of their sexuality. The much touted **safer sex** is more than sexual behavior that leaves one free of sexually transmitted diseases. It is also sexual behavior that leaves each partner free of psychological scars associated with feelings of guilt (Calderone & Johnson, 1981). Such decisions are best made within the context of long-range individual and couple goals.

After marriage, partners will have to decide how many children to have, if any; when to have them; and the necessary steps to take in accomplishing these goals. In keeping with their moral and religious values, couples must discern which contraceptive methods are most acceptable and the potential advantages and disadvantages of each method. Further, since modern contraceptive technology allows the separation of the reproductive function of sexual intercourse from that of pleasure, couples may choose the prominence that sexual intercourse will assume in their relationship.

Couples must also face the fact that an expanding knowledge base in human sexuality has led to changing perspectives and practices for women and men. As women have become increasingly knowledgeable about their bodies, the female sexual response, and their full potential as sexual beings, differing expectations are being communicated to men. Thus, women in search of greater physiological and psychological sexual satisfaction have ushered in what some have termed the new **sexual revolution** (Davidson & Darling, 1988b).

Perhaps the greatest battle being fought in the sexuality arena is not in the bedroom over sex but in the family room over gender. Women's and men's roles, once clearly defined, have been tilted if not turned upside down. Gender, or one's concept of femininity or masculinity, no longer definitively determines who plays which roles in marriage and family life. Although hormone differences are indisputable, ideology (firmly held doctrine of a particular philosophical group) appears to determine gender roles far more than hormones (Reiss, 1981). It is important that students in a marriage and family course be able to identify the biological and psychological differences in the sexes, the basis for these differences, and relate such implications to success in marriage.

Family Life Cycle: Adjustment and Conflict Management

Like individuals, families move through major stages within a life cycle. At each stage of the family life cycle, there are tasks that must be adequately completed to successfully move to the next. Each stage offers unique challenges for constructive family problem solving and growth. McGoldrick & Carter (1982) have defined six stages for the family life cycle: the unattached young adult, the newly married couple, the family with young children, the family with young adolescents, launching children, and the family in later life (see Table 1.1).

The quality of adjustments made at various stages in the family life cycle depends upon the psychological well-being of the couple's relationship, rooted in their ability to communicate. Such communication often involves learning a new language. Like the couple in Ingmar Bergman's play, *Scenes from a Marriage,* "they don't speak the same language. They must translate into a third language they both understand in order to get each other's meaning" (Beavers, 1985, p. IX).

Many young adults naively assume it is possible to go through life without having serious arguments with their marriage partner because they are so much in love. Despite their best efforts, they soon discover that problems are inevitable and that if their relationship is to succeed, they must learn to manage conflict. In fact, it is argued that the inability to constructively handle anger is the leading cause of marital failures (Mace, 1982). Therefore, marital partners need to learn effective methods of resolving problems in ways that leave them stronger as individuals and as a couple. Recognizing the developmental stages of the family life cycle and the dynamic aspects of relationships in each stage, including stress periods and desired coping strategies, can enhance such healthy family functioning.

Childbearing and Child Rearing

With the decision to have children, life is forever altered. Knowledge of the adjustment that parenting requires in the marriage relationship can lead to happier outcomes as partners and as parents. It is imperative that parents learn to engage in effective parenting skills

Table 1.1: Stages of Family Life Cycle

Stage	Emotional transition process	Second-order changes in family status
1. Between families: The unattached young adult	Accepting parent-offspring separation	a. Differentiation of self in relation to family of origin; b. Development of intimate peer relationships; and c. Establishment of self in work.
2. The joining of families by marriage: The newly-married couple	Committing to new system	a. Formation of marital system; and b. Realignment of relationships with extended families and friends to include spouse.
3. The family with young children	Accepting new generation of members into system	a. Adjustment to marital system including space for child(ren); b. Take on parenting roles; and c. Realignment of relationships with extended family to include parenting and grandparenting roles.
4. The family with adolescents	Increasing flexibility of family boundaries to include children's independence	a. Shift of parent-child relationships to permit adolescents to move in and out of system; b. Refocus on mid-life marital and career issues; and c. Begin to shift toward concerns for older generation.
5. The family with young adults	Accepting multitude of exits from and entries into family system	a. Renegotiation of marital system as dyad; b. Development of adult-to-adult relationships between grown children and their parents; c. Realignment of relationships to include in-laws and grandchildren; and d. Deal with disabilities and death of parents.
6. The family in later life	Accepting shifting of generational roles	a. Maintain own and/or couple functioning and interests in face of physiological decline; b. Support for more central role for middle generation; c. Make room in system for wisdom and experience of elderly; and d. Deal with loss of spouse, siblings, and other peers, and preparation for own death.

From M. McGoldrick and E. A. Carter, "The Family Life Cycle—Its Stages and Dislocations" in F. Walsh (ed.), *Normal Family Processes.*

to enable their offspring to successfully accomplish the various physiological, psychological, intellectual, and social developmental stages throughout life (Moore, 1985c). Because of the changing definitions and practices of gender roles in our society, it is becoming increasingly important that fathers as well as mothers learn specialized knowledge about the child-rearing process. Research indicates that both babies and fathers will profit from such experience. Increased fathering roles, like increased parenting on the part of new mothers, fosters ego integrity. Thus, more involvement in parenting can help new fathers cope with regressive attitudes that may develop from feeling left out of the parenting role (Spieler, 1982).

Child-rearing concerns are not of recent origin. The wisdom of the ages has promoted the welfare of children as lamented by Socrates.

If I could get to the highest place in Athens, I would lift up my voice and say; what mean ye fellow citizens, that ye turn every stone to scrape

CATHY Copyright 1989 Cathy Guisewite. Reprinted by permission of Universal Press Syndicate.

wealth together, and take so little care of your children to whom ye must one day relinquish all?
("Quotable Quotes," 1989, p. 1)

The study of parenting not only benefits one's children but also promotes advocacy for all children. American childhood is imperiled according to a congressional study that found more children than ever living in the streets or in families that have been shattered by divorce, drugs, or poverty. One fifth of all children, including 50% of black and one fourth of all preschoolers, live in poverty. Some authorities also estimate that more than 40% of America's children under age 13 go home from school each day to an empty house (Johnson, 1989). A large-scale study of eighth graders found **latchkey** children (children who are at home alone on a regular basis) to be twice as likely to abuse alcohol, tobacco, and marijuana as supervised children. This higher risk occurred across all families: two-parent, single-parent, affluent, and poor (Roark, 1989).

Knowledge about young children can also be a catalyst for personal growth. It may furnish university students valuable insight into their own experiences during childhood and youth and the continuing influence of the past on adult roles as marital partners and parents. Both personal insight and the latest knowledge about child growth, development, and guidance are the best possible base from which to make decisions about having and rearing children.

Family Resources

During the last 30 years, many private and public programs and agencies have emerged to assist with family needs and problems. The federal and local governments have at least partially funded such efforts (Clarke-Stewart & Friedman, 1987). Examples of community resources include such programs as Head Start; women's centers; crisis hotlines; family planning clinics; "meals on wheels"; and marriage, family, and child counseling services. Community-based networks provide a highly effective but modestly priced way of coping with the many concerns of day-to-day living as well as unexpected crises in the lives of individuals and families. However, there are calls for more extensive governmental intervention. In fact, the United States and South Africa are the only two industrialized nations without a comprehensive family policy (Moyers, 1989).

The National Coalition of Family Organizations (COFO), organized in 1975, has consistently promoted a family focus in policy making and social programs. The group, now called the consortium of Family Organizations, is composed of the National Council on Family Relations, the American Association of Marriage and Family Therapy, the American Home Economics Association, and Family Service of America. Their main agenda is to bring a family perspective to debates about specific legislation, to educate policy makers about family dimensions potentially affected by proposed legislation, to develop a reasoned position on family-related legislation, and to serve as a basis of advocacy (Feldman, 1989).

Students of marriage and family in search of helpful resources must recognize that ultimately they may be their own best resource. By maintaining a continuing interest and familiarity with research, personnel, and publications in the field of marriage and family, one can learn to critically analyze and select from the overpowering amount of information that which is most valuable for one's own use. Hopefully, this book will contribute to such motivation. To begin the process, it is important to briefly consider American families from an historical perspective before defining today's families, their structure, and functions.

The fancy footwork of these young graduates reflects no more exuberance than the smiles of this retired couple returning for their degrees.

American Families: Past and Present

"We fret ourselves to reform life, in order that posterity may be happy, and posterity will say as usual: In the past it used to be better, the present is worse than the past" (Chekhov, 1968, p. 510). It has been asserted that our day is the time of the parenthesis, the time between eras. Naisbitt (1984) pictures Americans as straddling the old industrial era that served our nation so well and the emerging electronics era of today. Although this time of parenthesis is characterized by great uncertainty, it also affords extraordinary leverage for change, both institutionally and personally. The crucial question becomes, do we not extend the past into the future at least as much as we separate from it (Marks, 1986)? A brief perusal of families in early America may furnish insight if not answers.

Families in Early America

Although "what's past is prologue," (Shakespeare, 1968, p. 509) its value is often obscured by sentimentality. This fact was illustrated in a once popular television program, "The Waltons," which depicted an ideal family from a bygone era. Several factors made the Walton family memorable. There were nostalgic depictions of rural life when such life was the norm. Principal characters were unsophisticated, and personal satisfaction depended on relationships rather than worldly attainments. Large families were viewed as being happier than small families, and religion was viewed as an essential part of goodness and happiness. This television program was popular because the Waltons were the kind of family that the American public wanted to believe existed historically, even though they were considered by some to be an "unreal family" (Roiphe, 1973). When we try to recall family life from the past, oftentimes our memories prove to be inaccurate, reinforcing an idyllic conception that existed largely in myth. Reality suggests that life in "the good old days" was not without problems and challenges.

Nevertheless, when people speak of the traditional family, they bring to mind an image of the family of an earlier era like the Waltons, one that is often used as a basis of comparison with the modern version. Probably the biggest difference between the modern family and its colonial counterpart is that the family today has more privacy. In 1790, the first national census found the typical household had 5.8 members, while in 1989 the average household had 2.5 members ("U.S. Household," 1989). More recent research has dispelled two myths about the ideal three-generational families in early America (Hareven, 1982). First, the great **extended families** with three generations co-residing in the same house rarely existed. Households did, however, frequently contain strangers or boarders. Second, the process of industrialization that increased the chances of family members staying together in the same place for longer time periods actually contributed to strengthening the family, not destroying it as often claimed by critics.

Essentially, the colonial family was organized around the nuclear unit with the father as the primary authority figure. Women could not own property nor were they considered to be legal guardians of their children. Marriage, which was largely based on economic considerations, required parental consent, notice of intention to marry, and registration. With geographical mobility and expanding frontiers, the authority of the father/husband was eventually weakened. When industrialization and urbanization transformed the family from a producing unit to a consuming one, work in the home assumed a different function and eventually opened the door to alternatives in family life-styles (Seward, 1978).

There also were reasons why earlier families were considerably larger than they are today. Aside from lack of contraceptive technology, the common law minimum ages for marriage, age 12 for girls and age 14 for boys, added to the probability of more offspring. In addition, children were considered members of the work force and therefore economic assets. Large families were needed to help assist with farming activities in a predominantly rural America (Hareven, 1982).

An important distinction between early and contemporary families is that formerly marriages were viewed as permanent relationships not to be broken by divorce. While divorce was permitted although discouraged in the northern colonies, it was actually prohibited in the southern colonies (Leslie & Korman, 1989). In fact, divorce did not become legally permissible in the state of South Carolina until 1948. In spite of historical data, there is widespread misinterpretation of the family as it was, a fact that clouds the issue of understanding the family as it is today.

Defining Marriage and Family

On the surface, defining marriage and family may appear to be easy. Upon further investigation, one is confronted with myriad definitions, each approaching the question from a slightly different perspective. In fact, few concepts have evoked more **aphorisms** (terse formulations of a truth or sentiment) than marriage and family.

Marriage

One recent maxim concerning the dichotomous nature of marriage evolved as therapist Karl Whittaker mused whether or not marriage could be thought of as a form of mental illness. "Marriage produces hateful demons out of perfectly nice people . . . while on the other hand, . . . it is the only way to get a Ph.D. in interpersonal relationships" (Beavers, 1985, p. vii). James Framo more seriously states, "Aside from its alleged inherent absurdity, marriage is an incredibly intricate phenomenon, simultaneously existing on multiple levels, stretching back to the past and built on uncommunicable experiences" (Beavers, 1985, p. vii).

Edward Westermarck (1891) in his classic, *The History of Human Marriage,* written a century ago, declared **marriage** to be a universal human institution that had been part of the social structure of all settled societies—a flexible institution existing in many forms. Westermarck also issued a now famous dictum, "Marriage is rooted in the family, not the family in marriage" (Mace, 1991, p. 7). Accordingly, marriage must be legally controlled and safeguarded by the community to assure continuity of the family.

Marriage has more recently been defined as a legally binding contract between a woman and a man that conveys certain rights and privileges including sexual exclusivity, legitimation of any children born of the union, and economic responsibilities. While most marriages involve an emotional commitment on the part of the two persons, this is not a requirement for a valid marriage. Additional characteristics that are usually ascribed to marriage include initiation through a public ceremony, need for a license, and the expectation that procreation will occur (Axelson, 1985).

Family

The **family** in all its variations is perhaps more difficult to define than marriage. Some believe that the family is best understood in the form of a metaphor (a figure of speech in which one object is likened to another):

> *If the family were a building it would be an old, but solid structure that contains human history, and appeals to those who see the carved moldings under all the plaster, wide plank floors under the linoleum, the possibilities.*
>
> *(Pogrebin, 1983, pp. 25–26)*

To understand concepts as complex as family one must begin with the *essence* or that which is pure and true. Pogrebin, in defining the *essence of family* as "who it is, how it feels and what it does," (1983, p. 26) suggests that families must be able to define themselves. Would metaphors used by students to define the family at the beginning of a marriage and family class differ significantly from those written at the end of the course? This is an interesting question that students may wish to explore.

In defining the family, Walters (1982) examines four aspects: biological factors, commitment, attachment, and mate selection. Commitment is the intention of a person to maintain a relationship while **attachment** is the bonding that causes feelings of at-homeness and ease when the other person is either present or easily accessible. Mate selection is a familial process whereby families stress the importance of selecting mates with similar attitudes, race, religion, social status, and values.

Thorne (1982) has characterized families as places of sexuality, eating, sleeping, and of close biological ties. The widely quoted U.S. Bureau of the Census definition is more narrow and legalistic: "two or more persons living together and related by blood, marriage, or adoption" (Engram, 1982, p. 5). But the family is believed to be far more than a collection of individuals occupying the same physical and psychological space. It is a natural social system with unique properties of its own, including "rules, roles, a power structure, forms of communication and ways of negotiating and problem solving that allow various tasks to be performed effectively" (Goldenberg & Goldenberg, 1985, p. 3). By such a definition, individuals are tied to one another by powerful, durable and reciprocal emotional attachments that may fluctuate but persist over the lifetime of the family. Entrance occurs only through birth, adoption, or marriage; and in spite of a sense of alienation from one's family, one can never truly leave except by death (Goldenberg, & Goldenberg, 1991).

The New York Court of Appeals in 1989 expanded the legal definition of family to include nontraditional relationships with a ruling that a gay couple who had lived together for a decade could be considered a family under New York's rent control regulations ("Definition of Family," 1989). Factors considered included exclusivity and longevity of a relationship, level of emotional and financial commitment, manner in which the parties have held themselves up to society, and the reliance placed upon one another for family services. The ruling was said to reflect a more functional approach to defining family than the structural view usually taken by courts in the past.

This ruling reflects the growing trend of many organizations to adopt a functional definition of family rather than one of form. The Family Service of America (FSA), a network of 300 local agencies providing counseling and educational programs for individuals and families, views families as follows: "Families . . . provide emotional, physical and economic mutual aid to their members. . . . Ideally, such families are characterized by intimacy, intensity, continuity and commitment among their members" (Sulima, 1989, p. 7). For the purposes of this text, a family will be defined as "two or more persons who share resources, share responsibility for decisions, share values and goals, and have a commitment to one another over time" ("A Force," 1978, p. 4). This definition, as delineated by the American Home Economics Association, emphasizes a network of sharing and commitments regardless of biological, legal, marital, or adoptive ties.

Family Types

It is important to understand the various ways in which family scientists classify families. The family into which a person is born is called the **family of orientation** and consists of self, sisters, brothers, and parents. When a person marries, she/he leaves the family of orientation to create a new **family of procreation** that is composed of self, spouse, and children, if any. The **nuclear family**, as the basic residential family unit in the United States, theoretically consists of two adults of the opposite sex living with their own and/or adopted nonmarried children (Leslie & Korman, 1989). Realistically, however, it may contain only one adult or no children. It also may include a stepparent and stepchildren through remarriage or other relatives. Thus, the nuclear family is the smallest kinship unit that appears in our society and which functions as an independent, self-sufficient unit. Murdock (1949) earlier argued that the nuclear family is the only universal human grouping that exists as a strong functional unit in every known society. But to attempt to define a typical nuclear family of the 1990s is to ignore the facts of diverse organizational patterns and styles of living. The **traditional family** structure of a conventional and intact nuclear family with full-time homemaker mother, dependent children, and sole wage-earner father represents no more than 10% of American families (Scanzoni, Polonko, Teachman, & Thompson, 1989). The common variations in family types today are illustrated in Table 1.2.

The extended family may be defined as wife, husband, nonmarried children, plus one or more other generations, such as grandparents, aunts, uncles, married children, or grandchildren occupying the same household (Hareven, 1987). While extended families were once more common in the United States, it has been

Table 1.2: Common Variations in Family Organization and Structure

Family Type	Composition of Family Unit
Nuclear family	Wife, husband, children
Extended family	Nuclear family plus grandparents, aunts, uncles, and/or other kin
Blended family	Wife, husband, plus children from previous marriage(s)
Common-law family	Woman, man, and possibly children living together as a family, although absence of legal marriage ceremony
Single-parent family	Household led by one parent (woman or man), possibly due to divorce, death, desertion, or never having married
Commune family	Women, men, and children living together, sharing rights and responsibilities, and collectively owning and/or using property, sometimes abandoning traditional monogamous marriages
Serial family	Woman or man having a succession of marriages, thus acquiring several spouses and different families over a lifetime but constituting only one nuclear family at a time
Composite family	Form of polygamous marriage in which two or more nuclear families share a common wife (polyandry) or husband (polygyny)
Cohabitation	More or less permanent relationship between two unmarried persons of opposite sex who share a household
Lesbian or gay couple	Two persons of same sex who develop and maintain a homosexual relationship and living arrangement

estimated that no more than 4% of American households today are composed of extended families (U.S. Bureau of the Census, 1990h). Despite geographical mobility in today's society, the extended family and family networks remain an important source of family aid (Cook & Weigel, 1983). In fact, a possible increase in this family form may occur because of today's high divorce rate and difficult economic circumstances (Sena-Rivera, 1979). Family networks include all members of the extended family, friends, and persons in the community with whom family members have emotionally significant, continuing relationships (Green, 1981). Such a definition acknowledges the interrelatedness of the family to other subgroups.

Family Functions

Historically, the functions of a nuclear family have included the following categories: reproduction of new members, sexual regulation, economic cooperation, and education (Murdock, 1949). These functions were expanded somewhat later to encompass protection and order, socialization of the young, and transmission of individual goals and societal values. Family scientists have long debated issues surrounding family functions. Some insist that today's family is becoming disorganized; others believe it is merely reorganized for different functions.

No one disputes that within recent years, family functions have changed. In our urban-industrial society, many functions once performed by the family, such as production of food and clothing and the educational and religious instruction of children, have been taken over by the state and other institutions such as factories, schools, and churches (Mace, 1991). These changes left the family freer to focus on the remaining functions for today's nuclear unit: bearing and rearing children and meeting the emotional needs of the family members (Parsons & Bales, 1955). A recent California Joint Select Task Force on the changing family identified five specific types of activity as the family's "basic function": "maintaining the physical health and safety of family members, providing conditions for emotional growth, helping to shape a belief system from which goals and values are derived, and creating a place for recreation and recuperation from external stress" (Sulima, 1989, p. 7). It is worthwhile to briefly consider contemporary family functions that have been divided into three categories: economic consumption, socialization of children, and meeting affective needs (Adams, 1986).

Economic Consumption

In order for a family to exist, goods and services must be produced and distributed among its members. Therefore, if economic cooperation does not exist within the family, its survival will be in question. Generations ago, the economic function meant that the family was expected to be self-sufficient by producing all of its own food and clothing. Today, however, at least one member of the family is expected to work, usually outside of the home, to produce income that will be used to carry out this economic function through consumer purchases. In fact, society fosters nuclear family values partially because the family unit plays so great a role in consuming goods from the marketplace (Adams, 1986).

Socialization of the Young

It has been said that it is no accident that in a million years of evolution, humanity has emerged with a particular form for the bearing and rearing of children—the human family (Bronfenbrenner, 1980). Reiss and Lee (1988) make it clear that nurturant socialization of the newborn is the key function of the family. **Socialization** is the process by which a child learns the ways of society so she/he can function within it (Elkin & Handel, 1989). The process explains not only how a person becomes capable of participating in a social group but also how social order itself is possible. Learning the rules of society is not confined to childhood but continues throughout life. As a child grows older, much of the responsibility for socialization is taken over by the schools and eventually the peers who become singularly influential during adolescence. But because of the significance of early experiences and primary relationships, the family remains the most important socializing agent in the child's life.

Fulfillment of Affective Needs

Because many societal tasks are performed outside the family group, family members can focus on meeting the affective needs of its members. This function is so crucial to family well-being that the ability of the family to furnish the needed affection and understanding will determine whether the family unit will persist or dissolve (Adams, 1986). When the major goal of life in the rural-agricultural society was economic survival and physical safety, the family fulfilled these functions. Now, however, our deepest need is for emotional security, for survival of our sense of personal worth in an impersonal world (Mace, 1991). This is the affective function of today's family.

Forces of Change

The ancients declared, "There is nothing permanent except change" (Heraclitus, 1968, p. 95). Although the concept is not new, the speed with which change is telescoped in time is unique to this century. Modern advocates differ in their predictions of how such drastic change will affect the home and family. A "third wave" society of the future in which the home once again would gain preeminence was postulated a decade ago (Toffler, 1990). Where the factory was the central institution for the "second wave" society created by the industrial revolution, the home was prophesied to be the central institution of tomorrow. The **electronic cottage** was pictured as the workplace of the future especially for clerical personnel, bankers, insurance agents, or others who create, process, and distribute information. However, others disagree, stating a "high tech/high touch" philosophy. Accordingly, the more technology in a society, the greater the need for people to be with others, to seek "high touch." This probability precludes the likelihood that, in the near future, the electronic cottage will become a reality for other than short-term options (Naisbitt & Aburdene, 1990).

All futurists, however, foresee the family greatly affected by technological developments such as bioengineering, artificial intelligence, and computer-based robotics with their potential to change intimate relationships, home management, and work roles (Moore, 1985c). Indeed, it is impossible to predict future home environments without acknowledging the impact of high-tech trends already on the drawing boards. What will "smart toilets" that measure blood pressure, pulse, urine, temperature, and body weight contribute to family self-sufficiency ("Toilets to Get," 1989)? Robot hamburger makers already programmed for fast-food franchises will surely find their way to America's kitchens, perhaps stemming the recent tide of eating out (Smith, 1989).

As automation moves into more areas of family life, the debate continues between the techno-enthusiasts and the technophobics concerning the relative merits of its effects. Some question the "Ideal of Progress" that emerged with industrialization proclaiming that scientific advances would always make life progressively better (Naisbitt & Aburdene, 1990). Spanier (1989) predicts that forces of change pertaining to family relationships will get more complicated before they simplify. He points to the fact that "it is now possible for a child to have five parents at birth: a sperm donor, an egg donor, the woman providing the womb for gestation, the man expecting to raise the child, and the woman expecting to raise the child" (Spanier, 1989, p. 5). Thus, family trees increasingly resemble inextricably intertwined vines of ivy when one considers all of the possible constellations of divorce, remarriage, stepparenting, and foster care. Of the many forces of change in the second half of the 20th century, none have more affected the family than shifting demographics, the modern women's movement, and changing values.

Demographics

Family scientists rely on demographers to bring into sharper focus the many statistical facts that portray family life in America and reflect its values. Since mid-20th century, many shifting demographic variables have both reflected and led to myriad relentless trends affecting families. Two trends of special significance are the baby boom and the aging of the population (Treas & Bengtson, 1987).

Legacy of the Baby Boom

The post World War II **baby boom** that peaked between 1946 and 1964 and the **birth dearth** (falling birth rates of the mid-1960s and early 1970s) continue to have major implications for many aspects of our society including births, marriages, and divorces ("Legacy," 1988). These dramatic changes in birth rates are depicted in Figure 1.1. One effect of the postwar baby boom was to create what is referred to as a **marriage squeeze** for women. Typically, women tend to marry men who are 2–3 years older than themselves. Therefore, women born during the baby boom reached marriageable age without equal numbers of eligible men available, thus creating the so-called "marriage squeeze" (Cherlin, 1981). Today's university students born in the post-Vietnam War era are a part of the so-called youth counterculture that is rapidly diminishing. A dramatic 9% drop in the teenage population aged 15–19 occurred between 1980 and 1988, while the population rose by 18% for those aged 25–34 and 38% for those aged 35–44 (U.S. Bureau of the Census, 1990b). Certainly, this change in the population structure will impact a wide range of family functions, particularly reproductive and economic ones. The conspicuous consumption of youth-oriented products such as records, cosmetics, and fashions is already changing as witnessed by the not-so-subtle advertising swing to an older clientele.

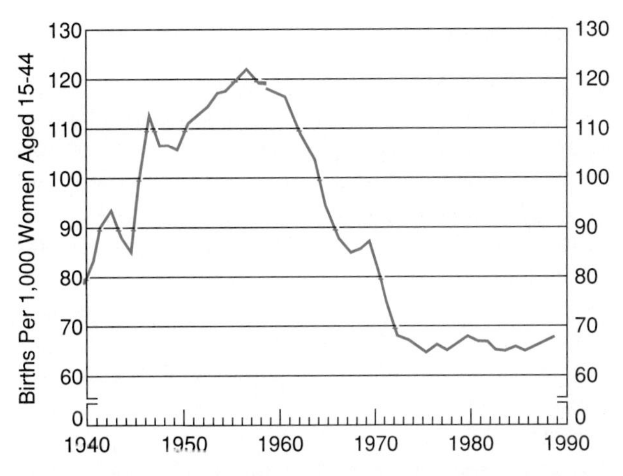

Figure 1.1 Births to Women Aged 15–44 by Rate Per 1,000 Women and by Year

Source: National Center for Health Statistics. "Annual Summary of Births, Marriages, Divorces, and Deaths: United States, 1989" in *Monthly Vital Statistics Report*, 38(13):3, 1990d. DHHS Publication No. PHS 90-1120.

The Graying of America

The combination of high birth and immigration rates in the late 19th and early 20th centuries and improved medical care have resulted in what has been called "the graying of America." The median age of Americans was 33.5 years for women and 31.2 years for men in 1988 (U.S. Bureau of the Census, 1990a). And in 1988, the life expectancy was 78.3 years for women and 71.3 years for men (U.S. Bureau of the Census, 1990s).

As the baby-boom **cohort** (persons in same group possessing common characteristics) grow older, the median age is projected to rise to age 42 over the next 40 years (Spencer, 1989). In the past 20 years, the proportion of persons age 65 and over has grown twice as fast as other age groups. This trend will continue until it peaks around 2030 when the aging baby boom generation will make up more than one fifth of our country's residents (Papalia, Olds, & Feldman, 1989). The largest growth group has been those age 85 and older whose numbers have increased 225% between 1960 and 1988 (U.S. Bureau of the Census, 1990c).

The implications of such an aging population extend to many areas of life. There will be an increasing burden on the Social Security system to pay for retirement benefits and Medicare services. While today five workers support one beneficiary, it is predicted that by the year 2030, three workers will be required to shoulder that load (Mann, 1977). Therefore, the percentage of disposable income for young families will continue to decline in the future if drastic increases are required in Social Security payments.

An older population in the voting booth and marketplace will likely effect changes in governmental programs, mass media, housing patterns, and demands for new products (Papalia, Olds, & Feldman, 1989). Most stressful for families, however, may be those controversial issues surrounding the end of life and decisions concerning elderly care and a person's right to die. Ethical dilemmas such as **active euthanasia** (merciful action to purposefully shorten a life) and **passive euthanasia** (withholding treatment that might extend life, allowing death to occur) will demand answers of today's students as they become tomorrow's caregivers (Schmeck, 1983).

The Modern Women's Movement

The modern women's movement is believed to be among the most influential factors affecting families in the 20th century. In the early 1960s, barriers that kept women from moving, working, and earning in the mainstream of society were challenged in Betty Friedan's (1963) expose, *The Feminine Mystique.* Of the two core messages that emerged from the ensuing women's movement, one urged an expanded identity for women, while the other demanded that a special value be afforded women's traditional role as maintainer of the fabric of daily life, a role that should be equally shared by men.

Feminists have challenged prevalent assumptions about the family by raising questions about family boundaries (Thorne, 1982). They have reopened the questions of what a family is, what its members do, and how they are affected by household and kin. Most of all, feminists have asked, what does the family do for women (Bridenthal, 1982)? In one survey among women under age 35, two thirds agreed with the goals of the women's movement and almost one half believed that it had made their lives better. However, three fourths of these same women indicated love and a good family life were necessary for fulfillment (LaFarge, 1983).

The women's movement has reverberated in the workplace and on the homefront. Women-men relationships have changed as have motherhood and fatherhood roles. Some family scientists view the most critical family-centered challenge of the 1990s to be how America accommodates, socializes, and cares for the children of increasingly egalitarian marriages in which both parents of young children work (Spanier, 1989). The demands of work and family life are so imposing that they cannot be solved by "succumbing to the culture of the overnight express delivery, the two-hour eyeglasses in one hour, . . . and the 28 second commercial that will change your life" (Russell, 1988, p. 2).

Shifting Values

During the 1980s, a number of changes in values associated with family life continued to escalate with a speed of change unknown before. Of the predicted trends for the 1980s that became a reality, none were more directly associated with value changes than those in the area of sexuality. For example, as predicted, "permissiveness-with-affection" has led to a greater percentage of single individuals participating in sexual intercourse at earlier ages. Such behavioral changes have precipitated myriad personal and social problems as illustrated by alarmingly high rates of teen pregnancies, abortions, and "babies having babies." In response, parents have been pressured to provide more adequate sex education and schools to incorporate sex education into their curricula (Johnson, Lay, & Wilbrant, 1988). Although, in some instances, school districts have implemented comprehensive sex education programs including school-based family planning clinics, such measures are still woefully inadequate.

Shifts in female/male roles are also fostering changing values. There is now more acceptance of behavior once considered taboo, such as women going into singles bars, initiating opposite-sex relationships, and sharing the expenses of dating. Increasing numbers of women working outside of the home, of single-parent families by choice, and of one-child families are all realities that reflect a shift in values related to families. Personal priorities are mirrored in shrinking households as families have fewer children, more young people establish their own homes, and the number of elderly who maintain their own households increases ("U.S. Household," 1989).

In what is being billed as the first-ever nationwide survey on family values, it was found that two high priority family values are being able to provide emotional support and respecting one's parents. The inability of parents to spend enough time with their

BOX 1.1 **Comics Increasingly Reflect Societal Problems**

While comics such as *Doonesbury* have always been known for their attacks on government and concerns about societal issues, other comic strips more noted for their humorous aspects are also beginning to reflect the effects of societal problems on relationships. The comic strip *Cathy,* for example, has dealt with the lack of adequate maternity leave in most American companies. The soon-to-be-mother, Andrea, is told by the personnel department, "Oh no. Like many American companies we treat giving birth to a human being just as we would if you skipped town for a bowling convention. No leave. No pay. No job when you come back." "I think I'm going to be sick," responds Andrea. "Better save it. You only have three days paid sick time coming," responds the boss.

Another cartoon strip vividly expressed the choices facing many of today's young women: "**No maternity leave?** You mean I have to **quit my job** to spend time with my newborn?" asks Andrea. "Don't be silly," notes the head of personnel. "You can quit . . . you can be fired . . . you can go broke hiring baby-sitters . . . or you can collapse from exhaustion trying to do it all!" When Andrea is asked by Cathy in the final frame, "What did you find out?" her grim reply is "We have options our mother never dreamed of."

Today Newsletters, Atcom Publishing, 2315 Broadway, New York, NY 10024. Reprinted by permission.

Role reversal or let's pretend? Dual-earner families may successfully balance responsibilities but powerful tapes inside of themselves are the greatest challenge.

children was perceived as the greatest threat to the family. However, the majority expressed that they would find it difficult to pass up a more lucrative or prestigious job even if it meant spending more time away from home (Reardon, 1989). These data agree with earlier findings that indicate that although most Americans wish to return to the values of a former era, they are unwilling to give up their new freedoms (Yankelovich, 1981).

Perhaps one way to gain a better perspective of the influence of changing values on marriage and family life would be to look at four overriding values that continue to affect many facets of day-to-day living in families. These values, identified as those cherished in American society, are individualism, self-actualization, new perspectives on life goals, and a sense of urgency (Blankenhorn, 1986).

Individualism

The roots of individualism in our society can be traced back to early colonial days, in which the individual was expected to stand on her/his own two feet and accomplish difficult tasks. It has been asserted that the basic building block of society is again shifting from the family to the individual (Naisbitt & Aburdene, 1990). To some degree the emphasis on mutual happiness in marital relationships has been replaced with an emphasis on individual happiness with people becoming more introspective and attentive to inner experience (Skolnick & Skolnick, 1989). When such individuals cease to be happy, they feel justified in seeking a divorce to end an unpleasant relationship. For this reason, some referred to the youth of the 1980s as the "me" generation.

Self-Actualization

During the 1970s, the word **self-actualization** (a person's realization of her/his full potential) came to be part of the vocabulary of most individuals (Skolnick & Skolnick, 1989). Although self-actualization is a genderless term, it has been especially used to describe the process whereby women have struggled to attain their potential through success in careers. A beneficial byproduct of the self-actualization movement has been the creation of a new perspective on goals for women and relationship potentials for men.

New Goals Perspective

With the increasing number of dual-career families, where both the wife and husband are gainfully employed, the range of possible goals for families has expanded. Changing values are reflected in college and university classrooms filled by women who earlier in their lives, because of economic circumstances, marriage, and/or children, either did not choose or were not able to enroll in institutions of higher education. However, while many middle-class and upper-class women have been able to expand their horizons by giving up domestic routines for a seat in the halls of ivy or a position on the corporate ladder, lower-class women still have fewer options for new perspectives (Blankenhorn, 1986).

Sense of Urgency

Americans are increasingly recognizing the need to focus on alleviating the causes of social ills and the interrelatedness of social problems to family well-being. An increasing sense of urgency associated with family life concerns such fears as possible nuclear holocaust and problems of poverty (Blankenhorn, 1986). Although the percentage of families classified as poor has declined substantially since 1959, 11% of all families and 29% of black families were below the poverty level in 1986 (Glick, 1989a). Further, 59% of families with children under age 18 in which a woman heads a single-parent household live below the poverty level today

BOX 1.2 The American Family—For Better or Worse?*

Americans are worried about the shape of the family; they don't think it's in good shape and they don't approve of some of the shapes it has taken: a stay-at-home parent is preferred, divorce is acceptable, gay marriages are not legitimate.

Is the American family better off or worse off than it was 10 years ago?

Worse 49%
Better 39%

Will the American family be better off or worse off 10 years from now?

Worse 42%
Better 42%

Which do you feel is more important for a family these days?

To make some financial sacrifices so one parent can stay home to raise children	68%
To have both parents working so family can benefit from highest possible income	27%

When husbands and wives with young children are not getting along, should they stay together for the sake of the children? Or should they separate rather than raise the children in a hostile atmosphere?

Separate 70%
Stay together 24%

Which one of these family concerns causes you to worry the most?

Finding and paying for good health care	21%
Keeping up with housing costs/payment	17%
Paying for children's college tuition	16%
Financing your retirement	12%
Getting good day-care for children	9%
Taking care of elderly, ailing parents	9%

Do you think the provisions and funding of government programs for the elderly, such as Medicare and Social Security, are adequate to meet your needs now or in the future?

Yes 28%
No 68%

Should unmarried couples, including homosexual couples, have the same legal rights as married couples?

	Yes	No
Unmarried couples	33%	61%
Homosexual couples	23%	69%

Based on *Newsweek* poll conducted by Gallup organization, which interviewed a national sample of 757 adults during October 1–4, 1989.
From J. K. Footlick, "What Happened to the Family?" in *Newsweek*, Winter/Spring 1989, p. 18.

(U.S. Bureau of the Census, 1990hh). No wonder so many feel an urgent need to solve problems such as population and arms control to assure a future in which they can better concentrate on quality of life.

In the midst of shifting values, Americans are worried about the shape of the family. Arlie Hochschild, a University of California at Berkeley sociologist, has stated:

> *Husbands, wives and children are not getting enough family life. . . . People are hurting. . . . We want it both ways. . . . We're glad we live in a society that is more comfortable living with gay couples, working women, . . . stepparents and single mothers, . . . people reaching . . . for self fulfillment. . . . But we also understand the value of a family life that will provide a stable and nurturing environment in which to raise children . . . in which personal goals have to be sacrificed.*
>
> *(Footlick, 1989, p. 18)*

How do we reconcile the drive for personal fulfillment and the quest for family stability? Hopefully, this text will provoke individuals to seek answers to this, one of life's significant questions.

Research and Theory in Family Science

Students of marriage and family should have some familiarity with the concepts inherent in research and theory. These tools will contribute to the accomplishment of the goal of understanding the institutions of marriage and family today. As early as 50 years ago, behavioral scientists discovered that sound **empirical** (reliance on experience or observation) research could be conducted on familial as well as other social behavior. At this time, they were already in the process of moving from asking "what" to asking "why" questions about various areas of family life (Nye, 1988). Research provides the basis for testing theories (frameworks of general ideas that permit a comprehensive view of concepts and facts). Theories can be useful in organizing assumptions into hypotheses or guesses that can be tested (Berger, 1988). Many clinicians speak of frameworks or perspectives rather than theories (Beavers, 1985). In clarifying the distinction between a conceptual framework and a theory, Klein (1980) defines a conceptual framework as a system of language and thought with two principal features: (1) a vocabulary of concepts and (2) rules for combining concepts and key suppositions called assumptions. The term theoretical perspective will be used in this text.

In spite of the quest for a general theory of the family, most theoretical perspectives in the family field are borrowed from other disciplines (Holman & Burr, 1980). The construct "family realm," recently advanced as a criterion for evaluating current theoretical perspectives, can increase effectiveness in borrowing, using, and doing research about theories in the family field (Beutler, Burr, Bahr, & Herrin, 1989).

Although many theoretical perspectives are relevant to the study of marriage and family, the authors have chosen to incorporate only three perspectives: family systems theory, developmental or family life cycle theory, and exchange theory. These theoretical perspectives were used as an underlying framework in the writing of this marriage and family text, although no attempt was made to specifically call attention to each perspective in the various chapters. Rather, they were used as a basis for the inclusion and discussion of various topics and as an overall organizing principle.

Systems Theory

Mortals are surrounded by systems: ecosystems, solar systems, systems of law, electronic systems, and more. A system exists when there are components that have common properties interacting and influencing each other in ways that produce a whole larger than the sum of its independent parts (Goldenberg & Goldenberg, 1991). Psychiatrist Murray Bowen developed Family Systems Theory in the 1950s based on his work in the family therapy field (Kerr, 1988). Unlike psychoanalysis, it viewed human beings, young or old, married or single, as elements in a structure of interlocking relationships rather than autonomous individuals. The 1970s saw the emergence of systems theory as one of the major theoretical frameworks in the study of marriage and families. Scholars suggest that systems theory may very well be the wave of the future. It can be particularly useful in describing many parts of the family that have not been seriously studied before and its systematic insights can be applied in practical settings (Holman & Burr, 1980).

A family is a system in which its members are organized into a group forming a whole larger than its separate elements. A variety of intricate relationships evolve in the family system; alliances and coalitions are formed as energy and information are exchanged. Subsystems with clear but permeable boundaries emerge. The most enduring subsystems are those of the spouses, siblings, and parent-child that all operate in some hierarchical order to maintain themselves and to sustain the system as a whole (Goldenberg & Goldenberg, 1985). For the family system to survive, it must be both flexible and stable. Otherwise, the family as a social system becomes dysfunctional (Melito, 1985).

Interrelatedness and adaptability are fundamental principles of family systems. Since change is circular, change in any member affects and is affected by change in any other. The family's adaptability or ability to reorganize as it moves through successive stages is a key to healthy family functioning (McFadden & Doub, 1983). Change or development in family systems may occur in three ways: by the day-to-day functioning of the family, adaptation of individuals within the system, and the system's adaptation to the individual's changes. These generational events taken together form a kind of "family life spiral" (see Figure 1.2).

Developmental/Family Life Cycle Theory

A second theoretical focus found in this book is the developmental/family life cycle framework. American family scientists began to use the concept of the family life cycle as an organizing principle in their study of the family in the 1930s (Duvall, 1988). When developmental theory was refined in the 1960s, most of its

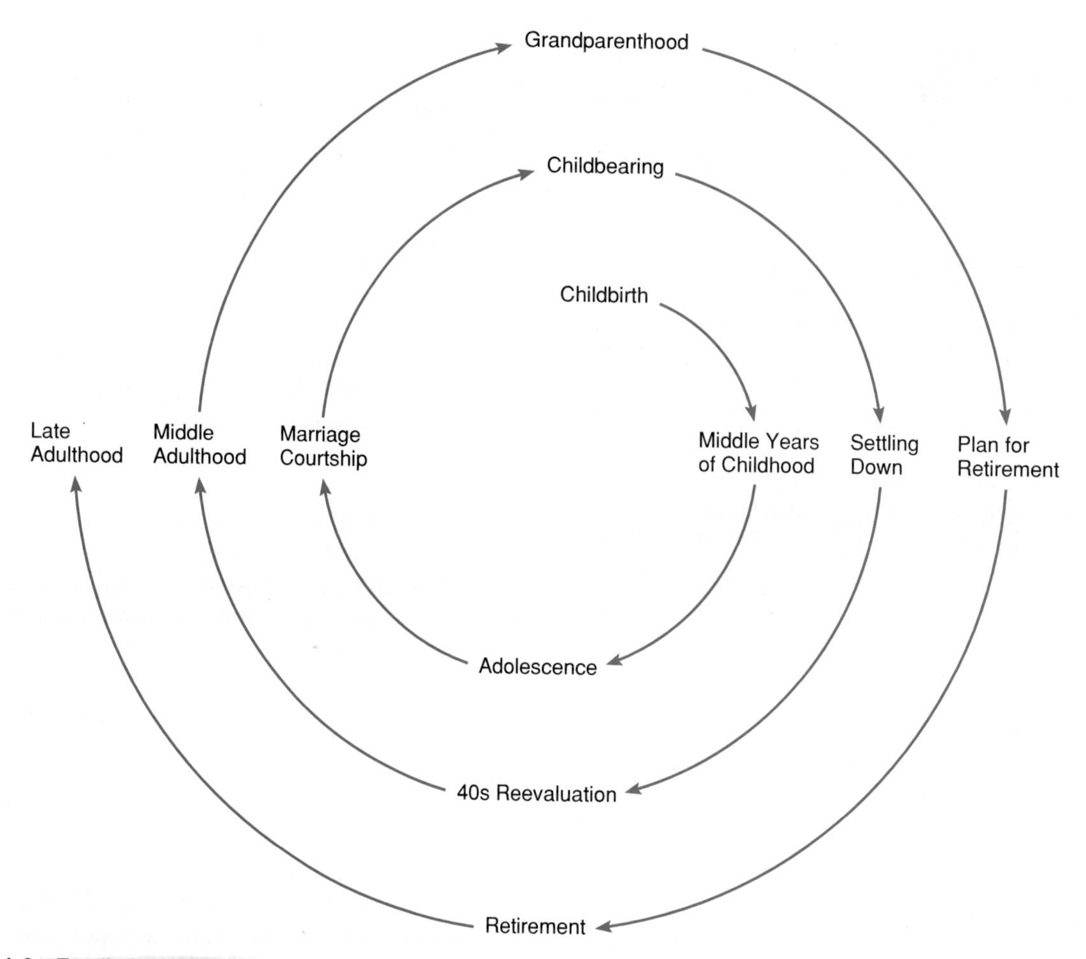

Figure 1.2 Family Life Spiral

emphasis was on life span issues (Holman & Burr, 1980). The developmental approach derives from a number of disciplines. Sociology furnished the family life cycle concept and ideas of social change that both influence and are influenced by families. Inherent in human development is the awareness of developmental tasks, critical periods, and the teachable moment. Learning theory and the interaction process flow from psychology. Finally, child development, family relationships, home management, housing, and family practice stem from home economics (Duvall & Miller, 1985). The family life cycle framework also has had a major impact on the way that family therapists conceptualize family functioning. In the past, the therapist's focus was on family psychopathology. From a family life cycle approach, a problem is viewed as a developmental impasse that occurs as the family negotiates a transition from one stage to the next (Breunlin, 1983).

Although families around the world differ enormously, there is evidence of the universality of the family life cycle (Hareven, 1974). Family life cycles also transcend varying family patterns. According to Ruben Hill, "The differences in paths of development of single-parent and two-parent families are seen primarily not in stages encountered but in the number, timing, and length of the critical transitions experienced" (1986, p. 28). Family career is a term that has been used to describe those structural changes over time (Aldous, 1978).

Exchange Theory

Another frame of reference is exchange theory that has been defined as a theoretical perspective whereby human beings seek to avoid costly behavior and seek statuses, relationships, interactions, and feelings that are personally rewarding in order to maximize their "profits" (Nye, 1988). Because it offers a relatively

simple focus on costs and rewards, it is particularly useful in understanding precarious human relationships such as sexual involvement of singles, courtship processes, marital satisfaction, and divorce (Holman & Burr, 1980). It is less effective when the exchange process becomes more complicated, subtle, long-term, or unconscious. Therefore, the exchange perspective would not be as useful when trying to interpret nonrational factors such as love, jealousy, self-esteem, values, and social norms (Murstein, Cerreto, & McDonald, 1977). One area in which exchange theory is particularly applicable is family power. Accordingly, the one who provides the most resources in the family has the most power (Adams, 1986). Also, couples may exchange different resources in a relationship such as beauty for money or sex for status. Such equity in relationships not only impacts the selection of a mate but also how two people will get along and how likely they are to remain together (Walster & Walster, 1978).

Marriage and Family in the 1990s

As we begin the last decade in the 20th century, what discoveries lie ahead for marriage and family life? There are decidedly more questions than answers at this point. Will the number of single-parent households continue to increase? Will the birth rate continue its decline, with a concomitant increase in the number of one-child families? Has the divorce rate stabilized? Will the percentage of voluntary childless marriages continue to increase? What will happen with regard to sexual attitudes and behavior in our society? Can we anticipate increasing acceptance of the standard of permissiveness with affection with an even further increase in premarital sexual intercourse among women and men? Will the concern about Acquired Immune Deficiency Syndrome (AIDS) as a sexually transmitted disease lead to a decline in the incidence of premarital and extramarital sex? Will the increasing availability of sex education result in a decrease in the percentage of infants born to single persons? And will a conservative governmental stance retrench more toward traditional values? Will marriage and childbearing continue to be postponed by many college-educated women who have promising future careers? What, if any, is the "new glue" for marriage now that self-sufficiency has reduced mutual dependency (Adams, 1988)? These questions and many similar ones continue to be the subject of great speculation among family scientists. Unfortunately, there are no crystal balls nor highly accurate measures of human behavior that will permit detailed predictions about the future of marriage and family in American society. However, taking our cues from past evidence, one thing is certain. Many changes in social attitudes and behavioral patterns that will inevitably occur will have tremendous effects on both premarital and marital relationships. Although there is little evidence to suggest that the American family will go out of existence, many historical facts indicate that it will continue to evolve structures and functions that meet the needs of its members.

With these perspectives in mind, it is hoped that readers will begin to have a deeper appreciation of the many facets of human relationships embodied in marriage and family. Further, it is believed that such awareness will lead to the accomplishment of personal goals for those who seek to improve their future choices in marriage and family relationships.

Summary

- Although both first marriage and remarriage rates declined and the divorce rate doubled during the 1970s, no evidence exists that suggests that marriage is losing its popularity.
- Major benefits from studying about marriage and family result from acquiring knowledge about marriage, family, and culture; self in marriage; marriage decisions; human sexuality; family life cycle; childbearing and child rearing; and family resources.
- A family is two or more persons who share resources, share responsibility for decisions, share values and goals, and have a commitment to each other over time. The functions attributed to families are economic consumption, socialization of the young, and affective dimensions.
- The major forces of change that have affected the American family since World War II are reflected in the postwar baby boom, the aging population, the women's movement, and the resulting changes in family values.
- Systems, exchange, and developmental/family life cycle theoretical perspectives underpin the writing of this book.
- From a systems theory perspective, the family system itself has three basic components: the structure of the family, the family undergoing development, and the adaptation of the family to changes in circumstances.
- Exchange theory can be defined as a perspective whereby human beings seek to avoid costly behavior and seek relationships, interactions, and feelings that are personally rewarding.
- The developmental or life cycle approach reflects that individual and family development continues throughout life.
- The family life cycle concept furnishes the overall organizing principle for the book's content.

Questions for Critical Reflection

1. After considering the several definitions of family given in this chapter, with which do you most agree? How does your own definition of family differ from this one?
2. What is meant by Westermarck's idea, "Marriage is rooted in the family, not the family in marriage"? Do you believe such a relationship is necessary for civilization to continue?
3. Change and continuity in the institutions of marriage and family are the key concepts in the book. Is one concept more significant than the other for the welfare of humankind? If so, why?
4. Can you identify any effects that the women's movement has had on your family of orientation?
5. What is meant by the French admonition, "Plus ça change, plus c'est la même chose," or translated, "The more things change, the more they stay the same"? How does this admonition apply to marriage and family?

Suggested Readings

Beavers, W. R. (1985). *Successful marriage: A family systems approach to couple therapy.* New York: W. W. Norton. Excellent overview of systems theory and attributes of the healthy couple.

Lewis, R. A., & Salt, R. E. (1986). *Men in families.* Beverly Hills: Sage. Research findings on men as husbands, fathers, and participants in kin and friendship networks in families.

Rubin, E. A. (1986). *The Supreme Court and the American family: Ideology and issues.* Westport, CT: Greenwood. A review of court decisions affecting the American family and family policy development.

Thorne, B., & Yalom, M. (Ed.). (1982). *Rethinking the family: Some feminist questions.* New York: Longman. Twelve original essays debating the future of the family by focusing on feminist critiques and defenses of the traditional family.

Willie, C. V. (1988). *A new look at black families* (3rd ed.). Dix Hills, NY: General Hall. Case studies that offer a window for viewing various patterns of affluent, middle-class, working-class, and poor black households.

CHAPTER 2

Changing Roles for Women and Men

As men seek for themselves the liberation that began with the Women's Movement, both men and women have to confront the conflict between their human needs—for love, for family, for purpose in life—and the demands of the workplace.
—Betty Friedan, 1983

OUTLINE

Probably no single facet of human behavior in the 20th century has had more impact on marriages and families than changing gender roles. A **role** is defined as a pattern of behavior that is expected of a person who has a certain function in a group (Zimbardo, 1988). While some role behaviors such as the formal duties of a professor are explicit requirements, others such as supporting the varsity football team may be implicit assumptions. The role assigned on the basis of common attributes related to gender is either female or male. A number of gender characteristics can be identified such as physical appearance, personality traits, role behaviors, and occupations (Lips, 1988). Understanding not only the roles of women and men in our society but also the intricate relationships between role behavior and societal and individual expectations is an important foundation for success in marriage and family.

Traditional Female/Male Roles

Traditional **gender roles** have emphasized women's childbearing functions and men's physical strength. These assignments reflect the necessity both to procreate and to defend family members in order to perpetuate the human species. Traditionally, the male role has emphasized dominance and permitted more sexual freedom than the female role, which has emphasized passivity and suppressed women's sexual freedom. In essence, the female role limited the function of women's sexuality to reproduction. This view, whereby sexual satisfaction for women has been frowned upon and actually regarded as being unimportant while considered for men an inalienable right, is part of what is called the "double standard." The **double standard** can be defined as a norm whereby premarital sexual intercourse is considered acceptable for men but not for women (Hyde, 1990). It is based on numerous factors including Freudian psychology and the female biological potential for pregnancy. Subscribing to the double standard has led to several myths associated with female sexuality, including the belief that women should not initiate sexual intercourse and that most women receive little, if any, physiological satisfaction during sexual activity (Faunce & Phipps-Yonas, 1979).

While data indicate that women have traditionally supported the double standard, it also suggests that they are beginning to reject such masculine definitions of "right" and "wrong" in sexual matters (Robinson & Jedlicka, 1982). In fact, research findings now support the idea that college students are shifting toward a single sexual standard: permissiveness with affection (approval of sexual activity between committed partners). Men, however, are still found to be more permissive in their sexual attitudes than women (Sprecher, 1989).

It is important to review how traditional gender roles have been developed in our society, both personally and historically. Personally, although biological orientation largely determines one's earliest behavior, by age 2 children are aware of their gender and have begun to exhibit a more socially influenced pattern of behavior (Cowan & Hoffman, 1986). As early as age 4 or 5, children have already begun to firmly embrace gender-role stereotypes (Shapiro, 1990). During adolescence, from about ages 14–18, one's psychological orientation, which is greatly influenced by peers, will affect gender-role behavior. By adulthood, social influence and psychological orientation have largely determined feminine and masculine behaviors (Renzetti & Curran, 1989).

Both hereditary and environmental factors influence personal gender-role development. Four identified determinants are biological factors, modeling behavior of others, rewards and punishments, and self-socialization (Flake-Hobson, Skeen, & Robinson, 1980). Supporting the biological influence, evidence suggests that variations in spatial and verbal abilities may be linked to differences in the organization of the female and male brains (Dworetzky, 1990). It is also well-known that by observing their parents, peers, and other significant persons in their social environment, children learn to imitate the gender role being modeled.

An even less than astute observer of children is aware that reward and punishment serve as vital links in gender-role development. Even in this age of enlightenment, little girls are often rewarded for looking pretty, while little boys are punished for crying. Finally, as gender-typed behavior emerges through interaction of the biological, modeling, and reward/punishment systems, children develop a set of organized rules based on what they see and hear in their social environments, a process known as self-socialization (Williams, J. H., 1987).

Historical Background

Prior to the 18th century, work that generated an income for the family was done in and around the family home by women as well as men (Tong, 1989). Gradually, forces of industrialism drew labor out of the home into the marketplace. Eighteenth century American

Dressed for the part—gender role socialization may be reinforced through play as children are typecast with toys and play clothes.

colonies operated under English law that placed married women under the control of their husbands, including ownership of their earnings and personal possessions. Wives could not appear in court, enter into contracts, inherit property without the approval of a male relative or guardian, or engage in philosophical arguments. Although community standards dictated that women should be able to read, write, and possess limited mathematical skills, they were admonished not to become too well-educated in order to avoid the "masculine-woman" image. Nevertheless, because of the informality of frontier conditions and economic needs of the colonists, women were often encouraged to engage in a wide variety of occupations such as soap making and cloth weaving (DePauw, 1975).

During the 18th and 19th centuries, the United States also adopted many English customs in order to become what it considered a more cultured society. This English standard of feminine behavior encouraged idleness, passivity, and gentility, thus developing women into "ladies" (Hafter, 1979). Therefore, by the 19th century, American women, intellectually limited by circumstances, were expected to be domestic and subservient to men (Tocqueville, 1972). An economic and political system that forced female dependence and an inferior education severely limited women's economic opportunities allowing them access to only low-paying jobs. Furthermore, since women did not receive the right to vote until the 20th century, they had little opportunity to participate in politics. With the construction of factories, the fathers of middle-class families emerged as sole breadwinners. As their work, which was performed outside of the home, gained respect, the work of mothers in the home was depreciated. Although married women, in general, tended not to be employed, evidence indicates that working-class, immigrant, and especially black women participated in the labor force. Economic factors demanded such a commitment to the "collective family economy" (Hareven, 1987). The traditional view of gender roles was supported by various organized religions, which approved of the domestic, pious woman clinging to the home and being subservient to her husband. Eventually, biblical warnings to women to obey their husbands worked their way into 20th century marriage ceremonies (Sklar, 1973).

In the first half of the 20th century, during two world wars, women were encouraged to take factory jobs as their part in the war effort. However, after the servicemen returned home, women were often demoted or transferred into less economically rewarding work. Thus, from the social fabric of this postwar era, the role of "true" womanhood was once again redefined. Women were persuaded that their appropriate place was in the home, serving as lay psychologists, educators, and nurturers of their children. With the invention of labor-saving devices for the home that made possible new social customs, women were encouraged to spend time in refined, cultural pursuits and social clubs (Cowan, 1976).

Female Passivity/Male Dominance

The widespread existence of male dominance in our society today is probably based on the long-held cultural view of male superiority. Data collected in the early 1970s depicted men as more aggressive and competitive but less emotional, and less likely to have their feelings easily hurt. Women, by contrast, were believed to be passive, noncompetitive, and illogical (Broverman, Vogel, Broverman, Clarkson, & Rosencrantz, 1972). Obviously great strides have been made since these data were collected. However, more recent studies have found little substantial change in the content of such gender stereotypes (Werner & LaRossa, 1985; Smith & Midlarsky, 1985). Positively valued traits attributed to women have been clustered into a factor identified as warmth-expressive while the positively valued cluster of traits for men are characterized as competence-assertion-rationality (Lott, 1987).

Other evidence of male dominance relates to occupational categories. The majority of women continue to be employed as secretaries, typists, nurses, and elementary school teachers. In 1988, 99% of secretaries and 95% of nurses were women while only 9% of dentists and 20% of lawyers and judges were women (U.S. Bureau of the Census, 1990aa). Income level is another index of gender inequality. In general, women of all races earn less than men of all races, with Hispanic women earning the least ("Wage Gap Continues," 1990). Full-time employed women earned only 70% of the weekly earnings of full-time male employees in 1988 (U.S. Bureau of the Census, 1990bb). While having a college degree increases a woman's salary, considerable disparity remains between women and men (see Table 2.1). Although technical professions are the most female-friendly occupations, the pay levels for female engineers are currently only 86%, and for computer programmers, 83% of the average of men's salaries (Russell, 1991). Having an M.B.A. degree also appears to substantially narrow the pay gap for women in select industries with only a 7% annual salary gap existing between women and men in marketing and 3%

Table 2.1: **Median Income of Full-Time Workers**

	1–3 years of college	4 years of college
Women, all races, ages 25–34	$16,152	$19,068
Men, all races, ages 25–34	$22,260	$25,754
Black women, age 25 and over	$15,795	$20,626
White women, age 25 and over	$17,114	$20,291
Black men, age 25 and over	$21,105	$25,110
White men, age 25 and over	$26,302	$32,022

Source: Data from U.S. Government Printing Office, Washington, DC, as appeared in *The Chronicle of Higher Education,* January 7, 1987, p. 23.

in finance ("The Pay Gap," 1990). Of all workers who were earning $25,000 or more in 1987, only 32% were women (U.S. Bureau of the Census, 1990gg).

Commercial television helps to perpetuate gender inequity by casting characters in stereotyped occupations. A study of television nurses concluded that they were usually single, child-free women who were dependent and subservient to physicians, most of whom were men. The general impression is conveyed that nurses contribute very little to the welfare of the patient (Kalisch & Kalisch, 1984).

The Viennese physician Sigmund Freud, considered to be the father of psychoanalysis, is believed to have played a significant role in perpetuating the concept of male dominance. One of Freud's most controversial ideas is the concept of penis envy, or the desire of women for male sex organs, which grew out of his stage theory of psychosexual development. This concept is frequently cited to support the assumption that Freud considered women to be biologically, sexually, and morally inferior to men (Shaw & Costanzo, 1970). Freud believed that when children discover that only boys have a penis, not only do girls worry that they lack a crucial body part, but boys conclude that girls must have had their penises removed and thus are biologically inferior. This erroneous thinking is said to occur during the phallic stage of psychosexual development, ages 3–6, which is characterized by a "family romance" when children "fall in love" with the opposite-sex parent (Papalia, Olds, & Feldman, 1989). In a broader sense, this thinking has come to represent the envy of women for the more valued characteristics, higher status, and societal advantages associated with men (Goldenson, 1970). Although largely unproved and discredited, Freud's assumptions still capture the imagination of many persons and continue to play a part in the support of male superiority in our society (Williams, J. H., 1987).

The Anatomy Is Destiny Controversy

Gender, the concept of femininity and masculinity, is based on biological sex, cultural conditioning, and the resulting gender self-identity. **Gender identity** has been defined as the private experience of the gender role that is everything a person does to indicate to others or to self that she/he is either female or male (Money, 1985). While society defines gender roles, an individual's interpretation of those expectations is her/his gender identity. In other words, a gender role is gender identity in action. So far, a number of stereotypical differences have been described for traditional female and male gender roles in our society. What is the origin of these role expectations? Many people, for example, have often assumed that men are "naturally" more aggressive and women more submissive. Some authors over the years have even cited so-called **maternal instincts** as a reason why many women prefer to stay at home and rear children (Rossi, 1984).

Years ago, developmentalists concluded that girls and boys differ on the basis of physical strength (Kagan, 1964). But does all of the difference in physical strength result from biological factors? Or do socialization experiences that neglect the development of muscular structure in women contribute to this difference?

Nature Versus Nurture

One way of addressing the issue of whether so-called feminine and masculine traits are biologically innate (nature) or socially learned (nurture) is to review research pertaining to differences and similarities between women and men. Research from the 1970s began to suggest that gender differences may result from a combination of biological/genetic factors and cultural learning experiences. As an example, a mother's ability to produce milk after childbirth was found to be influenced by her socially derived attitudes toward breast-feeding (Bardwick, 1971). Accordingly, social and psychological factors influence **hormone** secretion levels thus creating an interactive influence of genetics and learning on gender-linked attitudes and behavior (Rossi, 1977). However, the reviews are still mixed. Since the combination perspective is the prevailing view of the 1990s, it is important to understand both sides of the issue.

Innate Role Behaviors

Although it is not a particularly popular position today, there are many proponents of the nature/innate/biological heritage as determinants of role behaviors. Early studies concluded that female hormones created a greater potential for women to be nurturant, while male hormones created a greater likelihood for men to exhibit aggression. For example, male dominance was believed to be strongly related to the presence of the male sex hormone testosterone (Goldberg, 1973). Supporting this theory is a study of female infants whose mothers had accidentally received the male hormone androgen during pregnancy. As young girls, they were more likely to be tomboys and to be more career-oriented than marriage-oriented in comparison to those female children who were exposed to lesser quantities of androgen during their mother's pregnancy (Money & Ehrhardt, 1972).

From later research, there is considerable evidence for different female/male behavioral averages in three areas: play behavior, physical aggression, and thinking and reasoning (Hines, 1989). Play behavior of male children is typically rougher and more active than that of female children. And female and male children also prefer different toys (Carpenter, C. J., 1989). At all ages, male children in most cultures are more physically aggressive than female children (Campbell, 1989b). While there is no difference in the overall intelligence of female and male children, certain distinctions exist in the way in which they think and reason. **Cognition** (the ability to have ideas, solve problems, speak, read, calculate, and remember) involves two different abilities: verbal and spatial. Verbal skills are involved, for example, when one puts sounds together into words or sentences. Spatial abilities involve judging relationships between objects such as in mechanical manipulation or reading a map. Studies show significant differences between the sexes with girls excelling at verbal abilities and boys at spatial abilities (Epro, 1989).

Some of the most intriguing findings regarding the impact of heredity have come from studies of identical twins who were reared apart. If these individuals are quite similar as adults, heredity would then appear to be the causative factor. In fact, in a number of studies, there has been a tendency for identical twins reared apart to show very similar physical and psychological characteristics as well as comparable intelligence levels (Bouchard, 1983; Diamond, 1982; Lykken, 1982). When intellectual similarity of adopted children was compared to their biological and adoptive parents, genetic variability was found to be the most important influence in the development of individual intellectual differences. The adopted children resembled their biological mothers more than the adoptive parents who reared them from birth (Horn, 1983).

Since people's sexual status is defined by their external genital organs, when these organs are deformed, their gender role is affected (Money, 1985). One study describes a number of male infants born in Puerto Rico who at birth appeared to be female because they possessed a vaginal pouch and clitoris instead of a scrotum and penis due to a genetic-linked malfunction in their endocrine system. These male infants were successfully reared as female by their parents, who were unaware of any medical problem, a fact that seemed to support nurture as the primary factor in gender. However, at puberty there was a spontaneous hormonal change in their bodies that resulted in the development of a penis. This development produced a dramatic change in psychological orientation so that these male adolescents began to view themselves as males and to develop a sexual interest in female adolescents, thus strongly suggesting the primacy of nature in determining gender-linked behavior (Imperato-McGinley, Guerrero, Gautier, & Peterson, 1974). Much additional research still needs to be conducted to determine the interrelationship of biological and cultural factors in role acquisition.

Learned Role Behaviors

Evidence supports the idea that some dimensions of behavior are learned rather than inborn. Margaret Mead (1935) conducted a classic study of three primitive New Guinea tribes: the Arapesh, the Mundugumor, and the Tchambuli. Among the Arapesh, women and men exhibited traditional feminine traits—both were gentle, passive, and shared the responsibilities of child rearing. In contrast, both Mundugumor women and men behaved in ways considered masculine, showing aggression and combativeness. But perhaps the most surprising finding was that the Tchambuli possessed gender-role attributes that were the opposite of what we have identified in American women and men. More specifically, women were viewed as practical, powerful, and aggressive, whereas men devoted much of their attention to self-adornment, bickering and pouting, and exhibited frequent emotional ups and downs. Thus Mead concluded that these differences between the tribes, for the most part, were a function of their socialization.

A study of **hermaphrodites** (persons whose genital organs at birth cannot be clearly identified as being either female or male) concluded that socialization influences human behavior (Money & Ehrhardt, 1972). A different type of study concerned couples who were administered the Bem Sex Role Inventory (a measure of feminine and masculine traits) before and after they had completed a problem-solving skills training program. Both women and men scored higher on feminine qualities after completion of training. The men also indicated increased amounts of self-disclosure, a characteristic typically associated with women. Men may fail to learn self-disclosing skills because their environments are less conducive to it while growing up (Ridley, Lamke, Avery, & Harrell, 1982).

Some subscribe to the theory that gender-based attributes of motherhood are a product of our sociocultural experiences rather than the so-called "maternal instincts," which are thought to be genetically linked to gender per se (Rossi, 1984). This viewpoint is reflected by Money (1973) who maintains that only four biological differences exist between women and men: women ovulate, menstruate, gestate, and lactate, while men contribute only the sperm for impregnation after ovulation has occurred. Certainly the nature/nurture questions debated by social scientists for so many years are not intended to be answered in this text. However, it is the intent to furnish enough information in the two sections that follow to allow students to form their own opinions. It is upon such knowledge that many of life's decisions about significant relationships are made.

Biological Influences on Gender Identity

From the biological perspective, certain physiological processes occur during the embryonic and fetal stages that lead to the sexual differentiation of females and males. Further, research evidence suggests physical differences between women and men in terms of weight, height, and mortality (Hoyenga & Hoyenga, 1979). But to what degree are these variations genetically linked or culturally induced?

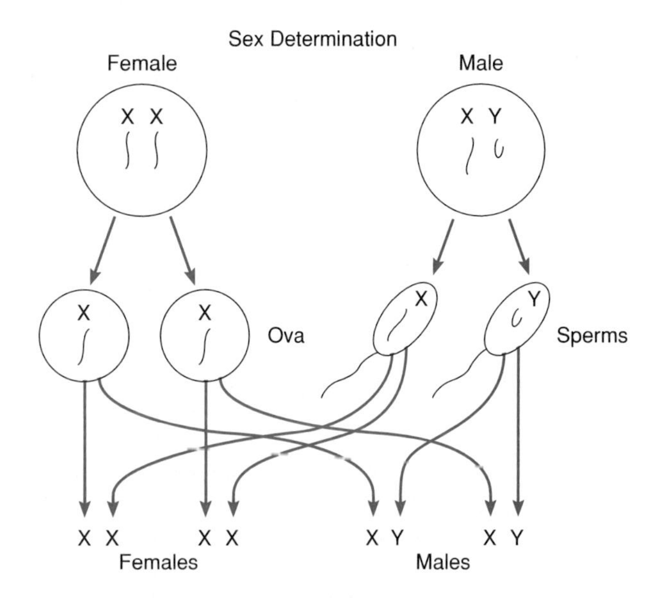

Figure 2.1 Chromosome Pairing

Sex Determination

What factors determine whether we are born female or male? To illuminate this question, the sex determination process and some of the physical variations in women and men will be examined. The complex process begins at conception with chromosomal sex and continues throughout fetal development under the influence of sex hormones (Hoyenga & Hoyenga, 1979).

Chromosomes

The process of human conception involves the uniting of an ovum (egg) and a sperm cell to form a zygote, each of which is different because of its unique chromosomes. A normal ovum contains 22 regular chromosomes and one X chromosome, whereas a normal sperm cell contains 22 regular chromosomes and one X or Y chromosome. The hereditary characteristics determined by the regular chromosomes include eye color, hair color, and body type, as well as predispositions to such abnormalities as color blindness and baldness (Hoyenga & Hoyenga, 1979).

Females have a pair of X sex chromosomes, and males have an X and a Y sex chromosome (see figure 2.1). Since the mother always contributes an X chromosome, if the fetus also receives an X from the father, it will develop as a female, XX. But if the embryo received a Y from the father, it will develop as a male, XY. Many people incorrectly conclude that the sex of the child is determined through the father. The father cannot consciously influence the process, of course, and it is more appropriate to say that the sex of the child is determined through the father (Allgeier & Allgeier, 1991). For reasons not yet understood, the process does not always work as clearly and simply as described. Occasionally, sex chromosomes may be either gained or lost during cell division. Chromosomal anomalies such as XYY, XXY, and even XXXY are known to occur and to result in aberrant sexual development (Money, 1975).

Hormones

The release of hormones (chemical substances secreted into the bloodstream by the endocrine glands) in varying quantities results in the development of a female or male embryo from the established chromosomal basis. In general, female and male embryos are virtually indistinguishable from each other during the first weeks of life (Denney & Quadagno, 1988). Both possess the external structures of a genital tubercle, genital folds, and genital swelling. Between the sixth and eighth weeks, the Y chromosome in the male causes the primitive gonads, or sex glands, to develop into testes (see Figure 2.2). In the absence of the Y chromosome, the primitive gonads develop into ovaries. After the differentiation of the gonads into testes, they begin secreting androgens (male sex hormones, including testosterone) in the third month of fetal development. One of the androgens causes the structures to continue to develop and differentiate into the male internal sex organs—the vas deferens, seminal vesicles, and ejaculatory duct (Crooks & Baur, 1990). If no male sex hormones are released, the structures develop into the female internal sex organs—the uterus, the fallopian tubes, and the upper part of the vagina (Francoeur, 1991). Around the fifth month of pregnancy, when the external genital organs begin to develop, if androgens are present, the genital tubercle becomes the glans penis, the genital folds form the penile shaft, and the genital swelling forms the scrotum. In the absence of androgens, the genital tubercle becomes the clitoris, the genital folds form the labia minora, and the genital swelling forms the labia majora (Denney & Quadagno, 1988). When puberty approaches the hormones once again sharply increase their productivity. At this time, testes and ovaries release the hormones necessary for the development of the secondary sex characteristics such as pubic and underarm hair, facial and chest hair in male adolescents, and breast development in female adolescents.

The distinction between genetic and environmental influences in this process remains somewhat hazy. Environmental influences begin to affect the fetus well before birth. The development of femaleness/maleness (biological sexuality) and femininity/masculinity (personality characteristics) are affected by hormones (Money, 1987). Unless the fetal testes secrete sufficient quantities of the male hormone androgen at a very critical period, the fetus inevitably develops as a female. Since it takes something extra to produce development as a male fetus, the process is more complicated and more subject to anomalies than development as a female fetus.

The interactions between chromosomal sex and hormonal influences are extremely complex. Many scientists believe that androgens may act upon the brain to produce one type of brain circuitry in female fetuses and another type in male fetuses (Hines, 1989). Thus, the masculine brain may be programmed for dominance, assertion, and high energy levels, with tender and caretaking behavior being somewhat inhibited (Money & Ehrhardt, 1972). If these scientists are correct, their findings indicate that limits may exist as to how far societies can successfully go in altering gender roles.

Social Influences on Gender Identity

By this time, it is apparent that gender identity (the person's persistent, unambiguous definition of self as either female or male) is the result of both biological sex assignment and socialization. The development of such a self-definition is crucial to the formation of later heterosexual relationships. It has been shown that environmental influences operate before birth. While it has been suggested that prenatal hormonal influences may predispose individuals to either feminine or masculine patterns of behavior, family scientists still cannot say how much, if any, of the childhood and/or adult behavior reflects prenatal influences. What is certain, however, is that the development of feminine and masculine behavioral patterns is greatly affected by the complex learning influences that begin to operate at birth (Hines, 1989). Regardless of the possible effects of hormones, human infants at birth are not psychologically differentiated as being either female or male. They do not know of their gender, their sexuality, or how girls and boys are expected to think, act, and feel differently. Female and male differentiation occurs during the process of socialization, which begins at birth and continues throughout life.

Process of Socialization

No single theory adequately explains how sex roles are acquired. Behavioral theory, insisting that environment determines behavior, contributes understanding of the

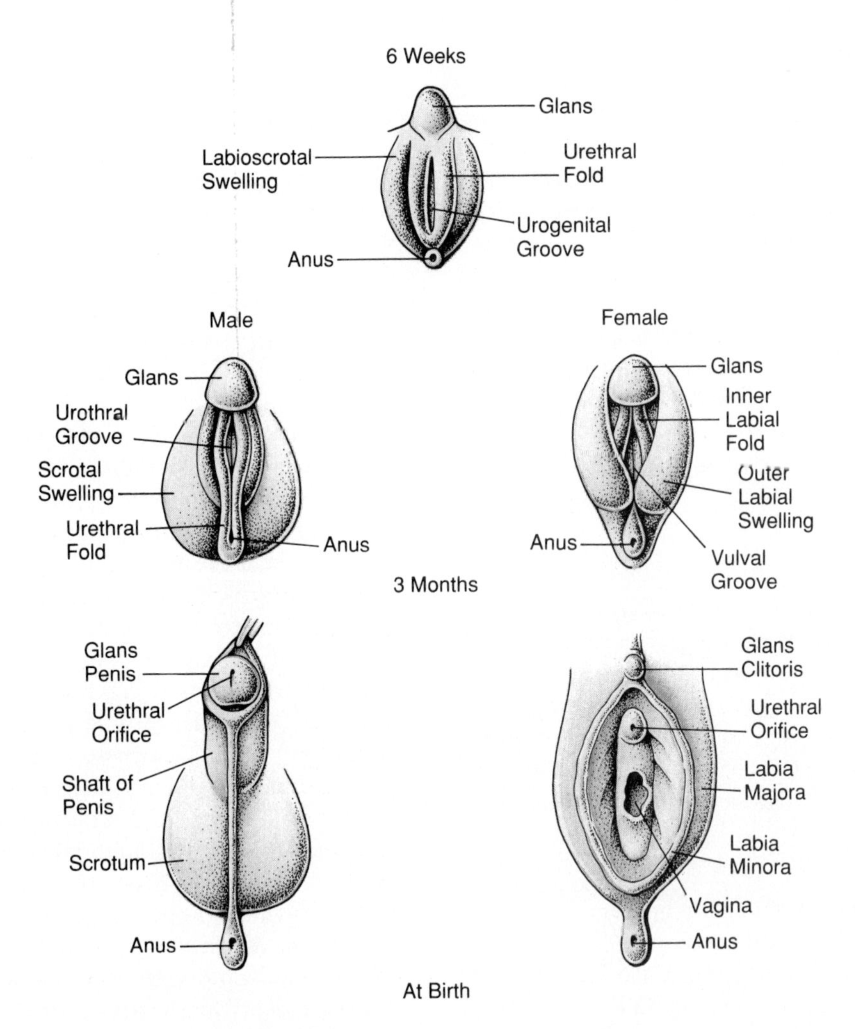

Figure 2.2 Stages of External Genital Differentiation

influence of different treatment of female and male children by parents and teachers (Kaplan, 1986). Social learning theory emphasizes the importance of imitation and observational learning from models. Biological factors such as maturational, hormonal, and genetic differences are indisputably influential. Finally, the importance of identification as stressed by the psychoanalytic approach or self-socialization proposed by cognitive-developmental theory cannot be ignored (Van der Zanden, 1989).

Since gender roles are learned, many people believe it is possible for society to alter its expectations and thus bring about changes in the behavior of women and men. Given the amount of support for the social learning theory as a basis of role behavior, it is important to review this process. There are at least three ways in which young girls and boys develop their gender-role identities through their cultural and social environments: imitation and modeling of others, social learning/self-socialization, and reward and punishment (Flake-Hobson et al., 1980). First, children learn gender-role expectations through the imitation and modeling of their parents, peers, and others. Freud believed that children identify with the same-sex parent out of fear of loss of love or fear of retaliation. Freud's interpretation of human behavior, centered around his belief that "biology is destiny," has continued to be very influential in research on gender differences (Bussey & Perry, 1982). Second, as children engage in social interaction, they rehearse their own gender roles as well as learn to anticipate attitudes and behaviors of the other sex (Cahill, 1983). A little girl playing with a doll and engaging in a make-believe game of caring for an infant's needs is learning the role of motherhood. Finally, through learning about the self in relation to others, the child engages in self-socialization, whereby she/he discovers that desired gender behavior is rewarded and undesirable gender behavior is punished (Richardson, 1988). For example, young girls may be discouraged from playing in "rough" games such as football because they may get hurt; and furthermore, it would be unladylike. If a young boy falls down and cuts his knee, the parental response may be for him to not cry but to be "tough." In each instance, "appropriate" behavior might be rewarded with praise and "inappropriate" behavior punished by withholding approval (Campbell, 1989b). However, not all parents perpetuate feminine/masculine stereotypes to this degree.

Sources of Socialization

Over the years, researchers have delineated a number of different sources of socialization in our society (Lott, 1987). Major socialization agents during infancy and early childhood include family, schools, peer groups, mass media, play activities, and religion. However, the most important influence in a child's life—the first and the longest lasting—is that of her/his parent(s).

Influence of Parents

From birth, parents intentionally and unintentionally begin to teach gender differences (Hunter College Women's Studies Collective, 1983). Parents begin the process in the nursery by choosing pink or blue decor depending upon the sex of the newborn infant. While no one would claim that the color of an infant's blanket is in itself a determinant of femininity or masculinity, color choice tends to reinforce the gender stereotypes that will inevitably influence such concepts. In the first few months of life, gender-based differences in treatment become evident. Both mothers and fathers are more likely to cuddle a female infant than a male infant. Male infants are more likely to be bounced around, shaken gently, and lifted over the parent's head. More physical reaction also is expected from male infants as a sign of infantile expression of toughness (Culp, Cook, & Housley, 1983). Mothers touch male infants more frequently than female infants during the first 3 months of life (Hunter College Women's Studies Collective, 1983). However, the reversal, which occurs at about age 6 months, is consistent with cultural norms and stereotypes: male children are expected to be more independent and thus are less restricted in their activities, and most female children learn at a very early age to respond to subtle verbal and nonverbal cues from adults that will bring them love and approval.

Research suggests that gender labels and their associated expectations are deeply ingrained. For example, in one study, most subjects incorrectly guessed the sex of the unidentified infant as male, justifying their choices on stereotypical cues such as strength or softness (Seavey, Katz, & Zalk, 1975). In a more recent study, although fathers gave daughters both trucks and dolls, most of them withheld dolls from their sons (Snow, Jacklin, & Maccoby, 1983). Although occurring in very subtle ways, it is quite evident that parents do contribute to gender-role socialization that begins at birth.

As children move from infancy into early childhood, girls gain security and learn to adjust by identifying with their mothers, being passive, and being dependent. Conversely, boys, who must give up their identification and dependence with their mother, develop independent attitudes more readily than female children (Bardwick, 1971). In contrast, male children must gain approval through achievement, first in peer competition and later in school and the workplace. Thus male children are more conditioned toward aggressiveness and independence than female children. During childhood, children witness various interchangeable feminine and masculine roles as played by parents. The mother may hold a job and the father may wash dishes and change diapers without either parent losing her or his gender identity. From these experiences, a child learns to assume the gender role of the same-sex parent and to respond to the gender role of the opposite-sex parent. The appropriate learning of gender roles does not depend on their content—that is, who does what around the house—but the ease and comfort with which the parents relate to one another and accept themselves as parents. At this stage, age 6 or 7, gender constancy is achieved (Emmerich & Shepard, 1982). This means the child can understand that an individual's gender is invariant over time across situations even with changes in activities.

Among older children, gender-role socialization is reflected in the amount and type of household chores that female and male children are asked to perform. In a study of children, ages 2–17, 84% had chores around the house and 40% had some type of paid employment outside of the home. For both kinds of work, parents reported that sons began working earlier than daughters. However, as daughters grew older, they put in substantially more hours of traditional housework such as cleaning, cooking, and washing dishes than sons did (White & Brinkerhoff, 1981b). More recently, parents indicated that only sons should be asked to mow the lawn, carry out garbage, and help with small repairs. In contrast, they believed that only daughters should be asked to perform household chores such as cleaning, cooking, grocery shopping, and doing their own laundry. Only in families with no sons did the number of daughters present cause a reduction in the gender-typing of male tasks (Brody & Steelman, 1985).

Finally, how does the mother's employment impact gender-role socialization? In two samples of high school seniors, taken 10 years apart, mothers who worked outside of the home possessed considerably more influence on gender roles, especially with daughters, than mothers who did not work. Further, the larger the family, the greater the influence exerted by the mother (Lueptow, 1980). These findings are of substantial importance because other studies have revealed that gender-role attitudes of mothers are more important than age, education, marital status, and occupational category in determining the gender-role attitudes of their daughters. College-educated mothers displayed a greater degree of gender-role similarity with their daughters than mothers who did not attend college, regardless of whether their gender attitudes were traditional or nontraditional (Smith & Self, 1980). In a study of employed mothers, daughters were more supportive of less traditional gender roles (Vanfossen, 1977). A later study found that sons of employed mothers also were more likely to have favorable attitudes toward women entering the work force than those of nonworking mothers (Powell & Steelman, 1982).

Since parents have begun to gain greater awareness of how childhood socialization occurs, many have attempted to minimize gender differences (Balswick & Avertt, 1977; Roper & LaBeff, 1977). Such parents try to accept tenderness and dependence in their young sons, believing that doing so will make their sons more able as men to give and accept love. Likewise, knowledgeable parents will encourage assertiveness and independence in their young daughters in hopes that such characteristics will best prepare them for a full complement of roles in their lives.

Influence of Schools

Schools generally reinforce and extend the femininity/masculinity differences that many female and male children learn in the home. Schools reinforce stereotypical gender behavior through the instructional materials that are used and by encouraging male students toward aggression and achievement and female students toward passivity and domesticity (Cahill, 1983). A study of 4-year-olds in a Head Start classroom demonstrated that teachers who believed that they were treating girls and boys in identical ways actually were encouraging different aspirations and self-images based on gender stereotypes (Chasen, 1977). In practice, teachers interact differently with girls and boys. They may seat boys on one side of the room only, form separate lines, organize teams, or assign different classroom chores according to a student's sex (Thorne & Luria, 1986). Such sex segregation prevents the sexes from working together cooperatively or comfortably and reinforces gender stereotypes (Lockheed, 1986).

With regard to academic performance, one study of fourth, sixth, and eighth-grade students found teachers were more likely to challenge male students to achieve academically. Boys were given more help in finding errors and correcting problems and were provided with more detailed instructions for completing a complex task (Sadker & Sadker, 1985). High school counselors often unintentionally reinforce gender stereotypes when female adolescents are counseled into secretarial science and English, while male adolescents are advised to take science and mathematics courses. Thus male adolescents are prepared for more prestigious careers, while female adolescents are channeled into traditionally female-dominated careers such as nursing and secretarial science (Weitzman, 1975). As has been previously pointed out, such choices have tremendous impact, hampering the acquisition of verbal skills by men and mathematical skills by women. Most people would agree that gender stereotyping is unfair and harmful. The human race is handicapped when one half of its population is discouraged from exploring many fulfilling and productive careers while the other half is impoverished by rigid, unyielding demands to place occupational goals above family cohesiveness.

Influence of Television

The influence of the mass media on gender-role socialization will be restricted to a discussion of television, although magazines, newspapers, radio, and recorded music also have similar impact.

An unusual experiment compared the effect of television on children from three Canadian towns, one of which had no television prior to 1974. Before the arrival of television, children in "Notel" were less likely to have sex-typed attitudes than children from the towns with television. Following the introduction of television, the "Notel" children showed a sharp increase in sex-role stereotyping. Girls were more affected in interpersonal relationships, and boys were influenced in perceptions of sex-appropriate employment (Kimball, 1986).

Children who watched television in the United States in the early 1980s found women occupying less than one third of all entertainment roles (Barcus, 1983). The majority of women portrayed were not employed but were in family or romantic roles (Signorielli, 1982). Women's personalities depicted by television tended to be passive, deferential, emotional, and weak whereas men were depicted as active, dominant, reasonable, and powerful (Downs & Gowan, 1980). These same sex-typed patterns are apparent in television advertisements directed toward children (Macklin & Kolbe, 1984).

As increasing numbers of prime-time television programs portray women as central characters, some gender-role stereotyping has diminished, but many stereotypes still remain. Nurses are increasingly portrayed as hostile and promiscuous and less as self-sacrificing and humanistic persons in comparison to earlier decades. In addition, employed, married women are more likely to be associated with unsuccessful or unsatisfactory personal lives (Durkin, 1985). Men are more likely to solve their own problems, but women are more likely to deal with problems of others while seeking assistance to deal with their own problems (Durkin, 1985). Finally, the amount of television watched may be influential. Children who are heavy television viewers (25 or more hours per week) are more likely to have stereotyped gender-role perceptions than children who view 10 or fewer hours of television per week (Ross, Anderson, & Wisocki, 1982). It is interesting that as adults, feminists watch less television than nonfeminists, although their childhood television-viewing habits are unknown (Lull, Mulac, & Rosen, 1983).

Influence of Play Activities, Toys, and Books

Sex-typing through play activity, toys, and books represent other important sources of gender socialization. Play activities can both teach and reinforce traditional gender roles. Even parents who have expressed belief in sexual equality and who expect the same behavior from their daughters and sons may inadvertently promote stereotyped gender roles through play. Despite egalitarian attitudes, parents tend to believe that sons are "naturally" more active, aggressive, noisy, and messy while daughters are "naturally" more gentle, quiet, neat, and courteous (Richardson, 1988). These beliefs, if reflected in the structure that parents provide for children's play such as the nature of toys and play environment, will affect what children do. By ages 2–3, female children move through space and explore less than boys and preschool-age female children spend less time outdoors than male children. By ages 3–4, girls and boys already differ in their play themes. Female children play-act homemaking, school, and organized social functions while play of the male children involves more adventure and fantasy themes (Lott, 1987).

Although at this time it is unclear what exact role is played by "nature" and "nurture" in the differences in children's play, replication of a classic toy study substantiates that adults do promote gender stereotyping by choice of toys (Stoneman, Brody, & MacKinnon, 1986). Little boys tend to be given toys that encourage aggression, adventuresomeness, and activities away from the home such as airplanes, guns, jeeps, sports equipment, and trucks. On the other hand, little girls tend to receive toys that encourage activities inside the home such as baby dolls, tea sets, and toy stoves. A perusal of any current toy catalogue will reveal the not-so-subtle messages that are reinforced by pictures. Little girls are most frequently shown with dolls or toy household appliances. The only dolls that little boys are pictured with are action figures such as Rambo or Masters of the Universe (Renzetti & Curran, 1989). Such stereotyping is also reinforced by pictures on toy packaging and by the arrangement of store stock in separate sections for girls and boys (Schwartz & Markham, 1985).

Books also have become subject to the gender-role socialization controversy. An analysis of award-winning picture books for children in the 1970s revealed that the image of girls was largely invisible by virtue of female under-representation in the titles, central roles, pictures, and stories (Weitzman, Eiffler, Hokada, & Ross, 1972). Most books were about boys, men, and male animals and dealt almost exclusively with male adventures. Adult women were stereotyped as passive, while men were active. Motherhood was represented in almost all books as a full-time, lifetime job, in spite of the fact that 90% of the women in this country will be in the labor force at some time during their lives. Significant improvement in the visibility of girls was noted in a more recent replication of the Weitzman research (Williams, J. H., 1987). However, while girls and boys were found to be about equally represented in their appearance in children's literature, the ways in which they were depicted remained virtually unchanged and entirely consistent with traditional gender roles. Another study concerning preschool children's books concluded that female characters continue to be depicted as passive, dependent, and in stereotyped gender roles portrayed in indoor activities,

Guns and dolls are the name of the game. Are these indelible scenes etched by nature or nurture?

service, and helping roles. This stereotyping image was as evident in female-authored books as in male-authored books (Kolbe & LaVoie, 1981).

Influence of Religion

Much debate has taken place in recent years over the impact of organized religion on maintaining traditional gender roles in our society. To date, only a small number of women occupy positions of leadership among Protestant and Jewish denominations, serving as ministers or rabbis. For example, as late as 1986, there were only five Conservative Jewish women rabbis in the United States (Cummings, 1986). Although women in the Roman Catholic faith do play various roles in church services, the official doctrines of the church still prohibit women from being ordained as priests (Renzetti & Curran, 1989). Virtually all Protestant churches now ordain women to their ministries (Weaver, 1985). In fact, since the late 1970s, the number of women ordained to full ministry in Jewish and Protestant congregations has more than doubled to over 20,000 (Loddeke, 1990). However, women clergy still confront discrimination in job assignments and salary (Briggs, 1987). One study found that even when the educational level of the clergywoman was higher than that of the clergyman, her average salary was $6,000 less ("Women in Clergy," 1984).

In assessing the influence of religion on gender roles, one study found that considerable experience with church activities and church attendance increases traditional views toward segregation of gender roles, including opposition to full-time employment for women. There were no significant differences between women and men with regard to their gender-role attitudes and their religious preference (McCandless, 1986). Other research involving college students found that those who were more religiously conservative exhibited more traditional gender-role attitudes. Women, however, scored higher on egalitarian attitudes than men (Larsen & Long, 1988).

Effects of Women's Liberation

The precise effects of the women's liberation movement on changing gender roles are very difficult to measure, but attitudinal surveys do help clarify the relationship. A national survey of high school seniors indicated that most female adolescents expected to be employed for the majority of their adult lives. In fact, 72% of female and 76% of male teenagers anticipated that work would be central to their lives (Deckard, 1983). By contrast, in a study assessing the effects of the women's liberation movement, the picture was somewhat different. These married mothers, ages 40–50, felt too old to have the chance to choose a career with society's approval, yet not young enough to work or return to school (Usher & Fels, 1985). Nevertheless, many people still feel that women have made tremendous strides in the last two decades toward achieving gender equity. In 1990, a national poll in Japan and the United States found that 44% of American women and 40% of American men believed neither sex was at an advantage in American society ("Poll: Japanese Women," 1990).

Evidence that changes are occurring in the status of women is contained in nationwide public opinion polls conducted at the beginning of the 1970s and the 1980s. In 1970, equal percentages of respondents (4 in 10) favored and opposed efforts to strengthen and change women's status in our society. By 1981, the percentage favoring efforts to change women's status had grown to two thirds, although one third still were opposed (Harris, 1981b). Many opponents of women's liberation believe that profeminists are seeking an androgynous society, whereby everything will be unisex. In fact, this argument was used to defeat the Equal Rights Amendment. However, a more recent study of married couples concluded that the widespread assumption that profeminists are androgynous is unsupported by research data (Wilkie, 1986).

Feminism for the 1990s is adjusting its battle for equality to fit the times. Such signs of the changing times are the publication difficulties of *Ms.* magazine and a *Time* magazine cover story, "Feminism for the 1990's," questioning the relevance of feminism to women in the emerging decade. A 1989 *Time*/CNN poll conducted by Yankelovich Clancy Shulman found that 58% of women did not consider themselves to be feminists and only 33% used this self-label (Wallis, 1989). Some suggest that the demand for sexual freedom and equal job opportunities has been superseded by the desire for maternity leave and child-care assistance. In fact, some feminist leaders believe that family issues such as child care, single-parent women living in poverty, and reproductive rights will help define the feminist agenda for the 1990s (Wallis, 1989). Pioneer feminist Mary Wollstonecraft (1972), a writer in the 18th century, argued that women should be educated the same as men and live in marriage as partners. That same message is echoed today, "Women need men for partners, not protectors; for equals, not oppressors; for someone to look across at, not up to" (Blumenthal, 1985, p. 84). These once radical ideas, now widely accepted, offer a base for moving beyond stereotyped gender roles to essential human rights for women, children, and men (Martin, 1989).

Table 2.2: Sex Differences in Development during Childhood and Adolescence

Physical Development

- **Rate of maturation.** Female children on faster developmental timetable, particularly during prenatal period and at adolescence.
- **Quality of maturation.** Physical growth of female children more regular and predictable, with fewer uneven spurts.
- **Strength and speed.** Little difference until puberty, when male adolescents become both stronger and faster, and develop larger percentage of muscle and smaller percentage of fat.
- **Heart and circulation.** At puberty male adolescents develop larger heart, lungs, and capacity for carrying oxygen in blood.

Cognitive Development

- **Cognitive structure.** No sex differences until adolescence, when male adolescents display somewhat higher incidence of formal operations thinking.
- **IQ.** No sex difference in total IQ.
- **Verbal skills.** Female children slightly faster in some aspects of early language; have better articulation and fewer reading problems; female adolescents better at verbal reasoning.
- **Mathematical skills.** Before adolescence, female children slightly better at arithmetic computation; male adolescents slightly but consistently better in mathematical reasoning.
- **Spatial ability.** Male children better at almost any task requiring spatial visualization with larger and more consistent differences at adolescence.

Social Development

- **Aggression/dominance.** Male children more aggressive and more dominant on virtually all measures, beginning in toddlerhood and continuing through adolescence.
- **Competitiveness.** Male children more competitive, although difference does not appear as early as aggression difference.
- **Nurturance.** No clear sex difference.
- **Sociability.** Female children typically have fewer but closer friendships beginning in elementary school and continuing through adolescence and adulthood.
- **Compliance.** Female children appear somewhat more compliant to adult requests in early childhood.
- **Identity.** No clear differences.

Overall Development

- **Vulnerability.** Male children more likely to show all forms of physical, emotional, and cognitive vulnerability to stress, as well as higher levels of deviant development.

Female and Male Differences

An objective review of the available research data, in which the stereotyped interpretations and biases have been controlled, identifies some differences between women and men in our society. Given the influence of the socialization process involving stereotypical gender-role expectations, it is often difficult to separate causative factors clearly and precisely (Losh-Hesselbart, 1987). However, the causes of these differences may be less important than the fact that they do occur, especially when one is contemplating signing a life contract with a person of the other sex! Understanding the apparent differences in the areas of physical characteristics, personality characteristics, and intellectual skills will contribute to success in marriage and family relationships. A summary of sex differences in development during childhood and adolescence is shown in Table 2.2.

Physical Characteristics

Despite the many similarities between women and men, some physical variations have been identified. These differences primarily relate to physiological body structure and mortality rates. Research suggests that such biological differences contribute to behavioral differences between women and men (Hines & Shipley, 1984).

Body Structure

Before birth the male fetus grows faster and at birth is heavier and has a larger head circumference (Williams, J. H., 1987). However, the female child grows faster from about 7 months until about age 4 but remains shorter and lighter in weight until about age 8 (Schickedanz, Hansen, & Forsyth, 1990). Differences also exist in the amounts of muscle and fat in the body.

Newborn male infants are more muscular and measurably stronger than female infants as evidenced by a stronger hand grip (Lewis, C., 1989). From infancy on, girls have more fat, and boys have larger, stronger muscles and seem to be more adaptive to vigorous activity (Papalia, Olds, & Feldman, 1989).

Men also have been found to carry more oxygen in their blood stream because of an increase in red blood cells that occurs at puberty. Therefore, both boys and men register a lower heart rate while resting and can better neutralize the metabolic effects of exercise and work. These gender differences in strength increase from about ages 11–17 and appear to be primarily the result of differences in androgens that increase muscle mass and estrogens that increase fatty tissue (Dworetzky, 1990). Typically, adult men are somewhat taller and weigh more than women. By adulthood, the average American woman is 5 inches shorter than the average man. Research suggests that this height variation is related to the greater production of estrogen in women, inhibiting the growth of long bones. Age at first menstruation has been correlated with adult height. Female adolescents who reach puberty later tend to be taller (Lott, 1987). If you compare women and men of a similar height, the men will, on average, weigh more than the women because of differences in body build. The body build of men makes it somewhat easier for them to engage in vigorous physical activities, such as running, throwing, and lifting. The center of gravity for women is around the hips, while the center of gravity for men is around the chest and shoulders. In addition, the angles of the arms and legs from the body tend to be more parallel in men and somewhat more flared in women (Gray & Drewett, 1977).

The sensory perceptions of female and male children also appear to differ. When given hearing tests, girls are generally found to be more hearing sensitive than boys (Shapiro, 1990). At all ages, female children are more bothered by loud noises and are more likely to respond to quieter sounds. Girls may also be more sensitive to touch than boys at age 3 months as they are more noticeably calmed by being picked up by a caregiver. Vision, which is based on two separate systems, rods for nighttime vision and cones for daytime vision, may also differ. Male children seem to have more sensitive cones because their daytime vision is superior, especially if the target is moving. The superior night vision of female children may be due to more sensitive rods (Epro, 1989).

The most difficult sex differences to investigate pertain to the brain. Human brains are physically divided into left and right halves (Epro, 1989). The left half is more involved in verbal activities at which girls excel, while the right half is concerned with spatial abilities at which boys are better. Some evidence exists that female children may have a larger band of nerve fibers that connect the two halves of the brain. This condition could account for women excelling in activities that involve communication: expressive use of words, empathy, recognizing faces, and understanding what the faces are communicating (Hines, 1989). It would seem that if women are better communicators, this circumstance may be partly based on differences in the brain that probably exist at birth (Epro, 1989).

Mortality Rates

In ways that are not completely understood, unequal numbers of females and males are conceived and there are unequal survival rates by sex. Estimates indicate that somewhere between 120 and 160 males are conceived for every 100 females (Money, 1975). Apparently, male fetuses are more vulnerable to death from the moment of conception than female fetuses. Since more male fetuses fail to survive until birth, the sex ratio is down to 100 females to 106 males by the time of birth. After birth, male infants continue to die in larger numbers than female infants. Women are believed to be healthier because the X chromosome carries genes for production of immunogenic agents. Additionally, the female hormones estrogen and progesterone stimulate certain blood cells to destroy infectious agents (Lips, 1988). Male infants are also more likely to inherit a variety of sex-linked disorders (Renzetti & Curran, 1989). Thus higher male death rates during infancy, childhood, and adolescence equalize the sex ratio by marriageable age.

Since there is evidence that greater stress is associated with the masculine role, the question arises as to what proportion of the higher death rates for men can be attributed to genetic factors and what proportion to the more active and hazardous lives that men often lead. Such gender-associated stress is reflected in the higher suicide rates and lower life expectancies for men. In one survey, men reported significantly longer work hours, more deadlines, and more occupational mobility than women. Further, men scored higher on measures of job absorption, patience, and hard-driving behavior in comparison to women (Sorensen et al., 1985). There are those who suggest that now that women have won their fight for equality on the career ladder, they too may begin to exhibit more male-like tendencies toward stress-related illnesses (Lips, 1988). Other research has confirmed that higher levels of stress were actually reported by women than men (Sorensen et al., 1985). But stress in women results in higher rates of mental illness and general illness, not in higher suicide rates (Gove & Hughes, 1979). Women report more nervousness, nervous exhaustion, migraine headaches, arthritis, and skin disorders (Sheldrake, Cromack, & McGuire, 1976). Although we have experienced major changes in gender roles in American society, to date there has not been a significant narrowing in the life expectancy gap with women still outliving men by 8 years.

Personality Characteristics

The two most frequently cited personality characteristics associated with gender-role differences are aggression and emotional display. The "Rambo" image depicts men as having superior physical strength, being aggressive in relationships, and being tough (Lips, 1988). This super tough "macho" image makes it extremely difficult for men to learn to express feelings of gentleness, kindness, and tenderness, which are the bases for future success as a family member. In fact, many men fear that such expressive qualities will be construed by women as being weak and passive. Such a stereotyped image will potentially affect the courtship process, the mate selection, and the future marriage relationship.

Some evidence suggests that American men are moving away from the masculine stereotype that many men have come to view as being a handicap. In a survey of 28,000 readers of *Psychology Today,* most men rejected the image of the macho man (Tavris, 1977). They appeared to favor the image of a man who possesses personal warmth, intelligence, and the ability to be tender and loving. At the same time, women were found to consider occupational success as essential for the "ideal man." These new and inconsistent demands that men be "tough on the outside" and "soft on the inside" will create new stresses for American men.

Aggression

In a review of 94 studies on aggression, Maccoby and Jacklin (1974) ascertained that in only five studies were female children and women found to be more aggressive, whereas male children and men were reported to be more aggressive in 52 studies. In general, male children and men displayed more physical than verbal aggression, a fact which has been observed in over 100 societies around the world. Of those adults arrested for violence in any year in the United States, approximately 90% are men (Campbell, 1989b). Statistics on crime indicate that men commit more murders and aggravated assaults than women. The only exception is in the case of child abuse where the battered child is most often victimized by its mother (Hoyenga & Hoyenga, 1979).

What accounts for these variations in aggressive behavior between women and men? Do parents and teachers discipline male children with corporal punishment more often than female children? (Campbell, 1989b). Could it be that women have more indirect outlets for aggression than men? Since women do not show aggression toward others, do they express their aggression toward themselves in such indirect ways as mental illness and suicide attempts?

While affirmative responses to these questions implicate social learning of gender roles, partial answers may also lie in prenatal biological circumstances. When daughters and sons born to women who had taken synthetic progestin to prevent miscarriages were compared with their unexposed siblings, significant differences were found between the two groups. Male children exposed to progestin were twice as high in physical aggression as their brothers, whereas three fourths of the female children scored higher on aggression than their unexposed sisters. Thus hormones were found to "flavor" individual gender behavior (Gelman, et al., 1981). Animal studies with mice and monkeys also substantiate that altered levels of male hormones at crucial periods when the brain is being differentiated can permanently affect levels of aggression (Campbell, 1989b).

However, some researchers feel that gender stereotyping, which has been reinforced by a male-dominated culture, has considerably more bearing on gender behavior than hormones. Implications are that aggression in the home leads to imitative behavior, especially among male children. Various studies suggest that television also fosters stereotypes about sex differences in violent behavior. Male children particularly are found to be influenced by programs that represent violence as "manly" and justifiable (Campbell, 1989b). It would be fair to say that current nature or nurture data fail to conclusively support either claim to causality (Rossi, 1984).

Emotionality

Personality differences of women and men as expressed in emotions have also been subject to considerable controversy. Fundamental issues concern what an emotion is, how many different emotions exist, and which emotions are basic. There is no precise definition of the word

Are the aggressive and passive games of life determined by destiny, design, or both? The debate continues.

emotion although it has been used widely by psychologists since the 19th century. The word *emovere,* which means to stir up, to excite, or to agitate, has been employed since ancient times to mean a reaction in self and others (Grigg, 1981). Most authorities recognize emotions to be a complex pattern of changes including physiological arousal, feelings, cognitive process, and behavioral reactions in response to personally significant situations (Zimbardo, 1988).

While some researchers identify emotions by expressive characteristics, others focus on the cognitive characteristics of emotion. Using expressive characteristics of facial expression, six basic emotions have been identified in early infancy: pleasure, distress, surprise, disgust, joy, and anger. Fear and sadness can be observed in infants by ages 8–9 months. More complex emotions such as affection and shame follow in the second year (Greenspan & Greenspan, 1985). Both the media and popular literature suggest that definite, narrow, and agreed upon gender roles prescribe female/male emotions (Goode, 1982). Among the commonly accepted stereotypes are that girls are to accept aggression directed toward themselves whereas boys must not display cowardice (Campbell, 1989b).

Male gender-role expectations dictate that men are not only supposed to be more aggressive and independent but also less emotional, less likely to cry, and less likely to express love, happiness, and sadness in comparison to women (Balswick, 1980; Lombardo, Cretser, Lombardo, & Mathis, 1983). Women are expected to be the emotional leaders in the family by providing warmth, empathy, and tenderness. Because of these stereotypes, men often have a great deal of difficulty in meeting the emotional needs of their wives and children, and the cycle seems to be perpetuated. Fathers have much more difficulty telling their sons than their daughters, "I love you." Men who certainly love their sons but consider it unmanly to express their love to a male child are unaware of the far-reaching implications of such omissions. There is documentation that if men do display their emotions, they may do so in a more forceful way than women (Kramarae, 1981).

Evidence suggests that men have learned to inhibit their tender feelings and overt expressions of affection. For example, among college students, women are more expressive of love, happiness, and sadness than men. While parental expressiveness is more likely to result in expressiveness on the part of both daughters and sons, when controlling for this influence, women are still more demonstrative of their feelings than men (Balswick & Avertt, 1977). More recent evidence suggests that age is a variable in the development of intimate feelings. In a study of college freshmen, seniors, and graduate students, it was found that male graduate students reported higher levels of intimate feelings than undergraduate men (Crown, 1985).

The traditional view of masculinity portrays men as tough, courageous, and aggressive, while forbidding them to display love, tenderness, or sentiment (Campbell, 1989a). What effect does such a masculine image have on a love relationship? The prospects are rather discouraging, since the man is often handicapped in his ability to give and receive affection, while the woman feels ambivalent about being loved and remaining a creative, productive person. However, today's women and men increasingly recognize that these stereotypes are the result of child-rearing practices, the sexual division of labor, the cultural definition of appropriate sex roles, and social pressures. Since these practices and roles have been created, they can also be changed (Goode, 1982). Thus it is the prerogative of today's young people to create a world of adult women and men who can express a full range of emotional experience in love relationships, work, and play.

Intellectual Abilities

As stated previously women are consistently reported to perform better in all verbal areas, including reading, whereas men tend to be less verbal (Renzetti & Curran, 1989). Based on standardized test performance as well as classroom performance, men tend to be somewhat better in mathematical skills, especially as related to problem-solving questions. After ages 11–13 male adolescents move ahead of female adolescents in mathematics achievement (Shapiro, 1990). However, analyses show that only 1–5% of the variation can be explained by gender (Hyde, 1981; Rossi, 1983). What accounts for these reported differences in verbal and mathematical abilities between women and men? Some researchers have linked performance in mathematics and science to **visual spatial abilities** (visual perception and location of objects and their relationships). This skill would include being able to mentally rearrange objects or figures (Lips, 1988). Gender differences favoring men in visual-spatial performance have been reported more consistently than any other cognitive difference (Connor & Serbin, 1985).

Other researchers have attempted to explain variations in intellectual skills by speculating that women are more dominated by the left (verbal) hemisphere of the brain and that men are more dominated by the right (visual) hemisphere. It has been hypothesized that men may be better able to coordinate the efforts of both hemispheres, thus enabling them to concentrate more effectively on problem-solving activities (McGuiness & Pribram, 1979). However, based on the available evidence, it is difficult to conclude that either verbal or mathematical abilities are exclusively sex-linked behaviors (Williams, J. H., 1987).

Sociological factors such as peer influence may furnish clues to differences in intellectual skills between women and men. High school female students are more likely to study with friends, while male students spend more time in activities requiring peer interaction such as playing sports. More male students wish they could work harder in school but fear what their friends would think. It is harder for male students than female students to study if their peers are "going out" with friends (Schneider & Coutts, 1985). Further, at all levels of school in which students are permitted to choose courses, female students are less likely to choose mathematics courses (Sherman & Fennema, 1977). Therefore, at a very early age, female students make choices that may preclude certain careers that require mathematical backgrounds. This difference in course preference is eventually reflected on standardized tests that measure mathematical performance. Thus the question remains, do female students succumb to the gender stereotype that it is feminine to do poorly in mathematics, or do their original choices reflect a lack of primary mental abilities in mathematics?

Because of early socialization experiences that promote the nurturing role of women, by the time they reach college age, women often value being liked and peer approval more than they value academic achievement. Although women have traditionally made better grades until late high school and have had a higher motivation to achieve, this achievement is quickly reversed after secondary school (Hunter College Women's Studies Collective, 1983). Some believe that traditionally, women fear success and equate high academic achievement with loss of femininity (Horner, 1972). In short, they appear to have been conditioned fairly effectively into the traditional feminine role in our society, a fact that may explain why until recently men were more likely than women to attend college. However, in the late 1980s, the number of women surpassed men on American college campuses. Women are much less concerned about conflicts of femininity and academic performance. In comparison to men, they are increasingly aspiring to obtain graduate degrees and to be hired into the highest status professions. These changes have led to an increased convergence of the educational and career goals of women and men, a major shift since 1970 (Fiorentine, 1988).

The Androgynous Person

The term **androgyny** has been popularized through recent efforts to reduce gender-role differences and to provide a new framework for thinking about sex and gender. Androgyny derives from the Greek term *andro* for man and *gyne* for woman. It refers to the psychological merging of the feminine and masculine. An androgynous person has reconciled femininity and masculinity within herself/himself. She/he will therefore exhibit both feminine and masculine qualities (Lott, 1987). Beginning in the 1970s, family scientists began to study the negative aspects of rigid sex-typing and the benefits of role flexibility. Research indicates that androgynous persons, when compared to masculine ones, are more at ease with babies and more sympathetic and supportive with new acquaintances. Androgynes were also more independent than feminine subjects (Lenney, 1989).

One may speculate that female/male sexual relationships would be related to androgyny. However, no differences were found in a study of the relationship of being either androgynous, feminine, or masculine to female sexual satisfaction. When adult women were asked to compare a sexually satisfying encounter with a sexually unsatisfying one that they had recently experienced, all categories of women indicated similar attributes in their unsatisfying sexual experiences: negative quality of the relationship, personal lack of involvement, and partner's lack of effort (Frank, Downard, & Lang, 1986). In a study of self-perceptions of gender roles, women perceived the ideal woman, ideal man, and themselves as androgynous. In contrast, men perceived the ideal woman as being traditionally feminine, while reporting themselves as being androgynous (Scher, 1984). In the discussion that follows, these differences in women and men will be seen in action through the roles that they play.

Roles of Women and Men

The traditional woman's role often limited women to the exclusive fulfillment of men's expectations. Before marriage, a woman was expected to cultivate her own

Reprinted with special permission of North America Syndicate, Inc.

beauty and feminine desirability in order to attract a man, while being careful to restrict his sexual advances. After marriage to a partner of appropriate wealth and attractiveness, she was expected to lose all sexual inhibition and continue to maintain her attractiveness, while devoting herself to her family's comfort and needs. To fulfill the traditional gender role, the American man was expected to be successful, self-assured, intelligent, unafraid, and to possess great strength. Living up to such expectations presupposed certain behaviors that include being occupationally successful, attaining wealth or fame, getting married to a well-dressed woman, belonging to the country club, or occupying leadership positions in community activities. The male gender role, in addition, placed great emphasis on adventure, the need to defeat one's enemies, and competitiveness in games (David & Brannan, 1976). These traditional masculine role concepts are increasingly being challenged as parents in the 1990s use more gender-neutral practices to socialize their young. These traditional role expectations will be examined in view of changing societal norms.

Family Roles

Regardless of the many changes occurring in women's lives today, the general expectation is still that women will marry and, in most instances, have children. Research does suggest that attitudinal changes are occurring regarding traditional family roles among today's women. Young women (18–34 years), in comparison to older women (over 60 years), attach much less importance to family-related tasks such as starting a family, rearing children, and managing a home (Merriam & Hyer, 1984). In a 1990 Yankelovich Clancy Shulman Poll of young adults, ages 18–24, 27% of women and 32% of men indicated their single most important goal was to have "a successful career." However, 39% of women and 30% of men reported "a happy marriage" as their most important goal ("What Youth Think," 1990). Whether more or less traditional, through marriage, the woman assumes the following roles: wife, lover, mother, and companion. Understanding the interface among the often contradictory roles may help the woman to become all that sne could be instead of being solely defined by self-limiting roles.

Although men are still choosing to include family in their formula for success, less time is currently invested in family functions than a generation ago. There has been a 43% reduction in the amount of time spent by men in family environments with young children since 1960 and a 49% increase in the amount of time spent outside of marriage-related activities. Further, college-educated men have spent considerably less time in families with children under age 6 but more time in marriages with no children (Eggebeen & Uhlenberg, 1985). Just as married women are expected to fulfill the roles of wife, mother, lover, and companion, men are expected to fulfill the comparable roles of husband, father, lover, and companion. Although some changes have occurred, much evidence of traditional roles remains in the different family roles of men.

Spouse

In traditional marriages, wives are expected to assist their husbands in career advancement by assuming responsibility for household and family management. In addition, they serve as hostesses during work-related functions and support decisions by their husbands. In such relationships, a woman's self-worth is often determined by how successful her husband is in his career or how attractive her daughters may appear to others, a fact that may lead to diminished self-identity (Hafter, 1979). Even in changing families, married women typically spend more hours performing household duties per week than married men. One study found that married women spend an average of 30.8 hours per week on household tasks, and married men only invest

19.4 hours. When compared, traditional men performed significantly less housework (8.7 hours) than nontraditional men (19.6 hours), but no significant differences were found between similar categories of women (Denmark, Shaw, & Ciali, 1985).

Since housewives appear to evaluate their happiness on the social acceptability of the housewife role, outdated feminine stereotypes of housewives "chained to routine tasks" and "uninterested in events outside their walls" may contribute more to poor mental health of today's housewife than the role itself. In terms of psychological health and the housewife role, one study found the lowest rates of depression symptoms among women who were married and working outside of the home and mild depression symptoms among married women not working. The highest rates of depression were found among those single and not working (Kandel, Davies, & Raveis, 1985). Social-class factors such as family income and husband's status are unrelated to housewives' reported satisfaction. However, social acceptability is correlated with higher reported satisfaction of housewives, regardless of their social class (Ferree, 1984).

While a generation ago the division of labor in most families was along stereotypical feminine and masculine lines, today the role of the modern husband includes assisting with household duties. The reality is that most husbands are neglecting this role. In a study of attitudes toward working wives, husbands agreed with their wives that husbands should do more household work. But the husbands only spent an average of 10 hours per week on household chores irrespective of their wife's employment status (Ferber, 1982). These findings are similar to another social survey that found that husbands with working wives contribute about the same amount of time toward family tasks as those married to nonworking wives (Pleck, 1984). In spite of changing family needs, traditional role definitions by men apparently are firmly rooted, resulting in less time being spent on household chores.

Lover

As lovers, women have traditionally been socialized to be romantic and nonsexual. Sexuality, when acknowledged, has been closely associated with love. Women were expected to teasingly display their sexuality, to be seductive, and to serve primarily as a source of sexual satisfaction for men. Most husbands expected their wives to automatically agree to requests for sexual intercourse when approached (Faunce & Phipps-Yonas, 1979). In recent years, there has been a growing acceptance of female sexuality, permitting women to have sexual activity for their own physiological and psychological pleasure, as well as experimenting with their sexuality within the context of marriage. For example, some women are exploring the possibilities inherent in differing types of orgasms and multiple orgasms (Darling, Davidson, & Conway-Welch, 1990).

One of the most highly valued roles of traditional men is their perceived sexual prowess as a lover. The traditional male image has often been defined in terms of the number of his sexual conquests rather than his ability as a lover from the woman's perspective. Apparently, today's views are changing at least for women. In one study that asked what changes women would desire in their sex lives, the majority responded that they would like more foreplay on the part of the man prior to the initiation of sexual intercourse (Darling & Davidson, 1986). As more women are becoming aware of the potential pleasure associated with physiological sexual arousal, they are establishing performance standards for their male sex partners (Faunce & Phipps-Yonas, 1979). Since women are beginning to expect men to better understand how the woman's body functions during sexual arousal and response rather than focusing primarily on their own physiological sexual satisfaction, men will undoubtedly respond—but how?

Companion

Women, as well as men, are expected to function as companions to their spouses throughout the life cycle. Companionship seems to be affected by the degree of equality existing in the relationship. A study of perceived equality in family roles revealed that both husbands and wives believed that, over time, the degree of inequity decreases. However, wives were more likely than husbands to perceive that an inequity existed with regard to the roles of housekeeping and companionship (Schafer & Keith, 1981).

Husbands are more likely than wives to be satisfied with the degree of companionship they receive from their spouse (Schafer & Keith, 1981). People learn to like each other if, when together, they experience positive outcomes. This quality is companionship (Lott, 1987). A companion, by definition, is "one who accompanies another." This role naturally presupposes that spouses must have time in order to accomplish this relationship expectation. Trying to fulfill all of the gender roles often leads to role conflict. For example, it is expected that men will be breadwinners and that their

Table 2.3: Earned Degrees by Level of Degree, Gender, and Year

Year	Bachelor's		Master's		Doctorate	
	Women	Men	Women	Men	Women	Men
1950	24%	76%	29%	71%	9%	91%
1960	35	65	32	68	10	90
1970	41	59	40	60	13	87
1975	43	57	45	55	21	79
1980	47	53	49	51	30	70
1987	51	49	51	49	35	65

Source: U.S. Bureau of the Census, 1990w, No. 274. "Earned Degrees Conferred, by Level of Degree and Sex: 1950 to 1987" In *Statistical Abstract of the United States, 1990,* 110th ed., p. 161. Washington, DC: U.S. Government Printing Office.

masculinity will be judged by the degree of success in their chosen occupation. Given the paramount importance of their economic provider role and competitiveness in the workplace, men often work long hours and on weekends. If parenthood is added to this equation, they may have great difficulties fulfilling all their roles but especially that of companion to their wives. For these reasons, among others, men have a high reported incidence of stress-related illnesses.

Parent

Acceptance of the motherhood role appears, at least in part, to be related to experiences as children with one's parents. Women are more likely to be child-oriented if they remember their parents as being nurturant toward them. In a study of attitudes toward child rearing, antiwomen's liberation women expressed greater personal interest in child rearing than proliberation women. Furthermore, liberal women were more likely to consider the population crisis before deciding to have children (Biaggio, Mohan, & Baldwin, 1985). In general, women with children report greater satisfaction with family life and health but less satisfaction with friendships and nonworking activities than child-free women (Charvrat, 1986). The role of mother today differs considerably depending on whether it is a parenting role shared with a husband or a single-parent role shared with a day-care institution. These issues will be more fully explored in chapter 16, "Dual Careers."

Traditionally, the role of father has been to provide only minimum assistance with child rearing but maximum assistance to the family as the breadwinner. This cultural expectation even became embedded in the laws of our society as evidenced by the father's legal obligations to financially support his family (Lopata, 1971). The fact that a man's identity is not as inextricably tied to the fatherhood role as is the woman's to motherhood is unquestionably related to both nature and nurture. The role of father was long neglected by many social scientists. In fact, it was not until the 1960s that a number of researchers began to study the father's role, and then it was usually to investigate the effects of father absence (Fein, 1978). The scene is quite different today, with both research and popular media frequently focusing on father-related issues. The resulting phenomenon is that fathering is becoming a new kind of verb—an active one—describing new father/child behaviors (Pogrebin, 1983). As children are discovering their "other parent," men are discovering their "other selves."

Women and Careers

Love and work were reportedly believed by Freud to be the two major sources of meaning in life ("Work and Family," 1983). The "myth of separate worlds," an unrealistic idea that work and family are separate entities, has existed since industrialization. This belief was based on a lifestyle where men worked outside the home to support their families, women were homemakers, and families adapted their living to the economic level of man's work. New patterns of work and family roles are necessary in a day when barely 7% of families fit this stereotype and when more than one half of all women, including those with children under age 6, work outside the home at least part-time. Women today are earning college degrees, getting jobs, and breaking barriers in the workplace. In fact, today more women than men are obtaining bachelor's and master's degrees (see Table 2.3). In the process, they are changing not only their lives but also the lives of the men they marry, the children they bear, and the world of work they help to shape.

Related factors that will be discussed in future chapters include the effects of working mothers on children and the influence of careers on self-esteem.

Changes in Job Opportunities

The status of women in the world of work has changed from the early 1960s when their employment opportunities were largely limited to the female-dominated service job market. Affirmative action and other federal regulations have promoted these changes with programs of child care and nontraditional job training needed to establish equality in the work force (Grefe, 1982). The following factors are believed to account for the substantial increase in labor force participation by women:

1. Increasingly, day-care for children made employment possible for mothers of small children.
2. Women seeking higher levels of education increased the probability of employment.
3. Technology decreased the amount of time for housework freeing women for employment.
4. A growing labor market increased job opportunities for women.
5. Women sought employment to enhance family income and to offset increases in costs of living and consumer demands (Ferber, 1982, pp. 458–460).

Some could argue that these factors are a complex mixture of cause and effect. For example, as many more women entered the labor force, more goods were demanded. Also, as technology reduced the time needed for specific household tasks such as washing clothes, standards and needs for fresh clothes increased.

Between 1970 and 1988, the female labor force increased from 30.5 million to 51.7 million women, representing 45% of the total labor force in the United States for 1988 (U.S. Bureau of the Census, 1985b, 1990aa). There also have been significant increases in the number of women employed in traditional male occupations (see Table 2.4).

Table 2.4: Select Occupations of Women in Work-Experienced Labor Force

Occupation	1970	1988
Administrators and Managers	18%	39%
Accountants and Auditors	25	50
Architects	4	15
Engineers	2	7
Lawyers and Judges	5	20
Mathematicians and Computer Scientists	17	33
Physicians	10	20
Elementary School Teachers	84	85
Computer Equipment Operators	42	66
Mechanics and Repairers	2	3
Construction Workers	2	2
Machine Operators	40	41
Motor Vehicle Operators	5	11

Source: U.S. Bureau of the Census, 1990aa, No. 645, "Employed Civilians, by Occupation, Sex, Race, and Hispanic Origin: 1988" in *Statistical Abstract of the United States, 1990,* 110th ed., pp. 389–390. Washington, D.C.: U.S. Government Printing Office.

Another phenomenon has been the increased number of women working in the print and broadcast media. By 1982, 97% of all local television newsrooms had at least one woman on their staff compared to only 57% in 1972. Although this higher visibility should help to eliminate gender stereotypes, it is readily apparent that inequities still exist. While more than one third of all news anchors were women, fewer than 10% were in positions of authority in the newsrooms (Schultz-Brooks, 1984).

Flextime is another workplace innovation that allows women as well as men to integrate their worlds of work and family. The flextime concept assumes a daily "core period" of time during which all employees must be at work. It allows wide variance in arrival and departure times as long as each worker fulfills a certain weekly total. This arrangement could allow for better melding of parents' and young childrens' schedules. Interestingly, flextime when used by men has been found to increase leisure time while for women it seems to extend time for family chores. A permanent part-time work week with full employee benefits such as medical and disability insurance, sick leave, and paid vacation is another option. A compressed work week of either four 10–hour days or three 12–hour days is still another option that would greatly enhance job opportunities (Pogrebin, 1983).

Gender-role identification appears to affect women's career achievement levels. In investigating the relationship between gender-role identification and career achievement, feminine women were found to have the lowest level of career achievement while women who subscribed to a masculine gender role had the highest level of career achievement (Wong, Kettlewell, &

Table 2.5: **Feminist Attitudes of Husbands**

Attitudes of Husbands	Employed Full-Time	Employed Part-Time	Keeps House, Employed Before	Keeps House, Never Employed
Vote for woman president	82%	88%	80%	73%
Allow wife to work	81	75	63	52
Women stay home, men run country	25	27	38	50
Men better suited for politics	38	39	43	44
Favor ERA	76	72	62	66
Working mother can be warm parent	57	43	27	21
Wife should help husband's career	36	38	67	72
Preschooler will suffer if mother works	59	72	86	82
Wife should take care of home	58	65	82	83
Allow wife to work, if jobs in limited supply	50	35	31	21
Wife may refuse to have children for husband	83	78	63	55

From T. W. Smith, "Working Wives and Women's Rights: The Connection between the Employment Status of Wives and the Feminist Attitudes of Husbands" in *Sex Roles,* 12:503. Copyright © 1985 Plenum Publishing Corporation, New York, NY. Reprinted by permission.

Sproule, 1985). It is also known that women who choose traditional male occupations such as police officer are more likely to have conflicts related to gender demands and the occupational role (Wexler, 1985).

Men and Careers

Even though the image of the husband as breadwinner has been firmly entrenched in our culture for at least 150 years, wives contributed to the family income directly through wages and indirectly through goods and services produced for exchange value. Especially during the 19th century, when a man's wife and children were considered his property, their labor was viewed as his. Therefore, the man was recognized as the sole provider, even though between 20–50% of the family's income was provided by his wife and children. Since 1970, with the increasing percentage of married women employed outside the home, this perspective is changing (Hood, 1986). However, as recently as the mid-1970s, over one third of wives and over one half of husbands indicated that the husband should be entirely responsible for family income (Slocum & Nye, 1976). Further, when another sample of married women from a 10-state area was questioned about who provides for the family's needs, 45% of the employed wives reported "husbands mostly" as compared to 96% indicated by the nonemployed wives (Scanzoni, 1978).

The man who subscribes to the breadwinner male ideal is likely to be unenthusiastic about anything he perceives as threatening to his future employment status. Consequently, husbands of employed wives are much more supportive of feminist positions than husbands of wives who keep house and have never been employed (Smith, T. W., 1985). As can be observed in Table 2.5, if wives keep house and have never been employed, their husbands are much less willing to "allow the wife to work," prefer women to "stay home and let men run the country," and are much less willing to allow their wives to work if there is a shortage of jobs in society. These attitudes may reflect perceived threats to full employment for men. Another perspective suggests the importance of working to men. While involuntary job loss is a tragic event for anyone, studies of unemployment during the Great Depression concluded that job loss was a much greater shock to men than to women. Despite the numerous references throughout time to man's virility and his desire to produce offspring, fatherhood appears to be a secondary role for most men while the primary role is breadwinner (Pleck, 1981).

A most dramatic shift in public opinion regarding married women working outside of the home occurred between 1938–1978. A Gallup Poll conducted in 1938 found that only 21% of those polled approved of a married woman working if she could be supported by her husband, but by 1970 the percentage of approval had risen to 60%. By 1978, 72% of the American public approved of a married woman working even if her husband was capable of providing support (Yankelovich, 1981).

The Movement Toward Neotraditional Role Attitudes

Evidence suggests that we are moving toward role versatility where solutions to practical problems often involve crossing the boundaries between what appear feminine and masculine (Lenney, 1989). Some family scientists have predicted instead a pattern of "neotraditional" gender attitudes, a growing acceptance by husbands of women working outside of the home so long as it does not interfere with the husband's career or normal routines. Wives receive approval for working outside of the home but are expected to continue to handle most, if not all, of the usual domestic responsibilities (Forisha, 1978). A study of married couples examined the perceptions of the spouse's role expectations with respect to child care, housework, money management, and earning income (Hiller & Philliber, 1986). The results indicate that marriage partners did not want to give up their own traditional gender roles, even though they were willing to participate in the traditional activities of the opposite-sex spouse, such as child care and housework. The degree to which the wives and husbands agreed that various jobs should be shared were child care, 84%; money management, 69%; and housework, 38%. With regard to the husband's attitudes toward their wife's employment, 74% of husbands with employed wives liked their wives to work, while an additional 11% did not care one way or the other. However, of those husbands with nonemployed wives, only 37% would like for their wives to work, whereas an additional 37% would not like them to work (Hiller & Philliber, 1986). Despite this approval level, many working wives still feel guilty about leaving their children and have difficulties finding what they consider to be adequate day-care facilities. Further, we can see that housework is still being perceived, to a substantial degree, by both wives and husbands as being woman's work.

BOX 2.1: The Difference Between a Businessman and a Businesswoman

A BUSINESSMAN is aggressive; a BUSINESSWOMAN is pushy.

He's good on details; she's picky.

He loses his temper because he's so involved in his job; she's bitchy.

When he's depressed (or hungover), everyone tiptoes past his office; she's moody, so it must be her time of the month.

He follows through; she doesn't know when to quit.

He stands firm; she's hard.

His judgments are her prejudices.

He is a man of the world; she's been around.

He drinks because of the excessive job pressures; she's a lush.

He isn't afraid to say what he thinks; she's mouthy.

He's close-mouthed; she's secretive.

He exercises authority diligently; she's power mad.

He climbed the ladder of success; she slept her way to the top.

He's a stern taskmaster; she's hard to work for.

NOW you know—the difference between a businessman and businesswoman!

Source: Anonymous, as appeared in J. A. Doyle, *Sex and Gender: The Human Experience,* 1985, p. 223.

As we enter the 1990s, certainly one could anticipate that married women will increasingly become a larger part of the labor force, as indicated by the growing percentage who intend to combine career with marriage. Just as surely, one could predict corresponding changes in the roles of men. As long as women and men play complementary roles, one position may not be changed without movement in the other. More and more, evidence will likely emerge to document the continued movement toward a redefinition and/or a refinement of the traditional gender roles in our society.

Summary

- Traditional gender roles, from an historical perspective, have tended to reflect the woman's childbearing functions and domestic responsibilities. Major factors that contributed to traditional gender-role patterns include early American political and social history, continued reinforcement of male dominance, and the double standard of sexual morality.
- The complex process of sex differentiation begins at conception with chromosomal sex (XX—female; XY—male). Hormones affect the development of femaleness/maleness (biological sexuality) and femininity/masculinity (personality characteristics).
- The same genetic factors that apparently cause men to be physically larger and stronger on the average than women may also cause them to be more vulnerable to illness and death.
- Gender identity develops during the beginning years of life as the child learns its biologically determined sex and is treated differently by others because it is female or male. By age 3, the child ordinarily has modeled after the parent of the same sex.
- The distinction between genetic and environmental influences remains somewhat hazy. Evidence suggests that although there are some genetically determined sex differences, most are not innate but have been learned through socialization.
- While a number of socializing agents have been identified such as family, schools, peers, mass media, play activities, and organized religion, parents are by far the most significant influence in a child's life.
- Women and men who play the roles of spouse, lover, companion, and parent may experience substantial role conflict with careers. They both are expected to exhibit personal warmth and tenderness, competitiveness, strength, and other characteristics leading to success in interpersonal relationships and occupations. These conflicting demands are creating stress for American women and men with further redefinition of gender roles likely to occur.
- Many parents have come to believe that the socialization of children for traditional female and male gender roles interferes with equality and satisfying marital and parental relationships. Such parents are trying to encourage the development of more gender-role versatility.

Questions For Critical Reflection

1. In the nature-nurture controversy concerning gender-role development, which side do you believe has the most convincing arguments? For what reasons?
2. Name two current TV programs, one that illustrates more traditional gender-role stereotyping and one that illustrates more gender-role versatility. Which one is your favorite? Why?
3. Who is the most androgynous person that you know? What characteristics of this person do you most admire?
4. Parents are said to be the most significant influence on gender identity. Which of your parents do you feel has most influenced your concept of gender identity? What are some specific examples that you can recall?
5. Do you think we should attempt to eliminate all femininity and masculinity in the child's persona? What would happen in a society in which all gender identity was neutralized?

Suggested Readings

Campbell, A. (Ed.). (1989). *The opposite sex.* Topsfield, MA: Salem House. A well-documented anthology on the differences and similarities between women and men.

Francoeur, R. T. (1991). *Becoming a sexual person* (2nd ed.). New York: Macmillan. An introductory level text in the field of human sexuality.

Hafner, R. J. (1986). *Marriage and mental illness: A sex role perspective.* New York: Guilford Press. An historical review of the social psychological processes involved in marital interaction and mental illness.

Lips, H. M. (1988). *Sex and gender: An introduction.* Mountain View, CA: Mayfield. An introductory level work on sex and gender issues in American society.

Williams, J. H. (1987). *Psychology of women: Behavior in a biosocial context* (3rd ed.). New York: W. W. Norton. An excellent resource on the psychological literature concerned with sex differences and gender roles.

PART II

PERSONAL CHOICES

Since success in marriage depends upon obtaining proper balance between individualism and couple bonding, students should be able to verbalize their own needs, attitudes, and values related to life choices concerning marriage and family. To that end, self and choice are the operative words in part 2. The significance of the self as the antecedent of success in marriage is a theme interwoven with responsible choices. Variations of this theme begin in chapter 3 with early courtship patterns forming a backdrop for understanding today's modern approaches to matchmaking. Date violence, including date rape, is also discussed.

The discussion of premarital sexuality in chapter 4 spotlights background issues of sex education and related early childhood experiences in seeking to answer the question, "Will the real sex educator please stand up?" Sociological factors affecting sexual standards are also explored. The personal dynamics of sexual involvement emphasize responsible sexuality and the continuing search for self-esteem with the right to say no or not now.

Is cohabitation in America considered to be a stage in the courtship process or, as in some Scandinavian countries, a "paperless" marriage? Exploring the costs, profits, and legal issues surrounding cohabitation in chapter 5 can help to clarify the issues inherent in the answer to this question. Additionally, the alternate life-style of homosexuality focuses on relationships among lesbians and gays as well as personal and societal issues impacting their parenting decisions.

America's favorite four-letter word, love, is defined, identified, and subjected to a search for its roots in chapter 6. Such an accomplishment, however, is without claim that love can ever be fully understood. Nevertheless, exploring the developmental tasks as a prelude to love, stages in love development, and styles of loving may lead to an expanded awareness of this most elusive of all emotions upon which marriages in America are based.

Finally, the choices of either mate selection or singlehood are viewed in chapter 7 as viable options for young persons in the 1990s. Sociological and psychological factors which propel the uninvited into homogamous relationship choices are explored as are interfaith, interracial, and interethnic issues surrounding heterogamous choices. To marry or not to marry? That is the question examined in the myths and realities of singlehood which highlights those factors affecting the decision. Special concerns of those who opt for the less popular choice are explored.

Ford

WE LOVE
ALL
OUR CHILDREN
GAY AND
STRAIGHT
PARENTS AND FRIENDS
OF LESBIANS AND GAYS
HOTLINE 472-3079

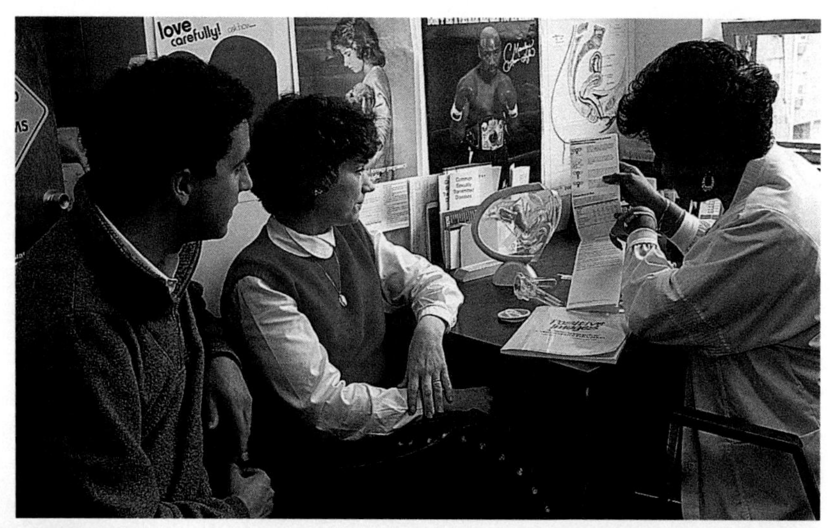
love
carefully!

CHAPTER 3

Dating

Although the search for someone to love—and ultimately to marry—takes place today in different settings from those of a century, or even a decade ago, it has not lost its urgency. . . . Now we talk about "relationships," not courtships; about boyfriends and roommates, not suitors and beaux.
Ellen Rothman, 1984

OUTLINE

The History of Dating in the United States
1. Background Factors • 2. The 1980s and 1990s • 3. Parental Influence Today • 4. Functions of Dating

The Dating Continuum
1. Casual Dating • 2. Steadily Dating • 3. Seriously Dating • 4. Engaged-to-be-Engaged

Early Dating Patterns
1. Early Adolescent Dating • 2. High School Dating

College Patterns
1. Traditional Norms • 2. Emerging Relationship Norms • 3. Interdating in Today's Society

Matchmakers: The Modern Approach
1. College Classes • 2. Friends • 3. Religious Activities • 4. Magazines and Newspapers • 5. Dating Services

Date Violence: A Growing Phenomenon
1. Changing Definitions • 2. Gender Differences • 3. Early Dating Violence • 4. College Dating Violence

Date Rape: A Special Case of Violence
1. Types of Date Rape • 2. The Gender-Role Model and Date Rape • 3. Factors in Date Rape • 4. Avoiding Date Rape

Summary

Questions for Critical Reflection

Suggested Readings

"Matchmaker, matchmaker, make me a match"—this melody, sung by the daughters of Tevye in "Fiddler on the Roof" may be familiar to young people in America today, but the message of this song is best understood by their foreign-born ancestors who commonly arranged their children's marriages (Ozick, 1988). Such practices, which placed no emphasis on romantic attachment, must certainly seem archaic to today's youth who orchestrate their own matchmaking based on romance and love. The current dating and courtship pattern in the United States evolved gradually as young people in a changing world increasingly gained autonomy and freedom from parental control (Reiss & Lee, 1988). The available data indicate a decline in dating research in the past 20 years (Murstein, 1980). However, a brief overview of historic pairing and dating customs can furnish needed insight into today's customs. Understanding dating patterns and challenges as well as the emerging concerns of date violence and date rape offers a knowledge base for healthy relationship choices.

The History of Dating in the United States

The 20th century brought forth a new social phenomenon called "dating," defined herein as a prearranged, planned social activity whose function is to meet and get acquainted with potential courtship partners. Dating is thought to have begun among college students in the United States after World War I. During the 1920s and 1930s, it became widespread on college campuses, eventually filtering down to high school and younger students during the 1940s and 1950s (Gordon, 1978).

In the beginning, dating was considered a form of recreation and only gradually assumed a direct relation to courtship or mate selection. Historically, there have been three approaches to mate selection and premarital heterosexual relationships: arranged, restricted choice, and open-choice marriages (Adams, 1986). Arranged marriages are found in those societies dedicated to fostering and strengthening kinship groups and economic benefits. For most immigrants to America, arranged marriage was a custom left behind in the old countries. In the new land of individual opportunity, rarely did parents formally determine their children's future mates. In contrast, restricted and open-choice marriages were based on individual decisions.

Restricted choice occurs in societies in which the family is considered paramount and individuals are believed to be the best possible decision makers. Prior to the 20th century, most courtship in America was by "restricted choice." Parents or older siblings chaperoned teenage social activities, and most young people lived at home until an early marriage (Rothman, 1983). It was not until the beginning of this century that premarital relations between the sexes became a "participant-run" or open-choice system (Reiss & Lee, 1988). Thus, dating eventually came to be an all pervasive aspect of premarital relationships.

Dating between members of the opposite sex was severely limited in past generations because of certain background factors. For instance, little leisure time was available for dating. When such time did occur, it was usually spent with one's own gender group or with family members. Another limiting factor was the lack of emphasis on romantic involvement and emotional commitment between persons contemplating marriage (Kett, 1977; Reiss & Lee, 1988). Thus, in a somewhat different world, the concept of an extensive courtship period was rare. But the dating game today is played quite differently. To best understand the process, one must look at the background factors that influence dating practices.

Background Factors

During the early 20th century, the American family began its gradual shift from a rural setting in which heavy emphasis was placed on the father as the authority figure to an urban society with greater emphasis on sharing between coequal spouses. Increasingly, American women entered a wider variety of occupations, received college educations, secured greater legal equality, and enjoyed more freedom in social relationships (Bell, 1983; Hareven, 1977). Changes occurring in education, including the movement to public schools and compulsory school attendance, resulted in more young people attending high school and eventually college. Such coeducational schools increased the opportunity for social interaction between young women and men.

Three other 20th century innovations uniquely influenced dating practices. Movies provided a socially approved location for unmarried persons of the opposite sex to be together in a dark environment, and the automobile transported them to unsupervised destinations. In fact, some family scientists have argued that the automobile was the one product from the Industrial

Tubing, a popular pastime, enables couples to drift into a relationship in today's less-structured dating society.

Revolution that did more to change American dating patterns than any other single phenomenon. Finally, the telephone significantly changed communication between couples, making it possible to "reach out and touch" without parental supervision (Leslie & Korman, 1989).

The 1980s and 1990s

A traditional date in which the man calls in advance to make a date, picks up the woman, returns her home at a prearranged time, and bears the expenses of the evening is rapidly disappearing (Murstein, 1980). In fact, decades of change, converging in the 1980s, ushered in new social trends in dating practices. As a result, dating today has considerably less structured female/male behavior and fewer rules to follow. Rather than having a formal date, many young people gather in groups at different "hangouts" such as their favorite hamburger, pizza, or drinking establishments. These group gatherings frequently lead to pairing when, later in the evening, individuals leave together as couples (Bell, 1983). Young couples not only have a greater number and variety of places to go on dates, but within the privacy of their own homes or apartments, a world of entertainment has unfolded in the form of prime-time television, Music Television (MTV), and video movies. Matters of manners are also changing. For example, it has become more socially acceptable for women to call men on the telephone or in some instances to initiate a date and share expenses (Korman, 1983). Although somewhat reluctant, most parents have become increasingly lenient regarding curfew hours and supervision. Colleges and universities have contributed significantly to dating freedom by permitting coed dormitories and/or extended room visitation privileges in residence halls. No longer do such officials consider themselves **in loco parentis** or the parent away from home whose duty it is to chaperon the young at organized parties and dances either on or off campus.

In spite of changing **mores** (folkways believed to be of compelling social importance by group members), some things about dating remain somewhat the same. When dating problems of university students in the 1980s were analyzed, the top five problems for women and men not only were ranked alike but were also reminiscent of earlier concerns (see Table 3.1). It appears that college students today, as always, worry about sexual pressures, where to go, communication, and money.

Table 3.1: Dating Problems of University Women and Men

Dating Problems	Women	Men
Unwanted pressure to engage in sexual behavior	23%	35%
Place to go	22	23
Communication with date	20	20
Sexual misunderstandings	13	17
Money	9	8

From D. Knox and K. Wilson, "Dating Problems of University Students" in *College Student Journal*, 17:225. Copyright © 1983 Project Innovation, Chula Vista, CA. Reprinted by permission.

Parental Influence Today

At first glance, dating in the 1990s appears to be a private matter between two people who freely select one another. However, it is suggested that this process is really role playing (Henslin, 1985a). Such expectations have been developed by others and accepted for themselves. In this process, no influence is greater than that of parents. Even if parents do not arrange their children's marriages or young men do not seek the father's permission to marry his daughter, the role of parental influence in dating and in the choice of a marriage partner should not be dismissed. In one study of university students, 60% of women and 40% of men reported that their parents had tried to influence their choices of dating partners. Further, three fourths of all students indicated that it was important to date the kind of person of whom parents would approve, with women more likely than men to express this concern (Knox & Wilson, 1981). Dating partners with a high level of involvement in their romantic relationships are more likely to perceive their family and friends as supportive (Parks, Stan, & Eggert, 1983). Young adults who are most committed to their dating relationship are more likely to inform their parents of its existence and try to influence their opinion regarding the relationship. Parents are more likely to support relationships in which their offspring are highly involved (Leslie, Huston, & Johnson, 1986). The fact that both parents engaged in higher levels of influence attempts and less support for daughters than sons may reflect fear of loss of the social roles that women are expected to play: the primary kin keepers and caretakers of the immediate and extended family.

For older students or college graduates who are living in their own apartment in a distant location from their family, dating choices tend to be less consciously influenced by parents. Certainly, persons who are divorced and again involved in dating would normally experience the least parental influence.

Parents may indirectly influence the dating patterns of their children in many ways with perhaps the most significant influence being at the subconscious level. In one study, the marital status of the parents appeared to be a significant factor. Children of divorced parents were found to date more frequently than those individuals whose parents were still married to each other (Booth, Brinkerhoff, & White, 1984). Others have investigated the relationship of parental divorce and perceived family conflict during childhood to dating experiences and social functioning of college students. Family background and conflict were associated with negative long-term social adjustment, with men not as well-adjusted as women (Slater & Calhoun, 1988). Research also suggests that poor father-daughter relationships may lead to more negative attitudes by daughters about men and about current and future dating relationships. Such daughters were more cautious about commitments to dating partners (Berger, 1988).

Functions of Dating

To understand the nature of dating, it is important to consider both the stages and specific functions of the dating continuum. From a review of pertinent studies, five functions of dating have been proposed:

1. *Recreation*—As a source of immediate enjoyment, dating is a form of recreation or entertainment.
2. *Socialization*—Dating serves as a form of learning about members of the opposite sex by providing interaction, playing of roles, and increasingly defining the self-concept.

3. *Ego Needs*—Satisfactory dating experiences may help young people in their struggle for independence and their need to be understood and to feel important.
4. *Status Placement*—By dating in a free-choice system, a person may raise their status within the peer group by sorting out prospective mates by status value.
5. *Selection of a Marriage Partner*—Dating is viewed as both a cause and effect in selecting a marriage mate (Adams, 1986, p. 181).

In one of the earliest sociological studies of dating, the distinction was made between dating as recreation and courtship as serious mate selection (Waller, 1937). It is argued that these concepts are no longer mutually exclusive and that dating appears motivated by serious as well as recreational purposes. Therefore, the dating continuum, with various identifiable stages, is suggested to be the heart of the courtship process today (Adams, 1986).

The Dating Continuum

Just as there are stages of development in individual growth that influence the timing and variations in dating, there are sequential steps in the dating process that determine the rules of the dating game (Petranek, 1981). For example, early dating experiences are likely to involve group activities, whereas older teens tend to become more exclusive and intimate. For some time now the continuum of dating has been delineated in the literature as four stages: casual dating, dating steadily, going steady/going with, and engaged-to-be-engaged (Duvall & Miller, 1985). Although the sequence of these stages has remained fairly constant over time, today's young people and their parents do not always speak the same language when communicating about the dating scene.

Casual dating may have been defined by parents in their day as "playing the field" whereby the person was dating a number of different people at the same time. Today it is called "going out with" or "seeing someone." **Steadily dating** describes the stage called "dating" today in which persons date each other frequently and decrease their dating of other persons. However, in this stage, there is no agreement to date each other exclusively. The term "seriously dating" has, to a considerable degree, replaced the term "steady dating," particularly among college-age individuals. **Seriously dating** usually means a commitment to date each other exclusively as well as an emotional commitment in the relationship.

The **engaged-to-be-engaged** status may be evidenced by a "sweetheart ring" or on some college campuses by being "dropped" whereby the man gives the woman a pendant as a symbol of their commitment to the relationship (Eshleman, 1988). Basically, this stage is often a prelude to a formal engagement. While it may involve an understanding that the individuals will eventually marry each other, there may be no public or formal declaration of this intent. In other cases, it indicates only that the couple is seriously dating and if the relationship continues, they will eventually progress to becoming engaged (see Figure 3.1).

Casual Dating

In recent years, labels such as "hanging around" and "going out" have been applied to contemporary dating patterns (Libby, 1978). These terms are intended to focus on activities with groups of women and men who may or may not be paired off when the get-together is initially arranged (Murstein, 1980). This phenomenon of less formal dating ("hanging out") often involves spur-of-the-moment activities contrary to a more formal date where one person initiates and pays for the event.

Since dating tends to enhance one's self-esteem, casual dating with a number of different partners could serve the function of promoting healthy development within the individual. However, there has been a decline in the total number of lifetime dating partners for women. The average number of different individuals dated reported by women was 54 in 1958, 25 in 1968, and 14 in 1978 (Bell & Coughey, 1980). Reasons for the decline in the number of dating partners include the following changes: dating practices making possible female/male interactions without structured dating; sexual standards, cited by those who claim to avoid dating because of sexual pressure; and family structure affecting when dating begins and its frequency (Gorney, 1982).

To partially address this last factor, the effect of single-parent family structure on dating behavior of older adolescents was investigated. Family structure was found to have no effect on the number of dating partners of adolescents in **nonintact** (a biological parent absent due to death or divorce) families. However, adolescents from these families began dating at earlier ages than those from **intact** (biological parents married to each other) families (Coleman, Ganong, & Ellis, 1985). Such data could imply that earlier dating may

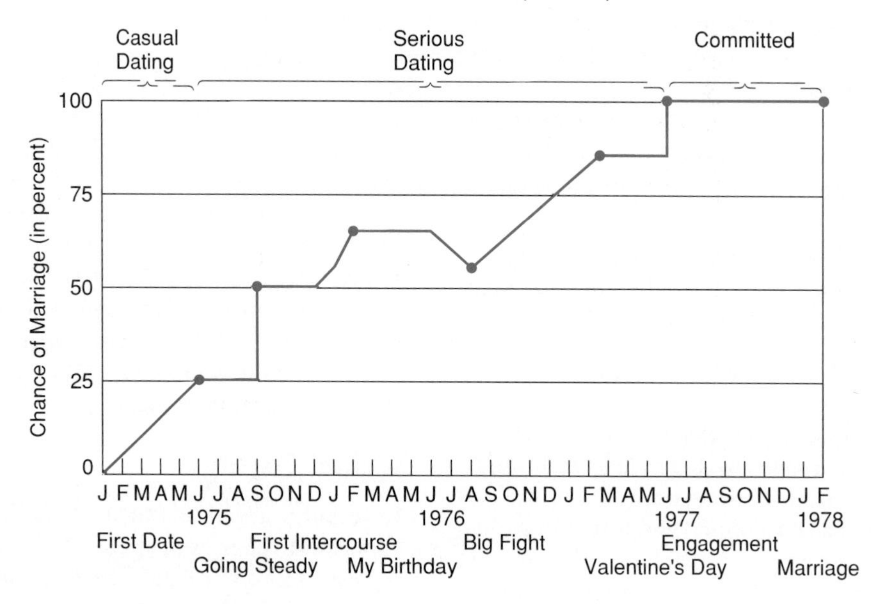

Figure 3.1 Turning Points in Relationship Development

have been used to help overcome feelings of inadequacy by adolescents living in a single-parent home. Or such parents may be so caught up in their own adjustment or financial problems resulting from singleness that they fail to exert the same influence on their teen's dating behavior as parents from an intact family.

Steadily Dating

The steadily dating stage involves dating the same person most of the time without a commitment to date each other exclusively. Having someone to "date" frequently may serve several functions for the young person. Aside from creating status in the peer group and providing a readily available date, it can serve as a source of emotional intimacy that may affect self-esteem. In a comparison of college women with and without boyfriends they dated steadily, those steadily dating reported higher self-esteem, placed a higher value on marriage, and were more sure of eventually marrying (Long, 1983). Since finding a mate and preparing for one's own family is a developmental task of this age, perhaps those in the process of achieving those tasks consequently felt better about themselves. If individuals are seeing each other on a regular basis and find that they are compatible, they will likely progress toward dating exclusivity in their relationship.

Seriously Dating

The "going steady" stage of dating, known today as seriously dating, serves to fill the void between recreational dating and engagement or marriage. As illustrated in Figure 3.1, there may be a natural progression from casual dating to serious dating, and finally, to marriage. Several factors have been identified that serve to enhance the degree of seriousness of the relationship. As a dating couple moves closer and closer to each other, their number of joint friends tends to increase. This expanded friendship network helps to stabilize the emotional closeness of the relationship (Milardo, 1982). The establishment of effective communication patterns and self-disclosure are also influential. When couples learn to communicate at all levels from exchange of daily information to the feeling levels of emotional intimacy, relationships are enhanced (Rubin, Hill, Peplau, & Dunkel-Schetter, 1980).

Another factor that can affect the progression of the relationship is perceived physical attractiveness between the partners. If the dating partners are about equal in physical attractiveness, the emotional intimacy is likely to intensify over time (White, 1980). During the early stages of dating, women and men are often insecure about their physical attractiveness, tend to rate their partners low in physical attractiveness, and feel that their partners would do likewise. At the stage of steady dating, men perceive their partners as an

Drawing by C. Barsotti; © 1988 The New Yorker Magazine, Inc.

idealized image of a woman in terms of beauty. For the women, however, the physical attractiveness of their male partner does not have to match an ideal in order for an intense dating relationship to develop (Bailey & Kelly, 1984). The influence of premarital sexual relationships on the couples' increasing emotional interdependence was measured at each of the four stages of dating. While the influence of love was found to increase with emotional interdependence, conflict was found to play a major role in predicting the occurrence of sexual intimacy in the early stages of dating (Christopher & Cate, 1988).

The percentage of high school-aged individuals who have ever gone steady (seriously dated) continued to increase between 1960 and 1984 (see Table 3.2). Among high school seniors in Connecticut, the majority who had gone steady had done so for the first time before their 15th birthdays. Further, female adolescents were more likely to be currently going steady, to have ever done so, and to be planning to marry their current steady dating partner (Gordon & Miller, 1984).

Engaged-to-be-Engaged

As a stage of dating, "engaged-to-be-engaged" is a rather ill-defined, subjective category. The percentage of individuals who classify themselves as being engaged-to-be-engaged at any given time tends to be small in comparison to the other dating stages. One study at a midwestern university found that only 13% of women labeled themselves engaged-to-be-engaged (Davidson, 1984). A later survey at the same university had similar results with 14% of women and 10% of men categorizing themselves as being engaged-to-be-engaged (Davidson & Moore, 1990). During this stage a couple discusses the prospects of marriage and usually reaches an understanding regarding a future engagement. It is anticipated that a formal engagement will occur, at which time there would be a public declaration to parents and friends, often involving the receiving and wearing of an engagement ring.

Early Dating Patterns

Dating patterns are usually established during the preteen and high school years. Most children develop a firm sense of self-identity as either female or male by age 3. This concept of femininity and masculinity or gender is a quality believed by some to be a master trait of personality (Henslin, 1985b). Certainly gender affects behavior throughout life but nowhere is this effect more apparent than in early adolescent involvement when a special interest in members of the other sex begins (Papalia, Olds & Feldman, 1989). Although sexual interaction at this stage is usually very limited, one of the facts of life is that preteens have begun a lifelong pattern of reacting differently to members of the other sex than they do to their own. While most girls and boys do not begin significant heterosexual interaction until much later, the personality foundations for such activity are established in the preteen years.

Table 3.2: **Patterns of Going Steady**

Patterns of Going Steady	Cameron and Kenkel (1960)	Poffenberger (1964)	Gordon and Miller (1984)
Currently going steady			
Women	38%	30%	58%
Men	43	27	38
Having ever gone steady			
Women	82	75	81
Men	71	58	70
Having gone steady more than 1 year			
Women	20	40	52
Men	16	28	42
Having gone steady only once			
Women	20	34	24
Men	20	34	24
Having gone steady eight or more times			
Women	6	7	4
Men	2	7	6
Planning to marry current steady			
Women	0	50	72
Men	0	40	38

From M. Gordon and R. L. Miller, "Going Steady in the 1980s: Exclusive Relationships in Six Connecticut High Schools" in *Sociology and Social Research*, 68:474.

Early Adolescent Dating

Courtship activities during early adolescence are such that the term "dating" may seem an inappropriate label. But by whatever name, evidence remains that the "pairing off" phenomenon is alive and well. During the early dating years, adolescents face awesome physical changes as well as increasing social pressures from peers and society. The personal meanings given these external influences by the individual will, to a large degree, determine their social and emotional maturity (McCabe, 1984).

The young adolescent has been learning lessons of femininity and masculinity since birth. It is only after increasing hormone levels trigger a heightened interest in sexuality that most adolescents become heterosexually oriented and emotionally involved with friends of the other sex (Henslin, 1985a). Differences in the timing of puberty affect interactions with members of the other sex. While most sixth grade girls have reached puberty, most boys have not. It is not until the seventh or eighth grade that the physically more mature girls and boys are likely to explore social relations in the form of dating (Petersen, 1987). Although dating is linked to pubertal status, there is no difference in the rates of dating for early or late maturers throughout early adolescence. In fact, when early maturers begin socializing with members of the other sex, the pattern quickly spreads throughout the entire peer group.

The beginning age of dating is increasing. While in 1958 the average age at first date was 13 years, 20 years later it had increased to 14 years (Bell & Coughey, 1980). Earlier research reported an interesting relationship between self-esteem and dating at early ages. Female students who were not dating or who dated infrequently were found to have higher self-esteem than those who were frequently dating. Further, those female students with the lowest self-esteem were more likely to have reached puberty earlier and to have dated earlier (Simmons, Blyth, Van Cleave, & Bush, 1979).

High School Dating

Although little recent research has been done on high school dating, an earlier study did identify gender differences in dating patterns. Of the male students, 15% had never dated, in comparison to only 8% of female students. These female adolescents also dated more frequently with about one third dating several times per

Early dating patterns may begin with hanging out with the gang.

week (Peters, 1980). Also, dating frequency and the influence of personal, social, and school adjustment among 10th-, 11th-, and 12th-grade students were investigated. Although no clear relationship was found between dating frequency and school adjustment, the frequent dater more often chose an academic-track curriculum and was more likely to look forward to a professional or semiprofessional career. Further, persons who were dating, in contrast to non-daters, had a greater sense of independence. Finally, the frequent dater also exhibited more peer orientation than parental orientation, which may suggest that dating contributes to the appropriate behaviors of separating from parents during adolescence (Williamson, 1977).

One reason for choosing to not date may be related to the process of asking for a date. For many, this emotionally threatening experience arouses a common fear of rejection that is generalized to a personal rejection (Harrington, 1988). An experience of this type may be one reason why, for the past two decades, American teenagers and young adults have become increasingly critical of the traditional dating system. As previously mentioned, pair dating is being replaced, to some extent, by groups of female and male adolescents getting together informally or "hanging out." Such activities often develop spontaneously with male adolescents feeling no responsibility for planning or paying for a date. The casualness and lack of explicit pairing-off in this arrangement help free both sexes of acceptance anxiety. Moreover, the emphasis is more on being together than on doing specific things. If attraction does develop between two people, they will pair off and participate in the group more as a couple, gradually withdrawing in order to have more private time together (Leslie & Korman, 1989).

Changing relationship norms were also reflected in the reasons for dating. Surprisingly, popularity or prestige, reasons previously given for dating, were not included in responses of high school students in the 1980s. Recreation was given by 49% of male and 36% of female respondents as their most important reason for dating. Socialization was reported second by 30% of female and 27% of male students. Characteristics desired in a date by both sexes, in order of mention, were cheerfulness, consideration, sense of humor, affection, good sportsmanship, well-dressed appearance, physical attractiveness, romantic qualities, and ambition (Peters, 1980). Male adolescents were more likely to list physical attractiveness as a desired characteristic of a dating partner than their female counterparts.

College Patterns

Most college students have grown up in subcultures that encourage competition, status striving, and sexual exploitation in female-male dating relationships. For some individuals, the transition to college dating has little direct effect upon their relationships with the opposite sex; while for others, substantial changes occur. This time of transition and change can be more easily accomplished by today's college students if they have the latest available knowledge. Therefore, the traditional norms associated with dating will be described before examining the relationships of the 1990s.

Traditional Norms

Turn-of-the-century norms reflected in the following 1905 rules governing female and male relationships at a normal school (teacher's college) sound archaic to people today:

> *During the afternoons and evenings of Saturdays and Sundays, students may, within proper bounds, make and receive social visits, but such visits may not extend later than 10 P.M. . . . The purpose which justifies the existence of the Normal is the preparation of young men and women to teach, not to afford opportunity to marry. Any marked indications that students are spending their time in courting, or in being courted, or in trifling about such matters, will be deemed sufficient for the prompt removal of such students from the Normal.*
>
> *(Brown, 1979, p. 12)*

On college campuses today, students encounter customs governing female/male relationships far removed from those of their ancestors. In fact, they are as different as the supersonic jet is from the horse and buggy. "Ladies, there are two things that you must never do on a date: wear a red dress or sit on a man's lap!" While such strange admonitions by the Dean of Women to college freshmen in the 1950s left a lot to the imagination, there was no doubt that they were sexual prohibitions. It is not surprising that parents and grandparents of today's college freshmen may be conflicted by coeducational dormitories with flexible curfew hours and lack of supervision by school personnel who no longer act in the role of in loco parentis. However, whether considering dating in the 1950s or the 1990s, the subject is inextricably tied to values.

Values in Dating

Many people of both sexes are consciously seeking certain values and qualities in their dating partners. By the time a person reaches college age, this process often has been fine-tuned enough that they are able to verbalize those qualities sought in dating partners and in a future spouse. Between 1976–1982, more than 1,100 University of Arizona students were asked to indicate the three most important qualities in a dating partner and the three most important qualities for a spouse (Jorgensen, 1986). The only common quality in the first four categories between date and spouse was "congenial personality" (see Table 3.3). Interestingly, physical attractiveness ranked last for spouse but first for dating partner. These findings are somewhat paradoxical as were those from an earlier study in which honesty was ranked last in a group of characteristics deemed important in a dating partner but fourth in terms of those characteristics deemed most important in a marriage mate (Hansen & Hicks, 1980). Obviously, more superficial qualities are accepted in a casual dating partner, while enduring virtues are desired in a potential wife or husband.

The most desired qualities after the college years were determined by a public opinion poll of American women at the beginning of the 1980s. Finances and social status were not deemed very important in terms of qualities most admired in a man. Instead, expressed preferences in order of importance were intelligence, sensitivity to the feelings of others, a sense of humor, gentleness, and self-control (Roper Organization, 1980).

The results of a replication study at the close of the 1980s confirmed that campus values in mate selection had not altered appreciably during the past decade (Goldberg & Hudson, 1989). Women and men still exchange different qualities and have conventional expectations for a mate. Specifically, greater importance is being placed on appearance by men and on financial and familial variables by women. The top six traits desired in a mate by both women and men were dependable character, emotional stability, mutual attraction, pleasing disposition, education/intelligence, and ambition/industriousness. Their rank order ratings were the same except for emotional stability, which women considered more important than mutual attraction. Results of a 1990 Yankelovich Clancy Shulman Poll question that changing gender roles influence those

Table 3.3: Desirable Qualities of Date and Spouse

Most Important Qualities in Date		Most Important Qualities in Spouse	
1.	Physical attractiveness	1.	Loving and affectionate
2.	Congenial personality	2.	Honest
3.	Sense of humor	3.	Congenial personality
4.	Intelligence	4.	Respectful
5.	Manners/being considerate	5.	Intelligent
6.	Sincere, genuine	6.	Mature/responsible
7.	Compatible interests	7.	Ambitious
8.	Conversational ability	8.	Loyal and trustworthy
9.	Fun to be with	9.	Physical attractiveness

qualities sought in a spouse. Essential requirements identified by these young adults were traditional feminine/masculine traits—41% for women and 72% for men, and physical attractiveness—19% for women and 41% for men ("What Youth Think," 1990).

Feminist issues emphasizing equality between women and men are also increasingly reflected in today's dating values. Using a sample of unmarried, undergraduate women at a large southeastern university, feminists and nonfeminists were compared to determine the incidence of date initiation during their college years. Feminists were more than twice as likely to be actively engaged in date-initiating behavior than nonfeminists. In addition, feminist perspectives also increase the chances of women sharing date expenses. Of the woman-initiated dates, 71% of the feminists but only 46% of the nonfeminists had shared the date expenses (Korman, 1983). Although there is evidence of change in the custom of men paying the dating expenses, 92% of the women in one survey indicated that men still paid for the date (Bowe, 1986). It is of interest that men have become even more supportive than women of role-reversals whereby women initiate and finance dates (Allgeier, 1981).

Another aspect of dating values relates to the issue of sexual involvement of singles. Evidence has already been cited that chastity is not viewed as a top priority in terms of qualities sought in dating and marriage partners. However, when investigating the effects of various levels of sexual experience on the evaluations of opposite-sex peers, it was found that most women and men, with the exception of highly experienced men, prefer partners with about the same amount of sexual experience as themselves. Specifically, highly sexually experienced women and men were perceived as less desirable partners than either sexually inexperienced or moderately experienced ones. Only highly sexually experienced women rated highly sexually experienced men more favorably (Istvan & Griffitt, 1980).

Relationships As Exchange

One way to look at interpersonal relationships, including dating, incorporates exchange theory, also called social choice theory. From this perspective, companions are sought who possess the qualities and resources necessary to provide the maximum amount of profits (pleasure) with the minimum amount of costs (displeasure) resulting from undesirable traits (Nye, 1988). These more or less explicit bargaining elements existing in dating relationships are more likely among those who subscribe to traditional sexual scripts. The young woman and man "trade" qualities and resources, as each seeks the best bargain or at least makes sure she or he does not feel "cheated." Men often bargain for sexual involvement, seeking to engage women in some type of sexual activity in exchange for their investments. According to these male concepts of exchange, the more time, money, and effort that have been invested in the dating process, the more sexual favors the man feels entitled to expect in return (Nye, 1979). Since traditional norms de-emphasized the sexual interests and needs of women, sexual activity was supposedly a bargaining commodity to be offered by women in exchange for other desired goals. Women, in this traditional context, were typically viewed as being interested in status to be obtained by dating only the most desirable men in order to marry as well as possible. This complex process, involving many choices and exchanges by both women and men, is obviously being reshaped by today's more egalitarian relationships (Korman, 1983).

It is postulated that some dating relationships, particularly first dates, are still far from egalitarian and are in fact based on the exchange system: "paying out" versus "putting out" (Pike & Hall, 1985). However, the women's movement and economic inflation have both affected dating norms as evidenced in these two comments:

> **Hers:** "I resent being expected to go to bed with my date especially after somewhere like Hardee's, and always feel like kissing him even when I don't."

His: "I hate having to blow my entire paycheck on my date just because girls think we can't have fun by doing something that doesn't cost a whole lot of money" (Pike & Hall, 1985, pp. 226–227).

One could speculate that the more recent substitution of group activities for traditional dating may have evolved as an avoidance of sexual obligations by women for payment of dates.

It should be emphasized that sex and status are not the only aspects of exchange related to relationships. Exchanges also involve the emotional and/or personality characteristics of the individual, one of which is self-disclosure. A study of self-disclosure conducted among Boston area college students who were dating each other exclusively found both sexes about equal in self-disclosure on such matters as general outlook on life, interests, tastes, and previous dating relationships. However, women were more likely than men to reveal information about things of which they were most afraid or ashamed (Rubin, Hill, Peplau, & Dunkel-Schetter, 1980).

More recently, it was hypothesized that satisfaction in dating relationships is associated not with strict reciprocity in personal exchanges but with the relative amount of disclosure exchanged between partners (Millar & Millar, 1988). Sex differences in perceptions of disclosure by self and others were examined. Men were less satisfied with interactions when they perceived themselves as disclosing more personal information while the reverse was true for women. When investigating variables that differentiated continuing and terminating dating couples, self-disclosure was found to be important to relationship satisfaction as were commitment, investment, self-esteem, and love attitudes (Hendrick, Hendrick, & Adler, 1988). Empathy, which includes understanding and sensitivity to feelings, is another emotional variable that appears to be positively correlated with satisfaction with one's dating partner (Mueller & Fiebert, 1988).

Another influence in exchanges relates to the **principle of least interest,** a term coined by the pioneer family scientists, Waller & Hill (1951) to indicate that one partner is more interested in continuing the dating relationship than the other one. This lack of balance may develop either from unequal status that results in uneven bargaining power of the partners or from unequal emotional involvement. Such unequal status may be based on social class, age difference, or any aspect of the relationship that leaves one partner more vulnerable than the other. Regardless of the cause, the stage is set for exploitation (use of someone for selfish ends). Exploitation itself is not gender specific in that both women and men exploit their partners. It has been theorized, however, that when men exploit, it tends to be for sexual reasons while for women it is more likely for status and economic advantages (Landis & Landis, 1977). Imbalance in a relationship often leads not only to exploitation but also to disillusionment and ultimately, to the end of the relationship. In one study, 54% of couples in which one member reported unequal relationship involvement had broken up, in comparison to only 23% of couples in which both members were equally involved (Hill, Rubin, & Peplau, 1976).

Emerging Relationship Norms

As indicated earlier, spontaneous, informal "hanging out" in heterosexual groups appears to be increasing at the college level as the trend continues toward a rejection of arranged dates for initial social encounters (Murstein, 1980). But because college students have both biological and societal pressures that propel them toward greater and more exclusive intimacy, pairing off as a couple is usually inevitable. Yet, few studies have focused specifically on the changes in this process in the past two decades. Identifying the combination of factors contributing to dating satisfaction is an important dimension in understanding the role of dating in the courtship process.

Changing Dating Patterns

A classic study of the 1960s, which identified dating patterns of Harvard University men, offers a baseline for interpreting changing patterns over the past four decades. Four distinct dating patterns emerged: companionship, instrumental, traditional, and intellectual (Vreeland, 1972). In the companionship pattern, a need to have a sympathetic listener as a friend was predominant. In these relationships, formal recreational activities were de-emphasized in favor of private and intimate dating activities. Usually, sexual involvement was present, but it appeared to be subordinate to searching for individual and paired identities. The instrumental pattern was evidenced by men seeking sexual conquests that would enhance their peer status. Dress and manners were emphasized along with taking their dates to popular places, sports events, and dances. The traditional dating pattern was most in line with the values that have previously been reported as desirable in dating partners. These men consciously sought wives to "take home to mother" who were of equal status,

religious, sexually conservative, and of good reputation. The intellectual pattern found among the very intelligent but socially inexperienced men emphasized the intellectual qualities of the woman and her ability to share ideas and questions (Vreeland, 1972).

In a later survey from the Harvard classes of the early 1970s, all four identified dating patterns were found, but significant changes had occurred. The greater variety of dating activities reported by those in the companionship group included concerts, sports events, and parties. However, the need for a sympathetic listener remained a priority. The instrumental pattern had changed the most; the formerly desired qualities of an effervescent personality, well-dressed appearance, and sexual attractiveness gave way to an interest in political activities, drug use, and making love. Preoccupation with sexual activity was still apparent, but the emphasis was on recreational sex. The traditional dating pattern had also been transformed; although some men were still looking for wives, the very traits sought in women earlier were devalued. Now women who were liberated and unconventional were highly desirable. The intellectual pattern of the 1960s remained relatively unchanged (Vreeland, 1972).

Research in the 1980s focused less on patterns and more on dating activities. A study of dating at a southeastern university showed considerable changes from a generation ago. A typical date was to go out to eat, attend a sports event, attend a party, and then go back to her or his dormitory room. The most frequent topics of conversation were "our relationship," school, and friends (Knox & Wilson, 1981).

When dating satisfaction was studied, a combination of factors were found to be important: confidence that one had found a future marital partner; more frequent, involved, and positive dating experiences; parental and peer support and approval; and absence of peer pressure. Predicting satisfaction for men were desirability as a date, access to a car, greater income, and attractive physical appearance. Dating satisfaction for women was linked to the social prestige and athletic ability of their dates (Riffer & Chin, 1988).

Changing Sexual Norms

Major changes occurring in sexual norms for dating relationships over the past three decades can be chronicled from university student data. Both women and men have become more liberal regarding acceptable degrees of sexual involvement in casual dating although women are still more conservative. Light to moderate petting has become much more acceptable during casual dating over the last three decades (Sprecher, McKinney, Walsh, & Anderson, 1988). In general, men expect sexual intimacy sooner in a relationship than women do. Using number of dates with partner as a measure of appropriateness for various sexual behaviors, five times (19%) as many men as women (4%) felt petting was appropriate on the first date. However, almost two thirds of women and one fifth of men thought that petting was appropriate only after six or more dates in this college sample (Knox & Wilson, 1981).

The use of alcohol and marijuana also play a role in achieving various degrees of sexual intimacy. In one study of graduate students, two thirds believed that marijuana functioned as an aphrodisiac (a substance that increases the level of sexual desire) and consequently increased their willingness to engage in sexual activity (Dawley, Winstead, Baxter, & Gay, 1979). However, the known fact is that marijuana is more likely to lower inhibitions rather than increase physical sexual desires. At the beginning of the 1980s, over one half of the students indicated in one survey that they had drunk alcohol on their last date, while 25% of men and 20% of women had used marijuana on their last date (Knox & Wilson, 1981). By the end of the 1980s, the growing movement toward substance abuse and addiction became a focus for campus reaction.

Over time, the campus sexual norms for steady daters have also become significantly more liberal, especially for women. When a more intense relationship involving affectionate feelings exists, women and men are likely to engage in more intimate sexual involvement including oral-genital sex and sexual intercourse. Of the women surveyed in a 1963 study, three fourths reported being virgins while in a 1978 replication study, only one third of the women surveyed were virgins (Sherwin & Corbett, 1985). As we moved toward the 1990s, a large-scale survey of college women in 1989 found that only 17% of seniors were still virgins (Davidson & Moore, 1990).

These changes reflect the impact of the sexual revolution. Although men have changed their sexual behavior very little in the latter half of the century, women have gone from virginity before marriage and monogamy afterward to a pattern resembling that of men (Ehrenreich, Hess, & Jacobs, 1986). The fact that sexual intercourse by single men has always been implicitly if not explicitly approved probably explains why the changes have been greater for women than men. Today the more commitment in the relationship, the more likely that the woman will participate in sexual intercourse. This perception of commitment seems to have become for many women the critical point replacing the exchange of marriage vows. The issue of changing sexual standards will be addressed in detail in chapter 4, "Premarital Sexuality."

Interdating in Today's Society

As the changing world increasingly becomes a "global village," it presents greater opportunities for interdating, whether interfaith, international, interethnic, or interracial. College campuses especially offer opportunities to choose dating partners from other religious, nationality, racial, or ethnic groups with varying rituals, customs, and languages. Ethnicity functions to transmit the native tongue, which is the instrument that preserves the fundamental beliefs and folkways of a group. As such, it is a powerful tool to maintain family bonds and therefore is not easily changed (Wilkinson, 1987). Although mixed relationships are not inherently good or bad, they are different. It must be recognized that should the relationship lead to marriage, the couple will face tougher challenges than those typically encountered by persons of similar backgrounds. Interfaith and interracial dating are usually the two most controversial forms of interdating.

Interfaith Dating

The old taboos against dating persons from another religious faith are breaking down gradually. Since dating often leads to marriage, virtually all representatives of organized religion have discouraged interfaith dating in the past because they are opposed to interfaith marriages. There are no accurate statistics on the proportion of people who have dated outside of their religious faith. In a *Seventeen* magazine survey on interfaith dating and religion, 97% of the teenagers reported that religion played no part in determining who they dated. Furthermore, three fourths indicated that they would not object to marrying someone of a different religious background (Kaplan, 1981). In most denominations, interfaith dating and marriage are no longer forbidden, and members of the clergy are willing to counsel with young people contemplating interfaith marriages. Jewish leaders maintain the most opposition, yet an increasing number of Reform rabbis will officiate at interfaith marriages. One estimate suggests that approximately one of every four Jews and one of every two Catholics and Protestants ultimately marry a person from another religious faith (Kaplan, 1981).

The religious devoutness of the individual, which is probably related to family religiousness, and the dissimilarity of religion are both important variables in the likelihood of interfaith dating (Marciano, 1987). People who are deeply involved in their denominational activities are more likely to regard interfaith dating as wrong or unwise since they are more likely to honor the official rules of their faith. However, many devout persons today are devoted to ecumenical ideals promoting worldwide religious unity. Such persons are more likely to accept interfaith dating as a means of bridging religious differences as long as there is a clear understanding that marriage cannot become an option. Further, many young people today consider religious rituals as less important than underlying moral values and principles (Kaplan, 1981).

For growing numbers of young people, interfaith dating is looked upon more as an opportunity for growth than as a problem. Jewish, Catholic, and Protestant young people, including those from many different denominations, consciously seek to learn and appreciate each other's traditions, beliefs, and outlooks. The rationale is that such contacts will broaden their awareness of the world and provide new insights into their own faith regardless of whom they ultimately marry. Just as placing restrictions on interfaith dating has been largely responsible for continuing religious prejudice, promoting interfaith dating offers the potential to decrease such prejudice in our society (Foderaro, 1984).

A substantial proportion of the dating among college students takes place away from the scrutiny of their parents and thus occurs in a generally more liberal atmosphere. In addition, many young people decrease their active involvement in organized religion while attending college. As a consequence, many young people involved in interfaith dating may never have to confront disapproval of parents and religious officials. If the dating relationship should become serious, these issues must eventually be faced. The topic of interfaith marriage will be considered in chapter 7, "Mate Selection."

Interracial Dating

Members of any race, whether black, white, or Oriental, who date someone outside of their group are involved in interracial dating. Generally, there is a lack of information about all but the black-white dating issue. One exception is a study of Hawaiian college students who were Caucasian, Chinese, Filipino, Japanese, and Hawaiian/part Hawaiian. Women were found to date within their own racial/ethnic group more frequently than men and were more likely to report stronger support from significant others for within-group dating. Female Caucasian and Japanese students more frequently dated within their own group. In general, Japanese male students were more likely to date within their own group in comparison to all other men (Johnson & Ogasawara, 1988).

Taboos against interracial dating have diminished significantly since the 1967 United States Supreme Court decision that held state laws prohibiting racially mixed marriages to be unconstitutional. Today, public opinion polls show that whites are less fearful and rejecting of marriage to a black person. Though not completely free of bigotry, young whites are now more likely to see blacks as their equals than are their parents. But with new levels of black pride, many blacks have developed strong political objections to interracial dating and marriage between blacks and whites. At the same time, more opportunities for social interaction between blacks and whites have emerged in public schools, colleges and universities, employment, and social organizations. In addition, the women's liberation movement has encouraged women and men to be freer in making their own decisions and choices regarding their dating preferences (Poussaint, 1983).

While interracial dating has become more apparent on college campuses, negative attitudes still remain toward the practice. Blacks who enter dating relationships with whites are considered by supporters of black power to be "consorting with the enemy," thus betraying the black cause. Black college women have a special resentment of black college men who date white women because proportionately fewer black men than women attend college, thus limiting their perceived pool of eligibles (Anson, 1981). Consequently, interracial dating couples are likely to experience some form of harassment or resistance in both black and white communities. The harassment can range from curious looks to violence. According to interracial couples, the "stare" is the most difficult reaction to which they must learn to adjust (Spaights & Dixon, 1984). Despite these circumstances, a growing number of young people are willing to try interracial dating.

Few studies of interracial dating among either high school or college students have been reported in recent years. One reason may be that interracial dating is still a limited practice, making it difficult to identify and gain access to potential respondents. One early study, conducted at a desegregated high school of some 3,000 students, found that white male students did not date black female students and black female students were pressured not to date white male students. Those black female students who were planning to attend college generally faced strong parental disapproval of interracial dating. They viewed white male students as being primarily interested in black female students for sexual reasons. Dating did occur between black male and white female students although it met with widespread disapproval. White female students who dated black male students were harassed, rebuffed, and regarded as immoral while black male students were verbally attacked by other blacks for lack of racial pride and for "thinking they were white." Black female students also resented the fact that white female students had access to both races (Petroni, 1974).

Some interdating is not across racial lines but ethnic ones. While a race is defined by physical inborn characteristics, ethnic identity derives from the racial, religious, or national collectivity of families of orientation. An **ethnic group** is a minority segment of society whose shared identity is based on a common ancestry and a common culture such as Irish or Italian. The group boundaries that are implied may impact dating choices (Elkin & Handel, 1989). There is little information on interethnic dating other than that which is also interracial. In one study concerned with interethnic college dating, two thirds of the respondents had also engaged in interracial dating. Of those who did date interracially, 20% reported only one such date, whereas another 50% indicated they had interracially dated several times (Lampe, 1981). Persons whose friends had engaged in interracial dating were much more likely to do so themselves. Further, men were more likely to engage in interracial dating than women irrespective of their ethnic status: Anglo (Caucasians of non-Hispanic origins), black, or Mexican-American (Lampe, 1981).

In an attempt to replicate a 1984 study, college students were asked to construct self-advertisements for dates. Ethnicity was conspicuous by its absence as a desired dating quality in the later study (LaBeff, Hensley, Cook, & Haines, 1989). This fact supports the contention that interethnic dating is becoming more commonplace and accepted among college students. From the foregoing evidence, the fact is clear that interracial dating has also become more commonplace in recent years. The practice is evidently sufficiently rewarding to some young women and men for them to withstand the social pressures that still prevail. When individuals reach their college and adult years, they become somewhat more independent and less vulnerable to external pressures.

Matchmakers: The Modern Approach

Looking for a dating partner today differs considerably from even a generation ago. As the single population has grown larger, older, more educated, and more sophisticated, dating partners are being sought in a variety of ways. Along with the more traditional ways of meeting a dating partner, many creative and innovative approaches have emerged: how-to workshops promoting "50 Ways to Meet Your Lover," singles nights at museums and supermarkets, personal newspaper advertisements, computer dating services, and video dating advertisements (Kantrowitz, Witherspoon, Williams, & King, 1986). However, probably the most productive approaches to meeting future dating partners are still through college classes, friends, and religious activities.

College Classes

The college admissions office has long been considered a matchmaker although just how often a class serves as the actual source of a dating partner is unclear. In one study, only about 1 in 14 women and men listed the classroom as a source for meeting dating partners (Knox & Wilson, 1981). Perhaps the college classroom was never the "pick-up spot" it was assumed to be or mass lecture classes may serve to create anonymity and thus less social interaction between students.

Friends

In the earlier cited study, friends (33%) were mentioned most often as sources of dates by women. While one third of men also listed friends, their most prevalent source was "other" (41%). As an indicator of the changing times, many women and men reported meeting their dates through parties (Knox & Wilson, 1981). An excellent way to meet dating partners is through friends because they can act as natural screeners for those who clarify in advance specific preferences such as height, personality characteristics, and smoking habits (Masello, 1982). Having friends who play matchmakers may strain the friendship, however. In order to avoid such stress, a wise friend makes it clear that the introduction does not include responsibility for the outcome of the dating relationship (Fein, 1984).

Religious Activities

If a person feels strongly about dating within her or his own religious faith, organized social activities through the local church or synagogue can serve as a source of dates. However, since religious participation declines during the college years, the number of eligible partners may be rather small. To combat this problem, Jewish synagogues have begun organized attempts to create social activities that will reportedly serve as meeting places for Jewish **Yuppies** (slang term for young upwardly mobile professionals). Their intent is to promote dating relationships and future marriages within the Jewish faith (Schneider, 1985).

Magazines and Newspapers

Even if dating has diminished on campus, it still thrives off campus in the noncollege or postcollege crowd. These young adults are more likely to use less traditional methods when connecting with partners (Murstein, 1980).

The use of advertisements in magazines and newspapers has existed in the United States for well over 130 years, including those advertising the settling of the West, the California gold rush, and the movement to Alaska. More recently, personal ads have become matchmakers. Typically, a person places an advertisement in the personals column of a newspaper and then waits for the responses to be sent to the newspaper publisher who, in turn, forwards them to the advertiser. In magazines, the customary practice is to pay a fee to the magazine in order to get the addresses and/or phone numbers of the persons placing the ads (Jedlicka, 1980).

Several researchers have conducted content analyses of advertisements that are seeking dating partners. One investigation determined that the exchange/bargaining system was very much in evidence. For example, each individual was willing to make an offer for something in return. More specifically, women were likely to offer attractiveness while seeking financial security with partners who were older than themselves. In contrast, men were more likely to be seeking attractive partners who were younger than themselves and to be offering financial security (Harrison & Saeed, 1977). Personal ads in singles newspapers have been characterized as a "heterosexual stock market," where the advertisers are trying to maximize their profits in exchange for their personal assets (Cameron, Oskamp, & Sparks, 1977).

Self-advertisements placed in the magazine *Living Single* illustrate some interesting gender differences. The traditional social exchange concept of dating was apparent for men but not for women. Men were seeking attractiveness and expressive personality traits in exchange for their own career status and attractiveness. On the other hand, women were interested in exchanging their own career, education, attractiveness, and expressive personality qualities for attractiveness and expressive personality qualities of the man rather than for his occupational and social status. Of the men, 40% required that the person responding to their advertisement submit a photograph in comparison to only 15% of the women advertisers (Bolig, Stein, & McKenry, 1984). Five years later, many of the same general patterns were still found. Respondents were, however, less traditional in their outlook with concerns regarding careers, family ethnicity, and religion being virtually absent from the advertisements. The traditional patterns of men exchanging social status for the expressive qualities of women also no longer existed (LaBeff, Hensley, Cook, & Haines, 1989).

Dating Services

Formal dating services operate either through computer-based searches using questionnaires or videotape cassettes. Most computer dating agencies advertise in women's and men's specialty magazines, newspapers, and by direct mail. The interested client fills out a questionnaire, which is then submitted along with a processing fee. Most data sheets seek personal information about appearance, race, age, hair color, eye color, physical measurements, religious preference, marital history, hobbies, income, and occupation. A limitation of the questionnaire is that, in most instances, only a specified number of predetermined answer categories exist for each question. Using these computer data, "matches" are made based on the participant's information including partner preferences (Jedlicka, 1981). Despite the application of modern computer technology to the selection of a dating partner, it is still a very difficult task to predict the success of future relationships. Just examining different background characteristics does not guarantee insight into the many unique qualities each person brings to a relationship. But computer dating services do provide an intriguing way of at least getting dating partners together for a first date.

The high-technology video approach to the selection of a dating partner involves the use of videotapes that have been made by the person seeking a dating partner. The videotape format usually includes an interview and a casual conversation (Kellogg, 1982). The cost of making the videotape is included in the membership fee for the dating service (Shostak, 1987). After the videotape is filed along with an autobiography and photograph, participants view the videotape and if interested arrange to meet a selected person (Jedlicka, 1980). The goal of using the video dating service is to appeal to one special person rather than expanding the pool of dating potentials. Since clients carefully compose a biographical sketch and select pictures of themselves, they are usually satisfied with the presentation of their own self-image but not always with those who select them. The most attractive feature of video dating is apparently the opportunity to prescreen dates. In video dating, the most frequently mentioned characteristics of ideal mates in rank order by women are humorous, successful, attractive, intelligent, and tall; and by men, attractive, intelligent, young, humorous, and tall (Woll & Young, 1989).

Video matchmakers are a nontraditional way to play the dating game.

Date Violence: A Growing Phenomenon

In recent years, considerable attention has been devoted to a tragic by-product of courtship: date violence. The variables of love, sexual intimacy, conflict, and violence seem to be closely interrelated. Violence, in fact, is more likely to occur as the couple becomes more seriously involved (Laner & Thompson, 1982). But what is known about factors that precipitate date violence? Acts of violence are most often precipitated by one or more of the following factors: personal stress, anger, jealousy, insults, deceit, disagreements, misunderstandings, teasing, childhood sexual abuse, loss of interest in the relationship, affairs, alcohol, or drugs (Laner, 1983). There appears to be no significant association between any of the types of abuse and race (Rouse, 1988). Major categories of violence among college students are pushing, slapping, and hitting with fist or object (Rouse, Breen, & Howell, 1988). In one survey, more than one third of men and one fifth of women indicated being either pushed, grabbed, or shoved at least once during their dating relationship. The most often reported locations for personal violence were residence, including home, residence hall, or apartment—51%, vehicles—22%, and out-of-doors—22% (Makepeace, 1981).

Studies in the early and mid-1980s agree that the incidence of date violence is increasing. Two studies, four years apart, found that almost two thirds of the college students had personal knowledge of someone who had been involved in courtship violence and one fifth had experienced at least one direct act of violence themselves (Bogal-Allbritten & Allbritten, 1985; Makepeace, 1981). These same two studies found that of those individuals who had been either aggressors or victims of violence, acts of violence had occurred on more than one occasion for one half of these women and men. When queried about the impact of the violence on their dating relationship, one half to two thirds indicated that the relationship had ended, and almost one fifth to one fourth had maintained the same degree of commitment to the relationship (Bogal-Allbritten & Allbritten, 1985; Makepeace, 1981). A more recent study corroborated that violence was not likely to lead to termination of the courtship relationship (Chin, Snyder, Forrestal, & McClure, 1988). Paradoxically, many violent dating relationships may eventually culminate in marriage between the partners. Following courtship violence, 29% of the subjects in one study reported becoming more deeply involved in the relationship (Makepeace, 1981). Since dating violence may have far-reaching implications for relationships of dating and marriage, it is important to understand changing definitions, gender differences, and general factors in dating aggression.

Changing Definitions

One of the unanswered questions relates to whether there has been an actual increase in dating violence in recent years or whether individuals have become more willing to report and discuss its existence. One plausible explanation is that events or actions that were formerly individually defined as nonviolent have come to be defined as acts of violence by today's standards. In other words, changing definitions of gender roles have resulted in former types of behaviors no longer being considered socially acceptable in a dating relationship. In addition, evidence is emerging that makes it possible to label some courtships as violent relationships (Chin et al., 1988). Earlier, in over two thirds of the cases where dating abuse had occurred, each dating partner had been both the victim and perpetrator of violent behavior at some point in the relationship. In only 1 in 10 cases was the male partner the sole abuser, while the female partner was the sole abuser in 1 in 5 of the dating relationships (Cate, Henton, Koval, Christopher, & Lloyd, 1982).

Gender Differences

Gender differences are reflected in the initiation of date violence. College men who have experienced violence themselves as children, as opposed to just witnessing violence between parents, are more likely to initiate dating violence in later life (Pirog-Good & Stets, 1986). In fact, the witnessing of parental fighting by college men while growing up actually decreases the odds that they will be hit by a dating partner. For women, the observance of violence between parents increases their likelihood of committing date violence (DeMaris, 1990). However, college women who have experienced violence themselves during childhood are less likely to initiate violence in dating relationships. Men are also more likely than women to view aggressive actions as nonviolent (Pirog-Good & Stets, 1986). Romanticizing relationships and traditional gender roles are related to dating violence among college students (Follingstad, Rutledge, Polek, & McNeil-Hawkins, 1988). Using the BEM Sex Role Inventory as a basis for measurement, more traditional, masculine men were more likely to report having abused their dating partners than those less clearly gender-role typed (Bernard, Bernard, & Bernard, 1985). Life events such as roommate problems, changes in personal habits, positive and negative changes in family relationships, or some major moral dilemma can be viewed as stressful circumstances in the lives of college students. Involvement in courtship violence has been found to be associated with the rate of such undesirable, nonhealth life event changes in men but not in women (Makepeace, 1983).

Early Dating Violence

Although the types of violence used in college are more severe, the pattern of date violence may begin in the early dating years of high school (Olday & Wesley, 1988). In a study of female high school students, 24% indicated that they had been victims of dating violence on one occasion and 15% on several occasions (Burcky, Reuterman, & Kopsky, 1988). Other high school-level abuse recipients interpreted dating violence as acts of anger (47%), confusion (47%), love (35%), and sadness (12%). Perhaps of greater concern is that when asked about the effects of violence on the couple relationship, 23% reported that it had led to an improvement in the relationship and 35% indicated the dating violence caused no significant change (Roscoe & Callahan, 1985).

Table 3.4: Violence in Heterosexual Relationships

Act	Abuser		Abusee	
	Women	Men	Women	Men
Slapped	34%	17%	20%	39%
Pushed, shoved	29	42	42	38
Threw something	27	18	20	31
Hit (or tried) with object	19	12	16	24
Kicked, hit, bit	18	9	13	28
Beat up	1	3	4	4
Threatened with knife/gun	1	2	3	3
Used knife/gun	1	1	1	0

From C. K. Sigelman, et al., "Violence in College Students' Dating Relationships" in *Journal of Applied Social Psychology,* 14:536. Copyright © 1984 V. H. Winston & Sons, Inc., Silver Spring, MD.

College Dating Violence

Research evidence indicates that dating violence has become a universal problem on college campuses regardless of racial or ethnic background (Kiernan & Taylor, 1990). A study of heterosexual violence among college students found that over one half of women and men had committed at least one physically abusive act toward their relationship partner. Most respondents who reported experience with violence had both committed and received dating violence (see Table 3.4). Women and men who abused their dating partners were more likely to have been abused as children. Such women were more likely to be rated low in socially desirable qualities while men had more traditional attitudes toward women (Sigelman, Berry, & Wiles, 1984).

Although it is a myth that substance abuse causes courtship violence, the use of alcohol is a significant variable in dating violence (Billingham & Henningson, 1988; Bogal-Allbritten & Allbritten, 1985). Of the abuse victims in one study, one third reported drinking before their violence experience, whereas one half of the abuse victims indicated that the perpetrator of the violence had been drinking (Makepeace, 1981). Use of drugs other than alcohol also has been reported to be associated with dating violence (Brodbelt, 1983).

Female and male college students involved with physical violence in their dating relationships are likely to report a significant amount of partner dominance and possessiveness (Rouse, Breen, & Howell, 1988). In one study, two thirds of such women and men reported that their dating partner monitored their time, while one half of women and two thirds of men indicated that their dating partner discouraged opposite-sex friends. In general, more women than men were perceived by their dating partners as being dominant and possessive, but there were no significant differences by gender on their physical violence scores. Although the level of dominance and possessiveness was found to increase as the level of sexual intimacy progressed from heavy petting to sexual intercourse, no relationship was found between physical violence and the degree of sexual intimacy (Breen & Rouse, 1986).

Finally, a substantial percentage of college women and men feel equally responsible for violent behavior that occurs in dating relationships. A survey of dating violence among college students in the Northeast found 42% of women and 48% of men perceived that they themselves were responsible for the violent behavior. Perhaps most revealing is the finding that violence in the dating relationship is often interpreted as love by both the abuser and the abused, and dating violence is not perceived as particularly unusual or necessarily unacceptable behavior (Matthews, 1984). These findings suggest that attitudes toward dating violence may be a product of circumstance. In other words, a person in a society that not only condones but promotes violence may come to view dating violence as socially acceptable. When young children are hit by parents who supposedly love them, when media and sports are saturated with acts of violence applauded by adults, is it any wonder that such socially learned behavior is much in evidence among America's youth today?

Date Rape: A Special Case of Violence

Evidence suggests that date rape and courtship violence in general are part of the normative structure of dating relationships in the United States (Scritchfield & Masker, 1989). A four-step continuum of sexual pressure has been found to exist among college dating couples: persistent physical attempts, positive statements, threats of force, and use of force (Christopher, 1988). Sexually experienced respondents are likely to be pressured into kissing and some form of fondling while casually dating and masturbation, oral-genital contact, and/or sexual intercourse while seriously dating.

By the mid-1980s, over one half of college men surveyed admitted to one or more forced sexual acts on a date (Murnen, Perot, Byrne, 1989). Further, by 1985, 57% of women in one sample described at least one sexual experience that was classified as date rape (Koss, 1985). While sexual coercion is a component of some dating relationships, it is not characteristic of most dating relationships involving sexual interaction. When disagreements arise over desired level of sexual involvement, most men do not use coercion to "convince" their date to engage in the desired sexual activity. Among sorority members at a large midwestern university, 40% had experienced unwanted sexual intercourse, while in college, due to physical threats or force by a dating partner. However, 68% of these women reported having had unwanted sexual intercourse due to "continual arguments and pressure" (Copenhaver, 1990). Thus, only men who misread or ignore the avoidance strategies of their female dating partners initiate unwanted sexual advances. Women who date men frequently may possess more effective strategies for stopping unwanted sexual advances. In addition, women may be at greater risks for sexual aggression in early stages of dating and when they are more romantically interested in their dates (Byers & Lewis, 1988). Many men interpret women saying no to their sexual advances as really meaning yes because stereotypically "nice" women are not supposed to appear too interested in sexual activity. Some researchers have found that sexual aggression among male university students is a socially learned behavior (Wilson, Faison, & Britton, 1983). These findings are inconsistent with the alternative theory that young men who rape are responding to feelings of powerlessness.

Rape is herein defined as engaging in sexual intercourse without consent through the use of or threat of force. Date rape has begun to receive widespread attention and is much more prevalent than formerly thought. Of all reported rapes, about 60% are date rapes (Seligmann, 1984). At the present time, it is not possible to determine whether this phenomenon is a new trend related to the increased acceptance of violence in our society or an experience that women have only begun to have the courage to report. Because jurors often believe that rape victims are consenting women who "changed their minds" afterwards, prosecution for this crime, in general, has only a 16% conviction rate. Consequently, date rapes are among the most difficult cases to prosecute (Barrett, 1982).

Types of Date Rape

Date rape can be divided into two categories: "early date rape" and "relational date rape." Early date rape occurs fairly soon in the dating relationship. It is believed to be correlated with the number of different men that the woman dates and her perceived sexual reputation. Relational date rape occurs during the "normal" social progression of the relationship. Research suggests that some men evidently perceive a greater degree of sexual interest than women actually have. These misunderstandings between women and men concerning sexual involvement are linked to relational date rape (Shotland, 1985). The least prevalent but most blatant form of date rape on college campuses is group rape ("gang bang" or "pulling train") usually attributed to fraternities or athletic teams (Barrett, 1982).

The Gender-Role Model and Date Rape

One explanation for date rape whether "early" or "relational" is the gender-role model (Murnen, Perot, & Byrne, 1989). This model suggests that traditional gender roles facilitate sexual behavior. Accordingly, men are sexually aggressive because they are taught to aggressively initiate sexual activity. Traditionally, feminine characteristics such as submissiveness and nurturance may adversely affect a woman's ability in dealing with unwanted sexual advances. A study of beliefs about rape and women's social roles found that college men were more likely than college women to subscribe to negative stereotypes concerning the woman's causal role and the issue of consent in rape. Further, men believed that women's social roles and rights should be more restricted than their own (Costin, 1985).

Rape crisis centers offer crisis intervention, counseling, and legal advocacy for survivors. They also provide community education and training for professionals.

Such beliefs suggest that this gender-role model does serve to perpetuate myths regarding sexual aggression.

In a survey of college date rapists, two thirds of the date rapist group and one fifth of the nonrapist control group had previously attempted to seduce a first date since entering college (Kanin, 1985). Their sexual exploitation techniques included attempting to intoxicate the woman with alcohol, 76%—rapists and 23%—controls; falsely professing love, 86%—rapists and 25%—controls; and falsely promising "pinning," engagement, or marriage, 46%—rapists and 6%—controls. Further evidence of the gender-role model for date rape is illustrated by the findings that almost all of the rapists and only one third of the controls indicated that their best friends would "definitely approve" of these sexual exploitation tactics for certain women. In fact, for many, these techniques had been suggested to them by their best friends as a way to achieve sexual success. If the woman was believed to be a "teaser" or economic exploiter, both the rapists and nonrapist control group were more likely to act sexually aggressive in a dating situation (Kanin, 1985). In general, men are more approving of male dominance and female passivity in dating than women. Thus, as a couple progresses from a first date to marriage, men gain support to violate their partner's consent while women lose support to assert their rights (Margolin, Moran, & Miller, 1989).

However, when assessing the roles of gender identity and self-esteem in both physical and sexual abuse, no support was found for the theory that abuse is the result of compulsive masculinity (Burke, Stets, Pirog-Good, 1988). In fact, among female and male midwestern university students, low self-esteem and abuse are related to the playing out of a more feminine identity for both women and men. Further, clear connection has been demonstrated between gender traditionality and perception of the female and male actor and the incidence of date rape. For both sexes, the more traditional their gender orientation, the more likely that they are to negatively evaluate the woman involved, excuse the behavior of the man, and define the rape incident as something other than rape (Scritchfield & Masker, 1989). Further, rape justifiability ratings are higher for men than women and for traditional than for nontraditional gender-role persons (Muehlenhard, 1988).

Factors in Date Rape

Date rapes are most likely to occur on weekends between 10 PM and 2 AM, are likely to last longer than stranger rape, and are less likely to involve a lethal weapon (Seligmann, 1984). Of the female rape cases in one study, about one half had been committed by first dates or by romantic acquaintances. Of those women who had been raped, one third did not discuss the experience with another person, and most (90%) did not report the incident to the legal authorities. The average age of the date rape victim was 18 years of age, which means that college freshmen, followed by high school seniors, are the most vulnerable women to date rape (Koss, 1985).

In reviewing the statistics on reported date rape among college women, most date rapists (82%) were college students. As for the location of the date rape, the assaults occurred in the male's residence (54%), the victim's residence (31%), and an automobile (11%). There also was a typical pattern in date rape cases. Some type of genital play immediately preceded a substantial number of the date rapes (84%), and most rape victims (90%) had been sexually intimate (including genital stimulation and sexual intercourse, in some cases) with the rapist prior to this particular date (Kanin, 1984). Men claim that it is difficult to take the women's rejections of sexual intercourse seriously, considering the high level of sexual intimacy that has already been achieved. Further, over 90% of men cited their partner's extreme sexual arousal as intensifying their own arousal, and therefore used this as their reason for committing the rape. They ignored the fact that the consent of the woman to engage in petting as a form of sexual intimacy did not give them the right to force participation in sexual intercourse (Kanin, 1984). Furthermore, usage of alcohol was cited as a factor in date rape by three fourths of college women (Copenhaver, 1990).

Reports of male sexual victimizations (usually by other men) have increased since the late 1970s. Because of the myth that men cannot be sexually exploited by women, the extent of this problem is possibly underreported. When male sexual abuse was explored among college students in the mid-1980s, 16% of men and 25% of women reported having been forced to have sexual intercourse by a dating partner (Struckman-Johnson, 1988). Follow-up data indicated that most women were physically forced into uninitiated sex while most men submitted due to psychological pressure. Women experienced more long-term emotional consequences than did men.

Table 3.5: Coping Response to Unwanted Sexual Intercourse

Coping Response	
Response to attack	
Accept	33%
Ignore	39
End relationship	11
Other	17
Person told about attack	
Nobody	50
Friend	44
Family member	6
Degree of contact with man after attack	
None	25
Brief	25
Are friends	25
Have dated	14
Maintain a sexual relationship	11
Self-blame for attack	
Some blame	48
Moderately to blame	23
Mostly to blame	23
All to blame	6
Blame directed to attacker	
None	12
Some blame	41
Moderately to blame	18
Mostly to blame	23
All to blame	6

Source: S. K. Murnen et al., "Coping with Unwanted Sexual Activity: Normative Responses, Situational Determinants, and Individual Differences" in *The Journal of Sex Research,* 26:97. Copyright © 1989 Society for the Scientific Study of Sex, Philadelphia, PA.

Persuasive and coercive techniques have been identified as primary methods used in unwanted sexual activity (Murnen, Perot, & Byrne, 1989). Responses to unwanted attempts at sexual intercourse indicate that the majority of victims accepted or ignored the attack, telling no one (see Table 3.5). However, Byers and Lewis (1988) have concluded from their investigation of disagreements among dating couples over desired levels of sexual intimacy that sexual coercion does not characterize the dating system to the degree suggested in the earlier research literature.

Avoiding Date Rape

Effective ways for handling sexual aggression in dating situations have begun to be identified. Such behaviors include avoiding risky situations, using alcoholic beverages only in moderation, and being assertive against unwelcome sexual overtures (Kiernan & Taylor, 1990). The most critical aspect of effective communication in conveying nonconsent for sexual intercourse is an early initiation of protest. In other words, it is possible, if women make it very clear to dating partners that they have no intent of engaging in sexual intercourse, the danger would be lessened. Physical tactics by the woman do not enhance either the clarity or the effectiveness of communicating the word no to sexual intercourse (Amick, 1986). However, responsibility for nonexploitative sexual behavior must be assumed by all. Both women and men should be educated for responsible use of their sexuality by promoting behavior that leaves both partners feeling stronger and better about themselves. This difficult task must counter the effects of a society that tolerates violence in many insidious ways. Needed changes would impact myriad aspects of life in America including changing sports images, television and media coverage, and addressing the role of alcohol and other drug use. Finally, student personnel staff and faculty must play an active role in the prevention of date rape on college and university campuses. Educational programs can raise the consciousness levels of students concerning the incidence of date rape and teach behaviors that would prevent its occurrence (Miller, 1988).

Nevertheless, when date rape does occur, student services personnel should encourage students to both report its occurrence and seek professional help. For example, a policy defining date rape as a campus offense punishable by the Undergraduate Student Court at the University of North Carolina Chapel Hill has been established (Wing, 1989). This unusual approach provides a different avenue for victims who feel uncomfortable pursuing the case in a criminal court. It also is imperative that victims of sexual assault receive therapeutic intervention to deal with the aftermath of rape: loss of control over their bodies and lives, psychological shock, flashbacks, nightmares, and other long-delayed reactions (Williams, 1981).

Summary

- The courtship system that developed in the United States during the early part of the 20th century places considerable emphasis on romantic involvement with substantial freedom from parental control.
- Early adolescent involvement begins very early as girls and boys begin to have romantic interests sometime between the fifth and seventh grades.
- For many high school students, formal dating produces anxiety. Spontaneous, informal activities are preferred by many teenagers as an initial introduction into the process of dating, with couples later pairing off.
- Both high school and college students consciously seek qualities in dating partners that they believe desirable in future marriage partners, such as honesty, ambition, intelligence, and congenial personality.
- There are bargaining elements (exchange theory) in traditional dating, such as exchanging sexual intimacy for status and money. When people date outside their own bargaining levels, exploitation may result from status differences or unequal emotional involvement.
- College dating patterns have changed significantly with resulting emphasis upon informality and sharing of time and activities. There appears to be less emphasis upon sexual conquest, and more emphasis on the romantic aspects of lovemaking. The sexually traditional woman coexists with the sexually liberated woman who subscribes to new campus sexual mores acknowledging increasing experiences of sexuality with relationship commitment.
- Increasingly, young people accept dating across religious lines as an opportunity to learn more about other people and other groups. Interracial or interethnic dating, which is becoming more commonplace, tends to be viewed more favorably by younger, better educated people, but is still strongly resisted by others.
- Many creative and innovative approaches to meeting dating partners have emerged such as computer dating services, personal advertisements, and singles nights at museums and supermarkets.
- In recent years, date violence has come to be viewed as a tragic by-product of the courtship process. Changing definitions of gender roles have resulted in former behaviors no longer being considered as socially acceptable in a dating relationship. Men appear to be more likely to initiate date violence, although they also experience it from their female partners.
- Date rape now accounts for over one half of all reported cases of rape. The gender-role model contributes to the likelihood of date rape. Educational programs are needed to raise the consciousness levels concerning date rape and to teach behaviors that could prevent the problem.

Questions for Critical Reflection

1. Since the American system of dating and courtship is a relatively recent phenomenon, how do you envision it changing by the mid-21st century?
2. What advantages would you perceive if your parents were to arrange your marriage? Name two ways that a partner your parents would choose might differ from one of your choice.
3. How common among your casually dating friends is the exchange system of "paying out" versus "putting out"? If a friend asked, how would you advise her/him to avoid such behavior?
4. Why do you believe empathy is more difficult for some people to achieve in relationships than it is for others?
5. Do you believe date violence is actually increasing or that there is just more reporting of such incidents? What would you do if a dating partner displayed violent behavior toward you?

Suggested Readings

Duck, S., & Gilmore, R. (Eds.). (1981). *Developing personal relationships (vol. 2).* London: Academic Press. A scholarly view of how personal relationships progress and develop.

Murstein, B. (1986). *Paths to marriage.* Beverly Hills, CA: Sage. A detailed consideration of the many components of dating including attraction and courtship.

Rothman, E. K. (1984). *Hand and hearts: A history of courtship in America.* New York: Basic Books. A contemporary view of courtship in the United States from 1770 to 1920.

Staples, R. (1981). *The world of black singles: Changing patterns of male/female relations.* Westport, CT: Greenwood. An excellent academic work on the courtship practices of American blacks.

Youniss, J., & Smoller, J. (1985). *Adolescent relations with mothers, fathers, and friends.* Chicago: University of Chicago Press. A social survey of middle-class adolescents and their interpersonal relationships.

CHAPTER 4

Premarital Sexuality

No aspect of human life seethes with so many
unexorcised demons as does sex. No human activity
is so hexed by superstition, so haunted by residual
tribal lore, and so harassed by socially induced fear.
Harvey Cox, 1977

OUTLINE

Premarital sexuality, a simple sounding phrase, is one which probably has engendered more debate in the mass media and research literature than any other topic of the so-called sexual revolution. In recent years, much controversy has surrounded the trend toward sexual involvement among adolescents at increasingly younger ages and the related issue of sex education (Reiss & Reiss, 1990). The list of unresolved questions about sex education in America is long and ominous: Who is the real sexuality educator and who should it be, what should be taught and when? These examples are only a few queries that fuel the debate. Today's startling statistics on sexually transmitted diseases (STDs), including genital herpes and Acquired Immune Deficiency Syndrome (AIDS), make yesterday's literature on STDs read like a Dick and Jane primer. In the 1990s, premarital sexual involvement has taken on new dimensions that definitely need to be explored by young persons today with their heads as well as their hearts.

The use of the term premarital when referring to sexual intercourse between unmarried persons creates terminological confusion since it literally means that which precedes marriage. Yet not all unmarried persons who engage in sexual intercourse with each other eventually marry. While the term nonmarital sexual intercourse might seem more accurate and thus appropriate, conventionality of usage in the research literature favors the term premarital sexual intercourse (Davidson & Leslie, 1977). Since the evidence suggests that the foundation for sexual attitudes and sexual behavior is built very early in life and that it is a process influenced by many sources, exploring the concepts of sexual knowledge and myths will contribute to understanding sexuality.

Sexual Knowledge and Sexual Myths

In spite of the blatant sexual themes in today's television programs, movies, and popular music, most young people as well as many adults are not well-informed about sexual matters. Neither can participation in premarital sexual intercourse be used as an index of sexual knowledge. Female and male college students with sexual experience are just as likely to believe in sexual myths as those without sexual intercourse experience. In fact, as their sexual guilt increases, so does the likelihood of subscribing to sexual myths (Mosher, 1979).

Level of Sex Knowledge

At the 1983 World Congress of Sexology in Washington, DC, Australian researchers revealed findings from a 4-year study with less than promising predictions for the United States (Cuniberti, 1983). Juliette and Ronald Goldman interviewed children, ages 5–15, from Sweden, Australia, England, and the United States. While the sample, restricted to white children living with both parents and a younger sibling, was less than representative of current American family life, it did provide a comparative index of sex education efforts in the four countries. Even though American youth date and have sexual intercourse at earlier ages, they know far less about the subject of sexuality than their peers in Sweden, England, and Australia. Not only were Americans found to be least knowledgeable, but there was a 3-year knowledge gap between American youth and their Swedish contemporaries. The fact that Sweden has had compulsory sex education in their schools for over 30 years may account for the fact that the incidence of teenage marriage, divorce, unintended pregnancy, abortion, and sexually transmitted disease ranks lowest in Sweden and highest in the United States. These appalling circumstances are suggested to be the result of Americans combining social precociousness with sexual ignorance (Cuniberti, 1983).

When considering sexual knowledge, sexual attitudes, and sexual guilt among college students, women were significantly more knowledgeable than men but also reported the highest levels of sexual guilt (Gunderson & McCary, 1980). Not only are college students with high sexual guilt less likely to be knowledgeable about contraceptives, they are less likely to use effective methods (Gerrard & Reis, 1989). Female high school students were also more knowledgeable than their male peers about reproduction, pregnancy, and contraception (Davis & Harris, 1982). However, only 9% of women and not a single man in another survey knew how to calculate the anticipated day of ovulation (Davidson & Darling, 1986). It is therefore not surprising that college men subscribe to more sexual myths than women. Among the myths are that sexual intercourse should be avoided during pregnancy to avoid injury to the fetus, pregame sexual intercourse weakens an athlete, conception is more likely to occur with simultaneous orgasms, and the absence of a hymen is proof of nonvirginity (Mosher, 1979). In summary, there is much support to document that most students, even those at the college level, are rather misinformed about many aspects of human sexuality, including their own bodies.

The teachable moment. Childhood curiosity is an important clue for parents who wish to optimize the timing for their children's sexuality education.

Sources of Sex Information

As stated before, two of the most controversial issues surrounding sex education in the past have been who shall provide sexuality education and what shall be taught. To date, formal sex education has tended to be minimal and to focus on the prevention of STDs and teenage pregnancy (Schickedanz, Hansen, & Forsyth, 1990). The central debate in sex education, however, concerns who is or should be the source of such knowledge. In a large scale study of sexual behavior and attitudes among college students, the first reported source of information about contraception was: teachers—57% for women and 44% for men, peers—28% for women and 45% for men, and parents—15% for women and 12% for men (Moore & Davidson, 1990; Davidson & Moore, 1990). But among American teens, the primary reported sources about contraception were school—37% and parents—17%. But the primary reported sources of information about masturbation were friends—32% and parents—12% (Coles & Stokes, 1985). Given the diversity of religious values represented in public schools, it is anticipated that the debate over compulsory sex education will continue, as will questions related to the appropriateness of various sexual topics. It is therefore important that today's college students, as future parents, school board members, and legislators, understand the sources of sexual information and the relationship of such education to behavior.

Parents

While both parents and professionals agree that parents bear the primary responsibility as their children's sexuality educators, the research to date indicates that most parents have abdicated their responsibility for information giving. Instead, peers and the media are the primary sources of sexuality information for America's children, a fact that has remained unchanged since the 1940s (Roberts & Holt, 1980). Many parents have tended to view sexuality as a problem area and a topic to be avoided. This may substantiate the belief that most American parents lack the necessary skills to provide adequate sex education for their children (Dyk, 1990). At the beginning of the 1980s, among 1,400 parents surveyed, only 15% of mothers and 8% of fathers indicated that they had even talked to their children about sexuality (Roberts & Holt, 1980). Although by the mid-1980s, 26% of mothers and 17% of fathers had told their children about contraceptives, this increase is surprisingly low considering that three fourths of these same parents indicated their own sex education was inadequate as a teenager (Leo, 1986b).

The fact that female college students are more likely to report their mothers as their first source of information about where babies come from may reflect the woman's vulnerability to pregnancy. The majority of mothers in one study had discussed menstruation and reproduction with their daughters. Yet less than 2% of either parent had discussed nocturnal emission, and only 10% had ever mentioned erotic behavior or its consequences to their children (Roberts, Kline, & Gagnon, 1978). Perhaps such revelations should come as no surprise to a nation known to have the world's highest rate of unmarried teen pregnancies.

Daughters are more often encouraged to learn about sexual matters as parents attempt to regulate their daughter's sexual behavior more than that of their sons. Parents are more likely to anticipate discussing masturbation and homosexuality with their sons than with their daughters, suggesting that the sexual double standard continues, with men expected to be more sexually active than women (Koblinsky & Atkinson, 1982). Educational level and parenting style predict sex education behavior of parents. For example, mothers with higher educational levels are more likely to discuss contraception with their daughters (Fox & Inazu, 1980). Also, parents who are more strict in child rearing are less likely to communicate with their children about sexual matters but more likely to rate sex education courses in schools as extremely valuable (Coreil & Parcel, 1983).

Most fathers rarely or never communicate with their children about sexual matters (Coreil & Parcel, 1983). Female and male university students who were asked to describe their family's participation in their sex education through their junior high school years indicated their fathers were especially uninvolved as sex educators. Less than one tenth of women and only one third of men indicated that their fathers had provided much sexual information (see Table 4.1). While twice as many women (50%) as men (25%) indicated that their mothers were their major source of first information about sexual matters, at least 86% of these students indicated independent reading as an important source of information regarding sexuality. The most frequently reported first sources of sexual information were mothers for pregnancy and same-sex friends for sexual intercourse (Mancini & Mancini, 1983).

If, as stated earlier, parents believe that they should be the primary sexuality educators of their children, what goes wrong between the belief and the practice? Several factors have been suggested that inhibit parents in their role as sexuality educators:

1. Parents perceive themselves to be uninformed.
2. Parents are often uncomfortable discussing sexual activity.
3. Parents lack skills since their parents did not serve as models.
4. Parents are unable to separate desire to control behavior and to give information.
5. Children may feel anxious and therefore act unresponsive.
6. Children and parents may have difficulty acknowledging each other as sexual beings particularly if parents are unsure about their beliefs and values concerning sexuality (Clark & Wilson, 1983, pp. 3–4).

The encouraging news is that, increasingly, parents themselves are attending sexuality education programs in an attempt to gain knowledge and skill in matters of sexuality education (Hale & Char, 1982). In so doing, they are not only confronting their own personal inhibitions, they are also offering the next generation of sex educators, their children, a positive role model to copy.

Thus far, parents have been considered as purveyors of sexuality information. However, their most

Table 4.1: Sources of Information about Sexuality

Source	Sexual Intercourse		Pregnancy		Menstruation		STD		Abortion	
	W	M	W	M	W	M	W	M	W	M
Mother	28%	9%	63%	39%	61%	11%	8%	4%	13%	8%
Father	1	9	2	9	1	7	1	5	1	2
Male friends	5	51	0	18	0	16	2	19	1	14
Female friends	32	6	8	3	6	9	9	1	17	3
Brothers	2	3	0	2	0	2	0	2	0	1
Sisters	4	0	2	1	3	4	1	1	2	1
Other relatives	2	1	1	1	1	0	0	0	0	0
Clergy	1	0	1	0	0	0	1	0	2	1
Teachers	8	4	10	6	16	25	51	41	21	23
Doctors	1	0	1	1	1	0	2	1	1	1
Independent reading	11	9	4	7	3	20	16	20	19	22
Experience or sight	0	2	2	5	2	3	0	1	1	2
Mass media	2	2	1	3	2	1	6	4	20	21
Mixed sources	5	4	4	5	3	3	3	2	3	2

Source: J. A. Mancini and S. B. Mancini, "The Family's Role in Sex Education: Implications for Educators" in *Journal of Sex Education and Therapy*, 9:19.

significant influence in their children's healthy sexuality must not be ignored. It concerns attitudes that are communicated long before children can understand verbal messages. From birth, daily lessons are imparted to children about their sexuality in both behaviors and attitudes of parents. These silent lessons in sex education, often masquerading as simple caring or noncaring techniques of parental behaviors, leave no neutral ground on which parents can stand. The manner in which the child's basic needs are met will teach either positive or negative messages about the self as a sexual being. For example, responsive parents impart gentleness and trust through touch as they lovingly care for the infant's bodily needs. If children are allowed by parents to like, enjoy, and become masters of their own bodies, when grown they will be able to experience closeness, warmth, and trust with another person (Calderone & Johnson, 1981). It is doubtful any significant degree of progress will be made in the areas of sexuality education until the parent is recognized, educated, and supported in this primary role.

Peers

Peers have always been reported as a major source of sexual information, although this source has declined somewhat over the last 40 years (see Table 4.2). Not only have peers been cited in the research literature as important sexuality educators since the 1930s, studies from the 1980s and 1990s suggest that they still may be the primary source for adolescents (Coles & Stokes, 1985; Davidson & Moore, 1990). A survey of over 1,000 school-age students confirmed that children do receive the majority of their sexuality information from peers. Additionally, as they grow older, adolescents tend to rely increasingly on one another for such information (Thornburg, 1981). Among female and male adolescents, the most commonly reported sources of sexual information were friends, schools, and parents, in that order. Further, friends remained the most often reported source regardless of gender, ethnicity, and urban or rural residence (Davis & Harris, 1982). While a later national investigation found that books and mass media were the primary sources of information about sexual techniques for one third of the respondents, more than one fourth indicated that friends played that role (Coles & Stokes, 1985). Of the various sources of sexual and contraceptive information that influence high school and college sexual behavior, the most important one for both women and men is reported to be their **significant other.** Interestingly, this source is more important for those who have experienced first sexual intercourse during high school than for those who are still virgins in college (Kallen, Stephenson, & Doughty, 1983).

Table 4.2: Peers as a Source of Sexual Information

Investigator	Year	Sample	Peers as Source
Exner	1915	College men	85%
Hughes	1926	Male adolescents	78
Kinsey et al.	1948	Wide age-range men	74
Thornburg	1972	College women and men	38
Gebhard	1977	College men	50

From C. A. Darling and M. W. Hicks, "Parental Influence on Adolescent Sexuality: Implications for Parents as Educators" in *Journal of Youth and Adolescence,* 11:233.

Unfortunately, sexual information that adolescents receive from peers is obviously without quality control and therefore likely to be misinformation (Scales, 1983). This fact may be significantly related to adolescent pregnancies, most of which are unintended and often linked to ignorance or misinformation concerning reproduction and contraception. Adolescents may be dependent on their peers for sexual information because of the different types of information that peers provide. For example, peers are the first source of information about female orgasm (Davidson & Darling, 1986). Educators, parents, and schools stress nonbehavioral physiological facts such as menstruation, conception, and sexually transmitted disease. Conversely, peers most often provide behavioral information on topics such as petting, sexual intercourse, masturbation, ejaculation, contraception, prostitution, and homosexuality (Chin & Dahlin, 1983).

School

Today's controversy over sex education in the schools is a natural progression of myriad evolutionary changes. Such factors have led to a shift away from the home and family as sources of sex education, decreasing influence of parents, and the simultaneous increasing role of public education (Francoeur, 1989b). Even though surveys have long shown that at least 80% of Americans favor sex education in the public schools, there is a deplorable lack of such programs. In 1986, Surgeon General C. Everett Koop changed the course of an ancient debate when, in response to the AIDS crisis, he stated, "There is no doubt that we need sex education in schools and that it must include information on heterosexual and homosexual relationships" (Leo, 1986b, p. 54). Following Koop's dramatic change of position, a national poll conducted by Yankelovich Clancy Shulman found that 86% of American adults wanted public schools to teach sex education. The vast majority, ranging from 72%–95%, wanted to include controversial subjects such as AIDS, other STDs, contraception, premarital sexuality, sexual intercourse techniques, homosexuality, and abortion. Only oral-genital sex and anal intercourse failed to receive a majority endorsement as subjects to be taught in public school sex education programs (Leo, 1986b).

Since the decision to include sex education in the curriculum is at the discretion of local school boards, it is difficult to assess the extent of programs across the United States. It is estimated that about 80% of public-school children in major cities receive some sex education (Leo, 1986b). However, only 13 states and the District of Columbia require sex education in all schools (Haffner, 1990). Further, some sexuality experts believe that even when programs are offered, only about 15% of American children receive good sex education (Leo, 1986b).

As shown in Table 4.1, teachers were most often reported by female and male respondents as their first source of information about fertilization and abortion. They also were the first source of information about STDs for women and for men, the topic of menstruation (Mancini & Mancini, 1983). But for women and men who experienced their first sexual intercourse in college, school classes were the third most useful source of sexual information following friends and books, respectively (Kallen, Stephenson, & Doughty, 1983).

In view of the tremendous controversy surrounding sex education in public schools, what conclusions can be drawn regarding the influence of sex education on sexual behavior? Available data indicate that participation in formal sex education has no detrimental effects. Researchers at Johns Hopkins University have found that there is no association between sexual activity and enrollment in courses that cover contraception. Further, they found that participation in sexual intercourse is not influenced by whether or not teenagers have been exposed to formal sex education in high school. However, they did conclude that female teens who are sexually active and who have been exposed to sex education are less likely to become pregnant (Kenney & Orr, 1984). When college students enrolled in human sexuality classes were compared to students in first aid classes, there was no significant increase in premarital sexual intercourse in either group at the end of the courses. But there was a significant increase in the percentage of human sexuality students who had participated in oral-genital sex (Dignan, Denson, Anspaugh, & C'mich, 1985). Further, researchers have reported a significant increase in the percentage of college women who engage in masturbation after completion of a family studies course with substantial human sexuality content (Davidson & Darling, 1990).

In summary, the following conclusions can be drawn concerning parents, peers, and schools as sexuality educators:

1. Parents and schools often do not provide sufficient or relevant sexual information to children.
2. Young people often look to peers for their information.
3. Most peers are themselves misinformed concerning sexual matters (Chin & Dahlin, 1983, p. 3).

Innovative Sexuality Education

There are so many problems in marshaling the various forces to enhance people's knowledge about sexuality that yesterday's tactics have fallen short of this goal. A concerted effort to reframe the problems as challenges and combine the best of all sources is called for in a day when failure to do so is so far-reaching. One such innovative attempt is peer education in which adolescents are trained as sexuality educators. They in turn facilitate the delivery of sexual information to other young people through peer education programs. These programs, usually sponsored by school systems or youth service agencies, have been successful (Chin & Dahlin, 1983). Their success lies in meeting adolescents' need for accurate information and guidance while enabling them in their struggle for independence from parents and other adults.

School clinics were another innovation of the 1980s. Usually located in or near public schools, these controversial health facilities spread rapidly. They are viewed by many professionals as a way to address some of the problems faced by adolescents in a cost-effective and medically sound manner (Kenney, 1989). They are claimed to save $25 for every $1 spent on preventing teen pregnancy. As of 1986, there were 72 clinics, found mostly in low-income neighborhoods of large cities. Of these facilities, 28% dispense contraceptives, while 52% prescribe contraceptives, and the others make referrals to family planning agencies. Opposed by conservatives, especially the Roman Catholic church and the National Right to Life Committee, such clinics have raised the voice of a vocal minority who fear their services will lead to promiscuity (Francoeur, 1989a). Although the facts are difficult to obtain, indications are that clinics may reduce birth rates to single mothers as well as postpone first sexual encounters. Activists cite St. Paul, MN where birth rates fell 40% in schools with clinics. Also, the Johns Hopkins study of two inner-city schools found a one third drop in the rate of pregnancies among teens with access to contraceptives at a school-based clinic (Leo, 1986b).

Any successful comprehensive program of sex education, whatever the source, must consider not only dispensing information or contraceptives but also the social and psychological factors. This is not a problem that can be solved with simplistic answers. Sex education is a continuous process that needs the concerted efforts of not only researchers, clinicians, educators, and clergy, but also of parents, who play the most significant role in their children's sexuality education.

Childhood Sexuality

Sexuality does not suddenly surface in adulthood. Instead, it is in the process of developing from the earliest stages of infancy through childhood and adolescence. What special significance does infancy and childhood play in this lifelong process? A new era of sex research began with the publication of the Kinsey Reports in 1948 and 1953. Based upon thousands of interviews conducted under the direction of Alfred C. Kinsey, these findings startled many people with their frank accounts of sexual behavior that directly challenged many cherished assumptions. One of the myths exploded concerned infant sexuality. Specifically, infants were found to be far from asexual beings as they had previously been considered. For example, orgasm-like responses were reported to have been observed in infants of both sexes as early as 4–5 months of age (Kinsey, Pomeroy, & Martin, 1948; Kinsey, Pomeroy, Martin, & Gebhard, 1953). In a later study, 20-week-old male infants were reported to have penile erections about 2.3 times per hour (Shuttleworth, 1959). Female infants also have been found to display an apparent sexual response as evidenced by the release of vaginal lubrication (Masters & Johnson, 1966). Certainly no conscious sexual awareness of infants is implied by these facts, but they do indicate the display of elementary sexual responses from birth. These two indicators, penile erection and vaginal lubrication, signal that the sexual response system is working normally (Calderone & Johnson, 1981).

The automatic functioning of the sexual response system at birth is programmed just as is the functioning of the reproductive system at puberty. Somewhat later in infancy the infant discovers its genitals and the active functioning of the sexual response system begins. This discovery initiates a process that will not reach maturity until puberty when the body is physiologically ready for normal sexual functioning with a sense of competence and pleasure (Calderone & Johnson, 1981).

Although the sexual response system is capable of functioning from birth to death, it does not always automatically function. Since both conscious and unconscious levels of the brain control sexual arousal, childhood events may interfere with sexual response in adulthood. Parents are therefore key figures in their child's healthy sexuality development making childhood sexuality a significant topic of concern.

Sexual Activity During Childhood

The Kinsey studies revealed that about one half of the subjects had experienced some type of sexual play during childhood, most commonly **masturbation** (pleasurable self-stimulation of the genitals). In fact, 1 in 10 women and 1 in 5 men had experienced orgasm via masturbation by age 12 (Kinsey et al., 1948; Kinsey et al., 1953). More recently, other researchers have concluded that these figures may actually be too low, because some adults may be unable or unwilling to recall their childhood sexual behavior (Simon and Gagnon, 1970). It is believed that at least three fourths of all persons engage in some sexual play during childhood. A study of over 1,400 parents of children ages 3–11 investigated the parents' knowledge, attitudes, and practices about masturbatory experience of their children. One fourth of mothers and about one half of fathers had masturbated as preteens. Further, mothers reported that one fourth of their daughters and one half of their sons had engaged in masturbation, as contrasted with the fathers who reported lesser degrees of such behavior. Most children were between ages 3–5 at the time parents discovered their masturbatory activity (Gagnon, 1985).

There is little research concerning the effects on children of parental attitudes and behaviors related to their children's sexual explorations. Conventional wisdom suggests that girls and boys are simply learning about their bodies and that childhood sex play is a problem only if parents make it one by incorrectly responding with punishment and shame (Fitzgerald, J. M., 1986). As in other areas of the child's life, parents may need to limit behavior, teaching her/him that sexual exploration is not something one does in public. However, it is important to do so in ways that do not attack the child's sense of self-worth or instill guilt. One of the main sources of failure to achieve sexual satisfaction in adult life is the impact of negative learning in the early years as children discover their own bodies as a source of sexual pleasure (Francoeur, 1989d). When sexually mature individuals engage in sexual activities, they must contend with any prior learning related to sexual guilt, which has been well-documented to affect adult sexual satisfaction (Darling & Davidson, 1987a).

During childhood, sexual activity usually is in the form of "play" rather than directed toward achieving orgasm. Children may stimulate their own genitals and engage in sexual play with members of both sexes (Katchadourian, 1980). Some of the earlier sexual play may involve siblings as illustrated by a survey of undergraduates at six New England colleges where 15% of women and 10% of men reported some type of sexual activity with a sibling. The most common activities were fondling and touching of the genitals (Finkelhor, 1980).

In general, boys are more likely to engage in sexual play than girls and to do so more frequently (Spanier, 1975). This finding raises a question of whether or not men have more compelling sex drives than women. Although the available data do not permit a final answer to this question, it is known that traditionally, boys are more likely than girls to have received more encouragement from their peer groups to engage in sexual play and less discouragement from parents. Among parents in one study, 44% wanted their sons to view masturbation positively during adolescence but only 35% wanted the same for their daughters (Gagnon, 1985). From such data, it is quite apparent that girls and boys receive very different kinds of sexual conditioning and that innate differences between the two in terms of sexuality may have been overemphasized. However, whether the result of nature or nurture, it quickly becomes apparent that girls and boys eventually differ considerably in their orientation to sexuality. Why do female adolescents eventually focus upon relationships and romance, while male adolescents tend to zero in on genital pleasure? Does this difference widen the gulf between the two sexes?

Even with the growing knowledge about the developmental aspects of sexuality unfolding, there are still more questions than answers. However, it is fully established that healthy sexual development depends on both normal biological development and a positive social scripting from family, ethnic, and cultural background; religion; and adequate nurturance (Francoeur, 1989d). Expanding our understanding beyond the childhood years to sexuality in the teen years will help in assessing later sexual involvement and adjustment.

Adolescent Sexuality

Two concepts, often incorrectly used interchangeably, are important to the understanding of teenage sexuality: puberty and adolescence. Puberty refers to the physical changes involved in sexual maturation as well as other bodily changes occurring during the teen years (Kaplan, 1986). Those bodily changes, directly related to sexual reproduction such as maturation of ovaries in girls and testes in boys, are called primary sex characteristics. Secondary sex characteristics such as breast development in girls and beard growth in boys further distinguish the sexes from each other. Puberty then is that time at which reproduction becomes possible. While menstruation in girls signals such an event, it is less easily determined in boys since puberty relates to the ability to ejaculate mobile sperm (Chumlea, 1982). Adolescence has been defined as a behavioral-cultural ripening that spans the time from puberty to adulthood (Krogman, 1972). In contrast to puberty which is physiological, adolescence is the psychological experience which bridges childhood and the adult years.

As puberty progresses and sex hormones flood the body, the individual's sex-role development becomes more focused on issues of sexuality, and the self and other are increasingly viewed as sexual beings (Santrock & Yussen, 1987). Although the drive to experience erotic sexual feelings is normally present at birth, at adulthood, sexuality asserts itself with strong physical drives that cannot easily be repressed (Calderone & Johnson, 1981). At this time, heterosexual relationships become the focus for most adolescents. Within this context personal decisions will be made about the use of one's sexuality from the range of possible expressions: masturbation, petting, and sexual intercourse. From the research on adolescent sexuality by the mid-1980s one could conclude:

1. Adolescent sexual attitudes have become quite liberal.
2. Adolescents seem to be more conservative in behavior than attitudes.
3. Male sexual attitudes are still more liberal than female attitudes.
4. Sexual intercourse is not viewed as a casual act (Kaplan, 1986, pp. 554–555).

Masturbation

Although masturbation is the most common type of sexual activity for teenagers, it is still considered by some societal members to be harmful, sinful, or mentally unhealthy (Davidson & Darling, 1989a). However, it is increasingly viewed by professionals, such as sexologists and sex therapists, as rehearsal for mature sexual involvement. These professionals believe that just as adolescents are constantly testing their bodies in sports or other activities, they also need to find out how their bodies perform sexually. Masturbation is viewed as a safe way to accomplish this goal since it does not involve another person (Allgeier & Allgeier, 1991).

Masturbatory Behavior

The age of the onset of masturbation varies by gender with proportionately more women reporting a later age at first masturbation. A survey of college students, for example, found that only 30% of women in comparison to 54% of men had begun to masturbate by age 13 (see Table 4.3). Studies indicate that regardless of religious affiliation or frequency of church attendance more than 75% of postcollege age women and 95% of postcollege age men masturbate at one or more periods in their lives (Calderone & Johnson, 1981). As women reach their late twenties, the likelihood of having engaged in masturbation increases. This is illustrated by a study of college-educated women in the health-related professions in which 89% of the never-marrieds (average age of 28.7 years) had engaged in such behavior (Davidson & Darling, 1989a). The incidence of masturbation among college students varies according to gender and race. Without regard to experience with sexual intercourse, the incidence of masturbation for college women ranges from 54% (Moore & Davidson, 1990) to 69%

Table 4.3: Age of Onset of Masturbation

Age	College Women	College Men
6	0.0%	0.2%
7	0.0	0.2
8	0.3	0.6
9	0.0	0.6
10	0.0	3.0
11	2.0	5.0
12	11.0	17.0
13	17.0	28.0
14	23.0	22.0
15	18.0	11.0
16	12.0	6.0
17	6.0	3.0
18	5.0	2.0
19	3.0	1.0
20	2.0	0.2
21	0.7	0.0
25	0.0	0.2

Source: J. D. Atwood and J. Gagnon, "Masturbatory Behavior in College Youth" in *Journal of Sex Education and Therapy,* 13:37. Copyright © 1987 American Association of Sex Educators, Counselors, and Therapists, Washington, DC.

(Pelletier & Herold, 1988). For college men, masturbatory experience ranges from 81% (Belcastro, 1985) to 92% (Story, 1982). Considerable differences have been found between black and white college students regarding the practice of masturbation. In one study, only one half of black women had engaged in masturbation, in comparison to two thirds of the white women. Similar differences in masturbatory practices were reported between black men—54% and white men—83% (Belcastro, 1985).

The variety of factors affecting the frequency of masturbation among never-married midwestern female college students included fatigue, opportunity, and privacy (Davidson, 1984). The reported frequency of masturbation among today's college students is 4.5 times per month for women (Moore & Davidson, 1990) and 6.3 times per month for men (Davidson & Moore, 1990). Among postcollege age women, the masturbatory frequency was found to be 3.5 times per month (Davidson & Darling, 1989a).

Masturbatory Attitudes

Masturbation and virginity are viewed as having negative sexual connotations by many female and male college students. A study was conducted in which subjects were asked to identify from photographs the woman considered most likely to be a virgin and the one most likely to engage in masturbation. Both female and male college students were significantly more likely to select a less attractive person as being both a virgin and more likely to engage in masturbation (Durham & Grossnickle, 1982). Formerly, persons who engaged in masturbation were considered to be lonely and deprived of opportunities for dating. However, one survey in the 1980s found that persons casually dating were more likely to participate in masturbation than those not dating. Respondents who had engaged in sexual intercourse were also more likely to masturbate and to do so on a more frequent basis than those who had never experienced sexual intercourse (Davidson, 1984).

Religious condemnation of masturbation as an inappropriate sexual outlet, especially by the Roman Catholic church, has evoked guilt feelings for a substantial number of individuals (Patton, 1985). Participation in masturbation does create guilt for some women; among college students, 9% indicate "frequent" guilt and 35%—"occasional" guilt (Darling & Davidson, 1987b). Among a sample of female health-related professionals, 8% reported "almost always" and 27%—"sometimes" experiencing feelings of guilt about engaging in masturbation (Davidson & Darling, 1989a). Further, those women who never experienced guilt about their own masturbatory practices were more likely to believe it to be a healthy practice; to approve of female acquaintances masturbating; to reject masturbation during marriage as a sign of poor sexual adjustment; and without shame, to admit to their female acquaintances that they engaged in masturbation (see Table 4.4). Today, the consensus among gynecologists and sex therapists is that masturbation can provide a harmless outlet for sexual needs, especially among persons who, for whatever reasons, lack other means of sexual expression. It may also help individuals learn more about their bodies and sexual arousal (Davidson & Darling, 1990). If such information is conveyed to a sex partner, increased sexual satisfaction in relationships may result.

Petting

The term **petting** has come to have a variety of meanings depending upon the degree of physical intimacy involved. More specifically, petting is physical contact that may lead to sexual arousal but does not involve sexual intercourse. The various degrees of petting include kissing on the lips, **French kissing** (tongue kissing), fondling and/or oral stimulation of breasts, and giving and/or receiving manual and/or oral-genital

Table 4.4: Attitudes toward Masturbation

Attitudes	Masturbatory Guilt Status			
	Almost Always	Sometimes	Rarely	Never
Approve/Female acquaintances/Masturbating				
Strongly disapprove	4%	1%	1%	1%
Disapprove	28	4	3	1
Approve	63	70	55	44
Strongly approve	5	25	41	53
Married person masturbates/Sign of poor sexual adjustment				
Strongly agree	2	0	0	0
Agree	22	6	5	2
Disagree	66	60	47	35
Strongly disagree	10	35	48	63
Masturbation/Healthy practice				
Strongly disagree	4	1	2	1
Disagree	35	6	3	2
Agree	49	64	48	38
Strongly agree	12	29	47	59
Ashamed admit/You masturbate/Female acquaintances				
Strongly agree	30	7	2	0
Agree	54	46	28	14
Disagree	14	38	50	50
Strongly disagree	2	9	20	36

From J. K. Davidson, Sr., and C. A. Darling, *Masturbatory Guilt and Sexual Responsiveness among Adult Women: Sexual Satisfaction Revisited,* paper presented at the meeting of the National Council on Family Relations, New Orleans, LA. Copyright © 1989 National Council on Family Relations, 3989 Central Avenue, N.E., Suite #550, Minneapolis, MN 55421. Reprinted by permission.

stimulation (Darling & Davidson, 1986b). Postcollege age adults are more likely to view petting as **foreplay** (a prelude to sexual intercourse).

Light Petting

Light petting is sometimes referred to as any sexual activity above the waist. This activity may include kissing and caressing of the lips, neck, and shoulders, as well as fondling the breasts through the clothing. In one study, less than one half of white (47%) and black female (48%) adolescents had experienced breast fondling through their clothes, whereas many more male adolescents, 67% of whites and 81% of blacks, reported having engaged in such behavior. Further, more than twice as many black and white male adolescents as female adolescents had participated in petting that involved uncovered breasts (Smith & Udry, 1985).

Female college students who had experienced sexual intercourse reported unclothed breasts kissed—97% and nipples orally stimulated—90%, in comparison to 71% and 46%, respectively, for those who had not experienced sexual intercourse (Darling & Davidson, 1986a). While the percentage of college students participating in light petting has continued to increase, especially among women, there have been even more dramatic changes in the rates of participation in heavy petting (see Table 4.5).

Heavy Petting

Technical virginity, a term that has been used by some authorities to describe the phenomenon of **heavy petting** or petting below the waist, is prevalent among today's college students. More specifically, **technical virginity** has been defined as all methods of oral and manual stimulation of the breasts and genitals, including sexual arousal to the point of orgasm but without sexual intercourse. Since religious beliefs emphasize the prohibition of sexual intercourse outside of

Table 4.5: **Petting Behavior**

Year and Degree of Petting	Women	Men
None		
1965	9%	2%
1970	1	2
1975	3	3
1980	2	3
Light		
1965	32	12
1970	20	9
1975	13	7
1980	13	7
Medium		
1965	24	15
1970	20	10
1975	17	10
1980	12	5
Heavy		
1965	34	71
1970	60	79
1975	73	80
1980	73	85

From I. E. Robinson and D. Jedlicka, "Change in Sexual Attitudes and Behavior of College Students from 1965 to 1980: A Research Note" in *Journal of Marriage and the Family,* 44:238. Copyright © 1982 National Council on Family Relations, 3989 Central Avenue, N.E., Suite #550, Minneapolis, MN 55421. Reprinted by permission.

marriage and the college environment emphasizes sexual experience, technical virginity provides an acceptable alternative to sexual intercourse for many students (Mahoney, 1980).

Just as in the case of sexual intercourse, women are much more likely than men to require love as a prerequisite for participation in oral-genital sex (Young, 1980). The term **cunnilingus** is used to describe oral stimulation of the female genital organs while **fellatio** is used to describe the oral stimulation of the male genital organs. In general, oral-genital sex is more likely to be engaged in by whites than blacks, by those who have experienced sexual intercourse, and to be received more often by women than men (Belcastro, 1985). Studies of university women have found the range of women who had given fellatio was 74% (Moore & Davidson, 1990) to 87% (DeBuono, Zinner, Daamen, & McCormack, 1990). The respective range for receiving cunnilingus was 80% (Moore & Davidson, 1990) to 84% (Pelletier & Herold, 1988). The experience of sexual intercourse is significantly related to these practices. In one study, 89% of those having experienced sexual intercourse had received cunnilingus, and 87% had given fellatio. Of those who had not experienced sexual intercourse only 38% had received cunnilingus, and 21% had given fellatio (Darling & Davidson, 1987b). Among black and white college students, more white women—50% had received cunnilingus than black women—33%, and more had given fellatio (80%—whites compared to 50%—blacks). The same percentage of black and white men had received fellatio (40%), whereas more white men—75% had given cunnilingus in comparison to black men—50% (Belcastro, 1985).

Premarital Sexual Standards

The Premarital Sexual Permissiveness Scale (Reiss, 1967) was based on premarital sexual standards proposed almost three decades ago by Reiss (1960). The four standards concern heterosexual premarital sexual attitudes and behaviors toward kissing, petting, and sexual intercourse:

1. *Abstinence*—Premarital intercourse is considered wrong for both sexes.
2. *Double standard*—Men are considered to have a greater right to premarital sexual intercourse.
3. *Permissiveness without affection*—Premarital sexual intercourse is right for both sexes regardless of the amount of affection present.
4. *Permissiveness with affection*—Premarital sexual intercourse is acceptable for both sexes in a stable relationship (Reiss, 1967, p. 19).

The dramatic shift in attitudes about premarital sexual intercourse that has occurred since the 1960s is illustrated by a longitudinal study of college freshmen. There has been a steady progression of approval for premarital sexual intercourse as the degree of affection increases between the potential sex partners (see Table 4.6). In 1967, 5% of women and 35% of men approved of premarital sexual intercourse if affection between the two partners existed. By 1982, almost two thirds of women and three fourths of men approved of sexual intercourse if affection existed between the couple (Walsh, Ganza, & Finefield, 1983).

A new version of the Reiss Premarital Sexual Permissiveness Scale was used in the late 1980s to measure the acceptance of sexual behavior by dating stages (Sprecher, McKinney, Walsh, & Anderson, 1988). Heavy petting was perceived as most acceptable followed by sexual intercourse and oral-genital sex. For

Table 4.6: Approval of Sexual Intercourse

Sexual Intercourse	1967 W	1967 M	1970 W	1970 M	1974 W	1974 M	1982 W	1982 M
Engaged	18%	53%	42%	65%	70%	87%	75%	84%
In love	16	46	37	62	67	84	74	80
With affection	5	35	22	48	51	79	61	75
Without affection	2	24	6	30	21	56	16	45

Reprinted from R. Walsh, W. Ganza, and T. Finefield, "A Fifteen-Year Study about Sexual Permissiveness" presented at MSS meetings, 1983.

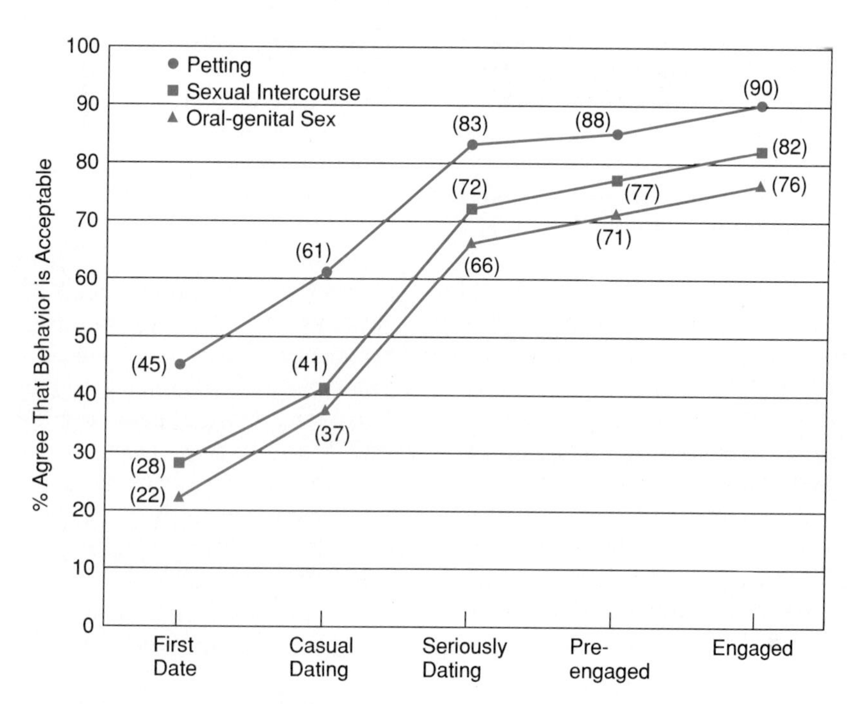

Figure 4.1 Acceptance of Sexual Activity by Relationship Stage and by Percent

some persons, oral-genital sex is considered a more intimate sexual activity than sexual intercourse. The relationship stage significantly affects the acceptability of all three sexual behaviors (see Figure 4.1). The greatest increase in acceptance of these sexual behaviors has occurred between the casual and serious dating stages. This finding is in keeping with the permissiveness with affection sexual script accepted by most young adults (DeLamater & MacCorquodale, 1979). Today, standards are still less permissive for teenagers and women than for young adults and men (Sprecher et al., 1988).

Factors Affecting Standards

In recent years, considerable concern has been expressed by parents, counselors, and the clergy over the changing sexual standards of American young people. The development of premarital sexual standards is influenced by a number of factors, including peers, parents, media, religion, pornography, and changing societal attitudes (Crooks & Baur, 1990).

The Influence of Peers

Premarital sexual standards are highly influenced by peers. One study found the best predictor of whether or not the woman or man had experienced sexual intercourse was the number of close female or male friends that she/he perceived as having had sexual intercourse. Further, for women, perceived approval from close friends for sexual intercourse was a major determining factor in their own decision (Sack, Keller, & Hinkle, 1984).

Women ages 15–19, whose views regarding sexual matters resemble those of their friends, have higher levels of premarital sexual intercourse experience. Moreover, single women who are influenced by their friends regarding sexual matters also are more likely to have a higher frequency of pregnancy than those who are more influenced by their parents (Shah & Zelnik, 1981). In a survey of college students concerning sexual attitudes and contraceptive behavior, the investigators found that female students had general attitudes about sexuality that were more correlated with the attitudes of their peer group than with those of their parents or church. Surprisingly, the sexual attitudes of male students were more correlated with the attitudes of their parents than with the views of their peer group. The use of contraception, however, was not found to be correlated with peers, parents, or church attitudes (Daugherty & Burger, 1984). Among black and white junior high school students in Florida, white adolescents were found to be influenced by the sexual behavior of their best female and male friends. Specifically, white, female adolescent virgins whose best friends of both sexes were sexually experienced at the beginning of the study were found to be extremely likely to have sexual intercourse themselves during the two years of the continuing study (Billy & Udry, 1985).

The Influence of Parents

In one group of college students who lived with both parents while growing up, perceptions were that parents seldom discussed sexual matters within the family and that female adolescents received parental sexual messages less frequently than male adolescents. The most often reported parental message by both female and male adolescents was "pregnancy before marriage can lead to terrible things." Of female adolescents, 44% also were admonished "no nice person has sex before marriage," while one third of male adolescents were told that "sex is a good way of expressing your love for someone" (Darling & Hicks, 1982). In general, mothers have a greater influence on the sexual attitudes of their daughters than of their sons (Thornton & Camburn, 1987). The interrelationship of peer attitudes and parental influence is demonstrated by the fact that daughters whose parents knew all or most of their friends were less likely to report being sexually experienced. Also, daughters whose parents had discussed sexual matters with them were somewhat less likely to have had premarital sexual intercourse. Finally, sons whose parents listened and discussed various decisions with them were somewhat less likely to be sexually experienced (Moore, Peterson, & Furstenberg, 1986). When characteristics of the family that may have been related to adolescent premarital sexual behavior were analyzed in one small-scale study, several implications emerged. Adolescents less likely to engage in premarital sexual intercourse lived with both parents, had only one or neither parent employed outside the home, had families who were less mobile, and had parents who attended school functions (Jacobson & Henegar, 1989).

In an investigation of the relationship between sexual behavior of the mother as an adolescent and the sexual behavior of her children, both female and male children were more likely to have had premarital sexual intercourse if their mothers reported a high level of experience with sexual intercourse during their own adolescence. Furthermore, mothers who were sexually experienced during adolescence were more likely to communicate with their daughters but less likely to communicate with their sons about sexual matters. Daughters and sons of mothers who were sexually experienced during adolescence perceived fewer sanctions about their own sexual behaviors than those of mothers with little sexual experience (Newcomer & Udry, 1984). However, the majority of adolescents believed their parents disapproved of premarital sexual intercourse (Thornton & Camburn, 1987).

The Influence of Mass Media

An indirect measure of the effects of mass media on the development of sexual standards is found in a study of college students. The study measured the effectiveness of commercials and programs with controversial sexual content. Although women were more angered than men by the programming with controversial sexual content, they were better able to interpret the message of the commercials. Apparently, such content adversely influenced the men's mental processing of the media messages (Bello, Pitts, & Etzel, 1983). Another study specifically concerned with adolescent viewing of sexually-oriented programming found that the more time spent watching the programming, the greater the degree of permissiveness of sexual attitudes and behavior (Sexton, 1984). Other evidence, however, suggests that the key factor is whether or not parents

Selling sex—The name of the game for Americans who live in a sex-saturated society.

discuss television programs with their children. Among teenagers who reported frequently talking with their parents about television programs, only 1% were sexually experienced, as compared to one fourth of sexually active teenagers whose parents did not discuss television programs with their daughters (Moore et al., 1986).

The Influence of Religion

Generally speaking, the greater the degree of religiosity, as measured by frequency of church attendance and strength of religious identification, the more conservative the person's attitudes toward sexual permissiveness, pornography, and contraception (Bock, Beeghley, & Mixon, 1983). A study compared virgins who were labeled adamant because of their unyielding stand on virginity, potential nonvirgins or those who expressed a willingness to engage in sexual intercourse, and nonvirgins. Only 9% of nonvirgins, 17% of potential nonvirgins, and 42% of adamant virgins attended church services one or more times per week (Herold & Goodwin, 1981a). Another researcher labeled female college students as "more religious" or "less religious" based on frequency of church attendance and traditional attitudes toward sex and religion. The "more religious" were less likely to engage in sexual intercourse when compared to their "less religious" contemporaries (Young, 1982). Further, in a survey of freshmen attending a college affiliated with a conservative religious denomination, these students were more religious and less sexually active than any other college sample reported in the research literature (Woodroof, 1985).

Changing Societal Attitudes

Public attitudes toward sexual behavior of adolescents and young adults began to liberalize substantially beginning about 1965. Evidence of this trend toward more liberalization of sexual attitudes can be found in national public opinion polls as well as in surveys of college students. Data collected from students at a major southeastern university between 1965 and 1980 clearly demonstrate the increasing acceptance of premarital sexual intercourse. In 1965, 70% of women and 33% of men believed that premarital sexual intercourse was immoral, but by 1980, only 25% of women and 17% of men agreed the practice was immoral. Although both women and men have become more disapproving of both sexes having multiple sex partners, there is still considerably less acceptance of this behavior in women than men, implicating the double standard. According to data collected in 1980, only 26% of college men believed that for a man to have sexual intercourse with a great many women was immoral; however, 42% believed that a woman was immoral if she had sexual intercourse with a great many men (Robinson & Jedlicka, 1982).

Although female rates of premarital sexual intercourse, which are traditionally lower than the male rates, increased throughout the 1960s, 1970s, and 1980s, sexual attitudes appear somewhat contradictory. One study found the sexual attitudes of women to be more conservative in 1983 than in 1973 (Kirschner & Sedlacek, 1987). Some authorities have suggested that a new double standard is emerging: not only do men expect stricter morality of women than themselves, but women, in turn, expect stricter morality of

Table 4.7: **Personal Sexual Code and Perception of Peer Sexual Code**

Sexual Code*	1972 W	1972 M	1983 W	1983 M	1987 W	1987 M
Personal code						
1	7%	5%	7%	3%	4%	2%
2	24	18	24	14	14	5
3	58	32	57	36	68	39
4	10	29	10	33	13	44
5	1	16	2	14	1	10
Perception of female code						
1	1	0	0	2	0	1
2	8	14	6	4	0	2
3	53	44	37	43	26	31
4	34	35	47	37	64	57
5	4	7	9	14	10	9
Perception of male code						
1	1	0	1	1	1	0
2	3	6	3	2	0	0
3	13	17	6	14	1	6
4	40	45	35	44	28	45
5	43	31	55	39	70	49

*Note: These sexual codes are based on absence or presence of commitment and/or attraction:
1 = No sexual intimacy
2 = No sexual intercourse
3 = Sexual intercourse only if emotionally involved
4 = Sexual intercourse if fond of and attracted to person
5 = Sexual intercourse if mutual attraction exists

men (Robinson & Jedlicka, 1982). Long-term trends are perhaps best illustrated by examining the sexual attitudes of incoming college freshmen at the University of Maryland over the last two decades (see Table 4.7). These findings indicate that both women and men perceived others as being more sexually liberal than themselves. A consistent pattern of increasing acceptance of premarital sexual intercourse in a committed relationship by women is reflected as well as increasing acceptance of fondness and sexual attraction as a basis for premarital sexual intercourse by men.

In 1985, a national poll by the Roper Organization found that only 49% of adult American women believed that sexual intercourse before marriage was immoral, representing a decline from 65% in 1970 ("Poll: Women's," 1985). While the outcomes of public opinion polls depend upon the wording of the questions asked and the population surveyed, it does appear that much of the harsh condemnation of premarital sexual intercourse that once existed has greatly diminished. Although proportionate changes have occurred in sexual standards, women were originally, and continue to be, somewhat more conservative than men with regard to sexual matters. In summary, changing sexual standards leading to rising rates of premarital sexual intercourse have been attributed to several changes in the American social structure:

1. The increasing number of years between puberty and marriage allows more time for premarital sexual intercourse to occur.
2. Prevalence of sexuality in the mass media serves to provide young people with role models about sexuality.
3. Greater freedom of young people due to the availability of automobiles, telephones, and living in urban areas provides more opportunity for sexual intercourse to occur.
4. Partial elimination of the double standard due to the gradual movement toward **egalitarian**

gender roles encourages sexual involvement during courtship.
5. Continued decline of the social norm of premarital sexual abstinence influences behavior (Beeghley & Sellers, 1986, p. 331).

Participation in Premarital Sexual Intercourse

Not only have attitudes changed concerning premarital sexual standards, behavior has followed. As people have become more approving of sexual intimacy, they are increasingly having sexual intercourse prior to their eventual marriage. While this statement is true for some younger adolescents, it is particularly so for college students and other young adults (Bachrach & Horn, 1985).

Prevalence of Sexual Intercourse

Numerous studies have been conducted regarding the incidence of premarital sexual intercourse, especially among college students over the past two decades. Considerably more of this research has reported the sexual activity among female rather than male students. It is important to cite a few earlier studies to accurately depict the current level of sexual activity among unmarried persons.

Although a random sample of almost 8,000 women, ages 15–44, revealed a general increase in premarital sexual intercourse from the early 1960s to the late 1970s, the rate of increase was greatest for white women. Of those who married between 1960 and 1964, 47% of white women and 88% of black women had experienced premarital sexual intercourse, as compared with 78% of white women and 95% of black women who married between 1975 and 1979 (Bachrach & Horn, 1985). As sexual attitudes become more liberal, the percentage gap between the levels of black and white sexual activity is rapidly disappearing (Forrest & Singh, 1990).

Degrees of involvement in the dating relationship and religious preference were variables affecting the increasing incidence of premarital sexual intercourse during the 1960s and 1970s. In the late 1970s, persons of the Catholic and Jewish faiths were less likely to have participated in premarital sexual intercourse during engagement than Protestants. But as dating relationships became more serious, it was more likely that persons participated in premarital sexual intercourse regardless of their religious preference (Bell & Coughey, 1980).

The trend toward early involvement in premarital sexual intercourse escalated during the 1980s despite heightened concerns over STDs and teenage pregnancy. A national survey by the Centers for Disease Control (CDC) found that the percentage of 15-year-old female adolescents who had premarital sexual intercourse increased from 5% in 1970 to 26% in 1988, and among 19-year-old women from 48% in 1970 to 75% in 1988 ("Number of Sexually Active," 1991).

The percentages of college women who experienced premarital sexual intercourse in the 1980s ranged from 53% (Earle & Perricone, 1986) to 87% (DeBuono et al., 1990). The likelihood of participation in premarital sexual intercourse increases with age. In a national sample of women ages 15–44, the reported percentages for participation in sexual intercourse by a given age were 15 years—13%, 17 years—35%, 19 years—71%, and 20 years—80% (Moore, Nord, & Peterson, 1989).

As might be anticipated, the incidence of premarital sexual intercourse is still somewhat greater among men than among women. The reported percentages for premarital sexual intercourse for college men range from 62% (Earle & Perricone, 1986) to 94% (Carroll, Volk, & Hyde, 1985). As the age of the man increases, the likelihood of participation in premarital sexual intercourse also increases. For example, in a national survey of men ages 15–44, the percentages of participation in sexual intercourse by a given age were 15 years—17%, 17 years—51%, 19 years—76%, and 20 years—85% (Moore et al., 1989). In terms of interracial premarital sexual intercourse, a survey of college students found that 40% of black male students had engaged in interracial premarital sexual intercourse, in comparison to only 13% of white male, 12% of black female, and 10% of white female students (Belcastro, 1985).

Frequency of Sexual Intercourse

In recent years, few studies of college students have addressed the issue of frequency of premarital sexual intercourse. One study found that, among sexually active never-married college students on a Midwest campus, the women reported engaging in sexual intercourse, on the average, 6.5 times per month (Moore & Davidson, 1990), while men indicated having sexual intercourse seven times per month (Davidson & Moore, 1990). Data from another survey of black and white college students reveal that while black students are more likely than their white contemporaries to have experienced premarital sexual intercourse, they do so less frequently. Data on number of times per month revealed these differences: white women—10 times, white men—9 times, black women—9 times, black men—8 times (Belcastro, 1985).

First Sexual Intercourse

While considerable research has documented increased participation in premarital sexual intercourse by young people, there have been relatively few recent studies that focus on the circumstances and reactions to their first experience with sexual intercourse. The risks of unintended pregnancy are more likely to be considered today as 65% of unmarried women, ages 15–19, in 1988 used a contraceptive during first sexual intercourse in comparison to only 48% in 1982 ("Condom Use," 1990). Although men are generally 2–3 years older than their dating partners, there has been a convergence of the age at first intercourse for women—17.2 years and men—17.6 years (Koch, 1988).

Gender differences in reactions to first sexual intercourse are exemplified by a study of teens in which personal feelings about first sexual intercourse were considered. Of the men, about two thirds were "glad" and one third "ambivalent," whereas about two thirds of the women were "ambivalent" and only one fifth "glad" about their first sexual intercourse (Coles & Stokes, 1985). Interestingly, another survey found that 14% of women and 28% of men did not have sexual intercourse with their first sex partner again, whereas 47% of women and 38% of men reported sexual intercourse 11 or more additional times with their first sex partner (Darling & Davidson, 1986a). With regard to dating status, two thirds of the women were either engaged to or going steady with their first sexual intercourse partner, with another one fifth steadily dating their first partner (Weis, 1983b).

Location

The circumstances under which the first premarital sexual intercourse occurs varies with the living situations of the participants, the year in which the data were collected, and geographical/climatic conditions. Among college students, one half of the women reported experiencing their first sexual intercourse in the home of either their parents or their partner's parents, while one fourth indicated their college dormitory or apartment to be the site. In fact, from 1973–1983, the percent of women experiencing their first sexual intercourse in an automobile dropped from 25% to 5%. About two thirds of these women indicated that their first sexual intercourse experience was spontaneous rather than planned. Their choice of location was probably affected by their dating relationship status (Weis, 1983b).

Level of Sexual Satisfaction

Levels of physiological and psychological sexual satisfaction among college students also have been studied. Substantial gender differences exist concerning physiological sexual satisfaction with first sexual intercourse (see Table 4.8). It is not surprising, given the socialization patterns and the nature of the male sexual response system, that an overwhelming majority of men indicated physiological satisfaction in contrast to only about one fourth of the women (Darling & Davidson, 1986a). These findings are similar to another investigation in which only 39% of college women reported feeling pleasure associated with their first sexual intercourse experience. The older that the woman was and the more heterosexual petting experience prior to first sexual intercourse, the more likely that she would perceive pleasure associated with her first sexual intercourse (Weis, 1983a).

Another variable in the woman's perception of pleasure in her first sexual intercourse is related to any physical discomfort that she may experience at the time. Folklore suggests that first sexual intercourse is painful for the woman. In a survey of college women, 28% experienced no pain with their first sexual intercourse, while 40% experienced moderate pain and 32% reported severe pain. The pain lasted less than an hour for most women and only a "few" minutes for 40%. The likelihood of undergoing pain with first sexual intercourse was associated with the following variables: conservative attitudes about sexuality, perceived low pleasure, high level of guilt, and feelings of exploitation (Weis, 1985). Other influential factors include actual physical structures such as size of penis, foreplay, and penetration techniques.

With regard to psychological sexual satisfaction, about one fourth of college women and two thirds of college men reported having psychological sexual satisfaction with their first sexual intercourse experience (see Table 4.8). A number of factors adversely affect the level of psychological sexual satisfaction for women during first sexual intercourse. These reported affective reactions include nervousness—76%, fear—51%, tension—48%, guilt—38%, embarrassment—31%, and sadness—24%. Women with liberal sexual attitudes and

Table 4.8: **Characteristics of First Sexual Intercourse**

Characteristics	Women	Men
Voluntary consent	91%	96%
Voluntary with pressure	39	9
Contraception usage	37	43
Psychological satisfaction	28	67
Physiological satisfaction	28	81
Feelings of guilt		
Never	44	60
Seldom	19	23
Occasionally	24	12
Frequently	7	3

From C. A. Darling and J. K. Davidson, Sr., "Coitally Active University Students: Sexual Behaviors, Concerns, and Challenges" in *Adolescence,* 21:411. Copyright © 1986 Libra Publishers, Inc., San Diego, CA. Reprinted by permission.

those who have acquired extensive heterosexual petting experience prior to their first sexual intercourse are much less likely to report various components of guilt and/or anxiety about their first sexual intercourse experience (Weis, 1983a).

Finally, concerning psychological sexual satisfaction among college students, 81% of women and 98% of men replied that they, on occasion, became aware of wanting and/or needing sexual intercourse. When asked about reasons for their desire or need, about two thirds of women but only one fifth of men replied that their need was based on emotional reasons rather than physical need (Carroll et al., 1985).

The Personal Dynamics of Sexual Involvement

Considerable attention is devoted in the literature to the percentages of women and men who engage in premarital sexual intercourse, the conditions under which it occurs, and the reactions/feelings afterward. However, these statistics fail to explain why individuals choose to participate in premarital sexual intercourse. What meaning does their sexual activity have in their lives? Two of the recurring themes in this book have called attention to the traditional heterosexual patterns that encourage the perpetuation of the sexual double standard and the new patterns of premarital sexual activity that are emerging. Several studies indicating that these old patterns survive, describe men still pursuing women for pure physical pleasure and boosting their masculine self-esteem by sexual conquests (Carroll et al., 1985; Darling & Davidson, 1986a; Sack, Keller, & Hinkle, 1984). Other studies show women to be more conservative about involvement in premarital sexual intercourse and more concerned about the possibility of exploitation and the risk of pregnancy (Hildebrand & Abramowitz, 1984; Weis, 1983a).

The Continuing Search for Self-Esteem

Many of today's young people, confronted with the search for **self-esteem,** mistakenly believe that it can be attained through premarital sexual involvement. The relationship of premarital sexual intercourse to self-esteem was indicated in a survey of never-married college women. Those from divorced and reconstituted families were much more likely to have engaged in premarital sexual intercourse than those from intact families (Kinnaird & Gerrard, 1986). In addition, sexually active female and male adolescents not reporting loneliness are much more likely to use contraception to avoid pregnancy and its potential for loss of self-esteem (Gates, 1985). In an earlier study where nonvirgins were found to have significantly higher self-esteem than virgins, their self-esteem was attributed not to sexual intercourse but to maturational variables, including years in school (Kallen, 1982). Such findings suggest a negative relationship between premarital sexual intercourse and self-esteem.

The Right to Say No or Not Now

Given the preoccupation with discovering how many young people are having premarital sexual intercourse and what their sexual adjustment problems might be, the fact that many students enter college as virgins is often overlooked. Furthermore, a number of persons still graduate from college without having had premarital sexual intercourse. College students tend to rationalize their own personal status and circumstances. In fact, some sexually liberated young people have not only rationalized their own life choices, but they also have convinced other college acquaintances that something must be wrong with them if they are not enjoying the pleasures of sexual intercourse (Darling & Davidson, 1987). College students may use the term "virginity" rather disdainfully, suggesting that this circumstance means either emotional immaturity or possible homosexual tendencies.

Human relationships, including those that involve sexual intercourse, are never simple and uncomplicated. Sexually active teenagers and young adults may experience ambivalences and anxieties that are concealed from outsiders. Many young women have doubts about whether or not they are emotionally ready for sexual intercourse with a particular man. They worry about the man really loving them, the possible discovery by their friends or parents, and the risk of becoming pregnant (Weis, 1983a). Men, too, often are unsure of themselves in their first sexual intercourse experience, although they may hide their uncertainty behind a screen of false sophistication. With their fantasies of the first sexual experience shattered, they often embark upon a compulsive round of further sexual conquests with other women to reassure themselves of their sexual adequacy. Because of this need to gain reassurance from other women, many men do not choose to continue having sexual intercourse with their first sex partners (Darling & Davidson, 1986a).

Premarital sexual intercourse is not necessarily a disappointing experience. What is unfortunate, however, is that some young people seek to allay their own anxieties by pressuring and/or coercing other persons into premature participation in premarital sexual intercourse. Data about first sexual intercourse among college students indicate that 39% of women and 9% of men felt pressured into their first sexual experience (see Table 4.8). Such pressures are reflected in the general trend in our society toward greater sexual permissiveness.

Currently, there is little clear-cut evidence concerning the relationship between premarital sexual intercourse and subsequent personal or sexual adjustment. Reflected in the literature, however, is a relationship between premarital sexual intercourse and intentions of engaging in extramarital sexual intercourse after marriage (Reiss, Anderson, & Sponaugle, 1980; Singh, Walton, & Williams, 1976; Weis & Slosnerick, 1981). Greater numbers of premarital sex partners and higher frequencies of premarital sexual intercourse were associated with college students being more likely to project that they would be involved in extramarital sexual intercourse in the future (Bukstel, Roeder, Kilmann, Laughlin, & Sotile, 1978). Sexual intercourse in a loving relationship is far more likely to be satisfactory than having sexual intercourse as a means of proving something to oneself or for gaining the approval of others. Engaging in caring sexual activity that does not violate the standards of either partner is most likely to strengthen the overall relationship.

Table 4.9: Most Important Reason for Women Not Having Premarital Sexual Intercourse

Reason	High School	College
Not ready for premarital intercourse	27%	29%
Partner not willing	0	1
Against my religious beliefs	4	13
Fear of parental disapproval	6	2
Fear of pregnancy	12	9
Believe intercourse before marriage wrong	18	22
Fear of damaging reputation	0	0
Have not met person wanted to have intercourse with	33	24

Herold ES, Goodwin MS. "Reasons Given by Female Virgins for Not Having Premarital Intercourse." *Journal of School Health.* 51, No. 7, September 1981, pp. 496–500. Copyright, 1981. American School Health Association, P.O. Box 708, Kent, OH 44240. Reprinted with permission.

What are the reasons for not having participated in premarital sexual intercourse? The fear of pregnancy has actually been ranked very low as a reason for not engaging in premarital sexual intercourse among high school and college students (see Table 4.9). No relationship was found between parental acceptance of premarital sexual intercourse and the reasons for abstaining from participation (Herold & Goodwin, 1981c). These findings are consistent with other research where young persons mentioned length of the relationship, the degree of intimacy, and possible loss of the relationship as reasons for abstaining from premarital sexual intercourse. Further, about two thirds of women and men believed their friends would eventually make the same decision that they had made regarding premarital sexual intercourse (Philliber & Tatum, 1982). Finally, a later study of college students, designed to determine the basic factors that virgins perceive will influence their future decision about engaging in premarital sexual intercourse, identified three factors: physical arousal, relationship, and circumstance. Women, in comparison to men, indicated that the relationship factor would be significantly more important in their decision-making process (Christopher & Cate, 1985).

Parents who wish to assist their daughter or son in saying no to participation in premarital sexual intercourse must be aware that simply telling their offspring, "do not have premarital sex," is not very effective. In fact, Carol Cassell, former president of the American Association of Sex Educators, Counselors, and Therapists recommends telling female adolescents to say not now instead of no in order to avoid experiencing guilt associated with their normal sexual feelings. Cassell believes that to say no promotes the double standard. "All this does is set up girls to feel guilty about their sexuality and pressure boys to go for intercourse whether they really want to or not" ("Urge Teenaged Girls," 1988, p. 59). On the other hand, some authorities feel that teaching an adolescent to say not now instead of no suggests that one does not have the right to say no or to hold to a standard at odds with that of their peers. To help their daughters and/or sons say no or not now to premarital sexual intercourse, Sol Gordon has suggested four steps that parents can take:

1. Create an atmosphere conducive to questions and discussion about sexuality and contraception.
2. Describe potential consequences such as unwanted premarital pregnancy and contraction of sexually transmitted diseases.
3. Try to eliminate the stereotype that participation in premarital sexual intercourse is a measure of manhood.
4. Recognize and acknowledge that peer pressure represents a very influential factor in the decision to engage in premarital sexual intercourse (Saline, 1986, pp. 166–167).

Possible Complications of Premarital Sexual Intercourse

Besides the potential emotional and relationship complications of participation in premarital sexual intercourse, there also are medical, social, and/or legal consequences (Trussell, 1988). In general, these possible complications include unintentional conception followed by either an abortion or single motherhood, an unanticipated marriage, or contraction of an STD. As will be seen in a later chapter, STDs, especially chlamydia, genital herpes, and AIDS, reached epidemic levels during the 1980s.

Conception and Single Mothers

Births to single mothers have become commonplace; three fourths of all abortion procedures are being performed on unmarried persons, and the percentage of premaritally conceived first births among married teens ages 15–19, remains high (Sternberg, 1989; Trussell, 1988). The risk of a premarital pregnancy is related, in particular, to choices of medically ineffective techniques for contraception and to inconsistent contraceptive usage patterns. As late as 1988, 21% of unmarried, sexually active women, ages 15–19, were still having sexual intercourse without using a contraceptive (Forrest & Singh, 1990).

The contraceptive of choice among college students tends to be, in order: condom, oral contraceptive, and **withdrawal** (Hale & Char, 1982). In a national survey conducted among women, ages 15–19, in metropolitan areas, slightly less than one half of never-married white respondents and two thirds of never-married black respondents had engaged in premarital sexual intercourse. However, only about one fourth of either group had been using a medically effective contraceptive technique (Zelnik & Kantner, 1980). A later study of young adult women at Columbia-Presbyterian Medical Center in New York City found the following contraceptive usage patterns: consistently—36%, spasmodically—46%, and never—19%. The consistent contraceptive users were more likely to have mothers who worked, to have parents who would help them to obtain an abortion, and to be willing to have an abortion if they should become pregnant (Jones & Philliber, 1983). Later reports have revealed conflicting data from never-married college students. Researchers have found that from 37% (Darling & Davidson, 1986a) to 55% (Moore & Davidson, 1990) of never-married college women and from 33% (Bishop & Lipsitz, 1988) to 57% (Davidson & Moore, 1990) of college men used a contraceptive during their first sexual intercourse.

The reasons reported by college women for not using contraceptives include fear of side-effects, feel embarrassed, don't like feeling prepared, and intend to abstain from intercourse (Hale & Char, 1982). A number of variables have been found to be associated with the failure of adolescents, in general, to consistently use effective contraception:

1. Age lower than 18 years.
2. Fundamentalist Protestant affiliation.
3. Absence of a committed dating relationship.
4. Sexual intercourse without prior planning.
5. Contraceptives unavailable when needed.
6. Lack of parental communication about contraceptives.
7. Trusting avoidance of pregnancy to luck.
8. High levels of anxiety about sexual activity.

9. Wrong assumptions about the "safe time".
10. Traditional gender-role attitudes (Chilman, 1980, p. 797).

A major reason for the lack of understanding about sexual matters and contraception is that friends are perceived as being the best sources of information for those who had their first sexual intercourse in high school or college. Consequently, considerable opportunity exists for sharing misinformation and ignorance among peers (Kallen et al., 1983).

Prevalence of Single Mothers

Births to single women continued to increase during the 1980s, especially among white women. In 1970, there were only 175,000 births to unmarried white women and 215,000 births to unmarried black women. By 1987, there were 499,000 births to single white women and 399,000 births to single black women. Approaching the question of births to single mothers from a different perspective, they accounted for 6% of all births to white women in 1970, and 17% of all births to white women by 1987. In 1970, 38% of all births to blacks were to single women and the percentage had increased to 62% by 1987 (U.S. Bureau of the Census, 1990l). If data are restricted to an analysis of teens, 66% of all births in 1987 were to unmarried teenagers. Consequently, 25% of all infants, without regard to age or race of the mother, were born to unmarried women in 1987 (U.S. Bureau of the Census, 1990l). If the current trend continues, researchers estimate that 40% of 14-year-old girls will be pregnant at least one time before they reach the age of 20 (Wallis, 1985b). It is somewhat incongruent that in a highly modernized society, America has the highest teen pregnancy rate among western industrial societies.

Consequences for Single Mothers and Their Babies

A substantial body of research evidence indicates that infants born to adolescent mothers, who frequently have inadequate prenatal care, may experience related consequences. They often have low birth weights, decreased rates of growth during childhood, suboptimal school achievement, and interactional difficulties with others (Zuckerman, Walker, Frank, Chase, & Hamburg, 1984).

The teen who gives birth is more likely to have prolonged labor and to have a cesarean section delivery. Women who begin their childbearing during their teen years have more children and are more likely to have the children closer together. Furthermore, about one fourth of unmarried teenagers who give birth are likely to have repeat pregnancies before the age of 20 (Leppert, 1984).

Other consequences of births to unmarried high school-age mothers also have been studied. Both teenagers and their parents perceive the effects to be limited, but school representatives believe that school-age motherhood has numerous, extensive, and long-term consequences. The consequences most often mentioned by the teenage mother were restriction of social activities and increased parent-daughter friction. The consequences most often perceived by parents were constriction of social activities for the teenage mother and delay and/or prevention of graduation (Henderson, 1980).

Contrary to popular opinions, at least during pregnancy, many adolescent expectant fathers maintain positive relationships with their girlfriend's family, contact with the expectant mother, and want to participate in naming the child. However, it is of substantial interest that in the majority of these cases, these same adolescents did not discuss the possibility of becoming pregnant during premarital sexual intercourse (Barret & Robinson, 1982).

While many fathers in two-parent families are playing a much greater role in the daily care of their small children than ever before, this is not true for most adolescent fathers who live apart from their infants (Lamb, Pleck, & Levine, 1985). Research indicates that the majority of such fathers contribute nothing to support their child(ren) regardless of income (Hunter College Women's Studies Collective, 1983). Therefore single mothers are often dependent on either their own parents or Aid to Families with Dependent Children (AFDC), a federally-funded and state-funded assistance program, to finance their infant's care.

Unanticipated Marriage

Of those women who became premaritally pregnant between 1955–1959, 55% married before the birth of the infant. However, of those women becoming premaritally pregnant in 1980–1981, only a little over one third married before the birth of the infant. Examining the variables of age and race in 1980–1981 data, some significant trends are apparent. Only 9% of black women, in comparison to one half of white women, who became premaritally pregnant married before the birth of the infant. Using the age variable, about one third of the women ages 15–17 who became premaritally pregnant married before the birth of the infant, whereas

Book bag or diaper bag? This mother and child portrait is a strong social commentary on teenage pregnancy in the early 1990s.

a little over one half of women ages 25 and over married before the birth of the infant (O'Connell & Rogers, 1984).

Despite the large number of young women becoming single mothers and those who choose abortion (about 750,000 per year), by the mid-1980s at least one fifth of all first marriages involved the woman being pregnant at the time of the marriage (U.S. Bureau of the Census, 1985a). While these marriages were, in many instances, formed to avoid single parenthood, their likelihood of success is substantially less than marriages not involving premarital pregnancies. A major question is likely to exist in the minds of the woman and man as to whether or not they would have married each other had the pregnancy not occurred. One study in the 1970s determined that about two thirds of teenage marriages involving a premarital pregnancy had broken up within 6 years after marriage (Furstenberg, 1976). It should be observed that parents, and especially fathers, may exert pressure and actually utilize coercion to pressure the expectant father into marriage. But under the laws of the various states, one cannot legally force a man to marry a woman even though he is the father of her baby.

Sexually Transmitted Diseases

Although STDs are contracted through the use of contaminated needles for intravenous drug injections, contaminated blood transfusions, or pregnancy/birth to an infected mother, they occur primarily from engaging in sexual activity with an infected person. The STD chlamydia, referred to as the disease of the 1980s, affects at least 4 million persons per year in the United

States. Other STDs such as trichomoniasis and gonorrhea are also rampant (Centers for Disease Control, 1990). In fact, there was a 30% increase in the reported incidence of gonorrhea among women, ages 15–19, between 1971 and 1976. In general, the incidence of gonorrhea tends to decrease with the increasing age of women (Bell & Holmes, 1984). These three diseases can be easily diagnosed and are curable with appropriate prescription medications. In the case of genital herpes, about 500,000 new cases are reported each year, and it is estimated that today at least 20 million Americans may have the disease (Centers for Disease Control, 1990). At the present time, genital herpes is incurable, but medications can reduce the severity of flare-ups.

The STD currently causing the most concern is AIDS, a fatal illness first reported in the United States in 1981. Of the 15,000 cases of AIDS reported between 1981 and 1986, 73% involved sexually active gay men; 17% were intravenous drug users; and 2% were blood transfusion recipients (Lord, Thornton, & Carey, 1986). However, a laboratory test introduced in 1985 now virtually eliminates the possibility of contracting AIDS via a blood transfusion, leaving intravenous drug use and sexual activity as the two main conduits of this fatal disease (Macklin, 1989). Of the 1989 cases, heterosexuals represented over one third of the total, and over 1,600 cases of pediatric AIDS were included in these figures (Kloser, 1989). As the 1990s began, gay men accounted for 68% of the reported AIDS cases in the United States (Ekstrand & Coates, 1990). According to the CDC over 147,000 AIDS cases had been reported by September 1990, representing a 66% increase since June 1989. Based on these statistics, the number of AIDS cases is growing at the rate of over 3,500 per month ("Number of AIDS Cases," 1990).

In today's changing moral climate with increased sexual freedom, young people, especially, must be educated that they represent a high-risk AIDS group. Vincent Fontona, M.D., medical director and pediatrician-in-chief at the New York Foundling Hospital, emphasized:

> *Sex these days can be risky, and ignorance is a common theme in the stories of many of the young people that have already died of AIDS . . . ignorance that their sexual behavior had put their lives at risk. . . . There is a tremendous amount of denial that "it can't happen to me". . . . It is no longer a matter of with whom one has a sexual encounter but with whom that person has engaged sexually in the last 7 to 10 years—the time it takes to develop AIDS after contracting the disease.*
>
> *(Prescod, 1987, p. 1)*

Much of the recent increase in STDs can be attributed to increasing sexual permissiveness and, to some degree, an increasing involvement with multiple sex partners. Loving partners in couple relationships, who have not previously had sexual intercourse, do not give each other STDs. But when one has sexual intercourse with a sexually experienced person, the risk of infection is always present. The more frequently that a person engages in casual sex, the greater that risk.

Some research is reflecting AIDS-related concerns among college students. In one study, 21% of women and 16% of men were extremely worried about getting AIDS through any contact, either sexual or social/casual (Adler & Sedlacek, 1989). However, over 40% of the students, while worried, did not believe that they would contract AIDS unless they had sexual intercourse or shared an intravenous needle with an infected person. The effects of these concerns over AIDS are also reflected in the sexual activity of unmarried college students. Over 40% of sexually active women and men in another study reported that being distressed over AIDS had affected their sexual behavior patterns. Among nonsexually actives, 15% indicated concerns about AIDS prevented them from engaging in sexual intercourse while only 3% of those formerly sexually active reported becoming celibate. However, 30% of those who were sexually active became more selective in their choice of a sex partner (Carroll, 1988). Despite these concerns, only 41% of college women at the end of the 1980s reported using condoms on a regular basis during premarital sexual intercourse (DeBuono et al., 1990).

Professionals believe that the fear of AIDS may be hastening an end to the sexual revolution that began in the 1960s. There is some anecdotal evidence that postcollege women and men are restructuring their sexual lives. Especially "one-night stands," casual sex, and mate swapping appear to be diminishing somewhat because of health fears rather than morality (Nordheimer, 1986). A detailed discussion of STDs will follow in chapter 11, "Birth Control and Sexually Transmitted Diseases."

Summary

- While infants display rudimentary sexual behavior, preschool children usually engage in explicit sex play. Male children are less negatively admonished about sexual play than female children. This and other differential treatment leads to the development of gender-specific sexual attitudes.
- Male adolescents are interested in sexual activity for its own sake, while female adolescents are more likely to view sexual activity within the broader context of relationships or love and romance.
- Studies show that many female and male adolescents masturbate fairly regularly, with or without involvement in other sexual activity such as petting and premarital sexual intercourse.
- Public attitudes toward sexual intercourse among unmarried people have become much less harsh in recent years, and the incidence of such behavior has steadily increased for both women and men. While there is less evidence of a sexual double standard today than in previous generations, it remains in the attitudes of many.
- Men still become involved in sexual intercourse somewhat earlier than women and are less likely to be in love with their first sexual intercourse partner.
- Most couples do not use effective contraception and thus greatly elevate the risk of pregnancy. Women, more often than men, suffer anxiety and guilt when involved in premarital sexual intercourse.
- New sexual patterns conflict with new values that place great importance on openness and honesty in interpersonal relationships. Although these patterns have relieved young people of some pressures, they have introduced new ones such as promoting sexual intercourse even if one is not socially or emotionally ready.
- Women and men today seem better able to become acquainted with one another as persons and not simply as dates and prospective sexual partners. When sexual relationships do develop, they tend to be serious, involved, and responsible.
- The new sexual permissiveness has brought some unpleasant consequences such as the aftermath of a broken relationship. In addition, a high rate of unintended pregnancies results in earlier marriages, abortion, or rearing infants as single parents. Further, sexually transmitted diseases have become epidemic among persons having casual sex.
- Childbearing during the teen years has substantial medical, social, and psychological consequences for the unmarried teen mother and her baby.

Questions for Critical Reflection

1. Compare your early sex education experiences with those of your best friend. In what ways were they similar? What do you believe accounted for the differences?
2. Since research documents that young people receive most of their sexuality information from peers, how do you account for the fact that parents are still the child's most significant sexuality educator?
3. In one recent survey, more unmarried college women had experienced sexual intercourse than had masturbated. What factors could explain such findings?
4. How "alive and well" is the sexual double standard among your friends and acquaintances?
5. Opposing opinions concerning the "right to say no" or the "right to say not now" are cited in your text. Which position do you support? Do you believe either approach represents effective sex education?

Suggested Readings

Anthony, J., Green, R., & Kolodny, R. (1982). *Childhood sexuality.* Boston: Little, Brown. Authoritative source about childhood and adolescent sexuality patterns.

Francoeur, R. T. (1989). *Taking sides: Clashing views on controversial issues in sexuality* (2nd ed.). Guilford, CT: Dushkin. Lively and thoughtful debates by articulate advocates on opposite sides of a variety of controversial sexual questions.

Macklin, E. D. (Ed.). (1989). *AIDS and families.* New York: Haworth Press. An anthology concerning the effects of AIDS on family relationships developed by the AIDS Task Force of the Groves Conference on Marriage and the Family.

Parrinder, G. (1980). *Sex in the world's religions.* New York: Oxford University Press. An outstanding and concise review of various religious approaches to human sexuality.

Reiss, I. L., & Reiss, H. M. (1990). *An end to shame: Shaping our next sexual revolution.* Buffalo, NY: Prometheus Books. A scholarly consideration of select cultural factors as precursors to an anticipated forthcoming sexual revolution.

CHAPTER 5

Alternative Life-Styles

In this era of experimentation we have
seen many alternatives proposed to the conventional
marriage and nuclear family—some to cause a
momentary flurry of interest in the popular press
and then fade from sight, others to remain as viable
options to be explored by thoughtful people
sincerely seeking personal fulfillment.
Nina S. Fields, 1986

Outline

Living Together without Marriage
1. A Typology of Cohabitation

Cohabitation as Courtship
1. Prevalence of Cohabitation • 2. Reasons for Increased Cohabitation Among College Students

Characteristics of Cohabiting Partners
1. Sociodemographic Variables

Relationship Issues
1. Sexual Division of Labor • 2. Sexual Satisfaction • 3. Financial Concerns • 4. Intimacy • 5. Attitudes toward Marriage

The "Costs" and "Profits" of Cohabitation
1. Improvement of Mate Selection • 2. Avoidance of Exploitation • 3. Cohabitation and Marital Satisfaction

Legal Considerations in Cohabitation
1. Community Property • (Box 5.1: Should You "Live Together"?) • 2. Inheritance

Homosexuality as an Alternative Life-Style
1. Definition of Homosexuality • 2. The Extent of Homosexuality

Societal Attitudes toward Lesbians and Gays
1. Legality of Same-Sex Practices • 2. Religion and the Homosexuality Issue

Dating and Courtship Patterns among Lesbians and Gays
1. The Stable Relationships of Lesbians • 2. Gays and "Cruising"

Lesbian and Gay Parents
1. Lesbian Mothers and Child-Rearing Practices • 2. Parenting Concerns of Gay Fathers

Summary

Questions for Critical Reflection

Suggested Readings

Made in heaven, settled in court, the title of a book addressing legal issues surrounding unmarried cohabitation, reflects American fascination with alternative life-styles (Mitchelson, 1979). The research on nontraditional family forms, which has increased dramatically since the 1960s, mirrors a period of rapid social change. The vast majority of Americans still marry, have children, live in single-family households and prefer heterosexuality and permanence with sexual exclusivity. Increasingly, however, as the evidence indicates, other life-styles are being chosen (Macklin, 1987). It is a mistake to believe that in the "good old days" there were no variations of the traditional nuclear family. The difference lies in the fact that in earlier times social and economic realities dictated alternate patterns, and free choice is exercised in such matters today. In this chapter, only unmarried cohabitation and homosexuality will be addressed as nontraditional family forms.

Unmarried cohabitation, hereafter referred to simply as cohabitation, is an alternative life-style which has become much more common in our society particularly among college students and postcollege young adults. Since 1970, the number of persons in the United States who have cohabited has increased by at least 495% (U.S. Bureau of the Census, 1990g).

Another alternative life-style also has emerged in our society with the decision of many lesbians and gays to "come out of the closet." However, as will be seen, it is very difficult to accurately determine the precise number of persons who are homosexual. One reason may be the stigma that society often imposes upon homosexuals. Further, because many persons have had one or more homosexual experiences but do not consider themselves to be homosexual, confusion of terminology has resulted.

Living Together without Marriage

Cohabitation (living together, "shacking up") has been defined as a living situation wherein an adult is sharing living quarters with one unrelated adult of the opposite sex. Children may or may not be present in the household, but no other adult may be living in the residence (Spanier, 1983). Although cohabitation exists in a variety of situations, this chapter focuses on cohabitation as an extension of a romantic relationship. Inherent in this definition is the assumption that sexual activity occurs between the cohabiting partners.

Today's college students may assume that cohabitation is of recent vintage since it is highly unlikely that their parents ever lived in such an arrangement. The fact is that the practice has been around since ancient times, existing in all types of cultures to varying degrees (Trost, 1979). In an analysis of cohabitation in his native Sweden and other countries, Trost makes the point that cohabitation has existed for centuries even though both the church and state made efforts to legally prohibit such behavior. Even in the United States the concept of alternative life-styles is not new. Judge Ben Lindsey spoke of a trial, or "companionate," marriage as long ago as 1927 (Russell, 1929). Later, during the 1960s, Vance Packard (1968) urged a 2-year confirmation period for marriage partners. By this time, Margaret Mead's (1966) proposal for a "two-stage marriage," consisting of an "individual" and a "parental" marriage, had already attracted considerable attention. Although both stages would require licensing, the first stage was characterized by a serious commitment, while the second one offered more permanence and allowed the option of children. Obviously none of these earlier proposals have gained cultural acceptance.

Although cohabitation itself is far from new, the trend escalating this type of behavior is fairly recent. What began in the 1960s in Sweden and Denmark had become an American trend by the 1970s. This era in the United States is remembered as the time of open marriages, communes, and group marriages. Of all these alternate life-styles, however, cohabitation is the one which still thrives today. It is important to understand that from the beginning, cohabitation in the United States differed considerably from that in Sweden and Denmark. While in America cohabitation is considered behavior that deviates from the norm, in Scandinavian countries with the world's highest cohabitation rates, it is considered an institution. The difference in perceptions of cohabitation in Sweden and the United States is illustrated in the findings of the Family Study Group at Uppsala University in Sweden. Both newly-married and cohabiting Swedish women and men overwhelmingly viewed the term cohabitation to mean "like being married" or "married indirectly." Of these couples, almost one half of women and the majority of men referred to their cohabitor as either wife/husband or fiancée/fiancé (Trost, 1979).

In Denmark, the practice is referred to as a "paperless marriage" and is also considered to be the "same as marriage" (Moore, 1986). Children born to the couples in these paperless marriages are neither a social stigma nor financial burden since Danish government support allows mothers to keep their children without great financial stress. However, according to Henrek Andrup, one of Denmark's leading divorce lawyers, there are new trends emerging among unmarried couples with children. Increasingly, legal documents are being drawn up to substantiate paternity and to establish the offspring as an heir. Therefore, Andrup believes paperless marriages are beginning to diminish because, "with children there is just as much paper work as in traditional marriages" (Moore, 1986, p. 103).

A Typology of Cohabitation

As the practice of cohabitation has become more widespread in the United States, several researchers have attempted to identify the motivations and/or functions of cohabitation. One such effort has resulted in the development of a typology of cohabitation based on the most common patterns identified among cohabiting couples. Four types of cohabitors were identified:

1. *Linus Blanket*—A "security blanket" relationship in which one partner serves as a buffer for a dependent-type personality who seeks refuge from living alone. This relationship often ends when the stronger cohabiting partner recognizes and resents being used.
2. *Emancipation*—Attempting to gain independence from parental influence and live according to one's own values, these cohabitors usually engage in a series of short-term, repeated relationships. A large proportion of women from this group come from strict, traditional backgrounds, with Catholics over-represented in this category.
3. *Convenience*—This type of cohabitation typically involves exploitation where the man's primary goals are usually sexual fulfillment and avoidance of domestic responsibilities. The woman supplies love and care in hopes that the relationship might lead to marriage, her primary goal.
4. *Testing*—For some, living together is to test the feasibility of marriage. Couples in a satisfying, intimate, physical relationship may be testing each other as a marriage partner or testing marriage itself (Ridley, Peterman, & Avery, 1978, p. 133).

Besides the above typology, still another category, "permanent or semi-permanent alternative to marriage," has been identified, whereby individuals are living together in a long-term, committed relationship but without the legal and religious sanctions usually associated with marriage (Macklin, 1983).

Regardless of the reasons to cohabit, most couples do not engage in elaborate planning to begin living together as might be the case for getting married; they drift into such an arrangement. Consider this familiar scenario: As sexual intercourse begins to occur on a regular basis, it becomes more and more inconvenient for one partner to get out of bed, dress, and go home, so she/he develops the habit of staying overnight. Chances are that the couple may already be eating some meals together, because it is cheaper than eating in restaurants. Other circumstances which may promote the drift into cohabitation occur when one partner loses her/his apartment or roommate. Among college students, especially in the initial stages, one partner only partially moves in with the other. Usually, both living spaces are retained allowing the mover to return at times to her/his own place to eat meals, to exchange clothes, and to pick up mail. This type of arrangement helps to hide the cohabitation from parents and enables the maintenance of close relationships with others. Further, it also provides a separate place for each to go in the event of a serious argument (Macklin, 1972).

Cohabitation as Courtship

Nonmarital cohabitation in the United States serves primarily as a part of the courtship process (Macklin, 1987). This function was substantiated in a study of southern college students among whom 63% indicated that they perceived cohabitation to be a new stage in courtship, and only 28% perceived it as a "trial" marriage. However, of those who were cohabiting, a much larger number (80%) perceived cohabitation as representing a new stage in the courtship process. Fewer than 1 in 5 of those cohabiting were engaged to be married (Preble, 1978). Yet, in a comparison of cohabiting and noncohabiting couples, cohabiting women had substantially higher expectations of eventually marrying their current partner than did noncohabitors. Cohabitation does not appear to threaten the institution of marriage. Most cohabiting relationships either terminate or progress into marriage within a year or two after their beginning (Macklin, 1980). Thus, cohabitation is not considered a long-term alternative to marriage (Risman, Hill, Rubin, & Peplau, 1981). The fact that women have been found to be more **monogamous** than men while in cohabiting relationships may reflect their more likely perception of the relationship as a prelude to marriage (Pietropinto, 1986).

Prevalence of Cohabitation

Accurate prevalence rates of cohabitation have been difficult to establish due to a lack of a generally accepted operational definition. Because cohabitation is a transition phenomenon, "currently cohabiting" rates are much smaller than those for "ever cohabited" (Macklin, 1987). Evidence suggests that cohabitation may be stabilizing. Only 33% of women, ages 15–44, from a 1988 national representative sample reported having ever cohabited (Forrest & Singh, 1990). Between 1960 and 1970 there was a gradual increase in the number of couples living together, but by 1980 that number had tripled. Although the total number of cohabiting couples was still a small proportion of all couple households (3.6% in 1980), it continued to rise during the 1980s (U.S. Bureau of the Census, 1990g). Further, earlier researchers concluded that cohabitation was more prevalent among college students than in the general population (Clayton & Voss, 1977). Even though it is more difficult to establish an accurate appraisal for the general population, it is known that in 1970, there were a total of over 0.5 million cohabiting couples in the United States. By 1988, the number had grown to 2.6 million (see Table 5.1). Further, over two thirds of the cohabiting couples had no children under age 15.

Table 5.1: Characteristics of Unmarried Couple Households

Characteristics	1970	1980	1988
Unmarried couples	523	1,589	2,588
Children			
None under age 15	327	1,159	1,786
Some under age 15	196	431	802
Age			
Under age 25	55	411	510
Ages 25–44	103	837	1,635
Ages 45–64	186	221	325
Age 65 and over	178	119	118

Note: Numbers refer to thousands.
Source: U.S. Bureau of the Census, 1990g, No. 54, "Unmarried Couples by Selected Characteristics, 1970 to 1987, and by Marital Status of Partners, 1988" in *Statistical Abstract of the United States, 1990,* 110th ed., p. 44. Washington, DC: U.S. Government Printing Office.

In a study of marriage license applicants, the prevalence of cohabitation at the time of marriage was found to have dramatically increased from 13% of all couples in 1970 to 73% of all couples in 1980 (Gwartney-Gibbs, 1986). A national survey of unmarried women, ages 20–29, found a much lower rate (30%) had engaged in cohabitation at least once in their lifetimes (Tanfer, 1986). Those with less than 12 years of education were more than twice as likely to have ever engaged in cohabitation in comparison to those women with one or more years of college. These data represent an interesting finding since the recent trend of cohabitation had its beginning among college students. It may reflect the previous lack of data from the general population or that cohabitation has become more acceptable.

When considering cohabitation among college students, some unique factors emerge. In a large-scale survey of the prevalence of cohabitation among college students, the percentages were found to vary considerably by gender and geographical region (Bower & Christopherson, 1977). The reported percentages of college women who have ever engaged in cohabitation have ranged from 6–25% (6%—Silverman, 1977; and 25%—Macklin, 1987) and college men from 14–34%

Co-ed dormitories and relaxed rules are a sign of the times in a day when universities no longer assume the in loco parentis role.

(14%—Silverman, 1977; and 34%—Bower & Christopherson, 1977). Cohabitation reportedly occurs most frequently in the Northeast and West, as well as in urban settings (Clayton & Voss, 1977; Glick & Spanier, 1980).

Reasons for Increased Cohabitation among College Students

Research suggests that there are at least three major reasons why there was a substantial increase in the percentage of college students cohabiting during the 1970s and 1980s. These reasons are new sex norms, especially among peers; increasingly tolerant attitudes by parents; and more convenient access to contraceptives. New sex norms and tolerant attitudes by parents, especially, have contributed to the increased participation in cohabitation by the general population.

New Sex Norms

While there is a difference in sex norms of college student-cohabitors and noncohabitors, as early as 1977 the majority of both groups, 90% and 52% respectively, had expressed a willingness to personally consider cohabitation in order to "test" a relationship. Further, 8 in 10 cohabitors and 4 in 10 noncohabitors were willing to cohabit without prior plans to marry the person (Bower & Christopherson, 1977). Most college students generally approve of cohabitation. When queried about what kind of relationship should exist before persons engage in cohabitation, most students in one study felt there should be an affectionate, preferably monogamous, relationship between the two partners (Macklin, 1983). Another survey of attitudes toward cohabitation at two universities determined that over one third of those in the Northeast and slightly fewer of those in the Midwest believed that cohabitation was appropriate if an affectionate relationship existed and contraception was going to be used (Silverman, 1977). Apparently, cohabitation is increasingly finding peer approval, especially among male college students. Further evidence of changing sexual norms can be found in a survey conducted by *The Chronicle of Higher Education;* only 12% of colleges and universities reported that they had policies which prohibited cohabitation (Middleton & Roark, 1981).

Parental Attitudes

One survey of college students found that among men, about three fourths believed that their mothers and fathers would disapprove if they cohabited. Of those who had actually engaged in cohabitation, less than one half believed that their parents were aware of their living arrangement (Bower & Christopherson, 1977). An earlier study determined that many female cohabitors feared discovery by their parents and felt guilty about deceiving them. After their parents learned of their cohabitation, many had received ultimatums to stop such behavior (Macklin, 1972). Although a *Time* magazine poll in 1978 found that one half of parents believed that it was not "morally wrong" for unmarried individuals to engage in cohabitation, many cohabitors felt they were acting contrary to parental attitudes and preferences (Yankelovich, 1981). It is interesting to note that cohabitors have reported receiving less sexual information as a child and to have mothers and fathers who were more conservative in their sexual attitudes in comparison to noncohabitors (Newcomb, 1986).

Influence of Contraceptive Availability

A survey of 400 physicians was used to assess the influence of modern contraception on the increasing number of unmarried couples living together. The responses indicated that contraceptives were believed to be very influential—41%, and significantly influential—37% (Pietropinto, 1986). In general, cohabiting couples are more likely to use oral contraceptives in order to achieve a higher level of security against an unwanted pregnancy (Hill, Peplau, & Rubin, 1983). One study of college couples found that over one half typically used oral contraceptives, while about 1 in 10 used a diaphragm or condoms. Prescription methods of contraception were more likely to be used by women whose fathers had graduated from college (80% versus 54%) and by non-Catholic women. A woman's prior sexual experience was said to increase the couple's use of contraceptives, whereas a man's prior sexual experience decreased the likelihood of contraceptive use as the dating relationship continued (Hill et al., 1983). Not only are contraceptives more easily available, their purchase, once an embarrassing situation, is unlikely to create much discomfort. Data from university students indicate that few female or male purchasers were made to feel uncomfortable by the contraceptive seller (see Table 5.2).

Table 5.2: Reported Feelings Generated by Seller during Contraceptive Purchase

	Women	Men
Uncomfortable	8%	7%
Like I was doing something bad	3	2
Like I was doing something good	7	7
Dirty	0	1
Stupid	1	3
Embarrassed	11	10
Pleasant	26	26
Neutral	79	81

Note: Respondents gave more than one answer so column totals equal more than 100%.

From D. J. Kallen and J. J. Stephenson, "The Purchase of Contraceptives by College Students" in *Family Relations,* 29:362. Copyright © 1980 National Council on Family Relations, 3989 Central Avenue, N.E., Suite #550, Minneapolis, MN 55421. Reprinted by permission.

Characteristics of Cohabiting Partners

Thus far, most of our attention has been devoted to cohabitation among college students. But a substantial quantity of evidence has emerged which shows that cohabitation is becoming much more prevalent among the noncollege population, both for persons in the postcollege years and for persons who have never attended college (Macklin, 1987). A clearer picture of this increasing percentage of persons living together will emerge with an examination of the sociodemographic and relationship variables associated with other populations as well as college students who are engaging in cohabitation.

Sociodemographic Variables

The likelihood of cohabitation has been found to be influenced by a number of sociodemographic variables including age, educational level, race, prior marital status, size of hometown, religiosity, and political conservatism/liberalism (Clayton & Voss, 1977). As cohabitation becomes more widespread, the differences between persons who have and have not cohabited become increasingly insignificant (Carpenter, W. D.,

1989). However, differing profiles of cohabitors and noncohabitors do emerge from the data.

Age

Although, as a group, cohabitors are somewhat younger than marrieds when comparing data from the decade of the 1980s, it is apparent that the age of cohabitors is increasing. Using data from the U.S. Bureau of the Census, equal numbers (38%) of cohabitors were found to be under age 25 and between ages 25–34 (Spanier, 1983). These findings are consistent with another study in which almost one half of women were under age 25, and nearly 40% were ages 25–34. However, fewer than one third of the men were under age 25, and one half were ages 25–34 (Gwartney-Gibbs, 1986). The fact that there were more younger women and older men probably reflects the social custom that most women tend to date and marry men who are slightly older than they are. By 1988, only one fifth of cohabiting women and men were under age 25 and about two thirds were between ages 25–44 (U.S. Bureau of the Census, 1990g).

Education

In examining the 1981 Census data for the educational level of never-married cohabitors, interesting gender differences are found. Almost two thirds of the women under age 35 had at least 12 years of education in comparison to slightly over one third of those older than age 54. Almost the same percentage of young male cohabitors under age 35 had 12 or less years of education. However, in comparison to women, the percentage of less educated men was more than double among those older than age 54. Surprisingly, almost two thirds of the older college-educated female cohabitors had never married (Spanier, 1983). From these data, it is apparent that as college-educated women reach age 55 and have never been married, they become more agreeable to establishing a cohabitation arrangement. However, as previously mentioned, it appears that the more educated woman is less likely to enter cohabitation than the less educated one. In a national survey of women in their 20s, almost one half of those with less than 12 years of education had cohabited in comparison to about one third of those with 12 years of education and still fewer of those with more than 12 years of education (see Table 5.3). It should be noted that the Census data reports persons currently cohabiting, whereas the Tanfer (1986) data includes persons who have cohabited during their lifetimes. Despite these seemingly contradictory data, it is likely that cohabitation is increasing in popularity among college-educated persons. For example, in a California study, the mean number of years of education completed for women cohabitors was 15.1 years and 14.5 years for cohabiting men (Newcomb, 1986).

Table 5.3: Demographic Characteristics of Never-Married Women Cohabitors

Characteristic	Currently Cohabiting	Ever Cohabited
ALL WOMEN	12%	30%
Age		
20–24 years	12	26
25–29 years	12	38
Race		
White	13	30
Black	10	29
Education		
Less than 12 years	23	46
12 years	15	36
More than 12 years	9	22
Religion		
Catholic	11	29
Non-Catholic	12	28
None	15	48
Residence		
Metro (SMSA)	12	32
Nonmetro (Non-SMSA)	12	22
Population		
100,000 or more	15	38
Less than 100,000	10	24
Region		
Northeast	9	28
North Central	12	25
South	11	29
West	20	44

From K. Tanfer, *Patterns of Premarital Cohabitation among Never-Married Women in the U.S.*, paper presented at the meeting of the Population Association of America, San Francisco, CA.

Race

Because of the uneven distribution of blacks in the general population, it is difficult to determine the racial composition of cohabiting couples. Furthermore, unpublished Census data provide only limited insights because the percentages are reported as total numbers of

Table 5.4: Cohabiting Couples by Marital Status, 1988

		Marital Status of Woman			
Marital Status of Man	Totals	Never-Married	Divorced	Widowed	Married/Husband Absent
Totals	2,588	1,364 (53)	875 (34)	177 (7)	172 (6)
Never married	1,401 (54)	968 (71)	300 (34)	62 (35)	71 (41)
Divorced	894 (35)	313 (23)	469 (54)	58 (33)	54 (31)
Widowed	80 (3)	19 (1)	21 (2)	35 (20)	5 (3)
Married/wife absent	213 (8)	64 (5)	85 (10)	22 (12)	42 (25)

Note: Numbers without parentheses refer to thousands, while numbers in parentheses refer to percentages.
Source: U.S. Bureau of the Census, 1990g, No. 54, "Unmarried Couples by Selected Characteristics, 1970 to 1988, and by Marital Status of Partners, 1988" in *Statistical Abstract of the United States, 1990,* 110th ed., p. 44. Washington, DC: U.S. Government Printing Office.

persons found to be cohabiting rather than the proportional distribution of blacks and whites (Spanier, 1983). However, a fairly accurate appraisal for women cohabitors by race can be found in Table 5.3. These data suggest that the percentages of white and black women who have cohabited are very similar (Tanfer, 1986). However, it is possible that college-educated black women may be less willing to engage in cohabitation than white women because of the pressures to find a college-educated black husband from a limited pool. But for men the picture is somewhat different. In a sample of 2,500 men, ages 20–30, taken from Selective Service registration records, almost twice as many black (29%) as white (16%) men had engaged in cohabitation (Clayton & Voss, 1977). Although blacks tend to have higher rates of cohabitation than whites, they represent only a small proportion of the total number of cohabitors (Glick & Spanier, 1980).

Former Marital Status

Fairly large numbers of formerly married persons engage in cohabitation in their subsequent love relationships. Two studies are remarkably similar concerning the number of cohabitors who were formerly married. According to 1988 Census data, 47% of female and 46% of male cohabitors had previously been married (see Table 5.4). These findings are similar to the Oregon study which found that 41% of both female and male cohabitors had previously been married (Gwartney-Gibbs, 1986). The formerly married may prefer to cohabit to help determine whether the new relationship will last. It is also probable that they may not be in a financial position to marry.

Place of Residence

Two studies from the 1970s and 1980s agree that size of town/city affects the likelihood of cohabitation. The Clayton and Voss (1977) study suggests that persons living in large urban centers are more likely to cohabit. They found that about one third of those who lived in a city with a population of 1 million or more had engaged in cohabitation in comparison to only about one sixth of those individuals who lived in cities under 25,000. Using different city-size categories, Tanfer (1986) also found that one third of women who lived in a city of 100,000 or more had cohabited, in comparison to only one fourth of those who lived in a smaller city (see Table 5.3). A larger city provides more anonymity for cohabitors since neighbors and employers may be less likely to become aware of the living arrangements.

Religion

Based on college data, Catholic and Protestant students are equally as likely to engage in cohabitation, while Jewish students are much more likely to do so (Silverman, 1977). These findings are similar to later ones for women, but no differences were found between Catholic, Jewish, and Protestant men (Newcomb, 1986). Regardless of religious preference, religion itself is a variable related to the likelihood of engaging in cohabitation, with those persons reporting no religion much more likely to cohabit (see Table 5.3). As might be expected, attendance at religious services was substantially less frequent for cohabitors than noncohabitors (Silverman, 1977). Regardless of educational level, if male cohabitors attended religious services at all, it was much less frequently than noncohabitors (Clayton & Voss, 1977). For postcollege, never-married women, only 1 in 10 of those who had engaged in cohabitation attended religious services more than once per week, in contrast to over one fourth of those who had never engaged in cohabitation (Tanfer, 1986). Thus, researchers have consistently found cohabitors to have lower rates of attendance at religious services as well as lower rates of religious affiliation.

Conservative/Liberal Orientation

In general, cohabitors more than noncohabitors tend to engage in unconventional behavior, perceive themselves as androgynous, and have liberal attitudes (Macklin, 1987). For example, college cohabitors are more likely than noncohabitors to have been in a dating relationship of three months or longer that involved sexual intercourse (Carpenter, W. D., 1989). Earlier data reported that male cohabitors were much more likely to have used marijuana, sedatives, heroin, opiates, and cocaine than noncohabitors. Further, male cohabitors were twice as likely as noncohabitors to have reported their age at first sexual intercourse as age 15 or younger (Clayton & Voss, 1977). A later national survey of unmarried women found that twice as many cohabitors had engaged in premarital sexual intercourse than noncohabitors prior to actual cohabitation. Further, only one fifth of the noncohabitors had been pregnant, in contrast to one half of those who had engaged in cohabitation. In this same study, the average age at first sexual intercourse was age 18 for noncohabitors but age 17 for persons who had cohabited (Tanfer, 1986). Another study found that women who had cohabited were more likely than others to report a greater number of sex partners, to have engaged in masturbation at an earlier age, and to masturbate more frequently. Cohabitors also have been found to score higher on political liberalism scales than noncohabitors (Newcomb, 1986).

In summary, one could picture the typical female cohabitor as never married; less educated; ages 25–44; equally as likely to be black or white; unlikely to be religious in affiliation or practice (if religious, likely to be Jewish); urban resident; more liberal, sexually and politically; and androgynous. The typical male cohabitor would differ on only one variable. He would more likely be black.

Relationship Issues

Although demographic data may furnish superficial information with which to sketch the profile of the typical cohabitor, it does not address the deeper issue of relationships. Initial studies, primarily of married college students, found few significant differences with regard to relationship issues between those who had and had not cohabited before marriage (Risman et al., 1981). With the exception of degree of commitment, few differences were found between married and cohabiting couples during the 1970s. More recently, however, research using broader populations has yielded significant differences (Macklin, 1987). Since many women and men cohabit for the purpose of testing relationship compatibility, it is important to review some of the potential sources of conflict that may exist for the couple.

Sexual Division of Labor

A comparison of gender-role-attitude scores determined that women who have never cohabited are more likely to exhibit traditional gender-role attitudes (Tanfer, 1986). Since cohabitors are likely to perceive themselves as more androgynous and liberal than noncohabitors, a more egalitarian division of household tasks would be expected (Newcomb & Bentler, 1980b). However, cohabiting and married couples are equally as likely to have traditional sexual divisions of labor. Although cohabiting partners generally share some chores, such as shopping and doing the laundry, the woman typically does most of the cooking and cleaning (Stafford, Backman, & Dibona, 1977). While in theory, cohabitors may hold more liberal attitudes, there is less behavioral egalitarianism (Risman et al., 1981). The liberal attitudes of men toward women's roles in the work force do not necessarily reflect an absence of patriarchal attitudes in the home. In fact, speculations are that it is the attitudes of women that are transforming the distribution of home labor rather than those of men (Hardesty & Bokemeier, 1989). As gender roles are gradually undergoing change, one would anticipate that change in traditional roles would occur among persons who choose to engage in cohabitation just as change in traditional roles is occurring for married persons in our society.

Roles and rules: Who makes them? Who breaks them?
Two pending questions in today's society.

Table 5.5: Sexual Behaviors and Satisfaction

Sexual Behaviors and Satisfaction	Sample 1		Sample 2		Sample 3	
	Cohabitor	Non-cohabitor	Cohabitor	Non-cohabitor	Cohabitor	Non-cohabitor
Sexual behaviors						
Age at first sexual contact[a]	13.2	16.0	13.4	14.2	13.2	13.5
Age at first intercourse[a]	17.3	18.5	16.9	17.9	18.0	17.3
Age at first masturbation[a]	15.5	12.5	—	—	—	—
Number heterosexual partners[b]	16.2	5.9	14.0	2.6	11.1	4.5
Times intercourse/month[b]	15.7	9.6	—	—	—	—
Times masturbation/month[b]	8.9	6.0	—	—	—	—
Sexual satisfaction						
Satisfaction with coitus[c]	7.2	7.1	8.2	8.3	7.6	8.1

[a]Mean number of years.
[b]Mean number of partners or frequency.
[c]Mean scores ranging from extremely repulsive = 1 to extremely satisfying = 9.
Source: M. D. Newcomb, "Sexual Behavior of Cohabitors: A Comparison of Three Independent Samples" in *The Journal of Sex Research,* 22:502–503.

Sexual Satisfaction

The popular perception of cohabitation implies that the primary motivation for couples choosing to live together is to provide either a greater or more convenient opportunity for sexual activity. Men are usually perceived as being more satisfied with the sexual part of the living-together arrangement than women (Pietropinto, 1986). As might be anticipated, the weekly frequency of sexual intercourse is substantially higher for couples living together in contrast to those couples who are going together (Risman et al., 1981). Further, cohabiting women and men are more likely to have experience with a greater number of sex partners, are less satisfied with their sexual experiences, and are more likely to have been involved in group sex than married respondents (Markowski, Croake, & Keller, 1978).

Another study, which reported significant differences between cohabitors and noncohabitors concerning age at initiation, frequency of sexual behaviors, and number of sex partners, found no difference in sexual satisfaction during sexual intercourse (see Table 5.5). Nevertheless, cohabiting women did report a higher percentage of orgasms occurring during sexual intercourse and with partner-related noncoital stimulation techniques (Newcomb, 1986). In an earlier study of cohabitors, it was found that about two thirds of women reported specific sexual problems. These sexual difficulties, in order of reporting, are different degrees of sexual interest, lack of orgasm, and fear of pregnancy (Ridley et al., 1978).

Financial Concerns

One survey found that two thirds of cohabiting women were in the labor force, and about one fourth were working at home on family-related tasks (Tanfer, 1986). It is obvious that whether or not both partners work there are many financial matters which should be taken into account when establishing a cohabitation relationship, some of which may have legal implications (Levinson, 1984). Decisions have to be made regarding household expenses such as utilities and food. Major purchases such as automobiles, appliances, furniture, and houses may be purchased and held jointly or separately.

Evidence suggests that premarital cohabitation is more likely to end in separation than in a subsequent marriage to the partner. Therefore, though unpleasant to consider at the beginning of the relationship, thought needs to be given to the division of any jointly-held property if the living-together relationship should end (Yamaguchi & Kandel, 1985).

Finally, few cohabiting couples share their finances completely. Although they are likely to share some of the expenses, each partner typically retains her/his own income. This separation symbolizes and helps

Table 5.6: Intimacy Expression

Intimacy Expression Variables	Women: Going Together	Women: Living Together	Men: Going Together	Men: Living Together
Frequency of interaction (seeing partner daily)	52.6%	100.0%	48.9%	100.0%
Frequency of intercourse (6+ times per week)	11.8%	37.5%	11.6%	43.6%
Closeness (9 = maximum score)	7.5	8.4	7.5	8.3
Love scale (9 = maximum score)	7.0	7.5	6.9	7.4
Self-disclosure given (34 = maximum score)	25.0	28.3	24.7	27.8
Self-disclosure received (34 = maximum score)	24.6	27.6	24.2	27.2

Note: Scores reported as means.
From B. J. Risman, et al., "Living Together in College: Implications for Courtship" in *Journal of Marriage and the Family,* 43:81.

to assure the woman's continued financial independence from the man (Stafford et al., 1977). As discussed in a subsequent chapter, financial difficulties are often a major source of dissatisfaction among married couples. It is not surprising that this same potential exists for cohabiting couples and may be somewhat magnified by the absence of matrimony.

Persons contemplating cohabitation would be wise to seek the advice of an attorney in the particular state in which they plan to reside, since laws and court decisions governing joint/community property vary substantially from state to state. This is particularly true in those few states which recognize **common-law marriages.** Both parties should be well aware of requirements for marriage without formalities (common law) in order to differentiate between conditions of marriage and cohabitation. In Texas, a common-law marriage state, when two persons of the opposite sex cohabit, the only two factors which differentiate their relationship from common-law marriage are the agreement of the couple to be married and the representation of themselves to the public in some way as wife and husband.

Intimacy

An important part of any living-together arrangement is the degree to which the partners feel that their intimacy needs are being met and the degree to which they experience a sense of satisfaction in this area of their lives. Both women and men in cohabiting relationships report higher levels of personal satisfaction than those who do not cohabit. Also, one follow-up study of dating couples has shown that cohabiting couples are no more likely to break up than noncohabiting ones (Risman, et al., 1981). Cohabiting couples, in an early comparison to couples who were going together, reported higher degrees of closeness and being in love and perceived that self-disclosure had been both given and received in the relationship (see Table 5.6). However, in a more recent study of relationship attachment, there were no significant differences between cohabitors and noncohabitors regarding loving feelings for the partner (Newcomb, 1986). Whether cohabitation is a cause or an effect of differing degrees of intimacy is unclear.

Attitudes toward Marriage

The majority of noncohabitors in one study indicated that they would personally consider cohabitation as a mechanism to test out a relationship for marriage. But twice as many (80%) cohabitors than noncohabitors indicated that they would cohabit without prior plans to marry (Bower & Christopherson, 1977). However, a vast majority (82%) of currently cohabiting women and never-cohabited women (84%) reported they were likely to eventually marry (Tanfer, 1986). In general, cohabiting women have higher expectations of eventually marrying their current partner than noncohabiting women who are currently going with someone (Risman et al., 1981). Women who were highly religious during adolescence were much more likely to marry their cohabiting partner than women who were only moderately or not religious (Yamaguchi & Kandel, 1985). It is also known that premarital cohabitors tend to delay first marriages longer than noncohabitors (Gwartney-Gibbs, 1986). Perhaps this issue is best placed in perspective by examining data concerning future marriage plans. In a study of never-married women, over one third of the currently cohabiting women wished they were married, compared to slightly more than one fourth of never-cohabited women (Tanfer, 1986). Many couples deny that living together means that they will eventually marry, indicating that permanent commitment is not common in this type of living arrangement. This argument lends support to the theory that cohabitation is a developing stage in the courtship process.

The "Costs" and "Profits" of Cohabitation

One way of approaching the decision of whether to establish a living-together arrangement with one's relationship partner is to evaluate the "costs" and "profits" that might result from cohabitation. Potential profits which have been identified are companionship, improvement of mate selection, sexual gratification, and economic gain. A potential cost is having to resolve conflict concerning property rights upon the termination of the relationship. Perhaps more importantly, cohabitors must be sufficiently stable in order to cope emotionally with the possible ending of the relationship. Many of the same kinds of feelings and concerns linked to a divorce could be associated with termination of a living-together arrangement. Additionally, there is an increased risk of exploitation, especially for female cohabitors who differ from men in expectations regarding marriage and maintenance of sexual exclusivity (Newcomb, 1979). Given the speculative nature of the supposed consequences of cohabitation, what are the chances for the improvement of mate selection, for exploitation in the living-together arrangement, and for increased marital satisfaction?

Improvement of Mate Selection

The research to date has not confirmed that married persons who have engaged in premarital cohabitation with each other have greater marital satisfaction or that their communication patterns are necessarily any better (Francoeur, 1991). However, the possibility exists that cohabitors could learn more about each other than would be possible under traditional courtship circumstances. Living together could also help partners to discover whether they are suited for marriage. But this probably depends upon their primary motives. Available research data clearly indicate that women are considerably more likely than men to anticipate that living together will ultimately culminate in marriage (Risman et al., 1981). Since sexual gratification is a major factor in the desire of many men to establish a living-together arrangement, the potentiality exists that the woman is exchanging sex for love and the man, love for sex. Thus, persons living together may actually impede the process of mate selection if they present facades to each other rather than presenting their real selves (Macklin, 1983). This possibility obviously exists in most dating relationships as well. No one really knows how long the average person can maintain such a facade before allowing their "true" self to become evident.

Another way to improve mate selection is to gain experience as a couple in problem solving. However, major questions are raised concerning whether or not living together actually is conducive to problem solving of issues such as equitable property rights, dealing with in-laws, the decision to have children, future marriage plans, sexual satisfaction, or self-actualization (Newcomb, 1979). Because many who live together maintain two residences, this arrangement allows one partner a place to go if a serious conflict should develop, which marriage and family experts believe discourages serious problem solving (Brothers, 1985). Thus, while the opportunity exists for premarital cohabitors to improve their chances for the selection of a marriage partner that will lead to a successful marriage, whether or not this actually happens continues to be debated.

Avoidance of Exploitation

Exploitation in relationships occurs when one person uses another to fulfill selfish needs. It frequently involves "hidden agendas"; even the exploiting person may be unaware of the underlying, unmet needs which drive her/his behavior. For those contemplating living together, there are probably at least two questions which may be of utmost importance: Are there ways to avoid being used? What are the effects of cohabitation on self-esteem?

Being Used

Some authorities suggest that when men get bored with having sexual intercourse with their cohabiting partners, they will leave for someone else. The average living together relationship lasted only about 9.5 months among one group of cohabitors (Brothers, 1985). Much earlier, a study of cohabiting college students revealed that women often felt they were being "used" both as a sexual outlet and to handle domestic responsibilities (Macklin, 1972). For these reasons, when the intended purposes are for the assessment of compatibility and/or trial marriage, some women establish a time limit for the living-together arrangement, stipulating that the relationship either must progress into marriage or end at a certain time.

Besides the use of sex and inequitable division of labor, partners may also be exploited for other reasons such as finances or status. The most important safeguard in avoiding exploitation of any kind is clarification of reasons for living together. If both partners are aware of their own motives and share them in open, clear communication, the likelihood of being used to meet their own or their partners neurotic needs is diminished.

Self-Esteem Considerations

Some opponents of living together have argued that it represents a misguided attempt to enhance one's self-esteem by making the person feel that she/he possesses qualities which would be desirable in an intimate love relationship. Further, they claim the person will suffer the opposite effect, a substantial loss of self-esteem, after the cohabitation ends. This outcome was suggested in a comparison of female cohabitors, both lifetime (ever cohabited) and current, and noncohabitors. The findings did not show any significant differences in self-esteem scores between current cohabitors and noncohabitors, but previous cohabitors did report slightly lower self-esteem scores than the noncohabitors (Tanfer, 1986).

Cohabitation and Marital Satisfaction

College students personally considering whether or not to cohabit may be concerned with the influence of premarital cohabitation on subsequent marital satisfaction. However, just analyzing whether respondents have or have not engaged in premarital cohabitation represents an oversimplification of the issue since there may be many other intervening variables. In fact, some have concluded that premarital cohabitation may not provide the kinds of learning experiences which are likely to alter a person's chances of success in marriage either in a positive or negative direction (Jacques & Chason, 1979).

Studies from the 1970s and 1980s yield somewhat different results. Based on her review of the research about cohabitation conducted during the 1970s, Macklin (1983) concluded that when married persons who cohabited before marriage are compared with those who did not, no significant differences exist with regard to marital satisfaction, amount of conflict, emotional closeness, degree of commitment, or degree of intimacy. In addition, no differences were found in the areas of communication, need satisfaction, relationship stability, and sexual satisfaction (Jacques & Chason, 1979). However, studies in the 1980s tend to support significant differences between cohabitors and noncohabitors in marital satisfaction. For example, one study found that those wives who had not cohabited reported higher degrees of consensus on marital issues and greater marital satisfaction than those wives who had cohabited prior to marriage. But there were no significant differences between male cohabitors and noncohabitors with regard to the degree of consensus on marital satisfaction (Watson, 1983). Similar findings were reported in another study where premarital cohabitation was significantly associated with a perceived lower quality of communication for wives and lower levels of marital satisfaction for both spouses (DeMaris & Leslie, 1984). Using data from a Canadian survey, premarital cohabitation was found to decrease marital stability. In fact, it would appear that persons who cohabit elevate their risk of marital dissolution by at least 50% (Trussell & Rao, 1989).

Some authorities suggest that persons who cohabit and later marry may have higher expectations for marriage than noncohabitors in terms of personal intimacy, sexual fulfillment, and shared experience (Spanier & Furstenberg, 1987). And, given the limited influence of religion in the lives of cohabitors, they may be more willing to dissolve an unsatisfying marriage (Francoeur, 1991). While premarital cohabitation increases the risk of marital dissolution, the effect of cohabitation appears to be related to amount of time that cohabitors have already spent in the relationship prior to marriage. More specifically, if couples with the same total amount of time invested in the relationship are compared, there is no difference in the rate of marital dissolution between cohabitors and noncohabitors (Teachman & Polonko, 1990).

Remarriage and Cohabitation

There is conflicting data regarding the effects of cohabitation on those who remarry. Divorced and/or widowed persons who premaritally cohabited and remarried reported significantly greater happiness, closeness, concern for partner's welfare, positive communication, family adjustment, and environmental support (Hanna & Knaub, 1981). However, it was suggested that these differences were related to the fact that younger children were in the homes. Later data failed to establish a relationship between cohabitation and marital satisfaction of remarried persons (DeMaris, 1984).

In summarizing the costs and profits of cohabitation, the research evidence to date does not support the contention that cohabitation will help persons select more appropriate partners, increase the odds of compatibility with a potential marriage partner, or improve subsequent marital relationships (Macklin, 1987). In fact, "trial marriage" has been termed a myth since cohabitors rarely try to work out problems to keep the relationship together as married couples are likely to do. One group of couples who lived together before marriage indicated that cohabitation did not better prepare them for marriage, concluding that living together was not a "true partnership" as was their original intent (Brothers, 1985).

Legal Considerations in Cohabitation

The practice of cohabitation is still illegal in a few states, so persons can be subjected to criminal prosecution for violation of laws concerning sexual conduct. For example, the Iowa State Supreme Court ruled that a state statute prohibiting cohabitation was constitutional. Further, no state recognizes cohabitation as a legal relationship creating the same rights and privileges for the partners as does marriage (Jorgensen, 1986). In fact, the California State Supreme Court has ruled that to grant unmarried cohabitors the same rights as married persons would seriously damage the state's support for the institution of marriage ("Unwed Couples," 1988). However, there are some legal implications in the practice of cohabitation: community property and inheritance.

Community Property

Since no state laws exist regarding the establishment of cohabitation as a legal relationship, any "rights" and/or "privileges" concerning community property have been established through court decisions. A review of several precedent-setting cases will illustrate that the effect of cohabitation on other social institutions such as the legal system has been profound, often requiring changes in public policy and procedure (Macklin, 1987).

In *McCullon v. McCullon,* the New York State Supreme Court held that the woman, who had lived with the man for approximately 28 years, was entitled to alimony as well as child support for their 18-year-old daughter. Circumstances in this case were somewhat different; the woman was "held out" or represented by the man to be his wife through their joint tax returns, bank accounts, and property title for their home. The court construed that the woman had made an implied promise to provide domestic services for the man and to not work in consideration of his implied promise to provide a residence and future financial support (Myricks, 1980).

However, in *McCall v. Frampton,* the New York State Supreme Court refused to enforce an oral contract because the court believed the contract was contrary to the common good of society (Myricks, 1980). A British rock star, Peter Frampton, was brought into court by his girlfriend, Penny McCall, who was seeking one half of his earnings between 1973–1978 plus one half interest in an estate in New York as well as a portion of his future earnings. The New York State Supreme Court decided that the alleged oral contract was contrary to the public policy because in its performance, **adultery,** which was illegal, had been committed. The **plaintiff** had left her husband and place of employment to live with Frampton and to share in his earnings and assets. The court ruled that such a contract would be a renouncement of her existing marriage and, therefore, was illegal (Myricks, 1980).

The Wisconsin State Supreme Court also has ruled in *Watts v. Evans* that living together without benefit of marriage does not prevent a former relationship partner from seeking a property settlement under the Wisconsin marital property law. Evans and Watts had lived together as wife and husband from 1969–1981 and had two children. The Court concluded that Evans was entitled to an equitable distribution of property because she had helped Watts to build his landscaping business ("Palimony Case," 1987).

Finally, the term "palimony" was generated by the news media in referring to the financial award given to Michelle Marvin after the ending of her living-together arrangement with the late movie star Lee Marvin. In *Marvin v. Marvin,* it was argued that Michelle had given up a potentially successful show business career to become Lee's live-in companion. After their relationship ended, the plaintiff maintained that her future earning potential had been substantially diminished because of her unemployed years while living with Lee. Therefore, a California court awarded Michelle Marvin a sum of money to be used to reeducate herself with new employment skills (Myricks, 1980).

In summary, the division of any property acquired during cohabitation remains subject solely to the judicial interpretation of laws of the state in which the cohabitors reside. Cohabitors may be more likely to avoid successful litigation concerning community property if they develop a written agreement prior to commencement of the cohabitation relationship which addresses any property acquisitions.

BOX 5.1	Should You "Live Together"?
Questions/Living Together	**"Good" signs and "Concern" signs**
Reasons for decision	**Good signs:** Each partner has given considerable thought to the decision including the advantages and disadvantages of living together. **Concern signs:** One or both partners have given little thought to the advantages and disadvantages of living together.
Goals to accomplish	**Good signs:** Each individual is concerned about learning more about self and partner through intimate daily living including degree of commitment to the relationship. **Concern signs:** One or both partners desire to live together for convenience only and/or to show independence from parents or peers.
Role expectations of self and partner	**Good signs:** Each individual's expectations of self and partner are compatible with those of partner. **Concern signs:** One or both individuals have given little thought to the role expectations of self and/or partner and/or disagree about their expectations.
Identification of partner's emotional and physical needs	**Good signs:** Each individual has a clear understanding of partner's needs, is motivated, and is able to meet most needs. **Concern signs:** One or both individuals are not fully aware of partner's needs and/or are not motivated or able to meet needs of partner.
Personal importance of relationship	**Good signs:** Partners care deeply for each other and view the relationship as a highly significant one. **Concern signs:** One or both individuals do not care deeply for the other partner and/or an emotional imbalance exists with one partner more involved in the relationship than the other.
Previous dating experiences with others	**Good signs:** Both individuals have had an extensive dating history with positive perceptions of self and opposite sex. **Concern signs:** One or both partners have had minimal dating experience accompanied by negative perceptions of self and/or of the opposite sex.
Reactions of parents and friends	**Good signs:** Family and friends are supportive of the cohabiting relationship, or couple has considered how they will deal with opposition. **Concern signs:** Family and friends would not be supportive of cohabiting relationship.
Ability to share feelings	**Good signs:** Each individual is usually able to express feelings to partner without difficulty. **Concern signs:** One or both individuals have difficulty expressing feelings to partner or do not believe expressing feelings is important.
Know partner's strengths and weaknesses	**Good signs:** Each individual is usually able to accept feelings of partner along with her/his strengths and weaknesses. **Concern signs:** One or both individuals are not able to understand and accept partner's strengths and weaknesses.
Ability to handle problems	**Good signs:** Individuals are able to mutually solve problems by expressing feelings openly and by understanding and accepting partner's point of view. **Concern signs:** Couple frequently avoids problems or fails to mutually solve them due to difficulty of expressing feelings openly or accepting partner's point of view.

From C. Ridley, et al., "Cohabitation: Does It Make for a Better Marriage?" in *Family Coordinator,* 27:135–146.

Inheritance

While historically, common-law marriage has had legal validity for the purposes of property and inheritance settlements, such is not the case for cohabitation (Thayer, 1989). If a person should die intestate (without a will), state laws will recognize family members rather than friends or cohabiting partners as the legally binding recipient of a deceased person's property and possessions. However, assuming the person is of sound mind, she/he may execute a legally valid will that specifies her/his possessions going to the cohabiting partner. Such a will needs to be drafted by an attorney and properly witnessed to avoid possible successful litigation by family members. In general, with proof of parentage, children born during the relationship would have inheritance rights.

Homosexuality as an Alternative Life-Style

Heterosexuality, homosexuality, and bisexuality are words that are alike in that they describe people's **sexual orientation.** However, they differ considerably in practice and acceptability within society. **Heterosexuality** (preference of sexual activity with persons of the opposite sex) is the accepted norm. **Homosexuality** (preference of sexual activity with persons of the same sex) and **bisexuality** (a sexual orientation in which sexual behavior with the same sex and the opposite sex are viewed as equally pleasurable) are both considered alternative life-styles (Crooks & Baur, 1990).

There has been much debate in recent years over an appropriate definition of homosexuality, especially among homosexuals themselves. Most heterosexuals tend to think of homosexuality in terms of the sexual act itself rather than correctly considering that a person may have a homosexual orientation even though she/he has never had an overt homosexual experience. Homosexuals themselves talk about sexual preference within the context of homosexual life-styles (Herdt, 1988). Further, male homosexuals prefer to be referred to as **gays,** whereas female homosexuals prefer to be referred to as **lesbians.** For the purposes of this chapter, the discussion shall be concerned with only those persons who consider themselves to be exclusively homosexual.

Definition of Homosexuality

Homosexuality may refer to sexual behavior, life-style, sexual preference, or sexual orientation. A homosexual person is defined as "an individual whose primary erotic, psychological, emotional, and social interest is in a member of the same sex even though that interest may not be overtly expressed" (Martin & Lyon, 1972, p. 1). Some homosexuals are more or less exclusively interested in same-sex partners since childhood, whereas others gradually conclude that their primary attraction/interest is for a person of the same sex (West, 1983). Support for this contention is found in a study that suggested that gays, prior to acknowledging their homosexuality, apparently view themselves as being different from their male peers and more similar to their female peers. Reportedly, as adolescents, they were romantically attracted to other male adolescents whom they viewed as more masculine than themselves. During adolescence, such men also were evidently excluded from homosocial bonding, feeling more accepted by girls than boys (Johnston, 1988). Contrary to popular **stereotypes,** most female homosexuals appear to be quite feminine in their appearance and actions, just as most male homosexuals appear to be masculine in dress, grooming, and recreational pursuits. In fact, one study found that those women who reported same-sex sexual experiences were more satisfied with their bodies and bodily functions, their sexual activities, and their general abilities in comparison to those women who had only had opposite-sex sexual experiences (LaTorre & Wendenburg, 1983). Further, contrary to earlier findings, a small-scale study concluded that lesbians are no more likely to have experienced child sexual abuse or rape by men than heterosexual women (Brannock & Chapman, 1990).

The Extent of Homosexuality

Given the controversial nature of the Gay Liberation Movement, along with discrimination against homosexuals in employment, housing, and the military service, it is very difficult to establish a precise count in our society of the number of persons who consider themselves to be exclusively homosexual (Crooks & Baur, 1990). A number of years ago, Ford and Beach (1971) concluded that approximately 10% of any societal population is homosexual, regardless of whether one considers societies that are permissive toward homosexuality or societies that react harshly toward homosexuality. Today, the accepted estimates for the incidence of an exclusively homosexual orientation range from 3–5% for adult women and 5–10% for adult men (Allgeier & Allgeier, 1991). However, findings from a 1989 national sample of adults indicate that less than 2% of women and men had experienced sexual activity with a same-sex partner during the past 12 months (Smith, 1990b). The fact that about one third of lesbians and one fifth of gays have been previously heterosexually married or are currently heterosexually married complicates their identification. Further, about one half of all gay married men have fathered children (Harry, 1983). Finally, a large-scale study of homosexuals in San Francisco found that 8 in 10 women and 6 in 10 men had engaged in heterosexual intercourse at some time during their lives. In fact, 24% of these women and 14% of these men had engaged in heterosexual intercourse within the past year (Bell & Weinberg, 1978).

Childhood sexual play such as playing nurse or doctor and, perhaps, pajama parties may include both opposite-sex and same-sex partners. These sexual activities usually represent sexual experimentation and do not constitute a homosexual orientation. Further, research indicates that an estimated 6% of female and 11% of male heterosexual adolescents have had at least one homosexual experience during their teen years. These reported homosexual experiences occurred with a younger person—24%, a same-age person—39%, an older teenager—29%, and an adult—8% (Sorensen, 1973). A survey of same-sex experience among heterosexual college students found that at least 1 in 7 women and 1 in 5 men had engaged in genital stimulation with a person of their own sex (Haynes & Oziel, 1976). The extent of adolescent same-sex experiences were much the same during the 1970s as had previously been reported in the 1940s and 1950s (DeLamater & MacCorquodale, 1979).

In summary, three points should be apparent concerning homosexuality:

1. It is very difficult to establish a precise figure as to the actual number of homosexuals in American society.
2. Just because a person has had a same-sex experience, does not mean that she/he is lesbian or gay.
3. The issue of bisexuality lacks definitive research.

Societal Attitudes toward Lesbians and Gays

During the 1970s, several surveys were conducted to determine public attitudes toward premarital sexuality, extramarital sexuality, and homosexual activity in the United States. No significant changes occurred during this decade, with about three fourths of the respondents still believing that homosexual relations were "always wrong" (Glenn & Weaver, 1979). Persons giving their religious preference as Jewish or as "no religion" were more than twice as likely as Protestants or Catholics to approve of homosexual relations. Further, persons who had attended college were more than twice as likely to approve of homosexual relations when compared to persons who were high school graduates only. While those persons who accept a strict interpretation of church teachings are more likely to have negative attitudes toward homosexuals, those with more education and who have a personal acquaintance or friendship with a homosexual are more likely to possess tolerant attitudes toward homosexuals (Turner, 1982).

Although both heterosexual women and men have negative views toward homosexuality, men's views are more negative (Kurdek, 1988a). Among high school students, male students are much more negative on such issues as permitting homosexuals to rear children, making homosexual marriages legal, homosexuals loving each other, placing homosexuals in supervisory positions, and living near a homosexual (Price, 1982). Among college students, less than one third of women and men were in favor of allowing a homosexual to adopt a child. Considering attitudes toward homosexuals working in various occupations, two thirds of women, in contrast to only about one half of men, were in favor of them working as teachers. Further, three fourths of the women, in comparison to only two thirds of men, favored allowing homosexuals to work as physicians (Leitenberg & Slavin, 1983).

Societal attitudes about homosexuality moving into the 1990s remain conservative. There is a growing national debate over whether or not homosexual couples should be allowed to declare themselves as "domestic partners" or become legally married and, thus, eligible for rights afforded to married couples. As of late 1989, long-term homosexual lovers in New York state had the same right as a surviving spouse to take over a rental apartment upon the death of their partner. At the same time, voters in San Francisco narrowly rejected a proposal that would have entitled gay couples to register their relationship with the County Clerk's Office (Francoeur, 1989c). Municipal employees in Berkeley and Los Angeles, CA and Madison, WI are eligible for sick leave to care for a domestic partner or bereavement leave to attend their partner's funeral. A few municipalities and private employers, including the American Psychological Association, offer health insurance to the domestic partners of their employees and members. However, the Internal Revenue Service has ruled that the cost of the insurance premium is taxable income for the domestic partner since they are not considered to be a family member (Lewin, 1990b). The debate over the civil and religious recognition of these alternate life-styles will undoubtedly escalate, forcing people to take a stand.

In a 1989 Yankelovich Clancy Shulman poll concerning attitudes toward homosexual rights, 65% of adult respondents replied that homosexual couples should be legally allowed to inherit each other's property and 54% indicated that they should be allowed to receive medical and life insurance benefits from a partner's policy. However, with regard to marriage and children, only 23% would permit marriages between homosexuals while just 17% would allow them to adopt children (Isaacson, 1989).

Legality of Same-Sex Practices

Legal discrimination against homosexuals is based on stereotyped beliefs that link homosexuality to participation in unnatural sex acts, the likelihood of seducing adolescents, and participation in child molestation. The belief that homosexual acts are unnatural has a religious basis that has been implemented into statutory law in the United States. As indicated earlier, only about 8% of adolescent homosexual experiences were with an adult. Furthermore, other studies reveal that most child molestation cases involve an adult heterosexual rather than an adult homosexual (Coleman, 1978). Nevertheless, in 1989, 24 states and the District of Columbia still had statutes carrying criminal penalties that prohibited sodomy between two consenting adults of the same sex (Allgeier & Allgeier, 1991). **Sodomy** is variously defined to include oral-genital sex and/or anal intercourse, depending upon the particular state. In addition, 18 of these same states have outlawed sodomy between two consenting adults of the opposite sex (Taylor, 1986).

Consensual marital sexual acts have tended to be protected by a long line of judicial decisions by the United States Supreme Court based on the notion of the right to privacy (Masters, Johnson, & Kolodny, 1988). Nevertheless, the state of Georgia prohibits heterosexual and homosexual sodomy ("any oral or anal intercourse") by classifying said acts as felonies with criminal penalties of 1–20 years in prison. In a 1985 test of the Georgia law, a man was arrested for having sexual activity with another man. Even though the district attorney's office dropped the charge before the case went to trial, the former **defendant** challenged the constitutionality of the Georgia law. In a landmark decision, the United States Supreme Court upheld the Georgia sodomy law in a five to four decision (Taylor, 1986).

Religion and the Homosexuality Issue

One of the most complex and troubling issues confronting American religious leaders today, especially among major Protestant denominations and the Roman Catholic church, concerns the position of the church on homosexuality. The Old Testament makes specific reference to male homosexuality being against Biblical teachings, but female homosexuality is not directly addressed (Byer & Shainberg, 1991). In spite of the fact that many Jewish leaders cite the Old Testament to substantiate their belief that homosexuality is an offense against God, more liberal attitudes toward homosexuality can be found among Jews. In fact, Reform Judaism, the largest and most liberal branch of Judaism, became the first major American denomination in the 1990s to sanction homosexual behavior ("Reform Judaism OKs," 1990). While declaring that heterosexual marriage is to continue as the Jewish ideal, same-sex relationships are deemed acceptable because "all Jews are religiously equal regardless of their sexual orientation" ("Gay Rabbis," 1990, p. 6). As for the clergy, lesbian and gay rabbis are being asked to remain discrete rather than celibate.

Generally, major Protestant denominations and the Roman Catholic church advocate the position that while homosexual acts are not permissible, it is not necessarily sinful to be lesbian or gay in terms of sexual orientation or preference. However, Quakers and Unitarians accept homosexual acts/behavior if they are practiced in a nonpromiscuous fashion. In 1972, the United Church of Christ became the first major denomination to ordain an avowedly homosexual clergyperson. They subsequently stated that a homosexual orientation was not a barrier to becoming ordained in their church (Ostling, 1989). During the 1980s, Lutherans, Presbyterians, and United Methodists had extensive debates over the issue of the ordination of homosexuals as ministers (Hyde, 1986). At the beginning of the 1990s, the United Methodist Church and Presbyterian Church (U.S.A.) were reexamining their opposition to homosexual clergy. In spite of the Evangelical Lutheran Church's policy against "homosexual erotic activity" among their clergy, a San Francisco Lutheran church in 1989 voted to call a lesbian couple as assistant pastors (Ostling, 1989). In 1988, the United Church of Canada approved the ordination of "homosexuals and others who have sexual relations outside of marriage" (Francoeur, 1989c, p. 254).

The Gay Liberation Movement has led to the establishment of homosexual religious organizations including churches, temples, and synagogues where lesbians and gays can practice their faith without harassment. The largest of these religious groups is the Universal Fellowship of Metropolitan Community Churches, which has churches in several major American cities. These churches have continued to sanction and to perform homosexual marriages, although such marriages are not legally recognized in any state. This

Although more visible today, lesbian relationships are still difficult to sustain in a society that largely disapproves of homosexuality.

religious organization's bid for membership in the National Council of Churches, the major American religious organization for Christian denominations, was rejected because of their ordination of homosexual ministers and marriage ceremonies for homosexuals (Hyde, 1986).

Dating and Courtship Patterns among Lesbians and Gays

Contrary to the popular beliefs of "straights" (heterosexuals), lesbians and gays engage in dating and courtship practices in a fashion somewhat similar to heterosexuals (Crooks & Baur, 1990). They engage in casual dating, one-night stands, and serious dating relationships. Lesbians and gays experience feelings of attraction, affection, love, and intimacy toward particular persons of the same sex. Some relationships even develop to the degree that the relationships culminate in "marriage" or a long-term commitment (Lockard, 1985). There are both differences and similarities between lesbians and gays in their courtship practices.

The Stable Relationships of Lesbians

Lesbian couples exhibit more equality of power and greater reciprocal expressiveness than gay couples (Kurdek, 1988b). The lesbian community has at least four distinct features which may encourage such factors: interacting social networks, a group identity based on sexual orientation, subcultural values which are essentially feminist in origin, and organizational settings for lesbian interaction (Lockard, 1985). Therefore, many structural opportunities are likely to occur which may lead to stable love relationships between lesbians. On the other hand, gays appear to be much more interested in casual sex rather than in stable relationships, although there are some gay marriages.

Lesbians and heterosexual women are more committed to maintaining their couple relationships than are gays and heterosexual men. Support for this viewpoint is found in a study of satisfaction and commitment in heterosexual and homosexual couple relationships. Both lesbians and heterosexual women reported having invested considerably more effort in their couple relationships than gays or heterosexual men (Duffy & Rusbult, 1986).

In an assessment of satisfaction in lesbian-couple relationships, high levels of love and satisfaction with current relationships were reported. The highest degree of satisfaction was associated with equal involvement and equal power in the relationship. Satisfaction was strongly related to the characteristics of the relationship itself rather than to individual attitudes or background features of the lesbian partners (Peplau, Padesky, & Hamilton, 1982). Factors involved in the breakup of past lesbian relationships included a desire to be independent, differences in interests, conflicting attitudes about exclusivity in the relationship, partner's desire to be independent, partner's dependence, and conflicting attitudes about sexual activity (see Table 5.7).

Table 5.7: Problems Reported in Lesbian Relationship Break Ups

Problem	Major Factor	Minor Factor
My desire to be independent	48%	12%
Differences in interests	36	26
Conflicts about exclusivity	29	24
Partner's desire to be independent	29	24
Partner's dependence on me	26	14
Conflicting attitudes about sex	24	21
My dependence on my partner	19	29
Living too far apart	19	17
Partner's feelings, being lesbian	19	12
Differences in background	17	31
Jealousy	17	29
Societal attitudes toward lesbians	14	10
My feelings, being lesbian	12	14
Differences in intelligence	10	12
Differences in political views	7	17

From L. A. Peplau, et al., "Satisfaction in Lesbian Relationships" in *Journal of Homosexuality*, 8:33. Copyright © 1982 Haworth Press, Inc., New York, NY. Reprinted by permission.

Evidence of the de-emphasis, to some degree, of sexual activity among lesbian couples can be found in a comparison of heterosexual and lesbian couples concerning their frequency of sexual activity. During the first two years of their ongoing relationship, 76% of lesbian couples and 83% of heterosexual couples engaged in sexual activity one or more times per week. However, after being in the relationship for 2 years, less than one third of lesbian couples, in comparison to three fourths of heterosexual couples, engaged in sexual activity one or more times per week (Blumstein & Schwartz, 1983).

Gays and "Cruising"

The term **cruising** has been used to characterize the process whereby homosexuals go out for the express purpose of looking for a person of the same sex with whom to engage in casual sex. In general, cruising tends to be primarily a social activity of gays. In a major San Francisco study of homosexuals, 17% of lesbian respondents had engaged in cruising activity during the past year, while 63% of gay respondents had been involved in cruising more than a "few times" per month.

Over one half of these gays had been cruising more than once per week. Cruising locations included gay bars, gay baths, streets, and tea rooms (public restrooms). Gay baths are used strictly for sexual purposes and have their heterosexual counterpart in the form of swingers' clubs. Of these gays, slightly over one half had utilized gay baths as a source of sexual partners (Bell & Weinberg, 1978). However, with the severe concern over the possible contraction of AIDS, most gay baths have closed, either by choice or by pressure from local health departments.

Dating patterns among gays in bars and discotheques suggest that gays judge prospective dating partners primarily on the basis of physical attractiveness. Regardless of the respondent's own physical attractiveness, the single determinant of how much he liked his dating partner and whether or not he wished to have another date with him was the physical attractiveness of the partner (Sergios & Cody, 1985).

The earlier cited study of homosexual and heterosexual relationships discovered some striking differences between lesbians and gays (Duffy & Rusbult, 1986). With regard to "costs" of the relationship, gays were much more likely to indicate the following costs: partner being sexually unfaithful, difficulty spending time together, and partner's inappropriate dependence (see Table 5.8). In terms of "alternatives" to the current relationship, gays were much more likely than lesbians to list availability of alternative partner. Further, gays were much less likely than lesbians to view their current relationship as monogamous or to consider themselves to be monogamous. Finally, the average duration of the longest courtship relationship for lesbians was 54.1 months, but it was only 29.6 months for gays (Duffy & Rusbult, 1986).

Despite the greater emphasis on casual sex among gays, there are still a number of gays who desire monogamous relationships. Those respondents living in closed relationships do not differ in their psychological adjustment from those respondents living in open homosexual relationships. However, gays living in closed relationships report having higher feelings of dependency, more favorable attitudes toward the relationship, and less tension toward the other partner in contrast to gay men living in open relationships (Kurdek & Schmitt, 1985). Data on gay couple relationships indicate that most men report that their current relationship is extremely close and personally satisfying (Peplau & Cochran, 1981).

Lesbian and Gay Parents

In view of the controversial issues surrounding surrogate motherhood and artificial insemination for lesbians and gays, consideration will be given to parenting children who were offspring from a prior marital relationship or heterosexual encounter. Lesbian mothers, as noted earlier, are much more likely to live in a couple relationship than are gay fathers. But many lesbians and gays have had their children taken away in child custody proceedings because the judge has felt that being homosexual automatically made a parent unfit (Coleman, 1978). With regard to child custody issues, very little research has been conducted concerning gay fathers because, regardless of sexual orientation, fathers are infrequently given custody of children after a divorce.

Lesbian Mothers and Child-Rearing Practices

Available estimates indicate that at least 1.5 million lesbians are mothers (Henry, 1990). When comparing single parents to heterosexual and lesbian mothers, both groups reported oppression in the areas of freedom of association, employment, housing, and child custody; however, the degree of perceived oppression was much greater for lesbian mothers. Among these women, 1 in 4 lesbian mothers, as compared to only 1 in 7 heterosexual mothers, did not have full custody of all of their children. Of the heterosexual mothers, only 13% indicated that they lived with a lover, whereas 60% of the lesbian mothers lived with lovers (Pagelow, 1980). These findings suggest that lesbian mothers perceive greater difficulties in adjusting to their life-style after divorce.

Another later study of currently unmarried lesbian mothers and heterosexual mothers found that three fourths of both groups of mothers would consider marriage. However, of these women, three fourths of lesbian mothers and only one tenth of heterosexual mothers were currently involved in a couple relationship with a person residing in their household. In addition, lesbian mothers were much more active in feminist groups than heterosexual mothers (70% versus 21%) and also much less likely to attend religious services (56% versus 15%). Further, it is of interest to note that 1 in 5 lesbian mothers and 1 in 2 heterosexual mothers planned to have more children (Green, Mandel,

Table 5.8: Rewards, Costs, Alternatives, and Investments by Sexual Orientation

	Homosexual		Heterosexual	
Rewards, Costs, Alternatives, and Investments	Women	Men	Women	Men
Rewards				
Partner's personality	7.80	7.57	7.92	7.96
Partners' attitudinal similarity	6.08	4.70	6.79	6.24
Partner's physical attractiveness	7.76	7.74	8.08	7.60
Partner's intelligence	8.12	7.70	7.88	7.72
Partners' shared interests	7.44	6.04	7.46	7.04
Respondent's sexual satisfaction	7.88	7.61	7.67	7.80
Partner's sense of humor	8.56	7.65	8.25	7.28
Costs				
Partner sexually unfaithful	2.92	4.54	2.56	3.44
Partner's unattractive personal qualities	3.28	3.33	3.56	4.24
Difficulty spending time together	3.52	5.13	3.96	4.24
Partner's inappropriate dependence	2.72	4.17	3.12	3.76
Respondent's loss of personal freedom	2.16	3.75	3.36	4.12
Partner's irritating habits	2.84	3.83	3.20	3.08
Financial costs	3.60	2.58	3.16	4.36
Partner's failure to live up to agreements	1.80	2.33	2.96	3.64
Alternatives				
Availability/alternative partner	4.92	6.08	5.12	6.00
Attractiveness/alternative partner	5.08	6.67	5.28	6.09
Anticipated satisfaction/alternative relationship	3.72	4.71	4.00	5.04
Confidence/finding alternative partner	5.08	5.92	5.68	6.00
Investments				
Exclusiveness	8.12	7.84	8.12	7.33
Mutual friends	6.88	6.16	6.04	6.58
Connection of social life with relationship	5.32	4.96	5.52	5.04
Shared events/experience	7.16	6.28	7.40	6.79
Emotional investment	8.20	7.36	8.40	7.50
Monetary investment	5.48	3.04	4.80	5.75
Self-disclosure	7.68	7.24	7.84	7.38
Shared material possessions	5.60	3.76	5.76	4.13

Note: Scores are reported as means and are based on 9-point scale with 1 = lowest value and 9 = highest value.
From S. M. Duffy and C. E. Rusbult, "Satisfaction and Commitment in Homosexual and Heterosexual Relationships" in *Journal of Homosexuality,* 12:13–14.

Hotvedt, Gray, & Smith, 1986). Finally, there is no evidence that being reared by a lesbian mother produces any sexual identity or peer group stigmatization for children (Green et al., 1986; Hoeffer, 1981). Children of lesbian mothers are essentially no different from other children in terms of gender-related problems, gender-role development, and general development (Pagelow, 1980). In general, lesbian mothers have been found to be quite similar to heterosexual mothers in life-style, maternal instincts, and parenting behavior (Kirkpatrick, 1982; Lewin, 1981).

Many persons, including former spouses, have negative attitudes toward lesbian mothers receiving custody of their children. However, today increasing

That not all gay fathers parade their gayness or parenthood status makes it difficult to research gay parenting issues.

numbers of lesbians are choosing to become pregnant outside of the traditional heterosexual family structure, often via artificial insemination. These future lesbian mothers have indicated a preference to receive prenatal care from a health-care provider that is staffed with lesbians or, more importantly, a health care provider with an open and supportive attitude toward lesbians giving birth to infants (Olesker & Walsh, 1984). While some adoptions by lesbians with live-in relationship partners are beginning to occur, opposition to homosexual adoptions is increasing. Because of state laws prohibiting homosexual marriages, the adoption placement is made to only one person in the couple relationship (Maddox, 1982). But despite the fact that at least 17 research reports have concluded that no major differences exist between children of homosexual and heterosexual parents, New Hampshire and Florida have recently passed laws banning homosexual adoptions (Dullea, 1988).

Parenting Concerns of Gay Fathers

A small-scale investigation of 18 gay fathers with custody of their children identified two major parenting concerns: disclosure of their gay identity and developing love relationships. Most gay fathers disclosed their homosexuality in the interest of clarifying their personal and social world for their children. The gay fathers generally believed that this disclosure permitted a more intimate relationship between themselves and their children. In most instances, children responded positively upon learning that their fathers were gay (Bozett, 1980, 1984). Since these gay fathers believed that it was very important to have a stable home environment, they tried to avoid having short-term relationships involving a live-in lover. The fathers expressed the view that two men could be affectionate with one another in front of children by hugging or by greeting with a kiss, although they indicated disapproval of overt displays of sexual behavior except in privacy. Examples of caring activities that were shared with their lover included helping with homework or putting the children to bed (Bozett, 1984).

Summary

- Cohabitation as an alternative life-style is becoming more common, especially among college students and postcollege age young adults. The major reasons for the increased incidence among college students are new sex norms, more tolerant parental attitudes, and convenient access to contraceptives.
- Female cohabitors are more likely to be never-married, to be less educated, to be over age 25, to reside in urban areas, to be nonreligious, and to have liberal social and political attitudes. While most male cohabitors view cohabitation as temporary, the majority of female participants hope that the relationship will eventually result in marriage.
- Among the potential sources of conflict for cohabitors are sexuality, finance, intimacy, and marriage attitudes. The potential profits of cohabitation include improvement of mate selection, and the costs include exploitation and lowered self-esteem.
- Evidence suggests that cohabitation, while meeting mutual needs, does not necessarily serve as a suitable test of partner compatibility for marriage. The major legal difficulties associated with cohabitation include sharing community property and inheritance concerns.
- It is difficult to determine the actual number of lesbians and gays in our society today. Further, no significant changes in societal attitudes toward homosexuals occurred during the past two decades.
- In general, being female, having a college education, being acquainted with a homosexual, or having a friendship with a homosexual increases the likelihood of a more positive attitude toward lesbians and gays.
- The issue of homosexuality is one of the most troubling questions to confront American religious leaders. The Roman Catholic church and most Protestant denominations advocate that homosexual acts are not permissible but that it is not necessarily a sin to have a homosexual orientation. Reform Judaism sanctions homosexual behavior in stable committed relationships.
- Gays appear to be more interested in casual sex, whereas lesbian women prefer more stable relationships. Although not legal, homosexual marriages do occur between lesbians and, at a lower rate, between gays.
- The research to date has not identified any adverse effects for children reared by lesbian mothers. While parenting by gay fathers is rare, their major concerns relate to disclosure of their gay life-style to their children and being able to develop relationships with lovers.

Questions for Critical Reflection

1. If you were chosen as the student journalist to write a feature article about cohabitation on your campus, what would you entitle your article? How representative do you believe your campus findings would be when compared to those from other colleges/universities? What factors might account for any differences?
2. Why is cohabitation considered a "paperless marriage" in Denmark but an alternative life-style in the United States?
3. From your personal experience or that of friends who have cohabited, have you witnessed any exploitation in the relationship? If marriage occurred following cohabitation, was this experience a better preparation for marriage than traditional courtship? Can you give some evidence to support your position?
4. Causes of the homosexual and hetcrosexual sexual orientations are undetermined in the research to date although there are various theories. What are your ideas concerning the origins of a person's sexual orientation? Is it important for scientists to continue their quest to unravel this mystery? Why?
5. Do you believe that a person's sexual orientation should be a factor in being allowed to adopt a child? What is the basis of your answer?

Suggested Readings

Barton, C. (1984). *Cohabitation contracts.* Brookfield, VT: Gower. A concise review of the major elements of cohabitation contracts.

Gochros, J. (1989). *When husbands come out of the closet.* New York: Haworth Press. Issues confronting wives upon discovery of their husband's true sexual orientation.

Loulan, J. (1984). *Lesbian sex.* San Francisco: Spinsters Ink. Comprehensive treatment of lesbian sexual activities, relationships, and life-styles.

Macklin, E. D., & Rubin, R. H. (Eds.). (1983). *Contemporary families and alternative lifestyles: Handbook on research and theory.* Beverly Hills, CA: Sage. A review of research and theory about alternative life-styles including cohabitation and homosexuality.

Schulenberg, J. (1985). *Gay parenting.* New York: Anchor Books. A practical and thorough guide to coping with becoming a gay parent, including child custody issues.

CHAPTER 6

Love: The Search for Fulfillment

Being in love is a good thing, but it is not the best thing. There are many things below it, but there are also things above it. You cannot make it the basis of a whole life. It is a noble feeling, but it is still a feeling. . . .
C. S. Lewis, 1958

Outline

Why study love? In a very real sense, to do so is an attempt to examine the unexaminable and to know the unknowable (Peck, 1978). There are even some who claim that studying it violates love's mystery. In the 1970s, Senator William Proxmire attacked the use of National Science Foundation funds to study love on such grounds:

> *I object to this . . . because no one can argue that falling in love is a science. . . . I don't want the answer. . . . I believe 200 million other Americans want to leave some things in life a mystery. . . . Leave that to Elizabeth Barrett Browning and Irving Berlin.*
>
> *(Walster & Walster, 1978, p. viii)*

There is no subject as central to the human experience and at the same time as incomprehensible as human love (Kazak & Reppucci, 1980).

Although considerable research has added to the body of knowledge about love in the last half century, scholars are continuing in their quest to unravel the mysteries of this elusive emotion. During the 1980s, investigators tended to focus on the subjective meaning of love and commitment, and on individual styles of loving (Surra, 1990). "What does it mean to love someone" (Sternberg, 1986, p. 119)? "What determines whether a relationship will function successfully" (Rusbult, Johnson, & Morrow, 1986, p. 744)? "What breaks down when a relationship breaks down" (Duck, 1984, p. 163)? What are the relationship variables that determine love, satisfaction, and staying together? These are just a few of the questions currently being explored by scientists to learn more about the nature of love and its implications for successful marriage and committed relationships.

The Meaning of Love

Long before love was "discovered" by family scientists, it was a favorite subject of philosophers and poets. The arts have frequently reflected the world's fascination with the meaning of love. For example, love songs have traditionally been a sign of the changing times. "Love and marriage go together like a horse and carriage." These words of the popular song of the 1950s reflected prevailing ideas about the interrelatedness of love and marriage in a postwar world. Indeed, "you could not have one without the other." The winds of change were apparent, however, when "Hello, I Love You, Won't You Tell Me Your Name," became the cry of the 1960s generation. By the 1970s, Glen Campbell's, "Gentle on My Mind," declared that romantic love can only survive in the absence of permanent commitment. It was not the ink-stained signatures on a marriage license that kept his bedroll stashed behind his lover's couch, it was the freedom to abandon her that kept her "gentle on his mind" (Latham, 1988).

Music of the 1980s revealed a strange turn of events. George Michael's blatant "I Want Your Sex" emphasized the directness of the times as well as the importance placed on physical gratification. Yet, for many, the decade of the 1980s was a musical trip "back to the future" to the era of the 1950s when people listened to songs by groups such as the Supremes or Buddy Holly and the Crickets, with words accurately depicting emotional love stories. For example, the number one record of 1987, "I Think We're Alone Now," by 17-year-old Tiffany, was a remake of a 20-year-old hit with "boy-meets-girl" simplicity. Perhaps this nostalgic journey reflected an attempt to deny present-day realities with the world of romance. While the greatest worry for lovers in the "prepill" world had been premarital pregnancy, their 1980s counterparts wrestled with the fear of AIDS. It has been suggested that as the younger generation turned back to old music, they also returned to old values and forms (Latham, 1988). Whether or not this proves to be true, experience suggests that the meaning of love will continue to evolve and find expression in this popular art form.

Love: The Name Game

Attempting to understand the nature of love is reminiscent of the tale of three blind men trying to describe an elephant. The answer depends upon one's hands-on experience in life. The question of semantics quickly surfaces as individuals try to unravel the meaning of love. People use the term "love" in a variety of ways. Love is used to describe an infant's helplessness and dependence upon parents as well as the tender, nurturant, selfless feelings of parents for their child. In addition, love is applied to the mutually supportive and cooperative relationships between friends. Perhaps most often, the same word is used to refer to an erotic bond, that passionate, romantic attraction two people have for each other. To further complicate the issue of understanding the meaning of love, this ubiquitous word is frequently heard when a person speaks of affection for, say, a Siamese cat or Silky Terrier dog, or even chocolate pie.

The ancient Greeks had no such problem. They used three words to distinguish between the various meanings of love: agape, philos, and eros (Crosby,

What Do You Look for in Your Relationship with Your Partner?

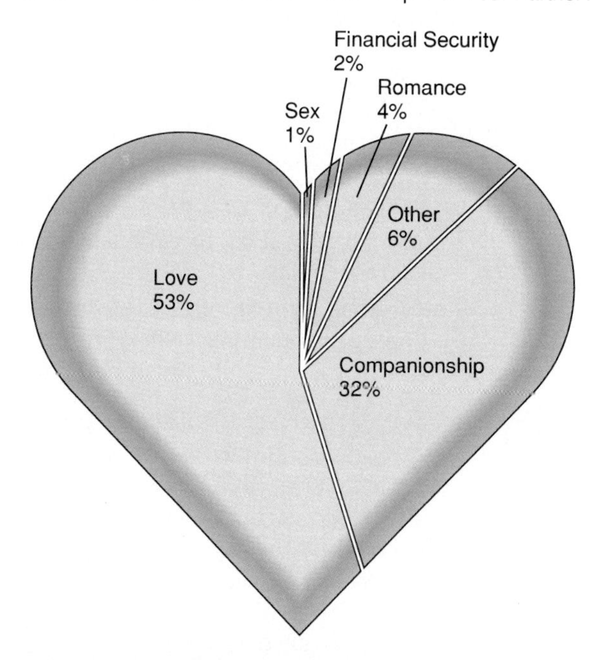

Figure 6.1 Qualities Sought in Partner Relationship

1991). Agape, the unconditional love, believed to represent the ideal, is perhaps best reflected in a parent's love for her/his child. It is love "in spite of" rather than "because of," love that is unearned and undeserved. Philos, the brotherly love, is one of friendship or love between equals. Eros, the sensual, physical emotion of lust, is the drive toward intimacy with another being. The focus of this chapter is the kind of love with which people can build a firm basis for marriage, one which combines the essence of all three components: unconditional acceptance, friendship, and erotica. Although the emphasis tends to change from passionate to compassionate love as persons grow older, love itself remains an important part of couple relationships, with the romantic symbols often remaining unchanged over the life cycle (Roden, Bulcroft, & Nordstrom, 1986). Love, by whatever name, is the most often sought quality in a relationship (see figure 6.1). Therefore, understanding how love develops, its role in commitment, and how it grows and changes over time is significant to healthy relationships. The exploration of this mystical quality, love, begins with its definition and identification.

Love Defined

Erich Fromm defined love simply: "Love is an art" (1956, p. 4). He proposed that in order to learn how to love, one must proceed with the steps necessary to learn any art: mastery of theory and mastery of practice. He perceived love as the overcoming of human separateness, the fulfillment of the longing for union. As such, it is an attitude or orientation of character that determines a person's relatedness to the world, not to one's object of love. "If I truly love one person I love all persons, I love the world, I love life" (Fromm, 1956, p. 39). In earlier definitions of love, Sullivan defined the state of love: "When the satisfaction or the security of another person becomes as significant to one as is one's own security" (1947, p. 20). Overstreet believed, "The love of a person implies not the possession of that person, but the affirmation of that person. It means granting him gladly the full right to his unique humanhood" (1949, p. 103). Both May (1969) and Peck (1978) include the concept of will in their treatises on love. Peck defined love as, "the will to extend one's self for the purpose of nurturing one's own or another's spiritual growth" (1978, p. 81).

During the 1980s, love was defined by Ridley as "a set of positive feelings targeted toward another person" and by Croake as "an emotion that follows from our decision to cooperate with our partner" ("Two Viewpoints," 1983, p. 166). In a survey of 12,000 readers of *Psychology Today,* 44% of women and 29% of men believed that sex without love was unacceptable, suggesting a possible resurgence of sexual conservatism. Love was perceived as including friendship, devotion, and intellectual compatibility but not passion-related elements. An interesting contradiction was identified in their responses. While two thirds of both women and men believed that love could last a lifetime, about one half agreed that their marriage might end in divorce (Rubenstein, 1983).

Romantic love has traditionally been viewed by family sociologists as a carefully conditioned social product (Waller & Hill, 1951). That is, people fall in love because they are socialized to do so. Although persons are socialized to idealize the loved one and to view her/him as a uniquely perfect individual, this period of euphoria inevitably results in conflicts and adjustments (Leslie & Korman, 1989). A classic definition of romantic love suggests that love exists at the point when a person's sentiment overcomes her/his objectivity (Waller & Hill, 1951). While logic seeks illumination, "romantic love is sustained by mystery and crumbles upon inspection" (Yalom, 1989, p. 15).

University of Southern California professor Leo Buscaglia developed and taught a pioneering "love" course. He declared that his classes never attempted nor were able to define love because, "We felt as we grew in love, that to define it would be to delimit it and love seemed infinite" (Hacker, 1985, p. 15E). However, his "love" students were able to formulate some generalizations about love in their attempt to clarify the concept. Accordingly, they concluded that love:

1. Is a learned emotion affected by her/his environment.
2. Is dynamic interaction.
3. Is something one "grows" in not "falls" in.
4. Must be lived in action.
5. Provides potential for growth in each person.
6. Is a process that gradually builds.
7. Is revealed differently in each person.
8. Cannot be bought, sold, or measured.
9. Lives the moment, not for the moment, which denies the past and future.
10. Is not afraid to feel but cries for expression (Buscaglia, 1972, pp. 59–74).

Fromm (1947) coined the term "productive love" to better define the word so often used ambiguously. Accordingly, the essence of productive love is the same whether it is a mother's love for her child, love of humankind, or an erotic love between mates. The basic elements that are characteristically in all forms of productive love are care, responsibility, respect, and knowledge. Fromm (1956) believed care and responsibility differentiate love from passion. Love is an activity that is expressed in concern for the growth of the loved one. Further, respect is that part of love that enables an individual to see a person as she/he is, to be aware of unique individuality. But all three—care, responsibility, and respect—are rooted in knowledge, without which there can be no love.

Love and Human Needs

In Daniel Prescott's classic article entitled, "The Role of Love In Human Development," he asked, "Is love a reality or a delusive romantic construct of our culture" (1952, p. 173)? The nature of love and its role in human development were also explored. Although love is accepted as a reality that markedly influences human development, behavior, and adjustment, many questions surround it. Unfortunately, both literature and research about love have focused on the negative effects of lack of love and its inappropriate use in relationships rather than the nature of love as a positive force. Nevertheless, the hypotheses proposed by Prescott concerning the role of love in human development have been well-affirmed by more than three decades of research. Accordingly, being loved serves many functions, it:

1. Affords human beings much needed basic security.
2. Makes possible learning to love self and others.
3. Facilitates belonging in groups.
4. Facilitates internalization through identification with parents, relatives, teachers, and peers.
5. Facilitates adjustment in situations involving strong, unpleasant emotions (Prescott, 1952, pp. 175–176).

Maslow's (1943) hierarchy of developmental needs offers additional insight into love as it relates to the satisfaction of human needs. The developmental needs are identified as physiological—hunger and thirst; safety—security and order; belongingness and love—affection and identification; esteem—prestige, success, and self-respect; and self-actualization—desire for self-fulfillment. According to this theory, not only is the sequence of needs invariant, but lower-order ones must be met before a person can successfully move to a concern for the next highest need. Maslow (1968) later characterized the first four need states as dependency needs and called them "D needs." The highest order needs for self-actualization were labeled as being needs and called "B needs." Thus, love can be described as either D-love that seeks happiness by taking love or B-love that achieves happiness by giving love. Accordingly, people who are primarily struggling with D needs are not good candidates for a successful marriage because of their dependence on others to meet these needs. Conversely, B lovers, characterized as independent, autonomous individuals with high self-esteem, would potentially be promising marriage partners.

Love is thus viewed as satisfying two human needs: legitimate needs that arise in the present rather than out of deficits from the past, and illegitimate needs that arise from past dependency needs and lead to feelings of self-doubt, unworthiness, and inadequacy (Crosby, 1991; Kernberg, 1978). Crosby (1991) concluded from the work of Erich Fromm and Karen Horney that dependency needs often masquerade under the guise of love. Thus, dependent personalities define the experience of finding someone to meet her/his deepest emotional needs as "being in love." Failure to understand one's own legitimate and illegitimate needs causes a person to confuse love with a neurotic need for affection (McCary, 1980).

The lessons of love are undisguised in the simple sharing of the moment.

Love Myths

In order to fully define love, one must not only understand what it is but also what it is not. To do that, some of the commonly held **myths** (beliefs that are held uncritically without examination) about romantic love need to be understood. From the many love myths, four of the more prevalent ones will be considered: there is only one right person, with real love all things are possible, there is love at first sight, and dependency is love.

Many persons believe that there is a "one and only" existing somewhere in the world with whom they could be extremely happy in a love relationship (Peck, 1978). Seeking such a love involves a sorting process with hopes that "Ms. or Mr. Right," the person that is "intended," will eventually be found. Those subscribing to this myth believe that since true love occurs only once in a lifetime, that they may never have another, even if the beloved is worthless, unloving, or already married (Ellis, 1962)! Certainly, the statistics regarding remarriage among persons who are widowed and divorced permits the conclusion that it is not only possible but probable that the ability to love again and again does continue throughout one's lifetime. This myth also intimates, at a deeper level, that the end result of love should be marriage; that love not only justifies marriage, it demands marriage (Crosby, 1991). Even when persons intellectually recognize the fallacy of such reasoning, it is apparent from the high rate of marriage failure that behavior often defies reason.

No matter how different individuals may be in terms of personalities, socioeconomic backgrounds, intelligence levels, and prior socialization experiences, if they are "truly in love," there are no insurmountable problems (Knox, 1983). This "all-things-are-possible" naive approach to love suggests that couples who are deeply in love will experience problem-free relationships. Regrettably, no matter how much two individuals may love each other, conflict is inevitable. Perhaps a more realistic measure of their love for each other is their willingness to work on resolvable differences.

The myth of "love at first sight" suggests that two persons will be instantly attracted to each other and know that they are destined to be one. The script implies that a person is seen across a crowded room and immediately becomes the object of love. This feeling, frequently described as "falling in love," is surely an unreliable basis for a permanent relationship. In fact, anything that one can "fall into," one can also "fall out of." Such first impressions of "love" could best be defined as **infatuation** or "lust at first sight." Unfortunately, these feelings of physical attraction and aroused sexual desires fail to offer any real insight into the person's suitability as a potential love partner (Rubenstein, 1986). It is true that falling in love is not an act of conscious choice. In fact, the experience may elude even those who eagerly await it or occur at times not sought (Peck, 1978). But it is also true that although discipline and will cannot create love, they can control the experience.

Another love myth is that dependency is love (Peck, 1978). This myth may be illustrated by the remark, "I could not live without my beloved." Such is not love at all but is **dependency** (the inability to experience wholeness or function adequately without being actively cared for by another). According to psychiatrist Scott Peck, dependency in a physically healthy adult is a sign of poor mental health. In fact, he classifies the passive dependent personality disorder as perhaps the most common of all psychiatric disorders. However, it is important that dependency be distinguished from dependency needs that everyone experiences throughout life. The desire, at times, to be nurtured and cared for by persons stronger than one's self is universal. Dependency needs are not harmful unless they are allowed to control one's life. In dependency where another person is required for survival, there is no free choice. Love is when two people are quite capable of living without each other but choose to live together.

Infatuation

Humorist Judith Viorst best described the difference between love and infatuation:

> *Infatuation is when you think he is as sexy as Robert Redford, as smart as Henry Kissinger, as noble as Ralph Nader, as funny as Woody Allen and as athletic as Jimmy Connors. Love is when you realize he is as sexy as Woody Allen, as smart as Jimmy Connors, as funny as Ralph Nader, as athletic as Kissinger and nothing like Robert Redford but you'll love him anyway.*
>
> *(Viorst, 1986, p. 131)*

Somewhat more seriously, infatuation has been defined as foolish, unreasoning love or passion. A person usually becomes infatuated with someone who appears to fit her/his image of sexual and/or social desirability. Consequently, infatuation often involves such "love" feelings as eye appeal, fantasy projection, and partner dependency (Hine, 1980). Most authorities consider infatuation to be unstable and short-lived, thus forming a poor basis for establishment of a long-term relationship (Miller & Siegel, 1972; Udry, 1974). This school of thought suggests that this irrational attraction, which is based on less than adequate knowledge of the person, will adversely affect the development of an interpersonal relationship. Since it is likely to be based on only one of a few characteristics, such as sex appeal or neurotic personality needs, infatuation cannot be expected to endure in a situation of continued intimacy such as marriage. Either the relationship will end or the nature of the love bond will change from infatuation and passion to devotion and companionship (Kazak & Reppucci, 1980).

When carefully analyzed, the question of infatuation becomes even more complicated. Parents and peers often use the label "infatuation" to discourage relationships of which they do not approve. For example, when a young woman or man becomes enamored with a person from a different religious, racial, or socioeconomic background, significant others are likely to describe the relationship as infatuation. This characterization is less likely if the person is attracted to someone considered to be a more suitable marriage partner. Also, if a relationship eventually has serious trouble and ends, then it was infatuation. But when a relationship is successful, it is believed to have started with infatuation and developed into mature love (Leslie & Korman, 1989). In other words, infatuation is often what one "was in," while love is what one "is in."

Idealization, an important element of infatuation, is the tendency to perceive loved ones more ideal than they actually are. Traditionally, the idealized woman was an incredibly beautiful, gracious, talented, and creative person, while the idealized man was a strong, brilliant, aggressive, and kind person. In today's relationships with less traditional gender roles, the woman may be idealized as being more aggressive and strong or the man as more creative and gracious than actually is the case. Regardless of the standards, the results are the same. With idealization, reality has been distorted (Leslie & Leslie, 1980). Contrary to popular opinion, idealization is not limited to relationships commonly defined as infatuation. Early in love relationships, substantial proportions of both women and men idealize their cherished partners. "Love is blind" is the phrase often used to express the fact that lovers see differently than others. This myopic condition is not correctable by medical science, but it has been noted that marriage may effect a cure (Chance, 1989)!

The Process of Identifying Love

After reviewing the various definitions of love and distinguishing between infatuation and love, it may well be concluded that being in love is a state of mind (Walster & Walster, 1978). Although it has been suggested that romantic love can be blind, it is also a reassuring buffer for needed relief in a stressful world (Kazak & Reppucci, 1980).

The Distinction between Loving and Liking Someone

There are differences in loving and liking. For most women, liking, loving, and having sexual intercourse are separate ideas. For many men, the idea of a close friendship with a woman is inseparable from the idea of becoming her lover. Since men associate strong liking and love with sexual activity, it is difficult for them to feel emotionally close to other men without considering these feelings to be indicative of homosexuality (Hill, 1989).

How does one distinguish between liking and loving someone? The depth of feelings and the degree of involvement may furnish clues since loving has been characterized as having feelings of great emotional intensity associated with a person (Murstein, 1980). It relates to the affection that one feels toward persons with whom their lives are deeply entwined. Liking, however, can be defined as the affection that a person feels toward a casual acquaintance. While liking is associated with respect or affection for someone, loving involves feelings of comfort, ease, warmth, and security in the presence of the other person. These perceptions about feelings of liking and loving are very different because people often like persons whom they do not love and occasionally love persons whom they do not particularly like.

Employing a loving/liking scale, dating partners were found to rate much higher on the love scale than best friends, whereas both dating partners and best friends received high liking scores. In general, women, when compared to men, were better able to distinguish between loving and liking someone (Rubin, 1973). Men who rate their partners high in love also rate them high for liking. Women, however, may rate high in one category and low in the other (Hill, 1989). Liking or companionate love, which has been characterized as sensible and rational, is said to increase in accordance with the partner's similarities. In contrast, loving or passionate

BOX 6.1: "I Love Her. What Does This Mean?"

I want her to exist for me and to exist for herself. I want her alive. I want her to be, and moreover, to be in the way that she chooses to be. I want her free. As she discloses her being to me, or before my gaze, my existence is enriched. I am more alive. I experience myself in dimensions that she evokes, such that my life is more meaningful and livable.

My beloved is a mystery that I want to make transparent. But the paradox is that I cannot make my beloved do anything. I can only invite and earn the disclosure that makes her transparent. I want to know my beloved. But for me to know, she must show. And for her to show her mysteries to me, she must be assured I will respect them, take delight in them. Whether the mysteries are the feel of her flesh against mine—something I cannot know until it happens—or what she is thinking, imagining, planning or feeling. Why should she disclose herself to me if I am indifferent, or if I plan to use her for purposes of my choosing that are concealed from her? She would know me, the one who claims to love her. If she would know me, then I must wish to be known. I must disclose my being to her, in dialogue, so that we know one another.

If I love her, I love her projects, since she is their source and origin. I may help her with them if she asks and wants my help; or I may let her struggle with them unaided, if this is meaningful to her. I respect her wishes in the matter. If I love myself, I love my projects, since they are my life. If she loves me, she confirms me in my projects, helps me with them, even if the help consists of leaving me alone. If she tries to control me, she doesn't love me. If I try to control her, I don't love her. I experience her as free and treasure her freedom. I experience myself as free and treasure my freedom.

I am a sexual being. So is she. Together, we can produce an experience that is exquisite for us both. She invites me to know her sexually, and I invite her to know me sexually. We share our erotic possibilities in delight and ecstasy. If she wants me and I don't want her, I cannot lie. My body speaks only truth in this way. And I cannot take her without her giving. Her body cannot lie. If I see and hear my beloved, I know her more than if I just see her. But if I touch, smell, and taste her, I know her still more. But she will not allow me to come that close, if she doesn't trust me or want me to know her.

Source: S. M. Jourard, "Some Dimensions of Loving Experience" in H. A. Otto (ed.), *Love Today: A New Exploration.*

love is less predictable because the passion often develops in irrational and illogical ways (Walster & Walster, 1978). Among married couples, passionate love was shown to decrease through time, whereas companionate love remained uniformly high no matter how long the couple had been married to each other (Cimbalo, Faling, & Mousaw, 1976).

Self-Labeling

If persons develop a conscious awareness of being in love, then indeed they are in love. When they reach the self-labeling stage, at least two things happen: they define themselves as being in love, and their actions confirm this fact (Bell, 1983). Schachter's two-component theory of understanding human emotional response has been applied to passionate love (Walster, 1971). Accordingly, arousal and appropriate cognition (thinking) are necessary for love to exist. Individuals will be incapable of experiencing love unless they are prepared to define their feelings in that way. This concept also can be applied to situations in which persons fall out of love. In other words, if a woman labels herself as no longer being in love, she is said to have fallen out of love. Whenever a person ceases to view the loved one as a love object, her/his actions will be influenced. The former love object may still be treated essentially as before only if important relationship rewards still exist (Bell, 1983). The research evidence suggests that three major areas of rewards are the most important reasons for remaining in a relationship without love:

1. Intrinsic characteristics of the other person such as inner beauty, sense of humor, and intelligence.
2. The other person's directly rewarding behavior such as sexual opportunity, attention, or consolation in times of stress.
3. The other person's ability to provide assistance in gaining access to desired external resources such as prestige or money (Casey & Matson, 1987, p. 12).

Measuring Love Attitudes

Folklore suggests that a person in love has difficulty sleeping, has a poor appetite, and is restless, all conditions that are more likely to be indicative of work-related problems or illness than love. Most persons are intrigued with love and its distinguishing characteristics. One of the most often asked questions in college courses about marriage and the family is, "How can I tell if I am in love?" Unfortunately, there is no precise scientific basis for categorizing a person as "being in love." A Love Attitudes Scale has been developed that is intended to measure the degree to which a person is romantic or realistic about love (Knox, 1983). Students can gain valuable insight into both personal and partner

Lovers at every age speak a special language of love, intelligible only by two.

qualities by use of this Love Attitudes Scale. Who is the realist, and who is the romantic? How much do we differ in ideas about love? On which answers do we least and most agree? Are these findings surprising, or were they anticipated? These are a few of the questions that the instrument may raise for partners in a love relationship.

Even in the absence of scientific proof, students can attempt to distinguish friendship, love, and infatuation, as well as to analyze such characteristics as exclusiveness, passion, and caring. Just knowing the research facts will not necessarily make a difference in personal relationships. However, knowledge is an essential first step for consciously changing behavior. For example, when persons know that love relationships, compared to friendships, are more likely to include greater degrees of passion, caring, ambivalence, and conflict, and to require more maintenance activities, they can better assess their own relationships. Knowing that the level of acceptance is lower and the readiness to criticize is higher among spouses and lovers than between friends, one can consciously choose to monitor the critical behavior (Davis, 1985).

BOX 6.2: The Love Attitudes Scale

This Love Attitudes Scale is intended to assess the degree to which you are a romantic or a realist in terms of love and does not relate to being a happy or mature person.

INSTRUCTIONS: Circle the response you believe is most appropriate: 1 = Strongly Agree (SA); 2 = Mildly Agree (MA); 3 = Undecided (U); 4 = Mildly Disagree (MD); and 5 = Strongly Disagree (SD).

		SA	MA	U	MD	SD
1.	Love doesn't make sense. It just is.	1	2	3	4	5
2.	When you fall head-over-heels-in-love, it's sure to be the real thing.	1	2	3	4	5
3.	To be in love with someone you would like to marry but can't is a tragedy.	1	2	3	4	5
4.	When love hits, you know it.	1	2	3	4	5
5.	Common interests are really unimportant; as long as each of you is truly in love, you will adjust.	1	2	3	4	5
6.	It doesn't matter if you marry after you have known your partner for only a short time as long as you know you are in love.	1	2	3	4	5
7.	If you are going to love a person, you will "know" after a short time.	1	2	3	4	5
8.	As long as two people love each other, the educational differences they have really do not matter.	1	2	3	4	5
9.	You can love someone even though you do not like any of that person's friends.	1	2	3	4	5
10.	When you are in love, you are usually in a daze.	1	2	3	4	5
11.	Love at first sight is often the deepest and most enduring type of love.	1	2	3	4	5
12.	When you are in love, it really does not matter what your partner does since you will love him or her anyway.	1	2	3	4	5
13.	As long as you really love a person, you will be able to solve the problems you have with that person.	1	2	3	4	5
14.	Usually there are only one or two people in the world whom you could really love and be happy with.	1	2	3	4	5
15.	Regardless of other factors, if you truly love another person, that is enough to marry that person.	1	2	3	4	5
16.	It is necessary to be in love with the one you marry to be happy.	1	2	3	4	5
17.	Love is more of a feeling than a relationship.	1	2	3	4	5
18.	People should not get married unless they are in love.	1	2	3	4	5
19.	Most people truly love only once during their lives.	1	2	3	4	5
20.	Somewhere there is an ideal mate for most people.	1	2	3	4	5
21.	In most cases, you will "know it" when you meet the right one.	1	2	3	4	5
22.	Jealousy usually varies directly with love; that is, the more you are in love, the greater your tendency to become jealous.	1	2	3	4	5
23.	When you are in love, you do things because of what you feel rather than what you think.	1	2	3	4	5
24.	Love is best described as an exciting rather than a calm thing.	1	2	3	4	5
25.	Most divorces probably result from falling out of love rather than failing to adjust.	1	2	3	4	5
26.	When you are in love, your judgment is usually not too clear.	1	2	3	4	5
27.	Love often comes but once in a lifetime.	1	2	3	4	5
28.	Love is often a violent and uncontrollable emotion.	1	2	3	4	5
29.	Differences in social class and religion are of small importance as compared with love in selecting a marriage partner.	1	2	3	4	5
30.	No matter what anyone says, love cannot be understood.	1	2	3	4	5

Note: 30 = Lowest possible score—the most romantic response; 150 = Highest possible score—the most realistic response.
Source: D. Knox, *The Love Attitudes Inventory*. Copyright © 1983 Family Life Publications, Saluda, NC.

Assessing Romantic Love: Female and Male Differences

Stereotypically, men are "lovers and leavers of women." The facts are that women are more tough-minded in assessing their love relationships, more likely to initiate a break-up, and more **resilient** (bounce back more easily) after parting (Hill, 1989).

Research over the past 25 years indicates that men are **romantic** or impractical, whereas women are pragmatic or practical whenever the question of love is considered (Lester, 1985). These gender differences are based, in part, on the fact that women and men differ in at least three areas with regard to expressing love: intimacy, caretaking, and stroking. Although men tend to consider intimacy more in terms of actions rather than in verbal expressions, women are more likely to evidence the caretaker role. For example, about 8 in 10 American women in couple-based households make the medical and health-care decisions for the family. Further, women play the major role in providing emotional stroking to soothe egos and to help reduce stress levels in their male relationship partner (Rubenstein, 1986).

Women as Pragmatists

A **pragmatic** or practical view of love means among other things that a person intellectually evaluates the appropriateness of her/his potential love object. Women with a high degree of self-esteem are more likely to use such objectivity as a basis for evaluating potential love relationships than women with low self-esteem (Prasinos & Tittler, 1984). However, when the term "romance" is used in the context of the **courtship** process, more women than men are likely to say romance is important to their relationship (Rubenstein, 1983).

Another basis for concluding that women are more pragmatic about romance relates to the earlier finding that women tend to express their inner feelings more directly, whereas men tend to rely on nonverbal communication. Women, when compared to men, are more likely to report experiencing both positive and negative emotions: contentment and joy as well as anger, depression, insecurity, and loneliness. They also underexpress their feelings of joy and liking for their partner while overexpressing sadness and hurt (Sprecher & Hatfield, 1986).

Sensations experienced when in love apparently differ for women and men (see Table 6.1). As illustrated, women were more likely than men to experience strong sensations when in love, with one exception: both women and men were equally nervous before dates.

Table 6.1: Sensations Experienced When In Love

Sensations When In Love	Women	Men
Floating on a cloud		
Strong	32%	24%
Moderate	31	31
Slight	36	45
Wanted to run, jump, scream		
Strong	26	16
Moderate	28	20
Slight	45	64
Trouble concentrating		
Strong	42	30
Moderate	27	23
Slight	31	47
Felt giddy and carefree		
Strong	22	16
Moderate	29	26
Slight	49	58
General feeling of well-being		
Strong	82	73
Moderate	12	18
Slight	6	9
Nervous before dates		
Strong	22	22
Moderate	24	20
Slight	54	59
Physical sensations: Cold hands, tingling spine, etc.		
Strong	21	18
Moderate	23	22
Slight	57	60

Source: E. J. Kanin, et al., "A Research Note on Male-Female Differentials in the Experience of Heterosexual Love" in *The Journal of Sex Research*, 6:67. Copyright © 1970 Society for the Scientific Study of Sex, Philadelphia, PA.

Further, women who reported strong romantic attitudes toward love generally tended to be more depressed. In addition, their romantic attitude was not associated with satisfaction of their basic needs in the relationship nor with liking their relationship partner (Lester, Doscher, Estrict, & Lee, 1984).

Men as Romantics

In various studies, men have been found to be more likely to fall in love, to do so more quickly, to fall into unrequited love, to have passions and crushes, and to characterize their partner as the "love of their dreams" (Rubenstein, 1986). Men may be less pragmatic and cautious in love experiences since love and marriage are, according to societal meaning, more important and serious matters for women than for men (Kazak & Reppucci, 1980).

A study of college students confirmed that men had more romantic attitudes toward love than women. At the time that these data were collected, about two thirds of women and one half of men reported currently being in love. Those persons currently in love possessed more romantic attitudes toward love than those individuals who had previously been in love or who had never been in love. Freshmen were more romantic than seniors, regardless of gender (Knox & Sporakowski, 1968). A later study detected similar attitudes, with women and seniors (regardless of gender) being more realistic toward love than men and freshmen (Knox, 1982).

The Origins of Love

Even if love can be defined and identified, is it universally attainable? What are the specific abilities needed to make a good lover, and how do we acquire them? The answers to these questions lie in the origins of love that begin with one's earliest life experiences. The search for answers begins with two basic assumptions concerning the ability to love that have survived the test of time for over a quarter of a century:

1. No one is born with the ability to love nor does love result from mere growth. Instead, it is a complex product of many life experiences.
2. Love in later life is affected by the quality of love in early life. Therefore, it is imperfect for adults because it was imperfect for them as children (Fromme, 1963, pp. 44–45).

The Ability to Love

Lessons of both love and nonlove are learned by children early in life. As infants grow into noisy, undisciplined children who threaten adult values such as orderliness and cleanliness, they are not always treated lovingly. Therefore they learn to feel unloved (Fromme, 1963). By making love conditional, adults teach children how to earn love, not how to give it. Obviously, if love can be earned, it is impermanent or conditional. Such unreliability is often expressed in new marriages. Although no parent purposefully teaches her/his child to not love, there are parental behaviors that inadvertently teach nonlove lessons. These early lessons have long-lasting implications for later love relationships:

1. When a parent's timing is off and they demand behavior of the child which is developmentally impossible, the child will equate inability to perform with frustration and nonlove.
2. Parents are often unjustly punitive, indifferent, unloving, or inattentive and, therefore, teach nonlove.
3. Overteaching ambition or to get ahead at any cost teaches a child to not love.
4. Unhealthy sexual attitudes of parents can cause sexual activity to be equated with shame or guilt rather than an expression of love.
5. Incorrect methods of punishment can cause a sense of unworthiness or guilt in individuals who will then seek not love but punishment from a mate (Fromme, 1963, pp. 44–45).

How, then, does a person learn to love? One of the ways is by simple imitation. Witnessing love between parents is perhaps the most valuable lesson in this life-long pursuit. But there are other more subtle ways related to child-rearing practices. If children are properly handled in childhood, if they are accepted at their own rate of development, if their biological needs are met, and if they are allowed as much freedom as possible within proper bounds of control, they will learn to love. Also, as persons developmentally mature, they become more capable of a dependable, consistent love (Fromme, 1963).

With this background in mind, one may wonder whether or not all adults are capable of having a successful love relationship. And how may one recognize such an adult? While there are many factors involved in the ability to love in adulthood, three deserve special consideration: level of self-esteem, ability to engage in self-disclosure, and acceptance of others.

Level of Self-Esteem

Self-esteem is a subjective evaluation that represents the feelings a person has about herself/himself and implies self-acceptance. In general, persons reporting high self-esteem have less difficulty in making friends, are less sensitive to criticism, and are less preoccupied with their own needs (Coopersmith, 1967). A person with low self-esteem is likely to approach a love relationship from a selfish perspective because she/he needs "to be made" to feel worthy (Kernberg, 1978). Without genuine self-esteem, she/he depends on the partner in a marriage to rescue and give needed praise (Crosby, 1991). Further, persons with low self-esteem can less easily interpret signs of interest from potential dating partners and are less able to respond in a positive manner to such overtures (Walster & Walster, 1978). Such persons often characterize themselves as having difficulty concentrating when in love and often feel that their lover does not pay enough attention to them (Hendrick & Hendrick, 1986).

Engaging in Self-Disclosure

As might be anticipated, persons who report low self-esteem find it very difficult to disclose personal information about themselves to others. In the interest of maintaining masculinity, men have been socialized to keep their innermost feelings to themselves. As a result, they are less likely than women to engage in **self-disclosure.** Also, when men do share information about themselves, they disclose less (Rubin, Hill, Peplau, & Dunkel-Schetter, 1980).

As self-disclosure occurs, the likelihood of an intimate relationship developing increases substantially. High degrees of self-disclosure between dating partners have been associated with high love scale scores among college-student couples (Rubin et al., 1980). Self-disclosure may intellectually yield a more accurate evaluation of potential lovers and appears more likely to lead to a successful love relationship (Prasinos & Tittler, 1984). In fact, Jourard states:

> *One who does not disclose himself truthfully and fully . . . can never love another person nor can he be loved. . . . Every maladjusted person is a person who has not made himself known to another human being and in consequence does not know himself (1964, p. 26).*

Accepting Others

As will be recalled from the definition of romantic love, there is a perception on the part of the lover that the partner is perfect and represents the ideal person. However, the lover soon discovers that the supposed ideal partner has more than one disliked quality. As reality asserts itself, the hard work in the relationship begins. Accepting the shortcomings or mistakes of others is an essential ingredient in the ability to love. The evidence suggests that a person must have high self-esteem in order to be able to accept others as they actually are rather than as they would like for them to be (Hendrick & Hendrick, 1986). In summary, a person who possesses high self-esteem, appropriate self-disclosing skills, and tolerance of others would have more potential to engage in a healthy adult love relationship than one who lacks these qualities.

Developmental Tasks as Prelude to Love

Well before marriageable age, even those persons who are not students of life-span development are quite aware that life is a series of biological stages. Having lived through several such periods, they also know that particular life stages such as infancy, childhood, adolescence, adulthood, and old age are associated with specific characteristics and problems. These invariant developmental stages and their tasks have two primary origins: physical and cultural. Because rates of physical maturity vary, as do cultural pressures and/or privileges, people's lives are highly individualized (Duvall & Miller, 1985). However, regardless of life circumstances, certain tasks will arise at or near a specific time in an individual's life that must be negotiated successfully in order to succeed with future tasks. The achievement of these developmental tasks facilitates the emotional and social progress of the individual from one life stage to another (Duvall & Miller, 1985).

Principles of Developmental Tasks

Since developmental tasks are subject to cultural variation, it is not possible to define precisely those developmental tasks that are appropriate for each life stage. But regardless of one's cultural values, developmental tasks do exist for each stage in the life of a person. Personal adjustment in all areas, particularly in the area of love, depends to a substantial measure upon the degree of success with which one is able to accomplish these developmental tasks. The person who fails to accomplish a given task or who becomes fixated at a certain level inevitably encounters frustration, unhappiness, and social disapproval (Havighurst, 1972).

Sequence of Gender Identity

The attainment of gender identity is an example of the sequence of achievement of a developmental task. As already seen, the development of gender identity in the very young child is crucial to later emotional growth. Unless a child establishes a firm sense of self in terms of the female or male gender, she/he will be severely handicapped later while attempting to build rewarding relationships with other children and adults. The successful establishment of gender identity depends first upon the child being able to establish a satisfactory love relationship with her/his parents. Once gender identity is established, the child must then form play relationships with other children to become a relatively happy, healthy, well-adjusted child by school age. After beginning school, the social adjustment to principals,

In the wonderful world of the preadolescent, peers of the same sex play an important role in the developmental stages of love.

teachers, and schoolmates becomes the next developmental task. Encouragement and support by family members and friends are essential for the completion of developmental tasks that the child might find too difficult to accomplish alone (Duvall & Miller, 1985).

Becoming attracted to members of the opposite sex and learning how to interact in socially appropriate ways begins early in childhood and persists, for most people, throughout adolescence. Eventually, successful social and emotional adjustment in college is usually accompanied or followed by courtship and selection of a potential marriage partner. These culturally derived activities, courtship and marriage, are appropriate developmental tasks for early adulthood. The phenomena of parenthood and grandparenthood extend the concept of developmental tasks into old age.

Stages in Love Development

The stages in the development of love are closely linked to an individual's overall personal growth (Orlinsky, 1977). Each major life stage has a corresponding stage in love development. Generally, these stages are differentiated according to the object of love as well as the time of life when they arise. However, there are no clear-cut steps from one stage to another; each one simply merges almost imperceptibly into the next. Drawing from the work of various authorities, the stages through which love develops can be described (see Table 6.2).

Table 6.2: Stages of Love Development

Object of Love	Time Period
Self	Infancy
Mother	Infancy
Family members and other children	Ages 3–6
Peers of the same sex	Childhood
Members of the other sex	Adolescence
One member of the other sex	Adulthood
Own children	Adulthood

Sources: S. Freud, *New Introductory Lectures in Psychoanalysis.* New York: W. W. Norton & Company, 1965; E. Fromm, *The Art of Loving.* New York: Harper & Row, Publishers, Inc., 1956; and D. E. Orlinsky, "Love Relationships in the Life Cycle: A Developmental Interpersonal Perspective" in H. A. Otto (ed.), *Love Today: A New Exploration.* New York: Dell, 1977, pp. 135–150.

Although during infancy the child receives love passively, this is an important stage in learning to give love later in life. It is usually parents who impart these early love messages through their nurturing care in daily routines as the baby is fed, bathed, clothed, cuddled, and held. As the infant begins to differentiate self from inanimate objects in her/his world, the first love object is identified as "I love me" and "I want my needs fulfilled." Since mother is usually the primary caregiver who supplies these needs, it is ordinarily she who becomes the first object of love outside of the ego-centered self-love. Between ages 3–6, the child's love cycle expands to include family members other than the primary nurturer(s) as well as other children. If early love experiences have been satisfying, the child is more likely to proceed successfully through successive stages. These experiences include teachers and other adult models in early childhood who help to bridge the span between home and the outside world. Peers of the same sex are the love objects during childhood and preadolescence, while members of the other sex begin to gain prominence during early adolescence. This period should involve relationships with a number of persons of the other sex if the young adult is to be prepared for the next stage, a committed love relationship with one person of the other sex.

Finally, the cycle of giving love begins anew with the stage of generativity in which young adults initiate the evolving process of love with their own children. With lengthening life spans today, this stage increasingly includes another dimension of love. The so-called **sandwich generation,** with responsibility for children and parents, must frequently modify their love for their own parent, whose aging creates more dependency needs. It is not, however, a complete reversal of roles. Part of this selfless love and nurturing process is allowing the aging parent to retain a degree of autonomy (Leslie & Leslie, 1980).

As has already been stated, arrestment at any stage of development in the love cycle could lead to difficulty in achieving successive stages. For example, a marriage may falter if one of the partners was arrested at the "I love me" stage and is incapable of moving beyond this ego-centered position. It is important to realize, however, that at no time in the cycle do former love objects become extinct. One must retain a healthy love of self on which to build all love relationships. And although one's love of mother is usually a lifelong affair, it becomes a touchstone yet does not remain the centerpiece of a mature adult's love life. The entire process is built on a series of essential building blocks that eventually lead to a mature love that enables healthy relationships.

Loving Styles: A Conceptualization of Love

Current research and theory on loving styles includes the triangular theory of love. This theory of love consists of three major components:

1. **Intimacy**—feelings of closeness, connectedness, and bonding that one experiences in loving relationships.
2. **Passion**—a drive that leads to romance, physical attraction, and sexual involvement.
3. **Decision/commitment**—short-term, a decision that one loves another person and long-term, the commitment to maintain that love with the love object (Sternberg, 1986, p. 119).

Accordingly, the amount and kind of love that one experiences in a relationship depends upon the strength of these three components. Through their interaction with each other, they will produce different kinds of loving experiences for the relationship partners (Sternberg, 1986). The way in which one person loves another person can take on many different attributes and characteristics. In recent years, much effort has been devoted to classifying the styles of loving and their characteristics.

Styles of Loving

Perhaps the most noted classification system appeared in a book entitled *The Colours of Love* in which terminology from classical literature was utilized to distinguish six styles/categories of loving: **storge, ludus, pragma, mania, eros, and agape** (Lee, 1973). More recently, another typology for styles of loving has been proposed by Lasswell & Lobsenz (1980) that appears to be based on this earlier work. This proposed classification contains the following categories: best-friends love, game-playing love, logical love, possessive love, romantic love, and unselfish love (Lasswell & Lobsenz, 1980). The latter classification system more clearly places the earlier discussion of love and love development in proper perspective.

Best-Friends Love (Storge)

This style of loving represents a comfortable degree of intimacy that has developed between good friends out of their close association with one another over a considerable period of time (Lasswell & Lobsenz, 1980). Their love involves companionship, assumption of permanency for the relationship, low degree of emotion, and more planning than spontaneity (Hatkoff & Lasswell, 1979). Women are more likely than men to display this style of loving. This may relate to women being more likely to exhibit greater interest and concern for the welfare of others, i.e., social interest (Leak & Gardner, 1990).

Game-Playing Love (Ludus)

Persons displaying this style of loving consider love to be fun. It is a game in which independence is sought in a series of short-lived relationships. Often, several persons are dated at the same time and the relationships are viewed as challenges to be enjoyed (Prasinos & Tittler, 1984). If there is sexual involvement between the two persons, it is typically self-centered and exploitative (Hatkoff & Lasswell, 1979; Lee, 1973). This type of self-centered love is more likely to be characteristic of men than women. Ludus has been found in later research to be negatively related to satisfaction in relationships (Hendrick et al., 1988).

Logical Love (Pragma)

In logical love, the person concentrates on the practical aspects of the relationship by rationally assessing the potential assets and liabilities of the partners (Lasswell & Lobsenz, 1980). Relationships that do not have substantial promise of becoming permanent are likely to be terminated. In general, women tend to be more logical in their love relationships when compared to men. Therefore, it is not surprising that a study of broken relationships revealed that women were more likely to have initiated the breakup (Rubin, Peplau, & Hill, 1981).

Possessive Love (Mania)

Since there is a need to possess the loved person totally and to be equally possessed by the other person, this category represents the most unfulfilling and emotionally disturbing style of loving (Lasswell & Lobsenz, 1980). The characteristics of this loving style include jealousy and an inability to sleep, eat, or think logically (Hatkoff & Lasswell, 1979). A fear of loss or rejection is always present along with an emotional dependency on the partner. This loving style also involves strong sexual attraction and emotional intensity with the lovers often alternating between euphoria and depression (Lee, 1973). Women are more likely than men to display characteristics of possessive love.

Romantic Love (Eros)

This loving style is characterized by a powerful sense of physical attraction between the two partners and typically is associated with love at first sight. A heavy emphasis is placed on physical appearance, passion, and sexual expression (Prasinos & Tittler, 1984). The lovers must be willing and emotionally capable of revealing themselves completely and committing themselves totally to the relationship (Lasswell & Lobsenz, 1980). In this instance, the ideal image of the perfect lover exists. But eventually the person employing the romantic-loving style may become disappointed if she/he discovers that the "real" person does not match the perception of an ideal person (Lee, 1974). This style of loving is more likely to be characteristic of a man than a woman. Eros has been found to have a positive affect on a relationship (Hendrick et al., 1988).

Unselfish Love (Agape)

The unselfish-loving style involves unconditionally caring, nurturing, giving, forgiving, and self-sacrificing for your relationship partner (Lasswell & Lobsenz, 1980). Persons who employ the unselfish love style typically have high self-esteem, ego strength, self-rated

Table 6.3: Love Styles

Variable	Eros	Ludus	Storge	Pragma	Mania	Agape
	Love Styles					
Gender						
Women	2.3	3.6	2.5	2.8	3.0	2.4
Men	2.3	3.1	2.6	3.0	3.1	2.3
Times in love						
None	2.5	3.1	2.6	2.8	3.2	2.8
One	2.2	3.5	2.4	2.9	3.0	2.2
Two	2.3	3.4	2.4	2.9	3.0	2.3
Three to five	2.1	3.4	2.6	2.9	3.0	2.3
Five and up	2.2	2.6	2.7	3.1	3.2	2.5

Note: Mean scores can vary from 1.0 to 5.0. The lower the mean, the greater the degree of agreement with the given love style.
From C. Hendrick and S. Hendrick, "A Theory and Method of Love" in *Journal of Personality and Social Psychology,* 50:398.

lovingness, and self-rated spirituality. It, therefore, requires a generous and nonpossessive attitude as a necessary ingredient (Prasinos & Tittler, 1984). This loving style can best be described as a kind of altruistic love with little desire for return other than the satisfaction of having loved and cared for someone else (Lee, 1973). No gender differences are reported with regard to the unselfish-loving style.

In examining the various styles of loving, many persons will probably conclude that they possess substantial elements of two or more loving styles. One of the most difficult aspects of any typology is trying to construct discrete categories that are mutually exclusive and avoid the classification of all persons into only one category.

Evaluation of Loving Styles

The theory of loving styles suggested by Lee has been retested with college students using a 42–item scale that attempted to capture the essential elements of each loving style (Hendrick & Hendrick, 1986). Although Lee (1973) did not find the agape style in full-blown fashion, these later findings suggest that it is a viable style of loving (see Table 6.3). Women were more likely to report evidence of the storge (best-friends), pragma (logical), and mania (possessive) love styles, whereas men were more likely to exhibit the ludus (game-playing) love style. There were no significant gender differences with regard to the eros (romantic) and agape (unselfish) loving styles. In addition, those respondents who had never been in love were more likely to report the ludus- and mania-loving styles. Without regard to gender, those respondents with high self-esteem were more likely to disclose the eros and ludus-loving styles, whereas those respondents with low self-esteem were much more likely to disclose the mania-loving style. The age of the respondents was not a significant factor in their loving style (Hendrick & Hendrick, 1986).

The Contributions of Love to Health

Persons who reported falling in love were earlier described as having problems with sleep, poor eating habits, and a general sense of nervousness. But if a person remains in love, she/he may come to possess feelings of security and psychological well-being. Further, the available evidence suggests that the physical health of persons in love may be better than the health of those persons who are not in love (Kemper & Bologh, 1981). This conclusion is supported by research that documents better physical health for married rather than unmarried persons (Glenn & Weaver, 1988).

Physical Health

In a study of postcollege age persons who had experienced the "broken-heart" syndrome, negative feelings associated with an ended love relationship, their feelings of loneliness and being unloved contributed to a higher incidence of heart disease and, in some instances, premature deaths (Lynch, 1977). A related study determined that when persons terminated a relationship, they were more likely to experience various health problems such as peptic ulcers and various other ill-defined symptoms (Peele & Brodsky, 1976). These findings are supported by a later investigation that found persons who had recently ended a love relationship were more likely to report a negative health status when compared to persons who were currently in love (Kemper & Bologh, 1981).

Another indicator of the negative health effects of a love relationship ending can be found in the higher death rates due to cirrhosis of the liver in widowed and divorced men in comparison to married men. Divorced men ages 25–35 were 11 times more likely to die from cirrhosis of the liver than married men (Gove & Tudor, 1973). However, since heavy alcohol consumption and cirrhosis of the liver are often related, one may argue that the real cause of the liver disease may have been alcohol rather than loss of love. On the other hand, one could argue that the problem could be cyclical with the loss of love leading to alcohol abuse or alcohol abuse leading to the loss of love.

Psychological Health

Perhaps the best evidence of the causal contributions of love to good psychological health can be found in data concerning recently divorced persons. The research suggests that most persons believe they are in love with their spouse at the time of their marriage. Since marriage represents a permanent commitment, a divorce is construed as a life failure for many persons. In a study of divorce, two fifths of both women and men characterized their divorce experience as stressful (see Table 6.4). Persons who are newly divorced are more likely to suffer from anxiety, loneliness, and personal disorganization than persons who are still married (Weiss, 1976). Therefore it is not surprising that a review of the data from 11 studies of divorced persons led to the conclusion that without regard to gender, divorced persons consistently exhibited higher mental disorder rates in comparison to married persons. Furthermore, in the majority of the studies, men had higher mental disorder rates than women (Bloom & Caldwell, 1981). These findings represent an indirect measure of the possible effects of a broken relationship on the psychological health and well-being of the person.

Table 6.4: Feelings after Divorce

Feelings after Divorce	Women	Men
Characterization of divorce		
Stressful but bearable	40%	40%
Traumatic, a nightmare	27	16
Unsettling but easier than expected	19	24
Relatively painless	14	20
Most difficult period		
Before decision to divorce	58	49
After decision but before final decree	20	25
Just after the divorce	19	23
Now	3	3

From S. L. Albrecht, "Reactions and Adjustments to Divorce: Differences in the Experiences of Males and Females" in *Family Relations,* 29:61.

The Role of Jealousy in Love Relationships

Jealousy is "a negative response to a real or imagined threat resulting from the actual or potential loss of an intimate partner" (Clanton & Smith, 1977, p. 153). This negative response may take the form of anxiety, anger, fear of partner loss, and/or vulnerability. The fear from jealousy is based on a devaluing of one's self and security (James, 1988). Margaret Mead is said to have perceived jealousy not as a barometer by which the depth of love may be determined but one by which the degree of the lover's insecurity is measured. Thus, jealousy is believed to be a negative, miserable state of feeling, having its origin in a sense of insecurity and inferiority (Walster, 1971).

Feelings of jealousy apparently exist, to some degree, for most persons who are engaged in love relationships. One study found that three fourths of women and men had experienced feelings of jealousy, while one half described themselves as "a jealous person" (Pines & Aronson, 1983). Jealous people may believe their reactions help to keep the love object sensitive to the fact that she/he is very deeply cared about and, therefore, are not a totally negative influence in a love relationship. The more prevalent view today, however, suggests that feelings of jealousy have their origins in insecurity and can potentially be very counterproductive for a love relationship. More specifically, extreme feelings of jealousy may result in severe depression, spouse abuse, or even homicide.

Factors Affecting Jealousy

Given the complex emotions involved in feelings of jealousy, it is a formidable task to clearly delineate those factors that may trigger jealousy in a love relationship. With this task in mind, five such factors have been identified: behavior of partner, lack of self-confidence in relationships, societal and cultural gender expectations, attitudes toward love, and opposite sex friendships.

Behavior of Partner

Jealousy may be elicited by certain behaviors. For example, the partner may behave in ways that convey feelings of disinterest toward the current loved one. If the partner constantly comments about the physical attractiveness or personal qualities of other potential love partners, it is likely to cause feelings of insecurity. Or if one's partner spends a disproportionate amount of her/his time with others, feelings of jealousy will likely arise. Such feelings may have a rational basis as indicated by the fact that a great majority of women and men whose spouse had had an extramarital affair reported general and specific feelings of jealousy (Buunk, 1982).

Insecurity in Relationships

Research on self-esteem and jealousy indicates that persons with low self-esteem are more likely to experience feelings of jealousy than persons with high self-esteem (Stewart & Beatty, 1985). Generally speaking, women are more likely to report feelings of jealousy than are men. Further, persons who are dissatisfied with their love relationship in general and those who are dissatisfied with their sexual lives in particular, are more likely to report feelings of jealousy (Hansen, 1983; Pines & Aronson, 1983).

Using hypothetical situations as a basis for gauging feelings of jealousy among college students, women were found to be more jealous than men over situations involving their partner spending time on a personal hobby or with his family members. A majority of women and men expected their dating partners to give up close friendships with members of the opposite sex as the relationship became more serious (see Table 6.5). Otherwise, jealousy can potentially generate feelings of insecurity and loss of self-esteem because of a perceived feeling that one's partner does not highly value the relationship (James, 1988).

Table 6.5: Reactions to Jealousy-Producing Events

Jealousy-Producing Event	Women	Men
1. Large portion of leisure time spent on personal hobby	4.4	3.8
2. "Night out with girls/boys"	3.7	3.6
3. Opposite-sex friend/co-worker gives emotional support	6.5	6.4
4. Solo participation in her/his family activities every Sunday	5.3	4.5
5. Business trip "one night stand" with person just met	9.8	10.0

Note: Reported as mean scores with responses ranging from 1 (extremely pleased) to 11 (extremely disturbed).
From G. L. Hansen, "Dating Jealousy among College Students" in *Sex Roles,* 12:717. Copyright © 1985 Plenum Publishing Corporation, New York, NY. Reprinted by permission.

Societal and Cultural Gender Expectations

Certain gender-role orientations are variables that have been consistently found to be associated with dating jealousy. Dating partners with traditional gender roles are much more likely to report feelings of jealousy (Hansen, 1982; Hansen, 1985). These jealousy feelings may represent a sense of lost pride, a threat to self-esteem, or a perception that one's property rights have been violated. In contrast, persons with nontraditional gender roles are more likely to perceive such circumstances as a boost to their own ego in that someone else would express interest in or give attention to their relationship partner.

Unrealistic Attitudes toward Love

Persons who possess unrealistic, romantic attitudes about love are much more likely to experience feelings of jealousy toward their relationship partner. In three separate studies of undergraduate college students, those persons indicating a romantic attitude about love had greater feelings of jealousy, higher jealousy scores, and were more irrational concerning their love relationship. However, their romantic attitude toward love was not found to be associated with self-esteem (Lester, Deluca, Hellinghausen, & Scribner, 1985).

Opposite-Sex Friendships

As more women are working outside of the home, social changes are resulting in primary relationships that have the potential to evoke feelings of jealousy. Such feelings may be a barrier to opposite-sex friendships when a person is involved in a couple relationship. A relationship partner may believe that it is wrong, shameful, or threatening to the relationship for the other partner to become friends with a member of the opposite sex. Further, many persons believe that the potentiality for sexual involvement will eventually develop between opposite-sex friends. Finally, if one or both of the opposite-sex friends are married, many persons interpret the opposite-sex friendship to mean that something must be missing from their marriage because of the rather common assumption in our society that all unmet needs should be provided by one's spouse (Bell, 1981).

Effects of Jealousy on Love Relationships

The presence of jealousy in love relationships, as indicated earlier, usually has negative consequences. Because feelings of insecurity and low self-esteem are associated with jealousy, persons who have overall dissatisfaction with their lives are likely to more frequently experience feelings of jealousy. Although experiencing jealousy seems to cause more pain and suffering in women, they are more likely to try to improve the relationship, whereas men are more likely to try to regain their self-esteem. Thus, men are much more likely to end a love relationship in which the woman has not maintained sexual exclusivity, in contrast to those cases where the man has not. Finally, women are much more likely than men to deliberately create jealousy feelings in order to obtain increased attention, to enhance their self-esteem, to test the relationship, and/or to seek revenge (Adams, 1980).

If a person is experiencing feelings of jealousy in a love relationship, it is very important that these feelings be shared with the partner. The circumstances that led to the jealousy feelings should be clarified. In some instances, the situation producing the jealousy may have been misinterpreted or misunderstood. In most instances, however, the jealousy and the humiliation that goes with it results from deep personal insecurity. Resolution of such destructive emotions requires more than cosmetic personality changes if the relationship is to be maintained (James, 1988).

Summary

- Mature love enhances the growth potential of both relationship partners and implies care, respect, responsibility, and knowledge, whereas infatuation consists of romantic illusions about an idealized relationship partner. Authorities consider romantic love as an inappropriate basis for a long-term relationship.
- It is important to distinguish between the myths and realities of love relationships. Three variables are associated with the ability to have a successful love relationship: level of self-esteem, ability to engage in self-disclosure, and acceptance of others.
- Developmental tasks are goals appropriate to particular stages in life, the achievement of which brings happiness and success in future ones. Formation of gender identity, development of a sexual orientation, falling in love, marriage, and parenthood are examples of developmental tasks related to love.
- Certain kinds of love relationships at each stage of the life cycle provide a foundation upon which to build mature relationships in adulthood.
- Based on physical attraction and sexual desire, romantic love propels individuals toward commitment, mate selection, and marriage. Passionate love may survive well into the married years but, gradually, if the marriage is to succeed, it must be replaced by a deeper love based upon shared experiences and commitment.
- Loving styles have been classified as best-friends (storge) love, game-playing (ludus) love, logical (pragma) love, possessive (mania) love, romantic (eros) love, and unselfish (agape) love.
- Being in love can contribute to a person's physical and psychological well-being. Feelings of jealousy in love relationships are usually based on insecurity.

Questions for Critical Reflection

1. If there is no such thing as love at first sight, how do you explain the fact that some people who married after a very short acquaintance have successful marriages?
2. What factors do you believe account for women being more pragmatic about love than men? Are these factors more related to sociological or personality variables?
3. What are the personality characteristics of a person with an inability to love? Are these characteristics hidden, or are they easily observable before marriage? Why are they frequently ignored in love relationships?
4. At which developmental stage of love are you? Do you know any married persons whose development was arrested at the "I love mother" stage or "I love me" stage? Do they have a successful marriage?
5. What role has jealousy played in your love relationships? How does the knowledge that jealousy is a measure of insecurity improve your odds of dealing with it in healthy ways?

Suggested Readings

Bell, R. R. (1981). *Worlds of friendship.* Beverly Hills, CA: Sage. A major work examining the origins, meanings, and functions of friendships.

Brehm, S. S. (1985). *Intimate relationships.* New York: Random House. An interesting analysis of love relationships between women and men.

Buscaglia, L. (1972). *Love.* Thorofare, NJ: Charles B. Slack. A sharing of practical and vital ideas, feelings, and observations about love.

Fromm, E. (1956). *The art of loving.* New York: Harper & Row. A classic work describing a humanistic approach to love.

James, J. (1988). *Women and the blues: Passions that hurt, passions that heal.* New York: Harper & Row. A woman's practical survival guide for understanding feelings and ending internal conflict.

Peck, M. S. (1988). *The road less traveled.* New York: Simon & Schuster. An important treatise on the interrelationship of discipline, love, and personal growth.

CHAPTER 7

Mate Selection or Singlehood: Options in the 1990s

When two people are under the influence of the most violent, most insane, most delusive, and most transient of passions, they are required to swear that they will remain in that exalted, abnormal, exhausting condition continuously until death do them part.
George Bernard Shaw, 1932

Outline

"If only I could marry the right person." This painful myth of everlasting passion fills the adolescent with hope (James, 1988). More mature persons are likely to reject the romantic idea of a one-and-only princess or prince with whom they are destined to fall in love. But even intelligent persons who fail to understand those principles that guide the probabilities in mate selection may enter into this phase of life at no less of a disadvantage than a star-struck teenager.

The alternative to mate selection, singlehood, is also an often misunderstood phenomenon. Since singles are one of the fastest growing segments of the population, there is a pressing need to understand the effects of such a life-style. Historically, singles have been viewed as self-centered and irresponsible, redeemable only by marriage. But most singles are socially, economically, and psychologically like everyone else. Only recently, however, has their status begun to be considered as worthwhile in its own right. For example, an in-depth coverage of singles in marriage and family texts is a recent phenomenon (Shostak, 1987). This chapter will explore the mate selection process and the option of singlehood.

Mate Selection

Although "free-choice" marriage is a hallmark of the American system, an observant visitor from another culture might well question the definition of free choice. In our culture, social approval is a particularly influential factor in determining mate choices. **Endogamy** (marriage within one's group) and **exogamy** (marriage outside of one's group) are two concepts that help to explain this selection system. Endogamous norms pressure persons to marry within their own social, religious, age, racial and/or ethnic, educational, and economic groups. Exogamy, on the other hand, pressures a person toward marriage outside a particular group (Hutter, 1988). Legal restrictions prohibiting marriage to one's kin and long-held incest taboos are both examples of exogamous norms. The process of mate selection involves a series of sociological and psychological filters that gradually eliminate persons from the pool of eligible mates, thus gradually narrowing a person's choices.

Sociological Factors

The initial attraction between two persons in the field of eligible dating partners occurs during the early period of their courtship and is based on factors such as physical appearance, competent behavior, agreement with one's attitudes, and positive responsiveness (Levinger, 1980). At that point, sociological factors become important. In one noncollege sample, economic and social factors were found to be more influential in mate selection than has been previously reported. Such research is usually conducted using college students who already are presorted on social and demographic variables, which will be overshadowed by love, affection, and compatibility (Davis-Brown, Salamon, & Surra, 1987). It is important to explore two sociological factors that significantly affect our free-choice mate selection: **propinquity** (physical nearness) and **homogamy** (similarity of characteristics).

Propinquity: Residential or Organizational Filter

In one major city 60 years ago, one half of persons applying for marriage licenses lived within 20 blocks of each other (Bossard, 1931). Historically, residential areas have tended to be somewhat segregated by social class, religion, race, and ethnic background, thus increasing the possibility that persons will come in contact with individuals who are similar to themselves. But as society becomes more mobile, the circumstances under which two people meet, become acquainted, and fall in love make the operation of propinquity much more complex (Adams, 1986). College student populations, for example, create residential propinquity. They bring together large numbers of students from differing locations with diverse religious, racial, or social backgrounds who live in dormitories, sorority and fraternity houses, and apartments.

Residential propinquity, however, may have become substantially less influential than organizational propinquity in mate selection (Leslie & Leslie, 1980). For example, college class projects or extracurricular activities bring into contact those who may not perceive each other as potential dating partners but who may form a serious relationship because of shared interests. Organizational propinquity also occurs in the workplace where an individual has an opportunity to become acquainted with persons in various capacities in their field of work. Also, work-related recreational activities and travel options may provide additional opportunities for becoming acquainted with potential marriage mates.

Homogamy as a Filtering Mechanism

The term "homogamy" refers to the fact that most persons select a marriage partner who resembles themselves in certain ways (Leslie & Korman, 1989). On

Why would royal marriages be least likely of all unions to result from organizational propinquity?

the other hand, **heterogamy** denotes differences rather than similarities. College students, in particular, often receive conflicting messages about these two factors. Their parents and acquaintances from home usually urge them to marry someone from their own circle of acquaintances, while their college peers may emphasize the importance of getting to know persons from widely different backgrounds. In the push toward homogamy, the influence of mothers is greater than that of fathers. But the father's influence is greater on his daughter's choice of a marriage mate than on his son's choice (Jedlicka, 1984). When one examines those attributes in a mate that are preferred by young persons themselves, it is obvious that homogamy is not a pressing issue, at least at the conscious level (see Table 7.1). There are a number of sorting factors that enable homogamous choices: social class, values, religion, occupation, sexuality, intelligence, education, age, and desire for children.

Social Class. A social class is a group of people with similar backgrounds in occupation, education, economic status, and general life experiences (Farley, 1990). Social class is more likely to limit a person's choice of a mate before they begin dating than to limit them at the stage of a deeper attraction (Adams, 1986). However, social differences are far less likely to be apparent when a dating relationship is initiated than, for example, racial or religious differences.

Traditional attitudes have maintained that a mating gradient exists in which men tend to date and marry downward in terms of their social class, whereas women tend to marry upward. However, research during the 1970s failed to confirm such a pattern. Using data from four national surveys, the concept of a mating gradient was found to be largely illusionary (Jorgensen, 1977). Evidence of considerable downward mobility for women in the mate selection process was also apparent, with parents being less successful in discouraging their daughter from marriage to a perceived

Table 7.1: Characteristics Sought in Marriage Mate

Rank	Characteristics Preferred by Women	Rank	Characteristics Preferred by Men
1	Kindness and understanding	1	Kindness and understanding
2	Intelligence	2	Intelligence
3	Exciting personality	3	Physical attractiveness
4	Good health	4	Exciting personality
5	Adaptability	5	Good health
6	Physical attractiveness	6	Adaptability
7	Creativity	7	Creativity
8	Good earning capacity	8	Desire for children
9	College graduate	9	College graduate
10	Desire for children	10	Good heredity
11	Good heredity	11	Good earning capacity
12	Good housekeeper	12	Good housekeeper
13	Religious orientation	13	Religious orientation

From D. M. Buss, "Human Mate Selection" in *American Scientist*, 73:47–51. Reprinted by permission of *American Scientist*, journal of Sigma XI, The Scientific Research Society, New Haven, CT.

undesirable marriage partner (Glenn, Ross, & Tully, 1974). One of the reasons may be that social class today is less rigidly structured than in previous decades. Also, most young couples tend to marry during the time that their social-class category is evolving, and, as they grow older, their social status tends to increase.

Values. **Values** refer to those elements that are important to human existence. They are the basic beliefs with which a person determines her/his life goals, interests, and behavior (Holman, Busby, & Larson, 1989). Understanding the process of valuing helps clarify the meaning of a value. This process involves freely choosing from considered alternatives, prizing the choice enough to affirm it publicly, and acting upon the choice repeatedly in life (Rath, Harmin, & Simon, 1966). Applying these criteria to a religion will enable a person to clarify whether or not she/he really values that which is claimed. For example, if one's religious faith was chosen freely from alternatives, is publicly acclaimed, and is implemented repeatedly in their life, it is valued. Values significantly affect all of the sorting factors used in selecting a mate. Therefore, substantial differences in personal values between partners can lead to potential conflict and marital instability. However, given the likelihood of persons from diverse backgrounds marrying, some value difference is inevitable.

Religion. Two studies among young, never-married singles suggest that religion is no longer considered highly important as a factor in mate selection (Epstein & Guttman, 1984). In fact, in the previously cited study of characteristics sought in a marriage partner, female and male college students ranked "religious orientation" the least important of 13 factors (see Table 7.1). Such findings probably reflect the increasing acceptance of interfaith marriages by most religions. The low ranking of religious importance may also be related to the developmental stage of young adulthood, during which resolution of religious issues is not as pressing a need as those more physiological in nature. The significance of religion in mate selection may also be gender related. In one survey of single women and men, ages 50–70, religion of mate was found to be twice as important for women as it was for men (Berkowitz, 1983).

Occupational Roles. Despite gains made toward egalitarian gender roles in our society, most men are still the primary family breadwinner. This is reflected in the perception of women who tend to place great importance on partner characteristics such as energy, working hard, and displaying physical strength, courage, and endurance (Laner, 1986). Further, women are significantly more likely than men to rank "good earning capacity" high as a characteristic sought in a marriage mate (Buss, 1985). Perception of female/male roles is a significant sorting factor in mate selection. Success in the relationship depends not on where the partners are positioned on the scale from traditionalism to egalitarianism but how far apart they find themselves. These ideas represent deeply held beliefs that are not easily changed.

Sexuality. Much debate exists over the issue of whether or not virginity is considered to be a desirable quality in the marriage market. It appears that college students use their own experience as a standard by which to judge others. In one study, sexually inexperienced women and men rated highly sexually experienced, opposite-sex peers as less desirable marriage partners. But the sexually experienced women and men rated all opposite-sex peers similarly in terms of marriage desirability (Istvan & Griffitt, 1980). Others found that both women and men preferred moderately sexually experienced partners for marriage regardless of their own sexual experience level. Further, women expressed a desire for a virgin marriage partner just as frequently as did men, thus offering no support for the traditional double standard (Jacoby & Williams, 1985).

Intelligence Level. People tend to want to marry others who are their intellectual equals. This factor, which relates to the level of education, may not only affect occupational roles but also leisure activities (Epstein & Guttman, 1984). Intelligence has been reported as the second most desired characteristic in a marriage partner by both women and men (see Table 7.1). Other research indicates that intelligence ranks first and second by college women and men, respectively (Laner, 1986).

Educational Level. Although educational level of spouses is usually equal, men with a higher educational level are considered more desirable as spouses than lower-educated men. But educational level is more of a marriage filter for women than for men (Dimaggio & Mohr, 1985). Generally, for men, additional education tends to attract a higher valued spouse, but for women it can potentially decrease their opportunities for marriage. Women with more education also tend to marry later (Boulier & Rosenzweig, 1984).

Age at Marriage. Contrary to popular opinion, there has been a gradual shift toward marital-age homogamy in this century. In 1900, 27% of wives were married to men who were 10 or more years older than themselves as compared to only 7% in 1980 (see Table 7.2). The age differential was approximately 4 years for 7 in 10 couples, whereas currently it is about 3 years. Today, husband-younger and/or husband-older marriages tend to be characterized by lower socioeconomic status on the part of one spouse when compared with same-age marriages (Atkinson & Glass, 1985).

Table 7.2: Marital-Age Homogamy/Heterogamy for Wives

Marital-Age Homogamy/Heterogamy	1900	1960	1980
Total husband older	47%	33%	27%
Husband older (5–9 years)	20	23	20
Husband older (10 + years)	27	10	7
Husband and wife same age (+ or − 4 years)	37	63	70
Total husband younger	16	4	3
Husband younger (5–9 years)	5	3	2
Husband younger (10 + years)	11	1	1

From M. P. Atkinson and B. L. Glass, "Marital-Age Heterogamy and Homogamy, 1900 to 1980" in *Journal of Marriage and the Family,* 47:687.

Desire for Children. A potential source of tremendous difficulty for future marital relationships involves differences in the desire for children. Men holding traditional gender roles are more likely to place greater importance on desire for children than women (Buss, 1985). A number of variables are associated with this issue, including choice of effective contraception, levels of sexual responsiveness/sexual satisfaction, and traditional versus egalitarian gender roles. In a study of never-married women, those wanting to have children rated their ideal marriage partner more highly on traditional masculine attributes than women who preferred to be voluntarily child-free in marriage. Regardless of attitudes toward having children, the factors "move ahead and improve economic status," "desire to save for future needs," and "keep materially ahead of others" were ranked important by all women (Callan, 1983).

Psychological Factors

Personality factors that operate in mate selection have been formed by the interaction of earlier life experiences with genetic endowment (Murstein, 1980). In this respect, parental impact on mate selection is believed to be more indirect than direct (Leslie, Huston, & Johnson, 1986). From among the theories concerning the influence of personality in mate selection, complementary needs and stimulus-value-role will be explored.

Complementary Needs Theory

A number of years ago, the **complementary needs theory** of more selection was developed using the principle that opposites attract (Winch, 1958). This theory suggests that individuals select marriage partners who are perceived to satisfy their unfulfilled personality needs. For example, persons with a need to be dominant are likely to select submissive marriage partners. Or one who has an unmet need to be nurtured will seek a person to take care of her/him. Complementary alliances may also exist when the personality needs of the two partners are somewhat the same, but their need levels differ markedly in intensity (Winch, 1958). This popular concept is consistent with common sense and, in fact, is substantiated by considerable clinical data from therapists (Crosby, 1991; Peck, 1978). However, others claim that accumulated scientific research fails to support the theory (Meyer & Pepper, 1977; Murstein, 1980).

Stimulus-Value-Role Theory

The **stimulus-value-role theory** (S-V-R) holds that persons are first attracted to one another on the basis of personal qualities (Murstein, 1980). In a free-choice situation, attraction and social interaction between two persons depend on the exchange value of the assets and liabilities that each individual brings to the situation. In this respect, Nye (1980) declares that the S-V-R Theory is Choice and Exchange Theory. In exchange theory, rewards are things wanted and costs are things to avoid. In mate selection, the rewards might occur physically, socially, or psychologically, while the costs would be any unpleasant consequences of these behaviors or attitudes. The profit is that which is left after the costs are subtracted from the rewards (Nye, 1979). Rewards include good looks, sex appeal, social status, and promising career prospects. Most individuals will only approach a person to whom they feel approximately equal, seeking to avoid persons who are "too attractive" for fear of being rejected. It is at this stimulus stage that the two dating partners are constructing a kind of balance sheet where not only the number of rewards but also their quality must be considered. Assuming the balance sheet is favorable for both partners, the relationship is likely to move to the value stage (Murstein, 1980).

During the value stage, the couple will determine whether or not there is compatibility of values and attitudes to support their initial attraction. If they like the other person's mental, physical, reputational, and social attributes they will likely remain together, at least for a time (Murstein, 1980). It is during this period that attitudes toward life, marriage, having children, and religion are discussed. Assuming their values are similar, the attraction will become stronger as each person receives positive reinforcement from the other person, thus enhancing their self-concepts. In most cases, only when attraction is combined with value compatibility will the couple move into the role stage (Murstein, 1980).

Roles are herein defined as expectations of self and partner as well as perceived fulfillment of these role expectations. As their range of behaviors broadens, partners are more likely to become conscious of how marriage roles might be handled. If the relationship continues, partners tend to focus more on their individual desires and preparedness for marriage (Leigh, Holman, & Burr, 1984).

The relationship partners going through the stages of stimulus, value, and role will, in most cases, have mentally constructed a balance sheet of both assets and liabilities in their relationship. They must decide whether their assets outweigh liabilities to accurately appraise the potential of the relationship for marriage.

Heterogamous Choices

Although, as previously suggested, most individuals marry persons who are similar in age as well as religious and racial backgrounds, much **intermarriage** does occur: age-discrepant, interfaith, interracial, interethnic, and interlinguistic (Adams, 1986). Many people are challenging traditional, homogamous standards by asserting both the right and desirability of marriage between persons of different groups. One study, for example, has examined interlinguistic and educational marriage patterns for native-born Americans (Stevens & Schoen, 1988). Cross-language marriages were more common for English-speaking women, many of whom married men with higher educational levels. Education was more important than language in marriage choices for those whose first language was French, German, Italian, or Polish. Linguistic homogamy was found to be more pronounced for women and men of lower educational status.

Age-Discrepant Marriages

The term **May-December** is used to describe age-discrepant marriages in which wives or husbands are years apart in age. As the prevalence and marital

BOX 7.1	Relationship Choice and Exchange Balance Sheet	
Equation: Rewards − Costs = Profits or Loss		
Behaviors	Rewards	Costs
Physical joining	1. Availability of physical affection	1. Fear of STD 2. No time for homework
Social coupling	2. Expansion of social circle	3. Lack time for old friends 4. Removed from dating circulation
Psychological bonding	3. Affirmation of self-esteem	5. Threatens independence 6. Jealous mate
Balance: 3 Rewards − 6 Costs = 3 Losses Since there are more costs than rewards in the relationship used in this illustration, it would yield a negative balance with more losses than profits for the individual. If either person perceives that the relationship's liabilities outweigh its assets, the relationship is likely to be discontinued.		

From F. I. Nye, "Family Mini-Theories as Special Instances of Choice and Exchange Theory" in *Journal of Marriage and the Family*, 42:479–482.

quality of age-discrepant marriages are analyzed, it should be noted that the typical woman is currently marrying a man who is, on the average, 2.3 years older than herself (Surra, 1990).

In examining the prevalence of age-discrepant marriages, several key points emerge. First, there is an increasing tendency in industrialized nations for women and men to select older partners as they marry later in life. In a survey of 55 industrial countries, 67% of women and 20% of men reflected this tendency (Bytheway, 1981). Second, there has been a decrease in the percentage of women marrying men 10 or more years older than themselves since the years 1948–1977, when the percentage of women marrying older men doubled from 7% to 14% (Veevers, 1984). Third, women are becoming increasingly willing to marry men who are younger than themselves. This is especially true for those who are single by virtue of having been widowed or divorced. A study of singles, ages 50–70, found that 8 in 10 women and men wanted to remarry with most men wanting to marry women at least 5–10 years younger than themselves. Most women, however, wanted to marry someone closer to their own age (Berkowitz, 1983). Fourth, age differences in marriages are more common among low-income families than among upper-income families (Vera, Berardo, & Berardo, 1985).

Marital Quality

A myth exists that persons involved in May-December marriages have a lower level of marital satisfaction when compared with marriages in which spouses are of similar ages. This was reflected in a study in which college and high school students rated marriages with large age differences as having the least chance of marital success (Cowan, 1984). But no significant differences in marital quality for couples with various age differences were identified. However, in those marriages in which the husband was 11 or more years older than his wife, marital problems concerning money, friends, extramarital sex, and spouse's mental health were more likely to be reported (Vera et al., 1985).

Interfaith Marriages

Traditionally, all major faiths have opposed **interfaith marriage.** However, since religion has been increasingly affected by trends in the larger society, religious opposition to interfaith marriages has been, to some degree, weakening (Barlow, 1977). Further, a decline in ethnic and cultural differences has also led to fewer religious prejudices and increasing numbers of interfaith marriages (Murstein, 1986).

Religious Policies

If a person's religion is valued, it is likely to be an influential factor in mate selection. Opposition to interfaith marriage often emphasizes value differences in

Unlikely unions sometimes work!

religious policies rather than their similarities. It is, therefore, appropriate to review official policies on interfaith marriages among three major religious groups: Roman Catholic, Jewish, and Protestant.

Fewer than 30 years ago, Roman Catholics who entered a religiously mixed marriage were threatened with excommunication. Church policy allowed interfaith marriages only under certain stringent conditions. The non-Catholic partner had to agree to attend sessions on Catholic doctrine and to be married by a priest. Both partners were required to sign an **antenuptial** agreement stating that artificial contraception would not be used and that any children would be baptized and reared as Roman Catholics (Gordon, 1964). The intent was to prevent religiously mixed marriages but failing in that, it was to protect the Catholic partner's faith and ensure that their children would be reared as Catholics.

It was not until 1970 that Pope Paul VI removed the necessity for a written antenuptial agreement as well as relieving the non-Catholic partner of the obligation to make promises or commitments (Duvall & Miller, 1985). However, Catholic partners in a mixed marriage still must promise to have any children born of the marriage baptized as Catholics, to rear the children as Catholics, and to follow the church policy regarding contraception and divorce. Further, non-Catholic partners need to be informed of these promises. Finally, the requirement for a Catholic ceremony has been eased, depending on the diocese. A dispensation for "serious reasons" to allow a marriage to be performed by a Protestant minister, a Rabbi, or even by a civil judicial official is now possible (Leslie & Leslie, 1980).

Although traditional Jewish opposition to interfaith marriage has its origins in the Old Testament, since the Holocaust, the American Jewish community of 5.9 million persons has become increasingly sensitized to its erosion through intermarriage and assimilation. Viewing intermarriages as a threat to Jewish survival appears well-founded based on the results of one survey where only 24% of children, ages 16–46, from such marriages considered themselves to be Jewish (Ostling, 1988). Of the four major branches of Judaism—Orthodox, Conservative, Reconstructionist, and Reform—the major distinction lies in the strictness with which the laws for Judaism found in the Old Testament are followed. There are two types of interfaith Jewish marriages: intermarriage and mixed marriage. An intermarriage involves a Jew and a Gentile who has converted to Judaism, whereas a **mixed marriage** occurs between a Jew and Gentile without conversion. Today, about one third of Jewish interfaith marriages are of the intermarriage type. Most Orthodox, Reconstructionist, and Conservative rabbis will not perform either mixed marriages or intermarriages (Schneider, 1985). However, it is estimated that nearly one half of Reform rabbis will perform a marriage ceremony if a Gentile partner converts. Consequently, the Union of American Hebrew Congregation's Outreach Program was started in 1982 to educate nonpracticing Jews about their religion, to encourage the conversion of nonaffiliated marriage partners, and to meet the needs of interfaith couples and their families ("Teaching Judaism," 1985).

Stating the Protestant position on interfaith marriage is rather difficult because of the great diversity of Protestant denominations. Protestantism actually constitutes something of a residual category; that is, people who are neither Catholic nor Jewish become labeled as Protestant by default. Discussion is further complicated by the fact that most Protestant denominations do not have the elaborate religious hierarchy of Roman Catholicism. Generally, Protestant denominations have opposed interfaith marriages on at least three grounds. First, interfaith marriages are more unstable than religiously homogamous marriages. Second, participation in religion by the respective partners will likely suffer. Third, fear that children born of the union will not be trained in their specific faith or any religious faith (Duvall & Miller, 1985).

Prevalence of Interfaith Marriages

Religious homogamy is still the pattern because Catholics, Protestants, and Jews marry within their own religious groups far more often than would occur by chance. Since there are unequal numbers in these major religious groups, the issues are somewhat complicated. In the United States, the following population distribution of religions exists: 55%—Protestant, 38%—Catholic, 4%—Jewish, and 3%—other (Hoffman, 1990). It is quite apparent that interfaith marriages have increased among Catholics and among Jews (see Table 7.3). These data suggest that about 18% of Catholics, 12% of Jews, and 7% of Protestants are marrying outside of their religion. About one third of those persons who indicated no religious preference have spouses who similarly reported. No extremely strong barriers against religious intermarriages existed, except for Jews. Among Protestants, persons of the Baptist, Lutheran, Pentecostal, and United Church of Christ denominations are most likely to marry a person within their own religion (Glenn, 1982).

Table 7.3: Homogamous and Heterogamous Marriages

Religion	1957	1973–1978
Protestants		
Married to Protestants	96%	93%
Married to Catholics and Jews	4	7
Catholics		
Married to Catholics	88	82
Married to Protestants and Jews	12	18
Jews		
Married to Jews	96	88
Married to Protestants and Catholics	4	12
Protestants, Catholics, and Jews		
Married to persons of same religion	94	90
Married to persons of different religion	6	10

From N. D. Glenn, "Interreligious Marriage in the United States: Patterns and Recent Trends" in *Journal of Marriage and the Family,* 44:557.

Based on the percentages of the major denominations represented within the United States, one would expect that 55% of Protestants, 38% of Catholics, and only 3% of Jews would marry within their own religious faith because the available marriage partners correspond to these percentages (Glenn, 1984). Actually, there is evidence of increasing interfaith marriages in a national survey of religious intermarriage that found 4 in 10 Jewish marriages between 1975 and 1985 involved a person from another religious denomination. Further, about one third of Catholic marriages occurring in large urban archdioceses involved a non-Catholic partner (Collins, 1985).

Religious Participation After Marriage

While limited data exist concerning the impact of interfaith marriage upon religious participation of marriage partners or religious upbringing of their children, some trends are evident. An interfaith marriage for many persons simply confirms that they have grown away from their formal religious ties. However, a comparison of Catholic-Catholic and Catholic-Protestant marriages determined that interfaith marriage did affect the degree of religiosity. Catholics married to non-Catholics reported attending mass and receiving communion less frequently when compared to Catholics married to Catholics. Further, the findings suggest that these differences are even greater for Catholics married to conservative Protestants rather than to liberal Protestants (Petersen, 1986). An Orthodox rabbi in pastoral counseling questions the wisdom of Jewish intermarriage:

> *It's difficult enough to merge two individuals in a good marriage when their values and customs are the same. Often couples refuse to face the reality that when the first child is born, one member of the couple has to give up his religion.*
> *(Ostling, 1988, p. 82)*

Interfaith Marriage and Marital Satisfaction

Persons in religiously homogamous marriages tend to have greater overall marital satisfaction. Religious involvement where spouses are of the same religious denomination is associated with high marital satisfaction (Heaton, 1984; Ortega, Whitt, & Williams, 1988). However, when comparing Catholic marriages to Catholic/non-Catholic marriages, two thirds of both groups reported high marital happiness. Religiosity, as measured by frequency of attendance at mass, was positively related to marital happiness among religiously homogamous, but not interfaith marriages (Shehan, Bock, & Lee, 1990). Religion, in general, tends to act as a deterrent to divorce. While the factors in the decision to divorce are very complex, past studies indicate that religiously homogamous marriages have lower divorce rates (Heaton, Albrecht, & Martin, 1985). Since persons who marry spouses of different religions tend to have more liberal attitudes toward divorce, they may be more likely to seek divorce if their marital satisfaction proves to be lower than anticipated (Jorgensen & Johnson, 1980).

Interracial and Interethnic Marriages

Interracial and interethnic marriages have increasingly resulted from mobility, new contacts in the workplace, and changing mate-selection practices (Wilkinson, 1987). The term "race" refers to the classification system of **Negroid, Caucasoid,** and **Mongoloid** delineated by many earlier anthropologists (Downs & Bleibtreu, 1972). And ethnicity is related to one's nationality and cultural heritage (Williams, 1990).

In order to understand the historic opposition to such intermarriage, it is necessary to clarify the concept of a minority. In such context, minority is a generic label referring to persons not simply small in number but a population who is socially, politically, and economically subordinated. The major minority groups in the United States today are blacks or Afro-Americans, Chicanos or Mexican-Americans, Puerto Ricans, Japanese, Chinese, and Filipinos (Wilkinson, 1987).

Pressures to attain racially homogamous marriages are even stronger than those supporting religiously homogamous marriages. One study found that black-white marriages were generally disapproved of by both women and men (Sones & Holston, 1988). When the relationship of gender and race to attitudes toward **interracial marriage** was studied in the 1970s and 1980s, results indicated more favorable attitudes held by blacks than whites and by men than women (Sones & Holston, 1988).

Traditionally, most states have prohibited interracial marriages, and few such marriages occurred. But since the United States Supreme Court ruled in 1967 that laws against racial intermarriage were unconstitutional, attitudes and practices have slowly been changing (Wilkinson, 1975). The court decision resulted in an interesting paradox complicating research on interracial marriage. Following the ruling, states removed the category of race from marriage registration forms, making it impossible to positively identify persons in interracial marriages. While issues of racial/ethnic homogamy include Asians, blacks, and whites as well as various ethnic groups, most available research data concerns black-white alliances (Adams, 1986). Therefore, the discussion in this chapter will be largely restricted to marriage between blacks and whites.

Prevalence of Interracial Marriages

Official statistics concerning interracial marriages today are highly suspect. First, it is well known that the U.S. Bureau of the Census fails to accurately enumerate all minorities. Second, since social stigma is still attached to interracial marriage in most geographic locations, such information may not be reported in the Census. Despite these data limitations, there were 310,000 interracial married couples in 1970 representing less than 1% of all married couples, and by 1988, there were

"I wish you'd think about it, son. Do you realize the potential social pressures of a mixed marriage?"

956,000 interracially married couples constituting 1.8% of all married couples. While the numbers of interracial marriages have increased, they still represent a very small percentage of total married couples. Only 23% of all interracially married couples in the United States are black-white marriages. Of these black-white interracial marriages, over two thirds involve a white wife and a black husband (U.S. Bureau of the Census, 1990f). Interracial marriage varies by geographical region. In the decade of the 1970s, 16.5% of the reported first marriages for black men in the Western region of the United States were interracial unions compared to 2.5% in the southern region (Tucker & Mitchell-Kernan, 1990).

Relationship Dynamics

Although earlier studies have been based upon small samples, the findings have generally been consistent. Persons in interracial marriages are more likely to be older at the time of marriage, to have been previously married, and to live in urban areas (Tucker & Mitchell-Kernan, 1990). The vast majority of interracial couples are attracted to one another through shared interests, ideals, and values, much the same as other couples (Porterfield, 1982). However, their experience of marriage may differ considerably from other couples. Great emotional pain may be inflicted by parents and other family members who refuse to accept the relationship, ostracizing the involved family member. In the past, white parents have tended to reject interracial marriage more than black parents (Porterfield, 1974). A white woman in an interracial marriage will often find her self-concept under attack from many sources—employer, coworkers, and landlords. However, this is less likely to occur in large cities where there may be enough anonymity to separate work from social life. Research in North Carolina and Virginia suggests that both black and white men are more likely than their female counterparts to choose interracial marriage partners with less education than themselves (Schoen & Wooldredge, 1986). This suggests an exchange of racial and socioeconomic status, since education is correlated with economic and social advantages. Evidence indicates that college-educated black men who marry interracially bargain their higher educational level for the perceived attractiveness of younger white women (Surra, 1990). Thus, black men, as is the case for their white counterparts, are likely to choose a marriage mate on the basis of physical attraction using the European standards of beauty—long blonde hair and blue eyes (Tucker & Mitchell-Kernan, 1990).

Regarding marital stability, interracial marriages are more likely to end in divorce than noninterracial marriages (Reiss & Lee, 1988). However, studies from the 1970s indicated that black-white marriages have lower rates than black marriages. In fact, divorce rates for black-husband and white-wife marriages were lower than for white couples (Monahan, 1970; Monahan, 1971). Not only are white-male/black-female marriages far less likely to occur, they are less likely to succeed than black-male/white-female marriages (Adams, 1986). It has been suggested that, given the unconventional nature of their relationship, interracially married couples may have difficulties in identifying a social network of support during times of crisis, which could potentially contribute to a high divorce rate (Reiss & Lee, 1988).

In general, social and psychological consequences of interracial marriages include difficulty finding appropriate places of residence, lack of close affectional ties with kin persons, and negative public

Interfaith weddings often occur in homes because many churches and synagogues do not allow interfaith ceremonies.

responses to the union (Golden, 1975). In addition, ambiguities in the self-concept development of children from such marriages have been identified (Wilkinson, 1987). Although skin color has generally been found to have no relationship with racial self-esteem, data suggest that light-skinned blacks still tend to choose a light-skinned marriage partner (Hughes & Hertel, 1990).

Moving toward Marriage

Once the choice of a marriage mate has been made, there are many social conventions and legal requirements to consider. Traditionally, various rituals and customs have been prescribed by society (Leslie & Korman, 1989). Many of today's couples anticipating marriage may choose alternate rituals or establish their own. Such was the case for 50 couples in Austin, TX who repeated a simultaneous "I Do" at a group marriage ceremony, Valentine's Day, 1991. This radio station promotional event was complete with family, friends, and formal reception ("I Do," 1991). For most couples, however, marriage means an engagement, a wedding ceremony, and, perhaps, a honeymoon.

Engagement as a Social Process

The engagement period is a time of adjustment when persons make the transition from a single to a couple life-style and begin to develop future marital attitudes. Also, since the idealistic views that a person has of her/his partner inevitably will fade, engagements provide a time to assess future chances of success in a reality-based marriage. Depending upon the status of the relationship, there may be either informal or formal engagements. In the case of informal engagements, individuals have a tentative agreement to marry which is sometimes called "engaged-to-be-engaged." This condition represents a more or less generalized understanding to marry each other. Their intended plans to marry may or may not have been conveyed to others, including parents, friends, and acquaintances. A **formal engagement** often involves the offering and acceptance of an engagement ring along with a public announcement of the intended marriage (Eshleman, 1988).

The intent of an engagement period is to provide an opportunity to get to know the future marriage partner and to be sure that each one wants to proceed with this life-changing event. It is a time to objectively evaluate the relationship and recognize any potential danger signals. However, with the current trend toward large weddings, formal engagements have become a time when more concern is directed toward planning the wedding than for assessing any potential deficiencies in the love relationship. Traditional anxieties have been replaced with issues such as the type of hors d'oeuvres to be served at the wedding reception or the color of the bridesmaids' dresses. Physicians are familiar with anxieties that are expressed in physical problems, such as acne, allergies, and irregular menstruation, by those about-to-be married. Sources of stress include personal relationship problems caused by disapproving family members and ethical and strategical problems associated with arriving at prenuptial agreements (Fowler, 1983).

Evaluating the Relationship

Engaged couples are becoming aware that it is difficult to realistically assess their relationship without outside assistance. Consequently, many premarital assessment programs have become available through colleges and universities, religious organizations, and marriage and family therapists. In fact, some religious denominations, including the Roman Catholic church, have begun to require a premarital assessment program prior to marriage. These programs have at least three goals: to enable the couple to examine themselves, their partner, and their relationship; to confirm their decision to marry by examining some of the frequent problem areas including finances, friends, in-laws, religion, and sexuality; and to develop more positive attitudes toward seeking professional help with any future marital problems (Buckner & Salts, 1985).

To assist in this evaluation process, **premarital inventories** have been developed to help engaged couples identify strengths and weaknesses in their relationship. One such tool is the PREP-M Inventory designed to assess premarital relationships. It helps people to better understand their personal values and expectations and to gain insight into their readiness for marriage (Holman, Busby, & Larson, 1989). The Premarital Personal and Relationship Evaluation (PREPARE) Inventory is another tool with which couples can explore issues and areas of compatibility and discord (Olson, Fourier, & Druckerman, 1982).

In a follow-up study to determine how well the PREPARE Inventory fared, three groups were surveyed 2–3 years after taking the test: those who had separated or divorced; those still married, although unhappy; and those happily married. Predictions of which couples would end up in which groups were accurate for 85% of those divorced/separated and 80% of those happily married ("Computerized Premarital," 1987). Other researchers have also compared couples who participated in a premarital-communications training and conflict resolution program with couples who did not participate. After 5 years of marriage, program participants were less likely to have engaged in destructive marital conflict and were more likely to have sought professional assistance in solving any emerging marital problems (Bader, Riddle, & Sinclair, 1981).

Such research points out the importance of premarital evaluations of relationships. Since most couples who are identified as having high-risk relationships do divorce, premarital counseling via computer inventories becomes a viable tool in marriage decision making. Many marriage and family therapists, however, believe that premarital counseling done shortly before the wedding is too late. To be most effective, it should be done when couples initially consider marriage.

Legal Requirements

Differences concerning state laws pertaining to marriages include minimum ages for marriage, requirements for blood tests, and waiting periods before and after the issuance of marriage licenses. With increasing attention being paid to family life in our society, many state legislators are continuously involved in reviewing and revising marriage laws. A review of the basic legal requirements for marriage in the various states indicates that all states require that persons reach a certain minimum age before being allowed to marry (Hoffman, 1990). Traditionally, the minimum age for men to marry has been older than for women. Persons also are permitted to marry at younger ages if their parents give written approval. The most common legal age for marriage in the United States, without parental consent, is age 18 for women and men. Several states, including Alabama, Texas, and Utah, permit female and male adolescents to marry at age 14 with parental consent. Further, New Hampshire will permit female adolescents who are age 13 to marry with consent of parents and the courts. Some states likewise have special provisions that permit marriage at even younger ages when a pregnancy exists if parental consent and/or a court decree is received.

In 1990, 33 states required a blood test as part of the marriage license application process. The primary purpose of a blood test is to determine whether either prospective marriage partner has a sexually transmitted disease, usually syphilis, in a communicable stage. No state required a test for genital herpes. Some states are considering expanding medical tests to include Acquired Immune Deficiency Syndrome (AIDS). A few states check for rubella (German measles) in women; Illinois checks for sickle-cell anemia; and North Carolina tests for infectious tuberculosis, mental incompetence, and rubella (Hoffman, 1990).

As of 1990, to discourage hasty marriages, 26 states and the District of Columbia impose a waiting period for the issuance of the marriage license that begins at the time of the initial application. The most common waiting period is three days, but it may be as long as five days as in Ohio and Minnesota. Further, three states impose a waiting period after the marriage license has been obtained prior to actual performance of the marriage ceremony. Finally, a number of states place limitations on the number of days a marriage license is valid once it has been issued. For many states, validity of the license ranges from 20–180 days (Hoffman, 1990). Apparently, the waiting period concept at least partially fulfills its function because a substantial number of couples who apply for marriage licenses never return to claim the issued licenses. Still others who have obtained marriage licenses allow the valid period to expire.

Prenuptial Agreements

Equitable distribution laws in at least 41 states separate property acquired during the marriage from property acquired before marriage so that only property acquired during the marriage would be divided after divorce. But separate marital property can easily become commingled with marital property during marriage (Kuntz, 1986). **Prenuptial agreements,** which supersede inheritance laws or wills, are intended to ensure the separation of individual property acquired before marriage if a divorce should occur (White, 1983). It is extremely important that both persons receive separate legal counsel before signing a prenuptial agreement, making it less likely that a judge would invalidate the agreement at her/his discretion (Kuntz, 1986).

The Elements of Prenuptial Agreements

Prenuptial agreements or marriage contracts have been used primarily by persons marrying for the second or third time who wish to protect financial assets accumulated prior to the impending marriage. Such agreements can reduce conflict over asset distribution at the time of death or marital dissolution through divorce. However, in the future, it is likely that persons entering their first marriage will increasingly make use of prenuptial agreements as their income-earning potential rises due to their college education. These prenuptial agreements were at one time disparagingly labeled as attempts to legalize prostitution under the namc of marriage. However, the concept has become so popular that the National Conference of Commissioners on Uniform State Laws has prepared national standards for such contracts (Gest, 1983). While courts have sometimes altered prenuptial agreements due to unanticipated circumstances such as a health problem that ends the other spouse's ability to produce income, prenuptial agreements have generally been ruled to be valid. Some couples are developing informal marriage contracts or agreements that include many items unrelated to property rights and financial matters, such as child rearing, custody of children, division of labor, domicile, family planning, names, and sexuality (Jeter & Sussman, 1985). Their value is largely in the communication that occurs during the drafting of such documents. They should be reviewed for change at frequent intervals with flexibility a key component.

Rituals as Customs

Groomal showers may be the new wave in marriage customs. They are only one of the many interesting and unique rituals associated with marriages in the United States. Although the symbolic meanings of marriage rituals are frequently not fully understood, they may eventually come to have an important and lasting effect upon the relationship (Chesser, 1980).

Nouveau options—Get me to the church on time! The wedding day . . . when childhood friendships and fantasies are reaffirmed before they begin to fade.

Marriage Rituals

Prior to marriage, it is common practice for a bride-to-be to have several showers given in her honor by friends and relatives. The traditional bridal shower is a "rite of passage" ritual that is intended to serve several purposes, one of which is to allow expressions of feelings of ambivalence toward marriage through jokes and games. A more tangible reward is receiving gifts to equip the home (Berardo & Vera, 1981). The recent emergence of celebrations for the groom, "groomal" showers, can be traced to egalitarian trends present in our society. This all-male occasion represents a kind of anti-ritual sentiment concerning the inequalities that are built into marriage customs. Consequently, the gift-giving component of groomal showers usually consists of gag gifts rather than items having practical value (Berardo & Vera, 1981).

There are a number of traditional rituals associated with the marriage ceremony in the United States, all of which are rooted in the customs of European ancestors. For example, the wedding ring symbolizes an unbroken circle of never-ending love for the couple, while the attendants for the bride and groom originally represented a legalization of the marriage. The inclusion of children in the wedding party symbolically encourages fertility, and white as the color for the wedding gown symbolizes virginity of the bride. Finally, the joint cutting of the wedding cake continues the ancient practice of "breaking cake" that represented the breaking of the bride's **hymen** to aid in first sexual intercourse and subsequent childbirth (Chesser, 1980).

The Honeymoon

Taking a honeymoon in our society generally represents a romantic interlude in the beginning days of a marriage. But, more importantly, it provides an opportunity to begin the adjustment transition to marriage. In a comparison of cohabiting and noncohabiting couples, 95% of couples who had not lived together took a honeymoon, whereas only 60% of those who had lived together prior to marriage took a honeymoon (Risman, Hill, Rubin, & Peplau, 1981). Some cohabiting couples believe that marriage does not represent a dramatic shift in their daily living patterns.

There are three suggested functions of a honeymoon. First, a honeymoon provides an opportunity for privacy that enables the couple to adjust from being separate individuals to becoming a couple who must share a common space and learn the intimacies of living together. Second, a honeymoon provides an opportunity for marital sexual activity and the achievement of sexual satisfaction. Third, a honeymoon allows for a period of recuperation from the stresses and fatigue associated with the preparation and "staging" of a large wedding and reception. Simply, it provides an opportunity for newlyweds to get better acquainted under extremely favorable and romantic circumstances (Coleman, 1984).

Responding to Reason

Wise counsel indicates that for everything there is a season, that timing is all important in life. Marriages should never be entered into as a response to a crisis precipitated by life change or an emergency. For example, if one suddenly makes the decision to marry at the time of college graduation, chances are that the decision is in response to feelings of discontinuity and uncertainty in life, not love. A delay in marriage plans can illustrate strength in the relationship. Ending relationships may likewise indicate maturity on the part of one or both partners (Crosby, 1991). This is illustrated by the ending of a love affair that has become too one-sided to be healthy.

Delaying Marriage

During the process of relationship assessment, circumstances may be identified that would warrant delaying the marriage. Or events may occur inside or outside the relationship that signal the wisdom of a postponement. Research has identified several such factors including inadequate financial resources, unintended pregnancy, and the recognition of an emotionally unhealthy basis for marrying (Buckner & Salts, 1985).

After carefully examining available financial resources, the couple may discover the reality of the popular cliché, "Two cannot live as cheaply as one." After realistically considering their employment status and the costs of living in their geographical area, they conclude that it would be extremely difficult to live on their current income(s). The couple could thus make a positive decision to delay marriage until their financial situation improves. Finances are known to be one of the top problem areas identified by couples. Couples who face economic distress are considerably more likely to blame their partner for marital problems unrelated to finances than couples not experiencing economic difficulties (Rosenblatt & Keller, 1983).

If an unintended pregnancy occurs during engagement, the couple typically wants to hasten the wedding date to try to avoid the appearance of sexual involvement during engagement. This action may not be in the best interests of the future marital relationship. Marriages which are precipitated by an unintentional pregnancy have a much greater risk of marital dissatisfaction and ultimate divorce than marriages not having a premarital pregnancy (Kraus, 1977). After marriage, one or both partners may contemplate whether or not they would have married if a premarital pregnancy had not occurred. Because of the higher divorce rates associated with premarital pregnancy, a Roman Catholic archdiocese in Michigan has prohibited its priests from marrying a couple in which the woman is pregnant. However, if the couple still wants to be married after the baby is born, the marriage ceremony can then be performed.

Persons sometimes become deeply involved in a love relationship that culminates in marriage in order to satisfy unhealthy emotional needs. These motives, which are not at the conscious level, were identified earlier as being based on neurotic or illegitimate needs (Fromm, 1956). There may be many such needs, but at least two common ones are rebellion and escape. First, some young persons may marry not in spite of but because of their parents' disapproval of the relationship. Any parental interference in the relationship is likely to increase the romantic attraction between the two persons, leading to the so-called **Romeo and Juliet effect** and further rebellion against the parents (Driscoll, Davis, & Lipetz, 1972). Second, if the primary reason one partner wants to get married is to escape from parental authority or to establish independence, this should be recognized as an unhealthy motivation for marriage (Rubin, 1976).

A primary motivation for getting married, in some instances, is economic advancement (Lott, 1987). Selection of a marriage partner on the basis of social connections in the business world may be viewed as promoting career advancement. Or she/he may be tired of working full-time outside of the home and would prefer to work part-time or not work at all, which would be possible in a financially secure marriage. The discovery of these types of motives should result in a marriage delay in order to properly assess the real meaning of the love relationship.

Ending Relationships

Despite the careful nurturance of a love relationship by one or both partners, relationships sometimes end. While social scientists might objectively view the ending of many relationships as being in the best interests of both persons, such conditions do not make coping easier. Hopefully, a better understanding of why relationships end, gender differences associated with terminating relationships, and guidelines for ending relationships will help to minimize the trauma and loss of self-esteem often associated with the loss of a love relationship (Murstein, 1980).

Reasons for Relationships Ending

External events may relate to reasons for the relationship to end. There are three specific times of the year when college couples are especially likely to break up: September/October, December/January, and May/June. These periods of time correspond to external changes such as the beginning and ending of the school year or the beginning of a new year (Hill, 1989). External events influencing the ending of relationships include issues such as schedules and living arrangements. Disagreements in these areas make it easier to end the relationship with buffers such as, "Let's date others while apart for the summer."

A study of college couples involved in serious dating relationships discovered that after 3 years, 4 in 10 had ended their relationship. The primary reason for ending the relationship was gradual loss of interest in the partner. The two major categories of factors associated with love relationships ending were partner differences and minimal involvement (Hill, Rubin, & Peplau, 1976). In those relationships with considerable differences in age, future educational plans, levels of intelligence, and/or physical attractiveness between partners, the couple was more likely to break up. Even though these individuals may have been attracted to each other for various reasons, differences in these areas were of sufficient importance to warrant ending their relationship. In one survey only 7% of the break ups had been by mutual agreement indicating that many persons are in relationships in which there is a difference in the degree of emotional involvement (Hill, 1989). The most deeply involved partner often finds herself/himself in a very vulnerable position because of their desire to maintain the relationship at any cost. In the previously reported study, couples who broke up typically had one partner who had less than equal involvement in the relationship. They did not date each other exclusively, had difficulty defining themselves as "in love," and were less likely to view the relationship as culminating in marriage (Hill et al., 1976).

In general, women are more likely to end relationships than men, and men are more likely to be emotionally traumatized by the break up (Hill, 1989). Relationship partners tend to remain friends after the break up if the man initiates it, but emotional feelings are usually least painful if the decision to end a relationship is a mutual one (Hill et al., 1976). Women who report ending a love relationship are less depressed, lonely, and unhappy afterwards than men (Rubin, Peplau, & Hill, 1981). It may be that the Women's Movement has served as a positive force, enabling women today to better handle disappointments over lost love.

Singlehood: A Personal Choice

Singlehood is a state that may or may not be chosen. In the past, it was largely considered to be the result of not having found a suitable mate and was often associated with negative connotations. Today's single may, however, represent a new age in which singlehood is a personal choice with positive features. While conceptually the term "single" may refer to never-married persons, widowed individuals, and divorced persons, throughout this chapter the term single will refer to the category of never-married persons. Singlehood, by virtue of being widowed or divorced, will be addressed in chapter 18, "Single Parents, Remarriage, and Blended Families."

Three factors indicated in the research of the 1970s contributed to the growth in singlehood: expanded opportunities for women in the world of education and employment, greater numbers of women than men of marriageable age, and social and sexual single life-style acceptance (Macklin, 1980). Further, the growth in numbers of single women has occurred to a large degree because of their widespread tendency to increasingly delay marriage ("Singles Account," 1986).

The decade of the 1980s was characterized by major changes in the attitudes of American women toward singlehood, sexual behavior, and childbearing. A national poll of women found that overwhelmingly (80%) they believed that single women should enjoy the same sexual freedom as men. While almost one half (49%) believed that sexual involvement while single was immoral, one half saw no reason why single women should not be able to bear and rear children on their own (Roper Organization, 1986). These ambivalent attitudes may partially account for the fact that childbearing while single has reached its highest level in history with one infant out of five being born to a single mother.

Tracing the underlying acceptance of singleness, one finds that the practice began to become more accepted in the mid-1950s. Survey data collected in 1957 and 1976 to determine attitudes toward persons who did not wish to marry found that while slightly less than one half of the earlier respondents described their attitudes as either "positive" or "neutral," two thirds of those in 1976 responded similarly (Thornton & Freedman, 1982). In a related study in the late 1980s concerning the importance of being married either now or in the future, more than one half of college students and nonstudents surveyed found it only "somewhat important" or "not too important" (see Table 7.4). These attitudes coincide with a change in behavior as indicated by a mid-decade report issued by the U.S. Bureau of the Census. Between 1970 and 1985, the proportion of American households composed of married couples fell from 71% to 58%, while the number of one-person households increased by 9% (Beckwith, 1985).

Table 7.4: Importance of Being Married Now or In Future

Degree of Importance	Student	Non-Student
Most important thing in my life	11%	11%
One of the most important things in my life	43	35
Somewhat important	31	33
Not too important	16	21

From Abbott Laboratories, *The Abbott Report: STDs and Sexual Mores in the 1980s*. Reprinted by permission.

Singles: A Growing Minority or Lengthening Life Stage

Family scientists are currently asking two questions in relation to the singles. Does the trend represent a growing minority who will never marry by choice or default? Or does this delay of marriage represent a lengthening of the life stage preceding marriage? To place the issue of singlehood in proper perspective, it is necessary to examine the marriage rate from an historical standpoint. While there have been some minor fluctuations in the annual marriage rate, with the exception of major changes related to World War II, it has remained around 10 per 1,000 persons since the 1950s, dropping to 9.6 per 1,000 by 1990 (National Center for Health Statistics, 1990b, 1990e).

There are two very important points to remember in understanding marriage in our society. First, the disparity between percentages of women and men in the never-married category at ages 20–24 suggests that men typically marry women approximately three years younger than themselves. Second, the popular media have created an impression that vast numbers of individuals are making the decision to never marry. But the marriage statistics, when broken down by age and

Table 7.5: Single (Never-Married) Persons

	Women		Men	
Age	1970	1988	1970	1988
Totals	**13.7%**	**18.7%**	**18.9%**	**25.4%**
18–19	75.6	89.3	95.1	96.6
20–24	35.8	61.1	54.7	77.7
25–29	10.5	29.5	19.1	43.3
30–34	6.2	16.1	9.4	25.0
35–39	5.4	9.0	7.2	14.0
40–44	4.9	6.2	6.3	7.5
45–54	4.9	5.1	7.5	5.6
55–64	6.8	4.0	7.8	4.9
65 and over	7.7	5.3	7.5	4.5

Source: U.S. Bureau of the Census, 1990e, No. 52, "Single (Never-Married) Persons as Percent of Total Population, by Age and Sex: 1970 to 1988" in *Statistical Abstract of the United States, 1990,* 110th ed., p. 44. Washington, DC: U.S. Government Printing Office.

gender, do not support that conclusion. It is true that in 1970, only 11% of all women and 19% of all men ages 25–29 had not married, and by 1988, those percentages had tripled for women and more than doubled for men (U.S. Bureau of the Census, 1990e). However, only slight change has occurred in the percentage of older persons, ages 45–54, who are in the never-married category. In fact, the percentage of women and men who were ages 40–44 and remained single in 1970 had not changed appreciably by 1988 (see Table 7.5). Generally speaking, since the large increases in percentages of singles occurred at the younger ages, they appear to be primarily a result of postponement of first marriage. This marriage delay is more likely to occur among blacks than whites as evidenced by the median age at first marriage, which is three years greater for black women than for white women (Surra, 1990). One interpretation suggests that singlehood should be viewed as a "stage" through which most persons pass prior to marriage (Cargan & Melko, 1982).

Prospects for Marriage

In 1988, only 5% of women and 5% of men age 65 and over had never married (see Table 7.5). The unknown variable at the moment is how many of the almost two thirds of American women and three fourths of American men under age 25 will decide to remain single. It has been estimated that of those women who were born between 1946–1966 (baby-boomers) and are single at age 30, only 20% will ever marry. Further, it was suggested that of those single at age 35, only 5% will marry (Salholz, 1986).

Since women tend to marry men older than themselves and since men die 5–7 years younger than women, there are obviously fewer marriage prospects for older women. Therefore, by the time women reach age 65, the number of available single men has declined substantially (see Table 7.6). Further, in 1970, the median age for first marriage was 21 years for women and 23 years for men. By 1986, the median age for first marriage had increased to 23 years for women and 25 years for men (U.S. Bureau of the Census, 1990u). These ages at first marriage represent the highest figures for women and men since the turn of the century (Beckwith, 1985).

In summary, the argument that increasing numbers of persons are choosing permanent singlehood is based on two facts. First, the proportion of young unmarried adults in the United States has increased greatly from 1970 to 1985; and second, there has been a substantial increase in median ages at marriage. However, upon closer examination, these arguments are inadequate to support the conclusion that a new lifestyle of permanent singlehood is emerging. Instead of a growing minority of never-marrieds, it is more likely that there is lengthening of the life stage preceding marriage. Also, some population experts believe that the increase in the proportion of young women who are single is a result of the high birth rate following World

Table 7.6: Marital Status of Population, 1988

Age	Never-Married	Married	Widowed	Divorced
Women, Totals	**18.7%**	**60.4%**	**12.1%**	**8.8%**
18–19	89.3	9.3	0.1	1.3
20–24	61.1	35.7	0.2	3.0
25–29	29.5	62.2	0.5	7.8
30–34	16.1	72.4	0.6	10.9
35–39	9.0	76.0	1.4	13.6
40–44	6.2	76.6	2.4	14.8
45–54	5.1	76.2	5.8	12.9
55–64	4.0	70.7	16.7	8.6
65–74	4.6	53.3	36.3	5.8
75 and over	6.2	24.9	66.1	2.7
Men, Totals	**25.4**	**65.1**	**2.7**	**6.8**
18–19	96.6	2.7	0.1	0.7
20–24	77.7	20.8	0.1	1.4
25–29	43.3	51.4	0.1	5.2
30–34	25.0	66.2	0.2	8.6
35–39	14.0	74.6	0.5	10.9
40–44	7.5	81.6	0.4	10.5
45–54	5.6	83.2	1.3	9.8
55–64	4.9	84.4	3.7	6.9
65–74	4.8	81.9	8.7	4.7
75 and over	4.2	69.7	23.7	2.4

Source: U.S. Bureau of the Census, 1990d, No. 49, "Marital Status of the Population, by Sex and Age: 1988" in *Statistical Abstract of the United States, 1990,* 110th ed., p. 42. Washington, DC: U.S. Government Printing Office.

War II. With more births each year and with women tending to marry men slightly older than themselves, a temporary surplus of women in the most marriageable-age categories was created as the number of births leveled off and began to drop after 1959.

The Myths and Realities of Being Single

In the late 1960s and early 1970s, the stereotype of unmarried persons shifted from "lonely losers" to "swinging singles" (Stein, 1975). Apartment complexes in metropolitan areas began to advertise a lifestyle centered around swimming pools and recreation rooms, featuring nightly cocktail parties with the presumption that sexual involvement was the norm. Popular magazines such as *Cosmopolitan, Ms., Playgirl,* and *Playboy* promoted such a concept of single life.

The Myths of Singlehood

Singles have often been described as being immature, lesbian/gay, irresponsible, socially inadequate, physically unattractive, neurotic, and/or workaholics. Among the myths of singlehood contributing to these erroneous conclusions are that singles are tied to mothers' apron strings, satisfied swingers, selfish, and affluent. It is also a myth that singlehood is an acceptable lifetime option for the majority (Cargan & Melko, 1982).

The popular stereotype of the daughter or son involved in an unhealthy emotional relationship with the mother or tied to her apron strings does not appear to be a major factor in influencing the decision to marry. In a study of never-married and married women and men, no differences were identified with regard to perceptions of warmth and openness with parents or degrees of parental conflict (Cargan & Melko, 1982). Also, there appears to be no documented influx of marriageable-age children providing full-time caregiving for their elderly parents today.

A general perception exists that singlehood confers a swinging singlehood status creating greater opportunity for more sexual involvement with a greater number of partners. A comparison of never-marrieds

and women and men in first marriages found that never-marrieds were more likely to have had 11 or more sex partners in their lifetime. However, the never-marrieds experienced sexual intercourse on a less frequent basis than the marrieds (Cargan, 1981). Further, the marrieds were more likely to report sexual satisfaction in their lives than the never-marrieds (see Table 7.7). Therefore, while singles may have more sex partners, evidently they derive less satisfaction from their sexual experiences. Since the ways of meeting persons have become more informal and impersonal, such as through singles bars, personal risks also are greater today. Along with increased risks for STDs is the growing phenomenon of date abuse. A survey of single women found that 40% reported some kind of physical or psychological abuse directed toward them through contacts at singles' bars (Simenauer & Carroll, 1982a).

Singles may worry that living alone will make them so selfish and inflexible that they will be unable to find an acceptable marriage mate (Simenauer & Carroll, 1982a). Some facts do contribute to this perceived selfishness, such as the fact that singles in comparison to marrieds are less likely to visit relatives. However, singles tend to place a greater value on friends than do married persons. Further, singles are more likely to be involved in community service projects than married persons, in part because they have more time (Cargan & Melko, 1982).

The perception that singles are more affluent, to a large degree, stems from comparisons that are typically made between singles without children and marrieds with children. However, because of the ability to pool financial resources, married persons often enjoy a higher standard of living when compared to single persons (Cargan & Melko, 1982).

It appears that singlehood is still not perceived as an acceptable lifetime option by the majority. Instead, singles feel greatly pressured to apologize for their status. In one study of singles, most women and men thought they would be married within the next 5 years (Cargan & Melko, 1982). Another survey reported that 75% of single women would prefer to be married rather than remain single (Simenauer & Carroll, 1982a). Thus for such individuals, singlehood would be viewed as a "stage" preceding marriage.

The Realities of Singlehood

Besides the fantasies of singlehood, the realities appear stark. In smaller communities, single adults often are discriminated against by employers and landlords who regard them as irresponsible and wild. Only in fairly

Table 7.7: Level of Sexual Satisfaction

Marital Status	Satisfied	Neutral	Dissatisfied
Never-married	49%	32%	18%
Divorced	61	22	17
In first marriage	78	16	6
Remarried	83	12	5
All singles	53	30	18
All marrieds	80	15	6

From L. Cargan, "Singles: An Examination of Two Stereotypes" in *Family Relations*, 30:383. Copyright © 1981 National Council on Family Relations, 3989 Central Avenue, N.E., Suite #550, Minneapolis, MN 55421. Reprinted by permission.

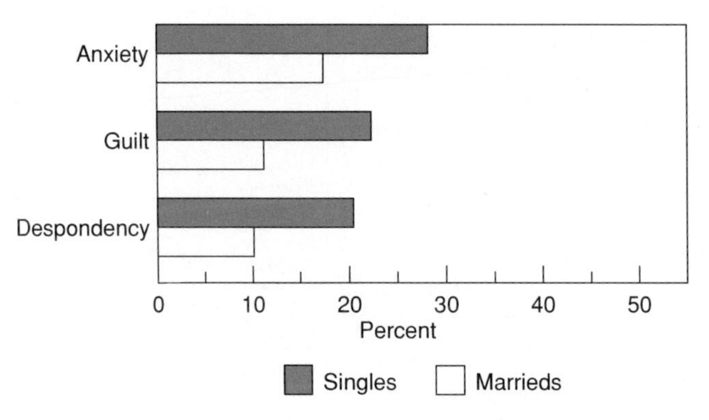

Figure 7.1 Psychological Stress and Marital Status

large cities are there likely to be special facilities catering to singles such as apartment houses and cocktail lounges. Even when these are a reality, the popular perception that large numbers exist is also misleading. Such establishments generally tend to be rigidly segregated by age and economic status. Middle-aged men will soon stop going to places where they are scorned by younger women, whereas middle-aged women may favor staying at home rather than being ignored by younger men. Further, it is likely to be the educated and professional persons who can afford the high rents, lavish entertainment, and clothes required for leading a "single" life-style (Cargan & Melko, 1982).

A major concern of parents is whether or not living away from home while single will cause young adults to change their attitudes, values, and expectations, thus drifting away from a traditional family orientation. A study of over 10,000 young women and men, over a 15-year period, concerning nonfamily living found that young women who lived independently were more likely to plan to be employed, to opt for smaller family size, to accept employment of mothers, and to develop more nontraditional gender roles than young women who lived with their parents (Waite, Goldscheider, & Witsberger, 1986). However, living away from parents during early adulthood appears to be a sign that appropriate developmental tasks are being accomplished. It prepares a person for getting along in a wider world than family. Living with persons other than family members also helps one learn both tolerance and an appreciation of solitude (Cassidy, 1985). To gain a more accurate picture of living as a single, realities related to personal happiness, leisure time, and loneliness should be understood.

Singleness itself does not confer happiness or unhappiness. Even the research does not agree concerning the relationship to personal happiness. Earlier, single women were found not likely to be very different than married women either in terms of personal or social adjustment (Spreitzer & Riley, 1974). Later research found singles to be more likely than marrieds to feel anxious, guilty, and despondent (see figure 7.1). It is likely that the interaction of singlehood and other variables produce varying life satisfaction. Some single women and men indicated that the factors that most affected their life satisfaction included self-esteem, degree of social support, and degree of emotional wellness. High levels of life satisfaction for women were associated with absence of emotional loneliness and availability of attachment relationships. For men, life satisfaction was more likely to be associated with high degrees of self-esteem and availability of social outlets (Cockrum & White, 1985).

Singles are much more likely to participate in social activities at least two or more times per week than marrieds. Singles also are more likely than marrieds to go to dances and night clubs and to bicycle (Cargan & Melko, 1982). The presence of children may explain the differences in recreational activities between married and single persons.

When considered as a group, singles are more likely to be lonely than are marrieds. Singles, for example, reported being more likely to feel lonely when dining alone or to feel depressed when alone than were married persons. However, feelings of loneliness are far greater for divorced singles than never-married singles, so one must be very careful about interpreting these findings (Cargan & Melko, 1982). Loneliness usually occurs when singles isolate themselves from social activities or relationships. They tend to be much more dependent on friend networks for companionship when contrasted with married persons (Harayda, 1986).

A Typology of Singles

Stein's (1981) examination of the factors associated with singlehood concluded that singlehood may be either voluntary or involuntary, temporary or permanent. Although his typology of singlehood may be applied to divorced, widowed, and never-married persons, this discussion is limited to never-married persons.

Voluntary temporary singlehood includes young never-marrieds who are merely postponing marriage. It also includes older never-marrieds who, if given the opportunity, would get married but who are not actively seeking a marriage partner. In addition, cohabitors who may eventually marry one another or someone else are included in this category. Never-married persons of all ages who intend never to get married constitute the voluntary stable singlehood group. Nuns and priests who have taken religious vows of nonmarriage are voluntarily single and stable. Cohabitors who do not accept the idea of marriage but consider themselves to be in a permanent relationship are also in this group.

The involuntary temporary singlehood group includes young, never-married persons who are actively seeking a future marriage partner. These individuals may have been seeking a marriage mate for a considerable period of time but have not identified a suitable marriageable person. The involuntary stable singlehood consists of older, never-married persons, especially women, who wanted to marry but have lacked the opportunity, thus resigning themselves to a life of singlehood. This grouping likewise includes never-married persons who perceive themselves as being handicapped in some way that lessens their perceived desirability as marriage partners.

Factors Affecting Decision to Marry or Not to Marry

Among those factors affecting the decision to marry, there are a number of debatable issues. Contrary to popular opinion, full-time employment for women has no effect on the likelihood of marriage. For men, however, full-time employment is the most important indicator that they will marry within the next year. Growing up in the South increases the likelihood that marriage will occur at a relatively young age, especially for men. Finally, being enrolled on a full-time basis in college decreases the likelihood of marriage until the mid-20s for both women and men (Kobrin & Waite, 1984). These data support the earlier argument that many postpone rather than reject future marriage.

In recent years, there has been considerable media attention about the growing number of college-educated, white women who are postponing marriage to the point of lessening their statistical likelihood of ever marrying. In fact, a controversial Harvard/Yale University report asserted that women who postpone marriage beyond their 20s may never find a husband. Such women were projected as having only one in five chances of ever marrying ("Stretching Their Options," 1987). However, a Census Bureau report sharply contradicts such claims. Their prediction is that fully two thirds of the age 30-plus, college-educated women will eventually marry. Even past age 40, 17–23% are predicted to still marry. The Census Bureau predictions, which are based on statistical analyses, show very little change over the past decade in rate of first marriages for women over age 25 ("Will Women," 1987).

Another problem with these reports is that only "marrieds" and "singles" have been considered, which disregards those women who are cohabiting, lesbians, or alone by choice. Media coverage implies that women must choose between a career and a husband/family, thus running the risk of being prosperous but desperate "old maids." This attitude reflects a larger attitude of sexism in our society, that women want to marry for sexual companionship and/or economic security (Pollitt, 1986). Nevertheless, women who have deferred marriage for educational and career goals may discover that by the time they want to marry, fewer prospective marriage partners are available. Many of the available men are unacceptable to these women, and the men that they would choose typically prefer to marry women who are younger than themselves (Greer, W. R., 1986).

The "biological clock" that defines the finite amount of time available for healthy childbearing is also at issue. This emerging concern of women who delay marriage but eventually wish to have children will be further addressed in chapter 12, "Decisions About Children."

Pushes and Pulls: Marriage or Singlehood

Over the years, a number of factors have been identified that "push" and "pull" women and men toward marriage or singlehood. An in-depth analysis of middle-class female and male professionals between ages 25–45, revealed a series of complex factors that enter into the decision to remain single or to marry (see Table

Table 7.8: Pushes and Pulls toward Marriage and Singlehood

Pushes (Pressures)	Pulls (Attractions)
Marriage	
Pressure from parents	Approval of parents
Desire to leave home	Desire for children and own family
Fear of independence	Example of peers
Loneliness and isolation	Romanticization of marriage
No knowledge of alternatives	Physical attraction
Cultural and social discrimination	Security, social status and prestige
Intolerance of singlehood	Social experiences
	Better jobs and promotions
	Social policies favoring the married
Singlehood	
Lack of friends, isolation, loneliness	Career opportunities
Restricted new experiences	Sexual availability
Suffocating one-to-one relationship	Exciting life-style
Obstacles to self-development	Freedom to change
Boredom, unhappiness, and anger	Self-sufficiency
Poor communication with mate	Sustaining friendships
Sexual frustration	
Influence of Women's Movement	

7.8). From these analyses, two factors warrant special attention: parental approval and career opportunities and goals.

A "pull" toward marriage results if parents approve of a potential marriage partner. If they exert pressure, this is a "push" toward marriage. On the other hand, if the potential marriage partner is a member of a religious or socioeconomic status group of which the parents disapprove, they may take an active role in discouraging marriage. If a daughter or son is involved in cohabitation and the parents strongly disapprove of this living arrangement, marriage may be promoted as a way of alleviating the situation (Stein, 1981). Persons who were reared in intact families experience considerable pressure to marry rather than engage in cohabitation or an extended period of singlehood (Kobrin & Waite, 1984).

Among women who were normative marriers—before age 25 and late marriers—after age 25, those who married later gave higher priority to their career goals than normative marriers. In addition, late marriers were more accepting of sexual intercourse while single and cohabiting, perceived more parental emotional and financial support for their careers, were closer to their parents, and assumed a more egalitarian approach to gender roles (Allen & Kalish, 1984).

Other evidence that women in their early 20s are increasingly postponing marriage can be found when comparing 1969 to 1975 data concerning attitudes of single women toward being "housewives." In 1969, 52% of white women and 37% of black women between ages 22–23 indicated they would prefer to be "housewives" at age 35. By 1975, those percentages had decreased to 27% for white women and 18% for black women. Single women who want to assume the housewife role are more likely to plan to marry in the near future than those who plan to be working outside of the home. The evidence also suggests that college attendance per se is not a deterrent to marriage, especially for older women (Cherlin, 1980).

Special Concerns for the Single Life-Style

The majority of singles have chosen to live in large cities because of greater privacy, closeness to other singles, and greater recreational opportunities. Smaller communities tend to be more family-oriented or couple-oriented (Jacoby, 1975). Singles may be discriminated against in the job market because of the myth that they are irresponsible. A survey of executives from 50 major corporations found that 80% believed that marriage was not essential for job promotion, yet only about 2% of their junior and senior executives were single. Further, about two thirds replied that single executives tended to make "snap" judgments, and one fourth believed that singles were "less stable" than married persons (Jacoby, 1975). Although there are a number of special concerns for persons having a single life-style, housing opportunities, sexual expression, and mental health are particularly pressing.

Housing Opportunities

In female-headed households, women tend to prefer a residential location close to the central business district in densely populated tracts (Cook & Rudo, 1984). Such living arrangements help prevent social isolation and ease the stress of travel to work. There is also some evidence of discrimination against single householders, forcing them to live in what some persons consider to be less desirable locations. Nevertheless, the National Association of Realtors reported in the mid-1980s that single women were buying 7% of all houses and 22% of all condominiums. This trend represents the fastest growing segment of the housing market. Since the passage of the 1977 Equal Credit Opportunity Act, women can more easily obtain financing for purchase of real estate. Before that time, one half of their income could be disregarded if they were in their childbearing years (Mithers, 1986).

Considerable speculation exists over the increase during the 1970s in the proportion of persons who are ages 18–29 and living with parents. The percentage of young adults living with their parents is greater for women than men at all ages (see Table 7.9). Of these persons, 89% of women and 94% of men were never-married, and two thirds were currently employed.

Table 7.9: **Young Adults Living with Their Parents**

Gender and Year	Age			Totals
	18–19	20–24	25–29	18–29
Women				
1940	68%	40%	19%	37%
1970	72	31	7	30
1984	75	37	11	31
Men				
1940	83	58	27	50
1970	83	44	12	39
1984	85	53	17	43

From P. C. Glick and S. Lin, "More Young Adults Are Living with their Parents: Who Are They?" in *Journal of Marriage and the Family,* 48:108. Copyright © 1986 National Council on Family Relations, 3989 Central Avenue, N.E., Suite #550, Minneapolis, MN 55421. Reprinted by permission.

Sexual Expression

In past generations, many persons chose marriage as a convenient avenue to alleviate their sexual frustrations and guilt. With the changing attitudes in our society toward sexual involvement by singles, many persons no longer feel that marriage is a prerequisite for fulfillment of their sexual needs. Depending upon personal values, levels of awareness, and concern regarding sexually transmitted diseases, singlehood may or may not lead to the exploration of one's sexuality with multiple sex partners (Stein, 1981).

Singlehood as a sexual life-style is beginning to be considered as an option to marriage by many persons in today's less sexually restrictive environment. In particular, upper-middle-class college graduates who have professional careers and who live in urban areas are choosing to remain single and have sexual involvement with multiple partners. For example, the mean numbers of lifetime sex partners in a study of highly educated career women in the nursing profession were 8.3 partners for never-married women and 10.5 partners for divorced/separated women compared to 5.0 partners for married women (Davidson & Darling, 1988b).

However, many women feel that excessive emphasis is being placed on the sexual aspects of relationships too soon after the initial dating experience. They deplore emerging social norms that have led many single women to assume that they must provide sexual favors in order to maintain a relationship. It is considered unfortunate that some single women may believe the only way to meet men is to be overtly sexual through revealing clothing and to immediately initiate sexual overtures (Silverman, 1981).

Changes in the number of sex partners for American singles reported in two studies are speculated to be the result of a number of factors including concern over STDs. In a 1984 survey of singles, ages 18–34, more than one third (38%) reported five or more sex partners for the previous 12 months, and 12% indicated more than 20 partners. Three years later, a similar survey revealed that only one fourth indicated having three or more partners during the 12-month period. Interestingly, men averaged twice as many partners as women (Abbott Laboratories, 1987).

Being Single and Mental Health Status

The data are inconclusive with regard to life satisfaction and singlehood (Veroff, Kulka, & Douvan, 1981). While some research indicates that single women and men report similar levels of happiness and overall satisfaction with their lives, other findings conclude that single women and men are less likely to report happiness than married persons (Campbell, Converse, & Rogers, 1976). A national survey found that one in four single women and one in five single men experienced feelings of loneliness as contrasted with only 1 in 10 married women and 1 in 17 married men (Weiss, 1981b). Although many persons living alone have feelings of loneliness, never-married women and men living alone have been found to exhibit higher levels of social interaction. This interaction includes more contacts with relatives as well as a greater number of neighbors and neighbor contacts than by never-marrieds living with other adults. Never-married women more often report networks of close, intimate friendships in comparison to married women (Alwin, Converse, & Martin, 1985). In addition, singles are much more likely to experience feelings of anxiety, guilt, and despondency than marrieds. Further, single persons, in general, have higher rates of mental illness than married persons, with single men suffering from mental illness much more frequently than single women (Gove, 1979).

Summary

- Mate selection tends to proceed through three stages. First, people are attracted to one another on the basis of external stimulus characteristics. Second, their initial attraction is either confirmed or discouraged through extensive verbal interaction, which establishes their degree of compatibility of attitudes and values. Third, continued intimacy encourages the adoption of roles that forecast what their marriage would be like.
- Although persons typically marry other persons who are similar in age as well as religious and racial backgrounds, age-discrepant, interfaith, and interracial marriages do occur. Religious intermarriage, particularly, has been rapidly increasing. Public approval of interracial marriages has been increasing for some time, but the numbers of such marriages are still relatively small.
- Engagement provides a period of transition from singlehood to a couple life-style, a time to assess future chances of marital success. Should serious problems arise, it is wise to delay marriage until they are resolved or to end the relationship.
- There are many variations of marriage laws among states, and all impose minimum legal ages for marriage. Some require blood tests that certify freedom from sexually transmitted disease or a waiting period before the marriage ceremony may be performed.
- Even though the mass media has created the impression that vast numbers of persons are making the decision to never marry, such a conclusion is not supported by statistics. The slight increase that is evident in the percentage of persons choosing singlehood is likely to be based on the unavailability of a suitable partner and the postponement of marriage to accomplish educational and career goals.

Questions for Critical Reflection

1. Has residential or organizational propinquity played a greater role in your choice of a (potential) marriage mate? Can you describe its influence?
2. Of the nine sociological factors of homogamy suggested to be filtering mechanisms for mate selection, what three factors would you consider to be most important in a present or future marriage? Why?
3. Why does the variable of religious differences seem to become more important to a married couple after children are born?
4. Do you agree that singlehood is really a free choice in today's world? What will important people in your life say if you have chosen or should choose to remain permanently single?
5. The text poses the question whether singlehood is a growing minority or a lengthening life stage. What is your opinion based on your circle of friends and acquaintances? Do women or men feel more pressure to marry at earlier ages today? Why?

Suggested Readings

Crester, G. A., & Leon, J. J. (Eds.). (1982). *Interracial marriage in the United States.* New York: Haworth Press. An anthology of scholarly works on various issues associated with interracial marriages.

Porterfield, E. (1978). *Black and white mixed marriages: An ethnographic study of black-white families.* Chicago: Nelson Hall. An excellent source for insights into black-white marriages.

Queen, S. A., Habenstein, R. W., & Quadagno, J. S. (1985). *The family in various cultures* (5th ed.). New York: Harper & Row. A highly readable classic work that includes a consideration of mate selection and other major facets of family life in diverse cultures.

Shostak, A. B. (1987). Singlehood. In M. B. Sussman & S. K. Steinmetz (Eds.), *Handbook of marriage and the family* (pp. 355–368). New York: Plenum Press. An authoritative review of current research and theoretical issues on singlehood in American society.

Simenauer, J., & Carroll, D. (1982). *Singles: The new Americans.* New York: Simon & Schuster. A social survey of 3,000 single adult women and men.

Weitzman, L. J. (1981). *The marriage contract: Spouses, lovers, and the law.* New York: Free Press. A comprehensive review of the rationale and common provisions of marriage contracts.

PART III

COUPLE CHALLENGES

"Marriage is not the answer, but the question!" This maxim becomes all too painfully apparent following the honeymoon stage of marriage. What are the challenges in achieving the optimum balance between couple bonding and individualism? This quest is pursued in the various chapters of part 3.

Many therapists agree that marriages that fail do so in their beginning period, regardless of when the divorce occurs. This is because couples who fail to make the necessary adjustment early in their relationship are seldom able to do so later. The narrative in chapter 8 confirms that if marital goals are to be attained, the role perspectives of the woman and man must, to some degree, converge. Unrealistic expectations of marriage are revealed as a major culprit in the failure to achieve marital adjustment. Health-promoting belief and interaction patterns are suggested as a base for achieving the couple tasks of early marriage: separating from parents and working out the relationship rules pertaining to intimacy and power.

The inevitability and even desirability of conflict are discussed in chapter 9. Since love cannot exist without effective communication, components of quality communication patterns and gender differences inherent in attaining communication goals are highlighted. If the relationship is to succeed, couples must adopt a positive approach to conflict resolution. Otherwise, misuse of power may be expressed through marital violence. Factors associated with spouse abuse and the emerging problem of marital rape need to be recognized in order to take preventive measures.

The challenges inherent in achieving sexual adjustment and satisfaction are considered in chapter 10. Healthy sexual adjustment in marriage is shown to evolve from healthy individual sexuality, that quality of being woman or man, which is developed as a part of one's total mental and physical makeup resulting from life experiences. Understanding the anatomy and physiology of reproduction and sexual response is basic to achieving the goals of sexual adjustment and satisfaction. Causes of sexual dysfunction and treatment modalities are offered as important pieces of the puzzle of sexual well-being.

Finally, the rationale and methods of birth control and issues surrounding abortion are explored in chapter 11. The magnitude and causes of sexually transmitted diseases in the 1990s are thoroughly documented as well as suggested safer sex strategies.

E.T.

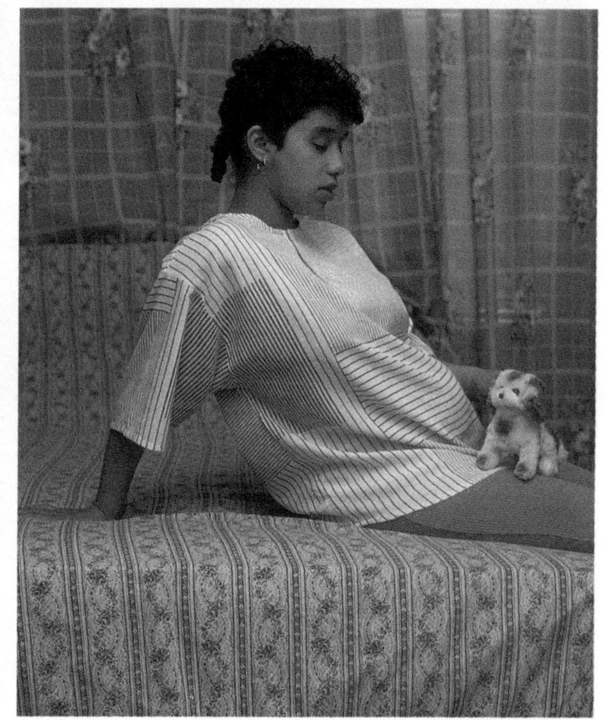

A.I.D.S.: WE NEED
RESEARCH,
NOT HYSTERIA!

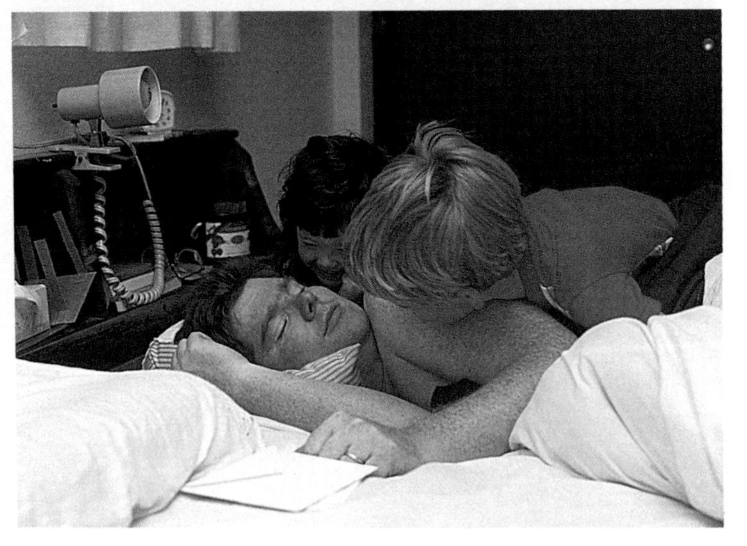

CHAPTER 8

Early Marital Adjustment

". . . The way society has structured the lives of men and women makes it difficult for couples to achieve the community of understanding necessary to a comradely marriage."
Robert S. Weiss, 1985

Outline

Early marriage is a significant stage in the family life cycle. It is a time of transition that blends the youthful romantic expectations concerning love and marriage with a more realistic acceptance of adult relationships and responsibilities. More than a mere passage, this initial period figures significantly in the success of the marriage. It may be the 2nd or 22nd year in which the divorce is granted, but its beginning is rooted in the failure to make the necessary relationship adjustments in the first stage of marriage. Early marriage is a time when many dreams may be fulfilled but also a time when problems must be identified and resolvable issues faced if successful passage is to be achieved. Ultimately, success depends upon the capabilities of the two individuals involved. Through childhood and adolescent socialization experiences, each of the partners has formed many expectations concerning marriage.

Expectations in Marriage

"After the romance" sounds like the title to a 1950s love song. But it may be too familiar to today's newlyweds. Couples typically experience their first major disappointments after a few months of marriage when characteristically the honeymoon ends and reality begins. By then they are aware of a number of "disagreeable issues," and disillusionment with the marriage is common (Stanush, 1991). Does this mean that romantic love disappears? Not necessarily! An adjustment toward a more mature, fulfilling love may begin if the couple realizes that it is not essential to agree on all issues. In fact, continued health of the relationship depends upon the recognition that differences are resolvable. At the base of early marriage disillusionments are differing role perceptions and unrealistic expectations about marriage.

Anticipated Roles

Perceptions of roles are fairly well determined by marriageable age. These individual expectations brought into the relationship will significantly impact marital adjustment, especially in the early stages of marriage. Therefore, it is important to understand how perspectives may differ for women and men.

Probably no social phenomenon has changed as much in the past several decades as women's attitudes toward what marriage should be like. The attitudes of men have changed, too, although not to the same degree as women's (Greenglass, 1985). Since these changing attitudes regarding marriage expectations are extremely important to the couple's adjustment throughout marriage, the woman's and the man's perspective will be analyzed as they relate to combining marriage, parenthood, and careers.

The Woman's Perspective

Most college-educated women today plan to combine careers with marriage and, in many cases, with having children (Shreve, 1987). But in reality, women's success in reaching such goals has been hampered by their inability to achieve equality with men in marriage as well as careers. Some authorities have argued that increased employment for married women outside of the home has indirectly been detrimental to their social and psychological status, because career women still tend to retain major responsibility for children and housework (Greenglass, 1985). Nevertheless, a study of female college students found that the wife/career role was perceived as most rewarding, while the wife/only role was perceived as least rewarding. The most problematic role was thought to be the combined wife/mother/career role (Bridges, 1987). Despite these ambiguous circumstances, a survey in the early 1980s of never-married, white college women found that all respondents planned to combine a career and motherhood. However, these women were more willing to delay their child-rearing plans than their career plans, with two thirds preferring to postpone the intended birth of their first child rather than give up their career (Granrose, 1985).

The combining of marriage, motherhood, and labor-force participation is most often found when more egalitarian views of gender roles are held during adolescence. Also, having a significant other with similar goal definitions and career aspirations as a role model is associated with the desire to combine motherhood and labor-force participation. Career aspirations of women are based on a number of factors, one of which is their adolescent socialization experiences. Such career goals are said to evolve from a two-stage process of decision making. The first stage occurs when decisions are made about desired family life and work roles, and the second stage occurs when a specific occupational goal is chosen (Corder & Stephan, 1984).

Women of the past who followed traditionally masculine occupations were considered by many to be social deviants. These women were viewed as having rejected womanhood and adopted masculine self-images. They were widely perceived to be poorly adjusted, more likely to remain single, and poor marriage risks if they did marry (Mueller & Campbell, 1977). A modern view now suggests that career-oriented women are persons who have been subjected to certain kinds of enrichment experiences during the process of growing up. The findings from one study strongly support the conclusion that especially women who want nontraditional careers have had socialization experiences that lead them to view themselves and the world in other than strictly family terms. Career-oriented women, when compared to noncareer-oriented women, differed in several ways. First, their mothers were more likely to be currently employed and to report enjoying their combined family and work roles. Second, these college women were more influenced by their professors and other persons in their chosen occupations than by their peers and family members. Third, career-oriented women had worked at more jobs and in more different kinds of jobs while enrolled in college (Spitze, 1978).

During the last two decades, many wives and husbands have embraced the trend toward egalitarianism in marriage without recognizing its full implications. As long as most women thought of outside employment in terms of a job rather than a career, they were more willing to bear additional responsibilities of being wife and mother. These wives would see that the house was clean, the children received adequate care, meals were prepared on time, and laundry was completed. They typically earned less money, subordinated the demands of their jobs to those of their husbands, and were ready to move to a distant location when their husbands received a transfer or promotion. However, the idea of equality has taken on new meanings. Today, more women want careers. They want to be full partners with their husbands in the world of work and expect their husbands to be full partners in the household (Kramer, 1991).

The Man's Perspective

Although considerable research has been conducted on changes in role expectations for women, relatively little attention has been paid to how these changes may be affecting men. It seems apparent that some men are better able to accept changing marriage expectations than others. On the whole, men tend to lag behind women in their awareness and adjustment to changing role expectations (Kramer, 1991).

As early as the 1970s, men's attitudes were beginning to change in regard to women working. A majority of a sample of Ivy League college men agreed that their future wives should be free to seek personal fulfillment through paid employment. However, a different picture was portrayed with their overall responses, which were categorized into four types: traditional, modified traditional, pseudofeminist, and feminist. The traditionalists (24%) intended to marry women who would not seek employment but rather would find sufficient fulfillment through family, civic, and cultural pursuits. Modified traditionalists (48%) anticipated their wives might work before children were born and again after children reached college age. Although these men were prepared to help their wives by hiring maids, they emphasized their unwillingness to clean or "do diapers." The pseudofeminists (16%) favored their future wives working, at least in the abstract. But when it came down to specific cases, they only wanted a working wife as long as the household ran smoothly and her job did not interfere with their career. Finally, feminists (7%) were willing to make significant changes in their own roles so that their wives might pursue careers without being unduly hampered by responsibilities of marriage and child rearing (Komarovsky, 1973).

Convergence of Perspectives

A review of the gender-role literature of the late 1970s and early 1980s revealed that generally husbands in dual-earner households did not have major responsibility for household tasks (Brubaker & Ade-Ridder, 1986). In fact, it may be no surprise that a traditional division of household labor was reflected in studies of dual-earner women, but the surprising fact was that many wives were pleased with such arrangements (Brubaker & Hennon, 1982). One study found that a group of faculty women at a major university did not want their husbands to share equally in housework (Yogev, 1981). But husbands and wives do not always agree. Two basic patterns have been identified among United States Air Force couples concerning traditional versus modern views of marriage: male-modern/female-traditional and male-traditional/female-modern. The greatest differences in attitudes between wives and husbands were found in male-traditional/female-modern couple relationships. In these cases, the man was unwilling to change and expected his wife to stay at home. The greatest number of marital problems appear to occur in these marriages (Bowen & Orthner, 1983).

Some believe that the emerging egalitarian family is really a myth and what has actually occurred is the

Role-strain may result from the options in the 1990s. Dual-earner couples are not always dual workers in the home.

emergence of the neotraditional family. In the neotraditional family, the wife has a "helping" economic position, while the man retains the status of provider (Poloma & Garland, 1971). The wife's income is typically used for luxuries such as vacations or private schools. Both wives and husbands view domestic responsibilities, including child care, as the woman's responsibility, although the husband may "help out." This quasi-egalitarian approach to dual careers encourages women to accept employment in positions such as public school teaching. Jobs of this type permit time in the afternoon to be with children, to prepare evening meals, and, in most instances, freedom for travel and leisure-time pursuits during the summer months.

In summary, women and men have differing conceptions of appropriate roles for wives and husbands to play, of what is fair and what is not fair, and what should be the proper division of labor. The adjustment to these differing role expectations and resolution of any serious differences constitutes a substantial part of learning to live together.

Unrealistic Expectations about Marriage

Marriage represents a process of change in which there will always be irresolvable tension between loving oneself and loving one's partner. The intimacy, closeness, and affection that develops depends upon the feelings that both partners have about themselves (Klagsbrun, 1985b). Gradually, as "Me" feelings are tempered with "We" feelings couples learn to trust each other and communicate. However, idealized thinking may interfere with this process. Such commonly held myths proclaim that wives and husbands must be each other's best friend, confessions of past life experiences are healthy for the relationship, marriage is a 50–50 partnership, children are essential for marital happiness, and there has been a disappearance of love with romance (Lazarus, 1986).

Wives and Husbands as Best Friends

It has long been advocated that in a good relationship wives and husbands will be each other's best friend. The inference is that no other "best" friends are needed. While friendship is an important dimension in the marriage, it differs considerably from other types of friend relationships. Friends do not usually live under the same roof or have a central focus as do marriage partners. Since marriage is a uniquely personal intimate relationship, it is considerably more complex than that which exists between best friends (Lazarus, 1986). The friendship aspect of love is only one dimension in the multifaceted phenomenon. Love blends friendship or philos with eros and agape. The most important facet of friendship, however, is that a person must be her or his "own best friend" as a basis for establishing healthy love relationships (Moore, 1976).

Confessions Healthy for Relationship

Some have argued that during engagement or early in marriage sharing information with your spouse about former indiscretions will improve the health of the relationship. This perspective is based on the idea that a person should share everything with her or his spouse. While guilt feelings may be resolved, a marriage partner may be devastated by such revelations. Thus, the best person to "confess to" may be a confidant other than your spouse (Lazarus, 1986). The need for discretion when revealing certain information about previous relationships suggests the merits of seeing a professional marriage and family therapist to work through such personal needs.

It is important to note that what is questioned here is the motivation for sharing, not the sharing itself. In fact, some past events may need to be shared with a lifetime partner. But how does one know? Ask yourself these questions: Why do I want to share? Do I just wish to "get even"? Is the information likely to affect our future together? Certainly, prior experiences that may impact the future of the relationship should be shared with one's mate. Examples of scenarios that may merit confession include having placed a baby for adoption who might one day appear, a felony conviction that precludes certain rights or privileges of citizenship, or having had a sexually transmitted disease creating the possibility of infertility. The bottom line questions are, "What will happen if I tell?," and "What will happen if I do not?"

Marriage as a 50-50 Partnership

Young married couples who believe marriage to be an equal partnership usually believe that all marital and household tasks should be divided equally. However, from a practical point of view, an equal trade-off or sharing of different tasks may be more logical, efficient, and beneficial than evenly splitting all tasks. Further, with some couples, one partner may prefer to take an unequal amount of tasks depending on the other's schedule and abilities (Lazarus, 1986). For marriages to work best, each partner must be prepared to give more than one half in the relationship. To do so occasionally is realistic, but to do so regularly is neurotic and self-depreciating. It is the balance of giving and receiving over time that is significant to successful marriages.

Children Essential for Marital Happiness

Many persons believe that marriages can be improved by having a child, since the wife and husband work together on child rearing. They idealize that the marriage will be strengthened as parents themselves grow by modeling kindness, empathy, and less self-centeredness. They insist that having a child will cause spouses to become more committed to solving relationship problems (Viorst, 1985).

Such thinking may head the list of wrong reasons to have a child. Adding a child to a failing marriage actually compounds the problem. For example, if the relationship does not improve and ultimately culminates in divorce, not only is the child at risk, but both parents must then cope with the additional responsibilities and complexities of custody issues. Couples should examine their motives very carefully before deciding to have a child. If the primary reason for desiring one is the hope that a poor marital relationship will improve, it represents an immature, unrealistic expectation.

Disappearance of Love with Romance

Romantic love involves the idealization of the love/marriage partner as being "perfect." Although it is a natural progression in the love experience, the intensity of romantic love usually fades after marriage. It then becomes necessary to make the transition of accepting something less than the idealized image of partner perfection (Lobsenz, 1981). Development of such disillusionment has been found to begin as early as the transition period from engagement to marriage. However, the positive aspects of romantic love need not be lost. With special care, it can be rekindled in marital relationships and eventually culminate in a much deeper love. Spouses should recall what was said or done to show love feelings during the early stages of courtship. In addition, the wife or husband should observe the things that their spouse does to make them feel loved. Finally, spouses should view changes in their relationship as not giving up something but as gaining new rewards or assets for both spouses (Lobsenz, 1981).

The Nature of Marital Adjustment and Marital Satisfaction

Although considerable research has been conducted regarding qualities associated with happy marriages, it is important to understand that positive emotional feelings concerning love and marriage are, to a substantial degree, shaped during childhood. Persons who have problems in adult love relationships and marriage tend to be products of homes in which their parents projected a hostile environment or presented highly inconsistent and unpredictable displays of affection (Goleman, 1985a).

Marital adjustment or marital satisfaction may also, in part, be related to age, gender, and the degree of social support received from the other spouse. For example, age and gender have been found to affect perceptions of subjective well-being in marriage. Men and younger couples perceive higher levels of marital satisfaction than do women and older couples (Haring-Hidore, Stock, Okun, & Witter, 1985). Among men, marital satisfaction usually remains fairly constant, whereas for women, marital satisfaction varies greatly over the life cycle. Marital satisfaction among women tends to be lowest when preschool children are present and highest after the children have left home. Further, men, in general, are more satisfied with their marital quality than are women (Rhyne, 1981). However, ratings of marital happiness appear to decline somewhat with the length of marriage (see Table 8.1). Adverse economic conditions, such as husband's employment instability, often lead to hostility and/or decreased warmth and supportiveness of husbands toward their wives. These changes in marital-interaction patterns typically result in lower reported levels of marital happiness and satisfaction for wives. In general, however, wives are found to experience less negative behavioral response to financial problems than husbands (Conger et al., 1990).

Measurement of Marital Quality

Interchangeable use of the terms "marital happiness," "marital adjustment," and "marital satisfaction" in the literature on marriage and the family potentially creates confusion (Broderick, 1988). The quality of marital relationships, by whatever name, continues to be one of the most widely studied topics in the family science field. Despite this circumstance, during the 1980s

Table 8.1: Rating of Marriage

Rating of Marriage	Years Married: Under 1	1–4	5–10	Over 10
Very good	62%	47%	41%	41%
Good	29	35	37	34
Fair	6	13	16	16
Poor	2	4	4	6
Very poor	0	1	1	3

From *Marriage and Family Interaction,* 6/E by Robert R. Bell © 1983 The Dorsey Press. Reprinted by permission of Wadsworth, Inc.

little attention was devoted to investigating marital quality for the duration-of-marriage effects beyond the early years of the transition to parenthood stage (Glenn, 1990). One study has, however, concluded that marital success, as defined by married persons reporting their marriages as "very happy," significantly spirals downward for at least the first 10 years of marriage and, perhaps, for 25 years or longer (Glenn, 1989). Measurement of marital quality continues to focus on the individual's perception rather than the couple's evaluation of the marriage (Glenn, 1990). The accuracy of such measurements are questioned since most persons have a tendency to oversimplify or misrepresent the true condition of their marriage when responding to questionnaire items, perhaps because they do not want to be viewed as being abnormal (Reiss & Lee, 1988). In addition, spouses in unhappy marriages are more likely to view the partner's behavior in question more negatively than spouses who perceive themselves as having happy marriages (Roberts & Krokoff, 1990). Further confusion results when measuring marital satisfaction if only one spouse is dissatisfied with an area(s) of the marital relationship. Since each marriage partner has a unique personality that has been largely molded by their prior socialization experiences, any assessment of marital adjustment/marital satisfaction is difficult. Therefore, it is suggested that research results be viewed as approximations rather than precise measurements.

Measurement of Marital Satisfaction

One study has attempted to determine the relative influence of perceived equity, equality, and reward levels on marital satisfaction. Using married couples with modern-egalitarian and traditional gender-role orientations, the major variable affecting marital satisfaction was found to be perceived reward level. In other words, a marital relationship must be perceived as personally rewarding for the wife/husband in order for her/him to experience a high level of marital satisfaction (Martin, 1985).

Couples who had taken a premarital inventory 3 to 4 months prior to marriage were surveyed after 2 to 3 years of marriage. Relationship consensus was more evident in the premarriage test results among those couples who later rated themselves as happily married than among those who were divorced/separated (see figure 8.1). These findings support the argument that marriages experiencing substantial problems during the first 3 years contain the "seeds" of distress from the very beginning of the marital relationship (Fowers & Olson, 1986). In a longitudinal study of marital satisfaction that began in 1936 and concluded in 1980, the major variables leading to marital dissatisfaction included **neuroticism** on the part of a spouse, wife's lack of emotional closeness with family of origin, husband's nonconformity to social ideals, and differences in desired frequency of sexual intercourse. Substantial differences in levels of education between spouses were found to affect marital satisfaction of only those couples who had been married for 20 or more years. Of the 43 couples in the study who divorced between 1935–1980 and for whom the major reasons for divorce could be determined, over one half reported sexual difficulties as a major factor in their divorce (Kelly & Conley, 1987).

Since rewarding marital experiences are based on diverse variables, a number of measurement instruments have been developed over the years to assess the quality of marriage. Among the most popular marital adjustment measures are the Dyadic Adjustment Scale (DAS), the Marital Adjustment Test (MAT), and the Revised Marital Adjustment Test (RMAT), which may be used by either distressed or nondistressed couples (Crane, Allgood, Larson, & Griffin, 1990). In many instances, these measurement instruments, such as the DAS, also can be used by persons in serious commitments such as engagement or cohabitation. These relationship assessment instruments can prevent marital difficulties by developing a relationship focus, identifying problem areas, promoting discussion, and confronting couple myths (Fowers, 1990).

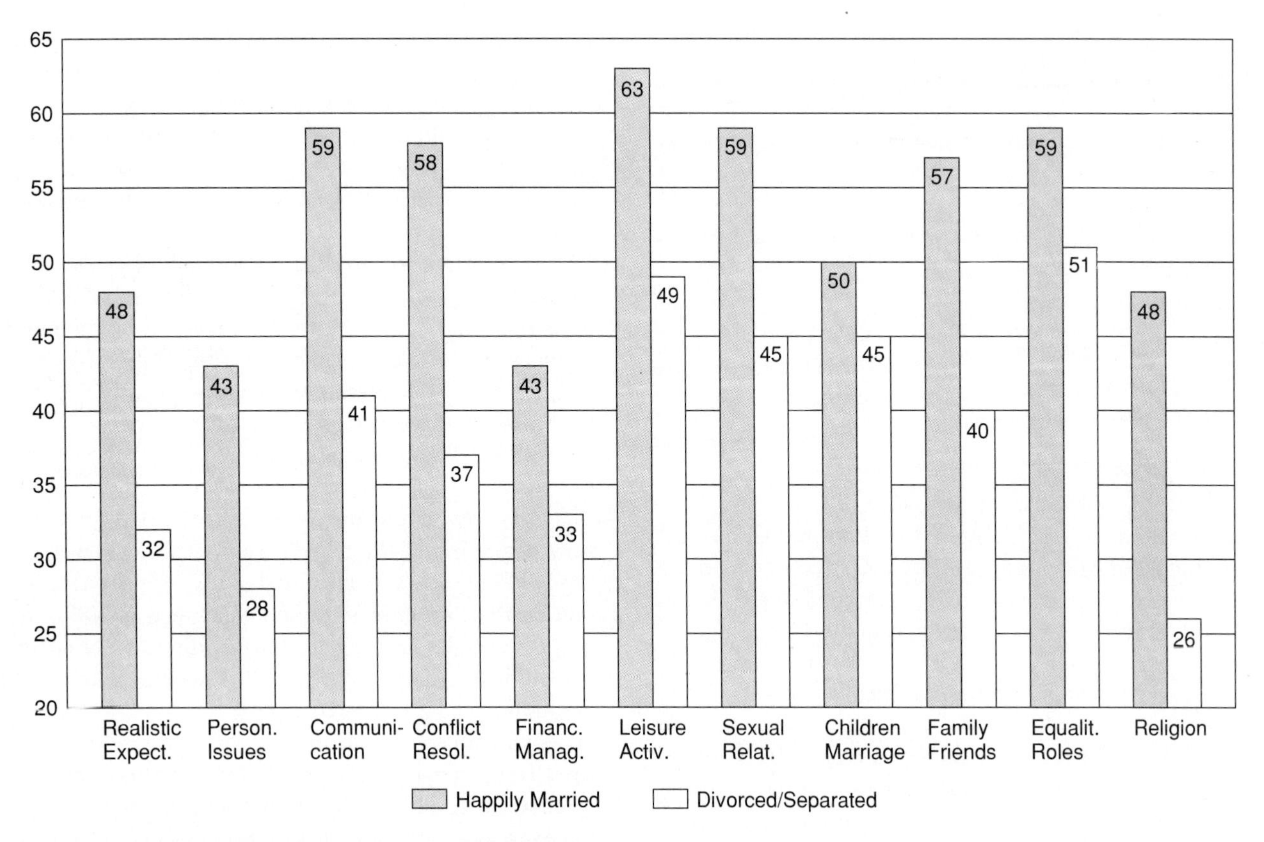

Figure 8.1 Happily Married vs. Divorced / Separated Positive Couple Agreement Scores by Percent

Qualities Associated with Marital Satisfaction

A *Redbook* survey of 17,000 readers found that two thirds of women married under 1 year rated their marriages as "very good," as compared with less than one half of those married over 10 years (see Table 8.2). The most important factor cited for a good marriage by happy couples was viewing their partner as a best friend. They reported liking her/him as a person and accepting each other's faults. While the importance of shared interests was stressed, each person was expected to have time for some separate activities (Lauer & Lauer, 1985).

Before determining the qualities of marital satisfaction it is appropriate to ask, what is a happy marriage? In a classic study defining typologies of marriage, a quality marriage was labeled an **intrinsic marriage.** Intrinsic spouses were said to be "near-perfect" companions, with an "all consuming interest" in their partnership for which they were willing to "heroically sacrifice" (Cuber & Harroff, 1965). By today's mental health standards such relationships could easily be viewed as highly neurotic rather than high quality. More attainable would be a healthy, close but not suffocating, companionship in which the relationship has top priority in life's total picture. The relationship would be a primary consideration in both thoughts and actions. Finally, the partners would be willing to make sacrifices as necessary for the sake of the partnership (Marks, 1989).

There are many specific qualities thought to be associated with marital satisfaction. Among these are job satisfaction, use of leisure time, and value similarity. A study of male **blue-collar** workers in traditional marriages determined that work satisfaction was related to marital adjustment. Surprisingly, the effect of work on marital adjustment was less related to a man's identity with his work than intrinsic factors such as job content, degree of challenge, variety, and degree of job recognition. Therefore, husbands who reported high levels of intrinsic work satisfaction tended to indicate higher levels of marital adjustment (Gaesser & Whitbourne, 1985).

BOX 8.1 **The Dyadic Adjustment Scale: A Self-Test**

Most persons have disagreements in their relationships. Indicate the approximate extent of agreement or disagreement between you and your partner for each item. A total of 218 married persons and divorced persons initially completed this 32-item scale. The average score for married persons was 114.8, and 70.7 for divorced persons. These scores will provide a basis to evaluate your current relationship.

	Always Agree	Almost Always Agree	Occasionally Disagree	Frequently Disagree	Almost Always Disagree	Always Disagree
1. Handling family finances	5	4	3	2	1	0
2. Matters of recreation	5	4	3	2	1	0
3. Religious matters	5	4	3	2	1	0
4. Demonstrations of affection	5	4	3	2	1	0
5. Friends	5	4	3	2	1	0
6. Sex relations	5	4	3	2	1	0
7. Conventionality (correct or proper behavior)	5	4	3	2	1	0
8. Philosophy of life	5	4	3	2	1	0
9. Ways of dealing with parents or in-laws	5	4	3	2	1	0
10. Aims, goals, and things believed important	5	4	3	2	1	0
11. Amount of time spent together	5	4	3	2	1	0
12. Making major decisions	5	4	3	2	1	0
13. Household tasks	5	4	3	2	1	0
14. Leisure time interests and activities	5	4	3	2	1	0
15. Career decisions	5	4	3	2	1	0

	All the time	Most of the time	More often than not	Occasionally	Rarely	Never
16. How often do you discuss or have you considered divorce, separation, or terminating your relationship?	0	1	2	3	4	5
17. How often do you or your mate leave the house after a fight?	0	1	2	3	4	5
18. In general, how often do you think that things between you and your partner are going well?	5	4	3	2	1	0
19. Do you confide in your mate?	5	4	3	2	1	0
20. Do you ever regret that you married? (*or lived together*)	0	1	2	3	4	5
21. How often do you and your partner quarrel?	0	1	2	3	4	5
22. How often do you and your mate "get on each other's nerves"?	0	1	2	3	4	5

BOX 8.1 *cont'd*

		Every Day	Almost Every Day	Occasionally	Rarely	Never
23.	Do you kiss your mate?	4	3	2	1	0

		All of them	Most of them	Some of them	Very few of them	None of them
24.	Do you and your mate engage in outside interests together?	4	3	2	1	0

How often would you say the following events occur between you and your mate?

		Never	Less than once a month	Once or twice a month	Once or twice a week	Once a day	More often
25.	Have a stimulating exchange of ideas	0	1	2	3	4	5
26.	Laugh together	0	1	2	3	4	5
27.	Calmly discuss something	0	1	2	3	4	5
28.	Work together on a projcct	0	1	2	3	4	5

These are some things about which couples sometimes agree and sometimes disagree. Indicate if either item caused differences of opinions or were problems in your relationship during the past few weeks.

		Yes	No
29.	Being too tired for sex.	0	1
30.	Not showing love.	0	1

31. The dots on the following line represent different degrees of happiness in your relationship. The middle point, "happy," represents the degree of happiness for most relationships. Please circle the dot which best describes the degree of happiness, all things considered, of your relationship.

0	1	2	3	4	5	6
·	·	·	·	·	·	·
Extremely *Un*happy	Fairly *Un*happy	A Little *Un*happy	Happy	Very Happy	Extremely Happy	Perfect

32. Which of the following statements best decribes how you feel about the future of your relationship?

5 I want desperately for my relationship to succeed, and *would go to almost any length* to see that it does.

4 I want very much for my relationship to succeed, and *will do all I can* to see that it does.

3 I want very much for my relationship to succeed, and *will do my fair share* to see that it does.

2 It would be nice if my relationship succeeded, but *I can't do much more than I am doing* now to help it succeed.

1 It would be nice if it succeeded, but I *refuse to do any more than I am doing* now to keep the relationship going.

0 My relationship can never succeed, and *there is no more that I can do* to keep the relationship going.

Table 8.2: Factors Contributing to Marital Happiness

	Women		Men
1.	My spouse is my best friend.	1.	My spouse is my best friend.
2.	I like my spouse as a person.	2.	I like my spouse as a person.
3.	Marriage is a long-term commitment.	3.	Marriage is a long-term commitment.
4.	Marriage is sacred.	4.	Marriage is sacred.
5.	We agree on aims and goals.	5.	We agree on aims and goals.
6.	My spouse has grown more interesting.	6.	My spouse has grown more interesting.
7.	I want the relationship to succeed.	7.	I want the relationship to succeed.
8.	We laugh together.	8.	An enduring marriage is important to social stability.
9.	We agree on a philosophy of life.	9.	We laugh together.
10.	We agree on how and how often to show affection.	10.	I am proud of my spouse's achievements.
11.	An enduring marriage is important to social stability.	11.	We agree on a philosophy of life.
12.	We have a stimulating exchange of ideas.	12.	We agree about our sex life.
13.	We discuss things calmly.	13.	We agree on how and how often to show affection.
14.	We agree about our sex life.	14.	I confide in my spouse.
15.	I am proud of my spouse's achievements.	15.	We share outside hobbies and interests.

From J. Lauer and R. Lauer, "Marriages Made to Last" in *Psychology Today,* June 1985:23.

The use of leisure time also has been determined to be associated with marital satisfaction. Married couples reporting greatest marital satisfaction spent more time together, spent leisure time together as well as alone, had their own interests, and did not feel the need to share every leisure activity with their spouse (Kotler, 1985). Finally, among couples married 20 or more years, similarity of specific values such as being honest, polite, and helpful were useful as predictors of marital adjustment (Medling & McCarrey, 1981). Overall marital quality measured among newlyweds indicated happiness to be the most significant dimension of marital well-being. Equity, competence, and control were also identified as important factors (Crohan & Veroff, 1989). It was speculated that young newlywed men who reported lower equity than women felt more "trapped" than their female counterparts. In addition, premarital cohabitation was negatively associated with happiness for blacks but unrelated to happiness for whites. Researchers predicted that marital commitment, even if absent in the first year of marriage, will emerge as a separate factor in later years.

Similarity of Sexual Needs

A nationwide survey of 12,000 persons indicated that fulfillment of sexual needs in terms of quantity and quality was very important to the well-being and happiness of a marriage (Blumstein & Schwartz, 1983). Generally speaking, relationship partners who are similar in gender-role identity are more likely to have a greater degree of sexual compatibility (Ewing, 1985). Concerning quantity, one study found that women today are also likely to complain about the low frequency of sexual intercourse, a typical male complaint. Wives have become especially concerned about the willingness of their spouses to devote sufficient attention to adequate foreplay as it relates to physiological sexual satisfaction including orgasm (Davidson & Darling, 1989b).

The frequency of sexual intercourse during the first year of marriage may become somewhat inflated due to ready availability of a sexual partner. The mean frequency of sexual intercourse reported in the early 1980s was 13.8 times a month for women and 14.4 times a month for men (see Table 8.3). After the first year of marriage, sexual intercourse frequency tends to decline because of reasons such as familiarity, work, and other responsibilities. Interestingly, the decline in frequency seems to be related to social class or occupational category. In one study, 59% of husbands employed in professional or white-collar occupations reported a decline in sexual intercourse frequency after 1 year of marriage in comparison to only 20% of husbands working in blue-collar occupations (Greenblat, 1983).

Table 8.3: Monthly Frequency of Sexual Intercourse During Early Marriage		
Frequency of Sexual Intercourse	Women	Men
1–4 times	8%	7%
5–8 times	21	18
9–12 times	21	32
13–16 times	19	11
17–20 times	17	21
21–24 times	8	0
25–29 times	2	0
30 or more times	4	11

From C. S. Greenblat, "The Salience of Sexuality in the Early Years of Marriage" in *Journal of Marriage and the Family,* 45:291. Copyright © 1983 National Council on Family Relations, 3989 Central Avenue, N.E., Suite #550, Minneapolis, MN 55421. Reprinted by permission.

Empathy for Partner

To avoid feelings of anxiety, jealousy, and depression during marriage, it is very important to be able to place oneself in the role of one's partner in order to understand the basis of her/his feelings. **Empathy** (the capacity to feel what another is feeling) allows one to understand the other person's needs and wants, to listen, and to provide positive support. It offers recognition or verification of feelings (Peck, 1978). Through this process, true intimacy should emerge from the passion created by romantic love (Goleman, 1985a). Such empathy is communicated, in part, through the friendship aspect of love.

Sense of Commitment to Relationship

Commitment is the foundation for any loving relationship. Although deep commitment does not guarantee the success of a relationship, when a relationship does succeed, commitment is the most important variable (Peck, 1978). High commitment to a marital relationship is associated with the interdependence of marriage partners. Such interdependence is usually found in couples with high marital satisfaction who have dealt effectively with relationship disillusionment in the beginning of marriage. Generally speaking, barriers to disillusionment become stronger the longer that a couple has been married (Sabatelli & Cecil-Pigo, 1985). With increasing commitment over the years, a deeper sense of intimacy may surface from the man. However, many men are afraid that deep intimacy may cause women to want to control them and make unreasonable demands. Fear of intimacy has been labeled as the number one male phobia (Kaplan, 1985). In the final analysis, it is the sense of commitment that makes possible the journey from falling in love to genuine love.

Age at Marriage

The average age at marriage has been increasing in the United States for the past 15 years for both women and men (Reiss & Lee, 1988). This apparent trend may portend well for the institution of marriage, since young age at marriage has typically been associated with lack of happiness or poor marital satisfaction. However, one study found no relationship between age at marriage and marital satisfaction. Evidence suggests that the major reasons why teen marriages are less happy are short acquaintanceship, less skill in assessing values and characteristics of partner, and fewer financial assets (Bahr, Chappell, & Leigh, 1983). These findings are supported by a later study that determined that those persons who dated only a short time before marriage reported less marital happiness than those who had dated for a longer period of time. While a longer period of dating was associated with a higher probability of happy marriage, it did not appear to be an absolute condition for happiness (Grover, Russell, Schumm, & Paff-Bergen, 1985).

Religiosity of Marital Partners

A high degree of religiosity has been identified as having a positive relationship with marital satisfaction for wives and husbands. In general, women engaging in religious activities and prayers with others had a higher degree of marital satisfaction than men, for whom participation in prayers with others was the strongest predictor (Hendershott, 1986). This finding raises an interesting question of the value of group interaction in a meaningful activity. But there is conflicting data, as another study found that church attendance and frequency of prayer did not contribute to marital satisfaction. The findings did, however, suggest that lack of consensus about religious practices may lower marital satisfaction, while spousal consensus may increase marital satisfaction (Hatch, 1986).

Self-Actualization

Self-actualization is an important factor in maintenance of a positive self-concept and self-esteem. The process of self-actualization can be defined as engaging in activities and pursuing one's goals to achieve the maximum use of one's skills and talents. If a spouse lacks self-esteem, she/he is more likely to blame the marriage partner or the marriage itself for her/his discontent (Bienvenu, 1986). The study of middle-age couples suggests that high regard for self alone does not contribute to marital quality. Rather, the perception of marriage partners that their mate has a positive image of themselves contributes to a positive evaluation of the marital relationship (Schafer & Keith, 1986). Considering the influence of self-esteem on marital adjustment, spouses who view each other as unique individuals have significantly greater marital adjustment than those spouses who have stereotyped views of each other. Furthermore, wives who perceived themselves possessing **conjugal power** (family power exercised between spouses) in the marital relationship were more likely to report high levels of self-esteem (deTurk & Miller, 1986).

Maintenance of Marital Quality

Newly married couples often hear, "The honeymoon is over and it's time to settle down." However, marriage must be viewed as a dynamic growth process in which marital happiness involves the ability to cope, change, and adapt to circumstances rather than as a time to settle down. In fact, to maintain a high level of marital happiness requires a constant day-to-day effort instead of taking the marital relationship for granted (Bienvenu, 1986). The question becomes, "How can couples maintain their marital happiness on the road from romantic love to married love?" Among those strategies identified as crucial to this process are honesty, listening, openness, physical affection, physical attractiveness, self-concept confirmation, sensitivity, supportiveness, and verbal affection. However, the association between marital quality and these or any other strategies is very complex. For example, if satisfaction with the marriage already exists, it is likely that the use of these strategies will further increase the satisfaction level (Bell, Daly, & Gonzalez, 1987). It is interesting that wives viewed themselves as using positive strategies more often than did their husbands and, in general, as being more responsible for maintaining marriage quality.

Ironically, maintaining the strength of a marriage depends upon the separateness of the partners. Ideally, marriage is a cooperative venture requiring great mutual contributions of care, time, and energy. However, a primary purpose of the relationship is to nurture each of the partners on their individual journey toward growth to the end that, "Male and female both must tend the hearth and both must venture forth" (Peck, 1978, p. 168).

Attributes of Healthy Couples

Relatively little has been written concerning clinical research with healthy couples. The research group at Timberlawn in Dallas, Texas, whose focus is on families that work rather than those who fail, is part of that pioneer movement (Beavers, 1985). Its research on healthy families found "no single thread" that accounted for optimal family functioning. Instead, there were many interwoven threads that contributed to healthy families (Lewis, Beavers, Gossett, & Phillips, 1976).

Using data that differentiated healthy families from dysfunctional ones, attributes of couples who are successful in maintaining a satisfying relationship over the years have been delineated ("Research On," 1989). Generally, such couples have a strong marital coalition of shared power and adapt well to changes in the individual and family life cycle. Specifically, attributes of such couples are evidenced in health-promoting patterns of attitudes and behaviors. These patterns fall into two groups: attitudes and beliefs and observable behavior or interaction (Beavers, 1985).

Health-Promoting Belief Patterns

Certain attitudes and belief patterns that promote couple health have been identified: relative, not absolute truth; people as basically neutral; human encounters as rewarding; a systems point of view; and purpose and meaning in life (Beavers, 1985). Successful couples believe that people are far from infallible and that relative, not absolute, truth exists. Therefore, honest differences offer opportunities for promoting growth through synthesis of ideas. Dysfunctional partners, however, believe truth to be absolute. Such beliefs lead to fear of encounter that may result in avoidance of conflict. This fear is usually derived from one's family of origin where either a revered or despised parent was the source of absolute truth, not to be questioned. In healthy couples, partners believe each other's motives are basically neutral. Such a belief allows people to make mistakes and even disagree without feeling abandoned. It assumes that sexuality, anger, willfulness, and ambivalence are natural conditions which, although not always good, are certainly not evil. They assume their partner is basically trustworthy. Further, optimism and hope are essentials for the healthy couple's basic belief that human encounters can be rewarding. Even when a spouse has behaved disappointingly, there is hope that hard work can restore the relationship (Beavers, 1985).

In addition, healthy couples understand that growth requires interpersonal relationships, that persons need a human system within which to define themselves. The family of origin is the first system in which the child learns interpersonal skills. With maturity, children grow up, leave home, and establish relationships in a new system. Open systems with clear but permeable boundaries that offer privacy allow healthy passage. Persons from closed systems with rigid boundaries and peculiar family rules find it harder to leave home and establish a new family. Healthy couples recognize that causes and effects are interchangeable and that human behavior is the result of many variables in the system. Dysfunctional couples instead seek oversimplified causes such as fate or destiny to explain problems. They also consider only one explanation for a problem and respond stereotypically (Beavers, 1985).

Healthy marital partners have an innate sense of purpose or meaning about life apart from their relationship. It may flow from religion or an embraced cause such as environmental protection or nuclear disarmament, but they have some kind of belief that directs their energy and provides community beyond their relationship. When couples depend entirely on each other to provide purpose in life, dysfunctional interaction results (Beavers, 1985).

Health-Promoting Interaction Patterns

It is important to understand how health-promoting attitudes and beliefs are implemented through positive behaviors. Six behavioral interaction patterns of healthy couples have been delineated: little overt power difference, capacity for clear boundaries, presence of operating strategies, respect for individual choice, skill in negotiating, and shared positive feelings (Beavers, 1985). Although no couple achieves absolute equality of power, the healthy couple experiences little overt power difference. Healthy partners respect each other's perceptions and are able to negotiate. They develop and maintain equal overt power through complementarity. Healthy couples may demonstrate many complementary roles through the years such as teacher and student, speaker and listener, and breadwinner and homemaker. Although such roles need not be stereotyped, both complementarity and role differentiation appear necessary to allow pleasant interaction with shared dignity (Beavers, 1985).

Healthy couples need to know where each boundary ends and the other begins. These boundaries should clearly establish what is inside and outside, yet be permeable enough to allow effective interchange with the outside world. In fact, healthy couples as well as dysfunctional ones can experience a loss of boundaries in passion, whether anger or ecstasy. Although the results of such merging may be either delightful or horrible, healthy couples can redefine the boundaries when passion cools, while dysfunctional ones remain enmeshed (Beavers, 1985).

Healthy couples interpret present operating strategies "in light of" the past, not "as" the past. They go beyond the repetitive drama of their pasts and develop healthier ways of relating (Kirschner & Kirschner, 1989). Many marital problems are based on legacies from the past where the world is experienced as it was in childhood. The healthy couple can use the past as a guide but not as a prophecy. They relate with relative ease to their own parents in ways that enhance the couple relationship. Dysfunctional couples relate to their families of origin by either continuing to operate as a child or making a radical break with parents. Acceptance of generational continuity is an integral part of healthy relationships in which some aspects are perpetuated, and needed changes are made in others (Beavers, 1985).

Healthy marital partners respect individual autonomy and choice. Their couple unity is based on the merging of two individuals who know what they feel and believe, take responsibility for personal behavior, and interact with others with reasonably clear choices. They have a system of rules that encourages the expression of personal perceptions and wishes. Dysfunctional couples have unresolved mixed feelings and, therefore, are unable to clearly define wishes and needs. They frequently try to fit themselves or their partner into stereotyped roles such as either a liberated or subservient wife or husband (Beavers, 1985). A creative balance between symbiosis and autonomy is vital to marital health (Kirschner & Kirschner, 1989).

Positive shared feelings are an observable quality of healthy couples. A mix of personal skill and good humor is needed to deal with the challenges inherent in couple relationships. Partners who share positive feelings are better prepared to cope with the realities of everyday living (Beavers, 1985). Finally, couples in a healthy marriage also have developed their skills in negotiating solutions to problems. All the former attributes of healthy couples are brought to bear in effective negotiating: boundaries are clarified, mixed feelings resolved, caring expressed, goals clearly defined, and decisions made in light of present facts (Beavers, 1985).

Tasks of Early Marriage

Couple tasks of early marriage emerged from the Timberlawn research with healthy families (Lewis et al., 1976). According to these findings, if marriages are not only to survive but also to nurture the individual involved, certain tasks must be achieved early in the marriage. These tasks have been identified as separating from one's family of origin and working out relationship rules concerning power and intimacy.

Separating self from parents does not mean to stop loving one's parents. It does imply, however, that persons in a new marriage must transfer their primary allegiance to their partner. In order to become an independent unit, other love relationships must become secondary. This approach obviously works best for individuals who have already achieved independence from parents. Marriage at later ages increases such a likelihood.

Working out rules by which the relationship will function is also an important early marriage task. Of the many relationship rules to be resolved, the two most significant ones involve needs of power, the capability of achieving desired goals or outcomes, and intimacy, the experience of being able to share one's innermost feelings and thoughts (Beavers, 1985; McDonald, 1980).

Intimacy Needs

Intimacy needs are psychological in nature. In marriages that work best, partners can communicate at intimate levels. People move through four psychological intimacy levels as they approach intimacy: clichés, information exchanges, everyday feelings, and private thoughts and feelings (Lewis et al., 1976). Clichés are the meaningless "How are you today?" exchanges that characterize much of communication in the day-to-day world of friends and acquaintances. Wives and husbands also engage in this mindless chatter at times. Information exchange is the next step toward intimacy. It is asking "What did you do today?" and receiving trivial information about the day's activities. The level of everyday feelings progresses to sharing not only facts but also feelings about life events. But all of these are based on less than full intimacy. In intimate communication, private thoughts and feelings are shared. Whether deepest fears or highest dreams, it is at this level, where one is truly vulnerable, that intimacy occurs. Marriages that work best have partners who discover and nurture this ability to communicate at intimate levels in the beginning years of marriage.

The emphasis on intimacy as a primary function in marriage is a 20th century phenomenon that emerged with changing family forms. By the 1960s, a psychological approach to life had heightened the concern for warm, intimate relationships. By the mid-1970s, this way of viewing the world in general and especially marital relationships had become commonplace (Veroff, Kulka, & Douvan, 1981). This accent on intimacy, characterized by tender loving care, came to be viewed as an expectation by many marriage partners, especially women. However, research indicates that women and men differ in their beliefs concerning intimacy. For example, women often believe that talking can be a great source of intimacy, whereas men tend to believe that intimacy is created through doing things together. Men appear to be more willing to talk about issues and problems during the courtship period than later during the marriage (Goleman, 1986). Given the emphasis on achievement and the provider role in our society, many men are ill-prepared to provide the feelings of tenderness, warmth, and intimacy desired by their wives. Men sometimes confuse their need for affection with unfulfilled sexual needs. As discussed in chapter 10, even though there has been a growing interest in physiological sexual satisfaction among modern women, sexual needs have not replaced the need for intimacy that comes through warm, tender expressions of affection.

Power Needs

Power needs are usually based on "parent tapes," those powerful messages received early in life from parents and other authority figures. Such "ought" and "should" messages at subconscious levels often dictate later behavior (Crosby, 1991). For example, when a child has been robbed of feeling powerful early in life, there may be so much leftover need for power that it will surface to damage marital relationships. With uneven power, when one partner dominates the decision making, both partners eventually tire of such inequity. They feel either controlled or tired of the decision-making role. In healthy couples, there is an equality of power based on respect for each other. Such equality rarely rests on absolute 50–50 decision making. Instead, it is based on use of individual strengths to achieve a balance of power. It is only with equal overt power that intimacy can be achieved.

In new marriages power involves relatively straightforward questions such as who will make decisions about where to live, shopping, savings accounts, buying a new car, and vacations. But marital power also embraces more subtle questions such as who tries to dominate the marriage and control the relationship. The allocation of power distribution may begin during courtship if one partner tends to dominate the relationship through a combination of social and personality characteristics (Harvey, 1986). Marriage usually just makes the power relationship that already exists more visible and systematic.

Bases of Marital Power. The popular press suggests that a number of attributes contribute to personal power, including beauty, charm, communication skills, cultural attainments, material assets, talents, and wit (Marcus & Smith, 1982). Family social scientists suggest coercion, influence, and/or the ability to persuade as bases for marital power. Gender also serves as a major determinant of power in view of the effects of traditional gender roles in our society (Nock, 1987).

In an attempt to clarify the various bases of marital power, a **typology** (classification) of conjugal power has been developed by social scientists (Raven, Centers, & Rodrigues, 1975). The classification of marital power had its origins in research concerned with the bases of social power, in general, and in later years, has been applied to studies of marital power. Accordingly, Raven et al. suggested six bases of conjugal power:

1. **Coercive power**—punish partner by acting or not acting in particular way.
2. **Reward power**—provide for partner's economic, psychological, or physical needs.
3. **Expertise power**—use of knowledge by marriage partner about particular subject or activity.
4. **Legitimacy power**—recognize certain wife/husband roles carry legitimate responsibilities.
5. **Referent power**—gain emotional satisfaction from thinking or behaving as spouse wishes.
6. **Informational power**—accept arguments of spouse concerning some issue or problem (1975, p. 219).

In view of these different bases of marital power, it makes sense to assign nonmajor decision making to one or the other of the marriage partners. This task-oriented approach, based on individual skills, is a popular method of sharing the power in a relationship.

Marital Power Patterns. Four general power patterns were identified in an early decision-making model: husband-dominant, **syncratic** (decisions negotiated together), and **autonomic** (each marriage partner makes decisions alone in certain areas based on perceived expertise), and wife-dominant. Among these couples, the vast majority of marriages were found to be autonomic, with over three fourths indicating being "very satisfied" with their marriage (Centers, Raven, & Rodrigues, 1971). However, the lowest level of marital satisfaction indicated was in wife-dominant marriages.

It has been suggested that the more resources possessed by a spouse, the more power that spouse has in the marital relationship. While early research found that husbands with higher education or occupational status had more power in the relationship than their wives, later studies have concluded that the decision-making power of wives increases as they enter the labor force (Osmond, 1978; Scanzoni, 1980). With the changing gender roles in our society, individual resources of wives have come to have more influence on marital power than individual resources of husbands (McDonald, 1980). Wives with high levels of education, income, and occupational prestige, when compared to those with low levels, were found to exert greater influence upon their employment decision making. However, husbands with higher levels of these same variables exerted very little influence over their wife's employment decisions (Rank, 1982). Employment of wives has obviously become a crucial power factor in marital relationships. In a comparison of dual-career couples and traditional couples with wife not working, dual-career couples reported using a greater number of power strategies associated with decision making than did traditional couples (Cate, Koval, & Ponzetti, 1984).

Marital Power and Marital Satisfaction. Perhaps of even greater importance is the relationship of wife-husband power and marital satisfaction. While there are problems associated with self-reporting data and the observational techniques used to investigate power interaction between wives and husbands, several significant findings continue to appear in various studies. First, marriages in which the wife is dominant are more likely to be unhappy. Second, egalitarian couples tend to exhibit the highest levels of marital satisfaction. Third, using coercive control techniques in marriages leads to marital dissatisfaction (Gray-Little & Burks, 1983).

Changing gender roles also affect decision making in families in which the wife is not employed. If the wife was a full-time homemaker, joint power sharing

was associated with greater marital happiness than a wife-centered or husband-centered authority structure. Further, whenever the actual use of authority approximated the couple's ideal pattern, the greater degree of marital happiness was reported by both wives and husbands (Mashal, 1985). There is an intervening psychological variable in the relationship between power and marital satisfaction. The "more in love" spouse has less marital power than the spouse who perceives herself/himself as being "less in love" due to fears about potential loss of her/his marital partner (McDonald, 1980). The use or abuse of power is highly significant to the well-being of a relationship as complex as marriage.

In-Law Relations

Most in-law relationships begin long before marriage occurs, and by the time a couple marries, a pattern of interaction has already developed. After marriage, it is important that the young couple becomes independent of their families of origin and develops a smoothly functioning marital unit. As their contribution, the families of the young wife and husband must encourage independence for the couple yet remain emotionally supportive. Available evidence suggests that conflict with or about in-laws is more likely to occur with young age at marriage for the wife and/or husband (Brenton, 1985).

Marital satisfaction of newlyweds has been found to be related to in-law support. Among first-married and remarried newlywed couples, spouses, friends, and family of origin have been frequently identified as providers of social support. In a study of the relationship of social support to psychological stress, remarrieds less frequently named families of origin and in-laws as providers of support (Kurdek, 1989b). However, marital satisfaction has been found to drop if relative/family visitation occurs more than once per week (Holman, 1981). The importance of kin opinions declines after marriage. In addition, the amount of disclosure about issues and events in personal lives decreases somewhat after engagement and even more substantially after marriage (Johnson & Leslie, 1982).

Background Factors

The likelihood that good in-law relationships will develop quickly between a young couple and their families depends in part upon the similarity of their familial backgrounds. A prospective spouse who comes from a similar financial and occupational background will be welcomed more quickly than one whose parents rank significantly higher or lower in social status. If differences in family backgrounds are substantial, each contact may only confirm the original objections by the parents (Burns, 1982). Religious background is important to most parents, regardless of their own religious participation. In addition, employment history, divorce, or substance abuse are family background factors of major concern to most parents (Brenton, 1985).

By the time children reach marriageable age, most parents have been employed 20 or more years and typically labored very hard to achieve their present station in life. Since parents usually hope that their children will achieve more in life than they did, a prospective mate for their child who is unambitious or lacking in social graces may be viewed as a potential future liability (Brenton, 1985). Such problems may arise because of differences between expectations and reality. Initial parental reactions are likely to be much more favorable if the prospective daughter-in-law or son-in-law fits their idealized image of a mate for their child.

Parent Problems

Parents are often influenced in their evaluation and/or acceptance of a mate for their child by issues that relate to their own problems as individuals or as parents (Jeffress, 1987). These problem areas include unresolved dependency on their daughter or son and loss of parental roles.

While some parents are mature, perceptive people who react unselfishly to their adult children's needs, others are not capable of fostering independence in their offspring. At first, children are totally dependent upon parents but gradually learn to become more independent. As children and adolescents seek independence, most parents increasingly relinquish their control. Some parents, however, have a strong need for their children to remain dependent, a fact which may become more evident as the young woman or man begins to date or goes away to college. This unresolved dependency is more likely to involve close mother-daughter ties (Brenton, 1985). The real fear is the loss of their child's love and dependence through marriage.

At least two major factors may produce this unhealthy emotional attachment between an adult child and her/his parents. First, a close relationship between the adult child and parent may be an attempt by the parent to compensate for an emotionally or physically absent spouse. Second, it may be an issue of control. The fact that a parent may not want to relinquish control over her/his child is significantly related to the use of harsh discipline in child-rearing practices (Jeffress, 1987).

The extent to which parents have invested time and energy in their roles as parents determines whether or not the marriage of their child will leave a vacuum to be filled. Given the nature of traditional gender roles, more mothers are affected than fathers because they have been immersed in daily child-care activities and spent more time listening to problems. Although parents may no longer play their familiar maternal and paternal roles, they may still feel very concerned and responsible for the welfare of their child. If children have not lived in the parental home for a considerable period of time before marriage, it is much easier for parents to adjust to the idea of their child's marriage (Brenton, 1985).

Handling Problems with In-Laws

One must be careful not to place oneself in an adversarial relationship with in-laws, because ultimately this circumstance is likely to escalate the conflict (Brenton, 1985). Initial small sacrifices to reduce in-law concerns often make no real difference in the long-term future plans of the young couple but will create a positive atmosphere by demonstrating consideration for the feelings of their in-laws.

To resolve conflict, it is important to first identify the problem and then meet with the in-law for a problem-solving discussion. In addressing the conflict, the following steps should be effective:

1. *Show mutual respect.* Try to understand the other person's point of view rather than exhibiting attitudes of rejection.
2. *Pinpoint the real issue.* Real issues often mask other factors brought to the conflict situation. The issue in an argument about a daughter-in-law working may actually relate to wishes of becoming a grandparent and fears that her biological clock will run down before conceiving.
3. *Seek areas of agreement.* There may be more agreement on problems with in-laws than initially realized. Through calm discussion, additional areas of agreement may be identified.

With marriage comes in-laws, for better or worse. Changes in in-law relationships that evolve over the family life cycle may be more sharply focused when grandchildren are added to the equation.

4. *Mutually work out solutions.* Conflicting parties should brainstorm and try to determine the best possible solution, and implement it as soon as possible (Brenton, 1985, p. 22).

Friendships and Marriage

When people marry, they do not cease to exist as separate individuals. No matter how much the marriage partners are in love or how committed they may be to one another, contacts with members of the opposite sex will continue. In the past, once the commitment to marry was made, each partner was supposed to either convert opposite-sex friendships into friendships that could be shared with the intended spouse or to discard the friendships in favor of new couple relationships (Bell, 1981). Any cross-sex friendships that were continued or formed after marriage were viewed as threats because of strong risks for emotional and/or sexual involvement. Also, in the past, women were viewed as being less vulnerable to the development of cross-sex friendships. With a high percentage of the labor force consisting of women, the opportunity is increasingly present for women as well as men to develop and maintain opposite-sex friendships. Therefore, the mix of friendship and marriage needs to be understood as it affects marital satisfaction.

Friendship Qualities

Early research not only determined that women disclosed more personal information about themselves to their female significant others but that female friendships were more spontaneous than those between men (Booth, 1972; Jourard, 1964). Women, when compared to men, have been found to converse more frequently about intimate topics, including daily and shared activities (see Table 8.4). Further, women reported greater depth of topics in personal and family conversations. Sports was the only topic that men were reported to discuss more frequently and in-depth.

When evaluating friendships, both women and men perceived cross-sex friendships as providing less help and loyalty than same-sex friendships. While men were more likely to view both types of friendships equally, women believed their cross-sex friendships provided less acceptance and less intimacy but more companionship than same-sex friendships (Rose, 1985).

Table 8.4: Depth of Conversation between Friends

	Woman-Woman			Man-Man		
Topic	In-depth	Somewhat in-depth	Not in-depth	In-depth	Somewhat in depth	Not in-depth
Family activities *	53%	44%	3%	33%	57%	10%
Family problems	49	39	13	29	49	22
Personal problems*	46	38	16	13	59	29
Doubts and fears	43	42	14	26	47	28
Reminiscences*	42	39	19	21	64	16
Friendship itself	40	40	21	24	47	29
Daily activities	37	53	10	23	54	23
Hobbies/shared activities	36	56	8	30	57	13
Religion and morals	34	48	18	28	42	30
Work*	29	49	22	38	55	7
Social/political issues	26	51	22	29	42	29
Community/civic affairs	23	63	14	29	52	19
Intimate relationship	23	56	21	16	41	44
Sex/sexual concerns	18	45	36	6	38	56
Sports*	16	22	62	21	56	23
Personal finances	14	41	45	16	49	36
Secrets about past	13	43	45	14	48	38

*Significant difference between women and men.

From E. J. Aries and F. L. Johnson, "Close Friendship in Adulthood: Conversational Content between Same-Sex Friends" in *Sex Roles*, 9:1190.

The Influence of Marital Status

Many persons believe that marriage should satisfy all of one's needs for friendship and in fact many partners are best friends. Some have found, however, that the majority of women and men do not consider their spouse as a "good friend" (Bell, 1981). Nevertheless, data do suggest that women are somewhat more likely than men to identify their spouses as good friends.

Gender differences in numbers of friends that have been identified appear to be related to the stages of the life cycle. Men have a greater number of friends from marriage to the **empty-nest stage** (children no longer home), whereas women have greater numbers of friends in the elderly stage, age 65 and over. Women who bear the responsibility for marriage, housework, and child rearing reduce their number of friends because less time is available for friendship. They report more friends than men after reaching age 65 because greater numbers of women lose their spouse through death than do men (Fischer & Oliker, 1983).

Competition to Marital Relationship

Whether or not having opposite-sex friendships while married is desirable is not really the issue. Whether or not cross-sex relationships are possible without an erotic component that leads inevitably to sexual involvement may be more to the point. One may argue that people are more than sexual beings and, thus, are capable of keeping their friendships on a platonic basis if they wish. On the other hand, many persons maintain that excluding sexual involvement from a woman-man relationship is itself a form of excessive emphasis on sexuality. However, despite the best intentions of friends, a sexual interest in the relationship will often surface as soon as empathy is established (Saline, 1975). While some persons will choose to abstain from sexual involvement because they fear that it will damage their marriage, others will choose to become sexual partners.

In an attempt to relate the number of friends to the life-cycle stage, married men under age 36, with and without children, were found to be much more likely to report a greater number of opposite-sex friendships among coworkers than were their wives (Fischer & Oliker, 1983). Since female cross-sex friends tend to be younger than their male friends, older wives may feel especially vulnerable. Husbands, on the other hand, may feel threatened because their wives are friends with an older man who may be higher in social, job, or financial status in comparison to themselves. The key to the maintenance of a healthy cross-sex friendship appears to be that both friends are quite aware of the nature of their relationship and clear with each other about the relationship boundaries. They can, for example, define the boundaries to exclude sexual involvement even though they find each other very sexually attractive (Saline, 1975). Many couples have concluded that cross-sex friendships are highly desirable. Successful friendships and marriage, like other areas of marital adjustment, depend on the maturity of the individuals involved and the ability to communicate concerns.

Summary

- Women's roles have changed greatly in recent years with most wanting careers, marriage, and children, and some wanting careers without marriage or to remain child-free. Traditional expectations of men that their wives will subordinate their work to the demands of home and family life often lead to marital conflict.
- Major qualities found to be associated with marital satisfaction are similarity of sexual needs, empathy for partner, sense of commitment to relationship, age at marriage, religiosity, and self-actualization of marital partners.
- The attributes of good couple relationships include promoting healthy belief patterns and healthy interaction patterns.
- Two significant tasks of early marriage have been defined for young couples: separating from parents and working out relationship rules of intimacy and power.
- Marital power has been defined as the capability of achieving desired goals or outcomes. Healthy couples agree on the distribution of power, with equality of power based on respect for each other.
- Intimacy needs are best met by couples who move through the stages of communication: clichés, information exchange, everyday feelings, and private thoughts and feelings.
- Before marriage the stage can be set for good in-law relationships.
- The mix of friendship and marriage needs to be understood as it affects marital satisfaction.

Questions for Critical Reflection

1. Do you believe it best to share everything about past love relationships with your marriage partner? If so, when? Can one have trust without complete honesty?
2. "Love makes the world go around" was the title of a once popular song to which someone added "but romance makes the trip worthwhile"! Do you think romance is a lasting reality in marriages that succeed? What evidence can you offer?
3. In what way does self-actualization contribute to marital satisfaction? As one becomes more self-actualized, is the couple unit threatened? Why?
4. A common belief is that in-laws cause a marriage to fail. Can you give reasons why this assumption is false?
5. A person who does not like any of your friends would be a poor risk as a marriage partner. What is the major reason for this risk?

Suggested Readings

Aldous, J. (1978). *Family careers: Developmental change in families.* New York: Wiley. A description of generational kinship relations through detailed analysis of family life cycle.

Crosby, J. F. (1991). *Illusion and disillusion: The self in love and marriage* (4th ed.). Belmont, CA: Wadsworth. Excellent self-help book on making love relationships better.

Greenblat, C. S., & Cottle, T. J. (1980). *Getting married.* New York: McGraw-Hill. A scholarly investigation of the transition from singlehood to marriage and the early period of marital adjustment.

Kimball, G. (1983). *The 50–50 marriage.* Boston: Beacon. A social survey of egalitarian marriages.

Pogrebin, L. C. (1983). *Family politics: Love and power on an intimate frontier.* New York: McGraw-Hill. A blend of personal experience and theoretical analysis describing ways in which society both glorifies and undermines the family.

Rubin, L. B. (1983). *Intimate strangers: Men and women together.* New York: Harper & Row. A description of differences between women and men and their effects on such critical issues as intimacy, sexuality, dependency, and work.

CHAPTER 9

Managing Marital Conflict

". . . The seemingly required condition—that couples be in serious trouble—means, inevitably, that help for many will come too late, especially since the way out of marriage is now an open door."
David Mace, 1987

OUTLINE

Marriage is the question in life—not the answer. Unless the question happens to be, "What is the name of the intimate relationship in which there is more potential for conflict than in any other?" In spite of 1.18 million marriages that ended in divorce in 1989, marriage is too often viewed as a blissful state in which two people find eternal happiness as their reward for finding the "right" mate (National Center for Health Statistics, 1990e). However, reality suggests that "good" marriages do not just happen. They require constant diligence on the part of each partner to make the relationship work harmoniously. This reality usually becomes painfully apparent early in the marriage when the first serious conflict arises. Young couples who are unprepared for the realities of marriage may believe that there is something drastically wrong with their relationship. Those fortunate enough to be forearmed with knowledge from the family science field recognize that conflict is inevitable in any close relationship. Creatively dealing with this conflict is not only a challenge, but a necessity, for success in marriage (Crosby, 1991).

Origins of Marital Conflict

Marriage creates a state of legalized intimacy between two persons who have professed their undying love for each other. No other relationship promises more than "till death do us part." Conflict in marriage results from two factors: the intimacy of the marital relationship and the different gender-role viewpoints of the spouses based on their background characteristics (Argyle, Henderson, & Furnham, 1985). Add to this equation basic human characteristics such as secretiveness along with inaccurate and inconsistent reporting, and the stage is set for mistrust and conflict between marital partners (Dhir & Markman, 1986). Even when spouses use the same information, they often draw different conclusions resulting in conflict.

Certainty of Conflict

The point has already been made that like death and taxes in life, conflict in marriage is inevitable. Research on satisfaction and conflict in long-term relationships, comparing spouse, close same-sex friend, work superior, and work associate, found that spouses scored highest as a source of conflict. But, paradoxically, spouses also scored highest as a source of satisfaction. The fact that younger spouses reported more conflict and less satisfaction suggests that effectively managing marital conflict is a long-term process (Argyle & Furnham, 1983).

It is helpful for young married couples to realize that marriage is a uniquely intense, emotional relationship in which a high level of conflict is normal. Formal education in marriage and family or participation in marriage preparation programs will, in some cases, lead to such realizations. In one Canadian study, Catholic couples who had participated in premarital preparation programs evidenced the traditional seven areas of marital conflict that have been reflected in the literature since the 1940s: sex, finances, children, in-laws, friends, social activities, and religion (Bader, Riddle, & Sinclair, 1981; Landis & Landis, 1977). By the mid-1970s, the areas of communication, household tasks, husband's job, and time differences had emerged. It was not until the 1980s that the wife's job, attention, and affection were added as areas of conflict (Bader et al., 1981). Interestingly, in spite of changing sexual mores, sex is no less of an adjustment problem than it was 50 years ago (Davidson & Darling, 1989b). In fact, sex, which was rated next to last in disagreements prior to marriage, was ranked third by the 5th year (see Table 9.1). Religious ritual, religious experience, and, to a lesser degree, religious belief have all been found to be significantly related to adjustment in marriage (Wilson & Filsinger, 1986). Therefore, one may question why religion was consistently ranked as the area of least disagreement in the Canadian study. Logically, it may be the one area in which there is less disagreement initially since the majority of marriages are religiously homogamous, as was especially true of this predominately Catholic sample. Also, if differences do exist, they are apparent prior to marriage and, therefore, are more quickly resolved (Shehan, Bock, & Lee, 1990). Overall, changes in the areas of marital conflict seem to reflect the increasing importance of meeting emotional needs in marriage relationships, a task that has only within recent years emerged as a fundamental function of marriage. These data suggest then that some conflict is inevitable in marital relationships, but is it desirable?

Desirability of Conflict

All conflict can be potentially destructive for a marital relationship as well as damaging to the individual marriage partners. Particularly if marital conflict is viewed as a chance to win an argument rather than as an opportunity to reach solutions to problems, it will be destructive (Crosby, 1991). However, if the conflict is handled in a constructive manner, the relationship may actually be strengthened. This is especially true if it occurs early in the relationship and forces the couple

Table 9.1: Disagreement Areas

Disagreement Areas	Premarriage	Six Months	One Year	Five Years
Husband's Job	74% (1)	75% (4)	68% (6)	76% (4)
Time and Attention	74 (1)	76 (3)	86 (2)	88 (1)
Household Tasks	66 (3)	87 (1)	91 (1)	88 (1)
Social Activities	66 (3)	51 (11)	71 (4)	65 (9)
Wife's Relatives	64 (5)	56 (9)	71 (4)	72 (6)
Handling Money	62 (6)	79 (2)	76 (3)	72 (6)
Husband's Friends	61 (7)	63 (6)	51 (12)	52 (11)
Wife's Job	56 (8)	63 (6)	62 (10)	53 (10)
Affection	56 (8)	65 (5)	67 (7)	76 (4)
Wife's Friends	54 (10)	50 (12)	46 (13)	42 (12)
Husband's Relatives	49 (11)	52 (10)	67 (7)	72 (6)
Children	44 (12)	48 (13)	54 (11)	42 (12)
Sex	41 (13)	62 (8)	64 (9)	78 (3)
Religion	25 (14)	21 (14)	19 (14)	28 (14)

Note: Numbers in parentheses refer to rank.
Source: Data from F. Bader, R. Riddle, and C. Sinclair, *Do Marriage Preparation Programs Really Help?*, paper presented at the 1981 meeting of the National Council on Family Relations Conference, Milwaukee, WI, p. 9.

to work on their relationship rules. Constructive conflict provides opportunities to clarify similarities and dissimilarities, to find methods for coping with future conflicts, to identify areas where greater communication and adaptation are needed, and to promote greater understanding of the other marital partner (Knapp, 1984).

Evidence of the need to engage in constructive conflict can be found in a study of divorced persons in which almost one half of the respondents indicated having seldom quarreled during their marriage. It could be argued that failure to communicate about sources of disagreement apparently contributed to the ending of their marriage (Hayes, Stinnett, & DeFrain, 1981). Persons who believe that positive marital outcomes result from their own efforts and abilities are likely to be effective problem solvers. Such couples report higher levels of general marital satisfaction (Miller, Lefcourt, Holmes, Ware, & Saleh, 1986).

Causes of Conflict

Establishing the causes of conflict is an intriguing task. One approach would be to identify specific problem areas within the marital relationship and frequency of occurrence. As previously stated, those problem areas currently cited in various studies most often include financial matters, use of leisure time, personal habits, child rearing, domestic responsibilities, career demands, in-laws, friends, and sexual matters (Knapp, 1984). But this identification-of-problems approach is rather superficial in nature because the often stated causes are symptoms of deeper, unresolved issues. The real sources of many disagreements are often hidden. From such a perspective, the four most common underlying sources of reported marital conflict are unrealistic marital expectations, role incompetence, external stress, and lack of partner similarity (see Table 9.2).

Undesirable Behaviors

Lack of partner similarity may be particularly evidenced in what is perceived to be undesirable behavior in a mate. Even if a person has annoying personal habits such as lack of neatness and odd eating or sleeping patterns, these habits will be a problem only if her/his partner does not value this behavior. Many disagreements emerge as marriage partners engage in their normal daily activities, behaving in ways that the other partner considers unwise and/or inappropriate. Examples of such behavior include handling of child-rearing responsibilities, spending of money, and allocating amount of leisure time spent with friends (Argyle & Furnham, 1983). Failure to achieve the necessary developmental tasks leading to adulthood may also underlie what is considered by some partners to be maladaptive or undesirable behavior. For example, a mate's nightly stop at the local tavern on the way home may simply evidence a cultural ritual, or it could indicate

Table 9.2: The 10 Most Common Sources of Marital Conflict

1. *Expectations*—unrealistic expectations about marriage.
2. *Role competence*—failure of partner(s) to perform expected role functions.
3. *External stress*—job stress, illness, environmental changes, and familial problems.
4. *Homogamy*—lack of partner similarity.
5. *Self-esteem*—low self-esteem leading to negative coping strategies.
6. *Family involvement*—conflicting loyalties between one's family and marital partner.
7. *Communication*—inadequate or deceptive communication skills.
8. *Children*—time, energy, and money devoted to children creates loyalty conflicts.
9. *Mental health*—presence of mental health problems in partner(s).
10. *Congruity of adult development*—unable to solve problems due to arrested development.

From O. J. W. Bjorksten, "Marital Conflict and Sexual Dysfunction" in S. F. Pariser, et al. (eds.), *Clinical Sexuality*.

having missed the developmental stage of adolescent peer approval. Again, the behavior itself is not necessarily damaging to the marital relationship, but differing partner perceptions of its appropriateness may cause problems. As indicated earlier, these may be symptoms of unmet needs. When persistent undesirable behavior reflects personal inadequacies or too great a difference in background factors, the marriage can be said to be at risk.

Discrepancies in Role Expectations and Performance

When one or both partners fail to perform expected roles, problems may arise. The wife, for example, may expect the husband to assist with household duties such as cleaning the kitchen and bathrooms, whereas the husband may prefer to read the newspaper at the end of his day. Or the husband may place great importance on his wife's role of entertaining his business clients, while she may not want to play the role of traditional homemaker/hostess. This may especially be true if she has her own career (Knapp, 1984).

Such discrepancies in role performance are usually based on expectations derived in families of orientation. Early patterns observed in family settings are powerful determinants of beliefs concerning who should enact certain roles. Finances are another area in which this issue quickly becomes apparent. If, when growing up, the wife's father paid the monthly bills, but in her husband's family, the mother assumed this duty, their assumptions of who will do so in their own marriage may clash. Conflict is unlikely only if family financial experiences were handled somewhat the same in both families of orientation.

Diverse Values

Religion and childhood socialization experiences can create a fertile ground for disagreements over the handling of various daily issues and behaviors within the marriage. Differences over sexual expression, child rearing, or the use of alcohol are examples of diverse values resulting in marital discord (Knapp, 1984). In a dual-career marriage, the issue of who, if either, will stay home during the early childhood years touches deeply held values about the rights and responsibilities of children and parents. When one's values and behaviors are incongruent, feelings of guilt may result. In such circumstances, one partner may attempt to switch the blame for her/his actions to the other spouse in order to justify their own behavior. Such responses may trigger feelings of bitterness, irritability, and/or jealousy (Warner & Olson, 1981).

Dependence/Independence Imbalance

Unrealistic expectations about marriage may tip the delicate balance of dependence/independence in a marriage. If partners believe their relationship should meet all of each other's needs, a relationship will result in which one or both will suffer the loss of individual identity. After marriage, some spouses become concerned over what they perceive to be a loss of their individual identity. Despite being very much in love, they do not wish to totally lose their sense of independence (Argyle & Furnham, 1983). Women who feel that they have less control over their lives after marriage are much more likely to have low marital satisfaction (Madden & Janoff-Bulman, 1981). Areas of conflict that result from perceived loss of independence may be reflected in career decisions, choice of friends, and perceived lack of privacy.

D needs or dependency needs have been defined as illegitimate developmental deficits. Since all deficiency needs must be satisfied in some manner, persons go to great lengths to do so, including distorting reality. For example, persons with low self-esteem resulting from a deficiency need may misinterpret their partner's willingness to meet their illegitimate needs as love. Abdicating the responsibility for meeting one's own needs is characteristic of a D-needs person. Marriages

Major messages are being transmitted by body language in this scenario. Do the clues indicate the problem to be inadequate communication skills or self-inadequacy?

based on such love usually involve unhealthy dependency. In his classification of marriages as dependent, independent, and interdependent, Crosby (1991) has referred to such a dependent state as an **A-frame marriage.** In such a relationship, as the structure of the A-frame marriage indicates, there is so much "leaning" on one's partner that the individuals are unable to stand alone. The **H-frame marriage,** on the other hand, is one of almost total independence. In fact, there is so much independence in an H-frame marriage that not enough couple identity develops. Finally, the **M-frame marriage** balances dependence and independence to form an interdependent relationship. In this marriage, healthy individual identity is retained, while meaningful couple identity is developed (Crosby, 1991). When one has achieved normal passage from early dependency on parents to and through the independence of adolescence, one is prepared for the interdependence required in a healthy marriage.

Communication Deficits

Most studies reveal a positive relationship between good communication and marital satisfaction (Noller, 1984). Conclusions are that good communication is a necessary precursor rather than the result of marital satisfaction. Marital communication is a process involving three elements: individuals; relationships; and environments, both inward and outward. The people, places, and things that make up the outward environment influence the values, goals, personal thoughts, and feelings of the inner environment. How are these elements of communication processed? First, the spouse creates meaning out of ideas, events, or experiences that are received from internal or external self-messages. Secondly, signals are transmitted to the mate that reflect personal meaning (Strong, 1983). Either inadequate communication skills and/or deliberate deception can sabotage the elements or the process of communication. By marriageable age, it is much easier to correct or change one's relationships and the outward environment than the inner self. Therefore, self-inadequacies such as low self-esteem or poor mental health are most likely to result in more serious communication deficits.

Developing Effective Marital Communication

Effective communication between spouses is the basis of all marital problem solving, including the resolution of serious conflict. In general, wives, who consistently report more difficulties and resentful feelings about marriage than husbands, have also indicated more desire for better communication and understanding (Voydanoff, 1985). In a survey of married couples, communication was one of two main marital problems indicated by the majority of respondents. The persistent issue of sexuality was the other (Renshaw, 1983). A survey of professional family therapists revealed that poor communication was viewed as the key to marital problems by 90% of their clients entering therapy. Even though therapists are aware that reasons stated for seeking help often camouflage the real problem, such an overwhelming response is noteworthy ("MDT Survey," 1986). In order to relate effectively, marriage partners must learn how to communicate with one another in ways that will reveal their deepest underlying feelings and needs. When wives and husbands feel that such self-revelations will be used in constructive ways to promote the well-being of the relationship, commitment to one another will be reinforced.

Communication: Life's Umbrella

The late renowned therapist, Virginia Satir, offered many insights into the process of communication. She pictured communication as a huge umbrella that covers and affects all that goes on between humans. "Once a human being has arrived on this earth, communication is the largest single factor determining what kinds of relationships he makes with others and what happens to him in the world about him" (Satir, 1972, p. 30). The contributions of Satir are often used by therapists to help couples clarify the concepts needed to understand communication. First, all communication is learned. Perhaps as early as age 5, a person has developed, through billions of communication experiences, many fixed ideas that will guide her/him throughout life. How a person sees one's self, what one can expect from others, and what seems either possible or impossible are likely to remain unchanged unless one has exceedingly unusual experiences. The insight that communication is a learned process is valuable to persons who may wish to change their ways of communication (Satir, 1972).

Everyday communication between marriage partners may occur via words—verbal or written; nonwords—symbols, sounds, or silence; facial expression—jeers or smiles; touch—no touch, nurturant touch, playful touch, or coercive touch; and behavior—a combination of these elements in a recurrent pattern (Renshaw, 1983). Added to these tangible elements are expectations based on prior experience and values, concepts of what one "ought" or "should" do (Satir, 1972).

Patterns of Communication

Satir delineated four seemingly universal, destructive patterns in communication from her work of thirty years. The roles enacted with these patterns are placater, blamer, computer, and distracter (see Table 9.3). The **placater** is characterized as a martyr-like "yes person" who always needs approval from others. The **blamer** is a fault finder, dictator, or superior who insists on cutting down everyone to enhance her/his own image. One who is seen as a very correct, reasonable person, using the longest words possible, and fearing feelings is labeled a **computer.** Finally, characteristics of the **distractor** include feelings of loneliness, purposelessness, being nonfocused, and internal dizziness (Satir, 1972). With any of these patterns, people unknowingly give double-level messages where words say one thing, but facial expression, body position, breathing, muscles, and voice tone say quite another. Double-level messages are used by persons who have low self-esteem, are fearful of hurting others, worry about retaliation from others, and fear loss of the relationship (Satir, 1972).

It is important for marriage partners to be able to recognize their own destructive patterns of communication. An effective way to do this is to identify such patterns used in their families of orientation. Chances are that these same patterns will reappear, especially under stress, in families of procreation unless a conscious effort has been made to eliminate them. With effort, partners can "unlearn" destructive behaviors and "learn" constructive skills for communication.

Communication: Closure vs. Disclosure

Besides abandoning destructive patterns, effective communication in marriage requires that the wife and husband disclose at equally high levels. This process will lead to a communication system in which there are equally high levels of understanding, esteem building,

Table 9.3: Universal Patterns of Communication

Pattern	Action	Example
Placater		
Words	Agree	"Whatever you say is okay"
Body	Pacifies	"I am a helpless being"
Feelings	Restrains	"I feel worthless"
Blamer		
Words	Disagree	"You never do anything right"
Body	Blames	"I am the boss"
Feelings	Restrains	"I am lonely and unsuccessful"
Computer		
Words	Ultrareasonable	"Careful observation will reveal the facts"
Body	Computes	"I am cool, calm"
Feelings	Restrains	"I feel vulnerable"
Distracter		
Words	Irrelevant	Nonsense words
Body	Imbalanced	"I am on the move"
Feelings	Restrains	"No one cares, what's the purpose?"

and respect for each other. Open disclosure rather than selective disclosure is associated with high levels of communication satisfaction among married couples. However, the majority of wives and husbands in one study preferred, and actually practiced, selective disclosure (Allen, Reisetter, & Strong, 1990). Whether open or closed, if there is imbalance in disclosure, the marital relationship is likely to be at risk of failure.

Marital Satisfaction and Disclosure Levels

Several studies on marital satisfaction in the 1980s focused on the role of self-disclosure. One study found that high levels of disclosure were associated with greater marital satisfaction (Jorgensen & Gaudy, 1980). Generally, self-disclosure and sensitivity to a spouse's feelings have both been found to be associated with greater marital happiness (Noller, 1984). Using a sample of married graduate students, researchers found that the more partners differed in terms of effective self-disclosure, the lower their marital adjustment. However, persons who indicated high levels of marital adjustment were suspected of exaggerating amounts of disclosures in order to eliminate distress from their relationships (Davidson, Balswick, & Halverson, 1983).

Both quantity and quality of self-disclosure appear related to marital satisfaction. Two studies have found both low quantity and low quality of self-disclosure to be detrimental to marital satisfaction, especially for wives (Hansen & Schuldt, 1984; Schumm, Barnes, Bollman, Jurich, & Bugaighis, 1986). A later study found wives' marital satisfaction to be related to their husband's use of self-disclosing skills such as sensitivity, spirituality, physical affection, self-inclusion, and honesty (Bell, Daly, & Gonzalez, 1987). A number of self-disclosing skills were evidenced in a typology of behavioral strategies developed to describe behaviors believed to be associated with maintaining and enhancing the **affinity** (close relation) in marriages (see Table 9.4). Another useful way of analyzing communication patterns is to classify married couples by their styles of communication. These communication styles might be said to be either low or high in terms of needs and problems disclosed.

Styles of Communication

Communication styles can be labeled as either closed or open. Research on communication among couples has identified two closed styles—controlling and conventional and two open ones—speculative and contactive. A **controlling style** of communication minimizes the importance of the other partner's experience and shows little awareness of respect for her/his needs. Mutual exploration of needs is likely to be discouraged

Table 9.4: A Typology of Behavioral Strategies to Maintain Affinity in Marriage

Strategy	Description	Example
Concede control	Spouse allows partner to exert dominance.	S/he lets partner decide what the two should do for recreation.
Conversational rule-keeping	Spouse converses politely with partner.	S/he does not interrupt partner.
Equality	Spouse presents self as partner's equal.	S/he does not act superior by issuing orders.
Faithfulness	Spouse is faithful to partner.	S/he does not engage in extramarital sexual relationships.
Honesty	Spouse is honest and sincere in interactions with partner.	S/he does not lie, cheat, or engage in pretense.
Inclusion of other	Spouse invites partner to participate in social activities.	S/he asks partner to go shopping with her/him.
Listening	Spouse is attentive to what partner says.	S/he demonstrates listening by being nonverbally responsive.
Openness	Spouse self-discloses to partner.	Spouse reveals her/his feelings, fears, and insecurities.
Physical affection	Spouse is physically affectionate with partner.	S/he frequently engages in sexual relations with partner.
Reliability	Spouse is dependable in carrying out her/his responsibilities to partner and family.	S/he promptly completes household duties.
Self-concept confirmation	Spouse tries to build partner's self-esteem.	S/he sincerely compliments partner.
Sensitivity	Spouse acts warmly, caring, and empathic toward partner.	S/he is sympathetic when partner faces problems.
Shared spirituality	Spouse and partner share spiritual activities.	They pray and attend religious services together.
Verbal affection	Spouse is verbally affectionate with partner.	S/he expresses loving messages to partner.

From R. A. Bell, et al., "Affinity Maintenance in Marriage and Its Relationship to Women's Marital Satisfaction" in *Journal of Marriage and the Family,* 49:448.

by the expression of strong feelings and intentions. In the **conventional style,** the person glosses over issues and needs through small talk on such topics as weather and politics, thus giving the appearance of communication while actually preventing disclosure of needs and problems. Using the **speculative style,** the partner is willing to explore issues and consider the other person's point of view but is unable to reveal her/his own feelings. Finally, the **contactive style** involves respect and appreciation for the needs of others as well as a revelation of the person's innermost needs. Using this pattern, partners work to resolve issues and fulfill their own needs as well as those of their partner (Hawkins, Weisberg, & Ray, 1977). A subsequent study, using these communication styles, found that both spouses perceived themselves as using more open than closed behaviors. Generally, wives characterized their husbands as "falling far short" of their preferred communication patterns. However, no significant differences were found between communication behavior claimed by wives themselves and the behavior attributed to them by their husbands (Hawkins, Weisberg, & Ray, 1980).

Gender Differences in Communication

A significant factor in effective marital communication relates to basic gender differences in the communication process. For example, when talking with others, women prefer expressions of empathy while men prefer "facts they can use." In a survey that illustrates this point, 63% of women but only 43% of men reported telephoning someone of their own sex "just to talk" (Sherman & Haas, 1984). Most men view themselves as more precise, dramatic, and impression-leaving in their conversations, while women consider themselves to be more animated and friendly during conversation. Men are also much more likely to exhibit dominance during marital communication than women. For example in conversation, men more frequently interrupt, talk more, talk simultaneously, and pause less often (Honeycutt, Wilson, & Parker, 1982). In general, women appear to be far better in sending and receiving nonverbal messages. Furthermore, wives often send out emotional messages based on their perceptions of their spouses' emotions, but husbands, on many occasions, fail to decode these nonverbal messages. This outcome may lead to frustration on the part of the wife or perceptions by the husband that his wife is too "emotional" (Notarius & Johnson, 1982). Such perceptions are based, in part, on the fact that emotional intimacy for women means talking things over, while for men it means doing something together. For these reasons, marriage may be actually perceived as less psychologically demanding by many men (Goleman, 1986).

In relationships, women are more likely to approach conflict in an indirect manner, taking an action independent of the partner. However, men are more likely to use direct approaches involving a give-and-take approach of bargaining or persuasion. Indirect strategies would include withdrawal or dropping hints whereas direct strategies would include asking or talking. But, men are more likely to withdraw from discussion of an issue during a high level of marital conflict, especially if the issue has been raised by the wife (Noller & Fitzpatrick, 1990). Evidence suggests that men often assume compliance from their female partner whereas women usually expect noncompliance from their male partner as they choose an approach to resolve a conflict (Falbo & Peplau, 1980). Nevertheless, satisfaction in communication for both wives and husbands is associated with feeling that their perspective had been understood during the communication process (Allen & Thompson, 1984).

Personal Factors in Effective Communication

Among the most important personal characteristics that have been identified for good marital communication are openness, relaxation, expressiveness, friendliness, and attentiveness (Honeycutt et al., 1982). There is evidence that certain feelings of competence are also important variables and that effective communication can only be established if the person believes that she/he can successfully perform the required or preferred response (Witkin, Edleson, Rose, & Hall, 1983).

A person's emotional state obviously affects her/his ability to communicate. A study of distressed and nondistressed married couples determined that distressed wives and husbands perceived words spoken and heard as more angry, critical, and unpleasant than nondistressed couples. However, both groups of spouses (distressed and nondistressed) reported sending messages that they believed to be more positive than the messages were perceived (Schachter & O'Leary, 1985). Among spouses receiving marital therapy, nondistressed spouses were more likely to attribute unselfish motivations, positive intent, and praise to their partner's behaviors. In comparison, distressed spouses were more likely to assign blame and to believe their partners had selfish motivations and behaviors (Fincham, Beach, & Baucom, 1987).

A comparison of communication practices of cohabiting and married couples found no significant differences in three areas of communication: verbal, nonverbal, and sexual communication. However, age was significant. The younger respondents, regardless of their life-style, were more likely to talk about personal problems, talk about disagreements, explain sexual disinterest, and tell their partner when sexual activity was enjoyable (Yelsma, 1986).

Components of Quality Communication

As indicated earlier, quality communication in marriage is the interpersonal process whereby marriage partners learn to achieve and maintain understanding of each other. Good communication uses various levels of thinking strategies. If the reasoning process that is used to interpret discordant messages is complex and abstract, the marital partner will be less likely to automatically react in anger. For example, in the case of home-management disputes, discord is usually settled through the use of generalized social norms that require low levels of thinking. More complex marital and communication problems, however, require a more involved process of higher level reasoning (Bruch, Levo, & Arisohn, 1984).

Since the need for good communication has been clearly established, it is appropriate to summarize from the literature some of its key ingredients. These components are applicable not only in marital relationships but also in love relationships in general. Therefore, the following elements can be used to access one's level of communication skills:

1. *Maintain a "safe" climate*—Both partners should be made to feel secure enough not to be threatened by what is said or worry about judgmental statements being made.
2. *Be a good listener*—Learn to not interrupt by saying, "Yes, but . . . ," so that feelings/meanings attached to both spoken and unspoken words can be determined.
3. *Self-disclose*—One must be willing to share her/his real feelings and thoughts about the issue under consideration.

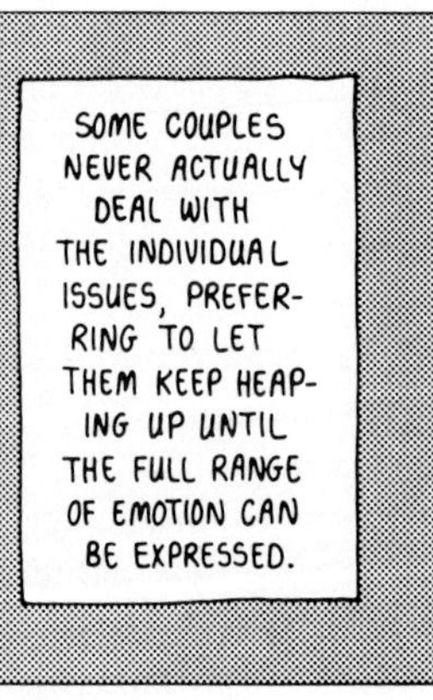

4. *Differ, argue, and confront*—Occasional recognition of a flaw, if handled constructively, can lead to problem resolution.
5. *Praise and recognize*—It is very important that attention, praise, and recognition be given to the other person so that she/he will feel worthwhile and be better able to cope with any stress being produced by a disagreement.
6. *Discuss touchy subjects*—While some topics may provoke anxiety or apprehension, in a caring, loving relationship, no subject should be off limits for discussion (Bienvenu, 1986, pp. 8–10).

Psychological Games in Relationships

Communication is often comprised of psychological games, even in marital relationships. A psychological game has been defined as "a recurring set of transactions, often repetitive, superficially rational, with a concealed motivation; or . . . as a series of transactions with a gimmick" (Berne, 1964, p. 11). In psychological games, there is no honesty, intimacy, or openness in relationships. James and Jongeward (1973), who pioneered the practical application of transactional analysis, declared that psychological games, as most games, are played to win, but those who are winners in life do not play! Since psychological games are programmed by the individual's ego states, to view game playing in a better perspective, one must first understand the application of transactional analysis to individual personality. Each personality has three facets that serve as sources of behavior: parent, adult, and child ego states. The **parent ego state** is that part of the personality that contains attitudes and behaviors from early authority figures, mainly parents. Its outward expression may be either judgmental, critical, or nurturing, depending on the balance of parent messages received. Inwardly, old parent messages influence the inner child to act, think, or feel as her/his parents did. The **adult ego state** is the computer part of the personality that gathers objective information. It is always the least developed state. When acting intelligently, adaptably, or realistically, one is in the adult state. The **child ego state** is comprised of all the natural instincts as well as **parent tapes** (mental recordings of parental messages). When acting impulsively, one is usually in her/his child state (James & Jongeward, 1973). A balance of nurturing messages in parent tapes results in spontaneous natural child actions. If the parent tapes are mainly critical or judgmental, the response will be that of either a compliant or rebellious child.

Psychological Marital Games

It has been suggested that because so little opportunity exists for emotional intimacy in daily life, the majority of our waking time is spent playing psychological games with our relationship partner. Over the years, a number of different terms have been employed to identify the many games played in marriage. Although the concept of psychological games has been applied by many different authors, it was originally popularized by Eric Berne (1964) in his book *Games People Play.* Only three games will be considered to illustrate the effects of game playing:

1. *Courtroom.* The psychological game of "courtroom" usually involves three players: the "plaintiff"—wife or husband, the "defendant"—other spouse, and the "judge"—therapist or friend. The plaintiff tells the judge what

the defendant did, while the defendant responds defensively, "This is what really happened." The wife and husband want the third party to judge her/him as "right," but any problems are not really solved. Although one marriage partner may believe she/he is actually wrong, she/he would never admit this possibility.

2. *Look how hard I've tried.* This psychological game is illustrated by the instance in which the husband wants a divorce, while his wife wishes to continue the marriage. The husband falsely claims that he does not want a divorce and agrees to see a therapist, but after a brief period of time, his behavior becomes worse than ever. The wife is then "forced" to file for divorce, and the husband considers himself blameless since the wife took the initiative to file for divorce. He can then say, "Look how hard I tried."
3. *Sweetheart.* This psychological game is typically played in social situations where one marriage partner very subtly depreciates the other partner in public. It may be a remark about her/his abilities that is so disguised that it does not appear derogatory. The spouse is then asked, "Isn't that right, sweetheart?" The psychological pay-off is that the spouse feels bad about herself/himself (Berne, 1964, pp. 96–109).

In many instances, persons acting as manipulators may not be consciously aware of their psychological game-playing behavior. Nevertheless, a person who becomes a skilled manipulator in using psychological games allows them to control her/his own life-style as well as to exploit or control others.

Learning to Manage Conflict

Many people, believing that quarreling or fighting in a marital relationship is an indication of personal failure, often attempt to hide such conflict from friends and other family members. This belief that anger and conflict should be absent from marital relationships is rooted in the premise that love represents a power opposite of hate (Crosby, 1991). When marital conflict escalates, the marital partners may actively challenge each other's weaknesses, often with devastating effects. Research evidence indicates that when wives and husbands disagree, they usually have different goals: Women want to resolve the problem in order to achieve emotional intimacy, whereas men simply want to avoid a blow-up (Goleman, 1986).

Barriers to Conflict Resolution

The distinguishing feature of a happy marriage is not how much conflict occurs but how well it is managed. However, rather than constructively dealing with conflict, many wives and husbands hope the problem will magically disappear. Fear of identifying the sources of marital conflict is a major barrier in resolving it. Some seem to believe that if they name the problem, it is somehow worse. In actuality, husbands are more likely to report higher marital adjustment when their wives have evidenced a high level of assertiveness related to identifying problems and resolving conflict (Reath, Piercy, Hovestadt, & Oliver, 1980). Failure to effectively manage conflict can result in negative consequences that will begin the slow progression toward serious marital and family discord (Gottman, 1979). Among mothers and fathers in distressed marriages and single-parent situations, partner conflict was found to be related to parenting stress, negative child behaviors, negative disciplinary approaches, and negative child-parent interactions (Webster-Stratton, 1989).

Undesirable Substitutes

Failure to manage marital conflict may also result when undesirable behaviors become substitutes for dealing with the actual anger aroused by the conflict. Among the undesirable substitutes are physical illness, depression, and alcohol abuse. The sick role has long been thought of as a means for women to sabotage their traditional gender roles (Connors, 1985). Stereotypically, "Not tonight, dear, I have a headache" has become the game some women play to avoid unwanted sexual overtures. A common myth exists that suggests many married women pretend illness to avoid the responsibilities of unrewarding domestic duties.

Depression is simply anger turned inward. As a substitute for anger, it is, at the subconscious level, a more socially acceptable response than displaying anger toward one's spouse. But chronic depression can serve as a barrier to establishing or maintaining emotional intimacy and can lead to serious illnesses (James, 1988). A note of caution is in order when comparing differences in reported rates of depression for women and men. Traditionally, women have been socialized to acknowledge emotional feelings associated with their problems including depression, guilt, and low self-esteem, whereas men have been taught to avoid any signs of inability to cope. Therefore, women may be more likely to be represented in statistics on depression and mental illness (Williams, J. H., 1987).

Persistent, unresolved marital conflict can lead to alcohol abuse as a form of escape. When alcohol abuse occurs, communication within the marriage becomes limited. The conflicts that develop between spouses lead to a reluctance to exchange feelings, and when communication does occur, it often leads to angry outbursts (Throwe, 1986). Fluctuations between episodes of sobriety and drunkenness cause much stress in a family. Oftentimes when a spouse becomes an alcoholic, the other marriage partner takes on her/his role and responsibilities within the family. Given the nature of our socialization experiences, if the wife assumes portions of the husband's role and responsibilities, her strength is likely to create even greater marital conflict since it threatens his masculine ego (Downs, 1982).

Defense Mechanisms

Defense mechanisms are cognitive devices or behaviors for tampering with reality to avoid emotional pain. They are behaviors for defending one's self-esteem. There is nothing inherently wrong with the use of defense mechanisms. All persons at some time use them to nurture wounded egos. They are dangerous only if used extensively to distort reality and when they interfere with other desired goals in relationships. While the mind uses these devices to cope with anxiety and stressful feelings, defense mechanisms may adversely affect conflict resolution (Goleman, 1985b). Five commonly used defense mechanisms are escapism, rationalization, projection, displacement, and intellectualization.

Escapism involves either direct or indirect denial that a problem exists. By departing either physically or mentally from too hurtful a situation, the person uses avoidance to escape from dealing with the problem. Such behavior may include escaping through recreational pursuits, abuse of substances such as alcohol or cocaine, or extended work activities (Goleman, 1985b). Through the process of **rationalization,** persons block out the true impulses behind their behavior. They falsely justify their behavior when the real reasons are too threatening to their self-esteem. For example, a spouse seeking to have an affair with a coworker justifies the action on the grounds that her/his spouse does not understand her/his sexual needs (Goleman, 1985b). Projecting one's feelings and/or behaviors onto someone else is another commonly used defense mechanism. **Projection** is inappropriately placing blame or attributing one's own unethical desires to others. By shifting the focus of attention, the other person is put on the defensive (Goleman, 1985b). Such actions typically create moods of hostility and defensiveness on the part of both partners (Magid, 1986). Through **displacement,** feelings and frustrations are replaced or transferred onto insignificant events. One spouse, for example, may be experiencing difficulties with her/his in-laws so any negative feelings are transferred to her/his marital relationship. Or a spouse who is reprimanded at work by her/his supervisor comes home and hits a pet (Brodsky, 1988). The threatening nature of an intimate relationship may cause persons to engage in **intellectualization** and to become cool, distant, and uninvolved. This game of detachment reduces one's commitment to the relationship and, thus, helps to ensure that one will not suffer emotional hurt if the relationship should end (Brodsky, 1988).

Establishing a Positive Approach to Conflict Management

Since resolving marital conflicts leads to higher levels of marital satisfaction, it is important to understand some approaches to marital problem solving. In one study, a group of married couples was categorized into two groups: "internals" and "externals." Internals, who reported significantly greater marital satisfaction than externals, believed that marital outcomes resulted from their own efforts and abilities, whereas externals accepted little personal responsibility for marital outcomes. The most effective problem-solving style was found to be an approach that combined an active involvement in issues with a positive, supportive approach to their spouse (Miller et al., 1986). Negative emotional patterns disrupt problem-solving outcomes, while staying on track enhances the ability to solve family problems (Forgatch, 1989). Therefore, directly dealing with problems as they arise can improve a relationship by increasing trust and confidence in the ability of the couple to handle conflict (Rempel, Holmes, & Zanna, 1985).

When couple consensus in joint decision making was evaluated, specific variables were found to contribute to higher levels of consensus. Husbands with patterns of previous cooperativeness during conflict and wives whose decision-making style was less coercive were more likely to achieve consensus. Spouses who demonstrated more equitable economic resources and greater control also were more likely to reach mutual decisions (Godwin & Scanzoni, 1989). Research has found that the rules that govern conflict in marriage cover a wide range of social behavior. These rules have resulted in prescriptions recognizable by most couples: give praise, avoid inflicting costs by hurting partner, control public behavior by not disagreeing in public over personal issues, and maintain intimacy (Jones & Gallois, 1989).

Family therapists have identified destructive and constructive communication strategies that marital partners frequently use to resolve conflict. The healthiest reported strategy was empathic understanding or attempting to take the other person's point of view (Fitzpatrick & Winke, 1979). Manipulation, nonnegotiation, emotional appeal, and personal rejection all represent destructive approaches to handling conflict (see Table 9.5). Everyone recognizes having used several, if not all, of the destructive tactics to resolve relationship conflicts. In fact, such behaviors seem to occur quite naturally as human nature after living many years among imperfect people. Couples who wish to resolve their problems in civilized ways, however, must learn better conflict-resolution strategies. Three such approaches to now be elaborated are empathic listening, ownership of problem, and negotiation.

Table 9.5: Destructive Communication Strategies and Tactics

Strategies	Representative Tactics
Manipulation	Be especially sweet, charming, helpful, and pleasant before bringing up subject of disagreement. Act so nice that person later cannot refuse when asked to allow partner her/his own way.
Nonnegotiation	Refuse to discuss or even listen to the subject unless partner gives in. Keep repeating personal point of view until partner gives in.
Emotional Appeal	Appeal to person's love and affection. Get angry and demand that partner give in.
Personal Rejection	Withhold affection and act cold until partner gives in. Make other person jealous by pretending to lose interest in her/him.

From M. A. Fitzpatrick and J. Winke, "You Always Hurt the One You Love: Strategies and Tactics in Interpersonal Conflict" in *Communication Quarterly,* 27:7. Copyright © 1979 Eastern Communication Association, Upper Montclair, NJ. Reprinted by permission.

Ownership of Problem

It is very important to establish ownership of any problem that arises. One of the best ways to determine who owns the problem is to use **"I" messages.** This is a skill that facilitates communication, since the two spouses talk directly to rather than about each other. Most significantly, by making an "I" statement, sometimes called "straight talk," one claims ownership of the problem. If an "I" message is a good one, the word "you" is avoided, since its use shifts the blame to the other person. Such "I" messages have three elements: a non-blameful description of the situation, tangible effects of the behavior, and the feelings evoked (Burr, 1990). It seems difficult and even artificial when one first begins to use "I" messages. However, each attempt furthers the principles of clear, unambiguous communication, a goal of successful relationships.

Empathic Listening

Effective communication consists not only of sending messages with "I" statements but also receiving messages. Successful conflict management involves a communication exchange in which each marital partner has equal time to express her/his point of view, while the other marriage partner listens with empathy and without constant interruption (Galvin & Brommel, 1982). First, it is important to hear without evaluating. This can be done by listening for the feelings behind the words spoken as well as for the meanings of what is not said during the conversation (Bienvenu, 1986). Second, persons need to let their partner know that they were heard by repeating what was said or restating it in their own words. Another technique is questioning for further clarification. Through training in active listening skills, partners can significantly improve their perceptual accuracy concerning attitudes and feelings of their spouse (Garland, 1981). However, one must not assume that listening-skills training will automatically enhance marital satisfaction. The skills must be applied!

Negotiating a Solution

In negotiating a solution to a problem, one must ask for a particular action or change. Specifically, one must not assume that their marital partner knows what they want. Oftentimes, persons hint at what they want rather than asking in a direct way (Bienvenu, 1986). Disparity between possession of marital power affects bargaining strategies as well as the potential bargaining outcomes. In addition, current negotiations and outcomes provide the context for future negotiations between spouses (Scanzoni & Polonko, 1980). Therefore, it is extremely important to develop adequate negotiation skills within the context of a marital relationship.

Constructive Marital Fighting

Establishing a constructive approach to marital fighting is of paramount importance. The term "fighting" here is assumed to be verbal interchange of some intensity. Since the point of resolving marital conflict is to lead to a more intimate and supportive relationship, maintaining a positive attitude during marital fighting and observing the principles of fair fighting become significant (Crosby, 1991).

In the beginning of a relationship, both marriage partners are more likely to give in and compromise because of a generosity that stems from their publicly professed feelings of love toward each other. Married couples need to learn how to express anger openly while avoiding name calling, sarcasm, blaming the other partner, hostile personal comments, and physical violence. It also can potentially be beneficial for children to see marital discord and the subsequent resolution of the conflict source. From these experiences, children can learn about the need to negotiate and compromise when disagreements occur (Cole & Laibson, 1982). However, some precautions need to be taken when arguing in front of children.

Marriage and family therapists stress that neither partner should win during marital fighting. When one spouse wins, the other inevitably loses. If the goal is for the relationship to win, each partner must be willing to negotiate. A marital dispute should always be handled as soon as possible. If resolution of the conflict is postponed until the next day, the issue is likely to seem even more serious. It is especially important that it either be resolved before going to bed or an agreement be reached to continue the dialogue at a specific later time (Appleton, 1983).

BOX 9.1	Precautions for Observation of Parental Conflict by Children
DO	
• Let children observe normal arguments about everyday things. • Let children see the end of an argument, or tell them that the fight was resolved. • Assure children that the fight is not their fault. • Be aware of information children are getting from an argu ment. • Call family conference if issues legitimately concern children. • Reassure children if they have reason to fear that fighting may lead to divorce. • Practice the rules for fair fighting.	
DON'T	
• Fight about money problems or relatives in front of children. • Fight about sexual problems in front of children. • Fight about child-rearing decisions in front of children. • Let children repeatedly see loss of control in fights. • Use children as referees or spectators in arguments. • Let children take sides in arguments. • Use verbal abuse or physical violence.	

Source: From J. Cole and H. Laibson, "When Parents Argue (and Kids Listen)" in *Parents*, September 1982:63. Copyright © 1982 Grunar & Jahr U.S.A. Publishing, New York, NY.

Principles for Fighting Fair

In the 1970s, psychologists, counselors, and marriage and family therapists began emphasizing "fighting fair" during marital conflicts. In order to engage in constructive conflict management/fighting, it is important that the self-esteem of both marriage partners be protected in the process. Therefore, in the interest of helping achieve this objective, the following principles of fighting fair have been adapted from the work of Crosby, *Illusion and Disillusion: The Self in Love and Marriage:*

1. *Avoid giving ultimatums.* Statements should be avoided that leave no room for negotiation and which cannot result in compromise and resolution of the issue/problem.
2. *Say what is really meant.* One should not make false representations about true feelings and thoughts nor should one withhold reservations about the source of conflict.
3. *Avoid making accusations and attacking.* Such statements will put the other spouse on the defensive and provoke a counterattack.
4. *Accept responsibility for one's own feelings.* Beginning statements with "I" rather than "you" avoids an accusatory tone i.e. "I feel disappointed," not "You disappointed me."
5. *Evaluate perceptions.* One should determine whether or not perceptions of the situation are accurate. Avoid assuming what the other person is thinking and feeling since this practice involves assigning motives and purposes.
6. *Repeat the message.* Repeating back messages is the practice of "active listening." This technique will force more careful listening.

7. *Refuse to fight dirty.* Avoid hitting a partner "below the belt" with past mistakes or things over which they have no control. Fight tactics to be avoided are using the silent treatment and name calling.
8. *Ask for a specific change.* Clearly and directly state the change desired in the other partner's behavior rather than manipulating them to create the desired behavior. However, one must be prepared for the possibility that her/his partner is unwilling or unable to change.
9. *Call time out.* A time-out period allows meditation regarding the issues and proposed solutions. Postponing the discussion does not preclude the need to renew the discussion at a later time.
10. *Closure.* One should try to reach a solution to a problem area as soon as possible after a misunderstanding or disagreement occurs. Stronger feelings of love are possible if the conflict is resolved quickly.
11. *No winner.* One should avoid having a winner or loser in a conflict situation. Good feelings of winning and bad feelings of losing will become intertwined with each other (Crosby, 1991, pp. 170–180).

Coping with Anger

Marriages fail when two people are unable to reach the goal of modern marriage, a close relationship of love and intimacy. The root of this problem, the inability to creatively deal with anger, is believed to be the reason behind all marriage failures.In fact, in marriage, there is the potential to generate more anger than in any other social situation. When anger is understood as a healthy emotion it can be resolved. Persons must remember that they are not responsible for anger, but that they are responsible for what they do with the anger as soon as they are consciously aware of it. The secret is to dissolve the anger through the process of working together rather than suppressing or venting the emotion (Mace, 1982). Venting or "letting it all hang out" is bad, but suppressing is worse. When persons suppress by pushing their anger down inside, they become incapable of tenderness, and the inner core of love withers away. To creatively deal with anger, both marriage partners must be willing to take these necessary steps:

1. Openly admit that anger is there, without penalty.
2. Agree to never again attack each other when angry.
3. Work together to discover the cause(s) of the anger and take corrective action (Mace & Mace, 1979, pp. 113–114).

Persons who become angry and hostile when confronted with a conflict situation need to learn to constructively deal with their emotions. Until that time they are a poor risk for a marriage partner. To evaluate their methods for coping with anger, students may want to consider completing the self-test, "Handling Anger Effectively." By sharing this information, partners can gain valuable insights into their possible reactions when disagreements occur.

Marital Violence: Misuse of Power

When attempts to compromise or accommodate fail in a relationship, the inevitable result is hostility. Inability to deal appropriately with such anger or hostility often leads to marital violence, the ultimate misuse of power. The issue of marital violence surfaced in research literature in the mid-1970s with publication of findings from a survey of college students who had been asked about physical violence between their parents. Of these students, 16% reported that, during their last year in high school, their parents had used physical violence against one another (Straus, 1974). Another exploratory study found that 30% of mothers and fathers had used physical violence to resolve conflict between themselves (Steinmetz, 1977). As shall be seen, the issue of marital violence has not abated with time. A 1985 survey of college couples found that 37% believed that physical violence improved the couple relationship, while 30% equated physical violence with being a sign of love (Pattison, 1985). And the majority of another sample of college students with traditional gender-role values believed that the husband, as head of the family, has the right to use violence to maintain his authority (Finn, 1986).

In a comparison of 1975 and 1985 National Survey rates for violence in black and white families, violence by women toward their husbands was found to increase. While the rate had remained the same for violence of husbands toward wives among blacks, it had decreased for whites (Hampton, Gelles, & Harrop, 1989). The researchers concluded that structural and economic changes in the family may explain such variations. Interspousal aggression is known to correlate

BOX 9.2	Handling Anger Effectively

Write your answers on separate sheets of paper. Use YES when the question can be answered *generally so* and NO when the answer is *seldom* or *never.*

1.	Can you admit you are angry when asked by your partner?	YES	NO
2.	Do you tend to be very critical of her (him)?	YES	NO
3.	Do you let your partner know when you are angry with her (him)?	YES	NO
4.	Does it upset you a great deal when your partner disagrees with you?	YES	NO
5.	Are you satisfied with the way the two of you settle your differences with each other?	YES	NO
6.	Do you disagree with your partner even though you feel she (he) might get angry?	YES	NO
7.	Do you tend to feel guilty over getting angry at your partner?	YES	NO
8.	When your partner is angry with you, do you automatically strike back with your own feelings of anger?	YES	NO
9.	When your partner hurts your feelings do you discuss the matter with her (him)?	YES	NO
10.	When you become angry, do you pull away or withdraw from her (him)?	YES	NO
11.	Do you have frequent arguments with your partner?	YES	NO
12.	Do you have an urge to hit her (him) when you are angry?	YES	NO
13.	Can you express your angry feelings to your partner without exploding?	YES	NO
14.	Do you have a tendency to take your anger out on someone other than your partner when she (he) is the one you are angry at?	YES	NO

Complete the following sentences:
WHEN MY FATHER GOT ANGRY HE ________________
WHEN MY MOTHER GOT ANGRY SHE ________________
Now exchange papers with your partner, study each other's responses, and then discuss your reactions.

Source: M. Bienvenu, Sr., *Strengthen Your Marriage through Better Communication* (pamphlet). New York: Public Affairs Committee, 1986, pp. 13-14.

with the frequency and severity of child problems. One study has confirmed that physical marital aggression contributes to the prediction of child misconduct and personality disorder, inadequacy-immaturity, and clinical levels of problematic child behavior (Jouriles, Murphy, & O'Leary, 1989).

Extent of Marital Violence

Health-care professionals today have learned to identify signs of a battered woman: frequent vague complaints related to stress, bruises and injuries that appear to be nonaccidental, nervousness, tearful references to unspecified marital problems, pain or unusual concern over gynecological problems, and fear of telling husband about any medical condition that would limit her household duties (Walker, 1987). Recognition of these signs by friends and family may increase the likelihood that marital violence will be reported to law enforcement officials.

The incidence of physical violence in marital relationships is far less than that of psychological abuse. One study reported that 67% of married couples cited instances of psychological abuse, whereas only 16% indicated any physical abuse. Further, 80% of those couples who were college-educated suffered from psychological abuse (Hornung, McCullough, & Sugimoto, 1981). However, later research suggests considerable disagreement between spouses as to what particular acts constitute marital violence. Husbands seem more likely to define particular incidents as evidence of physical violence than do wives (Margolin, 1987).

Wife Abuse

Using projection techniques, it was predicted that during the early 1980s at least 6 million wives per year would be physically abused by their husbands (O'Reilly, 1983). However, data from the National Crime Surveys conducted between 1978 and 1982 indicated the number to be closer to 2.1 million who actually had experienced domestic violence at least once per year. Further, they estimated that about one third of these women

Table 9.6: Perpetrators of Domestic Violence

Victim-Offender Relationship	Prevalence
Relatives	
Spouse	40%*
Ex-spouse	19
Parent or child	1
Sibling	2
Other relative	3
Close friends	
Boyfriend or ex-boyfriend	10
Friend	9
Other nonrelative	16

*Note: Represents percent of all cases in a given year.
Source: P. A. Langan and C. A. Innes, *Preventing Domestic Violence Against Women* (NCJ No. 102037). Washington, DC: Bureau of Justice Statistics, 1986, p. 3.

were victimized again within 6 months following the initial incident (Langan & Innes, 1986). Of the total reported incidents, 40% involved current spouses, and 19% involved ex-spouses (see Table 9.6). Despite this dismal picture, other data from 1975–1985 indicate that marital violence is on the decline. Between 1975 and 1985, there was a 27% decrease in husband-to-wife physical violence. Among the factors that led to this decrease were change in family structure, economic changes in society, alternatives for battered women, treatment for spouse, and deterrence/punishment (Straus & Gelles, 1986).

Husband Abuse

Given the macho image of American men, it is extremely difficult to obtain a reliable reading on the extent of physical abuse by wives directed toward husbands (O'Leary & Arias, 1984). Men are far less likely to report physical violence from their spouse than are women (Szinovacz, 1983b). In 1983, it was estimated that 282,000 husbands were beaten by their wives each year, a statistic that meant wives were at least 21 times more likely to be beaten by their husbands (O'Reilly, 1983). Evidence suggests that physical marital violence is reciprocal. A national survey found that 12% of both wives and husbands admitted to having committed at least one act of physical violence toward their spouse during the past year (Straus, Gelles, & Steinmetz, 1980). As the reported frequency of husbands striking their wives increased, the level of marital satisfaction reported by wives decreased. However, there was no relationship found between frequency of wives hitting their husbands and husband's reported level of marital satisfaction (O'Leary & Curley, 1986). These findings support the earlier contention that some men find violence to be an acceptable way of handling marital conflict or problem solving.

Factors Associated with Spouse Abuse

As more attention has been focused on spouse abuse, attempts have been made to identify plausible explanations. Three major avenues have been explored: psychiatric models emphasizing characteristics of the offender, social-psychological models stressing external factors, and sociocultural models highlighting learned social attitudes (Gelles, 1980). The search for reasons associated with spouse abuse is complicated by attitudes of professionals who come into contact with abuse victims. A study of interaction between battered women and hospital emergency department staff found that 40% of hospital staff members believed these women possessed "troublesome" qualities that made them personally responsible for their physical battering. Further, in only 1 case in 10 did hospital staff members take the battering seriously and believe that it was deserving of their time and attention (Kurz, 1987).

Other evidence suggests that the majority of abused wives had experienced physical violence during their courtship period (see Table 9.7). In fact, substantially fewer respondents reported experiencing physical child abuse as compared to courtship violence.

Personal Characteristics

The most often reported cause of marital violence is jealousy (Roscoe & Benaske, 1985). A psychological profile of a wife batterer suggests that the husband is pathologically jealous. He typically believes that his wife is having an affair or otherwise is receiving undue amounts of attention from a member of the opposite sex (Walker, 1979). Another survey of wife abuse among lower-middle class respondents found that about 50% of women and 20% of men replied that jealousy was highly problematic as a causative factor in their abusive marital relationship (Finn, 1985).

Earlier, alcohol abuse was revealed as a major factor in dating and courtship violence. It also has been disclosed as a frequent factor in physical abuse of wives by their husbands (O'Leary & Arias, 1984). The excessive use of alcohol was cited as a cause of physical violence by 56% of abused wives in one investigation (Roscoe & Benaske, 1985). However, caution must be

Table 9.7: Violence During Family Life Cycle of Abused Wives

Violence History	Childhood	Courtship	Marriage
Experienced Violence			
Yes	29%	51%	100%
No	71	49	0
Types of Violence Received			
Slapping	74	68	54
Hitting with object	65	33	26
Punching/shoving	43	75	60
Hitting with fist	35	62	57
Beatings	34	45	37
Kicking	30	38	33
Objects thrown	26	35	48
Choking	17	45	48
Biting	17	10	7
Other	17	11	12
Threatening with gun/knife	13	30	29
Throwing of victim	13	55	34
Trying to hit with object	9	18	16
Causes of Violence			
Jealousy		65	62
Alcohol		60	56
Money		40	41
Children		33	35
Drugs		30	20
Sexual denial		10	15
Other		10	12
In-laws		0	27
Types of Violence Performed			
Slapping		47	58
Punching/shoving		47	74
Objects thrown		26	53
Other		21	10
Trying to hit with object		21	37
Hitting with fist		16	26
Threatening with gun/knife		16	16
Kicking		11	37
Biting		0	26
Hitting with object		0	37

From B. Roscoe and N. Benaske, "Courtship Violence Experienced by Abused Wives: Similarities in Patterns of Abuse" in *Family Relations,* 34:421.

Table 9.8: Experience with Violence Among Wives by Educational Level

Experience with Violence	Less Than High School	High School Graduate	Some College/ College Graduate
Observed abuse in family of origin	41%	42%	59%
Abused in dating relationship	33	58	63
Abused as child	26	24	41
Abusive to husband	19	24	27
Abusive to dating partner	15	24	32

From B. Roscoe and N. Benaske, "Courtship Violence Experienced by Abused Wives: Similarities in Patterns of Abuse" in *Family Relations,* 34:422.

observed in the identification of cause and effect relationships in the case of alcohol abuse. One researcher suggested that alcohol abuse is used as a coping method for severe stress which in turn leads to wife battering as a further stress-coping mechanism (Walker, 1979).

Among abusive, satisfied, and discontented husbands, abusive husbands were more likely to have low self-esteem. Abusive husbands believed their wives behaved in a self-esteem debasing manner toward them (Goldstein & Rosenbaum, 1985). Further, abusive husbands scored lower on masculinity scales than those happily married and even those unhappily married who were nonabusive (Rosenbaum, 1986). Husbands who are abusers often use sexual activity as an act of aggression to enhance their own self-esteem, especially if they believe their virility is declining (Walker, 1979). Forcing their wives to engage in sexual activity evidently boosts their unhealthy ego and low self-esteem.

External Factors

Husbands with lower levels of education are considerably more likely to display physical violence toward their wives (Szinovacz, 1983b). On the other hand, women who have attended college are more likely to be physically violent toward their husbands in comparison to women who did not complete high school (see Table 9.8). As the educational level of the wife increases, she is more likely to have been abused in a dating relationship and to have been abusive to her dating partner.

Another external variable that may affect abuse is financial stress. Such stress may be caused by many factors such as low income, unemployment, or an unplanned pregnancy (Gelles, 1980; O'Leary & Arias, 1984; Yllo & Straus, 1981). There are conflicting reports of the influence of wife-based resources in the question of wife abuse. If the wife earns 40% or more of the total family income, spouse abuse was more likely (Szinovacz, 1983b). However, another study has reported that if a wife earns $30,000 or more per year, the likelihood of wife abuse disappears almost completely (Andrews, 1984).

Learned Social Attitudes

Although a Florida study of marital violence found that over one half of abused wives reported that their husbands had not witnessed any physical abuse between parents, and two thirds indicated that their husbands had not been abused as children, such findings are unsupported by other data (Andrews, 1984). Authorities on spouse abuse have argued that learned social attitudes are important. Observing spouse abuse during childhood or experiencing child abuse increases the likelihood of becoming subject to spouse abuse (Hamberger, Feuerbach, & Borman, 1990). A national investigation of intergenerational transmission of marital violence concluded that if a child observes her/his father hitting her/his mother, it greatly increases the likelihood that daughters and sons will be both perpetrators and victims of severe marital aggression (Kalmuss, 1984). Another study revealed that only 9% of abusive husbands indicated never experiencing child abuse (Pagelow, 1981).

Reasons for Continuation of Violent Marriages

Battered women are more likely to utilize inadequate and passive strategies in coping with stress than the general female population. They are less likely to use social support to reframe their lives, or to use spiritual support to cope with stress associated with experiencing physical violence (Finn, 1985). Despite this passivity, a survey of battered wives found that 6 in 10 wives had been advised by their relatives and friends to leave their husbands, whereas only 2 in 10 wives were advised to remain in the marriage. Surprisingly, only 1 in 20 were advised to call police to stop the physical abuse (Pagelow, 1981). Although most wives have concerns about adverse publicity regarding police involvement in domestic violence, later findings suggest that if the husband is arrested for wife battery, it substantially reduces the number of future occurrences (Berk & Newton, 1985). Reasons identified in the literature for continuing a violent marital relationship are sociocultural factors and personal characteristics.

Sociocultural Factors

Women in our society have been socialized to be dependent upon their husbands and to exhibit passivity, whereas husbands have been socialized to use aggression as a problem-solving technique. Historically, wives and children have been regarded as property of the husband. Therefore, striking the wife came to be considered not only a husband's privilege but also his duty (Kalmuss & Straus, 1982). A greater level of tolerance for marital abuse is found among wives with high marital dependency because they perceive no available alternatives. In the long run, increased gender equality will increase alternatives for wives. But in the short run, it may actually lead to violence being used more often by husbands as a last resort to prove their threatened power and authority (Kalmuss & Straus, 1982).

A survey of battered wives in 15 shelters throughout Texas found that economic dependence almost always ensured that the abused wives would return to their husbands. If the husband was the sole source of income, only 16% of battered wives intended to separate, whereas 82% planned to separate from their husbands if other sources of income existed (Aguirre, 1985).

Personal Factors

Many battered wives fear for their lives and rightly so. As revealed earlier in Table 9.7, over one half of victims have been hit with a fist, while others have been choked and threatened with a gun or knife (Roscoe & Benaske, 1985). Therefore, it should come as no surprise that fear may operate either in a direct or an indirect way to prevent wives from leaving their husbands (Strube & Barbour, 1984).

With time to contemplate their actions, husbands often, at least temporarily, regret their violent actions (Strube & Barbour, 1984). Consequently, the most often reported reason why abused wives continue their marriage is because the husband repents and promises to change his behavior. About three fourths of the wives in one survey indicated returning home to their husbands who professed to be sorry and promised to change (Pagelow, 1981). According to self-reports, calling the police reduced the incidence of repeated spouse assaults from 41% to 15% (Langan & Innes, 1986). But, wives who have already experienced physical violence are at substantial risk to have additional episodes, regardless of promises to change.

Coping with Marital Violence

In 1990, 41 states and the District of Columbia had laws under which a repeat spouse abuser could be held in contempt of court and subjected to arrest. Therefore, it is no longer necessary to file for divorce in order to obtain a civil protection order (Finn & Colson, 1990). However, as late as 1984, only 10 states had statutes that treated domestic violence as a separate criminal offense (Brozan, 1984). But is seeking relief through the criminal justice system necessarily the best alternative? This decision must be made by the victim depending upon her/his circumstances and the other alternatives available.

Attitudes and Responses of the Criminal Justice System

Of the female victims of marital violence who reported their victimization to police, 49% indicated that police were "concerned and helpful," and 22% replied that police were "concerned but not helpful." Further, women who viewed the police response as negative were more likely to report feelings of self-blame. Those women who reported that police explained their legal rights were much more likely to report "taking out" a warrant and to express a desire for "revenge." It is necessary in most states for the spouse to go to the district attorney's office to obtain a warrant for arrest if police did not observe the physical violence (Brown, 1984). Data from the National Crime Survey, involving 128,000 victims of domestic violence, indicate that victims called police in only one half of the incidents. The major reasons for calling police were to prevent future violence—37%, to prevent current violence from happening—24%, and to punish the offender—11%. In contrast, major reasons for not calling police were private or personal matter—49%, fear of reprisal—12%, incident not important enough—11%, and police "wouldn't do anything"—10% (Langan & Innes, 1986).

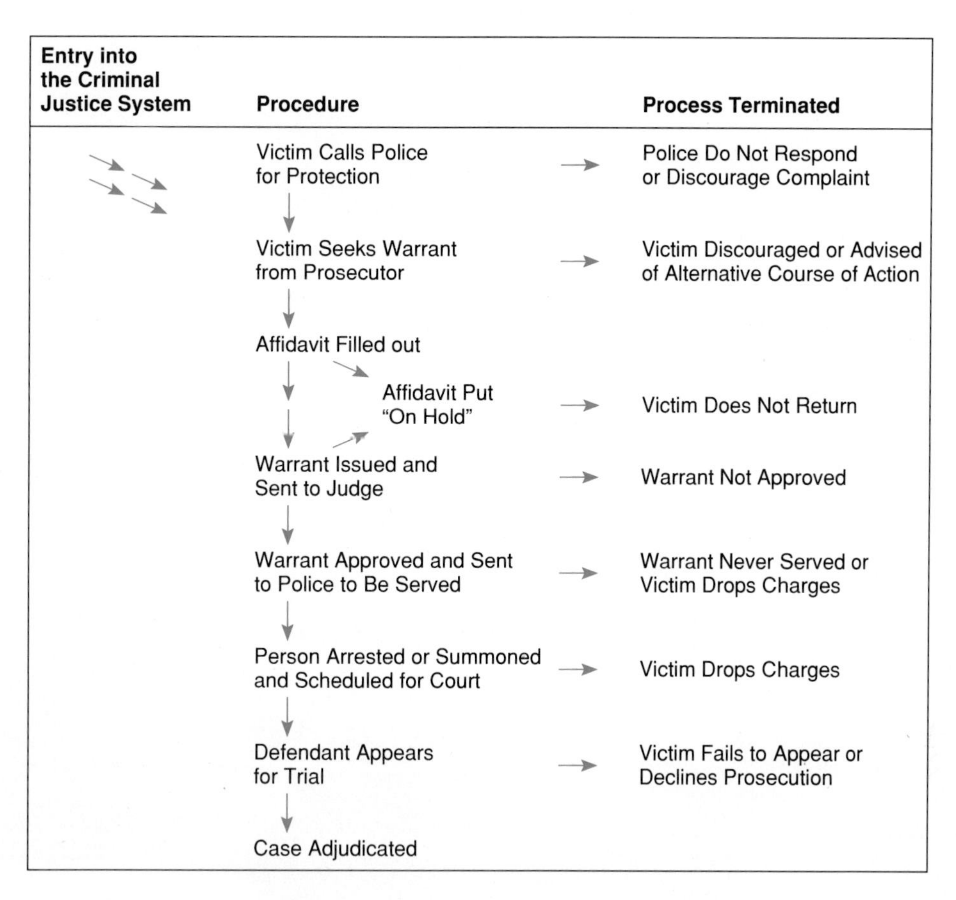

Figure 9.1 Schematic Diagram of Processing a Spousal Abuse Complaint

Unfortunately, there is some basis for wives feeling that the legal system "forgets" complaints because, in many jurisdictions, an affidavit regarding the nature of the marital violence may be put on hold. How does the victim's complaint proceed after she/he calls the police department for protection (see figure 9.1)? Depending on the particular state judicial system, discretionary power may exist to put the complaint "on hold" and allow a cooling-off period for a certain number of days to determine whether the victim wants to press charges. The reason for this procedure is to ensure that the victim wants to follow through with the complaint rather than beginning the process and then changing her/his mind. A review of misdemeanor conjugal battery cases revealed that three fourths of the cases involving abusive husbands were put on hold. Further, of those cases/affidavits put on hold, 78% of victims did not return and fill out a warrant to be issued so the husband could be arrested. In those instances where the husband was actually arrested, 80% of victims declined prosecution before the court date so the charges were dropped (Ford, 1983). During a 9-month period in Cleveland, Ohio, police received over 15,000 domestic violence calls, but reports were filed in only 700 cases, while arrests were made in only 460 cases (Saltman, 1986). Consequently, many police jurisdictions develop a less than positive attitude toward domestic-violence complaints.

Seek Help for Self and the Abusive Partner

To assist with the problem of wife abuse, at least 800 shelters for battered women have been established in the United States. These facilities provide a temporary haven for women and their children. In addition, professional counselors provide information concerning various options, including getting the husband into treatment and returning to live with the spouse (Saltman, 1986). In about one half of the cases, abusive couples live together while the husband is in treatment, but many husbands agree to go to therapy for the sole purpose of getting their wife to come back home (Feazell, Mayers, & Deschner, 1984).

Women's Centers have recently emerged in response to the rising tide of family violence and sexual abuse. Their counselors are especially trained to deal with sexual assault—including marital rape.

Basically, there are two types of treatment sources: service programs and service agencies. Service programs tend to have more funding and deal primarily with physical abuse cases, whereas service agencies tend to provide more diverse treatment and primarily deal with emotional abuse cases (Feazell et al., 1984). Therapy ideally begins with both the abuser and the victim seeing separate therapists, preferably of the same gender as the patient. Ultimately, this procedure should lead to joint therapy whereby both clients and both therapists are present. There must be an agreement to future nonviolence and development of protection plans so that alternatives to violent responses can be learned (Cook & Frantz-Cook, 1984). Group counseling is often indicated as desirable. Initial contacts with abusive husbands suggest that they are remorseful, guilt-ridden, and eager to change. But after breaking through this facade, these men are usually socially and personally inadequate, frustrated over unmet dependency needs, jealous, lacking in trust, and tend to deny or minimize the severity of their violence. Group counseling appears to be most effective because it helps to overcome social isolation, to develop an emotional support system, and to practice skills designed to control violence (Bernard & Bernard, 1984).

One successful approach that helps husbands end their physical violence toward wives or cohabitation partners involves group treatment sessions in four areas:

1. *Assertiveness training*—helps cope with criticism and develops empathy for the other person's feelings.
2. *Relaxation training*—develops techniques to reduce anger levels.

3. *Cognitive restructuring*—teaches the use of self-talk "coping" statements to prevent anger.
4. *Exploration of personal and social roots of aggression*—teaches that violence is partially a function of cultural conditioning (Saunders, 1984, pp. 350–352).

Obtain a Divorce

Women who do leave their husbands after being physically abused usually are employed, nonwhite, have tried other strategies to cope, and have been in the relationship for a relatively short period (Strube & Barbour, 1984). If the abusive spouse refuses to seek treatment or if the treatment does not prove successful, the victim may decide to obtain a divorce. However, if the abusive partner does not develop ways of controlling her/his violence, it may continue after the divorce. In one study, 37% of victims reporting physical violence to police were either separated from the spouse, had filed for divorce, or had divorced the violent partner (Ford, 1983). Therefore, it is very important, regardless of whether or not the marriage continues, for the abusive partner to seek treatment for her/his physically abusive behavior toward her/his spouse.

Marital Rape: An Emerging Problem

Marital rape has only recently been acknowledged by the legal system. As late as 1977, the Model Penal Code of the American Law Institute still was proposing a definition of rape that specifically excluded the possibility of a husband being tried for raping his wife: "A male who has sexual intercourse with a female *not his wife* is guilty of rape if . . . he compels her to submit by force or by threat of imminent death, serious bodily injury, extreme pain . . ." (MacNamara & Sagarin, 1977, p. 31). In general, state laws have defined rape as being an assault by a man upon a woman to whom he is not married. Oregon was the first state to change its legal definition of rape, thus permitting prosecution of rape charges in which the victim was a marital or cohabitation partner. The first Oregon prosecution of a husband for a rape ended with acquittal of the defendant by the jury. By the mid-1980s, the majority of the states had removed the "spousal exception" clause from their statuses, thus permitting the prosecution of one's spouse for rape (Allgeier & Allgeier, 1991).

Although there has been some tendency to view marital rape as less traumatic than stranger rape, it may actually be more traumatic due to feelings of betrayal and disillusionment for the victim (Weingourt, 1985). The limited research on marital rape has found that wives may blame themselves because their husbands use violence to engage in marital sexual activity. Part of this self-blame stems from the fact that women are socialized to be passive and private regarding their sexuality (Cherry, 1983). Many wives believe that marital rape occurs because they are sexually unresponsive or are perceived as not liking men. Still other wives believe marital rape occurs because of their refusal to engage in sexual activity at a particular time or their lack of an affectionate nature. But the assertion of self-blame by wives may be open to question. In one study, only four of 44 wives who had reported marital rape blamed themselves (Frieze, 1983). Thus, contrary to some professional opinions, only a very small percentage of wives may actually blame themselves for their marital rape. The issue is complicated because women no longer living in a violent relationship are much more likely to attribute responsibility for violence to their partner rather than engaging in self-blame. Of those women still living in a violent relationship, 53% reported current self-blame in contrast to only 14% of those no longer living with a violent partner (Andrews & Brewin, 1990).

Marital rape is considered to be less harmful by many persons because of the woman's prior sexual experience with her husband. In many states, if the wife is not physically injured, she may not file criminal charges for marital rape. The issue is further complicated by the fact that many persons consider marital rape as less serious than forcible rape by a stranger even if the rape involves persons who already are divorced. In a study of 1,300 women and men concerning their attitudes toward marital rape legislation, 45% of women and only 25% of men favored passage of marital rape laws. Of those women who favored marital rape laws, 59% were under age 40 (Jeffords & Dull, 1982). But despite such attitudes, changes in gender roles have led many legislators to conclude that such marital behavior is unacceptable. Marital rape has come to be defined as forcing an unwilling spouse to engage in sexual activity including sexual intercourse, fellatio, cunnilingus, and/or anal intercourse (Groth, 1979). By 1989, 31 states and the District of Columbia had passed laws permitting criminal prosecution of husbands who commit marital rape (Crooks & Baur, 1990).

Incidence of Marital Rape

The relatively low visibility of marital rape serves to prevent accurate reporting of meaningful statistics by most law enforcement agencies. Consequently, the incidence of marital rape reported in the research literature varies substantially from source to source (Cherry, 1983). Discounting other types of physical violence, it is estimated that 14% of all married women will be a victim of marital rape at some time during their marriage (Harman, 1984; Russell, 1982). The existing literature on marital rape suggests that it is most likely to occur in a relationship that involves other physical violence (Frieze, 1983). Therefore, if the consideration is restricted to women who have experienced other types of marital violence, the percentage who have been subjected to marital rape increases substantially (Walker, 1979). In one sample of women who had experienced other forms of marital violence, 23% indicated having experienced marital rape (Bowker, 1983). Other evidence of this pattern of marital violence can be found in data from the National Center on Women and Family Law which has concluded that at least one third of all clients who come to shelters for battered women have been raped by their husbands or cohabitation partners (O'Reilly, 1983). While many wives fail to report marital rape due to loyalty toward their husbands, the new laws appear to be very successful. The conviction rate of husbands accused of marital rape is about 85% as compared to about 4% for stranger rape ("New Laws," 1984).

Factors in Marital Rape

In general, marital rape victims appear to be more likely to have married at an earlier age, to have had a shorter period of acquaintance before marriage, to not be employed, and to be dependent upon welfare programs (Hanneke & Shields, 1985). But given the vast underreporting of marital rape, these findings must be considered tentative at best. Many wives do not report marital rape due to embarrassment, perceptions of hostility by police and/or the judicial system, fear of family reactions, fear of retribution by spouse, wish to avoid stigma of victimization, and refusal to admit to being raped (Hanneke & Shields, 1985).

From the existing literature, three types of marital rape have been identified: battering rape, nonbattering rape, and obsessive rape. **Battering rape** is said to be accompanied by a pattern of verbal and physical abuse by husbands. Typically, husbands are so angry that they yell, slap, shove, and otherwise physically abuse their wives. These battering episodes are often followed by marital rape. In the case of **nonbattering rape,** forced sexual activity occurs as a response to a continuing conflict or disagreement about either frequency and/or type of sexual activity. In this circumstance, the physical violence is usually not generalized to the remainder of the marital relationship. With **obsessive rape,** the wife is viewed as a sexual object who is to be used to satisfy excessive sexual needs of the husband upon his command (Finkelhor & Yllo, 1983).

Whether or not there is a distinct difference between marriages that involve marital rape and those that involve other physical violence remains open to considerable conjecture. Nevertheless, some consensus has emerged as to why some husbands engage in marital rape. Marital rape is more likely to occur in marriages with continuous disagreements over finances, friends, children, use of alcoholic beverages, use of drugs, and marital violence (Bowker, 1983). Three major categories of reasons have been set forth concerning why men rape their wives: anger, power/domination, and sadism (Russell, 1982). Some men equate engaging in sexual activity with power and as a display of their masculine virility. Still others view forcibly engaging in sexual activity as a form of debasing their wives. In other words, engaging in nonconsensual sexual activity will "teach her a lesson" (Groth, 1979). Given the patriarchal nature of our society, many husbands still believe that access to sexual activity is a marital right. Therefore, the husband feels that the wife has an obligation to engage in sexual activity whenever he desires to participate (Frieze, 1983). At the present time, additional research is needed to further clarify the causes of marital rape.

Seeking Professional Help

Despite serious attempts to reach resolutions of marital conflict, marriage partners may need to consider seeking professional help to address their difficulties. In general, the best source of such help is a professional marriage and family therapist. The profession of marriage and family therapists experienced tremendous growth during the 1970s along with substantial gains in credibility, thus becoming a viable treatment alternative for most mental health problems. During this time period, alternative perspectives of family therapy became identified as specific techniques, training centers, and more reliable assessment tools were developed, which led to much research about the effectiveness of therapy. Specialized professional areas, such as sex therapy, have emerged along with increased interest in preventive and enrichment programs for couples and families (Olson, Russell, & Sprenkle, 1980). During the 1980s, greater emphasis came to be placed on the interrelatedness of the individual, the family, and the social context as therapists gave more attention to cultural diversity and systematic approaches in addressing marital conflict (Piercy & Sprenkle, 1990). Couples seeking marriage and family therapy should remember that the role of the therapist is to point out aspects of reality and to serve as a facilitator, and not to resolve marital problems. They provide structure and guidance to allow the counselees to engage in self-discovery and develop accurate perceptions of reality (Sunbury, 1980). However, it is not the therapist's role to solve marital problems.

More married women are involved in receiving marriage and family therapy at any point in time than are men. This circumstance is primarily due to the traditional male socialization process and the belief by men that sharing problems with others is a sign of masculine weakness. One study of male participation in marriage and family therapy revealed that over one half of the men indicated that their wives had initiated the therapy sessions (Guillebeaux, Storm, & Demaris, 1986). However, if the therapy is to be successful, the husband's involvement is crucial.

Table 9.9: Criteria Used by Men to Choose Therapist

Factors	
Price	63%
Recommendation by friend	54
Therapist's education	51
Hours	47
Distance	46
Recommendation by professional	46
Therapist's reputation	37
Recommendation by relative	34
Type of center	34
Therapist's sex	8
Therapist's race	3
Activities	
Consulting professional	53
Consulting family member	49
Consulting friend	49
Talking to former clients of therapist	27
Checking on insurance	21
Checking credentials of therapist	17
Reading articles about choosing therapist	15
Meeting with prospective therapist	6

From F. Guillebeaux, et al., "Luring the Reluctant Male: A Study of Males Participating in Marriage and Family Therapy" in *Family Therapy,* 13:220.

Choosing a Marriage and Family Therapist

To help ensure minimal competency of the marriage and family therapist being selected, she/he should be a state-certified marriage and family therapist and/or a clinical member of the American Association for Marriage and Family Therapy (AAMFT). Unfortunately, only a few states currently certify persons as marriage and family therapists. Using the North Carolina marital and family therapy certification process, researchers found that certified or licensed marriage and family therapists possessed a greater level of knowledge about marriage and family therapy than those persons with graduate level course work about marriage and the family but who lacked certification (Markowski & Cain, 1984). Many people believe that clinical psychologists are excellent sources of marriage and family therapy, but a survey by the American Psychological Association in the early 1980s disputes this contention. Although clinical psychologists spent 40% of their time doing marriage and family therapy, only 1% of approved training programs for clinical psychologists included at least one course on marriage and family therapy in their graduate programs ("Embarrassing Fact," 1982).

An examination of factors and activities associated with choosing a marriage and family therapist ascertained that men rely most often on price of services, recommendations by friends, and advice from professionals (see Table 9.9). Further, when selecting a marriage and family therapist, it is indeed appropriate to inquire as to their primary therapeutic approach to marital problems. If a person selects a therapist and decides that she/he does not feel comfortable or satisfied with that therapist's approach, they should seek another therapist.

The Growth of Marriage Enrichment Programs

Marriage enrichment has emerged as a preventive approach to assist couples in making their marriage better. David Mace, a leading marriage enrichment advocate, argued that ". . . the knowledge we are steadily acquiring is not, of itself, capable of doing much to change human behavior; and programs for couples which do no more than educate are just not enough" (1987, pp. 183–184). Marriage improvement programs may take many different formats, including courses on marriage and the family, encounter groups, family and/or marriage enrichment weekends, consciousness-raising groups for women and men, communication workshops for married couples, sensitivity training, and sexuality workshops.

Marriage Enrichment Programs

By the beginning of the 1980s, over 1 million couples had already participated in marriage enrichment programs (Hof & Miller, 1981). These programs may be classified into three main categories: emotionally-oriented skill training programs including the Catholic Encounter, Christian Marriage Enrichment Retreat, and Conjugal Relationship Enhancement; reason-oriented skill training programs including the Family Evening Home—Mormon Church, Jewish Marriage Encounter, and the Jealousy Program; and action-skill training programs including Communication Skill Training (CST), Behavioral Exchange Negotiations, and Family Growth Group (Ulrici, L'Abate, & Wagner, 1981). Marriage enrichment programs usually are presented in one of three formats: a three-stage session involving introduction, practice, and a support group; an intensive session as a weekend with a follow-up support group; or spaced training. The goals of marriage enrichment programs include increased self-awareness and mutual empathy; mutual self-disclosure of thoughts and feelings; intimacy; and development of relationship skills in communication, problem solving, and conflict resolution (Hof, Epstein, & Miller, 1980).

Impact of Marriage Enrichment Programs on Marital Happiness

Ideally, marriage enrichment participants should already be involved in a happy marriage because enrichment programs are designed to enhance satisfaction. A review of several studies of marriage enrichment program participants suggests that pre-enrichment levels of marital satisfaction for participants are generally on a level of satisfaction somewhere between the extremes for couples who seek counseling and couples who report the highest marital satisfaction scores. Thus, all participants apparently are somewhat dissatisfied in reality (Powell & Wampler, 1982). One study of marriage enrichment and conjugal skills training programs found an immediate program impact on communication style for wives and communication content for husbands. In general, changes in relationship quality were reported earlier for wives than for husbands, but it changed significantly over time for both wives and husbands (Russell, Bagarozzi, Atilano, & Morris, 1984). A comparison of a weekend and a 5-week marriage enrichment program determined that both programs appeared to improve short-term and long-term marital adjustment. Wives demonstrated more positive results than husbands regardless of which program they had completed (Davis, Hovestadt, Piercy, & Cochran, 1982). Distressed couples actually may experience further deterioration of their relationship as a result of marriage encounter weekends. This conclusion was based on the belief by researchers that negative responses to marriage encounter weekends are more prevalent than previously reported (Doherty, Lester, & Leigh, 1986). Despite these negative effects, a review of evaluation research from the 1980s unequivocally concluded that marriage enrichment programs, on the whole, accomplish their intended goal: improvements of marital quality (Guerney & Maxson, 1990).

Summary

- All new marriages face a period of adjustment in which reality and disillusion replace fantasy and illusion. During this period, marital conflicts inevitably emerge that couples need to learn to resolve. All conflict is potentially destructive, but if it is handled constructively, relationships can be strengthened.
- Causes of marital conflict include undesirable behaviors, discrepancies in role-performance expectations, diverse values, and an imbalance in dependence/independence.
- Since resolution of marital conflict depends upon adequate communication between the partners, couples should strive for openness and high levels of disclosure. The major cause of psychological game playing may be fear of close, emotional intimacy.
- A positive approach to conflict involves establishing ownership of the problem, empathic listening, and negotiation of solutions. Since sharing personal feelings makes the marital partners vulnerable, self-esteem can easily be damaged. Consequently, learning how to fight fair and cope with anger is imperative.
- The incidence of reported marital violence has recently declined, but it remains a very serious problem. Wives are much more likely to experience physical spouse abuse than are husbands. Causes include jealousy, alcohol abuse, financial stress, negative family modeling, and low self-esteem.
- Reasons for marital rape are suggested to be more related to power than to sexuality. While in the past marital rape was viewed as less serious than forcible rape by a stranger, 31 states and the District of Columbia now permit criminal prosecution of marital rape.
- If problems continue to exist despite resolution attempts, couples need to seek professional assistance from a marriage and family therapist. Although debate continues regarding their overall effectiveness, marriage enrichment programs continued to expand during the 1980s.

Questions for Critical Reflection

1. Why would a diversity of values be more likely to lead to marital conflict than the other four causes listed in your text?
2. One has mused, "No matter what one is talking about, one is always talking about one's self." How does this cautionary note apply to marital conflict? What role do nonverbal messages play when one talks about "self"?
3. In the home in which you grew up, which defense mechanisms did you see being used most often in interpersonal relationships? Did the defense mechanisms interfere with effective communication? Do you use any of these same inappropriate interactions in your relationships?
4. Do you believe that personal or social factors contribute most to the rising violence in marriages today? What advice would you give a friend in an abusive marriage who sought your help?
5. When seeking professional help for a failing marriage, what are the advantages of choosing a marriage and family therapist rather than a psychotherapist or other mental health specialists?

Suggested Readings

Bradshaw, J. (1990). *Homecoming: Reclaiming and championing your inner child.* New York: Bantam Books. A practical work designed to help loosen the destructive hold of the past and awaken the healing potential of the inner self.

Goleman, D. (1985b). *Vital lies, simple truths: The psychology of self-deception.* New York: Simon & Schuster. A scholarly treatise on defense mechanisms and their detrimental contributions to interpersonal relationships.

James, M., & Jongeward, D. D. (1973). *Born to win: Transactional analysis with Gestalt experiments.* Reading, MA: Addison-Wesley. An excellent source on psychological insight into interpersonal relationships including an overview of transactional analysis and game playing.

Kaslow, F. W. (1987). Marital and family therapy. In M. B. Sussman & S. K. Steinmetz (Eds.), *Handbook of marriage and the family* (pp. 835–859). New York: Plenum Press. A technical yet excellent resource on the various approaches to marriage and family therapy.

Russell, D. (1982). *Rape in marriage.* Riverside, NJ: MacMillan. An authoritative resource for understanding the phenomenon of marital rape.

Straus, M. A., Gelles, R. J., & Steinmetz, S. K. (1980). *Behind closed doors: Violence and the American family.* New York: Doubleday. A landmark investigation of domestic violence.

CHAPTER 10

Achieving Sexual Adjustment and Sexual Satisfaction

"There are two great prerequisites to the art of love: an elementary knowledge of the structure and function of the sexual organs, and a realization that marriage is a great deal more than a mere matter of sex."
Theodor Bovet, 1969

Outline

The foundation for achieving healthy sexual adjustment begins long before conscious memory. As children discover their genitals and learn their proper or improper names, sexuality attitudes and behaviors are conveyed by parents and other family members. Regardless of whether these experiences are positive or negative, by marriageable age, everyone has fairly well-established sexual attitudes and ways of sexually interacting. Although some persons will have confined their premarital sexual activity to varying levels of petting, many will have had sexual intercourse. Since, in our society, marriage legitimizes sexual relationships and defines their expectations, there is the potential for considerable conflict between expectations and behaviors (Geer, Heiman, & Leitenberg, 1984).

Despite the open way in which sexual matters are discussed in today's sex-saturated society, most persons have never been exposed to formal instruction about human sexuality. A 1986 Yankelovich Clancy Shulman poll of American adults substantiated that only 9% of women and men had received information about sexuality from sex education courses (Leo, 1986b). Such sexual ignorance combined with sexual **precociousness** (premature development), which is usually promoted in our society, has resulted in a distinctive national formula with the potential for sexual disaster. Added to this equation are myriad sociological and technological changes that continue to affect sexual attitudes and behaviors. For example, the increasingly sophisticated 20th century contraceptive technology has allowed the separation of the procreation function from the recreation/pleasure part of sexuality. These and other changes have ushered in a new age of relationships between the sexes in which many women are just beginning to discover their full potential as sexual beings. Since a person's sexuality is an integral part of her/his personality, achieving sexual adjustment helps to promote well-being in all aspects of life. Such a task involves physical, psychological, and social factors.

The Meaning of Sexual Adjustment and Sexual Satisfaction

With recent advances in contraceptive technology and the advent of the women's movement with its increased emphasis on female sexuality, considerable attention has been focused on both sexual adjustment and sexual satisfaction. **Sexual adjustment** can be described as the extent to which an individual possesses an awareness and acceptance of her/his sexual nature as an integral part of her/his being (Sievers, Pocs, & Tolone, 1983). **Sexual satisfaction** can be defined as the perceived discrepancy between the level of aspiration and the level of achievement regarding physiological and psychological sexual fulfillment. This concept of sexual satisfaction implies an evaluation of the physiological and psychological qualities associated with the sexual experience. Personal standards used to determine whether or not sexual satisfaction has been achieved are based on personal needs, personal values, and the criteria imposed by one's peer group (Davidson & Darling, 1988b). Physical pleasure such as reaching an orgasm does not necessarily create psychological satisfaction. In a study of middle-aged wives, three fourths reported achieving orgasm during sexual intercourse, but only 42% stated that their sexual relations with their husbands were enjoyable. Sexual satisfaction also was unrelated to gender roles. Women with traditional gender roles were just as likely to report sexual satisfaction as those women with nontraditional role definitions (Jobes, 1986).

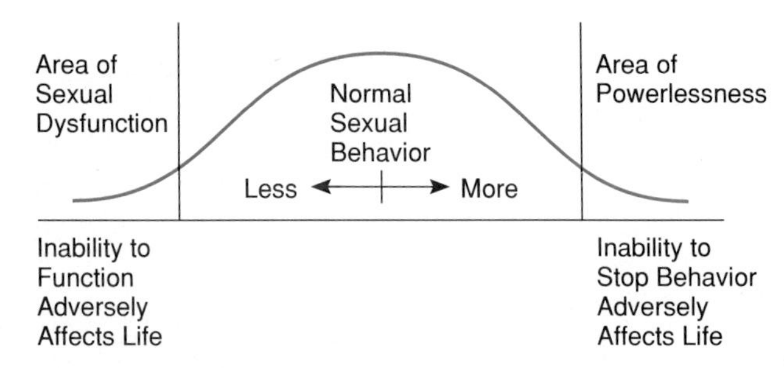

Figure 10.1 Continuum of Sexual Behavior

The Continuum of Sexual Behavior

One may better understand sexual adjustment by viewing the continuum of sexual behavior (see figure 10.1). The range of behavior labeled normal sexual behavior would include the vast majority of persons for whom sexual adjustment is a reality. In other words, those persons who are aware of and accepting of their sexual nature as an integral part of their being are considered to be sexually adjusted. **Sexual dysfunction** includes persons who have difficulty in sexual functioning. This may be expressed in impotency or lack of desire. Little attention has focused on the opposite end of the continuum, sexual powerlessness. These individuals are tinuum, sexual powerlessness. These individuals are unable to stop sexual behavior to the degree that it adversely affects their lives. They have lost the power to

A hug, a touch, a glance—expressing couple intimacy in everyday settings is more likely to lead to sexual satisfaction than much touted techniques for experiencing orgasm.

choose their sexual experiences, and sexual experimentation becomes their driving force to the detriment of other areas of their life. Sexual pleasure, rather than a rewarding experience, is a source of despair. Some authorities believe that such loss of ability to choose constitutes **sexual addiction** (Carnes, 1986). Many interrelated psychological factors may contribute to sexual addiction including childhood fears, deep-seated negative self-image, and undeveloped social skills (Earle & Crow, 1990). It is important to recognize that any pathological behavior needs to be dealt with professionally before sexual adjustment can be achieved.

Marital Satisfaction and Sexual Satisfaction

Marital satisfaction and sexual satisfaction may occur as very separate and distinct entities (Heiman, Gladue, Roberts, & LoPiccolo, 1986). The quest for sexual satisfaction is complex because lack of sexual satisfaction may signal a relationship issue rather than a sexual issue. Sexual dissatisfaction can best be described by the person who indicates "nothing else is wrong, yet something is missing" (Levine, 1983). Researchers have found that of those clients presenting for marital therapy, "sexual problems" were stated as a difficulty by 42% of wives and 37% of husbands. As might be expected, there were reported increases in marital satisfaction after undergoing marital therapy, but there also were increases in sexual satisfaction regardless of whether sexual issues had initially been described as a problem (O'Leary & Arias, 1983). Further evidence of the interrelation between marital and sexual satisfaction is found in other data from couples evaluated but not treated for sexual dysfunction. Over a 3-year period, marital satisfaction did not increase significantly for women or men, but women reported increased sexual satisfaction (De Amicis, Goldberg, LoPiccolo, Friedman, & Davies, 1984).

Essential Factors for Sexual Satisfaction

In order to accomplish the goal of sexual satisfaction, it is necessary for each person to possess strong emotional commitment to her/his partner; an attitude of caring, tenderness, and gentleness; and a willingness to learn the partner's preferences with regard to various stimulatory techniques in creating maximum sexual arousal (Hyde, 1986). Sexual intercourse should be perceived as a source of intimacy, pleasure, and personal enrichment for both persons (Kirkendall, 1976). This approach implies a sharing of the sexual experience and equal sexual pleasure for women and men.

While frequency of sexual intercourse and orgasm are certainly related to sexual satisfaction, they appear not to be the most important factors. One study found that the variables associated with sexual satisfaction include, in order, pleasure related to sexual activity with one's partner, level of couple happiness, absence of anxiety about sexual activity with one's partner, personal body image, and information about sexual functioning (Perlman, 1981). While relationship commitment is very important, other significant factors include consistency in achieving orgasm, frequency of sexual intercourse, and effectiveness of contraceptive techniques (Pinney, Gerrard, & Denney, 1987). Although no major studies were identified regarding the phenomenon of boredom in long-term sexual relationships, evidence suggests its existence. Although boredom with sexual activity may reflect general lack of excitement in the marital relationship, it also may be a function of unrealistically high sexual expectations that may have been generated by the mass media (Hyde, 1990).

While sexual dysfunction accounts for some sexual dissatisfaction, a substantial amount relates to unhealthy sexual attitudes including myths, unrealistic expectations, distorted view of sex partner, and projections of one's own sexuality issues onto one's sex partner (Jacobs, 1986). For these reasons, it has been suggested by sex therapists that a straightforward "back-to-basics" approach to achieving sexual satisfaction is needed (Botwin, 1985). Such a goal is best achieved by identifying and applying essential components for sexual satisfaction:

1. Adequate level of sex knowledge.
2. Comfortableness with one's body.

"There was a time when you indulged in a little tenderness during the commercials."

3. Acceptance of one's own sexuality.
4. Willingness to avoid constant state of fatigue.
5. Ability to communicate sexual needs and preferences.
6. Understanding the role of sexuality in interpersonal relationship.
7. Avoidance of performance standards and/or "spectatoring".
8. Availability of privacy for sexual activity.
9. Ability to vary time, location, and sexual activity to alleviate boredom (Botwin, 1985, pp. 148–150).

The Anatomy and Physiology of Reproduction and Sexual Response

The subject of human anatomy and physiology remains a mystery to many persons. This stems partially from the fact that much information about sexual matters has been obtained from uninformed peers. Furthermore, since most female anatomy is internal, a substantial segment of women and most men are rather ill-informed about how the female body functions during reproduction and sexual response. Understanding the facts about external and internal genitalia and their role in the physiology of reproduction and the sexual response is an essential building block for optimal sexual functioning.

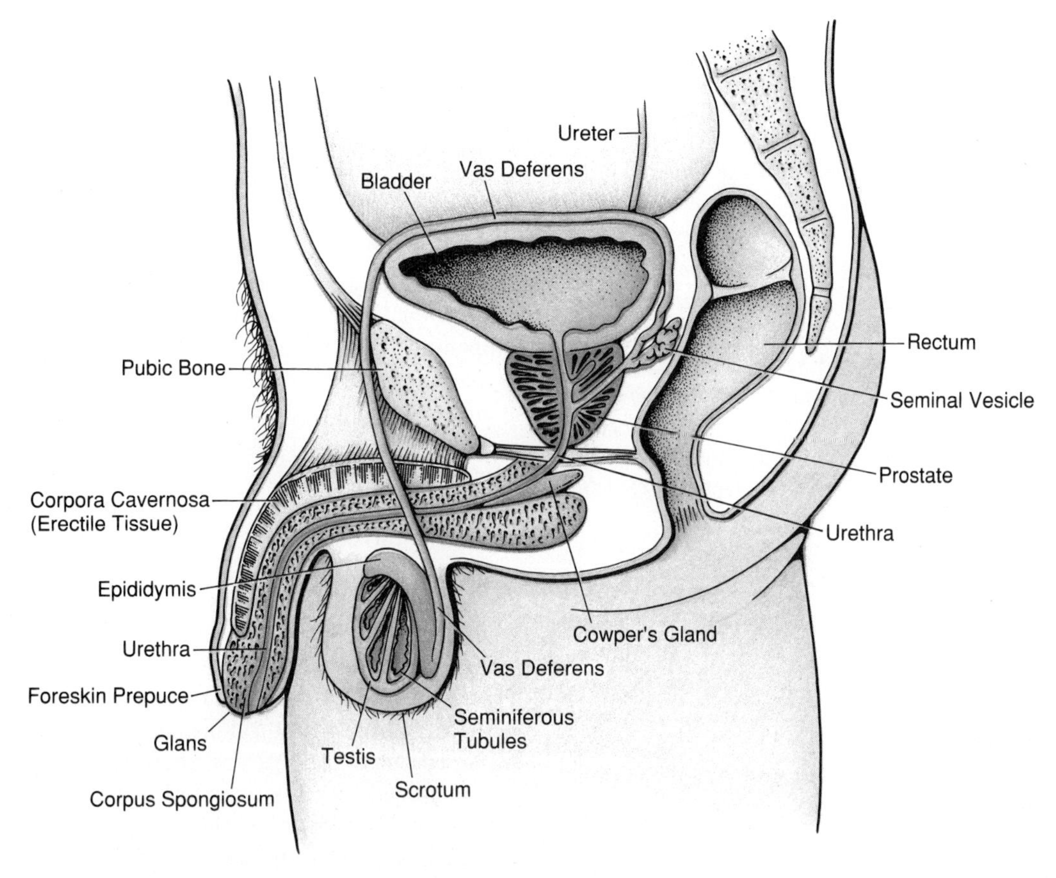

Figure 10.2 The Male Reproductive System, Side View

Male Anatomy and Physiology

Generally speaking, the male genitalia are more external and subject to immediate exploration than is the case for female genitalia. In addition, male physiological processes related to reproduction and sexual response are somewhat less complex than for women.

External Genitalia

The **penis** is an elongated shaft consisting of erectile tissue, numerous nerve endings, a large supply of blood vessels, and the urethra (see figure 10.2). In an adult man, a flaccid, or soft, penis ranges from 3.3″ to 4.5″ in length and about 1.3″ in diameter. When aroused, an erect penis ranges from 4.7″ to 9.2″ in length with an average diameter of 1.5″ (Geer et al., 1984). The penis actually consists of three parallel cylinders of spongy tissue covered by a thick membrane. During sexual arousal, this sponge-like tissue becomes engorged with blood, causing the penis to become erect. The head or tip of the penis is referred to as the glans penis. Although the entire penile shaft contains nerve endings, the greatest concentration is located in the glans penis. The **frenum** is a thin strip of skin connecting the glans penis to the penile shaft. It too is very sensitive to tactile stimulation (Masters, Johnson, & Kolodny, 1988).

The **foreskin prepuce** forms a sheath-like covering over the glans penis (Hyde, 1990). Today, the majority of American men have had all or a significant portion of the prepuce removed during circumcision as an infant. During the mid-1970s, the official position of the American Academy of Pediatrics (AAP) was that no medical indication existed for the routine circumcision of newborns. By 1987, only 59% of male infants were being circumcised (Francoeur, 1991). But, after two decades of debate and review of new research evidence, the AAP has reversed its position and adopted a new policy statement suggesting that male circumcision has some medical advantages (Crooks & Baur, 1990). For example, circumcised male children have substantially lower rates of urinary tract infections in comparison to those who are not circumcised (Herzog, 1989). Finally, the **scrotum,** a loose pouch of skin sparsely covered with pubic hair, containing the testes completes the male external genitalia.

Internal Genitalia and Physiology

The **testes** are two bean-shaped structures located in the scrotum whose functions are to manufacture sperm and the hormone testosterone (see figure 10.2). The **vas deferens** transport mature sperm cells to the area of the urethra where they are mixed with other body fluids to be released at ejaculation (Byer & Shainberg, 1991). **Semen** consists of secretions from the seminal vesicles, the prostate gland, Cowper's glands, and sperm. The average man releases about one teaspoonful of semen per ejaculation. The **seminal vesicles** are two small glands, located at the juncture of the vas deferens, that produce and secrete an alkaline fluid. This secretion contributes to sperm nutrition and motility and accounts for about 70% of the semen volume (Spring-Mills & Hafez, 1980).

The **prostate gland** is a chestnut-shaped gland located below the bladder that secretes an alkaline fluid. This secretion provides a favorable environment for the sperm and helps to reduce their destruction from acidity found in the vagina (Hyde, 1990). The two **Cowper's glands** are located below the prostate gland and empty directly into the urethra. They secrete a small amount of clear alkaline fluid during sexual arousal to lubricate the glans penis for ease of vaginal entry (Janda & Klenke-Hamel, 1980).

The **sperm** is the male counterpart to the egg in the woman. From the onset of puberty, a man generates billions of sperm each year. Sperm are produced in the seminiferous tubules, which consist of about 1,000 tightly coiled tubules in the testes (Hyde, 1990). A single ejaculation contains between 120 and 600 million sperm cells depending upon frequency of ejaculation (Masters et al., 1988). The **epididymis** consists of about 20 feet of tightly coiled tubing that forms a small crescent-shaped structure located on the top and side of the testes (see figure 10.2). Its function is to mature sperm cells and store them for up to 6 weeks (Francoeur, 1991).

Female Anatomy and Physiology

Although substantially different in outward appearance, female sexual anatomy has the same developmental origins as male sexual anatomy. For example, the same type of tissue develops into ovaries in women and testes in men (Katchadourian, 1989).

External Genitalia

The external female genitalia, commonly referred to as the **vulva,** are composed of the mons pubis, the labia majora, the labia minora, the vestibule, and the clitoris (see figure 10.3). The **labia majora** (outer lips) consist of two fatty folds of skin and a thin layer of smooth muscle tissue that encloses the vaginal opening. Their inner sides are covered with pubic hair and contain oil glands along with a rich supply of nerve endings that, when stimulated, contribute substantially to sexual arousal and pleasure. During the unstimulated stage, the labia majora are usually folded together at the midline, thus serving to protect the urethral and vaginal openings. The labia majora merge into the perineum, that region of tissue located between the vaginal and anal openings. Due to its abundant supply of nerve endings, many women find manual stimulation of the perineum to be pleasurable (Geer et al., 1984).

The **labia minora** (inner lips) have the appearance of curved rose petals and are enclosed within the labia majora. The labia minora also are richly supplied with blood vessels and nerve endings. During sexual excitement, the labia minora tend to flair outward, exposing the vestibule. The term **vestibule** refers to the area enclosed by the labia minora that contains both the vaginal and urethral openings. The entire area has copious nerve endings, and appropriate stimulation can lead to considerable sexual pleasure. The region over the pubic bone is called the mons pubis and consists of a cushion of fatty tissue covered by pubic hair. Stimulation of the numerous nerve endings in this region during foreplay also can help to achieve increased sexual arousal (Byer & Shainberg, 1991).

The most sensitive female sexual organ is the **clitoris,** which consists of three major parts—clitoral shaft, clitoral glans, and clitoral hood. The clitoral shaft or body of the clitoris consists of an elongated structure that is about 1″ in length and 1/4″ in diameter (Geer et al., 1984). The clitoral glans, or head, is typically the only portion of the clitoris that is readily visible during sexual arousal. In fact, the clitoral glans is so sensitive that many women prefer stimulation of the sides of the clitoral shaft rather than direct stimulation to achieve maximum sexual pleasure. The clitoral hood is formed by the meeting of the labia minora above the clitoral glans. It is filled with nerve endings and is the most sensitive portion of the clitoris. The clitoris, which contains erectile tissue, becomes engorged with blood when stimulated and may expand to twice its unaroused size. While the size of the clitoris may vary considerably among women, contrary to popular belief, a larger clitoris does not provide more intense sexual arousal (Masters et al., 1988).

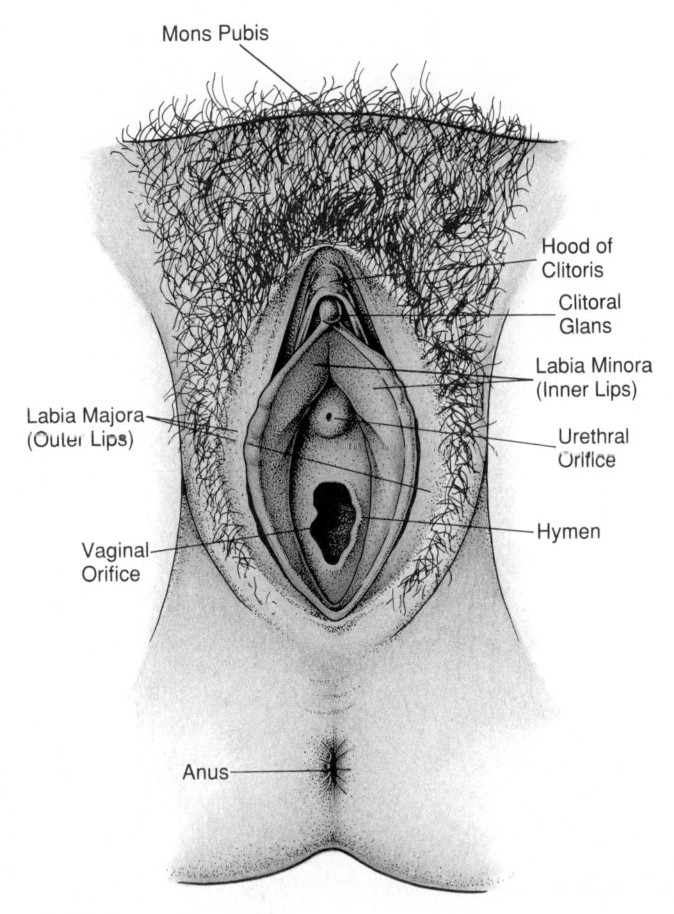

Figure 10.3 External Female Genitalia

The hymen is a thin tissue membrane that covers the vaginal opening. If it is too thick, a physician can cut or stretch the hymen during a physical examination to remove the possibility of discomfort during first sexual intercourse. A minority of women may still experience some pain and discomfort during their first sexual intercourse caused by involuntary contraction of vaginal muscles due to anxiety. While the rupture or stretching of the hymen, by tradition, has been associated with first sexual intercourse, it may occur when bicycling, horseback riding, masturbating, or using tampons. Typically, the hymen stretches across part but not all of the vaginal opening and varies in shape, size, and thickness (Hyde, 1990).

Internal Genitalia and Physiology

The female reproductive organs are located within the abdominal cavity and are protected by pelvic bones. The **vagina** is a muscular tube extending from the vaginal orifice and vestibule to the uterus (see figure 10.4). In the unaroused state, the vaginal barrel averages 3″ to 5″ in length. When the woman becomes sexually aroused, its diameter and length will increase at least 50% (Stewart, Guest, Stewart, & Hatcher, 1979). The vagina has both longitudinal and circular muscles, including a sphincter muscle that surrounds the external opening. As the woman becomes sexually aroused, glands located within the vaginal walls secrete a thin mucous to facilitate penetration. Although the vaginal barrel has long been thought to have few nerve endings, much attention during the 1980s was given to the so-called Grafenberg spot, a mass of sensitive tissue located in the anterior vaginal wall between the cervix and top of the pubic bone (Barbach, 1983). In two studies of the Grafenberg spot phenomenon, two thirds of the respondents have reported achieving orgasm via stimulation of this sensitive area without clitoral stimulation (Davidson, Darling, & Conway-Welch, 1989; Hoch, 1986).

The **uterus** is a hollow, muscular, pear-shaped organ approximately 3″ long and 2″ wide. Covering the inner walls of the uterus is the **endometrium,** which

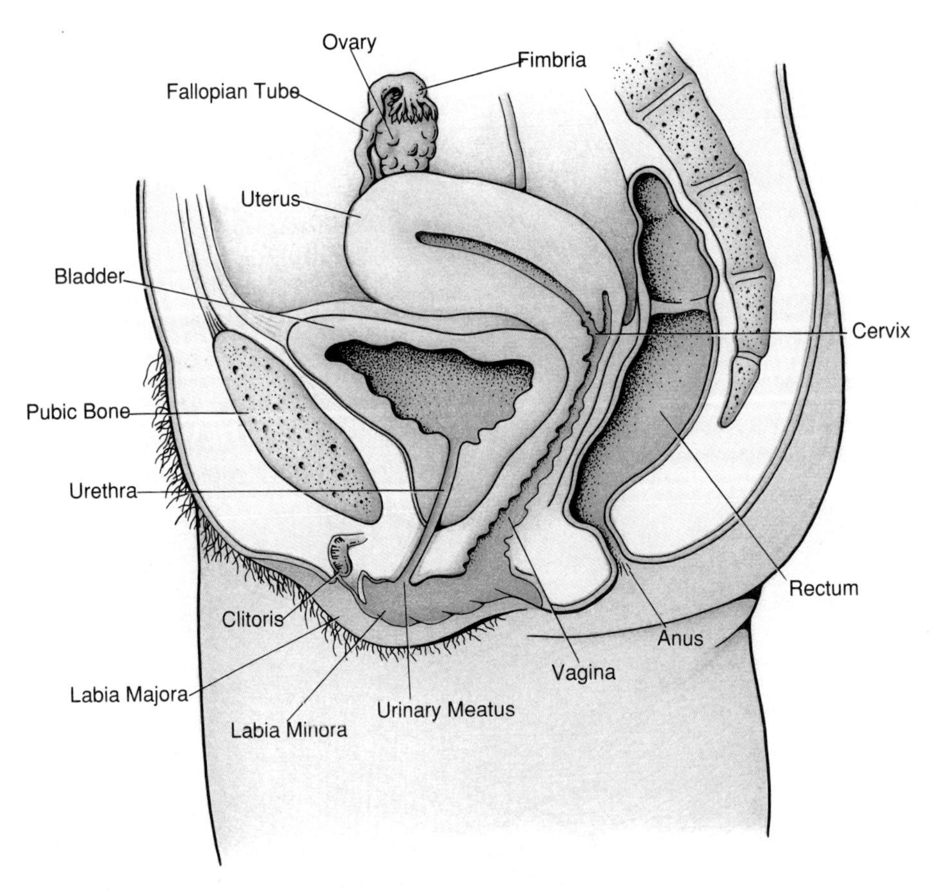

Figure 10.4 Internal Female Genitalia, Side View

undergoes various changes during the menstrual cycle and receives the fertilized egg for implantation at the beginning of pregnancy (see figure 10.5). The muscular wall of the uterus, referred to as the myometrium, serves to facilitate labor during childbirth. The tip or neck of the uterus that protrudes into the vagina is referred to as the **cervix.** The menstrual flow exits from the uterus through the vagina and sperm cells may pass into the uterus via the cervix. Since the cervix has no nerve endings, its surgical removal does not result in a loss of sexual responsiveness (Masters et al., 1988). The **fallopian tubes,** which are approximately 4″ in length, extend from the uterus toward the left and right side of the pelvic cavity. Their outer ends have the appearance of a funnel and contain finger-like projections called **fimbria** that almost touch each ovary. As the **ovum** (egg) leaves the ovary, the fimbria "pull" the egg inside the fallopian tube so that potential contact can be made with a sperm cell (Crooks & Baur, 1990).

The **ovaries** are located on either side of the uterus and are about 1″ in length and have the appearance of unshelled almonds. The ovaries produce the hormones estrogen and progesterone. In addition, they mature the ova that are released at ovulation. At the time of birth, a female infant has approximately 400,000 immature ova present in her ovaries, only 400–500 of which are released via ovulation prior to menopause (Allgeier & Allgeier, 1991).

Female Breasts

Breasts are considered to be part of the secondary sex characteristics rather than actual genitalia. In American society, there is a preoccupation about breast size, with large breasts often being linked to physical attractiveness. However, breast size does not relate to sexual responsiveness on the part of a woman. In fact, many women actually experience relatively little sexual arousal when their breasts and nipples are subjected to tactile stimulation. The arousal potential of breasts does not depend upon breast size or shape but rather upon personal preference and learned habit (Allgeier & Allgeier, 1991).

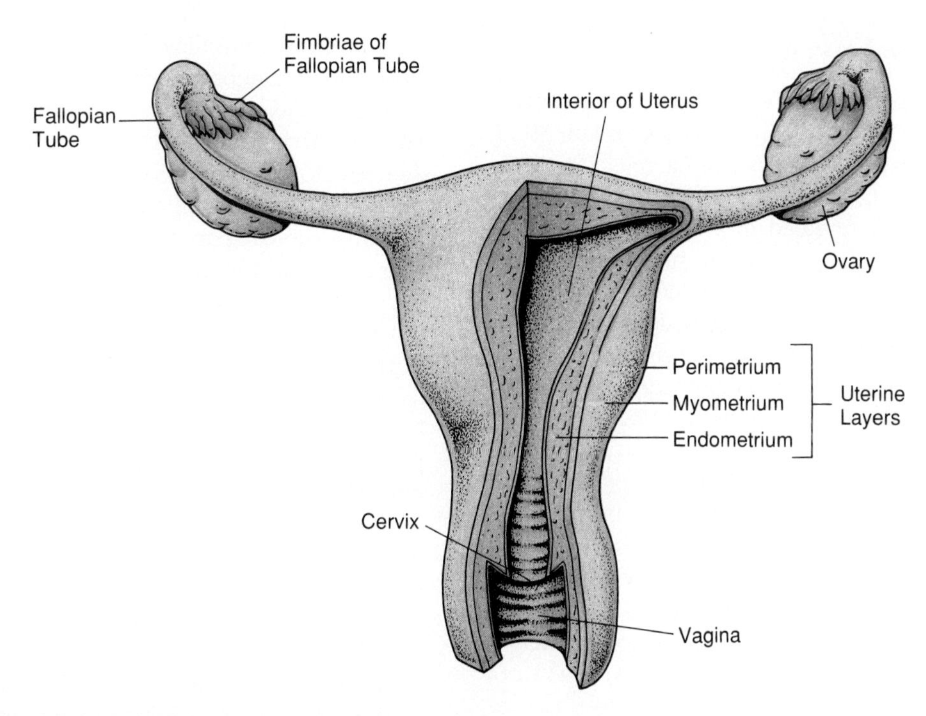

Figure 10.5 Internal Female Genitalia, Front View

BOX 10.1	**Breast Self-Examination**

In the shower

Examine your breasts during bath or shower; hands glide more easily over wet skin. With fingers flat, move your hands gently over every part of each breast. Use your right hand to examine your left breast, left hand for your right breast. Check for any lump, hard knot, or thickening.

Before a mirror

Inspect your breasts with arms at your sides. Next, raise your arms high overhead. Look for any changes in the contour of each breast: a swelling, dimpling of the skin, or changes in the nipple. Then, rest your palms on your hips and press down firmly to flex your chest muscles.

Lying down

To examine your right breast, put a pillow or folded towel under your right shoulder. Place your right hand behind your head—this distributes breast tissue more evenly on the chest. With your left hand, fingers flat, press gently in small circular motions around an imaginary clock face. Begin at the outermost top of your right breast for twelve o'clock, then move to one o'clock, and so on around the circle back to twelve. A ridge of firm tissue in the lower curve of each breast is normal. Then move in an inch, toward the nipple, and keep circling to examine *every part of your breast,* including the nipple. This requires at least three more circles. Now slowly repeat this procedure on your left breast. Finally, squeeze the nipple of each breast gently between thumb and index finger. Any lumps, thickening, or discharge, clear or bloody, should be reported to your doctor immediately.

Courtesy of the American Cancer Society.

The **nipple** consists of smooth muscle fibers along with a network of nerve endings, thus creating a considerable sensitivity to touch and temperature changes. The circle of dark skin surrounding the nipple is the **areola,** which contains many nerve and muscle fibers that allow the nipple to become erect. The areola contains **sebaceous glands** (oil-producing) that provide lubrication of the nipples during breast-feeding. The **mammary glands** typically produce milk in conjunction with childbirth. Since little variation exists in the glandular material found in the breast, differences in breast sizes are due to the amount of fatty tissue located within the breast (Crooks & Baur, 1990).

The Menstrual Cycle

Cultural traditions since biblical times have portrayed menstruation in a negative light. As a consequence, it is difficult to separate facts from fiction regarding menstrual discomfort (Siegel, 1985). The sensitive nature of menstruation is revealed in a survey of adults in which two thirds believed that the subject should not be discussed at work or socially, and one fourth did not believe that it should even be discussed between family members (Milow, 1983). When it is discussed, the word menstruation is used less often than "period," "friend," and "that time of the month" (Hays, 1987).

There are many social, cultural, psychological, and biological factors that interact, making it difficult to understand the complex relationship between behavior and the menstrual cycle. It appears that most women experience negative mood changes during the premenstrual week and menstrual period, which include an increase in feelings of anxiety and irritability (Dennerstein, Spencer-Gardner, & Burrows, 1984). In fact, pronounced symptoms such as these have been labeled **premenstrual syndrome** (PMS), a recognized medical condition. Symptoms of PMS include abdominal bloating, weight gain, acne, breast tenderness, constipation, headaches, irritability, fatigue, anxiety, and depression ("Can Hormones," 1982). The percentage of women suffering from severe PMS has been found to range from 10%–20% of all menstruating women with an additional 30%–50% reporting mild to moderate symptoms (Woods, Lentz, Mitchell, Lee, Taylor, & Allen-Barash, 1987).

The Physiology of Menstruation

A complete menstrual cycle includes the proliferative phase, the secretory phase, and the menstrual phase (Katchadourian, 1989). A brief review of this complex phenomenon will provide insight into this physiological process.

During the proliferative phase, the pituitary gland increases production of the **follicle stimulating hormone** (FSH), which causes the **Graafian follicle** to mature an ovum and to produce several types of estrogen. **Estrogen** has a number of functions including the thickening of the vaginal and uterine linings, producing cervical mucus at the time of ovulation, production of vaginal mucus, increasing fluid retention, and providing feedback to the brain to regulate the cyclical release pattern for FSH and the **luteinizing hormone** (LH). Release of LH by the pituitary gland causes a mature Graafian follicle to rupture and to release an ovum. Ovulation occurs about 14 days prior to the beginning of the next menstrual period irrespective of the number of days in the menstrual cycle (Katchadourian, 1989). Normally, only one ovum is released, but sometimes two follicles rupture releasing ova, potentially resulting in multiple births if a pregnancy occurs (Stewart et al., 1979).

The secretory phase involves continued secretion of LH by the pituitary gland causing the remaining cells of the Graafian follicle to develop into a mass of cells called the **corpus luteum.** The function of the corpus luteum is to secrete **progesterone,** which inhibits reproduction of cervical mucus during ovulation. Progesterone along with estrogen causes the endometrium of the uterus to thicken and to become filled with blood in anticipation of receiving a fertilized ovum for implantation. If there is no fertilized ovum, the pituitary gland increases its production of LH and FSH. These chemical changes bring about a sloughing off of the endometrium during the menstrual phase (Stewart et al., 1979). Imbalances in progesterone and estrogen have been linked to premenstrual syndrome symptoms such as irritability, anxiety, depression, and menstrual migraine headaches (Clare, 1985).

During the menstrual phase, the inner layer of the endometrium breaks down and is discharged as part of the menstrual flow. Typically, the menstrual flow is composed of mucus, blood, and tissue from the endometrium. Since the body naturally cleanses itself a woman should not use a douche at any time unless medically advised to do so by her gynecologist. Unnecessary douching will disturb the vaginal **ecosystem** (organisms and their environment) and potentially lead to gynecological disorders (Stewart et al., 1979). The pituitary gland begins to release FSH which causes the maturation process of the Graafian follicle to start and the menstrual cycle to begin anew (Byer & Shainberg, 1991).

Menstruation and Sexual Activity

Although from a medical point of view, there is no reason why women should abstain from sexual intercourse during menstruation, 56% of women and 51% of men in a national survey believed that persons should abstain (Research Forecasts, 1981). However, many women who experience orgasm during menstruation report that uterine contractions during the orgasmic response help to alleviate menstrual cramps (Masters et al., 1988).

Among wives and husbands, a lower incidence of sexual intercourse during menstruation occurs primarily due to a lack of sexual desire on the part of the woman. This lack of desire for women is thought to be attributable to hormone changes occurring during menstruation (Morris & Udry, 1983). When asked about their feelings toward having sexual intercourse when their sex partner was menstruating, only 31% of a national sample of men reported enjoying sex "as much as at other times" (Pietropinto & Simenauer, 1977). Those persons having menstrual cycle lengths in the normal range (26 to 34 days) are more likely to engage in sexual intercourse at least once per week. Data suggest that regularity of sexual activity may serve to streamline the functioning of the reproductive system, thus regulating the length of the menstrual cycle (Cutler, Garcia, & Krieger, 1980).

The relationship between physiological sexual arousal and menstrual cycle phase is unclear. Highest levels of physiological arousal were found to occur during the postmenstruation and postovulation portions of the menstrual cycle in one study. But no significant relationship was found between levels of hormone concentrations in the bloodstream and the levels of sexual arousal (Schreiner-Engel, 1980). However, other researchers found no significant changes in self-reports of sexual arousal, vaginal blood volume, or labia temperature elevation associated with the menstrual cycle phase (Hoon, Bruce, & Kinchloe, 1982). It is possible that levels of sexual arousal during the menstrual cycle may be more a function of psychological or social factors than physiological ones.

The Pelvic Examination

A pelvic examination can provide a woman with important information about the health of her reproductive anatomy and physiology. However, many young women wait to have a pelvic examination until they suspect an infection, contract a sexually transmitted disease, or experience severe menstrual discomfort. Today, most reproductive tract problems can be treated successfully if they are diagnosed early. By age 17, women should have an annual pelvic examination or at an earlier age if sexual intercourse has been initiated. Further, a woman should immediately have a pelvic examination if she is bothered by vaginal itching, redness, soreness, sores, swelling, odor, unusual discharge, burning sensation during urination, unusual vaginal bleeding, or if the possibility of pregnancy exists. To assure that the vaginal ecosystem remains in its usual condition, it is important that a woman avoid douching, use of tampons, and sexual intercourse for 24–48 hours prior to having a pelvic examination (Stewart et al., 1979).

BOX 10.2 **Men, Lovemaking, and Menstruation**

In sexually intimate couple relationships, a man who cares about a woman's period may help to avoid misunderstandings and build intimacy. He may ask his partner if she gets cramps, but pain is not the only consideration. The bloated feeling caused by water retention may not hurt, but it can be fairly uncomfortable. A man can do several things to help a woman deal with dysmenorrhea: a cup of soothing herbal tea—chamomile and mint teas may be especially effective—or massage her lower back or abdomen.

Try to discuss how a partner feels about making love premenstrually or during her period. Some women prefer not to: discomfort can interfere with the undivided attention lovemaking deserves. Other women say lovemaking right before or during menstruation helps alleviate cramps. During orgasm, the uterus contracts and the cervix opens, thus speeding the menstrual flow and reducing the duration of cramps. Men should bear in mind, however, that this is not an experience shared by all women. Also, ask about breast tenderness and keep it in mind during sensual explorations.

For couples who do make love during a woman's period, there are several things to keep in mind. Menstruation may change a woman's natural vaginal lubrication. Menstrual fluid irritates some penises, but a man can use a condom if this is a problem. A diaphragm or cervical cap can be used to catch the flow. If a couple would rather not have genital intercourse, there are other satisfying ways to make love.

From Michael Castleman, *Medical SelfCare* Magazine, Spring 1981. Reprinted by permission.

The Human Sexual Response Cycle

Using data from a classic investigation of sexual physiology obtained via direct laboratory observation of over 10,000 episodes of sexual activity involving 382 women and 112 men, four stages of the human sexual response cycle were delineated: excitement, plateau, orgasmic, and resolution (Masters & Johnson, 1966). While the sexual response cycle suggests a consistent pattern of progression, the actual patterns of sexual response may vary widely from time to time. On occasion, a person may move rapidly from the excitement stage to orgasmic stage, whereas on other occasions, sexual excitement may develop over a period of several hours, for instance, while taking a romantic, scenic boat ride. At other times, a person may reach the plateau stage only to have her/his high level of arousal reduced back to the excitement stage. It is important to keep in mind that the human sexual response consists of two primary physiological reactions: **vasocongestion,** in which an increased supply of blood is concentrated in the genitalia and female breasts; and **myotonia,** an increased neuromuscular tension from buildup of energy in the nerves and muscles (Allgeier & Allgeier, 1991).

The Female Sexual Response

While the clitoris is considered the primary female **erogenous zone** (body areas particularly responsive to sexual stimulation), it is only one of the many sensitive areas that are more widespread in women than in men. These primary erogenous zones include the entire vulva, **mons pubis** or **veneris,** inner thighs, and the breasts particularly the nipples, along with the lips, mouth, ears, and neck (Geer et al., 1984). Secondary erogenous zones refer to any other areas of the body, though less endowed with nerve endings, which have developed erotic potential via sexual conditioning. For example, if one's partner tenderly kissed the back of the neck with each sexual encounter, this area could potentially become a powerfully erogenous zone. Thus, each person possesses their own erogenous body map (Crooks & Baur, 1990).

The Excitement Stage

During sexual arousal, the entire breast becomes swollen increasing in size by as much as 25%. The areola becomes engorged with blood, partially concealing the continuing erection of the nipples persisting through the orgasmic stage. At the same time, the clitoris is responding by becoming erect, but its small size and the fact that it is partially covered by the clitoral hood causes its response to be visible in only a few women. The vaginal barrel also begins to lubricate and becomes coated with a thin film. As it dilates and begins to increase in length, its color changes from its usual deep red to an uneven deep purple. The uterus begins some minor muscular contractions, becomes engorged with blood, and starts to elevate, creating a kind of ballooning effect in the upper two thirds of the vaginal barrel (see figure 10.6). The labia minora gradually become thicker and help to lengthen the vaginal barrel, while the labia majora, depending upon the woman's childbearing history, become thin, flat, and flair away from the vaginal orifice (Byer & Shainberg, 1991).

The Plateau Stage

During the plateau stage, genital reactions that began during the excitement stage continue to occur. The muscular tension increases dramatically as the woman approaches orgasm. There also is an increase in heartbeat, blood pressure, and respiratory rates (see Table 10.1). The most pronounced physiological reaction during the plateau stage is that the labia minora change from pink to bright or dark red which signals an impending orgasm. During the plateau stage, the clitoris withdraws from its normal overhanging position and recedes back deeply beneath the clitoral hood. Prior to orgasm, the clitoral shaft may decrease in length by almost one half its original size (Masters et al., 1988).

The Orgasmic Stage

While the vast majority of men usually experience **orgasm** with every episode of sexual intercourse, this is not true for women. Over the last two decades, the reported percentages of women who experience orgasm "always" or "most of the time" range from 59% (Bell & Bell, 1973) to 63% (Tavris & Sadd, 1975) to 69% (Davidson & Darling, 1988a). Since most men consider a woman's orgasm as symbolic of their prowess as a lover, many women perceive tremendous pressure to reach orgasm during sexual intercourse. Consequently, a majority of women sometimes pretend to experience orgasm during sexual intercourse. One study found that three fourths of the divorced and separated, about two thirds of the never-married, and over one half of the married women, occasionally pretended to reach orgasm (Darling & Davidson, 1986b).

Factors that are of crucial importance for women to reach orgasm during sexual intercourse include "right" position, receiving adequate stimulation, concentrating on genital sensations, fantasizing about sexual activities, "right" rhythm/speed, concentrating on area of stimulation, and moving with partner (Sholty et al., 1984). The onset of orgasm is accompanied by strong involuntary contractions of muscles located in the uterus, perineum, anus, and outer one third of the vaginal barrel. Usually there are at least three to four strong contractions of the vaginal barrel which come about 0.8 seconds apart. Depending upon the degree of sexual arousal and continued stimulation, there may be 10 or more vaginal contractions. After the first few, these contractions become less strong and less frequent.

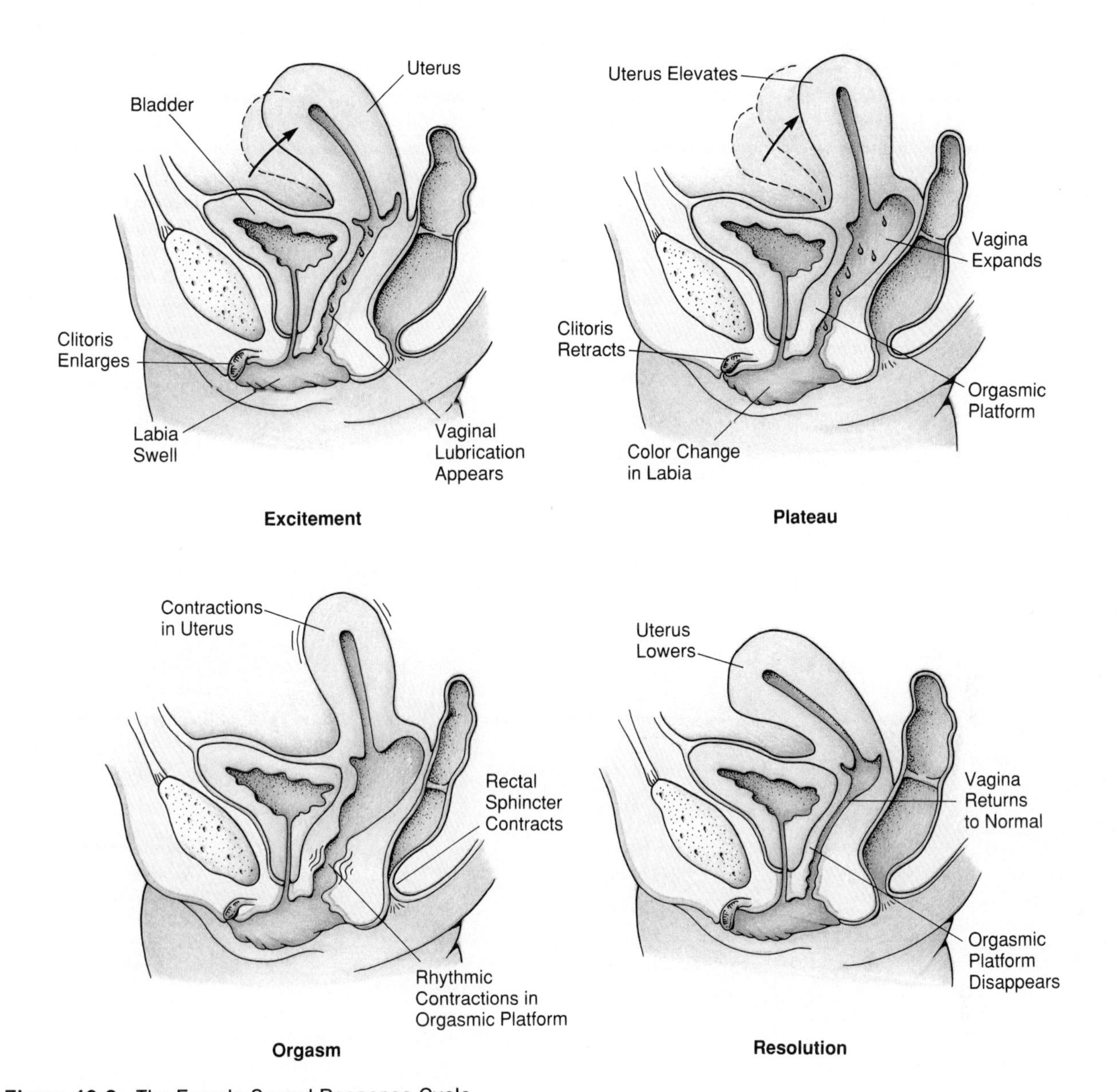

Figure 10.6 The Female Sexual Response Cycle

During the orgasmic stage, the heart rate continues to elevate, more so during masturbation than sexual intercourse. Blood pressure rises, less than a man's, and increases in the breathing rate are proportional to degree and duration of sexual arousal and stimulation (Masters et al., 1988).

The Resolution Stage

Within about 5 minutes after sexual stimulation ceases, the muscular tension disappears and the breasts return to their normal size and shape. The heart rate, blood pressure level, and breathing rate also return to their normal condition very quickly (see Table 10.1). The vaginal barrel returns to its original size within 5 to 15 minutes, while the uterus is somewhat slower to return to its usual size and location. Although the clitoris returns to its regular overhanging position almost immediately after vaginal contractions cease, it may not completely lose its erection until 5 to 30 minutes after orgasm. The labia minora resume their light pink color almost instantly, but the labia majora require somewhat longer to return to their original size and position, particularly among women who have had vaginal childbirth deliveries. For these women, the labia majora

Table 10.1: The Sexual Response Cycle of Women and Men

	Excitement Phase	Plateau Phase	Orgasmic Phase	Resolution Phase
Breasts	Nipple erection; increase in breast size in females only	Nipples becomes hard, further increase in breast size, areolae engorgement	No changes	Blood leaves areolae, erection of nipples disappears, decrease in breast size
Sex flush	Appearance of rash in late phase; first appears on upper part of abdomen, then on breasts	Well-developed; may have widespread body distribution	Reaches peak of color	Rapid disappearance of rash
Myotonia	Voluntary muscles of arms and legs tense; involuntary muscles become tense	Further increase in voluntary and involuntary muscle tension; may be grimaces of facial muscles, tension in neck muscles, and involuntary contractions in hands and feet	Loss of voluntary control; involuntary contractions or spasms of muscle groups	Muscles return to relaxed state within 5 minutes after orgasm
Rectum	No change	No change	Involuntary contractions of rectal sphincter occurring at same time as contractions of orgasmic platform and ejaculation	Return to normal
Hyperventilation	None	Occurs late in this phase	Respiratory rates as high as 40/minute	Return to normal
Tachycardia	Heart rate increase begins	Recorded rates average from 100–175 beats/minute	Recorded rates range from 100–180+ beats/minute	Return to normal
Blood pressure	Increase begins	Increased elevation	Greater increases	Return to normal
Perspiration	No change	No change	No change	Appearance of widespread film of perspiration

Reproduced by permission from Denny, Nancy W., and Quadagno, David: *Human Sexuality,* St. Louis, 1988, Times Mirror/Mosby College Publishing; modified from Masters and Johnson, 1966.

may not return to their original state for 1 to 2 hours after sexual stimulation ceases (Masters & Johnson, 1966). Since the refractory period for women is not as pronounced as for men, if sexual stimulation is resumed during the resolution stage, most women will return to the plateau stage. Many women may quickly progress to additional orgasms, which they often report as being more physiologically intense than their first orgasm (Hyde, 1990). Orgasms have been reported to differ in their physiological intensity as well as their degree of psychological satisfaction depending upon their source (Davidson & Darling, 1989b).

The Male Sexual Response

Given the preoccupation with penis size in our society, a man's self-esteem and sense of identity may actually be influenced by how he perceives his penis size. While some women find the pressure and stretching of the vaginal barrel by a large penis to be very arousing, others may find deep penetration or extensive vaginal stretching to be painful rather than pleasurable (Allgeier & Allgeier, 1988). For younger men, the sight of an attractive woman, daydreaming, or a suggestive picture may psychologically induce sexual arousal. But as men move into their 30s and 40s, psychological factors produce sexual arousal less and less frequently. Although there are differences between the female and male sexual response, the four stages are quite similar in many ways.

Very early during the excitement stage, the penis becomes erect, the testes draw up near the body, and the skin ridges of the scrotum become smooth (Masters et al., 1988). Erection of the penis is accompanied by

BOX 10.3 On the Trail of the Big O

Ralph: Quiz time, dearest. What moves around more often than Elizabeth Taylor, the QE2 and the wandering albatross?

Wanda: I give up, Ralph. What?

Ralph: The female orgasm. In the old days, it used to be in the vagina. Then they moved it to the clitoris, where it remained stationary for a decade. Now it seems to be on the move again. Just restless, I guess.

Wanda: Ralph, what on earth are you talking about?

Ralph: The Great Traveling Orgasm, my pet. Under the majestic scepter of science, not to mention the cattle prod of sexual politics, the Big O is thrashing about once again. It's gone from vagina to clitoris and now seems headed for the brain and back to the vagina. One never knows where tomorrow's sexual climaxes will be located.

Wanda: I am about to have an out-of-body experience, Ralph. But I suppose I could remain here with you and your monologue if a fact or two happened to intrude.

Ralph: Facts are the backbone of good argument, my beloved. I hold here in my hand the current winter issue of the *Journal of Sex & Marital Therapy* from which I quote: "From recent empirical studies it can be concluded that most (and probably all) women possess vaginal zones whose tactile stimulation can lead to orgasm." Apparently the long tyranny of the clitoris is coming to an end, dearest. At least until the next dramatic breakthrough of sexual science or the next wave of feminism.

Wanda: You argue like a rogue elephant runs, Ralph. Look, Masters and Johnson showed that the clitoral-vaginal debate was irrelevant. There is only one kind of orgasm and it almost always involves stimulation of the clitoris. It's just that orgasms without that stimulation are rarer and milder than those with it.

Ralph: Manfully argued, my pet. But let us cast a practiced eye at the politics of orgasm. Freud thought that truly mature women always shift their focus from the clitoris to the vagina, so women who needed clitoral stimulation were made to feel like retards or perverts. The feminists just reversed that. It was a much-loved way of downgrading penis-vagina sex and upgrading masturbation. Clitoral enforcers like Shere Hite were sent out to mop up any remaining opposition: the poor deluded women who said they had vaginal orgasms and thought they were enjoying them. But no, the clitoral-pride movement got so strong it became somewhat embarrassing to admit that you owned a vagina or a penis. For all we know, women who used to fake vaginal orgasms for their hubbies began to fake clitoral ones for the women's movement. But do women really have to limit themselves to politically correct orgasms?

Wanda: Your argument has only one minor flaw, Ralph: it's totally wrong. The clitoris is the normal center of women's sexuality, and it is not our fault that it happens to be located in a spot that men find inconvenient. I bet that the article in the *Journal of Sex & Marital Therapy* is just more woolgathering about the G spot.

Ralph: Wrong, beloved helpmate. In fact, the author of the journal's piece, says that his own studies show no evidence of any such sexually sensitive tissue in the vaginal wall where the G spot is alleged to be. These are dark days for G spotologists, my dear. Ernst Grafenberg discovered this spot in the late 1940s. But, who says sexologists should be able to locate a major sexual organ after only 40 years of searching? Anyway, the G spot people say the sensitive spot is usually found between 11 o'clock and 1 o'clock on the vaginal wall.

Wanda: Let me tell you a little secret, Ralph. Who cares about the technology of orgasm? Sex is supposed to be part of a relationship, not a high school biology course. Some women have orgasms without contractions, and the white coats smile down and say, "Sorry, we can't count those because we can't measure them." Same old stuff of males using science to define and control women.

an increase in heart and blood pressure rates. For at least one half of men, their nipples become erect and some muscular tension is apparent. Although men often move through the excitement stage very quickly, by continuing foreplay, it is possible to prolong this stage almost indefinitely as they partially lose and regain their erection (see Table 10.1).

As sexual arousal continues in intensity, the glans penis increases still more in size with the testes swelling to as much as twice their unstimulated state. During the plateau stage, a small quantity of a clear fluid, which is thought to be secreted from the Cowper's glands, is released to assist with penetration of the vagina. Further, most men report the sensation of internal warmth and pressure that comes from vasocongestion of the prostate gland and seminal vesicles. A generalized increase in neuromuscular tension occurs in the buttocks and thighs accompanied by increases in heart, breathing, and blood pressure rates. As orgasm nears, the testicles continue to elevate toward the body but also rotate forward so that firm contact is established with the perineum (Byer & Shainberg, 1991).

The orgasmic stage occurs actually in two separate stages for men. During the first stage, the vas deferens, prostate gland, and seminal vesicles start a series of contractions that transport semen into the **ejaculatory duct,** which connects with the urethra. At this point, the man experiences a sense of "ejaculatory inevitability," because at this point ejaculation cannot be stopped (Masters et al., 1988). During the second stage of orgasm, contractions of the urethra and penis along with those of the prostate gland result in semen spurting from the urethral orifice. These rhythmic contractions occur at approximately 0.8 second intervals for approximately 3 or 4 seconds. During orgasm, the heart rate may double along with an increase in breathing rate that may be characterized by a gasping for air accompanied by an even higher blood pressure level. In addition, there may be severe involuntary muscular tensions throughout the entire body. To avoid the possibility of urine mixing with semen, the neck of the urinary bladder is tightly closed (Francoeur, 1991). Under certain circumstances such as prior to puberty, physiological damage to the prostate gland, or repeated episodes of sexual intercourse in a short period of time may lead to orgasm without ejaculation (Masters et al., 1988). Physiologically, the male's experience of orgasm is one of intense pleasure and relief. Although it is generally acknowledged that the psychological satisfaction may be somewhat less for men than women, the reasons for such differences are still debated.

Under most circumstances, the penis begins to immediately lose its erection during the resolution stage. Depending upon degree and length of preorgasmic arousal, the loss of erection may occur more slowly. Assuming no further stimulation occurs, the penis may remain partially erect for several minutes after orgasm. Most men go through a **refractory period** (time during which further sexual arousal is not possible) lasting from a few minutes to an hour or more before regaining a full erection to continue sexual intercourse. After loss of erection, the heartbeat, blood pressure, breathing rate, and muscular tone return to their pre-excitement levels. In addition, the testes return to their normal size and the scrotum assumes its wrinkled appearance (Crooks & Baur, 1990).

Differences Between Female and Male Sexuality

There are many myths about male sexuality that apparently are based on earlier experiences during the teenage years. These myths include: men have a greater sex drive than women, love is not a prerequisite to have sexual intercourse, and men can always "perform on demand" (McCoy, K., 1985). In recent years, much narrative has been written about gender differences in the sexual response. Accordingly, many reported variations in sexual response are related to social and cultural factors rather than biological differences. For example, in an earlier study of arousal levels for women and men while watching film portrayals of marital sex, casual sex, and sexual activity with a prostitute, both women and men were most aroused by the depiction of casual sex. However, levels of arousal between women and men were equal (Fisher & Byrne, 1978). At this juncture, only two differences between female and male sexuality will be considered: the refractory period and the multi-orgasmic response.

The Refractory Period

Research suggests that the male sex desire dissipates very rapidly after sexual intercourse, whereas the female sex desire may actually increase. After their first orgasm, it is possible for women to immediately desire another orgasm, while men undergo a refractory period (James, 1984). The level of sexual desire is a function of the neuroendocrine system, thought processes, and motivation to engage in sexual activity. These three factors vary from women to men as well as across the life span (Levine, 1987). Although most men require a refractory period before another orgasm may occur, it should be noted that some men can achieve another erection and continue pleasuring the woman even though they will not immediately experience another orgasm. The length of the refractory period, which ranges from a few minutes to a number of hours, becomes longer with each ejaculation occurring within a 24-hour period and with age (Masters et al., 1988). Some men also have reported several mild orgasmic peaks followed by ejaculation as well as sustained pelvic contraction occurring after the release of semen (Zilbergeld, 1978).

The Multi-Orgasmic Response

Another major difference between sexual response patterns of women and men relates to the question of orgasmic capacity. Women have the physiological capacity to be multi-orgasmic; in other words, they have the capability of having two or more orgasms during a single sexual episode. Assuming continual interest and adequate stimulation, the vasocongestion of the vagina remains at a high level between orgasms (Amberson & Hoon, 1985). A 1970 survey of *Psychology Today* readers found that 16% of women reported having multiple orgasms (Athanasiou, Shaver, & Tavris,

1970). More recently, a survey of college-educated female nurses found that 49% had experienced multiple orgasms during masturbation and 48% during sexual intercourse (Darling, Davidson, & Jennings, in press). Despite these findings, women should not consider multiple orgasms to be the goal of their sexual encounters.

Researchers have suggested that social and psychological factors related to the sex partner are extremely important in the way in which physiological orgasmic responses will be perceived (Snyder & Berg, 1983). The quality of orgasmic response is influenced by mood, timing, depth of involvement with partner, environment, and other subjective factors such as memories, experiences, emotions, thoughts, guilt, and anxiety (Roberts, 1983; Wells, Lucas, & Meyer, 1980). Adequacy of foreplay, willingness, relaxation, and the ability to concentrate on genital sensations are more likely to induce the maximum sexual pleasure from orgasms (Levine, 1983). The psychological factors inhibiting orgasm include trying too hard, worrying about not achieving orgasm, and anxiety associated with the partner's attitude toward one's ability to achieve orgasm (Snyder & Berg, 1983). Physiological factors also inhibit the orgasmic response including inadequate clitoral stimulation, ineptness of sex partner, and inconsistency in approach to genital stimulation (Davidson & Darling, 1989b).

Foreplay as Prelude

Foreplay is herein defined as a number of different activities such as kissing, caressing, manual and oral stimulation of breasts, and oral-genital stimulation in which the intended purpose is to heighten the degree of sexual arousal for the person receiving stimulation. Women especially enjoy kissing and caressing as a prelude to other sexual activity because it permits expression of affection between partners. In a survey of married couples, 80% of wives reported engaging in kissing and caressing "every time they have sex" (Blumstein & Schwartz, 1983). To illustrate a gender difference, when asked what sexual activity gives the most pleasure during foreplay, only 37% of men in a national survey replied "kissing and caressing" (Pietropinto & Simenauer, 1977).

The most often reported preferences for foreplay techniques by women, excluding oral-genital stimulation, include oral and manual stimulation of the breasts and nipples, manual stimulation of the clitoral area and clitoris, and manual stimulation of the vaginal opening (Davidson & Darling, 1989b). However, one must remember that individual preferences do exist with regard to foreplay so some women may not enjoy or respond to all foreplay techniques. The importance of foreplay is demonstrated by the changes in sex life desired by college-educated women: more tenderness by partner—25%, more manual stimulation of clitoral area—23%, more oral stimulation of the nipples—23%, and more manual stimulation of breasts—20% (Darling & Davidson, 1986b). In a comparison of college-educated professional women, almost one half reported the desire for more foreplay during sexual activity regardless of their marital status (Davidson & Darling, 1988c). Thus, many women perceive the quantity of foreplay in their sex lives as being insufficient to satisfy their needs.

Not only does foreplay serve as a medium of affection between sex partners and increase vaginal lubrication, it also elevates the level of arousal to a sufficient degree in women to activate an orgasmic response. Among married women, the two most often reported inhibitors of orgasm are lack of foreplay and fatigue, whereas lack of foreplay is most often reported by never-married and divorced/separated women (see Table 10.2). In addition, foreplay, in the form of manual clitoral stimulation by one's partner, was found to be an important source of orgasm for three fourths of the women in another study (Darling & Davidson, 1986b).

Oral-Genital Stimulation

If both sex partners are psychologically comfortable with oral-genital contact, the physiological and psychological feelings of giving and receiving oral-genital stimulation may be a highly pleasurable experience (Crooks & Baur, 1990). Cunnilingus can be a very effective method of precipitating orgasm for many women. An important consideration for persons giving fellatio involves individual preferences regarding ejaculation of semen into the mouth. Among the reported reservations about engaging in oral-genital stimulation are religious beliefs, fear of vaginal odors, fear of ejaculation into mouth, and legal status of oral-genital stimulation between heterosexual partners in some states (Geer et al., 1984).

Despite the reservations expressed by some persons, the percentage of those participating in cunnilingus and fellatio has continued to increase as women and men experiment and learn to enjoy this activity (Kitzinger, 1985). Participation in oral-genital sex by women today appears more likely if they are married. A study of college-educated women employed as health

Table 10.2: Inhibitors of Orgasm for Professional Women

Inhibitors of Orgasm	Never Married	Married	Divorced/Separated	Totals
Lack of foreplay	62%	63%	83%	66%
Preoccupation	46	62	56	56
Fatigue	33	63	56	52
Conflicts with partner	28	43	44	38
Premature ejaculation	54	28	39	38
Difficult to sexually arouse	18	26	28	24
Lack of interest-foreplay	20	17	39	21
Lack of vaginal lubrication	33	17	11	21
Desire to perform well	20	14	39	20
Lack of tenderness	10	15	39	17

From J. K. Davidson, Sr., and C. A. Darling, "The Stereotype of Single Women Revisited: Sexual Practices and Sexual Satisfaction among Professional Women" in *Health Care for Women, International,* 9:328. Copyright © 1988 Hemisphere Publishing Corporation, New York, NY. Reprinted by permission.

care-related professionals in the United States and Canada found that 84% of never-marrieds had engaged in cunnilingus and 81% in fellatio, whereas 96% of marrieds had engaged in cunnilingus and 95% in fellatio (Davidson & Darling, 1988a). Other evidence suggests that most married couples use fellatio and cunnilingus as an alternative pattern in their love-making rather than experiencing these practices each time they engage in sexual activity. In fact, only about 6% reported using the practice every time (Blumstein & Schwartz, 1983). Generally speaking, persons who are college-educated and who hold professional/managerial positions are more likely to engage in oral-genital stimulation than working class persons. But men, regardless of their socioeconomic status, reported "more oral sex" as the second most preferred change in their sex life, with different positions for sexual intercourse being the most desired change (Shostak, 1981).

Anal Intercourse as an Alternative Practice

Since the anus and anal sphincter are richly endowed with nerve endings, some heterosexual couples find anal intercourse to be a pleasurable alternative to penile-vaginal intercourse (Allgeier & Allgeier, 1991). Although manual stimulation of the breast, clitoris, or vagina may occur during anal intercourse, some women report experiencing orgasm solely through anal intercourse. Further, most men report more physical pleasure because the anal orifice is usually smaller and tighter than the vaginal orifice (Delora, Warren, & Ellison, 1981).

Available evidence today suggests that participation in anal intercourse is an infrequent occurrence among most heterosexual couples. In the early 1970s of those married couples under age 35, only 25% had experienced anal intercourse, whereas only 14% of those married couples over age 35 indicated having engaged in anal intercourse (Hunt, 1974). In a *Redbook* study of 100,000 women, 22% of these women had tried anal intercourse "once" (Tavris & Sadd, 1975). By 1986, a survey of 26,000 women found that 43% had tried anal intercourse, but only 12% reported enjoying the sexual experience (Rubenstein & Tavris, 1987). Others in the mid-1980s reported that 25% of women occasionally engaged in anal intercourse while 10% did so on a regular basis for reasons of physiological satisfaction (Bolling & Voeller, 1987). As the 1990s began, among never-married college students, 18% of women and 15% of men report having experienced opposite-sex anal intercourse (Davidson & Moore, 1990).

Potential Harmful Effects Associated with Anal Intercourse

If anal intercourse is to be attempted, a commercial lubricant such as K-Y Jelly should be used because the anal sphincter ordinarily tightens when it is stimulated (Allgeier & Allgeier, 1991). To avoid injury, the anal sphincter should be manually dilated prior to penile insertion. But even a well-lubricated penis, if large, can result in tissue laceration in the rectum.

Acquired Immune Deficiency Syndrome (AIDS) is less likely to be transmitted through vaginal than anal intercourse where the risk is much greater for laceration of the mucus membranes contained in the rectum.

Further, the sexually transmitted diseases of gonorrhea, genital warts, and genital herpes also may be transmitted through anal intercourse. If persons choose to engage in anal intercourse, the penis should be thoroughly washed before vaginal insertion to prevent transportation of bacteria from the anus and rectum to the vaginal tract. Ideally, condoms should be used during anal intercourse to prevent vaginal infections because all bacteria may not be removed from the penis prior to beginning penile/vaginal intercourse (Agnew, 1986).

Marital Sexuality

Among laypersons and professionals, much attention in recent years has been focused on the changes in premarital sexual activity. However, marital sexuality also appears to be changing. Evidence suggests that as women have become sexually liberated in terms of acceptance of their sexuality, the importance of achieving sexual identity and experiencing sexual pleasure has increased. As evidence of this change, the practice of masturbation has come to be accepted as a sexual outlet by many married women.

Sexual **abstinence** is another example. In a survey of married couples, one third of those under age 45 had previously stopped having sexual intercourse for periods ranging from 2 months to over 1 year. Among the reasons cited for **celibacy** (voluntarily abstaining from sexual intercourse) were marital discord, illness, and decreased interest. However, stress and increased work pressure were reported as the most common causes. It should be noted that sexual abstinence was desired by only one of the marriage partners in over one half of the reported cases (Pietropinto, 1987). With so much emphasis on the importance of sexuality, it is crucial to explore several dimensions including the incidence of sexual intercourse, masturbation, and sexual fantasizing in marriage.

Frequency of Marital Sexual Intercourse

In attempting to assess the frequency of sexual intercourse among married persons, the process is influenced by a number of factors: age at marriage, duration of marriage, religiosity, presence of children, cohabitation prior to marriage, educational level, gender-role orientation, level of marital happiness and/or satisfaction, and fatigue (Donnelly, 1990). For example, among wives under age 30, the frequency of sexual intercourse decreased from 10.0 times per month to 7.8 times per month over a period of 5 years. As the educational level of the wife increased, the reported decrease in frequency of sexual intercourse was greater. One could wonder if this is true because increased levels of education are related to other influential factors: being older and being married longer (Udry, 1980).

A further indication of the complex nature of the question comes from a 6-year study of 2,000 couples who had been married between 1 month and 25 years. For these spouses, frequency of sexual intercourse began decreasing from their wedding day, reaching its lowest level about 2 to 3 years later, thereafter increasing to reach its peak at about 6 to 10 years after the wedding (Jasso, 1985). Perhaps this point is best illustrated by the steady decline in mean monthly frequency of marital sexual intercourse over time: 15 times per month in 1st year of marriage and only 6 times per month after 6 years (Greenblat, 1983). However, a decline in frequency of sexual intercourse was much more likely to be reported if the husband's occupation was professional rather than blue-collar and if he had married at age 25 or older. Work demands, child rearing, fatigue, and sexual familiarity were cited as reasons for this decline.

Confirming popular opinion, one study found that divorced and separated women experience sexual intercourse more often than never-marrieds. Unexpectedly, however, frequency of sexual intercourse for the divorced and separated women also exceeded that of married women. The reported frequencies for this sample of college-educated women in the health professions were never-marrieds—7.4 times per month; marrieds—7.8 times per month; and divorced/separateds—8.6 times per month (Davidson & Darling, 1988a).

Masturbation Among Married Persons

Although many changes have occurred with regard to sexual attitudes and sexual behavior over the last two decades, masturbation among married persons remains a closely guarded secret. While masturbation can be used to provide a sexual outlet during partner absence or as a supplemental source of sexual pleasure, much guilt surrounds the practice (Davidson, 1984). Masturbation among married persons is more frequent among men, in general, and among younger women and men as well as among college-educated spouses of either gender (Aldridge, 1983). A study of married couples between ages 18–32 found that 100% of wives and husbands engaged in masturbation. However, it is of interest to observe that 92% of husbands in this study believed that their wives did not engage in masturbation (Aldridge, 1983). Investigating the monthly mean frequencies for masturbation among married persons, researchers found 2.5 times for wives and 11.0 times for husbands (Davidson, 1985; Davidson & Hoffman, 1986). Further, another survey of college-educated women in the health professions found masturbation to occur more frequently among never-married and divorced/separated women: 5.6 times per month—never-marrieds, 5.1 times per month—divorced and separateds, and 3.6 times per month—marrieds (Davidson & Darling, 1988a).

Reasons for Masturbation

Masturbation among married persons is becoming a common practice despite some negative religious attitudes as well as personal feelings of guilt toward the practice. Guilt often stems from a perception that married persons should not have the need to engage in masturbation (Aldridge, 1983). These feelings of guilt arise from several sources. Some persons believe that wives or husbands with an option for sexual intercourse who engage in masturbation have abnormally high sexual appetites. Others consider that engaging in masturbation will deprive their marital partner of the opportunity for sexual activity. On the contrary, masturbation may actually heighten a person's sexual awareness through exploration of her/his body and lead to more sexual intercourse rather than less (Gordon, 1985). The reported reasons for married women engaging in masturbation include husband absent—38%, to relax tensions—31%, enjoyable addition to sexual intercourse—31%, sexual intercourse not satisfying—18%, and sexual experimentation—16% (Tavris & Sadd, 1975).

The Utilization of Sexual Fantasies

Sexual fantasies are mental experiences arising from either imagination or life involvement which usually occur during daydreams, masturbation, or sexual encounters with a partner (Crooks & Baur, 1990). In the late 1950s and early 1960s, utilization of sexual fantasies during sexual intercourse by married persons ceased to be viewed as deviant behavior. Having sexual fantasies while engaging in sexual intercourse with one's spouse gradually became related to good rather than poor marital adjustment (Kelly, 1978). Although some therapists believe that private fantasies during sexual activity with a partner may lessen the trust and intimacy in a relationship, they agree that fantasies may serve as psychological safety valves to eliminate inner tensions and needs (Byrne, 1977). Deficits in erotic fantasies have been related to low sexual desire and slow arousal (Nutter & Condron, 1983). However, their presence has been found to help many women experience arousal and orgasm (Davidson & Hoffman, 1986).

As for incidence of sexual fantasies, the reported percentages for married women range from 88% (Davidson & Hoffman, 1986) to 94% (Crepault, Abraham, Porto, & Couture, 1977). Of married women reporting sexual fantasies during sexual intercourse with their spouse, the percentages range from 37% (Davidson & Hoffman, 1986) to 75% (Fisher, 1973). Among married men, 96% reported having ever engaged in sexual fantasizing in general (Davidson, 1985). Of those married men reporting sexual fantasies during sexual intercourse with their wife, the percentages range from 56% (Davidson, 1985) to 63% (Hessellund, 1976).

Function of Sexual Fantasies

The two major reasons for fantasizing are to achieve sexual arousal and to help achieve orgasm (Stock & Geer, 1982). Without regard to marital status, about three fourths of women and men have reported using sexual fantasy to enhance their sexual arousal (Zimmer, Borchardt, & Fischle, 1983). However, only one fourth of married women indicated their spouses were aware of their sexual fantasies, and less than one half thought their husbands would be accepting of such fantasies (see Table 10.3). Further, of these wives, one third reported feeling guilty about their sexual fantasies. Among married women who reported sexual fantasies during sexual intercourse, two thirds indicated their fantasies helped them to reach orgasm. Interestingly, the use of sexual fantasies was not related to satisfaction with current sex life (Davidson & Hoffman, 1986). For those married men reporting fantasies during sexual intercourse, 91% used fantasies to achieve sexual arousal and 74% employed fantasies to achieve orgasm. Again, no relationship was found between experiencing sexual fantasies during sexual intercourse and satisfaction with their current sex life (Davidson, 1985).

Sexual fantasies of married women tend to be more romantic in nature in comparison to married men. Five favorite sexual fantasies for married women, in order, were reliving previous memorable sexual experience, extramarital sex, current sex partner, new sex partner, and different positions for sexual intercourse (Davidson & Hoffman, 1986). The five favorite sexual fantasies during sexual intercourse for married men, in order, were different positions for sexual intercourse, new sex partner, oral-genital sex, extramarital sex, and female as sexual aggressor (Davidson, 1985).

Table 10.3: Perceived Reaction of Husband to Wife's Sexual Fantasies

	Rating of Current Sex Life		
Perceived Reaction of Husband	Satisfied	Neither*	Dissatisfied
Acceptance	50%	39%	33%
Try harder to please	27	30	33
Feel hurt	25	22	33
Damaging to ego	24	35	33
Partner jealous	19	9	33
Feelings of inadequacy	15	30	17
Sexual arousal	14	17	17

*Neither satisfied nor dissatisfied.
Source: J. K. Davidson, Sr., and L. E. Hoffman, "Sexual Fantasies and Sexual Satisfaction: An Empirical Analysis of Erotic Thought" in *The Journal of Sex Research,* 22:199. Copyright © 1986 Society for the Scientific Study of Sex, Philadelphia, PA.

Sexual Dysfunction

Sexual dysfunction has been described as a condition in which there is impairment of ordinary physiological responses of sexual excitement or orgasm (Masters et al., 1988). Until fairly recently, very little scientific research had been conducted to assist in the understanding of sexual dysfunction. The landmark work of Masters & Johnson (1966) has provided baselines for the range of normal physiological sexual responses. A review of routine sexual histories taken by physicians found the following sexual dysfunctions among women: lack of sexual desire—27%, **anorgasmia** (absence of orgasm)—25%, and **dyspareunia** (pain during sexual intercourse)—20%. For men, the dysfunctions were premature ejaculation—14%, lack of sexual desire—13%, and erection difficulties—12% (Ende, Rockwell, & Glasgow, 1984).

Causation: A Complex Issue

While many sexual disorders are thought to be caused by inhibitions, lack of emotional commitment to sex partner, fear of intimacy, and/or fear of the opposite sex, the question is much more complex (Hirsch, 1986). To ascertain the cause of sexual dysfunctions is a difficult and intricate problem for two reasons. First, while a particular sexual dysfunction may have been identified, it may be difficult to determine the specific cause due to the many varied personal experiences and influences that contribute to sexual response. Second, it is also difficult to establish a specific and consistent cause-and-effect relationship because what produces a sexual dysfunction in one individual may have absolutely no effect on another person (LoPiccolo, 1985). For example, the effects of alcohol consumption on sexual performance are at least twofold. Alcohol consumption may serve to lower inhibitions about engaging in various sexual activities such as oral-genital stimulation or anal intercourse, resulting in a more assertive or aggressive role for women during their participation in sexual activity (Klassen & Wilsnack, 1986). In contrast, women who drink socially have reported that as their blood alcohol levels rise, they have reduced orgasmic intensity, less vasocongestion of the labia and vaginal barrel, and less vaginal lubrication. Further, alcoholic women have indicated a variety of other sexual concerns including orgasmic difficulty, **inhibited sexual desire,** and painful intercourse (Pinhas, 1987). In men, ingestion of small amounts of alcohol decreases **tumescence** (swelling of penis at erection) by about 10%, while consuming large amounts of alcohol decreases tumescence by as much as two thirds due to its anesthetizing effects on nerve endings contained in the glans penis. In addition, men under the influence of alcohol will take longer to ejaculate (Price & Price, 1983).

Contrary to popular opinion, in a survey of drug users, only 14% of women and 32% of men reported a belief that utilization of cocaine enhanced their orgasmic intensity (Seecof & Tennant, 1986). With regard to marijuana usage prior to sexual activities, over one half of men but only one third of women in one study reported that marijuana usage enhanced the quality of their orgasms. However, it is possible that the sensations of the orgasmic experience are distorted by direct effects of the marijuana on brain centers that control sexual activity (Weller & Halikas, 1984).

Female Sexual Dysfunction

During the past two decades, the traditional view that women are less sexual than men has been largely discarded, and sexual needs of women have come to be recognized and accepted. Consequently, a woman today who perceives herself as being sexually unresponsive oftentimes becomes embarrassed or confused (Masters et al., 1988). The three major types of female sexual dysfunction are inhibited sexual desire, anorgasmia, and dyspareunia.

Inhibited Sexual Desire

Inhibited sexual desire is defined as a condition characterized by little or no interest in initiating and engaging in sexual fantasy and/or sexual activity (Crooks & Baur, 1990). It is estimated that primary inhibited sexual desire, which relates to general aversion to engaging in sexual activity, occurs in only about 1–3% of women. However, secondary or situational inhibited sexual desire, which occurs only under certain circumstances, is estimated to involve from 33–48% of all women (Nathan, 1986). A survey of counselors and therapists ascertained that the most often reported client sexual dysfunction was inhibited sexual desire (Kilmann, Boland, Norton, Davidson, & Caid, 1986). The emotional state of a person is a very important component of whether or not they will experience pleasure and sexual arousal during sexual activity. If a certain situation is perceived as pleasant, sexual desire will be higher which will likely produce a high level of sexual arousal (Mehrabian & Stanton-Mohr, 1985).

The causes of primary or chronic inhibited desire may be psychological issues such as power struggles fueled by the changing role of women, unresolved childhood anger at parents, and intimacy and communication problems. Biological causes may include depression, alcoholism, substance abuse, and hormone imbalance (Kaplan, 1987). Origins of situational inhibited sexual desire are more likely to be related to a partner or a particular type of sexual activity. For example, inhibited sexual desire may be a way of psychologically distancing oneself from one's sex partner. Or a sex partner may insist on a sexual practice that the other partner finds distasteful. Fatigue also may be the origin of situational inhibited sexual desire (Schover, 1986). In a group of married working and nonworking women who had sought therapy for sexual dysfunction, almost one fourth of those women who were characterized as career women and working for both psychological and financial rewards reported inhibited sexual desire. But of those women who were either working for financial reasons only or who were not employed, only 11% indicated inhibited sexual desire. These data suggest that fatigue associated with heavy job demands may play a significant role in inhibited sexual desire (Avery-Clark, 1986b).

Anorgasmia

Primary anorgasmia refers to a condition in which a woman has never experienced orgasm either by masturbation, through manual or oral stimulation by her partner, or during sexual intercourse. Situational anorgasmia refers to a circumstance where the woman has experienced orgasm but can do so only under certain conditions such as while masturbating or during oral or manual genital stimulation by her partner (Hyde, 1990). Surveys of sexually active adult women suggest a range of 5–15% of women reporting primary anorgasmia with the percentage being lower among married and highly educated women (Nathan, 1986). The incidence of situational anorgasmia is difficult to establish because of the circumstances surrounding its cause. However, one study of ex-therapy clients found that situational anorgasmia had been indicated by 1 in 5 women (Kilmann et al., 1986).

The inability to reach orgasm during sexual intercourse, without supplemental manual or oral clitoral stimulation, is the most common sexual complaint among women (Kaplan, 1987). In a study of sexual responsiveness, only 44% of women reported "always" experiencing orgasm during sexual intercourse without simultaneous manual clitoral stimulation (Ellison, 1980). Consequently, most sexologists have concluded that indirect clitoral stimulation provided by sexual intercourse may not be sufficient to produce orgasm in the majority of women. Such women, nevertheless, report sexual intercourse to be highly pleasurable. Thus, sex counselors and therapists do not perceive a sexual difficulty to exist if the woman enjoys sexual intercourse and achieves orgasm through some means other than sexual intercourse (LoPiccolo, 1985).

Anorgasmic women, when compared to orgasmic women, are more likely to report greater discomfort in communicating with their partner about those sexual activities involving direct clitoral stimulation (cunnilingus and manual stimulation by partner), more negative attitudes toward masturbation, greater endorsement of sexual myths, and greater sexual guilt (Kelly, Strassberg, & Kircher, 1990). The cause of primary anorgasmia appears to be rooted in the personal lack of permission to enjoy sexual activity. Several factors may be operating, such as the traditional cultural conditioning that "nice girls" are not supposed to exhibit sexual feelings, sexual guilt created by conflicts between personal values and sexual response, fear of sexual feelings, religious attitudes, and afraid to "let go" during heightened sexual arousal (Francoeur, 1982). Situational anorgasmia may result from lack of adequate knowledge about the female sexual response cycle, lack of sufficient clitoral stimulation, fear of urination during sexual arousal, short duration of sexual intercourse, and ineffective oral, manual, or sexual intercourse stimulation techniques by partner (Jayne,

1985; Newcomb & Bentler, 1980a). Further, anorgasmic women are more likely to have a traditional feminine gender identity whereas orgasmic women are more likely to be androgynous or neutral in their gender identity (Weil, 1985). This may relate to the fact that in some studies, androgynous women have been found to have more positive attitudes toward sexuality than those with traditional gender identity (Walfish & Myerson, 1980). Nevertheless, it is important that women not conclude that it is an absolute necessity to experience an orgasm during sexual intercourse in order to achieve sexual satisfaction.

Dyspareunia

Dyspareunia is the third most often reported sexual complaint among women. Two types exist: primary dyspareunia—pain present from initial sexual intercourse and secondary dyspareunia—later development of discomfort after initial pain-free sexual intercourse. Further, this dysfunction may be categorized as either complete (occurs during all episodes of sexual intercourse) or situational (occurs only when using certain positions or with certain sex partners) (Glatt, Zinner, & McCormack, 1990). The actual incidence of dyspareunia is subject to considerable speculation. Clinical data suggest that about 15% of sexually active adult women experience dyspareunia at least a few times each year, with 1–2% of women estimated to have dyspareunia on more than an occasional basis (Masters et al., 1988). In survey data from college-educated women in their 30s, 34% reported having persistent dyspareunia while another 27% indicated having had dyspareunia at some time in their sex lives. Of those women currently reporting dyspareunia, 55% had occasional discomfort whereas 24% had frequent discomfort (Glatt et al., 1990).

Psychological causes of dyspareunia may include hostility, anger, or resentment directed toward sex partner, or fears associated with experiencing sexual intercourse (Francoeur, 1982). Inadequate vaginal lubrication also may produce discomfort at the entrance to the vaginal orifice or deep inside the vaginal barrel. This lack of vaginal lubrication may be a function of inadequate stimulation, level of sexual arousal, or insufficient estrogen production. If painful sexual intercourse occurs during deep thrusting, it may be caused by jarring of the ovaries or stretching of the ligaments that suspend the uterus. Such discomfort may only be experienced when using certain positions for sexual intercourse or at certain times during the menstrual cycle. Or deep pelvic pain during sexual intercourse may be associated with endometriosis, a physical condition in which the endometrium begins growing in other locations within the abdominal cavity (O'Shaughnessy, Zuspan, Pariser, Nelson, & Boutselis, 1983). This condition may prevent the internal reproductive organs from moving about freely during sexual intercourse, thus creating discomfort. Further, inflammation of the vaginal wall may be produced by such conditions as yeast and bacterial infections which may result in dyspareunia. Sexually transmitted diseases such as gonorrhea and chlamydia, which will be discussed in chapter 11, can cause infections in the vaginal barrel or uterus, thus producing dyspareunia (Crooks & Baur, 1990).

Male Sexual Dysfunction

Since male sexual performance is considered a benchmark for measuring masculinity, men suffering from sexual dysfunction may be extremely embarrassed or depressed since this condition will be perceived as challenging their manhood. Inhibited sexual desire and dyspareunia occasionally occur among men, but the incidence is considered somewhat rare (Masters et al., 1988). Men who do report difficulties with sexual desire are much more likely to be concerned about the discrepancy that exists between their level of sexual desire and that of their female sex partner. Only two dysfunctions will be considered: erectile dysfunction and premature ejaculation.

Erectile Dysfunction

Erectile dysfunction is defined as the inability to achieve or maintain an erection, on a more than occasional basis, for a sufficient period of time so as to engage in sexual intercourse. Primary erectile dysfunction is used to describe the inability of a man to achieve an erection of sufficient quality for engaging in sexual intercourse with a partner. However, this same man may be able to achieve an adequate erection for masturbation. Secondary erectile dysfunction is a condition in which a man has previously had an adequate erection with his current or previous partner but at the present time is unable to achieve an erection sufficient for engaging in sexual intercourse (Francoeur, 1991).

Given the anxiety associated with erectile dysfunction, it is difficult to precisely establish its prevalence. Using clinical records, the incidence of secondary erectile dysfunction is estimated to be about 10 times more frequent than primary erectile dysfunction (Kolodny, Masters, & Johnson, 1979; Kilmann et al., 1986).

In fact, it has been projected that at least one half of all men have experienced secondary erectile dysfunction on one or more occasions (Kaplan, 1974). One survey of sexually active men found that 98% could maintain an erection long enough to have sexual intercourse "most or all of the time," although 15% indicated erectile dysfunction in the past (Spector & Boyle, 1986). When couples seeking sex therapy were interviewed, in three fourths of the cases there were discrepancies in their assessment of the problem. In most cases, the male patient's partner indicated her lover had an erectile difficulty, but the man failed to indicate this fact (Tiefer & Melman, 1983). These findings suggest that men are reluctant to label themselves as having erectile dysfunction.

In the past, it was thought that about 90% of all erectile dysfunction problems were attributable to psychological factors. However, it is now estimated that 50–60% of all primary erectile dysfunction difficulties are partially or totally caused by physiological factors such as illicit drugs, some prescription medications, severe diabetes, and alcoholism (Crenshaw, 1984; Maatman & Montague, 1985). Organic conditions, including damage to the nerves and blood vessels controlling the tumescence process, also cause erectile dysfunction (Wespes & Schulman, 1985). Psychological factors such as sexual guilt, anxiety, anger, boredom, and relationship problems with either a current or a past sex partner also may result in secondary erectile dysfunction (Miller, 1983). Further, as more women demand equality in terms of sexual pleasure and sexual arousal, there has been a significant increase in the reported frequency of secondary erectile dysfunction among younger men due to their anxiety about their partner's performance standards during sexual intercourse (Francoeur, 1982).

Premature Ejaculation

Premature ejaculation, or rapid ejaculation, may be defined as lack of voluntary control leading to the unintentional release of semen during attempts at vaginal entry or very soon after sexual intercourse begins. This does not allow sufficient time for the woman to become sexually aroused, experience vaginal lubrication, and/or reach orgasm (Masters et al., 1988). The American Psychiatric Association (1980) has suggested the need to take into account various factors affecting the duration of the excitement stage such as age, "novelty" of the sex partner, and frequency of sexual intercourse when establishing whether premature ejaculation exists. Nevertheless, it is estimated that 15–20% of adult men have at least a moderate degree of difficulty controlling rapid ejaculation. Further, of the total reported cases of premature ejaculation, only about 10% involve ejaculation while trying to penetrate the vagina (Kolodny et al., 1979). However, these estimates may be somewhat low, because a more recent study of 218 husbands seeking treatment for sexual dysfunction found that one fourth reported premature ejaculation (Avery-Clark, 1986a).

Although premature ejaculation is probably the most common sexual dysfunction for which men seek sex therapy, it is the female partner who is more likely to complain about its occurrence (Masters et al., 1988). Its cause may be either physiological or psychological in nature. Among the physiological causes of premature ejaculation are unusual nerve sensitivity of glans penis, enlargement or infection of the prostate gland especially in men over age 50, and tight uncircumcised foreskin (Francoeur, 1982). Psychological causes of premature ejaculation include traumas associated with prior sexual experiences, poor foreplay, anxiety, fear of unwanted pregnancy, and anxiety over adequate sexual performance (Byer & Shainberg, 1991; Perelman, 1980).

Seeking Treatment for Sexual Dysfunction

Depending upon the nature of the sexual dysfunction, sometimes expansion of one's knowledge base about the female and male sexual response cycles through reading, human sexuality workshops, and/or self-help groups prove to be extremely beneficial in the resolution of certain types of sexual dysfunctions (Meldman, 1981). However, causes of inhibited sexual desire, dyspareunia, erectile dysfunction, and premature ejaculation are complex and often related to other aspects of the partner relationship rather than the sexual arena. Therefore, sexual dysfunction should be treated in a relationship context rather than on an individual basis (Fish, Fish, & Sprenkle, 1984).

There are a number of approaches to the treatment of sexual dysfunction depending upon whether the causes are physiological/organic or psychological in nature. In recent years, the use of group treatment for primary and secondary anorgasmia in women has become popular. Through sharing their experiences with other women, treatment outcomes indicate increased levels of sexual arousal, more frequent orgasms, higher self-esteem, and better communication with their sex partners (Cotten-Huston & Wheeler, 1983). For men with organic-based dysfunctions due to disease or injury, an inflatable penile prosthesis such as Scott's Model 700 is available (Gregory & Purcell, 1987). Another promising medical advance appropriate for the treatment of either organic or psychologically-based erectile dysfunction is the utilization of self-injections of papaverine-phentolamine into the penile shaft to produce an immediate and sustained erection. To date, no long-term complications or side effects have been identified other than prolonged erections (Trapp, 1987).

Given the variety of causes of sexual dysfunction, it is imperative that the person have a complete medical examination by a physician who specializes in treatment of sexual dysfunctions. They can be found within the fields of internal medicine, endocrinology, gynecology, and urology. If the sexual dysfunction is thought to be psychological in nature, the individual should seek professional help from a person who is a certified clinical member of the American Association for Marriage and Family Therapy specializing in treatment of sexual dysfunction or from a person certified as a sex therapist by the American Association of Sex Educators, Counselors, and Therapists. Marriage and family therapists may not necessarily be qualified to handle the treatment of sexual dysfunctions (Schiller, 1981).

Extramarital Sexual Relationships

As persons marry, social and occupational contacts with members of the opposite sex will continue to occur. Since the women's movement began, more women are working outside the home. In the world of work, women and men are often thrown into contact with attractive members of the opposite sex, under conditions that often encourage emotional sharing. Because of these and other changes in our modern world, couples are increasingly facing the fact that not all of a person's needs can be met by a wife or husband. Thus spouses, and women in particular, ask whether it is possible and desirable for both marital partners to share personal interests and concerns with friends but not with spouses (Saline, 1975). As empathy is established in such relationships, sexual interest may surface, so it is important for opposite-sex friends to be completely frank with one another about the relationship boundaries. Part of the problem is that there are no recognized rules regarding friendships of the opposite sex that exclude the spouse. Consequently, what starts out as a socially approved friendship may become a socially disapproved extramarital relationship (Lampe, 1985).

The three most prevalent types of extramarital sexual relationships are recreational extramarital sex, the affair, and swinging (Reiss & Lee, 1988). **Recreational extramarital sex** refers to nonconsensual or secretive extramarital sexual intercourse, often without emotional commitment, with an emphasis on the pleasure aspects of sexuality. **Extramarital affair** is a term used to describe secretive sexual involvement in which an emotional commitment exists between the extramarital partners along with an emphasis on the pleasurable aspects of sexuality. **Swinging** refers to a form of consensual extramarital sexual involvement that is shared by a couple whereby the wife and husband engage in sexual activity simultaneously and in the same location without emotional involvement (Crooks & Baur, 1990).

Since considerable secrecy is associated with engaging in extramarital sexual intercourse, the reported statistics should be considered as estimates and not generalized to the whole population. When women of all ages, education levels, and varying durations of marriage were surveyed, the reported percentages of married women engaging in extramarital sexual intercourse range from 22% (Blumstein & Schwartz, 1983) to 69% (Wolfe, 1981). Among men, the reported percentages participating in extramarital sexual relations range from 30% (Blumstein & Schwartz, 1983) to 66% (Hite, 1981). These data can be contrasted with a large-scale study of highly-educated British respondents in which 66% of women and 68% of men reported having experienced extramarital sexual intercourse. However, the researcher cautioned that it was not possible to conclude from this sample whether or not a minority or majority of married persons engage in this behavior (Lawson, 1988).

Attitudes Toward Extramarital Sexual Involvement

In a study of gender differences with regard to extramarital sexual involvement, only 11% of women reported having extramarital sexual relations that included emotional commitment in comparison to 44% of men. Further, women felt more guilty about participating in extramarital sexual relations and reported a greater amount of marital dissatisfaction than men (Glass & Wright, 1985). And among female and male graduate students, only 15% of women and men approved of extramarital relationships if sexual intercourse was a component. Factors associated with acceptability of extramarital relationships included number of premarital sexual partners and attitudes toward premarital sexual permissiveness (Weis & Slosnerick, 1981). Those persons with more sex partners and those who approved of premarital sexual intercourse considered extramarital relations as more acceptable than did others.

During the decade of the 1970s, combined data from four national surveys conducted by the National Opinion Research Center (NORC) suggested that only about 30% of respondents "sometimes" approved of extramarital sexual relationships. Permissive responses (approval) by religion were Protestant—16%, Catholic—23%, no religion—53%, and Jewish—55%. In terms of educational level, 38% of respondents with one or more years of college education also gave these permissive responses (Glenn & Weaver, 1979). By 1989, only 7% of respondents in a NORC survey "sometimes" approved of an extramarital sexual relationship (Smith, 1990a). Using national data from the 1970s and 1980s, researchers found that as the size of community increased and the degree of religiosity decreased, the degree of approval for extramarital sexual relations increased (Weis & Jurich, 1985). In general, women seem to be more disapproving of extramarital sexual relations because of the perceived detrimental consequences (Thompson, 1984). Finally, concerning the variable of marital satisfaction, in a study of married dentists, real estate agents, and housewives, those persons reporting high levels of marital and sexual satisfaction were less likely to approve of extramarital sexual relations (Saunders & Edwards, 1984). Gender continues to be an important variable as women who engage in extramarital sexual relationships are viewed in more negative terms than men. This finding is related to the continuation of the double standard of sexuality in our society (Salzman, 1983).

Factors Associated with Extramarital Sexual Involvement

In general, there appear to be three major motivations for engaging in extramarital sexual relationships: compensation for an inadequate marriage, long periods of separation from spouse, and unwillingness to accept a monogamous life-style. However, men are considerably more likely than women to engage in extramarital sexual relations even if their marriage is rated as satisfactory. Some researchers have found the most often cited reason for engaging in extramarital sexual relations is sexual dissatisfaction within marriage. If people engage in extramarital sexual intercourse in search of sexual fulfillment, their reasons are likely to include curiosity about their capacity for sexual fulfillment, sexual boredom, reassurance about their own sexual identity, and revenge against their marital partner (Pestrak, Martin, & Martin, 1985). Marital problems are reported by still others to be the primary reason for participation in extramarital sexual relations (Spanier & Margolis, 1983). Middle-class employed women reporting extramarital sexual involvement indicated dissatisfaction with both the emotional and financial aspects of their marital relationship (Schneiderman, 1990). Consequently, the motivation for an ongoing extramarital relationship may be to experience emotional closeness with the extramarital partner and/or to establish distance from the spouse (Marett, 1990). Extramarital sexual relations appear to be associated with certain characteristics: male gender, age 40 or older, one or more years of college education, infrequent attendance at religious services, no reported religious denomination, low level of marital satisfaction, working outside home, approval of extramarital sexual relationships, and participation in premarital sexual intercourse (Reiss, Anderson, & Sponaugle, 1980).

The impact of extramarital sexual involvement on marriages has long been studied. Some intriguing questions have emerged concerning meanings for those involved. In one study during the mid-1970s, 50 "feminist-oriented" women were interviewed about their extramarital sexual relationships. Selected from a pool of 300 women who had answered an ad in *Ms.* magazine, the majority reported curiosity and desire for personal growth as their major motivations for engaging in extramarital relationships rather than marital unhappiness. Most (93%) reported increased feelings of self-esteem, self-confidence, or resourcefulness (Atwater, 1982). The change in self-confidence was said to result mainly from the women feeling more physically appealing because someone was interested in them. The researcher cautioned, however, that women who have positive extramarital sexual experiences may be more likely to volunteer as subjects, thereby, yielding more positive findings than may randomly occur in the general population. Short-lived relationships that are not discovered by the other spouse may have no detectable effects upon the marriage. However, long-term involvements increase the probability that the other spouse is likely to learn of the relationship. Upon discovery, the feelings of guilt, shame, and betrayal could be so great as to destroy the marriage (Ruben, 1986).

Summary

- Sexual adjustment can be described as the extent to which an individual possesses an awareness and acceptance of her/his sexual nature. In contrast, sexual satisfaction is the perceived discrepancy between the level of aspiration and level of achievement regarding physiological and psychological sexual fulfillment.
- The male reproductive system is comprised essentially of the penis, testicles, Cowper's glands, seminal vesicles, and prostate gland.
- The primary female genital organs involved in the sexual response and reproductive process are the clitoris, labia minora, vagina, uterus, ovaries, and fallopian tubes. Ordinarily, a mature ovum is released from an ovary during each menstrual cycle and travels through the fallopian tubes where conception may occur.
- While the entire vulva is highly erogenous, the clitoris is the major locus of sexual sensation. A sensitive area inside the vagina known as the Grafenberg spot has been identified as an additional locus of sexual sensation.
- The menstrual cycle consists of the proliferative phase, the secretory phase, and the menstrual phase.
- For women and men, there are four stages in the sexual response cycle: excitement, plateau, orgasm, and resolution. The two primary physiological reactions are vasocongestion in the genitalia and female breasts and increased neuromuscular tension in nerves and muscles.
- While a refractory period exists for most men, many women can return almost immediately to the plateau stage and experience repeated orgasms.
- Foreplay permits expression of affection between partners and elevates their level of sexual arousal to allow ease of vaginal penetration during sexual intercourse.
- In recent years, masturbation has come to be recognized as a sexual outlet during spousal absence or as a supplemental source of pleasure. Further, sexual fantasies have come to be viewed as a psychological safety valve to release sexual tensions and to assist in sexual arousal or achievement of orgasm.
- Sexual dysfunction is the inability to react psychologically and physiologically to sexual arousal in ways deemed adequate for a healthy woman or man.
- The three major female sexual dysfunctions are inhibited sexual desire, anorgasmia, and dyspareunia. Among men, the two major sexual dysfunctions are erectile dysfunction and premature ejaculation.
- The major motivations for extramarital sexual relationships are compensation for inadequate marriage, long periods of separation from spouse, and unwillingness to accept a monogamous life-style.
- In general, public attitudes toward extramarital sexual involvement are negative.

Questions for Critical Reflection

1. Parents prematurely buying training bras for little girls is one example of promoting sexual precociousness. What such instances do you remember occurring among your childhood friends? Why do you think sexual precociousness is said to be linked to sexual disaster?
2. Some authorities believe the loss of ability to choose one's sexual behavior constitutes sexual addiction while others believe there is no such thing as sexual addiction. What do you believe? What three points substantiate your belief?
3. Does an understanding of the female/male sexual response systems contribute more to sexual satisfaction or sexual adjustment? Can one be sexually adjusted without being sexually satisfied or sexually satisfied but not sexually adjusted? Why or why not?
4. In a society in which 87% of persons surveyed view extramarital sex as wrong, what could explain the fact that of the 50 feminist-oriented women in Atwater's study from the mid-1970s, 93% indicated increased feelings of self-esteem from extramarital relationships?
5. Erica Jong's book about emotional addiction, *Any Woman's Blues,* suggests that sexual liberation for women may offer not freedom but servitude . . . that freedom is attained only from within oneself through self-knowledge. Do you agree or disagree? What personal experience supports your answer?

Suggested Readings

Allgeier, E. R., & Allgeier, A. R. (1991). *Sexual interactions* (3rd ed.). Lexington, MA: D.C. Heath. Excellent comprehensive text on all aspects of sexuality.

Atwater, L. (1982). *The extramarital connection: Sex, intimacy and identity.* New York: Irvington. A thoroughly documented but highly readable description of women's feelings about love, sex, and their extramarital connections.

Boston Women's Health Book Collective. (1985). *The new our bodies, our selves.* New York: Simon & Schuster. Outstanding nontechnical guide to understanding contraception, physiology of reproduction, and the sexual response.

Calderone, M. S., & Johnson, E. W. (1981). *The family book about sexuality.* New York: Harper & Row. A creative interpretation of all aspects of human sexuality in a family setting.

Kaplan, H. S. (1987). *The illustrated manual of sex therapy* (2nd ed.). New York: Brunner/Mazel. A clear, concise explanation of the various techniques used in the behavioral treatment of the six major sexual dysfunctions.

Masters, W. H., & Johnson, V. E. (1975). *The pleasure bond.* Boston: Little, Brown. A consideration of sexual activity in the context of a long-term commitment rather than a short-term emphasis on self-pleasure seeking.

CHAPTER 11

Birth Control and Sexually Transmitted Diseases

Every time a new contraceptive or a new treatment for infertility is introduced, certain segments of the population raise their voices in protest. In part, this protest has nothing to do with fertility control itself and everything to do with a general resistance to change.
Lynn S. Baker, 1981

OUTLINE

Modern contraceptive technology has provided women and men with the ability to determine when or if they will exercise their social and personal right to have children. Effective family planning not only serves to improve the health status of the woman but also the well-being of her baby and partner (Maine, 1981). These benefits ultimately accrue to a society in which childbirth is by choice and children are truly valued. When sex partners are freed from concerns about an unwanted pregnancy, sexual satisfaction and sexual adjustment are more likely to be achieved. Conversely, an unplanned pregnancy often has social and psychological consequences as well as physical complications such as spontaneous abortion, premature birth, stillbirth, or postpartum difficulties.

The concept of birth control was first widely promoted in the United States during the early 1900s by activist Margaret Sanger, pioneer of the Planned Parenthood Movement. Even so, the sale of contraceptives was prohibited in some states as late as 1965 (Allgeier & Allgeier, 1991). Although the terms birth control and contraceptive are often used interchangeably, they are not synonymous. Birth control or fertility limitation, which includes contraception, **sterilization,** and abortion, refers to the prevention of the occurrence of a live birth. In contrast, **contraception,** one method of birth control, uses a technique, device, or drug to permit sexual intercourse between fertile partners while preventing **conception** (McCary & McCary, 1982).

The sexual behavior patterns of individuals also affect the likelihood of their contracting sexually transmitted diseases (STDs). Medical evidence indicates that sexual activity that is anonymous, casual, with multiple partners, and/or with high-risk partners, substantially increases this likelihood. Choosing to remain a virgin, limiting one's sexual experiences to a single, noninfected partner, and the use of barrier contraceptive methods will help to protect a person from acquiring STDs (Hatcher et al., 1988). With the growing concern in American society about STDs, it is important that all persons understand how STDs can be transmitted and learn methods of safer sexual practices. They also need to be able to recognize symptoms of STDs, and to become familiar with methods for treatment.

Reasons for Failure to Use Contraception Among Unmarrieds

Since the evidence suggests that 90% of fertile women having regular, unprotected sexual intercourse will become pregnant within one year, an obvious question emerges (Hatcher et al., 1986). Why do persons who wish to avoid a pregnancy fail to use a method of contraception? In one study, of those persons currently using no contraceptive method, one half reported negative attitudes toward contraception which included concerns about negative side effects and "just didn't like to practice" (Silverman, Torres, & Forrest, 1987). Despite the need for and ready availability of contraceptives, many sexually active unmarried persons consciously choose not to use contraceptives or to only use them in a spasmodic fashion. One survey of sexually active college women found that one fourth had not used a contraceptive during their last sexual intercourse experience, and only one third consistently used contraceptives (Herold & Goodwin, 1981b). A later study of sexually active women, ages 18–35, found 94% of women had used contraceptives, but 25% were currently not doing so (Silverman et al., 1987).

The likelihood of using a contraceptive is associated, in part, with age of the person (Silverman et al., 1987). But the variety of age ranges of respondents in the various studies makes it difficult to determine the precise percentage of sexually active women at various ages having unprotected sexual intercourse. The strongest evidence, that a high percentage of sexually active never-married women, ages 18–29, are not using contraception, is reflected in the 1988 finding that 22% of all births to women in this age group were to never-marrieds (U.S. Bureau of Census, 1990n).

Negative Self-Feelings

Although attitudes are changing concerning contraceptive availability, promotion, and use among unmarried persons, such issues are still controversial. Fear of discovery, lower self-esteem, and guilt feelings are personal factors impacting the use of contraceptives. Among a number of the single, female teenagers seeking contraceptives at a family planning clinic, parental discovery was also apparently an issue. Of these teens, only slightly over one half of their mothers and one fourth of their fathers were aware of their intention to seek contraception. Generally, parental approval for seeking contraception was much higher among young black women than young white women (Nathanson & Becker, 1986). A survey of never-married undergraduate students found that, for the majority, no major barriers existed that would make contraceptive purchase a particularly difficult or embarrassing experience. Most respondents (90% of women and 80% of men) indicated that convenience was the major reason for their choice

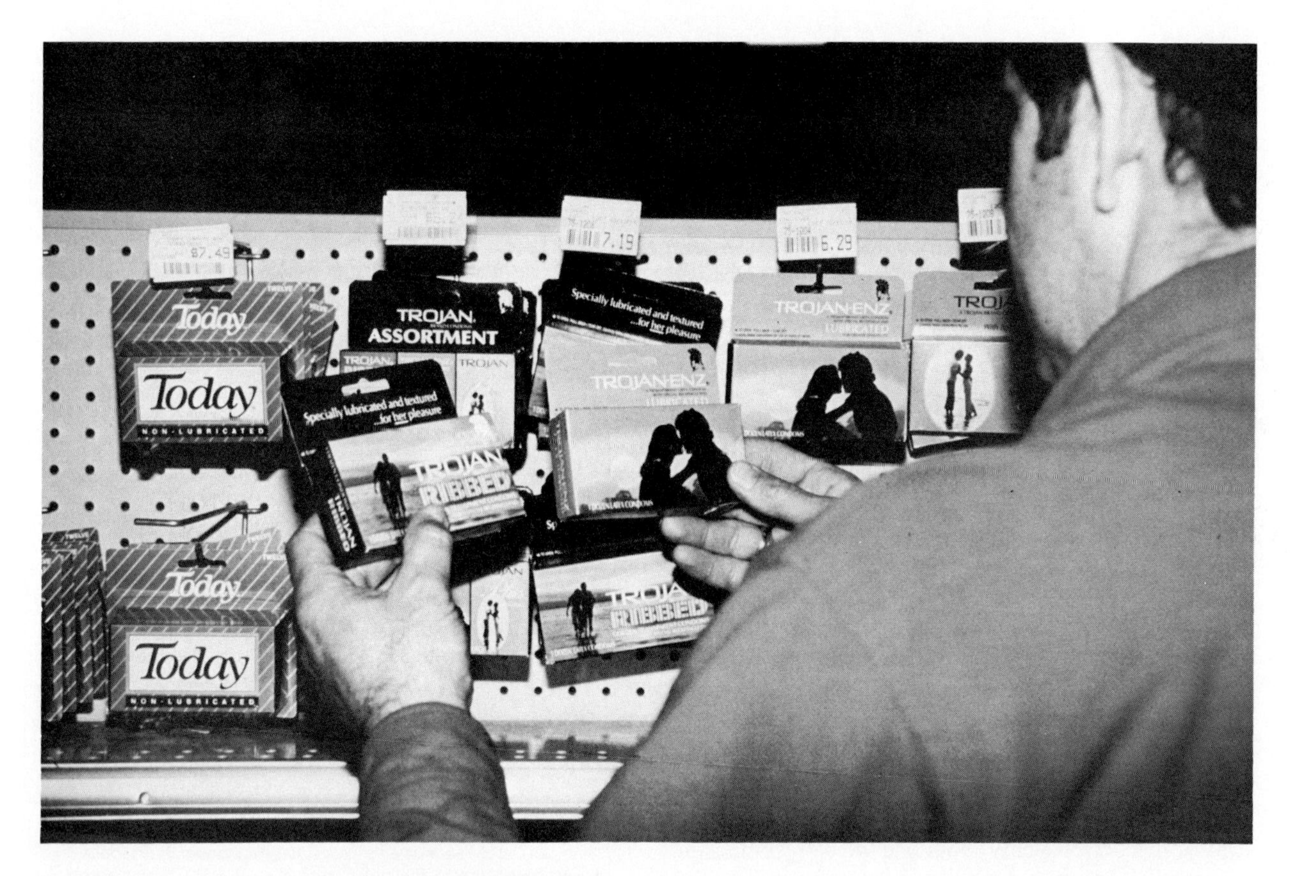

Plan ahead and follow the plan! Sexually active women and men who wish to avoid an unwanted pregnancy must both act responsibly.

of location for purchasing contraceptives. However, the fact that women were more likely to purchase nonprescription contraceptives away from their university campus raises the question of fear of discovery (Kallen & Stephenson, 1980).

Sexually active unmarried women and men with positive self-concepts and body images are much more likely to have used contraceptives and to have used them on a consistent basis (McKinney, Sprecher, & DeLamater, 1984). Apparently, most persons with poor self-images believe they have little control over their lives, and thus avoid advance planning when engaging in any activity that would include contraceptive usage.

The percentage of sexually active college women using effective contraceptive methods has actually increased. It has been suggested that the change occurred because women who now engage in sexual intercourse are those who feel less guilty and thus choose to use an effective contraceptive (Gerrard, 1987). Findings confirm that, at least for female college students, experiencing contraceptive shame has led to inconsistent contraceptive usage as well as choosing less effective methods (Jung, 1983). In general, college women with high sexual guilt rarely use contraceptives. They typically wait longer than others to begin contraception after initiating sexual activity and are poor users of contraceptives because their use is considered to be a commitment to have sexual intercourse. Such women are embarrassed to go to family planning clinics because of having to acknowledge their sexual activity and disclose their sexual involvement (Herold & Goodwin, 1981b). The negative emotions of fear, shame, and disgust are further increased by contraceptive techniques that require touching of the genitals. Consequently, women with high levels of masturbatory guilt rarely use diaphragms, condoms, or foam (Mosher & Vonderheide, 1985). Persons having religious scruples against premarital sexual activity and masturbation are also more likely to have a negative attitude toward contraception. Overall, sexual attitudes and beliefs play a major role in the decision to use contraceptives and the choice of contraceptive methods (Miller, 1986).

Indifference and Lack of Knowledge: Two Crucial Factors

Generally speaking, emotional intimacy and commitment in the dating relationship leads to more consistent contraceptive usage during sexual activity (McKinney et al., 1984). When a dating relationship grows more serious, individuals begin to give more thought to the possibility of an unplanned pregnancy and the resulting consequences for the relationship. From such concerns, responsible decision making about contraception often emerges. But unmarried sexually active persons with many sex partners apparently develop an indifferent attitude toward contraceptive use. Even though the risks are seemingly greater, such persons are less likely to use contraception than persons with a single partner or few sex partners (Miller, 1986).

Women who exhibit knowledge about sexual matters including contraceptive methods are significantly more likely to use contraception and to use it more consistently than less knowledgeable women (Jung, 1983; Levinson, 1986). However, a survey of midwestern college students found that only 7% of women and no men knew how to correctly calculate when **ovulation** was most likely to occur. Of these sexually active persons, only about one third of women and men or their sex partners were currently utilizing contraceptives during sexual intercourse (Davidson & Darling, 1986).

BOX 11.1 — **Choosing Contraception: Questions to Ask Yourself**

The time for a rational approach to birth control is before the need arises. Step one is to clarify your needs by posing questions:

- Why am I using (planning to use) contraception?
- How important is it for me to avoid pregnancy?
- Under what circumstances would I be (have been) most likely to "take a chance" and not to use a contraceptive?
- If my contraceptive method failed, would I consider abortion or continue pregnancy to term? What would be the implications for my life/feelings in either course of action?
- Under what circumstances might I wish to be pregnant?
- To what extent do I know my partner's attitudes and how do they influence the kind of contraceptive method I choose?
- How do I feel about taking medication in general?
- How do I feel about having physical control over my body?
- Would I be more comfortable with a contraceptive method permitting spontaneous sexual intercourse or one used only at the time of sexual intercourse?
- How predictable is the setting and timing of sexual intercourse?
- How long do I plan to use contraceptive method X?

Source: P. Lowry, "Birth Control: Questions to Ask Yourself" in S. Hendricks (ed.), *The Women's Yellow Pages: Original Sourcebook for Women* (West Virginia Edition). Copyright © 1979 The Public Works, Boston, MA.

Factors Associated with Contraceptive Selection

From an ideal perspective, couples should jointly decide upon their choice of contraception prior to initiation of sexual intercourse. The average sexually active adult woman has tried at least three separate methods of contraception: over three fourths have tried oral contraceptives; more than one half have tried condoms; but less than one third have tried chemical spermicides (Forrest, 1987). Women, ages 35–44, are less likely to use oral contraceptives and white women are more likely to insist on the use of condoms than black women (U.S. Bureau of the Census, 1990q).

The 1982 National Survey of Family Growth found that 53% of never-married women were using oral contraceptives. Among married women, significant changes in contraceptive choice occurred in the 1970s and 1980s. In 1973, a little over one third of married women practicing contraception were using oral contraceptives as compared to only one fifth by 1982. In addition, the percentage of women reporting sterilization as their birth control method had almost doubled by 1982 (Bachrach, 1984). Of those currently married women who reported sterilization as their birth control method in 1988, about two thirds had been sterilized themselves in comparison to only one third of their husbands (see Table 11.1).

The husband's attitude with regard to desired number of children plays a very important role in contraceptive choice. Couples who have similar attitudes about family size are more likely to use "joint" methods that require cooperation such as condoms or the rhythm method. Couples who have different attitudes regarding the number of children desired are more likely to place responsibility with one partner, namely the woman, and the method of choice is likely to be oral contraceptives (Asis, 1986a).

Religious Values

Religion continues to play an important role in the lives of women and men in our society. Therefore, it is important that a person evaluate her/his religious beliefs

Table 11.1: Birth Control Methods Used by Women, Ages 15–44, in 1988

Method	Total	Never Married	Currently Married	Formerly Married
Sterilization	39%	8%	49%	55%
Female	27	6	32	51
Male	12	2	17	4
Pill	31	59	20	25
IUD	2	1	2	4
Barrier	21	25	21	11
Diaphragm	6	5	6	5
Condom	15	20	15	6
Foam	1	NA	1	NA
Periodic abstinence	2	NA	3	NA
Withdrawal	2	NA	2	NA
Other	2	7	2	5

Note 1: NA indicates data not available.
Note 2: For never-marrieds and formerly marrieds, the category "other" includes foam, periodic abstinence, and withdrawal.
Source: W. D. Mosher, "Contraceptive Practice in the United States, 1982–1988" in *Family Planning Perspectives,* 22:198–205.

regarding the question of contraceptive usage. Perhaps the best-known religious position on contraception is that of the Roman Catholic church. In 1968, Pope Paul VI rejected the majority report of the church's special commission on birth control and contraception by reaffirming that periodic abstinence or the **rhythm method** was the only acceptable approach to contraception for Roman Catholics (Francoeur, 1982). In spite of this official stance, by the 1980s, 88% of Protestant and Roman Catholic women were using artificial contraceptive methods (Bachrach, 1984). The Mormons, who have had a long history of high birth rates, have traditionally supported the idea that educational, economic, or professional aspirations are not legitimate reasons for limiting the number of children. By the early 1980s, Mormons who were parents were using artificial contraception about as often as white Protestants. There was a difference, however, in the timing of their contraceptive use. About one half of Mormons delayed contraception until after the birth of their first child and one fourth waited until after the birth of their second child (Heaton & Calkins, 1983).

Health Considerations

There has been increasing concern about the possibility of detrimental side effects occurring from the use of certain contraceptive methods. In the case of the oral contraceptive, the concern has centered on preexisting conditions in the contraceptive user. These medical conditions require assessing the personal and family history for cardiovascular problems and breast cancer. Other concerns relate to **pelvic inflammatory disease** (PID), use of the intrauterine device (IUD), and vaginal lining inflammation associated with use of chemical spermicides in susceptible women (Hatcher et al., 1986). Although there are many important considerations regarding medical conditions and contraceptive choice, much conflicting information about contraceptive safety exists in our society. For example, while many physicians believe that an association exists between diaphragm use and incidence of urinary tract infections, a study that controlled for the frequency of sexual intercourse found no significant relationship between diaphragm usage and urinary tract infections. Since the action of sexual intercourse facilitates the entry of bacteria into the bladder, this researcher believed higher frequencies of sexual intercourse were likely to lead to urinary tract infections regardless of contraceptive method (Hsiao, 1986).

In a study of sources of information about oral contraceptives, magazine articles were found to influence both women and men in their beliefs about in the safety of oral contraceptives. Surprisingly, magazine sources were perceived as being more credible than reports by physicians about the safety of oral contraceptives (Halpern & Blackman, 1985). As can be observed in Table 11.2, there are many kinds of voluntary risk-taking behavior that are considerably more likely to lead

Table 11.2: Voluntary Risk-Taking Behavior by Death Chances in One Year

Risk Behavior	Death Chances
General Activities	
Smoking	1 in 200
Motorcycling	1 in 1,000
Automobile driving	1 in 6,000
Playing football	1 in 25,000
Having sexual intercourse (PID)	1 in 50,000
Canoeing	1 in 100,000
Using tampons (toxic shock)	1 in 350,000
Preventing pregnancy	
Using barrier methods	None
Using natural methods	None
Oral contraception-smoker	1 in 16,000
Oral contraception-nonsmoker	1 in 63,000
Using IUDs	1 in 100,000
Undergoing sterilization	
Vasectomy	None
Hysterectomy	1 in 1,600
Laparoscopic tubal ligation	1 in 20,000
Continuing Pregnancy	1 in 10,000
Terminating pregnancy	
Nonlegal abortion	1 in 3,000
Legal abortion	
After 16 weeks	1 in 10,000
Between 13–16 weeks	1 in 25,000
Between 9–12 weeks	1 in 100,000
Before 9 weeks	1 in 400,000

Source: Robert Hatcher, et al., *Contraceptive Technology 1986–1987*, 13th rev. ed. Copyright © 1986 Irvington Publishers, Inc., New York, NY.

to death than employing an effective contraceptive method. However, since there are possible serious consequences, no method should be employed before first considering the known risks. It is very important that contraceptives that do involve potential medical risks be used only under the supervision of a physician along with regular physical checkups.

Personal Concerns: Effectiveness Level and Ease of Use

It is important to assess the effectiveness and ease of use of various forms of contraception. An important factor in such assessments relates to personal motivation. First, it must be understood that a difference exists between the theoretical and user effectiveness rates of any method of contraception. The theoretical rate is calculated on the presumption that the user carefully follows the instructions for the contraceptive method as well as uses the method at each instance of sexual intercourse. The user effectiveness rate, which is based on actual use, reflects user error and lack of motivation. It is always lower than the theoretical effectiveness rate (Hatcher et al., 1986). For these reasons, considerable variation exists in the reported failure rates of various contraceptives. In general, women with higher educational levels report substantially lower failure rates with diaphragm usage than women with lower levels of education (Condelli, 1986). When considering the question of effectiveness levels, one should obviously take into account the influence of religious values as a motivating factor in the use or nonuse of contraceptives. In addition, any preexisting medical conditions that could affect the efficacy of the contraceptive must not be ignored. In a survey of women undergoing abortion counseling to determine the cause of their contraceptive failure, one half reported incorrect and/or inconsistent usage of contraception. Further, 20% used no contraceptive method, and 19% reported product failure. Inconsistent contraceptive usage was most often associated with oral contraceptives (Sophocles & Brozovich, 1986).

Systematic contraceptive usage is also related to ease of use. Important considerations are lack of interference with spontaneity for sexual intercourse; perceived interference, if any, with physiological sexual satisfaction; comfortableness with handling the genitals; and any feelings of perceived messiness including ease of personal hygiene after sexual intercourse. These factors might best be summarized under the heading of convenience. After weighing the foregoing factors, most women continue to rank oral contraceptives first in terms of ease of use (Condelli, 1986).

Contraceptive Methods

The prevention of an unwanted pregnancy has been a concern of women and men for centuries. Bizarre attempts to control impregnation have long been recorded. For example, eating a testicle or hoof shavings from mules were contraceptive methods in 6th century Greece. During the 1600s in Western Europe, vaginal sponges soaked in various solutions were inserted into the vaginal barrel. And during the 1700s, animal membranes tied at the base of the penis were believed to be effective contraceptive methods (Crooks & Baur, 1990). From the 1950s to the 1980s, tremendous advances were made in contraceptive technology (see Table 11.3).

Table 11.3: Advantages and Disadvantages of Contraceptive Methods

Method	Theoretical Failure Rate	Actual Use Failure Rate	Advantages	Disadvantages
Combined birth control pills	0.5%	3.0%	Highly effective; easy to use	Daily use required; continuing cost; slight medical risk; side effects
Progestin-only minipill	1.0	2.5	Highly effective; easy to use	Irregular menses; daily use required
IUD	0.5–3.0	6.0	Needs little attention; no expense after insertion	Side effects; possible expulsion; may perforate uterine wall; some incidence of PID
Condom	4.0	12.0	No side effects; easy to use; easy to obtain; helps prevent disease	Continuing expense; must use every time; may interrupt continuity of intercourse
Cervical cap	8.0	18.0	Can be left in place for several days; uses no hormones; no side effects	May be dislodged by intercourse; requires skill in insertion
Sponge (with spermicide)	14.0–28.0	18.0–28.0	Easy to obtain and use; uses no hormones; no side effects	May be inadvertently expelled; requires skill for removal; may create dry vagina
Diaphragm (with spermicide)	2.0	18.0	Easy to obtain and use; uses no hormones; no side effects; helps prevent disease; prescription required	Continuing expense; requires high motivation to use consistently with each intercourse
Spermicide agents (foams, creams, jellies, and vaginal suppositories)	0.0	21.0	Easy to obtain and use; no prescription required	Continuing expense; requires high motivation to use correctly and consistently with each intercourse
Withdrawal (coitus interruptus)	7.0	18.0	No preparation or cost; no hormones or chemicals	May be frustrating to full enjoyment of intercourse; low effectiveness
Natural family planning (calendar, basal body temperature, ovulation, sympto-thermal methods)	8.0–14.0	20.0	Acceptable to those who object to devices or hormones/chemicals	Requires much motivation and cooperation between partners
Chance (no protection)	89.0	89.0	No preparation; no hormones/ chemicals	High risk of pregnancy; provides little peace of mind

Source: Robert Hatcher, et al., *Contraceptive Technology 1988–1989,* 14th rev. ed. Copyright © 1988 Irvington Publishers, Inc., New York, NY.

Oral Contraceptives

The most commonly used oral contraceptive is a combination pill that contains synthetic estrogen and a progesterone-like synthetic substance called **progestin.** This oral contraceptive must be taken for 21 days beginning on the fifth day of each menstrual cycle. This medication prevents pregnancy by disturbing the normal output of the follicle stimulating hormone (FSH) and the luteinizing hormone (LH) by the pituitary gland, thereby preventing ovulation. The presence of progestin also makes implantation of a fertilized egg difficult by impeding the development of the uterine lining as well as thickening the cervical mucus and reducing the possibility of sperm entering the uterus (Masters, Johnson, & Kolodny, 1988).

Women who use oral contraceptives report shorter and more predictable menstrual periods and a sense of relief from anxiety about becoming pregnant (Harding, Vail, & Brown, 1985). Further, the use of combination oral contraceptives reduces the risk of ovarian and endometrial cancer by at least 50% (Tyrer & Kornblatt, 1983). This protection lasts for at least 15 years after pill usage is concluded ("Pill Appears," 1987). There is also evidence that the risks of PID and benign breast

BOX 11.2 **Contraindications to Combination Oral Contraceptives**

When considering use of the oral contraceptives for women with strong relative contraindications, it is extremely important to weigh its risks and benefits and to carefully consider other alternatives.

Absolute contraindications:

1. Thromboembolic disorder (or history thereof)
2. Cerebrovascular accident (or history thereof)
3. Coronary artery disease (or history thereof)
4. Known or suspected carcinoma of the breast (or history thereof)
5. Known or suspected estrogen-dependent neoplasia (or history thereof)
6. Pregnancy
7. Benign or malignant liver tumor (or history thereof)
8. Known impaired liver function at present time

Strong relative contraindications:

*9. Severe headaches, particularly vascular or migraine
10. Hypertension with resting diastolic BP of 90 or greater, or a resting systolic BP of 140 or greater on three or more separate visits, or an accurate measurement of 110 diastolic or more on a single visit
11. Diabetes
12. Active gall bladder disease
13. Mononucleosis, acute phase
14. Sickle cell disease (SS) or sickle C disease (SC)
15. Elective major surgery planned in next 4 weeks or major surgery requiring immobilization
16. Long leg cast or major injury to lower leg
*17. Forty years of age or older, accompanied by a second risk factor for the development of cardiovascular disease
*18. Thirty-five years of age or older and currently a heavy smoker (15 or more cigarettes a day)

*Refers to a contraindication to combination oral contraceptives which MAY NOT be a contraindication to progestin-only pills or may be LESS of a contraindication to progestin-only pills.
Source: Robert Hatcher, et al., *Contraceptive Technology 1986–1987*, 13th rev. ed. Copyright © 1986 Irvington Publishers, Inc., New York, NY.

disorders can be reduced significantly with the use of oral contraceptives (Tyrer & Kornblatt, 1983).

A new issue emerged with introduction of the **multiphasic pill** in 1984. This pill provides varying hormone dosage levels during the menstrual cycle whereas the older type of pill maintains a constant dosage level. By 1987, this new pill was being prescribed for about 90% of all new oral contraceptive users. However, evidence now suggests that the multiphasic pill may be associated with an increased incidence of benign (noncancerous) ovarian cysts whereas the older type of oral contraceptive has been found to actually reduce the risk of benign ovarian cysts ("Pill May Raise," 1988).

The most often reported reasons for discontinuing oral contraceptive use are weight gain and nausea (Pratt & Bachrach, 1987). Whether or not sexually active women age 30 and over should continue to use oral contraceptives remains the subject of considerable medical debate. Those women ages 30–34 who stop using the oral contraceptive take longer to conceive than younger women or women who have had at least one birth. However, one study found that 87% of women ages 30–34 had conceived within 72 months after going off the pill, placing this age group within the normal range for women who try to conceive ("Pill Users," 1986).

Spermicides

Spermicides include foams, suppositories, creams, and jellies containing a chemical substance that immobilizes and destroys the sperm cell provided that the spermicide comes in contact with said sperm cell. They are available without prescription, have no serious side effects, and typically are found on pharmacy shelves along with feminine hygiene products. Contraceptive **foam,** the most commonly used product, is white in color and comes in pressurized cans somewhat resembling shaving cream. It is inserted into the vaginal barrel using a plastic applicator prior to initiation of sexual intercourse. **Vaginal contraceptive suppositories** have an oval shape and are somewhat more difficult to insert and dissolve. Further, they are more likely to leave a sticky residue in the vagina. Since contraceptive creams and jellies are intended to be used with diaphragms, their level of effectiveness is substantially lower than foam. Consequently, many medical authorities do not recommend their usage without a diaphragm.

There is a need to wait 2–3 minutes after the application of contraceptive foams, jellies, and creams before beginning sexual intercourse. A woman must be certain to initiate sexual intercourse within 30 minutes after having applied a contraceptive spermicide, otherwise its effectiveness will be substantially lowered. The issue is further complicated by the fact that vaginal suppositories take approximately 20 minutes to completely dissolve, therefore making it necessary to postpone immediate initiation of sexual intercourse (Crooks & Baur, 1990). As is the case for diaphragms, women must be sufficiently comfortable with their sexuality to handle their genitals during the application of chemical spermicides. The fact that chemical spermicides must be reapplied before each act of sexual intercourse could complicate love making (Stewart, Guest, Stewart, & Hatcher, 1979).

Barrier Methods

Barrier methods of contraception are mechanical devices that serve to physically block the passage of sperm into the vagina and/or uterus (Denney & Quadagno, 1988). Today, most physicians recommend that the older barrier methods (condoms, diaphragms, and cervical caps) be used in conjunction with a spermicide (Allgeier & Allgeier, 1991). Understanding these various contraceptive methods will lead to their proper selection and usage.

Condom

The **condom** is a sheath that, when unrolled to be placed on the erect penis, has the appearance of a long, thin balloon. To provide adequate space for the semen upon ejaculation, about ½ in. of space should be left at the tip of the condom during its application (Byer & Shainberg, 1991). To assist with ease of vaginal penetration, many condoms today are lubricated and may also be coated with the chemical spermicide, nonoxynol-9, to further reduce the risk of pregnancy (Adams, Fliegelman, & Grieco, 1987). Condoms are made either of thin latex or animal tissue. Those made of animal skin, while more expensive, permit more sensation because they allow the transfer of heat between the vagina and penis during thrusting (Allgeier & Allgeier, 1991). However, animal-skin condoms supposedly provide less protection against acquisition and/or transmission of STDs, especially Acquired Immune Deficiency Syndrome (AIDS), because of the apparent presence of microscopic holes (U.S. Public Health Service, 1988).

A substantial body of evidence exists which concludes that consistent use of condoms will greatly reduce the likelihood of contracting a sexually transmitted disease. One study of male condom users found that only about one fourth who used condoms all the time contracted sexually transmitted disease as compared to approximately one half of those who never or inconsistently used condoms. It is important to note that of those men who always and correctly used condoms, 4% still contracted gonorrhea and 2% contracted trichomoniasis (Rein, 1985).

Diaphragm

The **diaphragm** is a round, dome-shaped device made of thin rubber that contains a rubber-coated rim of flexible steel. This prescription device, which fits tightly over the cervical area, is inserted into the vagina prior to initiating sexual intercourse. To achieve maximum effectiveness, a chemical spermicide should be applied to the rim and surface that fits against the cervix. After sexual intercourse is completed, the diaphragm must remain in place for at least six hours to prevent any sperm cells from accidentally entering the uterine cavity (Hyde, 1990). The diaphragm, which is considered to be the first modern method of contraception, was the method of choice for many women in the 1940s and 1950s prior to the advent of the oral contraceptive. Women are more likely to choose a diaphragm and foam if they possess a positive self-image (McKinney et al., 1984). In the 1980s the use of the diaphragm regained popularity because of concerns about the side effects of oral contraceptives and IUDs. In 1986, one study of diaphragm users found that three fourths were ex-oral contraceptive or IUD users (Kovacs, Jarman, Dunn, Westcott, & Baker, 1986). Nonetheless, the diaphragm is only recommended as a means of contraception for those women who are extremely dedicated to its proper usage.

BOX 11.3	How to Talk about Condoms with a Resistant Partner
If partner says:	**You can say:**
"I'm on the Pill, you don't need a condom."	"I'd like to use it anyway. We'll both be protected from infections we may not realize we have."
"I *know* I'm clean (disease-free); I haven't had sex with anyone in X months."	"Thanks for telling me. As far as I know, I'm disease-free, too. But I'd still like to use a condom since either of us could have an infection and not know it."
"I'm a virgin."	"I'm not. This way we'll both be protected."
"I can't feel a thing when I wear a condom; it's like wearing a raincoat in the shower."	"Even if you lose some sensation, you'll still have plenty left."
"I'll lose my erection by the time I stop and put it on."	"I'll help you put it on—that'll help you keep it."
"By the time you put it on, I'm out of the mood."	"Maybe so, but we feel strongly enough for each other to stay in the mood."
"It destroys the romantic atmosphere."	"It doesn't have to be that way."
"Condoms are unnatural, fake, a total turnoff."	"Please let's try to work this out—an infection isn't so great either. So let's give the condom a try. Or maybe we can look for alternatives."
"What kinds of alternatives?"	"Maybe we'll just pet, or postpone sex for a while."
"This is an insult! Do you think I'm some sort of disease-ridden slut (gigolo)?"	"I didn't say or imply that. I care for you, but in my opinion, it's best to use a condom."
"I love you! Would I give you an infection?"	"Not intentionally. But many people don't know they're infected. That's why this is best for both of us right now."
"Just this once."	"Once is all it takes."
"I don't have a condom with me."	"I do." or "Then let's satisfy each other without intercourse."
"You carry a condom around with you? You were planning to seduce me!"	"I always carry one with me because I care about myself. I have one with me tonight because I care about us both."

From R. Adams, E. Fliegelman, and A. Grieco, "Patient Guide: How to Use a Condom" in *Medical Aspects of Human Sexuality,* 21(7):75, 1987. Reprinted by permission.

Sponge

The contraceptive **sponge** is shaped like a mushroom cap and is made of polyurethane. The sponge, which is saturated with a chemical spermicide during its manufacturing process, is inserted into the vagina in front of the cervix prior to initiation of sexual intercourse. This device not only serves as a physical barrier to prevent sperm from entering the uterus but the spermicide will kill sperm upon contact. The sponge may be inserted up to 24 hours prior to beginning sexual intercourse and must be left in position for at least 6 hours after concluding sexual intercourse. Because of concern over **toxic shock syndrome,** the Food and Drug Administration recommends that the contraceptive sponge not remain in the vagina for more than 24 hours. The Centers for Disease Control have estimated that 1 per 10,000 contraceptive sponge users will develop toxic shock syndrome in comparison to 1 in 350,000 women who will develop toxic shock syndrome from tampon usage (Kleinman, 1985; Hatcher et al., 1986). The contraceptive sponge appears to be as effective as the diaphragm for women who have never been pregnant. However, women who have been previously pregnant are twice as likely to become pregnant again when using a contraceptive sponge as compared to previously pregnant women who are using a diaphragm (McIntyre & Higgins, 1986). A major advantage of the sponge is that it is available without prescription.

Cervical Cap

The **cervical cap** is a thimble-shaped device made of plastic or rubber about 1½ in. in diameter. It is fitted tightly over the cervix prior to sexual intercourse and remains in place due to suction (Masters et al., 1988). Like the diaphragm, for fitting purposes, it is available only through a prescription. Since the cervical cap is more difficult for some women to insert than the diaphragm because it must fit snugly over the cervix, the patient is typically taught how to insert the device. Physicians recommend that this contraceptive method be utilized in conjunction with a chemical spermicide. If used with a chemical spermicide, the effectiveness level of cervical caps is thought to be similar to that of the diaphragm (Boehm, 1983). An advantage of the cervical cap over the diaphragm is that the device can be left in place for up to 48 hours, which can serve to enhance the spontaneity of sexual intercourse (Toufexis, 1988).

Although the cervical cap enjoys widespread acceptance in Europe, it has not gained popularity in the United States due to its limited availability. The cervical cap was finally approved by the FDA as a female contraceptive method in 1988 after a decade-long campaign by feminist health leaders. Based on clinical tests for safety and effectiveness with more than 40,000 women, no immediate health risks were identified. However, women using the cervical cap were found to have a higher rate of abnormal PAP tests, which would suggest the possible existence of infection or cervical cancer, in comparison to diaphragm users. Consequently, the FDA recommends usage only by women with normal PAP tests and that PAP tests should continue to be performed on a quarterly or semi-annual basis after usage of the cervical cap begins (Toufexis, 1988).

Intrauterine Device

The **intrauterine device** is a small plastic object that is inserted into the uterus for contraceptive purposes. Precisely how the IUD functions as a contraceptive method is uncertain. Many medical experts believe that it produces cellular and biochemical reactions in the endometrium which will interfere with implantation of a fertilized ovum (Katchadourian, 1989). If this explanation is accepted, then the IUD is really a means of birth control rather than a contraceptive method.

Given the potential for major side effects of the intrauterine device including PID and sterility, it has been reconsidered in recent years as a viable method of contraception. In fact, the IUD was largely withdrawn from the American market due to the millions of dollars of court-awarded damages to users of the Dalkon shield, one brand of IUD (Allgeier & Allgeier, 1991). Although it has been estimated that at least 88,000 women may be unable to give birth due to irreparable damage to their reproductive systems from use of IUDs, an estimated 2.2 million women were using IUDs when most brands were withdrawn from the market (Haney, 1985).

By the mid-1980s, about 5% of married women and less than 1% of never-married women were still utilizing this contraceptive method (Hatcher et al., 1988). However, in 1988, a new version of the Copper T IUD was introduced. The first IUD to be entirely copper clad, it must be replaced every four years. Like other IUDs of the past, the side effects may include PID, bleeding, cramping, ectopic (tubal) pregnancy, perforation of the uterine wall and, in some cases, inability to become pregnant in the future ("Copper IUD," 1988). However, despite the negative publicity surrounding usage of IUDs, a study concerning contraceptive methods used by sexually active female physicians found that those who were **obstetricians/gynecologists** were using the IUD more often than other female physicians (Zbella, Vermesh, & Gleicher, 1986).

Fertility Awareness with Periodic Abstinence

The fertility awareness method of contraception is often called natural family planning since it does not involve the use of chemicals or mechanical devices. Fertility awareness with periodic abstinence ("rhythm") is based on the assumption that ovulation occurs 14 days plus or minus 2 days before onset of the next menstrual period. Since this concept requires abstinence from sexual intercourse during the fertile segment of a woman's menstrual cycle, the "safe" period must be carefully calculated. Therefore, it is important to consider the various techniques that can be used for this purpose. The variations include calendar method, basal body temperature method, and cervical mucus method.

For the calendar method, records of menstrual periods are kept for at least 8 months to determine the shortest and longest menstrual cycles. A woman can then determine the first and last fertile day of her menstrual cycle and subsequently plan to abstain from or engage in sexual intercourse, depending upon couple goals. Since the sperm can live 3–5 days, abstinence may be required a few days prior to anticipated ovulation for those wishing to avoid conception.

The basal body temperature, the lowest temperature reached by a healthy person during their waking hours, usually occurs after awakening from a night of sleep. Approximately 12–24 hours prior to ovulation, in most women, a drop in basal body temperature occurs followed by a sustained rise for at least 3 days. Using preprinted charts, a woman can enter her basal body temperature each day for a period of 8 months to determine her patterns of dropping and rising temperatures. Assuming regularity of the menstrual cycle, the elevation in basal body temperature should occur at approximately the same time during each menstrual cycle. Since it is assumed that ovulation occurs on the day after the drop in temperature, a woman who wished to avoid pregnancy would abstain from sexual intercourse during the days that ovulation is most likely to occur (Stewart et al., 1979).

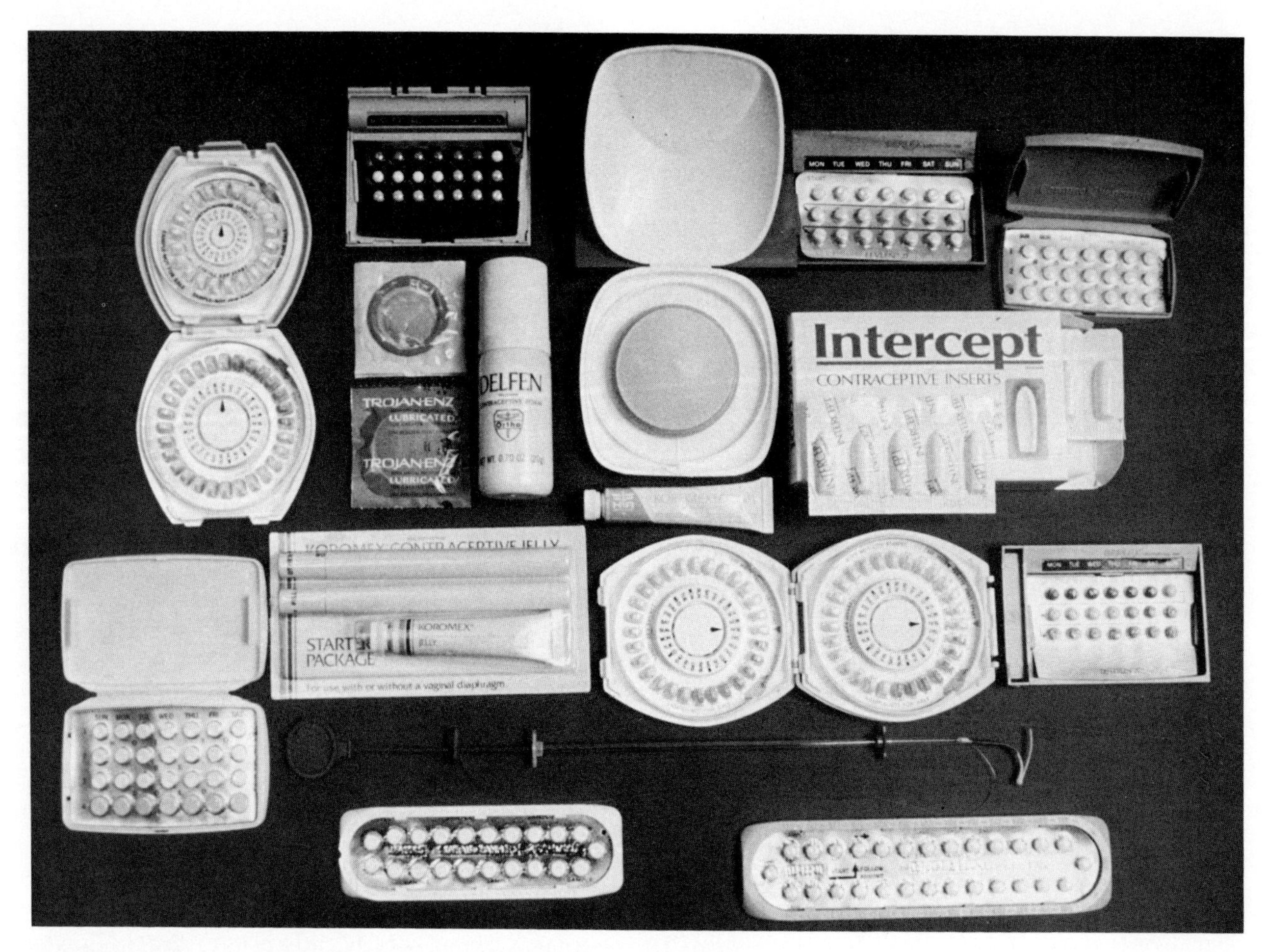

This wide array of contraceptives does not include the recently FDA-approved hormonal implant, Norplant. This new method of contraception is believed to be the most significant advance in preventing pregnancy since the advent of the "pill."

The cervical mucus method of natural family planning involves attempting to identify changes in vaginal discharge patterns. After menstruation and prior to ovulation, most women experience a slight vaginal discharge that is cloudy, yellowish, white, thick, and sticky. A few days before ovulation, the volume of vaginal discharge increases and turns to a clear, slippery "raw-egg" white appearance. Ovulation is thought to occur about 24 hours after the peak day of this slippery vaginal discharge. The woman again would abstain from or engage in sexual intercourse during those days that ovulation is likely to take place depending upon couple goals (Denney & Quadagno, 1988).

There are differences in medical opinion regarding how long the sperm lives after ejaculation and the ovum after ovulation. Considering these factors, along with the incidence of irregular menstrual cycles, many persons, after learning more about these methods, discontinue their usage. A survey of wives and husbands who had received complete instructions about fertility awareness found that less than one half of the couples continued to rely solely on this method. Non-Catholics and those less religiously oriented were somewhat more likely to discontinue sole reliance on fertility awareness methods (Daly & Herold, 1985).

Sterilization

Examination of female contraceptive usage patterns by age, race, and marital status indicates that about two thirds of all women today ages 35–44 are classified as being sterile either through surgery for contraceptive or noncontraceptive purposes, or due to illness, accident, or congenital conditions (U.S. Bureau of the Census, 1990q). The actual number of sterilization procedures performed each year in the United States is subject to debate due to lack of adequate reporting mechanisms, but one thing is certain: more women have sterilization procedures performed each year than men. The 1982 National Survey of Family Growth found that 1 million women but only 325,000 men had received sterilization operations during each of the three prior years. However, other estimates place the figures as high as 1.3 million women and 880,000 men receiving sterilization operations each year (Orr, Forrest, Johnson, & Tolman, 1985). Regardless of which estimate is correct, sterilization is the most widely used form of birth control among married couples and formerly married women in the United States (Mosher, 1990).

Sterilization differs from other ways of preventing conception due to its potential irreversibility. The person depending on contraceptive methods does so with the knowledge that usage can be discontinued if a pregnancy is desired. But those persons who choose sterilization may not be able to have a child with their present or future partner even if, because of changing life circumstances, they should wish to do so. Given the relatively early ages at which most persons are seeking sterilization coupled with the high divorce rates and the possibility of early widowhood, a relatively permanent decision becomes an important consideration. However, medical progress in the use of microsurgery techniques has led to considerable improvement in the success rate of restoring fertility in cases of tubal ligation for women and vasectomies for men. The percentages of pregnancies leading to live births following reversal of tubal ligations ranges from 50–70% (Liskin, Rinehart, Blackburn, & Rutledge, 1985). In the case of men, the percentages of conception following vasectomy reversal range from 35–82% (Goldstein, 1986). A crucial factor in the success rate appears to be the length of time between the actual vasectomy and the reversal procedure. The longest reported successful conception occurred 9 years after the initial vasectomy surgery (Aldridge, Bueschin, Lloyd, & Burns, 1985).

Three major variables in the decision to undergo sterilization were identified in a study of 9,300 couples choosing sterilization: age, education, and religion. Protestants were most likely to undergo sterilization with Roman Catholics being least likely. If the woman was older than the man, sterilization was more likely to be chosen as the birth control method. In general, blacks were more likely to choose sterilization for the woman rather than the man. But as the level of education increased for the woman, the likelihood that the man would choose to have a vasectomy increased (Bean, Williams, Opitz, Burr, & Trent, 1987).

Sterilization by any method should be based on clear reasoning and should never be undertaken as a solution to sexual or marital problems. Among major reasons reported by women and men for sterilization are wanting more time for leisure activities and by women, general dissatisfaction with other contraceptive methods (Burnell & Norfleet, 1986a). It is also interesting to note that in another study only one fifth of the women reported joint responsibility between themselves and their husbands regarding the decision to have a tubal ligation (Abell, 1987). These data suggest that many women want to retain control over their bodies by avoiding an unwanted pregnancy.

Tubal Ligation

Laparoscopic sterilization refers to a tubal ligation or salpingectomy ("tying tubes") that is performed by using a **laparoscope** (a tube-like instrument with fiber optics)that is inserted through a tiny incision in the abdominal wall. Typically, a second tiny incision is made at the pubic hairline to insert the instrument that is used to cauterize (burn) about 1–2 in. of the fallopian tube, within about 2–3 seconds of application (Stewart et al., 1979). The small incisions are made in or near the navel to eliminate the possibility of large scars.

Physiological and Psychological Effects of Tubal Ligations

A **tubal ligation,** which can be performed, in most instances, on an outpatient basis, has a very brief recovery period. The woman will be able to resume normal activities including sexual intercourse within 2–3 days after any physical discomfort has subsided. There is no impairment of the menstrual function, although some women have reported increased premenstrual tension following a tubal ligation (Bledin, Cooper, Brice, & MacKenzie, 1985).

Studies in the 1970s and 1980s suggest that tubal ligations do not necessarily result in an improvement in either the marital relationship or the overall sexual relationship. While most women reported no change in either area, from 86–95% had "no regrets" (Kjer, 1990; Philliber & Philliber, 1985). However, in two studies, the percentage of women who perceived their sexual lives had improved, ranged from 25% (Bredin, Cooper,

MacKenzie, & Brice, 1984) to 44% (Kjer, 1990). One study also found that 1 year after a tubal ligation, about two thirds of the women reported more positive self-perceptions along with feeling more relaxed during sexual intercourse, free of the fear of pregnancy (Abell, 1987).

Vasectomy

The **vasectomy** is a surgical procedure in which the vas deferens is cut and/or cauterized, thus preventing sperm cells from mixing with the other semen components and being released during ejaculation. A small incision is made in the scrotum well above the testes, and the vas deferens is either cut and/or cauterized. Vasectomies that are performed using the cauterization method have a failure rate of 0.2 of 1% versus 1–6% for the cutting and tying method (Denniston, 1985). The procedure, which is typically performed in a physician's office under local anesthetic, takes about 15–20 minutes. The man can resume sexual intercourse within 2–3 days, but a conventional contraceptive method should be used until the ejaculated semen is free of sperm which is usually 6–8 weeks later (Masters et al., 1988).

Physiological and Psychological Effects of Vasectomies

A question that remains foremost in the minds of many men concerns the possibility of changes in sexual functioning as a result of a vasectomy. The simple answer is that there are no changes that are physiologically based. Evidence indicates that the volume of ejaculated semen, the male hormone level, and the secondary sex characteristics remain the same. In addition, the ability to have an erection or the level of sexual desire are also unaffected. The only change is that sperm cells being produced by the testes die and are absorbed by the body, a process that has no bearing on sexual functioning ("Vasectomy Facts," 1987). Further, no major complications are usually reported from a vasectomy with only minor hemorrhaging and some pain occurring at the incision site. In general, men have indicated that a vasectomy generates a feeling of freedom from contraceptive worry (Marsidi & Wise, 1983).

With regard to impact on overall sexual relationships, studies conducted in the 1970s found the percentages of men reporting "better" overall sexual relationships ranged from 61–75%, whereas the percentages reporting a positive impact on the marital relationship ranged from 36–85%. While the issue of regret has remained a debate in some circles, the percentages of men reporting "no regret" about having a vasectomy ranged from 97–100% (Philliber & Philliber, 1985). It appears that men are considerably more likely than women to perceive their sterilization as having a positive impact on their sexual and marital relationships.

The Search for New Contraceptive Methods

The quest continues for the ideal method of contraception that is safe, simple to use, reversible, and does not require daily action on the part of the user. Consequently, a variety of promising new methods of female and male contraceptive methods are being considered. But even after an effective method has been identified, a number of years are required to evaluate its possible long-term side effects before approval by the FDA can be obtained as illustrated by the case of the cervical cap. For men, it is estimated that no effective male contraceptive other than the condom will be commercially available prior to the year 2000 (Allgeier & Allgeier, 1991). Part of the reason is that only 8% of the research monies for the development of new contraceptive techniques are being devoted to male-type methods (Atkinson, Lincoln, & Forrest, 1986). The revolutionary contraception methods for women being investigated include a 21-day vaginal ring containing progestin which fits around the cervix and a nasal spray containing progestin (Welles, 1985). Further clinical trials also have begun for a new disposable female condom (Krieger, 1988). The main reasons for the slow development of new contraceptive technology stem from the cost of product liability insurance that discourages testing and marketing of new contraceptive medications or devices (Lollar, 1987).

Female Methods

The earlier concept of a postcoital contraceptive or so-called "morning after" approach utilized high dosage levels of estrogen to prevent implantation of a potentially fertilized ovum (Potts, 1983). More recently, the introduction in French medical clinics of **RU—486** (an abortion-inducing pill) for use during the early stages of pregnancy has received considerable attention. This medication, which inhibits production of progesterone, is intended to be taken only four times a month rather than the minimum of 21 days per cycle as in the case of conventional oral contraceptives ("France Approves," 1988). Based on data from 10,000 French women who had used the drug to induce an abortion, the reported failure rate was 4% ("Controversial Pill," 1991). Since this drug is considered to be an abortifacient (causes abortion), it is facing extremely heavy opposition from pro-life groups in the United States (Allgeier & Allgeier, 1991). As a consequence, the FDA has issued an "import alert," which bans the importation of the medication for personal use even though medical scientists have stated that no medical evidence exists that indicates that RU-486 is unsafe (Wheeler, 1990). Conversely, medical research demonstrates that RU-486 will slow or stop the growth of some types of breast-cancer tumors and has the potential to be used in the treatment of endometriosis. In addition, it has been prescribed in France for the treatment of Cushing's Syndrome, a serious endocrine disorder. However, a government policy in the United States currently blocks federal support for any medical research involving this medication ("Controversial Pill," 1991).

At the present time, the newest female contraceptive is the **Norplant system** involving the use of silicone pellets about the diameter of matchsticks that contain progestin. Six pellets are usually inserted under the skin of the upper arm in a daisy pattern, and the hormone Levonorgestrel is continuously released into the bloodstream for at least five years. The progestin thickens the cervical mucus to impede sperm penetration as well as inhibiting ovulation by suppressing the natural production of progesterone ("5-Year Contraceptive Implant," 1985). The failure rate for the Norplant system is said to be 0.4 of 1% (Trussell, Hatcher, Cates, Stewart, & Kost, 1990). The Norplant system, which has been available in 16 foreign countries, was not approved for usage by the FDA until December, 1990 (Purvis, 1990). It supposedly delivers the lowest dosage of hormones used in any hormonal contraceptive. Also, it does not contain estrogen, the hormone with the most apparent serious side effects. The major potential side effects of the Norplant system are menstrual irregularity, headaches, nervousness, skin rashes, and changes in appetite or weight (Okie, 1989). Initial side effects include irregular breakthrough bleeding reported by 75% of users along with menstrual periods ranging from 3–7 weeks apart and averaging 8 days in length. According to the manufacturers, these side effects should diminish after the first two years following implantation (Purvis, 1990).

Male Methods

Considerable interest has been generated by the possible use of **Gossypol,** a derivative of cottonseed, as a male oral contraceptive. Chinese researchers have found that Gossypol has a 99.9% efficacy rate in preventing the production of sperm cells with supposedly minimal side effects. Gossypol must be taken orally on a daily basis for 2 months and then a monthly maintenance dosage is required. Fertility is usually fully restored within 3 months after discontinuation ("Gossypol," 1981). However, Gossypol is classified as a toxic substance by the American Chemical Society. Furthermore, research in the United States has shown that it is associated with liver damage and depletion of needed potassium, and 10–20% of men who use Gossypol apparently are permanently sterilized (Goldstein, 1986).

Another question exists regarding whether men will utilize a male oral contraceptive if such a product should become available. In a study of white husbands, of whom over one half were college graduates, only 31% indicated they would be "very likely" to use a male oral contraceptive (Marsiglio, 1985). Husbands expressing egalitarian gender-role preferences were more likely to report that they would use a male oral contraceptive. But wives were less likely than their husbands to believe that they would use a male oral contraceptive (Marsiglio & Menaghan, 1987).

An earlier approach in male contraceptive research involved the long-term administration of the luteinizing hormone-releasing hormone to decrease sperm production. However, side effects included decreasing the libido or sex drive and problems with erectile dysfunction (Ziporyn, 1984). Research efforts also have been directed toward using an injection of testosterone which causes the pituitary gland to cease its own production of testosterone, thus depressing production of sperm. However, several potential side effects have been identified including possible prostate, heart, and kidney disorders (Goldstein, 1986).

Abortion

Abortion may be the most controversial legal and moral issue confronting American society today. This issue is viewed as a dilemma by both pro-choice and pro-life advocates. "It is a dilemma because it involves an unwanted pregnancy, that poignant predicament in which the best choices have already been foreclosed" ("Abortion Debate," 1986, p. 1). Advocates of the pro-life position stress the ethical and moral issues whereas pro-choice advocates stress the economic, political, and personal facets of the issue as it affects the pregnant woman.

It is important that abortion not be confused with a method of contraception. A contraceptive prevents conception whereas abortion destroys the product of conception. Abortion on demand, that is legal abortion for any reason, is rarely endorsed as a universal right to be exercised freely. Rather, societal approval is dependent upon the circumstances surrounding the abortion (Breslau, 1987).

Numerous religious denominations including Evangelical Lutheran, Eastern Orthodox, Roman Catholic, Lutheran (Missouri Synod), Mormons, Southern Baptists, and various conservative Evangelical denominations reject abortion (Cronell, 1988). Until the middle of the 19th century the Roman Catholic church permitted abortions for the first 40 days following conception since the church believed that the embryo had no soul until the 41st day (McLaren, 1981). In addition, American Baptists have now shifted away from their position of abortion being a "matter of responsible personal choice" and officially accept neither the pro-life nor pro-choice position (Harris, 1988). However, several major Protestant denominations such as the United Methodist, Episcopal, United Church of Christ, and Christian (Disciples of Christ) support freedom of choice on the abortion question (Cronell, 1988). Generally speaking, the various branches of Judaism also are supportive of freedom of choice (Ebaugh & Haney, 1980).

Despite varying religious attitudes toward abortion, it is considered one of the oldest existing medical procedures practiced throughout history (Tietze & Lewit, 1978). The liberalization of abortion laws has been based on three premises:

1. Recognition that illegal abortion constitutes a public health threat.
2. Belief that social justice requires equal access to abortion for the poor.
3. Support for rights of women to control their bodies (Allgeier & Allgeier, 1991, p. 371).

Table 11.4: Legal Abortions—Select Characteristics

Characteristic	1973	1985
Age of woman		
Less than age 15	2%	1%
Age 15–19	31	25
Age 20–24	32	35
Age 25–29	17	21
Age 30–34	10	12
Age 35–39	6	5
Age 40 and over	2	1
Race of woman		
White	74	68
Black and other	26	32
Marital status of woman		
Married	29	17
Unmarried	71	83
Number of prior live births		
None	55	55
1	15	22
2	14	15
3	8	5
4 or more	7	3
Number of prior induced abortions		
None	NA	60
1	NA	26
2	NA	14
Weeks of gestation		
Less than 9 weeks	38	51
9–10 weeks	30	27
11–12 weeks	18	13
13 weeks or more	15	9

Note: NA indicates that data are not available.
Source: U.S. Bureau of the Census, 1990r, No. 101, "Legal Abortions, by Selected Characteristics: 1973 to 1985" in *Statistical Abstract of the United States, 1990,* 110th ed., p. 71. Washington, DC: U.S. Government Printing Office.

Incidence of Abortion

During 1983, approximately one third of all female adolescents who became pregnant in the United States terminated their pregnancies through abortion (Henshaw, 1987). Data for 1988 indicate that 1.37 million legal therapeutic abortions occurred, which represents the highest level ever reported ("Abortion Increases," 1990). For women who obtained abortions between 1973 and 1985, two major changes are evident: the percentage of married women obtaining abortions decreased by almost one half during this period and the percentage of women having abortions at fewer than 9 weeks of gestation increased by one third (see Table 11.4). It is also of interest to note that about two thirds of all abortions were performed for women ages 15–24. Generally speaking, when compared to older women the frequency of sexual intercourse among young unmarried women is rather low, but they are extremely

Abortion is an issue without an answer. There are well-meaning persons on both sides of the abortion issue. Where do you stand?

fertile and, therefore, at a much greater risk of becoming pregnant. Consequently, teenagers have an abortion rate that is about 10 times greater than older women (Trost, 1986).

Legal Status of Abortion

On January 22, 1973, the United States Supreme Court in *Roe v. Wade* rendered its famous "woman's right to choose" abortion decision. The Court interpreted the Constitution to mean that the full protection of the lives of fetuses was reserved for only those fetuses that were capable of surviving outside the uterus, which, at that time, was considered to be 24–28 weeks of pregnancy (Adler, 1982). The Court concluded that during the first trimester (1–3 months) of pregnancy, the decision about whether to have an abortion was left entirely to the discretion of the woman and her physician. During the second trimester (4–6 months), states could impose reasonable standards and regulations for abortion which were related to the preservation of the hygiene and health of the pregnant woman, but they could not prohibit abortion. Finally, states could legally prohibit abortion during the third trimester (7–9 months), even if needed to save the life of the woman (Liss, 1987).

In mid-1989, the United States Supreme Court in the *Webster v. Reproductive Health Services* decision upheld a Missouri law that prohibits public employees, including doctors and nurses, and public hospitals or other tax-supported facilities from performing abortions that are not necessary to save the woman's life. In addition, this law requires that a medical viability test be performed on any fetus thought to be in at least 20 weeks gestation prior to the abortion ("The Court Edges," 1989). While this court decision permits states to impose restrictions on the performance of abortions for purposes other than to save the life of the woman, its future impact on the abortion option is unclear at this time. Findings from a 1989 national *Time*/CNN poll indicate that 61% of Americans disagree with the Court's ruling on the Missouri law and 57% were opposed to an overturning of the *Roe v. Wade* decision ("Most Oppose Ruling," 1989).

The central point of disagreement that has continued to surround the abortion controversy is the question of whether or not the fetus is a person. Pro-life advocates believe that a person is created at the moment of conception. Despite this argument, the United States Supreme Court has used the concept of viability, that is, the stage of fetal development when the fetus may live outside the uterus by natural or artificial life-support systems (Liss, 1987). But with the increasing sophistication of medical technology, the likelihood of survival for a fetus during the early months of pregnancy has increased somewhat thus raising the ethical issue of whether or not a need exists to lower the age whereby viability is thought to begin. Medical data now indicate that the fetus is fully formed by the end of the 3rd month. Its heartbeat can be heard by the 4th month; it responds to sound and sleeps during the 5th month; and opens its eyes during the 6th month (Berger, 1988; Masters et al., 1988; Snow, 1989). In fact, the age of viability has now been established as sometime between the 20th and 26th week after conception. At this point, the fetus is said to have a slight chance of survival outside the uterus if expert health care is provided through high-level medical technology (Parmelee & Sigman, 1983). One such case occurred in 1983, when a 20 oz baby girl was born 16 weeks early against enormous odds for survival. One year later, the infant had grown into a healthy toddler, weighing close to 20 lbs (Berger, 1988).

Although other kinds of elective surgery for minors require parental consent, abortion constitutes a special case in medical and legal circles. The United States Supreme Court in *H. L. v. Matheson,* in 1981, found that since the role of parent in child rearing is so basic to our society, physicians, if possible, should notify the parents of a minor who is seeking an abortion. However, the Court went on to conclude that if the minor was not living at home, was mature, or had hostile parents, the question was left open as to whether parental notification was necessary (Liss, 1987). The United States Supreme Court decision suggested that minors are vulnerable to severe or permanent psychological aftereffects of abortion and questioned the ability of minors to make reasonable decisions. Therefore, the Court concluded that parental counseling was both desirable and in the best interest of the minor.

By 1990, 23 states had passed parental consent laws, while 11 states had passed parental notification laws. There is evidence that parental-involvement laws restrict access to abortion. For a 20-month period after a parental-consent law went into effect, 1 in 3 teenage abortions in Massachusetts was obtained out-of-state while those perfomed in state decreased by 43% (Carlson, 1990). But parental-involvement laws are currently operating in only 12 states due to court orders enjoining their operation or adverse legal opinions regarding their constitutionality ("Parents and Abortion," 1990). In 1990, the United States Supreme Court ruled in *Hodgson v. Minnesota* that the legal requirement to notify both parents is constitutional since an alternative exists for a judicial by-pass hearing. The court also found in *Ohio v. Akron Center for Reproductive Health* that Ohio's requirement of notification of one parent was constitutionally valid, but the question of a judicial by-pass procedure with notification of only one parent was not addressed (Greenhouse, 1990). Most state laws permit a local court to bypass parental consent and/or notification if, in the judgment of the court, the minor is sufficiently mature to make the decision about abortion (Bonavoglia, 1988). Generally, those teenagers who do not wish to involve their parents are age 16 or older. The major reasons cited for not notifying parents are to avoid hurting the mother's feelings and the antiabortion attitudes of parents (Melton, 1987). Female adolescents who had good communication with their father, including being open about sexual matters, poor communication with their mother, and frequent attendance at religious services, were unlikely to notify either parent about their abortion (Blum, Resnick, & Stark, 1990). Despite the intense debate over the issue, the majority of Americans favor requiring parental consent as a condition for a person under age 18 to obtain an abortion. A 1990 *Time*/CNN poll of adults found that 69% favored requiring parental consent for a minor to have an abortion (Carlson, 1990).

Public Attitudes Toward Abortion

Immediately after the 1973 Supreme Court decision, approval of abortion by the public for reasons of poverty, unmarried status, and no desire for children increased. However, after Congress, in 1978, decided to limit Medicaid payments for abortion to those cases involving incest, rape, or the woman's health, there has been an increase in public approval of abortion among persons age 18–29 and among women generally. Disapproval of abortion has actually decreased among persons age 50 and older and for those persons who are religiously affiliated (Moldanado, 1985). In a survey of college students, three fourths of female respondents and about two thirds of male respondents favored legalized abortion (see Table 11.5). It is important to observe that acceptance of abortion, regardless of gender, is dependent upon the reason for the abortion (Finlay, 1981). A higher educational level also tends to correlate with a more favorable attitude toward abortion. As for religious preference, as already stated, Jews are the most liberal denomination on the abortion issue followed by Protestants and Catholics (Ebaugh & Haney, 1980). However, persons who frequently attend any type of religious service are more conservative in their attitudes toward abortion regardless of their denomination (Plutzer, 1986).

Although overall public attitudes toward abortion have become more favorable in the last decade, the pro-life movement has been gaining strength since 1978. Several factors are related to attitudes toward abortion. The influence of religion is reflected in the fact that Roman Catholics and Fundamentalists who frequently attend religious services constitute the majority of pro-lifers. Geographically, persons living in the South are generally more conservative in their abortion attitudes than persons living in the rest of the United States (Church, 1989). It is of importance to observe that national public opinion polls have not found any significant differences between women and men with regard to favorable attitudes toward abortion. However, two large-scale surveys of American obstetricians and gynecologists in the mid-1980s found female physicians to have more favorable attitudes toward abortion than male physicians (Weisman, Nathanson, Teitelbaum, Chase, & King, 1986). Contrary to other findings, one study has found no correlation between maternal employment and a positive attitude toward abortion (Plutzer, 1986).

The crucial fact remains that a person's attitude toward abortion is strongly influenced by the reason for seeking an abortion. In general, these reasons can be placed in two categories:

1. "Hard Reasons"—when the woman has no control over the reason such as pregnancy placing her health in jeopardy, incest, or sexual assault.
2. "Soft Reasons"—when the woman has more control, such as not wanting any more children or not wishing to be an unmarried mother (Ebaugh & Haney, 1980, pp. 493–494).

Fewer people are in favor of abortion for "soft" reasons as compared to "hard" reasons. Gallup polls conducted since 1975 have found that the majority of Americans believe that abortion should be legal only under certain circumstances. For example, a 1985 Gallup poll for *Newsweek* determined that 58% of respondents wanted abortion legal only in cases of rape, incest, or threat to the mother's life. And, only about one fourth of the respondents in the various polls agreed that a person should be able to obtain an abortion regardless of the reason ("Split Verdict," 1985). By 1990, another Gallup poll found that 31% of Americans believed that abortion should be legally available for any reason with only 12% indicating that it should be illegal under all circumstances ("Public Opinion," 1990). And, an attempt to pass a city charter amendment in Corpus Christi, Texas declaring that "human life begins at conception" was defeated at the polls by a margin of 62% to 38% ("Abortion Foe Says," 1991). Given the wide diversity of opinion on the abortion issue, the controversy is likely to remain in American society for many years.

Table 11.5: Acceptance of Reasons for Abortion

Reasons	Acceptance Level
Pregnancy is the result of rape	90%
Woman's life endangered by pregnancy	90
"Woman" is an unmarried 14-year-old	69
Woman had German measles/fears baby affected	68
Woman feels she cannot afford another baby	47
Woman is unmarried 25-year-old	42
Woman simply does not want another baby now	38
Woman wants abortion/husband disapproves	25

From B. A. Finlay, "Sex Differences in Correlates of Abortion Attitudes Among College Students" in *Journal of Marriage and the Family,* 43:574. Copyright © 1981 National Council on Family Relations, 3989 Central Avenue, N.E., Suite #550, Minneapolis, MN 55421. Reprinted by permission.

Medical Procedures for Induced Abortions in First and Second Trimesters

The type of abortion procedure is largely determined by the length of pregnancy and the general health of the patient (Masters et al., 1988). The costs and complexity of the abortion procedure as well as the risks of complications increase considerably the longer a woman waits before having an abortion.

Generally speaking, first trimester abortions, which account for about 91% of all abortions (U.S. Bureau of Census, 1990r), place less physiological stress on the woman's body than second trimester abortions (Masters et al., 1988). There are two first trimester abortion methods: vacuum aspiration and the older dilation and curettage (D & C) method. In the **vacuum aspiration** procedure, a physician dilates the cervix with metal dilating rods and inserts a soft plastic vacuum tube with a hard plastic curette (spoon-shaped instrument) attached to its end into the uterus. The amniotic sac and part of the thick uterine lining from the pregnancy are removed with the electric vacuum pump. This procedure is typically performed under a local anesthetic on an outpatient basis and accounts for 95% of all abortions and 98% of all first trimester abortions (Stewart et al., 1979). Another first trimester technique is the **dilation and curettage** (D & C) procedure which involves dilation of the cervix and scraping the walls of the uterus. This method, which has a greater risk of hemorrhaging, has largely passed into obscurity with the advent of the vacuum aspiration method. The D & C is used mostly if a complication, such as an ectopic pregnancy, exists (Allgeier & Allgeier, 1991).

Because of the advanced development of the fetus, abortion in the second trimester of pregnancy is much more complicated both in terms of physical and psychological perspectives. In fact, it has been estimated that the risk for abortion increases about 50% for each week beyond the first trimester (Tyler, 1981). The primary reasons for second trimester abortions include discovery of genetic abnormalities of the fetus, exposure to medications or measles, an impending divorce, or unexpected financial hardships (Allgeier & Allgeier, 1991). There are two second trimester abortion procedures: dilation and evacuation (D & E) and amniotic injection.

The **dilation and evacuation** (D & E) procedure is used primarily during 13–15 weeks of pregnancy. The D & E procedure is generally performed in a hospital because local or general anesthesia is required due to the length of the pregnancy (Hatcher et al., 1986). This method requires greater dilation of the cervix and a larger curette to remove the greater quantity of fetal tissue in comparison to vacuum aspiration. While this procedure accounts for about 85% of all abortions performed for pregnancies that are 13–15 weeks in duration, few abortions occur this late (Allgeier & Allgeier, 1988). The mortality rate for having an abortion performed in the second trimester is much greater than in the first trimester.

The other primary method of induced abortion during the second trimester involves an **amniotic injection** of either saline (concentrated salt solution) or prostaglandins. Saline injections account for 2% of all 13–15 week abortions, while prostaglandins account for 1% of all such abortions (National Center for Health Statistics, 1990a). These amniotic injections are more likely to be used when the pregnancy is 16 weeks or more in duration. Major complications are about two and one half times more likely to occur than with the D & E procedure (Tyler, 1981). Under a local anesthetic, a hollow needle with a tube attached is inserted into the amniotic sac (amnion) and saline or prostaglandins are injected into the amniotic fluid. These substances cause uterine contractions to occur which will expel the fetus. Such a procedure usually requires an average of a 24–hour hospital stay (Stewart et al., 1979). Risks from saline abortions include accidental injection into the uterine muscle, blood vessels, or abdominal cavity; infection; or absorption of the saline solution into the bloodstream. The most common side effect from prostaglandins is vomiting, which occurs in most women (Hatcher et al., 1986).

Aftereffects of Abortions

Much attention has come to be focused on the question of aftereffects (results that follow the initial effects of a cause) of an abortion on the woman's physiological and psychological health. At the present time, considerably more is known about the subsequent physiological health of the woman than the psychological aftereffects of having an abortion. The prevailing view in medical circles is that a legal first trimester abortion is as safe as being given a penicillin shot (Cates, Grimes, & Smith, 1978). After an 18-month study of the research, the United States Surgeon General concluded that sufficient scientific evidence does not exist to condemn abortion as psychologically harmful (Carlson, 1989). Even so, a major thrust of the pro-life movement is concern over the issue of regret and long-term emotional effects of abortions. Consequently, it is important to look at the major findings on the physiological and psychological aftereffects of abortions.

Physiological Aftereffects of Abortions

The most common short-term complications associated with a first trimester abortion are infection, retained products of conception, cervical or uterine injury, and hemorrhaging. **Hemorrhaging** (excess bleeding) can be easily controlled through the use of medication and by massaging the uterus. However, this complication affects less than 1 in 100 women having a first trimester abortion. Often, infections have sources other than abortion-related circumstances such as preexisting gonorrhea. Perforation of the uterus and/or laceration of the cervix rarely occur if a skilled physician performs the procedure. The short-term post-abortion difficulties can generally be alleviated through proper medical treatment and proper precautions during the abortion procedure (Hatcher et al., 1986).

Various studies have found that a previous abortion does not impair the future ability of the woman to conceive. A study of 3,000 women who had received abortions over a 3-year period concluded that 40% of all women had become pregnant within 30 months with no significant difference between abortion and nonabortion recipients. The fact that those women who had three or more abortions were twice as likely to have conceived again suggests a higher degree of fertility among these women ("Abortion," 1985). Finally, it must be observed that much of the data relating to long-term post-abortion complications are contradictory, thus preventing firm conclusions about the issue. However, there is increasing evidence that early first trimester abortions performed by vacuum aspiration may cause few problems. In fact, the risk of dying from a legal abortion is very slight, with the death rate being .8 of one death per 100,000 abortions if the vacuum aspiration or D and E methods are used (Hatcher et al., 1986).

Psychological Aftereffects of Abortions

Research reveals conflicting data concerning the psychological effects of abortion. One body of research reports that adolescents who choose abortion are more likely to be independent, have more realistic views about pregnancy, have begun sexual intercourse at a later age, have a better future-time perspective, and have the lowest need for external approval of their actions (Biro, Wildey, Hillard, & Rauh, 1986). An earlier study also indicated that most women who had abortions reported an absence of resentment, guilt, or sorrow over the decision as well as feelings of relief. Further, almost all respondents indicated that if necessary, they would still choose an abortion (Shusterman, 1979). In a later study, women who had recently undergone an abortion reported increased satisfaction with their lives and little guilt over their decision to abort (Burnell & Norfleet, 1986b). However, reactions appear to depend on the amount of support from significant others. For example, support from friends and parents as well as the male sex partner reportedly contributes positively to feelings of self-esteem and self-worth after receiving an abortion (Robbins & DeLamater, 1985; Chilman, 1980).

Contradictory data in the research literature indicate that, at the time of the abortion, many may have concerns regarding the disapproval by family or friends, the partner's reaction, not being able to have another child, becoming a mother, and having an abortion. In addition, feelings of anger may be directed toward the sex partner for not using an effective contraceptive or toward one's own parents for providing inadequate information about contraception. Mood swings and intense feelings that surface may vary from guilt to relief—from being happy not to be pregnant, to being sad about aborting the fetus (Francoeur, 1991). Persons who are Roman Catholic or a member of a Fundamentalist denomination and attend religious services on a frequent basis are more likely to feel guilty after having an abortion (Plutzer, 1986). After an extensive review of the studies, researchers have concluded that the period of greatest stress is before the abortion and the severe negative psychological reactions after an abortion are rare. Findings suggest that those women who lack support from their partner or parents, are less sure of their decision beforehand, or desire to maintain the pregnancy may be at somewhat higher risk for negative consequences (Adler et al., 1990).

The impact of abortion on men has been largely neglected in the research arena. One study does indicate that many men try to approach the abortion decision in an abstract, intellectual way. However, they indicate later finding themselves faced with feelings of hurt, guilt, or anger (Shostak, McLouth, & Seng, 1984). Post-abortion counseling is important to address the problems of loss and grief experienced by men as well as women following an abortion. Such emotional aftercare can help relieve guilt and regret that may lead to depression or similar problems later in life (Katchadourian, 1989). It is not uncommon for marriage therapists to uncover guilt or hostility toward self or a partner resulting from an earlier abortion. Of course, such is hardly ever verbalized as the "presenting problem" in therapy but rather emerges as the couple explores past unresolved issues (Boran, 1988).

In one interesting study, women in the process of deciding whether to terminate an unwanted pregnancy were interviewed and reinterviewed one year later (Belenky & Gilligan, 1979). The analysis focused on Kohlberg's (1969) levels of moral reasoning that were used by the women in reaching a decision. Results indicated that those in the "gain" group (life circumstances 1 year later improved) resolved the issue with higher stages of moral reasoning. Although they experienced the highest degree of conflict, they were most likely to emerge from the crisis more mature, having reevaluated their concepts of self and morality. The "stable" group (life circumstances 1 year later unchanged) tended to show less conflict and evidenced less change in their stages of moral reasoning. Those in the "loss" group (repeated, unwanted pregnancies 1 year later) resolved the pregnancy with a lower stage of moral reasoning. They typically reported going through the abortion "not thinking and not feeling" (Belenky & Gilligan, 1979).

Depending upon one's religious and moral values, the question of whether or not to obtain an abortion must be carefully weighed against the advantages and disadvantages of all available options. As in other areas of life, one cannot deny the influence of the values of those persons close to them when making significant decisions (Kelly, 1976).

Sexually Transmitted Diseases (STDs) in the 1990s

Probably more media attention was directed to the issue of sexually transmitted diseases (STDs) during the 1980s than any other single news topic. Although there was speculation concerning its impact, such widespread coverage is apparently an important source of information about STDs (see Table 11.6). Emerging problems in the 1990s have raised new issues. One evolving dimension of sexuality relates to sexual etiquette. For example, how does one say "I love you but can I ask a question?" (Goode, 1988). A person today may not only question but even visually inspect their potential sex partner prior to initiation of sexual activity. There is also apparent avoidance of some forms of sexual activity during the early stages of acquaintance (Grieco, 1987). Legal rights are also being redefined. Persons who have contracted STDs have begun to seek monetary damages from their sex partners through civil courts. In the case of genital herpes, for example, some state courts have tried civil suits based on the legal concepts of fraud, battery, and negligence. While proving a case is difficult since it involves one person's word against another's, juries have awarded monetary damages. Some insurance companies even have covered the amount of the damage awards under provisions of homeowner's insurance (Margolick, 1984).

Table 11.6: Sources of Information about STDs

Source	%
Magazines	51%
Television	48
Newspapers	40
Personal Physician	33
Friends	27
Books	24
Clinic	17
School	15
Parents	12
Sex Partners	10
Hospital	9

From Abbott Laboratories, *The Abbott Report: STDs and Sexual Mores in the 1980s*. Reprinted by permission.

Magnitude and Causation of the Problem

The breadth of the problem is reflected in the following statistic: Each day in the United States, 33,000 persons contract STDs and each year, 2.5 million teenagers become infected with an STD (Centers for Disease Control, 1990). STDs can cause pain, sterility, abnormal pregnancies, brain damage, and even death in the cases of acquired immune deficiency syndrome (AIDS), syphilis, and chlamydia (Breo, 1986). The highest reported annual rates of STDs are for women ages 20–24 and the second highest rates are for women ages 15–19. The most common STDs based on estimated annual cases are chlamydia—4 million cases, trichomoniasis—3 million cases, gonorrhea—1.4 million cases, nonspecific urethritis—1.2 million cases, genital warts—750,000 cases, and genital herpes—500,000 cases (Centers for Disease Control, 1990). In fact, it is estimated that 20% of all sexually active adolescents and 10% of all college students have chlamydia (Greene, 1987; Wallis, 1985c). Although gardnerella vaginitis is not a reportable STD, it is thought to be as prevalent as trichomoniasis (Fiumara, 1986c). Syphilis and AIDS appear to be growing more rapidly in terms of percentage increase from year to year. Between 1985 and 1989, the rates for syphilis increased by 176% among black women and by 106% among black men. The rates for white women remained relatively unchanged, decreased for white men, and decreased for Hispanic women and men ("Syphilis Surging," 1990). Based on the first nationwide survey of AIDS on college campuses, it is estimated that between 25,000–35,000 college students, or 1 in 500 are infected with AIDS ("AIDS Shows Up," 1990). As of October 1990, the Centers for Disease Control (CDC)

What appears to be child's play is really rehearsal for responsible use of sexuality later in life.

reported 89,761 deaths had been attributed to AIDS, an increase of 69% over the previous 12-month period ("AIDS: The Human Toll," 1990). However, since experts believe it may take an average of 9 years for the **human immunodeficiency virus** (HIV) to progress to serious illness, most persons currently infected with the virus are not presently ill. The CDC estimates that 1.5 million Americans are infected with the HIV (Centers for Disease Control, 1990).

The major reasons for the significant increases in STDs relate to the rise in premarital sexual intercourse, decreased use of condoms with the advent of oral contraceptives, increased incidence of multiple lifetime sex partners, and increased casual sex (Crooks & Baur, 1990). The comparative effectiveness of contraceptives in preventing STDs suggests that if a person chooses to be sexually active, the condom provides the overall best protection for women and men. In fact, use of oral contraceptives actually increases the risk of chlamydia and genital warts, if exposure occurs, by establishing a growth-enhancing environment in the reproductive tract (Cates, 1987).

Types of STDs

The causation of STDs is primarily either bacterial or viral (Francoeur, 1991). An understanding of the potential risks that exist in today's society concerning STDs is essential.

Chlamydia

The disease **chlamydia** is caused by a bacterium that is transmitted during vaginal-penile sexual intercourse or oral-genital contact. The incubation of the bacterium usually takes from 1–3 weeks before any symptoms appear. Symptoms of men may include a pus-like discharge, burning during urination, inflammation of the scrotal skin, and painful swelling along the sides of the testicles. Women are more commonly asymptomatic (no symptoms), but may exhibit signs of a urinary tract infection (Crooks & Baur, 1990). Chlamydia is treated with the antibiotics tetracycline or erythromycin. But it is important to know that the common antibiotic penicillin is not an effective treatment (Keith, Schink, & Berger, 1985). If men go untreated for this infection, they will experience no lasting effects but can continue infecting any sex partners with the disease (Wallis, 1985c). Although often undetected, chlamydia is a major cause of acute cervicitis, an infection accompanied by redness and swelling of the cervix and purulent discharge (Rosenwaks, Benjamin, & Stone, 1987). If chlamydia goes untreated and uncured in women, it will become a very serious illness, leading to severe abdominal pain, elevated temperature, nausea, and vomiting, and can cause infertility, abnormal pregnancies, pelvic inflammatory disease (PID), and death (Allgeier & Allgeier, 1991). In fact, it is three times more likely to cause sterility in women than gonorrhea. Further, it increases the risk of ectopic pregnancies, stillbirths, premature delivery, and newborn deaths if conception should occur (Brody, 1984).

Gonorrhea

Gonorrhea is caused by a bacterium that is spread through vaginal-penile sexual intercourse, fellatio, cunnilingus, or anal intercourse. While the period of incubation ranges from 1–14 days, the average time is about 3–5 days after contact. Symptoms for men may include increased frequency of urination, painful urination, and a pus-like discharge within 24 hours. Failure to seek immediate treatment also may result in inflammation of the scrotal skin and swelling of the testicles. The symptoms for women include painful urination, pus-like cervical discharge, red and swollen cervix, and some intermenstrual spotting and bleeding. However, about three fourths of women infected with gonorrhea remain asymptomatic. The usual mode of treatment for gonorrhea is penicillin (Fiumara, 1987a). However, during the 1970s, a mutant strain of gonorrhea (PPNG) emerged from Southeast Asia. This bacterium is resistant to penicillin, thus necessitating the use of a different antibiotic for treatment (Hook et al., 1989). Another gonococcal bacterium mutation has also occurred that is resistant to both penicillin and other antibiotics (Boslego, 1987). If a woman has a "one-night stand" with a man infected with gonorrhea, the chances of becoming infected are 80% (Spagna & Prior, 1983).

Syphilis

Syphilis is caused by a bacterium that is transmitted via open lesions during vaginal-penile sexual intercourse, fellatio, cunnilingus, or anal intercourse. It also is possible to spread syphilis through kissing a person who has a syphilitic oral lesion. Usually in primary syphilis, a painless chancre or ulcer appears on the genitals, oral cavity, and/or breasts. The length of incubation for primary syphilis is usually somewhere between 10–90 days. In general, about three cases are reported in men for each case reported in women. If untreated, syphilis moves to the secondary stage with such symptoms as low grade fever, patchy hair loss, and skin rash on the palms and soles of feet. During the secondary stage, a light red rash will start on the trunk, shoulders, and arms and then move to the face, chest, and abdomen. If a person is exposed to syphilis in the secondary stage, they will usually develop the infection after about 6 weeks. During the 1st year of infection, syphilis will be spread to about 90% of a person's sexual contacts; but by the 2nd year, it is spread to only about 5%; and after 4 years, the infected person can no longer spread the disease. The recommended treatment for primary and secondary syphilis is benzathine penicillin (Fiumara, 1987b). If the infection remains untreated, the tertiary stage of syphilis will be characterized by impaired speech, concentration, and memory; trembling of lips or hands; and eventually death (Keith et al., 1985).

Genital Herpes (Herpes Genitalis)

Genital herpes is caused by the Herpes Simplex Virus Type II (HSVII), a member of the same virus family as HSVI that causes fever blisters and mouth ulcers. Although each are distinct viruses, during oral sex, Simplex I can be transferred to the genital area and Simplex II to the mouth (Crooks & Baur, 1990). The genital herpes virus is primarily transmitted via penile-vaginal intercourse, cunnilingus, fellatio, or anal intercourse through direct contact with the blisters or open sores. In addition, medical scientists have now established that the virus can live for 2–4 hours in tap water, on toilet seats, and on moist, plastic-coated surfaces such as seats at a health spa, swimming pool, or gym (Francoeur, 1991). Length of incubation for genital herpes is between 2–12 days before the appearance of the blisters that will eventually turn into lesions. Symptoms include painful blisters on the genitals, buttocks, thighs, or within the urethra. Those blisters that occur in the vagina or cervix are usually not painful and may go unnoticed. Other symptoms include a burning pain or itching of the affected area along with skin inflammation. This eruption period usually lasts from 2–10 days. In addition, low abdominal pain and fever are frequently associated with the primary infection (Byer & Shainberg, 1991). The lesions eventually go away and the disease becomes dormant, although it can reoccur due to physical or emotional stress with younger people being most likely to experience these reoccurrences. Persons with genital herpes may continue to have safe sexual intercourse unless the virus is in an active state. There is no known cure for genital herpes, but the primary symptoms and discomfort may be alleviated with the use of **acyclovir** applied directly to the lesions. In addition, acyclovir is also available as an oral preparation (Fiumara, 1986d). Some have suggested that diet and rest may also affect the likelihood of reoccurrence.

In a survey of college students who had contracted genital herpes, both women and men believed that the disease had ruined their sex lives. Of these respondents, three fourths avoided any sexual contacts for a long period of time and 9 in 10 believed that it would be difficult to find a future marriage mate. Most indicated that they discussed genital herpes with a new partner prior to sexual intercourse, and two thirds decided to seek sexual relationships only with persons who had genital herpes (Mirotznik, Shapiro, Steinhart, & Gillespie, 1987).

Trichomoniasis (Trichomonas Vaginalis)

The cause of **trichomoniasis** is a protozoan parasite that is passed on through penile-vaginal sexual intercourse and sometimes by using the towel, toilet seat, or bathtub after an infected person. This protozoa can survive for 24 hours in tap water, 3 hours in urine, and for about 45 minutes on a toilet seat. The average length of incubation for trichomoniasis is about 7 days. The disease is especially prevalent among women ages 15–40. Symptoms among women include a white or yellow, frothy vaginal discharge with an unpleasant odor, increased frequency of urination, burning sensations during urination, and soreness and itching of the labia. The symptoms for men may be only genital itching or a slight yellowish discharge. Most men and about one fourth of women, however, are asymptomatic. The drug metronidazole has proved to be very effective in the treatment of trichomoniasis (Fiumara, 1986f).

Genital Candidiasis (Yeast Infection)

While yeast infections are present in women and men who are celibate, they are often spread via sexual activity with others and thus need to be understood in this context. *Candida* fungus sometimes occurs when there is a disturbance of the chemical balance in the vaginal barrel due to pregnancy, diabetes, oral contraceptives, antibiotics, vaginal-penile sexual intercourse, or oral-genital sex with a sex partner having the chemical imbalance. This fungus is normally present in the vagina and on the glans penis. However, if the vaginal chemical balance is disturbed, its growth becomes accelerated. The incubation period usually lasts less than a week. Although this is not a reportable disease, it is estimated that more than 3 million women suffer from **genital candidiasis.** Symptoms in women range from a slight vaginal itching to irritation and soreness of the labia, a burning sensation following urination, a lack of vaginal lubrication during sexual arousal, and a white, "cheesy" discharge (Bingham, 1986). For men, the glans penis may itch and there may be a painful skin irritation, but oftentimes men are asymptomatic. Yeast infections have typically been treated by vaginal suppositories or a medicated cream such as nystatin and miconazole available via a physician's prescription (Fiumara, 1986a). Because an estimated three fourths of all women experience yeast infections at sometime during their lifetime, the news that the medication Gyne-Lotrimin will no longer require a prescription has been well-received ("Yeast Infection," 1990).

Nonspecific Urethritis (Nongonococcal Urethritis—NGU)

The cause of **nonspecific urethritis** is unclear, but it is thought to be a bacterium that seems to be primarily transmitted via penile-vaginal sexual intercourse. It is usually diagnosed following a negative test for gonorrhea using standard laboratory tests. Nonspecific urethritis develops primarily in persons between ages 15–29 with an incubation period ranging from 7–21 days (Keith et al., 1985). Usually women are asymptomatic, while men suffer from frequent urination, urethral itching, and experience a thin, clear urethral discharge in the mornings (Fiumara, 1986e). If nonspecific urethritis goes untreated, it may cause inflammation of the epididymis and potentially cause infertility in men and pelvic inflammatory disease in women ("Cinderella," 1978). The usual mode of treatment for nonspecific urethritis is the drug tetracycline or erythromycin (Denney & Quadagno, 1988).

Gardnerella Vaginitis (Hemophilus)

While the presence of some gardnerella vaginalis bacteria in the vaginal flora is considered normal, its overgrowth leads to the development of **gardnerella vaginitis** (Ching, Borchardt, Smith, & Beal, 1988). Asymptomatic men are believed to harbor the bacteria in their urinary tract, thus transmitting the organisms during penile-vaginal sexual intercourse (Watson, 1985). The time of incubation for this STD is less than 1 week. For women, as the acidity level of the vagina increases, a grayish-white vaginal discharge with a fish-like odor may appear along with redness and soreness of the labia and painful urination (Keith et al., 1985). The recommended method of treatment is for the infected woman and her sex partner to be treated with either metronidazole, ampicillin, or tetracycline (Fiumara, 1986c).

Genital Warts (Human Papillomavirus)

Genital warts are caused by a virus that is spread through penile-vaginal intercourse, anal intercourse, or oral-genital sexual activity. It primarily affects women and men usually between ages 15–40 (Fiumara, 1986b). Although genital warts are not a reportable disease in the United States, it is thought to be one of the most common STDs in the world. Between 1981–1986, private physicians observed a 46% increase in genital warts ("Another Sexual," 1988). Genital warts may not appear until 1–20 months after contact with an infected sex partner. The symptoms are characterized by single or multiple soft, pink cauliflower warts that appear around the vaginal orifice, labia, anus, penis, urethral orifice, and/or perineum (Denney & Quadagno, 1988). It is anticipated that between 5–15% of persons with persistent warts will develop cancer of the cervix, vulva, vagina, anus, and/or penis. Several factors appear to be required to trigger the development of cancer: smoking, oral contraceptives, and genital herpes ("Another Sexual," 1988). Modes of treatment may include topical agents such as podophyllin, cauterization, freezing, surgical removal, or vaporization by a carbon dioxide laser (Crooks & Baur, 1990). However, the FDA in 1988 approved the use of the genetically engineered drug Alpha interferon that is injected directly into the wart ("Drug OK'd," 1988).

Acquired Immune Deficiency Syndrome

Acquired immune deficiency syndrome (AIDS) is a new STD that has grown into a serious world health problem since it was first recognized in America in 1981. The AIDS virus is believed, by some authorities, to have evolved in Central Africa more than a century ago (Francoeur, 1991). It is a fatal disease in which the body's immune system fails to function properly, thus allowing life-threatening, opportunistic infections to occur from bacteria, fungi, parasites, viruses, and some cancers. The HIV may also produce milder illnesses called **AIDS-related complex** (ARC). So far only a minority of those with ARC have progressed to the stage of AIDS (AIDS Foundation Houston, 1986).

Two diseases often seen in persons with AIDS (PWA) are Kaposi's sarcoma (KS), a type of skin cancer and pneumonocystis carinii pneumonia (PCP), a type of lung infection (Denney & Quadagno, 1988). Among the AIDS symptoms are high fever, night sweats, swollen glands, unexplained weight loss, diarrhea, yeast infections, persistent cough, fatigue, and loss of appetite (U.S. Public Health Service, 1984). Since there is no known cure for AIDS, medical treatment is limited to treating the symptoms (Masters et al., 1988).

Without symptoms, carriers can only be identified by a blood test for the presence of an antibody to the AIDS virus. The ELISA test is used in the initial screening for infection and the Western Blot test for confirmation of a positive test result (Macklin, 1989). A positive test only indicates that the person has been exposed to HIV, not whether she/he has or will develop AIDS. However, it is important that all persons with positive tests regard themselves as carriers of the virus and take appropriate precautions to protect others (American College Health Association, 1986).

AIDS is known to be transmitted via blood and semen through vaginal and anal intercourse, transfusions of infected blood, sharing of unsanitary needles by intravenous drug users, and from an infected mother to unborn child. The top risk groups for AIDS have been identified as homosexuals, bisexuals, and intravenous drug users (Conrad, 1986). Most heterosexual transmission of AIDS is from men to women because women apparently may be less efficient transmitters (Wallis, 1985a). However, categories of sexual orientation do not always accurately reflect behavior or risk for the HIV infection since many heterosexuals and homosexuals live in overlapping communities of risk. Recent Kinsey Institute data from lesbians indicate that a significant percentage of these women had previously engaged in high-risk sexual behaviors with men. These behaviors included unprotected penile-vaginal intercourse, vaginal intercourse during menses, anal intercourse, and **analingus** (oral stimulation of anus). This high rate of risk-taking sexual behavior among lesbians raises questions concerning the AIDS risk for heterosexual women as well. The point is that it is behavior, not group membership, that confers an at-risk status for the HIV infection (Reinisch, 1988).

Studies of undergraduate students' knowledge, attitudes, and behavior regarding AIDS reveal that many college students deny being at personal risk for contraction of AIDS (Gray & Saracino, 1988). Even persons who are knowledgeable about AIDS still tend to think the disease is someone else's problem (Stanley, 1989a). Although the reviews are mixed, some evidence suggests there are changes in sexual behavior due to concern about STDs (Abbott Laboratories, 1987). However, in a study of heterosexual singles, 81% indicated that no major changes had been made in their sex lives due to the AIDS scare (Lord, Thornton, & Carey, 1986). A medical survey of over 16,000 students at 19 universities was conducted in early 1989 by the CDC to determine the prevalence of HIV on college campuses. Of those students tested, 2 in 1,000 were found to be carriers of HIV. Some authorities have questioned the representativeness of this sample from a population who sought general medical services at a university health center. Nevertheless, CDC officials believe that aggressive efforts are needed to prevent the spread of AIDS on college campuses where premarital sexual involvement is common (Stanley, 1989b). Increasingly, the social significance of AIDS is also being recognized, especially as it relates to families. National and state organizations are emphasizing the need for social policy that responds to the needs of families as the primary caretakers of PWA (Macklin, 1988).

The Best Defense Against STDs

Nowhere is the age-old adage, "the best defense is a good offense" more applicable than in the case of coping with STDs. Since all STDs are "behaviorally related" and "personally transmitted," it makes good sense for each person to consciously and carefully choose her/his behavior from all available options. The concepts of safer sex and responsible sex must become synonymous. The following risk reduction behaviors offer guidelines for making responsible decisions and taking actions for safer sex:

1. Have sexual contact only with persons not infected with an STD.
2. Know your sex partner well enough to trust answers to STD questions.
3. Agree to mutual medical exams prior to sexual intercourse if uncertain about STD status.
4. Avoid sexual contacts in which body fluids are exchanged.
5. Reduce number of sex partners.
6. Avoid using intravenous drugs or sharing needles.
7. Avoid use of inhalant recreational drugs such as "poppers," which can weaken the immune system.
8. Avoid mixing alcohol and mind-altering substances ("drugs") with sexual encounters.
9. Avoid sharing razors or toothbrushes.
10. Inspect genitals of partner prior to sexual intercourse.
11. Use a condom in any sexual activity.
12. Urinate after sexual intercourse.
13. Use a chemical vaginal spermicide during sexual intercourse.
14. Promptly and thoroughly wash genitals with soap and hot water after sexual contact (American College Health Association, 1986, p. 5; Crooks & Baur, 1990, pp. 676–679).

Safer Sex Strategies

A "safer sex" strategy that is recommended involves simply asking one's partner about her/his sex history and mind-altering substance background. However, this approach may provide a false sense of security. One cannot always assume that potential sex partners will accurately disclose their risk for STDs. In one study, almost one half of women (42%) and men (47%) said they would indicate fewer past sex partners than was the case. Further, 1 in 10 women and 2 in 10 men replied they would never disclose their prior sexual involvement with someone else to a new partner. Perhaps most disturbing was the fact that only 4 in 10 women who asked partners about AIDS risk also insisted that their partner use a condom (Cochran, 1988). The message of such findings would indicate that simply asking one's partner about her/his sexual and drug history is not necessarily "safer sex." It is safe only if one is with a partner who is truly trustworthy.

In order to encourage the "safer sex" techniques so vital in today's age of AIDS and other STDs, it is important to be "sex positive." One such creative suggestion is to eroticize condoms. Teaching people to view putting on a condom as a stimulating sexual act itself is a sex-positive approach to changing behavior. Other ways include learning more about "outer course" rather than "inter course" wherein caressing, fondling, and/

or other noncoital experimentation is used (Hawkins, 1987). Finally, arming oneself with reliable knowledge may be the most important safer sex strategy. Appendix A includes hotline numbers for select STDs, including AIDS, as well as additional sources of information.

Summary

- The reasons that unmarrieds do not use contraceptives include negative self-feelings along with indifference and lack of knowledge.
- Available contraceptive methods include oral contraceptives, condoms, diaphragms, chemical spermicides, and fertility awareness methods with abstinence. With concerns about STDs and possible side effects of oral contraceptives, the condom and diaphragm appear to be gaining in popularity.
- Tubal ligations and vasectomies are becoming the birth control technique of choice among middle-aged couples.
- In the developmental stages for men are a possible oral contraceptive and injections of testosterone. The Norplant system is the latest available contraceptive for women.
- The United States Supreme Court ruled in 1973 that a state cannot interfere with a woman's right to terminate her pregnancy through abortion during the first trimester. Although the majority of Americans support freedom of choice on the abortion issue, many persons remain opposed to the idea.
- While much of the data are contradictory about physiological and psychological aftereffects of abortion, there is increasing evidence that early first trimester abortions performed by vacuum aspiration cause few physiological problems.
- Despite the adverse publicity over the dangers of STDs, the annual rates of increase suggest that little change is occurring in sexual behavior patterns.
- Safer sex practices can greatly reduce the risks of contracting an STD. The greatest number of reported cases of STDs today are for chlamydia, genital warts, and trichomoniasis, but the percentage of AIDS cases appears to be growing most rapidly.

Questions for Critical Reflection

1. A 1990 National Academy of Sciences study concluded that research has contributed little to contraceptive techniques since the pill and the IUD in the early 1960s; the United States is years behind European countries in such development. Fear of product liability lawsuits, unduly strict FDA regulations, and the antiabortion movement have all been blamed. Which of these do you believe to be most influential? What might be other reasons?
2. Sterilization is now the most popular form of birth control among married persons, with two thirds of all couples choosing this method of birth control within 15 years of marriage. Why do far fewer men elect such surgery than do women for whom the process is more costly and risky? What major factors would be important to you in making such a decision?
3. Based on the experience of any women you know who have had an abortion, what can you add to the contradictory research findings concerning the psychological aftereffects of abortion?
4. If you were compiling a list of myths concerning STDs believed by your friends, which three would top the list? What nonthreatening source of information could you share with them?
5. What major message is inherent in the statistics confirming a 43% increase in teen AIDS cases between July 1988 and August 1989 and the fact that only six states require AIDS education in public schools? Why is this your problem?

Suggested Readings

Dornblasser, C., & Landy, U. (1982). *The abortion guide: A handbook for women and men.* New York: Berkley. A nontechnical resource on all aspects of abortion including its aftermath.

Hatcher, R. A., Stewart, F. H., Trussell, J., Kowal, D., Guest, F. J., Stewart, G. K. & Cates, W., Jr. (1990). *Contraceptive technology 1990–1992* (15th rev. ed.). New York: Irvington. A comprehensive, up-to-date medical guide to contraception, sterilization, abortion, and sexually transmitted diseases.

Parish, L. C., & Gschnait, F. (Eds.). (1988). *Sexually transmitted diseases: A guide for clinicians.* New York: Springer-Verlag. A technical but authoritative source on diagnosis and treatment of sexually transmitted diseases.

Tribe, L. H. (1990). *Abortion: The clash of absolutes.* New York: W. W. Norton. A nonpartisan, scholarly consideration of the abortion controversy from a constitutional law perspective.

Ulene, A. (1987). *Safe sex in a dangerous world.* New York: Random House. A highly readable overview of the AIDS threat and suggestions for ways of practicing safer sex.

PART IV

PARENTING DECISIONS AND BEYOND

The decisions about children are perhaps among the most difficult and complex issues in today's society. A mythical "children by choice" society is one in which every child will be truly wanted and, therefore, valued. However, young persons need to be aware of today's reality: There are healthy and unhealthy reasons for desiring children as well as advantages and disadvantages of parenthood. In chapter 12, child-free couples of the 1990s are said to be seeking more freedom to pursue careers and an unrestricted life-style. Infertility, its causes, treatment, and alternatives such as artificial insemination, in-vitro fertilization, and surrogate motherhood offer new answers to old problems. Also, clarification of adoption issues leaves many decisions clearly in the hands of tomorrow's adoptive parents.

One needs not only to understand the physiology of conception and stages of pregnancy addressed in chapter 13 but also to realize the emotional responses to pregnancy. The health issues and risks cited for congenital defects are sobering knowledge needed prior to pregnancy. Familiarity with the process of childbirth, including alternative methods and the advantages of breast-feeding, arms future parents for wise decisions. Transitions to parenthood include information about postpartum depression and for employed mothers and fathers, emerging work-parent role conflicts.

The need for preparation for parenting, stressed as a basis of coping with the challenges and concerns of child rearing, is explored in chapter 14. A framework for successful parenting is used as an organizing principle. Contributions of others to socialization are examined, such as early childhood education and television. When parenting goes awry, the stage is set for child abuse and in some instances incest, the well-guarded family secret, both of which are chapter topics.

When children are added to the family equation, financial responsibilities increase. In chapter 15, financial management is viewed as a crucial factor in family success. Nutritional facts and fantasies need to be separated in order to make the most effective food choices in the market and on the table. Housing, including the advantages and disadvantages of owning or renting, must be considered by families, especially today with limited housing dollars. Insights are offered into adequate health care, life insurance, banking procedures, the use of credit, and estate planning, all of which are significantly related to family financial success.

Traditional expressive and instrumental roles are juxtaposed with those in dual-career or dual-earner marriages in chapter 16. It is important for today's young person contemplating briefcase, baby, or both to comprehend the barriers and costs inherent in such decisions: child-care options, role-overload conflict, and the effects of maternal employment on children. Finally, a consideration of marital stability in dual-career marriages and commuter marriages offers today's generation food for thought.

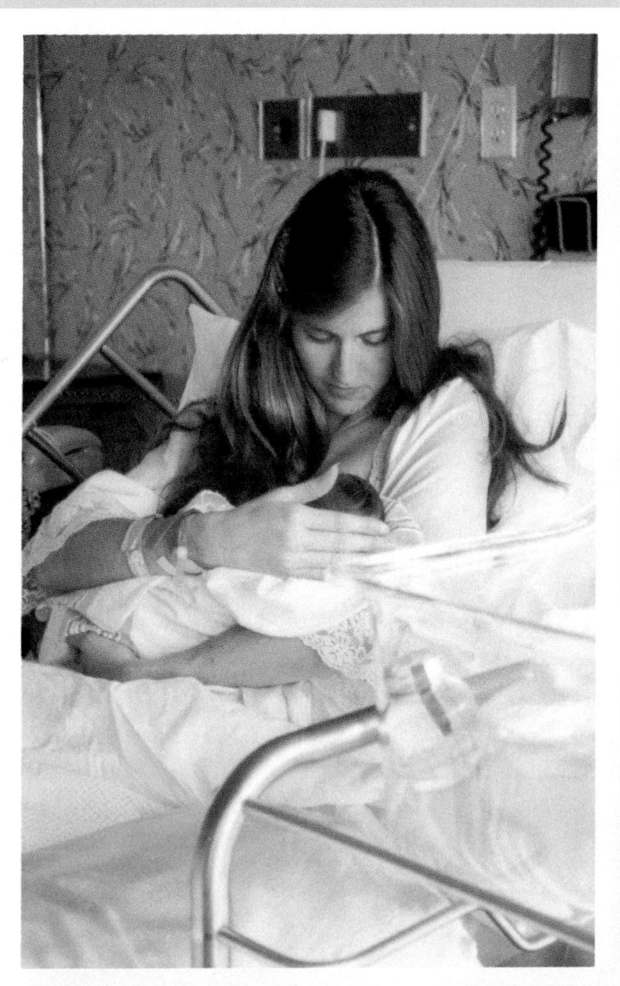

GO!

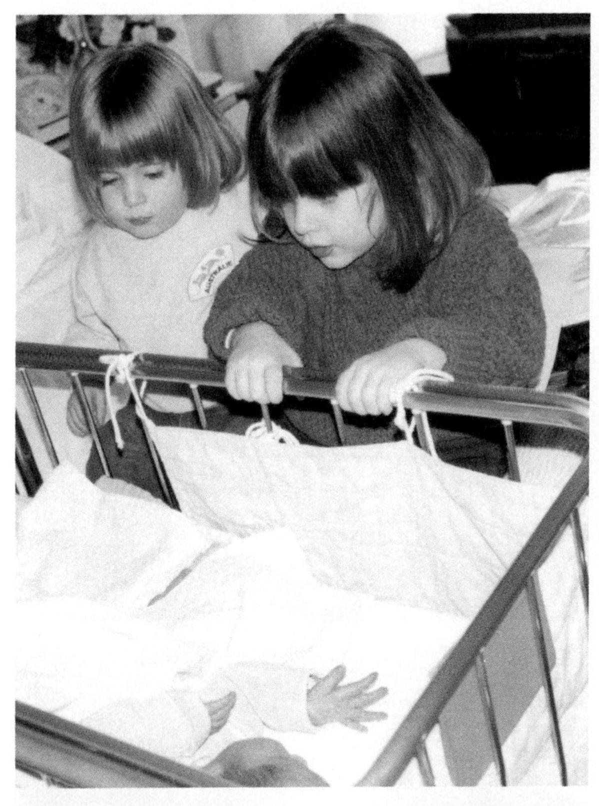

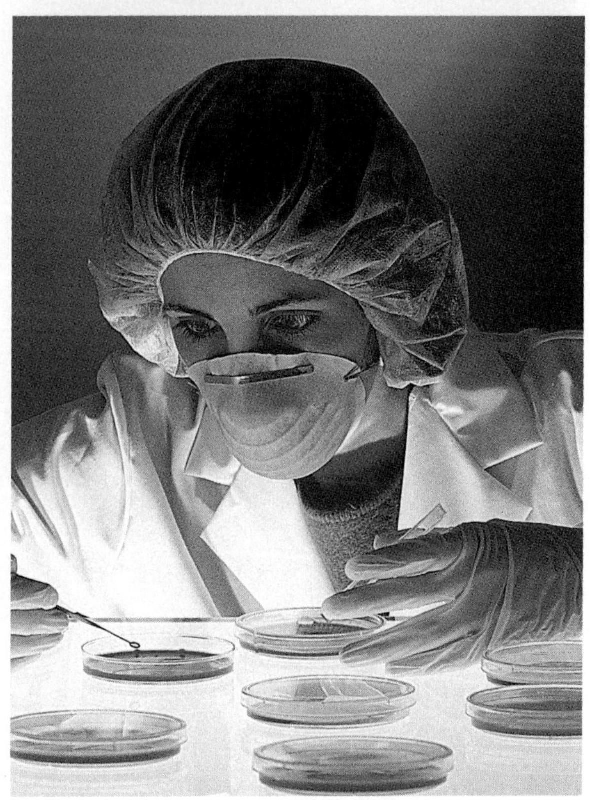

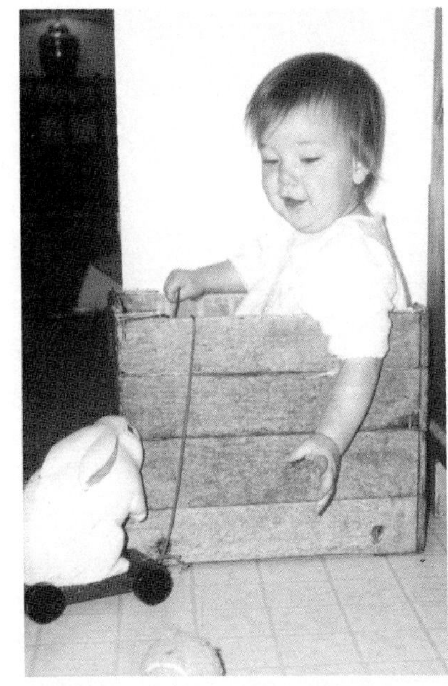

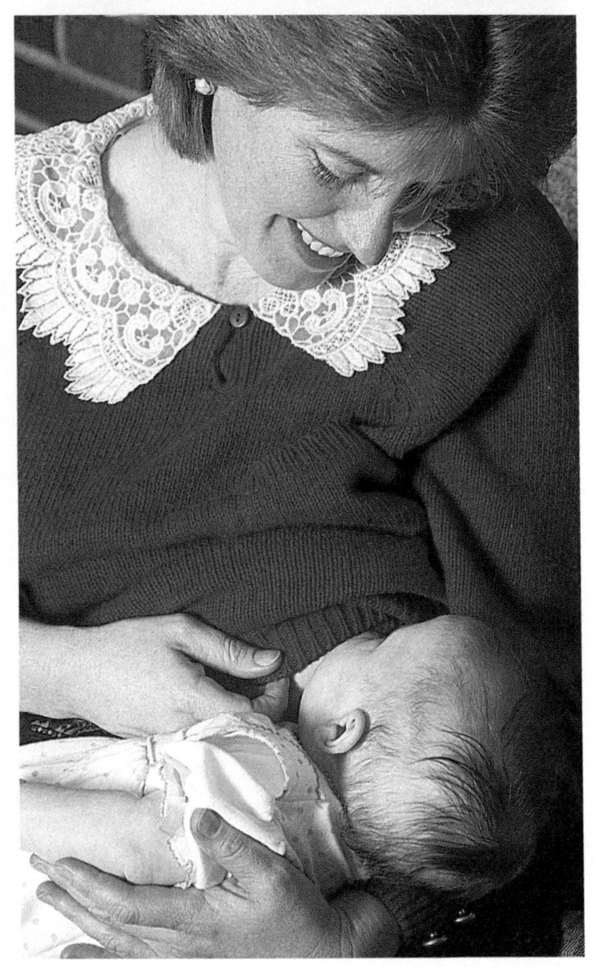

CHAPTER 12

Decisions about Children

Decisions about having or not having children have a great bearing on whether adult life is going to be happy and successful or not . . . A decision to have or not to have them has far-reaching consequences.
Joanna Magda Polenz, 1981

OUTLINE

Marriage by choice, children by choice, theories of choice and exchange: family historians may record the second half of the 20th century as the "age of choice." At no previous time have more options been available in marriage and family. Until recently, however, the inevitability of wives bearing children was accepted without question. It is only within the past several decades that the idea of choosing not to have children has even emerged. The possibility of limiting the size of traditionally large families began with the advent of effective and available contraceptives during the 1920s and 1930s (Wells, 1988). The idea of choosing to remain childless did not gain widespread acceptance until the 1980s. The sexual revolution and the women's movement as well as issues of overpopulation and environmental pollution have added impetus to this once nondebatable question.

During the 1950s and 1960s, a commitment to parenthood was a strong factor in choosing a marriage partner, and few college women were willing to sacrifice marriage and motherhood for occupational success. But major shifts in attitudes toward childbearing occurred during the 1970s and 1980s (Neal, Groat, & Wicks, 1989). Much to the surprise of their parents, a majority of young women and men began to reject the idea of childbearing as a moral obligation (Yankelovich, 1974). In 1972, a survey of white middle-class college women found that over one half believed that refusal to have children was a legitimate reason for a divorce, whereas by 1979, only about one fourth thought that refusal to have children should be a basis for divorce. Further, about three fourths of these women did not feel that children were essential for a happy marriage (Cook, West, & Hamner, 1982).

Childbearing for women in the United States peaks between ages 20–24 and typically begins to decline by age 30. However, there has been an increase in first births after age 30 which has been attributed to delayed first marriage and childbearing especially among women who work outside the home (Teachman & Polonko, 1985). According to Census Bureau data, between 1980–1988, the proportion of women who remained child-free between ages 35–39 has increased slightly from 8% to 12%. In this age span, white and Hispanic women are almost twice as likely as black women to remain child-free (U.S. Bureau of the Census, 1990o).

Decision to Have Children

In general, married women with traditional gender-role orientations are more likely to bear children. While it has been assumed that participation in the labor force decreases the likelihood of childbearing, a crucial factor appears to be not whether women work outside the home but, rather, their occupation. Women who work in professional or managerial positions are less likely to bear children than women working in lower-paying positions (White & Kim, 1987). Among the reasons cited by couples today for postponing childbearing are to achieve personal maturity, to gain financial security, to determine stability in marriage, and to establish a career (Soloway & Smith, 1987). It is important to observe that not all reasons for having children are necessarily healthy ones. For example, some couples have a child in order to relive a deprived childhood. While providing material advantages which they never had for their child may appear selfless, it is an unhealthy base for childbearing. Other questionable reasons would be to hold a marriage together and to help a spouse "grow up" (Paluszny & Thombre, 1987). With the availability of modern contraceptive methods, married couples today can make a conscious choice to parent or not to parent. However, there are many personal and external factors that affect the decision to have children.

Advantages of Parenthood

While various social surveys suggest decreased cultural support for parenthood, the data indicate that careers, marriage, and childbearing remain strong interests for women today. In the mid-1980s, a survey of undergraduate women concluded that over three fourths expected to marry, two thirds expected to bear one or more children, and over one half expected to work outside the home while engaging in parenting. In terms of number of children desired, their expectations were two children—51%, three children—20%, four children—13%, and only one child—5%. When asked to describe their ideal family and career pattern, about two thirds chose "two children and a half-time job" (Straits, 1985). Available research suggests that unresolved personal identity issues interfere with the decision-making process regarding when to begin a family. It contends that the question "Who am I?" needs to be answered before making the decision to become a parent (Soloway & Smith, 1987).

CATHY Copyright 1985 Cathy Guisewite. Reprinted by permission of Universal Press Syndicate.

Personal Motives Affecting Decision to Have Children

Assuming relative maturity, there are still varied personal reasons for choosing to parent. From the many personal motives for having children, four common ones are that children serve as a source of love and affection, fulfill personal needs, provide for immortality, and convey adult status. The **altruistic** pleasure of having children is often mentioned first on the list of reasons. The feelings of love and affection associated with giving birth to a wanted child can produce intense personal pleasure. A child is perceived as a lifelong source for both giving and receiving expressions of affection and love (Burnell & Norfleet, 1986a). Childbearing also appears to be a creative experience of bonding. In fact, in a survey of noncollege adults, "creating a new person with someone you love" was reported as the most important reason for having children by women and second most important by men (see Table 12.1).

More purpose and fulfillment in life as well as a higher sense of achievement are reported by parents as major satisfactions from having children (Callan, 1987; Hoffman & Manis, 1979). Giving birth to a child may be viewed as a way of providing deep personal satisfaction to an otherwise dreary life. In Table 12.1, it is shown that men were more likely than women to perceive that a child would "make their life richer." In a comparison of mother's and daughter's values, children were not as valued by daughters for their future economic benefit but rather for psychological reasons (Callan & Gallois, 1983).

Having a child may be perceived as a way of carrying on the family name or perpetuating those self-qualities that are deemed worthy of preservation. A sample of college students ranked "having someone to carry on a part of oneself" as the most important reason for having a child (Asis, 1986b). Despite recent changes in gender roles, the desire to have a male child to maintain the family name through "eternity" remains an important variable in influencing the decision to have a child (Soloway & Smith, 1987).

Table 12.1: Reasons Given for Having Children

Reasons for Having Children	Women	Men
Create new person with someone you love	60%	56%
Make life richer	52	62
Important part of being married	42	42
Someone to share things with	38	53
Enjoy being with children	36	31
Experience raising child	30	27
One of life's greatest accomplishments	23	18
Feelings about continuation of life	19	26
Part of being a real woman or man	13	1
Someone who loves you	9	15

From G. M. Burnell and M. A. Norfleet, "Psychosocial Factors Influencing American Men and Women in Their Decision for Sterilization" in *The Journal of Psychology,* 120:116. Copyright © 1986 Heldref Publications, Washington, DC. Reprinted by permission of the authors.

Persons concerned with the problem of teen pregnancy have known for some time that having a child may be perceived as a symbol of adult status for many teenagers. Some believe that only through parenthood is one considered a real woman or man. However, in one survey among adult women with children, 35% of black women and only 40% of white women believed that having a child symbolized their achievement of adulthood (Hoffman & Manis, 1979). However, it is somewhat surprising that this reason was given by only 13% of women in a later study (see Table 12.1).

Disadvantages of Parenthood

Nowhere is the concept of choice and exchange more applied than in the process of parenting. While the vast majority of married couples embrace the role of parents as one of life's most meaningful experiences, childbirth is not without its costs (Umberson & Gove, 1989). The birth of a child irrevocably alters life for the parents. This is especially true if it is the birth of their first child. Not only does the birth affect day-to-day living patterns but couple relationships also change. A review of research findings from the 1970s and 1980s suggests that childbirth brings increased personal responsibility for housework, some restrictions on social activities and personal pursuits, lost opportunities, and lack of social support (Callan, 1987).

Evidence suggests that college students are becoming more realistic about the decision to have children. In one survey, two thirds of the college students cited drastic changes in life-style and financial costs as disadvantages of parenthood (see Table 12.2).

Table 12.2: Disadvantages of Having Children

Having children causes drastic change in life-style	68%
Financial cost of children too great	65
Children cause worry and tension	49
Caring for children takes too much time	47
Having children makes it difficult for women to work	42
Having children adds to population problem	35
Children cause disorder in household	26
Having children endangers one's health and stamina	20

Source: M. M. B. Asis, The Involuntarily Childless: Is There Support for Them in American Society? Paper presented at the meeting of the Midwest Sociological Society, Des Moines, IA, 1986b, March, p. 8.

The birth of a first child often has a tremendous impact on the household budget especially if the wife plans to discontinue working after childbirth. Budget categories that usually undergo reductions include recreational pursuits, clothing allowance for parent(s), investment/savings programs, and vacation locations. In the typical family, about 20% of the annual family income is spent on children (Bloom & Bennett, 1986). It also is important to remember that household expenses will increase regardless of whether the wife remains employed or discontinues her career, at least for the time being.

After the birth of the first child, the welfare of a third person must constantly be considered in such areas as susceptibility to illness, regular eating schedule, and reduction in spontaneous decisions about use of leisure time (Lamanna, 1977). The altering of the daily routine is not a short-term consequence of having a child but rather it is a continuing task and responsibility which does not end with infancy or early childhood. A parent of a preteen or teenager sometimes wonders if the role of parent will ever end!

The arrival of a child in the household will reduce the amount of time that spouses have for each other due to their increased family responsibilities. In general, wives continue to have responsibility for most domestic tasks. Thus, mothers report feeling fatigued and emotionally depleted due to stress associated with parenting (Paluszny & Thombre, 1987).

External Factors Affecting Decision to Have Children

It is paradoxical that even in this age of choice, some persons still believe that biologically, socially, and psychologically, we have little choice in childbearing (Callan, 1986). Such persons cite the biological imperative or **instinctual** urge to reproduce as well as the myth perpetuated by the majority within our society that reproduction is necessary to fulfill one's destiny.

However, beginning in the 1970s, considerable debate has emerged over whether or not American society has shifted its attitude toward childbearing to the extent that persons were actually being discouraged from having children. Concern was expressed that college-educated women may have to choose their profession over motherhood in order to ensure continued career advancement (Friedan, 1978). Corporations are viewed in some circles as being primarily committed to the profit motive to the detriment of families and childbearing (Hunt & Hunt, 1986). Despite these concerns, socialization experiences and perhaps other factors still push in the direction of becoming parents after marriage (Straits, 1985).

Costs of Parenthood

While most couples do not carefully consider the financial costs of childbearing and child rearing before deciding whether or not to have a baby, many people are becoming aware that the costs can be substantial. The ultimate decision to limit the number of children

The skyrocketing cost of a college education is high on a parent's list of financial pressures.

often reflects an awareness that too many children can result in a lower standard of living for the family. In general, both society and individuals tend to choose a higher standard of living over a number of children (Weeks, 1989). Surveys conducted in 1972 and 1979 indicated that the majority of persons believed that family economic considerations were the most important factors in the decision of whether or not to have a child (Cook, West, & Hamner, 1982). In 1977, it was estimated that the direct cost of rearing a first child in a middle-class family through 4 years of college was $64,000 (Belkin, 1985a). Eleven years later with inflation and the escalating costs of education, that figure had risen to $227,000 including 4 years at an in-state college/university or $310,000 if one chooses private schooling (Peterson, 1990). While direct costs may vary substantially by geographical region and the standard of living of parents, this figure is a dramatic increase. To put these figures in better perspective, the 1987 median household income for families in which the head of household had 4 or more years of college was $50,908 for whites in contrast to only $43,382 for Hispanics and $36,568 for blacks (U.S. Bureau of the Census, 1990ff). In addition, the indirect costs of lost economic opportunities for wage earning and investments which mothers often give up during child rearing also must be considered. For example, many working women who decide to become mothers may experience interrupted career advancement which is then reflected in their annual salaries (Waite, Haggstrom, & Kanouse, 1985a).

Parental and Peer Pressures

Although one survey found that female college students disagreed with their mothers over the issue of having children as a primary function of marriage and a way of achieving womanhood, the parents of a couple can create considerable pressure to have grandchildren (Callan & Gallois, 1983). Both indirect and direct hints may be given to married daughters and sons regarding their desire to become grandparents. Parental pressures may derive from the desire to have grandchildren in order to perpetuate the family line. In addition, grandchildren are viewed as a source of recognition and prestige in the social milieu of grandparents (Cherlin & Furstenberg, 1986). Such pride is frequently expressed in a favorite activity: displaying photographs of grandchildren to friends and acquaintances.

Subtle pressures from peers may also influence the decision to have children. At social gatherings involving young mothers, the topic of conversation often centers on various aspects of child rearing related to the age of their children. Married women without children may feel somewhat awkward in such conversations. Or a man may be made to feel left out of father/son recreational activities in which his male peers participate (Soloway & Smith, 1987). Some women and men, thus, may decide to become parents to alleviate such subtle pressures.

Religious Values

Religious values, which have traditionally played a major role in the decision to have children, still influence the choice of parenthood today (Neal, Groat, & Wicks, 1989). Since 1950, national surveys of childbearing patterns have continued to demonstrate that a person's religion is a key factor in childbearing rates. Traditionally, Roman Catholics having the highest rates and Jews having the lowest rates. A review of data from the 1973 and 1976 National Family Growth Surveys revealed that Hispanic and Anglo-Catholics reported the greatest number of wanted pregnancies (Mosher & Hendershot, 1984). The theological position that childbearing is an important facet of marriage is also reflected in the continued opposition of the Roman Catholic church to artificial contraception.

While population data from the late 1980s suggest that birthrates for Roman Catholics have converged with those for Protestants, women who are high on the religiosity scale, as measured by frequency of attendance at religious services, from both denominations have higher birthrates than those who are less religious. Further, Mormons, as evidenced by the state of Utah having a birthrate that is 50% above the national average, have much higher birthrates than either Catholics or Protestants (Weeks, 1989)

Children and Marital Satisfaction

A longitudinal study conducted during the 1970s concluded that marital dissolution for child-free couples is about three times as high as for couples with children. A more recent 10-year longitudinal study suggests that the actual number of children in the family may be a more important variable than the presence or absence of children per se. For example, the risk of marital separation was 50% less in families with three preschoolers in comparison to those with only one child (Fergerson, Horwood, & Lloyd, 1990). It is speculated that married couples with children are more likely to avoid divorce in comparison to child-free couples because of the much greater costs of a divorce (Waite, Haggstrom, & Kanouse, 1985b). While the birth of a child may increase marital stability, it also tends to create added stress which may affect the actual level of marital happiness. Although the evidence is clear that having a child in marriage may be a source of deep personal satisfaction, the influence of a child on a marital relationship is subject to considerable controversy. In the transition to parenthood research of the 1970s, satisfaction as well as dissatisfaction was found to result from having children (Russell, 1974).

Research in the 1980s suggests that couples who feel best about themselves prior to parenthood tend to be most satisfied after childbirth, while those who report fewer coping skills tend to feel most dissatisfied. The researchers concluded that how couples negotiate the decision to parent, arrange their lives as lovers and parents, and solve problems affects how they will feel about themselves (Cowan & Cowan, 1989).

Levels of Marital Satisfaction

Earlier studies documented the satisfactions of parenthood in which children were among the only sources of satisfaction listed by low marital-satisfaction couples (Luckey & Bain, 1970). Parenthood is related to diminished levels of depression (Kandel, Davies, & Raveis, 1985). In addition, it leads to a reduction of negative health behaviors (Umberson, 1987). Both of these tendencies have the potential to positively affect marital satisfaction. Although characteristics such as gender, age, race, income, and education may affect the association between parenting and marital satisfaction, the parent-child relationship appears most important (Umberson, 1989). The content of parent-child relationships, particularly when positive, is significantly related to parental well-being.

Married couples report that the happiest times during their marriage were before the birth of their first child and after the last child had left home (Breskin, 1986; Nock, 1979). After becoming parents, wives and husbands typically engage in fewer activities together and share less decision making because of the demands on their time as parents (White, Booth, & Edwards, 1986). The impact of the first child on marital happiness begins with the first knowledge of the pregnancy when marital satisfaction decreases while marital conflict increases. A major source of conflict relates to the handling of daily living routines with each spouse expecting the other spouse to handle a greater share of the household responsibilities. Generally speaking, husbands report a greater degree of unhappiness than wives (Breskin, 1986; Cowan et al., 1985). Earlier

BOX 12.1 Having a Baby Rating Scale*

Positive aspects of having a baby		**Positive aspects of not having a baby**	
Enjoyment	____	Freedom of life-style	____
Growth through child rearing	____	Financial freedom	____
Sharing parenthood with spouse	____	Career opportunities	____
Total Positives	____	Total Positives	____
Negative aspects of having a baby		**Negative aspects of not having a baby**	
Career problems	____	Loneliness	____
Physical-emotional stress	____	Lack of growth	____
Curtailing activities	____	Lack of sharing	____
Total Negatives	____	Total Negatives	____

*Rate each item on a scale of 0 (least) to 3 (most) and add to determine the total positives and negatives for each category. Subtract the total negative rating from the total positive rating on the left side of the scale; repeat the same operation on the right side of the scale. Is having a baby rated as more positive and is not having a baby rated as more negative?

From M. Paluszny and M. Thombre, "Pregnancy and the Female Physician" in *Medical Aspects of Human Sexuality,* 21(7):66, 1987. Reprinted by permission.

studies explored the relationship between marital happiness and the number of children. The crucial factor concerned agreement between number of children desired and actual number of children in a marriage. The lowest level of marital happiness was reported by those couples who had more children than they had desired (Figley, 1973; Heath, Roper, & King, 1974).

In a comparison of college-educated, married working mothers and nonmothers, child-free women reported a higher level of marital satisfaction in the areas of both affection and sexuality. Mothers with preschool male children reported the lowest levels of marital satisfaction. The reason cited for this gender difference is that boys were viewed as being more fussy, active, and difficult to handle than girls leading to excessive role demands on mothers (Abbott & Brody, 1985). A review of national data from the General Social Surveys during the 1970s indicates that having children generally had a negative effect on the overall happiness of married white women. In addition, well-educated white and black men reported adverse effects of becoming a father on both global happiness and life satisfaction including friendships, nonwork activities, and family life. Therefore, the researchers concluded that "present young adults should not decide to have children on the basis of expectations that parenthood will lead to psychological rewards in the later stages of life" (Glenn & McLanahan, 1981, p. 419).

The possibility exists that insufficient attention has been paid by researchers to the level of marital satisfaction prior to birth of the first child. When a high degree of marital satisfaction exists prior to the birth of a child, more positive changes are likely to occur in the marital relationship than when a low level of marital satisfaction exists prior to childbirth (Harriman, 1986).

Child-Free Marriages

Until fairly recently, persons who chose to have a child-free marriage tended to be defined as **deviant** (abnormal), self-centered, or immature (Houseknecht, 1987). A study of female and male college students perceived that women who were child-free by choice were generally less liked as persons. Further, husbands with children were viewed as less likely to have psychological disturbances than husbands who were child-free (Calhoun & Selby, 1980). Never-married female and male students who anticipated marrying and becoming parents rated voluntarily child-free and involuntarily child-free couples on a series of personality attributes including loneliness, loving, and personally happy. The voluntarily child-free couples were viewed least favorably although the life-style benefits of their choice were recognized. Those perceived benefits included being more career-oriented and not being restricted in their daily activities (Callan, 1985b). Although research suggests that voluntarily choosing to have a child-free marriage can be a desirable state, some couples may seek child substitutes such as pets. However, when investigating the social meaning of pets, families with children were found more likely to have pets than child-free couples; but more of the child-free couples (one half) placed their pets in a childlike role in the household (Veevers, 1985).

Decision to be Child-Free

In 1975, 5% of wives who were ages 30–34 indicated "none" for lifetime birth expectations. Thirteen years later, that expectation of "none" was 7% for the same age group (U.S. Bureau of the Census, 1990p). Obviously, the precise number of couples who have voluntarily decided to remain child-free at any one time is subject to considerable speculation. A survey of students in 28 Southern schools located in poverty level areas revealed that only 1 in 6 female students and 1 in 4 male students wished to have child-free marriages. Those female students who wanted no children had higher educational and occupational goals for themselves in contrast to male students (Kenkel, 1985).

While some women may choose early in life to remain child-free, most women reach this status by postponing childbirth until they have finally established a child-free life-style (Holahan, 1983). The available evidence suggests that while a few persons may make the decision to remain child-free prior to marriage, most persons arrive at a final decision only after postponing childbearing during the early years of marriage (see figure 12.1). Most couples move through four successive stages in the decision-making process. First, parenthood is postponed for a specific period of time, which is the case for most newly marrieds. Second, couples progress to an indefinite period of postponement until they can "afford" or "feel ready" for a child. In the third stage, the emphasis shifts to the advantages of remaining child-free, which include more money, more opportunities, and fewer restrictions. It is at this point that couples openly consider the possibility of remaining permanently child-free. The fourth stage involves making explicit and irreversible decisions to remain permanently child-free (Veevers, 1973).

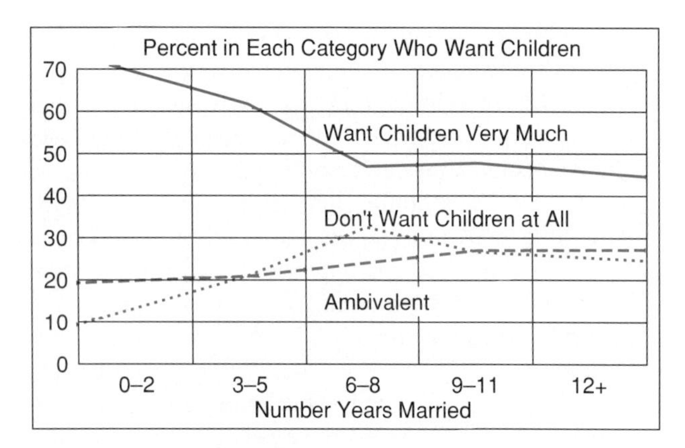

Figure 12.1 Level of Desire for Children by Years of Marriage

Based on a 29-study profile, the rationales for child-free marriages, in order of mention, included freedom from child-care responsibility/greater opportunity for self-fulfillment, more satisfactory marital relationship, wife's career considerations, monetary considerations, concern about population growth, general dislike of children, and early childhood socialization experiences (Houseknecht, 1987).

A comparison of young marrieds who wanted children with those who did not want children found no evidence of selfishness on the part of couples who desired to remain child-free. However, child-free spouses were more likely to be loners, to prefer solitary occupations, and to have less interest in spending time with other persons besides their marriage partner. Further, child-free wives were much more likely to have professional occupations and to report that their careers weighed heavily in their decision not to have children (Silka & Kiesler, 1977). Child-free couples generally place greater emphasis on personal goal attainment. The pursuit of a career is a strong motivation for women, especially, to remain child-free. Further, women who expect to remain child-free in marriage earn more money than women who expect to have children (Bloom, 1984). The woman who assumes the child-free role is more likely to be an achievement-oriented individual, perhaps a first-born child in a family of several children (Nason & Poloma, 1976). Some research indicates that husbands who prefer to remain child-free tend to be more confident about their decision whereas women tend to be more ambivalent. Husbands in egalitarian marriages appear to enjoy their freedom and the additional monetary resources that exist in a child-free marriage (Scanzoni, 1976). However, more recent findings indicate high degrees of ambivalence on the part of the husband (Baber & Dreyer, 1986).

Wives in child-free marriages have reported being somewhat stigmatized in having to justify their decision to other family members and to friends (Veevers, 1975). While child-free wives are generally satisfied with their decision, they nevertheless experience considerable pressure from a disapproving society to become a mother (Ory, 1978). Making the decision of whether to remain child-free or to become a parent can be a positive experience if the positive and negative aspects of remaining child-free and becoming a parent have been examined honestly and thoroughly (Holahan, 1983). It is a sobering decision without certainty "and as those who've made the wrong choice—either way—know only too well, babies aren't exactly returnable, and adoption in later life is a long, trying process" (Wells, 1988, p. 144).

Being Child-Free and Marital Happiness

Renowned psychologist Erik Erikson believes that it is important that people who decide to remain child-free know what they are *not* doing (Iaconetti, 1988). This admonition rests on his belief that repressing the frustration and loss that comes with rejection of **procreation** may have its own costs. Erikson suggests that with childlessness unconscious repressions may emerge just as did the sexual repressions of the Victorian age. Even if one does not believe Erikson's theory that an instinctual wish to have children exists, it is harder to dismiss his thought-provoking concept that women and men who fail to procreate may be cutting themselves off from a major experience in adult development (Wells, 1988). But, generativity or instinct to nurture does not have to be directed toward one's children, or even toward children at all; there are numerous ways to satisfy this need. The channeling of the procreative drive into creative expression through arts, political action, or volunteer work are examples of healthy sublimation. Erikson's point, however, is that such overt expression is more than fulfilling; it is necessary (Iaconetti, 1988).

Should a married couple disagree over the decision to remain child-free due to prior socialization experiences, the wife will most often accept the preference of the husband (Marciano, 1979). This area of disagreement which is basically a values issue is fertile ground for marital conflict which, if not resolved successfully, may ultimately lead to divorce. The majority of child-free couples, however, resolve the question of whether or not to have children without disruption to their marriage. The research reveals certain characteristics of child-free couples. In a comparison of couples with children and child-free couples, both groups

Table 12.3: Women's Ratings of Satisfaction with Life Concerns by Parenthood Status

Life Concerns*	Infertile Wives	Mothers	Voluntarily Childless Wives
Marriage and family			
Your husband	8.00	7.20	7.40
Your marriage	7.84	6.96	7.37
Close adult relatives	6.73	6.10	6.09
Self			
Extent you are achieving success	5.50	5.94	6.37
What you are accomplishing	5.96	6.14	6.50
Life-style			
How interesting each day is	5.58	6.08	6.40
Amount of beauty in your world	6.49	6.74	6.68
Way you spend spare time	6.18	5.52	6.34
Levels of creativity and freedom			
Time for things you want to do	6.03	4.28	5.40
Chances of relaxation	6.56	4.62	5.65
Amount of independence and freedom	6.69	4.90	6.46
Respect from others			
Amount of friendship and love in life	7.43	6.72	6.90
How sincere and honest you are	7.20	6.40	6.40
How much admired by others	6.07	5.58	6.18

*Higher mean indicates higher level of satisfaction.

From V. J. Callan, "The Personal and Marital Adjustment of Mothers and of Voluntarily and Involuntarily Childless Wives" in *Journal of Marriage and the Family,* 49:852.

had similar levels of self-esteem; but persons with children were more likely to express traditional attitudes toward women than child-free persons. In addition, while there were no differences in terms of levels of marital satisfaction, child-free couples reported having more social interaction with their spouses (Feldman, 1981). Other researchers have found that child-free couples, in general, report better marital adjustment and the wives view themselves as being less sex-typed and have outstanding careers (Hoffman & Levant, 1985; Holahan, 1983).

Perhaps the influence of parenthood versus remaining child-free can best be placed in perspective by examining data from **infertile** wives, mothers, and voluntarily child-free wives. When considering various indicators of happiness and personal well-being, all three groups were generally similar (see Table 12.3). Mothers and voluntarily child-free wives were similarly satisfied with their lives. Involuntarily child-free spouses were more understanding of each other, more affectionate, more satisfied with their spouse, and less likely to have experienced extramarital sexual intercourse. They were generally more satisfied with marriage than mothers or voluntarily child-free wives. Although infertile wives expressed frustration, anger, and unhappiness over the loss of control over their ability to have a child, they still valued their freedom. Voluntarily child-free wives rated themselves slightly higher than did mothers in the areas of creativity and freedom, self-satisfaction, and satisfaction with respect from others. Further, voluntarily child-free wives are slightly more satisfied with their husbands and with their marriages than mothers (Callan, 1987).

Establishing Childbearing Plans

For the last 30 years, the birth rate in the United States has continued to decrease. The development of greater confidence in contraceptive measures has been accompanied by a decrease in the number of children that women indicate they want and expect to have. For example, only 9% of women desired 4 or more children in 1988 as compared to 12% in 1975 (U.S. Bureau of the Census, 1990p). While new contraceptive technology is obviously a major factor, it does not account for the total picture.

Number of Children

While it is rather difficult to establish an absolute causal relationship, the decrease in the number of children appears to be related to women having redefined their marital roles (Stolzenberg & Waite, 1977). However, women are more likely than men to take family custom, tradition, and social factors into account when reaching a decision about family size (Johnson & Freymeyer, 1987). Furthermore, the number of children desired will be affected by financial circumstances, religious convictions, circumstances of childhood, and biological or medical conditions (Coles, 1984). Usually, children learn social norms concerning family size from their parents and thus tend to have similar numbers of children. Factors such as happiness, satisfaction, and closeness also are key factors in determining family size (Johnson & Freymeyer, 1987).

Current population statistics suggest that the size of the average American family has decreased considerably since 1940. This trend is partially accounted for by the increase in the percentage of couples desiring only one child and the number of couples who decide to remain child-free ("Demographers Miscalculate," 1989). A 1986 Gallup poll reported that 59% of parents believe that two children represent an ideal family size (Harder, 1987).

Some very interesting differences have been identified between voluntary one-child mothers and mothers with one child who desire more children. Voluntary one-child mothers were more likely to be working full-time (73%) as compared to the other mothers (30%). In addition, voluntary one-child mothers were less likely to believe having a child would fulfill their role as women, provide proof of femininity, provide fulfillment to their marriages, create feelings of being needed, or create emotional closeness with their husbands. Further, voluntary one-child mothers were more likely to believe that child care was boring and tedious while working outside of the home was more important than motherhood (Callan, 1985a).

Timing of First Births

The timing of the birth of the first child is a complex question involving a number of factors including whether the couple is Catholic or non-Catholic, degree of religiosity, and age and work history of wife before marriage (Teachman & Polonko, 1985). Other factors that influence the decision include status of career, financial situation, and biological considerations (Bloom, 1984). Catholic couples tend to be older at first birth

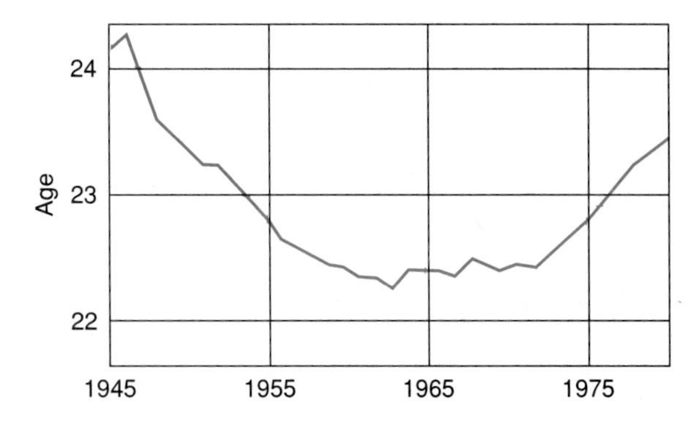

Figure 12.2 Age of Woman at First Birth by Year

because they tend to marry later. Women living in the South, in a rural environment, and/or whose father had a lower occupational status are more likely to have an earlier first birth (Rindfuss & St. John, 1983). The literature suggests at least three major factors associated with timing of first births: age of wife, number of years married, and career goals of wife.

The initiation of childbearing at a later age is associated with greater levels of marital happiness and higher levels of affectionate feelings of daughters, but not sons, for their mothers (Heuvel, 1988). Women who delay the birth of their first child are more likely to be highly educated and pursuing a career. Substantial evidence exists which suggests that many wives decide to have children only after their professional goals have been met (Soloway & Smith, 1987). Of women born between 1940 and 1944, about two thirds of those working in professional occupational categories were still child-free at age 28 in comparison to only one fourth of sales workers and service workers (Wilkie, 1981). As we will see in chapter 16, many women are working because of the intrinsic psychological rewards received from their career. Therefore, such women may be concerned about any adverse effects of childbirth on their future career opportunities.

Since the early 1960s, the average age of women giving birth to their first child has continued to rise from age 22.5 in 1965 to age 23.5 in 1985 (see Figure 12.2). Of all births to women ages 30–44 in 1988, 21% were first births as compared to 18% in 1980. Although no comparable statistics are available for 1980, 5% of births to women ages 40–44 in 1988 were first births (U.S. Bureau of the Census, 1990m). A major intervening variable as to why the age at first birth has increased for wives is that increasing levels of education are related to delayed marriage and a shorter average period of childbearing years (Spanier, Roos, & Shockey,

1985). However, it should be noted that the longer women postpone their first birth, the lower will be their chances of conceiving. Further, the older that a woman is at the time of pregnancy, the greater probability that the problems of **toxemia** (hypertension disorder) and **Down's syndrome** may occur (Bloom, 1984). Other complications include premature detachment of the placenta, prolonged second stage of labor, and the risk of a cesarean section (Witwer, 1990a). Consequently, a major factor that influences the birth of the first child is the woman's perception of her biological time clock (Soloway & Smith, 1987). Nevertheless, there are still many women in their 30s who are giving birth to healthy infants without medical complications. In fact, researchers have concluded that first-born infants of mothers, age 35 and over, were not at greater risk for low birth weight, small size for gestational age, or perinatal death than first-born infants of mothers in their 20s (Wittwer, 1990a).

In her first marriage, a woman is approximately four times more likely to give birth to a child within the 1st year than 5–6 years later (Teachman & Polonko, 1985). However, it is important to remember that highly educated women and career women are likely to postpone entering marriage. Thus, these women will be older when having their first child and more likely to have a smaller number of children over the duration of their marriage (Marini, 1981). It would appear that persons who have postponed marriage are more likely to enjoy their freedom and privacy. Thus, while these women have reached a stage in their life where they choose to marry, they may be reluctant to further alter their life-style by immediately giving birth to a child ("Motherhood Put On," 1989).

Timing of Subsequent Births

Generally speaking, younger women are less likely to experience short birth intervals. Previously identified differences in birth spacing attributable to the educational level of the mother have largely disappeared due to the diffusion of effective contraceptive usage throughout all socioeconomic groups (Wineberg & McCarthy, 1989). There are sound reasons for desiring another child, and there are questionable reasons. The questionable reasons include giving into pressure, wanting a playmate for another child, wanting a child of a different gender, or wanting a child to reclaim one's youth (Andrews, 1985). Among women with at least 1 year of college, their last child is likely to be born at a later age than women with high school diplomas only (Koo, Suchindran, & Griffith, 1987). Religion and degree of religiosity also play a significant role in the likelihood of rapid, repeated childbirth. Rapid, successive births are considerably more likely among Catholics than non-Catholics. In addition, the impact of a high degree of religiosity on timing of second births is much greater among Catholics (Heckert & Teachman, 1985).

Although many people believe that two years of space between children is optimal, a longer period of time is actually more desirable because it allows for the development of the child's independence and sense of self (Andrews, 1985). The age of the mother at birth of the first child plays a major role in the timing of the second birth for blacks and Hispanics. Further, Hispanics are much more likely than blacks or whites to have a second child very soon after the birth of the first child. Other factors include marital status at birth of the first child and the degree to which the first birth was desired (Mott, 1986). The influence of birth order on childhood socialization will be considered in chapter 14, "Child Rearing: Challenges and Concerns."

The Father's Role: Silent or Salient?

Research on fertility decisions has generally focused on the women involved and how their educational and career goals impact family plans. Their male partners in such decisions have been virtually ignored by researchers with few exceptions. Very little is known about the male's contribution to the decision-making process and the factors related to his readiness for parenthood. However, such factors may affect not only the man's future emotional development but also the pregnancy outcome and parental adjustment of his spouse as well as the father-child role (Baber & Dreyer, 1986). For example, delaying fatherhood has been found to be associated with greater marital happiness for the fathers and greater affectionate feelings of sons for their fathers (Heuvel, 1988).

In one of the rare studies of first-time fathers, three factors were identified as important in signaling readiness for the parental role: stability in the couple's relationship, relative financial security, and a sense of closure to the child-free period. Variables influencing the attainment of closure were the intention to have a child and the degree to which a child was actually wanted. Wives were found to exert more influence in the couple's childbearing decisions than husbands. Men's responses to various questions about childbearing decisions revealed ambivalence. There was a striking lack of readiness to commit to either parenthood or a child-free life-style (Baber & Dreyer, 1986).

Timing of subsequent births may offer positive rewards to couples and their children. Unless families have unlimited psychological and economic resources, such factors should be carefully considered.

While men are moving toward increased participation in the childbearing and child-rearing process, these data suggest their interest and desire to parent is as varied as their female counterparts.

Infertility in Marriage

Some couples begin marriage practicing contraception only to discover that they are unable to conceive when they decide to have a child. In other instances, even though conception occurs, the woman is unable to carry the pregnancy long enough for a live birth. Infertility is defined as the inability to conceive after 1 year of sexual intercourse on a regular basis without contraceptives or the inability to carry a pregnancy for a sufficient period of time to permit a live birth (Porter & Christopher, 1984). It should be noted that even for fertile women, as their age increases, the probability of conception within a given year decreases (see Table 12.4).

When the possibility of infertility is first confirmed, most child-free couples who wish to conceive are likely to view this information as deeply disturbing. Men, however, tend to be more fatalistic about infertility, viewing the circumstances as disappointing but hardly tragic. Infertility generally tends to be seen primarily as the wife's problem. Consequently, wives have a tendency to take a leadership role in decision making regarding a possible solution (Greil & Leitko, 1986). Often, infertility has a significant impact on the marital relationship just as does pregnancy and parenthood. Identity shock also may be experienced by those

Table 12.4: **Probability of and Time to Conception among Fertile Women**

Age	Probability of Conception—1 Month	Probability of Conception—1 Year	Mean Time to Conception—Months
Early 20s	20–25%	93–97%	4–5
Late 20s	15–20	86–93	5–7
Early 30s	10–15	72–86	7–10
Late 30s	8–10	65–72	10–12

Adapted with permission of Charles Scribner's Sons, an imprint of Macmillan Publishing Company, from *How to Get Pregnant* by Sherman J. Silber. Copyright © 1980 Sherman J. Silber.

who have a great commitment to parenthood and find themselves to be infertile (Matthews & Matthews, 1986).

Incidence of Infertility

Since the woman is only fertile for 24–48 hours each month, the precise extent of infertility is subject to some speculation (Hyde, 1990). Estimates of the prevalence of involuntary child-free couples range from 1 in 12 to 1 in 5 couples (Kim & Friedman, 1983; Matthews & Matthews, 1986). The National Center for Health Statistics has reported that 14% of all married couples are infertile (Sabatelli, Meth, & Gavazzi, 1988). Available data indicate that the number of infertility cases has tripled in the past 20 years (Francoeur, 1991). Although the evidence is unclear, some authorities believe that infertility has increased in recent years due to increases in sexually transmitted diseases and women postponing childbirth, thus leading to an expanded opportunity for fertility impairment to develop prior to the beginning and/or conclusion of childbearing (Matthews & Matthews, 1986).

Causes and Treatment of Infertility

The medical literature suggests that 40–50% of infertility cases involve female-related causes, 30–40% involve male-related causes, while 10–15% involve a combination of female and male-related causes (Mazor, 1980; Porter & Christopher, 1984). In general, it is easier to diagnose and treat female-related infertility than male-related infertility (Porter & Christopher, 1984). Of those couples who choose to go through the long and expensive process of ascertaining the source of infertility, about 90% eventually have the causes identified. If the infertility is based on genetic or chromosomal factors, little can be done to enable the couple to conceive and have a child. Thus, successful treatment for infertility is only available for about one half of the diagnosed infertility problems (Allgeier & Allgeier, 1991). An intriguing aspect of the infertility issue relates to findings from a follow-up study of infertile couples in which the pregnancy rate was found to be 41% among treated couples, but 35% among untreated couples (Collins, Wrixon, Janes, & Wilson, 1983).

Female Infertility

The major causes of female infertility are blocked fallopian tubes—50%, failure to ovulate—33%, and "hostile" cervical mucus—17% (Berkow, 1982). Blocked fallopian tubes are usually caused by formation of scar tissue due to failure to treat gonorrhea, chlamydia, or pelvic inflammatory disease in time (Allgeier & Allgeier, 1991). In those cases where the fallopian tubes are only partially blocked, conception may occur but the fertilized ovum may lack sufficient space to pass from the fallopian tube into the uterus, thus resulting in an ectopic pregnancy. Depending upon the degree of obstruction, a blocked fallopian tube can sometimes be successfully treated by microsurgery techniques. The scar tissue obstruction can be removed, and the healthy portions of the tubes sewn together; but this technique is only successful for about 30–50% of women with blocked fallopian tubes (Masters, Johnson, & Kolodny, 1988). In the remaining cases, successful medical treatment is not possible at this time.

The absence of or irregular ovulation may be caused by a number of conditions such as anemia, malnutrition, vitamin deficiency, and psychological stress. Successful treatment of these conditions frequently results in normal ovulation (Armstrong, 1986). Another major reason for failure to ovulate is hormonal imbalances. Hormonal imbalance problems may be treated by using the drug Clomid, a synthetic follicle-stimulating hormone (FSH), or a drug such as Pergonal that will stimulate ovulation. Using Clomid will result in ovulation in about 70% of cases with a 30% conception rate (Andolsek, 1990). While Pergonal will result in conception for most women, the incidence of multiple births using this medication is 1 in 4 births (Rosenwaks, Benjamin, & Stone, 1987) in comparison to only 1 in 8 births using Clomid (Andolsek, 1990). An elevated prolactin level, or hyperprolactinemia, which suppresses ovulation, accounts for approximately 20% of infertility cases in women. Many women with elevated prolactin levels also suffer from premenstrual tension and/or amenorrhea. The drug Bromocriptine can be used to reduce the prolactin level, which results in a restoration of normal reproductive functioning in 80–90% of women (Rosenwaks et al., 1987). Modest success has been achieved by treating these women with high dosage levels of vitamin B-6, which apparently reduces the prolactin level.

For some not totally understood reasons, the cervical mucus may begin to develop antibodies that "attack" sperm cells as though they were a foreign protein substance. These antibodies may ultimately come to be present in either the cervical mucus or the semen resulting in infertility (Rosenwaks et al., 1987). The cervical mucus also will become hostile to sperm cells due to infections associated with gonorrhea, chlamydia, and pelvic inflammatory disease (Curran, 1980). One recommended solution is using condoms for several months prior to attempting to conceive which may reduce the level of sperm antibodies sufficiently to allow conception to occur (Fraser, Radonic, & Clancy, 1980). Another approach that has met with some limited success involves inserting sperm cells directly into the uterus, thus bypassing the hostile mucus (Denney & Quadagno, 1988).

Male Infertility

Although medical evaluation of men with infertility problems, in general, is considerably less expensive and less complex than for women, many men resist evaluation and treatment because it is viewed as a threat to their masculinity (Ross, 1986). Most male infertility is related to low sperm count and less often to abnormal sperm cells. Abnormal sperm cells usually have impaired ability to swim with sufficient action to reach the ovum (Porter & Christopher, 1984). The average male ejaculation contains 200–400 million sperm cells which account for only about 1% of semen composition. Although a sperm count of 40 million per ejaculation is considered below normal, conception is still possible with as few as 20 million sperm cells per ejaculation (Masters et al., 1988).

A **varicocele** (enlarged, damaged blood vein) in the testes or vas deferens will impair sperm production by allowing blood to accumulate in the scrotum, thus, elevating the scrotum temperature (Crocket & Cosentino, 1984). It is estimated that varicoceles account for about one half of all low sperm count and sperm motility cases. Corrective surgery performed on an outpatient basis can remove the varicoceles leading to 60–70% improvement in semen quality and typically a 50% pregnancy success rate (Ross, 1986). Medical research also has suggested that environmental pollutants such as chemicals used in the manufacture of electrical equipment (PCBs) and Tris (a flame retardant) are associated with low sperm count (Allgeier & Allgeier, 1991). Other impairments to sperm production include hormonal disorders, prostate infections, mumps, and overexposure to radiation (Porter & Christopher, 1984).

Other Medical Avenues for Coping with Infertility

Since only about 1 in 2 of infertile couples may be successfully treated through medical intervention, what alternatives do untreatable couples have regarding their desire to become parents? Modern medical technology has made three alternatives available: artificial insemination, in vitro fertilization, and surrogate motherhood (Porter & Christopher, 1984). Many unanswered questions surround these alternatives for human reproduction. These questions include the psychological well-being of persons who choose these options and the relationship of these medical technologies to individual rights, freedom of choice, and personal happiness (Zimmerman, 1982). Further, a series of legal issues have emerged along with many ethical and moral concerns. Among the legal concerns are the following issues: availability of medical and genetic screening for sperm and ovum, payments to donors and surrogates, and legal rights of the biological mother (Donovan, 1986).

A survey of college women and men at a state college and a church-related college found significant differences in their attitudes toward artificial insemination, in vitro fertilization, and surrogate motherhood. Students at the church-related institution were much less likely to support artificial insemination as contrasted with those at the state college. It is also of interest to observe that women, regardless of their religious feelings, were considerably more willing to choose artificial insemination as a way of dealing with infertility in comparison to men. Further, about one half of students in the religiously affiliated college were willing to use in vitro fertilization as compared to two thirds of those enrolled at the state college. Finally, only one third of women and one fourth of men at the church affiliated college were willing to consider surrogate motherhood as compared to about one half of women and men at the state college (Kallen, Powell, Popovich, & Griffore, 1986). Nevertheless, the latest medical advances for coping with infertility offer potential solutions for women and men (Figure 12.3).

Artificial Insemination

The procedure for **artificial insemination** involves the clinical injection of sperm, usually obtained through masturbation, near the cervix or into the uterus at the anticipated time of ovulation. Artificial insemination is of two types: artificial insemination using donor's semen (AID) and artificial insemination using husband's semen (AIH). Donors must be willing to provide semen specimens at the time of the patient's ovulation and must be available on each day of a scheduled insemination (Donovan, 1986). If intracervical insemination is used, a cup-like device is filled with semen and is placed around the cervix and left for three to four hours (Olshansky & Sammons, 1985). Many physicians prefer to use intrauterine insemination because it has been found to have a pregnancy rate per injection that is 2.5 times greater (10% vs. 4%) than the intracervical method (Byrd et al., 1990). However, placing semen directly into the uterus can cause severe cramping, bleeding, and inflammation. The pregnancy success rates are 70% when using fresh sperm and 50% when using frozen sperm (Olshansky & Sammons, 1985).

As of 1986, approximately 300,000 children had been born as a result of AID in the United States. With regard to its legal status, 28 states signify that a child conceived by AID with consent of the husband is considered a legal offspring of the couple (Donovan, 1986). When AID is used, the identity of the donor remains anonymous due to confidentiality associated with the sperm collection process and the mixing of semen from several donors (Zimmerman, 1982). Sperm donors typically are screened for sexually transmitted diseases, genetic diseases, physical status, and health history based on their willingness to provide such information. However, only Oregon, Idaho, and New York City require that donors be screened for genetic abnormalities and infectious diseases such as syphilis or AIDS. Further, an estimated three fourths of physicians maintain no records on AID donors to ensure confidentiality (Donovan, 1986).

There are religious and ethical issues associated with artificial insemination. The Roman Catholic church opposes all artificial insemination due to its unnaturalness and separation of sexual intercourse from procreation (Annas, 1981).

In Vitro Fertilization

In vitro fertilization involves the removal of mature ova from the ovary and fertilizing them in a laboratory petri dish using sperm cells from the husband. Usually, several fertilized ovum are placed in the uterus in hopes that one will become implanted and develop into a healthy fetus. As a consequence, the chance for twins is 20% and for triplets, 5% (Crooks & Baur, 1990). Given the complicated nature of this procedure, the costs run as high as $7,000–$10,000 per procedure. Since three or four fertilized ovum implantations may be necessary before a successful pregnancy is begun, the total costs may run as high as $28,000–40,000 (Buell, 1990). For the same reason, multiple ova are usually obtained and fertilized in a petri dish. The extra fertilized ova are then frozen for future use, if needed. Eventually, these unused fertilized ova are destroyed, thus raising the question of abortion among pro-life advocates (Allgeier & Allgeier, 1988). So far, this procedure appears to have a 15–25% success rate among viable couples (Hyde, 1990). This method of coping with infertility is opposed by feminists and anti-abortionists on the grounds that it challenges and destroys the meaning of motherhood and fatherhood by using women as human incubators. However, a 1978 Gallup poll found that 60% of all respondents and 56% of Roman Catholics approved of this medical procedure (Zimmerman, 1982).

Surrogate Motherhood

Surrogate motherhood is defined as artificial insemination of a volunteer woman using sperm cells from the husband of an infertile woman or a woman who is at risk of transmitting a genetic defect. The surrogate woman who volunteers to conceive and give birth to a child receives a fee for her services. If the surrogate mother is married, the newborn child is legally the child of the surrogate and her husband. A typical procedure involves signing of a contract which specifies that the surrogate mother will receive a fee, usually a minimum of $10,000, and agrees to allow the sperm donor and his wife to adopt the child (Taub, 1985). The mother's pregnancy-related expenses also usually are paid by the prospective adoptive parents. Presently, at least 24 states prohibit women from accepting payment, except for medical expenses, in placing a child for adoption.

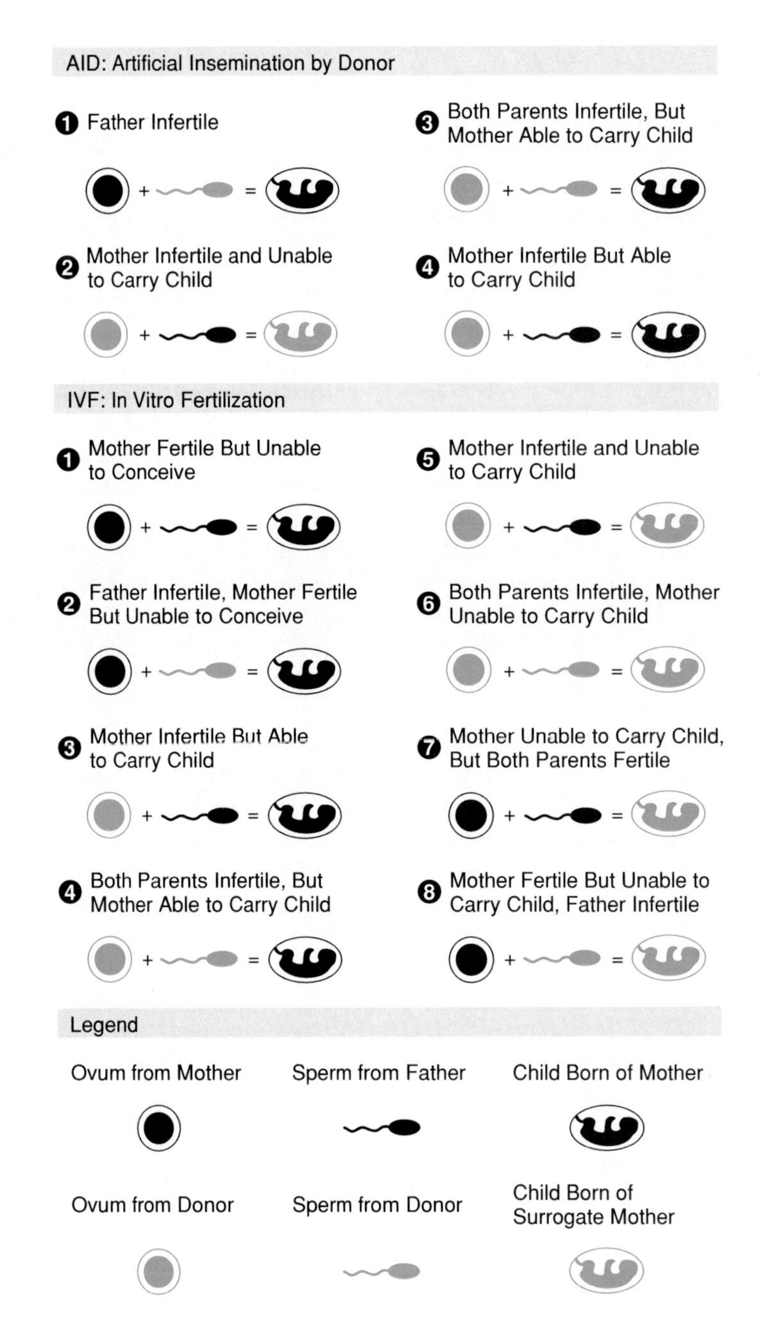

Figure 12.3 High Technology Babies

It is unclear as to whether or not these laws apply to cases of surrogate motherhood. The issue has become a hotly contested debate in state legislatures where there is substantial sentiment to prohibit payment to surrogate mothers for childbearing (Donovan, 1986). At least four states have outlawed surrogate-mother contracts, including any payment for services (Francoeur, 1991). In the Baby M case, the New Jersey Supreme Court upheld the surrogate motherhood contract, although the surrogate mother professed her desire to retain custody of the baby girl. A major factor in the decision centered around the question of whether or not the surrogate mother was a fit mother and what would be in the best interests of the child (Lacayo, 1987). In a subsequent decision in this case, the Supreme Court of New Jersey granted gradually expanding, unsupervised visitation rights to the surrogate mother over the vigorous objections of the adoptive parents ("Baby M's," 1988).

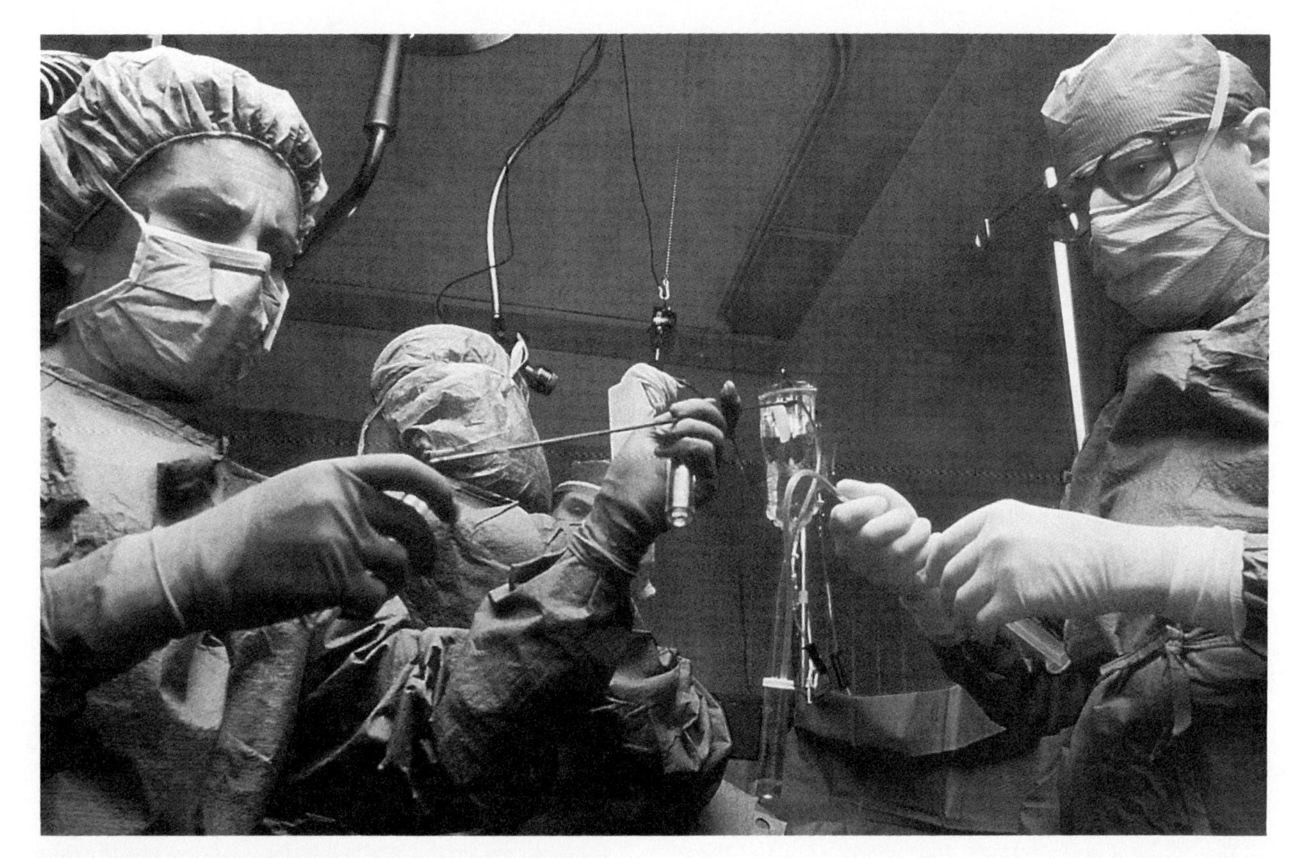

Some children have difficulty dealing with two parents! The child born of a surrogate mother may have as many as five parents: a sperm donor, an egg donor, the woman providing the uterus for gestation, and the woman and man expecting to rear the child.

In other states, a substantial possibility exists that if the surrogate mother changes her mind about placing her baby for adoption, the courts would permit the surrogate contract to be breached (Taub, 1985).

Psychological Adjustment to Infertility

Infertile couples commonly suffer from feelings of shame, guilt, embarrassment, anger, depression, and frustration. These feelings often transfer into anxiety associated with their sexual performance (Kim & Friedman, 1983). One reason for this anxiety is that the revelation of possible infertility creates a sense of loss of control over the most private aspect of their life: their sexual relationship. After learning of their infertility, 56% of the wives in one study reported a decrease in sexual intercourse and 59% indicated a decrease in their sexual satisfaction (Sabatelli et al., 1988). The feelings of guilt and shame are partially the result of one or both partners waiting to see who is to "blame." In practice, about 1 in 10 couples never discover the actual cause of their infertility (Matthews & Matthews, 1986). In terms of psychological adjustment, 37% of women and 31% of men involved in infertile marriages exhibited signs of psychological disturbance. In general, women who were younger and who had not received a diagnosis regarding the cause of the infertility were more distressed. Wives perceived being involuntarily child-free as less-acceptable and reported more stress associated with infertility than husbands (McEwan, Costello, & Taylor, 1987). But, husbands who were the source of the infertility indicated less satisfaction with expressions of affection and sexual activity in their marriage than fertile husbands (Ulbrich, Coyle, & Llabre, 1990). Further, women who gave their religious preference as Protestant showed better psychological adjustment than women of other religious faiths (McEwan et al., 1987).

The process of coping with infertility involves three stages. The first stage includes disbelief, denial, guilt, helplessness, poor self-esteem, and unworthiness. A person's job, friendships, and marital relationship may suffer during this stage. If treatment is unsuccessful during the first stage, the second stage emerges in which some persons will experience feelings of depression and mourning. The couple also may feel isolated because other persons may not be aware of their problem. In the third stage, spouses accept the outcome and plan for the future. They develop new friendships and establish new interests while deciding whether or not to remain involuntarily child-free. Typically, there is a return of energy, optimism, and humor for the spouses (Porter & Christopher, 1984).

The Decision to Seek Adoption

For many infertile couples, artificial insemination, in vitro fertilization, or surrogate motherhood are not feasible solutions to their child-free condition due to medical, religious, or costs reasons. Therefore, a number of couples turn to adoption as a possible resolution of their infertility status. However, some members of society believe that adoptive parents cannot love a child as much as biological parents and believe that too many risks exist regarding the child's genetic background and family ancestry (Miall, 1987). There is a dearth of children for adoption, with those who are available often being physically or emotionally handicapped, or of minority ethnic or racial heritage (Flynn & Hamm, 1983). A survey of Midwest and West Coast college students found that although most women and men preferred to adopt a healthy American baby, they would be willing to adopt a baby with a minority heritage (Kallen et al., 1986). Despite this apparent willingness, in practice, the race of the mother differs from that of the child in only about 8% of adoption cases. And, most of these adoptions involve children born outside the United States (Bachrach, Adams, Sambrano, & London, 1990). Most women who adopt a child tend to be between ages 25–34 and married. Most adopted children are first children although some couples may become infertile after having their first child and choose the adoption alternative for a second child (see Table 12.5). A real dilemma faces prospective adoptive parents because only about 5% of unwed teen mothers are placing their babies for adoption (Bachrach, 1986). As a result, only 1.3% of married women report having ever adopted an unrelated child (Bachrach et al., 1990). However, no accurate figures on the number of annual adoptions are available because the federal government stopped keeping records in 1975 (Gibbs, 1989).

Table 12.5: Select Characteristics of Women Who Adopted Unrelated Child

Age	
15–24	18%
25–29	47
30–34	29
35–44	6
Parity	
0 births	70
1+ births	30
Marital status	
Currently married	99
Not currently married	1

From C. A. Bachrach, "Adoption Plans, Adopted Children, and Adoptive Mothers" in *Journal of Marriage and the Family,* 48:247. Copyright © 1986 National Council on Family Relations, 3989 Central Avenue, N.E., Suite #550, Minneapolis, MN 55421. Reprinted by permission.

Agency Adoption Versus Independent Adoption

During the early 1970s, adoption agencies handled about three fourths of all adoptions, whereas by the mid-1980s they handled only about one half of all adoptions (Rule, 1984). Independent adoptions are usually arranged directly between adoptive parents and the biological mother or her agent such as a lawyer or physician. The cost of an independent adoption ranges from $6,200 to $18,600 depending upon the need for a caesarean section and/or payment of the mother's living expenses (Gibbs, 1989). Most adoption agencies have age restrictions for potential adoptive parents and are often unwilling to accept applications from persons over age 35. Adoption agencies usually screen prospective parents to determine reason for adoption, willingness to adopt an older child or one with handicaps rather than an infant, ability to provide a stable financial and housing environment, and physical and psychological assessments of the potential for parenthood (Rule, 1984).

Independent adoptions arranged by physicians or lawyers are illegal in at least six states (Gibbs, 1989). A major disadvantage of independent adoptions is that few legal rights exist for the adoptive parents if the biological mother should change her mind. If the biological mother should assert at a later time that she was exploited or coerced into placing her baby for adoption, a state court may overturn the adoption even after several years (Cohen, 1985). This possibility certainly exists according to one study in which two thirds of unmarried women who placed their infants for adoption later had negative attitudes about their decision (Grow, 1979).

Telling Child About Adoptive Status

Contrary to adoption agency recommendations, some adoptive parents choose to conceal the adoptive status of their child. The major reasons are failure to come to terms with infertility and fear of personal rejection by child and/or by society (Miall, 1987). While authorities differ concerning the precise age that a child should be told that she/he is adopted, the general rule is to tell as soon as the child is able to understand the meaning of adoption. Although psychiatrists and psychologists tend to agree that a child lacks sufficient cognitive and personality development to comprehend and accept their adoptive status prior to age 4, this circumstance does not mean that the parents should wait until then to bring up the subject.

The process of telling the child about being adopted should be gradual and continual. In other words, the child should not be overwhelmed with information but rather parents should respond to questions as they are asked (Berman, 1987). Most parents prefer to tell a child of her/his adoptive status at a very young age in hopes that when the child is old enough to understand about being adopted, no traumatic effects will result.

The Issue of Sealed Adoption Records

Among the most controversial issues associated with adoption is the question of open birth records for the adoptive child. The term "open adoption" has come to be defined as a written agreement prior to adoption enabling the child to have continuing contact with one or more members of her/his birth family after adoption. A model state adoption law prepared by the Department of Health, Education, and Welfare in 1980 includes a provision that open adoption is permissible provided that it is approved by the court at the time of the adoption (Amadio & Deutsch, 1984). By 1989, only three states (Alabama, Alaska, and Kansas) had implemented completely open records for adoption that were available to adoptees age 18 and over (Taylor, 1989). Older adoptive parents are much more opposed to open birth records than younger adoptive parents. Of adoptive parents, only one half supported open birth records if agreeable to the birth mother and adoptive parents (Geissinger, 1984). However, some authorities believe that open adoptions can be damaging to the psychological and emotional health of the birth mother (Kraft, Palombo, Woods, Mitchell, & Schmidt, 1985). Still others believe that open adoption could result in substantially greater numbers of unmarried, teen mothers placing their babies for adoption because they would have more input in the adoption process and more information about the adoptive parents (Kallen, Griffore, Popovich, & Powell, 1990).

Contrary to popular opinion, of those adoptees searching for their birth mother, three fourths reported having positive relationships with their adoptive parents. The most common reasons given by adoptees for starting a search for their birth mother were genetics, genealogy ("roots"), and curiosity (Geissinger, 1984). After passage of the Minnesota Open Birth Record Law, over three fourths of the adoption agencies were successful in procuring genetic information, and one third were successful in organizing meetings between birth mother and child in cases of adoptee searches (Simpson, Timm, & McCubbin, 1981). Adoptees who were older at the time of their adoption are more likely to initiate a search for their birth parents. A major reason for not initiating a search for the birth parent is not wanting to hurt the feelings of the adoptive parents (Sobol & Cardiff, 1983).

Summary

- Although marriage and childbearing remain strong interests for young people today, many couples choose to postpone their childbearing plans to establish personal maturity, financial security, stability in marriage, and a career.
- Personal motivations to have children include source of love and affection, fulfillment of personal needs, provision for immortality, and symbol of adult status. External social factors such as the costs of parenthood, parental pressures, peer influence, and religious values also impact the decision of childbearing.
- Although having a child in marriage may be a source of deep personal satisfaction, the influence of a child on a marital relationship is debatable. If a high degree of marital satisfaction existed prior to the birth of a child, chances are that positive changes will occur in the marriage.

- A child-free marriage has come to be viewed positively for those who make this choice. Child-free marriages are more likely to end in divorce, while those that survive are happier than marriages with children.
- Factors such as happiness, satisfaction, and closeness are key factors in determining family size as is the redefinition of marital roles by women.
- The timing of the birth of children is influenced by the age of the wife, age at first marriage, career goals of wife, level of education, degree of religiosity, and religious denomination.
- Involuntarily child-free couples often suffer from feelings such as guilt, embarrassment, anger, and depression.
- Major causes of infertility in women are blocked fallopian tubes, failure to ovulate, and hostile cervical mucus. Low sperm count and abnormal sperm cells contribute to infertility in men.
- Artificial insemination, in vitro fertilization, and surrogate motherhood have emerged as ways of coping with infertility.
- Due to religious, medical, or costs reasons, many couples seek to adopt a child. Agency adoptions appear to provide more safeguards for the biological mother and the adoptive parents than independent adoptions.
- If adoptive parents do not inform an adopted child of its adoptive status at the appropriate time, psychological trauma may result.

Questions for Critical Reflection

1. Of the several unhealthy reasons for having children, which have you observed most frequently among your friends? What percent of your couple friends who have had children have done so by choice?
2. In vitro fertilization is said to be opposed by feminists and antiabortionists because it uses women as human incubators. What is the commonality leading to agreement between these two groups with usually divergent opinions?
3. Agency versus independent adoptions and open versus closed adoptions are issues facing many potential adoptive parents. What are the advantages and disadvantages of each that you could outline for friends seeking to adopt a child?
4. Activist Gloria Steinem contends that a "cultural baby strike" has occurred with some women choosing to not have children at all or to delay childbirth because of the inequities involved in parenting. However, a recent "baby boomlet" has occurred. How can you reconcile these apparent contradictions?
5. "I can put the wash on the line, feed the kids, get dressed, pass out the kisses, and get to work by 5 of 9—cause I'm a wo—man." This TV jingle for Enjoli, "the 8-hour perfume for the 24-hour woman," typifies the marathon supermom. Some believe this depiction is a myth and that women really can't have it all—at the same time. What do you think?

Suggested Readings

Andrews, L. B. (1989). *Between strangers: Surrogate mothers, expectant fathers, and brave new babies.* New York: Harper & Row. A consumer's guide to the legal issues surrounding surrogate motherhood and modern reproductive technology.

Arditti, R., Klein, R. D., & Minden, S. (Eds.). (1984). *Test-tube women: What future for motherhood?* London: Routledge & Kegan Paul. An anthology of feminist essays on modern reproductive technology including artificial insemination, in vitro fertilization, and surrogate parenthood.

Cohen, J. B. (1985). *Parenthood after 30?* Lexington, MA: D.C. Heath. A review of the major considerations in the postponement of parenthood.

Lewis, R. A., & Salt, R. E. (Eds.). (1986). *Men in families.* Beverly Hills: Sage. A collection of articles summarizing research on the central roles that men play in contemporary families, including decisions about fertility matters.

Lindsay, J. W. (1987). *Open adoption: A caring option.* Buena Park, CA: Morning Glory Press. A nonscholarly resource that helps adoptive parents, birth parents, and counselors understand the trend toward more openness in the adoption process.

Walter, C. A. (1986). *The timing of motherhood.* Lexington, MA: D. C. Heath. A scholarly work on the effects of timing of motherhood including mother role, dual careers of motherhood and employment, and interpersonal relationships.

CHAPTER 13

Conception, Pregnancy, and Childbirth

*"Pregnancy provided an in-depth, full force,
no screens-up experience of myself. It was ecstatic,
primal, scary, rough, revealing. . . . It was real.
More real than anything before it. Everything since
happens at a deeper level."*
Jean Marzollo, 1975

Fertilization of the ovum begins a process as old as humanity, yet one which, in many ways, remains a mystery. Understanding the developmental stages of the prenatal period requires familiarity with words such as zygote, blastocyst, embryo, and fetus. Such knowledge, however, does not preclude the greater need to understand at a deeper level the awesome significance of such an occurrence. Despite the dramatic changes in medical technology, pregnancy and childbirth are the only available means through which we are able to insure continuation of the human species. In addition, the event of childbirth signals the creation of additional roles of mother and father for women and men. As pregnancy progresses and childbirth approaches, the parents-to-be begin to construct for themselves a perception of social reality which includes their future infant as a separate entity or other person (Stainton, 1985). In short, the act of conception has created and changed their lives forever.

The Physiology of Conception

At the time of ovulation, the ovum is released and is "pulled" into the fallopian tube by the fimbria. When fertilization of the ovum occurs, it is usually in the upper portion of the fallopian tube (Masters, Johnson, & Kolodny, 1988). Although it is estimated that between 100–500 million sperm are released into the vagina during ejaculation, only a few hundred sperm are thought to actually reach the proximity of an ovum (Allgeier & Allgeier, 1991). During the fertilization process, only one sperm cell penetrates the ovum and a hard outer protein coat is formed to prevent any other sperm cells from penetrating the ovum (Schatten & Schatten, 1983). The fertilized ovum is initially called a **zygote.**

Within about 36 hours after fertilization, the zygote begins to undergo cell division as it is moved forward along the fallopian tube toward the uterus at a speed of about one inch per 24 hours. This cell mass, which is referred to as a **blastocyst,** reaches the uterus in 3–5 days after fertilization (see Figure 13.1). Within 2 days after entering the uterus, the blastocyst implants itself into the uterine wall (Denney & Quadagno, 1988).

Predetermining Sex

Changes in attitudes toward gender roles apparently have impacted the sex choice for first offspring. In a survey of women in the third trimester of their first pregnancy, 58% had no sex preference for their first offspring while 24% desired a girl and 18% desired a boy. Although about one half of these women indicated they would not be willing to use a medical preselection process to determine the sex of their future child, medical researchers continue in their efforts to make it possible to do so (Steinbacher & Gilroy, 1985). In one such process, liquid albumin (a protein substance found in blood that is similar to egg whites) already has been used to separate the faster swimming Y sperm cells from X sperm cells. This laboratory procedure permits sperm recovery for use with artificial insemination to increase the probability of a male conception (Glass & Ericsson, 1982).

Although the X-bearing sperm cell is slower moving, it travels longer distances and is larger in comparison to the Y-bearing sperm cell. A gelatinous material has also been used by medical researchers to collect X sperm cells for use in artificial insemination to try to increase the probability of a female conception (Hewitt, 1987). Such medical research has been characterized by some feminists as being the most outrageous sexist activity yet developed by the medical establishment (Powledge, 1981). Recommendations for sex preselection without medical intervention include timing of sexual intercourse during the menstrual cycle, using an alkaline or acid vaginal douche, varying the depth of vaginal penetration at the moment of ejaculation, and position selection for sexual intercourse (Shettles & Rorvik, 1970).

The Phenomenon of Multiple Births

The likelihood of conceiving twins is 1 in 90 births whereas the chances of triplets are 1 in 8,000 births, and for quadruplets, the odds are 1 in 700,000 births (Meeks & Heit, 1982). Fetal mortality is about four times as high for twins as for single pregnancies with the major cause of death being prematurity. However, the survival rate for twins increases after 36 weeks of gestation when the birth weight is likely to be 4.2 lbs or more (Oxorn & Foote, 1975).

Fraternal Twins

Fraternal twins, which may be two female infants, two male infants, or a female and male infant, account for about three fourths of all twin births (Francoeur, 1991). Generally, a genetic tendency toward fraternal twins is inherited from the maternal family. In addition, fraternal twins are more prevalent among older women, women with previous multiple births, and black women

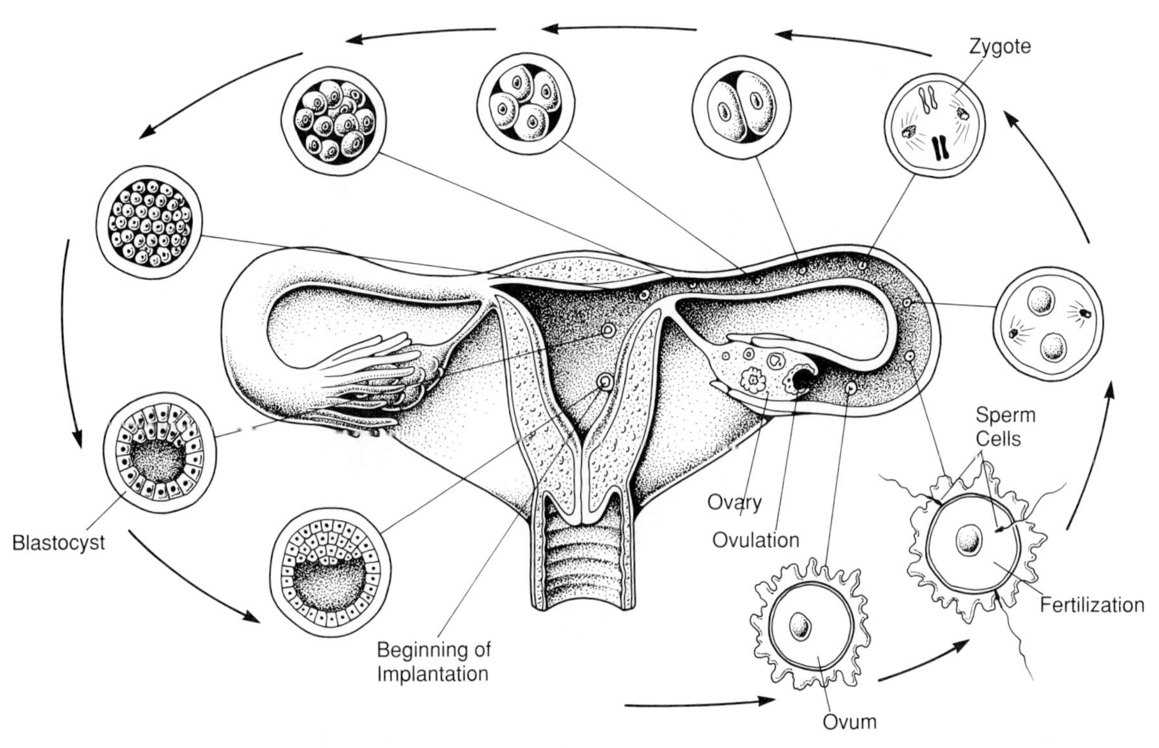

Figure 13.1 The Process of Fertilization

(Oxorn & Foote, 1975). During the conception process, fraternal twins result from fertilization of two separate ova by two separate sperm cells. They are called dizygotic twins because they come from two (di) zygotes. Each twin will develop a separate placenta and **amnion** (see Figure 13.2). The **placenta,** which is connected to the fetus by the umbilical cord, serves as a major life support system for the fetus. It furnishes nutrients from the mother and removes waste products of the fetus via the bloodstream of the pregnant woman. The amnion or amniotic sac serves as a protective covering for the fetus and contains amniotic fluid which serves to insulate and further protect the fetus during its development in the uterus (Allgeier & Allgeier, 1991).

Identical Twins

Identical twins evolve from a single ovum that has been fertilized by one sperm cell and are called monozygotic (one zygote) twins. As the blastocyst continues to develop, it divides into two separate cell masses very early. While the twin fetuses share one placenta, each twin has its own amniotic sac. By definition, identical twins are the same sex, look alike, and share all other inherited characteristics (Berger, 1988). The incidence of identical twins does not appear to be influenced by the factors of heredity, race, or maternal age (Francoeur, 1982).

Pregnancy

Pregnancy is characterized by ambivalence as expressed in the word "wonder." The "wonderment of nature" begins with the uniting of the tiny ovum and sperm cell, which develops into a fully-formed fetus that moves within the uterus. Wonder also describes concerns that a woman may have about her body: Will it ever return to its physical appearance? Will the weight gain and body distortion associated with 9 months of pregnancy disappear? (Sils & Sils, 1980).

Diagnosis of Pregnancy

While some women may experience a light menstrual flow or "spotting" after conception, the typical first presumptive sign of pregnancy is a missed menstrual period (Crooks & Baur, 1990). This time-honored indication of pregnancy is not wholly reliable because there are many emotional and physical conditions that also can delay the onset of menstruation. In fact, such stressful conditions can even cause a woman to skip a

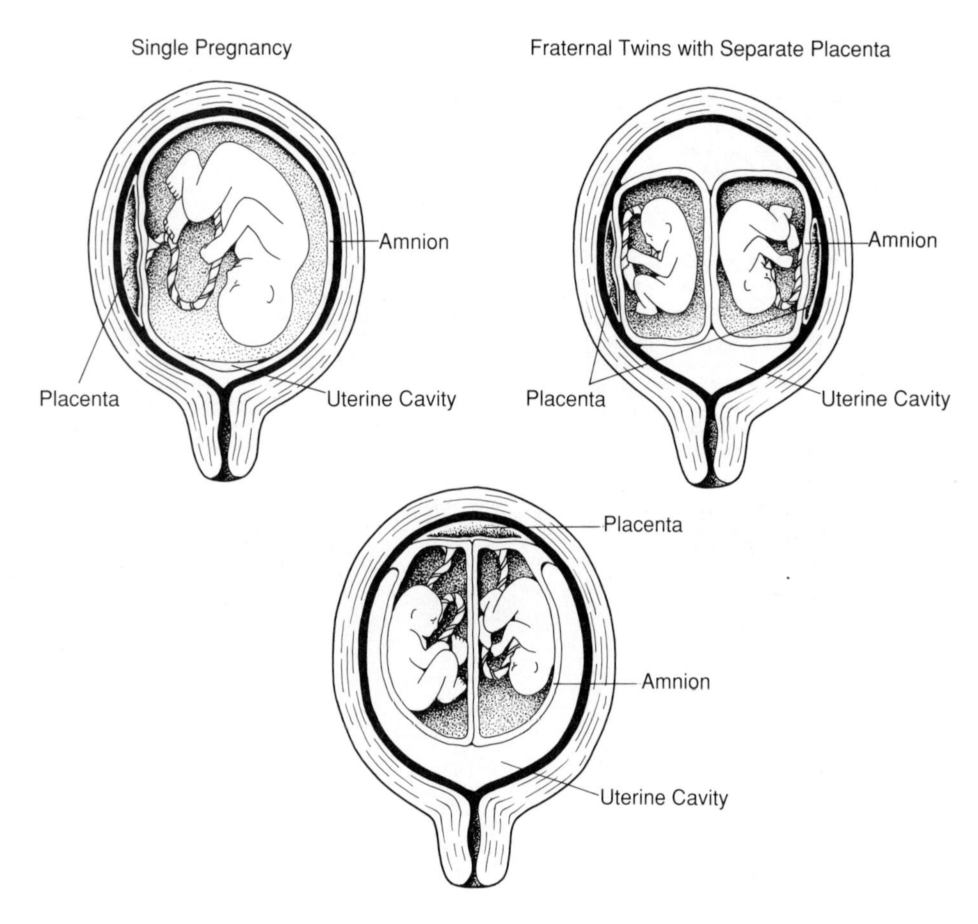

Figure 13.2 Single Pregnancy, Fraternal Twins, and Identical Twins

menstrual period altogether. In addition to the absence of the menstrual period, other presumptive signs of pregnancy include the physiological symptoms of breast tenderness, "morning sickness" (a tendency toward nausea and vomiting upon wakening), tiredness, change in appetite, slightly elevated body temperature, unusual food cravings, and increased frequency of urination (Crooks & Baur, 1990; Stewart, Guest, Stewart, & Hatcher, 1979).

If a woman believes that she is pregnant, she should immediately obtain a pregnancy test by a physician or through a medical clinic. Early diagnosis of the pregnancy will allow the woman to avoid certain drugs and possible exposure to certain infectious diseases that could harm the developing fetus. Also, pregnancy-like symptoms in a woman who is not pregnant may be an indication of serious medical disorders such as benign or malignant reproductive tract tumors and cysts (Allgeier & Allgeier, 1991). All pregnancy tests attempt to detect the presence of human chorionic gonadotropin (HCG) in the blood serum or urine of a pregnant woman (Hybritech Incorporated, 1985). This hormone begins to be secreted by the placenta in increasing amounts about ten days after fertilization occurs. The majority of the clinical pregnancy testing relies on a 2-minute urine slide test that can detect pregnancy within 42 days after the last normal menstrual period. Morning urine should always be used for the pregnancy test because HCG will be more concentrated than later in the day. A blood serum test also can be used which is accurate within 22–24 days after the last normal menstrual period. This test should be used by women who have a history of diabetes, hypertension, or kidney disease (Stewart et al., 1979).

An in-home pregnancy test that measures the amount of luteinizing hormone (LH) in urine has been developed. This over-the-counter test takes about 20 minutes to complete (Worth, 1986). Although in-home

Couples who joyfully anticipate the birth of their baby can best withstand the stress a new person introduces into the family.

tests for early pregnancy detection are readily available, they have a relatively high level of false negatives. In other words, the test incorrectly indicates that the woman is not pregnant. A medical survey found that reports of false negatives, even 20 days after a missed menstrual period, range as high as 20% (Doshi, 1986). A false negative outcome may result if urine is tested too early or too late, tested incorrectly, is too diluted, or is left too long at room temperature. False positive results, indicating a non-pregnant woman is pregnant, are sometimes also found. The reasons for false positives include testing on the day of ovulation; blood or protein in the urine; and the use of aspirin, antidepressants, hypertension drugs, or marijuana (Stewart et al., 1979).

After confirmation of pregnancy, one of the first things prospective parents usually want to know is when their baby is likely to be born. The length of the pregnancy averages about 266 days counting from the time of conception or 280 days from the first day of the last menstrual period, assuming a 28-day menstrual period. Predicting when conception occurred is a very difficult task because many women do not have regular 28-day menstrual cycles. Nevertheless, the gestation period is usually considered to be 9 calendar months. Physicians use the following formula to calculate the expected due date: add 7 days to first day of last menstrual flow, subtract 90 days from this date, and add 365 days. About two thirds of all births will occur within 5 days of this calculated date. In most instances, first births tend to occur slightly later than the anticipated due date. However, this circumstance may be attributable to calculation errors associated with the due date (Denney & Quadagno, 1988).

Emotional Responses to Pregnancy

Uncertainty and conflict about becoming pregnant are related to low marital satisfaction prior to the pregnancy. Factors associated with higher marital satisfaction during pregnancy include whether the child is wanted, intentional pregnancy, and consensus between wife and husband on deciding to become pregnant

BOX 13.1	Parental Reactions to Pregnancy
Mother's Reactions	**Father's Reactions**
First trimester	
Informs father secretively or openly	Differ according to age, parity, desire for child, economic stability
Feels ambivalent toward pregnancy; anxious about labor and responsibility of child	Acceptance of pregnant woman's attitude or rejection and lack of communication
Is aware of physical changes; daydreams of possible miscarriage	Is aware of own sexual feelings; develops more or less sexual arousal
Develops special feelings for mother, forms own mother identity	Accepts, rejects, or resents mother-in-law
	May develop new hobby outside of family as sign of stress
Second trimester	
Feels movement of fetus, incorporates into self	Feels for movement of baby, listens to heartbeat, or remains aloof, with no physical contact
Dreams partner will be killed, telephones often for reassurance	May have fears and fantasies about himself being pregnant; may become uneasy with feminine aspects in himself
Experiences distinct physical changes; sexual desires increase or decrease	May react negatively if partner is too demanding; may be jealous of physician's importance to partner and her pregnancy
Remains regressive and introspective; problems with authority figures projected onto partner; becomes angry if he exhibits lack of interest	If he can cope, will give her extra attention she needs; if he cannot cope, will develop a new time-consuming interest outside of home
Continues to deal with feelings as a mother; looks for baby furniture as concrete expression	May develop a creative feeling and a "closeness to nature"
May have other extreme of anxiety and wait until ninth month to look for baby furniture and clothes	May become involved in pregnancy and buy or make furniture
Third trimester	
Experiences more anxiety, tension, and physical awkwardness	Adapts to alternative methods of sexual contact
Feels much discomfort and insomnia from physical condition	Becomes concerned over financial responsibility
Prepares for delivery, assembles layette, picks out names	May show new tenderness and concern; treats partner like doll
Dreams often about misplacing baby or not being able to deliver it; fears birth of deformed baby	Daydreams about child as if older and not newborn; dreams of losing partner
Feels ecstasy, excitement, and spurts of energy during last month	Renewed sexual attraction to partner
	Feels he is ultimately responsible for whatever happens

(Snowden, Schott, Awalt, & Gillis-Knox, 1988). The most important task confronting a woman with her first pregnancy is the acceptance and emotional incorporation of the fetus into her daily life. In a comparison of pregnant married, single/partnered, and single/unpartnered women, married women who reported a high degree of family task sharing, such as shopping for groceries or cleaning, had a greater level of psychological adjustment during pregnancy. Women in the unpartnered group with greater numbers of close friends were more likely to be psychologically adjusted during their pregnancy (Liese, Snowden, & Ford, 1989). Emotional closeness between daughters and mothers during the daughter's pregnancy was closely associated with perceptions of equity in exchanges of psychological support and/or tangible goods and services. However, in actual practice, these exchanges averaged only about once every two months (Martell, 1990). Pregnant women often reconcile any differences with their own mothers during their pregnancy. Failure to achieve maternal reconciliation may adversely affect the relationship with their future child. Research suggests that the failure of the pregnant woman to conduct routine tasks such as acquiring baby clothes and bassinet accessories may indicate a lack of commitment to the fetus as an individual. As prospective fathers adjust to the fetus, the couvade syndrome may be experienced whereby the physical symptoms of pregnancy are reported including nausea, vomiting, appetite loss, abdominal pain, bloating, and heartburn (Valentine, 1982).

Women tend to undergo more anxiety and depression during their first pregnancy than in subsequent pregnancies. In fact, women giving birth for the second time are more likely to experience the positive

Table 13.1: **Embryonic and Fetal Growth Changes**

End of Month	Approximate Size and Weight	Representative Changes
First Trimester		
1	1/4 inch	Backbone and vertebral canal form; leg and arm buds begin; heart forms and starts beating; body systems start to form.
2	1 inch	Eyes form far apart; eyelids fuse, nose flat; ossification of bones begins; limbs become distinct as arms and legs; fingers take shape; major blood vessels form; internal body systems continue to develop.
3	3 inches 1 ounce	Eyes develop underneath fused eyelids; nose bridge takes shape; external parts of ears form; arms and legs are fully formed; nails start to develop; heartbeat can be detected.
Second Trimester		
4	6 1/4 inches 4 ounces	Head is much larger than rest of body; face takes on human features; hair appears on head; joints begin to form between bones.
5	9 1/2 inches 11 ounces	Head becomes less disproportionate to rest of body; fine baby hair all over body; body systems show rapid development.
6	12 inches 1 1/2 pounds	Head becomes birth size; eyelids separate and eyelashes form; skin still wrinkled and pink.
Third Trimester		
7	14 inches 2 1/2 pounds	Head and body become more proportionate, premature baby now capable of survival.
8	16 inches 3 1/2 pounds	Fat deposited under the skin; skin less wrinkled; testes descend into scrotum in male; bones in head still soft; five-and-a-half-pound fetus considered full term.
9	20 inches 7 1/4 pounds	Additional fat accumulates under skin; baby hair shed; nails extend to tips of fingers or beyond; further time in uterus mainly causes baby to be heavier.

Source: Data from C. O. Byer and L. W. Shainberg, *Dimensions of Human Sexuality*, 3d ed. Copyright © 1991 Wm. C. Brown Publishers, Dubuque, Iowa.

emotions of interest and joy toward pregnancy at the postpartum rather than at the predelivery stage (Rosenberg, Darby, & Robinson, 1984).

Fetal Development

The product of conception has various names depending on the period of gestation. It is called a zygote prior to implantation, an **embryo** during the first 8 weeks of development, and a **fetus** after that time. The average length of pregnancy, 38 weeks or 9 months (266 days), for medical convenience, is divided into three 3-month segments called **trimesters** (Byer & Shainberg, 1991).

Stages of Pregnancy

During the first trimester, the embryo will grow to about one fifth of an inch during the 1st month. The cardiovascular system is the first organ system to function with the heart beginning to beat in the 4th week (Moore, 1982). Embryonic growth becomes more rapid during the 2nd month with formation of major blood vessels and initial development of arms and legs. By the end of the 3rd month, all the major organs have completed their formation including stomach, heart, lungs, and kidneys. Thus, at the beginning of the second trimester, the fetus is fully formed. External body parts such as fingernails, eyelids, and eyelashes become clearly visible. And by the end of the 5th month, the legs will have achieved their final relative proportion (Jones, 1984). During the last trimester, brain development is appreciable (Parmelee & Sigman, 1983). Although the fetus will have achieved a weight of approximately 1½ lbs by the end of the 6th month, its survival rate at this stage is low (see Table 13.1). An infant born prematurely at the end of the 7th month has only a 50% survival rate (Francoeur, 1991).

Physical movements of the fetus can be detected in the 4th month (Jones, 1984). If the mother-to-be is not working outside of the home or engaging in strenuous physical exercise, she is more likely to notice the characteristics of fetal movement. Rubbing or patting the fetus through the abdominal walls seems to have a calming effect on the movements (Stainton, 1985).

Since the fetus can hear sounds after 24 weeks, it will respond with vigorous activity to angry voices or unfamiliar sounds.

By the beginning of the third trimester, fat deposits have begun to form under the skin which give the characteristic chubby appearance to the fetus (see Table 13.1). If an infant is born prematurely in the third trimester, the chances of survival are: by the 7th month—50%, 8th month—90–95%, and 9th month—99% (Francoeur, 1991). At the end of 9 months, the fetus is full-term and usually is positioned upside down to begin the actual birth process.

Health Issues for Pregnant Women

After confirming the existence of a pregnancy, the physician will take a complete medical history to determine whether or not any unusual circumstances warrant special medical management of the woman's pregnancy. Of particular interest will be restrictions on the use of substances associated with congenital defects and developmental problems. Presence of diseases or abnormal medical conditions, hormone levels of the woman, and blood compatibility will also be determined (see Table 13.2). The pregnant woman will usually be advised to avoid a variety of prescription and nonprescription drugs and medications; alcohol; tobacco products; large quantities of caffeine; and radiation exposure (Snow, 1989). Since inadequate nutrition during pregnancy may cause low birth weight or mental deficiency, it is also important that nutritional facts be communicated. In fact, there are a number of important health issues related to pregnancy.

Weight Gain

Generally speaking, women with ideal body weight prior to pregnancy should gain 20% of their current weight during pregnancy. All women should gain some weight since fetal development is not dependent upon stored fat but rather is based upon food currently eaten by the pregnant woman. Nevertheless, a major concern during pregnancy is the issue of weight gain. General medical standards suggest that the average weight gain for most women during pregnancy should range from 20–25 lbs. This normal prenatal weight gain includes fetus—7.7 lbs, placenta—1.4 lbs, uterus—2.0 lbs, breasts—1.5 lbs, interstitial fluid—2.7 lbs, maternal blood—4.0 lbs, and amniotic fluid—1.8 lbs (Allgeier & Allgeier, 1991).

Sexual Activity

Depending upon the medical condition of the woman and her individual comfort levels, sexual intercourse can continue during pregnancy. Although the frequency of sexual intercourse may remain at the same level throughout the pregnancy, the frequency of sexual intercourse decreases for most women during the third trimester (White & Reamy, 1982). The most often reported reason for this decrease is physical discomfort which develops as the uterus enlarges due to fetal growth. Other reasons for less frequent sexual intercourse include fear of injuring fetus, lack of sexual desire, feelings of awkwardness during sexual intercourse, feelings of unattractiveness, and physician's recommendation (Solberg, Butler, & Wagner, 1973; Walbrochl, 1984). Wives, compared to their husbands, are twice as likely to attribute the decline in sexual activity during pregnancy to decreases in their physical attractiveness (LaRossa, 1979).

Assuming a normal pregnancy, women who engage in sexual intercourse during the third trimester have no reported increases in incidence of premature rupture of amnion, low birth weights, or amniotic fluid infections (Mills, Harley, & Harley, 1981). Therefore, in the absence of breakthrough bleeding or uterine contractions, sexual intercourse during the third trimester of pregnancy remains a personal option (Page, Villee, & Villee, 1981; Reamy & White, 1985). However, because of research possibly linking infections with sexual intercourse in the last month of pregnancy, sexual intercourse at this time should be discussed with the obstetrician (Calderone & Johnson, 1981). Other forms of sexual activity may be preferred during the third trimester such as mutual genital stimulation (Rosen, 1980). However, it is extremely important that air not be blown into the vagina during cunnilingus as fetal and maternal deaths from air embolisms (bubbles) have been caused by blowing air into the vaginal orifice (Fyke, Kazmier, & Harms, 1985).

As discussed in chapter 10, if insufficient vaginal lubrication develops for sexual intercourse due to inadequate sexual arousal, it can lead to dyspareunia. During pregnancy, dyspareunia has been found to be associated with the following factors: unhappiness about being pregnant, fear about gestation/labor/delivery, and perceived unattractiveness to spouse. Women reporting anxiety, fear or unhappiness about the pregnancy, or concern about labor and delivery are more likely to report dyspareunia during the first and second

Table 13.2: Medical Factors That May Affect the Fetus

Factors	Effects
Drugs	
Alcohol	Small head size, defective joints, congenital heart defects, mental retardation
Nicotine	Low birth weight, prematurity, stillbirth, spontaneous abortion, nicotine dependency at birth associated with sudden infant death syndrome, hyperactivity, and increased respiratory infection during 1st year of life
Aspirin—moderate use	May prolong labor and lengthen clotting time for both mother and baby, increasing the risk of hemorrhage
Vitamin A—excessive use	Cleft palate, neural tube defects
Tetracycline	Liver, bone, and tooth damage, discolored teeth, abnormally short arms or legs, webbed hands
Heroin	Low birth weight, maternal toxemia, postpartum maternal hemorrhaging, altered neonatal sleep patterns, fetal addiction/withdrawal, respiratory depression
Methadone	Low birth weight, hyperirritability, respiratory depression
Caffeine	Low birth weight
Marijuana	In animals, reduced growth rate, spontaneous abortion, low birth weight
Cocaine	Neonatal intoxification
Diseases or medical conditions	
Rubella virus	Deafness, blindness, cataracts, heart malformations
Diabetes	Maternal toxemia, abnormally large fetus, stillbirth, spontaneous abortion, respiratory difficulties
Syphilis	Malformations, mental retardation, syphilitic infant, deafness, blindness, spontaneous abortion, stillbirth
Herpes Type II	Neonatal death, spontaneous abortion, prematurity, neonatal herpes infection, congenital abnormalities
AIDS	Postnatal death from opportunistic infections
Radiation	Microcephaly, mental retardation, skeletal malformations
Hormones	
Androgens	Females—masculinization of internal and/or external genitals
Estrogens	Females—clitoral enlargement, labial fusion, congenital abnormalities
Progestins	Cardiovascular abnormalities
DES	Females—abnormal vaginal or cervical growth, reproductive tract cancer, masculization; Males—semen and testicular abnormalities, reduced fertility
Oral contraceptives	Suspected but unconfirmed reports of physiological difficulties including anal, cardiac, kidney, and limb abnormalities

trimesters of pregnancy. If women believe their husbands perceive them as being more attractive prior to their pregnancy, dyspareunia is more likely to be reported (Reamy & White, 1985).

Proper Nutrition

Since the developing fetus receives its nutrients and food from the woman via the placenta, it is extremely important that good nutrition habits be practiced during pregnancy. Ordinarily, the daily intake from the basic food groups should increase during the last 6 months of pregnancy. Otherwise, serious impairment of fetal development may occur which can lead to premature childbirth, low birth weight, higher risk of infant mortality, and mental retardation (Katchadourian, 1989).

Among the crucial nutrients during pregnancy are protein, iron, calcium, and folic acid (Winick, 1985). An extra 30 g of protein per day is recommended for pregnant women to prevent low birth weights and decreased head circumference (Sweeney, Smith, & Foster, 1985). Using nutrition counseling along with individual protein and caloric prescriptions, a group of pregnant women experienced major increases in total weight gain during their pregnancy along with an increase in their infant birth weights (Sweeney et al, 1985). A 50% increase in calcium intake per day is needed to help develop the fetal skeleton and to regulate muscle contraction, blood coagulation, heartbeat, and nervous system function. In addition, iron is needed to form hemoglobin for the fetal circulatory system and because maternal blood volume increases up to 30% during pregnancy. Most pregnant women should begin taking iron supplements under the direction of their physician. Finally, vitamin B-6 is necessary for tissue growth and cell multiplication during the embryonic and fetal stages (Alfin-Slater, Aftergood, & Ashley, 1982).

Substances to Avoid

As a result of an exhaustive review of the scientific literature, a number of medications were labeled as high risk during pregnancy. For example, Accutane, the extensively used medication for acne, can cause heart defects and deafness. The antidepressant lithium is also problematic. Two studies found that 7% of those infants exposed to lithium in the first trimester of pregnancy had heart defects. Metronidazole (an antibiotic used for treatment of protozoa-based diseases such as trichomoniasis) and tetracycline were also found to pose threats to the fetus (Winick, 1985). Two other commonly available and widely used substances, nicotine and alcohol, have been found to be significantly related to the health of the fetus.

Fetal alcohol syndrome (FAS) is a combination of mental, motor, and growth retardation accompanied by facial abnormalities often occurring in children of mothers who heavily consumed alcohol during pregnancy (Golden, Sokol, Kuhnert, & Bottoms, 1982). In fact, FAS is the third most frequent cause of mental retardation in the United States (Papalia & Olds, 1990). Heart and skeletal defects and hyperactivity have also been related to FAS (Abel, 1983). Even though infants of mothers who drank some, but less than 2 oz of alcohol a day while pregnant, did not evidence FAS at birth, they were later found to have abnormal brain waves (Ioffe, Childiaeva, & Chernick, 1984). Moderate social drinking may also result in low birth weight and infant learning problems (Barr, Streissguth, Martin, & Herman, 1984). Furthermore, a single episode of binge drinking during the latter part of pregnancy or while a mother is breast-feeding may affect brain development, and cause motor impairment and learning disabilities (Papalia, Olds, & Feldman, 1989). Thus, with the current research suggesting development of FAS as well as more subtle effects of alcohol consumption, both the March of Dimes Foundation and the Surgeon General of the United States recommend that women completely avoid alcohol intake during pregnancy (Berger, 1988).

With regard to the effects of nicotine, women who smoke during pregnancy have increased risks for premature birth, stillbirth, lower birth weight, and infant mortality (Baird & Wilcox, 1985; Neiberg, Marks, McLaren, & Remington, 1985). In addition, a longitudinal study found that many common childhood problems including asthma and temper tantrums are more common in children of mothers who smoked during pregnancy (Butler & Golding, 1986). In spite of such findings, 1 in 4 pregnant women still smokes, ignoring the possibility of a smaller, more vulnerable infant (Berger, 1988).

The Rh Factor

Approximately 1 in 200 pregnancies is affected by the Rh factor or blood incompatibility of the mother and the fetus. The Rh factor is a protein substance found in the blood of most people. However, if the prospective mother does not have this protein in her blood, she is said to be Rh negative. Since blood type is controlled by the genes, if the prospective father is Rh positive, the blood of the fetus may also be Rh positive (Snow, 1989). Although the blood of the woman and fetus are separated by the placenta, during the prenatal period and at birth, some of the fetal blood leaks into the woman's blood causing an allergic reaction. The development of antibodies will destroy the red blood cells of the fetus, leading to anemia, brain damage, or even death (Masters, et al., 1988). Infants with the Rh negative condition can be treated with repeated blood transfusions even before birth (Papalia & Olds, 1990). Normally, antibodies do not develop in sufficient quantities during the first pregnancy to cause problems, but successive pregnancies are at risk. If untreated, the chances of fetal problems with the Rh factor are 1 in 10 for a second pregnancy, 1 in 5 for a third pregnancy, and 1 in 3 for a fourth pregnancy. After the birth of the first baby, an injection of Rh antibodies (RhoGAM) into the bloodstream of the woman will block any future manufacture of additional antibodies (Snow, 1989).

Risks and Identification of Congenital Defects

Available evidence suggests that **congenital** (present at birth) defects occur in about 3% of all live births and in a much higher percentage of all products of miscarriages or **spontaneous abortions** (Wilson, 1977). Congenital defects appear to be a causative factor in about

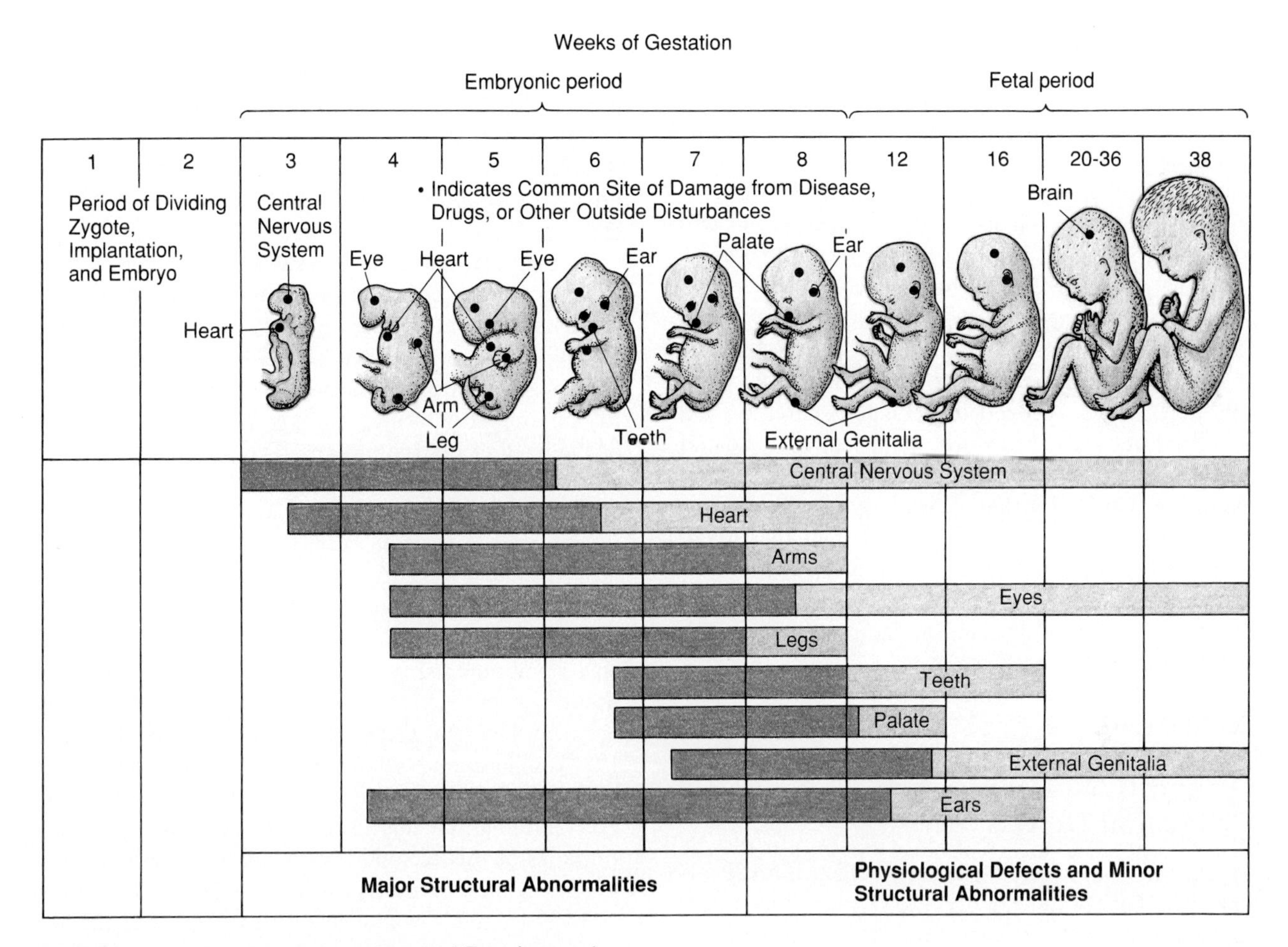

Figure 13.3 Critical Periods of Prenatal Development

two-thirds of all spontaneous abortions (Rosenwaks, Benjamin, & Stone, 1987). Birth defects may either be due to hereditary or environmental factors such as **teratogens** (substances that can cause congenital defects). Teratogens have been classified as the "3 Ds": disease, drugs, and diet (Bee, 1989). During the first 12 weeks of pregnancy, the fetus is at much greater medical risk from adverse factors (see Figure 13.3). It is estimated that 20% of congenital defects are **inherited** (transmitted by parental genes); 3–5% are the consequence of chromosomal abnormalities; 2–3% are attributable to infections; and about 5% are due to maternal drug use or exposure to toxic environmental chemicals. However, in the majority of congenital defect cases, no precise reason can be established (Wilson, 1977).

Common Congenital Defects

Among the more common congenital defects are Down's syndrome and Tay-Sachs disease. **Tay-Sachs disease,** found among northeastern European Jews, is a hereditary enzyme deficiency that makes it impossible to break down fatty materials (lipids). Lipids build up in fetal cells causing the infant to be born blind, deaf, and mentally retarded. The Tay-Sachs child usually will die by ages 2–5 (*Dorland's Illustrated,* 1988). The most prevalent type of congenital defect is Down's syndrome which affects about 1 in 1,000 live births. It is an abnormality that is caused, in 95% of the cases, by either the ovum or sperm cell having an extra chromosome for a total of 47 chromosomes instead of the normal 46. The extra genetic material causes physical and mental abnormalities such as small head, flat nose, cardiac defects, and mental and physical retardation (Allgeier & Allgeier, 1991). There is a high mortality rate associated with Down's syndrome with about 50% of affected infants dying within the 1st year after birth (Levitan & Montagu, 1977). If serious, untreatable congenital defects such as Tay-Sachs and Down's syndrome diseases are detected during pregnancy, many women will obtain therapeutic abortions.

Age of Mother as Factor in Congenital Defects

Of the many factors thought to be associated with various congenital defects, the age of the mother is currently most affected by societal changes. It is estimated that the number of births to women ages 35–44 will increase by about one half by 1995. Women who become pregnant after age 35 are more likely to have postpartum hemorrhaging, inadequate uterine contractions resulting in slower labor, and increased likelihood of uterine or ovarian tumors interfering with pregnancy (Harris, B. A., Jr., 1987). Further, chromosomal abnormalities are seven times more likely to occur if the pregnant woman is age 45 rather than age 35 (Simpson, 1981). Further, Down's syndrome is three times more likely to occur at age 35 than at age 26. For example, the odds at age 20 are 1 in 1,923 that the birth will result in Down's syndrome, while at age 41 the risk has climbed to 1 in 85 (Simpson, 1981). The reasons for greater numbers of infants with congenital defects born to older women remain a matter of considerable speculation.

Diagnostic Procedures for Congenital Defects

A prenatal test for possible genetic defects is medically indicated if one or more of the following conditions exist: maternal age over 35 years, familial background that suggests a significant risk for chromosomal abnormalities, previous Down's syndrome infant, or previous infant with severe spinal cord defects (Crooks & Baur, 1990). Of those women who undergo prenatal testing, about 95% of the tests will prove to be negative (Strong & DeVault, 1988). However, it should be noted that normal chromosomal results and normal biochemical results do not eliminate the possibility that the fetus may have congenital defects or mental retardation due to other causative factors (Tucker, 1978). Today, there are three primary diagnostic procedures for congenital defects: amniocentesis, ultrasound scanning, and chorionic villi sampling.

The procedure of **amniocentesis** involves the withdrawal of amniotic fluid that contains cells from the fetus. Amniocentesis is usually conducted at about 16–20 weeks of gestation if needed. Without benefit of an anesthetic, a thin needle is inserted through the abdominal and uterine walls into the amniotic sac, and a small quantity of amniotic fluid is withdrawn. Chromosomes and body secretions from this specimen are examined to determine whether any genetic diseases or chemical abnormalities are present in the fetus. Usually, a 3–4 week waiting period is necessary before obtaining the results (Snow, 1989). This test also reveals the sex of the fetus, which is valuable information if an X-linked genetic disease is likely (Berger, 1988). Fetal injury is estimated to occur in 2–3 cases per 100 tests (Kaiser, 1982).

First introduced in the 1960s, ultrasound, which is considered to be much safer than other techniques, is the most commonly used prenatal assessment (Snow, 1989). While amniocentesis can detect chromosomal abnormality, **ultrasound scanning** can be used to identify missing or deformed limbs or gross malformations of the head or internal organs. The procedure involves sending sound waves through the uterus to produce a screen image of the fetus. Since neither the woman nor the fetus are exposed to radiation, ultrasound scanning or ultrasonography can be performed several times during pregnancy (Cohen, 1985).

Chorionic villi are thread-like tissue protrusions on a membrane that surround the embryo or fetus. This tissue, which eventually becomes the placenta, is genetically identical to the fetus ("New Prenatal Test," 1988). Chorionic Villi Sampling (CVS) is conducted by inserting a tiny catheter through the vagina and cervix to obtain a small sample of this tissue. The advantages of this technique over amniocentesis include the availability of results within 6–24 hours rather than 2–3 weeks, and it can be performed as early as the 8th week of pregnancy rather than at 16–20 weeks (Cadkin, Ginsberg, Pergament, & Verlinski, 1984). Although expensive, this newest safe and accurate procedure is becoming more widely available in cities with large medical facilities.

The Process of Childbirth

Before the 19th century, childbirth was primarily handled by midwives and was accompanied by a relatively low incidence of maternal deaths. However, in the 19th century, the birth process began occurring in hospitals. At that time, puerperal or childbed fever, believed to be caused by physicians using dirty hands and nonsterilized surgical instruments, resulted in a maternal mortality rate of 20%. By the 20th century, physicians believing that women were too nervous and inefficient for childbirth began using general anesthesia, forceps to extract the fetus, and extensive episiotomies (Eagan, 1985). An **episiotomy** is an incision made from the vaginal orifice toward the anus to prevent tearing of tissues during childbirth (Allgeier & Allgeier, 1991). It

BOX 13.2 **Preventing Mental Retardation**

Experts estimate that more than one half of all mental retardation in infants and children could be prevented by observing the following precautions:

1. Before planning a pregnancy, have a blood test to determine susceptibility to measles. If susceptible, get inoculated at least 3 months prior to conception.
2. See physician as soon as pregnancy is suspected due to importance of good prenatal care and nutrition.
3. Don't smoke or drink alcohol while pregnant.
4. Ask physician before taking any medication—even vitamins or aspirin.
5. Stay away from animal (especially cat) feces and avoid people who have German measles, chicken pox, or other contagious diseases, especially during first 3 months of pregnancy.
6. Tell physician or dentist about pregnancy before submitting to X rays; agree only to those absolutely necessary.
7. If Rh negative, be immunized with RhoGAM immediately after each pregnancy.
8. Test newborn infant for all four metabolic disorders, including PKU.
9. Have child inoculated against childhood diseases at proper times.
10. Prevent child from swallowing or chewing on lead-based painted surfaces to avoid brain damage.
11. If future child predisposed to genetic abnormalities for any reason, seek referral to genetic counseling center.

From J. Wilson, "Preventing Mental Retardation" in *Town & Country*, August 1982:82–83.

is now known that relaxation, proper breathing and pushing techniques, physician patience, and freedom of leg movement can eliminate the routine need for an episiotomy during childbirth (Crooks & Baur, 1990).

Natural, Prepared, or Gentle Childbirth

A growing number of people object to what they believe to be excessive medical intrusion into a phenomenon that is viewed as a natural biological experience for both mother and baby. Some women object to being given so much anesthetic that they remain semiconscious during the entire delivery process. Further, concerns exist regarding the effects that various medications and anesthetics may have on the baby during and after delivery.

The concept of natural childbirth was popularized by Grantly Dick-Read during the 1930s in his book *Childbirth Without Fear.* This treatise promoted the philosophy that childbirth itself is a natural process, and that without fear which results in muscular tenseness with increasing pain and stress, there is no pain during childbirth. The importance of attitude, nutrition, and physical exercises to relieve muscular tension was stressed. Women who embrace such concepts often find that they are able to give birth without the use of anesthetics during labor and delivery. Such women not only can assume a more active role during labor and be totally aware of the birth process, but they can also protect their infant from the added risk involved in the use of anesthesia (Dick-Read, 1972).

Preparation for natural childbirth typically includes both classes and exercises. Childbirth classes are designed to allay the woman's anxiety about impending childbirth, to provide instructions about exercises that will tone her muscles, and to encourage following the instructions provided by medical personnel during childbirth. Prospective fathers are encouraged to participate by sharing the experience of the woman and by providing assistance during the exercises. Couples who attend childbirth classes are more likely to have upper-middle class backgrounds and to attend during their first pregnancy. Further, husbands who participate in childbirth classes are more likely to have less traditional gender attitudes and roles, higher levels of marital happiness, and equal dominance in decision making. Wives have reported lower levels of pain and more enjoyment during the birth process if their husbands actively participated during labor (Block, Norr, Meyering, Norr, & Charles, 1981).

Does natural childbirth make the birth experience easier? A review of clinical studies concluded that natural childbirth effectively reduced subjective pain perception and increased pain endurance. In addition, women use fewer medications and anesthetics, express greater satisfaction with childbirth experiences, and report less **postpartum depression** than women who use traditional hospital birth methods (Conway, 1980).

The Lamaze and Leboyer Approaches

Developed by French obstetrician Fernand Lamaze, the Lamaze method of prepared childbirth teaches women to disassociate their pregnancy in response to pain from their intrauterine contractions (Clarke-Stewart & Friedman, 1987). By adopting various body positions and breathing techniques during labor, it is thought to be possible for a woman to terminate most pain and

Hospital birthing centers, which often resemble luxuriously furnished hotel suites, offer an alternative to the delivery room.

anxiety often associated with uterine contractions (Lamaze, 1970). Controlled breathing provides a distraction from pain during labor, while deep breathing relaxes muscles and helps to prevent **hyperventilation** and holding of breath. Exhaling while pushing the fetus downward during labor is much less exhausting than forced pushing of the fetus with held breath. Some medical authorities believe that the on-the-back position during childbirth actually slows labor and reduces the oxygen supply for the fetus. Therefore, a "semi-squatting" position is considered superior for natural childbirth (Eagan & Lieberman, 1984). A study of Lamaze users found that the childbirth process represented a joint partnership and shared experience. The parents indicated a strong desire to use this method for subsequent births (Lowe & Frey, 1983).

French obstetrician Frederick Leboyer, believing that the birth process is traumatic for the infant and may potentially lead to emotional difficulties later in life, promoted "birth without violence." Gentle births are designed to eliminate shock and pain experienced by the fetus during the childbirth process by replacing these negative conditions with peace, comfort, and happiness (LeBoyer, 1975). The technique includes low indirect lighting, minimal talking during childbirth, placement of baby on abdomen of mother while umbilical cord is still attached, gentle massage of baby's body, and emersion of baby in warm-water bath (Young, 1982). A comparison of Leboyer and conventional deliveries found that Leboyer women had significantly shorter first stage labor, but no differences were found with regard to satisfaction with birth, amount of time that newborn infant spent crying during 1st hour, and infant behavior at 24 or 72 hours after birth (Nelson, Enkin, & Saigal, 1980). A later study reported "gentle-birth" infants during the 1st year of life to be either the same or "slightly easier" in temperament than others delivered by conventional methods (Maziade, Boudreault, Cote, & Thivierge, 1986).

Alternatives to Conventional Hospital Delivery

Women have become increasingly concerned about the quality of health care, questioning the impersonal assembly-line delivery room approach found in most modern hospitals. They have argued that hospital labor and delivery rooms are designed for the obstetrician and not the pregnant woman and her spouse (Mead, 1975). While some women have advocated a return to home deliveries, less than 1% of all reported births in 1987 occurred in nonhospital settings (U.S. Bureau of the Census, 1990j). In a study of alternative birth environments, most persons reported a desire to feel in control of the birth process regardless of whether they chose a maternity center, traditional hospital, or home birth (see Table 13.3). Couples using home births were more likely to report anxiety toward separation from the child, whereas couples choosing traditional hospitals were more likely to have concerns about infant and maternal safety.

Maternal birthing centers, which may be located within hospitals or may exist as separate facilities, are also an alternative. In-hospital birth centers usually include a bedroom, bathroom, and family sitting room with home-like furnishings. The birthing room approach to childbirth is flexible, allowing family members and close friends to be present (Young, 1982). In these birthing centers, childbirth is viewed as a normal, healthy process to be assisted by physicians or nurse-midwives in a home-like environment. **Nurse-midwives** (certified registered nurses with considerable additional training regarding the handling of childbirth cases) are likely to have administrative and clinical responsibilities in the maternity birth centers located in hospitals (American College of Nurse-Midwives, 1978). These birthing centers are likely to utilize a birthing chair rather than a delivery table to assist with the labor process (Strong & DeVault, 1988). Delivery tables, introduced by obstetricians in the 20th century, are believed by many to be for physician convenience rather than the woman's welfare (Wertz & Wertz, 1977). Women who select a birthing center are more likely to report support from others and to consider choosing different delivery positions (Sacks & Donnenfeld, 1984). However, 85% of friends and relatives of pregnant women in one study gave some negative reactions to the choice of a birthing center (Annandale, 1987).

The advantages of birthing centers include emphasis on psychological and social needs of family, lower cost, earlier discharge with home care, and pediatric examination and care conducted in presence of the family. Other advantages include atmosphere and environment focused on wellness and normality, continuity of care provided by one birth practitioner throughout the birth process and postpartum, and immediate availability of obstetrical backup and care if complications develop (Young, 1982).

Table 13.3: Priority Considerations for Selection of Birth Environments

Priority Consideration	Maternity Center	Hospital	Home Birth
To feel in control	90%	85%	68%
To avoid separation from child	85	66	82
To avoid excessive obstetrical management	72	32	68
Support of others	62	45	36
To freely choose those present at delivery	54	77	50
To breast-feed immediately	44	43	55
To have utmost safety	21	81	32
Fear of hospitals	18	6	27
Least discomfort	13	32	14
To be able to choose delivery position	13	6	14
To avoid high costs	10	6	23
To feel taken care of	10	28	18
Past negative experience	5	6	14
To be prepared for indicated complications	0	15	0

From S. R. Sacks and P. B. Donnenfeld, "Parental Choice of Alternate Birth Environments and Attitudes toward Childrearing Philosophy" in *Journal of Marriage and the Family,* 46:472.

Labor and Delivery

As the anticipated delivery date approaches, most women are more than ready to conclude their pregnancy. They yearn to be relieved of the physical discomforts associated with their condition including increased frequency of urination and difficulties in finding a comfortable position for sleeping. While the woman may have attended childbirth classes, she remains anxious about the pain that may be associated with childbirth and is eager to make sure that the baby will be normal and healthy (Allgeier & Allgeier, 1991). The four critical factors in the process of labor and delivery have been identified as the passage, the passenger, the powers, and the psyche. The "passage" refers to the size of the pelvis and ability of the cervix to dilate during birth. The "passenger" relates to fetal head size, presentation, and position whereas "powers" has to do with frequency, duration, and strength of the uterine contractions. The "psyche" includes prior physical preparation for childbirth such as breathing exercises and various social customs associated with childbirth (Olds, London, & Ladewig, 1984).

Rise In Cesarean Births

A **cesarean section** is a surgical method of childbirth in which an incision is made through the abdominal wall and the uterus. Cesarean sections originally were used only to extract a live fetus upon the death of the mother (Eagan, 1985). In 1970, 6% of all deliveries in the United States were cesarean births, but by 1987, that number had grown to 24% of all deliveries (U.S. Bureau of the Census, 1990k). In 1987, 35% of the cesarean procedures were done only because mothers had experienced previous cesarean births (Taffel, Placek, & Moien, 1989). In recent years, many health care advocates and feminists have come to question the need for repeat cesarean deliveries. In Norway, for example, almost one half of the women who have initial cesarean deliveries undergo vaginal deliveries for future pregnancies, whereas only 10% of women in the United States do so (Downey, 1989; "Rise in Cesarean," 1987). These are interesting statistics when compared to a 1990 survey of over 2,200 American obstetricians who concluded that at least 60% of women with a previous cesarean section were able to deliver vaginally in a subsequent pregnancy ("Vaginal Delivery," 1990).

Three risks have been noted in the argument against cesarean sections:

1. It has all the risks of major surgery, including complications with anesthesia, blood transfusions, and infection.
2. Maternal mortality is twice as high for women who have repeat cesarean sections.

3. Infants are at increased risk for respiratory problems and distress caused by anesthesia (Thompson, 1988, p. 103).

The 1982 Guidelines for Vaginal Delivery After Cesarean Childbirth prepared by the American College of Obstetricians and Gynecologists indicated that 50–60% of women could have a vaginal delivery after a cesarean birth (Young, 1982). Why then has cesarean childbirth become so popular in the United States? In 1988, new guidelines for cesarean births were issued in which the following reasons for choosing cesareans were cited:

1. Advanced fetal monitoring is more sensitive to fetal distress.
2. Trend is toward larger babies who are more difficult to deliver vaginally.
3. More requests exist from women exhausted by labor.
4. Doctors want to protect themselves from malpractice suits.
5. Cesareans take less time in the delivery room (Thompson, 1988, p. 103).

It appears that the degree of emphasis during obstetrical residency training is a significant factor in the rise of cesarean deliveries (Young, 1982). Further, many women who have had a previous cesarean section appear to choose this procedure for their second birth (Placek, Taffel, & Moien, 1983).

Despite concerns, there are several medical reasons why a cesarean procedure is sometimes warranted. The medical indications for a cesarean section are pelvic contractions accompanied by abnormal labor, **malpresentation** (abnormal position for delivery) of fetus, previous uterine surgery, hemorrhaging, fetal distress such as irregular heart beat, fetal death in earlier pregnancy, diabetes, poor elasticity of cervix, small pelvis, age of woman, prolonged labor, abnormal pelvis, and fetus too large for the vaginal passageway (Oxorn & Foote, 1975; "Rise in Cesarean," 1987). As a woman becomes older, the stress of labor and a vaginal delivery creates the possibility of complications during labor and delivery. Therefore, women who are age 35 or older having their first child are especially good candidates for a cesarean section (Placek et al., 1983).

Positioning of Fetus

During the last weeks of pregnancy, the fetus ordinarily moves into the cephalic (head first) position for labor. This presentation accounts for 96% of all cases. Since the head of the fetus is the largest part of its body, once the head has emerged from the birth canal, the rest of the delivery typically goes smoothly. A few deliveries involve a breech presentation (pelvis first) in which the presenting part may be the buttocks, feet, or knees. Since breech deliveries are more difficult, the physician may attempt to manually turn the fetus to a normal presentation (Meeks & Heit, 1982). In very rare cases, there may be a transverse presentation in which the fetus is situated crosswise in the uterus so that the presenting part could be the arm, back, abdomen, or side (Olds et al., 1984). If fetal rotation is not possible, the fetus must be delivered via a cesarean section. In a breech or transverse presentation, there is a danger that the umbilical cord could become entangled and/or knotted, thus cutting off the oxygen supply to the fetus. An absence of fetal oxygen during the delivery process will cause permanent brain damage (Oxorn & Foote, 1975).

Use of Medication during Childbirth

Substantial controversy surrounds the use of medications for pain reduction during labor and delivery. Those women who have undergone natural childbirth training report a great deal of energy and euphoria several hours after delivery. Such patients are usually able to move around some after childbirth, but women who have utilized anesthetics are likely to indicate feelings of grogginess and fatigue (Avard & Nimrod, 1985). Since some medications tend to impede the progress of labor whereas others may have temporary negative effects on the fetus/infant, a woman and her physician should discuss the options and her preferences before labor begins (see Table 13.4). Although relief from pain and discomfort has obvious psychological and physiological benefits, some women report guilt feelings if they used pain relievers during childbirth. Such women feel inadequate as women because they took the easier avenue by using medication during childbirth (Masters et al., 1988).

There is evidence that labor and delivery anesthetics and prepartum medication influence behavior and interaction between mothers and their infants. For example, the degree of touching and smiling after delivery were found to be reduced for both mothers and infants when anesthetics were used. As the dosage level was increased, there likewise was less spontaneous infant behavior during the first months of life (Hollenbeck, Gewirtz, Sebris, & Scanlon, 1984). Another study found that infants whose mothers did not utilize any medications during labor and delivery exhibited more

Table 13.4: Effects of Various Methods for Pain Reduction in Labor and Delivery

Method	Effects on Mother	Effects on Fetus
	Analgesics	
Tranquilizers		
Valium or Vistaril	Physical relaxation and reduced anxiety; takes the edge off pain	Minimal
Barbiturates		
Nembutal, Seconal, or Amytal	Drowsiness and reduced anxiety; may slow progress of labor	Can depress nervous system and breathing
Narcotics		
Demerol, Dolophine, or Nisentil	Reduces pain and elevates mood, but may inhibit uterine contractions; cause nausea or vomiting	Can depress nervous system and breathing
Amnesics		
Scopolamine ("Twilight")	Does not reduce pain but causes woman to forget birth experience; may cause physical excitation and wildness	Minimal

Method	Effects on Mother	Effects on Fetus
	Anesthetics	
Local		
Paracervical	Blocks pain in uterus and cervix, but relatively short-lasting and ineffective late in labor; can lower blood pressure	Causes slowing fetal heartbeat—about 20% of cases
Pudendal	Blocks pain from the perineum and vulva in about 50% of cases	Minimal
Regional		
Spinal, Epidural, or Caudal	Blocks pain from uterus, cervix, and perineum; highly effective, but can cause serious drop in blood pressure or seizures	Generally does not affect fetus but requires forceps delivery more often
General		
Nitrous oxide (laughing gas) or Halothane	Used only in last few minutes of labor to eliminate pain completely, but may cause vomiting or other complications; leading cause of maternal death	Can depress nervous system and breathing

behavioral changes and greater sensitivity to stimuli than infants of mothers in the medication group (Hill & Smith, 1984). Thus, use of medication during labor and delivery may adversely affect bonding between mother and baby which begins when mother and infant have first contact outside the uterus (Klaus & Kennell, 1981). Further, if anesthetics are used during delivery, the infant may show less responsiveness and alertness (Richards, 1981).

Stages of Labor

Women having their first child often worry about whether they will know when actual labor begins. Uterine contractions, which represent the essence of labor, actually occur throughout most of the pregnancy, but they are not strong enough to be felt until the last few weeks of pregnancy. These so-called **Braxton Hicks contractions** (false labor) serve to exercise the uterus for the eventual labor process (Snow,

1989). Braxton Hicks contractions also assist during actual labor to dilate the cervix. Among the preliminary signs of labor are persistent backache, increase in vaginal secretions, and loss of weight caused by increased frequency of urination. In addition, about 2 to 3 weeks prior to the onset of labor, "lightening" occurs as the fetus settles into the lower portion of the uterus (Oxorn & Foote, 1975).

There are three signs that indicate the onset of actual labor. First, there is the regularity and frequency of uterine contractions. Initially, uterine contractions will occur at 15–20 minute intervals and last between 30–60 seconds. When the contractions begin approaching 5-minute intervals, most physicians advise that the woman should immediately depart for the hospital (Jones, 1984). A second sign of labor is the appearance of the **show,** which is a small bloodstained mucus plug that has served to block the cervix preventing infection from entering the uterus. The expulsion of the mucus plug from the vagina indicates that delivery is near (Jones et al., 1985). Third, the amnion may rupture (breaking of the "bag of water") releasing a trickle or gush of amniotic fluid from the vagina. However, the amniotic sac breaks in about 1 in 10 pregnancies prior to the onset of labor (Jones, 1984). Although many women have increased anxiety with the onset of labor, maternal deaths associated with complications from pregnancy and childbirth occur rather infrequently—only about 6.5 maternal deaths per 100,000 live births (National Center for Health Statistics, 1990f).

The Major Events of Labor

Once labor has begun, there are three perceptible stages. The first stage of labor (dilation) lasts from the onset of labor until the cervix dilates sufficiently to permit passage of the fetal head. This stage of labor usually lasts anywhere from 6–18 hours for first pregnancies with an average length of 13 hours. And for later pregnancies, it lasts an average of 8 hours (see Figure 13.4). Strong pains begin in the back and pass to the front of the abdomen and upper thighs as the cervix shortens and begins to dilate about 10 cm (Masters et al., 1988).

The second stage of labor, which in essence is the expulsion of the fetus, lasts from the time of complete cervical dilation to birth. The duration of the second stage of labor ranges from 30 minutes to 2 hours with expulsion of the fetus occurring much sooner in women who have had previous vaginal deliveries (Jones, 1984). Uterine contractions become more frequent; pain is at its peak level; and the woman is asked to "bear down" with her abdominal muscles. An episiotomy will be done, if necessary, to prevent tearing of vaginal or anal tissue. This procedure is typically performed on 60–90% of women in their first pregnancy who deliver vaginally. However, no apparent differences exist in the recovery time for women who undergo an episiotomy and those who experience a perineum tear. Therefore, many medical authorities have begun to question the routine use of the procedure (Abraham, Child, Ferry, Vissard, & Mira, 1990). Crowning occurs when the largest diameter portion of the fetal head passes through the vaginal orifice. Next, the shoulders will be delivered when the woman bears down during a strong uterine contraction. The body trunk and lower limbs will then slip out of the dilated vagina very easily. At this point, the umbilical cord typically is tied, and the baby's eyes are treated with silver nitrate (an antiseptic) to prevent **Ophthalmia neonatorum** (an eye infection) that could potentially lead to blindness (Oxorn & Foote, 1975).

The third stage of labor (expulsion of placenta) usually lasts from 15–30 minutes. The placenta separates from the uterus within 5 minutes after birth occurs. It is then expulsed from the uterus as the woman bears down with her abdominal muscles. As shown in Figure 13.4, a large **hematoma** (blood clot) is formed as a result of bleeding from the separation of the placenta from the uterus, but only about 8 oz of blood is typically lost during delivery. If an episiotomy has been performed, the incision is sutured and closed at this point (Jones, 1984).

The Return of Breast-Feeding

During the 1970s, with the emphasis on physical fitness and health, there was a resurgence of interest in breast-feeding of infants. In 1970, about 1 in 10 mothers were breast-feeding their infants for 3 or more months after birth; whereas by 1980, one third of all mothers were breast-feeding for at least 3 months. The educational level of the mother and geographical region appear to be major variables in the decision to breast-feed. By 1981, only 16% of mothers with less than 12 years of education were breast-feeding for 3 or more months as compared to over one half of mothers with at least 1 year of college. Further, mothers from the West were twice as likely to breast-feed than those from the Northeast and South (U. S. Bureau of the Census, 1989a).

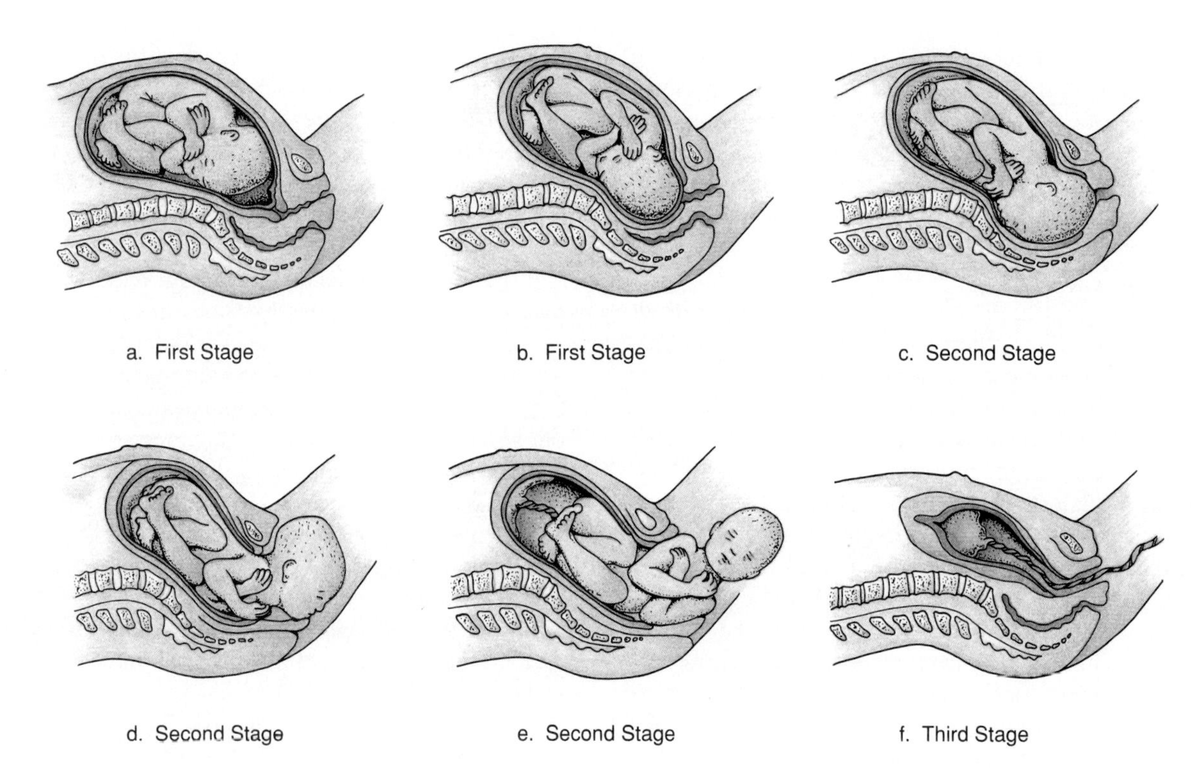

Figure 13.4 Stages of Labor

Since **lactation** or milk production begins on the 2nd or 3rd day after childbirth, women need to make early decisions regarding breast-feeding. If a woman chooses not to breast-feed, she may choose to have estrogen injections during the third stage of labor which will suppress lactation and help the uterus to begin shrinking (Jones, 1984). Research suggests that many women decide rather early to breast-feed. A survey of mothers who were breast-feeding found that 53% of mothers chose breast-feeding prior to their pregnancy while an additional 28% decided to breast-feed during the first trimester (Gavinski, 1985). Given the availability of breast pumps to collect and store milk along with bottle feeding as a supplement, women who are working outside the home need not reject breast-feeding because of employment. In general, lack of knowledge about breast-feeding and its benefits seems to lead to a low incidence of its adoption (Joffe & Radius, 1987).

Advantages of Breast-Feeding

Those women who choose to breast-feed believe that the practice enhances bonding between infant and mother (MacLaughlin & Strelnick, 1984). Other reasons cited for breast-feeding include breast milk being more nutritious and easier to digest, increased release of hormones that shrink the uterus back to normal size, and pleasurable physiological sensations during breast-feeding (Lott, 1987). Women who experience these pleasurable feelings as sexual need to be reassured that such a response is a natural physiological reaction. In fact, women who become sexually aroused during breast-feeding are more likely to be successful at breast-feeding (Williams, N. D., 1987). Although about 98% of mothers are able to breast-feed, some women are unsuccessful and for no apparent physiological reason experience a lack of milk release.

There are several important nutritional and immunological advantages in breast-feeding an infant. As a nutritional benefit, human milk contains more vitamin C, vitamin E, vitamin D, thiamine, and riboflavin than cow's milk as well as less fat and fewer calories (Ewy & Ewy, 1975). Further, human milk protein is more easily digested than cow's milk protein (Snow, 1989). Breast-feeding also has important immunological and health benefits leading to lower incidence of allergies and respiratory diseases, fewer dental problems, and less diarrhea (Gavinski, 1985). While the ideal length of breast-feeding remains debatable, nutritionists believe that by the time an infant reaches age 6 months, breast milk alone will not provide sufficient protein intake to ensure good health. Therefore, solid food should be introduced into her/his diet at that time (Waterlow & Thompson, 1979).

Bonding, the wondrous reciprocal process of nature, occurs through the senses.

Breast-feeding also provides psychological and physiological benefits for lactating mothers. First, **oxytocin** (a pituitary hormone) secretion, which is caused by the infant sucking its mother's breast, results in milk being released from milk glands into the milk ducts. Oxytocin also causes uterine contractions that help the uterus to return to its normal, nonpregnant shape (Denney & Quadagno, 1988). Second, emotional and psychological satisfaction is associated with breast-feeding because the woman feels that her womanhood is being reaffirmed by providing assurance that she is capable of sustaining the life of an infant (Ewy & Ewy, 1975). Working women who were breast-feeding reported feeling good about themselves because they were both working and breast-feeding. But one half of these women still reported guilt feelings due to their perception that they were not doing a good job at breast-feeding or at work. Among the reported problems with breast-feeding were milk leakage; increased milk supply; and less support from friends, family, and co-workers (MacLaughlin & Strelnick, 1984). Third, given the concern that some women have about their breast size, many women who were breast-feeding indicated feeling more physically attractive because of their breast enlargement. Further, although many women indicated feelings of embarrassment about milk leakage, their husbands often found their milk leakage to be erotic, especially if it occured during sexual activity (MacLaughlin & Strelnick, 1984). Nevertheless, many other American women choose not to breast-feed because of inconvenience, tenderness of nipples, inhibitions about nursing their babies, and inadequate milk supply (Gavinski, 1985).

Adjusting to Parenthood

The arrival of an infant is likely to be a peak time of excitement and joy especially for those individuals who have become parents for the first time. Once the infant is safely asleep in its crib, the new parents can relax for a moment, at peace with themselves and the world. But the mother and father also must suddenly confront their new roles as parents. Newborn infants demand attention at all hours. When crying begins at 2 or 3 AM, each parent may feign sleep and hope that the other parent will change or feed the baby, but one or both persons must get up. So no matter how considerate the new parents may be toward each other, elation at having a baby typically gives way to fatigue and frustration. It is indisputed that the birth of a first child can be one of the most significant and stressful life events experienced by a couple (Glass, 1983). The first 4–6 weeks after the birth of the first child is labeled the "parental honeymoon" by proponents of this philosophy. Then a "crisis" period follows, lasting from 1–8 months, whereby the parents must learn to make adjustments to their new roles (Harriman, 1983). During this period, wives are likely to indicate concerns about their physical appearance, fatigue, and general nervousness; whereas husbands are more likely to have concerns about perceived interference with baby care by in-laws, interruption of their sleep patterns, and plans for the baby (Russell, 1974).

A significant change in attitudes usually occurs over the course of pregnancy and childbirth. In general, older mothers adjust better to parenthood because as their age increases, parenthood becomes more attractive. At this stage women are likely to have better social support networks with more friends already having children (Glass, 1983). In addition, the first child brings more changes in parental lives than later children (Harriman, 1983).

Coping Strategies for Transition to Parenthood

Social networks are an important source of help, especially for mothers, in coping with the newly acquired status of parent. The frequency of contacts with families of origin and with other parents tends to increase over time from the last trimester of pregnancy through the 9th month postpartum. Further, the amount of emotional and material support received from families of origin is likely to be greatest at 3 months postpartum than either during the third trimester or at 9 months postpartum especially for first time parents. Geographical proximity to one's family of origin increases the quantity of extended family contacts as well as the degree to which baby-sitting services are provided. But this support does not affect the amount of emotional and material support received by the new parents nor the degree to which relatives are considered to be significant others (Belsky & Rovine, 1984).

Research indicates that prior to the birth of a first child, mother-daughter strain seems to be based on the mother's criticism of the daughter as a person, whereas mother-in-law strain tends to be based on home management issues and "intrusion" into the marriage. After the birth of a first child, the mother-daughter bond tends to become closer with more contact and greater likelihood that daughters will ask for advice, thus reducing the strain level. However, in-law relationships often become more strained due to differing child-rearing philosophies and unwanted advice given by mothers-in-law. Mothers tend to give more help to their daughters, whereas mothers-in-law tend to give more things to the baby or the family (Rischer, 1983).

Mothers are more likely than fathers to seek social support and self-development as a means of coping with becoming a parent. In addition, mothers are more likely to report being religious, thankful, and content as coping strategies associated with being a parent. Generally speaking, reliving the past, wishing the baby were not here, and believing life would be better without the baby are least helpful as coping behaviors (Ventura & Boss, 1983). Further, the ability to balance social life and mothering is positively correlated with better total adjustment to life, more freedom-in-life changes that occur, more acceptance of changes, prior marital satisfaction, and greater freedom from parental responsibilities and restrictions (Myers-Walls, 1984).

Women and Motherhood

Most authorities agree that attachment of the infant to its mother is of major importance in its social and cognitive development. Reactions such as crying, clinging, smiling, and vocalizing by infants will occur while the child is physically close to its mother or other significant caretaker. Through these repeated interactions with the attachment figure, infants develop their understanding of social reality (Bowlby, 1988). Given this influential role in the life of a child, how do mothers perceive themselves as managing their parenting tasks? In assessing the five stages of parenting—infancy, toddlerhood, preschool, school age, and adolescence—mothers feel least comfortable about their effectiveness as a parent during the stage of adolescence. Mothers of adolescents are concerned with the child's moodiness and growing independence as well as matters of discipline. During infancy, mothers feel uncomfortable about bottle- or breast-weaning and financial pressures of motherhood; and during toddlerhood, their concerns center around toilet training, "stubborn no's," and eating habits (Ballenski & Cook, 1982).

Perhaps the greatest stress is perceived by those women who combine motherhood with careers. They often experience an intense sense of obligation, recurrent guilt, anger, and resentment over their traditional roles. Mothers are torn between providing safe and adequate infant care and having to work. In an attempt to juggle their job and household responsibilities, women have little time to accomplish personal errands and tasks (Ventura, 1987). Evidence suggests that middle-class women do not define the role of motherhood as quickly or as stereotypically as working-class women. In fact, women with husbands who are more involved in child care actually have lower self-evaluations of themselves as mothers than women with husbands who are less directly involved in child care (Reilly, Entwisle, & Doering, 1987).

Postpartum Depression

The excitement and suspense of pregnancy are suddenly over, and the fantasies of idyllic parenthood have to be replaced by a seemingly endless succession of late night feedings and dirty diapers. While not all mothers experience an emotional letdown during the first few weeks after childbirth, many women do experience symptoms of depression often called postpartum "blues." After the birth of a child, relationships among family members must be renegotiated, a fact that unsettles many previous living patterns. In our culture, there has been a diminished emphasis on parenting skills or lack of validation for the caretaker role, which greatly contributes to the new mother's stress level. It is estimated that between 50–70% of all new mothers experience some alteration in mood or depression, which usually starts about the third day after childbirth. This condition is characterized by crying, anxiety, insomnia, headache, and irritability (Kraus & Redman, 1986). In more severe postpartum depression, which occurs in about 10–20% of women within three months of childbirth, the symptoms are exaggerated and may lead to an inability to cope with everyday living, especially with a baby. In severe cases, suicidal thoughts could lead a mother to harm herself or her child (Reamy, 1991). Treatment may involve drugs to elevate mood, to aid sleep, and to control agitation; or hospitalization in severe cases (Kraus & Redman, 1986).

A major cause of stress in new mothers seems to be the infant's fussy behavior associated with feeding and the mother's inability to soothe the baby (Ventura, 1987). Other factors associated with the infant's adaptation to the family's life rhythm include sex of child (female infants are more rhythmic), age of infant, mother's feelings of confidence, and absence of behavior problems with older siblings (Sprunger, Boyce, & Gaines, 1985).

Generally speaking, women tend to experience more anxiety and depression with their first pregnancy than with subsequent pregnancies. Further, there is a considerable fluctuation of emotions prior to delivery, 1st week postpartum, and 3 months postpartum. The positive emotions of interest, joy, and surprise usually reach their peak during 1 week postpartum (Rosenberg, Darby, & Robinson, 1984). While support from a social network does not significantly change the level of psychological distress, high levels of marital intimacy are associated with reduction in such stress (Stemp, Turner, & Noh, 1986). Mothers who are classified either as androgynous or masculine in terms of gender roles tend to have lower levels of psychological distress than feminine mothers. These findings suggest that new mothers who possess what is frequently thought to be masculine characteristics of assertiveness, independence, and leadership are more likely to experience adequate mental health than mothers who lack these attributes (Bassoff, 1984).

The Issue of Parental Leaves

By mid-1990, 15 states had unpaid parental leave laws, and an additional 30 states had considered similar legislation (Lewin, 1990a). The state of Rhode Island, for example, provides up to 13 weeks of either paid or unpaid leave for the birth or adoption of a child for its state employees. Connecticut allows its state employees to take up to 24 weeks of unpaid leave for the birth or adoption of a child ("States Study," 1987). A parental leave bill, passed by the United States Congress in 1990, was vetoed by President Bush on the grounds that it represented "unwarranted intrusion of the government into business affairs." This proposed law would have required employers of 50 or more persons to provide three months of unpaid leave for workers with new babies or for those providing care to immediate family members (Lewin, 1990a). As indicated by

Harris poll, three fourths of Americans favor the passage of a law guaranteeing a woman up to 12 weeks of "unpaid parental leave" (Holmes, 1990).

The Pregnancy Discrimination Act of 1978 requires that pregnancy be treated like any other temporary disability. Therefore, the United States Supreme Court ruled in 1987 that a California law guaranteeing pregnant workers up to 4 months of maternity leave and job reinstatement rights was constitutional and valid. However, in another related case, the Court ruled that a state may deny unemployment compensation to pregnant women who take leaves of absence but who will find their jobs available at the time that they plan to return to work ("Status of Cases," 1987). This case illustrates a major concern that many women have about being able to return to their prior job after childbirth. Most women who plan to continue their careers would like to spend several weeks or months with their newborn infants prior to returning to work. But without any guarantees of reemployment in the form of an official, extended maternity leave, most women are reluctant to take the risk of losing their jobs.

In a survey of 1,300 major corporations, only one quarter of management personnel indicated they favored the idea of extended maternity leaves (Langway, 1981). In light of the United States Supreme Court decision, states may require businesses to provide maternity leave and job security. However, only about 40% of working women were receiving such protection through their employers in 1987 (Wallis, 1987).

BOX 13.3 Negotiating a Maternity Leave

The following elements of a maternity leave to negotiate with an employer are suggested:

1. Decide the best length and timing of leave.
2. Determine degree of flexibility in hours after return to work.
3. Ascertain if leave to be paid or unpaid.
4. Determine the possibility of extension by using vacation time.
5. Determine if same or different job will be available after return to work.
6. Evaluate feasibility of choosing full- or part-time work.

In preparation for negotiations, these steps are recommended:

1. Read company manual and compare leave policy with needs and preferences.
2. Have goals and potential compromises clearly in mind.
3. Talk with colleagues at work about employer flexibility.
4. Discuss interpretation of leave policy with supervisor at the first meeting to prevent misunderstandings.
5. Emphasize hard to replace special skills to supervisor.
6. Give suggestions for covering personal assignments during absence.
7. Deal with unspoken feelings by supervisor.
8. Give serious consideration to issues that supervisor raises.

Men and Fatherhood

The transition into fatherhood is actually more abrupt, traumatic, and life altering for men than their transition into marriage. By the mid-1980s, men were noted to have become more attached to their family roles, including the nurturing aspects of fatherhood, than had previously been reported in documented research. But higher levels of role attachment to fatherhood has not led to behavioral change. The workplace still restricts men in their progress toward more active familial roles, while social norms and values restrict psychological involvement of men in fatherhood roles (Cohen, 1986).

Traditionally, fathers have tended to roughhouse with their infants and to encourage exploratory behavior more than mothers. They tend to engage in more physically-arousing play with their infant children than mothers who tend to interact through verbalizing, smiling, and social play (Ricks, 1985). Research suggests that fathers have begun to hold and rock their infants more than mothers if they have access to their newborn infants in the hospital. However, the degree to which a father enjoys and participates in care-giving for his child depends on a good marriage, feelings about his own father, and adequate avenues for breadwinning (Muenchow & Bloom-Feshbach, 1982).

Fathers can serve as objects of attachment for infants that are age 7–8 months and older (Ricks, 1985). They can also provide an extra source of stimulation to enhance a child's cognitive and social competencies. However, fathers view the teaching of cognitive development, social skills, norms, and values as major responsibilities more often for their male children than

Is this baby a girl or boy? While toys and clothes are traditional signs of sex typing, research now confirms that the ways in which fathers touch and hold their babies also furnish clues.

female children. Fathers also seem to feel more responsibility toward male children than female children whereas mothers feel similar responsibilities for both. Thus, female children are likely to be placed at a disadvantage because fathers typically encourage the development of behaviors and attitudes consistent with the traditional male role. Such actions continue to perpetuate the differences between women and men, which persist throughout adulthood (Gilbert, Hanson, & Davis, 1982).

If a man has decided against having children, he may be more reluctant to accept the pregnancy or be involved in child rearing. A study of first time expectant fathers suggests that timing is a crucial variable in acceptance of the pregnancy. The wife and husband's decision to bear children was influenced by the expectant father's perception of a stable couple relationship, relative financial security, and his acceptance of ending a childless life-style. Generally, expectant fathers who were younger than 25 felt more strain and discomfort over pregnancy and were more likely to engage in rejection behaviors whereas expectant fathers who were age 34 and over tended to be more accepting and flexible regarding children (May, 1982).

Participation by Father in Child Care

In a study designed to assess use of social networks for parenting advice, about one half of the fathers reported three or more sources of child-rearing advice. Both groups, those receiving greater and lesser amounts of advice, reported more nonkin persons than kin in their social network. Fathers receiving less advice were more likely to seek information about parenting from nuclear family members and were less likely to seek such information from neighbors (Riley & Cochran, 1985). Among working-class fathers of preschoolers, social networks include more coworkers rather than neighbors and relatives. But they do not typically ask peers for help with child care or housework and, in fact, they ridicule other men who help with housework. These husbands also perceive that their wives' employment and their increased personal participation in housework are symbolic of relinquishing the breadwinner responsibility (Lein, 1984). Middle-class and upper middle-class families suggest a similar pattern. In general, mothers spend more time on child care than fathers, performing such tasks as child discipline, communication, nurturance, housework, and meal preparation. However, fathers are more likely to perform outdoor and repair/maintenance tasks whether or not the mother is employed outside the home (Levant, Slattery, & Loiselle, 1987).

As for parent-child interaction and performance of child-care tasks, few fathers are responsible for such tasks as "take to doctor" or "buy clothes" and home chores such as cooking and cleaning. In fact, only one third of the fathers indicated responsibility for any child-care tasks and substantially fewer (7%) performed home chores. Of the total interaction time spent with children, mothers spent an average of 45 hours per week, and fathers spent an average of 30 hours per week. However, if the mother was employed outside the home, the amount of father interaction time increased, but the father's performance of child-care tasks or perceived "feminine" home chores did not significantly increase (Barnett & Baruch, 1987).

However, other findings suggest that as the educational levels of mothers and fathers increase, participation of fathers in child-care activities in the home increases. Although one third of mothers indicated that responsibility for child care was equal between parents, mothers were more likely to provide physical care and religious training, whereas fathers were more likely to be responsible for child discipline and financial support (Atkinson, 1987). One of the reasons for differential participation of fathers in household tasks and child care relates to gender-role definitions that lead many men to label such tasks as cooking and child care as either leisure or partially leisure-time activity rather than work for the female task performer (see Figure 13.5). For example, men are more than twice as likely as women to perceive cooking as a form of leisure-time activity.

Parenthood and Marital Adjustment

Couples with planned pregnancies are more likely to report a higher level of marital adjustment; but wives, in general, tend to feel relationship changes are more intense. Low marital adjustment was associated with a feeling that numerous marital changes occurred after parenthood, whereas high marital adjustment was related to an overall positive attitude toward parental adjustments. Husbands were more likely to report "not having enough time for yourself" whereas wives were more likely to indicate not having enough time to "get everything done" regardless of their level of marital adjustment. Usually, sexual relationships were reported to suffer the most ill-effects from new parenthood due to fatigue over other time demands (Harriman, 1986). The single best predictor of postpartum marital adjustment is the level of marital adjustment during the pregnancy. Thus, it is possible to predict which marriages are likely to decline in quality after childbirth and which ones will improve (Belsky & Rovine, 1990). In general, both wives and husbands reported the highest level of marital adjustment at one month postpartum, while indicating a level of marital adjustment at six months postpartum significantly below that which existed during the pregnancy (Wallace & Gotlib, 1990).

Another factor relates to expectations regarding the child's effect on the marriage prior to childbirth as compared with reality. Wives, generally speaking, are more positive about how the baby will and does influence relations with friends and neighbors, but the effects on the marital relationship are usually more negative than either the wives or husbands expected. In particular, fathers help less in caregiving than their wives expect. Thus, most negative marital changes are due to violated expectations regarding the child's effect on the lives of the couple. This factor remains as most powerful from the third trimester of pregnancy through the 3rd month postpartum (Belsky, 1985).

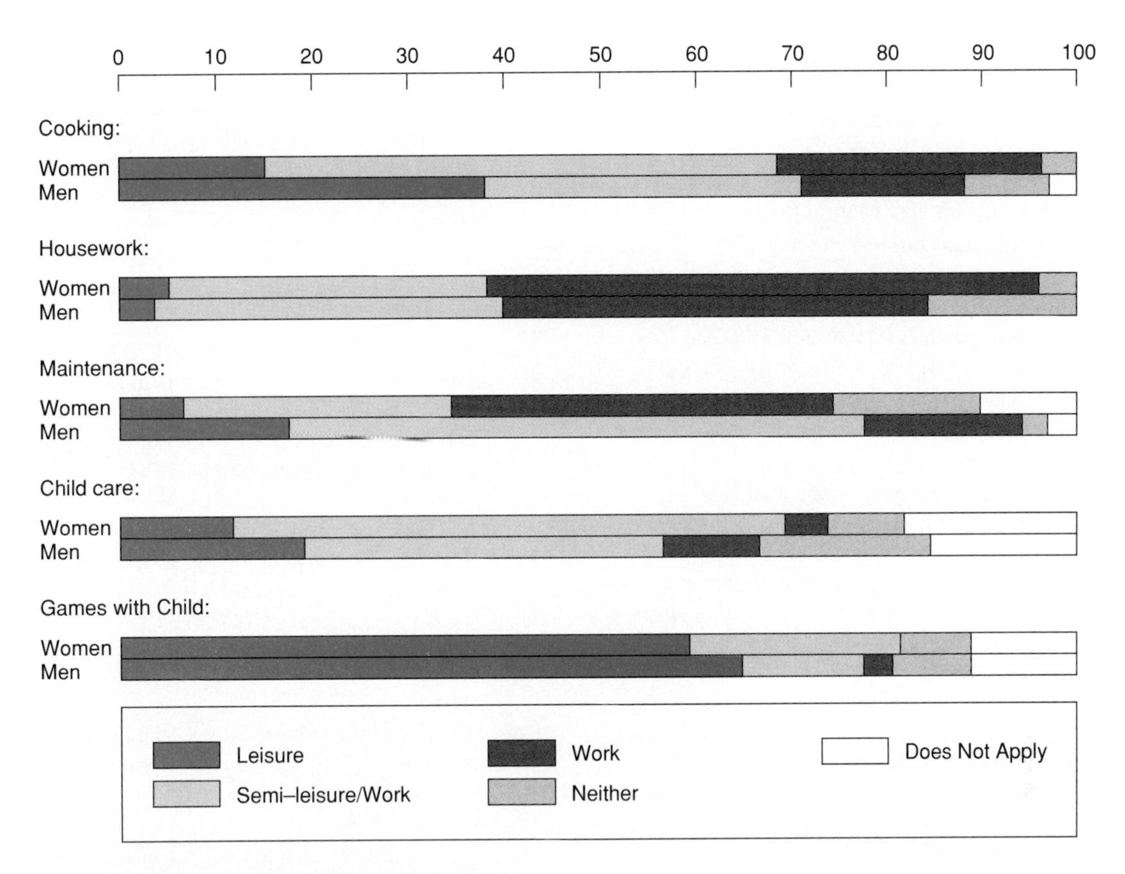

Figure 13.5 Perceptions of Select Homemaking and Child-Care Activities, by Gender and by Percent, in 1987

Summary

- Fertilization of the ovum begins a process that affects far more than the life begun. A missed menstrual period is only presumptive of pregnancy, but a pregnancy test can confirm the fact.
- The most important task confronting women during their first pregnancy is the acceptance and emotional incorporation of the fetus into their daily lives.
- Since the fetus receives its nutrients and food from the woman, it is extremely important that good nutritional habits exist during pregnancy.
- Pregnancies are divided into three 3-month segments called trimesters.
- After confirming a pregnancy, the medical management of the pregnancy will likely involve restrictions on the use of prescription and nonprescription medications; determination of the presence or absence of diseases, abnormal medical conditions, and the Rh blood factor; and the hormone levels of the woman.
- Congenital defects are more prevalent among infants born to women over age 40, with the most common types being Down's syndrome and Tay-Sachs disease. The diagnostic procedures for congenital defects include amniocentesis, ultrasound scanning, and chorionic villus sampling (CVS).
- The use of hospitals and general anesthesia for childbirth were popularized in the late 19th and early 20th century. Recent concerns about excessive medical intrusion into the natural process of birth have led to methods of natural or prepared childbirth and maternal birthing centers.
- Use of various medications during labor and delivery to alleviate pain poses a risk for the infant and influences the degree of interaction between the mother and the newborn.
- The overuse of cesarean sections, which now account for over one fifth of all births in the United States, is an emerging concern.
- The first stage of labor lasts from the onset of labor until the cervix dilates sufficiently for passage of the head. The second and third stages of labor involve the expulsion of the fetus and the placenta.
- Breast-feeding has gained in popularity with over one third of all mothers now breast-feeding their infants for 3 or more months. Advantages include enhancement of bonding between infant and mother, nutritional benefits for infant, reduction of uterus size, and psychological reaffirmation of womanhood for the mother.
- Social networks provide an important source of support for coping with stress related to the birth of a first child. Coping strategies for role conflict must be developed when mothers work outside the home.
- The transition into fatherhood is more traumatic and life altering for men than transition into marriage. With the changing gender roles in our society, men are assuming a greater degree of responsibility for child care.
- In general, marital satisfaction remains at the same level after the birth of a child as that prior to childbirth.

Questions for Critical Reflection

1. The sex of the unborn baby is frequently discerned through medical tests, yet some parents do not wish to know the results. How would you feel about this decision? Why?
2. The Grantly Dick-Reed book, *Childbirth Without Fear,* purports that without fear there is no pain and therefore no need for medication during childbirth unless complications arise. How does this fit with your beliefs or experience about childbirth? Are you aware of the basis of your feelings?
3. Knowing both the advantages of breast-feeding and the problems inherent for working mothers who breast-feed, what would you tell a friend who asked your opinion?
4. "Children change things!" Cite three examples of change you have witnessed in the relationship of a couple who recently became parents. Are there more positive or negative changes?
5. In Sweden, where 60% of women with children have jobs, the government provides day-care for children through the 9th grade. They also pay 90% of the parent's salary for a year so mom or dad can stay home. How can the United States, as the world's most technologically advanced society, defend its lack of support for families who have children? Whose problem is this?

Suggested Readings

Cunningham, F. G., MacDonald, P. C., & Gant, N. F. (1989). *Williams obstetrics* (18th ed.). Norwalk, CT: Appleton & Lange. A highly technical, but continuing classic, work in the field of obstetrics.

LaRossa, R., & LaRossa, M. (1981). *Transition to parenthood: How infants change families.* Beverly Hills: Sage. A longitudinal study of couples from pregnancy through 1st year with infant.

LeBoyer, F. (1975). *Birth without violence.* New York: Random House. A popular work that addresses traumatic effects of traditional childbirth procedures on infants.

Lyon, J. (1985). *Playing God in the nursery.* New York: Norton. A treatise on ethical issues associated with sustaining infants with severe congenital defects on life support systems.

Messenger, M. (1982). *The breast-feeding book.* New York: Van Nostrand Reinhold. A practical guide about breast-feeding.

Samuels, M., & Samuels, N. (1986). *The well-pregnancy book.* New York: Summit. An excellent and readable source about all facets of pregnancy.

CHAPTER 14

Child Rearing: Challenges and Concerns

Most people would never expect someone to perform a job as comparably complex as that of being a parent without substantial instruction. It would be like placing a third-grader in an atomic energy lab and expecting him to carry on research.
Jerry Bergman, 1985

OUTLINE

Preparation for Parenthood
1. The Need for Parent Education • 2. Parent Education • (Box 14.1: Dialogue with Bill Moyers and T. Berry Brazelton)

Framework for Successful Parenting
1. Parenting Perspectives

Defining Parenting Roles
1. Transition to Parenthood Role • 2. Role of Parents in Attachment • (Box 14.2: Differences between Securely and Insecurely Attached Children)

Clarifying and Attaining Parenting Goals
1. Influential Factors in Attaining Goals • (Box 14.3: Bringing up Fathers)

Principles of Child Development
1. Theoretical Perspectives • 2. Developmental Perspectives

Principles of Child Guidance
1. Methods of Child Guidance • 2. Child Discipline • (Box 14.4: General Guidelines for Noncorporal Punishment)

Contributions of Others to Child Rearing
1. Early Childhood Education Options • 2. Television as an Agent of Socialization

Child Abuse: Trends and Resolution
1. Prevalence and Risks of Child Abuse • 2. Predisposing Factors: Family Stress and Childhood Abuse

Incest: A Family Secret
1. Prevalence and Risk Factors of Incest • 2. Signs of Incest • 3. Types of Incest • 4. Aftermath of Incest

Summary

Questions for Critical Reflection

Suggested Readings

Quiz any parent: Is parenting a joy, a dilemma, a reaffirmation, or a stressful experience? Seasoned parents readily respond, "All of the above." Seldom, if ever, are young persons fully prepared for the ambivalence of parenthood. In fact, few persons are formally educated at all for this most awesome of life's tasks. For the vast majority of people, parenting is one of two significant life roles learned through on-the-job training with the role of spouse being the other. And even for those who are fast learners, by the time they begin to feel accomplished as a parent, a large part of their job is completed. This phenomenon is only a part of the paradox of parenting. Consider yet another absurdity. In no other role in life does success breed unemployment. When parents attain their goal of producing independent children who form new relations outside of the family, they work themselves out of a job (Moore, 1985d). Such is the nature of parenting.

The word **parenting** is often used interchangeably with acculturation, socialization, or **child-rearing practices.** It is the rearing of children within a family to conform to the social group in which they were born (Brink, 1982). The process, which involves complex attitudes and behaviors, is a composite of role, process, task, and skill. It is a role with prescribed functions; a process that involves nurturing; a task of creating an environment in which children can learn responsible social behavior; and a skill in the creative use of knowledge, experience, and technique (Horowitz, Hughes, & Perdue, 1982). The word "process" emphasizes that parenting is a continuous interaction between parent and child that changes both individuals. Thus, the parenting relationship is described as a social system since it is bidirectional with the child and parent each influencing the behavior of the other (Brooks, 1987).

Since parents and early childhood experiences within the family are most important in shaping the personality and behavior of a child, logic dictates that the parenting role is highly significant to the welfare of individuals. Family historians argue that what happens in child rearing influences not only the child but also what happens historically in society. In fact, child-rearing practices have been identified as the central force for change in history (McCoy, E., 1985). Nevertheless, the role of parenthood is not assigned a correspondingly high priority in our society as evidenced by lack of social support for parents (LeMasters & DeFrain, 1983). Advocates of a national family policy believe that public attitudes are changing and that by the end of this century it will be "conventional wisdom to invest in our children" (Footlick, 1989, p. 20).

Preparation for Parenthood

Those who question the need for formal education to perform a practice as natural and as old as humanity itself argue that countless generations have reared families successfully without parent education. Such an assumption is only partially correct. While there have always been healthy families as well as unhealthy ones, neither happens by accident. The way that children are reared and the way that future parents learn about child rearing are two basic functions in our society that have recently undergone dramatic change (Karpowitz, 1980). Children who formerly grew up in a world of continuity where the home was the workplace learned to parent by observing the process in action. In today's technological society, with its breakdown in cultural traditions and changing family forms, the functions of the family have been altered to the extent that it is no longer feasible to learn all that one needs to know about parenting through modeling and experience (Ellwood, 1983; Papalia & Olds, 1990).

Another related fact is that, presently, there is a great storehouse of knowledge about child rearing upon which parents can base their decisions. This knowledge results from more than a century of research in the science of child development. In this respect, today's parents can be expected to do a better job than their parents. However, since a multitude of societal factors impinge upon the ability to succeed in parenting, young people today may justifiably claim their job to be far more difficult because of an increasingly complex and changing society (Hamner & Turner, 1990). Discovering facts about child development and those sociological factors affecting parenting is not enough. This knowledge must be communicated to parents of all socioeconomic, ethnic, and racial backgrounds who live in widely varying family forms. Such responsibility is the task of parent education. There has long been a concern about the lack of preparation for parenthood (Rossi, 1968). Sadly, the amount of information in our children's educational process concerning successful family life, including sex education, child care, interpersonal competence, and empathy, is still woefully inadequate.

The Need for Parent Education

Among the early proponents of parent education, English educator A. S. Neill declared that **delinquency** may have its origins in the nursery:

But how can we blame such parents when their entire education never touched the most important job in the world—the job of bringing up children. . . . If every therapist in the world were to do nothing but educate parents about child psychology, telling them primarily what not to do with their children, there would be little need for adult therapy of any kind (1964, pp. 174–175).

Research has long substantiated the seminal role of parents in providing life experiences that contribute to the social-emotional adjustment of their child. However, it was not until the 1970s that scientists widened their focus to study the relationship between a child's intellectual development and methods of child rearing. A review of 12 observational studies of mother-infant interaction points to the positive role played by attentive, warm, stimulating, responsive, and nonrestrictive mothering in fostering intellectual development (Belsky, 1981). One study revealed several aspects of mothering during the earliest periods of childhood to be related to IQ: providing appropriate play materials in the home, avoidance of restriction and punishment, variety in daily stimulation, and organization of the environment (Bradley, Caldwell, & Elardo, 1977). Others found that as the level of mother and infant interaction increases, the infant's IQ or development score likewise tends to be higher (Clarke-Stewart, 1977). From a review of numerous studies, one authority concluded that the father's influence may at times exceed that of the mother in certain areas of development such as quantitative skills (Hamilton, 1977). Fathers exert a particularly strong influence on competence in problem solving (Easterbrooks & Goldberg, 1984). Researchers at the Princeton Educational Laboratory, studying methods of child rearing and the intellectual development of infants, concluded:

A course in every public high school in the United States covering current work in this field [parenting] might do more to raise the intellectual level and emotional well-being of the next generation of children than any other single improvement in education.

(Fremon, 1971, p. 85)

Over the past two decades many behavioral and social scientists have urged that family life training should become a required course for every student, female and male (Fantini & Cardenas, 1980; Jensen & Kingston, 1986). Although more people become parents than any other "occupation," it appears that most educational institutions have never felt the need to stress parent education. In many schools, hundreds of hours of mathematics instruction are given to children, while not one hour is devoted to understanding human relationships. It is puzzling why schools require training in other living skills such as driver education, while neglecting an area that so profoundly influences the emotional health of individuals within a society (Moore, 1989). This practice is difficult to justify since accumulated research not only substantiates the indisputable need for parent education but also attests to the efficacy of good programs (Harman & Brim, 1980; Sheek, 1984). A parent's knowledge of child development has repeatedly been found to be positively related to her/his abilities to provide an environment for the child that promotes healthy development (Stevens, 1984). It is important to understand what education for parenthood is and the part that parent-training programs play in fulfilling the needs of parents today.

Parent Education

Parent education, one component of family life education, is defined as "instruction to develop an understanding of physical, mental, emotional, social, economic and psychological aspects of interpersonal relationships . . . between persons of various ages" (Sheek, 1984, p. 1). Areas within family life education which are highly interrelated with parenting competencies include communication, human growth and development, understanding self, marriage and family dynamics, human sexuality, values, decision making, and management of resources (Sheek, 1984). The goal of parent education, enabling parents to rear happy, healthy children who become fully functioning, productive adults, is important for individuals and society. In accomplishing this aim, parent education acts as a catalyst to effect change in parents' performance of their roles. It is true that parents most often "do unto their children what was done unto them" without exploring options or consequences. But with education in guidance techniques, parents may consciously choose different methods. For example, a "time out" may be used to deal with their child's misbehavior rather than to instinctively spank. Acquired knowledge helps parents replace behavior that is guided solely by internalized values and cultural traditions with a carefully chosen rational role. In determining this rationale, parents need not ignore the collected wisdom of their cultural heritage or personal experience. However, parents do need to carefully examine their backgrounds for

BOX 14.1 Dialogue with Bill Moyers and T. Berry Brazelton

Renowned television journalist Bill Moyers talks with the widely acclaimed "Dean of American Pediatricians," T. Berry Brazelton, professor of Pediatrics at Harvard University, and chief of the Child Development Unit at Boston Children's Hospital. Brazelton has authored the Brazelton Behavioral Scale, a test for newborns, and books for parents which have been used around the world.

Moyers: You started your career caring for babies as individuals, but in the last couple of years you've been concerned with the families in which babies live. Why have you changed your emphasis?

Brazelton: Families are really suffering. The family is where we've got to turn to try to give kids a different future than the one we've provided in the past.

Moyers: It now takes two full-time wage earners to buy essentially what one check would buy up until the early 1970s. This is not altogether just a matter of choice, is it? There is an economic imperative that drives both parents out into the market now.

Brazelton: I think 50% of the women in this country don't have a choice; they have to work. Another 20–30% might have a choice."

Moyers: You still believe that women should be with their newborns for at least the first year. Yet you've said that for economic reasons they have to get out into the marketplace. That seems to be an irreconcilable contradiction.

Brazelton: It is at this point. But it wouldn't be if national and state governments, individual businesses, and families were willing to share the cost of making it possible for women or men to stay home long enough to know, "That baby is my baby."

Moyers: Why are those first few months so important?

Brazelton: First, they're terribly important to adults. Adults about to have a baby go through a real inner turmoil: "Will I ever get to be a parent? I sure don't want to be like my parents." And then, of course, they always are.

Moyers: Is the family that bonds early more likely, as the years come and go, to function together?

Brazelton: I would think so, wouldn't you? What I'm saying, though, is more subtle than that. Bonding is falling in love, but attachment is hard work.

Moyers: What does the child miss if she or he doesn't bond with the mother and father?

Brazelton: What a child needs is this: Every time they do something, somebody should be there to say, "Hey, that was great." This helps a child to have an inner sense of having achieved something, like learning to walk. If somebody's there to say "You are great!" she/he gets a double-barreled shot of, "Wow, I am important." All of that contributes to a sense of competence in the child. If she/he doesn't have that through infancy, she/he never gets that later on and grows up with a sense of, "It doesn't matter what I do." They expect to fail. We can see a sense of failure in kids as early as nine months of age. Those kids, we can predict, will become difficult in school; they'll never succeed in school; they'll make everybody angry; they'll become delinquents later.

Moyers: What would happen to society if Harvard produced parents with the same skill, zeal, and financial support with which it produces MBAs?

Brazelton: I've been over at the Business school for the past two or three years, teaching the second-year class. It's 50% women now. So I show them a baby, and I show them this period when the baby and mother get locked in with each other, and the father gets locked in. At the end of that class, all of these kids are sitting forward, and they're saying, "Oh my God! We're on the fast track. How are we going to do this with our kids?" If they really think about it, they can figure out how to nurture and still be on the fast track. I don't think we're going to have to give up the fast track, but I think we have to balance it.

Moyers: Fundamentalists say, "Woman, get back in the home." Feminists say, "Woman, get out there in the marketplace, go for it like everyone else." I've heard both groups damn you.

Brazelton: That's right, I have, too. But you realize what you're saying—we're an either/or society, and we don't look for the compromise. We're an either/or society because we've left everything up to the individual. We're going to have to look at our governments as supplementing families, not pushing them to make either/or choices.

learned parenting behaviors and delete any that may be counterproductive to achieving overall goals for their child. Parenting strategies that lead to negative results are behaviors that are usually contrary to scientifically established facts (Mead, 1976). Everyone has a list of "things I will never say to my child." The irony is that unless patterns are consciously changed, these very words will survive to surface under stress. But beyond eliminating detrimental behaviors, parents must learn appropriate ways to accomplish their goals. This is the role of parent education.

Progress began in educational programs for parents just prior to this century as several social movements contributed to the breakdown of cultural traditions in child-rearing practices. Such factors included change in status of women, decline of intergenerational family relations, and social mobility of different ethnic and socio-economic groups with contrasting concepts of child rearing (Jensen & Kingston, 1986). At that time, child development research furnished burgeoning evidence of better ways of rearing children, and parent education became an area of academic concern. Thus, the stage was set for a variety of nonschool parent-education programs to emerge. Although parents learn from many informal methods including group participation, lectures, books, films, radio, newspapers, and television, parent-training programs are a more formal approach to parent education (Hamner & Turner, 1990). Highly-educated women are more likely than women with lower education to prepare for parenthood by taking courses and reading books. However, no relationship has been found between a father's educational level and the likelihood of knowledge acquisition about successful parenting (Simons, Whitbeck, Conger, & Melby, 1990).

"The first problem I see is one of communication. . ."

From *Family Therapy Today*, 4(4):10. Copyright © 1989 PM Inc. Publishers, Van Nuys, CA. Reprinted by permission.

Parent-Training Programs

The major strengths of parent-training programs are their preventive approach and the focus on problems common to all parents (LeMasters & DeFrain, 1983). The goal of these programs is simply to enable children and parents to relate to each other (Fritz, 1985). Two of the more widespread parent-training programs are Parent Effectiveness Training (P.E.T.) and Systematic Training for Effective Parenting (STEP).

Parent Effectiveness Training (P.E.T) uses parent-training groups to teach parents how to listen to their children through use of the language of acceptance and active listening. For example, if a child indicates that she/he does not feel like eating because her/his stomach hurts, the parent may respond with the language of acceptance by saying, "You are feeling sort of tense today?" Through active listening, the parent identifies the actual source of difficulty and works toward its resolution. P.E.T. emphasizes a positive **self-concept** for the child as well as self-actualization for both child and parents (Gordon, 1970). Mutual encouragement and support of peers, often occurring outside the parent-training group, helps to bring about positive and lasting results (Fritz, 1985). Criticisms of P.E.T. include the charge that the "no-lose" method of conflict resolution, which teaches negotiation, may prove to be unrealistic if the issue at hand is not readily amenable to compromise. Others believe that it fails to adequately account for value conflicts that may exist between children and parents (Knox, 1988).

Systematic Training for Effective Parenting (STEP) programs establish parent study groups to discuss and practice the essential skills for good parent-child relationships. Skilled STEP parents encourage the child to make her/his own decisions and to manage life constructively, participate in effective communication with child, engage in effective listening, acknowledge feelings of child, and use "I" messages (Dinkmeyer & McKay, 1976a). It will be remembered that an "I" message shows ownership of the problem and avoids placing blame. The STEP goal is the establishment of a democratic family atmosphere whereby the parent(s) present(s) the child with choices for which the child must accept the logical consequences. Essential elements suggested for building positive relationships with a child include displaying mutual respect, taking time for fun, encouraging progression toward maturity, and communicating love (Dinkmeyer & McKay, 1976b).

Framework for Successful Parenting

There has been a movement away from simplistic explanations of unidirectional cause and effect in parent-child relationships. Children are now viewed as important determinants of their parents' behavior (Lerner & Spanier, 1978). In fact, "from birth, infants and parents begin the process of socializing each other for a relationship that will be of primary importance throughout their lives" (Walters & Walters, 1980, p. 810). While parent-child relationships were formerly thought to be exclusively a function of parental guidance, in reality, there are a variety of physiological, psychological, and societal influences. Nevertheless, it is parents who orchestrate this process called socialization.

Since the aim of parenting is socialization, parents need to understand this seminal process through which the child learns to function in society. The socialization process depends upon a number of interrelated factors including learning and communication. Learning is the **developmental change** in the organism that occurs over time through interaction with significant others. Communication occurs in emotionally significant relationships and is shaped by social groups. Universally, socialization must accomplish two things: competence and commitment (Elkin & Handel, 1989). In every society, the young must be taught the skills to enable competent participation in life. But these skills alone are insufficient. A society will fail unless its young are motivated to a commitment to sustain responsive participation in the society. Although socialization teaches the child to behave in socially acceptable ways, such as appropriate times and places to dress and undress, to laugh, or to cry it is more than merely imparting rules of behavior. It also teaches children about themselves and their culture (Fantini & Cardenas, 1980). This process through which the child's biological potentialities are melded with social realities is best described by Erik Erikson's (1980) eight stages of psychosocial development to be considered later in this chapter.

Parenting Perspectives

In today's complex world, there are no simplistic prescriptions to assure the success of parents in the socialization process. It is an enormous task with which parents are charged: to choose from the many alternate systems of child rearing, a workable one for them—a dynamic approach open to change and based on the latest available knowledge. Faced with an awesome amount of information, parents are often overwhelmed. But they do not have to be "superpersons" to do a good job of parenting. Fortunately, ordinary people will do (Hymes, 1985). A proper perspective is easier if parents remember two truisms: patterns of parental behavior are more meaningful to outcomes than isolated single events, and children are resilient. Fortunately for less than perfect parents, children can endure more than a few mistakes and still emerge as healthy adults (Chess, 1983). Above all else, the parents' pilgrimage with their child should be based on a mix of science and art which combines the best of both—head and heart.

In the absence of magic formulas, there are six basic competencies which provide a framework to enhance such possibilities (see Table 14.1). From those basic competencies identified in the literature as enabling parents to accomplish their goals, several will be used as organizing principles for the remaining sections of this chapter.

Self-Awareness and Self-Acceptance

Earlier chapters have emphasized the importance of the attainment of **self-awareness** to healthy adjustment. The same principles of adjustment which enhance one's chances of success in marriage also apply to parenthood. Regardless of the roles played in life, whether spouse, parent, child, or others from a vast array of possibilities, success is largely related to how one feels about self. To "know thyself," being able to realistically assess one's strengths and weaknesses, begins the journey toward emotional maturity. To accept the less than perfect self is the second step (Moore, 1976). Parents must first answer the question "Who am I?" before they can facilitate self-awareness in their offspring.

Many persons are emotionally mature and ready for parenthood, having been reared by parents who were themselves mature and able to foster a sense of self-worth and social responsibility in their children. However, for those less fortunate, a greater sense of self-worth and emotional maturity may still be attained. While acquiring such qualities in adulthood is more difficult and time-consuming than in childhood, it can be done.

The process of self-awareness and self-acceptance can be facilitated by attending to three inner tasks: allow emotions to be felt without denial; trace the origin and meaning of feelings, using as clues one's innermost fears and desires; and consciously choose to act or not act while expressing feelings in appropriate ways (Crosby, 1979). Although the literature is replete

Table 14.1: Basic Competencies for Parents

Self-awareness and acceptance	Understanding and accepting self, parents can fulfill personal potential and best facilitate child's life.
Role definition	Defining role and understanding significance of relationship with child enables wiser parenting decisions, making parenting easier and more pleasant.
Goal clarification	Clarifying personal and societal goals for child enables parents to better attain them. In haste to "humanize" child, parent(s) must not neglect to nurture child's creativity.
Principles of development	Applying principles of development and essential needs that govern behavior at each stage makes child's job of growing up easier and more pleasant.
Principles of guidance	Understanding purposes and principles of guidance and using appropriate techniques enables parents to achieve ultimate goals for child. Parents cannot undo mistakes but can modify attitudes and behavior by changing environment and experiences.
Philosophy of parenting	Developing a flexible philosophy of parenting enables parents to learn from mistakes and choose more valid methods based on latest available knowledge.

Source: N. B. Moore, "As the Twig is Nurtured" in *Beginnings: For Parents of Babies, Creepers, and Toddlers*, 5(3):4–5, 1986c.

with various prescriptions for improving how one feels about self, three admonitions appear repeatedly: accept responsibility for self-growth, recognize and reaffirm the significance of interpersonal relationships, and learn and use the skills of good communication (Moore, 1976). Such accomplishments should be priorities for parents who wish to model principles of good mental health for their children. Beyond this base of good personal adjustment, persons must have a clear awareness of their parental role in order to succeed as a parent.

Defining Parenting Roles

The Danish philosopher Kierkegaard once said that it is a satire on mankind that Providence has endowed almost every child richly because it knew in advance what was to befall the child: to be brought up by parents, to be made a mess of in every way (Rasmusson, 1970). The family has long been viewed as the keystone of mental health. L. K. Frank, often called the father of the parent education movement, lamented, "The family is so crucial in personality development that it can be and so often is destructive. . . . The parents did not seek maliciously and intentionally to ruin their children and indeed are often horrified and crushed by the outcome" (1956, p. 613).

The special significance of early experiences on later human development and the crucial role of parents in their child's life has remained a substantive research issue transcending the passage of time (Walters & Walters, 1980). As a result, there has been a growing conviction that the parent is the child's first and most important teacher (Hymes, 1985). It is accepted that the home is the laboratory of life in which parents are the master teachers and the child is the apprentice. Most sobering for parents, however, is the idea that no neutral lessons exist, that either positive or negative lessons are learned daily. Since the role of the parent is crucial to successful outcomes for the child, clarifying this role is essential (Moore, 1985a).

Transition to Parenthood Role

Defining boundaries within the mother-father-child triangle can ease the tension in relationships precipitated by the transition to parenthood roles. It has been demonstrated that with parenting, the emphasis in a couple's relationship is likely to change from a romantic to a practical partnership because of diffusing time demands (Belsky, Spanier, & Rovine, 1983). This ability of the marital or family system to change its role relationships, power structure, and relationship rules in response to situational and developmental stress is called adaptability (Olson, 1982). **Cohesion** (emotional bonding) and adaptability are two crucial behaviors in family interaction that affect family well-being, especially at transition points.

The balance between individual **autonomy** and couple mutuality, developed during the initial period of marriage, is believed important in establishing healthy parenting roles. The quality of parent-child relationships and the extent of gender-role segregation of duties between parents are both affected if proper balance of individual needs and couple cohesion are not attained (Rossi, 1968). Although the arrival of a baby can create marital stress, it can also lead to a sense of fulfillment. For most couples, the parenthood role adds new meaning and strengthens the bonds between wife and husband. There are, however, obvious differences in becoming a parent when age, martial status, and financial conditions vary. For example, the stress of single parenting at age 16 is quite different from that experienced by a couple in their early 30s. Effective parenting can be adversely affected by such factors as depression, employment instability, marital dissatisfaction, and the child being perceived as difficult. For example, mothers who report satisfying, supportive relationships with their husbands are more likely to be sensitive and responsive to the needs of their children. (Simons, Whitbeck, Conger & Melby, 1990).

Nevertheless, the coping strategies for the period of transition to parenthood role are somewhat the same, regardless of circumstances: being adaptable, integrating shared responsibilities with usual nonparenting activities, using social supports, and looking to the future (Miller & Sollie, 1985).

The first of two unique characteristics of the parenthood role is that healthy parental behaviors necessarily will change with the developmental needs and stages of growth for the child. For example, protective mother or father behaviors, essential for an infant, may no longer be needed and, therefore, inappropriate and detrimental for an autonomy-seeking toddler. A second unique feature of the parental role is that its termination is not signaled by any specific act. In fact, there are few cultural prescriptions dictating when the authority or obligations of a parent end. For the most part, with the birth of a child, one assumes an irrevocable role. There are ex-spouses and ex-in-laws but no ex-children or ex-parents (Hamner & Turner, 1990). Socialization is a lifelong process that parents increasingly share with persons and agencies outside the family (Mead, 1976). However, the role that parents play in this process is seminal. No life event or circumstance more significantly affects their child's success in later life than do parents.

Role of Parents in Attachment

Historically, attachment theory developed as a variation of object-relations theory. Over thirty years ago, British psychiatrist John Bowlby revolutionized the understanding of human development by scientifically demonstrating that the nature of early bonds with parents plays a crucial role throughout life. According to attachment theory, if parents provide a secure emotional base, while encouraging and supporting their child to seek autonomy, she/he will grow up psychologically stable and able to make the most of life's experiences (Bowlby, 1988). During the 1970s and 1980s, attachment theory was elaborated by numerous researchers using clinical procedures to assess infant-parent attachment (Belsky, 1990). Infants and toddlers with secure attachments are more sociable and ready to interact with friendly, unfamiliar adults and agemates. Preschool and early elementary-age children with secure attachment histories behave more confidently when challenged, are more active and independent in exploring new settings, are less emotionally dependent on teachers in preschool, and are less likely to be judged by parents and/or teachers to have serious behavior problems (Belsky, 1990). Infant-to-mother affection, which is believed to slowly develop in the 1st year of life, is called attachment. This process is said to involve "trustful focused relationships to specific pepople, marked by preferences or contact seeking, separation protest, greeting and the desire to be held" (Lamb, Pleck, & Levine, 1985, p. 143).

For optimal development during the 1st year of an infant's life, a secure attachment with another person, usually the mother, must be formed (Ainsworth, 1979). Conditions necessary for the development of this attachment are adequate affectionate and sensitive responses to the baby's signals from a caregiver. This requires a person who accepts the child's natural behavior, is aware of their own individuality, and is thus capable of orchestrating harmonious interactions between self and infant (Belsky, 1990). Although "adequate" is not yet clearly defined, observations of "normal" families reveal that as the level of interaction characterized by affection and responsiveness increases, the better will be the results (Papalia & Olds, 1990). The evidence also suggests that attachment develops more easily if there are only a few caregivers who continue for a substantial period of time. Therefore, when alternative child care is used at this age, parents should be especially sensitive to the quality of their limited interaction with the child and the quality of care provided by the substitute caregiver (Clarke-Stewart, 1982). Although the amount of time is less significant than the quality of time between the attachment figure and the infant, indisputably a certain amount of time is required to assure quality time.

Bonding is the name for the mother-to-infant attachment that is also highly significant to the infant's well-being (Clarke-Stewart & Friedman, 1987). It has been characterized by T. Berry Brazelton as "falling in love" with the infant (Moyers, 1989). This strong emotional attachment allows mothers to better tolerate the stress inherent in child rearing and to provide the loving care so essential to the child's development (Crawford, 1982). Since research suggests bonding is related to the birthing process, including initial contact and early interaction with the infant, maternity procedures may

BOX 14.2 | **Differences Between Securely and Insecurely Attached Children**

Sociability with peers. Up through age 6, securely attached children show consistently higher rates of social behaviors and greater popularity with peers.

Self-esteem. Securely attached children have higher self-esteem at ages 4–5.

Flexibility and resourcefulness. Securely attached children rate higher in "ego resiliency" at ages 4–5.

Dependency. Insecurely attached children show more "clinging" attention seeking as well as "negative attention seeking" (getting attention by being "bad") in preschool years.

Tantrums and aggressive behavior. Insecurely attached children show more evidence of negative, aggressive behaviors.

Compliance and good behavior. Securely attached children easier to manage.

Empathy. More empathy toward other children and adults by secure children.

Behavior problems. At age 6, behavior problems more common among boys who were insecurely attached as infants.

Self-recognition. At age 2, insecurely attached children show earlier self-recognition in mirror suggesting that they may be more individuated than attached.

Sociability with strange adult. Securely attached children show faster and smoother interaction with strange adult during preschool years.

Problem solving. Securely attached toddlers show longer attention span in free play and more confidence in attempting solutions to tasks involving tool use.

Symbolic play. Secure children show more mature and complex play at ages 18–30 months.

Sources: As appeared in H. Bee, *The Developing Child,* 5th ed. New York: Harper & Row, Publishers, Inc., 1989, p. 413. Data from Easterbrooks and Goldberg, 1987; Lewis, Feiring, McGoffog, and Jaskir, 1984; Lewis, Brooks-Gunn, and Jaskir, 1985; Londerville and Main, 1981; Lutkenhaus, Grossman, and Grossman, 1985; Matas, Arend, and Sroufe, 1978; Pastor, 1981; Slade, 1987; and Sroufe, 1983.

foster or impede such development. **Rooming-in** arrangements whereby the newborn stays with the mother instead of in the nursery have been found to contribute positively to such attachments (Klaus & Kennell, 1981). While some mothers have been found to achieve closer bonding with their infants after early extended contact, other research has failed to confirm the theory of a "critical period" for bonding (Papalia & Olds, 1990). Even so, the fascination with and belief in early bonding remains a strong impetus for research (Morrison, 1990). Both the resiliency of the human organism and social learning theory, which maintains that human learning is more complex than simple conditioning, offer a balanced perspective to the questions of attachment. Since the first few months are crucial for the development of the parent's bonding, full-time daycare during this period would not be advisable for parents who have an option (Moyers, 1989).

Parent-Child Interaction

Observations and analyses of parent-infant interactions began less than 50 years ago. Studies have now moved from analyses of single behaviors and discrete time units to more global approaches (Brazelton & Cramer, 1990). The 1980s trend of examining the behaviors of the mother and father as a system is thought to offer a better understanding of influences impacting infant development. However, to date, remarkably consistent findings indicate that sensitive caregiving is the most significant variable enabling the infant to develop the trust necessary for optimal development.

Belsky (1990) concluded from his review of research during the 1980s that data consistently documents associations between early infant-mother attachment security and subsequent competence. In terms of the mother-child dyad, children who are securely attached to their mothers during infancy tend to score higher on measures of initiative, skill, and getting along with other children in nursery schools as compared to insecurely attached children (Cassidy & Main, 1984; LaFreniere & Sroufe, 1985). A child's popularity is also related to appropriate parenting attitudes and skills of mothers and, to a lesser degree, those of fathers. Children who are rejected and isolated by their peers tend to be from families in which mothers have low self-confidence in their parenting skills (Peery, Jensen, & Adams, 1985). Conversely, more positive and less disagreeable mothers who focused conversations with their first-grade children on feelings had more popular offspring (Putallaz, 1987). A large number of studies also underscore the importance of parents' emotional support and sensitive responsiveness in the socio-emotional development of children (Belsky, 1990). Longitudinal studies furnish evidence that the effects of supportive and unsupportive care may extend well

Infancy: "That magical period in life when the view from the top feels safe and secure."

beyond childhood. One study began with female third-graders who experienced rejection, authoritarian parental care and/or failed to identify with their parents. These subjects had higher levels of depression at age 19 and lower levels of ego development at ages 30–31 (Dubow, Huesmann, & Eron, 1987).

A major factor in the lack of more caregiving by fathers is related to the assumption that mothers are natural, expert caregivers and that infants are capable of forming attachments only to their mothers (Kabatznick, 1985). Conversely, studies over the past 2 decades have confirmed that infants typically form attachment to both parents at about the same time, ages 6–8 months. However, there were preferences for the mother when infants were distressed and have a choice between the two parents (Belsky, 1979; Lamb, 1976). Where a secure parent-child relationship exists at age 3, children are equally likely to initiate social exchanges with their mothers or fathers and to remain securely attached throughout adolescence. They are also more curious, persistent, and enthusiastic (Clarke-Stewart & Hevey, 1981; Lamb, Pleck, & Levine, 1985). Studies comparing mother-infant behaviors to father-infant behaviors have discovered more similarities than differences even though fathers do tend to engage in more vigorous motion play (Ricks, 1985). The range of behaviors of fathers toward their infants is wide—caregivers, teachers, playmates, or strangers—though the significance of their involvement in infant care has only recently begun to receive attention from developmental psychologists (Clarke-Stewart & Friedman, 1987). If fathers provide extra stimulation during infancy, the infant is more likely to discriminate faces and sounds at an earlier age, to develop a greater tolerance for fear-arousing stimuli, to have an easier time when establishing trusting relationships, and to possess increased cognitive capacities. Achievement motivation, self-confidence, and more flexible attitudes toward female-male roles also result from father-child attachment (Lamb, 1981). Infants have been found to have higher IQ's at age 1 if their fathers have been significantly involved in their care. This IQ gain is also documented at age 7 when the child performs better in school and has a heightened sense of humor (Moyers, 1989). The importance of father-child interaction is not dependent upon the quantity of time spent together but rather a sensitivity on the part of the father and infant to each other's behavioral signals and paternal playfulness (Lamb, Pleck, & Levine, 1985).

Men, however, need encouragement in this nurturing process since their socialization experiences generally hamper the development of such skills. Mothers should avoid "gate keeping" or subtly closing out fathers. This may occur with remarks like "Darling, that's not the way to diaper a baby" or "Hold her this way, not that way." An already vulnerable father may internalize such messages as "I knew I couldn't do it right" and eventually with enough interference, quit trying (Moyers, 1989).

Clarifying and Attaining Parenting Goals

Clearly delineated goals are necessary not only to determine direction in life but also to provide a base line from which to measure their accomplishment. At no time is this task more essential than in parenting. What is known about goals and parenting? Certain general assumptions can be made: parenting goals are both personal and societal in nature, determining goals requires ethical decisions while attaining them depends on scientific answers, and multiple factors influence goal attainment (Moore, 1985b).

All parents have personal goals for their child growing out of their own composite life experiences. Although parents are supposedly free to choose goals for their children they are not always able to do so. Their own cultural backgrounds and other life circumstances such as health, economics, natural disaster, or war may limit their ability to choose (Papalia & Olds, 1990). Equally as influential as personal goals of parents are societal goals: expectations based on the norms and values within our society. For instance, certain characteristics are expected of individuals by adulthood. In a democracy, it is assumed that a mature person will be a law-abiding, loyal citizen with democratic values (Elkin & Handel, 1989).

Understanding the duality of both short-term and long-term goals helps parents attain them. Although personal goals vary, most parents agree that the short-term goal is a healthy, coping child in the present environment, while the long-term goal is a happy, healthy, fully functioning adult. The complex challenge is to select methods of guidance leading to attainment of both goals (Moore, 1985b). For example, in the interest of short-term goals, it is far easier for parents who are obviously older and wiser to make all of the daily decisions for their child. However, if the child is eventually to become a fully functioning adult who can make wise decisions, she/he must have some practice in making age-appropriate decisions and experiencing their logical consequences.

If parents are to achieve ultimate, long-term goals for their child, they must also affirm creativity, the flip side of the coin of socialization. **Creativity** is the ability to see things in a new way; to see problems no one else has recognized; and to solve them with unusual, effective solutions (Hargreaves, 1989). Since the future of society may well depend upon such innovative characteristics, it is important for parents to nurture their child's creative expression as the wellspring of self-actualization in adulthood. To do so, parents must supply enough love and security to allow the child to venture beyond social norms and guidance methods of "freedom within controls." Specific strategies are suggested to foster creativity in young children: demonstrate to the child that creative thinking is valued by openness to new ideas, allow the child to make mistakes without recriminations, encourage constructive expression of nonconforming, independent behavior, encourage **divergent** (moving outward in different directions) as well as **convergent** (move toward same conclusion) thinking, and nurture child's capacity for fantasy until it matures into creativity (Moore, 1971).

While scientific research in child development makes possible the attainment of the various goals parents and society have for children, determining goals remains an ethical question with answers rooted in personal values. Educational achievement, religion, manners, and morals are examples of specific areas in which parents' values influence their children. The circular effect of parent-child socialization is evidenced when parenting itself raises value issues that individuals have not previously clarified. Therefore, parenting may evoke values clarification, leading to personal change and growth (Mead, 1976).

Once goals are determined, established scientific facts can be useful in attaining them. For example, if parents value emotional security for their child, knowledge of related research facts offers valuable guidance. Finding that parental warmth positively relates to a child's social and emotional development may prompt a change in parenting behaviors (Quinton & Rutter, 1984). Or since studies have identified the most effective parenting pattern for facilitating school success and intellectual development, knowledgeable parents may consciously choose to adopt such practices. If so, they would therefore be nurturing, responsive, and stimulating without being too restrictive, overly controlling, or too directive (Turner & Harris, 1984). In addition, research in the field of mental health has provided scientific evidence concerning the relationship of extremes in parental practices to distorted personalities in children. Given such information, parents could avoid rejection, domination, over-protection, and over-indulgence which respectively can lead to insecure, immature, dependent, and selfish child behaviors (Maccoby & Martin, 1983). However, scientific evidence must always be applied with caution. While certain parenting styles are found to be associated with certain child characteristics, they do not demonstrate causality. Children, parents, the family unit, and the larger environment are all developing, changing organisms which influence each other (Jensen & Kingston, 1986).

Influential Factors in Attaining Goals

Both child and parent(s) bring certain characteristics to the process of parenting that will affect outcomes. The infant comes complete with inborn sexual characteristics, patterns of growth, birth-order position, and temperament (Brooks, 1987). The unique individual that parents take home from the hospital may be modified by many factors such as a pink or blue blanket but never completely changed. Personalities of parents and other family members also substantially affect the attainment of goals for children. Ordinal position, whether an only, first, middle, or last child, is another influential factor which has been studied. Finally, although the total character of home, siblings, family size, socioeconomic, and cultural background factors influence the outcomes of socialization, none do so more than child-rearing practices (Mead, 1976).

Influence of Temperament

Genetic endowment is known to account for considerable variance of personality as exhibited in early **temperament.** Temperamental qualities are inborn characteristic ways of reacting to the world (Brooks, 1987). Three broad categories of infant temperament patterns have been delineated: easy, difficult, and slow-to-warm-up (Chess & Thomas, 1984). An easy infant displays a positive mood, adapts readily, does not react negatively to small discomforts and frustrations, and gets hungry and sleepy at about the same time each day. In contrast, a difficult infant cries often, has very irregular feeding and sleep schedules, has considerable difficulty adapting to new people and places, and is typically described as having a negative mood. Finally, a slow-to-warm-up infant takes longer to adjust to new people or places, follows a moderately irregular feeding and sleep schedule, withdraws at first when someone approaches, and typically displays a mildly negative mood. These three temperament patterns are found to exist without regard to social class, child-rearing style, or infant sex (Chess & Thomas, 1984). New parents who perceive their infant as difficult are less likely to feel in control of their lives than before childbirth occurred (Sirignano & Lachman, 1985). Further, if the child is difficult as an infant, mothers will put less effort into teaching the child as she/he grows older (Maccoby, Snow, & Jacklin, 1984).

Influence of Birth Order

Birth order affects both parent-child relationships and sibling characteristics. The uniqueness theory suggests that first-born and last-born children enjoy an inherent uniqueness in birth order, facilitating status, recognition, and attention by parents and other siblings (Bee, 1989). Parents treat first-born children differently than later borns. With first-born children, parents are not only more anxious, but they also use more achievement pressure, coercive discipline, and restrictive methods of child rearing. They provide more child-centered environments with more total and complex language, especially during infancy. With the birth of a second child, there is usually less interaction between wife and husband as well as the mother and the newborn infant (Dunn, 1983). Findings suggest that of all ordinal positions, middle-born children need to be given more attention by parents (Bell & Avery, 1985).

Numerous studies have found that birth order affects personality development regardless of social class, sex of siblings, or size of families (Schiamberg, 1988). Firstborns have been found to be more achievement-oriented, conscientious, prone to guilt feelings, conforming to social pressures, cooperative, and responsible. They are also typically more dominant (Henderson, 1981). Middle children tend to be liberal, revolutionary, and subtle. They tend to have lower self-esteem and perceive less emotional support (Andrews, 1985). Youngest children, as the most pampered, may become manipulative charmers who get others to serve their needs (Jensen & Kingston, 1986).

The impact of birth order, however, depends upon the number of siblings, child spacing, and sex of the siblings. For example, the first-born, male child with only female siblings will have higher self-esteem than if he has siblings of both sexes. Negative behaviors are more likely between same-sex siblings (Minnett, Vandell, & Santrock, 1983). Further, the effect of birth order will be stronger if the siblings are spaced closer together and if there is a large number of siblings (Kidwell, 1982). As the number of siblings increases, the degree of social success in getting along with other children climbs proportionately for each child except for the youngest. No relationship has been found between academic achievement and birth order in multiple-child families by some researchers (Steelman & Powell, 1985). However, others report first-born and only children are more likely to go to college, to do better in school, to be National Merit Scholars, to earn a Ph.D., to score higher on IQ tests, and to be listed in *Who's Who in America* (Papalia & Olds, 1990).

Only children are a growing segment of the population due to the increasing social phenomenon of people marrying and bearing their first children later. The rising cost of child rearing is also a factor. In 1989, about 20% of families had only one child (Sifford, 1989). A review of 141 studies conducted between 1926 and 1985 concluded that only children were more motivated to achieve than those with siblings. However, no significant differences were found between only children and others in terms of character, social ability, and personal control. Further, there is no support for the idea that only children are less well-adjusted socially due to sibling deprivation. But the heightened parental attention given to only children may lead to greater expectations for performance along with more opportunity to observe and reward their achievements. Increased parental contact may also positively influence a child's self-concept and self-confidence, resulting in a higher achievement level. Only children may compensate for their lack of siblings through interaction with their parents (Polit & Falbo, 1987). However, only children perceive their parents as being more intrusive into their lives than do other children (Bell & Avery, 1985).

Influence of Socioeconomic Factors

Early research of social-class variations in child-rearing patterns and their effects on personality and behavior of children generally reflected considerable differences that were assumed to be caused by social-class variation (Bigner, 1985). By the 1950s, these earlier findings began to be refuted by studies reporting diminishing differences (Bronfenbrenner, 1958). The increasing similarity in child-rearing patterns between social groups was believed to be related to the advent of television with its middle-class values and upward mobility of lower-class families.

Although the gap has narrowed between social classes leaving most parents with common goals for their children, certain socioeconomic differences in values are reflected in children's behavior. This is because the behavioral choices of parents are guided by their value system, which is rooted in their social class. For example, low socioeconomic-status parents stress obedience, respect, cleanliness, and staying out of trouble. Therefore, they use parenting behaviors that are controlling and are more likely to use physical punishment. Conversely, high socioeconomic-status parents stress happiness, independence, ambition, and self-control. Their parenting behaviors are more often democratic, warm, and affectionate, using reason and complex language (Jensen & Kingston, 1986). Even though such differences seem to hold across race and culture, it must be emphasized that they are based on averages (Maccoby, 1980). Others have concluded from a review of numerous research studies that although social-class differences exist, they are not very large (Van der Zanden, 1981).

Influence of Family Interaction

A national survey of over 8,000 students and parents concluded that parents today still serve as role models. Daughters are more influenced than sons by parental modeling, with the effects of modeling being stronger in white-collar families than in blue-collar families. In general, mothers and fathers are fairly equal in their degree of modeling influence on both female and male adolescents (Cohen, 1987). Although the primary caregiver is the most important source of learning for infants and young children, findings indicate that parents are often unaware of how their words and actions affect their children (Culp, Cook, & Housley, 1983). Data on interaction patterns among intact families suggest that for three fourths of families, social activity is combined with eating and almost all shared activity occurs within the home setting. Surprisingly, the factors of maternal employment and socioeconomic status have no influence on the number of family interaction episodes. However, fathers as compared with mothers do have fewer interaction episodes with their children (Davey & Paolucci, 1980).

Children from divorced families usually report more conflict and less enjoyment from family activities, perhaps resulting from a limited attachment to the custodial parent. However, development of self-concept is known to be heavily influenced by a child's perception of her/his family relationships regardless of their reality. Children who perceive conflict resulting from interaction with their divorced parents are likely to have lower self-esteem (Cooper, Holman, & Braithwaite, 1983).

Next to parents, siblings are the most important socializing agents because of their daily interactions with each other. Since older siblings may serve as role models, younger children may develop faster in some ways than the first or only child (Garrett, 1982). Babies begin to interact with their sisters and brothers as early

BOX 14.3	Bringing up Fathers

It is both unfair and unrealistic to expect a young man of 25 to automatically "father" when his life experiences have skillfully isolated him from learning how. Rarely, if ever, do boys respond to the question, "What do you want to be someday?" by enthusiastically exclaiming, "A daddy!" Fathers cannot be blamed for this inability—even unwillingness—to nurture due to the unfortunate fact that boys traditionally have been removed from nurturing activities at the earliest age possible—usually around age 5 or 6. Tragically—our society has kept boys away from any type of domestic activity—other than perhaps yard work or carrying out the trash—under the pretext that they need to develop their masculinity as early as possible.

Fathers, like mothers, need to be trained for their roles from an early age. Boys benefit by recognizing that nurturing qualities do not detract from masculinity but rather add a richer, far less pressured dimension. When a young boy expresses a desire to nurture a doll family, or openly conveys affection, homophobic fears are aroused. Since he is not interested in "boy" things, parents fear that he might be developing homosexual tendencies.

Children learn to be adults by watching adults. Effective parents display an egalitarian approach to marriage by sharing the responsibilities of home and family. As boys as well as girls observe positive parenting models, they receive far more realistic "signals" about what boyhood, fatherhood, manhood, and masculinity are all about.

From an early age, boys must be given opportunities to interact with babies—whether siblings, friends of the family, or in learning environments. In addition to observing their own fathers nurturing, boys should witness other men receiving and giving nurturance to infants. As girls observe boys nurturing, they learn that boys possess these natural capabilities, and they need not bear the total responsibility of child rearing.

as age 6 months. Siblings typically begin to demonstrate interest in each other by engaging in activities together, and learning from each other, oftentimes by imitation (Dunn & Kendrick, 1982). Most siblings attempt to entertain younger sisters and brothers as well as to provide comfort when they cry or are upset (Brody, Stoneman, MacKinnon, & MacKinnon, 1985). Although sibling relationships are very different from parent-child relationships, older siblings often play the role of teacher for their younger siblings. Older sisters, especially, appear to be good teachers because they can adapt instructions to the level of the child better than parents (Minnett, Vandell, & Santrock, 1983).

The most commonly reported positive qualities of good sibling relationships by 6th graders were companionship, admiration of sibling, and affection. Children were more likely to feel closer to same-sex siblings if they were similar in age. Although older children tended to provide greater nurturance, they also were more likely to exhibit dominance over their younger siblings (Furman & Buhrmester, 1985). In one study reporting sibling rivalry, there were no significant gender differences in number of fights between siblings in homes with or without fathers present (Prochaska & Prochaska, 1985).

Principles of Child Development

One of the most priceless gifts a parent can give a child is the gift of understanding. Such a gift is made possible when parents themselves understand human development and the essential needs which govern behavior at each stage of life. Today, there is an almost overpowering amount of information in the area of child development, all of which no parent can be expected to know. Therefore, knowledge of the basic theories and principles of human development is the key.

Theoretical Perspectives

Although most parents are unaware of the philosophical basis of their child-rearing practices, all parents have definite ideas about the nature of human beings. In order to develop a workable philosophy of parenting, mothers and fathers will have to choose from the many alternative systems the one that works best for them (Moore, 1985b). A review of select theoretical perspectives of human development offers parents an opportunity to clarify their ideas about children, including their development and guidance.

Theories provide a framework for general principles. Although each theorist interprets human development from a different perspective, the goal is to

Table 14.2: Freud's Psychosexual Developmental Stages

Stage	Emphasis	Age
Oral	Pleasure obtained by stimulation of mouth during sucking, eating, and biting.	Birth–18 months
Anal	Pleasure obtained by urination and expulsion or retention of feces.	18 months–3 years
Phallic	Sexual curiosity with genitals represents primary source of pleasure; sexual fantasies about parent of opposite sex (Oedipal).	3–6 years
Latency	Sexual urges submerged; energies devoted to acquisition of social skills; identifies with parent of same sex.	6 years–onset of puberty
Genital	Emergence of attempts to satisfy heterosexual desires; love objects become primary source of pleasure.	Adolescence

provide insight into individual experience and behavior (Berger, 1988). There are basically four perspectives through which one may view the basic nature of human beings and from which theories of child development evolve: the mechanistic, organismic, psychoanalytic, and humanistic perspectives.

1. Mechanistic—This perspective views the person as reactive rather than active. Change is quantitative or measurable with the focus being observable behaviors. Behaviorist B. F. Skinner, emphasizing rewards and punishments, and social learning theorist, Albert Bandura, are two such theorists who support this perspective (Jensen & Kingston, 1986).
2. Organismic—From this viewpoint, people are portrayed as active contributors to their own development which is believed to occur in a series of qualitatively different stages. The focus is more on process than product. Jean Piaget, cognitive theorist, and Lawrence Kohlberg, who conceptualized the stages of moral development, represent this viewpoint (Schiamberg, 1988).
3. Psychoanalytic—Using this perspective, some developmentalists purport that individuals are in a stage of conflict between natural instincts and societal constraint. Sigmund Freud's psychosexual stages and Erik Erikson's psychosocial stages exemplify psychoanalytical thinking (Dworetsky, 1990).
4. Humanistic—Employing this point of view, individuals are perceived to have within themselves the ability to take charge of their own lives and to develop in healthy ways. Carl Rogers and Abraham Maslow are two theorists of this persuasion (Berger, 1988).

Freud

Sigmund Freud, the Viennese physician who originated psychoanalysis, believed that people are in a state of conflict between their instincts and societal constraints. The nature of this conflict depends upon a person's stage of development (Schiamberg, 1988). Freud named his five psychosexual stages of development for those body parts that are primary sources of gratification for each phase: oral, anal, phallic, latency, and genital (see Table 14.2).

Freud postulated that personality was made up of the **id** (unconscious desires based on pleasure), the **ego** (reason or common sense), and **superego** (conscience which incorporates morals of society). According to Freud, personality differences result from the various ways in which people deal with their fundamental drives (Berger, 1988). A continuing battle between the id in its search for gratification and the superego which insists on doing what is morally right is moderated by the ego, the reality-based aspect of self. When the battle between the id and superego becomes too great for a compromise, the ego employs defense mechanisms to defend itself against conflict. The most basic ego defense, repression, involves pushing conflicts created by the id impulses from conscious awareness to the unconscious mind (Zimbardo, 1988).

Table 14.3: Erikson's Psychosocial Stages

Stages	Age	Essential Strengths	Lasting Outcomes
Trust vs. Mistrust	1st Year	Learn to trust environment; to have needs met; and to be loved, and accepted	Drive and hope
Autonomy vs. Shame and Doubt	2nd–3rd year	Learn to make choices; to control and trust self	Self-control and willpower
Initiative vs. Guilt	4th–5th year	Initiate an idea, carry it out; and develop conscience	Direction and purpose
Industry vs. Inferiority	6th year–puberty	Develop sense of industry, curiosity, eagerness to learn, and loyalty to gang	Method and competence
Identity vs. Role Diffusion	Adolescence	See self as unique and integrated individual; gain peer acceptance	Devotion and fidelity
Intimacy vs. Isolation	Young Adulthood	Know how to love and commit to another person	Affiliation and love
Generativity vs. Stagnation	Adulthood	Have and care for children; devote self to work and common goals	Productivity and care
Ego Integrity vs. Despair	Maturity	Become assured that life has been meaningful; face death with acceptance and dignity	Renunciation and wisdom

From E. H. Erikson, *Childhood and Society,* 2d ed. Copyright © 1963 W. W. Norton & Company, Inc., New York, NY.

Erikson

Erik Erikson used the Freudian concept of ego (reason or common sense) as the basis of his psychosocial development theory. While Freud focused on biological and maturational factors, Erikson emphasized social and cultural influences. The results were eight ages or stages of psychosocial development, each of which depends upon the successful resolution of a crisis (Erikson, 1963). Achievement or failure in these tasks influences the personality of the individual. The stages are trust versus mistrust, autonomy versus doubt and shame, initiative versus guilt, industry versus inferiority, identity versus role confusion, intimacy versus isolation, generativity versus stagnation, and ego integrity versus despair (see Table 14.3).

Piaget

Much of our knowledge about how children learn is based on the work of Jean Piaget, the Swiss **epistemologist** (one who studies the nature of knowledge). He was a cognitive-developmentalist whose theory assumed change to be an inherent, internal part of life (Piaget, 1967). The central assumption in Piaget's theory is that it is the nature of the human organism to adapt to its environment. This process of adaptation involves assimilation, accommodation, and equilibration. When the child encounters an object, person, or experience, **assimilation** occurs. Thus, the child notices, recognizes, and takes the experience in and relates it to earlier experiences or categories. **Accommodation** involves changing the mental categories, actions, or concepts (schemes) to fit the newly assimilated experience. Finally, **equilibration** is the motive to stay in balance and to achieve an overall understanding or mental structure that fits the experience (Bee, 1989). The four stages of cognitive development are a key feature of Piaget's theory: sensorimotor, preoperations, concrete operations, and formal operations (see Table 14.4).

Developmental Perspectives

Human development is a process of change in which an undifferentiated infant becomes a complex, differentiated adult. More than simply change, it is a particular type of change that is developmental in nature. In order for change to be classified as developmental, three criteria must be met: the change must be orderly or sequenced; it must result in permanent alteration of behavior; and it must be more advanced, adaptive, or useful than previous behavior (Schiamberg, 1988).

Table 14.4: **Piaget's Stages of Cognitive Development**

Stage	Activities and Achievements	Age
Sensorimotor	Discover world through sensory impressions, and motor activities; development of coordination.	Birth–2 years
Preoperations	Learn to think in images and symbols and to form mental representations of objects and events.	2–7 years
Concrete Operations	Learn to understand logical principles that apply to concrete, external objects.	7–11 years
Formal Operations	Begin to think in abstract terms; learn to work in probabilities and possibilities.	11 years–adulthood

Development occurs when growth, quantitative change such as numbers of words, inches, or pounds, is accompanied by maturity, qualitative change such as higher levels of organization or complexity. A simple expression of this formula is **growth** (quantitative change) × **maturation** (qualitative change) = development.

But development does not occur in a vacuum. The socialization and child-rearing approach to the study of young children stresses the importance of external factors in the child's development (Schickedanz, Hansen & Forsyth, 1990). A child inherits more than a genetic endowment. She/he also receives an acquired endowment: a set of parents, natural or adoptive, who will determine the environment for development. Accordingly, the process that results in change in a person's behavior requires a complex series of interactions between the individual (including previous experiences and current interpretations of events) and her/his environment (Lauter-Klatell, 1991). Thus, another simple formula can be used to express this equation: development (nature) × environment (nurture) = unique individual (Moore, 1985d).

The nature-nurture controversy of old centered on the relative importance ascribed to heredity and environment in effecting change. Researchers today recognize that the two factors are symbiotic and that understanding each one is essential to an explanation of the child's development. While development is the sum of quantitative and qualitative changes over time, each person is much more than the sum of her/his own parts. Quantitative change is far easier to observe since it involves changes in amount, such as weight, height, or vocabulary. Conversely, qualitative changes in type or kind, such as moral reasoning levels that reveal the changing nature of the individual, are more difficult to assess (Neubauer & Neubauer, 1990).

Fundamental Principles That Govern Growth

When parents who had just had their first child were asked what all parents should know about infants, over one third of mothers and fathers indicated developmental milestones such as the time for the baby's first word or first step (Kliman & Vukelich, 1985). There are four fundamental principles underlying such knowledge about human growth and development. Although they are easier to recognize in the young child whose behavior is less guarded by defenses, these principles remain applicable to all ages. Accordingly, growth is continuous, interrelated, nonuniform, and patterned (Langford & Rand, 1975). These processes are related to changes in social, physical, intellectual, emotional, and moral domains throughout life (Schiamberg, 1988).

Growth is a continuous process from conception to death. Throughout life, inborn forces continue to interact with experiences provided by the environment. Sometimes children's growth is observable; more often it is not. Although there may not always be outward signs, the child is growing daily. For example, unseen cognitive change enables more complex intellectual functioning which propels the child from Piaget's sensorimotor stage of discoveries to the world of images and symbols around age 2 (see Table 14.4). As muscles become firmer, bones become harder, and as legs grow longer, the child is enabled to walk. Fortunately for parents, the impetus for growth is inside the child. The parent's role is to guide, to remove obstacles, and to furnish emotional nurturance in order to enable optimal growth (Hymes, 1985).

Findings suggest that parents believe that physical development, intellectual development, and acquisition of social behavior occur independently (Lawton,

Schuler, Fowell, & Madsen, 1984). However, development is an interrelated process involving all areas of growth: physical, emotional, social, and intellectual (Papalia & Olds, 1990). For example, a growth of several inches in height during adolescence greatly influences the child's development in other areas. Such a growth spurt may signal other changes in, for example, coordination. A basketball player who suddenly begins tripping over her/his own feet may experience not only diminishing athletic prowess, but such change may also affect feelings about self, dating opportunities, or even ability to concentrate in the classroom.

The fact that the tempo or rate of growth is uneven means that development is a nonuniform process. There are **plateaus** (stages of leveling off), spurts, and even possible regressions for each child who grows in her/his own unique way. The unevenness of the developmental rate is perhaps most apparent in the area of physical growth; but it also occurs in the social, emotional, and intellectual areas. Unless parents are aware that growth is not uniform from child to child, they may be particularly concerned if their child is not as advanced in development as other children (Schiamberg, 1988). Sudden regressions as well as stages when growth seems to be at a standstill may also be disconcerting for parents, but understanding that such patterns are likely to be necessary for successive development to occur can relieve anxiety.

Given the actuality that growth follows an orderly sequence means that it is a patterned process. What is perhaps one of the first patterns in physical development is noted in the embryonic stage when growth proceeds according to two directional principles **cephalocaudal** (from the head downward) and **proximo-distal** (from the center, outward). Examples of the cephalocaudal pattern can be observed in the infant's later development when arms are more fully developed before legs and head before trunk (Kaplan, 1991). The fact that patterns can be determined enables the prediction of development. In physical development, for example, the baby crawls, then walks; in language development, the baby babbles, then talks. In social development, she/he plays alone before progressing to parallel play and eventually group play. The sequence of development is more apparent for physical functions than for social and intellectual development but no less a reality (Clarke-Stewart & Friedman, 1987). Stages and critical periods are two additional concepts related to the predictability of development.

Stages and Critical Periods

The concept of stage, a genetically programmed sequential pattern of change, was introduced in child development literature by Arnold Gesell (1940), who emphasized the biological aspects of developmental patterns in physical characteristics such as body size and shape. His classic work *The First Five Years of Life* was filled with numerous timetables for "Ages and Stages" based on norms established in research at the Gesell Institute. While such work has made an invaluable contribution to learning about "normal" development, it also has prompted parental concern about those "below average" or "behind" children (Bee, 1989).

When considering "ages and stages," parents should differentiate between their child's chronological and developmental ages. A child's **chronological age** (age in years) should not determine parental expectations of her/his behavior. Instead, a child's developmental age, the level of development that a child has reached regardless of chronological age, should be the standard (Langford & Rand, 1975).

A stage has specific characteristics. Each is qualitatively different and more mature than the preceding stage, universal with everyone passing through the same stage, and part of an invariant sequence (Schiamberg, 1988). A rigid age and stage sequence is no longer in vogue; but the concept of stages, although difficult to delimit, is still widely used in various theories. A shift in stages is believed to precede changes in skills or physical characteristics as well as changes in underlying anatomical structures. The child then approaches tasks differently and is interested in different issues (Bee, 1989).

A critical period in a person's life is an identifiable segment of time that is crucial in the development of the individual. It is a time when the potential for growth and development as well as damage from the environment is maximal. These periods are often called critical because the effects that occur during that time are irreversible. Critical periods are most clearly demonstrated in prenatal development by certain periods of vulnerability during which damage may occur to the fetus. For example, if during the first 3 months of pregnancy the woman is exposed to rubella (German measles), her baby is far more likely to be born with congenital defects than if the disease occurs later in pregnancy (Schiamberg, 1988).

In postnatal development, critical periods have been proposed for acquiring gender-role identification, trust, and other personality characteristics (Brophy, 1977). Although the concept is still controversial, brain research even suggests the idea of a critical period for language development (Snow, 1989). Some believe these postnatal periods should be called "sensitive" rather than "critical" since the results are not so irrevocable (Bee, 1989).

A sensitive period in the attachment process of infants is also suggested. This attachment is believed to begin about 6 weeks after birth and to last until 7–8 months after birth when the infant evidences a secure attachment by exhibiting separation anxiety when separated from the caregiver (Brophy, 1977). The predictability of human development is also apparent in the essential needs and developmental tasks.

Essential Needs and Developmental Tasks

Until the 19th century, the main concern of parents was the physical survival of their child. Now that survival is no longer an overriding issue, all facets of a child's growth are nourished as parents protect and guide them through the course of development (Brooks, 1987). A principal assignment for parents today may be helping their child negotiate that delicate balance in life between their innate needs and societal demands.

Developmental tasks represent cultural expectations and therefore vary from culture to culture; essential needs of children do not vary but represent inherent human needs (Schiamberg, 1988). There are four essential needs that have been identified: *physical*—all children need food, shelter, and opportunity for activity; *emotional*—love must be supplied by the parent(s) to fully nurture the child; *social*—positive experiences within the family are basic for success in later relationships with others; and *intellectual*—learning occurs as the child experiences her/his environment through the senses of touch, sound, sight, smell, and taste (Kaplan, 1991).

Developmental tasks are growth responsibilities faced by all persons from birth to death. They arise from societal expectations, but are influenced by physical and personal motivation (Duvall, 1988). A developmental task represents a midpoint between an individual's need and a societal demand. Robert Havighurst defined a **developmental task** as:

> *A task which arises at or about a certain period in the life of an individual, successful achievement of which leads to his happiness and success with later tasks while failure leads to unhappiness in the individual, disapproval by society, and difficulty with later tasks (1972, p. 2).*

Although these tasks do not explain why individuals develop in particular ways, they do offer a framework for understanding the sequence of development in six chronological stages of life: infancy, middle childhood, adolescence, early adulthood, middle age, and later maturity (see Table 14.5). The stages in the developmental tasks sequence are not invariant nor exhaustive. In fact, several life span researchers have proposed other stages. A stage has been suggested that divides old age into young-old and old-old. One might speculate that in the future, the preteen group, a large target audience for advertising, might also become a designated life-span stage (Simons & Irwin, 1986).

Principles of Child Guidance

"Our earth is degenerate . . . children no longer obey their parents." Child development students are surprised to find that this 20th century-sounding adage was inscribed in stone by an Egyptian priest over 6,000 years ago. They wonder if indeed it is true, the more things change, the more they stay the same! Family historians have documented various techniques of guidance used throughout the centuries to attain socialization of the young (Aries, 1960/1962). However, parents in the latter half of the 1900s are the first to have a large body of scientific data available from which general principles of child guidance can be derived.

Various techniques of guidance have been used through the centuries to attain socialization of the young. One of the first tasks in understanding these principles of guidance is to differentiate between two words often incorrectly used synonymously: discipline and guidance. **Discipline** is what one does *to* a child and it is just one part of the total parent-child relationship. **Guidance,** on the other hand, is what one does *with* or *for* a child, and it encompasses the total parent-child relationship. It will be remembered that the immediate purpose of guidance is the optimal and happy adjustment of the child to her/his present environment while the ultimate goal is for the child to grow into a happy, healthy, fully functioning adult (Langford & Rand, 1975). Burton White (1975) who directed the exten-

Table 14.5: Select Life-Cycle Developmental Tasks

Infancy: birth–6 years
- Learn to walk.
- Learn to take solid foods.
- Learn sex differences and sexual modesty.
- Learn to relate emotionally to parents, siblings, and others.

Middle childhood: 6–12 years
- Learn to get along with age mates.
- Learn appropriate sex role.
- Develop fundamental skills in reading, writing, and calculating.
- Develop conscience, morality, and a scale of values.

Adolescence: 12–18 years
- Accept one's physique and sex role.
- Achieve emotional independence of parents and other adults.
- Select and prepare for a vocation.
- Prepare for marriage and family life.

Early adulthood
- Select mate.
- Start family.
- Start occupation.
- Take civic responsibility.

Middle age
- Establish and maintain an economic standard of living.
- Assist teenagers to become responsible and happy adults.
- Accept and adjust to the physiological changes of middle age.
- Adjust to aging parents.

Later maturity
- Adjust to decreasing health and strength.
- Adjust to retirement and reduced income.
- Adjust to death of mate.
- Establish satisfactory living arrangement for age level and needs.

From R. Havighurst, *Developmental Tasks and Education,* 3d ed.

sive Harvard Preschool Research Project on Parenting believes that while such goals are ambitious, perfectly average people can accomplish them. Essentials for doing a good job of child rearing are a strong feeling of love for the child, a great deal of patience and stamina, some degree of knowledge about developmental processes, and strategies for direct and indirect guidance (White, Kaban, & Attonucci, 1979). Even corporations are beginning to recognize that parents who have well-adjusted, happy children are more productive and report greater job satisfaction. Thus, more than 1,000 "family-friendly" companies nationwide now offer seminars to help parents "manage" their children (Roel, 1990).

Methods of Child Guidance

When parents of firstborn infants were asked their first choice for sources of information about child rearing, most mothers indicated their own parents while a number of fathers reported medical professionals. Books and magazines were less popular sources of information on guidance and child development (Kliman & Vukelich, 1985). Even well-read parents are frequently at a disadvantage because of all of the conflicting messages—too many prescriptive "how to's" and fads. The Department of Health, Education and Welfare bulletin *Infant Care,* which was distributed broadly to families for most of this century, is a case in point. An historical analysis of its contents indicate that recommendations to parents continually shifted to whatever ideas were prevalent in child development research at the time. One authority reported contradictory advice from experts over the years concerning discipline: 1910—spank them, 1920—deprive them, 1930—ignore them, 1940—reason with them, 1950—love them, 1960—spank them lovingly, 1970—to heck with them (Kephart, 1981)!

So, what methods of child guidance should parents use? To help answer this question the Harvard Preschool Research Project sought to determine differences in the child-rearing practices of mothers in three groups of children with varying levels of cognitive and social competence. Mothers whose children were most competent ("A" children) were more able to design the child's world, to serve as a consultant for their child, and to exert the right amount of control over the child. These mothers generally had positive attitudes about life, enjoyed being with their child, and were firm and consistent while showing love and respect. In contrast, mothers who were rearing the least competent children ("C" children) exhibited signs of being overwhelmed by life, ran chaotic households, and were too absorbed by daily struggles to spend much time with their child. Although physically present, the mothers rarely made actual contact with their child apparently because they did not enjoy it. These mothers were overprotective, confined the child to a crib or playpen, spent too much or too little time with them, and pushed them to learn (White et al., 1979). Since parenting styles are known to be of considerable importance in determining methods of child guidance, it is important to learn the effects of the various parenting styles that have been identified over the years in the research literature.

Parenting Styles

The research of Diane Baumrind is perhaps the most widely cited in the field of parenting styles. Her classic contribution was the categorization of parenting styles related to child behavior: authoritarian parents and a conflicted-irritable child; permissive parents and an impulsive-aggressive child; and authoritative parents and an energetic, friendly child (Baumrind, 1967).

The **authoritarian parent** is always in control, intent upon making rules without any discussion with the child. If rules are not followed, the consequences are likely to be physical punishment, often severe. In such an environment, the independence of the child is discouraged and overt behaviors as well as attitudes, beliefs, and values are targeted for control (Baumrind, 1971).

Parents who frequently use power-assertive techniques and are punitive in their actions have children who display higher levels of aggression (Patterson, 1982). And children who are punished for aggressive behavior have higher levels of such behavior. In fact, authoritarian-parenting styles are more often associated with juvenile delinquency, illegal drug use, and runaway teenagers (Jurich, 1978).

Authoritarian parenting is associated with children who are socially less competent than their peers, have lower self-concepts, are withdrawn and lack initiative and an internal locus of control. These children show a lesser degree of conscience and display an external moral-judgment orientation. Thus, one could speculate that authoritarian parenting is likely to be associated with low levels of both self-awareness and appropriate assertiveness in children. Outcomes of this parenting style are believed to be the opposite of a self-actualized person (Moore, A. J., 1985).

Permissive parents give little or no guidance to their children. The parents accept the child's impulses, desires, and actions without judgement; and few demands for responsibility are made of the child, who is allowed to regulate her/his own behavior (Baumrind, 1966). Overt power or punishment is not used by the parents, but rather reason and manipulation are used to control behavior. Such parents believe that children should make their own decisions. This parenting style has been labeled "the parent as pal" style (LeMasters & DeFrain, 1983).

Early research found that nursery school children of permissive parents lacked independence and social responsibility, and, at ages 8–9, were low in both cognitive and social skills (Baumrind, 1971). Studies since the 1970s have confirmed that permissive parenting is likely to produce children who are impulsive, aggressive, and lacking in independence and the ability to take responsibility (Moore, A. J., 1985).

Consistent discipline and high maturity demands are hallmarks of an **authoritative parent** (Baumrind, 1967). This type of parent values open communication, explains the reason for decisions to the child, and invites the child to discuss the situation. It is important to this parent that the child be autonomously self-willed but able to conform to situations appropriately. Thus reason, power, and shaping are used rather than coercive measures of control (Baumrind, 1966).

Children reared in an authoritative environment are more competent and independent than their peers. Preschool boys tend to be more socially responsible and both females and males, ages 8–9, have shown high social and intellectual self-assertion (Baumrind, 1971; Baumrind, 1978). Children have higher self-esteem when parents' decisions are fair and reasonable and when parents are helpful in a suggestive way rather than a direct way (Loeb, Horst, & Horton, 1980). Since the authoritative parent, by definition, encourages the child to be self-willed, such parenting should be associated with intrinsically motivated behavior and higher potential for self-actualization. Most experts agree that authoritative parenting, which encourages children to work hard at developing their own potential and talents, is best for assisting with the social development of the child (Lawton et al., 1984). Generally, younger parents are most likely to follow authoritative parenting strategies (Carter & Welch, 1981).

Gender Roles and Parenting

The debate continues concerning characteristics of those parents most likely to embrace the authoritative style of parenting. It has been claimed that androgynous persons, when compared to sex-typed (traditionally feminine or masculine) persons, exhibit greater gender-role flexibility, higher self-esteem, and function more effectively at home and at work (Bem, Martyna, & Watson, 1976). Consequently, androgynes of both sexes were hypothesized to be more likely to be authoritative parents whose children were predicted to be assertive, socially responsible, and highly competent. However,

other research has yielded somewhat conflicting results concerning these predictions:

1. Androgynous women differed from feminine women on only one child-rearing variable: They used more negative reinforcement.
2. Androgynous men were more similar to androgynous women than masculine men in their child-rearing practices.
3. Sex-typed feminine mothers were responsive, and sex-typed masculine fathers were firm.
4. Androgynes were not more likely to be authoritative but tended to be child-centered in their approach to child rearing.
5. Children of sex-typed parents were somewhat more competent than those of androgynous parents (Baumrind, 1982, pp. 54–69).

Baumrind concluded, "Since behavioral data have not been accumulated to support their claim, androgyny researchers should refrain from promoting the androgyne as the new American ideal" (1982, p. 44). Beyond recognizing their parenting style, parents need to be aware that there are not infinite but few basic methods for teaching desired behavior.

Teaching Desired Behavior

Parents may more easily teach a child desired behavior if they recognize that there are general principles pertaining to what is taught and how. Young children learn about life in a three-step sequential process involving performance, role, and attitude. But these steps are seldom taken simultaneously. First, the "how to do it" or proper performance is learned. Second, the child must understand "when to do it" or the playing of approved social roles. Third, unless the child is taught "why to do it" or the attitude/values facet of behavior, the process is incomplete. Without comprehending why a specific behavior is important, children are unable to internalize a rationale for its performance (Moore, 1985c).

The methods that parents use to teach their child desired behavior must be appropriate to achieve the desired result. Some things, such as staying off a busy street, are best learned by directed teaching, whereby the child is told or shown how to do it. Other behaviors are most effectively learned by trial and error, as long as the child does not hurt herself/himself or others in the process. Learning to share toys with age mates is one lesson best learned by doing. However, the preferred method of learning, when appropriate, is through identification, whereby parents offer the child a stable model to copy with a minimum of variation (Moore, 1985c). Manners and morals are examples of lessons that are best learned by modeling.

Child Discipline

Discipline is only one part of the total guidance scheme. Parents who understand discipline to be a system of rewards as well as punishments can more easily accomplish its aim: helping the child to ultimately become a self-disciplined person (Bigner, 1985). Discipline, from the root word "disciple," indicates the child is a disciple who follows the parent as a master teacher. Therefore, as parents reward desired behavior and teach by example, it is far easier for the young child to become a disciplined person (Moore, 1985d). Familiarity with the reasons for misbehavior by young children, and positive strategies for coping with undesirable behavior enables parents to choose appropriate methods of guidance/discipline.

Reasons for Misbehavior

It may be difficult for parents to realize that the reasons for their child's misbehavior and their own responses to it are far from infinite. Understanding these basic reasons for misbehavior and appropriate responses by parents not only simplifies the role of disciplinarian, it greatly improves the odds of succeeding. The four most frequent reasons for misbehavior in young children, age level of child, unsatisfied need inside child, the present environment, and lack of knowledge about appropriate behavior, have long been identified and reaffirmed, (Hymes, 1955; Hymes, 1985). By recognizing the various causes of misbehavior, parents can choose the most effective coping strategies.

When the age level of a child is the cause of misbehavior, it is easily recognized by those parents who are aware of normal, age-level behavior and who can appropriately gauge the developmental level of their own child. The best response to this type of misbehavior is to tolerate it when possible, remembering that such behavior may be essential for growing up. Even so, at times when age-level behavior is inappropriate for the occasion or the adult is unable to tolerate it, channeling the behavior into some form of more desirable behavior is suggested. If neither method works nor is appropriate, the last parenting technique is to actually stop the misbehavior (Hymes, 1985). For example, responsible parents will stop a 2-year-old who runs in a public library. This action protects the rights of others and teaches the child that there are appropriate and inappropriate places to run. However, a wise parent recognizes that running is an age-level behavioral need and later provides an appropriate space to do so.

Misbehavior resulting from unsatisfied needs of the child can be recognized because it is more developmentally appropriate for younger children. If the misbehavior persists in spite of efforts for control, it likely represents a hidden hunger from an earlier unmet need in the child's life. Adults can help the child to satisfy this emotional hunger by supplying in healthy ways, the needed affection, attention, or approval for whichever unmet emotional need exists (Hymes, 1985). This approach must be skillfully used in order to avoid rewarding the misbehavior. Admittedly, such a task is not accomplished easily nor quickly. It has been suggested that if the child is age 3, it took 3 years for the hunger to develop so, therefore, it may take 3 years to feed the hunger.

The environment often causes misbehavior when it is not suited to the needs of young children. Their space may be too restrictive or filled with too many or too few people or objects. Restrictions may be in the form of too many no's in the child's life. It may be easier for parents to cope with this misbehavior since it relates to environmental causes that may be controlled. By simply altering the timing, activity, grouping, or restructuring the child's world to include more yes responses and fewer no's, positive goals may be attained for both parent and child (Hymes, 1985).

If the child's misbehavior is characteristic of a younger age, this is a clue that the child may lack knowledge about appropriate behavior. Such misbehavior is asocial (without social knowledge) as opposed to antisocial where the child knowingly disobeys the rules. Asocial behavior should not be punished, but the child should be taught what is appropriate by simply telling or showing the child what to do (Hymes, 1985). Such learning occurs best when the lesson is couched in positive "to do" words rather than negative "don't do" ones.

Punishment

Much of a young child's misbehavior stems from age-level developmental needs. Therefore, even parents who have optimally structured their child's environment and rewarded desired behavior must ultimately decide on appropriate forms of punishment (Clarke-Stewart & Friedman, 1987). Frequently, parents employ **corporal punishment** (physical) simply for lack of a well-thought-out plan of discipline (Moore, 1985a). Issues associated with corporal punishment and more positive forms of punishment need to be clarified to assure informed decision making by parents.

Corporal Punishment. "They spank you." These words were the most frequent response given by children, ages 3–4, when asked in a preschool readiness test "What do mothers do?"; "What do fathers do?"; "What do teachers do?" (Moore, 1972). The use of corporal punishment remains an unresolved issue in both homes and schools in the United States. Authorities remain divided over the appropriateness and/or detrimental effects of occasional use of physical punishment such as spanking on the hand or the buttocks (Clarke-Stewart & Friedman, 1987). Not all nations are so divided. The Swedish Parliament passed a law in 1979 that states that parents may not strike their children or treat them in any other humiliating way.

Poland, in 1783, abolished corporal punishment in its schools. It is also prohibited in all other Communist countries as well as France, Finland, Sweden, Denmark, the Netherlands, Israel, and Japan. By contrast, in the United States, at least 19 states since 1972 have passed laws permitting the use of corporal punishment in schools (Kersey, 1983). However, numerous school districts across the country have abolished corporal punishment, and at least 19 other states now prohibit its use in schools ("Kids: You Can't," 1989). While many organizations and publications are concerned with ending corporal punishment in public schools, the current climate of fundamental conservatism appears opposed to change in some states.

Parents also appear to be sharply divided over the issue of using corporal punishment. Of those women and men replying to a *Psychology Today* survey, 49% believed that children should never be physically punished whereas 51% felt that a simple "spanking" on the buttocks would be appropriate (Stark, 1985). There is some evidence that parents with higher levels of educational achievement tend to spank their children least often. Among those who had attended graduate school, only 2% spanked "frequently" while 29% spanked "sometimes." By comparison, 5% of those with a high school education or less spanked "frequently" while 47% spanked "sometimes" (Greer, K., 1986).

Decisions about punishment should be made with full awareness of the short-term results and the long-range consequences of the chosen form of punishment. One short-term result of spanking is that it usually does stop the undesirable behavior and may even temporarily reduce the chances of the child repeating the behavior. However, the undesirable behavior is only suppressed, leading to long-range consequences. A second short-term result is that the parent is reinforced to spank again since a spanking was successful in stopping the behavior (Bee, 1989). However, even for those parents who consider these outcomes to be short-term benefits, they appear less desirable when the other immediate side effects are considered: immediate high aggressiveness, less compliance with adult requests, and troubled peer relationships (Bandura, 1973; Power & Chapieski, 1986).

Based on a review of the research literature, three long-term consequences of corporal punishment were identified:

1. *Spanking serves as a model of violence*—When the child observes physical force being used as a method of solving problems, the odds are greatly increased that she/he will choose aggression/violence to resolve differences with siblings and peers.
2. *Spanking erodes positive influence of parent*—By repeatedly being paired with the unpleasantness and pain of spanking, the parent often finds their positive value to the child is undermined. Eventually, praise or affection becomes less powerful in influencing the child's behavior.
3. *Spanking creates a family climate of rejection instead of warmth*—Emotionally powerful messages of anger, rejection, and dislike are likely to be communicated. The child easily generalizes this rejection to self rather than the misbehavior itself (Bee, 1989, pp. 474–475).

Another authority advances additional arguments against spanking, citing five negative effects. Spanking lowers child's self-esteem; fails to teach appropriate behavior; promotes dependency on external rather than internal control; damages parent's self-concept because of losing control of emotions; and conveys only reasons for not misbehaving, rather than giving child reasons for appropriate behavior (Kersey, 1983).

Noncorporal Punishment. If the goal of discipline is to help the child profit from mistakes and to avoid repeating behaviors that are self-defeating, punishment methods other than corporal punishment need to be chosen. The most effective punishment produces long-term changes in the child's behavior without negative side effects. Such punishment has three distinct qualities: it is employed early in the sequence of misbehavior, it uses the mildest level of punishment, and it is accomplished with the lowest possible level of emotion (Johnston; 1972; Patterson, 1975). Parents can learn to cope with misbehavior from their child by using positive strategies:

1. Be sensitive to the child's rhythms and introduce changes at the least disruptive time.
2. Warn child of upcoming changes in activity or requests.
3. Allow time before repeating request.
4. Give child choices when possible.
5. Use "time outs" by removing adult attention from child's presence when intense misbehavior is exhibited (Haswell, Hock, & Wenar, 1981, pp. 443–445).

BOX 14.4	General Guidelines for Noncorporal Punishment

1. **Ignore irritating behaviors if possible.** Walk, look, or move away. Learn art of silence. Children want and need attention, but learn quickly that misbehavior will not lead to these goals.
2. **Watch for appropriate behavior.** Call attention to desired behavior with special privileges, smiles, affection, and appreciation.
3. **If behavior is dangerous, destructive, embarrassing, or an impediment to learning, DON'T ignore it.** Take action to STOP undesired behavior.
4. **Best ways to stop behavior.** Stop misbehavior in the least reinforcing way—with glance, look, or shake of head. If necessary, use words, "Stop it," or nonverbal action such as taking child by hand and moving away from scene.
5. **Don't confront child in public.** Take child to a private place and communicate that behavior must be stopped.
6. **Make sure that message is clear.** Might be necessary for child to sit in chair or spend few minutes alone to get control of self.
7. **Allow child to return, if she/he understands parental message.** Make sure that behavior is not repeated. If misbehavior reoccurs, repeat process more firmly with more "time out." Give as little attention as possible to misbehavior but enough to correct situation.

Source: K. C. Kersey, *The Art of Sensitive Parenting: The 10 Keys to Raising Confident, Competent and Responsible Children.* Copyright © 1983 Acropolis Books Ltd., Washington, DC.

Having consistent expectations that are enforced and setting limits also appear to be significant variables. When inquiring about discipline techniques, most children indicate that they prefer that their parents set limits rather than having a permissive approach to discipline (Siegal & Barclay, 1985).

Contributions of Others to Child Rearing

Childhood socialization necessarily encompasses influential factors other than parents such as schools, peer groups, and mass communication. Television, movies, magazines, and other forms of mass media do not involve interpersonal interaction as is the case for other agents of socialization. However, they cannot be considered in isolation from family or peer groups which exert considerable influence in the child's selection from the wide array of possibilities (Elkin & Handel, 1989). Only early childhood education and television are addressed in this chapter while the influence of day-care is addressed in chapter 16, "Dual Careers, Marriage, and Parenthood."

Early Childhood Education Options

From birth to age 5, a child undergoes rapid emotional, physical, intellectual, and social development. Although family members are key figures in the child's early development, other children begin to play an important role around age 3 when social interaction with peers becomes a priority need. If there are limited neighborhood children of appropriate ages available, preschool programs may help fill this need. Preschools include Head Start programs, nursery schools, parent cooperatives, play groups, and drop-in centers (Hamner & Turner, 1990). Since they are usually half-day programs from 2–5 days a week, preschools do not meet the needs of full-time working parents.

Although some educational activities are provided in a quality preschool program, the emphasis is on the child's total growth and development. A child-centered curriculum includes a stimulating environment, opportunity for acquisition of skills, development of social attitudes, and growth of conceptual understanding (James, 1984). Such programs are frequently known as developmental preschools to differentiate them from group baby-sitting programs where the level of professional care may be substantially lower (Wallis, 1987). Due to the cost of preschool, its accessibility is primarily limited to children in the upper-middle socioeconomic class and those from lower-class enrolled in the federally-funded Head Start programs (Hofferth & Phillips, 1987).

In a preschool, children receive and share information as well as gain self-esteem by learning to cooperate in group play in a relaxed, noncompetitive atmosphere (Cartwright, 1987). Some authorities maintain that preschool experience can result in improved intellectual performance in early childhood as well as better scholastic achievement throughout the school career including higher graduation rates (Schweinhart & Weikart, 1985). While such claims may have some validity, early childhood education is the prime time for development in all areas of a child's life and play is the medium through which this growth occurs. The excessive pressure from parents and teachers for children to achieve academically and the idea that "faster is necessarily better" is decried by many child developmentalists (Jensen & Kingston,

1986). In his book *The Hurried Child: Growing Up Too Fast Too Soon,* David Elkind (1981) objects to excessive pressure for children to read, participate in sports, or become socially and sexually mature at an early age.

> *It is important to see childhood as a stage of life, not just as the anteroom to life. Hurrying children into adulthood violates the sanctity of life by giving one period priority over another. . . . In the end, a childhood is the most basic human right of children.*
>
> *(Elkind, 1981, pp. 199–200)*

As of 1988, 90% of all 5-year-olds were enrolled in public school kindergartens with over one third in all-day programs. Further, 26 states had free kindergarten programs for 4-year-olds within the public school system (Besharov, 1988). However, most programs were targeted for children that were expected to be "at risk" for failure in school, which was defined by family income, individual screening, and/or low level of English language proficiency (Hofferth & Phillips, 1987).

Television as an Agent of Socialization

Adversaries promote being "TV Free," bumper stickers proclaim "Just Say No to Television," and authors sell books condemning the television habit. Yet Americans watch an average of almost 7 hours of television per day, according to a 1989 Nielsen Report (Greth, 1990). Authorities believe the more a child is engaged in imaginative play during the formative years, the more her/his potential for competence will be realized. Those opposed to television believe it leaves a "sticky coating" on the imagination—that it pacifies a child's intellect, imagination, and body. Others, although agreeing that television is a problem, advise that excluding TV viewing from a child's life might result in social isolation—alienating her/him from peers—an even worse problem than TV addiction (Greth, 1990).

Although many facets of the mass media may influence the family, none is more significant than television (Christopher, Fabes, & Wilson, 1989). Largely unknown half a century ago, TV is in virtually all American households with more than one half having two or more sets. Television has significantly affected many facets of family life: sleeping patterns and meal time have changed for more than one half of families, and over three fourths use television as an electronic baby-sitter (Liebert & Sprafkin, 1988). Since the advent of television, social gatherings away from home, community activities, personal correspondence, conversation, and household care have decreased for most Americans (Robinson, 1981; Williams & Handford, 1986).

Between ages 2–12, children watch an average of 25 hours of television per week ("Reports on Television," 1987). In fact, by age 6, most children have spent more time watching TV than they will spend talking to their father in a lifetime (Berendson, 1987). Further, by age 18, a child will have spent more hours watching TV than in school or any other single activity besides sleep (Liebert & Sprafkin, 1988). While authorities are in agreement that TV is a significant socialization agent for children, conflicting evidence exists regarding whether or not its negative contributions outweigh its positive contributions.

Television: Friend or Foe?

There are those who would label television as user friendly. Television is the single major recreational pursuit most often shared today by parents and children, accounting for almost one fourth of the time spent together each week (Fischman, 1986). Children learn more from TV when viewing it with an adult as the child's comprehension and retention of information is enhanced. However, adults can either inhibit or intensify the child's imitative responses to TV programs. For example, mothers' comments were found to counteract the influence of TV commercials regarding various food products (Messaris & Kerr, 1984). Fears raised concerning the negative effects of TV watching on intellectual development are purported by some to be overblown (Fischman, 1986). In fact, a 1979–1980 study of academic achievement in California public schools found that as children watched more TV, their academic performance actually increased ("Reports on Television," 1987).

Research on **prosocial behavior** (socially desirable behavior that in some way benefits another person or society) suggests that children learn from television, and that what they learn depends on what they watch. When prosocial programs are viewed, children are more likely to become friendly, self-controlled, and generous. Therefore, some authorities envision TV as a potential force for good (Pearl, Bouthilet, & Lazar, 1982). In addition, the Project on Human Sexual Development considers TV to be an important agent for sexual learning. These professionals have sponsored workshops and seminars for television producers, writers, and network executives to heighten their awareness of appropriate portrayals of sexuality in television programming (Liebert, Sprafkin, & Davidson, 1982).

T.V. time together—One way parents in the 1990s transmit values to their children is by choice of television programs and reactions to the program's content.

Many authorities believe there are more negative than positive effects of television on children. They charge that television provides an unrealistic portrait of the world to children. Divorce is depicted casually as being legal and moral, lifetime marriage rare. Drugs, alcohol, and sexual activity are often glamorized; everyone is depicted as thin; and most people smoke, but no one develops lung cancer (LeMasters & De-Frain, 1983). Some professionals also maintain that TV viewing by children has led to a shortening of their attention span, an eroding of their linguistic powers, and a declining ability to manipulate mathematical symbols ("TV's 'Disastrous' Impact," 1981).

Early Exposure to Sexuality and Violence. Prior to the 1970s, the use of words such as pregnant and sexual intercourse on television were taboo, and married couples were depicted as sleeping in separate beds. Today, frequent references to sexual intercourse occur through descriptions and innuendos or behavioral cues that a sexual act will take place. However, in 1975, the Family Viewing Time Code went into effect prohibiting sexual and violent content in TV programs between 7–9 P.M. Thus, the prime-time viewer should not be exposed to depictions/allusions to **exhibitionism, fetishism,** or **voyeurism.** However, during a typical evening of prime-time viewing, one can experience at least one reference to sexual intercourse, homosexuality, prostitution, rape, transvestism, and/or pornography (Liebert & Sprafkin, 1988). When adults rated 15 prime-time programs, about two thirds concluded there was too much sexuality content on TV. Most believed that many sexual topics were unsuitable for the average child or teenager, while some thought certain sexual topics such as child molesting, rape, and homosexuality were even unsuitable for adults. The five topics rated most unsuitable for the average child were prostitution—72%, rape—71%, extramarital sexual relationship—69%, premarital sexual intercourse—69%, and homosexuality—61%. The five topics deemed most inappropriate for the teen were striptease, rape, extramarital sexual relationship, prostitution, and child molesting (Liebert et al., 1982).

Content analyses of television programs reveal that the frequency of sexual references and the degree of sexual explicitness continued to increase during the 1980s. But despite these concerns, studies of the effects of sexual content on adolescents are scarce. The limited data suggest that adolescents who rely on TV for information about sexuality are more likely to have extreme ideals about female beauty and to believe that premarital and extramarital sexual intercourse with multiple partners is socially acceptable (Brown, Childers, and Waszak, 1990).

Exposure to television violence is also believed by some to be detrimental to children. Male adolescents and working-class children are more likely to have a preference for TV violence than female adolescents and middle-class children. Specific effects of TV violence are thought to be related to the issues of violence arousal and violence value shaping. Evidence suggests that a child may act more aggressively for several days after being aroused by television violence and that such violence may be imitated. If "admired characters" such as Fred Dryer of "Hunter" behave in aggressive or antisocial ways, such behavior may be viewed as appropriate and desirable among children (Liebert & Sprafkin, 1988).

Despite these claims, one study found that geographic areas with the largest audiences for violent television programs had the lowest rates of violent crimes. Plausible explanations were that frequent TV watchers are less likely to report crime, watching TV violence acts as a catharsis to reduce the likelihood of overt aggression, and/or high rates of TV viewing may decrease opportunities for household criminal victimization (Messner, 1986). Another study found that adolescents exposed to large amounts of TV violence were no more likely to exhibit aggressive actions than individuals not exposed to such material. However, adolescents who frequently played video games reported more aggressive behavior (Benson, Williams, & Johnson, 1987).

The overall relationship between television violence and aggressiveness during adolescence suggests that regular or frequent viewing of violent television programs may cause aggressive behavior. Persons who already exhibit aggressive tendencies may be even more influenced by TV violence. Although TV violence is only one of many factors that may lead to aggressive behavior, its influence should not be ignored (Lowery & DeFleur, 1983). Summarizing 20 years of research, authorities concluded that TV violence can provide instruction in antisocial and aggressive behavior. The value-shaping effects of TV violence appear to be widespread, suggesting that it can work in subtle and insidious ways to adversely influence youth and society (Liebert & Sprafkin, 1988).

Child Abuse: Trends and Resolution

Child abuse is the ultimate expression of parental rejection. It most likely occurs when parents have inadequate abilities to control their impulses to punish the child or when they receive an emotional payoff from the abuse. Such an emotional payoff results when anger is used to relieve depression about other problems (Salter, Richardson, & Martin, 1985). **Child abuse** may be defined as a circumstance in which a child under age 18 experiences nonaccidental, serious physical and/or mental injury, sexual abuse or exploitation, or serious physical and/or emotional neglect resulting from acts of omission. Child neglect, a result of an act of omission, means failure by the parent or caregiver to provide for the child's basic needs such as food, clothing, shelter, medical attention, or supervision ("Understanding Child," 1985). The most underreported form of neglect may be nonorganic failure to thrive which occurs when a child under age 3 stops growing. During 1987, the National Committee for the Prevention of Child Abuse estimated that over 1,100 children died in the United States as a direct result of child abuse. Authorities believe that the number of fatal cases may be considerably higher because numerous reported deaths are attributed to other causes such as illness or accident (Esper, 1988). For example, the repetitive and violent shaking of a young child often leads to head injuries such as retinal and intracranial hemorrhages, which can result in death without any visible signs of external trauma. Evidence suggests that violent shaking of children is often preceded by other forms of abuse and neglect (Alexander, Crabbe, Sato, Smith, & Bennett, 1990).

Prevalence and Risk Factors of Child Abuse

Today, one can report a suspected case of child abuse without giving her/his name and be legally protected from civil or criminal liability ("Understanding Child Abuse," 1985). In fact, in most states, it is illegal for certain professionals such as teachers and physicians to not report child abuse. Consequently, there has been a threefold increase in the estimated number of reported child abuse and neglect cases since 1976. In 1987, there were over 2.2 million child abuse cases reported in the United States (Flanagan & Maguire, 1990). Since the

Table 14.6: Parent-to-Child Violence

Type of Violence	Rate per 1,000 Children Ages 3–17*	
	1975	1985
Minor violence acts		
Threw something	54	27
Pushed/grabbed/shoved	318	307
Slapped or spanked	582	549
Severe violence acts		
Kicked/bit/hit with fist	32	13
Hit, tried to hit with object	134	97
Beat up	13	6
Threatened with gun or knife	1	2
Used gun or knife	1	2
Violence indexes		
Overall Violence (1–8)	630	620
Severe Violence (4–8)	140	107
Very Severe Violence (4, 6, 8)	36	19

*For two-caretaker households with at least one child, ages 3–17 at home.
From M. A. Straus and R. J. Gelles, "Societal Change and Change in Family Violence from 1975 to 1985 as Revealed by Two National Surveys" in *Journal of Marriage and the Family,* 48:469. Copyright © 1986 National Council on Family Relations, 3989 Central Avenue, N. E., Suite #550, Minneapolis, MN 55421. Reprinted by permission.

reported rates of child abuse are actually increasing, a question arises concerning interpretation of data. Is child abuse actually increasing, or is it more likely to come to the attention of law enforcement and/or social service agencies? Comparing national representative samples of families from 1975 and 1985, two leading authorities on family violence, Murray Straus and Richard Gelles (1986), concluded that a substantial decrease in child abuse occurred between 1975 and 1985. According to their data, there was a significant reduction in both severe and very severe violence (see Table 14.6).

Predictive factors most likely to lead to child abuse and/or neglect include an unplanned pregnancy where the father did not want the child, complicated and painful childbirth, absence of mother-infant bonding, strict and harsh parenting techniques, and dislike of the child in comparison to other children in the family (Oates, Davis, & Ryan, 1983). Family circumstances often associated with child abandonment are evidence of sexual **promiscuity,** alcoholism, and/or parent-child conflicts. Child-neglect factors include intellectual inadequacy of parent, temporary financial problems, physical problems such as illness of parent, too many children for size of income, and/or physical defect or illness in child (Martin & Walters, 1982).

Predisposing Factors: Family Stress and Childhood Abuse

Family stress resulting from socioeconomic status is a predisposing factor in child abuse; children from low-income families are more likely to be victims of physical abuse or neglect (Lieshman, 1983). Both affluent blacks and whites have low rates of child abuse although low-income whites have a higher level of child abuse than low-income blacks (Bergdorf, 1981). Whether or not an impoverished group engages in physical child abuse is more likely to depend upon the special social resources that each group possesses. However, one must be careful with data interpretations which suggest that the largest number of child abusers come from low-income families. Such cases are more likely to be reported to human service agencies by low-income families who have contact with these agencies. Nevertheless, there is a strong relationship between stress and lack of money in the family. Physical child abuse is almost twice as likely to occur in families where the husband is unemployed (Zigler & Rubin, 1985). It is unclear as to whether or not physical abuse is a consequence of increased psychological stress, being exposed to children for more time each day, or inability to obtain child care (Krugman, Lenherr, Betz, & Fryer, 1986).

Alcohol abuse by the parent or caretaker is also associated with physically abused, sexually abused, and neglected children. One survey of abused children found that over one half had at least one parent with a history of alcoholism (Femularo, Stone, Barnum, & Wharton, 1986). Unmarried pregnancy is another family characteristic that is related to child abuse. As the number of live births to a teen mother increases, the likelihood that she will engage in child abuse increases substantially. Teen mothers lack social support, material resources, and knowledge about child care resulting in a heightened stress level (Zuravin, 1988). Abusive families are usually isolated from the community, have few friends, and lack extended family support systems—all of which contribute substantially to the likelihood of child abuse (Zigler & Rubin, 1985). Finally, violence itself is a family characteristic that begets violence (Martin, Schumm, Bugaighis, Jurich, & Bollman, 1987). For example, mothers who come to shelters for battered women are much more likely to have engaged

Anatomically-correct dolls, which are frequently used by therapists who work with sexually abused children, may also serve as educational tools for parents and teachers.

in child abuse in comparison to mothers from a national representative sample (Giles-Sims, 1985).

Childhood abuse has also been determined to be a predisposing risk factor in child abuse. About one third of all parents who were abused or extremely neglected during childhood will subject their children to the same types of maltreatment (Kaufman & Zigler, 1986). Further, among high risk, low-income mothers, one third of those mothers who themselves had a history of severe childhood abuse also abused their own children (Egeland & Jacobvitz, 1984). However, the unqualified acceptance of the idea that child abuse is transmitted from generation to generation can lead to a self-fulfilling prophecy for parents with a history of childhood abuse. Characteristics associated with parents who have not repeated the abusive behavior pattern from their own childhood include having had one parent or foster parent who loved and supported them, present involvement with a supportive spouse or partner, experience of fewer current stressful life events, and attainment of a greater awareness of their abuse history (Kaufman & Zigler, 1986).

Incest: A Family Secret

Child sexual abuse has been defined as involvement of dependent, psychologically immature children and adolescents in sexual activities that they do not fully comprehend and for which they are unable to give informed consent (Endert & Daniel, 1986). Although each state mandates that suspected cases of child sexual abuse must be reported, in many states such sexual activity is not included within the incest law unless vaginal penetration by the penis occurs. Legally, **incest** is defined as an illicit sexual relationship between persons who are within prohibited degrees of kinship (Edwards, 1987). As in the case of sexual assault of adult women, incest represents the sexual expression of nonsexual needs (Conte, 1985). However, incest is not just an exercise of power domination, but rather it involves other components such as desire to express hostility, create dependence, and find emotional fulfillment. Therefore, the sexual activity always occurs in conjunction with other motives (Stark, 1984). While incest is sometimes a nonviolent means of pathologically expressing affection, in most cases coercion and violence are involved (Ledray, 1984).

The greatest threat of child sexual abuse comes from within the nuclear family, especially from fathers and stepfathers (Endert & Daniel, 1986). The most commonly reported form of incest involves biological fathers and daughters, whereas mother-son sexual abuse is rarely reported (Edwards, 1987). It is a myth that incest perpetrators differ from other types of child sexual abusers. In one group of incestuous fathers, 44% were found to be abusing other female children outside the home and 11% were also sexually abusing other male children (Conte, 1985).

Prevalence and Risk Factors of Incest

To attempt to gauge the actual prevalence of incest is a formidable task because of its very nature. For example, one survey of adult women in San Francisco found that 16% had been incest victims (Russell, 1986). Others have estimated that about 50% of all teen runaways, 60% of all psychiatric inpatients, and 83% of all women in sex therapy have experienced incest (Foster, 1988). Regional variations in the rates are suggested by findings at a major southern university in which a much higher percentage (one fourth) of the women reported experience with incest than the national average (Alexander & Lupfer, 1987).

Whenever incest occurs, every member of the family makes a psychological contribution to its development and maintenance (Conte, 1985). Such abuse is more likely to occur in families with parent-child conflicts, a promiscuous and alcoholic father, a younger female child, or an emotionally disturbed child (Martin & Walters, 1982). Risk factors specific to father-daughter incest include unavailability of mother due to employment, disability, or illness and the existence of a conflict-ridden marriage (Finkelhor & Baron, 1986). Other family factors, in descending order of occurrence, are broken family, insufficient or misuse of income, inadequate housing, family discord, and physical abuse of spouse (Vander Mey & Neff, 1984). Fathers who engage in incest tend to be middle-aged, heterosexual, employed, a disciplinarian with low self-esteem, religious, possibly alcoholic, and married to a passive wife with whom sexual intercourse rarely occurs (Foster, 1988). When compared to biological fathers, stepfathers who engage in incestuous activity are more likely to have been sexually abused as a child, to have an antisocial personality, and to engage in excessive brooding and acting-out behavior (Erickson, Walbek, & Seely, 1987).

Signs of Incest

Many suspected cases of incest, based on clinical signs, are reported by pediatricians, social workers, schoolteachers, counselors, and principals (Endert & Daniel, 1986). Even when there are obvious signs, fear and disbelief may prevent incest from being reported. At least one fifth of the mothers of incest victims in one study refused to believe their daughters, and another one fifth indicated fear of their spouses prevented them from reporting the incest (Pierce & Pierce, 1985). The signs of incest may be physical or behavioral. Physical signs are often evidenced as medical problems while behavioral ones are more likely to be noticed in school-age children than younger children (see Table 14.7).

Types of Incest

Although most child sexual abusers are men, only one third of all incest cases involve the biological parent (Watson, Lubennow, Greenberg, King, & Junkin, 1984). The increased incidence of incest in stepfamilies may be due to common adjustment problems and lack of childhood caretaking (Erickson et al., 1987). Other data on incest suggest that about one fourth of the cases occur within the nuclear family and one third within the extended family (Alexander & Lupfer, 1987).

Parent-Child

Approximately 85–90% of incest victims are female children and 98% of the offenders are men (Foster, 1988; Stark, 1984). About 75–85% of all cases of incest are thought to involve father-daughter incest including stepfather or mother's cohabitation partner (Ledray, 1984). Other studies suggest a range of 2–40% for biological fathers and 16–23% for stepfathers, adoptive, or foster parents who are likely to have sexual contact with their daughters (Finkelhor, 1983; Foster, 1988; Pierce & Pierce, 1985; Russell, 1986). Father-daughter incest usually begins with daughters between ages 6–11 and usually lasts about 2 years (Stark, 1984). Stepfathers are more likely to continue their incestuous behavior than biological fathers. Women who are sexually abused by their stepfathers also are more likely to be sexually abused by other men, especially by friends of the stepfather (Erickson et al., 1987).

Many incestuous fathers make initial sexual overtures to their daughters at about age 10, but most do not actually have sexual intercourse with their daughters until the onset of puberty (Peretti & Banks,

Table 14.7: Signs of Incest

Physical

Sexually Transmitted Diseases
- —Genital candidiasis
- —Gonococcal infection in urethra, rectum, or vagina
- —Herpes genitalia
- —Nonspecific urethritis
- —Trichomoniasis

Medical Problems
- —Blood on underwear
- —Changes in appetite
- —Chest pains
- —Enuresis (bed-wetting)
- —Gastro-intestinal complaints
- —Lax rectal tone
- —Premarital pregnancy

Behavioral

School-Related Problems
- —Anxiety
- —Inability to concentrate
- —Inadequate examination preparation
- —Late arrival or departure
- —Late assignments
- —Sudden drop in grades

Personal Problems
- —Alcohol and substance abuse
- —Fearful
- —Guilt
- —Loss of self-esteem
- —Provocative dress
- —Runaway
- —Seductive behavior
- —Self-depreciation
- —Sexual promiscuity
- —Sophisticated sexual knowledge

Interpersonal Problems
- —Inability to make friends
- —Lack of trust
- —Nonparticipation in social activities
- —Poor peer relations
- —Rebel against mother who failed to protect
- —Withdrawal

Source: From P. C. Alexander and S. L. Lupfer, "Family Characteristics and Long-Term Consequences Associated with Sexual Abuse" in *Archives of Sexual Behavior,* 16:239–242, 1987; S. Foster, "Counseling Survivors of Incest" in *Medical Aspects of Human Sexuality,* 22(3):119–120, 1988; C. M. Endert and W. A. Daniel, Jr., "Intra-Family Sexual Abuse of Adolescents" in *Pediatric Annals,* 15:769, 1986; K. C. Finkel, "Sexual Abuse of Children: An Update" in *Canadian Medical Association Journal,* 136:248–249, 1987; and D. Finkelhor, "Sex Among Siblings: A Survey On Prevalence, Variety, and Effects" in *Archives of Sexual Behavior,* 9:178–189, 1980.

1984). Detrimental effects of incest tend to increase with time as daughters develop degrading and self-depreciating attitudes toward themselves and beliefs that their fathers perceive them only as sex objects (see Table 14.8). The mother often realizes that her daughter is fulfilling the sexual needs of the father but is relieved that she no longer has to do so (Endert & Daniel, 1986).

Father-son incest has received little attention in the research literature, which partially explains the sizeable variations in the estimated prevalence when compared to data on father-daughter incest. The estimated percentage of male-child incest cases involving the biological father or stepfather ranges from 6–50% (Ellerstein & Canavan, 1980; Pierce & Pierce, 1985). Although sexual involvement of a father with his son is related to both homosexuality and incest, few studies of incest have addressed these problems. The limited data on father-son incest suggests that at least one half of the victims display evidence of psychological disturbances, frequent educational problems, continual sexuality problems in later life, and in some instances thoughts of suicide (Pierce, 1987).

The reported incidence of mother-child incest suggests that it is the least common form of all incest. Of the identified cases of incest, only 1–2% typically involves the mother of the child (Rowan, Rowan, & Langelier, 1990). Some experts believe that mother-child incest goes largely unreported because it can be disguised during bathing or dressing of the victim and because children are unlikely to report a mother. However, most children are usually very perceptive in distinguishing an affectionate touch from an inappropriate touch that is sexual in nature. Male children, who apparently are more likely to be victims of mother incest, are less likely to report incest (Russell, 1986). In addition, **neonatal incest** (applying oral or manual stimulation to infant's genitals) is likely to go unreported unless the infant suffers injury. It is thought to be motivated by loneliness or alienation from a sex partner (Chasnoff et al., 1986).

Sibling

Sibling incest is not as thoroughly researched or clearly delineated as other forms of incest. Circumstances leading to sibling incest are thought to include situational pressures, personality dysfunctions, and assumption of inappropriate roles within the family system. Some authorities also believe that both siblings may willingly engage in the behavior in an attempt to cope with unmet needs for affection and to release tension (Ascherman & Safier, 1990). However, casual sex play

Table 14.8: Adverse Psychological Reactions of Father-Daughter Incest Victims

Anxiety	88%
Fear	83
Humiliation	80
Guilt	73
Self-devaluation	63
Value-conflict	61
Sexual meaninglessness	54
Sexual frigidity	49
Heterosexual aversiveness	39
Suicide contemplation	27

Source: P. O. Peretti and D. Banks, "Negative Psycho-Social Variables of the Incestuous Daughter of Father-Daughter Incest" in *Child Psychiatry Quarterly,* 17:17. Copyright © 1984 Community Mental Health Center, Indira Health Home, Andhra Pradesh, India.

occurring between very young siblings does not constitute incest. Even when it involves older children, most researchers consider incest between siblings with less than a 5-year age difference as nonabusive and victimless (Finkelhor & Baron, 1986). About 4 in 10 women and 2 in 10 men have reportedly experienced sibling incest (Finkelhor, 1979). However, a survey of about 800 undergraduate students at New England universities found that only 15% of women and 10% of men had engaged in some type of sexual activity with a sibling. About two thirds of the sibling sexual activity consisted of only touching and/or fondling the genitals regardless of age at occurrence with only 18% attempting or actually engaging in sexual intercourse (Finkelhor, 1980). Similar findings from a later study indicate that one fourth or less of the cases involved sexual intercourse while the majority involved fondling of genitals and/or oral-genital contact (Smith & Israel, 1987). This behavior is more likely to involve sister-brother than sister-sister participation (Fortenberry & Hill, 1986).

Sister participants in sister-brother incest are more likely to feel exploited than brothers (Finkelhor & Baron, 1986). Data suggest that about one half of women are very upset about the sexual experimentation with their brother, and some have long-term negative effects. It is common for participants in sister-brother incest to report a more ambivalent or positive response toward the sexual encounter in comparison to other incest victims. However, such feelings are often replaced by more substantial negative reactions later in life (Russell, 1986). Thus, long-term ill effects are more likely to occur as the siblings become older (Endert & Daniel, 1986).

Aftermath of Incest

The tragedy of incest is that it can have adverse effects on those involved for the rest of their lives. The extent and duration of emotional damage to an adolescent victim of sexual abuse is related to the identity of the offender, the use of force, and the age of the abuser. Because disclosure of incest represents a betrayal of the parent, the sexually abused child often refuses to disclose the incest. Instead, they may show intense loyalty to the parent because they fear court removal from the home. In fact, many children use various defense mechanisms in an unconscious attempt to protect themselves from the pain and anger associated with their incest experiences (Solin, 1986). For example, three fourths of sexually abused adolescents reported psychosocial complaints associated with incest whereas only about one half complained if they had been sexually victimized by nonfamily members. Most incest victims display feelings of depression, guilt, and helplessness; negative attitudes toward sexuality and sexual behavior; and poor self-images (Orr & Downes, 1985). The type of sexual act is the most accurate predictor of the distress level among female, adolescent incest victims. Sexual intercourse is more often associated with lower self-esteem, higher levels of depression, and greater frequency of antisocial and self-injurious behavior than any other form of sexual contact (Morrow & Sorell, 1989). Untreated adults who were incest victims in childhood may display feelings of depression, low self-esteem, feelings of powerlessness, lack of trust, impulsivity, self-destructive behavior, and difficulty in parenting and in opposite-sex relationships (Lowery, 1987).

Incest can be prevented by educating parents in responsible parenting and educating children in their rights over their bodies and the right to say no. Children need to be reassured that open channels of communication with responsible, caring adults always exist. And, finally, mothers and fathers should be allowed and encouraged to share the responsibilities and rewards of nurturing their children and their family (Foster, 1988).

Summary

- Most parents have no training for the most difficult and complex task they will ever do, being a successful parent.
- Since it is no longer feasible to learn all that one needs to know about parenting via modeling and experience, formal education is essential.

- A variety of physiological, psychological, and societal factors affect socialization.
- For optimal future development, during the 1st year of an infant's life, a secure attachment with another person, usually the mother, must be formed.
- The self-concept of a child is heavily influenced by the child's perceptions of her/his family relationships.
- Attaining parenting goals is influenced by multiple factors including temperament, birth order, socioeconomic factors, and family interaction.
- Theories of child development are based on four theoretical perspectives: mechanistic, organismic, psychoanalytic, and humanistic.
- Effective methods of child guidance involve designing the child's world, serving as consultant, teaching desired behavior, and exerting the right amount of control over the child.
- In order to accomplish desired discipline goals, parents need to understand the reasons for misbehavior and appropriate methods of punishment.
- Quality preschools may contribute to childhood socialization.
- Television is a significant socialization agent for children about which there is substantial concern over exposure to violence and sexuality.
- Child abuse can involve serious mental or physical injury, sexual abuse or exploitation, or serious physical and/or emotional neglect.
- Predictive factors of child abuse include unplanned pregnancy, absence of mother-infant bonding, having been abused as a child, and unhappy marital relationship.
- Incest is the sexual expression of nonsexual needs such as desire to express hostility, to create dependence of another person, and to find emotional fulfillment.
- Most incest victims have symptoms of depression, feelings of guilt and helplessness, poor self-images, and negative attitudes toward sexuality and sexual behavior.

Questions for Critical Reflection

1. America was once considered the world's most child-centered nation, yet Dr. T. Berry Brazelton has said, "We don't value children and we certainly don't value their parents, so we're paying a big price now." How do you resolve this contradiction? What is the price that we are paying?
2. A recent conference on the family at Stanford University explored the increasing self-centeredness of the "me-generation" parents who leave children behind in their rush to get ahead. What is your reaction to these ideas?
3. Which parenting style(s) did your parent(s) use most in rearing you? Did this style differ considerably from that used by their parents? How? If you have children, will (do) you use the same, a modified, or a different parenting style?
4. Based on your personal experience and knowledge of research concerning television, which of the following bumper stickers would you distribute to couples in a parenting class? "Just Say No to Television"; "No Baby-sitter for Me—I've Got TV"; or "TV: Accentuate the Positive and Moderate!" Devise an alternative slogan that embodies your own ideas about TV and children.
5. Dr. Urie Bronfenbrenner argues no hard evidence exists that day care has a negative effect on children, and Dr. Lee Salk believes that parents who anticipate not providing enough time for one-to-one contact in the first 3 years should reconsider the idea of having children. With such conflicting advice from experts, how can parents make informed choices with which they can live comfortably? What would you do if faced with this decision today?

Suggested Readings

Bee, H. (1989). *The developing child* (5th ed.). New York: Harper & Row. A balanced presentation of theory, research, and practical applications in child development.

Bowlby, J. (1988). *A secure base: Parent-child attachment and healthy human development.* New York: Basic Books. A major contribution to clarifying the role of parent-child attachment in establishing a healthy personality for the child.

Brazelton, T. B., & Cramer, B. G. (1990). *The earliest relationship: Parents, infants, and the drama of early attachment.* Reading, MA: Addison-Wesley. A widely-acclaimed book on understanding and caring for children, which focuses on pregnancy and the earliest stages of infancy.

Kempe, R., & Kempe, C. H. (1985). *Child abuse.* Cambridge, MA: Harvard University Press. A consideration of the causes of child abuse and neglect along with recommended prevention and treatment protocols.

Liebert, R. M., & Sprafkin, J. (1988). *The early window: Effects on children and youth* (3rd ed.). New York: Pergamon Press. An updated account of the theory and research on television and children's attitudes, development, and behavior.

Maltz, W., & Holman, B. (1987). *Incest and sexuality: A guide to understanding and healing.* Lexington, MA: Lexington Books. A self-help book designed to assist adult victims in understanding the effects of incest on their sexual attitudes and behavior.

CHAPTER 15

Family Finances

The hallmarks of a healthy approach to money are virtually indistinguishable from those marking a satisfactory sex life within marriage. These hallmarks are: openness, trust, mutual respect, and attentiveness to detail.
N. S. Fields, 1986

OUTLINE

On any given day, children and adults are bombarded with advertising for products from such diverse sources as newspapers, magazines, television, radio, direct mail, and outdoor billboards. In 1988, it was estimated that $1.18 billion was spent on advertising consumer products in the United States (U.S. Bureau of the Census, 1990ll). Newly married couples may quickly conclude that they need an apartment or house; furniture; automobile; health, fire, and automobile insurance; new clothing; and the list goes on. Despite careful planning, a wife and husband often discover that their perceived needs far outweigh their level of financial resources and that financial contentment constantly eludes them as they struggle to balance income with cash outflow.

The complexity of financial issues is evidenced by statistics concerning how disposable personal income is spent by consumers. In 1988, nondurable goods purchased included clothing and shoes—$186.8 billion, food away from home—$176.6 billion, tobacco products—$36.9 billion, and housekeeping supplies—$30.9 billion (U.S. Bureau of the Census, 1990cc). The average weekly household expenditure for food purchased away from home in 1987 was $30.10 compared to $6.56 for housekeeping supplies (U.S. Bureau of the Census, 1990dd). By any measure, family financial management is a crucial area requiring compromise, planning, and efficient use of available financial resources. Thus, the search for marital satisfaction cannot be separated from economic issues (Crosby, 1991). In one study, the most important predictor of satisfaction with quality of life for married men was income satisfaction followed by marital satisfaction. Their wives, however, reversed the importance of these two crucial factors (Berry & Williams, 1987). While financial problems are thought to be more prevalent among lower-class marriages, economic reverses, inflation, and loss of jobs create severe financial problems in middle-class marriages, often leading to divorce (South, 1985). However, couples should not buy into the myth that marriages fail because of money. Although the abundance or lack of financial resources undeniably impact a relationship, the underlying issue in money disputes is one of values. Two unique individuals from two quite different families will inevitably attach different meaning or value to the use of financial resources. Thus, a fertile ground is spawned for marital conflict. Anticipating such differences and forearming oneself with financial knowledge offers a sound basis for successful family financial planning.

The Family and the Economy

As parenting has become optional, there is an interesting phenomenon emerging: class differences between parents and nonparents. Child-free partners with combined resources can buy more luxury items than can those with children. For example, it is estimated that the family food bill will go up at least 20% after the birth of the first child (Trunzo, 1985). In 1988, approximately one half of all married couples had children. These families had a median annual income of $34,000, only $3,000 more than child-free couples. Of female-headed households with children, about two thirds had a median annual income of only $11,000 compared to $21,000 for child-free women (Waldrop, 1988).

Divorce and economic difficulties are far too often synonymous. Although single parenting is becoming more common, with roughly one fifth of all households headed by a single parent, it is becoming less and less economically feasible (Hunt & Hunt, 1986). Financial problems for single-parent families arise for many reasons. Child-care costs are not the least of these, considering the fact that 84% of single mothers with children under 18 are in the work force compared to 73% of married mothers (U.S. Bureau of Census, 1990y). One authority suggests that mothers who are college graduates will lose an average of $53,000 in salary due to lost time at work associated with parenting by the time that the first child reaches age 14 (Espenshade, 1983). The cost of child care involves a number of factors including geographical region, level of living, presence of other children, and the inflation rate (U.S. Department of Agriculture, 1988). The single greatest cost for children is that of providing adequate housing (see figure 15.1).

Medical care for growing families is also stretching the family dollar. And the so-called "sandwich" generation is frequently pressed from both sides as their own parents reach old age, develop frail health, and require increasing medical services. A survey of university extension home economists found that escalating medical costs was ranked as the leading public policy issue for families followed by pay equity for women and costs of preschool child care (Kobbe, 1985).

Inflation and the Consumer Price Index

Inflation can best be described as across-the-board increases in the cost of goods and services (Garman & Forgue, 1988). It simply means the dollar does not buy

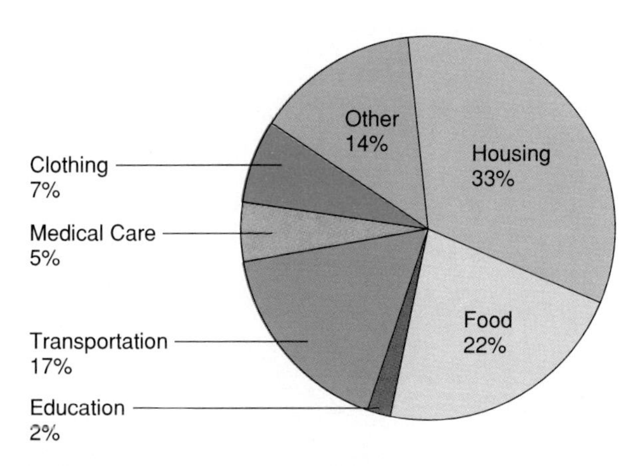

Figure 15.1 Relative Expenses of Rearing Child to Age 18

Source: *Family Economics Review* No. 2, K. S. Tippett, editor. Washington, DC: U.S. Department of Agriculture, p. 35, 1985.

as much as it once did. The **Consumer Price Index** (CPI) is an economic indicator that measures the impact of inflation over time as stated in terms of the percentage change of the average price of a basket of goods and services that the consumer might purchase and use (Lang, 1988). The major groups of items contained in the CPI include food, shelter, fuel oil and coal, energy, apparel and upkeep, transportation and services (U.S. Bureau of the Census, 1990ii). The **rule of 72** can be used to determine the effect of inflation on future prices. By dividing 72 by the expected rate of inflation, one may estimate how many years it will take for prices to double. For example, with a 4% inflation rate, it would take 18 years (72/4) for the price of an automobile to double from $11,000 to $22,000 (Lang, 1988).

The rate of inflation as measured by the CPI was characterized by major fluctuations during the 1980s. But despite increasing demands for consumer products, both inflation and prices remained relatively low partly due to foreign competition (Berger, 1987). By late 1990, the annual rate of inflation was the worst in 9 years, 6.1% in comparison to only 4.6% in 1989 ("Consumer Costs," 1989; "Inflation Rate," 1991). If family wage increases lag behind consumer price increases, the family is less well-off financially; they will have less income to make similar purchases than in previous years.

Consumer Prices

The cost of living continued to rise throughout the 1980s. Data from the United States Bureau of Labor Statistics indicates that consumer prices rose 28% between 1980 and 1985 ("Upcreep of Prices," 1986). During the 1980s, consumer price increases for food and housing were the greatest in the Northeast and West (U.S. Bureau of the Census, 1990jj). The major groups of items that exhibited the lowest price increases were food and apparel (U.S. Bureau of the Census, 1990ii). Due to shifting priorities throughout the life cycle, rises in consumer prices means that persons are constantly trying to assess the impact of inflation on their personal financial planning. Couples should anticipate the rate of inflation to prepare for future major expenses such as college tuition and housing (Lang, 1988).

Household Income Levels

Despite rises in inflation reflected in the CPI, median family incomes increased by only modest amounts in relationship to inflation during the 1980s. Using **constant dollars** (dollar value adjusted for inflation), median family income for those families in which the wife was in the paid labor force increased by a total of 10% between 1980–1988. In contrast, the CPI rose by a total of 51% during the same time period (U.S. Bureau of the Census, 1990ii). In 1990, the median family income for a married couple with a nonworking wife was $23,764 as contrasted to about $46,904 if the wife was in the paid labor force (U.S. Department of Labor, 1991). However, the dollar values for median family income do not represent **disposable income,** that is, after tax income. For example, a suburban, home-owning family of four earning $46,000 per year pays $9,938 in income, real estate, and sales taxes. Thus, this family actually has only about $36,000 in disposable income ("Cost of Living," 1986).

The Role of Money in Family Life

Over the years, considerable efforts have been devoted to trying to understand the relationship between money and marital happiness. A 1987 poll of almost 1,000 American women found that 42% rated sexual activity as more important to a marriage than money, whereas 35% believed that money was more important. In general, younger women were more likely to pick sexual activity over money in terms of importance ("Money Takes," 1987). Money represents a medium of exchange for goods and services, but inwardly, most people attach values to money. Family backgrounds often help explain money "personalities" and symbolic values (Goode, 1988). Symbolically, money may represent control, self-esteem, love, and security (Weinstein, 1986).

Money matters! Negotiations in financial decisions can strengthen couple commitment.

Gender Roles and Money Management

Although money remains a considerable point of disagreement for couples, as it has been over the years, financial roles have undergone substantial changes. Today, wives often earn as much income as their husbands, and thus may have more definite ideas about how money should be handled. In fact, women now often define their independence through financial autonomy. However, because of traditional beliefs about gender roles men may be reluctant to acknowledge the financial contributions of their wives to the marriage (Weinstein, 1984). Therefore, the financial disagreements that surface in the achievement of family goals are issues about responsibility, commitment, and self-worth (Goode, 1988).

A crucial issue related to the success or failure of marriages is not so much the amount of family income but rather the money management techniques employed by couples (Blumstein & Schwartz, 1983). In a comparison of divorced and happily married couples a greater influence by the wife in paying bills, looking after household expenditures, and deciding to obtain cash was reported by happily married couples. They were also more likely to spend money for recreational vehicles, appliances, and down payments for houses. Couples whose marriages ended in divorce more often spent money for stereo equipment, living room furniture, and television sets (Schaninger & Buss, 1986). The purchases of happily married couples seem to suggest long-term planning, while those of couples who later divorced relate more to immediate pleasure. Factors that increase the involvement of wives in financial management include increases in wife's job earnings and family's net worth. Other related factors are large family size, belief that wives should make career plans, and decrease in marital satisfaction (Fitzsimmons, 1987).

Effective Money Management

The inevitable question in a newly formed family is who should manage the money? Problems that arise in seeking answers may be due to differing money management practices observed in their respective families. If in their families of orientation, the wife's mother and the husband's father paid the bills, each partner may have unexamined assumptions of how bills "should" be handled. Ideally, money management should be a shared responsibility with each partner contributing to the process that they do best. In practice, women tend to purchase household items and those items that are consumed by other family members, whereas men are usually the chief buyers of insurance and automobiles (Miller, 1987).

While there are many systems for effective money management, their efficacy rests on three essentials: communication on a regular basis about money matters, continued involvement of both spouses in money issues, and agreement on both short-term and long-term financial goals (Goode, 1988). Marriage partners should jointly decide financial goals. The process includes resolving philosophical differences, drawing up a budget, and establishing a savings cushion of at least 2–3 months' salary for emergencies (Weinstein, 1984). If problems arise regarding money management plans, family financial counseling services can help. Areas where financial management skills are needed include identifying realistic goals, exploring alternative behavioral strategies, and selecting new financial management techniques (Bagarozzi & Bagarozzi, 1980). Such assistance is typically available from credit unions and consumer credit counseling services supported by insurance companies, banks, labor unions, and many large corporations.

Developing a Financial Plan

A financial plan involves determining the total amount of income and devising a complete plan of spending for a specific period (Lee & Zelenak, 1987). Financial plans must be based on available income and contain a summary of all essential and nonessential items. They include expenditures for taxes, social security, and pension plans. Families may not have financial plans because of several reasons: good consuming practices may mask the need for one, the benefits of preparing one may not be immediate or tangible, or a financial plan may require a greater level of family cooperation than that which exists (Lee & Zelenak, 1987). A financial plan should be established in consultation with all family members to ensure cooperation in the development of spending and saving priorities including cash for emergencies (Harris, 1983).

A primary advantage of developing a financial plan is that it forces a more realistic assessment of how the family money is actually spent. By keeping track of the various categories, most people find that they tend to underestimate how much money they spend on many items such as gifts for birthdays, holidays, and other special occasions (Stauffer, 1988). The specific benefits of a financial plan include:

1. Encourages rational use of income while minimizing influence of custom, conspicuous consumption of latest fashions, and advertising.
2. Proves helpful when family income increases or decreases substantially.
3. Assists in planning major expenditures over several years.
4. Helps to assure that essential goods and services will be given priority in light of family goals and values.
5. Provides mechanism to more easily adjust to changes in family size.
6. Helps in allocating **discretionary income** (disposable income remaining after paying taxes and for essentials).
7. Helps to identify unnecessary family expenditures (Lee & Zelenak, 1987, pp. 261–263).

Stages of Financial Planning

The development of a sound financial plan necessitates careful thought. Recognizing that inflation can have a dramatic impact, any family financial plan may require periodic adjustment to accommodate the rising prices in the economy (Lee & Zelenak, 1987). Financial planning involves sequential steps including analyzing resources, establishing goals, and designing and executing the plan followed by an evaluation of the process (Lang, 1988).

The process in financial planning is more important than the product. A financial plan should be considered as a spending guide rather than an absolute, inflexible budget. As circumstances change, many persons find that readjustments are necessary because of consistent overspending or underspending (Lee & Zelenak, 1987). It is helpful if the financial plan is set up

Table 15.1: Budget Allocation Components for Four-Person Family

Budget Allocation Components	Lower	Intermediate	Higher
Total family consumption	**79%**	**72%**	**65%**
Food	30	23	19
Housing	18	22	22
Transportation	9	9	8
Clothing	6	5	5
Personal care	2	2	2
Medical care	10	6	4
Other family consumption	4	5	5
Total nonconsumption	**21**	**28**	**35**
Other items	4	4	5
Social Security and disability	7	7	5
Personal income taxes	10	17	25

Source: C. Hefferan, "Family Budget Guidelines" in *Family Economics Review,* U.S. Department of Agriculture, 1987, October, p. 2.

in a ledger including individual expense categories such as groceries, toiletries, and linens rather than broad categories such as household expenses. In addition, a daily journal used to list out-of-pocket expenses will facilitate income tax preparation (Stauffer, 1988). Although entries should be accurate, figures may be rounded to the nearest whole dollar.

Considerations to determine allocations for expenditures include geographical region, size of community, number of children in family, number of household earners, and level of living. The percentages for budget allocation categories for a four-person family in an urban area provide insight (see Table 15.1). As the level of living increases, the percentage of disposable income that goes for food and medical care decreases substantially while the percentage for personal income taxes increases dramatically (Hefferan, 1987).

Budget Tasks

The major components of a budget are net income and expenses including housing, personal maintenance, obligations, and savings and investments. Most people mistakenly assume that a budget is a plan for saving money. In actuality, it is a plan for spending money in such ways that personal and family goals may be achieved. Making a budget requires analyzing previous spending trends. This may be accomplished by keeping records in terms of fixed expenses (i.e. mortgage payment, rent, insurance) and flexible or variable expenses (i.e. clothing, food) for at least 2 months. The next task is to balance fixed and flexible expenditures with available disposable income. To be successful in financial planning, one must maintain somewhat detailed records of cancelled checks, receipts, and other pertinent data (Miller, 1987). An annual budget worksheet is illustrated in Table 15.2.

Rational Consumer Decision Making

Americans appear to be shopping not only less but less compulsively than before. A 1990 Louis Harris Poll found almost one half of those surveyed were spending less time shopping than five years ago. Further, only 16% of these consumers reported that shopping gave them a sense of pleasure or excitement ("Shoppers Are," 1990). By making rational consumer purchases, families can maximize their satisfaction from their invested time and money resources. Financial goals usually determine consumption behavior. Therefore, persons with long-term goals may work hard and spend little money at the present time, while others may engage in conspicuous consumption, purchasing goods and services to demonstrate their social worth. Finally, customs related to holidays, ceremonies, and leisure time activities influence purchases. Thus, rather than engaging in impulse or habit buying, persons should buy according to a spending plan and limit their purchases to items that are affordable (Miller, 1987).

Knowledgeable consumers obtain information regarding price and quality of merchandise. There are several consumer publications for this purpose. One valuable source of such information is *Consumer Reports* published by Consumers Union, which purchases, tests, and evaluates various products. In order to preserve its objectivity, this magazine does not accept

Table 15.2: An Annual Budget Worksheet

Net Income

Sources				
Sources ____________	Annual	$ ______	Monthly	$ ______
____________		$ ______		$ ______
____________		$ ______		$ ______
____________		$ ______		$ ______
	Total Annual	$ ______	Total Monthly	$ ______

Expenses	Annual		Monthly	
	Now	Goal	Now	Goal
Housing				
Rent, home loan payment				
Property taxes, assessments				
Property insurance (homeowner, tenant)				
Maintenance, repairs				
Utilities				
Gas, electricity				
Other fuel				
Telephone				
Water, sewer				
Cable TV				
Garbage collection				
Home furnishings				
Other (such as homeowners' association dues, household help *other than* child care)				
Personal Maintenance				
Food				
Clothing				
Purchases				
Laundry, drycleaning, repairs				
Self-improvement				
Education				
Books, magazines, newspapers				

Table 15.2: *cont'd*

Expenses	Annual Now	Annual Goal	Monthly Now	Monthly Goal
Entertainment & recreation				
Vacations				
Other (including movies, sports, restaurants, hobbies)				
Transportation				
Gas, oil				
Repairs, maintenance				
Parking, tolls				
Auto insurance				
License registration				
Public transportation				
Gifts & holiday expenses (*other than* Christmas Club accounts)				
Child/dependent care (including babysitters, nursery school fees, convalescent care)				
Health care				
Health insurance				
Doctors' visits				
Prescriptions, medicine				
Personal care (including barber, hairdresser, cosmetics)				
Obligations				
Regular payments to others (including alimony, child support, other court-ordered payments)				
Contributions & dues (voluntary, including those deducted from your paycheck)				
Debt payments				
Installment loan payments (for vehicles, furniture, etc.)				
Credit card, charge accounts				
Savings & investment				
Short-Term savings (including Christmas Club, emergency fund)				
Long-Term savings (including company or private pension)				
Life insurance				
Investments (including stocks, bonds, real estate)				

Source: As appeared in R. L. Miller, *Economic Issues for Consumers*, 5th ed., pp. 140–141, 1987.

advertising from manufacturers. At least six major types of products plus automobiles are reviewed in each issue ("Put to the Test," 1982).

The Secrets of Defensive Shopping

Today's shopper is increasingly confronted with advertisements featuring competing products at a wide variety of prices, and salespersons trained to enhance their sales quota for the week. Salespersons learn to use various sales techniques such as authority— the seller is perceived as an expert, scarcity—there is a limited quantity, social consensus—other persons are buying item, and reciprocation—free gift encourages purchase (Krucoff, 1985). Therefore, learning to be a good shopper involves, among other things, being aware of standard sales techniques and key considerations in the purchase of clothing and food as well as use of bargaining principles for major purchases such as appliances, furniture, and automobiles.

In order to become more skillful at bargaining with the seller, the following principles should be applied: know precisely the product desired in terms of make, model, and frills before obtaining competing prices; divide opponents by obtaining competing prices from a number of sources; and show a little inflexibility which provides psychological advantage to potential purchaser (Seixas, 1985). If asked, for example, to make an offer for an automobile or house purchase, the suggested purchase price should be below what the seller is likely to accept but not so low that the offer appears ridiculous.

Finally, by watching the calendar, a good money manager learns that appliances; furnace and air conditioning systems; recreational, home, and lawn equipment; building and decorating materials; furniture; housewares; sporting goods; and automobiles have peak sales periods and promotions which tend to run in off-seasons. For example, the last week of the year is the best time to buy a large major appliance whereas fall is the peak sales period for electronics equipment so it should be purchased in spring or late winter (David, 1985).

Food: Nutrition and Cost

Generally, family food expenditures represent about 15% of personal disposable income. However, the proportion varies from 50% of total income for households with a before-tax income below $5,000 to 9% for those families with incomes of $40,000 and over (Dunham, 1987). Food costs will continue to increase because people with fast-paced lives are tending to eat more meals in restaurants. In 1989, almost 134 million Americans ate out daily with more than 16 million choosing McDonald's. On an average day, Americans eat more than 24 million hot dogs, along with 524 million servings of Coca-Cola. Almost 1 million of these Cokes are drunk for breakfast along with 3 million Dunkin' Donuts (Monson, 1989). Further, food consumed at home includes greater quantities of convenience food items such as frozen entrees. In addition, grocery stores are adding in-store bakeries, salad bars, and delicatessens with more plastic and microwave containers being used for food sales (Parlett & Lipton, 1987).

Besides costs, the crucial factor of the nutritional value of food cannot be ignored. Available evidence suggests that the nutrient levels in the body of the average American are declining. For example, an assessment of the iron status and dietary iron intake among healthy, menstruating women concluded that one fifth were depleted in iron stores due to their low intake of meat and dairy products (Izviak, Dop, Galan, & Hercberg, 1986). A partial explanation is that much misleading and confusing information about the nutritional value of foodstuffs is conveyed via advertising (Miller, 1987). In 1988, the advertising expenditures for food products in magazines was $377 million and $1.6 billion on network television (U.S. Bureau of the Census, 1990mm, 1990nn). In the early 1980s, over one half of all television commercials directed at children were for sugared foods. Mothers who watched Saturday morning cartoons with their children were unlikely to discuss the nutritional values of the foods being advertised (Brody, Stoneman, Lane, & Sanders, 1981).

The fact that many Americans suffer from malnutrition due to an overconsumption of fats, simple sugars, and cholesterol is uncontested. What is not known is whether this circumstance is due to a lack of nutritional knowledge or its application ("75 Tips," 1983). National Survey data suggest that the majority are uninformed about important nutritional issues, such as fats and **cholesterol.** For example, less than one half of the respondents could identify the food sources of cholesterol or link its high levels to heart disease (Schiller et al., 1989). Diets could be improved for most persons with little effort and less money if individuals would arm themselves with basic nutrition facts.

The Four Basic Food Groups

The most significant information needed about food pertains to neither costs nor preparation. Unless a person is knowledgeable about the functions of key nutrients, one may not be motivated to select a well-balanced diet. There are five categories of essential nutrients:

1. *Carbohydrates*—provide energy and dietary fiber.
2. *Fats*—provide energy, cushion organs, help maintain body temperature, promote healthy skin; and carry fat-soluble vitamins.
3. *Proteins*—promote growth, repair body cells, and provide energy.
4. *Minerals:*
   Calcium—builds and strengthens bones and teeth; regulates muscle contractions, transmission of nerve stimuli, and coagulation of blood.
   Iron—combines with protein to form **hemoglobin** (a substance in red blood cells that transports oxygen throughout body).
5. *Vitamins:*
   Vitamin A—prevents night blindness; promotes growth, bone development, and healthy skin and mucous membranes.
   Vitamin B Complex (Thiamin, Riboflavin, and Niacin)—releases energy from food and aids in metabolism.
   Vitamin C—maintains structure of bone, cartilage, teeth, skin, and blood vessels; promotes wound healing (National Live Stock & Meat Board, 1987, p. 1).

Since about 50 nutrients are needed daily by both children and adults for body growth and maintenance, selecting a balanced diet can be an inordinate task (American Dietetic Association, 1981). To assist consumers in making proper decisions, the concept of **recommended daily allowance (RDA)** was developed by the National Academy of Sciences to measure the nutritional value of different foods (National Research Council, 1980). This continuously updated key resource reflects the work of dietitians who are constantly reevaluating new information on food composition; dietary requirements; and the relationships among diet, health, and disease (Monsen & Owen, 1985). The best way to ensure a well-balanced diet is to consume a wide variety of foods each day from the different food groups as established by nutritionists (Christian & Greger, 1988). Foods commonly consumed are conveniently arranged into four basic groups: milk, meats, fruits/vegetables, and grain or seed products (see Table 15.3). While each person needs the same nutrients, the number of calories vary. Adults need fewer calories than teenagers, and women require fewer calories than men. Persons who have **sedentary** (inactive) life-styles do not need as many calories as people who are physically active. Women, when pregnant or lactating, need larger caloric intake (Christian & Greger, 1988).

Ways of Controlling Food Costs

As might be expected, food costs vary substantially depending upon the care with which one shops and the degree to which convenience foods are used. Further, projected family food costs can be expected to decline slightly once women and men reach age 51 (see Table 15.4). These projected food costs assume that all meals and snacks are purchased at a store and prepared in the home. In recent years, many persons have attempted to obtain relief from rising food prices by growing their own food products; buying directly from farmer stands; going directly to fields to pick their fruits and vegetables; redeeming discount food coupons; and buying **generic** (nonbrand) foods (Diggs, 1982). However, many such options may not exist for the typical working wife and husband.

Cost-Cutting Strategies

A wise shopper will buy according to the cost of the basic unit of measurement. While it is cheaper per cup to purchase a 1/2 gal of milk than 1 qt, it may not be cheaper to purchase the larger size container of rice or peanut butter because of the increased cost of the larger container. In addition, the unit cost can be used to compare the costs of prepared foods such as grated cheese and shredded cabbage to the costs of foods in their natural form (Morrison, 1986).

In order to reduce costs of food, some stores have implemented self-service bulk-food bins whereby shoppers measure and package their own purchases. When buying food products such as rice, beans, nuts, and dried fruits in bulk, the consumer can save up to one third by avoiding packaging costs. Bulk foods are usually supplied by name-brand processors or by companies that package generic or in-house brand products and are often comparable, but less expensive than packaged food. Advantages given for bulk food purchasing include the ability to purchase only the quantity needed,

Table 15.3: Basic Food Groups

Food Group	Serving Size	Recommended Number of Servings[1] Children 1–10	Teenagers and Young Adults 11–24	Adults 25+	Pregnant Women	Breast-feeding Women
Milk		3	4	2	4	4
Milk	1 cup					
Yogurt	1 cup					
Cheese[2]	1 oz					
Cottage cheese[2]	1/2 cup					
Ice cream, ice milk, frozen yogurt	1/2 cup					
Meat		2	2	2	3	2
Cooked, lean meat, fish, poultry	2–3 oz					
Egg	1					
Cooked, dried peas, dried beans	1/2 cup					
Peanut butter	2 tbsp					
Nuts, seeds	1/4 cup					
Fruit-Vegetable[3]		4	4	4	4	4
Juice	1/2 cup					
Vegetable, fruit	1/2 cup					
Apple, banana, orange	1 medium					
Grapefruit	1/2					
Cantaloupe	1/4					
Dried fruit	1/4 cup					
Grain[4]		4	4	4	4	4
Bread	1 slice					
English muffin, hamburger bun	1/2					
Ready-to-eat cereal	1 oz					
Cooked cereal, rice, grits	1/2 cup					
Pasta	1/2 cup					

[1]These servings supply only about 1,200 calories.
[2]Count cheeses as serving of milk OR meat, not both simultaneously.
[3]Dark green, leafy, or orange vegetable and fruit are recommended 3 or 4 times weekly for vitamin A. Citrus fruit is recommended daily for vitamin C.
[4]Whole grain, fortified, or enriched grain products are recommended.
Guide to Good Eating (5th edition), 1989, Courtesy of NATIONAL DAIRY COUNCIL.®

Table 15.4: Average Weekly Food Costs in 1987

Individuals	Thrifty Plan	Low-cost Plan	Moderate-cost Plan	Liberal Plan
Child				
Ages 1–2	$10.30	$12.50	$14.60	$17.60
Ages 3–5	11.10	13.70	17.00	20.40
Ages 6–8	13.70	18.20	22.80	26.60
Ages 9–11	16.20	20.70	26.60	30.80
Woman				
Ages 12–19	16.90	20.30	24.60	29.80
Ages 20–50	17.00	21.20	25.70	33.00
Age 51 and over	16.80	20.50	25.40	30.40
Man				
Ages 12–14	17.00	23.40	29.30	34.30
Ages 15–19	17.60	24.30	30.10	34.90
Ages 20–50	18.80	24.00	30.20	36.40
Age 51 and over	17.10	22.90	28.20	33.80

Source: K. L. Lipton and J. King (eds.), *National Food Review* (No. 37). Washington, DC: U.S. Department of Agriculture, 1987, p. 30.

nostalgic return to the "good old days," and knowing precisely what is being purchased. On the other hand, there are disadvantages of bulk purchases: greater susceptibility to contamination, less potential sanitation, and the extra time and trouble needed to bag bulk food and restore in containers at home (Hunter, 1985). Observations of bulk-food shoppers in large California supermarkets found that 1 in 7 shoppers tasted food from the bins and 1 in 5 used their hands rather than the bin scoops, thus raising the issue of sanitation problems (Bozzi, 1986). In most cases, it is cheaper to buy beef and pork in bulk and have the meat custom cut into desirable portions prior to placing in the freezer ("50 Ways," 1983).

As most shoppers have observed, supermarket aisles are filled with displays of weekly specials. Large stores may have several specials each week that are called **"leaders"** (items priced below wholesale cost to retailer in order to attract customers). Selective purchase of such items can result in significant cost savings provided the item is needed and its quality will be retained through long-term storage. If the food package is dated, persons should purchase the most advance-dated package so that the food will remain fresh for a longer period of time. Further, fresh fruit purchased out of season is usually more expensive (Morrison, 1986). In summary, there are many recommended strategies for cutting costs when food shopping:

1. Assess the amount of income spent for food.
2. Consider weekly food specials.
3. Use discount coupons only for needed items.
4. Prepare meal plans (menus).
5. Shop for groceries from a list of planned needs.
6. Avoid grocery shopping when hungry.
7. Avoid impulse purchases.
8. Use warehouse stores where foods are in boxes.
9. Buy in bulk when possible and practical.
10. Evaluate name and generic brands.
11. Develop understanding of unit pricing.
12. Shop during slower business hours—mornings or after dinner (Morrison, 1986, pp. 126–127).

The cost-cutting strategies for the handicapped may be limited because of fewer monetary or physical resources.

Housing: Seeking Basic Shelter

Based on available data, the cost of obtaining shelter represents one third of the total family expenditures each year for both single-parent and two-parent families with at least one child under age 18 (Lino, 1990). Therefore, the selection of housing should be based on family space needs, available financial resources, and the mortgage market as well as personal tastes and preferences. A national quality of life survey concluded that parents of lower socioeconomic status living in crowded homes have more dissatisfaction with family life, use of leisure time, and parenthood. They also reported more problems with controlling children. The most dissatisfaction was found among parents living in higher density homes with older children (Baldassare, 1981). Most families with children do not ever fully adjust in terms of space and number of bedrooms during the child-rearing cycle. Couples with toddlers and/or couples with older children do not purchase significantly larger homes than couples without children (McLeod & Ellis, 1983).

Owning or Renting

The question of whether to buy or to rent a home is affected by a number of factors including marital status, tax laws, number of children, income level, and financial goals and objectives. Some experts are beginning to discourage persons from buying homes and suggesting that their intended down payment be put into tax-free bonds that will yield a greater return on their investment. Further, unless used home prices rise substantially more than the rate of inflation, purchasing a home does not necessarily lead to a quick profit after its resale (Schiffres, 1986).

In 1988, the national median price of a used single-family home was $89,300 (U.S. Bureau of Census, 1990pp). As might be anticipated, new housing is somewhat higher. The median sales price for a new single-family home was $112,500 with the lowest median sales price found in the South—$92,000 and the highest median sales price found in the Northeast—$149,000. By late 1989, the median national sales price had risen to $120,000 (U.S. Bureau of the Census, 1990oo).

Numerous rental units in the United States prohibit children or place restrictions on the number and/or age of children. An adults-only housing policy has been upheld to be constitutional by the Florida State Supreme Court, but a similar policy was declared to be unconstitutional by the California State Supreme Court (Press, Prout, & Pedersen, 1984). Therefore, the legality of having children in upscale-priced rental units remains a problem in identifying appropriate housing.

Many families believe that purchasing a home will ensure financial security, social status, stability, and desirable living conditions (Kennedy & Stokes, 1982). Research suggests that if total housing costs are compared over the years, homeowners only gain about a 1–2% financial advantage over renters in terms of a long-term investment. Although renters tend to pay out less money with regard to cash flow, homeowners, in most instances, will eventually experience an increase in the value of their home (Block, Peavy, & Thorton, 1988). But, the perceived advantages of renting versus buying are subject to debate, depending on the long-term prognosis of the real estate market (see Table 15.5). If a couple purchases a $100,000 home with a 10% mortgage rate and an $800 monthly payment, their annual investment **equity** (market value minus mortgage balance) would be 5.1% if real estate values increased by 2%. The rate of return on equity geometrically increases as the value of real estate rises ("To Buy," 1990).

Alternative Approaches to Housing Purchases

Cooperatives, condominiums, and mobile homes have become increasingly popular for busy career persons. They offer alternative ways of coping with maintenance responsibilities as well as access to leisure-time facilities such as swimming pools and tennis courts. A cooperative is an apartment building in which each apartment dweller owns a proportionate share of the nonprofit corporation. The owner has a legal right to lease the unit she/he occupies, accepts financial responsibility for her/his payments, and must pay a monthly assessment for maintenance and taxes. The purchasers vote to elect a board of directors to manage the cooperative and must obtain approval before remodeling, renting, or selling their units (Miller, 1987). A condominium is an apartment house or complex in which the owner purchases a living unit and shares joint ownership in common facilities such as swimming pools and tennis courts. Each purchaser arranges her/his mortgage and tax payments individually, but separate assessments must be paid for maintenance and other related services. A condominium owner votes to elect persons to supervise the property, but one does not assume financial responsibility for the other units. In

Table 15.5: Advantages of Renting Versus Buying Housing

Renting	Buying
Easy mobility	Pride of ownership
Apartment amenities (pool, tennis courts, laundry facilities)	Higher status for home owners
No maintenance or repairs	Better credit rating
No large down payment, only a deposit	Monthly payment relatively constant
Fixed rent easier to budget	Income tax deduction for mortgage interest and taxes
No chance for large financial loss	Potential for home to increase in value
Low moving-in costs	Owner forced to save by making payments
	Owner can borrow against own equity
	More space available
	Freedom to make home improvements

Garman, E. T., and R. E. Forgue, *Personal Finance*, Second Edition. Copyright © 1988 by Houghton Mifflin Company. Used with permission.

addition, the condominium may be refinanced, sold, or remodeled without seeking any type of approval from other owners (Garman & Forgue, 1988).

A mobile home is a factory-assembled housing unit that has a maximum width and length of 14′ x 70′ and is designed to be towed. Double-wide mobile homes have now become available whereby two units are connected side by side. Since mobile homes usually are equipped with appliances, furniture, carpet, and curtains, the building cost per square foot is only about one half of the cost for a single-family home. Further, most mobile homes today are sold to owners who may, in the future, move their unit to a new location. However, mobile homes rarely increase in resale value in comparison to other forms of housing; in fact, they often depreciate in value (Garman & Forgue, 1988).

Home Financing

The largest single expenditure that a family will typically make during their lifetime will be the purchase of housing. Because of the escalating costs of housing, 86% of first-time buyers and 74% of repeat buyers are dual-income families. By 1987, the average monthly mortgage payment in metropolitan areas was $939 including principal, interest, taxes, homeowners insurance, and private mortgage insurance (Reeves, 1988). There are two basic types of mortgages: fixed-rate mortgages and adjustable-rate mortgages. With a **fixed-rate mortgage,** the interest rate and amount of the monthly payment are fixed throughout the life of the mortgage. Typically, the consumer pays a higher interest rate and larger monthly payment for a fixed-rate mortgage (Sloane, 1985). A person obtaining a $100,000 fixed-rate mortgage for 30 years can anticipate paying over $229,000 in interest charges for the duration of the mortgage plus payment of the principal (see Table 15.6). However, if the lending institution will permit payment of an additional sum toward the principal each month without penalty, the total interest charges can be substantially reduced.

An **adjustable-rate mortgage** permits the interest rate to rise and fall based on financial market conditions over the duration of the loan. Generally, the interest rate is lower than for a fixed-rate mortgage. But if there are drastic changes in the inflation rate, the interest rate can soar under this arrangement unless the lending institution has agreed to place a cap on the interest rate. In other words, the interest rate will not increase beyond a certain amount over the life of the loan (Block et al., 1988). Due to the relatively higher interest rates for fixed-rate mortgages, consumers have continued to shift toward adjustable-rate mortgages which presently account for almost two thirds of all home mortgages (McQueen, 1987). The final decision about the details of a loan package should include consideration of present income, future income potential, the pros and cons of adjustable-rate mortgages versus fixed-rate mortgages, and the preferred type of payment plan ("Budgeting for Your," 1986).

Among the new mortgage options that can save the consumer money are biweekly payments whereby the home purchaser pays one half of the monthly payment every 2 weeks and ends up making 26 payments per year or the equivalent of 13 monthly payments. By making one extra payment each year, at the end of the 12th year, the length of the mortgage will have been cut by 1 year, thus saving considerable interest. In addition, shorter term mortgages of 10–15 years instead of 30 will result in lower interest rates and substantial savings in terms of long-term interest costs ("How to Build," 1988). Most lending institutions require that the monthly payment for principal, interest, taxes, and insurance cannot exceed 30% of the gross monthly income (Reeves, 1988). For example, if a person who wanted to buy an $80,000 home could get a 30-year fixed rate loan of 8% and pay down $16,000, she/he would need a gross income of $21,000 to qualify for the loan.

Table 15.6: Cost of $100,000 Fixed-Rate Mortgage

Type of Mortgage	Interest Rate	Months Paid	Monthly Payment Amount	Total Finance Charges
10-year	10.25%	120	$1335	$ 60,247
15-year	10.25	180	1090	96,191
20-year	10.25	240	982	135,594
30-year	10.50	360	915	229,306

Obtaining Adequate Health Care

Today, the concepts of prevention, maintenance, and risk reduction are more effective in ensuring good health care than treatment of illness with increasingly expensive technology. Therefore, frequent medical checkups, proper nutrition, and avoiding risk-taking behavior go hand-in-hand with obtaining adequate health care (Spencer, 1987). When family members decide to seek outside medical help, they may choose to use standard insurance programs or **health maintenance organizations (HMO).** This crucial decision requires consideration of such factors as family health care needs and previous patterns of health plan satisfaction so that the most appropriate health care plan may be chosen (Doherty & McCubbin, 1985).

The medical field has substantially changed, especially with the emergence of the medical specialty of **family practice.** As the level of physician involvement with families has increased, there has been a shift away from biomedical issues as the sole focus of patient care. Physicians serve as a source of ongoing medical information and advice; offer support to family development stages and reactions of family to stress; and provide systematic assessment and planned intervention by supporting, reframing, and helping the family system (Doherty, 1985).

Generally, there are four categories from which persons can select a primary care physician: family practice, internal medicine, obstetrics and gynecology, and pediatrics. The family practitioner deals with preventive health care and most types of medical problems. **Internal medicine** practitioners serve as primary care physicians or specialize in areas such as **cardiology** (treatment of heart disease). Obstetricians serve as primary care physicians for women during pregnancy and childbirth while gynecologists deal with diseases of the female genital tract. **Pediatricians** specialize in childhood diseases but may care for young persons until they reach age 21 ("Shopping For," 1986).

While family members, friends, and acquaintances can provide information about the bedside manner of physicians, such information is usually of modest assistance. In addition, a person may consult the *Directory of Medical Specialists,* which provides a listing by specialty, city, and state for physicians who have been certified by their specialty board ("Doctor's Guide," 1984). It is most important that persons select a well-qualified physician with whom they feel comfortable and who meets their personal needs.

Health Insurance Plans

At least 33 million people in the United States, two thirds of whom are heads of households and hold full-time jobs, have no health insurance (Farrell, 1990). Women, in particular, have a higher chance of being without health insurance, especially after age 40, due to marital transitions and/or losing temporary and/or low-paying jobs. The most prevalent type of comprehensive health insurance coverage is either employer-paid or employer-subsidized. Most new employees are able to enroll in group health insurance programs without evidence of insurability. Individual health insurance coverage, as opposed to group coverage, should only be considered as a last resort because of the high premium costs (Card, 1985). Standard health-care insurance allows a person to have a personal physician of their choice to ensure continuity of health coverage. Further, it permits coverage for children who are away in college, especially if they are attending an out-of-state college or university (Donahue, 1986). If existing health insurance coverage provides payment for less than two thirds of physicians' fees and hospital charges, supplemental insurance should be considered (Trunzo, 1985).

Some persons with high health risks such as hypertension and back problems and those who have high risk occupations such as a race car driver may have trouble finding individual health insurance coverage. If a person is rejected for insurance coverage, the company may not be required to provide an explanation. In some states, Blue Cross/Blue Shield insurers have open enrollment for 1–2 months each year when persons that they otherwise might reject are accepted for insurance coverage (Card, 1985). But these persons are vulnerable to "substandard" health policies that charge higher premiums, exclude preexisting conditions for the first 12 months of the policy, and have deductible clauses which are much less generous than regular health insurance policies. Although at least 11 states now offer health insurance through a state high risk plan, the premiums are usually one and one half times higher than regular health insurance coverage (Lawrence, 1986).

Health Maintenance Organizations

Health maintenance organizations are based on the concept of prepayment for health care that requires members to go to a designated health care center(s) for treatment. This concept differs from **preferred provider organizations** (PPOs) which direct insured members to a list of "preferred" health providers for treatment at discounted rates (Donahue, 1986). By 1986, 16% of the insured population was covered by HMOs whereas 10% was covered by PPOs (Donahue, 1987).

Major reasons why millions of persons have joined HMOs are government changes in Medicare reimbursements, some allow patient to retain her/his personal physician, more aggressive advertising, and coverage offered as fringe benefit option by employers ("HMO Rolls," 1987). However, many physicians argue that HMOs will ruin traditional doctor-patient relationships and foster less than adequate health care (Donahue, 1987).

Available evidence suggests that families who enroll in HMOs differ from families with traditional health insurance coverage. HMO families tend to have younger children, lower levels of education, and lower occupational prestige. The perceived incentives for enrolling in HMOs are immediate accessibility to health care, comprehensiveness of health care, and relative cost of health care (Monroe, Garand, & Price, 1985).

HMOs do appear to have the following advantages: patients go to the hospital on a less frequent basis than with other traditional insurance plans, mental health coverage ranges from $750–$1,500 maximum per year, and fewer deductibles for surgical and hospital costs exist. In addition, a person's medical records will be in a central place readily available to all physicians. Further, subscribers will not encounter paperwork and reimbursement delays that occur when other physicians file insurance claims. Finally, an emphasis on preventive health care surpasses conventional insurance plans in terms of checkups, other medical exams, and free health education classes and exercise clinics (Stickney, 1985). Despite these advantages, many see disadvantages in HMO use: premiums often cost as much or more than conventional health insurance coverage, oftentimes must give up a current physician and select new one from an HMO list, and lack of coverage for emergency health care out of geographical area (Schaeffer, 1987). Also, patients may see a physician outside the HMO only if the plan cannot provide the necessary medical treatment or when an HMO physician gives a referral (Stickney, 1985).

Buying Life Insurance

Most persons would agree that a $3 million asset needs protecting. Yet, few college graduates are aware that a $25,000 annual salary with a 6% yearly increase will accrue to $3 million before the age of their retirement. Protecting such an asset may be the most important part of any family financial planning program. Life insurance is often described by financial planners as the base of the pyramid on which family security is built (Rosenbloom, 1987). Major advertising campaigns promote the concept of life insurance as a financial instrument or a high yield investment. But the evidence suggests that, in most instances, life insurance should be considered as protection against lost income and not as a tax-sheltered investment program (Harris, D., 1987).

Since the major purpose of life insurance is to protect dependents, persons with no one depending upon them have the least need for life insurance. In fact, most people do not consider buying life insurance until marriage or the birth of a child when they realize that if they should die, their family would potentially suffer severe financial distress. The key is to provide enough life insurance to ensure that the family does not suffer from financial hardship at a premium cost that will not create undue financial strain on family resources (Donoghue & Shilling, 1987).

Several concepts are basic to understanding life insurance. A premium is the amount of money that is paid each year to keep an insurance policy in force. An insurance policy is issued at a standard premium rate for persons whose chances of dying are average compared to others in their age group with no significant health problems, or hazardous occupations or hobbies. A substandard risk means that the person has a greater than average chance of dying because of occupation, previous medical history, or hazardous behavior such as using tobacco products or narcotics. Such persons would pay higher premiums. Insurance companies measure risk by assessment of medical history and by an investigative report which confirms information on the insurance application such as the policyholder's driving record. Conversations with spouse and friends furnish information about the applicant's personal habits. The Fair Credit Reporting Act enables a person to review her/his files, if she/he chooses, to make sure that all information is accurate ("Are You," 1986).

Some persons may be intimidated by the complexity of the subject of life insurance, and therefore fail to address their needs. Certain steps can make the somewhat difficult task less confusing. Such manageable steps include selecting an insurance/financial advisor, determining needs, deciding appropriate amount of protection, choosing proper type of life insurance policies, and reviewing insurance needs periodically as personal and family circumstances change (Rosenbloom, 1987).

Decisions: How Much Insurance?

The question, "How much life insurance does a person really need to adequately sustain her/his family over a long period of time?" is not easy to answer. A consumer advocacy group concluded that the average married man carries $101,000 of life insurance but actually needs an additional $100,000 in coverage ("How Much Life," 1986). To determine the amount of life insurance that a family needs, the loss of income principle should be applied. The family should determine how many years they will need a yearly income and in what amount. Several expenditure categories are to be considered: immediate expenses such as estate taxes, probate costs, funeral expenses, and medical expenses; future family living expenses with emergency fund of 2–6 months after-tax income; child care and educational funds adjusted for inflation; and debts including mortgage loan, car loan, and credit card purchases. A competent insurance/financial advisor can help determine the appropriate income-replacement needs for these circumstances (Rosenbloom, 1987).

Types of Life Insurance

There are three basic types of life insurance contracts: term, endowment, and whole life. Due to the changing interest rates and strong competition among insurance companies, a number of interest-sensitive type policies have been introduced such as variable life and universal life policies (Block et al., 1988). Since the three basic types of contracts serve different purposes, each one may be useful at particular stages of a person's life. The role of an insurance/financial advisor is to guide a person in making appropriate choices.

Term Life Insurance

Term insurance is designed to give the most protection for the money. However, there is no savings element involved in this type of policy since it pays a death benefit only if the person dies during a limited, specified period of time (Miller, 1987). Some companies have an extremely low 1st-year premium, but the premium increases substantially during the subsequent years. Persons purchasing term life insurance need to make certain that it is both renewable and convertible. Policies are usually renewable on an annual or a 5-year basis without evidence of insurability while the amount of coverage remains constant. But the cost goes up as the policyholder increases in age at each renewal point ("Term Insurance," 1986). It is possible with some companies to convert from a term policy to a whole life policy that builds cash value. However, the purchaser will receive less coverage for the same premium level if converted to whole life. When converting insurance policies, the old policy should be continued until the new policy has been approved and conveyed to the policyholder ("Should You Switch," 1986).

Whole Life Insurance

The whole or straight life insurance policy provides a savings program along with protection up to an agreed upon amount throughout a person's lifetime. This coverage is considered to be permanent as long as the premium continues to be paid. The cash value of the policy accrues according to a predetermined annual schedule on a tax-deferred basis (Sloane, 1985). The amount of premium that is paid each year to keep the policy in force usually remains constant from the date of purchase. Whole life premiums are typically higher as illustrated by an example of a man who, at age 35, would pay $2,000–$3,000 per year for a $200,000 whole life policy, but he pays only $250 per year for a top-rated term policy of the same amount. Consequently, the market percentage for whole life insurance shrunk from 61% of all policies in 1970 to only 35% in 1984 ("Life Insurance," 1986a). However, whole life builds cash reserves, offering potential borrowing power not available with term insurance. Nevertheless, buying a whole life insurance policy strictly as an investment would appear to be analogous to opening a savings account without knowing what interest rate the bank will pay ("Life Insurance," 1986a).

Limited pay life insurance is a form of whole life insurance that permits premium payments to cease at some point prior to reaching age 100. The two most common forms are 20 years-pay life and paid-up at age 65 policies. When the time period for premium payments concludes, the individual will have a specified amount of paid-up life insurance. Annual premiums for these types of policies are considerably higher in comparison to straight whole life policies (Garman & Forgue, 1988). Limited-pay policies are most suitable for persons whose incomes will be higher during their early adult years such as entertainers and professional athletes or for persons whose incomes after age 65 will decline drastically so they will be unable to continue paying insurance premiums.

Endowment Life Insurance

Endowment life insurance provides protection for a specified period of time and allows persons to accumulate savings (Sloane, 1985). The premium level will remain constant throughout the policy period. Although this type of policy may be useful in meeting known future expenses such as college tuition for children, it is the most expensive form of life insurance per dollar on the basis of coverage and premiums. This is because the insurer has only a limited time to collect premiums in order to earn monies for paying the face amount of the policy at the endowment date (Garman & Forgue, 1988).

Variable Life Insurance

Variable life is a type of insurance in which a policyholder may choose investments made with cash value accumulations of her/his premiums and share in the investment gains and losses. The base amount of the policy for a death benefit may increase to a guaranteed minimum, depending on the performance of the investment portfolio in which the funds are placed. The cash value of the policy also will vary with investment performance but without a guaranteed minimum cash value (Miller, 1987). Since holders of this type of policy maintain control over the investments made with their premiums, persons who are unfamiliar with the stock market would find variable insurance policies a poor option. Costs of such policies, which include management fees and transaction charges, are deducted from investment returns (Garman & Forgue, 1988). Variable life insurance policies are categorized as a moderately risky investment (see figure 15.2).

Universal Life Insurance

Universal life insurance policies combine the purchase of annual policies with an investment program. This type of policy must be purchased in initial face amounts of $25,000 or more at prevailing interest rates tied either to the financial market or, more commonly, as dictated by the company (Garman & Forgue, 1988). It matures at a specified date with a part of the premium being used to pay for the yearly renewal of term insurance, while the remainder of the premium is invested in a fund consisting of short-term, high yielding securities (Sloane, 1985). A major disadvantage of this type of policy is that interest rates can range from very low to very high. Buying a universal life insurance policy is similar to buying term insurance and investing the rest of the premium money in the business operations of the insurance company ("Life Insurance," 1986b). Whether or not this choice represents the "best" alternative depends upon an individual's financial goals and objectives (see Table 15.7).

Selecting an Insurance Advisor/Agent

Just as the choice of a physician is significant to the physical welfare of the family, selecting an insurance advisor/agent is an important step in sound financial management. Since insurance needs vary throughout the family life cycle choosing a knowledgeable agent with professional integrity is the greatest assurance that those needs will be met. Such professional guidance will be based on the consumer's changing needs rather than the agent's desire to sell a specific product. Some persons may prefer an advisor who has access to many types of financial planning services such as tax shelters, real

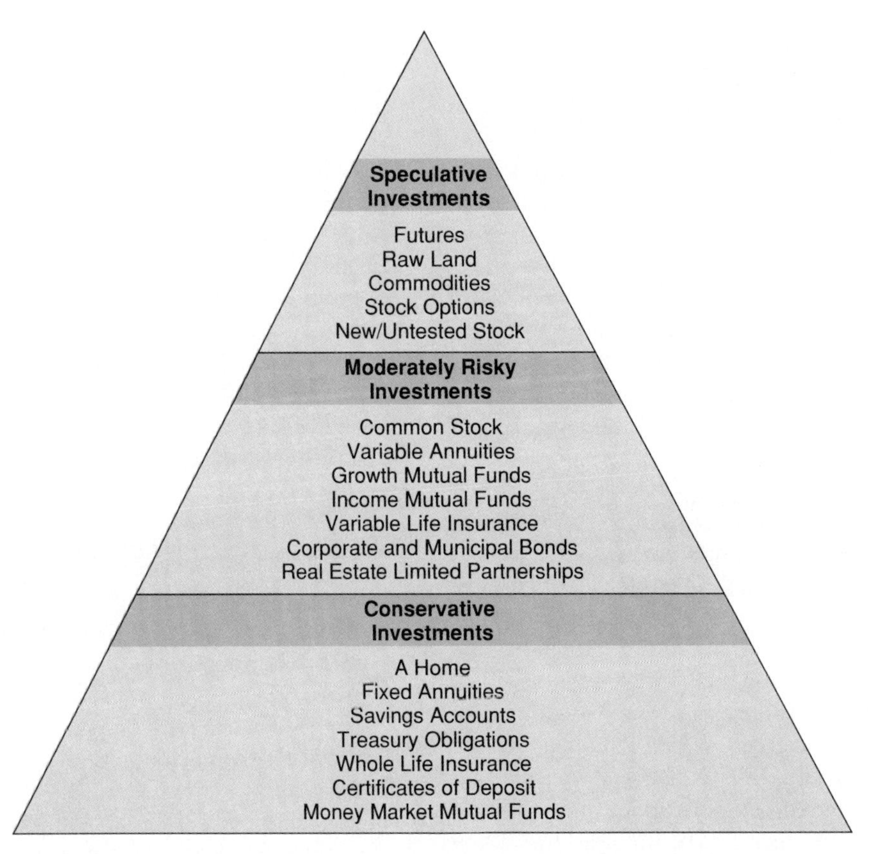

Figure 15.2 The Investment Pyramid

estate, and investments, and who, therefore, can incorporate their life insurance needs into an overall financial plan. Others may prefer a life insurance specialist (Rosenbloom, 1987).

The two preferred professional credentials for life insurance agents are Charter Life Underwriter (CLU) and Chartered Financial Consultant (ChFC). To earn these designations, an agent must pass national examinations plus participate in periodic continuing education. Although there are well-qualified agents who do not possess either designation, a person with one or both credentials is more likely to be up-to-date on insurance matters (Block et al., 1988). It is advisable to check for professional credentials and to ask friends and associates about their insurance advisors/agents.

Banking: Checking and Savings Accounts

Another important decision that must be made concerns the choice of institution to handle various kinds of financial transactions. When selecting a financial institution, the following factors should be considered: safety of assets, convenience, fees, interest rate structures, and services ("Banking 101," 1986). To ensure safety of assets, financial institutions should be insured by the Federal Deposit Insurance Corporation (FDIC) in the case of commercial banks or the Federal Savings and Loan Insurance Corporation (FSLIC) for savings and loan associations. These federal agencies guarantee individual deposits up to a maximum of $100,000. Availability of automatic teller machines and length of time required for a deposit to be held by the bank before the money is accessible are convenience factors. The issue of services relates to features such as overdraft checking privileges and traveler's checks (Garman & Forgue, 1988). A final question in the selection of a financial institution is whether or not the fee and interest rate structures are competitive.

Checking Accounts

Because banks consider regular checking accounts as a service rather than as an income-producing mechanism, many banks now require a major bank credit card in order to open a regular checking account (Card,

Table 15.7: A Comparison of Insurance Policy Types

Feature	Term Insurance	Whole Life Insurance	Universal Life Insurance
Face amount	Fixed or declining during term of policy; changeable at renewal	Fixed	Variable
Premiums	Low with increases at renewal	High and fixed	High but variable within limits
Cash value accumulation	None	Fixed	Variable as premium and interest rate vary
Rate of return on cash accumulations	Not applicable	Fixed	Variable with interest rates in economy or as specified by company
Cost of death benefit portion	Low and fixed	Unknown	Known but can vary and may be partially hidden
Expense charge	Low but unknown; hidden in premium	Unknown; hidden in premium	Known; may be high

The careful choice of a qualified, trustworthy insurance agent may be a young couple's most important insurance decision because insurance companies are usually competitive in both price and options.

1986). Although the original intent of savings and loan associations was to serve as savings repositories and to provide home loans, most such institutions today have also become involved in other kinds of commercial banking activities such as checking accounts (Garman & Forgue, 1988). However, a survey of 100 commercial banks and savings and loan associations concluded that checking accounts were over one third cheaper at a commercial bank ("You and the Banks," 1985). There are three basic types of checking accounts: regular, NOW, and Super NOW.

A regular checking account provides unlimited checking services, and the cost depends upon the number of transactions per month and the minimum balance maintained throughout the month. The minimum account balance required to avoid payment of fees ranges from $200–$1,000 and interest is paid on this monthly balance. If the minimum balance falls below this amount, there will be a monthly service charge ranging from $3–$10 per month plus 20–25¢ for each check written during that month (Block et al., 1988). NOW accounts (negotiable order withdrawal) require a high minimum balance ($750–$2,000) and usually pay a fixed interest rate on this monthly balance which ranges from 4.5%–5.5% per year. A monthly service charge for failure to maintain the minimum balance ranges from $5–$15 plus a charge of 25–50¢ for each check written (Rinzler, 1986). A Super NOW account requires a higher minimum balance than a NOW account, usually $1,000–$2,500; but unlike NOW accounts, it does not have a fixed maximum interest rate. The interest rate is allowed to fluctuate with the financial marketplace. At most banks, if the minimum balance drops to the level of a NOW account, no monthly fees will be assessed and the interest rate will be paid at the NOW account level ("You and the Banks," 1985). Still other banking institutions charge penalties or often pay no interest if the balance goes below the minimum level ("Banking 101," 1986).

Savings Accounts

Accumulation of savings is another aspect of financial planning and budgeting. Money that is systematically placed into a savings account provides protection in case of emergencies. It can also be used for eventual major purchases such as automobiles and furniture either without incurring finance charges or by controlling finance charges to a reasonable limit. The percentage of individual savings placed in savings accounts tends to fluctuate with the inflation rate and the economy (Tippett, 1985). In 1987, the percentage of annual personal income being saved by individuals was only 3.8%, the lowest annual rate since 1947. Factors that have affected the savings rate are percentage of population in 25–44 age bracket, which saves little and borrows a lot of money; changes in percentage of personal income represented by farm and interest incomes; and changes in stock prices (Koretz, 1988). The three major types of savings accounts are passbook account, certificates of deposit, and money market account.

A passbook savings account permits frequent deposits and withdrawal of funds without penalty. The term "passbook" originated from the days when a bank customer's transactions were recorded in a bank book passed to a teller. Today, most financial institutions have printed receipts to indicate account transactions, having discarded the bank passbook. Because of the lack of a minimum deposit and the ability to withdraw without penalty, the interest rate for passbook accounts is the lowest rate for any savings account (Garman & Forgue, 1988).

The certificate of deposit (CD) is a savings account in which the consumer agrees to leave the money for a specified period of time ranging from 3 months–5 years with a fixed interest rate. Generally speaking, the longer the money is left on deposit, the higher the interest yield rate. There is a premature withdrawal penalty, typically forfeiture of the first 90 days of interest with the interest compounded on either a monthly, quarterly, or annual basis (Donoghue & Shilling, 1987). The interest rate depends upon the amount of the initial deposit, which ranges from $500–$10,000. Many CDs permit withdrawal of earned interest on a quarterly or annual basis without penalty (Sloane, 1985). The usual financial strategy is to purchase a short-term certificate for a period of 1 year or less in case the interest rates should rise in the future (Weiss, 1987).

A money market account pays a higher interest rate than a savings account but a lower rate than a CD. The outstanding feature of this type of account is that funds can be deposited and withdrawn without an early withdrawal penalty within certain limitations. However, the depositor must agree to maintain a minimum account balance, which is often double the minimum amount for a CD (Donoghue & Shilling, 1987). A money market account is not the same concept as a standard money market fund, which invests in stocks and bonds and is not federally insured ("Banking 101," 1986).

The Use of Credit: Issues and Insights

By 1988, American consumers had accumulated $629 billion of outstanding installment credit obligations including credit cards and bank credit which represented about one fifth of the annual disposable personal income ("Attention Shoppers," 1988). Almost three fourths of all families have at least one credit card including 77% from banks and 86% from department stores (U.S. Bureau of the Census, 1989c, 1990kk). Today, there are myriad credit options which have become part of the fabric of our society including installment purchases, bank credit cards, credit unions, and home equity loans.

Determination of Credit Ratings

Credit worthiness is the probability, as perceived by a lender or debtor, that a person will be able to repay a loan or credit card balance (Block et al., 1988). Credit worthiness is determined by evaluating the ability and willingness to repay an incurred debt by examining available financial resources and willingness to repay previous debts. The willingness to repay a debt encompasses, among other factors, personal stability and responsible financial habits (Turco, 1979). It is wise to establish a good credit rating. This can be done by incurring a series of small, manageable debts and meeting all financial obligations in a timely manner (Donoghue & Shilling, 1987).

Creditors use a behavior scoring system to track a customer's bill-paying reliability. Banks and retail establishments consider factors such as length of time needed to pay bills, percentage of balance paid off each month, number of times account becomes delinquent, and whether or not the account balance grows over time without significant reduction. Further, factors of occupation, residence, income, assets, and established credit are considered (Johnson, 1983). Such information is used to develop a score that may be used to warn other creditors, increase the customer's credit limit, or freeze her/his credit line (Quinn, 1988). Among the valid reasons for rejecting a credit application are insufficient income, inadequate **collateral** (security for debt), insufficient credit history, delinquent credit obligations, poor credit references, excessive obligations, and incomplete credit application (Block et al., 1988).

If a person believes that she/he has been denied credit unjustly, the Equal Credit Opportunity Act and the Fair Credit Reporting Act provide mechanisms to address this problem. The Equal Credit Opportunity Act was passed in 1975 by Congress to prevent creditors from discriminating on the basis of sex or marital status when evaluating a credit application. The legislation was further amended in 1977 to prohibit discrimination based on age, race, religion, or national origin (Block et al., 1988). Therefore, lenders cannot insist that a woman's husband sign her loan application, and wives are entitled to have a separate credit history from that of their husband (Sloane, 1985).

Credit bureaus collect and report financial data for use by bankers, retailers, credit card issuers, insurance companies, employers, and landlords. The Fair Credit Reporting Act of 1970 requires that if a credit report adversely affects a person's chances for a job or a credit application, a free copy may be obtained and any information found to be inaccurate must be deleted or corrected. Even if the information is correct, an explanation of any extenuating circumstances may be inserted into the credit report file (McGrath, 1987).

Choosing to Use Credit

Using consumer credit to make purchases has become as much a product of American life as baseball, apple pie, and denim jeans. Consumer debt is defined as nonbusiness debt used by consumers for purchases other than home mortgages. There are two types of consumer credit: installment credit and noninstallment credit. In the case of installment credit, the consumer agrees in writing to repay the amount of debt in a specified number of equal payments, typically on a monthly basis. Noninstallment credit includes single-payment loans, such as paying for having used electric services for a month, and open-ended credit. In the case of open-ended credit or revolving credit, the purchaser may choose to repay the entire debt in a single payment or to make a series of equal or unequal payments. Most credit cards and department store accounts use this system (Block et al., 1988).

A number of factors enter into the decision to choose credit over cash to obtain goods and services. Consumers may choose to use credit for several reasons:

1. *Emergencies*—to cover unexpected expenses such as emergency medical care or automobile repairs.
2. *Consumption*—to provide immediate consumption of products such as a compact disk player.
3. *Convenience*—to establish detailed record of purchases and as leverage in disputes with retailers.

4. *Education*—to assist with the increasing costs of higher education for self or children.
5. *Offsetting Inflation*—to take advantage of lower prices prior to a rise in product price due to inflation.
6. *Free Credit*—to take advantage of free credit for short periods of time such as using credit cards, depending upon the timing of purchase.
7. *Identification*—to have credit cards available for such activities as renting an automobile or cashing a check (Garman & Forgue, 1988, pp. 142–143).

While the foregoing reasons for credit usage seem financially sound, individuals must be careful not to overburden themselves with debt, which can affect their sound financial management.

BOX 15.1 — You Should Stop Buying on Credit If . . .

Debts amount to 15–20% of take-home pay (not counting mortgage).

Credit being used to meet expenses of daily living, such as food and electricity costs.

Credit being used to buy things with a short life span, such as toothpaste or panty hose.

Payments so far behind on bills that creditors seeking payment.

No cash reserve available.

Revolving charge accounts never paid up.

Payments continually less than amount actually due.

Things get so bad that debt-consolidation loan considered.

Overextension of Credit Obligations

An overextension of credit often becomes a real problem for many credit users. Credit card users easily get into serious debt because as long as they continue to pay the monthly minimum balance, the creditors will not complain. Many people overestimate their buying power by looking at their salary prior to taking out taxes and mortgage payments. Further, overspending by some people is a psychological problem. That is, people buy something to make themselves feel good, and then they begin to feel the need to buy. In addition, many people overspend to project a higher status image or to provide things for their children. Evidence suggests a disproportionate amount of credit card spending occurs among persons ages 25–40 who may be trying to start their new households at the same level as their parents (Barrett & Greene, 1986).

If a person has installment debts that amount to at least one fifth of her/his monthly take-home pay, she/he can be labelled as being seriously in debt (Garman & Forgue, 1988). In general, it is recommended that spending on credit should be limited to no more than 10% of take-home pay (Weinstein, 1984). After losing control of debts, many persons have to adjust to a standard of living that is lower than that to which they have become accustomed. To help cut credit costs, a person should keep track of all expenses and ask themselves whether or not they really need an item. In addition, debt-prone persons also should avoid situations that trigger compulsive spending along with trying to cut fixed costs such as heating and electricity. Nonprofit counseling services also are available that can assist a person in preparing a budget plan and negotiating with creditors. Credit counselors can accomplish the same task, but a fee is charged for their services. As a final resort, a person can file for a Chapter 7 bankruptcy wherein the court handles all debts by splitting her/his assets among the creditors. Under these circumstances, a person may retain a minimum quantity of their assets. However, filing for personal bankruptcy will establish a bad credit record for at least 10 years (Schurenberg, 1987).

Credit Cards: Convenience and Costs

Most large retail establishments offer a charge account, the cost of which is included in the sales price of their merchandise. In fact, customers who pay cash often help to pay for the cost of maintaining credit operations. While most stores offer a free 30-day charge privilege, most retail establishments such as Macy's and Sears also offer revolving credit accounts.

Another type of credit card is a bank card such as MasterCard or Visa. For the standard bank card, the line of credit is usually $1,200 (Hitchings, 1987). Lower socioeconomic groups use bank credit cards as a form of installment credit so that less than the full monthly balance can be paid, whereas higher socioeconomic groups use credit cards for convenience. The increasing demand for bank credit cards is due to less loyalty to particular stores especially among younger shoppers (Hawkins, Best, & Coney, 1986).

A major segment of the credit card industry involves travel and entertainment cards such as American Express and Diners Club which have become general purpose credit cards for charging not only hotel, restaurant, and airline fares, but also a wide variety of other goods and services. Generally, the entire account balance must be paid within 30 days as for American Express accounts. Travel and entertainment cards are somewhat more difficult to obtain as less than 15% of American families have this type of card. Thus, a key element in their advertising campaigns relates to the prestige factor (Garman & Forgue, 1988). Another type of potential travel card is the gasoline company credit card which is used for automobile-related goods and services. To compete with Visa and MasterCards, the American Express Optima card has been introduced with a variable interest rate on the unpaid balance tied to the prime lending rate, as listed in the *Wall Street Journal,* plus 5.75% (American Express Centurion Bank, 1988).

The Convenience Factor

Credit card users may be categorized as *revolvers*—minimum payments as low as 2.5% of monthly balance, *average users*—alternate between paying full monthly balance and the minimum balance, and *convenience users*—always pay balance in full ("Your Most Fantastic," 1987). The advantages of credit cards include instant credit, summary of purchases, less need for carrying cash, and ease of resolving disputes. A person also can travel without carrying a large amount of cash because it probably would be less traumatic if the loss of a credit card occurred. And due to federal laws, the charges placed on a stolen credit card are not the responsibility of the consumer if the lost card has been promptly reported (Barrett & Greene, 1986). Furthermore, credit cards provide a means of instant credit to take advantage of unanticipated sales merchandise and travel expenses (Hawkins et al., 1986). New federal income tax rules require separation of food and hotel-related travel expenses for the purposes of tax deductions. Therefore, travel and entertainment cards, especially, can provide a summary of travel expenses for expense account reports and income tax records (Garman & Forgue, 1988). Finally, if consumers are dissatisfied with a purchase or a billing error occurs, they may have the card issuer credit their account for the disputed amount. The credit card issuer cannot change a person's credit card rating for withholding payment while the amount is being disputed. To resolve billing errors, however, the credit card issuer must be notified of the disputed charges within 60 days of the date that the statement was mailed ("Hidden Power," 1987).

Costs of Credit Cards

Most banks charge annual fees for their bank credit cards as does the travel and entertainment card industry which may range from $10–$50 ("Hidden Power," 1987). Credit cards typically provide grace periods that give the consumer a specific time period within which to pay the balance in full before incurring a finance charge. But only about one third of MasterCard and Visa holders pay their entire balance each month (Dennon, 1986).

The annual interest rate for retail charge cards and bank cards ranges from 12%–22% (Lamaute, 1987). Contrary to a popular myth, a person can shop for credit. A person seeking bank credit cards should shop for the cheapest annual fee rates and the lowest interest rates including options offered by out-of-state banks (Dennon, 1986). During the 1980s, credit card interest rates increased substantially prompting states to impose ceilings on these interest rates.

Sources of Consumer Loans

Depending upon circumstances, the costs of borrowing money directly may be cheaper than using installment contracts or credit cards. Loans are typically paid off in monthly installments although other loan terms can sometimes be arranged. Savings and loan associations have expanded their services to include secured loans for such consumer durables as television sets, ranges, washers, and dryers (Garman & Forgue, 1988). But interest rates vary as much as 2%–3% between commercial banks and savings and loan associations (Marsa, 1987).

Alternative Approaches to Consumer Loans

As persons have sought to expand their sources of credit, other options have developed over the years. Alternative sources of loans include credit unions, finance companies, and insurance companies. Credit unions, typically associated with a company or governmental agency, usually limit membership to its sponsor's employees. In 1986, one half of the adult population in the United States had access to credit unions and about one

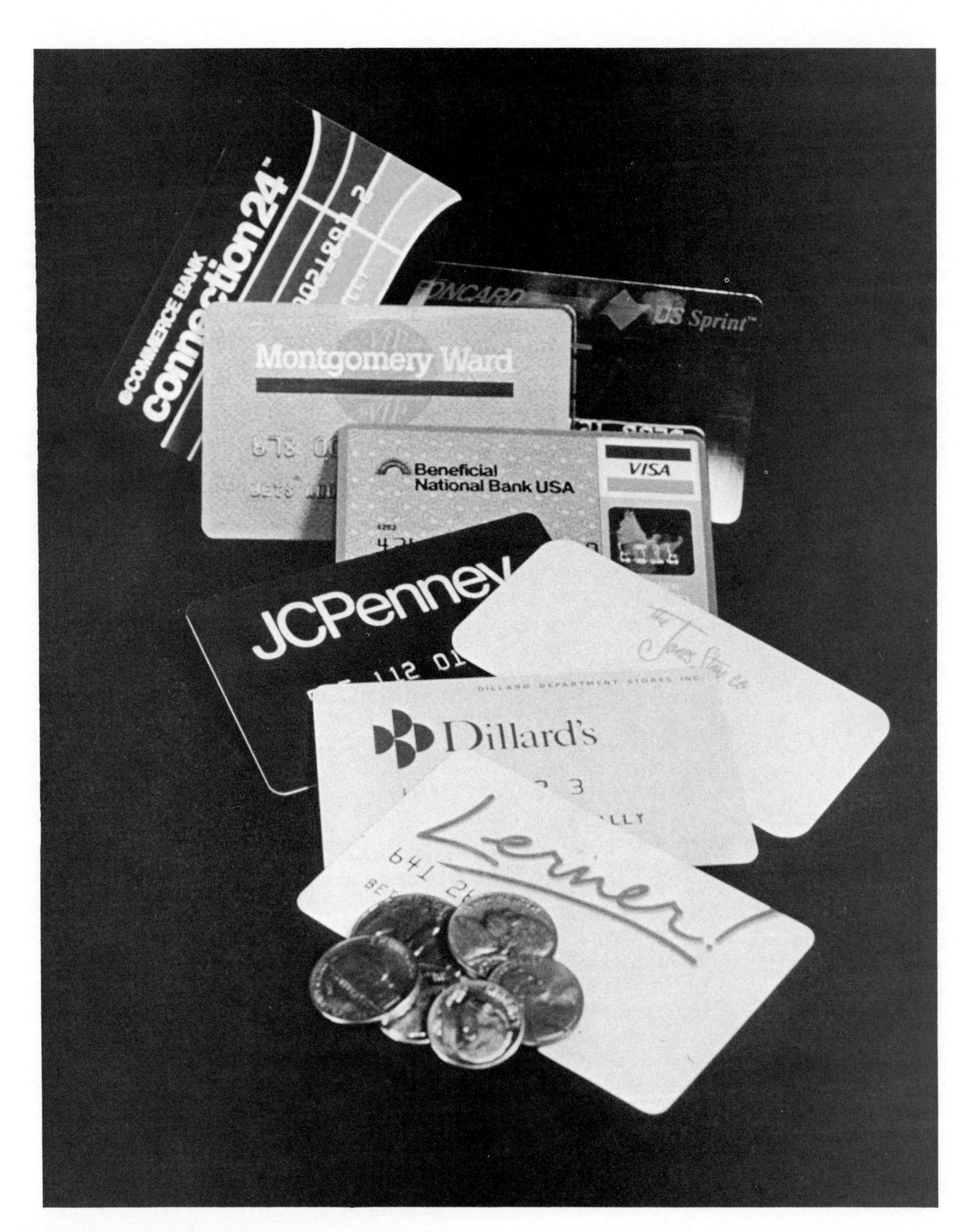

Credit-wise consumers distinguish between the use and abuse of credit. In today's economy, the common variable in personal bankruptcy is not unemployment but overextension of credit.

fifth of all eligible employees were members. Advantages of using a credit union are personal service, inclusion of persons with an unfavorable credit rating who can sometimes qualify for a loan, and slightly lower interest rates than banks. If a borrower should die, the credit union loan is likely to be forgiven. However, credit unions specialize in small loans that are spread out over many individual borrowers which reduces the lending risk for a particular loan ("Credit Unions," 1986).

Consumer finance companies often make loans to persons without an established credit history or persons who are poor credit risks, unable to obtain credit from other established sources. Oftentimes, consumer finance companies can provide borrowed funds on the same day as the loan application, but these types of loans are much more costly than loans from other sources. While their interest rates are regulated by state law, interest rates may range from 12%–36% per year including hidden finance charges supposedly because the loan default rate is much higher than for other lenders (Block et al., 1988).

Another source of consumer loans is borrowing against a personal whole-life insurance policy. The amount available for borrowing is usually up to the cash surrender value of the insurance policy with an interest rate usually ranging from 8%–11%. Further, there are no loan origination fees for borrowing against an insurance policy. The disadvantage of such loans is that if the loan is not repaid, the amount of the loan will be deducted from the insurance payment at the time of death (Goodman, 1986).

Home Equity Loans: A Trend

At the present time, home equity loans are being promoted as a way to consolidate debts and to cope with new income tax laws which have greatly reduced the amount of consumer interest that can be used as tax deductions (McCormally & Spellman, 1987). Typically, home equity loans involve borrowing 70%–80% of the equity in your home. The interest rate for this type of loan is variable rather than fixed, plus the consumer may have to pay for the real estate appraisal. A consumer must realize that pledging one's home for a second debt is risky business (Goodman, 1986).

Planning for the Future: Pension Plans and Wills

Despite the increased life expectancy for women and men, two stages of the life cycle are inevitable: retirement and death. The Social Security retirement program was developed in the 1930s when many persons lost their life savings and earnings due to the Great Depression. Now, many persons also have employer-funded or joint employer-employee funded pension plans. In addition, many individuals have private pension plans such as IRAs and Keogh plans (Feldstein, 1986). Perhaps, because of the unpleasant thoughts generated by contemplation of death, about two thirds of all Americans do not have wills (Trunzo, 1985). To prevent unpleasant circumstances and potential legal problems, a will should be drawn up.

Two Options: Individual Retirement Accounts and Keogh Plans

Individual retirement accounts (IRAs) permit many persons to deposit and accumulate funds for retirement on the same tax-deferred basis as regular employer pension plans. The IRA has been granted a deferred tax status so that earnings from IRAs are not taxable until retirement age when the person will have decreased income, thus placing herself/himself in a lower tax bracket (Wallace, 1985). A person must start withdrawing these funds by age 70.5; and they can be withdrawn prior to age 59.5, but there is a penalty of at least 10%. An IRA reduces taxable income depending upon the person's income level, and will provide a supplemental retirement income (Stephens, 1987). The Tax Reform Act of 1986 permits only individuals who are not active participants in employer-sponsored retirement plans with adjusted gross income levels below a certain amount to make tax deductible contributions to IRAs. Single persons earning over $35,000 and married couples earning over $50,000 who file joint tax returns are no longer eligible to make tax deductible contributions to IRAs. However, persons whose income levels exceed the designated levels may make nontax deductible contributions up to a maximum of $2,000 to an IRA (Lieberman, 1987). Although annual IRA contributions are limited to $2,000 per employed family member, a person not covered by a pension plan can take a full IRA deduction regardless of her/his income level (Block et al., 1988).

A person who is self-employed can set up a Keogh plan. A Keogh plan may involve either a profit-sharing option, which represents a variable annual contribution of up to $30,000 for businesses with fluctuating profits, or a money-purchase Keogh in which there is a fixed percentage contribution. Once a Keogh plan is established, the percentage contribution under the money-purchase plan can be increased, but it can never be decreased. Keogh plans can be set up as trust funds as a straight or variable rate nontransferable annuity contract purchased from a life insurance company, or as a custodial account set up with a bank or mutual fund company. Keogh plans also provide a deferred tax status mechanism for accumulating resources (Donoghue, 1986).

BOX 15.2	Family Records Locator

Responsible partners, whether in business or marriage, both need adequate information about the location of important financial records and legal documents. A Family Records Locator file with the following information will yield great dividends:

1. Names of resource professionals with whom either spouse deals, such as accountants, lawyers, insurance agents, and real estate agents.
2. Social Security numbers and cards.
3. Birth certificates, marriage licenses, divorce decrees, and records of previous marriages.
4. Insurance Policies: accident, automobile, dental, disability, homeowners or renters, liability, life, and medical.
5. Employment and military service records.
6. Bank account records.
7. Keys to safety deposit boxes.
8. Documentation of separately-owned assets such as annuities, bonds, coin collections, jewelry, pension funds, real estate, and silver.
9. Wills and the names and addresses of attorneys who wrote them.
10. Income tax returns for the past four years.

The Need for a Will

In some states, if a person dies **intestate** (without a will) and the state courts divide the assets, the surviving spouse will be eligible to get only 33%–50% of the assets with the remainder going to any children. However, in community property states, the surviving spouse would receive 100% of the assets. In some states, the surviving spouse may have to share the personal property with brothers-in-law, sisters-in-law, nieces, and nephews ("Providing a Will," 1986). However, any joint property held by spouses will automatically pass to the surviving spouse without a will. In order for a will to be valid, it must be signed by **testatrix/testator** (person making will) and by witnesses. Most states require either two or three witnesses who must be persons who would not be beneficiaries under the will or have a conflict of interest if they should be called to testify as to its validity (Donoghue & Shilling, 1987).

The will may contain provisions for specific disposition of property such as X dollars to sons John and Stephen or formula dispositions of property such as 10% of the gross estate to each child. If there are dependent children, a guardianship provision should be included to cover the possibility that both parents might die simultaneously in an accident. In addition, an executor must be named to be responsible for carrying out the provisions of the will (Donoghue & Shilling, 1987). After a will is signed, the person may later make changes by either creating a new will or by adding a **codicil** (change in will) to the original will. If a codicil is used, new witnesses must be used and persons who would lose assets of value under the earlier will must be notified. A will should be reviewed when a person moves to a new state or when there is a significant change in her/his financial station in life. Wills should be kept in a safe, fireproof location. But it should be noted that in many states, a person's safety deposit box is sealed upon her/his death; and a court order is required to gain access to its contents. Therefore, a person should consider having a copy of the will at her/his lawyer's office ("Providing a Will," 1986).

Summary

- Money management techniques are of crucial importance to the success or failure of a marriage.
- The development of a financial plan should be viewed as a spending guide rather than an inflexible budget.
- Major considerations concerning food are escalating costs and lack of applied nutritional knowledge.
- In seeking adequate housing, ownership versus renting and selection of affordable housing should be considered.
- Families must make decisions about medical and hospital insurance, health maintenance organizations, and selection of physicians.
- The purpose of life insurance is to provide for dependents when the breadwinner(s) die(s). The basic types of life insurance contracts are term, endowment, and whole life with variable life and universal life as newer types of policies.
- For most couples, a decision must be made regarding selection of a financial institution to handle monetary transactions. Two major options are commercial banks and savings and loan associations.
- The types of checking accounts are regular, NOW, and Super NOW, while major types of savings accounts are passbook, certificates of deposit, and money market.
- Available credit options include installment purchases, home mortgages, bank credit cards, credit unions, and home equity loans.
- Credit worthiness is the probability that a debtor will be able to repay a loan.
- Sources of consumer loans include commercial banks and savings and loan associations, credit unions, finance companies, and insurance companies. Department store, bank, travel and entertainment, and gasoline credit cards represent other credit sources.
- Individual Retirement Accounts (IRAs) and Keogh Plans provide ways to accumulate funds for retirement, often on a tax-deferred basis.
- Since persons who die intestate will have their assets divided by a state court, the writing of a will insures that a deceased person's assets will be distributed according to their desires.

Questions for Critical Reflection

1. Consider your personal (or if married, couple) financial objectives determining where you want to be 1 year, 5 years, and 10 years from now. What is your overall financial goal?
2. Keeping a fair percent of what you earn is harder than earning it! How do today's economic uncertainties complicate the issue of saving money?
3. Why, as a rule, do young children and college students have the least need for life insurance? Which type of college student would be the exception?
4. Do you feel children should be included in family financial decisions? If so, in what ways? Did you receive an allowance as a child? What will you do differently with your own children in regard to money?
5. A common thread in the lives of persons filing for personal bankruptcy is overextension of credit. When is credit use most risky? Are there safeguards for using it wisely? How does one best protect her/his credit rating?

Suggested Readings

Christian, J. L., & Greger, J. L. (1988). *Nutrition for living* (2nd ed.). Menlo Park, CA: Benjamin/Cummings. A comprehensive guide to the various aspects of nutrition including basic food groups and vitamins.

Garman, E. T. (1991). *Personal finance* (3rd ed.). Boston: Houghton Mifflin. A comprehensive work on all aspects of financial planning.

Hawkins, D. I., Best, R. J., & Coney, K. A. (1986). *Consumer behavior: Implications for marketing strategy* (3rd ed.). Plano, TX: Business Publications. An excellent source of information concerning the influence of advertising on consumer behavior.

Lister, H. J. (1985). *Your guide to IRAs and 14 other retirement plans.* Glenview, IL: Scott, Foresman. A resource tool for planning your financial future during the retirement years.

Miller, R. L. (1990). *Economic issues for consumers* (6th ed.). St. Paul: West. An excellent scholarly work about the influence of economic issues on family life.

Nader, R., & Smith, W. J. (1990). *Winning the insurance game: The complete consumer's guide to saving money.* Beverly Hills, CA: Knightsbridge. A user-friendly guide to purchasing auto, health, home, and life insurance.

CHAPTER 16

Dual Careers, Marriage, and Parenthood

Years of struggle and conflict over new roles and new rules in the family have taught us that changing who works inside the house, who outside, and balancing those responsibilities more equitably is only part of the problem. . . . The deeper issues lie in the struggle to change what happens inside ourselves.

Lillian B. Rubin, 1983

OUTLINE

The current generation of young Americans differs significantly from its predecessors. One obvious distinction is that more young people today than ever before have grown up in families where mothers worked outside of the home. By 1986, over two thirds of all married couples were part of dual-earner families ("Half of All," 1989). Consequently, many young adults today have been socialized to believe in gender equality and the rights of women to full participation in the world of work.

Traditional Marriages: An Overview

In traditional marriages, the husband was the main provider, authority figure, and decision maker concerning such issues as money and education. However, contemporary marriage has gradually shifted from a partnership based on economics and childbearing to one based on companionship (Richmond-Abbott, 1979). Evidence suggests that traditional roles of the woman as housekeeper and the man as **breadwinner** have continued to diminish since women entered the labor force in large numbers during World War II. However, even though both marriage partners may be working outside the home, traditional gender-based distribution of household tasks remains the norm ("Marriage: Traditional," 1987). This pattern may relate to the fact that many wives still hold traditional beliefs about gender roles, and, therefore, do not assert their marital power ("Half of All," 1989).

Wives and the Homemaker Role

One of the earliest researchers to address this issue, Jessie Bernard (1974), concluded that despite contrary opinions, the traditional homemaker role is not considered to be an occupation. According to economists, an occupation requires an application for the job, a pay scale, and an organized standard by which to judge performance, and the possibility of being fired. Without such requisites, housewives are not considered to be part of the labor force and are not directly paid for their efforts in spite of the economic value of homemaker services. Low status is afforded housework because it is noncompetitive in nature, its timing does not correspond with schedules in the outside world, and work is performed on the basis of love and/or duty rather than for pay (Bernard, 1974). How do these facts affect the personal well-being of full-time homemakers?

It appears that the majority of homemakers are happy with what they do. One survey revealed that if money were no consideration, almost two thirds of homemakers would prefer to continue caring for their families whereas the majority of working women would prefer to work only part-time (see Table 16.1).

The perceived rewards of full-time homemaking include more time for children, housework, and oneself while the perceived advantages of working outside of the home are interacting with adults, getting out of the house, and having something interesting to do. It is a myth that nonemployed wives are more likely to be depressed than employed wives (Shehan, 1984). However, research does indicate that women who are homemakers rate themselves lower on aggression, ambition, intelligence, and ability to work well under pressure. They also hold more conservative values and traditional views about gender roles than women who work outside of the home (Stokes & Peyton, 1986). One study found that employed women are more dissatisfied with their lives than homemakers, posing an interesting question. Is not such disenchantment related to liberal attitudes toward gender roles and unrealistic expectations that "they can have it all—at the same time?" Women employed outside the home may have goals which are more personal in nature than homemakers, and are, thus, more likely to be dissatisfied if they fail to achieve these personal expectations (Stokes & Peyton, 1986).

Many women today are not only comfortable in the traditional roles of wife and mother but believe them to be equally as challenging as other careers. Such a philosophy is reflected in a national newsletter written specifically for mothers who choose to stay home. A new mother is emerging who sees herself neither as the media's stereotypical "housewife of the 50s" or as the "working mother of the 70s": a mother who has decided to put her family first without putting herself last (Burton, 1986). For today's women who may have many attractive options, it is possible to consciously choose to devote their exceptional skills and minds to nurturing their families while widening their personal and professional horizons. Particularly, this perspective may be found among educated women who interrupt or postpone a career to devote themselves to child rearing during the significant early years of their children's lives (Ehrlich, 1989). However, the views of those who value the significance and excitement of rearing a family are largely devalued by pressures from highly competitive and achievement-oriented women. Some authorities have suggested that the hardest question for today's young mothers may be "which job is most important."

Table 16.1: **Employment Status Preferences Among Working Women**

Employment Status Preference	Executive/Professional/ Manager	White Collar	Homemakers
Work part-time	51%	38%	18%
Work full-time	19	14	4
Work at home	18	33	61
Do volunteer work	12	15	14
Other	1	1	3

Even some liberated women and men believe that now that a woman can "have it all," if she makes the wrong decision, her family has a lot to lose (Greiff & Munter, 1980). The real issue is that one may not really have a clear concept of which choice was best until the children are grown (Stein, 1984).

Husbands and the Provider Role

The provider role of the husband has been traditionally expressed through economics with success as a good provider increasing his status in the community while failure created frustration and humiliation. Regardless of the tremendous pressures for most men to be perceived as a good provider, this role has greater benefits than costs. With the entry of women into the work force, changes in family roles have led to more demands being placed on men to become involved with family life. These demands include more intimacy and nurturance along with greater sharing of household responsibilities and child care. As more women have come to share the provider role, some men feel relieved; others feel degraded by this shared responsibility (Bernard, 1986). Even men who want to take part in family decisions and spend time with their children are realizing that this task is difficult to combine with full-time work (Weiss, 1985).

In today's society, economic conditions, couple preferences, and family needs have created many two-provider families. Three types of two-provider families have emerged: main/secondary providers, co-providers, and ambivalent co-providers (Hood, 1986). In the main/secondary provider family, the family relies on the second income for improving the quality of life. The possibility always exists that the wife can or will quit work in the future. The co-provider family pools the two incomes and expenses. The couple admits that the wife cannot quit work because her income is needed to sustain their desired standard of living. Finally, ambivalent co-providers accept dependence on the wife's income, but have ambivalent ideas about who is and who should be responsible for providing for family needs. Wives are more likely than husbands to perceive themselves as co-providers rather than having a duty to provide for the family (Hood, 1986). These changes have obviously altered not only economic functions of marital partners but psychological relationships as well.

Dual-Career or Dual-Earner Marriages

Family scientists define dual-career families as a variation of the nuclear family in which both wife and husband pursue an uninterrupted, lifelong career while establishing and developing a family life-style that often includes children (Gilbert, 1985). A career is defined as an occupation or position requiring special education and training that is undertaken or engaged in as a life work. Careers typically require a high degree of personal commitment and often provide the individual with a sense of continuous and progressive achievement either through promotions or other recognitions of one's accomplishments or special skills. On the other hand, a job may be performed with a high degree of commitment, but little opportunity may exist for personal development or advancement in either pay or status. Ideally, dual-career families are supposed to share homemaking and paid work roles in a relatively egalitarian manner (Gilbert, 1985).

Some authorities prefer to use the term **dual-earner marriage** to describe the much larger population in which both wife and husband are employed in the labor force. The argument is that the term **dual-career marriage** should be restricted to the small proportion of the population in which the wife and husband both

Table 16.2: Labor Force Participation for Women

Year and Marital Status	Participation Rate					
	Ages* 16–19	Ages 20–24	Ages 25–34	Ages 35–44	Ages 45–64	Age 65 and Over
1960: Married	25.3%	30.0%	27.7%	36.2%	34.2%	5.9%
Single	25.3	73.4	79.9	79.7	75.1	21.6
Widow/Divorced	37.3	54.6	55.5	67.4	58.3	11.0
1970: Married	36.0	47.4	39.3	47.2	44.1	7.9
Single	39.5	71.1	80.7	73.3	67.8	17.6
Widow/Divorced	46.5	59.7	65.1	67.9	60.7	9.9
1980: Married	47.7	60.5	59.3	62.5	46.9	7.2
Single	49.0	72.2	84.2	78.5	62.8	12.0
Widow/Divorced	51.0	68.5	77.1	76.4	59.5	8.6
1988: Married	46.8	65.9	68.6	72.7	52.7	7.4
Single	48.7	74.8	81.8	81.5	65.2	10.9
Widow/Divorced	64.5	67.7	76.3	81.5	62.6	8.2

*Ages 14–19 category used in 1960.
Source: U.S. Bureau of the Census, 1990x, No. 634, "Labor Force Participation Rates, by Marital Status, Sex, and Age: 1960 to 1988" in *Statistical Abstract of the United States, 1990,* 110th ed., p. 384. Washington, DC: U.S. Government Printing Office.

have professional or managerial positions. Using this definition, only about one fourth of dual-earner marriages could be also classified as dual-career marriages (Hiller & Dyehouse, 1987). One survey of dual-earner wives and husbands found that only 13% of couples were both professionals and/or in managerial positions whereas two thirds were dual nonprofessionals (Moen & Dempster-McClain, 1987). Other researchers use the term "dual earner" to indicate that the wife's job is subordinate to the husband's job or career (Hicks, Hansen, & Christie, 1983). While recognizing that most marriages are technically dual-earner marriages, for our purposes, the term dual-career marriage will be used in keeping with popular usage.

The Establishment of Dual-Career Marriages

Although women have long worked outside the home, the establishment of dual-career marriages is a fairly recent phenomenon. The percentage of married women working has gradually increased so that by 1988, two thirds of all married women ages 20–34 were at least part-time labor force participants (see Table 16.2).

Several critical factors have promoted the formation of dual-career marriages: desire to achieve a higher level of living, reinforcement for women from the **feminist** movement, technological advances freeing women from constraints of homemaking, and desire for security in the event of husband's job loss or indiscriminate job relocation (Greiff & Munter, 1980). Early career entry, continuous employment throughout early family stages, orderly job sequences, and favorable industrial locations tend to be associated with the highest salaries and/or wages for career women (Van Velsor & O'Rand, 1984).

Women, Marriage, and Career Patterns

In examining dual-career marriages, the variables of age at first marriage and timing of first birth appear to be associated with career patterns of women. The most often reported reasons for leaving the labor force are either to get married or to give birth to the first child. Of those women who reported leaving the labor force, two thirds indicated "birth of a child" as the primary reason. Women who married at age 23 or older also were more likely to leave the labor force at the birth of their first child or at the time of their marriage (Sorensen, 1983). However, in comparison to their mothers, more young women today are choosing to continue their careers after their first child is born. In the early 1960s, only 17% of women returned to work within 12 months after the birth of their first child compared to 53% in the mid-1980s (Witwer, 1990b). Evidence suggests that a woman who gives birth to a first child early in her career may later experience advantages in the job market. As she progresses in her career, the children become older and require less care, thus allowing her more time to devote to her job. By choosing early motherhood, she may receive rewards for dedication to her occupation as well as increased earnings (Hanson, 1983).

Married women exhibit different career patterns due to a variety of circumstances. Four career types have been identified: regular career, interrupted career, second career, and modified second career (Poloma, Pendleton, & Garland, 1982). In the regular career pattern, a woman begins full-time work after completing her education. Although somewhat limited by family demands while the children are young, she continues working with minimal interruptions. Oftentimes, these women become even more involved in their careers after their children leave home (Poloma et al., 1982). Regular career pattern women are much less likely to perceive that child care must be exclusively maternal (Morgan & Hock, 1984).

When a regular career pattern is interrupted after several years, usually for childbirth and child rearing, it is an interrupted career (Poloma et al., 1982). Many mothers leave the labor market or attempt to work part-time during the child-rearing stage resulting in what some believe to be long-term negative effects on their careers (Ting, 1988). Such women typically earn less than wives employed during every stage of the life cycle. However, women with interrupted careers will still earn more than women who have delayed careers (Van Velsor & O'Rand, 1984). In a comparison of work careers for women and men, three fourths of women had experienced work interruptions for 6 or more months as contrasted with only one fourth of men. Of these women, two thirds said family was the primary reason for their work interruption. Substantially fewer women with college degrees experienced family-related work interruptions. This pattern may be related to job commitment, which is correlated with a college education ("Work Interruptions," 1985).

The second career pattern is used to describe a married woman who completes her college education after divorce or after the children are grown and about to leave home. Such women typically start out with more momentum in their careers because they have fewer family demands and obligations (Poloma et al., 1982). Level of education is the most important determinant of salary level for those mothers who enter the labor force after completion of their childbearing (Van Velsor & O'Rand, 1984).

A modified second career pattern involves completing professional training and initiating career involvement after children are old enough not to need full-time mothering. Wives in this category tend to begin their career commitments slowly and increase the momentum as their children grow older (Poloma et al., 1982). In general, the more education a mother possesses, the more likely she is to go back to school while her youngest child is still a preschooler (Hicks et al., 1983).

Working Wives and Working Mothers: Choices and Benefits

Since 1975, over 20 million new jobs have been created of which over two thirds have been filled by women. However, because many new jobs are in the lower paying sectors of the economy, it is anticipated that the average wages of women will rise to only about three fourths of those paid to men by the year 2000. In fact, women in elite positions such as lawyers, physicians, college professors, and management professions are more likely to be single, married with no children, or divorced. These higher salaried positions accounted for less than 1% of all married women in the labor force in 1982 (Benenson, 1984). Because women are having fewer children, they also are spending more time at work rather than at home (Pennar & Mervosh, 1985). Wives are more likely to be in the labor force if they have no young children, a high level of education, a decreased need for housework due to changing technology, an increased opportunity in the labor market, and an increased need to purchase household commodities (Ferber, 1982).

Factors Affecting Employment Decision

Generally, the decision of married women and mothers to seek employment is influenced by many factors such as changes in societal attitudes toward working mothers, perceived rather than real need to work for financial reasons, and need to work for reasons other than financial ones (Eggebeen, 1988).

Educational Level of Wife

The likelihood that a woman will be employed after marriage increases with the amount of her education. The number of years that a woman is likely to have worked since marriage is correlated with her educational level (Ferber, 1982). Highly educated wives usually have a smaller family and more favorable attitudes

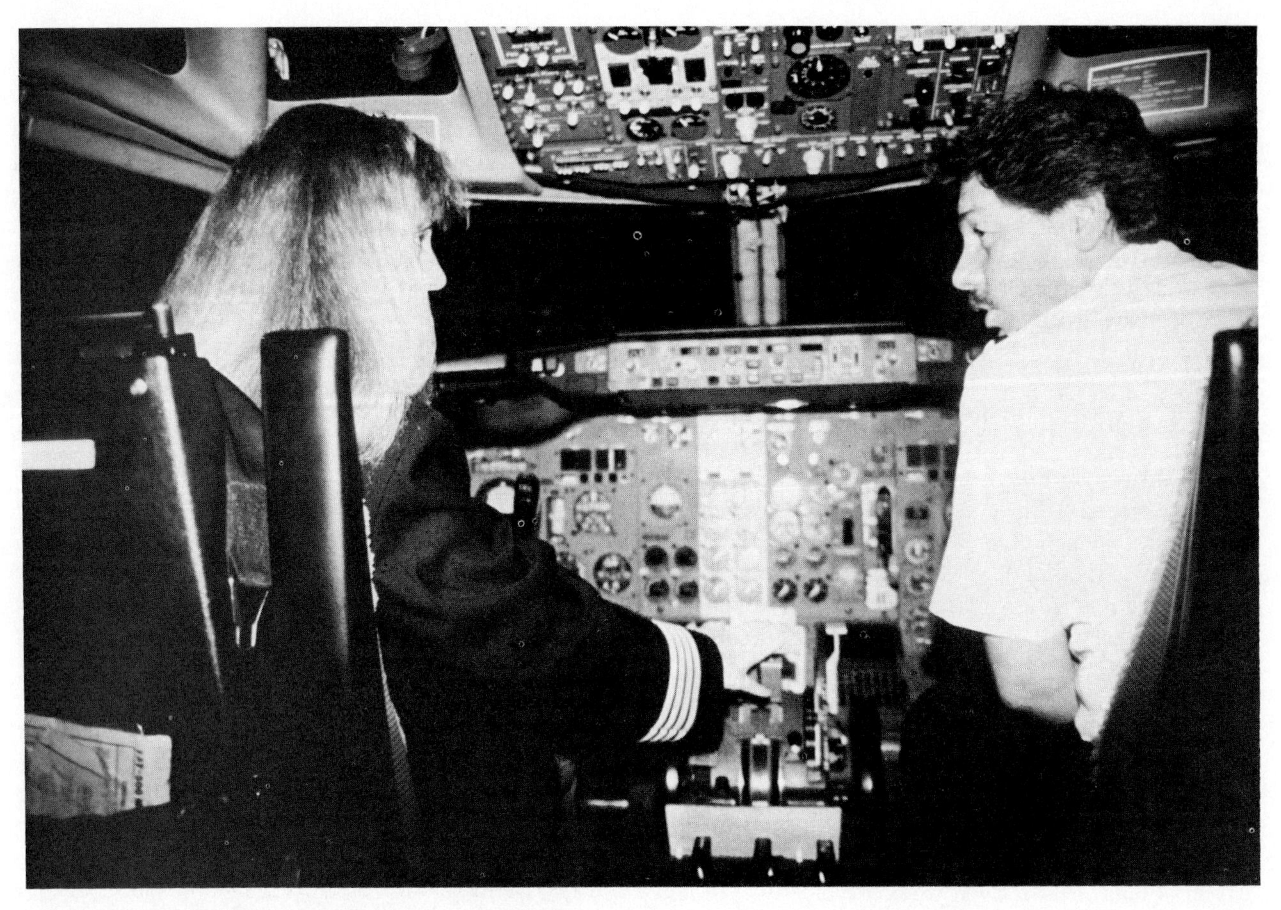

Indeed, we have "come a long way" since 1968 when Lillian Cazalet became the first female airline captain.

toward wives and mothers working outside the home (Shapiro & Shaw, 1982). Support for this argument is found in data which indicate that nonemployed wives have more children and younger children than full-time employed women (Glass, 1988). Thus, being married and having younger children decreases the likelihood of being employed outside the home (Rexroat, 1985).

Pink Collar Occupations: Economic Realities

The term pink collar occupation has been used to label occupations held mainly by women such as typist, secretary, bookkeeper, and store clerk (Fox & Hesse-Biber, 1984). Many so-called female occupations entail clerical skills or nurturant skills related to preserving social relations. Such occupations require more clerical perception, less spatial perception, and slightly less form perception while so-called male occupations tend to require slightly more motor coordination, substantially more physical strength, and greater complexity in dealing with things (England, Chassie, & McCormack, 1982). Such culturally induced norms have led to women being overrepresented in certain occupations such as food, health, and clerical positions (Pennar & Mervosh, 1985). Whether or not a man's mother was employed outside the home apparently makes no difference with regard to the man's perception of the employment status of women. However, men employed in low prestige occupations are more likely to perceive working women as a greater personal threat (Crosby & Herek, 1986).

By 1987, over one third of the approximately 13 million executive, administrative, and management positions in the United States were held by women. And, the number of women graduating with business degrees had increased by over 300% since 1977 (Fisher, 1987). However, in terms of administrative positions, today's women fare less well than before. When only 4% of the Masters of Business Administration (MBA) degrees granted in 1972 were to women, they held 20% of the management and administrative jobs. In 1987, with 33% of the MBA's going to women, they still held only 37% of such positions (Baum, 1987). Nevertheless, women are moving up the corporate ladder in fields such as commercial banking, retailing, advertising, and publishing.

The Equal Pay Act of 1963 called for **comparable worth** whereby women and men must be paid equally for the same job requiring similar skills, effort, and responsibility. Even with such legislation and the trend toward egalitarian gender roles, substantial variations in hourly wages and salaries still exist between women and men (Arnold, 1985). By 1988, women still earned only 65¢ for every dollar earned by men. In 1988, the median weekly earnings for married women was $324 in contrast to $500 for married men (U.S. Bureau of the Census, 1990bb). Furthermore, the average hourly wage for employed women is almost $4 less per hour than for men. In 1988, that figure was $7.80 for women compared to $11.24 for men (Bernstein, 1988). Men working in "women's jobs" earn less than men in "men's jobs," but women working in "men's jobs" experience no significant increases in their pay. Even when controlling for work experience, education, and family status, women are still unlikely to receive comparable salaries (Coverdill, 1988). However, some women may choose lower-paying jobs with less responsibilities to enable them to spend more time with their children (Bernstein, 1988).

Part-Time Work Option

In the past, companies were reluctant to hire part-time workers because they believed such individuals would have poor work habits and would contribute to a lack of continuity in the workplace. However, many employers hire part-time workers to their economic advantage since part-time employment does not usually include health insurance or pension benefits (Forbes, 1987). This trend may be one reason why the part-time work force has increased four times as rapidly as the full-time work force during the past two decades. By 1988, 26% of all employed women were working part-time (U.S. Bureau of the Census, 1990z).

Married women who are working part-time are more likely to have children than women who are employed full-time (Statham, Vaughan, & Houseknecht, 1987). The advantages of part-time employment for the married female professional with children include more freedom, more ability to interact with other people, high visibility, and more growth opportunities (Brown, 1986). A 1990 survey found that 46% of large-corporation executives and 69% of MBA students believed that corporations should provide a separate career track for women executives to work part-time without sacrificing professional careers or motherhood (Gudridge & Byrne, 1990). Psychological stress may be lowered by part-time employment for women with children in the home since it allows them more control over their lives. Such women, as opposed to full-time employed or nonemployed women, have a greater sense of power and relatively lower outside demands (Rosenfield, 1989).

Working part-time may be the best option for married women who choose to work after their children reach school age since it allows mothers to be home when the children return from school. A national survey of working mothers found that two thirds of those mothers working full-time would prefer to work part-time. Paradoxically, mothers who spent the least amount of time with their children were more likely to prefer working fewer hours (Moen & Dempster-McClain, 1987).

Psychological Benefits of Being a Working Wife

In the early 1960s, when most Americans thought the only "proper" role for a woman was to be a wife, mother, and homemaker, Betty Friedan (1963) verbalized the gathering winds of change which challenged this assumption. In *The Feminine Mystique,* she argued that the traditional view of women stifled their personal and intellectual growth; in so doing, it worsened marriage and family life for all. In her view, women as well as men could be strong and happy only if they could express themselves outside as well as inside of the family (Friedan, 1963). Since this important impetus to the modern women's movement, many women have succeeded in forging their own identities and in attaining equal opportunities in the world of work.

However, a new generation of American women face other important issues. Friedan (1981), who later examined the social revolution that she helped to create in another book, *The Second Stage,* clarified the emerging questions of women in the 1980s. Addressing the practicalities of liberation, she concluded that the real and most basic question has still to be asked:

> *Must-can-women now meet a standard of performance in the workplace set in the past by and for men who had wives to take care of all the*

details of living and—at the same time—meet a standard of performance at home and with children set in the past by women whose whole sense of worth, power and mastery had to come from being perfect housewives and mothers? Or will the women's new experiences create new standards at home and at work that permit a more human and complete life not only for themselves but also for men?

(Friedan, 1980, p. 47)

Job Satisfaction and Happiness

Among female executives, most women (86%) reported working for reasons including accomplishment/achievement, whereas less than one half mentioned money as the primary reason for working. These women who gave priority to their careers were still able to integrate marriage into their lives although three fourths had no children (Keown & Keown, 1985). Employment of mothers is viewed by some as a positive activity because it offers an alternative source of social and psychological rewards which can help overcome the isolation perceived to be inherent in the motherhood and household roles (Pleck, 1985). In fact, 8 in 10 working mothers reported higher personal confidence levels because of the realization that they could combine work and parenthood and still be a good mother (McKaughan & Kagan, 1986).

Job satisfaction for married women depends upon the degree of occupational status, work schedule, and absence of problems with family income. The lack of maternity benefits and leaves are likely to adversely affect job satisfaction (Moore, H. A., 1985). Other key factors are their level of education and income. Women employed in low status jobs who reported positive job moves were more likely to report marital satisfaction, satisfaction with other family relations, and a positive job mood. Women in high status jobs with job security and intrinsic job satisfaction indicated satisfactory family relations. However, their positive moods were related to lower levels of satisfaction with family relations (Piotrkowski & Crits-Christoph, 1982).

An earlier study found that working wives who were happy with their jobs were more likely to be happy with their marriages. Conversely, job satisfaction correlated with overall happiness, with marital happiness being the strongest determinant of life happiness (Houseknecht & Macke, 1981). Later, researchers found that being happily married and satisfied with work does not create as much overall happiness for working wives as it does for their husbands. Husbands were happiest when there were no children in the home and unhappiest during the child's preschool years because of decreased attention from their wives (Benin & Nienstedt, 1985).

Influence of Career on Self-Esteem

In one study, more married professional women working outside the home felt better about themselves and their marriages than women with children living at home, who felt unfulfilled in terms of career opportunities (Crossman, 1987). Another comparison of employed and nonemployed mothers with preschool children found employed mothers to be relatively well-adjusted psychologically in spite of their role overloads. This may occur because their jobs provide social interaction with other adults and interesting daily activity. However, no significant differences in overall life satisfaction were found between working and nonworking mothers (Shehan, 1984).

Evidence suggests that career women have a higher self-concept than women in general (Baker, 1985). Working outside the home has the potential to free women from dependence on men, and, therefore, increases their well-being, self-esteem, and sense of identity (Toman, 1983). Working mothers feel more socially connected and goal-oriented than nonworking mothers (Lovell-Tray, 1983). Further, middle-aged, married working women with or without children exhibit greater feelings of achievement and pleasure in their lives which they attribute to high self-esteem and a feeling of control over their lives (Baruch, Barnett, & Rivers, 1983). However, there are psychologically stressful issues, that affect the self negatively, which must be handled if the psychological rewards of employment are to outweigh the costs. This perception is more likely true for the professional woman whose self-esteem is enhanced through career achievements rather than for one who just holds a job. In a comparison of women in traditional and nontraditional careers, women in nontraditional careers such as accountants or managers who engaged in high levels of traditional male activities had much lower levels of self-esteem. In contrast, traditional career women such as teachers and nurses who engaged in few traditional male activities reported the highest levels of self-esteem (Reinhardt, 1985). A well-formulated sense of gender role identity, which obviously influenced the initial occupational choice, may partially account for these differences in self-esteem.

Careers for Wives and Mothers: Barriers and Costs

Working wives must have enormous reserves of energy for myriad tasks: handling overloaded schedules, making decisions effectively and quickly, being flexible, managing guilt feelings associated with being unavailable for their spouse, and coping with potential lack of mutual support from their spouse (Greiff & Munter, 1980). Since wives are expected to have primary responsibility for child care, their chances of career advancement through promotion and higher salaries may be jeopardized (Rexroat, 1985). Perhaps, for this reason, 37% of women in one study believed that motherhood had slowed their career advancement, whereas 25% indicated no effect. Some also had changed to jobs that were more challenging—27% and to jobs with more flexible hours—25% (McKaughan & Kagan, 1986). In fact, an earlier investigation found that as the number of preschool children in the home increases and as the age of the wife decreases, it becomes less likely that the woman will ever be employed outside the home (Hiller & Philliber, 1980).

One of the barriers to working mothers is societal attitudes. Despite increasing numbers of working mothers, there are many negative attitudes toward mothers working outside the home. In a national poll of women and men, more than one half believed that children are neglected to some degree when the mother works (Wallis, 1987). In addition, a California poll found that about two thirds of women and men agreed that a mother with small children should not work outside the home if the husband is able to provide a good income ("Both Sexes Agree," 1986). Similar findings were obtained in a *Redbook* study in which about three fourths of nonworking mothers and one half of working mothers believed that children almost always suffer when both parents work outside the home. But two thirds of working and one half of nonworking mothers thought their own children would not suffer if good substitute child care were available. Interestingly, 39% of nonworking mothers reasoned that most mothers worked outside the home because they did not like the everyday responsibilities associated with taking care of their children (Gaylin, 1986).

Motherhood Responsibilities: Choosing Between Competing Demands

Attempting to balance the competing demands of motherhood and careers often leads working mothers to feel guilty for not living up to impossible standards: "perfect mother" and "superwoman." The "perfect mother" represents the stereotyped mother of the 1950s and early 1960s who understood everything about being a mother and who stayed at home for the happiness of her children. Today, "superwoman" has come to represent a woman capable of meeting all demands including being a successful worker and an all-knowing mother. Although little evidence exists which suggests that maternal employment itself has direct detrimental effects on children, the working mother often experiences guilt feelings. Such guilt feelings may lead to the conclusion that her employment is responsible for any problems her child may have including those in developmental areas such as walking, talking, and toilet training (Sanger & Kelly, 1987).

Some authorities argue that career and family involvement have never been very easily combined within the same person. They believe that highly educated, career-centered married women will be more likely to remain child-free because having children will mean scaling down their aspirations and settling for a "job" instead of a career. Working mothers are predicted to have a lower standard of living than those who are child-free because family demands will prevent them from competing for the highest salaried positions. Thus, they will more likely be financially disadvantaged when compared to child-free women or men (Hunt & Hunt, 1986). Actually, many managerial and professional women are searching for new ways to balance career goals and motherhood by leaving the "fast track" for the "mommy track." Their employers, worried about losing top producers as well as attracting talented women in the future, are beginning to reshape the work setting to help women rear families. These career alternatives range from extended leave and flexible hours to **job sharing** and telecommunication systems connected to the employee's home. The premise is that women can slow down their career pace for a few years to get their children launched and then reenter the full-time work force without penalty. However, some women, notably feminists, believe that by accepting the "mommy track" women would be giving up the fight for family-related social change that would help mothers have full-time careers while fathers share more nurturing responsibilities (Ehrlich, 1989).

Statistics on childbearing indicate that many couples delay having children in order to first establish careers. Another way to balance commitments is to sequence careers so that only one partner's career is a priority at a given time. This approach avoids an overlap of peak family work demands (White & Botkin, 1989). Finally, having fewer children will enable couples to invest less time, energy, and resources in child rearing (Glass, 1988).

Returning to Work After Childbirth: A Major Decision

When mothers return to work after childbirth, the ability to balance a career and mothering is associated with high scores on good adjustment to life, greater freedom from pregnancy, and high marital satisfaction (Myers-Walls, 1984). Among married women with children under 3 years of age, three factors appear to determine whether they are likely to become employed wives or full-time homemakers: prior work experience, work plans, and husband's attitudes toward wives working. Studies indicate that white women who are working and who are not doing so out of financial need are more likely to have been employed prior to childbirth, to be comfortable with their employment status, to have husbands who are supportive of their careers, and to have feelings of personal satisfaction. In contrast, black women are more likely to be working out of financial need, to be employed full-time, and to be working with or without their husbands' approval (Avioli, 1985).

Returning to work after childbirth is related to whether or not mothers have chosen to breast-feed their infant. In the mid-1980s, a survey of mothers who were breastfeeding found that about one half used breast pumps so that a caregiver could provide breast milk from a bottle. On the average, mothers who breast-fed returned to work about 10 weeks after childbirth. Although three fourths of these mothers indicated their co-workers were supportive of their choice, almost one half had guilt feelings about working and breast-feeding (MacLaughlin & Strelnick, 1984). Mothers who make arrangements to have their infant brought to them at work may find their employers opposed to such a practice. But if they spend considerable time away from their infant, they may have difficulties breast-feeding (Lott, 1987).

With the exception of self-employed, working mothers who care for their children at work, other mothers who decide to return to work must make arrangements for child care. Highly educated women are most likely to take their children to day-care centers or to the home of a baby-sitter. Further, preschoolers are more likely than infants to be in group care centers or nursery schools ("Child Care," 1987). A frequent source of concern of a working mother is related to whether a sick child is obtaining proper care while she is at work. As of 1987, working mothers were losing an average of 8 days of work per year because of child-care problems, a fact that has led over one third of them to consider quitting their jobs (Wallis, 1987). Mothers commonly report being ill themselves in order to stay home with their sick child. Most day-care centers are unwilling to accommodate sick children because of the extra attention required and the possibility of legal liabilities (Levine, 1988).

What about the child-care role of fathers? A national survey of working mothers in dual-career families found that the average mother spent 3.5 hours per day in child care if she was working full-time and 4.7 hours per day if she was working part-time. However, fathers spent only 2.3 hours per day in child care regardless of working either full-time or part-time (Moen & Dempster-McClain, 1987). If there were two or more children under age 5 in the family, three fourths of fathers reported providing some child care. And, as might be anticipated, fathers were more likely to provide child-care assistance if the mother worked full-time at night (Presser, 1988). Although mothers are least likely to work full-time at night, when they do, mothers and fathers often participate in joint child care. But even under these circumstances, fathers are still less likely to be the sole child-care provider (Presser, 1986).

Domestic Responsibilities for Working Mothers

Family science professionals have estimated that non-employed women spend at least 50 hours per week doing household chores: preparing and cleaning up after meals, washing clothes, cleaning the house, taking care of children and other family members, shopping, and maintaining household records (Hartmann, 1981). If a wife was formerly employed in a high-status occupational position, she is less likely to report satisfaction with housework than those wives who previously held lower-status jobs (Ferree, 1984). Family household tasks have been found to be strongly segregated by gender with about three fourths of all housework being done by the working mother while the husband and children share the remainder (Kalleberg & Rosenfeld, 1990). In fact, the husband spends about the same amount of time doing housework regardless of the number of children or age of the youngest child in the family. Whether or not the wife is employed outside the home makes little difference in terms of the total number of hours that the husband contributes to housework (Hartmann, 1981). While working mothers today spend less time doing household work, they still spend an average of 10 hours more per week engaging in household work than fathers (Shelton & Firestone, 1987).

Attitudes of Husbands toward Working Wives and Mothers

The husband's encouragement for a wife to work is the single best predictor of the wife's employment outside the home. Wives not employed outside the home receive the least encouragement from their husbands whereas wives who are employed full-time typically receive the most (Glass, 1988). One survey found that even though a husband approved of his wife working at the time of their marriage, if she continued to work, as the marriage progressed, his attitude became less positive (Ferber, 1982).

As the occupational status and educational level of the wife increases, the chances are greater that the husband will approve of his wife working (Hiller & Dyehouse, 1987). A national survey suggests that whether or not the wife works outside the home is not problematic for the marriage but that spousal disagreement is the issue. But if one or both partners are "work-centered," the amount of attention paid to various aspects of their marriage and to each other will be reduced (Blumstein & Schwartz, 1983).

Since perceived adequacy as a breadwinner is a main component of men's mental health, it is not surprising that husbands of working wives were found to have poorer mental health and feel less satisfied with their work and home life compared to husbands of nonworking wives (Mehren, 1986). While the increase in family income from the wife's earnings improves her evaluation of the marriage, it decreases the husband's rating (Simpson & England, 1982). As has been reported in a previous chapter, the mother's employment during this age period is generally believed to be less desirable for the child than later employment.

Women are more likely to believe that their husbands oppose their employment if either the husband or wife has a low educational level and the wife works part-time. Men who oppose their wife's employment are more likely to feel depressed than those who are supportive, especially if their own earnings are low. But husbands will feel less depressed if their own earnings are higher than those of their wives (Ulbrich, 1988). The husband's income will be highest in those families in which the wife is not employed and will tend to be lowest in families in which the wife is employed full-time (Glass, 1988). Men also report more stress when married to a more educated woman while women indicate more stress when married to a less educated man (Wampler & Kingery, 1985).

Lack of Corporate or Governmental Support

During the 1980s, much debate centered around the issue of corporate obligations for special types of benefits for working mothers. The three general types of family support benefits provided by some companies are more time for parenting through parental leave, flexible hours, sick-child care, and job sharing; assistance with child care through employer-provided child care, information, referral service, and financial substitutes for child care; and parental education programs contributing to better parenting and family relations which lead to less role strain (Raabe & Gessner, 1988).

It is not surprising with the number of women working during the childbearing years that 80% of all working women will become pregnant during their working lives. Although many employers are unenthusiastic about the prospects of female employees being pregnant and on leave, the 1978 Pregnancy Discrimination Act requires employers to treat pregnancy as a short-term illness/injury. Consequently, an employer cannot refuse to hire a pregnant woman or require a pregnant woman to use up all her vacation time before receiving sick pay/disability benefits. In addition, a pregnant employee cannot be forced to take an unpaid leave for a minimum number of weeks. While this legislation addressed maternity leave and as such is limited to women, another policy issue receiving attention is parental leave and family leave. **Parental leave** is work absence for the purpose of caring for a newborn, sick, or adopted child, while **family leave** encompasses the care of seriously ill family members such as spouse or parent (Wisensale & Allison, 1989).

Neither federal nor state governments had a family leave policy prior to 1987, although the concept of maternity benefits has been documented in other countries as early as 1880. In fact, almost all Western industrialized countries had such policies in place well before mid-20th century with 135 countries having established maternity benefit programs by 1985 (Wisensale & Allison, 1989). By 1986, five American states required companies to provide short-term disability benefits and some paid leave to pregnant workers

Table 16.3: Family-Oriented Programs and Policies of Select Companies

Programs and Policies	Practices and Attitudes		
	Currently Have	Are or Would Consider	Would Not Consider
Part-time work	61%	25%	10%
Maternity leave	57	25	16
Sick child leave	38	30	27
Flextime	35	34	28
Maternity and paternity leave	16	32	48
Contract with outside agencies	9	35	52
Job sharing	8	42	44
Flexible benefits	6	49	41
Resource and referral	6	49	40
Printed materials	4	70	21
Worksite seminars	1	44	49
Consortium child care benefits	1	47	47
On-site child care	1	14	80
Subsidized parent-selected child care	1	18	76

From R. L. McNeely and B. A. Fogarty, "Balancing Parenthood and Employment: Factors Affecting Company Receptiveness to Family-Related Innovations in the Workplace" in *Family Relations*, 37:191. Copyright © 1988 National Council on Family Relations, 3989 Central Avenue, N.E., Suite #550, Minneapolis, MN 55421. Reprinted by permission.

(Brophy, 1986). Yet, a Bureau of Labor survey in 1988 found that only 33% had unpaid maternity leave and 2% had paid maternity leave. While 28 states introduced parental and family leave legislation in 1987, only Connecticut, Rhode Island, Oregon, and Minnesota actually enacted legislation for parental leave. Connecticut broadened its act to include elderly parent care, thus embracing the family leave concept ("Third of Workers," 1989). And, Wisconsin now requires large-company employers to grant unpaid family leave for the birth or adoption of a child or to care for a seriously ill family member. Federal family-leave legislation, requiring employers with 50 or more employees to provide up to 12 weeks of family leave, was passed in 1990 by the United States Congress. However, it was vetoed by President Bush on the grounds that leave policies should be negotiated between workers and employers (Roel, 1991). Various studies have indicated that working women, in addition to meeting various other family and job-related responsibilities, are also the primary caretakers of their elderly family members (Brody & Schnoover, 1986; Brubaker, 1984). Therefore, the family and workplace issue is now an intergenerational one. With decreased fertility and increased longevity, the average married couple may expect to spend more years caring for aging parents than children (Preston, 1984). Today, a woman will spend at least 17 years caring for a dependent child and 18 years providing assistance to elderly parents (U.S. House Select Committee on Aging, 1987).

A survey of 276 companies found that while a slight majority of companies (57%) had provisions for maternity leave, strong opposition to on-site child care existed (see Table 16.3). Industrial companies and heavily unionized companies were less receptive to job sharing, part-time work options, sick child leave, and parental leave (McNeely & Fogarty, 1988).

An evaluation of personnel records of working mothers with young children revealed that they are more likely to miss work, arrive late, leave early, and deal with child-care issues while at work (Raabe & Gessner, 1988). As a result, many employers have "formal" and "informal" policies concerning work schedules and personal holidays. One survey of companies identified only two cases of formal policies which permit job sharing and provide parent education seminars, counseling for family matters, and/or child care in the workplace (Raabe & Gessner, 1988). Nevertheless, a 1987 national poll found that over one half of women and almost one half of men believed that businesses should provide day-care (Wallis, 1987).

The Dual-Career Family: Problems and Issues

A career person who is a spouse and/or parent plays multiple roles which can result in role overload and family problems which can in turn create interference in the job setting. Lack of time is a major problem for working women. There is more likely to be a time shortage when certain conditions exist in the family: presence of working mother, presence of school-aged children, acceptance of new job(s) which may involve relocation, and wife having a higher status job than husband (Voydanoff & Kelly, 1984). These same family-related factors also contribute to job tension in the work environment. Specific family variables influencing one's job include presence of one or more preschool children in family and serious illness of family member (Kelly & Voydanoff, 1985).

Career Decisions in Dual-Career Families

In dual-career families, consideration must be given to career priorities. Among the questions the wife and husband must answer is their willingness to make moves for career purposes. Particularly for high level professional and/or managerial opportunities, career advancement is related to willingness to be geographically mobile. Wives are generally less willing to accept a transfer to another location even though it usually means career advancement (Markham, Macken, Bonjean, & Corder, 1983). If couples do move, they usually move for the husband's career rather than for the wife's career. Further, such wives are more likely to engage in part-time work at the new location (Statham et al., 1987).

If husbands have flexible jobs, earn less than their wives, and have nontraditional gender-role attitudes, they are more willing to follow their wife's career and relocate when she receives a job transfer or promotion (Wampler & Kingery, 1985). In general, husbands who relocate tend to be younger in age, better educated, more likely to be employed in professional positions, and earn higher annual salaries than husbands in nonmigrating families (Lichter, 1982). Only if the wife earns a substantial percentage of the family income and if she has more egalitarian role preferences will her job be influential in the family decision to move. Wives are only willing to move for a better job/position for themselves if their husbands receive satisfactory job offers prior to the proposed move. However, husbands will accept a job offer for a better position if it is only plausible that their wives will find employment after moving (Bird & Bird, 1985). These findings support the assumption that family moves are more often initiated to advance the career of the husband.

As reported earlier, if the wife has a job with higher status or income than her husband, their relationship may be adversely affected. Their sex life may suffer and feelings of love diminish with a higher risk of mutual psychological abuse likely leading to divorce (Rubenstein, 1982). Thus, married, working women are caught in a dilemma. If they are highly career-oriented, such motivation may potentially damage their marital relationship.

Career Priorities

In most dual-career marriages, husbands devote more hours weekly to their careers than wives (Yogev, 1981). The husband's career usually takes priority over the wife's career because of his good-provider role and her family role, which is often considered more important than her professional one (Earle, Harris, Pearson, Perricone, & Smith, 1988; Ulbrich, 1988). In fact, there are obvious negative sanctions for men who opt out of the breadwinner role (Wampler & Kingery, 1985). Regardless of the wife's level of education or employment status, her support for her husband's career depends upon his length of involvement with the work organization and their life-style satisfaction. Marital and personal adjustment do not affect the degree of support directly, but they do affect overall life satisfaction (Pittman & Orthner, 1988). During the 1980s, women and men became more alike in their evaluation of money, power, prestige, and recognition as motivators for occupational advancement. However, men are still more likely to have a career-centered life-style preference in comparison to women (Regan & Roland, 1985).

Female college seniors in the 1980s were twice as likely as their 1970 counterparts to prefer a career-centered pattern rather than having a family-centered life-style (Benenson, 1984). However, among married, college-educated career women, only 4 in 10 reported feeling equal to their husbands in terms of their potential for professional success. Although their husbands devoted less time to housework, three fourths of working wives with young children thought that their husbands were doing their fair share of child care. In addition, some working wives perceived themselves and their husbands as having equal ability to handle household

Role reversals may be revolutionary as in the 1960s or evolutionary as in the 1990s. Some couples respond to the priority of parenting by Dad staying home for the child's early years.

decisions and problems (Yogev, 1981). These findings support an egalitarian model of marital relationships for dual-career couples. Among such couples engaged in "role sharing," their reasons for choosing this lifestyle were to avoid burdening the husband with all of the provider responsibilities and its resulting anxiety and stress. They perceived this arrangement as offering greater financial security since the wife's income was used for general family expenses rather than just for purchasing luxury items (Haas, 1980). If marriage and family life is secondary to the wife's job or career, the following circumstances are likely to exist: flexibility of husband's job, absence of children in home, and a traditionally male job held by the wife (Atkinson & Boles, 1984). With more women working, more women in male-dominated occupations, and the increase in egalitarian norms for women and men, the wife's career may become more of a priority. Further, as the percentage of family income earned by the working wife rises, the likelihood also increases for an egalitarian career emphasis (Bird & Bird, 1985).

Marital Costs

Husbands are usually more dissatisfied with their marriage when their wife has a higher-status occupation. They tend to be even more stressed by their wives' superior salaries than by her superior occupational prestige (Fendrich, 1984). Underachieving husbands who have wives who are overachievers are about 11 times more likely to experience premature death from heart disease. Further, the rate of divorce for women who hold traditional male jobs is twice as high as for those women who hold traditional female jobs. Finally, underachieving husbands are more likely to report personal problems with sexual satisfaction, friends, finances, unhappy marriages, and to have lower self-esteem than husbands who are at the same salary level or who earn more than their working wives (Rubenstein, 1982). Since career women typically have strong egos and high needs to achieve, such characteristics may present problems such as competitiveness in their marital relationship. With dual careers, over time there will be shifts in achievement, power, rewards, and costs for each marital partner (White & Botkin, 1989).

Child-Care Options

Since over one half of children under age 6 and three fourths of children who are ages 6–17 today have mothers who work at least part-time in the labor force, child-care options are an important issue (U.S. Bureau of the Census, 1990y). Further, by 1995, it is anticipated that two thirds of all preschool children will have mothers who are employed outside the home (Hofferth & Phillips, 1987). The continuing high rate of divorce fuels the fastest growing family form, the single-parent family, whose preschool children are more than twice as likely to be enrolled in day-care centers than their peers from two-parent homes (Turner & Smith, 1983). In 1987, a U.S. Census Bureau survey found that 60% of employed mothers with children under age 5 used nonparental child care: home-based day-care (primarily nonrelative)—36% and group day-care—24%. Of these working mothers with preschool-age children, 56% made cash payments for child care in comparison to only 16% of mothers with school-age children (Turner, 1991). The relative most likely to be the primary caregiver is the child's grandmother. School-age children are usually cared for by relatives or at family day-care centers (Presser, 1986).

In order to gain a balanced perspective of the day-care issue, it should be noted that of the married working mothers of children under 6, only about one fourth are employed full-time for the entire year. Those mothers who work less than full-time have markedly different child-care needs. Although the political debate is over licensed center-based care, two thirds of preschool children of working mothers are cared for in their own homes or another home because of the more flexible hours of home-based care. This figure is particularly sobering since as much as 94% of home-based care is unlicensed, and therefore unregulated according to safety, health, and other state child-care standards (Besharov, 1988).

Families find that the economic cost of weekly child care for preschool-age children is substantial. For a family with two children, costs for child care can be the second largest family expense, ranging from $2,000–$5,000 annually per child (Besharov, 1988). A 1987 survey of child-care costs in Boston determined that the costs ranged from $35–$70 per week for family-based day-care to $260–$340 per week for care provided within the child's home ("Child Care," 1987). Nationally, in 1987, the average cost of child care for preschool-age children was $55 per week in contrast to $35 per week for school-age children (Turner, 1991).

Attitudes toward Day-Care

A 1987 national public opinion poll found that 53% of women and 61% of men believed that it was bad for children if their mothers worked outside the home (Wallis, 1987). Nevertheless, if child care is available,

Table 16.4: Attitudes of Mothers toward Career and Child Care after Birth of First Child

	Strongly Agree		Somewhat Agree		Disagree	
Attitudes toward Career	T1	T2	T1	T2	T1	T2
More than any other adult, I meet my child's needs best.	59%	65%	32%	24%	9%	11%
My child is happier with me than with baby-sitters or teachers.	50	39	36	39	14	21
I am better at keeping my child safe than any other person.	23	28	30	28	46	44
A mother just naturally knows how to comfort a distressed child.	12	23	24	30	64	46

Note: Time 1 = mother in hospital and Time 2 = infant—age 3 months.
From E. Hock, et al., "Mothers of Infants: Attitudes toward Employment and Motherhood Following Birth of the First Child" in *Journal of Marriage and the Family,* 46:427. Copyright © 1984 National Council on Family Relations, 3989 Central Avenue, N.E., Suite #550, Minneapolis, MN 55421. Reprinted by permission.

employed mothers tend to work even more hours (Presser, 1986). In a survey of attitudes toward employment and motherhood after the birth of the first child, most mothers believed that they could meet the child's needs better than any other adult and that the child would be happier with its mother rather than with a baby-sitter (see Table 16.4). Further, three fourths of these women would not regret postponing their career in order to be able to stay home with a child. If the infant was age 3 months, three fourths of the mothers would still choose to stay home rather than working full-time (Hock, Gnezda, & McBride, 1984). It is important to understand what research has to offer concerning the effects of day-care on children.

Effects of Day-Care on Children

In the absence of longitudinal studies which indicate the long-term effects of day-care on infants and children, much debate continues to surround the issue. The central question in determining the effects of day-care on children relates to the formation of attachment, an affectional bond that exists between two people (Bowlby, 1988). The primary argument against day-care is that a sustained one-to-one relationship with the primary caregiver during the first 2–3 years of life is essential for the child's emotional development if she/he is to emerge with a secure and nurturing personality.

The fundamental issue of day-care has to do with the long-term consequences about which no definitive answer exists. A whole generation of American children is being reared in a way that has never happened before in our history. Edward Zigler, a national authority on child care, believes that it is exactly this unknown factor which is frightening to people (Wallis, 1987). The debate began in the 1960s when researchers and psychoanalytic theorists warned of the potentially damaging effects of the young child being separated from its mother (Bowlby, 1988). Although research in the 1970s failed to substantiate such negative effects, by the 1980s, a number of studies indicated possible negative effects of separation from attachment figures on the emotional development of children (Barglow, Vaughn, & Molitor, 1987; Belsky, 1987; and Vaughn, Gove, & Egeland, 1980). Studies documented that infants who enter full-time day-care in the first year of life have higher levels of insecure attachment than those who are reared at home or even those whose mothers work only part-time. These data involved almost 500 infants of low-income and middle-class families. Of those mothers who were employed more than 20 hours per week, over one half of their infants were securely attached as compared to three fourths of the infants whose mothers were not employed or who worked less than 20 hours (Belsky & Rovine, 1988). However, it should be noted that some research in the 1980s found no differences in the rate or type of security and/or attachment between home-reared or day-care infants (Chase-Lansdale & Owen, 1987; Jaeger, Weinraub & Hoffman, 1987).

Burton White, noted child development researcher and former director of the longitudinal Harvard Preschool Project, asserts that researchers may be asking the wrong questions. Instead of asking if there is any emotional damage to the child involved, he believes the question should be, is using day-care the best way to rear a child (Davis, 1989)? Psychologist Lee Salk, perhaps the most outspoken professional critic of day-care, agrees:

> *The most common problems of people in therapy—the inability to form meaningful relationships, difficulties in being able to love and be loved, problems of hostility and dependency stem from a lack of fulfillment of their needs in the early stages of development. . . It just might be that people who can't organize their lives to provide sufficient time for their children would be better off if they didn't have any.*
>
> *(Stein, 1984, p. 149)*

Authorities agree that it is premature to draw final conclusions about day-care at this point because several interpretations exist for the current research findings. Possibly, there may be a significant risk of insecure attachment among infants placed in full-time care during the first year of life, which has been described as the window of vulnerability (Belsky, 1987). This vulnerability appears to be greatest at ages 6–12 months, the time noted for forming the strongest first attachment. Or, as others suggest, the infant response of withdrawal from or avoidance of the mother may wear off especially if the mother and father can maintain responsive and supportive interactions (Bee, 1989; Blanchard & Main, 1979). Alison Clarke-Stewart, a child development authority, maintains that the crucial factors determining emotional vulnerability are not age entered, number of hours spent, or quality received in day-care but rather the mother's attitude toward the baby, her confidence as a mother, and her desire for independence (Davis, 1989).

Professionals have also sought to determine if social and intellectual development are affected by day-care attendance. Some studies suggest that day-care children may later become more aggressive, argumentative, and less compliant with peers and teachers (Haskins, 1985; McKinney & Edgerton, 1983). In contrast, other research has revealed heightened passivity (Schwartz, 1983). However, the evidence is unclear as to whether or not it is day-care itself or a specific day-care environment which produces such results (Bee, 1989). Research on intellectual development indicates that high-risk infants and those children from families in which lower IQ scores are typical can profit most from quality day-care. On the other hand, middle-class children rarely show either positive or negative intellectual effects (Caldwell, 1986).

Despite these concerns, many career women assert that their need to work is at least as powerful as any other need and that by choosing day-care they are no less devoted to their children's welfare. In fact, they often regard full-time mothers with the same implicit contempt with which men have traditionally viewed working mothers (Stein, 1984). For those mothers and/or fathers who do choose or have no option but to work during the beginning period of attachment, the most important consideration is quality child care. Research suggests that good child care will help to alleviate the guilt feelings that mothers often experience over leaving their children while working (Ross & Mirowsky, 1988). Such care would include a nurturing, responsible individual who will be available for an extended period of time (Gorney, 1987).

Day-Care Facilities

Even though there are over 60,000 professional day-care centers in the United States, of which approximately 50% are nonprofit, day-care problems are legion. Because of the demand for services and lack of adequate staffing, at least 33 states have lowered their standards and reduced their enforcement procedure for licensed day-care centers. And, day-care staffers rank among the lowest 10% of all wage earners which contributes to an average staff turnover rate of over one third per year (Wallis, 1987).

Home day-care is generally the least expensive for working parents (Hofferth & Phillips, 1987). Many family-based day-care facilities are run by women who are primarily supported by their husbands but who earn extra income by caring for their children and someone else's simultaneously. Although extra income is earned, problems with other children can threaten the woman's self-concept as a good mother and may be self-defeating (Nelson, 1988). By 1987, only eight states had training requirements for family-based day-care. The number of infants per adult in family-based facilities varies from 2–12 children with costs averaging about $40 or less per child per week (Wallis, 1987). A comparison between day-care centers and family-based day-care determined that day-care center personnel talk to parents more. They discuss learning, social development, behavior problems, and peer relationships with parents more frequently than family-based care persons (Hughes, 1985).

BOX 16.1 **How Young is Too Young?**

Jay Belsky is a Pennsylvania State University child psychology professor, noted for his day-care research and as a former full-time day-care proponent. In 1987, he was quoted in *Time Magazine* and *The Wall Street Journal* as saying: "Babies placed in child care for more than 20 hours a week run the risk of long-term psychological difficulty." The following is an excerpt from an interview with Belsky in *Parenting* magazine.

Parenting: You've been described as having executed a major about-face on the issue of infant day-care. Why did you change your mind?

Belsky: Ten years ago, nearly all research was drawn from high-quality, university-based centers with a well-paid, stable, experienced staff. At that time, few if any risks seemed to be associated with extensive child care. Recent evidence suggests that extensive nonparental care in the first year of life is associated with increased rates of insecure infant-parent relationships and with increased aggressiveness—hitting, kicking, fighting. There's also an increase in noncompliance which means refusing to cooperate, playing with things you're not supposed to, and not heeding instructions.

Parenting: Is it clear that day-care is the main cause of the trouble?

Belsky: It seems to be, in those instances where kids are receiving more than 20 hours a week of nonparental care.

Parenting: What were the conclusions of your first major study that found no problems associated with day-care?

Belsky: The first review focused mainly on high quality, research-oriented day-care centers. There was very little to suggest that day-care undermined kids' development when delivered in a high quality manner. There was some promising news that high quality care, particularly in centers, seemed to benefit children growing up in economically impoverished circumstances. Other evidence suggested that preschoolers developed some real social skills. They seemed more empathetic and more cooperative. But some studies did point out that children in day-care might be more noncompliant, more aggressive, and more disobedient. So there was a mixed message.

Parenting: And subsequent studies began to clarify your thinking?

Belsky: Yes. A 1980 study indicated that babies who started day-care in their first year were "anxious-avoidant" with their mothers; that is, when reunited with their mothers after a separation of any length, they behaved in a way that showed insecurity—looking or moving away, avoiding contact. Other children studied had started in ideal infant day-care during their first year and continued through their preschool years. These children in kindergarten and first grade, compared to children who started in day-care after the first year of life, were more aggressive, though seemingly more intelligent.

Parenting: Imagine I'm a new mother. And I have to go back to work. What do you say to me?

Belsky: I say to you, do two things, given what you can afford to pay. First, find a person who can care for that baby who's going to be responsible, sensible, and nurturing. More important is who that person is as a human being—that's more important than all the materials in the world. Second, make certain the caregiver is going to be around for a substantial period of time. What I think probably breeds risk is frequently changing day-care arrangements.

Parenting: Your article and subsequent discussions have not expressed any concern about day-care after the first year.

Belsky: If we look at good, quality day-care that's initiated after the age of 18 months, there's no evidence of anything to be concerned about.

Corporate day-care is still in its infancy, but it is growing. In the mid-1980s, only 120 corporations and 400 hospitals had begun to provide child-care centers at or near the work site. Further, about 1,800 employers out of 6 million businesses provided financial assistance for child care to their employees (Hofferth & Phillips, 1987). By early 1991, 64% of large-company employers in the United States offered some form of child-care assistance as part of their fringe benefits package (Gunn, 1991). Businesses that have invested in child care attest that it yields high dividends in lower rates of employee absenteeism and turnover. Research also suggests that companies reduce use of sick leave due to less stress-related illnesses and that corporate child care engenders unusual company loyalty (Wallis, 1987).

Choosing A Day-Care Site

A survey of general problems associated with day-care found that the most often reported difficulties are finding suitable care for ill children or for young infants, and costs that are too high (Fuqua & Labensohn, 1986). A national survey by the Centers for Disease Control found that children under age 18 months placed in day-care experienced 60% more colds and other respiratory illnesses than children cared for at home

(D'Alessio, 1991). With regard to quality of care, almost one half of parents reported care was inadequate, and one third indicated that their child was not properly supervised. While the majority of parents expressed satisfaction with their child-care arrangement, a large percentage replied that they would prefer some other form of child care than that which they were presently using if it were available and affordable (Fuqua & Labensohn, 1986).

Unfortunately, adult needs often take precedence over the needs of the child in selecting day-care. This conclusion was drawn from an assessment of child care by working parents where the most important considerations for mothers were, in order of importance, flexible hours for child care center, quality of provider, and convenience of location. Convenience of location was ranked even higher by fathers because they most often provided the transportation to day-care centers (Atkinson, 1987). When selecting day-care, 77% of parents reported depending upon friends and neighbors for recommendations, 43% used advertisements in newspapers and telephone books. But ironically, only 15% of parents took the time to check with the state Department of Human Services (Fuqua & Labensohn, 1986). However, the primary factor in selection of a day-care facility should be the quality of care (Turner & Smith, 1983). Many characteristics of the day-care facility will determine its quality of care. None are more important than the amount of personal contact with a caring adult who is knowledgeable about children's development (Bee, 1989).

BOX 16.2 **Day-Care Characteristics That Affect Outcomes for Children**

Teacher/child ratio. Lower ratios usually better, with 15:1 and higher being much less desirable.

Number of children per group. The smaller the number of children cared for in each assigned group, the better for the child.

Amount of personal contact with caregiver. In general, the more time child spends in one-to-one interaction with an adult, the better.

Richness of verbal stimulation. Greater complexity and variety of language used with the child leads to faster language and cognitive development.

Space, cleanliness, and colorfulness. More creative play and exploration occurs in colorful, clean environments adapted to child play. Expensive toys not critical, but there should be engaging activities and space for children to move around freely.

Caregiver's knowledge of child development. Adult guidance and children's development are better in centers or homes in which caregivers have specific training in human development.

Dual-Career Family Stress

A significant feature of dual-career life-styles is family stress. Tension may develop between marriage partners when either partner becomes so highly involved in her/his career that family obligations are not fulfilled. Such tension may eventually precipitate depression. Professional women who perceive their work, marital, and parenting roles as conflicting are more depressed and dissatisfied as parents even though they derive satisfaction from their multiple roles (Tiedje et al., 1990). Typically, wives experience the impact of role strain more, although husbands with working wives report less life satisfaction and perform their role responsibilities less effectively (Skinner, 1980). If job or family-oriented demands are low, employed women report significantly fewer symptoms of anxiety and depression than their male counterparts (Rosenfield, 1989). Women and men who are younger and who have more children at home experience greater work-family strain than older persons with few or no children. In fact, work-family strain is the most often reported source of depression among men (Keith & Schafer, 1980). For most women, especially those who are younger and combining marriage and motherhood, employment in managerial positions is associated with stress and depression. As the level of depression for working wives grows, they are more likely to perceive that their husbands oppose their employment. Wives who have been employed full-time are able to reduce their depression by becoming employed on a part-time basis (Ulbrich, 1988).

Among college-educated working wives, as the perceived conflict between home and work roles increased, several symptoms of depression were likely to be reported: appetite and sleep disturbances; inability to "get going"; lack of feelings of happiness, hopefulness, and enjoyment of life; and feelings of loneliness and sadness. Those women who worked for financial reasons only and who were dissatisfied with their pay level, experienced greater numbers of depression symptoms. Women with young children at home who reported performing more child-care tasks alone also had more symptoms of depression (Krause & Geyer-Pestello, 1985). Despite these findings about strain and depression among working wives and mothers, wives who desire to work but are not doing so are more likely to be depressed than working wives who desire not to work (Benin & Nienstedt, 1985). In fact, as the number of children grows, nonworking mothers who are depressed become more disenchanted with homemaking (Ross & Mirowsky, 1988). Stress and depression among dual-career couples appear to be related to work overload and role conflict.

Role Overload Conflicts

The most striking feature about dual-career couples is how their lives become filled with stress from demanding occupations, parenting, and work-related responsibilities. Although dual-career wives devote only one half as much time to housework as full-time housewives, realistically the same work in the home must be done (Berardo, Shehan, & Leslie, 1987). Division of labor in the home is affected by time demands of wife's employment, power of husband and wife in relationship, and husband's values relating to division of labor (Ross, 1987). Time is especially problematic for dual-career couples. Time-related strains and role conflicts include work-family conflict, time pressure, and time shortage. Work scheduling plays a more important part in time allocation than the actual number of hours worked. Working women seem to have more difficulties than men dealing with conflicts in daily routines. Transportation appears to be a problem with women in two-car families experiencing less time strain than those in one-car families (Cannon, 1987).

Role overload for employed women develops due to the wide range of child-care and housework activities which they are expected to assume within limited time. Working mothers identified lack of time for children, their own needs, housework, and social life as factors in role conflict (Pleck, 1985). However, evidence suggests that if women avoid role overload by limiting their work hours, they may hurt their chances of occupational mobility as well as curtail their earnings in the labor market.

Working Wives and Family Tasks

The fact that working mothers experience more work and family role strain than their spouses may relate to the attitudes of employers toward working mothers. When working mothers were viewed as being more responsive to family concerns, male supervisors were less likely to depend on them and less likely to promote them (Wiley & Eskilson, 1988). Earlier research suggests that the stress of being a working mother may be substantially offset by increased financial resources, privileges associated with careers, and an increased sense of personal growth (Hicks et al., 1983). The chances for high marital adjustment are also much greater if family members are willing to make accommodations for the fact that the mother/wife is employed outside the home (Houseknecht & Macke, 1981).

Research indicating that gender-role expectations impact work overload documents that women in dual-career families take primary responsibility for family tasks. They are most likely to implement task sharing by remembering when things need to be accomplished, making assignments, and checking on progress (Schnittger & Bird, 1990). A gender-specific task of working wives appears to be the expressive role of being **kin keeper** (someone who works to keep family members in touch with one another). In about three fourths of families, this position is filled by wives. The role of kin keeper includes telephoning, writing family members, visiting, and organizing or holding family gatherings (Rosenthal, 1985).

In those instances in which wives and husbands worked the same number of hours, almost one half of the wife's time at home was spent with family responsibilities in comparison to only one fifth of the husband's time (Condran & Bode, 1982). A 1986 national poll found that among dual-career families, the household chores were equally divided in only one fourth of families with wives performing all household chores in another one third of the families ("Both Sexes Agree," 1986). Data indicate that about two thirds of employed wives with children had sole responsibility for grocery shopping, cooking, and washing clothes (see Table 16.5). In contrast, with exception of washing dishes, nonemployed mothers had sole responsibility for all major domestic tasks.

Income and housework appear generally related. As the husband's income level rises, the home responsibilities of the wife increase even if she is working outside the home (Ross, 1987). Likewise, if the employed wife's income or prestige level rises substantially, her home responsibilities will decrease and the husband's participation will increase in tasks such as meal preparation and cleaning (Bird, Bird, & Scruggs, 1984). The optimum level of sharing domestic responsibilities between spouses appears to occur in those dual-career families in which the annual salaries of spouses are similar (Maret & Finlay, 1984).

Table 16.5: Sole Responsibility for Domestic Tasks among Married Mothers

	Employment Status	
Domestic Task	Employed	Not Employed
Grocery shopping	64%	68%
Child care	39	56
Cooking	65	81
Washing dishes	34	49
Cleaning house	42	57
Washing clothes	66	79

From E. Maret and B. Finlay, "The Distribution of Household Labor Among Women in Dual-Earner Families" in *Journal of Marriage and the Family,* 46:360.

Husbands as Dual Workers in the Home

In two-career families, the degree to which the husband assists with housework and child-care responsibilities largely determines the extent of the wife's role overload. The total amount of housework in dual-career homes performed by husbands ranges from 19% (Barnett & Baruch, 1987) to 23% (Kalleberg & Rosenfeld, 1990). Husbands of working wives indicated that the factors that most influenced the amount of time they spent on "feminine" home chores were number of hours their wives worked and attitudes toward male roles. However, for husbands of nonemployed wives, other variables were more influential. Those fathers who had younger and larger numbers of children spent more time in sole charge of them. Fathers also were more likely to be solely in charge of male children if their wives held more liberal attitudes toward male roles (Barnett & Baruch, 1987).

Evidence suggests that during the 1970s, men under age 30 began to increase the amount of time spent doing housework. This time proportionately decreased, however, as the amount of time increased that they spent in leisure activities such as playing golf, fishing, hunting, and spectator sports (Coverman & Sheley, 1986). The typical husband spends about 12 hours per day on the weekend in leisure activities in comparison to about 8 hours for wives. For nonemployed wives and employed wives, there are no significant differences between their average amount of weekday leisure time (Shaw, 1985). This may be because husbands tend to contribute about the same amount of time on family tasks regardless of whether or not their wives are employed outside the home (Pleck, 1984). In addition, the presence of children does not substantially increase the amount of time that husbands in dual-career marriages devote to housework. Lack of participation in household tasks by husbands may stem from the fact that they perceive their wife's standards for housework to be too high (Hartmann, 1981). If wives want their husbands to handle more housework and child care, his refusal to do so has an extremely negative impact on both family adjustment and psychological well-being of the mother/wife (Pleck, 1985). How do couples manage to balance the work and family role?

Coping with Role Overload

In coping with role overload, couples in dual-career marriages may either redefine or expand their roles. One of the reasons that women, more than men, find balancing a career with a family more stressful is that they have not reallocated the traditional responsibilities to the degree to which time, energy, and resources have been assigned to their career. When they simply expand rather than redefine their earlier role, role overload oftentimes occurs. Even when wives attempt to reassign responsibilities, the attitudes of many men have been found to be more egalitarian than their actions (White & Botkin, 1989).

Women in dual-career marriages should be encouraged to recognize that role conflict results from both internal sources (self-confidence and attitudes about life roles) and external sources (job flexibility and spouse support). These factors occur both within their family and at the societal level (Cox, 1986). Therefore, they should evaluate the influence of social roles and social norms on their personal experience. Further, it is helpful to clarify what family members consider to be major and minor parental role responsibilities and which parent is expected to fulfill these roles. Even though women who try to expand their roles to accommodate all demands report higher role conflict, they also indicate more spouse support and greater life satisfaction with the maternal role. In addition, women who choose role expansion obviously place much greater importance on the maternal role than women who redefine their role. Those women who try to redefine their roles must alter externally imposed expectations and/or change their own role expectations and behaviors. Both coping strategies can lead to women experiencing guilt feelings about neglecting various aspects of their maternal role (Gilbert, Holahan, & Manning, 1981).

"Your mom's a very special person."

Despite the consequences of dual careers, wives and husbands can adopt successful coping strategies to deal with work overload and role conflicts. Reframing some of the issues can help couples achieve more positive outcomes:

1. Define dual-career patterns as favorable or advantageous.
2. Establish priorities within various roles.
3. Compartmentalize work and family roles.
4. Compromise career aspirations to meet other role demands.
5. Hire outside help for child care and domestic work.
6. Establish friendships with couples who lead similar life-styles.
7. Negotiate possible changes in work arrangements such as job sharing and flexible schedules (Skinner, 1980, pp. 478–479).

The Effects of Maternal Employment on Children

A 3-year-old girl, whose mother is a professional described by colleagues and friends as so well-organized that she is something of a "superwoman," announces one morning that she wants to be a father when she grows up. "Why?" asks an adult friend. The girl has no trouble answering: "Because mommies work too hard" (Shreve, 1987, p. 126). The work-family conflict as it relates to the care of children was a central issue in an earlier national survey conducted for *The General Mills American Family Report.* The vast majority of those surveyed believed that the trend toward both parents working outside the home has had negative effects on families. However, perceived changes in quality of parenting was a greater source of worry than the issue of working parents per se. The quality and amount of

Table 16.6: **Labor Force Participation for Women**

Year and Marital Status	Participation Rate		
	No Children under age 18	Children ages 6–17	Children under age 6
1960: Married	34.7%	39.0%	18.6%
Separated	(NA)	(NA)	(NA)
Divorced	(NA)	(NA)	(NA)
1970: Married	42.2	49.2	30.3
Separated	52.3	60.6	45.4
Divorced	67.7	82.4	63.3
1980: Married	46.0	61.7	45.1
Separated	58.9	66.3	52.2
Divorced	71.4	82.3	68.3
1988: Married	48.9	72.5	57.1
Separated	60.1	69.3	53.0
Divorced	73.0	83.9	70.1

NA = Not Available
Source: U.S. Bureau of the Census, 1990y, No. 636, "Married, Separated, and Divorced Women—Labor Force Status by Presence and Age of Children: 1960 to 1988" in *Statistical Abstract of the United States, 1990,* 110th ed., p. 385. Washington, DC: U.S. Government Printing Office.

guidance, discipline, and attention children receive were specific concerns while more self-reliance and independence in children were perceived as positive benefits of both parents working (Harris, 1981a). As previously noted, more mothers are increasingly employed outside of the home. Between 1960 and 1988, there was a dramatic increase in the percentage of employed married women with children under age 18. By 1988, 57% of married women with children under age 6 were employed. The percentages of separated and divorced mothers who are employed are even greater (see Table 16.6). Further, by 1987, one half of all women with newborns were either working part-time or seeking employment compared to less than one third of such women in 1976 ("Half of All," 1989).

The changes in work and family are more than simply an increase in the number of working women. It is the emergence of a trend: a new working woman who no longer endures a job for the sake of family welfare but enthusiastically embraces a career. Such a fundamental change raises myriad political, economic, and social questions with long-range consequences. Family science professionals as well as parents are asking: Will children of dual-career families as adults be better persons and parents or will they be conflicted by so many options? Will gender stereotypes be erased or reinforced? Perhaps the most often asked question is, will the pressures from the world of work force mothers to abandon their time-honored role of nurturer? While today's children can have one person as their achieving and their nurturing model, many child development specialists believe that it is important for the children's welfare that the nurturing role be a priority for at least one parent (Shreve, 1987).

Remaking Motherhood

As burgeoning numbers of working women begin to "remake motherhood," researchers are busy studying the effects that this change may have on their children (Shreve, 1987). Which effects of dual-career parents may be positive and which may be negative no one knows for sure. According to the theory of choice and exchange, what is certain is that one does not make a choice without exchanging something in return. It is unrealistic to argue that children will be unaffected when both parents work outside the home in full-time careers permitting only intermittent contact with each other and their children. This pattern is a basic change from the traditional pattern of family life. Therefore, the task is one of discerning not *if* but *what* the effects are and seeking to maximize the positive ones and minimize those which are negative (Greiff & Munter, 1980).

Child development specialists believe that one of these positive changes may be that children who grow up in homes with career mothers may not see feminine and masculine traits as being so irreconcilable. Some studies already suggest that independent and achieving androgynous mothers have daughters with higher career aspirations and greater self-esteem than mothers who do not work outside of the home. However, although such mothers also encourage nurturing behavior in their daughters, they do not encourage similar behavior in their sons. These findings have led to speculation that the next generation may be one of androgynous women and traditional men (Shreve, 1987). Acquisition of gender roles by children of working mothers is influenced by the occupational prestige level of the mother and the home setting in which the mother was reared. However, the mother's educational level and her specific occupation apparently do not affect the children's view of traditional and nontraditional gender roles (Levy, 1986).

The research seems to suggest that people will support the choices that they have already made. For dual-career families with first-born only children, two thirds of employed mothers and three fourths of fathers indicated that the impact of maternal employment on the mother-child relationship was positive. In contrast, two thirds of nonemployed mothers and their husbands anticipated that maternal employment would have negative effects upon the child (Easterbrooks & Goldberg, 1985).

Children's attitudes toward their mothers' employment have been studied. In the American Chicle Youth Poll, 6 in 10 children who were ages 8–17 preferred a mother who worked outside the home rather than a mother who stayed at home and took care of the family ("American Children," 1987). Older children, female children, and children who stay at home alone after school tend to feel more negative toward their mothers' employment. Further, the attitudes of children also are greatly influenced by their perception of how their mothers feel about their job. Apparently, the more interest mothers exhibit toward their children and the more positive they feel about working, the less negative impact their employment will have on their children. Generally speaking, first-born children feel more negatively affected by their mothers' employment and female children more so than male children (Trimberger & MacLean, 1982).

General Adjustment and Academic Performance

Some authorities have concluded that elementary-age children of working mothers have higher I.Q.s, obtain better grades, and receive better ratings from their teachers in comparison to children of nonworking mothers. Further, as the family income of working mothers increases, the children demonstrate more skills in the performance of school-related tasks (Hales, 1987). Still others have found conflicting results. Considerable evidence collected between the 1930s and 1980s indicate that although a mother's working outside the home resulted in positive effects on daughters, it had a negative influence on the development of sons. Boys of middle-class families especially were more likely to attain lower academic rankings (Bronfenbrenner & Crouter, 1982). But it is not really possible to conclude whether or not any of these differences are related to maternal employment or to other factors such as educational level of mother, why she works, her job satisfaction, adequacy of child care, or socioeconomic status of the family. Finally, little attempt has been made to assess long-term achievement and the mental health of children in relation to their mother's employment (Easterbrooks & Goldberg, 1985; Moore & Sawhill, 1984).

Assignment of Household Tasks to Children

Children may be asked to assist with household tasks for various reasons: to develop character and responsibility, encourage working together as a family, give parents needed help, develop skills, and occupy the child's time. Among Nebraska families polled, over three fourths of female and male children were required to perform household chores with the weekly average number of hours progressing with the child's age (White & Brinkerhoff, 1981a). The most common household tasks assigned to children are housecleaning, food preparation, and dishwashing. Female children are somewhat more likely to perform housecleaning and food preparation and are twice as likely to help with dishwashing as male children (Cogle & Tasker, 1982).

Female children of employed mothers spend substantially more time than other children doing housework. Adolescent daughters of full-time employed mothers were found to spend 10.2 hours per week performing household chores in comparison to 8.2 hours for daughters of nonemployed mothers. However, adolescent sons spent only 2.8 hours doing household chores in employed-mother families, but 7.3 hours in nonemployed-mother families (Benin & Edwards, 1990). Consequently, female children of working mothers may be likely to resent their mother's employment. If asked to devote a disproportionate amount of time to household tasks, less time is left for school-related activities or socializing with their peers (Cogle & Tasker, 1982). The problem is compounded if older

Reconnecting at the end of a busy, but separate, day reaffirms the parent / child bond.

children are asked to provide child care for their younger siblings after school while their mothers are working.

Allocation of Time for Children

Mothers can express maternal love in ways other than staying at home and children of working mothers can develop healthy personalities and experience adequate socialization. Some research evidence suggests that most nonworking mothers spend the majority of their time doing housework so that, in actuality, they spend about the same amount of time in social interaction with their children as working mothers (Sanger & Kelly, 1987). But in a comparison of working mothers and nonworking mothers, working mothers spent about one fourth less play and educational time with their children than nonworking mothers during workdays. However, after children reach school age, mothers spend very little time playing, educating, talking, and providing direct care for their children regardless of whether or not they work outside the home. Working mothers employed during the day, especially after school hours, spend the least time with their children. But fathers in dual-career families have, on the average, 2 hours more contact with their children on Sundays than husbands of nonemployed mothers (Nock & Kingston, 1987).

Parents in dual-career families need to recognize the increased vulnerability of their child to separation and loss (Bowlby, 1988). Communication on a frequent basis with their children may help them deal with any anger, hostility, rebellion, or negative feelings of being abandoned because both parents have careers. Sometimes, children of working parents conclude that it is necessary to compete with their parents' careers in order to receive adequate time and attention. Therefore, dual-career parents should make special efforts to pay attention, listen, and react to their children's thoughts and feelings and at the same time share their own feelings (Greiff & Munter, 1980).

Latchkey Children: A Growing Concern

The term latchkey child has been coined in recent decades as a byproduct of the burgeoning numbers of working mothers. The image portrayed by media depicts a small child with a large key returning to an empty house each day. Latchkey children are more likely to be from homes of middle and upper-income white mothers living in suburban or rural areas with no other adults in the household (Cain & Hofferth, 1989). For latchkey children, about three fourths of the time spent alone is in the afternoons after school (Cole & Rodman, 1987). Differences of opinion exist between family scientists regarding the actual number of latchkey children ("Census Bureau Estimate," 1987). The Census Bureau estimates that daily at least 22% of children, ages 5–15, come home from school to an empty house because their parent(s) is working (Turner, 1991). However, other research suggests that as many as 20%–25% of school age children are left unsupervised (Ross & Mirowsky, 1988). As the working mother's level of education, occupational prestige, and income level increases, the probability increases that the child will not be supervised by an adult after school ("Child Care," 1987). Working mothers from low-income families more frequently rely on family members to provide child care than working mothers from higher-income, dual-career families. However, difficulties with finding adequate child care are often associated with higher rates of depression among working mothers with low annual incomes (Ross & Mirowsky, 1988).

Although among professionals there is grave concern over latchkey children, relatively little research has been conducted on either the long-term or short-term effects of being a latchkey child (Schickedanz, Hansen, & Forsyth, 1990). Two surveys have indicated that such children did not appear adversely affected by being left alone. Comparing self-care, adult-care, and mother-care children, no differences were found in academic achievement, fear of going outdoors alone, self-esteem, and ratings by teachers on social adjustment in interpersonal relations (Galambos & Garbarino, 1983; Rodman, Pratto, & Nelson, 1985). Conflicting evidence from other researchers indicates that a majority of latchkey children reported negative experiences from being home alone (Long & Long, 1983). Further, a content analysis of telephone calls to an after-school hotline revealed that one fourth of latchkey children were bored or lonely and another one fourth wanted to talk to someone (Guerney & Moore, 1983). And, a study of adjudicated juvenile delinquents in one Maryland county found that 90% were latchkey children (Long & Long, 1983). While such large numbers cannot be ignored, neither should casuality be solely attributed to the latchkey experience. Obviously great care should be exercised by parents in making the decision to leave a child alone. In assessing readiness for self-care, children need to show physical, emotional, cognitive, and social readiness. Physical readiness includes the abilities to manipulate locks for doors and to operate any safety equipment to which they have access. Emotional readiness involves several abilities: tolerating separations from adults, following rules, handling unexpected situations without fear, and not being withdrawn or self-destructive. Cognitive readiness relates to capabilities of understanding and remembering verbal instructions, reading well enough to take messages, and solving problems adequately. Finally, social readiness is apparent when the child can get help from friends and neighbors, maintain friendships with other children and adults, and understand the roles of police and fire personnel in emergency situations (Cole & Rodman, 1987).

BOX 16.3 Safety Tips for Latchkey Children

1. Tell children not to tell anyone (other than trusted adults, such as relatives, a neighbor, or a teacher) that they're home alone.
2. Have children call parent as soon as they get home. Keep emergency numbers and number of a close neighbor by telephone, where children can easily see them.
3. Teach children to pay attention to anything unusual, such as repeated telephone calls from a stranger, or barking dogs, but **never** go outside alone to investigate suspicious circumstances or noises.
4. Tell children **exactly** what they may or may not do until a parent arrives home, especially with regard to the use of appliances.
5. Enroll children in safety courses available through YMCA, Boy Scouts or Girl Scouts, schools, and other community groups.
6. Teach children fire safety: to leave home immediately in case of fire and to call for help from a neighbor's telephone; to **never** try to fight a fire themselves; and to stop, drop, and roll on ground if their clothes catch on fire.

Marital Stability in Dual-Career Marriages

Attempting to assess marital stability in dual-career marriages is a formidable task because of the number of conflicting variables that may impact the marital relationship. For example, male professionals have a lower divorce rate than the general population, but female professionals have a higher divorce rate. Since most professionals marry other professionals, are dual-career marriages at greater or less risk of failing? A number of studies have documented the relationship between a woman's higher level of education, higher earnings, and strong commitment to career and higher rates of divorce. One study which monitored marital behavior over a period of years concluded that the likelihood of divorce is greater if wives have access to an independent source of income (Moore & Sawhill, 1984).

Support for the theory that divorce occurs because the wife wants to experiment with choices missed earlier in her life is found in a survey of women who had received professional or graduate degrees to become physicians, dentists, lawyers, or college professors. Those women who completed professional or graduate school after marriage were much more likely to be divorced or separated from their spouses. Two major reasons cited for the higher rate of divorce were failure of husband to support their careers or to help with housework. However, marriages fail more often among professional women who marry early and who have established traditional family roles (Houseknecht, Vaughan, & Macke, 1984). If the wife is employed in a traditional occupation, the likelihood of divorce is less than for those in nontraditional work (Philliber & Hiller, 1983). However if the husband is willing to move or to leave his job to support the wife's career, the probability of marital disruption declines substantially (Houseknecht et al., 1984).

Level of Marital Satisfaction

Does the wife's employment adversely affect marital satisfaction? Some evidence suggests that employment of the wife per se or the degree of her interest in work activity has no effect on either marital adjustment or companionship (Locksley, 1980). In fact, some authorities maintain that employment of the wife actually has positive effects on marital solidarity as perceived by both wives and husbands (Simpson & England, 1982). Others suggest that if both spouses are very career-oriented, tension in the marriage will be inevitable even though both marital partners support gender equity. Such tension has the potential to destabilize marriages by improving the bargaining power and rights of wives, unsettling the lives of their husbands, and increasing excessive competitiveness overall (Moore & Sawhill, 1984; White & Botkin, 1989). Thus, while the wife's employment is generally thought to have negative effects on the personal marital adjustment, research has shown negative effects only for wives employed full-time in low-prestige jobs, with low socioeconomic status, or with preschool children (Pleck, 1985; Schumm & Bugaighis, 1986).

The level of marital satisfaction among dual-career couples appears to be related to attitudes toward gender roles, willingness of husband to help with household tasks, and quality of the marital relationship itself. Working wives who value their work report high marital satisfaction provided that the husband is family-oriented rather than work-oriented (Pleck, 1984). A review of 27 prior investigations of the relationship between wife's employment status and marital adjustment examined five categories of variables: overall marital adjustment, tensions and regrets, communication, companionship, and sexual variables (see Table 16.7). The conclusion was that for most wives and husbands, having a dual-career marriage has little, if any, effect on marital satisfaction or marital adjustment (Smith, D. S., 1985).

Factors Associated with Marital Quality in Dual-Career Marriages

High marital quality is more likely among dual-career couples with adequate family standard of living, approval of wife working by husband, objective communication between spouses, presence of emotional gratification between spouses, and perception of relationship compatibility (Thomas, Albrecht, & White, 1984). A major contributing factor to marital satisfaction or dissatisfaction in dual-career marriages is the issue of time allocation. The more time that a couple spends together, the greater likelihood that the marriage will be rated as satisfactory. However, overall satisfaction with the amount of time spent together depends on the hours worked, the work schedule, and the way that time is spent together. The more time that is spent in leisure activities such as eating, playing, and conversation, the more satisfied that the spouses will be with their marriage (Kingston & Nock, 1987). But simply "doing things together" without a high level of perceived communication apparently does not contribute to marital satisfaction. Further, as the amount

Table 16.7: A 27–Study Review of Effects of Wife's Employment on Marital Adjustment

	Effects on Marital Adjustment		
Adjustment Variable	Favor Employed Wives	Show No Difference	Favor Nonemployed Wives
Global/Overall	5%	86%	9%
Companionship	14	59	27
Sexual	8	60	32
Communication	7	72	21
Tensions and Regrets	4	82	14

From D. S. Smith, "Wife Employment and Marital Adjustment: A Cumulation of Results" in *Family Relations*, 34:485. Copyright © 1985 National Council on Family Relations, 3989 Central Avenue, N.E., Suite #550, Minneapolis, MN 55421. Reprinted by permission.

Table 16.8: Influence of Wife's Employment Status on Household Decisions

	Working Wife			Nonworking Wife		
Household Decisions	Wife	Both	Husband	Wife	Both	Husband
Who mainly influences wife working?	34%	60%	6%	21%	62%	17%
Who decides how much cash to get?	27	56	17	23	49	28
Who decides about leftover money?	16	77	8	12	73	14
Who makes decisions when to buy?	4	78	17	6	61	33

From M. A. Ferber, "Labor Market Participation of Young Married Women: Causes and Effects" in *Journal of Marriage and the Family*, 44:465. Copyright © 1982 National Council on Family Relations, 3989 Central Avenue, N.E., Suite #550, Minneapolis, MN 55421. Reprinted by permission.

of time spent by each spouse in individual leisure time activities increases, the level of reported marital satisfaction decreases. In general, the proportion of time spent in joint leisure time activities is more important for the marital satisfaction of wives than for husbands (Holman & Jacquart, 1988). If the husband makes substantial sacrifices for his wife's career, it will substantially elevate the reported level of marital adjustment (Houseknecht & Macke, 1981).

Gender-Role Identity

Compatible gender-role identity is an important factor in marital satisfaction for dual-career couples. When a wife with a traditional feminine identity attains a higher occupational level than her husband conflict may result. She may feel that she has failed to support her husband's career or blame her husband for inadequate performance of the provider role. Similarly, a husband with a traditional masculine gender identity, is more likely to believe that he has failed to perform the provider role if the occupational attainment of his wife's career accomplishments exceed his own. If such feelings by the wife or husband precipitate dissatisfaction, there will either be pressure for a change in the wife's role performance or for a disruption of the marital relationship (Hiller & Philliber, 1982). In fact, women who are employed in nontraditional managerial or professional positions and are married to men in similar status occupations are more likely to leave the labor force, shift to a traditional occupation, or move to a lower status occupation (Philliber & Hiller, 1983).

It appears that the wife's work status affects household decisions. Working wives were more likely to take part in decisions about when and how money would be spent in comparison to nonworking wives (see Table 16.8). Since some dual careers do lead to role conflict which creates a barrier to intimacy and healthy management of conflict, it is essential for couples to develop effective negotiating and bargaining techniques to accommodate individual needs. Further, personal flexibility is of greatest importance in achieving a high level of marital satisfaction in a dual-career marriage (Thomas et al., 1984).

Career Competitiveness Between Spouses

Since some career sacrifices are inevitable in dual-career marriages, the question arises whether or not the partners tend to resent limitations which may be placed on them. Successful dual-career couples involve persons who have learned how to handle their competitiveness and to minimize its disruptive effects on their relationship. However, if the competition for salary, for example, remains strong, then the likelihood of marital disruption is very great (Hopkins & White, 1978). As previously indicated, husbands with employed spouses feel more distress in their lives if their wives' salaries are greater than their own salaries. Surprisingly, as the husband's reported annual income rises, the greater will be the negative impact of the wife's employment on his self-esteem (Fendrich, 1984). Women who are not particularly concerned about getting ahead also report less life dissatisfaction as the prestige of their husband's occupation increases. Overachieving women indicate their lives are more satisfying, but at the same time they are more dissatisfied with their marriages. In contrast, occupational overachievement for men is more likely to be associated with more satisfying marriages (Hornung & McCullough, 1981).

Commuter Marriages: A Dual-Career Compromise

A **commuter marriage** is a dual-career marriage in which the marital partners maintain separate residences in order to accommodate the career demands of both spouses (Gross, 1980). By 1985, it was estimated that at least 1 million commuter marriages existed (Kantrowitz, 1985). While commuter or two-location marriages represent popular topics for office and party conversations, little research exists regarding this living arrangement. Thus, no precise statistics can be identified regarding the number of commuter marriages in the United States. The few empirical studies which are available involve small, nonrepresentative samples. Therefore, analysis of responses may only, at best, generate insight into a complex life-style (Gross, 1980; Gerstel & Gross, 1983).

A major source of difficulty for commuter marriages relates to the fact that the couple is trying to live a life-style for which few societal structures or cultural supports are provided. The cultural definition of marriage includes the concept that wives and husbands live together under the same roof (Kirschner & Walum, 1978). Relatives and friends may find it difficult to understand or accept a couple's decision to live apart because of career demands (Maynard & Zawachi, 1979). Spouses in commuter marriages tend to have higher educational levels, to be employed as professionals or managers, and to have above average median family incomes. Women are perceived to be the prime beneficiaries of the commuter marriage arrangement with wives reporting the ability to pursue educational and career opportunities as the chief advantage of such marriages (Gerstel & Gross, 1984). However, it should be remembered that other research has found that women are generally less willing to move for job advancement and are twice as likely as men to mention family ties as the major reason for not wanting to move to a new job (Markham & Pleck, 1986). Therefore, women in dual-career commuter marriages are breaking with traditional social norms. What are the advantages and disadvantages of commuter marriages? What is known about the circumstances in which they work best, and what are the long-term effects on the marital relationship? These are important questions without precise answers, but tentative conclusions can be drawn from the available research.

Choosing Commuter Marriage: Pros and Cons

Living apart is a life-style that is difficult at best, one endured to attain certain career goals but hardly one that is embraced enthusiastically. Couples are, however, able to identify advantages such as the obvious freedom this life-style allows for each spouse to pursue her/his career goals and to devote long and uninterrupted hours to one's work (Gross, 1980). Persons in commuter marriages have a greater opportunity to compartmentalize their work and family roles since they work in separate locations from their spouses (Gerstel & Gross, 1984). Most spouses in commuter marriages report that it is easier to get work done because of the heightened intensity for achievement in their careers (Kirschner & Walum, 1978). Therefore, the opportunity for career advancement for persons in commuter marriages seems substantially greater because of the reduction of daily family pressures and the ability to devote major uninterrupted blocks of time, including nights and weekends, to their job (Maynard & Zawachi, 1979).

However, there are some perceived disadvantages to commuter marriages. Persons in commuter marriages may experience feelings of isolation and develop a strong tendency toward becoming a workaholic. In fact, many commuting spouses often put in

12–14 hour workdays to occupy their time (Maynard & Zawachi, 1979). However, some marriage partners who live apart, at least initially, may waste time and not be able to concentrate as well in the work setting in comparison to noncommuters. Family members and younger children especially may not comprehend why a parent would attach such significance to career goals that she/he would move to another city disrupting traditional family life (Gross, 1983).

In most instances, finances are problematic for married couples, but they may be especially so for commuting couples. Commuter marriages are very expensive because it means establishing two separate households. Therefore, additional expenses may quickly offset any monetary gains made by taking a better position in another geographical area ("Commuting," 1978).

Previously established friendship and support systems also may be more difficult to maintain in a commuter marriage due to a lack of understanding and the discomfort level of others. It appears easier for women to find support systems in their new job location especially among those in the women's movement who have encouraged other women to take advantage of better career opportunities (Kirschner & Walum, 1978). As the length of time increases between spousal visits, the level of dissatisfaction with commuter marriage typically increases. Commuters who do not reunite on weekends usually experience greater separation pains (Gross, 1983).

Contributing Factors to Adjustment in Commuter Marriages

A commuter marriage is likely to be least stressful for those couples who possess high career commitment for each other as well as themselves, recognition of importance of wife's career by husband, financial resources to meet expenses of maintaining two households including extra child expenses, short geographical distance between location of other spouse's job, and long established patterns of communication (Kirschner & Walum, 1978). Other factors which affect the ease in adjusting to commuter marriage include how often spouses see each other, length of time married, number of children, employers' attitudes, work flexibility, and coping abilities of each spouse (Gerstel & Gross, 1984). In general, couples who are established in their marital, parenting, and work lives have the fewest strains while engaging in a commuter marriage (Kantrowitz, 1985).

Those couples who see each other on a regular schedule and more than once a month appear to function more effectively in commuter marriages. Further, most spouses in commuter marriages prefer to spend their weekend time together rather than fulfilling duty-related social obligations associated with the workplace or friends (Gerstel & Gross, 1984). Thus, older couples who have been married longer, where one spouse has an already established career and who are freed from child-rearing responsibilities, are most likely to succeed in commuter marriages (Gross, 1980).

Finally, dual-career couples who live apart have problems which differ according to their age-type. Younger couples are classified as "adjusting" and older couples as "established" in their career. For younger couples who spend more time adjusting, there is more career ascendancy conflict concerning whose career should dominate. Among older couples who are more likely to have children, more conflict arises over child-care and domestic responsibilities, but overall their commuter marriage is less stressful since they are more established in their chosen careers (Gross, 1980).

Long-Term Effects of Commuter Marriage on Marital Relationship

Most people think that commuting couples have weak marriages, but often the opposite is true. Persons in commuter marriages often put more time, money, and effort into their marriage than noncommuting couples (Belkin, 1985b). In fact, a commuter marriage actually allows a couple to reevaluate their marriage and to consider appropriate changes in the marital relationship, if any, that might be implemented upon being reunited. Contrary to popular opinion, commuter marriages appear to be less likely to end in divorce because the couple is more committed to the marriage, otherwise they would not bother with the extra efforts of maintaining their marriage. However, if the marriage is already weak, then it might fail (Kantrowitz, 1985). On the other hand, a commuter marriage also can intensify existing marital problems. Women especially suffer greater role strain and risk associated with loss of self-image. Further, men are more likely to be emotionally dependent upon their wives and have trouble coping without their physical presence. Another major problem for some commuter marriages is an unwillingness of the wife and/or husband to adapt to different roles (Rhodes & Rhodes, 1984). Finally, there is some evidence that a person in a commuter marriage is no more likely to engage in an extramarital sexual relationship than persons who do not live apart (Gerstel & Gross, 1983).

Summary

- Employed wives/mothers are part of social reality even though husbands/fathers continue to be the main providers, authority figures, and decision makers in most marriages.
- Factors in forming dual-career marriages include desire to achieve economic advantages, reinforcement of women from feminist movement, technology that lightens household tasks, and desire to protect against husband's job loss and indiscriminate relocation.
- Research suggests that part-time employment represents a "best" option for married mothers.
- Women embracing traditional gender roles and employed in traditional female occupations have higher levels of self-esteem than those employed in nontraditional occupations.
- While job satisfaction is associated with overall happiness among working wives, marital happiness is the strongest determinant of overall life happiness.
- Barriers to careers for wives include motherhood and domestic responsibilities, attitudes of husbands toward women working, and lack of support for mothers in the workplace.
- Three general types of family support benefits are offered by companies: more time for parenting via parental leaves, flexible hours, sick child care, and job sharing; employer-provided or financially-assisted child care and referral; and parent-education programs.
- Career priority is often given to the husband's career because most persons hold traditional ideas of women's family responsibilities.
- Dual-career family issues are child care, where to live and work, work overload and role conflicts for women, and lack of housework by husbands.
- Family-based, professional, or corporate day-care facilities are child-care options. Conclusions about the effect of day-care on young children are contradictory.
- The effects of maternal employment on children is unclear. Apparently, the more positive mothers feel toward their employment, the less negative impact it will have on their children.
- The evidence is contradictory concerning the effects of a dual-career marriage on either marital adjustment, companionship, or marital satisfaction.
- Opportunities for career advancement of partners are an advantage of commuter marriages, but financial costs of operating two households are a disadvantage.

Questions for Critical Reflection

1. Family Scientist Pauline Boss has accused technology of a double-cross: Rather than delivering more leisure time and the promised easier life, it has resulted in periods of high stress for both women and men, especially in dual-earner families. Evaluate her remarks.
2. If it were possible to enter a magic time machine, in which time period would you choose to begin a marriage—the earlier, less technologically advanced or the present, more stressed one? Why?
3. The impact of working women, creating major changes in family functioning, has been cited as the most important thing to happen to American families in the 1980s. What would you entitle a feature article about this issue? What three major points would you make to substantiate your choice of title?
4. Therapist Carlfred Broderick proposes that to succeed, families of the 1990s will need to be as competent in teaching the skills of connection as earlier families were in teaching the skills of individuation. Economist Sylvia Ann Hewlett believes there are costs to unlimited individualism citing the divorced and workaholics as casualties. Are you aware of examples where individualism is more important than commitment among any of your friends? How do you evaluate their success in life and love thus far?
5. During most of the daylight hours, most days of the week, most children are at one place and their parents at another. How do these circumstances of work and family life affect children and their parents? Does society have an obligation to help families balance jobs and family life?

Suggested Readings

Burton, L. (1986). *What's a smart woman like you doing home?* Washington, DC: Acropolis Books. An exploration of the factors making child rearing a major priority for many young women.

Gerstel, N., & Gross, H. (1984). *Commuter marriage.* New York: Gilford Press. A highly readable work on commuter marriages in American society.

Ogden, A. S. (1986). *The great American housewife: From helpmate to wage earner, 1776–1986.* Westport, CT: Greenwood. A historical tracing of the housewife role in American society.

Pleck, J. H. (1985). *Working wives, working husbands.* Beverly Hills, CA: Sage. An interesting analysis of the allocation of domestic responsibilities in dual-earner families.

Shreve, A. (1987). *Remaking motherhood: How working mothers are shaping children's future.* New York: Fawcett. A well-researched, realistic look at children of working mothers and the mothers themselves.

Vannoy-Hiller, D., & Philliber, W. W. (1989). *Equal partners: Successful women in marriage.* Newbury Park, CA: Sage. An examination of the influence of high-achieving women on family patterns and processes.

PART V

DISRUPTIVE CHANGE AND REAFFIRMATION

Hamilton McCubbin, a well-known family-stress researcher, equates change to stress. He defines family stress in terms of individuals who experience change, all having to adjust to each other (McCubbin & Figley, 1983). Generally, change evolves in response to adjustment to circumstance, much of which occurs during normal family life cycle transition such as births, marriages, and empty-nest periods. In chapter 17, disruptive change is described as resulting from marital dissolution.

Although it is important to determine the demographics of divorce, they alone do not tell the story. Influential societal and individual factors implicated in divorce must also be explored. The actual process of divorce and transition stages require clarification. For those women and men who have felt its impact or for children affected in life-changing ways, all are shown to need help from family and friends in reestablishing an emotional balance.

Single parenting, remarriage, and blended families are examples of disruptive, stressful change explored in chapter 18. Although there are special issues for single parents, financial problems are paramount for the majority, especially for women. Remarriage after divorce is more problematic for those with children than for those without children. Blended families, which have been billed as the most difficult of all family forms to accomplish successfully, may fall prey to the stepparent myth which often precludes establishing workable relationships with stepchildren.

The developmental tasks of marriage and family in the middle and later years are examined in chapter 19. The "nesting" phenomenon, adult children living at home, offers a new twist to the empty-nest syndrome. The role of grandparents is depicted as a new evolving pattern since more of today's children have living grandparents. Sexual satisfaction in the middle years is considered along with the life-transition stage of female menopause. And, attention is given to financial and psychological adjustment during the retirement years.

Caring for elderly parents with one hand and children with the other has led "mid-life persons" to be characterized as the sandwich generation. Maintaining health and achieving life satisfaction, including the often neglected sexual dimension, are key issues for the elderly. Finally, adjusting to the death of a spouse must be faced, as well as eventual alternate living arrangements. Inherent in human mortality are attitudes toward death and dying, which inevitably must be reconciled for peace of mind. The book's final pages are devoted to illuminating these significant life-cycle transitions surrounding the "last of life for which the first was made."

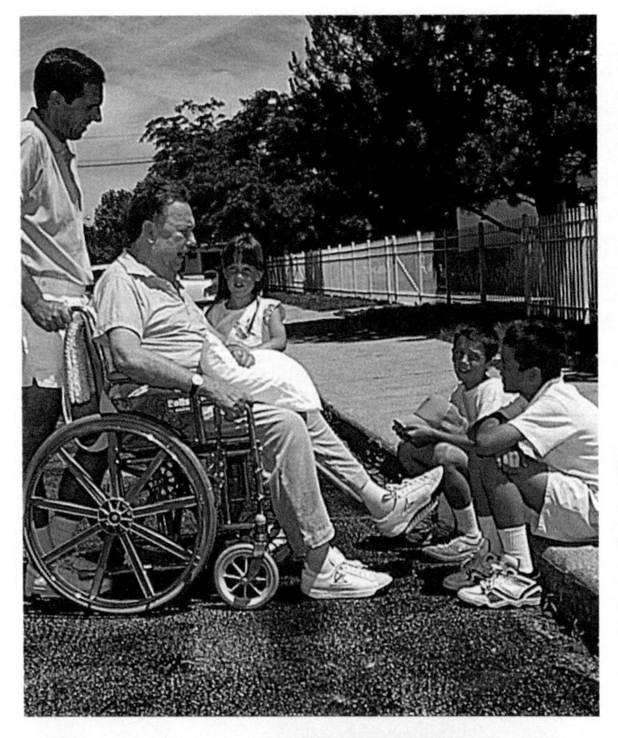

CHAPTER 17

Marital Dissolution

For years now, social scientists have been placing much of the blame for the steady increase in divorce on the great importance our society gives to romantic love. Encouraged by poems, books, songs and movies, the sweethearts float away into a make-believe world that has little connection with the everyday world they will inhabit.
Francine Klagsbrun, 1985a

Outline

Historically in America, relationship termination for most adults occurred because of death; whereas today, divorce is the leading cause of marital dissolution. Such change is not necessarily true in other industrialized countries. In Japan, for example, where 40% of all marriages are still arranged, they have two thirds fewer divorces than in the United States (Hutter, 1988). Despite the best of intentions at the time of marriage, many persons eventually find themselves in unhappy situations that they believe can only be resolved by divorce. In fact, a 1990 Yankelovich Clancy Shulman poll found that three fourths of women and men, ages 18–24, believed that having a good marriage was difficult ("What Youth Think," 1990). While there are myriad social and psychological factors leading to marital dissolution, the reasons frequently cited by couples themselves include financial disagreements, physical and mental abuse, alcohol abuse, life-style conflicts, communication breakdowns, drifting apart, and "falling" out of love ("Divorce," 1986). Divorce continues to be an important issue since it affects about 1.17 million families each year, more than one half (52%) of which involve children (National Center for Health Statistics, 1990c). Since divorce represents a failure for many persons, women and men often have difficulties coping with its multiple dimensions such as returning to singlehood and/or performing the responsibilities of single parenthood.

Table 17.1: Divorces for Select Years

Year	Number	Crude Rate
1920	170,505	1.6
1940	264,000	2.0
1950	385,144	2.6
1960	393,000	2.2
1970	708,000	3.5
1975	1,036,000	4.8
1980	1,182,000	5.2
1986	1,159,000	4.8
1987	1,157,000	4.8
1988	1,183,000	4.8
1989	1,163,000	4.7
1990	1,172,000	4.7

Source: M. S. Hoffman (ed.), *The World Almanac and Book Facts 1988.* New York: Random House, p. 809; National Center for Health Statistics, 1990d, "Annual Summary of Births, Marriages, Divorces, and Deaths: United States, 1990" in *Monthly Vital Statistics Report,* 38(13). DHHS Publication No. PHS 90–1120. Hyattsville, MD: Public Health Service, p. 5; National Center for Health Statistics, 1990e, "Births, Marriages, Divorces, and Deaths for June 1990" in *Monthly Vital Statistics Report,* 39(6). DHHS Publication No. PHS 90–1120. Hyattsville, MD: Public Health Service, p. 2.

Divorce in Today's Society

During the 1980s, considerable controversy was generated by projections that over one half of women ages 25–29 would eventually end their first marriage by divorce (Weitzman, Lachs, & Tucker, 1986). In general, such predictions are based on predisposing factors toward divorce. For example, women who marry in their teens, who marry after a premarital birth, or who conceive their first child prior to marriage are more than twice as likely to have their marriage end in divorce (London & Wilson, 1988). What are the current divorce rates and the probability of obtaining a divorce?

Divorce Rates

The crude divorce rate is the number of divorces per 1,000 persons in the population, whereas the refined divorce rate is a comparison of the number of divorces each year to the number of married women (Crosby, 1980). Available evidence suggests that the rate of marital dissolution probably reached its highest peak during the late 1970s and early 1980s with a new normative level subsequently being established (see Table 17.1). The divorce rate appears to be stabilizing due to fewer marriages, older first-time brides and grooms, and possibly less extramarital sexual involvement due to fear of AIDS ("Divorce," 1987). Difficult economic conditions, such as unemployment, produce extra strains on marriage so it is not surprising that divorce rates rise during peak periods of unemployment rates. However, women who are not involved in labor force participation are less likely to seek a divorce even if poor economic conditions have lowered the family income and standard of living (South, 1985).

In general, the divorce rate has fluctuated very little since the mid-1980s (see Figure 17.1). The rate has been found to be influenced by age at first marriage, mother's age at first childbirth, low family income, wife's work status, wife's income level, number and ages of children in household, race, and educational attainment of head of household (Smith & Meitz, 1985). The most frequently offered reasons for the substantial increase in the divorce rate during the 1960s and 1970s were the increase in female labor force participation and the state of the economy (South, 1985).

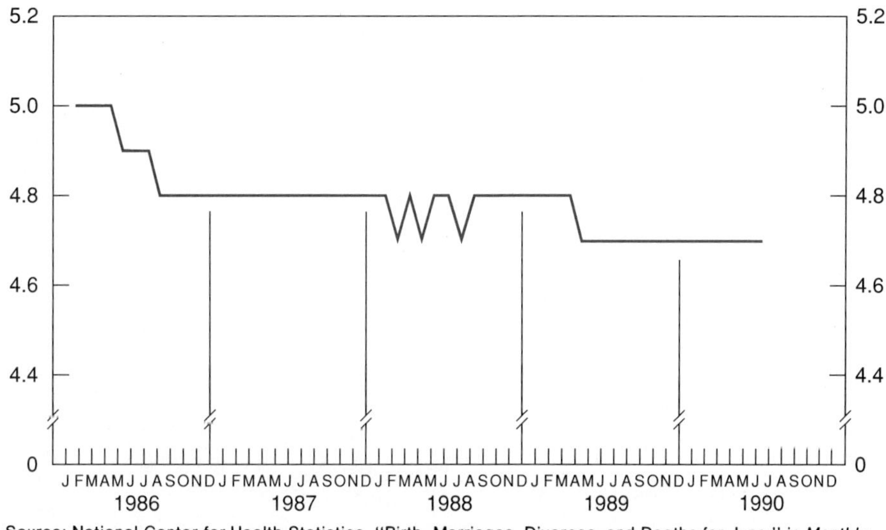

Source: National Center for Health Statistics. "Birth, Marriages, Divorces, and Deaths for June," in *Monthly Vital Statistics Report,* 39(6):4, 1990e. DHHS Publication No. PHS 90–1120, Hyattsville, MD: Public Health Service.

Figure 17.1 Divorce Rates Per 1,000 Population by Month and by Year

However, there are believed to be at least eight major factors that have served to maintain a high divorce rate:

1. Incompatibility of gender roles.
2. Differences between women and men in problem solving due to prior socialization.
3. Demands of life such as time and energy.
4. Boredom with everyday married life.
5. Changes in functions of marriage and family.
6. Increased emphasis on emotional fulfillment.
7. Increased institutional support for divorced women including less stigma and more economic independence.
8. Unreasonable demands of traditional social roles for wife and husband (Henslin, 1985c, p. 424).

Probability of Divorce

Attempts at divorce predictions for the future are probably conservative because the U.S. Bureau of the Census bases its estimates on persons who have divorced in the past. During periods of rapid social change, divorce rates may undergo significant increases. Further, the Census Bureau bases its estimates of future divorces on persons under age 55 even though it is the number of divorces for persons in the middle and later years which have been escalating (Weitzman, 1981). Attempts have been made to predict future likelihood of seeking a divorce. One such prediction was that among those married couples ages 25–34 in 1980, about one half would eventually terminate their first marriages through divorce. However, of those couples ages 45–54, only about one fourth were expected to divorce (Glick, 1984a). With remarriage becoming more common, about two thirds of divorced women eventually will remarry by age 54. Of these women, approximately one half will ultimately obtain a second divorce ("Women in 30s," 1986).

Many factors affect the likelihood of obtaining a divorce. Divorce rates generally tend to be higher in the West and in the Southwest due somewhat to higher rates of residential mobility (Glenn & Supancic, 1984). The lowest rates are found in northeastern states, partially due to the high percentage of Roman Catholics in that area ("Divorce," 1987). While the divorce rates have traditionally been higher in urban than in rural areas, the differences are becoming much less pronounced. High rates of residential mobility increase the likelihood that persons with dissimilar backgrounds will marry. In addition, changes in the membership of social groups to which a married person belongs may result in that person viewing her/his marriage in less favorable terms (Glenn & Shelton, 1985). Data regarding the influence of socioeconomic status and income level on the likelihood of divorce appear contradictory. While having a high median family income is associated with a lesser likelihood of obtaining a divorce, being employed in the professional field does not appear to deter the likelihood of divorce (Breault & Kposowa, 1987).

While 1.1 million children per year are involved in divorces, the average number of children per divorce dropped to less than one by 1980 due to declining birth rates and an increase in the number of child-free marriages (U.S. Bureau of the Census, 1990v). In general, the more children present in a marriage, the less likelihood that the wife and husband will divorce. The total number of children is a more important variable than number of preschool children in delaying divorce. Couples at greatest risk for divorce are those with short-term marriages with one child. This underscores the need for couples to seek help early in their marriage, especially if they begin to encounter difficulties after the birth of their first child (Fisher, 1987).

The Demographics of the Divorced

Statistically speaking, the typical divorced couple, wife age 32 and husband age 35, has one child (London & Wilson, 1988); there are over 16.5 million divorced women in the United States (Lester, 1990); and, 6.9 years is the median length of time between first marriage and divorce (U.S. Bureau of the Census, 1990v). Divorce is not only most likely to occur in the sixth or seventh year of a first marriage, but also at various pressure points of a first marriage. These pressure points include birth of a first child, financial difficulties, a seriously-ill child, or when children leave home ("Divorce," 1987).

Educational Level

Persons who are less educated in our society have a greater tendency to divorce than those with more education (Smith & Meitz, 1983). However, the variable of education is a complex issue. In general, women with higher levels of education have less stable marriages whereas men with higher levels of education have more stable marriages (Hanson & Tuch, 1984). If the wife has a high level of education, it substantially increases the probability that she will be employed outside the home in positions of responsibility. Therefore, she may experience role overload, especially if the marriage also involves motherhood. Marital stability is greatest with either least or most amounts of education. Women and men who have completed 0–8 years of school, for example, are least likely to obtain a divorce in comparison to all educational levels. By comparison, persons with 16 or more years of education are less likely to obtain a divorce than persons who have completed only 9–15 years (Maneker & Rankin, 1985). While there is a link between early marriage and lower educational attainment, some researchers have questioned the actual influence of education on divorce. Having a college education increases the likelihood of a person having a higher income level which, in turn, may serve as a deterrent to divorce (Witt, Davidson, Sollie, Lowe, & Peek, 1987).

Relationships between duration of marriage and education among women presents an interesting picture. The variables of home ownership, time period during which wife attained higher education, and number of hours that the wife works interact with marital duration to affect the likelihood of divorce. More specifically, if a woman obtained a college degree during the early years of marriage, she is much less likely to obtain a divorce than if her college education was completed later in the marriage. Possibly the fact that a woman returns to school in later marriage to acquire career skills may suggest that she desires an alternative to an unwanted life-style. There is also some evidence that a highly educated woman is more likely to find a more desirable relationship partner in her later years (South & Spitze, 1986). Those women who completed their college education or obtained a professional degree in the later years of their marriage are more likely to have experienced substantial changes in their perceptions of social reality as it relates to fulfillment of their needs.

Race as a Factor

First marriages of blacks are substantially less stable than first marriages of whites, with the blacks about one and one half times more likely to divorce than whites (Glenn & Supancic, 1984). Although black women are more likely than white women to have had a premarital birth or conception, being a parent is less related to obtaining a divorce among blacks (Teachman, 1986).

Since black women have a more restrictive field of eligibles, as discussed in chapter 7, they are more likely to marry less educated men. And marriage and family life among blacks is often associated with economic problems and social discrimination which may make it somewhat more difficult for blacks to provide for their families (Ball & Robbins, 1986). A substantial body of evidence suggests that although blacks have a higher rate of divorce than whites, if black and white couples are compared within the same income level, the differences in divorce rates are negligible (Price-Bonham & Balswick, 1980).

Influential Factors in Divorce

Given the nature of the American courtship and mate selection process along with the gender-role changes in society, the task of delineating the causes of divorce is perplexing. Causes can be sought by exploring certain structural and demographic variables such as age at marriage which has long been found to be related to divorce. Another method involves asking the marital partners themselves about the reasons for their divorce (Burns, 1984). Structural/demographic variables and perceptions of marital partners concerning the causes of marital dissolution are interrelated. When reviewing positive and negative factors leading to success in marriage, major blocks to a successful marriage were unrealistic expectations, false assumptions that problems will disappear after marriage, poor communication, and lack of problem-solving skills ("Computerized Premarital," 1987). Conversely, key behaviors in avoiding divorce are gaining **rapport,** developing self-disclosure, achieving accurate perceptions of role expectations, and fulfilling role obligations during courtship and dating (Edwards & Saunders, 1981).

A person is likely to seek dissolution of the marriage when the actual results of couple interaction are less rewarding than those in some alternative interpersonal arrangement. However, if no attractive alternatives exist, the person will tolerate the marital relationship even if it is unsatisfactory (Edwards & Saunders, 1981). Even though many persons may contemplate divorce for a variety of reasons, they may decline to seek one. One survey, for example, found that 1 in 3 wives and 1 in 5 husbands had thought about obtaining a divorce. Thoughts of divorce by wives increased if they were employed outside the home, their youngest child was aged 6–11, and they possessed egalitarian attitudes toward housework. For husbands, thoughts of divorce also escalated if the wife was employed outside the home and if she possessed egalitarian attitudes toward housework (Huber & Spitze, 1980).

Societal Factors

Persons have long lamented the fact that societal factors contribute substantially to divorce. Several major social trends implicated in the increasing divorce rate are decline in social stigma attached to divorce, increased life-style alternatives, economic options for women, and rising standard of happiness for marriage. For example, persons may hesitate to remarry if they have nontraditional gender-role attitudes thus viewing divorce as a time of personal growth. Finally, many persons find that the new standards for personal happiness in marriage make it hard to justify remaining in a bad marriage (Weitzman, 1981). Men especially tend to look for influences outside the marital relationship to explain their divorce rather than to personal factors involving interaction with their wives. Thus, they more often than women perceive mental illness, in-laws, religious differences, financial problems, women's liberation, and drugs to be reasons for their divorce (Cleek & Pearson, 1985).

Employment of Wife Outside Home

If wives are employed outside the home, they have greater financial independence and are more likely to be able to support themselves whenever necessary (Weitzman, 1981). Therefore, women today are less willing to tolerate an unhappy marital relationship than in previous generations. Some economists believe that married women work more hours now than in past generations because they believe their marriages will eventually end in divorce ("Divorce Concerns," 1986). For couples who embrace traditional gender roles, if the wife earns more than her husband, the probability of divorce is enhanced (Moore & Hofferth, 1979). On the other hand, a working wife may actually reduce the probability of divorce due to increased availability of financial resources (Hanson & Tuch, 1984). While the wife's salary can increase the standard of living for the family and potentially increase marital stability, her employment outside the home can make divorce more feasible for an unhappy husband (Weitzman, 1981). The stability of marriage often appears to be eroded by the effects of wife's income along with some combination of spousal disagreement and lower marital satisfaction especially if she works more than 40 hours per week. Unemployment also may lead to spousal disagreement because of the necessity to reorganize family life. It is speculated that since so few married persons today grew up in dual-career families, the impact of the wife's employment on marital instability is greater than it may be in future generations (Booth, Johnson, White, & Edwards, 1984).

Fewer Moral and Religious Sanctions

The tolerance for divorce appears to have substantially increased over the past 40 years with divorced persons no longer characterized as being sinful or engaging in wrongful behavior. Attitudes both reflect societal influence and predict future behavior. The divorce attitudes of husbands are more related to their perceptions of overall marital quality whereas wives are more influenced by presence of dependent children. The most liberal attitudes toward divorce, found among child-free wives, may be related to the fact that the majority of these wives are in the labor force and thus less economically dependent on their husbands (Jorgensen & Johnson, 1980). In spite of more liberal attitudes, social sanctions still exist. More than two thirds of divorced persons reported societal disapproval of their divorce, and most felt socially stigmatized, especially by their married friends (Gerstel, 1987).

Although religious teachings of the Roman Catholic church disapprove of divorce, attitudes of young Catholics toward divorce are similar to those of nonfundamentalist Protestants. However, Catholics are still less likely to divorce than Protestants (Glenn & Shelton, 1985). Persons who hold church membership are less likely to obtain a divorce in comparison to persons who are nonmembers (Breault & Kposowa, 1987). For example, women who attended church services frequently were found to be less approving of divorce and less likely to have changed their attitudes toward divorce over the years. Consequently, they had the lowest probability of divorce (Thornton, 1985). Likewise, men who never attended religious services were three times more likely to obtain a divorce than those men who frequently attended religious services (Glenn & Supancic, 1984).

Parental Divorce

Various studies exploring children of divorce suggest that those persons with divorced parents have a greater probability of obtaining a divorce themselves. Composite data from the General Social Surveys between 1973 and 1985 suggest that black and white adults from divorced families obtained divorces with greater frequency than those who lived with both parents during childhood. Although children from divorced homes tend to have a lower commitment to marriage, they are oftentimes strongly attracted by the idea of marriage (Glenn & Kramer, 1987). However, they feel highly apprehensive about their own future marriage. Having already experienced the aftermath of divorce, those children who later find themselves in an unhappy marital situation are less likely to refrain from divorcing. Adults from divorced homes report their childhood and adolescence to be the most unhappy times of their lives. Men are more likely than women to indicate long-term problems and marital difficulties, although many women and men from divorced homes do report marital satisfaction ("Do Effects Last?," 1986).

Individual Factors

In reviewing causes of their divorce, three fourths of women and men blamed their spouse. Women had a significantly greater number of complaints about the

Table 17.2: **Divorced Women, Their Age at First Marriage and Duration of First Marriage**

	Duration of First Marriage					
Age at First Marriage	0–5 Years	6–10 Years	11–15 Years	16–20 Years	21+ Years	Median Years before Divorce
Under age 20	41%	25%	15%	9%	9%	7.3
Ages 20 to 24	39	25	15	9	12	7.6
Ages 25 to 29	40	26	13	11	11	7.5
Age 30 and over	47	24	14	8	8	6.1

From A. J. Norton and J. E. Moorman, "Current Trends in Marriage and Divorce Among American Women" in *Journal of Marriage and the Family,* 49:10.

personality, authority, drinking, and extramarital sexual involvement of their husband and his desire for "going out with the boys." Complaints by men were more likely to relate to extramarital sexual involvement of wife and conflict over gender roles. Persons with higher educational levels were more likely to mention change in interests, value conflicts, gender-role conflict, lack of communication, and work commitment. In comparison, those with lower educational levels were more likely to mention use of threats, physical abuse, conflicts over children, and "hanging out with the girls/boys" (Kitson & Sussman, 1982).

Premarital Factors

Over the years, cohabitation, age, and premarital pregnancy have emerged as important variables in marital stability. These factors appear to make persons more prone to having marital difficulties and subsequently more likely to obtain a divorce (Reiss & Lee, 1988).

Cohabitation. Since many women agree to engage in cohabitation with hopes that it will lead to marriage, the ultimate question may be, will it lead to marriage stability? Although cohabitation among college graduates has increased dramatically within the past 20 years, emerging evidence indicates that it has spread most rapidly among those with the least education. Further, 60% of those who remarried between 1980 and 1987 were found to have cohabited prior to marriage (Barringer, 1989). Bumpass and Sweet, using data from a 1987–1988 national survey of 13,000 respondents, have discredited the theory of those family scientists who predicted that cohabitation would result in fewer divorces by sorting out unstable relationships before a final commitment. Within 10 years of their wedding, 38% of premarital cohabitors had divorced compared to 27% of noncohabitors (Barringer, 1989). Further, a Swedish study has concluded that women who cohabit premaritally with their future spouse are almost twice as likely to obtain a divorce than those women who do not cohabit (Bennett, Blanc, & Bloom, 1988). The available research, however, does not permit a definitive answer on how cohabitation influences the likelihood of divorce.

Age at Marriage. The age at which one marries is believed to be an influential factor in the risks of divorce. Based on data from the National Center For Health Statistics, younger people are more likely to divorce with the highest rates for teenaged wives. They are more than twice as likely to divorce than wives ages 35–39 and almost 12 times as likely as wives ages 55–59 (London & Wilson, 1988). Some evidence suggests that a late age at marriage increases the likelihood of divorce throughout the first 15 years of marriage (Booth, Johnson, White, & Edwards, 1986). Women who married before age 20 had higher divorce rates than those marrying later, while those who married in their mid-to-late 20s tended to have higher divorce rates than women who married in their early 20s (see Table 17.2). Therefore, marital instability appears highest for those persons who marry early and late in their lives.

While having children under age 2 appears to serve as a deterrent to obtaining a divorce, it may not do so for adolescent parents. Adolescent spouses, immature themselves, may feel threatened by the birth of a child who competes for time and attention. Adolescent parents may also be less aware of the potential negative consequences of divorce on young children (Rankin & Maneker, 1985). Persons who marry early may lack the skills necessary to cope with an intimate relationship, leading to dissatisfaction with the way in which their spouse fulfills certain marital obligations. In contrast, those who marry later often lack agreement on life-style and companionship. Since persons

Table 17.3: **Premarital Birth or Conception Status of First Marriages Ending in Divorce**

	Premarital Birth or Conception		
Age	None	Conception	Birth
Under age 20	6%	0%	0%
Ages 20–29	18	21	20
Ages 30–39	29	35	34
Ages 40–49	29	36	35
Ages 50–59	23	28	29
Age 60 or older	16	16	18

From A. J. Norton and J. E. Moorman, "Current Trends in Marriage and Divorce Among American Women" in *Journal of Marriage and the Family,* 49:10.

who marry later have a smaller pool of eligibles from which to choose, they are more likely to marry someone with different attitudes and life-style (Booth & Edwards, 1985).

Factors which contribute to likelihood of divorce are known to have their greatest impact during the first few years of marriage. These factors include lack of faithfulness to spouse, lack of understanding from spouse, lack of agreement about important things in life, and lack of companionship (Heaton, Albrecht, & Martin, 1985). The developmentally younger spouse is more vulnerable to these issues than a more mature spouse.

Premarital Pregnancy. Divorced women ages 30–49 are much more likely to have had a premarital birth or premarital conception than divorced women ages 20–29. This reflects the increased availability and use of contraceptives and abortions (Norton & Moorman, 1987). Women whose first child was conceived or born premaritally are more likely to experience significantly higher rates of divorce than those women who marry before their first pregnancy. Couples who marry after a premarital pregnancy tend to have lower family incomes and less wealth over the duration of their marriage (O'Connell & Rogers, 1984). Today's single woman who becomes premaritally pregnant is less likely than before to marry or give birth. However, women at every age who have had a premarital conception or birth are still more likely to have their first marriage end in divorce than women who conceive after marriage (see Table 17.3).

Post-Marital Factors

Statistics reveal who divorces but not always why. Even those endless compilations of causes provided by family scientists may list symptoms, not reasons. Causes of divorce may differ, depending upon when in the marriage it occurs (Burns, 1984). The three time periods when divorce is most likely are early stage, mid-stage, and late stage marriage (McLanahan, Wedemeyer, & Adelberg, 1981). When divorce occurs during the first few years, it may be that there was a wedding but never a marriage. These couples are viewed by marriage therapists as seeking permission to divorce without having been "married." They fail to realize that in the absence of bonding, they were never emotionally married. Such divorces are usually by mutual consent. Mid-stage divorce, which occurs after 7–10 years, may result from a marriage that "neglected itself to death." These persons fail to realize that it takes hard work to make even the best marriages succeed. The woman is likely to initiate a mid-stage divorce often to "discover herself." Such women are frequently attempting to establish a new identity in perhaps a career or professional role. When divorce happens in the late stage, after 20 or more years, the couple has usually grown apart. It may be that the nest is empty and a common bond no longer exists. Often the woman has sacrificed her own self-identity in the marriage. Husbands are most likely to initiate divorce during this stage. Four specific post-marital factors related to cause of divorce are spousal behavior, inability to manage conflict, sexual incompatibility, and perceived marital quality.

With regard to spousal behavior, in one study concerning the causes of divorce, almost one half of the wives and over one fourth of the husbands believed that lack of time at home by the husband was a major factor in the marriage breakdown. In addition, about one third of the wives and one fifth of the husbands reported extramarital sexual involvement and drinking by husband as major causes of the divorce (Burns, 1984). Other researchers have cited male alcoholism along with financial and sexual problems as key variables in increasing the likelihood of physical abuse of the wife (Cleek & Pearson, 1985). Drinking and lack of time spent at home by husband are more commonly cited among Roman Catholics, and least often by couples reporting no religious affiliation (Burns, 1984).

The inability to deal with anger is believed by some to be the single most important cause leading to marital failure (Mace, 1982). If intense marital conflict develops involving verbal or physical abuse, extramarital sexual involvement, or alcoholism, it will often lead to divorce (Fitzgerald, R. V., 1986). Communication is a frequently reported cause of divorce (see Table 17.4). A lack of communication impacts all aspects of the marital relationship thus making it very difficult to resolve problem areas (Burns, 1984). Oftentimes, couples who deserve an equal amount of blame for marital problems fail to acknowledge their own weaknesses or failures which is a prerequisite for negotiating.

Complaints about sexual incompatibility typically emerge during the early years of the marriage. Generally men are more likely to complain about sexual difficulties in marriage than women. However, women with no religious affiliation more often report sexual incompatibility as a cause of marriage breakdown (Burns, 1984). With increasing acceptance of their sexuality, married women are becoming more willing to express their dissatisfaction with marital sexual life. A comparison of never-married, married, divorced, and separated professional women found almost one half of married women reported the desire for more foreplay in their sex lives (Davidson & Darling, 1988c). Men often perceive sexual problems in marriage as contributors to numerous other problems in the marital relationship, many of which do not have a direct connection with sexual satisfaction (Cleek & Pearson, 1985).

Available research suggests that marital quality is more important to women than men. With the emphasis on individual happiness in our society, if a person concludes that their marital relationship is no longer personally satisfying, their marriage will likely end. In fact, basic marital unhappiness was the second most often reported cause of divorce by women and men (Cleek & Pearson, 1985). Attractive alternatives to marriage increase the likelihood of divorce. However, if there are external pressures to remain married such as religious sanctions, a higher level of marital quality will be perceived (Green & Sporakowski, 1983).

Table 17.4: Perceived Causes of Divorce

Perceived Cause	Women		Men	
Communication problems	70%	(1)*	59%	(1)*
Basic unhappiness	60	(2)	47	(2)
Incompatibility	56	(3)	45	(3)
Emotional abuse	56	(4)	25	(6)
Financial problems	33	(5)	29	(5)
Sexual problems	32	(6)	30	(4)
Alcohol abuse—spouse	30	(7)	6	(14)
Infidelity—spouse	25	(8)	11	(9)
Physical abuse	22	(9)	4	(15)
In-laws	11	(10)	12	(8)
Children	9	(11)	4	(16)
Religious differences	9	(12)	7	(12)
Mental illness	5	(13)	7	(11)
Drug abuse—spouse	4	(14)	1	(17)
Infidelity—self	4	(15)	6	(13)
Women's lib	3	(16)	14	(7)
Alcohol abuse—self	1	(17)	9	(10)

*By rank.

From M. G. Cleek and T. A. Pearson, "Perceived Causes of Divorce: An Analysis of Interrelationships" in *Journal of Marriage and the Family,* 47:181.

Progression Toward Divorce

Couples with many alternatives to marriage such as financial independence or remarriage have a greater chance of divorcing than persons with fewer options. For example, husbands who believe that maintaining their current level of living will be difficult, are less likely to perceive divorce as a realistic alternative. If remarrying is a strong possibility, wives may be more likely to perceive divorce as a positive alternative (Udry, 1981). Persons who are considering divorce tend to have less financial security, less religious attachment, a shorter marriage, an earlier age at marriage, and preschoolers at home (Booth & White, 1980). During the period preceding separation and divorce, about three fourths of wives and husbands reported not showing any love during the final months of marriage, and one half indicated disagreements about expressions of affection and sexual intercourse (Thompson & Spanier, 1983).

In examining the amount of time that women take to progress from making a decision to obtain a divorce to actually filing a divorce petition, some interesting patterns were revealed. Those quick to separate and to reach the divorce petition stage were likely to be less educated, least in favor of separation, in a marriage of long duration, and most likely to blame their spouse for the separation. In contrast, women who were slow to separate and to file a divorce petition tended to be highly educated, to favor separation, to report having been "boss" in their marriage, and to perceive themselves or both parties as being at fault for their marital problems. Those women who felt most in control over the divorce process perceive themselves as being better adjusted after the divorce (Melichar & Chiriboga, 1985).

Costs of Divorce

When there are few perceived rewards in marriage and the emotional and economic costs of dissolving a marriage are perceived as small while alternative relationships are viewed as desirable, the probability is high that divorce will occur (Yoder & Nichols, 1980). Most persons contemplating divorce evaluate their personal qualities and assets in terms of the available alternatives along with any barriers associated with obtaining a divorce. As the attractiveness of the alternatives increases and the commitment to the marital relationship decreases, the likelihood of a positive outcome for the marriage is lowered (Edwards & Saunders, 1981). While there are many costs in seeking a divorce, the goal of personal happiness is an important motive in the dissolution of marriage. Three potential costs of divorce are presence of children, financial considerations, and loneliness.

In spite of the fact that one of the greatest worries for parents is whether or not divorce will damage the emotional and social well-being of their child(ren), over 1 million children per year are involved in divorces (U.S. Bureau of Census, 1990v). Persons with fewer children and child-free persons are more likely to divorce. If there are children present in the household, divorce is perceived as being more "costly" for several reasons: social stigma, problems with custody and visitation rights, psychological costs for children, resistance to divorce by children, and mother usually having sole responsibility for child care (Rankin & Maneker, 1985).

Although both parents are responsible for supporting their children, a major financial consideration is usually whether or not the noncustodial parent will meet her/his child support obligations. A Census Bureau study found that of those women awarded child support, only 65% regularly received any money. A contributing factor was that only three fourths had a formal child-support agreement specifying the payment amount (Peterson & Nord, 1990). The incomes of the parents are the basis of the amount of child support payment ordered. Other Census survey data indicates that the average child support award increased from $4,043 in 1981 to $4,829 in 1987 (Lester, 1990). Other major financial considerations include **alimony** (spousal maintenance) and property settlements. Alimony is becoming rare unless the spouse is unable to meet her/his own reasonable economic needs.

Divorce is economically more damaging to women and children over the duration of their lives than to men (Wishik, 1986). In general, children from economically disadvantaged homes are the least financially protected following divorce in terms of the likelihood of their mother receiving a child support award and the size of the award (Teachman, 1990). In comparing annual family income before and after divorce, if the annual family income was $40,000 or more, the wife's per capita income after divorce was only 42% of family income before divorce (Weitzman, Lachs, & Tucker, 1986). In California, women were found to have experienced a 73% average decrease in their standard of living after divorce while men reported a 42% rise in their standard of living (Weitzman, 1985).

Most persons find that a major adjustment of living alone after divorce is loneliness, the greatest problem of singlehood. Such loneliness has been described as the absence of anyone who is emotionally close to a person. It is not just a desire for company or social loneliness but rather a yearning for a certain type of relationship. Therefore, some may mistakenly believe that the solution to loneliness caused by a divorce is to quickly find another emotional attachment. Women are generally perceived to be more lonely because men are more likely to socialize in same-sex groups, whereas many women consider themselves social failures if they do not engage in social activities with a man (Simenauer & Carroll, 1982b). Loneliness after divorce can be damaging not only to one's emotional health but to physical health as well (Lynch, 1980). Access to social networks can help to alleviate symptoms of anxiety and depression associated with loneliness (Weiss, 1981b).

Who Seeks the Divorce

Persons with a high level of attachment to their spouse are much less likely to first suggest obtaining a divorce (Kitson, 1982). Women are almost twice as likely to initiate a divorce as men. In 1987, 61% of the divorce petitions were filed by wives compared to 33% by husbands (National Center for Health Statistics, 1990c). This pattern may reflect the fact, reported from various studies, that women are more often dissatisfied with their marriages than men. Whether the wife or the husband files for divorce is determined by the strength of the desire to end the marriage and social norms regarding who should initiate legal proceedings. Husbands are more likely to initiate the divorce if their income is higher or if they are unable to reach an agreement with their wife on the divorce settlement including division of property, spousal support, and/or child custody (Dixon & Weitzman, 1982). If the marriage lacks companionship and harmony, husbands are more likely to claim that they initiated the divorce. However, wives more frequently take credit for initiating the divorce if the marriage has been characterized by great companionship, marital harmony, and personal commitment to the marriage (Thompson & Spanier, 1983).

Male initiators of divorce had more complaints about their spouses regarding finances, job or school commitments, and problems with children. Female initiators complained more about their husband being demanding, bossy, nagging, and not loving them. Apparently initiators of divorce experience more change and disruption in their lives and they are less in favor of reconciliation than noninitiators. Contrary to what might be expected, no significant differences were found between initiators and noninitiators in stress-related symptoms at any point in the postseparation period nor in perceived quality of life at 18 months after the divorce (Pettit & Bloom, 1984). However, another study found that women tended to perceive higher levels of disruption because of feelings of fear, moodiness, and insecurity (Buehler, 1987a).

Transitions in Divorce

Society does not provide a prescriptive way to deal with relationship termination. It is probably the only major turning point in life for which there are no normative means or social rituals for coping (Pocs & Walsh, 1985). However, if divorce can be understood as a series of transitions which occur as the family system changes from a married to a divorced state, it can more successfully be negotiated (Ahrons & Rogers, 1987).

"Oh no you don't, Gladys! I was going to leave first!"

From Joe Buresch, as seen in *Medical Aspects of Human Sexuality*, 22(3):113. Copyright © 1988 Joe Buresch. Reprinted by permission of Joe Buresch.

Marital Separation

Some marriage and family therapists are beginning to suggest that couples may be able to work out their differences if they temporarily separate. However, being separated may discourage resolution of marital problems since the individual begins to relearn the phenomenon of single living. Trial separations, however, do permit essential trust and commitment between the marital partners to remain intact. Typically, the husband will move out and the wife will stay in the home with the children (Brooks, 1985).

Marital separations may be of two types: legal separation or temporary separation. Legal separation, like desertion, does not terminate a marriage and the data are not included in divorce statistics (Crosby, 1980). After 4 years of separation from their husbands, 4 in 10 women in one study had divorced while only 2 in 10 had reconciled with their spouse. A high family income prior to separation increases the likelihood of divorce (Morgan, 1988). In general, marital separations have a greater probability of occurring for persons with no college training, with children under 18, and with family incomes under $20,000 (Kitson, 1985).

During the preseparation stage, women generally report poorer psychological adjustment whereas men typically have a harder time adjusting during the post-separation period. Preseparation difficulties of married women may be associated with their greater dissatisfaction within the marriage, but after the separation occurs, they may begin feeling the positive effects of the separation. In contrast, men may not be dealing with the issues associated with marital separation (Bloom & Caldwell, 1981).

Transition Phases

When divorce is inevitable, there are many changes/transitions that the family must go through in order to survive this traumatic experience. Mental health professionals believe that the anxiety experienced by children after the divorce of their parents is second only to the emotional upheaval caused by a parent's death ("Divorce is Changing," 1986). Understanding the nature of these phases will help spouses and children in negotiating the painful process.

1. *Individual cognition*—Beginning long before the issue of divorce is dealt with openly, spouses may deny the existence of marital problems, blame the other spouse, and emotionally withdraw. **Emotional divorce** (withdrawal of emotional investment in marital relationship by at least one partner) inevitably precedes physical divorce.
2. *Family metacognition*—The family recognizes that the marriage is disintegrating, initiating a period of ambivalent feelings including love, hate, euphoria, and sadness.
3. *Physical separation*—Highly disruptive to the family system, separation results in ambiguous roles and boundaries. Children who usually remain with the mother experience the father's departure as a terrifying event.
4. *Family reorganization*—The family experiments with new roles and redefines relationships. The relationship between former spouses determines whether the family will reorganize in functional or dysfunctional ways.
5. *Family redefinitions*—Families begin to think differently about themselves. Decisions are made about child custody often leading to the non-custodial parent developing a less intimate child-parent relationship (Ahrons, 1980, pp. 535–538).

Of the children in divorced families, only 10% were relieved with the divorce decision. For younger children, early visits with fathers were very important to help allay fears (Wallerstein & Kelly, 1980b). When recoupling by remarriage or recommitment of one or both parents occurs, the family must broaden its view from a nuclear family with two parents in one household to include a binuclear family made up of two separate but interrelated households (Ahrons, 1988).

Among divorced persons, about one half indicated spending a lot of time thinking about a former spouse, feeling depressed, and regretting that the divorce occurred (Thompson & Spanier, 1983). McGoldrick & Carter (1982) have charted the dislocation of the family life cycle which requires individuals to take certain steps to restabilize and proceed developmentally in a divorce and post-divorce family (see Table 17.5).

The Process of Divorce Today

During the 1980s, state legislatures and courts became increasingly aware of the need to establish gender equity for issues relating to marital property and the bases for divorce (Gest, 1983). Before 1950, most states were "title states" whereby the spouse who held the property title would retain the property after divorce; and the courts could only provide for spousal and child support. Today, all states have either equitable or equal distribution of marital or community property. Further, marital fault as the basis for divorce is no longer considered a significant factor by courts in division of property (Samuelson, 1988).

Divorce laws in the United States have been strongly influenced by English legal traditions. By 1900, most states had adopted divorce laws containing four major elements: perpetuation of gender-based division of roles and responsibilities, requirement of grounds for divorce, establishment of adversarial proceedings for granting divorce, and association of financial terms for divorce with determination of fault (Weitzman & Dixon, 1988). To grant a divorce, the traditional adversary system required that one marital partner be guilty of violating some legal grounds for divorce and that the other partner be innocent. The plaintiff (person petitioning for divorce) had to prove that the defendant

Table 17.5: **Divorce and the Family Life Cycle: Steps and Developmental Issues in Restabilizing**

Phase	Steps Required to Restabilize in Transition Process	Developmental Issue
1. Decide to divorce	Accept inability to resolve marital tensions	Accept one's part in failure of marriage
2. Plan breakup of system	Support viable arrangements for all parts of system	Work cooperatively on problems of custody, visitation, finances; and deal with extended family about the divorce
3. Separate	Continue cooperative co-parental relationship; and work on resolution of attachment to spouse	Mourn loss of intact family; restructure marital and parent-child relationships and living arrangements; and realign relationships with own and spouse's extended family
4. Divorce	Continue work on emotional divorce: overcome hurt, anger, and guilt	Mourn loss of intact family and give up fantasies of reunion; retrieve hopes, dreams, expectations from marriage; and stay connected with extended families
5. Postdivorce single parent (custodial)	Maintain parental contact with ex-spouse and support contact of children with ex-spouse and family	Make flexible visitation arrangements with ex-spouse and family; and rebuild social network
6. Postdivorce single-parent (noncustodial)	Maintain parental contact with ex-spouse and support custodial parent's relationship with children	Find ways to continue effective parenting relationship with children; and rebuild social network

From M. McGoldrick and E. A. Carter, "The Family Life Cycle—Its Stages and Dislocations" in F. Walsh (ed.), *Normal Family Processes*.

committed a marital offense. If the guilty spouse was able to establish that the other spouse was also at fault, the divorce might not be granted so that both spouses could be punished (Weitzman & Dixon, 1988).

The Emergence of No-Fault Divorce Laws

During the 1970s, many states began to adopt no-fault divorce legislation which eliminated the adversarial process. Since it was believed that the legal process generated hostility between spouses, the language of the proceedings began to be changed to more neutral terms such as "dissolution" for divorce and "respondents" for plaintiffs and defendants (Samuelson, 1988). The fault-based grounds for divorce were eliminated and irreconcilable differences or irretrievable breakdown became the new standards by which divorces were to be granted. Responsibilities of wives and husbands came to be redefined on the basis of gender equality with the financial aspects of the divorce decided on the basis of equity and economic need holding both parents equally responsible for child support (Weitzman, 1985).

Every state has some version of a no-fault divorce law. While these laws make divorce less traumatic, the division of assets often does not take into account such intangible assets as future earning capacity, professional education, and health insurance (Lacayo, 1986). Another central problem is that many divorced persons do not earn enough income to support two households.

California was the first state to initiate a no-fault divorce law. When the law's impact on divorce was assessed, the percentage of husbands filing for divorce was found to have increased (Welch & Price-Bonham, 1983). However, the no-fault divorce law per se did not lead to any real increase in the divorce rate. Although the divorce rate grew steadily in California, the same was true for the rest of the United States. Further, there were no differences with regard to whether couples separated or filed for divorce early in their marriages or later. In general, the pattern of custody requests and child support awards remained essentially unchanged. However, the number of petitioners asking the court to divide their debts declined considerably as did the percentage of petitioners requesting spousal support for the wife (Dixon & Weitzman, 1980).

A later study involving the states of California, Georgia, and Washington determined that since implementation of no-fault divorce, alimony had been awarded less often, and if awarded, it was likely to be for a lesser amount and not permanent. Under the no-fault system of divorce, child support awards usually end before the child reaches age 21 (Welch & Price-Bonham, 1983).

Grounds for Divorce and Annulment

Although all states have now passed no-fault legislation for divorce, many states have maintained one or more of their previous grounds for a divorce. For example, Georgia, Texas, and Virginia retained adultery as a grounds for divorce while Illinois, Mississippi, and Oklahoma kept impotence as a grounds (see Table 17.6).

An **annulment** means that no valid marriage ever existed from a legal perspective. Among the legal grounds for annulment are underage at marriage, impotence, bigamy, and force or duress (Hoffman, 1988). In contrast, a religious annulment in the Roman Catholic church (and other denominations that grant annulments) means that a marriage is considered to be invalid from a theological viewpoint even though the couple is legally married in the eyes of society (Farrell, 1984). For the past two decades, the number of Roman Catholic marriages annulled has grown from 300 to over 59,000 on an annual basis. But this number is still small considering the fact that by 1985 there were over 8 million divorced Roman Catholics in the United States (Young & Griffith, 1985). A religious annulment represents an affirmation by religious authorities that a person of faith has made a human mistake and puts an official end to a relationship, which may have become unbearable. It supposedly leads a person to forgiveness with themselves or by their spouse, requires confrontation of the problem and acceptance of responsibility for the marital failure, and permits remarriage for a practicing member of the faith (Brunsman, 1985). Religious annulment requests can only be considered after a civil divorce has been obtained. Some Catholic officials have estimated that between 40%–80% of divorced Roman Catholics could successfully acquire a religious annulment (Young & Griffith, 1985).

Division of Marital Property

Some states have begun to revise their no-fault divorce laws to provide judges with more specific guidance about equitable division of marital property (Lacayo, 1986). However, substantial variations still exist between states with regard to the division of marital property. By 1988, at least nine states including Texas and Wisconsin used the concept of community property under which the couple jointly owns all property acquired during the marriage (Samuelson, 1988). Community property states require that property be divided equitably at divorce. In the case of separate marital-property states, the spouse who holds the property title is allowed to retain the property at the time of divorce (McGrath, 1986). Some states follow common law rules in most other matters but reserve the right to require an equitable distribution in a divorce. States without a community property law may divide assets based on such factors as length of marriage; ability of each spouse to find job; and each spouse's relative age, health, income level, wealth, and contributions to economic assets of the marriage ("What You Should," 1981).

Prenuptial agreements are not always so formal or friendly. In the process, couples may experience their first serious disagreement.

Table 17.6: Grounds for Divorce and Annulment

	Residence	Adultery	Cruelty	Desertion	Alcoholism	Impotency	Nonsupport	Insanity	Pregnancy at marriage	Bigamy	Separation	Felony conviction or imprisonment	Drug addiction	Fraud, force, duress
AL	6 mos.	Yes	Yes	1 yr.	Yes	No	2 yrs.	5 yrs.	Yes	A	1–2 yrs.	—	Yes	A
AK	—	Yes	Yes	1 yr.	1 yr.	A	No	18 mos.	No	A	No	Yes	Yes	A
AZ	90 da.	No	No	No	No	No	No	No	No	No	No	No	No	A
AR	60 da.	Yes	Yes	1 yr.	1 yr.	A	Yes	3 yrs.	No	Yes	3 yrs.	Yes	A	A
CA	6 mos.	No	No	No	No	No	No	Yes	No	No	No	No	No	A
CO	90 da.	No	No	No	No	No	No	No	No	A	No	No	No	A
CT	1 yr.	Yes	Yes	1 yr.	Yes	A	1 yr.	5 yrs.	Yes	A	18 mos.	—	No	Yes
DE	6 mos.	No	Yes	No	No	A	No	A	No	A	6 mos.	No	A	A
FL	6 mos.	No	No	No	No	A	No	No	No	No	No	No	No	No
GA	6 mos.	Yes	Yes	1 yr.	Yes	Yes	No	Yes	Yes	A	No	—	Yes	Yes
HI	6 mos.	No	No	No	No	No	No	A	Yes	A	2 yrs.	2 yrs.	No	A
ID	6 wks.	Yes	Yes	1 yr.	1 yr.	A	1 yr.	3 yrs.	Yes	A	5 yrs.	Yes	No	A
IL	90 da.	Yes	Yes	1 yr.	2 yrs.	Yes	No	No	Yes	Yes	2 yrs.	Yes	2 yrs.	No
IN	6 mos.	No	No	No	No	A	No	2 yrs.	Yes	A	No	Yes	No	A
IA	1 yr.	No	No	No	No	A	No	A	Yes	A	No	No	No	No
KS	60 da.	No	No	No	No	No	Yes	2 yrs.	A	A	No	No	No	A
KY	180 da.	No	No	No	No	A	No	No	No	No	No	No	No	A
LA	1 yr.	Yes	No	No	No	No	No	No	No	A	1 yr.	—	No	No
ME	6 mos.	Yes	Yes	3 yrs.	Yes	Yes	Yes	7 yrs.	No	No	No	No	Yes	No
MD	None	Yes	No	1 yr.	No	No	Yes	3 yrs.	No	A	1 yr.	—	No	No
MA	None	Yes	Yes	1 yr.	Yes	Yes	Yes	No	No	A	No	No	Yes	A
MI	180 da.	No	No	No	No	No	No	No	No	A	No	No	No	No
MN	180 da.	No	No	No	No	No	No	No	No	No	No	No	No	A
MS	6 mos.	Yes	Yes	1 yr.	Yes	Yes	No	3 yrs.	Yes	Yes	No	No	Yes	A
MO	90 da.	No	No	No	No	A	No	A	No	A	1–2 yrs.	No	No	A
NE	1 yr.	No	No	No	No	A	No	No	No	A	No	No	No	A
NV	6 wks.	No	No	No	No	No	No	2 yrs.	No	A	1 yr.	No	No	A
NH	None	Yes	Yes	2 yrs.	2 yrs.	Yes	2 yrs.	No	No	No	2 yrs.	—	No	No
NJ	1 yr.	Yes	Yes	1 yr.	1 yr.	A	No	2 yrs.	No	A	18 mos.	18 mos.	1 yr.	A
NM	6 mos.	Yes	Yes	Yes	No	No	No	No	No	No	No	No	No	No
NY	1 yr.	Yes	Yes	1 yr.	No	No	No	No	No	A	No	Yes	No	No
NC	6 mos.	No	No	No	No	A	No	3 yrs.	No	A	1 yr.	No	No	No
ND	6 mos.	Yes	Yes	1 yr.	1 yr.	A	1 yr.	5 yrs.	No	A	No	Yes	1 yr.	A
OH	6 mos.	Yes	Yes	1 yr.	Yes	Yes	Yes	4 yrs.	No	Yes	1 yr.	Yes	No	A
OK	6 mos.	Yes	Yes	1 yr.	Yes	Yes	Yes	5 yrs.	Yes	No	No	Yes	No	Yes
OR	6 mos.	No	No	No	No	No	No	No	No	No	No	No	No	A
PA	6 mos.	Yes	Yes	1 yr.	No	No	No	3 yrs.	No	Yes	3 yrs.	Yes	No	No
RI	1 yr.	Yes	Yes	5 yrs.	Yes	Yes	1 yr.	No	No	Yes	3 yrs.	No	1 yr.	No
SC	1 yr.	Yes	phys. only	1 yr.	Yes	No	No	No	No	No	1 yr.	No	Yes	No
SD	None	Yes	Yes	1 yr.	1 yr.	A	1 yr.	A/5 yrs.	No	A	No	Yes	No	A
TN	6 mos.	Yes	Yes	1 yr.	Yes	Yes	Yes	No	Yes	Yes	No	Yes	Yes	A

Table 17.6: *cont'd*

	Residence	Adultery	Cruelty	Desertion	Alcoholism	Impotency	Nonsupport	Insanity	Pregnancy at Marriage	Bigamy	Separation	Felony Conviction or Imprisonment	Drug addiction	Fraud, Force, Duress
TX	6 mos.	Yes	Yes	1 yr.	—	A	No	3 yrs.	No	A	3 yrs.	Yes	No	No
UT	3 mos.	Yes	Yes	1 yr.	Yes	Yes	Yes	Yes	No	A	3 yrs.	Yes	Yes	A
VT	6 mos.	Yes	No	Yes	No	No	Yes	5 yrs.	No	A	6 mos.	Yes	No	A
VA	6 mos.	Yes	Yes	1 yr.	No	A	No	No	A	A	1 yr.	Yes	No	No
WA	Bona fide res.	No	No	No	No	No	No	No	No	No	90 da.	No	No	No
WV	1 yr.	Yes	Yes	6 mos.	Yes	A	A	3 yrs.	A	A	1 yrs.	Yes	Yes	No
WI	6 mos.	No	No	No	No	No	No	No	No	A	1 yr.	No	No	A
WY	2 mos.	No	No	No	No	No	No	2 yrs.	No	A	No	No	No	No
DC	6 mos.	No	No	No	No	A	No	A	No	A	6 mos.–1 yr.	No	No	A

Note: A = Grounds for annulment
The World Almanac and Book of Facts, 1991 edition, copyright © Pharos Books, 1990, New York, NY 10166. Reprinted by permission.

In 1986, Wisconsin became the first state to enact a uniform marital property law that gives an equal share of assets to each spouse regardless of who had original title to the asset/property. Under its provisions, any income produced through inherited assets is considered community property. If an individual spouse wishes to retain ownership of select assets, a contract can be signed prior to or after the marriage. But in the absence of a contract, couples automatically come under provisions of the uniform marital property act at the time of marriage. Many states also consider vested and nonvested pensions as marital property subject to division at the time of divorce. In addition, California, New York, and Wisconsin consider a specialized professional degree as an asset to be divided if the degree was received through the financial support of the spouse. In such cases, a professional degree or license has monetary value that is considered part of community or marital property (McGrath, 1986). Women are usually more likely than men to express satisfaction with property settlement arrangements under these conditions (Albrecht, 1980).

Alimony: The Tie That Binds

The term alimony comes from the Latin word "alimonia" which means nourishment or sustenance. The concept of alimony is linked to the ancient tradition that in return for a wife's services in the home, she is entitled to support by her husband ("What You Should," 1981). Under common law, the traditional rationale for alimony was to force the husband to continue his obligation by providing for the wife's needs so she would not become dependent upon society. It also was used to punish wrongdoing and reward virtue in marriage, to support the idea that wives were entitled to the same standard of living after divorce, to compensate the wife for labor during marriage, and to reinforce marrriage as a sharing partnership (Weitzman, 1985). But under the no-fault divorce approach, the intended purposes of alimony are to provide transitional support for women to adjust to new situations, to become self-supporting, and to support women divorced after a long marriage who are perceived as incapable of supporting themselves and/or as too old to be retrained. A further change brought about by no-fault divorce laws is the granting of many more time-limited alimony awards. Thus, by 1977, the median duration of alimony was only about 2 years (Weitzman, 1985).

Under the Uniform Marriage and Divorce Act, alimony is only to be awarded if a spouse lacks sufficient property to provide for reasonable needs and is unable to support herself/himself through appropriate employment. Although alimony is intended to provide for reasonable needs, it is sometimes used as a form of bribe between spouses to promote divorce in those cases where only one spouse wants a divorce. In addition, it can be used to provide a mechanism to encourage cooperation between spouses for the long-term welfare of children (Oster, 1987). Further, the United States Supreme Court has ruled that alimony statutes have to be gender neutral so men can be awarded alimony payments from their wives. If the recipient remarries or the payer dies, alimony payments usually cease ("What You Should," 1981).

Changes in tax laws which lead to more reliance on property settlements and larger child support payments have decreased the attractiveness of alimony. Now considered a part of the recipient's income, alimony must be taxed whereas the payment is considered tax deductible for the payee (Rankin, 1986a). In 1987, only 17% of divorced women were awarded alimony at the time of the divorce, while 27% received a one-time cash payment (Lester, 1990). In 1985, the average annual payment received by a divorced woman from a former spouse was $3,733, which increased her average annual total money income to $17,780 (U.S. Bureau of the Census, 1989b). A Census Bureau survey for 1987 indicated that white women (18%) were twice as likely as black women (9%) to receive alimony. Older women, those without children, and college graduates also were more likely to receive alimony (Lester, 1990). Although the frequency of alimony awards has dropped since the advent of no-fault divorce, most women were not awarded alimony even before that time (Weitzman, 1985).

Divorce Mediation: A Solution

Mediation may be described as a conflict resolution process whereby two disputing parties meet with a third-party mediator who facilitates communication or impartially guides negotiations. A successful mediator must have skills in power balancing, conflict management, negotiation, agreement drafting, and interpersonal communication (Kaslow, 1984). This method has advantages over the traditional adversary process because it is informal, less structured, and conducted in private, encouraging openness not possible in a public setting. In mediation, spouses retain control over the outcome rather than turning the decisions over to a judge (Vroom, Fassett, & Wakefield, 1982).

The use of mediation in divorce cases is an attempt to reduce hostility, aggression, and retaliation between the marriage partners. The goals are to encourage cooperative problem solving in reaching an equitable distribution of assets and in determining financial and living arrangements for the children. The mediator tries to establish a working relationship between parents by overcoming financial and emotional marital dependencies through focusing on parenting issues. In other words, the intent is to reach a mutually acceptable divorce agreement with the least possible distress. Most divorce mediation cases require 6–12 sessions (Kaslow, 1984).

While mediation is not intended as therapy, it is unclear how much exploration of mental health issues occurs (Stier, 1986). While the mediator assists in developing an agreement, each spouse must prepare an individual budget and arrive at workable solutions with responsibility for her/his own life (Grebe, 1986). In fact, mediation has become one of the fastest growing approaches to resolving conflicts at numerous times throughout the family life cycle (Vroom, Fassett, & Wakefield, 1982).

Adjusting to Divorce

At the end of most marriages, a sense of bonding still persists regardless of whether the marriage was happy or unhappy. This attachment generates varying reactions in different persons. For example, a person can be drawn to the former spouse after divorce by a dependent emotional bond similar to one that children have for their parents. Men are more likely than women to maintain a sense of attachment for their ex-spouses (Gerstel, Riessman, & Rosenfield, 1985). Further, the degree of distress experienced does not depend upon which spouse initiated the divorce. In fact, feelings of continued attachment on the part of either partner may lead to a desire to rejoin the former spouse causing even greater distress and intense anger (Weiss, 1981a).

Since marriage is more likely to be a source of economic support for women and emotional support for men, it is not surprising that divorced women have adjustment problems in the area of household management while men tend to have more problems with personal ties. Generally, women and men from egalitarian marriages, where a division of wage and domestic labor exists, typically are less distressed over divorce and have fewer adjustment problems than those from more traditional marriages (Gerstel et al., 1985). Wives report more trauma and stress associated with divorce than husbands, with many describing their divorce experience as a "nightmare." However, both women and men indicate that the most difficult period is before the decision to divorce (Albrecht, 1980).

Coping with Parents, Friends, and Community

Divorce is believed to be the only family crisis during which social support falls away (Wallerstein & Blakeslee, 1990). Since social support systems play a major role in adjustment to divorce, the reaction of the parents of divorcing spouses is crucial. In one study, less than one half of women and men reported that parental response to their divorce could be classified as positive. Among the harmful parental behaviors to divorce adjustment are punishing the adult child, psychologically repossessing the adult child, denying the divorce, focusing solely on the problems of the grandchildren, and personalizing the divorce. Adult children can attempt to change parental attitudes and behavior toward the divorce by demonstrating self-sufficiency, confronting their parents, explaining the circumstances of the divorce, and establishing a new love relationship (Lesser & Comet, 1987).

The issue of relationships with friends after divorce is another complex question. Some divorced persons dread telling friends about their divorce while many others want to give friends their personalized account of the divorce to avoid blame. One researcher revealed depressing facts about friends and divorce: 4 in 10 women and 5 in 10 men indicated that their friends took sides with their former spouses. Divorced persons felt excluded by married friends who were threatened by the divorce, often feeling like "a third wheel" at social events. Also, many opposite-sex married friends were believed to be concerned about sexual competition for their own spouse. Therefore, divorced persons tended to pull away from their married friends and to seek out other persons like themselves who were single. In fact, almost one half of women and men reported that they could not maintain friendships with married persons (Gerstel, 1987).

After divorce, other factors such as changes in employment, residence, and child care may cause persons to either be added or dropped from social networks. Divorced mothers with a close-knit social network of kinspersons and co-workers reported more emotional support and assistance from these sources than other divorced persons. About a year and a half after divorce, most women began to find their social network limiting and felt the need to have more time away from friends (Leslie & Grady, 1985). Changes in the social network following divorce will tend to increase stress resulting from the divorce and decrease the quality of the person's adjustment to the crisis. Persons reporting high levels of adjustment indicated that more of their relationship needs were met by fewer persons after divorce while low adjustment persons had twice as much assistance from others usually in the form of financial or physical help (Daniels-Mohring & Berger, 1984). The change in contacts with friends after divorce may be related to decreases in income level for divorced women since little change was reported in contacts with relatives or participation in clubs and organizations (see Table 17.7).

Table 17.7: Changes in Life-Style after Divorce

Changes in Life-Style	Women	Men
Participation in clubs and organizations		
More participation	39%	35%
No change	39	50
Less participation	22	15
Contact with relatives		
More contact	37	25
No change	52	60
Less contact	10	15
Post-divorce income		
Much lower	48	7
Somewhat lower	18	12
About the same	27	57
Somewhat higher	6	17
Much higher	1	7

From S. L. Albrecht, "Reactions and Adjustments to Divorce: Differences in the Experiences of Males and Females" in *Family Relations,* 29:63.

Reestablishing Emotional Balance

Most persons experience a period of mourning after divorce during which they withdraw from social contacts and have intense feelings of personal failure and confusion. A period of anger often follows in which they have feelings of betrayal or hostility toward their former spouse. A gradual period of readjustment then begins as individuals realistically give up their relationship with a former spouse (Kressel, 1980). Remarrying or remaining single after divorce does not affect the level of grieving that is experienced over the divorce. Further, personal adjustment is not related to gender, being a parent, remaining single, or remarrying after divorce (Saul & Scherman, 1984).

Psychological factors causing emotional stress after divorce include frequently feeling an inability to give love as a spouse or parent and intense painful feelings about a former spouse. More tangible nonpsychological sources of stress include change in residence, usually for the husband; less frequent contact with children by noncustodial parent; and severe economic decline in life-style for the wife (Kressel, 1980).

Some researchers have found that divorced persons are much more likely to exhibit higher levels of depression than married and never-married persons (Vega, & Warheit, & Meinhardt, 1984). One study reported that they are twice as likely to feel depressed about being alone with almost one half of divorced persons having no one with whom they could discuss issues and problems (Cargan & Melko, 1982). However, other research suggests that if divorced and married persons are equated in terms of economic problems, decline in their economic condition, and availability of personal support systems, the differences in depression become insignificant. A major variable in the likelihood of depression among divorced persons is whether or not they have personal support systems and their current perceptions of personal difficulties. In other words, divorced persons who do not perceive a high level of personal difficulties are much less likely to report symptoms of depression (Menaghan & Lieberman, 1986). After divorce, the most important factor in improving one's self-concept appears to be the establishment of a satisfying, intimate interpersonal relationship. Most divorced persons with high levels of distress are more willing to acknowledge their negative feelings and to accept assistance, whereas those with low levels of distress tend to deny any negative feelings associated with their divorce (Berman & Turk, 1981).

If divorced persons feel psychologically good about themselves, they are more likely to be physically healthy. As was reported earlier in chapter 9, failure to manage marital conflict and existence of depression can cause physical health problems (Hanson, 1986a). Available evidence suggests an increased risk of physical illness due to suppressed immunological functioning associated with the stressful conditions of divorce (Kitson & Morgan, 1990). Among divorced persons, frequent physical health problems include respiratory tract disorders, diabetes mellitus, tuberculosis, and alcoholism (Segraves, 1985). Attempting to link the causation of these health problems directly to divorce is extremely difficult. However, it is thought that the life-style of divorced persons plays a major role, increasing the risk for these diseases.

What are the gender differences in emotional adjustment to divorce? Emotional problems after divorce are initially more severe for men, but they remain more sustained for women. Although men indicate loneliness as being the most pervasive problem during the separation period prior to divorce, after the divorce significant improvement in coping with loneliness is usually reported (White & Bloom, 1981). Many family therapists believe that loneliness and continued anxiety about living alone among women are linked to persisting anger toward the former spouse (Wallerstein, 1986). Social and interpersonal involvements are related to increased life satisfaction after divorce as well as development of independence from the former spouse. In one study, in which divorce appeared to improve psychological functioning of women, about two thirds indicated such improvement, whereas only about one sixth of men did so. Despite these findings, almost one half of women but only one fifth of men were still angry toward their former spouse after 10 years. Further, women were more reluctant to accept responsibility for the marital failure with over one half claiming no responsibility at all. Regardless of gender, persons who initially sought a divorce were more likely to improve the quality of their lives in contrast to those persons who were opposed to a divorce (Wallerstein, 1986).

Fulfillment of Sexual Needs

The ending of a socially sanctioned opportunity for sexual intercourse represents a major area of adjustment for most divorced persons. They also may feel anger and frustration over still being sexually attracted to their former spouse (Price-Bonham & Balswick, 1980). Almost two thirds of men indicated that even during the period of separation prior to divorce, they experienced severe difficulties in coping with their sexual needs. However, after their divorce, most men were able to adequately meet their sexual needs (White & Bloom, 1981).

Although there has been a growing acceptance of nonmarital sexual intercourse for single women, many inhibitions, stereotypes, and false premises continue to exist regarding sexual expression (Newcomb, 1985). Among professional women in academe, divorced and separated women reported an average of 19 lifetime sex partners in contrast to 7 sex partners for marrieds and 14 sex partners for never-marrieds (Davidson & Darling, 1988c). Other findings from college-educated women in the health professions corroborate that divorced women have at least twice as many lifetime sex partners as married women and one and one half times as many partners as never-married women. Further, divorced women experience sexual intercourse more frequently than either never-married or married women (Davidson & Darling, 1988b). But divorced women were almost three times as likely to report that lack of tenderness by their sex partner served to inhibit them from experiencing orgasm in comparison to never-married and married women (Davidson & Darling, 1988c). And among post-college age women, about three fourths of divorced women as compared to only one half of marrieds and two thirds of never-marrieds pretended to experience orgasm, at least occasionally, during sexual intercourse (Darling & Davidson, 1986b).

Establishing Social Boundaries with Former Spouse

Following divorce, the relationship with a former spouse is usually characterized either by avoiding contact altogether or by keeping any social contact emotionally distant (McCollum, 1985). When there are children, the relationship between former spouses will determine if the family reorganizes in functional or dysfunctional ways. Therefore, it is very important to carefully reestablish contact with the former spouse in ways that do not regenerate feelings of hostility and anger which could result in further distancing (Ahrons, 1980). In reviewing social interaction patterns of divorced families, five relationship styles with former spouses have been identified:

1. *Perfect pals*—Former spouses are able to maintain strong friendships with mutual respect and high quality shared-parenting arrangements. Extended family relationships are maintained.
2. *Cooperative colleagues*—Parents cooperate to minimize the trauma of divorce for the children but are not good friends.
3. *Angry associates*—Former spouses feel bitter about the divorce, fights ensue over child custody, visitation rights, and financial matters with children caught in the middle.
4. *Fiery foes*—Legal battles over child custody and property settlements continue for years interfering with the ability to co-parent. Children siding with one parent diminishes contact with the other.
5. *Resolved duos*—Former spouses discontinue contact and one often moves from the area. Withdrawal creates the true "single-parent family" with absent parent existing only in memories and fantasies of children (Ahrons & Rodgers, 1987, pp. 114–121).

Establishing amicable social boundaries between former spouses is an important link in successfully rebalancing lives after a divorce.

Spousal interaction after divorce is important to the welfare of both former partners and any children involved. However, establishing healthy boundaries may be difficult.

Although many persons may consider friendship after divorce to be pathological, contact with an ex-spouse is very important to some. This desire is especially true for women who did not make the decision to divorce. Factors increasing the likelihood that a couple will remain friends after divorce include quality of the relationship prior to divorce, couple's attitude toward the divorce, circumstances under which the marriage ended, and absence of other emotional issues (Stark, 1987). The frequency of contact between former spouses appears to be related to length of marriage with those having had shorter marriages reporting less contact with their former spouse. Most contacts take place as the former spouses spend time together discussing such topics as finances, property settlement, and current lives. In the early months after divorce, friends also play a more important role in bringing former spouses together. The frequency of contact between the former spouses usually decreases between 6–18 months after the divorce (Bloom & Kindle, 1985).

Research assessing parental interaction after divorce found that less than one half of wives and husbands wanted to relate to each other about their children. After three years, only one third wanted to continue a co-parenting relationship. In the case of coparental interaction, only 1 in 5 couples had relatively high degrees of interaction with former spouses regarding such matters as addressing the child's personal, school, and medical problems; planning special events in the child's life; and talking about child-rearing concerns. By three years postdivorce, only 1 in 10 couples had maintained a high degree of interaction (Ahrons & Wallisch, 1987).

As the level of attachment to the former spouse increases, so does the level of distress after divorce (Kitson, 1982). The greatest quantity and highest quality of spousal interaction are reported by those who have not remarried and who have joint custody of children. They have the highest levels of psychological closeness, attachment, and positive feelings toward their former spouse (Ahrons & Rodgers, 1987). If the divorced person remarries and has confidence in the new spouse along with a high quality marital relationship, she/he is much more likely to remain friends with the former spouse. In fact, the more contact a woman has with her former spouse, the happier her new marriage is likely to be so long as her new spouse agrees with the continuing contact (Stark, 1987).

Therapists stress that couples can write their own "scripts" for the future relationships that they would like to have with former spouses to avoid the traditional hostile interactions. There are some instances where continued interaction may be ill-advised such as cases in which there is a history of spouse abuse or serious alcohol or other substance abuse problems (Stark, 1987).

The Impact of Divorce on Children

In most crises, parents instinctively reach for their children, gathering them to safety. However, when divorcing, parents put children on hold while they attend to their own problems (Wallerstein & Blakeslee, 1990). Such diminished capacity to parent may be an important key to the impact of divorce on children. An in-depth study found that when children initially learned that their parents were divorcing, their typical reactions were to express shock, surprise, and denial. They were frightened about what would happen to them; angry with their parents; and visibly sad, depressed, and moody. Most children typically found themselves caught between their parents because of conflicting loyalties, and fantasized that their parents would eventually reconcile (Wallerstein & Kelly, 1980a). These initial reactions of children to divorce, a result of acute stress, were expected to disappear in the first year after divorce. However, 5 years after the divorce, one third of children still suffered from depression and experienced low learning capacities in school, difficulties with peers, explosive anger, and preoccupation with the divorce (Wallerstein, 1985). Differences in the reactions of children may vary considerably depending on factors such as the child's personality or age. Since children of various age groups are working on different developmental tasks, the added stresses of a parental divorce may impact each child distinctly (McCoy, 1984).

Is the real source of difficulty for children of divorce the fact that their parents are divorcing? Some suggest it may be because many parents are so deeply troubled during and after divorce that they are unable to provide their children with the emotional support and stability that is needed. Authorities are searching for answers. In one study, parents who had experienced less marital conflict, including verbal abuse, physical abuse, or nagging, had better relationships with their children after separation. In addition, children from such homes were found to have better emotional and behavioral adjustment after separation (Tschann, Johnston, Kline, & Wallerstein, 1989). For whatever reasons, the period following divorce is often the most stressful period in the life of a child (Wallerstein, 1985).

Changes in Behavior

As might be expected, divorced mothers work outside the home more frequently than nondivorced mothers. However, researchers have found that children from divorced families do not have any greater number of household or child-care responsibilities than other children. But children from divorced families more often assume a confidant role with their mothers and rate themselves as being lower in social competence. Maternal employment among divorced women also seems to decrease participation of children in athletics and activities with friends (Devall, Stoneman, & Brody, 1986). These findings may reflect the time overload and lack of money often experienced in nonintact families. Such variables may also account for children in divorced families tending to be less sociable, to have fewer close friends, to spend less time with friends, and to participate in fewer shared activities (Demo & Acock, 1988).

For the most part, mental health ratings assigned to intact-family children are higher than ratings assigned to children from divorced families. Children from divorced families also tend to exhibit more anxiety behaviors, hostility toward adults, nightmares, and aggression toward friends and siblings (Guidubaldi & Cleminshaw, 1985). Other research suggests that children of divorced families have greater distractibility, more acting out behaviors toward parents, and higher levels of aggression. However, inadequacy of family income and stressful parental life events are related to child maladjustment irrespective of the child being from a divorced or intact family (Hodges, Tierney, & Buschbaum, 1984). Further, children of lower socioeconomic status are much more likely to use their divorced mothers as scapegoats for their frustrations with poverty (Ambert, 1982).

In reviewing the effects of divorce on children, many studies support the contention that male children are more at risk after divorce than female children, and younger children are more at risk than older children (Johnston, 1990). Further, male children take longer to initially recover than female children. Within 2 months after divorce, the behavior of preschool female children from divorced families was similar to that of children from intact families; but male children tended to be more aggressive. Two years after divorce, the behavior of female children was still similiar, whether from divorced or intact homes, while male children were still behaving in a somewhat hostile and aggressive manner. However, during adolescence, female behavior problems appeared to catch up to the male level. Female adolescents from divorced families more often engaged in promiscuous sexual behavior as well as evidenced more bitter conflict and arguments with their mothers than female and male adolescents from intact families (McCoy, E., 1985).

Despite these findings, evidence from a longitudinal study of children from divorced families suggests that general satisfaction with the behavior of children generally increases over time. Children living with their mothers eventually showed a substantial reduction in anger or rudeness as well as fewer threats to move out and live with their fathers (Ambert, 1984). Good mental and physical health for the custodial parent is associated with good mental and physical health in children (Hanson, 1986a).

Children at Risk: A Continuing Debate

Research continues to center on the serious question of whether or not children will necessarily be adversely affected by divorce. Earlier, some researchers believed there was no strong evidence that established a clear link between divorce and maladjustment of children from divorced families (Lowery & Settle, 1985; Nock, 1982). More recently, studies have found that children from divorced families perform worse than children from two-parent families on a wide variety of academic, social, physical, and health measures (Hanson & Sporakowski, 1986). However, although divorce is acknowledged as a major stressful life event for children and adolescents with frequent negative effects on health and well-being, it may be less harmful than other events (Guidubaldi & Perry, 1985). There is evidence that high levels of conflict and family distress in families who stay together may be more damaging to children than a time-limited "acute distress syndrome" following divorce (Shaw & Emery, 1987). "It's better to come from a broken home than to live in it," expressed one experienced teenager (Greer & Keating, 1983, p. 358). Various studies have corroborated this fact. Adolescent well-being in intact families with high conflict is significantly lower than that of adolescents living in divorced families with low conflict (Mechanic & Hansell, 1989; Slater & Haber, 1984). Parents who had less marital conflict reported better relationships with their children after separation and more adaptive child functioning. Although children with difficult, uneven temperaments evidenced more emotional adjustment problems, they had more positive relationships with their fathers (Tschann, Johnston, Kline, & Wallerstein, 1989). High levels of family conflict are related to low self-esteem, greater anxiety, and less inner control for the adolescent regardless of whether or not family dissolution has occurred. Thus, adjustment of teenagers may not be related to divorce itself but rather to the conflict level in the family (Slater & Haber, 1984).

Socioeconomic conditions also appear to be a major determining factor in the effects of divorce on children as single-parent families tend to have lower family incomes as well as overall poorer economic conditions. Persons reared in single-parent families are more likely to have their first child at a younger age themselves, to be a single parent, to receive welfare assistance, and to go without material necessities (Mueller & Cooper, 1986). However, most studies have concluded that family structure is unrelated to self-concept in that children from divorced families suffer no losses in self-esteem unless their family situation is socially stigmatized. While adolescents in mother-only families tend to be more socially deviant, the misbehavior appears related to a lack of parental control.

Considerable disagreement exists as to how long the effects of divorce last. Based on the first longitudinal study of its kind, Wallerstein suggested that while behavioral and academic problems often do not last, feelings do. She concluded, "It's quite clear that for the children, divorce has been the main event of their childhood and adolescence—that although most accept and even approve—a sense of loneliness seems to endure" (cited in McCoy, 1984, p. 198). These feelings of loneliness may relate to data from the General Social Surveys (1972–1983) suggesting that daughters and sons of divorced parents marry earlier than children from intact families. Those children living with a divorced mother who had not remarried, married at even younger ages. Daughters of divorced parents were also twice as likely to obtain a divorce as daughters from intact families (Keith & Finlay, 1988).

The impact of marital disruption is less severe for preschool-age children than for school-age children (Demo & Acock, 1988). Children who were older at the time of divorce (age 9 and up) seemed to be more troubled 10 years after the divorce with vivid memories of their suffering and concerned with the unreliability of relationships (Wallerstein, 1985b). A critical factor appears to be whether or not a close relationship exists between the noncustodial parent and the child. If such a relationship does exist, both female and male children are likely to exhibit good adjustment (Wallerstein & Kelly, 1980a). However, the National Survey of Children found that almost one fourth of children had no contact with their fathers during the previous 5 years following the divorce, and in only one fourth of the cases did the noncustodial father spend at least 24 days per year with his children. Yet, children in divorced families were found to be no better adjusted if they saw their fathers more regularly (Furstenberg & Morgan, 1987). In a comprehensive 15-year follow-up study of families after divorce, many children emerged as compassionate, competent, young adults (Wallerstein & Blakeslee, 1990). However, a number of ill effects were also identified for children of divorce. Among the findings, two thirds felt rejected by at least one parent and almost one half entered adulthood as worried, underachieving, self-deprecating, and sometimes angry individuals. Several key generalizations emerged from this research:

1. Divorce is almost always more devastating for children than for their parents.
2. Divorce is not an event that stands alone but a continuum beginning with an unhappy marriage, and extending through separation, divorce, remarriage, and/or subsequent divorce.
3. The effects of divorce are often long-lasting because what children witness and experience becomes a part of their inner world view.
4. Almost all children of divorce view their childhood and adolescence as over shadowed by the divorce (Wallerstein & Blakeslee, 1990, pp. 297–298).

More research data is needed regarding the effects of divorce on children including age differences, gender differences, conflict between custodial and noncustodial parent, life changes related to divorce, custody arrangements, and visitation arrangements (Lowery & Settle, 1985).

Child Custody: Trends and Issues

Probably no other aspect of the divorce generates more frustration, anger, and ill-will than the issue of child custody. Custody decisions delineate parental rights and responsibilities following a divorce with legal custody determining which parent(s) makes decisions concerning the welfare of the child. Although judges must approve the final custody arrangements, they usually endorse the proposed agreements of the parents (Buehler, 1989). In fact, the great majority of divorcing parents decide, with their lawyer's advice, which parent will have custody (Levy, 1988). In many cases, however, the court has to make a determination as to which parent receives custody because parents bitterly contest this issue. Among the unhealthy, often subconscious, reasons why parents contest custody are to hold the marriage together, reinvolve the uninterested spouse, or get revenge on a spouse. Other attempts may be to validate one parent's self-worth, justify one's position regarding divorce, and/or hold onto a child to provide emotional stability (Scheiner, Musetto, & Cordier, 1982). The changing roles of women and men and increasing social acceptance of women's careers has led to a modest increase in child custody being awarded to fathers (Weiner, 1985).

Among divorced parents with some college education, two thirds were in complete agreement about the custody decision. The most often mentioned factors influencing their decision about custody were ability to provide financially for child, and sense of responsibility by parent for child's well-being. Emotional quality of parent-child relationship, continuity in child's environment, and amount of time parent would spend with

BOX 17.1	Child Custody: A Sense of Injustice?

It wasn't that we were ashamed of our display of affection, it was just that we didn't think about it, this man-boy of mine and myself. We unabashedly hugged, kissed, cried and clung to each other in the courtroom hallway. I can remember the tough, hardened Marines surrounding us. They turned away, lest they display the same gut emotion as my son, their fellow Marine.

The unemotional ruling of the judge in district court had just ended a phase of my grown son's life. His boy, the son of my son, would forever be in the care of my daughter-in-law. There were to be only scant weeks during the year when my son could exercise "visitation rights" and hold and hug his son to his heart's content. It wasn't only the devastation of separation that made my son cry that day; it was frustration before a system of justice that he would, and has, put his life on the line to protect. Did the fact of his fatherhood mean nothing to the judge who struck his gavel and, in doing so, severed my son's physical attachment to his only son? Apparently not.

During the four days of the divorce trial, as we waited through a number of recesses and delays, we talked of my son's own growing-up years. In that darkened courtroom hallway, my son revealed to me, albeit unwittingly, how little I and my wife had prepared our only son for the reality and heartbreak of divorce. I learned for the first time how important all those Pop Warner football games were a decade or so ago. There were the nights of watching television, those darkened evenings he and I sat in the television room secretly watching "Rat Patrol." His mother wouldn't let him watch it. We both disagreed with her opinion that it was too violent a program for an 8-year-old. Jim renewed his sobs in the realization that he wouldn't be sharing similar times with his own son. His son would now be like Joe and all the other boys from broken homes. My son talked of the ship models that we built together, the fishing lures we made, and the times we just sat on the dock at the river watching the boats pass. But, nobody let him see, nobody told him in so many words, how marriage required give and take and that both parties had to work hard to make it work.

The tough Marines were still looking the other way, each of them wrapped in his own thoughts as they had sat in the courtroom after having had done their best testifying in my son's behalf. But what is it that makes a judge, an old-fashioned, country, Southern-style gentleman judge, decide that a mother, no matter what her habits or reputation, is a better parent than his father to rear a son? What is it that goes through a judge's mind when he hands down visitation rights that begin at noon on Christmas Day, half a continent away? Or 9 A.M. on Thanksgiving morning, in a far-off section of the country? And I silently wondered as I held this strong young Marine's head to my shoulder and felt his tears on my neck, how such happiness of youth could lead to such devastation in maturity.

child were also indicated (Lowery, 1985). Surprisingly, parenting skills did not show up as a criterion in the decision-making process by mothers or fathers.

Types of Custody Arrangements

The trend toward equal treatment of women and men in divorce and changes in parenting styles have led to three types of custody arrangements: sole or exclusive custody, joint custody, and split custody. **Sole custody** involves one parent caring for children on a daily basis with assumption of all decisions and responsibilities. In **split custody,** two or more children are actually divided between the parents with each parent taking sole responsibility for the child(ren) in her/his care. However, with **joint custody,** both parents share in the decisions and responsibilities for the child(ren). Joint custody arrangements can be as flexible as the parents desire, but the parents usually must live in the same geographical area. This arrangement works best when the parents are on friendly terms and enjoy open communication. Parents may share children every other week, month, or season (Carter & Leavenworth, 1985). Whatever the terms, detailed and explicit joint-custody agreements decrease the potential for conflict generated by ambiguous language or conditions (Ferreio, 1990).

Nationally, about 90% of the divorces involving children result in the mother being awarded sole custody (Peterson & Nord, 1990). A survey of four Vermont court districts found the following distribution of custody arrangements: sole custody to mother—79%, sole custody to father—11%, split custody—5%, and joint custody—5% (Wishik, 1986).

Judges, however, are becoming increasingly willing to recognize the concept of joint custody because of the greater participation in child rearing by fathers and the recognition of the crucial influence of the father on childhood socialization (Melli, 1986). Consequently, 34 states now specifically refer to joint custody arrangements in their child custody laws (Ferreio, 1990). Other states may permit joint custody, but no actual reference is contained in their custody laws. Of particular significance is the fact that only a few states permit the noncustodial parent to have access to a child's medical records by law if the custodial parent does not give permission. Grandparent visitation rights are permitted in a majority of states (Howell & Toepke, 1984).

Joint custody may involve one parent having physical custody of the child and sharing in the decision making with the noncustodial parent. Or joint custody arrangements may mean that both parents share

Though ill-prepared to play the parts of both Mom and Dad, divorced fathers with custody of their children may discover a rare relationship with their children is their reward.

an equitable, though not necessarily equal, amount of time in actual physical custody of the child. Joint custody can be court awarded or implemented by parents outside of the court. The media has promoted the impression that joint physical custody is a common occurrence and a modern solution to the problem of children and divorce. However, available data indicate that joint legal custody is granted in only a very small number of all divorce cases (Phear, Beck, Hauser, Clark, & Whitney, 1984).

The arrangement of joint custody may help to eliminate some of the stress associated with the divorce and separation process by producing fewer potential changes in the life of the child. Through this approach, the child may continue to have similar financial resources available, access to a familiar community, and constant physiological and emotional access to both mother and father (Lowery & Settle, 1985). Awarding of joint custody balances the parental power and increases the rights and responsibilities of both parents as well as increasing contact between the former spouses. It also provides an opportunity for each parent to be involved with the children, while still having time for her/his own life. However, children may feel insecure about where they belong because of living in two homes and having to adjust to different living schedules (Hayden, 1986). Complications also may develop if the parent remarries, has more money and a better home, and/or tries to have the joint custody agreement modified after remarriage (Scott, 1983). Unfortunately, this system does provide an opportunity for parents to use their children as pawns against one another (Hayden, 1986).

In a comparison of joint custody fathers and noncustodial fathers, two thirds of joint custody fathers spent at least 2 days and nights per week with their children in comparison to only one fourth of noncustodial fathers. Where parental conflict was evident, the degree of shared parental responsibilities substantially decreased although it did not affect the amount of time that a father spent with his children (Bowman & Ahrons, 1985).

Basis of Awarding Custody

Most states award custody based on the best interests of the child. Judges are given broad discretionary power to interview children, appoint guardians to represent children in court, and use domestic relations investigators and mental health professionals in arriving at their decision (Pearson, Munson, & Thoennes, 1983).

The Uniform Child Custody Jurisdiction Act has been added to all state codes except Massachusetts which has similar legislation. This law provides that the state with the "closest attachment" to the divorce case decides custody which means the state in which the divorce petition was filed and the initial custody decision made. The purpose of this legislation is to prevent controversies over child custody, keep the child's environment stable, deter child abductions, and promote interstate assistance in child custody matters (Freed & Foster, 1984).

Despite the passage of the 1980 Parental Kidnapping Act, by the mid-1980's, there were still as many as 100,000 children being kidnapped per year, with most being abducted by the noncustodial parent (Weiner, 1985). Thus, a determination of custody made in a child's home state is valid in all 50 states. About one half of the states specify that neither parent is preferred for custody and three fourths specify that the wishes of the child must be considered (Howell & Toepke, 1984).

The Family Law Section of the American Bar Association has established the following standards for awarding child custody:

1. Custody shall be awarded to either parent according to the best interests of the child.
2. Custody may be awarded to persons other than the mother or father if such an arrangement serves the best interests of the child.
3. If the child is of a sufficient age and capacity to reason or form an intelligent preference, her/his wishes regarding custody should be considered and given appropriate weight.
4. The custody award shall be subject to modification or change whenever the best interests of the child requires or justifies such action.
5. Reasonable visitation rights shall be granted to the noncustodial parent and to any other person interested in the welfare of the child at the discretion of the court. However, visitation rights must not be detrimental to the best interests of the child (Watson, 1981, pp. 474–475).

Findings suggest that judges, in the case of interracial marriages, will award custody to the parent who is of the same race as the child. The rationale is that recognizing a child's racial identity is important to the child's self-image and adjustment in the world of work (Myricks & Ferullo, 1986). Some states such as Colorado, Illinois, and Kentucky stipulate that courts shall not consider the behavior of the proposed custodial parent if said conduct does not affect their relationship with the child (Freed & Foster, 1984). For example, unless the act of cohabitation adversely affected the parent-child relationship it could not be used to withhold custody rights. Although the wishes of the child may be taken into account, the amount of weight given to the preference of the child is determined by the age of the child and her/his emotional maturity (Watson, 1981). While fathers today are gaining custody more frequently, one survey found that in about two thirds of the cases where the father gained custody, the mother did not desire custody. Further, two thirds of the custodial fathers reported that they did not initiate the divorce. The two major reasons why the fathers gained custody were by mutual agreement with former spouse and children chose the father (Greif, 1985b).

In most states, changes in custody, visitation, and support cannot be made for at least 2 years after the first decision unless the child's present environment seriously endangers her/his mental, physical, or emotional health. The major reasons for custody changes are remarriage of custodial parent, desire of child to spend more time with noncustodial parent, deterioration in health of custodial parent, or noncustodial parent upset by other parent's life-style (Weiner, 1985).

"The Best Interests of the Child" Doctrine

The "tender years" doctrine, which maintains that it is better for custody to be awarded to the mother during the early years of the child's life, was used for many years. In 1925, Judge Benjamin Cardozo in the New York Court of Appeals first suggested that a judge should do what is in the best interests of the child (Ramos, 1979). This best interests concept, that a child has rights and needs independent of her/his parents, did not have an immediate impact because most judges were biased in favor of mothers. Fathers had little chance of gaining custody unless the mother was unfit for motherhood. The best interests of the child involve a consideration of the interrelationships of the child with her/his parents, siblings, and any other person who may significantly affect the child as well as the child's adjustment to her/his home, school, and community environment (Langelier & Nurcombe, 1985). Courts also evaluate the ability of each parent to provide stability for child, and whether or not the custodial parent will encourage visitation with the noncustodial parent (Weiner, 1985).

While the "best interests of the child" doctrine has been implicitly or explicitly adopted by every American court jurisdiction, many judges still fall back on the "tender years" doctrine (Weiner, 1985). Judges often are skeptical about whether or not children, especially younger children, can make rational custody decisions. Since judges rarely get feedback about the outcomes of cases, they are unsure whether their decisions are harmful or beneficial to the child. Therefore, judges often are unwilling to take any action that is not required or that would lengthen the court proceedings (Pearson et al., 1983).

Child Support and the Noncustodial Parent

In 1987, 82% of divorced women with custody of children were awarded child-support payments at the time of the divorce with the average annual child support payment being $3,000. However, women with four or more years of college received an annual payment of $4,310 in comparison to $2,595 for those with some college. In addition, 41% of custodial mothers had health insurance included as part of their child support award (Lester, 1990).While child-support payments are nondeductible for the payee, they are not considered taxable income for the recipient (Rankin, 1986a). The parent who contributes more than one half of a child's support is entitled to claim the child as a dependent for tax purposes. Not just fathers pay child support, but at least 14% of mothers without child custody do so. Mothers who pay child support are more likely to be more involved with their children, to be living in another geographical location, and to be consulted about the children more frequently than mothers not contributing child support. In general, the amount of child support paid is about the same for both women and men (Greif, 1986).

Unpaid child support payments represent over $3 billion each year (Nuta, 1986). Of those women who were supposed to be receiving child support, only about one half actually received the full amount due, while one fourth received no payment at all (Lester, 1990). There is no correlation between father's income and the likelihood that he will pay child support. If noncustodial fathers live in the same state as their child(ren), the frequency of their visits and the amount of child support increases. However, as the amount of time since the divorce increases, both visits and payments decrease (Seltzer, Schaeffer, & Charng, 1989).

In 1984, federal legislation concerned with child support enforcement required states to tighten their collection procedures if they wanted to continue receiving federal money for Aid to Families with Dependent Children (AFDC). Among the provisions are mandatory wage withholding, authorization to intercept income tax returns, and expedited court procedures. Wages and salaries can be withheld without going to court if persons fail to meet their child-support obligations. Child-support payments now take priority over all other debt obligations except federal income tax payments. State child-support enforcement agencies can, in many instances, locate a former spouse and arrange for wage withholding (Rankin, 1986b). However, intrusion by a government agency may drive the parent who owes child support away from the family. In order to protect the children, the custodial parent also may be unwilling to help find the other parent if she/he is a criminal or child abuser (Sussman, 1983).

Summary

- The substantial rise in divorces during the 1960s and 1970s was related to the increase in labor force participation by married women and economic prosperity.
- Societal factors implicated in divorce include employment of wife outside of home, fewer moral and religious sanctions, and parental divorce. Individual factors involved in divorce are cohabitation, age at marriage, and premarital pregnancy. Postmarital variables contributing to marital dissolution include spousal behavior, inability to manage conflict, sexual incompatibility, and perceived marital quality.
- The transition stages of divorce are individual cognition, family metacognition, physical separation, family reorganization, and family redefinition.
- The fault-based grounds for divorce have been eliminated and irreconcilable differences is the new standard by which divorces are granted.
- In no-fault divorce, marital property is more equitably distributed between spouses and alimony is awarded only if the spouse is unable to provide for her/his needs.
- A major factor in successful adjustment to divorce is a supportive response from parents and from married friends especially if children are involved. Emotional problems after divorce are initially more severe for men but remain longer for women.
- Life-style is thought to play a major role in the cause of physical illness among the divorced.
- In general, male children appear more vulnerable to the stress of divorce and take longer to adjust than female children. Female adolescents from divorced families are more likely to engage in premarital sexual behavior than those from intact families.
- There is evidence that divorce is more devastating and the effects are longer lasting for children than for parents.
- The trend toward equal treatment of women and men in divorce and changes in parenting styles have led to three types of custody arrangements: sole or exclusive custody, split custody, and joint custody.
- Most states award custody based on the "best interests of the child" standard.
- Both mothers and fathers are responsible for child support with the specific amounts based on ability to pay and level of living prior to divorce, although only about one half of custodial parents receive a full payment for child support.

Questions for Critical Reflection

1. In the 1980s divorce rates largely stabilized. How will changes in the economy, religion, and politics affect the 1990 rates?
2. Therapist John Crosby cites the commonality and acceptance of divorce as a major family issue of the 1990s. He believes that perhaps one half of divorcing couples probably could make it with help; too many "bail-out" too soon. If you were composing a list of ways to avoid a premature bail-out, what would be your first three suggestions?
3. How will the reality of marital dissolution reshape and redefine the American family by the year 2000? How are the ripple effects of divorce extending beyond the family into society? Should society shape a different family or the family shape a different society?
4. The first long-term study on the effects of divorce revealed that divorce is not only a short-term trauma but also a long-term life changing event. What do you think a leading therapist meant when he said, "When there are children, there really is no such thing as divorce"?
5. The 15–year Wallenstein study of divorce found that many children from upper-middle class families are not going to college because child support stops at age 18. How will a high divorce rate and rising college costs converge to affect not only the individuals involved but society as well?

Suggested Readings

Francke, L. B. (1983). *Growing up divorced.* New York: Simon & Schuster. A description of the experiences and psychological reactions of children to divorce.

Lupepnitz, D. A. (1982). *Child custody.* Lexington, MA: Heath. A comparative study of mother custody, father custody, and joint custody.

Spanier, G. B., & Thompson, L. (1984). *Parting: The aftermath of separation and divorce.* Beverly Hills: Sage. A scholarly work describing adjustment of women and men to divorce and separation.

Vaughn, D. (1986). *Uncoupling turning points in intimate relationships.* New York: Oxford University. A sociological analysis of the separation and divorce process.

Wallerstein, J. S., & Blakeslee, S. (1990). *Second chances: Men, women, and children a decade after divorce.* New York: Ticknor and Fields. A 10-year follow-up study of 62 divorced families including representative case analysis.

Weitzman, L. J. (1985). *The divorce revolution: The unexpected social and economic consequences for women and children in America.* New York: Free Press. A major contribution to understanding the social and economic aftermath of divorce.

CHAPTER 18

Single Parents, Remarriage, and Blended Families

"But one lives, suffers and forgets, and begins again—perhaps even thinking that this time, this new time, is to be permanent."
Clark E. Moustakous, 1961

OUTLINE

Samuel Johnson's familiar quote, "remarriage is the triumph of hope over experience," attests to the fact that Americans love marriage even if they do not always love the one to whom they are married (Ganong & Coleman, 1989). The almost 1.5 million people who remarry each year represent more than 17% of all families in the United States. Of those who remarry, almost one half (48%) have children under age 18 (Glick, 1989b). In such a family, if there are children who were born before the remarriage occurred, it is called a **stepfamily** or by newer terminology, a reconstituted or blended family. Major problems exist in the midst of these changes, the greatest of which may be that there are no socially prescribed rules or norms governing life in remarriage. In fact, remarriage has been labelled an incomplete institution because of such omissions (Cherlin, 1978). Nevertheless, during the period after divorce, new roles emerge for family members, relationships are redefined, and new rules are established as family reorganization occurs (Ahrons, 1988). The aftermath of divorce involves restructuring a living routine; coping with loneliness; and often, being a single parent. Nearly one fourth of America's children currently live with just one parent, but it is estimated that as many as 60% of today's children will spend at least some time in a single-parent household before adulthood ("More Children Lead," 1988).

Since society considers marriage to be the normative life-style with social life organized on the basis of couples, those single parents who do not conform by getting married or remarried may be perceived to be challenging traditional social values. Consequently, many divorced persons feel a sense of failure which can only be relieved by subsequent remarriage. Further, for some, remarriage affords social prestige if they progress to a more attractive marriage partner just as moving up in a new job offers greater financial security (Goetting, 1982). However, there are healthier reasons to remarry.

A small number (10%) of remarriages follow the death of a spouse (Glick, 1989b). When the marriage is involuntarily ended through death of the spouse, there are different problems. The period of bereavement may last for a few weeks or months; and for some, it may extend to several years or even a lifetime (Caplan, 1981). For the majority of divorced and widowed persons, remarriage represents a viable alternative to remaining unmarried. However, even for those persons who choose to eventually marry again, many have to cope with life as a single parent prior to remarriage.

Single-Parent Families after Divorce

In our society, single-parent families are often portrayed as a root cause of many social problems such as substance abuse, juvenile delinquency, unmarried motherhood, and school failure. Obviously, any family can experience these same difficulties. Approximately 40% of women who were in their late 20s in 1984 can expect at some time in their life to establish a single-parent family involving children under age 18 (Norton & Glick, 1986).

Although single parents are most often women, as the age of the divorced parent and child(ren) increases, there is a greater likelihood that the father will maintain a single-parent family. Further, after divorce, male children are more likely than female children to live with their father. For the most part, single-parent families tend to have a higher rate of poverty, greater geographical mobility, and a lower level of education for the head of household (Hanson & Sporakowski, 1986). Family form may not have as large an impact on children as lack of adequate social support systems and the methods of socialization in single-parent families (Bilge & Kaufman, 1983).

In considering the single-parent family, the reported data oftentimes makes no distinction between single-parent families created via divorce/separation and never-married mothers and fathers. Attention in this chapter will focus on single-parent families generated through divorce, since they represent three fourths of all single-parent families (Hanson & Sporakowski, 1986). In 1988, 79% of all white children and 39% of all black children under age 18 were living with both parents. And 8% of white and black children were living with divorced mothers, while about 3% were living with divorced fathers (U.S. Bureau of the Census, 1990i). Consequently, divorced mothers and never-married mothers account for most single-parent families (Gelman et al., 1987a).

Single Mothers: Making It Alone

Marriage and family therapists have identified three potential reactions to separation and divorce which occur among women: separation distress, **euphoria** (a sense of freedom, well-being, and relief), and recovery—usually lasting 2–4 years. When motherhood is added to this equation, long-term decreases in self-esteem also are typical (Johnson, 1986). Female-headed families are more likely to experience greater levels of

Table 18.1: Time Spent Per Week by Parent on Work and Family-Related Activities by Parent*

Work and Family Related Activities	Married Woman	Single Woman	Married Man	Single Man
At Work	40	39	41	43
Home Chores	22	18	13	14
Child Care	24	19	13	8
Total Work/Family	86	76	67	65

*Numbers refer to mean hours.

From D. S. Burden, "Single Parents and the Work Setting: The Impact of Multiple Job and Homelife Responsibilities" in *Family Relations,* 35:40. Copyright © 1980 National Council on Family Relations, 3989 Central Avenue, N.E., Suite #550, Minneapolis, MN 55421. Reprinted by permission.

stress due to negative self-images and negative views about the future due to lack of social support. Single-parent mothers reported significantly more child behavior problems and personal stress when compared to two groups of married mothers: those who felt supported and those who felt distressed (Webster-Stratton, 1989).

While a lack of social support and psychological resources contribute to the stress of being single, the divorce itself is the main culprit. For instance, 3 years after divorce, the amount of stress in a single-parent home was no greater than that in a two-parent household (McLanahan, 1983). Divorced parents who maintained regular involvement in their child's life, such as sharing "good times" together and listening as the child shares details of her/his day, reported high self-esteem and life satisfaction. However, if coercive discipline techniques were used in the parent-child relationship, divorced mothers were much more likely to report self-doubts, low self-esteem, and life dissatisfaction (Buehler, 1987b). As the number of children at home increases, the divorced mother perceives family life to be less organized, more complicated, and less sharing-oriented (Amato & Partridge, 1987).

In the past, many employers were reluctant to hire divorced mothers for fear that their parenting activities would adversely affect their job performance and career advancement. However, research shows that both married and single mothers exhibit equally high levels of job satisfaction along with no significant differences in the rate of absenteeism. Further, single, employed mothers spend fewer hours per week on home chores and child care than married, working mothers (see Table 18.1). Regardless of employment status, mothers in single-parent families spend less time on household tasks than mothers in two-parent families (Sanik & Mauldin, 1986). Nevertheless, the greatest amounts of stress in handling multiple role responsibilities of job and home are still reported by single mothers (Burden, 1986). Divorced mothers are less likely than divorced fathers to share responsibility for housework with their children. They also experience more discipline problems with sons, especially younger sons (Risman & Park, 1986).

Single Fathers: Coping with Parenthood

The majority of single fathers in one study gained custody through the consent of the mother with only about one fifth obtaining custody through a legal battle. Those fathers seeking custody perceived a more positive interaction with their children than fathers who agreed to assume custody. The quality of the single father-child relationships were equal to or better than those in two-parent families (Hanson, 1986b). Although people tend to sympathize or admire single-parent fathers, most single fathers are neither extraordinary supermen because they perform all household duties nor bumbling "Mr. Moms" who need help. Most men find that being a full-time parent who is the major caregiver requires a surprising amount of time, so much so that three fourths of the fathers in one survey had altered their work schedule because of parental responsibilities (Kabatznick, 1985). Finding it difficult to balance career and family, single fathers may have to curtail job responsibilities; and consequently, they experience a decrease in income (Meredith, 1985). Nevertheless, over three fourths of the fathers believed that single parenting did not hinder the attainment of their life goals (Smith & Smith, 1981).

Parenting skills are reportedly more difficult for single fathers to learn than household chores. While many men report having problems communicating with their older children, they have an easier time rearing younger children. Although one comparison of single mothers and fathers found no significant differences in the quality of parenting, some researchers believe that children living with opposite-sex parents are more apt to be immature, dependent, anxious, and have lower self-esteem (Meredith, 1985).

Single fathers in the upper-income brackets often hire a housekeeper to assist with home duties. However, over 80% of fathers in one study reported personal responsibility for all housekeeping tasks (Risman, 1986). While most fathers learn to manage household tasks within a few months to a year after divorce, as the children grow older, they increasingly provide help (Greif, 1988). Fathers receive the most assistance from female adolescents. Some fathers limit the children's participation in housework in order to prove their competence as a parent, to make transition from two-parent to single-parent household easier, and to accommodate for lack of time due to visitation with mothers (Greif, 1985a).

Most fathers handle topics concerning sexuality and personal hygiene with their sons, but they ask female friends or teachers to explain hygiene and sexuality to their daughters (Greif, 1988).

Special Issues for Single Parents

After divorce, many single-parent families move into less expensive housing because of their reduced income. This move often means changing school districts for the children and a potential loss of frequent contact with their friends. The aftermath of divorce is much easier on children when the parent copes with the situation in a realistic manner by dealing openly and honestly with issues and does not try to be too protective (Porter & Chatelain, 1981).

Studies indicate that divorced women who are single parents have higher depression and anxiety rates than women of any other marital status category. The reason may be that single parents are more vulnerable than others to stressful life events and everyday strains while having fewer resources for coping with stress. Women may adapt to single parenthood by reuniting with the family of origin, establishing new friendships, and reestablishing a relationship with a man who can be a major provider of emotional support (McLanahan, Wedemeyer & Adelberg, 1981). Single-parent families, especially those headed by mothers, can reduce stress by setting goals, adjusting the standard of living, exploring other resources, and redefining role expectations. Those single-parent families with high stress levels may need to temporarily block out decisions about the future in order to reduce stress. Oftentimes, small changes that involve very low psychological risks can be made to reduce stress (Buehler & Hogan, 1980). For example, car pooling with neighbors and allowing older children to assume a greater role in sibling care would both provide stress reduction benefits.

Single-parent families must go through a process of role redistribution to adequately adjust. If the mother perceives the family as being incomplete without a husband/father, this role may be kept open. In fact, a father's presence in the form of fantasies after divorce may serve as a barrier toward reorganizing the family system. A mother can fulfill instrumental personal qualities such as independence, competitiveness, and self-confidence more easily if she has androgynous gender-role attitudes (Boss, 1980).

Single, divorced mothers and fathers indicate that good communication is the key to success in their roles of parent and friend to their child. The majority of single parents express no guilt about their care of their children and feel they are doing reasonably well as a single parent. And, although they would prefer to have a two-parent family, they do not regret the divorce (Defrain & Eirick, 1981). However, as might be expected, divorced mothers perceive a lack of power and control over their daily lives. Therefore, the need for social network and support systems is evident. Divorced women living with children are more likely to have contact with friends than never-marrieds or married persons with children (Alwin, Converse, & Martin, 1985). Further, contrary to popular perceptions, employed mothers in single-parent families spend more time in volunteer work than employed mothers in two-parent families (Sanik & Mauldin, 1986).

Maintaining Contact with Noncustodial Parent

A major concern about contacts with the noncustodial parent is one parent contradicting or excluding the other parent from decision making. The most basic form of parental sabotage is an emerging power struggle which exists between the custodial and noncustodial parent. Thus, many custodial parents become very stressed and anxiety ridden over periodic contact by the child with her/his noncustodial parent (Goldberg, 1988). Noncustodial mothers may be classified as warm and loving—basically the same as before the divorce; angry and hostile—feeling that children deserted or betrayed her; or ambivalent—exhibiting a combination of guilt, anger, love, and longing for the children. The type of noncustodial mother that a woman becomes is largely determined by whether the custody decision was the woman's choice, the couple's choice, or ordered by the court. The process is further complicated by the fact that most noncustodial mothers believe that society disapproves of the noncustodial mother (Fischer, 1983). Nevertheless, the vast majority of noncustodial mothers in one survey maintained contact with their children with about one half visiting their children at least biweekly (Greif, 1988). Noncustodial mothers spent substantially more time with their children in terms of visitation and telephone contacts than noncustodial fathers (see Table 18.2). Some custodial fathers fear that the children will not want to return after a weekend visit while others fear that noncustodial mothers will eventually attempt to seek custody. Another common concern of custodial fathers is that "an old-fashioned" judge will reverse the custody decision (Greif, 1988).

Table 18.2: Contact History and Types of Noncustodial Parent Contacts with Child

Noncustodial Parent Contacts	Mothers	Fathers
Contact history		
When child last saw outside parent		
1–30 days ago	64%	40%
31–365 days ago	29	18
1–4 years ago	4	7
5+ years ago	3	35
Contacts in a typical month		
Number of times child sees outside parent		
Never	42	64
1–3 days	39	16
4+ days	18	20
Number of times child sleeps over at outside parent's home		
Never	42	80
1–3 days	40	12
4+ days	18	8
Child talks with outside parent on telephone		
Never	18	55
1–3 times	39	23
4+ times	43	22

From F. F. Furstenberg, Jr., and C. W. Nord, "Parenting Apart: Patterns of Childrearing After Marital Disruption" in *Journal of Marriage and the Family,* 47:895. Copyright © 1985 National Council on Family Relations, 3989 Central Avenue, N.E., Suite #550, Minneapolis, MN 55421. Reprinted by permission.

Financial Problems

Divorce brings about a reduction of income in every income category (high, middle, and low) with the reduction being greatest in those cases where the family income has been the highest. Researchers have found that at the upper-income level, a divorce reduces the annual income to about one half of the amount during the last year of marriage. In comparison, at the lower-income level, the annual income level is reduced to about three fourths of what it was during the last year of marriage. To help with expenses, many lower-income and middle-income mothers receive financial help from relatives (Weiss, 1984).

Families that are headed by young, divorced mothers are more likely to be at the poverty level than other families. In 1985, of those mothers who had been awarded child support, 23% were below the poverty income level (U.S. Bureau of the Census, 1989b). By way of contrast, analysis of income data from members of Parents Without Partners found that the average income of single fathers was about twice that of single mothers (Kabatznick, 1985). Another study concluded that almost one third of all women experienced an income loss of more than $8,000 per year after their divorce while the annual incomes of many former husbands improved (Pett & Vaughan-Cole, 1986). The distribution of income sources for custodial mothers and fathers indicates that the primary income sources for women are self-employment, businesses, dividends, child support, AFDC payments, and food stamps whereas primary sources for single fathers are self-employment, businesses, and dividends (see Figure 18.1).

In assessing the financial aspects of child rearing after divorce, almost two thirds of children received no money from their fathers during the previous year for schooling or for other purposes (Furstenberg & Nord, 1985). Consequently, divorced mothers in comparison to widows tend to have a lower level of material well-being including size of home, amount of income, and ability to afford luxury purchases. But as the educational level of divorced mothers rises, they are more likely to report increased income, to move less frequently, and to have help available for child care (Amato & Partridge, 1987).

Sexual Involvement and the Single Parent

Single parents receive no positive reinforcement of their social and sexual worth in our society; and, in fact, they may be warned of dire effects on their children if they

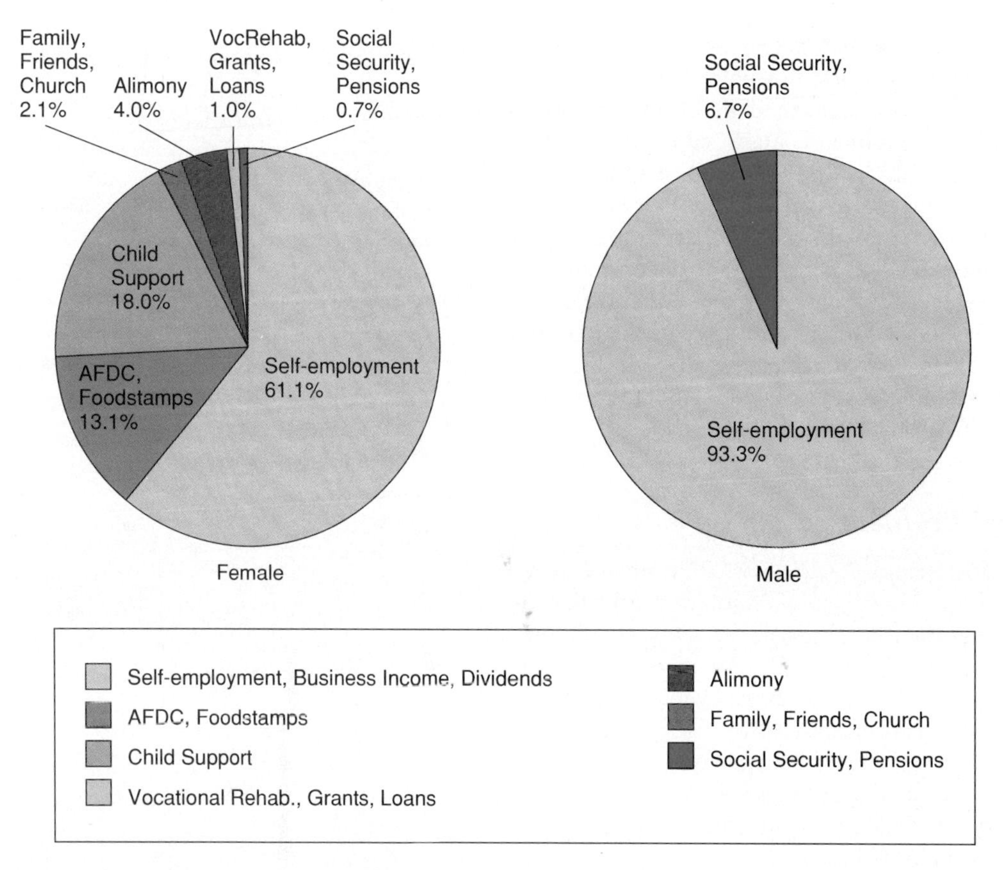

Figure 18.1 Sources of Income for Custodial Parents by Gender and by Percent

become sexually active without remarriage. Many sexually active, single mothers feel that they are violating societal standards; and thus, they have trouble communicating sexual values to their children (Jones, 1981). Somehow single parents must develop a new moral standard that satisfies their own sexual needs and can be transmitted to their children. Research suggests that both female and male adolescents from a single, divorced-mother household are more likely to initiate sexual intercourse earlier than adolescents from intact families (Newcomer & Udry, 1987). In a comparison of female and male preadolescents, ages 10–12, 25% of those from nonintact families had experienced sexual intercourse in comparison to only 11% from intact families (Flewelling & Bauman, 1990).

Initially, divorced parents may be hesitant to date because they fear that a new relationship would be similar to their previous marriage. They may even develop general anger toward the opposite sex. Many single parents also worry about their children's reactions to their dating activities or the persons whom they date. Further, the former spouse may use the custodial parent's dating as a basis to renegotiate custody or support arrangements (Weiss, 1979). Despite these concerns, 80% of divorced mothers and fathers in a Nebraska study were dating and 90% of their children were aware of the dating activities. However, about one fourth of the children had negative feelings about their parent dating (Defrain & Eirick, 1981).

Many women are reluctant to admit having sexual needs and may even suppress such feelings while men seem to accept the idea that sexual deprivation will produce sexual tension. This sexual need can increase the loneliness of the single parent and a desire for a new sex partner (Weiss, 1979). Thus, a popular image exists that divorced persons, especially noncustodial parents, adopt the "hummingbird" syndrome by moving from sex partner to sex partner in order to reaffirm their sexual attractiveness. However, the majority of mothers and fathers with child custody perceived single parenting as directly restricting their sexual lives. It reduced the amount and quality of sexual activity due to being too tired or the risk of intrusion by children. About one half of the mothers and fathers believed that if

Developing a new moral standard that satisfies the single parent's sexual needs while communicating moral values to children can be a complicated challenge.

sexual activity were noticed by the children, it would have negative effects. They do not wish to cause emotional trauma to the child, create a negative image of the parent, or serve as an inappropriate role model. Despite these concerns, 95% of these women and men accepted partner-related sexual activity as being appropriate for a single parent (Greenberg, 1979).

Remarriage after Divorce

People remarry for many of the same healthy and unhealthy reasons that they married for the first time. Men with older children may be motivated to marry a younger woman to make themselves feel young. Many other people remarry because they desire a family. Persons who may have been deeply in love with their former spouse may subconsciously choose an unsuitable second spouse and end the second marriage in divorce in order to feel that they have remained "faithful" to their former spouse (Sager et al., 1983). The transition from divorce to remarriage is a developmental process involving five stages:

1. *Survive divorce and become a whole person again*—Cope with everyday living and perhaps, establish a single-parent family.
2. *Get back into circulation*—Cope with dating, sexual encounters, and learning to love again.
3. *Initiate courtship*—Establish an intimate relationship with a new partner, which may involve a period of cohabitation.
4. *Make plans for remarriage*—Face decisions concerning wedding and living arrangements.
5. *Remarry*—Move from being a divorced, single person to a remarried person; adjust to a new partner; and, perhaps, organize a blended family system (Whiteside, 1982, pp. 59–60).

Probability of Remarriage for the Divorced

Until the 1920s, almost all remarriages involved persons who were widowed. By 1975, 84% of women and 86% of men remarrying were divorced rather than widowed (Cherlin, 1981). By mid-20th century, persons under age 45 who had divorced were products of an era in which divorce was not disapproved of as much as in the past (Glick & Lin, 1986b).

What is the probability of remarriage among divorced persons? Between 1975 and 1980, the proportion of women divorcing in their 20s and 30s increased, thus creating a substantial pool of marriageable-age women ("Women in 30s," 1986). In 1986, the remarriage rate of divorced women was 80 per 1,000 divorced women in comparison to the first marriage rate of 60 per 1,000 women. Further, the median age for remarriage of divorced women was age 33, and for divorced men was age 37 (U.S. Bureau of the Census, 1990u). The remarriage rate after divorce is highest for those under age 25 and sharply declines as the older age brackets are reached. For example, Census data indicate that 75% of divorced women, ages 20–24, had remarried (Glick & Lin, 1986b). Further, less than one half of black women eventually remarry after divorce in contrast to three fourths of white women (Bumpass, Sweet, & Martin, 1990). And, Hispanics are less likely to remarry than either blacks or whites (Coleman & Ganong, 1990).

The probability of remarriage among women increases at a regular rate with about two thirds having remarried by the fifth year after divorce. Young women who remarry after their first marriage tend to do so rather soon. The longer that women remain divorced, the smaller their chances of remarrying (Glick & Lin, 1986b). The number of years between first divorce and remarriage has increased for women and men. In 1970, the median interval between divorce and remarriage was 1.0 years for women and .9 years for men, but by 1987, it was 2.5 years—women and 2.2 years—men (National Center for Health Statistics, 1990b). However, these figures are subject to considerable misinterpretation because they only refer to those divorced persons who remarry in a given year. The median interval before remarriage for all divorced persons who ever remarry at some point in their lives is 7 years (Bumpass et al., 1990).

Having children, higher levels of education, and job dissatisfaction decrease the probability of divorced women being able to remarry (Bumpass et al., 1990; Mott & Moore, 1983). Of those women with children, it is projected that 40% of those with three or more children and 25% of those with 1–2 children will never remarry (Bumpass et al., 1990). In 1986, among women with less than a high school education, over three fourths had remarried after divorce whereas less than one half of those women with 17 or more years of education had remarried ("Women in 30s," 1986).

Those women who are not working or who are disenchanted with their jobs are more likely to remarry than other women (Mott & Moore, 1983). Although the remarriage rates are higher for those in managerial occupations than professional occupations, rates vary

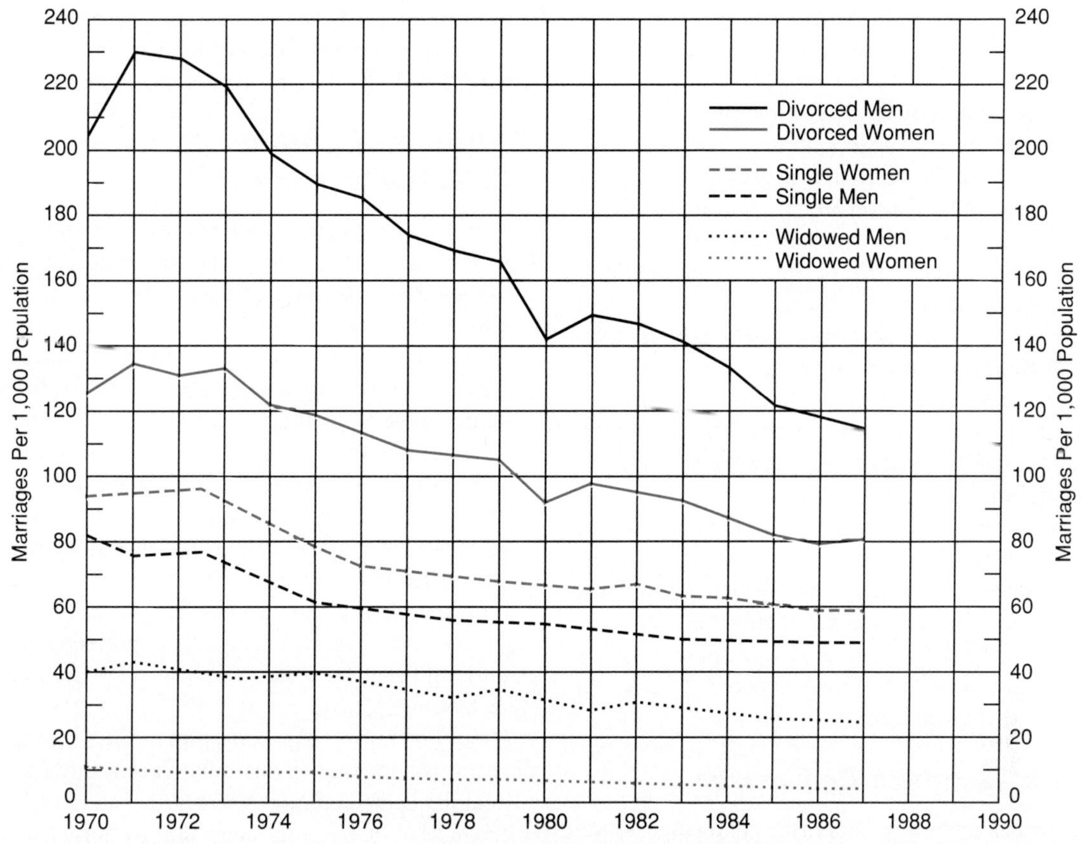

Source: National Center for Health Statistics. "Advance Report of Final Marriage Statistics, 1987" in *Monthly Vital Statistics Report,* 38(12):3, 1990b, Supplement. DHHS Publication No. PHS 90-1120, Hyattsville, MD: Public Health Service.

Figure 18.2 Marriage Rates by Previous Marital Status and Gender by Year

widely in the various professions. Teachers below the college level, physicians, and registered nurses have relatively low rates of remarriage while social scientists, social workers, writers, artists, and entertainers have higher ones. Gender-related differences are reflected in the relatively low rates of remarriage among men in the engineering and legal professions compared to higher rates evidenced by women employed in these traditionally male professions (Glick, 1989b).

Although almost 1 million (991,000) divorced women and men remarried in 1987, the remarriage rate for divorced persons has dramatically decreased over the years (see Figure 18.2). For example, it is now estimated that 70% of women who divorce in their 40s will never remarry (Bumpass et al., 1990). The divorce, remarriage, and second divorce rates evidently peaked in the late 1970s and probably will stabilize at a slightly lower rate (Norton & Moorman, 1987). Nevertheless, in 1987, 27% of the women and men who married had previously been divorced (National Center for Health Statistics, 1990b).

Costs and Profits in Remarriage: The Issue of Exchanges

Many remarriages involve children from the previous marriage of one spouse, but few marriages begin with children from both spouses. In general, the proportion of couples who have children living elsewhere from both previous marriages is small because most mothers retain custody of children after divorce. Therefore, far fewer households have stepmothers as contrasted with stepfathers (Cherlin & McCarthy, 1985).

Social exchange theory suggests that the children's effect on a remarriage depends on the level of costs associated with children, the value that the new partner holds for children, and the costs and rewards in the new relationship. The greater degree of relative costs that a person brings to a remarriage, the less power and greater dependence in the relationship. When adjustment problems are great, those marital partners with greater power and less dependence will seek alternatives sooner. Therefore, the more similar costs and rewards in the marital relationship, the greater will be the chances of success for remarriage (Giles-Sims, 1987).

Another consideration is the double standard of aging among divorced women and men. Men will have a higher rate of remarriage and a greater chance of marrying younger and never-married women (Giles-Sims, 1987). In seeking a relationship, men tend to concentrate on the weight, shape, and physical build of their partners. Further, men are much more likely than women to report that a decline in partner attractiveness affects their level of sexual desire. Thus, attractive men tend to seek someone who is younger, at least in appearance, than themselves (Margolin & White, 1987). Consequently, women who divorce in their 40s are substantially less likely to remarry because the marriageable men are interested in younger women as marriage partners. Women who have a kind, protective, and secure relationship tend to develop a more positive attitude about changes in their appearance due to aging. But divorced women are more apt to have low self-esteem and to be particularly concerned about the aging process (Berkun, 1983).

Economic Factors in Remarriage

Family income generally increases following remarriage but remains slightly lower than the level that existed 2 years prior to divorce, even if wives work more hours and at a higher rate of pay. Women with higher levels of educational attainment are more likely to marry a similarly educated husband with a high status occupation (Jacobs & Furstenberg, 1986). Financial security appears to influence the likelihood of remarriage by women. Financially-secure, divorced women do not have a lesser desire to remarry but may be more cautious about selecting a marriage partner since they feel that ample opportunities exist to meet prospective marriage partners. Researchers have found that financially-secure women are more likely to be dating and to have a regular dating partner. They also report more varied dating activities and more power to choose such activities. Less financially-secure women are often approached just for sexual reasons and feel exploited by men (Ambert, 1983).

Another economic factor relates to voluntary stepchild support. Unlike biological-child support, it can often be terminated at will. However, if the stepparent assumes in loco parentis, legal obligations for continued stepchild support can be created. If a stepparent becomes disabled or reaches retirement age, having been in loco parentis for at least 1 year, the child will continue to receive Social Security benefits when the parent and stepparent divorce (Kargman, 1983).

Attitude of Children toward Potential Stepparent

The introduction of a courtship partner into the family system may raise loyalty issues in relationships. If the new courtship partner displaces the child as a primary source of emotional support for the custodial parent, the child may resent this loss of special status. On the other hand, the child may actually feel relieved to no longer have this emotional responsibility (Rodgers & Conrad, 1986). If there is not a commonly agreed upon term or name to describe the courtship partner or her/his new social role, the nature of and legitimacy of the relationship may be called into question. In a single-parent family that has worked out sharing of household responsibilities, decision making, and emotional support roles, the children may experience difficulty in making room for a new adult in their lives (Bernstein & Collins, 1985).

The remarriage courtship process may also result in a crisis for the noncustodial parent-child system, especially if the coping resources are inadequate. The introduction of parental courtship to family life may be seen as an additional stress factor or it may be viewed as a resource. Since the self-esteem of the courting partners is likely to be enhanced, the courtship process may have a positive overall effect on the parent-child relationship. A new interpersonal relationship may bring additional financial assistance to the family. However, the courtship process can also cause stress over whether or not remarriage will have future adverse effects on children (Rodgers & Conrad, 1986).

Selecting Another Marriage Partner

Persons seeking to remarry tend to be more suspicious of romantic love, cautious in selecting their marriage mate, and willing to enter into a second marriage with less lofty expectations (Furstenberg & Spanier, 1984b). Available research suggests that the decision of women to remarry comes from their desire for companionship even though they are able to function alone. In general, women place greater emphasis on companionship in their second marriage than first marriage. Men, however, tend to emphasize companionship in both first and second marriages and consider sharing an important quality of companionship (Smith, Goslen, & Byrd, 1987).

Assessment of Attitudes about Previous Marriage

Attitudes or feelings from the past can adversely affect remarriage, especially if too little time has been spent in the adjustment and mourning process. An important facet of coping with the anger, depression, and guilt associated with divorce is to reevaluate the prior marriage to avoid quickly entering into another relationship that possesses the same potentialities for unhappiness (Beatrice, 1979). Therefore, bitterness and other adverse reactions related to the partner who initiated the divorce should be worked out prior to remarriage. Many times, the legal ties that exist between the noncustodial parent and the child may further serve to create emotional attachments to the past. Such ties may intensify the need to deal with and resolve the hostilities that were generated during the divorce process (Bernstein & Collins, 1985).

Even though the first marriage may have been of poor quality, it is likely that some bonding occurred between the partners. Consequently, these bonding emotions need to be loosened so that the person can move on to a new relationship. In addition, any unpleasant emotional experiences from other love relationships between the time of divorce and remarriage also need to be processed and any remaining feelings of attachment resolved (Chilman, 1983). The success of remarriage will be, to a large degree, determined by the factors that lead to the divorce and the completeness of the mourning process associated with marital dissolution. Many couples believe they are well-prepared for remarriage even though they have not worked through the unresolved problem areas from their first marriage (Rolfe, 1985).

Differences the Second Time Around

Researchers have observed a significant reduction in the average length of courtship between first and second marriages—from 5 months–1 year. Women with higher socioeconomic status who were college-educated tended to engage in courtship activity longer before their second marriage than less-educated women of lower socioeconomic status. Further, women and men under age 30 tended to date longer before their second marriage than persons over age 30. However, there were no significant differences in the average length of courtship before second marriage between women and men (O'Flaherty & Eells, 1988).

Women are more likely to be upwardly mobile in second marriages because after divorce they often attain a higher educational level and thus are able to obtain a better job (Jacobs & Furstenberg, 1986). For a remarriage partner, men tend to select a woman who is younger than themselves and who has never been remarried (Giles-Sims, 1987). Therefore, most remarriages tend to be less homogamous than first marriages in terms of age, religious background, religiosity, and educational level (Price-Bonham & Balswick, 1980). Both women and men who first married someone from their own ethnic group are likely to remarry within the same group while those who married outside are also likely to do so again (Jedlicka, 1987). The longer that one waits to remarry, the less their marital relationship will be homogamous.

Persons seeking to remarry hope to avoid the mistakes made in their previous marital relationship; but they often have fears that the same guilt, hurt, and stress could happen again (McGoldrick & Carter, 1980). If the second spouse is similar to the first spouse, the problems of the first marriage are likely to reoccur (Jedlicka, 1987). This probability relates to the fact that the courtship partners are attempting to develop a love relationship in a time of considerable confusion, guilt, stress, and mixed feelings about the previous marriage.

Preparation for Remarriage

Remarriages are faced with complexities beyond the typical stress of first marriage. Not only must couples deal with the normative issues such as sex, compatibility, finances, and in-laws but also with the unique issues of blending families. A review of seven studies conducted during the 1980s revealed several areas of frequent conflict in blending families: disagreement over stepchildren, relationship with former spouses, lack of social rules for stepfamily roles, merging two different life-styles, legal issues, and blurred boundaries or lack of clear distinction of self and others (Ganong and Coleman, 1989). Most of the problems encountered in blended families are not due to individual psychopathology but to potentially preventable situations (Stanton, 1986). Responding to such apparent risks of blending families, professionals have emphasized the need for educational intervention designed to prevent problems before they occur (Miller, 1985).

How do people actually prepare for remarriage? Although little factual information is known about this issue, one study found that the primary way that individuals prepared for remarriage was by living together (59%) whereas counseling was received by 38% of women and 25% of men (Ganong & Coleman, 1989).

Table 18.3: Source and Value of Advice Sought Regarding Remarriage

	Women		Men	
Source of Advice	Sought Advice	Rated Helpful	Sought Advice	Rated Helpful
Written material	47%	80%	34%	67%
Friends	25	81	20	57
Counseling	17	63	16	53
Educational/support groups	12	67	4	30

From L. H. Ganong and M. Coleman, "Preparing for Remarriage: Anticipating the Issues, Seeking Solutions" in *Family Relations*, 38:30. Copyright © 1989 National Council on Family Relations, 3989 Central Avenue, N.E., Suite #550, Minneapolis, MN 55421. Reprinted by permission.

When asked about seeking advice, women were more likely to seek advice and evaluate the source as helpful (see Table 18.3). Couples indicated the two most often discussed issues prior to remarriage were stepchildren and finances. Surprisingly, there was little reported discussion of any of the other common problems encountered in blended families (Ganong & Coleman, 1989). In fact, in one study, one third of the couples indicated being so swept up in the courtship process and family involvement that neither conscious thoughts about nor preparation for family life after remarriage had occurred. And, in 41% of the cases, at least one partner entered the marriage believing that the close bonding that exists in nuclear families would develop. Thus, it should come as no surprise that three fourths of these couples later reported disappointment over the degree of bonding in their blended family (Pill, 1990).

Prenuptial Contracts in Remarriages

Premarital agreements are emerging as a common practice in second marriages to provide each person with a way of controlling her/his assets especially in the event of death or another divorce. However, too much emphasis on protecting one's own independence and not sharing assets can damage a loving relationship (Bernstein & Collins, 1985). Prenuptial contracts were considered in chapter 7, "Mate Selection or Singlehood: Options in the 1990s." However, they deserve further consideration in view of the special issues and responsibilities of a new marriage partner to help stepchildren and to dispose of assets at the death of the spouse (Weitzman, 1981).

People entering remarriages have different concerns from those entering a first marriage. Most persons still have responsibilities from their first marriage such as child support and/or alimony. Further, they are apt to be older, possess more assets, and be more concerned with how assets will be handled after their death. If both wife and husband should remarry, they will have to reallocate their support responsibilities for their common children and may have to share responsibilities for stepchildren. Therefore, persons entering a second marriage should consider obligations to both existing and prospective children of their former and prospective spouses (Weitzman, 1981). Children often worry about what will happen to their inheritance because these assets may represent all that is left of their former family life. Thus, prenuptial contracts can require both parties to set aside assets for their biological children (Carter & Leavenworth, 1985). Because of these special concerns, prenuptial contracts for remarriages tend to have unique features:

1. Establishment of trusts to protect surviving spouse.
2. Use of homestead or other assets for life of spouse in second marriage, or for a given period following death or divorce with deceased spouse's estate retaining ownership.
3. Funds for education of spouse or stepchildren.
4. Rights of reimbursement if joint property is used to improve separate property of one spouse or if separate property is used to increase value of separate property of other spouse in a community property state (Bernstein & Collins, 1985, p. 13C).

Marital Satisfaction and Stability in Remarriage

Remarriages are at a higher risk of dissolution than first marriages, especially if children from a prior relationship are in the home (Ishii-Kuntz, 1985; White & Booth, 1985). It is estimated that about 50% of remarriages end in divorce (Coleman & Ganong, 1990). This estimate coincides with the forecast in the early

1980s by one authority that 50% of women and 60% of men who had remarried would eventually experience another divorce (Glick, 1984b). Second marriages for whites are more stable than first marriages for blacks. Black women in second marriages, compared to first marriages, are less educated, less likely to be Roman Catholic, and have more liberal attitudes toward divorce (Teachman, 1986).

Couples in second marriages may be somewhat more predisposed to leave an unhappy marital relationship than those in first marriages because they have a somewhat different outlook on marital stability and are less inclined to remain in an unhappy marriage (Furstenberg & Spanier, 1984b). Among those persons who remarry, the quality of their second marriage appears to be positively related to their general sense of well-being. Remarried persons seem to have a greater sense of well-being than recently divorced persons because they have had a longer time to recover from their divorce. In addition, persons who remarry are more likely to have better psychological health than those who are still divorced (Spanier & Furstenberg, 1982).

The available evidence on marital satisfaction in remarriage is somewhat contradictory. An early study of remarried couples found that 60% of women and 70% of men reported being very happy in their remarriage (Glenn & Weaver, 1977). However, when remarried women and men were asked to compare their level of happiness in remarriage with their first marriage, only 50% of women and 40% of men reported currently being very happy (Weingarten, 1980). More recently, however, no significant differences were identified with regard to marital satisfaction between persons in first marriages and those in remarriages. Further, persons entering a remarriage were more likely to have cohabited than persons entering a first marriage. However, cohabitation was not found to be associated with lower marital satisfaction of remarrieds (DeMaris, 1984). Spouses in remarriages indicate their second marriages are different and improved from their first marriage because they try to communicate differently, make alterations in the way they make decisions, and implement modifications in division of household labor. However, since remarriage partners are aware of the possibility of failure, they may hedge their commitment to marriage more than those married for the first time (Furstenberg & Spanier, 1984a).

A review of 34 studies of marital satisfaction and remarriage was conducted during the 1970s and 1980s. Intriguing conclusions were drawn regarding gender differences and children:

1. No differences in degree of marital satisfaction existed between stepmothers and stepfathers.
2. No differences in marital satisfaction were found between remarried couples with or without stepchildren at home.
3. Remarried men, in general, were more satisfied with their marriage than remarried women.
4. No differences in marital happiness existed in remarriages regardless of whether one or both marriage partners was a stepparent.
5. Persons in first marriages reported greater marital satisfaction than those in remarriages, although the differences were not substantial (Vemer, Coleman, Ganong, & Cooper, 1989, pp. 721–723).

Factors Contributing to Marital Instability among the Remarried

Divorce is more prevalent in remarriages even though the marriage partners are usually older, more mature, and often in a better financial position than those persons marrying for the first time. Earlier studies suggest several explanations as to why remarried couples seem to have less unity than first-marriage couples including possible personality disorders in one or both marriage partners. However, a survey of family counselors and remarried couples concluded that difficulties in remarriage stem from a lack of institutionalized guidelines for dealing with many everyday problems among remarried persons. If neither spouse has children from a previous marriage, the lack of institutionalized support is less serious than if the remarriage involves children (Cherlin, 1978). Evidence suggests that the presence of children may have a negative effect on marital quality, especially for stepfathers who devote little time to parenting. The time and energy demands required for preschool children and the warming up of adolescents to stepfathers, which occurs more slowly, are cited as problems (Kurdek, 1990). Several stress factors have been associated with remarriage:

1. Leadership role-sharing by biological parent and stepparent.
2. Distribution of resources such as space, time, and affection.
3. Ambiguous nature of the stepparent role.
4. Possible sexual tension between stepsiblings.
5. Existence of conflicting life-cycle stages due to age differences in spouses.

6. Existence of biological and stepparents of the same sex (Crosbie-Burnett, 1987, pp. 3–4).

Thus, stability of remarriage may be a product of societal support and interpersonal interaction between wife and husband. Since spouses in second marriages tend to be more independent in their decision making, remarried couples are less likely to be dependent upon each other than couples in first marriages. In addition, the possibility exists that remarried persons may be less committed to their marriage than persons in first marriages (Ishii-Kuntz, 1985).

Several variables contribute to a decline in marital satisfaction according to data on parent and spouse relations during the first years after remarriage. Those variables found to be most significant were partner's evaluation of the division of household labor, relationship of each partner to father's child, and perceptions of former wife. These couples usually identified the children's mother as the major source of stress in their remarriage (Guisinger, Cowan, Schuldberg, 1989).

Additional insights can be gained by examining differences between happily and unhappily remarried couples regarding children, financial considerations, household tasks, outsiders, and spousal interpersonal relationship. When happy and unhappy remarried couples were compared, happily remarried spouses were more likely to clearly perceive their agreement on various issues. All of the happily married group and none of those in the unhappy group perceived agreement on children, finances, household tasks, friends, in-laws, time spent with spouse, and sex life (Pasley, Ihinger-Tallman, & Coleman, 1984). Relationship quality for both wives and husbands in stepfather families has been found to be related to satisfaction with social support and degree of expressiveness. However, the quality of the relationship was only reported as high by couples in which it was a second marriage for both partners (Kurdek, 1989a).

Relationships between Former Spouses after Remarriage

The remarriage of a former spouse often activates old conflicts for the spouse who is not remarrying. If the noncustodial male parent is remarrying, financial issues and feelings of jealousy often emerge. Conflict between former spouses may limit access to the children by the noncustodial parent. Such action could damage the noncustodial parent-child relationship since the child may have resentment or anger toward the noncustodial parent for remarrying. With remarriage, social distance is created between parent and child which will likely end any fantasies of parental reconciliation. The spouse responsible for ending the previous marital relationship, however, may actually feel a sense of relief when her/his former spouse remarries. Further, if both former spouses remarry, even greater social distance will be generated between them (Rodgers & Conrad, 1986). Nevertheless, remarriage contributes to feelings of rejection by former spouse, competition for affection of children, and a further fear of losing the children. In addition, living close to a former spouse after remarriage may interfere with establishment of new family roles. Friends and in-laws from a previous marriage may serve as disruptive influences in the relationship with a former spouse (Nelson & Nelson, 1982). Many times, the former spouse is referred to despairingly in a mistaken attempt to demonstrate loyalty to the new spouse and to enhance the current relationship (Furstenberg & Spanier, 1984a).

Former spouses almost always have a very low level of involvement with either marital partner in remarriage especially if there are no children from the first marriage. If children are present, involvement is usually confined to matters pertaining to child rearing. Nevertheless, the relations with the former spouse usually produce some emotions that are carried forth into the second marriage (Furstenberg & Spanier, 1984a). The likelihood of contact with a former spouse after remarriage depends upon whether or not contact with former in-laws is maintained. However, only custodial parents who have developed a smoothly functioning coparental relationship with the former spouse are likely to maintain friendly relationships with the former in-laws. Child-free, divorced persons were much less likely to report friendly relationships with former in-laws after remarriage. About 1 in 10 persons reported frequent telephone conversations with their former in-laws whom they considered to be a source of help (Ambert, 1988).

Remarriage after Widowhood

Although an increasing number of widowed persons are remarrying, remarriage during widowhood is among the least researched topics in family science. Nevertheless, age at widowhood is known to be a significant factor in remarriage. Widowhood at age 65 is known to precipitate quite different problems than those widowed at age 35 or 40 (Neugarten & Neugarten, 1986).

BOX 18.1	Myths about Remarriage and Blended Families

1. **Myth:** Things must work out—this time, it's "really" love. **Fact:** Research indicates that many remarriages end in divorce.
2. **Myth:** Stepparent should always consider everybody else first—before self and any children. **Fact:** Biological parent and children are often considered first in stepmother families, thus placing stepparent in precarious situation.
3. **Myth:** Keep criticism to oneself and focus on positive conditions/circumstances. **Fact:** Children may be unnaturally "good" in presence of stepparent and hide real feelings.
4. **Myth:** If things are not going well, focus on what went wrong in past and make sure it does not happen again. **Fact:** Reason(s) why first marriage ended in divorce often incorrectly assessed.
5. **Myth:** "What is mine is mine, what is yours is yours." **Fact:** Approach lacks an "our" orientation and is much less satisfactory if financial contributions to remarriage are blatantly unequal.
6. **Myth:** "If you love me, you will love my children." **Fact:** Requires extraordinary effort to love a stepchild who blatantly ignores the stepparent's existence or is constantly rude.

Reprinted from M. Coleman and L. H. Ganong, "Remarriage Myths: Implications for the Helping Professions" in *Journal of Counseling and Development*, 64:117–118, 1985.

Several barriers to remarriage among older persons include existence of children, societal norms, and misunderstanding of sexuality (Streib & Beck, 1980). Education and finances operate differently in shaping probabilities for women and men. Greater financial and educational resources act as a barrier for remarriage opportunities for women but as an enhancer of options for men (Horn & Meer, 1987).

Dating and Courtship during Widowhood

Researchers found that among widowers, about two thirds reported loneliness as their biggest problem. Their strategies for coping with loneliness included establishing relationships with peers, participating in organizations, and dating (Clark, Siviski, & Weiner, 1986). Available survey data from a Midwest singles club suggest that older women and men dating seemed to tolerate the shifting norms for dating roles but still exhibited some traditional behavior. Further, while there was a low emphasis on romance in dating relationships among older persons, women placed more value on symbolic romanticism. Their dating activities appeared more varied than for college students including trips, camping, dances, card parties, and participation in voluntary social organizations. Among sexually active women and men, sexuality seems to be a vital part of their dating relationships. One study found that sexual intercourse was expected by both women and men. And, if it did not occur by the fourth or fifth date, a new dating partner was usually sought. However, long-term commitment and monogamy were the social norms in dating (Bulcroft & Bulcroft, 1985). Other evidence of the monogamous nature of dating during widowhood relates to the number of close, opposite-sex relationships. Among widows, two thirds had limited themselves to one dating partner with only 1 in 10 women having had more than two serious dating relationships (Lopata, 1979).

Among single women and men age 60 and older, the majority of whom were widowed, the major reason given for dating was the hope of finding a new marriage partner. Yet, research suggests that few persons marry their dating partners because it is difficult to meet their romantic ideal and to mesh extended family ties. Companionship is a major motive for dating partly due to the increased leisure time and loneliness of older persons. For women in this age group, dating also provides a source of social prestige since few men are available. On the other hand, dating for men furnishes an opportunity for self-disclosure whereas women can usually share their feelings with female friends (Bulcroft & O'Connor, 1986). Consequently, dating contributes to life satisfaction among older persons in several ways:

1. Dating partner takes on role of friend by sharing interests and recreational activities to protect each other from loneliness.
2. Dating partner acts as confidant, especially for women.
3. Dating partner becomes a lover, although role of lover is not valued as highly as role of companion.
4. Caregiver role is not emphasized in such areas as finance, health, or home chores (Bulcroft & O'Connor, 1986, pp. 399–401).

"Sweet sixteen" courting skills may be a distant memory during widowhood. For some, maturity enhances romance the second time around.

Therefore, dating becomes an end in itself because, despite the desire on the part of some to marry, many older persons do not wish to remarry (Bulcroft & O'Conner-Roden, 1986).

Probability and Reasons for Remarriage of the Widowed

The United States has one of the highest rates for remarriage of persons over age 60 in the Western world. However, widows are 14 times less likely to remarry than divorced women whereas widowers are 4 times less likely to remarry than divorced men (National Center for Health Statistics, 1990b). Among older people, remarriage is a male prerogative. For example, after age 65, men are eight times more likely to marry than women (Horn & Meer, 1987). Much higher percentages of women are found in the widowed category, but the absolute numbers of older married men greatly exceed those of widowers. The reasons are that women live longer on the average than men and the nearly universal tendency of men at every age to marry women younger than themselves (Torrey, Kinsella, & Taeuber, 1987). The remarriage rates for the previously widowed in 1987 were 10.9 per 1,000 widows for widows ages 45–64, and 1.8 per 1,000 for those age 65 and over. By comparison, for widowers, the remarriage rates were 53.9 per 1,000 widowers for those ages 45–64 and 15.4 per 1,000 for those age 65 and over. Or viewing this issue another way, only 25% of widows who remarried were age 65 and over in contrast to 43% of widowers (National Center for Health Statistics, 1990b).

In general, widowed blacks have a lower probability of remarriage than whites. Widows have the highest probability for remarriage if they are under age 45. Beyond this age, the probability of a widow remarrying decreases sharply and is considerably less than that of her male counterparts (National Center for Health Statistics, 1990b). The scarcity of older single men means that many older women who wish to marry may be unable to find partners (see Figure 18.3). Consequently, few widows and widowers remarry (Coleman & Ganong, 1990).

Loneliness is a major factor in the decision to remarry. Most widows and widowers desire to return to a social role that has been rewarding for many years, namely that of a marriage partner. When men lose their main source of emotional support, they find it more difficult than women to reveal their feelings to another person (Smith & Zick, 1986). Data from couples in which one partner was age 75 or older indicated that elderly wives and husbands shared household responsibilities. However, the majority of husbands were primarily responsible for "masculine" tasks while their wives were responsible for most "feminine" tasks (Brubaker, 1985b). Thus, it appears that widowers who remain less prepared to do housework and widows who have difficulties managing instrumental tasks may seek to replace a complementary partner.

The "pooling" of financial resources may also serve as a motivating factor for remarriage of widows. Many women live on about one half of their available income prior to being widowed. In fact, about one third of the widows in one study received income from a family member; and only one third reported income from savings, dividends, stock, and bonds (Lopata & Brehm, 1986). In contrast, the annual income of the widower is usually higher than the widow (Hooyman & Kiyak, 1991). In 1986, the median annual income for widows was $6,993 in comparison to $9,258 for widowers (U.S. Senate Special Committee on Aging, 1988).

Some widowed persons prefer to remain single. There are at least three reasons for choosing not to remarry:

1. *Desire to retain independence*—For women, this period of their life may be the first time on their own.
2. *Absence of motive*—No motivation exists to begin a new life or start a family.
3. *Possibility of deteriorating health*—A person would not want to become a caregiver for an ill spouse (Bulcroft & O'Conner-Roden, 1986, pp. 68–69).

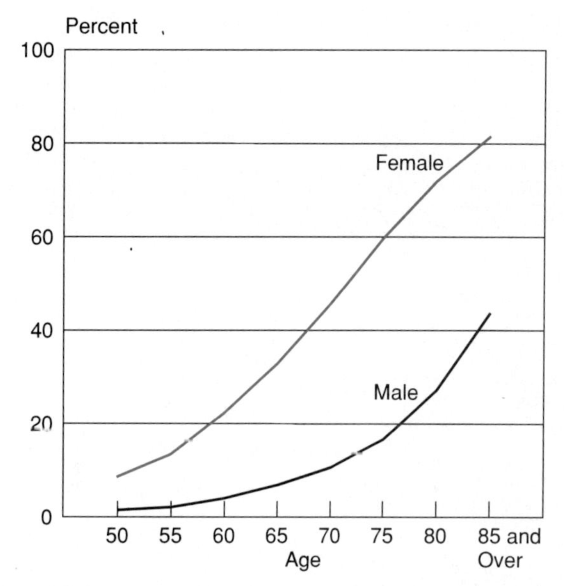

Source: B. B. Torrey, et al., *An Aging World.* International Population Reports Series P-95, No. 78, p. 27, 1987. Washington, DC: U.S. Government Printing Office.

Figure 18.3 Widowhood by Age and Gender by Percent

Reactions of Children to Remarriage of Widowed Parent

Although most persons choose to live alone after the loss of a spouse, they are not isolated from their children. Widows tend to have closer relationships with their children and are more likely to live closer to their children than widowers (Horn & Meer, 1987). In a study of remarried widowed parents, over one half received only positive reactions from their children concerning remarriage. The typical reaction was that the children were happy because their parent was happy about being remarried (Vinick, 1978). Evidence suggests that widowed persons need the support of their children when they remarry to help them overcome the various social pressures and attitudes about remarriage. Generally, children who do oppose their parent's remarriage often voice their complaints in words similar to those used by parents to complain about their own children's choice of marriage mates (Berger, 1988).

Children's concerns that an older parent may fail to protect their estate oftentimes creates opposition to the parent's plans for remarriage. However, these concerns can be put to rest by development of a prenuptial contract. Such a legal agreement that would protect

the interests of both spouses since chances are that both persons will bring assets to the marriage (Weitzman, 1981).

Marital Satisfaction among the Older Remarrieds

Remarriage in late adulthood tends to be happier than remarriage at earlier ages. This pattern may be because both partners are usually widowed, not divorced. Their lifetime experience of a love relationship that worked is a better base for a new relationship than a failed marriage. Also, the fact that most of the time any children are grown and no longer in the household may serve to ease the stress of a new family system (Campbell, 1981). In a comparison of remarried and unmarried widowed persons, the remarrieds indicated less stress, more self-esteem, more life satisfaction, better feelings about friendships, and more positive resolution of grief (Burks, Lund, Gregg, & Bluhm, 1988). The identified factors that predict marital success among remarried widowed persons include partners being well-acquainted before marriage, approval of friends and relatives especially children, living in a home that did not belong to either partner before remarriage, and having an adequate income (Streib & Beck, 1980). Remarriage for most widowed persons is better than the alternatives. It is less expensive and less lonely while providing, for many, needed sexual affirmation (Berger, 1988).

Blended Families: The Trend of the 90s

During the 1970s and 1980s, family scientists used several different terms to refer to the formation of new families through remarriage after divorce and widowhood including blended families, reconstituted families, remarried families, and stepfamilies (Sadler, 1983). Since the ultimate goal is to establish a new cohesive family unit through remarriage and since society delineates various types of kin relationships after remarriage, the terms blended family and stepfamily seem especially appropriate.

Despite the widespread interest in blended families, existing research has been described as limited in quantity, characterized by inconsistent findings, and flawed with serious methodological problems (Esses & Campbell, 1984). Popular magazine articles published on stepparenting during the 1970s and 1980s focused on needs of stepchildren and ambiguity of the stepparent role with little attention being given to financial and legal issues. Of the articles examined, over one half were based on personal accounts that served to support stepparents but did little to educate them about stepparenting issues and techniques (Lagoni & Cook, 1985). Most popular magazine articles about stepfamilies either had an overly optimistic or a neutral tone with about two thirds combining personal and professional experience with advice. The most frequently mentioned problem areas during the 1970s were stepparent or parent-child relations followed by marital relations, prior marriage, and material resources (Pasley & Ihinger-Tallman, 1985).

While issues of blended families and stepparenting are very important, it should be observed that only about 5–8% of children under 18 are living with a biological parent and a stepparent at any point in time (Coleman & Ganong, 1990; U.S. Bureau of the Census, 1990h). In 1990, researchers estimated that 69% of all children were living with parents in comparison to 85% in 1970 (Coleman & Ganong, 1990). Nevertheless, it was estimated that about one third of the children born during the 1980s could expect to live with one biological parent and a stepparent for at least 1 year before reaching age 18 (Glick, 1989b).

Blended Families Differ from First Marriage Families

In spite of claims to the contrary, blended families do differ from first marriage families. It is erroneous to conclude that a blended family can function like a nuclear, biological family or that stepparents and stepchildren will love each other in a similar fashion as biological kin (Dolan & Lown, 1985). For the most part, **complex stepparent** (both spouses with children from prior marriage) families have significantly lower rates of positive nonverbal behaviors during marital discussions. Further, stepfamilies with a more complex structure exhibit lower marital quality than **simple stepparent** (only one spouse with children from prior marriage) families (Clingempeel & Eulalee, 1985).

Family members need to understand that attaining the previous boundaries of the nuclear family is usually not possible. This is due to the fact that the relationship between former marital partners as well as the relationship with the children creates boundary ambiguity (Clingempeel & Eulalee, 1985). Family boundaries is a concept derived from Family Systems Theory, wherein boundaries refer to system rules regarding participating members. **Boundary ambiguity** is the uncertainty of family members concerning their perceptions of who is and who is not a family member and who is performing what roles and tasks (Pasley & Ihinger-Tallman, 1989). This lack of clarity concerning family membership has been suggested to increase stress in overall family functioning (Boss, 1987). In general, more boundary ambiguity has been found in stepmother families, with children in these families said to be at greater risk for behavioral problems (Pasley & Ihinger-Tallman, 1989; Brand & Clingempeel, 1987).

To place the discussion of blended families in proper perspective, it is important to call attention to six structural differences that have been identified as distinguishing a blended family from a first marriage:

1. Most members of blended families have lost an important primary relationship with a parent or spouse which may generate anger and hostility.
2. One biological/adoptive parent typically lives outside the current household generating feelings of jealousy between stepparent and noncustodial parent.
3. The close bond between custodial parent and her/his children may impede the establishment of a successful marital relationship.
4. Children who live in blended families as a member of two households may react to altered family patterns with unpredictable behavior.
5. Children in blended families typically have at least one extra pair of grandparents who may play conflicting roles.
6. One parent is not legally related to the children and thus is not responsible for their financial support (Visher & Visher, 1979, pp. 29–33).

Blended Families: The Perspective of Children

A by-product of stepparent/stepchild relationships is a **division of loyalties** (feelings of disloyalty that children have for one parent because of positive feelings for the other parent) experienced by children between the biological/adoptive parent and the stepparent. Divided loyalty is often generated by one parent talking negatively about the other parent. Consequently, the child may feel that she/he has to choose between the two parents which can lead to anxiety and negative feelings. The same kind of divided loyalties also may be experienced with regard to grandparents and toward biological/stepsibling relationships (Sager et al., 1983). Of adolescents living in stepfamilies, three fourths reported feelings of divided loyalty that were very stressful. In fact, over one half of the adolescents liked their stepparent more than their biological parent of the same sex (Lutz, 1983). In some stepfamilies, problems arise over loyalty issues as well as the distribution of resources (Ihinger-Tallman & Pasley, 1987).

Most adolescents adjust to living with a new set of rules from the stepparent and accept her/his discipline. Only about one third of the adolescents experienced stress related to which household they should visit for holidays and special occasions. Further, most adolescents indicated that it was not especially stressful to explain about living in a stepfamily, to have a different family name than other family members, or to have others find out about a stepparent. The perceived level of stress was much higher if the stepfamily was formed after the death of a biological parent rather than through divorce (Lutz, 1983).

If a parent in a blended family is perceived to favor specific children, it is typically the stepparent. According to one survey, of those adolescents who felt rejected, it was usually by both parents. And interestingly, stepdaughters desired to emulate stepmothers more often than daughters tried to emulate their biological mothers who had remarried. In addition, children living in stepmother households were more apt to report being closer to their fathers than children living in stepfather households (Ganong & Coleman, 1987).

Establishing Blended Family Relationships

Following a single-parent and two-parent family, the third most common family form in which children live is the stepfamily. This living arrangement, which represents a challenge for children and adults, may depend upon a number of factors. What happened in the previous marriages is of great significance. Also, the ages of the children will affect outcomes with stepfamilies having adolescents being much different than those families with preadolescents. While the new stepparent is interested in establishing closeness and building a positive relationship, the adolescent is interested in independence. To ensure proper emotional development, the adolescent in the stepfamily needs to feel supported and close to the different family members. In general, more problems are found in stepparent-stepdaughter relationships than in stepparent-stepson relationships. Female adolescents typically have more difficulty than male adolescents relating to stepfathers, since the remarriage is often considered a threat to the relationship with her noncustodial father (Clingempeel, Brand, & Ievoli, 1984).

Many fathers feel guilty about leaving children from a previous marriage to become a stepfather to new children. These guilt feelings oftentimes make it very difficult for the stepfather to deal with the rivalry for attention between his stepchildren and new wife. While children in first marriage families usually try to help keep their parents together, blended family relationships frequently become more fragmented because stepchildren may consciously or unconsciously want to separate the biological and stepparent in hopes of reuniting their biological parents (Nelson & Nelson, 1982). Stepparent relationships may be more central to family happiness in blended families than the marital relationship itself. The establishment of mutually suitable relationships between the stepfather and stepchildren is a more basic issue for stepfamilies than discipline or nurturance between blended family members. The relationship between stepfathers and stepchildren seems to have the most positive or the most negative effects on family happiness. In fact, nurturance may not even be a necessary part of the stepparent relationship (Crosbie-Burnett, 1984).

Blended families do not differ significantly from first-marriage families in terms of the ideals desired for their families. However, family members in blended families usually describe their families as being less cohesive and adaptable than intact families (Pink & Wampler, 1985). In comparison to intact families, blended family members do tend to display lower levels of functioning on most dimensions including cohesion, flexibility and openness, interaction skills such as problem-solving communication, and affective responsiveness. Women are generally more likely than men to characterize their blended family as more communicative, more affective, more responsive, and better at problem solving (Peek, Bell, Waldren, & Sorell, 1988).

In most cases, with diligent work, effort, and time, family happiness can occur in blended families (Scales, 1985). There are several key elements that appear to undergird strong blended families:

1. Accepting the realities of a blended family and the development of positive, realistic expectations.
2. Realizing that time is needed for trust and love to develop and for healing of wounds left by dissolution of the former marriage.
3. Focusing on positives when difficulties occur and developing a sense of responsibility for own problems.

Table 18.4: Blended Family Formation

Step	Prerequisite Attitude	Developmental Issue
1. Entering new relationship	Recovery from loss of first marriage	Recommitment to marriage and to forming family with readiness to deal with complexity and ambiguity
2. Conceptualizing and planning new marriage and family	Accepting one's own fears and those of new spouse and children about remarriage and forming stepfamily; and accepting need for time and patience for adjustment to: multiple new roles; boundaries: space, time, membership, and authority; and affective issues: guilt, loyalty conflicts, desire for mutuality, and unresolvable past hurts	Work on openness in new relationship; plan for maintenance of cooperative co-parental relationships with ex-spouses; plan to help children deal with fears, loyalty conflicts, and membership in two systems; realignment of relationships with extended family to include new spouse and children; and plan maintenance of connections for children with extended family of ex-spouse(s)
3. Remarriage and reconstitution of family	Final resolution of attachment to previous spouse and ideal of intact family; and acceptance of different family model with permeable boundaries	Restructuring family boundaries to allow for inclusion of new spouse-stepparent; realignment of relationships throughout subsystems to permit interweaving of several systems; and making room for relationships of children with biological (noncustodial) parents and grandparents

4. Learning stress management skills in order to detect early indicators of tension in self and others.
5. Establishing joint activities, goals, and traditions along with frequent expressions of appreciation, encouragement, and love (Quick & Quick, 1986, pp. 1–3).

Achieving Family Integration

Persons contemplating the establishment of a blended family need an ability to develop new attitudes and role definitions along with a willingness to deal with many complex and ambiguous developmental family issues. The most important prerequisite is the recovery from loss of the first marriage partner (McGoldrick & Carter, 1980). Thus, the formation of a blended family usually involves three essential steps: entering new relationship, conceptualizing and planning for new marriage and family, and remarriage itself along with reconstitution of the family unit. In each step, there are prerequisite attitudes to be dealt with and developmental issues to be solved (see Table 18.4).

It can be helpful for persons entering a remarriage to recognize that, in a sense, they are embarking upon not one but six remarriages. The various tasks that will be required to successfully accomplish a blended family have been categorized under emotional, psychic, community, parental, economic, and legal remarriage (Goetting, 1982). In an emotional remarriage, one reestablishes attraction bonds, feelings of commitment, and trust with another person. Psychic remarriage changes one's identity from being an individual to being couple-oriented. This requires relinquishing personal freedom and autonomy as well as reestablishing a lifestyle as a married person. Community remarriage implements changes in order to establish friendships with peers, while parental remarriage attempts to establish the stepparent role. Economic remarriage reestablishes a household as a unit of economic productivity and consumption, and legal remarriage resolves issues of alimony, child support, and property settlement along with allocation of resources among a variety of individuals (Goetting, 1982). Perhaps the greatest value of familiarity with these developmental tasks is the awareness that blending families is a process which cannot be accomplished without adequate time and skill.

Decision to Have Another Child

Childbearing after remarriage is a frequent occurrence. Using Census Bureau data, 48% of black and white women were found to have given birth to another child after remarriage. In fact, about one fourth gave birth within 18 months after remarrying (Wineberg, 1990). A mutual child is more likely to be born in a stepfather-biological mother marriage if the stepfather is younger and had no children prior to the marriage (Ganong & Coleman, 1988). Among child-free women who enter their second marriage before age 40, about two thirds will have their first child in these marriages. However, there is a relatively low probability of a first birth for highly educated women in remarriages, which suggests that the postponement of childbearing leads to an emerging commitment to a life-style without children (Griffith, Koo, & Suchindran, 1984).

Some authorities have suggested that having a mutual child in a blended family helps to cement the family bonds. On the surface, making the decision to have a new baby in a blended family would seem to have positive effects on the new family by providing a "blood tie" and helping to clarify parental responsibilities. Consequently, a new baby could be viewed as a unifying force in a blended family (Sager et al., 1983). However, the presence of a mutual child seems to have no significant effect on the marital relationship nor on the positive feelings felt for other stepfamily members. While a mutual child does not seem to strengthen emotional bonds in the blended family, 40% of parents indicated that the birth of a mutual child created problems with their other children (Ganong & Coleman, 1988). Other authorities see negative effects such as adding emotionally, physically, and financially to the stress level of the blended family, and in some instances, even threatening family stability. When the family does decide to have a new baby, other children, whether living at home or not may feel threatened and left out of the family environment (Lief, Sholevar, Furstenberg, & Isaacs, 1988). And as might be anticipated, findings suggest that both wives and husbands in blended families have more positive relationships with their shared/mutual children than with "her" or "his" children (Hobart, 1988).

Handling Finances

Children in blended families indicated the most frequent sources of disagreement for their stepparents were money and finances, home matters, social matters, insufficient money, and a lack of respect for privacy and personal space (Ihinger-Tallman & Pasley, 1987). Other data from remarried families suggest that three areas of conflict in the marital relationship are related to discipline and handling children, financial difficulties, and interpersonal concerns (Knaub, Hanna, & Stinnett, 1984).

Financial problems in remarriage often have to do with continuing ties from the previous marriage, especially if remarried fathers are paying child support. Other financial difficulties may relate to secrecies about money, bonds and securities, and financial obligations which may convey the impression that the spouse is hesitant about making a commitment to the new marriage (Price-Bonham & Balswick, 1980). The fewer ties that men have with their prior marriage, the less likely that they will have money conflicts and its attendant stresses in remarriage (Robinson & Barret, 1986). Persons marrying for the second time are usually more careful in their financial planning than persons marrying for the first time. Data indicate that at least one half of remarried couples pool their money and resources ("Money Side," 1985). Combined accounts may seem simple to manage; but, on the other hand, they require good communication between spouses.

In second marriages, each partner is likely to have an independent source of income. Consequently, two patterns of financial management in remarriages have been identified: "common-pot" blended families and "two-pot" blended families. In the common-pot blended family, the mother and father pool all available resources and distribute these resources to family members according to need, regardless of any biological relationship. For many families, one marriage partner may have a former spouse who cannot or will not contribute financial resources to her/his biological child. Therefore, child support may be sporadic and minimal. So the total family resources are oftentimes limited and are used for current domestic needs. This expedient approach means commitment to a common goal in which

Reprinted by permission of UFS, Inc.

family unity and solidarity are placed above self-interest and personal autonomy (Fishman, 1983). As for the two-pot blended family, financial resources are distributed to family members primarily according to their biological identity with only secondary consideration given to expressed or perceived needs. For example, the biological mother provides financial resources only to her biological child. This family structure usually includes the involvement of at least one noncustodial parent who contributes financially to the support of her/his biological children. Typically, each marital partner contributes a specific amount toward the ongoing maintenance of the household. Under these arrangements, the stepparent may provide income for use in making investments or the purchase of luxury goods (Fishman, 1983).

Coping as a Stepparent

The most dramatic transition to the role of stepparent usually occurs shortly after remarriage as new stepparents learn that they may need to change their parenting strategies. During this period, children may feel abandoned by their biological parent as attempts are made to put their marital relationship first, in order to make the marriage work. For the most part, children have more difficulty with stepmothers than stepfathers. But given the situation of having a stepmother present with the biological father as noncustodial parent, it is hard to determine causality of the difficulties. Being a stepparent is a role that is not automatic but has to be achieved as the stepparent deals with issues of divided loyalties. A complicating factor in blended families is that a parent with more previous experience in child rearing may criticize the practices that the other spouse uses with her/his own children (Lief et al., 1988).

Stepparents, especially stepmothers, prefer that stepchildren live with them as opposed to living with the other parent. Yet, over one half of those stepparents with stepchildren living with the other biological parent felt that they would get along better with their spouse if there were no stepchildren. However, stepmothers who lived with their stepchildren indicated a higher level of marital happiness and satisfaction than those women whose stepchildren lived with the other parent. Stepmothers were more attached to their live-in stepchildren when their own children lived in the same household (Ambert, 1986).

Stepparents often have unrealistic expectations of instant love and family feelings without realizing that time is needed to develop mutual trust, affection, and a feeling of closeness. Consequently, stepparents may try too hard in the role of stepparent because of their own insecurities. Depending upon their age, some stepchildren also have difficulty adjusting to the idea of a sexual relationship between their biological parent and another person. Problem areas that are most often mentioned by stepparents are discipline, adjustment to habits and personalities of children, and difficulty in gaining acceptance of the children (Kompara, 1980).

Closely related to discipline is the initial problem of what to call each other. Children themselves are more likely than adults to use the "step" label for stepkin. But even among children, a certain degree of awkwardness is reported with regard to the "step" label (Dahl, Cowgill, & Asmundsson, 1987).

Stepmothers and Stepfathers: Lingering Stereotypes

One of life's early messages of nonlove occurs for many young children when they encounter the story of Cinderella and her wicked stepmother. However, myths are not confined to fairy tales nor to children. Among stepfamily myths that developed are that love occurs instantly, a stepfamily can duplicate a biological family, remarriage is smoother after death than following divorce, children of divorce are forever damaged, stepfamily integration occurs quickly, and children adjust more quickly if the noncustodial parent withdraws (Visher, 1984).

Research suggests that the more positive a stepfather feels about his new marriage, the more positive that he will be perceived by his stepchildren (Brand & Clingempeel, 1987). Further, living with stepfathers is associated with less stereotyping of women because children from stepfather homes are evidently better able to appreciate the difficulties of being a mother. However, children living in both stepmother and stepfather households hold stronger stereotypes of stepmothers than stepfathers (Fine, 1986). Nevertheless, many stepfathers have difficulty with stepparenting. The most frequently mentioned stepchild-related problems are uncertainty about degree of authority, amount of affection to give to stepchildren, conflicts with discipline and enforcement of rules. Other sources of stress include guilt over biological children, loyalty conflicts between stepchildren and biological children, the potentiality of sexual conflicts, and conflict over surname (Robinson, 1984). As the amount of time spent in the blended family household increases, stepdaughters living in blended families have less positive perceptions of the stepdaughter-stepfather relationship (Clingempeel & Segal, 1986).

In stepmother households, over three fourths of adolescent stepchildren felt either fairly close to their stepmothers in comparison to nearly two thirds of adolescents living in stepfather households (Ganong & Coleman, 1987). To combat the "wicked stepmother" stereotype, a stepmother may overcompensate and pay more attention to her stepchildren than biological children. As a result, her biological children may feel left out or ignored and thus may become angry causing additional strain in spousal relationships as well as leading to resentment of the stepchild by the stepmother (Nelson & Nelson, 1982). If female children are present in stepmother families, more frequent visiting by the biological mother is associated with less positive relationships with the stepmother. However, positive stepmother-stepchild relationships are more likely to develop the longer that the father and stepmother live together (Clingempeel & Segal, 1986). In stepmother families, as the level of marital satisfaction increases, the less positive the stepmother-stepdaughter relationship will become and the reported level of psychological adjustment for stepdaughters will decline. In contrast, for stepmother families with stepsons, higher levels of marital satisfaction are related to more positive stepmother-stepson relationships and better psychological adjustment of the stepson (Brand & Clingempeel, 1987).

One survey of female and male adolescents living in blended families concluded that the overall stress level related to family issues is not very high. The reasons may be that divorce and remarriage are so common and acceptable in society or that family issues play a less significant role in social interactions within peer groups (Strother & Jacobs, 1984). Nevertheless, tension can develop from stepfathers and stepchildren having different surnames. Some stepchildren may want to be adopted in order to feel like they are part of the blended family, to help them in relations with other family members, and to prevent embarrassment. However, other stepchildren may not wish to be adopted because of fears that they will not be allowed to visit their biological parent (Robinson & Barret, 1986).

Establishing Workable Relationships with Stepchildren

The establishment of workable relationships with stepchildren is complicated by several factors. First, the stepparent role is not fully understood or comfortably accepted in our society. Second, the task is difficult because biological parents outside of the stepfamily influence what happens in the lives of their children. Third, children often have difficulty adjusting to visitations between two households where life-styles and rules may differ considerably. Fourth, stepchildren bring many background differences to the blended family such as values and beliefs, and possible loss of friends. Fifth, courts and laws often fail to recognize and support persons in the role of stepparent (Visher, 1984).

Although the wicked stepmother myth has been refuted, in stepparent families in which only one parent has a child(ren) the most positive parent-child relationship is with the biological parent. In a dual stepparent family when both spouses have children there

Remarriage 1990s: the best man is frequently the "best" son.

is an equal but less positive parent-child relationship (Peek et al., 1988). To establish good stepchild-stepparent relations, the stepparent should set long-term goals that are based on the needs of all members of the family with input from children. Further, a stepparent should encourage the child's relationship with her/his biological parent of the same sex in the "other" household. In blended families, many parents tend to focus on disagreements which can be detrimental in the development of a positive relationship with their stepchildren. If one parent is entirely in charge of setting and enforcing rules for their biological children, the possibility exists that different rules for different sets of children may develop. In this case, ill-will can be generated between stepsiblings (Mills, 1984).

The available research suggests that other than finances, the most frequently reported problem area for blended families is children. Further, in a survey of remarried persons, approaches to discipline and meeting their children's needs were the two most frequent sources of disagreement between marital partners (Knaub et al., 1984). Discipline is a common problem with stepchildren. It can be very difficult, especially for stepfathers, to enforce rules and implement discipline with stepchildren while maintaining a friendly relationship. A part of the difficulty relates to the fact that many times the stepfather does not know how to act like a father. Some stepchildren will test their stepfathers to determine what they are able to get away with, whereas others are shocked that their stepfather is assuming the father role. Many mothers also become protective when the stepfather disciplines her children (Robinson & Barret, 1986).

Some research suggests that a typical pattern in blended families is for the stepparent to be frozen out of the parental role function. Under these circumstances, the biological parent usually sides with the children thus worsening the situation (Price-Bonham & Balswick, 1980). It is not unusual for adolescents striving for control and independence to rebel against discipline. When they do not succeed in other life activities, it is especially difficult to accept discipline from a stepparent. Although occasional discipline was viewed as a significantly stressful part of blended family living for stepparents, it was not perceived as a very stressful life event by stepchildren themselves (Strother & Jacobs, 1984).

Table 18.5: Parent-Child Problems in Stepparent Families

Specific Problems	1960s	1970s
Stepparent-child adjustment	29%	28%
Child's reaction to stepparent	15	19
Discipline	15	15
Loyalty issues	15	11
Parent sides with own child	7	3
Age/sex of child	5	7
Lack of prior parenting experience	3	5
Other	3	9
Stepparent feels like outsider	5	3
Stepparent resents child	3	3

From K. Pasley and M. Ihinger-Tallman, "Portraits of Stepfamily Life in Popular Literature: 1940–1980" in *Family Relations,* 34:532.

Adjustment of Children in Blended Families

Children of remarried parents seem to have more short-term problems than those in nondivorced families. However, remarriage of a custodial mother is often associated with an increase in behavioral problems for female adolescents and a decrease in behavioral problems for adolescent male children (Hetherington, Cox, & Cox, 1985). At the 6-month stage of the blended family, a better relationship with the noncustodial father was found to be associated with better behavioral adjustment for male children, but not until the 2.5–year stage for female children (Bray & Berger, 1990). To children, remarriage means changes in their lives including adjustment to the response of the biological parents to each other as previous marital partners. Their level of stress also depends on which parent remarries; expectations regarding visitation and financial resources; stepsibling relations; cultural and religious factors; and change of residence, school, and/or peer group (Sager et al., 1983). Since children may not be well-acquainted with the stepparent at the time of remarriage, the former spouse and her/his parents (grandparents) may give unwelcome input concerning the remarriage. Because children are able to expand their family boundaries, they may end up serving as messengers back and forth between custodial and noncustodial parents (Ihinger-Tallman & Pasley, 1987). A comparison was made of children living in intact families, single-parent families with mother custody, and blended families with mother custody. Children in all families were equally as likely to report that their mothers talked to them a lot, were interested in their activities, provided assistance with homework, and helped with personal problems (Amato, 1987).

In the 1960s and 1970s, the most often mentioned problem area within the stepparent or parent-child relationship was stepparent-child adjustment (see Table 18.5). In an environment where parents fail to meet the children's needs, siblings will often increase their dependency upon one another thus becoming more tightly bonded. However, sibling-stepsibling bonding depends upon access to one another, degree of shared experiences, perceived membership in the family group, availability of conditions that foster intimacy and privacy, and perceived status differences (Ihinger-Tallman, 1987). Despite the many adjustments necessary for living in a blended family, most children seem to do fairly well in this new family environment.

Summary

- The aftermath of divorce involves restructuring a living routine, coping with loneliness, and often being a single parent.
- Major issues for single parents are maintaining contact with noncustodial parent, financial problems, lack of social support systems and community participation, and fulfillment of sexual needs.
- Remarriage rates after divorce are highest for those in the youngest age group.
- The greater degree of costs that a person brings to remarriage after divorce, the lower their power in the marital relationship.
- Alimony and child support payments may affect money flow in remarriage.
- Persons remarrying tend to be more suspicious of romantic love, more cautious in selecting their marriage mate, and more willing to enter a second marriage with lower expectations than the first time around.
- Remarriages, for which a higher divorce rate exists, tend to be less homogenous than first marriages for such factors as age, religious background, and educational level. The evidence on marital satisfaction among the remarried is contradictory.
- Although an increasing number of widowed persons are remarrying, barriers to remarriage include existence of children, societal norms, lack of eligible partners due to differences in life expectations between women and men, and misunderstandings about sexuality.
- Reasons for remarriage among widowed persons are having companionship, obtaining a socially approved sexual outlet, and securing assistance with household chores and cooking.
- Having a mutual child in a blended family may cement the marital bonds, but it also adds emotional, physical, and financial stress.
- Children in blended families have more short-term problems than children from intact families. Problems identified include uncertainty about degree of authority, amount of affection to give stepchildren, conflict over discipline and enforcement of rules, and time spent with biological children versus stepchildren.
- Finances and child discipline are the most often mentioned problem areas in blended families.

Questions for Critical Reflection

1. Women and children were the high-profile members of society in the 1980s. In the 1990s, single fathers may lead the way, encouraging men to "have it all" in careers and nurturing relationships. List all of the ways that it is both easier and more difficult for single fathers to cope with parenthood.
2. In a remarriage following divorce, a person usually wants the relationship to be different, while if the remarriage follows death of the spouse, they want it to be the same. Which expectation has the greatest potential for failure? Why?
3. As growing numbers of older adults remarry, their adult children are faced with quite different issues than are younger children. What would be some of the questions raised by the realities as well as the emotions of the new relationship?
4. Some family scientists have deplored the fragmentation of divorce, the incredibly impossible task of co-parenting, and the loss of traditional models. Others believe that having multiple ways to be a family opens up many exciting opportunities. With whom do you most agree? Why?
5. In the blended family life cycle, why are permeable boundaries needed? Are they more important to blended than intact families? What factors influenced your answers?

Suggested Readings

Burns, C. (1985). *Stepmotherhood: How to survive without feeling frustrated, left out or wicked.* New York: Times Books. A useful guide to coping with the role of stepmother.

Cherlin, A. (1981). *Marriage, divorce, and remarriage.* Cambridge, MA: Harvard University Press. A major contribution to scholarly work on divorce and remarriage.

Ihinger-Tallman, M., & Pasley, K. (1987). *Remarriage.* Newbury Park, CA: Sage. A comprehensive review of the research literature on remarriage.

Maglin, N. B., & Schniedewind, N. (Eds.) (1989). *Women and step-families: Voices of anger and love.* Philadelphia: Temple University Press. A collection of essays, journal entries, letters, and poems written by women from their stepmother, stepdaughter, or stepgrandmother perspective.

Ware, C. (1984). *Sharing parenthood after divorce.* New York: Bantam Books. A practical book on co-parenting for divorced couples.

CHAPTER 19

Marriage and Family in Middle and Later Years

. . . And we ourselves shall be loved for a while and forgotten. But the love will have been enough; all those impulses of love return to the love that made them. Even memory is not necessary for love. There is a land of the living and a land of the dead, and the bridge is love, the only survival, the only meaning.

Thornton Wilder, 1939

OUTLINE

This century has brought profound demographic shifts affecting the shape of family life. One such change is an increase in life expectancy (Hagestad, 1988). An estimated one half of the women who marry today at age 24 may expect to reach age 68 before either they or their husband dies. This phenomenon represents 44 years of living together compared to 31 years a century ago (Glick, 1989a). As the life expectancy of women and men has continued to increase, much attention has been focused on life in the middle and later years. While the terms middle years and later years defy an exact definition, in his stages of the life cycle, Erikson (1982) uses the term maturity for persons ages 45–70 and older age for persons age 70 and over. A less precise definition describes families in the middle years as lasting from the time that the last child has left home until retirement or death of one of the spouses. Aging families are those where the wife and husband near their mid-sixties and enter into retirement (Duvall & Miller, 1985). Still others define the middle years as between ages 40–60 (Berger, 1988; Wantz & Gay, 1981). Although the exact span of years for each category is subject to debate, in this chapter the middle years will be defined as ages 45–64 and later years as age 65 and over.

Regardless of which ages constitute the latter stages of the family life cycle, the patterns of change and growth for the individual are continuous and interrelated in all areas: physical, social, intellectual, and emotional. Although authorities do not agree concerning the degree of stability of personality traits, longitudinal research has revealed significant continuity of many personality characteristics (McCrae & Costa, 1984). However, people do change as reflected in the fact that behavior in women and men often becomes more similar with age. Many women in the middle and later years evidence increased assertiveness and dominance, more aggressiveness in social relations, and desire for personal growth through self-expression in new activities. In contrast, men in the middle and later years exhibit decreased aggressiveness while displaying more reflective and nurturing behaviors (Zube, 1982). Thus, women and men may grow to be more similar in behavior. Of course, if spouses change too far in opposite directions, conflict may arise due to heightened insecurities. The changes that occur during the latter life-cycle stages also give rise to many myths about sexuality in the later years which influence both attitudes toward sexuality as well as sexual activity (Zube, 1982).

Family Life in Middle Years

Although more attention has been focused on the early stages of marital life, aging populations will necessitate more knowledge about significant later developmental phases ("Marriage in Later," 1988). These stages, which have been variously described, include the preretirement or active stage, sometimes called the empty nest or launching stage in which the couple enjoys life after children; the early retirement or dwindling stage in which one or both partners experience less energy and/or physical infirmities; and the late retirement or dependent stage when both partners are forced to rely on each other for help (Swensen, 1983).

The rising life expectancy of women and men means an increase in the length of the "empty nest," period (Glick, 1989a). Thus, wives and husbands will have the opportunity to focus more attention on their marital relationship. In a quality marriage, these years can be extremely satisfying as spouses have expanded time to do things together without child care responsibilities. However, research implies that this period can lead to the development of either a more harmonious or discordant marital relationship (Allgeier, 1983). If unhappiness already exists in the marriage, the costs and profits of seeking alternative sources of life satisfaction may be carefully examined and marital dissolution even contemplated at this time (Goetting, 1982).

Developmental Tasks in Middle Years

Whether or not couples successfully negotiate the developmental tasks of middle and later years depends upon having satisfactorily achieved the preceding ones involving communication, self-esteem, sexual needs, conflict resolution, and problem-solving (Cole, 1986). Developmental tasks of these later years call for couples to address certain life areas:

1. Correct imbalances in separateness and togetherness.
2. Redefine and realign relationships with children and grandchildren.
3. Redefine and realign relationships with siblings and family members of own generation.
4. Cultivate and maintain support network of friends (Cole, 1986, pp. 395–396).

Given the changing needs of both partners, it is very important to reevaluate and redefine their relationship before and after retirement (Beavers, 1985).

A vital part of this process should concern a retirement plan for shifting health and financial needs. Health and energy changes will call for establishing predictable daily routines in simplified life-styles. Healthy habits of eating, taking vitamins, exercise, and sleep as well as mental stimulation are believed essential for optimal functioning in the later years. Couples may also need to rebalance work loads to reflect changing energy levels. Finally, they must implement a financial plan to be able to live on a fixed income (Hennon & Burton, 1986). Ultimately, one's own mortality must be faced along with the handling of unfinished financial and emotional business. Facing the eventual death of the marital partner, saying goodbye, and reaffirming what the relationship has meant are the most difficult aspects of the aging years (Cole, 1986).

The Empty Nest: A Period of Transition

"Bittersweet" may best describe this ambivalent period in the life cycle characterized by both joy and sadness. The basic reason for such conflicting feelings is that the empty nest precipitates a transition: a life change involving personal shifts in role involvements and social identity (Hagestad, 1988). All transitions are not self-initiated. While some transitions involve ascribed roles, some are produced by the life changes of others and are thus known as counter transitions. For example, counter transitions in marriage lead to in-law roles; in parenthood, to grandparenthood; and in divorce, to "ex-relationships" (Hagestad & Neugarten, 1985). Family stress researchers have defined such family developmental transitions as normal crises because such events are experienced by most families. They are defined as crises because families may become disorganized and dysfunctional when their coping resources are inadequate to deal with changes in roles, expectations, and behaviors (McCubbin & Patterson, 1983).

Many wives and husbands who engage in the process of parenting for a number of years look forward to the day when their offspring will be launched into full adulthood by leaving home. Authorities believe that this period of life has many positive psychological rewards for a mother because she can devote herself to a career or other projects such as returning to school or community service (Berger, 1988). Ironically, children leaving home seems to be somewhat synchronized with the period of failing health on the part of the spouse's aging parents (Pillemer & Wolf, 1986). Just as the child-rearing role diminishes and parents begin to appreciate the financial and psychological freedom of the "empty nest," they frequently find themselves confronted with health problems of aging parents (Stueve & O'Donnell, 1984). However, most daughters and sons feel more rewarded than disturbed by such family obligations (Troll, 1986).

Research indicated that parents were less likely to expect their children to establish an independent residence before marriage than were the children themselves. Young people from mother-only families were less likely to have conflict over this issue than those from intact or blended families because they anticipated delaying marriage. Also, traditional families were more likely to expect premarital residential independence (PRI). The fact that stepparent families expected greater PRI may reflect a pattern of low intergenerational closeness in such families (Goldscheider & Goldscheider, 1989). A Canadian study found that 61% of children in stepfamilies left home before age 20 in comparison to 52% in single-parent and 44% in intact families. And women were more likely to leave at an earlier age than men (Mitchell, Wister, & Burch, 1989).

The Effects of an Empty Nest

Most people generally manage the transition of a child leaving home reasonably well. However, the major changes in relationships required at the time may precipitate a family crisis (Anderson, 1988). Family difficulties associated with negotiating the leaving of home by a child are reflected in adolescent **schizophrenia,** college maladjustment, substance abuse, and suicide (Anderson, 1988). Although the majority of mothers and fathers surveyed seemed to enjoy the empty nest and suffered no permanent loss, some parents reported deep unhappiness over their last child leaving home. The impact was more negative for mothers who had been overinvolved or overprotective of their children (Lewis, Volk, & Duncan, 1989). Further, when the last child's leaving home is related to being "off schedule" such as a sudden, unexpected departure for military service, it is more traumatic for mothers (Barber, 1981). Reportedly, for fathers, the last child leaving home is most disturbing if he has missed knowing his child intimately, or if he is more nurturing, has fewer children, is older, is retired, and has lower marital quality (Lewis et al., 1989). The two reasons given most frequently for leaving home by rural youth were to marry and to establish independence (see Table 19.1).

Table 19.1: Reasons for Rural Children Leaving Home by Family Status

Reasons	Farmer 1983	Farmer 1985	Nonfarmer 1983	Nonfarmer 1985
Marry	56%	25%	45%	22%
Establish independence	26	28	21	34
Enter educational program	8	44	17	27
Join armed service	4	3	13	6
Could not live with family rules	3	0	2	4
Cohabiting	2	0	0	2
Died	1	0	1	3
Institutionalization	0	0	0	2
Other	0	0	1	0

From R. A. Lewis, et al., "Stresses on Fathers and Family Relationships Related to Rural Youth Leaving and Returning Home" in *Family Relations,* 38:177.

An investigation of parental stress and coping during the leaving-home transition found a significant relationship between parent role stress and family system resources. In families with existing resources such as open and effective communication along with a sense of emotional connectedness and support, there was less vulnerability to stress. Parents who could reframe the situation viewed their family as strong, confident, and able to accept the unexpected. By finding some positive elements in these situations, they were able to report less role stress following the departure of the child (Anderson, 1988).

"Nesting": Adult Children Living at Home

While most young adults tend to leave home in their late teens or early 20s, some choose to stay and commute to work or college and still others return home because of job loss, marital dissolution, or unwed parenthood. The adult child living at home with or without a spouse present has been called a "nester" (O'Kane, 1981). **Nesting** is an interesting phenomenon requiring family adjustment to the unexpected returning home of an adolescent or young adult who was thought to have left permanently. The number of young adults ages 18–34 living with their parents between 1970 and 1983 increased by 85% (Clemens & Axelson, 1985). By 1988, of those parents with unmarried children or stepchildren, 47% had an adult child residing in their household. Younger parents were more likely to have an adult son than an adult daughter residing in their household (Aquilino, 1990). Major reasons for this occurrence are suggested to be economic even though divorce, separation, or widowhood may be underlying factors (Shehan, Berardo, & Berardo, 1983). Data from the 1980 Current Population Survey indicate that two thirds of young adults living with their parents were employed, and most nesters were in the never-married category. Of the ever-married daughters and sons living with their parents, almost one half had their spouse present (Glick & Lin, 1986a).

Young adults who choose to stay at home with their parents often create stressful parental relationships, and those who choose to return home may find that parental relations become less cordial. The term "returning adult syndrome" describes the situation where despite the parental expectation that a young adult will leave home, there has been one or more attempts by the young adult to separate, followed by a return home. This pattern involves continued economic dependency on parents because of a failure to launch a "career." Parents are more likely than young adults to identify a "crowded nest" instead of an "empty nest" as a problem. Returning young adults may perceive few benefits from assuming adult roles in a family that allows sharing parental resources rather than encouraging independence. Such nesters may be unaware of their parents' income and financial obligations and thus remain insensitive to parental financial problems (Schnaiberg & Goldenberg, 1986).

Although their children may be employed, some parents feel guilty about asking them to pay room and board. One survey found that about two thirds of those nesters who were working full-time paid room and board. These nesters should be distinguished from

From *Family Therapy Today,* 3(7):10. Copyright © 1988 PM Inc. Publishers, Van Nuys, CA. Reprinted by permission.

summertime college nesters who usually do not have money for room and board but contribute by doing chores at home (O'Kane, 1981). However, parents and young adults typically have their own expectations for economic independence which may offset these comforts, so most returning young adults eventually move out again (Schnaiberg & Goldenberg, 1986).

Among the identified advantages of nesting are that nesters can relate views and excitement from their academic and career lives to parents, share in family recreational activities, save money, and become known as adults. There also are several disadvantages: lack of consideration for others' needs such as space, time, possessions, and peace (absence of annoying music or telephone calls); communication gaps over clarification of expectations and rules; and stress on parental marriage bond (O'Kane, 1981).

Some research suggests that having adult children in the home results in lower marital satisfaction for both mothers and fathers and great strain on the coupled relationship (Clemens & Axelson, 1985; Lee, 1988). Since the **launching period** (when children leave home) has frequently been followed by greater marital quality, it is reasonable to assume that failure of children to leave home or their decision to return home may have detrimental effects on marriages of older couples. Yet, other evidence suggests that the presence of adult children has no effect on the parent's degree of marital conflict (Suitor & Pillemer, 1987).

Marital Satisfaction in Middle Years

Earlier research on marital satisfaction has consistently reported a U-shaped pattern over the marital career with the greatest satisfaction in the beginning and ending periods of marriage and the least when the oldest child is an adolescent (Steinberg & Silverberg, 1987). Others who have discovered no such relationship caution that much of the early research was flawed because of the tendency to assess the partner's perception of the marriage rather than actual satisfaction. Employing cross-sectional research designs that ignored what happened over time has also been criticized

(Spanier & Lewis, 1980). Further, although marital satisfaction in any life-cycle stage differs according to cultural diversity and norms within families, such variables have not been carefully considered to date. One researcher has proposed assessing family life satisfaction on the basis of the family's own values rather than those of the researcher (Bowen, 1988).

A successful marriage at any stage is related to the ability of each spouse to be empathic, to adapt, and to adjust to changes in the marital relationship as needed. Marriage during the middle years is characterized as a time when spouses come to rely more on each other for companionship and support. Those spouses who report high levels of trust are apt to have greater marital satisfaction and sexual satisfaction. In general, women tend to have a more overall positive view of husbands during the middle years than men have of wives (Fields, 1983). Among the characteristics associated with higher life satisfaction and marital happiness at this stage are greater gender equality and increased sharing of couple-oriented activities. Greater marital dissatisfaction is reported by those middle-aged women who are seeking more psychological fulfillment (Zube, 1982). Is marital satisfaction in the middle years better or worse than in the early years? What are the factors associated with marital satisfaction in the middle years?

Factors Associated with Marital Satisfaction: Middle Years

"For better or for worse" is a phrase that can be defined by any couple who has reached the middle years of their marriage. Spouses who can be the greatest source of life satisfaction, can also be the greatest source of conflict. When spouses report being very close, they have greater marital satisfaction and less conflict. Among the factors contributing to marital satisfaction in the middle years are living close to children and anticipated financial security. Sources of conflict include extramarital sexual involvement and problems with in-laws. Based on a review of 23 studies conducted over two decades, most persons gave positive rather than negative ratings to marital satisfaction in the middle years (Duvall & Miller, 1985).

An examination of studies since the early 1980s reveals alternate sources of emotional satisfaction. Women reported considerably more life satisfaction from friends and family members who provided emotional support whereas men received more life satisfaction from spouses and work (Argyle & Furnham, 1983). When asked to name a close confidant, two thirds of women and almost one half of men chose someone other than their spouse. For the most part, those who confided in their spouse perceived the highest level of marital satisfaction (Lee, 1987). For persons in the middle years, length of marriage was not significantly related to marital satisfaction of either spouse. But husbands with a high frequency of attendance at religious services and a large number of grandchildren tended to have higher levels of marital satisfaction (Lee, 1987).

Little evidence has been found that indicates participation in nonmarital roles creates role conflict and strain among middle-age couples, at least to the degree that marital satisfaction is likely to be reduced (Lee, 1988). To break the stereotype of marital boredom in middle years, couples need to emphasize setting aside couple-time, to increase frequency of social interaction and sexual activity, and to commit time and energy to the marital relationship and sexual activity (McCarthy, 1982).

Grandparents in Today's Society

Grandparents have been characterized as "America's forgotten resource." While the aging population is increasing, the role of grandparents in families is decreasing ("America's Forgotten," 1984). The likelihood of having a living grandparent is higher than at any previous time in history with approximately 48 grandparents per 100 parents compared to only 14 per 100 in 1900 (Sanders & Trygstad, 1989; Serow, 1981). Oftentimes, the intergenerational tie between living forebearers and their descendants may span as many as four or five generations (Barranti, 1985). However, as more persons are becoming grandparents at younger ages and spending more of their total lives in the role of grandparent, there is less consensus concerning guidelines about being a grandparent than ever before (Cherlin & Furstenberg, 1986). Emotional attachments between a grandparent and a grandchild do not contain the elements of emotional intensity and responsibility that exist in parent-child relationships. Consequently, grandparents may provide an unconditional love that parents, because of their responsibilities, are unable to offer to their child (Kornhaber & Woodward, 1981). Those who participate in grandparenting and identify with the role have an increased sense of well-being and morale (Kivnick, 1982).

Grandparent Roles: New Evolving Patterns

Many factors influence the role that a grandparent plays: age, gender, marital status, employment status, education, and economic resources. The number of grandchildren, frequency of contact, social resources (interaction with friends and community ties), personal resources including health and personality, and experience with own grandparents are also important contributors (Barranti, 1985). The research literature suggests several roles for the grandparent:

1. *Centrality*—The grandparent role is central to the life of grandparents, an important facet of their identity.
2. *Valued elder*—Grandparents are viewed as wise and esteemed elders from whom grandchildren can learn.
3. *Immortality through clan*—By having grandchildren, feelings of immortality are experienced.
4. *Reinvolvement with personal past*—Grandparents are able to relate relevant aspects of their own life history to grandchildren.
5. *Indulgent*—Grandparents use resources to provide gifts to grandchildren they were not able to give to their own children (Kivnick, 1982, p. 61).

Childhood experiences that persons have with their grandparents greatly influence how they will fulfill their role of grandparent. For example, a positive experience as a grandchild could result in a grandmother perceiving her role as a valued elder, or it may cause a grandfather to spoil his grandchildren (Kivnick, 1982).

For the most part, grandparenting styles fall into two categories: active and passive. In the active category, grandparents take an active role in the life of their grandchildren including visiting on a frequent basis, providing child care on a temporary or regular basis, and serving as a confidant for the child. In contrast, nonactive or passive grandparents exhibit infrequent visitation or communication with their grandchildren due to personal choice or geographical distance (Cherlin & Furstenberg, 1985). Parents are mediators of the relationship between grandchildren and grandparents, a role which weakens when the children reach young adulthood (Sprey & Matthews, 1982).

Grandmothers who possess the centrality role usually suffer deprivation in the social/emotional, maternal, and physiological aspects of life, but they receive life satisfaction from frequent contact with grandchildren. In contrast, grandfathers who assume the valued elder role often demonstrate strength and satisfaction in the social and emotional areas. They also have more confidence which is expressed through advice and help to the younger generation (Kivett, 1985). While grandmothers reported high levels of satisfaction with grandparenthood, they typically gave weak endorsement to caretaking responsibilities for grandchildren. Finally, grandfathers indicated less satisfaction in bonding with their grandchildren than grandmothers (Thomas, 1986).

Most grandparents exaggerate the amount of emotional closeness between themselves and their grandchildren. If grandparents and grandchildren live relatively close to each other, they are more likely to interact. About three fourths of grandfathers indicated that they interacted most with the grandchild of the daughter/son with whom they have the most social contact. If contact with grandparents was limited, it usually centered around holidays, birthdays, and other special occasions (Kivett, 1985).

Sexual Satisfaction in Middle Years

Sexuality has at least three major functions in the marital relationship: to share pleasure and positive reinforcement, to facilitate intimacy, and to reduce tension (McCarthy, 1982). Some spouses find that the mundane demands of a long-term relationship lead to a dulling of their eroticism toward each other. However, for many others, the relief from contraceptive hassles and fear of pregnancy may lead to a heightened enjoyment of erotic capabilities (Sarnoff & Sarnoff, 1989). Security of their relationship and increased leisure time with departure of children can also lead to new heights of sexual satisfaction (Allgeier, 1983). But failure to establish and maintain good communication increasingly affects the sexual aspects of marriage (Zube, 1982).

In general, sexual activity tends to remain relatively stable from middle years to older age (see Table 19.2). Of persons in their 50s, 9 in 10 women and men remained sexually active either with a partner or through solitary masturbation compared to 8 in 10 women and 9 in 10 men in their 60s (Brecher, 1984). Persons who prefer sexual intercourse over masturbation have higher levels of life satisfaction, greater pleasure from sexual activity, higher levels of sexual desire, and more interest in sexual activity (Turner & Adams, 1988).

Table 19.2: **Distribution of Sexual Activity Patterns by Age and Gender**

	Women			Men		
Sexual Activity Patterns	Age <56	Ages 56–65	Age 65>	Age <56	Ages 56–65	Age 65>
Stable activity	61%	55%	34%	66%	63%	43%
Decreasing activity	11	8	0	11	8	3
Continuously absent	5	6	33	0	10	12
Some activity to no activity	5	22	33	5	7	18
Increasing activity	2	0	0	3	1	0
No activity to some activity	2	3	0	2	3	9
Other	14	6	0	13	8	15

From L. K. George and S. J. Weiler, "Sexuality in Middle and Late Life: The Effects of Age, Cohort, and Gender" in *Archives of General Psychiatry*, 38:922.

As women and men grow older, physiological changes do occur that affect sexuality. Some women report less vaginal lubrication and elasticity whereas some men indicate a need for more direct and forceful penile stimulation to induce firmer erections and orgasm, longer refractory periods, and more episodes of sexual intercourse terminating without ejaculation (Brecher, 1984). However, it should be noted that older women and men in deeply committed love relationships are often more accomplished lovers (Sarnoff & Sarnoff, 1989). They may even achieve a more heightened state of arousal than during their earlier years. Women, for example, can still have ample vaginal lubrication and men have the potential to experience several erections over a brief time period (Allgeier & Allgeier, 1991). Even if such men are unable to have repeated ejaculations, they may receive immense physiological and psychological satisfaction from pleasuring their partner through sexual intercourse as well as manual and oral stimulation.

Women and Sexuality in the Middle Years

Women tend to be less satisfied sexually with their spouses than men. Reportedly, although women who worked during marriage seemed to be more likely than nonemployed wives to experience orgasm and to enjoy sexual activity, they tended to report less personal satisfaction with their sexuality in general (Jobes, 1986). According to one survey, two thirds of married women in their 60s were sexually active with many indicating that they enjoyed sexual activity as much as they did when they were young. Of those women who were not sexually active, 60% blamed their husband's lack of interest. Husbands gave the "number one" reason as either impotence or fear of impotence ("Women in 60s," 1989). Thus, for women, the cessation of sexual activity is dependent, to a substantial degree, upon the availability and willingness of a male sex partner (George & Weiler, 1981). In terms of frequency of sexual activity, about 70% of women in their 50s, 60% in their 60s, and 50% over age 70 engage in sexual activity with a partner or alone at least once per week (Brecher, 1984). Among married women, ages 50–59, the reported annual frequency of sexual intercourse was 46 times, slightly less than once per week (Smith, 1990b). As women age, they report a decreased level of enjoyment with sexual activity, a change that may be partially attributed to the unavailability of a sex partner. An unexplained desire for an extramarital sexual relationship at this age is believed to be related to several factors: fear of aging, sexual inexperience, unfulfilled sexual needs, need for personal growth and change, and lack of successful careers relative to their husband's career (Squire, 1984).

Since the risk of pregnancy still exists for premenopausal women in their 40s, contraceptive methods are available that will prevent conception as well as provide hormonal replacement as a woman's ovarian hormones begin to wane. Sterilization, of course, is the surest way of preventing an unwanted pregnancy at this stage in life and may be a viable alternative depending upon one's religious values (Upton, 1986).

Table 19.3: Select Physical and Emotional Symptoms of Menopause

Physical Symptoms		Emotional Symptoms	
Hot flashes	80%	Irritability	93%
Muscle/joint pain	72	Fatigue	91
Headaches	68	Tension	91
Increased weight	65	Nervousness	88
Lightheadedness	58	Depression	86
Breast sensitivity	56	Lack of concentration	82
Increased appetite	50	Short temper	81
Dizziness	49	Lack of motivation	77
Constipation	45	Early awakening	77
Numbness and tingling	45	Insomnia	77
Vaginal discharge	40	Loss of memory	75

From E. Anderson, et al., "Characteristics of Menopausal Women Seeking Assistance" in *American Journal of Obstetrics and Gynecology,* 156:430.

Menopause: A Life Transition

About one third of every woman's life is spent in the postmenopausal years which begins, on the average, at age 51. The symptoms of **menopause** for women will begin to appear when the estrogen and progesterone levels start to fall during their 40s (Lalich & Scommegna, 1988). Women with high levels of educational attainment and sexual knowledge about physiological changes tend to perceive menopause positively (Seymour, 1987). Significant physical symptoms are more frequently experienced than psychological symptoms at the onset of menopause (Anderson, Hamburger, Liu, & Rebar, 1987).

Physiological and Psychological Symptoms During Menopause. Declining estrogen levels can cause many different kinds of medical problems for menopausal women. The most often reported symptom during menopause is hot flashes followed by muscular/joint pain, headaches, and increased weight (see Table 19.3). Other symptoms include senile vaginitis, **osteoporosis** (brittleness of bones), urethral changes that lead to **urinary incontinence** (involuntary loss of urine), **dysuria** (painful urination), and increased frequency of urination. **Arteriosclerosis** (hardening of the arteries) also seems to increase with a diminishing supply of estrogen, but some studies indicate conflicting findings (Lalich & Scommegna, 1988).

While hot flashes, urogenital atrophy, and osteoporosis all respond very well to estrogen replacement therapy; there are some risks associated with this treatment. Endometrium cancer, stimulation of existing breast cancer, and gallstones are inherent risks (Lalich & Scommegna, 1988). Nevertheless, using estrogen replacement in conjunction with a progesterone regimen can control the physical symptoms of menopause as well as reduce or eliminate the potential risk of endometrium cancer, breast cancer, and **cardiovascular** disease. If a minimal dosage of estrogen is administered vaginally rather than a higher dose taken orally, it can elevate the level within the body sufficiently (Wu, 1985). Another mode of delivery involves the use of a skin patch containing transdermal estradiol (synthetic estrogen). The patch, which is placed on the abdomen, buttocks, upper arms, or lower back, must be changed weekly (Youngkin, 1990). This approach avoids a high concentration of estrogen in the liver and is effective in preventing vaginal atrophy and hot flashes. But, it has not been proven to alleviate osteoporosis (Rosenwaks, Benjamin, & Stone, 1987). In addition, exercise and nutritional substances such as calcium and vitamin D are essential for postmenopausal women (Wu, 1985).

The term **postmenopausal** means that a woman has not menstruated during the past 12 months (McKinlay, McKinlay, & Brambilla, 1987). Upon reaching postmenopause, women should conduct monthly self-breast examinations and receive an annual examination to detect breast or cervical cancer. A general physical examination is needed at least every 3 years from the middle years to age 65. Postmenopausal women also should have routine blood pressure and cholesterol level checks as well as an annual examination for cardiovascular disease since they are at increased risk (Piscitelli & Parker, 1986).

The most prevalent psychological symptoms reported with the onset of menopause include irritability, fatigue, tension, nervousness, and depression (see Table 19.3). Some medical authorities assert that the empty-nest syndrome is related to menopausal symptoms among full-time homemakers who have less demands on their time. In general, mothers who work outside the home do have lower reported levels of psychological menopausal symptoms than those who do not work. Yet, women without children experience more psychological symptoms than women with children which suggests a possible physiological origin (Nolan, 1986). Research findings indicate that widowed, divorced, and separated women with less than 12 years of education experience the most depression during menopause. However, women who have experienced a **hysterectomy** (surgical menopause) are twice as likely to have depression in comparison to women who went through natural menopause. Although many medical authorities believe depression results from menopausal-related changes in the body, the data suggest that depression is strongly related to events that occur in mid-life but are unrelated to menopause itself (McKinlay et al., 1987). Researchers have concluded that natural menopause appears to have no negative mental health consequences for the majority of middle-aged healthy women (Matthews et al., 1990).

Effects of Menopause on Sexual Response. The reported decreases in frequency of sexual intercourse during the menopausal years may be triggered by physiological changes in the body rather than changes in sexual desire per se. Estrogen deficiency caused by menopause is related to low levels of vaginal lubrication and sexual desire. Sexual motivation factors such as frequency of sexual fantasies and level of arousal also appear to be associated with estrogen deficiency among postmenopausal women (Bachmann, 1991). A longitudinal comparison of the premenopausal and postmenopausal stages found decreases after menopause in frequency of sexual intercourse, **libido** as reflected by decreased sexual thoughts and fantasies, and sexual responsiveness as reflected in the quantity of vaginal lubrication. Although there were no differences in the frequency of orgasm during sexual activity, there was a drop in the perceived enjoyment (McCoy & Davidson, 1985). Of women attending a menopausal clinic, 1 in 4 reported loss of sexual desire while 1 in 3 indicated a loss of clitoral feelings and sensation along with vaginal dryness (Sarrel & Whitehead, 1985).

Social and cultural factors such as unavailability of the marital partner due to death or separation, more single women than men in this age group, and traditional expectations of sexual nonassertiveness on the part of women may also affect sexual behavior during the postmenopausal years. Finally, age-related physiological changes affecting men's sexual responsiveness may also affect the sexual responsiveness of their spouses (Iddenden, 1987). For some women, removing the fear of pregnancy elevates their level of sexual interest and creates a need for even greater sexual fulfillment. And, regular weekly sexual intercourse is associated with the decrease or total absence of hot flashes (Davidson, 1985).

Men and Sexuality in the Middle Years

Men are especially vulnerable to a **mid-life crisis** after age 40, when they often start to check their sexual performance for any signs of aging. They compare their performance capabilities to those from their early 20s. Some men turn to younger women and blame any sexual problems on their **perimenopausal** (irregular menstruation) or postmenopausal wives. Men in their late 50s have often become less assertive while women have become more assertive. For some couples, this change means that wives become increasingly sexually aggressive in comparison to their husbands who become more attendant and better able to incorporate more affection into their sexual overtures and techniques (Masters, Johnson, & Kolodny, 1988).

Because of the male's greater ego, women who are disappointed with the sexual skills of their husbands are reluctant to initiate sexual activity or to experiment during sexual activity. Sometimes, discussing the male's sexuality capabilities makes it more difficult for him to either achieve or maintain an erection (Masters et al., 1988). Men during the middle years tend to have either very high or very low expectations regarding sexuality. They either believe that their sexual experiences will be very intense during every episode of sexual activity or that their sexual experiences will become boring after a short time with the same person regardless of intensity (McCarthy, 1982). Some authorities have speculated that sexual burnout may affect at least one fifth of all men during the middle years. Sexual burnout stems from boredom with the same sexual routine and results in physical depletion, emotional emptiness, and a negative sexual self-concept. When experiencing sexual burnout, men may feel that

This May–December scenario depicts behavior of those who mistakenly equate sexuality with youth.

nothing can be done to bring back their sexual pleasure. However, most persons recover spontaneously over time (Kolodny, 1983).

Family Life in Later Years

The life satisfaction of persons in the later years, if they have children, is related to several aspects of parent-child interactions. These factors include similarity of role expectations between parents and child, perceived quality of role performance, and personality dispositions of persons in the later years. Emotional support from adult children is more important and satisfying for elderly persons than financial support. The overall quality of the contact between the elderly mother and her children is particularly important to life satisfaction (Houser & Berkman, 1984). Health seems to have the greatest effect on the morale of elderly parents followed by the quality of their marital relationship including expressions of affection and communication patterns. If elderly parents engage in social networks outside of the home, they usually have higher expectations of their children (Quinn, 1983).

The Aging of the Population

By 1988, the life expectancy was 78.3 years for women and 71.5 years for men (National Center for Health Statistics, 1990f). The percentage of persons in the population who are age 65 and older is projected to exceed 11% by the year 2000 (Gelman et al., 1987b). Some predict by the year 2005, that percentage will increase to 13% with the absolute numbers rising from 29 to 36 million persons. When the baby boomers mature by the year 2025, the elderly population will have increased to 59 million persons with those age 80 and over being the fastest growing population segment (Torrey, Kinsella, & Taeuber, 1987). By 1990, over 7 million persons were in this age category (Atchley, 1991). The number of three-generation and four-generation families has increased because of a shorter

Elderhostel programs that enable persons in their later years to continue learning are significant to an era in which knowledge is power.

gap between generations and longer life expectancy (Streib & Beck, 1980).

The Retirement Years: A Time of Reflection and Adjustment

The term retirement has come to mean the withdrawal of women and men from active, paid employment. Some persons look forward to the prospect of retirement after having waited years to gain the freedom to live the life-style that they want without having to go to work each day. For others, retirement means a drastic decline in disposable income; loss of a meaningful social status; and the uncertain effects of being with their spouse all day, every day. Persons who have social and economic plans for retirement are likely to have little resistance toward retirement. For many, the impending loss of a job also may be outweighed by the successful accomplishment of having reared a family (Johnson & Price-Bonham, 1980).

In our society, older persons have less power, prestige, and privileges because such a high value is placed on self-reliance. Therefore, elderly persons expect to continue their own separate lives until they become physically disabled (Ishii-Kuntz & Lee, 1987). Further, the work ethic labels work as virtuous and has given high esteem to such traits and habits as diligence, initiative, industriousness, competitiveness, and self-reliance. Consequently, the work ethic has been translated into the "busy" ethic whereby retirees come to hold the expectations, along with society, that their lives should be "active and earnest." The media describes elderly persons as being active depicting them golfing, bicycling, and swimming. The "busy" ethic serves to legitimatize leisure retirement, defends retirees against being obsolete and useless, defines the retirement role, and assists in adapting to prevailing social norms. Although pensions allow retirees to receive income without working, they are still able to retain self-respect because the pensions were earned through their former work activities (Ekerdt, 1986).

Coping with Reduced Financial Resources

By 1987, the median household income for families in which the head of the household was age 65 or over was only $14,334. Further, of these families, about one third had family incomes of less than $10,000 (U.S. Bureau of the Census, 1990ee). Elderly persons tend to spend larger proportions of their incomes on food, home, medical care, and utilities than younger families. Further, federal budgetary initiatives during the 1980s reduced benefits and tightened eligibility requirements for Medicaid, food stamps, and other welfare programs that provide benefits to older persons (Clark & Sumner, 1985). However, major changes in Social Security and Medicare benefits have greatly reduced the threat of catastrophic health care costs depleting the life savings of retired persons ("Determining How," 1988).

Retirement brings a substantial economic loss for women especially among the unmarried. Women have lower incomes, retire earlier, receive reduced Social Security benefits, are less likely to be covered by private pensions, and have fewer assets than men (Szinovacz, 1983a). Married couples without adequate incomes after retirement are less likely to express well-being and more likely to have problems in adapting to changing times (Ferraro & Wan, 1986). In a survey of retired college professors, about one third indicated that changes in their life-style had been made due to cost of living increases since retirement. Some retirees also reported having to help their children through financial difficulties (Milletti, 1987).

Adjusting to Retirement

A favorable view of retirement by significant others in the elderly person's life will lead to her/his successful adjustment to retirement. Further, if an individual has a positive preretirement attitude, then the adjustment to retirement is likely to be successful (Cox & Bhak, 1987). Participation in preretirement programs can facilitate both spouses learning and sharing their concerns about retirement, thus enhancing understanding between marital partners. In addition, such programs foster social contacts which can decrease social isolation in old age (Johnson & Price-Bonham, 1980). After retirement, retirees lose meaningful segments from their lives: institutional role (prestige and authority), institutional work setting, atmosphere with professional friendships and acquaintances, and resources to keep up with their profession. Compensating mechanisms to replace the segments of the retiree's life include volunteer work activities and part-time consulting work (Milletti, 1987).

The adjustment of women to retirement has been a neglected concept in the research literature because until recently the empty nest and widowhood have been considered the major life cycle changes for women. Women are more likely than men to experience retirement as a stressful life event because many women go or return to work to escape the empty-nest syndrome or to gain life satisfaction and achievement recognition. The negative effects associated with retirement for women include feelings of wasting time, being cutoff and useless, boredom, loneliness, missing people at work, and difficulty doing household chores (Szinovacz, 1983a). Nevertheless, working married women seem to prefer to retire before age 65 (Brubaker, 1985a).

It is important that both women and men maintain social contacts and meaningful interests following retirement to avoid social isolation and guilt feelings. Persons with high levels of education, more income, and better health are less lonely and have higher morale in the retirement years. Social interaction with friends and participation in volunteer associations contribute to high morale for women, whereas social interaction with neighbors and church attendance contribute to high morale for men. However, social interaction with family members has essentially no effect on alleviating loneliness (Lee & Ishii-Kuntz, 1987). Sources that provided the strongest meaning in life to elderly persons were twice as likely to be relationships including friends and family members in contrast to maintaining physical and mental health. Further, in all previous studies, the most popular category of contribution to the meaning of life has been "relationships and friends" (Ebersole & DePaola, 1987).

Those individuals reporting the least satisfaction during retirement are those with a strong work ethic who do not think their activities are useful. Persons maintaining meaningful interests can cope with retirement by either relinquishing their strong work values or by being involved in substitute work-like activities. In a survey of retired persons, the more activities in which a person participated, the greater likelihood that she/he reported life satisfaction (Hooker & Ventis, 1984). Perhaps, these individuals misunderstand the meaning of leisure. Leisure does not mean an absence of activity but rather the freedom to determine the choice of activities. Many persons use retirement to expand their hobbies or engage in new activities that have been postponed due to lack of time (Milletti, 1987).

Retired persons who continue working part-time at a job that they consider meaningful will prevent loss of habits and skills associated with the worker role, maintain their productive role in society, and enhance their self-image contributing to greater satisfaction with daily life (Gregory, 1983). Elderly women are more likely to report enjoyment of nontask-oriented family maintenance activities such as getting together with family for a meal, telling stories to grandchildren, or going to a park or zoo with grandchildren. Task-oriented activities consisting of meal preparation, cleaning, laundry, and sewing are less enjoyable (Hildreth, Van Laanen, Kelley, & Durant, 1980). Older persons who live with their spouse have more negative attitudes toward caregiving than elders living with their children or grandchildren (Dunkle, 1985).

The Retirement Years and Marital Satisfaction

Evidence suggests that employed wives with retired husbands experience lower marital satisfaction than wives in dual-retired relationships (Lee & Shehan, 1989). The influence of retirement on marital satisfaction is, in part, related to the degree of support that the retiree receives from her/his mate. The quality of marriage prior to retirement helps to determine the dynamics of marriage after retirement (Brubaker, 1985a). Major factors contributing to life satisfaction of wives after retirement of their husbands are good health of husband, adequate income, joint decision making about entertainment and leisure time use, and participation of husband in housework activity (Hill & Dorfman, 1982). Among wives of retirees, two thirds perceived retirement as an opportunity for increased companionship from their husband whereas one third indicated that their husbands did not have enough to do with their time (see Table 19.4).

Older couples may feel the need for increased emotional support if they believe life events represent challenges. But for the most part, the amount of social support provided by one's spouse decreases with age. Women are less likely than men to indicate that they provide emotional support to their spouse, but wives also perceive themselves as receiving less emotional support from their husbands. Spouses do not receive the desired amount of emotional support because of limits in personal resources and nurturing skills, and less respect, affection, and compatibility with their spouse over the duration of their marriage (Depner & Ingersoll-Dayton, 1985). If couples have not previously been supportive of each other, it is unlikely this pattern will be changed at this point in their lives.

Table 19.4: Attitudes of Housewives toward Retirement of Husband

Positive Aspects	
Time available to pursue interests	81%
Increased companionship	67
Flexibility offered by retirement	33
Increased participation of husband in household tasks	28
Decrease in own home responsibilities	22
Husband happier after retirement	22
Negative Aspects	
Financial problems	36
Husband does not have enough to do	31
Too much togetherness	22

From E. A. Hill and L. T. Dorfman, "Reaction of Housewives to the Retirement of Their Husbands" in *Family Relations,* 31:197. Copyright © 1982 National Council on Family Relations, 3989 Central Avenue, N.E., Suite #550, Minneapolis, MN 55421. Reprinted by permission.

Caring for Elderly Parents

Although many older people are poor, both older parents and their children still believe that elderly parents should live independently for as long as health circumstances permit. When asked who should care for the elderly, over one half of women and men ages 30–39 mentioned family members. But only about one third of those persons ages 18–29 preferred family sources in contrast to such nonfamily sources as public assistance and private agencies (Sanders & Seelbach, 1981). A survey of female triads involving a grandmother, mature daughter, and young adult granddaughter found that three fourths of each generation believed that adult children did not provide as much care for their elderly parents as in previous generations (Brody, Johnsen, Fulcomer, & Lang, 1983). But contrary to the widely held belief in American society that the elderly are alienated from their children, at least 80% of their home care is provided by family members. Consequently, many younger families drain their financial, social, and emotional resources in caring for elderly parents (Montgomery, 1982). The process is further complicated by the fact that only about 3% of American companies have personnel policies that assist employees in caring for their elderly family members (Beck, 1990).

If daughters and sons are in excellent health themselves, they are more likely to have a positive attitude toward the social value of the elderly (Rakowski, Barber, & Seelbach, 1983). Among elderly families, those who interact often with their children usually exchange assistance. However, those parents who are healthy and highly educated are more likely to help their children but less likely to receive assistance themselves (Lee & Ellithorpe, 1982). For the most part, older persons give help with activities such as baby-sitting and housework more often than they receive help with shopping, laundry, and food preparation. Of those elderly who receive help, the major sources are children, other relatives, and friends/neighbors (Stoller, 1985).

The degree of involvement of daughters and sons in caring for their elderly parents is related to the influence of traditional gender roles. An attitude survey of three-generation families found agreement among most members of each generation on a number of beliefs about care for elderly parents. The findings indicated that sons should share equally with daughters in their care, and both sons and daughters should help with everyday activities, household tasks, and provide financial aid as necessary. Further, the respondents believed that it is better for a working woman to hire someone else to give care rather than to leave her job to provide care herself (Brody et al., 1983).

In spite of these attitudes, one study found that regardless of the amount of time available, personal attitudes toward familial obligations, or the availability of external resources, women provided more care than men (Finley, 1989). Evidence of the influence of traditional gender roles in providing care for elderly parents is exemplified by findings that sons are more likely to help their mothers with financial management and household repairs but are much less likely to provide emotional support in comparison to daughters (Houser, Berkman, & Bardsley, 1985). Other evidence is found in attitudes toward responsibilities of daughters and sons in caring for an elderly mother. Both women and men believed that it was more appropriate for sons to help with yard work while daughters should help with housework and carry meals to the mother's home (see Table 19.5). In general, as mothers increase in age, they perceive greater attachment for their daughters than daughters perceive toward their mothers. However, a mutual dependence remains between daughters and

Table 19.5: **Perceptions of Responsibilities toward Mother**

Item	Responsibility of Daughter	Responsibility of Son
Encourage mother to get better medical attention	1.36*	1.42
Encourage mother to become active in senior citizens' activities	1.39	1.34
Drive mother to shop, church, and social events	1.46	1.44
Help mother do her housework	1.56	2.07
Advise mother on financial affairs	1.75	1.62
Do yard work for mother	1.92	1.59
Give mother extra spending money	1.94	1.98
Take over management of mother's finances	2.54	2.61
Insist mother come live with child	2.95	3.07
Tell mother if dislike her friends	3.15	3.14
Place mother in nursing home	3.30	3.24

*Mean score: 1 = definitely should; 4 = definitely should not.
From L. L. Roff and D. L. Klemmack, "Norms for Employed Daughters' and Sons' Behavior toward Frail Older Parents" in *Sex Roles,* 14:366.

mothers based on their early reciprocal experiences and continuing interaction over the years (Thompson & Walker, 1984).

With the increase in the number of child-free marriages, there will be more and more elderly persons who will not have children to provide assistance during their later years. Major concerns are that the elderly will live in social isolation, have unmet essential daily living needs, and permit their health to deteriorate without receiving proper medical attention. Research suggests that elderly persons without children frequently live alone and go without social contact for long periods of time (Bachrach, 1980). Other findings suggest that elderly child-free persons are also less likely to have face-to-face contact with other family members in comparison to those who are elderly parents. But child-free persons and parents did not differ with regard to experiencing feelings of loneliness or their appraisals of life satisfaction. Although social isolation among the child-free elderly is linked with negative attitudes about death, regular association with relatives and close friends leads to a more positive attitude toward it (Keith, 1983). In general, child-free elderly persons are in better health, more satisfied with their health, and report greater satisfaction with their income and standard of living in comparison to elderly parents. Despite these findings, other studies confirm that both parents and child-free elderly are satisfied with life (Rempel, 1985).

Maintaining Health in Later Years

Declining health conditions are both normal and predictable with advancing age. While modern medicine has increased life expectancy, it has not necessarily increased the quality of life for elderly persons. Today, many elderly are able to survive for years despite having had strokes, cancer, emphysema, arthritis, or Parkinson's disease. Women who reach age 65 are likely to live for another 18 years on the average in comparison to an average of another 14 years for men (Beckham & Giordano, 1986). Contrary to what might be expected, as the physical impairment of an elderly person progressed, there was no increase in the quantity of contact with her/his social network. Yet, after hospitalization, children were twice as likely to maintain daily contact with a widowed parent in contrast to a married parent (Johnson, 1985).

For married couples, physical illness can cause various difficulties in the marital relationship. Usually, it is the husband who becomes ill and the wife who becomes the caregiver. Almost one half of all widows cared for their husband during his final illness and one fifth provided nursing care for over 1 year. The healthy marital partner may have to assume additional responsibilities such as preparing meals, shopping, and housekeeping. The spouse who becomes a caretaker may develop physical or psychiatric symptoms from unexpressed anger and then she/he experiences guilt feelings over this anger toward their disabled spouse.

Eventually, declining physical health may cause a reduction in sexual interest, desire for travel, ability to do household work, and interest in maintaining mutual friends (Beckham & Giordano, 1986).

Physical Health in Later Years

Older women who were judged to be physically attractive rated themselves more favorably on a number of mental, physical, and social well-being dimensions. They perceived themselves to be healthier; to have less illness; to possess a more positive outlook on life; to enjoy a greater feeling of well-being; and to be more cheerful, less depressed, and better adjusted (Kligman & Graham, 1989). In support of the adage, "use it or lose it," most mental skills as well as physical health remain intact provided that an older person keeps mentally and physically active. While it is true that older persons perform such tasks as dialing a telephone or typing more slowly, they are able to substitute experience for speed. Thus, they can maintain skills for many types of problem solving and other mental activities. Further, forgetting is not a sure sign of **senility** or of **Alzheimer's disease.** It may be caused by incorrect medication, depression, or other physical and mental problems that can be dealt with by medical treatment (Meer, 1987).

Chronic pain is a major health problem among the elderly which often leads to depression and reported marital dissatisfaction. The disruption of marital support for a chronic pain problem actually contributes to depression more than the experience of pain itself (Kerns & Turk, 1984). Arthritis is the most common chronic pain condition for older women, whereas older men suffer much less from arthritis pain but tend to have more heart attacks, strokes, respiratory diseases, and urinary tract disorders. Nevertheless, older women tend to have more chronic health problems and greater physical limitations than older men (Verbrugge, 1984). However, researchers found that women who frequently attended church services and met people were less likely to become physically disabled and depressed. In contrast, minimal displays of public religiousness by men, as defined by church attendance, was associated with less physical disability and depression (Idler, 1987).

Mental Health in Later Years

Due to increased life expectancy, more persons must cope with less energy, greater physical illness, and diminished abilities, all of which may affect mental health. An estimated 1 in 5 elderly persons find that they cannot deal with everyday living and may stop eating and/or misuse their medication (Nissenson, 1987). Men more often than women become depressed during retirement because it may represent losses instead of new opportunities. Major causes of depression among male retirees are lack of preretirement planning, failure to adjust to aging process, lack of life satisfaction, major personal losses in later life, and certain diseases (Charatan, 1983). The suicide rate for men, ages 65–74, is about six times greater than for women in this age group (Harris, 1990).

Although persons age 65 and over are twice as likely to be hospitalized for a mental disorder than younger persons, they are still very underrepresented in the total number of people receiving psychiatric care in any given year (Hooyman & Kiyak, 1991). Many elderly persons do not seek psychological counseling or psychiatric treatment because of the stigma attached. This fact may also be attributed to the earlier Freudian philosophy that it is inappropriate to try to treat patients age 50 and older (Nissenson, 1987).

Mental status at any age is a composite of external life events such as job, family, health, and internal images such as self-esteem and sexuality (James, 1988). Estimates for the prevalence of psychiatric disorders among those elderly living in the community range from 5–45%, depending upon the type of disorder being evaluated (Hooyman & Kiyak, 1991). For men, the conditions of poor physical health, lack of social support, and occurrence of undesirable life events are related to poor mental health. In contrast, for women, the variables are number of medical conditions, poor housing quality, lack of social support, and undesirable life events (Himmelfarb, 1984). Some evidence also suggests that women have increased vulnerability to mental health problems due to the empty-nest syndrome (Nissenson, 1987). Other findings suggest that women have higher levels of anxiety than men with peak levels occurring at ages 75–79 and ages 85–89. Anxiety, in particular, is associated with lack of quality housing and a small number of rooms in the residence (Himmelfarb & Murrell, 1984).

Coping with Loneliness and Depression

Depression among the elderly appears to be related to conflict between expected and actual roles (Sinnott, 1984). Older married women reported loneliness if they did not see their closest family member often as well

Homecoming Queen or Coming Home Queen, the need for self-esteem continues throughout life.

as stress over emotional inequity in their marital relationships (Essex & Nam, 1987). If a chronically ill or impaired older person is able to make a noneconomic contribution to the household, either while living with a caregiving spouse or with a child, she/he is substantially less depressed (Dunkle, 1985). Some older persons have the problem of learned helplessness; that is, they perceive little control over their environment and thus feel that little can be done to change their degree of life satisfaction. In addition, many elderly persons have trouble telling others about their problems, in part, because others may find someone else's medical history or mental health problems too depressing (Nissenson, 1987).

Many communities have formed support groups to assist the elderly to cope with medical and social service agencies, to communicate with their family, and to adjust to retirement. These support groups can be of major importance because they provide a new source for social networks, letting elderly people help each other and experience feelings of belonging (Nissenson, 1987).

Sexual Satisfaction in Later Years

Although sexual functioning may decline over the years, over one half of elderly persons remain sexually active (Rotberg, 1987). During the later years, some may prefer to engage in petting or masturbation rather than sexual intercourse. Those who prefer sexual intercourse tend to have higher life satisfaction, greater pleasure from sexual activity, a higher level of sexual desire, and more interest in participating in sexual activity. Physical changes in the body and availability of a sex partner are the two major factors that result in changes in preferred sexual activity. A large majority of the elderly decrease their frequency of sexual activity over time but still remain at high levels of sexual satisfaction. Men, in comparison to women, continue to report high levels of subjective sexual pleasure (Turner & Adams, 1988). However, the absence of sexual activity is not related to life satisfaction among elderly men (Johnson, 1987).

Variations in the level of sexual activity among the elderly can be partially explained in terms of their level of sexual functioning in their younger years, the age and gender of the elderly person, and their subjective health ratings. The health and life-styles in middle to old age which promote healthy sexual functioning include no smoking, moderate use of alcohol, control of blood pressure and weight, balanced diet, regular exercise, and adequate rest (Butler & Lewis, 1987).

The Impact of Aging on Sexual Response

Normative sexual changes for persons in the later years should not be stressful unless anxiety develops due to misinformation leading to unrealistic and unattainable expectations (Renshaw, 1984). Reasons why the elderly abstain from sexual activity include societal views, lack of available sex partner, illness, and residency in nursing home (Hobson, 1984). Physical health and attitudes about sexuality which prescribe socially-sanctioned sex partners are determining factors regarding sexual satisfaction and participation for elderly women. A woman's ability to engage in satisfying postmenopausal sexual activity is not totally dependent upon hormones since emotional and psychological factors can affect the level of sexual satisfaction more than physical factors (Rotberg, 1987).

For many elderly women and men, there is reduced objective intensity of orgasm along with decreased frequency of sexual intercourse. Alcohol, when taken either alone or with needed medications, may result in sexual difficulties. In addition, many pharmaceuticals such as antihistamines, hypertension medications, cardiac medications, and some **diuretics** (drug to maintain adequate urination) may cause sexual dysfunction. Further, mild tranquilizers that induce muscle relaxation may interfere with experiencing orgasm (Renshaw, 1984).

Aging and Sexuality in Women and Men

Physiological changes in female sexual response due to aging include menopause and its accompanying symptoms, decrease in production of vaginal lubrication, gradual shrinking of the uterus to the degree that it becomes less involved in sexual response, and some shrinkage of breast tissue (Allgeier & Allgeier, 1991). As the vaginal walls become thinner and less elastic, discomfort may occur during sexual intercourse (Hobson, 1984). If the vaginal barrel becomes **atrophied** (wasted away), it becomes distorted in shape and size, and dyspareunia results. Further, the time required for vaginal lubrication increases as does the susceptibility to vaginal infections (Bachmann, 1991).

Since genital changes in women appear to be reversible with estrogen replacement therapy, the physiological sexual response may be related to the estrogen deprivation (Semmens & Wagner, 1982). Sexually active elderly women exhibit much less overall vaginal atrophy than sexually inactive women. For example, the release of vaginal lubrication appears to lessen the tendency toward vaginal atrophy. Those with less atrophy have significantly higher levels of androgens and gonadotropins and are less likely to have pubic hair loss, atrophied labia, and vaginal mucosa (Leiblum, Bachmann, Kemmann, Colburn, & Swartzman, 1983). However, medical evidence suggests that estrogen replacement therapy does not always resolve complaints due to menopause such as low level of sexual desire, anorgasmia, inadequate vaginal lubrication, and decreased vaginal elasticity.

Physiological changes in the sexual responsiveness of aging men include reduction in size and firmness of testicles, lower sperm production, weaker

BOX 19.1 **The Fountain of Eternal Youth**

The slim young man I married
Has slowly gone to pot;
With wrinkled face and graying pate,
Slender he is not!
And when I meet a mirror,
I find a haggard crone;
I can't believe the face I see
Can really be my own!
But when we seek our bed each night,
The wrinkles melt away:
Our flesh is firm, our kisses warm,
Our ardent hearts are gay!
The Fountain of Eternal Youth
Is not so far to find:
Two things you need—a double bed,
A spouse who's true and kind!

—74-year-old wife

Table 19.6: Perceptions of Sexual Functioning among Older Men by Status

Perceptions of Sexual Functioning	Status		
	0	1	2
Frequency of spontaneous erection	65%	6%	28%
Frequency of masturbation	59	16	25
Sexual satisfaction	39	30	31
Frequency of intercourse	36	11	53
Strength of erection	36	23	41
Responsiveness to partner's caressing	32	6	62
Sexual desire	14	43	43

Note: Status categories are 0 = absent; 1 = decreased; 2 = unchanged.
From R. Weizman and J. Hart, "Sexual Behavior in Healthy Married Elderly Men" in *Archives of Sexual Behavior,* 16:42. Copyright © 1987 Plenum Publishing Corporation, New York, NY. Reprinted by permission.

contractions of prostate gland during ejaculation, and less forceful expulsion of semen during ejaculation (Allgeier & Allgeier, 1991). These changes result in longer refractory periods and reduction in quantity of semen during ejaculation (Hobson, 1984). Neurological changes specifically related to the penis include a loss of sensation in the glans penis and decreased sensitivity to light touch. Arterial changes in the penis also occur with aging which prevent an adequate flow of blood into the penile shaft, thus playing a major role in the decline of the erectile function (Mulligan & Katz, 1988). Aging men experience a gradual increase in the amount of stimulation required to achieve an erection and ejaculation. Further, they undergo a decline in the degree of rigidity and duration of their erections (Crooks & Baur, 1990). Researchers also have found that elderly men are likely to report less sexual desire, decreased frequency of spontaneous erections, a weakened strength of erections, and less sexual satisfaction (see Table 19.6).

About one fourth of men who are age 65 and one half of those age 70 develop physiologically-based erectile dysfunction from endocrine, vascular, pharmacologic, or neurologic causes (Rousseau, 1986). Diabetes mellitus and other endocrine disorders may produce erectile dysfunction as can neurologic disorders such as spinal cord disease, **prostatectomy** (removal of prostate gland), and chronic degenerative nerve disorders (Rousseau, 1988).

Sexual Attitudes and Behavior among the Elderly: A New Perspective

Variations in sexual capacity and performance among the elderly are greater than among persons in young or middle years. The double standard defines a man's sexual value according to his power and status (Klinkenborg, 1990). Consequently, physical aging is less of a crisis for men than for women whose physical appearance, smooth skin, slim physique, and firm breasts define their sexual value (Allgeier, 1983). A high level of sexual activity in earlier years tends to ensure sexual adequacy in old age, given the availability of a sex partner (Winn & Newton, 1982). Three fourths of sexually active elderly men reported sexual activity benefitted their health (Martin, 1981).

Two "nonsexual senior" myths among the elderly are that sexual activity is not prevalent and that it is wrong. Many older people, some of whom have a history of unsatisfactory sex lives, accept these myths in order to avoid sexual issues. Although many people believe that the elderly lose their sex drive, in reality, sexual needs do not change abruptly with age; and the potentiality for sexual expression continues until death (Rotberg, 1987).

Research suggests that societal attitudes toward sexuality among the aging population is changing. Content analysis of the treatment of sexuality and romance in advice books for the elderly published before 1970 concluded that about one fourth of the advice approved of sexual activity. In books published after 1970, the amount of sexual information had almost tripled and about two thirds approved of sexual activity among the elderly (Arluke, Levin, & Suchwalko, 1984).

Nevertheless, professionals indicate that the widespread disapproval of sexual activity among older persons that still exists can harm the elderly if they are led to believe that their sexual feelings are abnormal. Most medical students in one survey believed that a sexually active person living in a nursing home would be unpopular with the nursing home staff (Damrosch & Fischman, 1985). Similarly, nursing home staff members were only moderately knowledgeable about the sexuality of older persons and highly restrictive in their attitudes toward elderly sexuality. The most negative attitudes were held by supervisors and administrators who believed that they were responsible for protecting elderly women from all sexual advances from elderly men (Glass, Mustian, & Carter, 1986). Service providers can be sensitive to the sexual issues associated with the elderly by considering their sensual, sexual, affectionate, and companionship needs (Genevay, 1986).

Sexual Activity and the Elderly

Reports of masturbation in older age are more common among the unmarried than among the married elderly. Only about 20% of women and 10% of men regarded masturbation as their preferred sexual activity. Church attendance was found to be unrelated to masturbation among men. However, women who did not attend church services were four times more likely to report masturbation in older age in comparison to those who attended church services (Adams & Turner, 1985). Data on frequency of masturbation indicate that about one third of postmenopausal women engaged in masturbation one to two times per month (Bachmann et al., 1984). In comparison, about one half of elderly men who masturbated did so four or more times per month (Weizman & Hart, 1987). Among elderly married men, there was an increase in the frequency of masturbation with a decrease in sexual intercourse (see Table 19.7). In the absence of sexual intercourse, masturbation appears to be helpful in maintaining continued production of vaginal lubrication as well as vaginal elasticity (Leiblum et al., 1983).

Among married persons, ages 70–74, 43% of women and 58% of men reported being sexually active (Dionko, Brown, & Herzog, 1990). For married elderly persons who do experience a decrease in sexual intercourse, it may be due to a decline in physical health. However, among older singles who are more likely to abstain from sexual intercourse, the reason may be the unavailability of an acceptable sex partner (Gurian, 1986). For persons age 70 and over who classified themselves as being sexually active, 50% of women and 60% of men participated in sexual intercourse at least once per week (Brecher, 1984). Another survey of sexually active postmenopausal women with available sex partners found the frequency of sexual intercourse to be 1–2 times per week with 28% engaging in oral-genital stimulation and over one half in manual-genital stimulation (Bachmann et al., 1984).

A comparison of men in their early 50s and in their late 60s revealed little difference in levels of sexual activity and confirmed that sexual vigor is not necessarily related to age. Almost one half of men, ages 66–71, continued to have sexual intercourse five or more times per month (see Table 19.7). For elderly men, the frequency of sexual activity appears to be unrelated to marital adjustment, the number of times married, or age of their current wife. Instead, increased frequency is related to visual stimuli such as observing attractive women in public situations and seeing female nudity (Martin, 1981). Nevertheless, aging does appear to have its effects as both women and men over age 80 reported their most frequent type of sex activity, in order of occurrence, was touching and caressing, masturbation, and sexual intercourse (Bretschneider & McCoy, 1988).

Table 19.7: Sexual Activity among Elderly Married Men

Sexual Activity	Age 60–65	Age 66–71
Sexual Intercourse		
Never or once	9%	23%
2–4 times	27%	30%
5 or more times	64%	47%
Masturbation		
Never or once	45%	38%
2–4 times	22%	12%
5 or more times	33%	50%

From R. Weizman and J. Hart, "Sexual Behavior in Healthy Married Elderly Men" in *Archives of Sexual Behavior,* 16:43. Copyright © 1987 Plenum Publishing Corporation, New York, NY. Reprinted by permission.

Coping with Death of a Spouse

For the elderly, bereavement is a part of life because losses of loved ones occur much more frequently than for persons of younger ages. The death of a spouse is very difficult because it means the loss of a companion, sex partner, partner in decision making and oftentimes a best friend. With the death of a spouse, the widow or widower assumes a single status and may feel uncomfortable in activities involving couples. If there were either excessive dependence in the marital relationship or a high ambivalence toward the marriage, the grieving process may require more difficult adjustments. Adjustments may also include reduced income for the widow and the necessity to move to a new home (Osterweis, 1987).

As women age, they face extensive loss: their motherhood roles, their careers, and eventually their spouses. Although women outlive their husbands, at least two thirds of wives in one survey never considered the possibility of widowhood prior to their husband's death (O'Laughlin, 1983). In 1988, there were 11.2 million widows and only 2.3 million widowers in the

United States (U.S. Bureau of the Census, 1990d). Thus, the chances are about five times greater for a woman to experience widowhood during her lifetime (Torrey et al., 1987).

Adjusting to Being a Widow

A review of the research conducted during the 1980s identified no significant differences between widows and widowers in terms of feelings, coping behaviors, or eventual adjustment to bereavement (Brubaker, 1990). However, some research does indicate that older widows adjust better to widowhood than younger widows (Balkwell, 1985). There is no apparent relationship between length of marriage and amount of psychological distress associated with becoming a widow. However, widows who make preparations prior to their spouses' death are more likely to experience less distress after their death (Roach & Kitson, 1987). But the more grief and anger associated with becoming a widow, the greater degree of psychological distress likely to be experienced (Kitson & Zyzanski, 1987). Thus, providing social support to a widow may be more or less helpful to her psychological well-being depending upon such factors as stage in the adjustment process, type of support given, and source of support (Bankoff, 1983). Older widows, in particular, are likely to set apart memories associated with their late husband as being sacred (Lopata, 1981).

Losing a spouse may take years to resolve and is often characterized by guilt, rage, and disabling loneliness (Gelman, 1983). Older women who have been widowed for only a short period of time are lonelier than those who have been widowed for a longer period of time (Essex & Nam, 1987). Widows who have unsatisfactory interaction within their social networks experience greater feelings of loneliness than others. Being too open or not open enough with acquaintances results in substantial loneliness and discomfort in social interactions (Rook, 1987). Widows typically turn to adult children when they are worried or feel depressed but turn to friends to overcome loneliness (Anderson, 1984). However, after the death of a spouse, most widows lose friends because many social activities are couple-oriented. Consequently, support groups such as Widowed Persons of the American Association of Retired Persons offer widows social events where an escort is not considered a social necessity (Doan, 1985).

Coping with feelings of guilt and loneliness may magnify financial concerns (Osterweis, 1987). Elderly widows who may know little about financial management are suddenly faced with budgeting and making difficult decisions such as whether or not to move out of the family home. The economic status of a woman is usually worse after the loss of her husband. A substantial loss of income and a lower standard of living leads to widows having the lowest household income of any segment of our population. There is usually a change in the major source of income with widows often having to rely more on reduced Social Security payments and less on their late husband's pension payments (Hooyman & Kiyak, 1991). Many widows are ineligible to continue receiving income from their spouse's pension while others receive reduced benefits. For example, in 1987, the average annual Social Security payment was $9,234 for retired couples but only $5,616 for surviving spouses (Atchley, 1991). And, it is estimated that only 25% of widows receive their full benefits from Social Security and/or pensions due to lack of information or misinformation about obtaining these funds (Hooyman & Kiyak, 1991). However, poverty is more likely to be related to one's past economic position than one's advanced aged. In fact, researchers have reported that one half of all widows fall below the poverty line for at least 1 year during the first 5 years of their widowhood. Yet, in dual-career families, widowers may be just as likely as widows to experience economic hardship because of the subsequent cessation of the wife's Social Security payments (Smith & Zick, 1986). Also, a widow in her 50s or 60s who obtains personal health insurance may pay twice as much in premiums but receive only one half of the benefits that might have been available under an employer-subsidized insurance plan (Doan, 1985).

Widowers: Coping with Loss

Men appear to be less able to endure widowhood than women because they generally are more dependent on their wives for psychological and sexual needs. Consequently, widowers are more likely than widows to die soon after the death of their spouse (Gelman, 1983). Some widowers may feel that they have no time left to make adequate life changes and often experience low self-esteem. But for many other men, widowhood restructures their remaining years by defining their social identity. Men who successfully reorganize their lives usually find replacements for the roles and activities of their wives especially for the role of confidant. And the person who becomes their confidant also is likely to become a sex partner (Rubinstein, 1986). Life-styles that develop among older men prior to retirement have more influence on their social participation level than loss of a spouse. Thus, if the level of social participation was high prior to retirement, it is likely to remain high during retirement and widowhood (Wan & Odell, 1983). Although widowers usually have greater financial resources than widows, oftentimes they are more depressed. This depression may stem from the fact that it is harder to make and maintain friendships in old age. As widowers grow older, they also seem to have an increasing need for physical touch but often have no one with whom to express or satisfy this need. Such circumstances may be related to widowers in their 80s having a very high suicide rate because their self-esteem decreases as a result of their social isolation (Hogstel, 1985).

Given the traditional gender roles in our society, many men have substantial difficulties coping with everyday living. The major problem areas identified in a survey of widowers were loneliness, need for help with housework, and desire for help with cooking (Clark, Siviski, & Weiner, 1986). Attending to these problems enhances the daily lives of widowers.

Coping with loneliness is a major task as indicated by two thirds of widowers in one study. To cope with loneliness, about one half reported seeing their child(ren) at least once per week, and over three fourths had a close relationship with at least one child. In addition, over three fourths of these widowers socialized at least once per week with friends. Other coping skills cited were reading, keeping in physical shape, and believing in God (Clark et al., 1986).

Many widowers who have never performed household chores such as cooking, laundry, and cleaning are unprepared to perform housework. Even if wives and husbands share household responsibilities, the majority of men typically are responsible for so-called masculine tasks with wives responsible for most so-called feminine tasks (Brubaker, 1985b). Of those widowers who sought help with domestic work, approximately two thirds hired part-time cleaners, and over one third received help from family members (Clark et al., 1986).

Elderly persons generally experience more nutritional problems than younger adults since they are especially vulnerable to the effects of poor nutrition. Dietary problems contribute to and result from chronic diseases that affect at least 85% of all persons age 65 and over (Glanz & Scharf, 1985). Even if men have chronic conditions such as **hypertension,** heart disease, and diabetes which require special diets, it usually is the wife who purchases and prepares the food (Osterweis, 1987). Difficulties in preparing food are sometimes due to physical limitations such as arthritis and poor vision. However, obtaining and consuming an adequate diet is further limited by inadequate income, lack of transportation, and traditional gender roles (Glanz & Scharf, 1985). A survey of elderly widowers determined that their food intake included less than two thirds of the required daily allowances for vitamins and nutrients. Almost one half of those with low incomes consumed less than one serving from each food group on a daily basis (Davis, Randall, Forthofer, Lee, & Margen, 1985).

Living Arrangements for the Elderly

Elderly persons who have experienced widowhood value independent living. Even those widows and widowers who want to live nearby to be able to see their children and grandchildren prefer to maintain a separate home. While the proportion of elderly persons living with their children has decreased, the proportion of those living near their children has increased. Further, elderly parents who live alone are just as likely to have regular contact with their children as those who live with their children (Shanas, 1980). Women with few children have fewer alternatives in deciding where to live after widowhood (Thomas & Wister, 1984). Although widowers may want to move out of their home because of too many painful memories, they may not be able to afford other housing. Further, these men would have great difficulty depending upon their adult children for support after having been the main source of household income (Hogstel, 1985).

It is estimated that before the year 2000, over one half of all elderly women will be living alone due to the disparity of life expectancy between women and men (O'Bryant & Nocera, 1985). While living alone has formerly been associated with higher mortality rates, data from the National Senior Citizens survey suggests that widows and widowers living alone are in better health than those living with family members (Lawton, Moss, & Kleban, 1984).

Elderly widows, when compared to elderly women in general, tended to be much more attached to their homes because of greater investments in memories and family traditions. In fact, their home may become more meaningful to them after the death of their husband (O'Bryant & Nocera, 1985). For widowers, if the level of grief is still high, the home represents contact with the previous marriage. However, for those who have worked through their grief, living alone may represent

Adult congregate living centers offer a welcome alternative to nursing homes, which too often are viewed as half-way houses—from life to death.

a successful reorganization of their lives and enable them to get away from others after a busy day to enjoy a pleasant environment that they can control (Rubenstein, 1986).

Living with Children

The incidence of widows and widowers living with an adult child may be somewhat lower than is generally assumed. Of those parents who are 75 and over, only about 8% of mothers and 25% of fathers live with an adult child (Atchley, 1991). Due to the advantages of having a live-in child-care giver, some widows and widowers live with their adult children. Widowed persons choosing to live with their children tend to have high quality housing. But they are more likely to have poor health, less contact with friends, less life satisfaction, and lower morale when compared to those who live alone. Widowers especially have proportionately less satisfaction with family relationships if they live with their children (Lawton et al., 1984).

Alternative Residential Facilities

Although increasing numbers of elderly persons are moving to retirement communities, those who choose to live in retirement communities are less likely than their friends to have adult children. And if they do have adult children, the children often live a great distance away. Since community residents have age, life-style, and needs in common, mutual support within the retirement community is available. Yet, less than one fourth of retirement community residents indicated that they would turn to other residents for long-term support if it were needed (Sullivan, 1986). Widowers have significantly fewer primary relationships in retirement communities than widows (Longino & Lipman, 1981).

Another option, adult congregate living facilities (ACLF), has emerged as an alternative for elderly persons who need limited care but not full-time nursing care. In this type of facility, the elderly person takes care of many of her/his own needs. Typically, residents eat their meals in a common dining room, and professional staff members are available to provide care in emergencies and to monitor their health status. Persons who enter an ACLF are usually elderly persons who find their present living environment inappropriate to their needs. Of those residents living in one ACLF facility, over two thirds had been referred by a member of their former social network and over one half had been referred by relatives. Most residents believed ACLF to be a better alternative than a nursing home (Bear, 1988).

Contrary to popular opinion, only about 5% of the elderly population lives in nursing homes (Atchley, 1991). At the present time, a major deterrent to a larger number of elderly persons living in nursing homes is the costs. In 1988, about 70% of the 1.5 million nursing home residents depended upon Medicaid to help pay for their care (Pear, 1988). Almost three fourths of all private nursing homes are losing money due to the failure of Medicaid to keep pace with rising health care costs. Consequently, nursing homes that are heavily dependent upon state and federal Medicaid payments tend to provide the lowest quality care. In fact, a 1987 federal audit of nursing homes in 5 states found that 41% failed to meet one or more requirements that were most likely to adversely affect the residents' health and/or safety (Freudenhem, 1988).

The most powerful variable determining whether or not an elderly person will be placed in a nursing home is the family caregiver's attitude toward nursing home care. Other factors are the level of family burden created by the elderly person and the caregiver's perceptions of quality of care in the specific nursing home. Caregivers themselves reported twice as many health problems after placing an elderly relative in a nursing home. This finding suggests that a great burden exists in their lives associated with trying to provide adequate caregiving to their elderly relative and cope with guilt feelings surrounding the issue (Deimling & Poulshock, 1985). Data from relatives of nursing home patients indicate that having a positive family attitude toward nursing homes is a crucial factor in their level of satisfaction with nursing home care. Most caregivers reported that placement of their relative in a nursing home made their lives easier (Braun & Rose, 1987).

Facing Death and Dying

Death has changed from colonial times in that today it is likely to be predictable, take place at an older age, and follow a period of chronic illness. Further, death usually occurs in hospitals, and the deceased person's body is handed over to strangers (Marshall, 1986). Society tends to deny death, in part, due to increased life expectancies and better medical technology which has relegated death to old age (O'Laughlin, 1983). Although death is a natural life event for an old person, conflicting societal attitudes exist about death. For example, some believe that death rituals are unimportant and tend to be morbid. Others purport that major social and medical resources should only be used to save or prolong the lives of the young. Since these social attitudes are not well-supported by empirical evidence, greater expectations are being placed on caregivers as society has come to believe that elderly persons cherish their lives (Kastenbaum, 1987).

Due to a number of factors including dietary habits, lack of exercise, and the stresses of coping with attempts at upward occupational mobility, the leading cause of death among the elderly is heart disease (National Center for Health Statistics, 1990d). However, the proportion of the death rate attributable to heart disease has declined by one third for women and men since 1970 (U.S. Bureau of the Census, 1990t). Other causes of death are depicted in Table 19.8.

The suicide rate for men ages 75–84 is about seven times higher than for women of a similar age (U.S. Bureau of the Census, 1990t). The death rate for women, in general, is lower in comparison to men. This statistical variation is created by the longer life expectancy of women (National Center for Health Statistics, 1990f).

Attitudes toward Death

In the past, some religions provided a justification for death as being God's judgment. Now that death is more predictable and religiosity has declined somewhat, our society does not share a common belief about its meaning. In the "happy death movement" of the 1980s, people came to regard death as a normal part of the life cycle. An awareness of **finitude** (a recognition of limitations) or that death is drawing near usually starts around the middle years and is strong by age 70. This heightened awareness that one will not live forever initiates a process of preparation for death which helps to reduce death anxiety (Marshall, 1986). Such preparation for death may involve three stages that have been couched in metaphorical terms:

1. *Legitimize biography*—Persons approaching death focus on the past and are preoccupied with

Table 19.8: Causes of Death in 1989

Cause of Death	Rank	Rate	Total Deaths
Diseases of heart	1	296.3	34.1%
Malignant neoplasms	2	200.3	23.1
Cerebrovascular diseases	3	59.4	6.8
Accidents and adverse effects	4	38.2	4.4
Chronic obstructive pulmonary diseases	5	34.0	3.9
Pneumonia and influenza	6	30.3	3.5
Diabetes mellitus	7	18.8	2.2
Suicide	8	12.6	1.4
Chronic liver disease and cirrhosis	9	10.6	1.2
Homicide and legal intervention	10	9.3	1.1
Human immunodeficiency virus (AIDS)	11	8.6	1.0
Nephritis, nephrotic syndrome, and nephrosis	12	8.6	1.0
Aterosclerosis	13	7.7	0.9
Septicemia	14	7.7	0.9
Conditions originating/perinatal period	15	7.5	0.9

Source: National Center for Health Statistics, 1990d, "Annual Summary of Births, Marriages, Divorces, and Deaths: United States, 1989" in *Monthly Vital Statistics Report,* 38(13). DHHS Publication No. 90–1220. Hyattsville, MD: Public Health Service, 20–21.

their own identity. Since they are in the last chapter of their autobiography, they would like for it to be noteworthy.

2. *Legitimatize death*—Most persons who would like their life stories to have good endings try to make sense out of their eventual death.
3. *Assume authorship*—Persons take responsibility for their life in an attempt to control the situation (Marshall, 1986, pp. 139–143).

For the most part, persons with high levels of life satisfaction are more accepting of the inevitability of death (Flint, Gayton, & Ozmon, 1983). In addition, older persons are less anxious and less fearful about death than younger persons. Most persons want to know about a terminal illness and prefer to die a natural death rather than to have their life artificially prolonged. Thus, the fear of physical impairment may be greater than the fear of death itself. In some ways, adjustment to the death of friends may be more difficult than for family members, because a friend's death is a reminder of one's own vulnerability to death. Religion also strongly influences the way that people feel about their own death. One survey found that about two thirds of elderly persons expressed a strong belief in an afterlife (O'Laughlin, 1983).

Dying with Dignity

Preparing for death is still considered a major task for the elderly, even as their life expectancy increases. Although about 95% of the elderly population does not live in institutions, most elderly persons will die in some type of institutionalized medical setting. Among the problems for elderly persons who are spending their final days in an institutionalized setting are stigma associated with institutions, loss of individual identity, and weakened self-esteem due to fewer social contacts within the larger community. Once a person has been labeled as "dying," these problems will become intensified (Kastenbaum, 1987). Consequently, most dying persons experience five stages: denial and isolation, anger, bargaining with fate, depression, and acceptance (Kübler-Ross, 1969).

Reactions of dying persons are very complex. While positive attitudes about death are now becoming popular along with the pervasive optimism in our society, reading about the "happy" side of death can cause persons to feel anxious, scared, and inadequate about facing death. Further, it may have been easier to feel calm about death in the past when more people firmly believed in the afterlife. The new attitudes about death may place a burden on the dying person to "die correctly" (Wasow, 1984).

The world's first modern **hospice** (home for the dying), St. Christopher's in London, was established in 1967 by Cicely Saunders who had been trained at different times as a nurse, social worker, and physician. History suggests that the Greeks probably originated the concept of a place to go to die before 1000 B.C., while the modern roots for hospices can be traced to Dublin, Ireland, and London in the late 19th century (Brand, 1988). Although most dying patients prefer to be in their homes, available data indicate that most persons die in hospitals (Atchley, 1991). Oftentimes, after being labeled as dying, terminal patients in hospitals may experience a lack of communication and eye contact with hospital staff members and physicians. When nothing more can be done for a patient, the nursing staff often feels inadequate and treats the patient as if she/he were already dead. In other words, the patient moves into a kind of "social" death (Shanis, 1985).

The hospice offers an alternative way of dying which allows the terminal patient with 2–6 months to live to die with dignity in a familiar environment as in the patient's home, a special building, or hospital wing. A hospice environment has no bureaucratic rules like visiting hours, restrictions on pets, or personal possessions. A patient also usually has a primary care provider such as a relative, friend, or nurse. The hospice team consists of professionals including nurses, social workers, physicians, clergy, and volunteers who guide, instruct, and assist the patient and the informal network of supporters. Hospice team members fulfill the roles that the patient no longer can perform by helping the family to reorganize and adjust their lives around the patient. Control is given to the patient in contrast to the hospital where the patient has no control over her/his life (Shanis, 1985).

Euthanasia refers to the practice of a friend, a relative, or an incurably ill person herself/himself asking the physician to withhold treatment and allowing the person to die. Instead of being kept alive by machines, many persons would prefer to die in this painless manner with dignity, honesty, and compassion. Thus, by 1987, the Euthanasia Society, which advocates letting a person die with dignity, had grown to over 50,000 members (Sage, 1987). Active euthanasia involves increasing the dosage level of a medication that would be fatal in large quantities. In contrast, passive euthanasia relates to withholding treatments that merely serve to prolong the life of the patient rather than cure her/him of the terminal illness. Further, euthanasia may be either voluntary or involuntary. In the case of voluntary euthanasia, the patient requests that a physician, friend, or relative end her/his life, whereas involuntary euthanasia involves a friend or relative making the decision herself/himself regarding euthanasia. In general, both active and involuntary euthanasia are perceived more negatively than passive or voluntary euthanasia (Sugarman, 1986).

A survey of elderly patients in nursing homes found that only one fourth wanted to die if their medical situation became hopeless. In contrast, a national survey of college students ascertained that over one half approved of euthanasia under certain circumstances. But perhaps the most controversial finding is contained in data from members of the American Association of Professors of Medicine in which 4 in 5 physicians had actually practiced passive euthanasia (Sage, 1987).

Summary

- During the middle and later years, women tend to become more aggressive and intent on personal growth whereas men exhibit decreased aggressiveness and more nurturing behaviors.
- Young adult children who "nest" at home may create stressful parent-child relationships.
- Marital happiness in middle years is associated with presence of children, anticipation of financial support in old age, and a sexual outlet.
- Since emotional attachments between a grandparent and grandchild lack the intensity and responsibility that exists in parent-child relationships, grandparents are better able to offer unconditional love to a grandchild.
- Security of relationship, increased leisure time with departure of children, and absence of concerns about pregnancy enhance sexual satisfaction.
- Menopausal women report physiological symptoms that may be alleviated by estrogen-replacement therapy.
- Retirement may mean a drastic decline in disposable income, loss of meaningful social status, and potentially negative effects of being with one's spouse every day.
- While modern medicine has increased the life expectancy for elderly persons, it has not increased their quality of life which depends to a great degree upon a person staying active.
- Over one half of the elderly continue to be sexually active with any decline in sexual activity being attributable to their health status and lack of available sex partner.
- The reasons for greater numbers of unmarried widows are that women live longer, men marry younger women, and widowers are more likely to remarry.
- Major problems of adjustment for widows are decreased financial resources and coping with loneliness; and for widowers, loneliness, inability to perform household tasks, and poor nutrition.
- Retirement communities and adult congregate facilities represent new living options for elderly persons.
- The major cause of death for women and men is heart disease.
- Problems confronting the terminally-ill elderly in hospitals or nursing homes are loss of identity, self-esteem, and dignity as well as stigma of institutionalization.
- Voluntary euthanasia and the hospice movement have emerged as proposed ways of dying with dignity.

Questions for Critical Reflection

1. Mid-life crisis has been described as an issue that comes with a slogan but no real understanding. Since this last uncharted territory in human development is now being studied, do you believe the findings will most affect individuals, families, or society? Why is mid-life the beginning of dysfunction for some and not for others?
2. If writing a letter of thanks to your favorite grandparent for her/his gifts of life to you, what sights, sounds, and smells would be evoked? If they are not still living, what major messages would you give them that you were never able to express during their lifetime?
3. A female writer characterized retirement as that time when she saw more of her husband and less of his money. What problems, if any, have you observed in relationships due to adjusting to retirement among your own family or friends? Who seemed to have the most trouble adjusting?
4. What experiences in life have best prepared you to confront your own mortality? What epitaph would you choose for yourself?
5. "Grow old along with me, the best is yet to be" and "the last of life for which the first was made" are two familiar phrases. Based on your observation of older persons, do you believe these sayings are idealistic or realistic? For what reasons?

Suggested Readings

Asso, D. (1983). *The real menstrual cycle.* New York: Wiley. An excellent review of the menstrual cycle and menopause from the physiological and psychological perspective.

Atchley, R. C. (1991). *Social forces and aging: An introduction to social gerontology* (6th ed.). Belmont, CA: Wadsworth. A well-written, comprehensive textbook on the study of aging.

Bergtson, V., & Robertson, J. F. (Eds.). (1985). *Grandparenthood,* Beverly Hills, CA: Sage. A collection of essays and research articles on the symbolic role of grandparents in American society.

Bould, S., Sanborn, B., & Reif, L. (1989). *Eighty-five plus: The oldest old.* Belmont, CA: Wadsworth. A sociological analysis of the health status, economic and personal coping resources, and caregivers for persons age eighty-five plus.

Brecher, E. M. (1984). *Love, sex, and aging.* Boston: Little, Brown. A comprehensive and technical work on aging and sexuality.

Kübler-Ross, E. (1969). *On death and dying.* New York: Macmillan. A classical narrative on the stages of adjustment to death.

Appendix A

Sources of Assistance

A

AIDS Hotline
United States Department of Health and Human Services
3700 East-West Highway
Hyattsville, MD 20782

Toll Free: 1–800–342–2437

Serves as a source of general information about AIDS and makes referrals to physicians, clinics, and counselors by geographical area.

Al-Anon Family Groups
P.O. Box 862, Midtown Station
New York, NY 10018–0862

Phone: 212–302–7240

Acts as a fellowship for relatives and friends of alcoholics who help each other by sharing their own experiences.

Alcoholics Anonymous (AA)
468 Park Ave. South
New York, NY 10016

Phone: 1–800–356–9996

Represents a voluntary fellowship of men and women who meet to attain and maintain sobriety.

American Association for Marriage and Family Therapy
1717 K St. NW, Suite 407
Washington, DC 20006

Phone: 202–429–1825

Provides information about marriage and family therapy and a directory of certified marriage and family therapists.

American Association of Sex Educators, Counselors, and Therapists
11 Dupont Circle, Suite 220
Washington, DC 20036–1207

Phone: 202–462–1171

Strives to provide education in human sexuality and standards for sex education, counseling, and therapy programs; publishes a newsletter and the Journal of Sex Education and Therapy.

American College of Nurse-Midwives
1522 K St. NW, Suite 1120
Washington, DC 20005

Phone: 202–347–5445

Provides a directory of certified nurse-midwives and information on accredited university-affiliated nurse-midwifery programs.

American Dietetic Association
430 N Michigan Ave.
Chicago, IL 60611

Phone: 312–280–5000

Provides a directory of registered dietitians and information on nutrition for general and therapeutic situations.

The American Fertility Society
2140 Eleventh Ave. South, Suite 200
Birmingham, AL 35205–2800

Phone: 205–933–8494

Provides current information on infertility, reproductive endocrinology, conception control, and reproductive biology.

American Foundation for AIDS Research
40 W 57th St., Suite 406
New York, NY 10019

Phone: 212–333–3118

Promotes fund-raising efforts for AIDS research.

The Association for Couples in Marriage Enrichment
P.O. Box 10596
Winston-Salem, NC 26108

Toll Free: 1–800–634–8325

Promotes activities to strengthen marriages by offering weekend retreats, local chapter meetings, workshops, and conferences throughout the United States and Canada.

Association for Voluntary Surgical Contraception
122 East 42nd St.
New York, NY 10168

Phone: 212–573–8350

Promotes female and male sterilization as a method of birth control.

B

Bankcard Holders of America
383 Pennsylvania SE
Washington, DC 20003

Phone: 202–543–0805

Offers information on lowest annual interest rates for bank cards.

Birthright
1001 N Broad St.
Woodbury, NJ 08096

Phone: 609–848–1818

Provides information for pregnant women; maintains pro-life stance.

C

Center for Auto Safety
2001 South St. NW, Suite 410
Washington, DC 20009

Phone: 202–328–7700

Identifies and evaluates safety problems in automobiles associated with manufacturing defects.

Centers for Disease Control
Freeway Park 1680, Room 203
Atlanta, GA 30333

Phone: 404–639–2575

Answers inquiries concerning communicable diseases, including sexually transmitted diseases.

Child Welfare League of America
440 First St. NW
Washington, DC 20001

Phone: 202–638–2952

Supports the rights and interests of children.

Clearinghouse on Child Abuse and Neglect Information
P.O. Box 1182
Washington, DC 20013

Phone: 703–821–2086

Provides information on child maltreatment issues to professionals and concerned citizens.

Consumer Information Center
P.O. Box 100
Pueblo, CO 81002
Phone: 719-544-0075
Furnishes lists of available booklets on various topics including careers, children, health, housing, money, and many others.

Consumer Product Safety Commission
5401 Westbard Ave.
Bethesda, MD 20207
Toll Free: 1-800-638-8326
Evaluates the safety of products sold to the public; answers questions, and provides information on different aspects of consumer product safety other than drugs, prescriptions, warranties, advertising, repairs, or maintenance.

D

Divorce Mediation Services
Association of Family and Conciliation Court
1227 Spruce St.
Boulder, CO 80302
Phone: 303-447-8116
Provides information about divorce mediation services.

F

The Fatherhood Project
c/o Bank Street College of Education
610 W 112th St.
New York, NY 10025
Phone: 212-663-7200
Center for field research and literature review providing free resources on male involvement in child rearing.

FDA Consumer Affairs Office
5600 Fishers Lane
Rockville, MD 20857
Phone: 301-443-5006
Provides information and referrals on food products, pharmaceutical drugs, and cosmetics.

Federation of Parents and Friends of Lesbians and Gays
5715 16th St. NW
Washington, DC 20011
Phone: 301-439-3524
Offers information and support for those who care about lesbians and gays.

G

The Gladney Center
2300 Hemphill St.
Ft. Worth, TX 76110
Toll Free: 1-800-452-3639
Provides comprehensive maternity and social services, including adoption, to birth mothers, children, and adoptive parents.

Gray Panthers
311 S Juniper St., Suite 601
Philadelphia, PA 19107
Phone: 215-545-6555
Works to eliminate ageism and discrimination against older people.

H

Health Care Financing Administration
200 Independence Ave. SW
Washington, DC 20201
Phone: 202-245-0923
Answers questions on child health, social security, and all aspects of Medicaid and Medicare; provides referrals including listings of local public assistance offices.

Herpes Resource Center
P.O. Box 100
Palo Alto, CA 94302
Phone: 919-361-2120
919-361-8488
Supplies information about coping with Herpes Simplex Type I and Type II virus.

J

Joint Custody Association
10606 Wilkins Ave.
Los Angeles, CA 90024
Phone: 213-475-5352
Serves to support parents involved in joint custody of children.

L

La Leche League International
P.O. Box 1209
Franklin Park, IL 60131-8209
Phone: 312-455-7730
Provides advice and support for nursing mothers.

M

Make Today Count
P.O. Box 222
Osage Beach, MO 65065
Phone: 314-348-1619
Offers telephone counseling and referrals to local chapters for terminally ill patients, their families, and friends.

The Missing Children Network
1612 Prosser Ave.
Dayton, OH 45409
Toll Free: 1-800-235-3535
Serves as clearinghouse for information on missing children.

N

National Abortion Rights Action League
1101 14th St. NW
Washington, DC 20005
Phone: 202-371-0779
Directs efforts to make abortion "safe, legal, and accessible" for all women.

National Center for Missing and Exploited Children
1835 K St., Suite 700
Washington, DC 20006
Phone: 202-634-9821
Toll Free: 1-800-THE-LOST
Serves as a national hotline for missing children.

National Child Abuse Hotline
P.O. Box 630
Hollywood, CA 90028
Toll Free: 1-800-422-4453
Skilled child abuse counselors provide information and locate emergency shelters 24 hours a day.

National Clearinghouse for Alcohol and Drug Information
P.O. Box 2345
Rockville, MD 20852
Phone: 301-468-2600
Provides referrals, answers inquiries on alcohol and drug-related subjects and gathers and distributes information free of charge.

National Clearinghouse on Marital and Date Rape
2325 Oak
Berkeley, CA 94708
Phone: 415-548-1770
Provides information, referrals, seminars, and speakers covering numerous aspects of marital and date rape for a nominal charge.

The National Coalition Against Domestic Violence
1500 Massachusetts Avenue NW, No. 35
Washington, DC 20005

Phone: 202–347–7017

Coordinates private, nonprofit programs for battered wives and their families in 50 states, Washington, DC, Puerto Rico, and the Virgin Islands.

National Coalition Against Sexual Assault
Sexual Violence Center
1222 W 31st St.
Minneapolis, MN 55408

Phone: 612–824–2864

Strives to understand and to eliminate sexual violence in society.

National Committee for Prevention of Child Abuse
332 S Michigan Ave., Suite 950
Chicago, IL 60604–4357

Phone: 312–663–3520

Supports prevention of child abuse through educational programs, materials, and self-help groups for parents.

National Council on Aging
600 Maryland Ave. SW
W. Wing, Suite 100
Washington, DC 20024

Phone: 202–479–1200

Cooperates with other organizations to promote concern for older persons and develop resources for meeting their needs.

National Down's Syndrome Congress
1800 Dempster St.
Park Ridge, IL 60068

Phone: 312–823–7550

Serves as source of information and support for parents of children with Down's Syndrome.

National Foundation for Jewish Genetic Diseases
250 Park Ave., Suite 1000
New York, NY 10177

Phone: 212–682–5550

Strives to determine cause and cure for Tay Sachs disease.

National Gay and Lesbian Task Force
80 5th Ave., Suite 1601
New York, NY 10011

Toll Free: 1–800–221–7044

Provides information and referrals on lesbian and gay issues and rights.

National Health Information Center
P.O. Box 1133
Washington, DC 20013

Toll Free: 1–800–336–4797

Refers consumers to health information resources.

National Hospice Organization
1901 N Fort Myer Dr., Suite 307
Arlington, VA 22209

Phone: 703–243–5900

Provides information and referrals for support and care of persons in the final phase of terminal disease.

National Information Center for Children and Youth with Handicaps
P.O. Box 1492
Washington, DC 20013

Phone: 703–893–6061
Toll Free: 1–800–999–5599

Provides referrals for parents of disabled children; distributes publications free of charge.

National Organization for Women
425 13th St. NW
Washington, DC 20004

Phone: 202–347–2279

Supports full equality for women in equal partnership with men; promotes social change through research, litigation, and political pressure.

National Parents' Resource Institute for Drug Education
100 Edgewood Ave., Suite 1002
Atlanta, GA 30303

Toll Free: 1–800–241–7946

Provides drug information and referral services.

National Right to Life Committee
419 7th St., NW, Suite 500
Washington, DC 20004

Phone: 202–626–8800

Works through education, public affairs, and lobbying to promote a pro-life perspective concerning abortion, euthanasia, and infanticide.

National Runaway Switchboard
2210 N Halstad St.
Chicago, IL 60614

Toll Free: 1–800–621–4000
Toll Free (Illinois only):
1–800–972–6004

Provides services for young runaways, those considering running away, and parents.

National Save-A-Life League
4520 4th Ave., Suite MH3
New York, NY 11220

Phone: 212–492–4067

Provides referral services and information on suicide prevention.

National Sudden Infant Death Syndrome Foundation
8200 Professional Place, Suite 104
Landover, MD 20785

Phone: 301–459–3388
Toll Free: 1–800–221–SIDS

Provides emotional support to families who have lost a child to sudden infant death syndrome; supports research into SIDS; and provides free crisis counseling, referrals, and information.

North American Adoption Congress
P.O. Box 44040
L'Enfant Station
Washington, DC 20026

Phone: 206–481–6471

Serves as a clearinghouse for information about search and support groups for persons seeking their birth mother and "roots."

North American Council on Adoptable Children
1346 Connecticut Ave. NW, Suite 229
Washington, DC 20036

Phone: 202–466–7570

Provides information and support services to parents and adoption agencies.

O

OURS, Inc.
3307 Hwy. 100 North, Suite 203
Minneapolis, MN 55422

Phone: 612–535–4829

Provides problem-solving assistance to adoptive individuals and families.

P

Parents Anonymous (PA)
7120 Franklin Ave.
Los Angeles, CA 90046

Toll Free: 1–800–421–0353
Toll Free (California):
1–800–352–0386

Provides support for parents who abuse or fear they may abuse their children.

Parents United
P.O. Box 952
San Jose, CA 95108

Phone: 408–280–5055

Self-help organization for all family members affected by sexual abuse.

Parents Without Partners
8807 Colesville Road
Silver Springs, MD 20910

Phone: 301–588–9354

Acts as mutual support group for single parents and their children, offering educational programs and literature, low-cost recreation, and member benefits.

Permanent Families for Children
c/o Child Welfare League of America
440 First St. NW
Washington, DC 20001

Phone: 202–638–2000

Provides information about adoption and makes referrals to appropriate agencies and organizations; serves as advocate for minority placements and single-parent adoption.

Planned Parenthood Federation of America
810 Seventh Ave.
New York, NY 10019

Phone: 212–541–7800

Provides information, counseling, and medical services related to reproduction and sexual health.

Project Focus
250 Church St., Rm. FAS-1316
New York, NY 10013

Phone: 212–941–6130

Offers information on services to adults who need protection from abuse.

R

Recovery
802 N Dearborn St.
Chicago, IL 60610

Phone: 312–337–5661

Sponsors group meetings for people with mental health problems and makes referrals to local chapters.

Resolve, Inc.
5 Water St.
Arlington, MA 02174

Phone: 617–643–2424

Focuses on the problem of infertility, makes referrals to local chapters, provides fact sheets on female and male infertility, and publishes a directory of infertility resources.

S

The Samaritans
500 Commonwealth Ave.
Kenmore Square
Boston, MA 02215

Phone: 617–247–0220

Maintains a worldwide, nonreligious organization of trained volunteers who talk with anyone who is suicidal, lonely, or depressed.

San Francisco AIDS Foundation
333 Valencia St.
San Francisco, CA 94103

Phone: 415–863–2437

Promotes AIDS education and provides information and emotional support to families and those with AIDS.

Sex Information and Education Council of the United States
32 Washington Place
New York, NY 10003

Phone: 212–673–3850

Promotes healthy sexuality as an integral part of life, provides information and referrals, and maintains extensive library and computer database.

Single Mothers by Choice
P.O. Box 1642
New York, NY 10028

Phone: 212–988–0993

Supports single mothers and single women who are considering motherhood; offers workshops and support groups; and maintains bibliographic information about artificial insemination and adoption.

STD Hotline
(American Social Health Association)
P.O. Box 100
Palo Alto, CA 94302

Toll Free: 1–800–227–8922

Provides information on all aspects of sexually transmitted diseases.

Stepfamily Association of America
602 E Joppa Road
Baltimore, MD 21204

Phone: 301–823–7570

Offers information and emotional support for persons living in stepfamilies.

W

Widowed Persons Service
American Association of Retired Persons
1909 K St. NW
Washington, DC 20049

Phone: 202–872–4700

Provides information about services to widowed persons.

Z

Zero Population Growth
1400 16th St. NW, Suite 320
Washington, DC 20036

Phone: 202–332–2200

Works to achieve a sustainable balance between earth's population and its environment and resources.

GLOSSARY

A

abstinence: voluntarily refraining from indulgence in sexual intercourse (p. 263).

accommodation: adjustment of old ideas to adapt to newly assimilated experience (p. 372).

Acquired Immune Deficiency Syndrome (AIDS): a fatal sexually transmitted disease in which the body's immune system fails to function properly (p. 298).

acyclovir: antiviral drug that, in ointment or pill form, is often highly effective in the management of genital herpes (p. 297).

adjustable-rate mortgage: interest rate permitted to rise and fall based on financial market conditions over the duration of the loan (p. 405).

adult ego state: computer-like component of the personality which gathers objective information (p. 226).

adultery: voluntary sexual intercourse of a married person with someone else other than her/his spouse (p. 127).

affinity: close relation (p. 223).

A-frame marriage: a marital relationship in which one partner is too dependent upon the other (p. 221).

agape: an unselfish form of love involving unconditional caring and self-sacrificing (p. 154).

AIDS-Related Complex (ARC): an AIDS-related syndrome with less severe symptoms; often develops into AIDS (p. 298).

alimony: monetary payments from one ex-spouse to the other for maintenance of her/his economic needs (p. 468).

altruistic: unselfish regard for the welfare of others (p. 309).

Alzheimer's disease: a degenerate disease usually in persons over age 60 who experience serious memory loss and inability to concentrate (p. 531).

amniocentesis: withdrawal of amniotic fluid to examine chromosomes to determine presence of genetic abnormality (p. 338).

amnion: thin membrane forming a sac which surrounds the embryo (p. 329).

amniotic injection abortion: a second trimester method of abortion in which saline or prostaglandins are injected into the amniotic fluid resulting in uterine contractions expelling the fetus (p. 292).

androgyny: exhibiting both feminine and masculine traits and behaviors in more or less equal degrees (p. 46).

anilingus: oral stimulation of the anus (p. 298).

annulment: marital dissolution through either proving that no valid marriage ever existed from a legal perspective; after civil divorce, may be religious annulment to declare marriage invalid for theological reasons (p. 472).

anorgasmia: the inability to experience orgasm (p. 265).

antenuptial: prior to marriage (p. 168).

aphorism: terse formulation of a truth or sentiment (p. 15).

areola: circle of dark skin surrounding the nipple that contains many nerve and muscle fibers, which produce nipple erection; site of sebaceous glands, which provide lubricant to nipple during breast-feeding (p. 253).

arteriosclerosis: hardening of the arteries (p. 523).

artificial insemination: fertilization of the ovum by introduction of semen into the uterus or oviduct by other than natural means (p. 321).

assimilation: the process of integrating a new object, experience, or concept into existing cognitive structures (p. 372).

atrophied: wasted away; decreased in size (p. 533).

attachment: bonding in the early months of life between an infant and the primary caregiver; that endures over time (p. 16).

authoritarian parent: pattern of parental behavior characterized by high levels of directiveness and low levels of affection and warmth (p. 377).

authoritative parent: pattern of parental behavior characterized by consistent discipline, high maturity demands, and high warmth (p. 377).

autonomic: a power pattern in which each marriage partner makes decisions alone in certain areas based on perceived expertise (p. 210).

autonomy: state of being self-governing or morally independent (p. 363).

B

baby boom: refers to a sustained cycle of increased birth rates between the mid-1940s and mid-1960s (p. 19).

battering rape: sexual assault accompanied by episodes of verbal and physical abuse by the offender (p. 240).

birth dearth: falling birth rates of the mid-1960s and early 1970s (p. 19).

bisexuality: a sexual orientation in which sexual behavior with the same sex and the opposite sex are viewed as equally pleasurable (p. 129).

blamer: a response pattern of a person who is a fault finder, dictator, or superior cutting everyone down to enhance her/his own image (p. 222).

blastocyst: a cluster of cells formed from the division of the fertilized egg which implants itself into the uterine lining on the 6th day after fertilization, ending the first prenatal or germinal stage (p. 328).

blue-collar: class of wage earners whose duties require wearing work clothes or protective clothing (p. 202).

bonding: process of forming a close, personal attachment in a relationship (p. 364).

boundary ambiguity: the uncertainty of family members concerning their perceptions of who should perform what roles and tasks (p. 505).

Braxton Hicks contractions: false labor during pregnancy, assists during actual labor to thin and dilate the cervix (p. 345).

breadwinner: a family member whose salary/wages provides the primary means of family livelihood (p. 422).

C

cardiology: treatment of heart disease (p. 406).

cardiovascular: involving the heart and blood vessels (p. 523).

casual dating: going out with someone or "playing the field" (p. 65).

Caucasoid: a major racial division of the human species, sometimes referred to as whites, characterized by light to brown skin coloring (p. 170).

celibacy: abstinence from sexual intercourse (p. 263).

cephalocaudal: a pattern of physical development in the infant occurring from the head downward (p. 374).

cervical cap: thimble-shaped contraceptive device made of plastic or rubber which fits tightly over the cervix (p. 282).

cervix: neck of the uterus which protrudes into the vagina (p. 252).

cesarean section: surgical method of childbirth in which an incision is made through the abdominal wall and the uterus to extract the fetus (p. 342).

child abuse: nonaccidental, physical and/or mental injury, sexual abuse or exploitation, or emotional or physical neglect (p. 384).

child ego state: part of the personality comprised of natural instincts and recordings of early experiences (p. 226).

child-rearing practices: methods of guidance used to rear children (p. 358).

child sexual abuse: involvement of dependent, psychologically immature children and adolescents in sexual activities (p. 386).

chlamydia: a sexually transmitted disease caused by a bacterium; male symptoms include pus-like discharge, inflammation of the scrotal skin, and painful swelling along the testicles; women may develop signs of a urinary tract infection (p. 295).

cholesterol: abundant steroid in body tissues that may build up in the arteries leading to arteriosclerosis (p. 399).

chorionic villi: thread-like tissue protrusions on membrane that surrounds the fetus (p. 338).

chronological age: age in years (p. 374).

clitoris: most sensitive female sexual organ consisting of clitoral shaft, clitoral glans, and clitoral hood (p. 250).

codicil: change in a legal will (p. 418).

coercive power: acting in such a way as to punish your partner (p. 210).

cognition: the ability to have ideas, solve problems, speak, read, calculate, and remember (p. 32).

cohabitation: an arrangement in which an unmarried couple lives together in an intimate sexual relationship (p. 114).

cohesion: emotional bonding (p. 363).

cohort: persons from the same age group (p. 19).

collateral: security for debt (p. 413).

common-law marriage: marriage without formalities of ceremony recognized in some states as legal when parties cohabit and agree to publicly proclaim themselves married (p. 124).

commuter marriage: a dual-career marriage in which the marital partners maintain separate residences in order to accommodate the career demands of both spouses (p. 449).

comparable worth: concept suggesting that women and men must be paid equally for the same job requiring similar skills, effort, and responsibility (p. 427).

complementary needs theory: based upon principle that opposites attract, and that an individual selects a marriage partner who satisfies unfulfilled personality needs (p. 166).

complex stepparent: blended family in which both spouses have children from a prior marriage (p. 505).

"computer": a response pattern of an overly correct and reasonable person who uses the longest words possible and fears feelings (p. 222).

conception: the act of becoming pregnant; fertilization of the ovum by a sperm resulting in a zygote (p. 274).

condom: a sheath, often made of rubber, worn over the penis to prevent conception or contraction of a sexually transmitted disease during sexual intercourse (p. 281).

congenital: present at birth (p. 336).

conjugal power: family power exercised between spouses (p. 207).

constant dollars: dollar value adjusted for inflation (p. 393).

Consumer Price Index (CPI): an economic indicator which measures the impact of inflation over time (p. 393).

contactive style: respect and appreciation for the needs of others as well as a revelation of the person's innermost needs (p. 224).

contraception: deliberate prevention of conception (p. 274).

controlling style: minimizes the importance of the other partner's experience and shows little awareness for the other's needs (p. 222).

conventional style: glossing over issues, using small talk which prevents disclosure of needs and problems (p. 224).

convergent: to move toward the same conclusion or result (p. 367).

corporal punishment: physical punishment involving spanking or hitting (p. 379).

corpus luteum: mass of cells produced from the remaining cells of the Graafian follicle with the function of secreting progesterone (p. 254).

courtship: period of social activities leading to engagement and marriage (p. 149).

Cowper's glands: glands located below prostate gland that empty directly into the urethra, and secrete alkaline fluid during sexual arousal to lubricate the glans penis for ease of vaginal entry (p. 250).

creativity: the ability to see things in a new way; to see problems no one else has recognized; and to solve them with unusual, effective solutions (p. 367).

credit worthiness: the probability, as perceived by a lender or debtor, that a person will be able to repay a loan or credit card balance (p. 413).

"cruising": process whereby homosexuals go out for the express purpose of looking for a person of the same sex with whom to engage in casual sex (p. 133).

cunnilingus: oral stimulation of the female genital organs (p. 98).

D

D needs: deficiency needs, such as those resulting from low self-esteem, seen as illegitimate developmental deficits by therapists (p. 220).

decision/commitment: a cognitive component of the triangular theory of love that addresses decision-making about the existence of and commitment to a loving relationship (p. 153).

defendant: person required to respond in a legal action or lawsuit (p. 131).

defense mechanisms: cognitive devices or behaviors distorting reality to avoid emotional pain (p. 228).

deferral syndrome: the increasing delay of marriage (p. 11).

delinquency: conduct which is unacceptable; those acts which are against the law (p. 358).

dependency: the inability to experience wholeness or function adequately without being actively cared for by another (p. 144).

developmental change: orderly or sequenced change that results in a permanent alteration of behavior that is more advanced, adaptive, or useful than previous behavior (p. 362).

developmental task: a task which arises at a certain period of life whose achievement leads to happiness and success because of approval from society (p. 375).

deviant: abnormal (p. 313).

diaphragm: dome-shaped contraceptive device made of thin rubber that is inserted into the vagina fitting snugly over the cervix prior to sexual intercourse (p. 281).

dilation and curettage (D & C): a first trimester method of abortion in which the cervix is dilated with a metal instrument followed by the scraping of the uterine wall (p. 292).

dilation and evacuation (D & E): a second trimester method of abortion requiring anesthesia and a greater dilation of the cervix to remove a large amount of conception product (p. 292).

discipline: use of instruction, control, rewards, or punishment in order to train or correct, with goal of instilling self-discipline (p. 375).

discretionary income: disposable income after paying taxes and for essentials (p. 395).

displacement: a defense mechanism in which feelings and frustrations are replaced or transferred onto insignificant events (p. 228).

disposable income: money which is available after taxes have been removed from the paycheck (p. 393).

distractor: a response pattern of a person who comments irrelevantly because of feeling lonely, purposeless, and nonfocused (p. 222).

diuretic: drug to maintain adequate urination (p. 533).

divergent: moving outward in different directions; deviating from the norm (p. 367).

division of loyalties: feelings of disloyalty that children have for one parent because of positive feelings for the other parent (p. 505).

double standard: norm whereby premarital sexual intercourse is considered acceptable for men but not for women (p. 28).

Down's syndrome: congenital condition characterized by mental deficiency, slanting eyes, and broad short skull; caused by defect in chromosome 21 (p. 317).

dual-career marriage: a marriage in which the woman and man are heavily committed to their careers (p. 423).

dual-earner marriage: a married couple with wife and husband in the labor force, but not necessarily employed in professional positions (p. 423).

dyspareunia: painful sexual intercourse (p. 265).

dysuria: painful urination (p. 523).

E

ecosystem: organisms and their environment (p. 254).

egalitarian: a belief in human equality with demands for social, political, economic, legal, and cultural rights (p. 102).

ego: the part of personality which represents reality (p. 371).

ego boundary: psychological self-boundary that differentiates oneself from the rest of the world (p. 10).

ejaculatory duct: a duct formed by the joining of the duct from the seminal vesicle with the vas deferens through which semen is ejaculated (p. 260).

electronic cottage: home as a workplace for those who create, process, or distribute information (p. 18).

embryo: the human organism from about 2–8 weeks of prenatal development beginning when the blastocyst implants itself into the uterine wall (p. 333).

emotional divorce: withdrawal of emotional involvement in marital relationship by at least one partner (p. 470).

empathy: the capacity to feel what another is feeling (p. 206).

empirical: reliance on experience or observation (p. 23).

empty-nest stage: period in the family life cycle beginning when children leave home to become independent (p. 214).

endogamy: marriage within one's social, religious, age, racial, ethnic, or educational group (p. 162).

endometrium: mucous membrane comprising the inner uterine wall (p. 251).

engaged-to-be-engaged: stage during which couples discuss the prospects of marriage and agree to a future engagement (p. 65).

epididymis: a crescent-shape structure of tightly coiled tubing on the top and side of the testes which stores and matures sperm cells (p. 250).

episiotomy: an incision made from the vaginal orifice toward the anus to prevent tearing of tissues during childbirth (p. 338).

epistemologist: one who studies the nature of knowledge (p. 372).

equilibration: the motive to stay in balance and to achieve an overall understanding or mental perspective that fits the experience (p. 372).

equity: market value of housing minus mortgage balance (p. 404).

erectile dysfunction: the inability to achieve and/or maintain an erection of sufficient quality for engaging in sexual intercourse (p. 267).

erogenous zone: areas of the body particularly responsive to sexual stimulation (p. 256).

eros: a romantic love style characterized by a powerful sense of sexual attraction between the two love partners (p. 154).

escapism: a defense mechanism that involves either direct or indirect denial of a problem (p. 228).

estrogen: hormone present in both sexes but primarily considered a female sex hormone; maintains lining of vagina, produces breast growth, and controls menstrual cycle (p. 254).

ethnic group: segment of society whose shared identity is based on common ancestry and common culture (p. 75).

ethnocentrism: belief in the superiority of one's own cultural group (p. 8).

euphoria: a sense of freedom, well-being, and relief (p. 488).

euthanasia (active): merciful action to purposefully end a life (p. 19).

euthanasia (passive): withholding treatment that might extend life in order to allow death to occur (p. 19).

exhibitionism: act of exposing oneself indecently for own sexual pleasure (p. 383).

exogamy: marriage outside of one's social, religious, age, racial, ethnic, or educational group (p. 162).

expertise power: power based on the perception that more knowledge is possessed about one particular subject or task than another (p. 210).

extended family: wife, husband, unmarried children, plus one or more other relatives occupying the same household; vertical extension includes three or more generations (grandparents or grandchildren) while lateral extension includes same generations of kin such as aunts, uncles, cousins, and married siblings (p. 15).

extramarital affair: secretive sexual involvement outside of marriage in which emotional commitment exists between the extramarital partners (p. 269).

F

fallopian tubes: tubal structures extending from the uterus to the left and right sides of pelvic cavity providing a pathway for the ovum to travel to the uterus (p. 252).

family: two or more persons who share resources, responsibility for decisions, values, and goals, and have a commitment to each other over time (p. 15).

family leave: work absence for the purpose of caring for family illness or other emergency (p. 431).

family of orientation (family of origin): family that a person is born or adopted into consisting of self, parent(s), and any siblings (p. 16).

family of procreation: family established by self, spouse, and any children (p. 16).

family practitioner: physician trained to deal with preventive health care and most types of medical problems (p. 406).

fellatio: oral stimulation of the male genital organs (p. 98).

feminist: one who believes in the equality of the sexes (p. 424).

fetishism: erotic interest and sexual satisfaction derived through devotion or fixation to a particular object (p. 383).

fetus: the human organism from 8 weeks of prenatal development until birth (p. 333).

fimbria: finger-like projections at the outer ends of the fallopian tubes which "pull" the egg inside the tube so that contact may be made with a sperm cell (p. 252).

finitude: quality of being limited in existence (p. 539).

fixed-rate mortgage: interest rate and amount of the monthly payment remain fixed throughout life of the mortgage (p. 405).

foam: contraceptive spermicide in pressurized cans that is inserted into the vagina with a plastic applicator prior to sexual intercourse (p. 280).

follicle stimulating hormone (FSH): causes the Graafian follicle to mature an ovum during each menstrual cycle and to produce estrogen (p. 254).

foreplay: kissing, caressing, stimulation of breasts, and/or oral-genital stimulation to heighten the degree of sexual arousal; a prelude to sexual intercourse (p. 97).

foreskin prepuce: a layer of skin forming a sheath-like covering over the glans penis often removed during circumcision of an infant (p. 249).

formal engagement: often involves the offering and acceptance of an engagement ring along with an announcement of the impending marriage (p. 172).

French kissing: tongue kissing (p. 96).

frenum: a thin strip of skin that connects glans penis to the penis shaft (p. 249).

G

gardnerella vaginitis: a sexually transmitted disease caused by a bacterium; men remain asymptomatic while women experience a fish-like odor discharge, soreness of the labia, and painful urination (p. 298).

gay: a male homosexual (p. 129).

gender identity: the person's persistent, unambiguous definition of self as either female or male; how one feels about self as female or male (p. 10).

gender roles: traits, behaviors, and attitudes socially prescribed for women and men in a given culture (p. 28).

generic: nonbrand (p. 400).

genital herpes: a sexually transmitted disease with no known cure; symptoms include painful blisters on the genitals, buttocks, thighs, or within the urethra (p. 296).

genital warts: a sexually transmitted disease caused by virus; symptoms include pink cauliflower warts near external genitals or anus (p. 298).

gonorrhea: a sexually transmitted disease caused by a bacterium; symptoms include painful urination and pus-like discharge (p. 296).

Gossypol: a toxic cottonseed derivative used in China to prevent sperm cell production (p. 287).

Graafian follicle: an ovarian follicle that serves to mature an ovum for release at ovulation and to produce estrogen (p. 254).

growth: quantitative change (p. 373).

guidance: what one does with or for a person in order to enable adjustment to the environment (p. 375).

gynecologist: a physician who specializes in the treatment of diseases of the genital tract in women (p. 283).

H

H-frame marriage: a relationship of total independence in which very little couple identity develops (p. 221).

health maintenance organization (HMO): uses prepayment for health care that requires members to go to designated center for treatment (p. 406).

heavy petting: sexual activity below the waist including kissing and fondling on genitals (p. 97).

hematoma: blood clot (p. 345).

hemoglobin: a substance in red blood cells which transports oxygen throughout the body (p. 400).

hemorrhaging: excess bleeding (p. 292).

hermaphrodite: a person whose genital organs cannot be clearly identified as being either female or male at birth (p. 33).

heterogamy: differences in characteristics (p. 163).

heterosexuality: preference for sexual activity with persons of opposite sex (p. 129).

homogamy: similarity of characteristics (p. 162).

homosexuality: preference for sexual activities with persons of same sex (p. 129).

hormone: chemical substance secreted into the bloodstream by the endocrine glands (p. 32).

hospice: residential facility for the dying; typically affiliated with a hospital (p. 541).

Human Immunodeficiency Virus (HIV): virus which causes AIDS and ARC (p. 295).

hymen: a fold of mucous membrane, partly closing the vagina, which stretches or ruptures at first sexual intercourse if not previously stretched through strenuous exercise (p. 176).

hypertension: abnormally high blood pressure (p. 537).

hyperventilation: excessive rate of respiration leading to abnormal loss of carbon dioxide (p. 341).

hysterectomy: removal of the uterus by surgery (p. 524).

I

"I" messages: a communication skill in which partners avoid the word "you," speak directly to rather than about each other in order to avoid placing blame, and show ownership of problem (p. 229).

id: a component of the personality made up of unconscious desires based on the pleasure principle and characterized by desire for immediate gratification (p. 371).

idealization: the tendency to perceive a loved one as more ideal than they actually are (p. 145).

incest: illicit sexual relationship between persons who are within prohibited degrees of kinship (p. 386).

infatuation: romantic illusions which involve the idealization of a partner (p. 144).

infertile: not capable of reproduction (p. 315).

inflation: across-the-board increases in the cost of goods and services (p. 392).

informational power: power based on ability to persuade due to possession of relevant information (p. 210).

inherited: transmitted by parental genes (p. 337).

inhibited sexual desire: a condition characterized by little or no interest in engaging in sexual activity (p. 265).

in loco parentis: in the place of parent(s) (p. 63).

instinctual: inherited tendency to respond to the environment without involving reason (p. 310).

intact family: a family in which the biological parents are married to each other (p. 65).

intellectualization: a defense mechanism in which one becomes cool, distant, and uninvolved to avoid the threatening nature of an intimate relationship (p. 228)

interfaith marriage: a marriage in which wife and husband are of different religions (p. 167).

intermarriage: marriage between a Jew and a Gentile who has converted to Judaism (p. 166).

internal medicine: physician trained to serve as primary care physician or to specialize in a particular area such as cardiology (p. 406).

interracial marriage: a marriage in which the wife and husband are of different races (p. 170).

intestate: without a will (p. 418).

intimacy: feelings of closeness, connectedness, and bonding which one experiences in loving relationships (p. 153).

intrauterine device (IUD): a plastic device inserted in the uterus by a physician and left to prevent a fertilized egg from implanting into the uterine wall (p. 283).

intrinsic marriage: one in which the spouses are near-perfect, have an all-consuming interest in the partnership, and are willing to make heroic sacrifices (p. 202).

in vitro fertilization: removal of mature ova from the ovary and fertilizing them in a laboratory petri dish using sperm cells (p. 321).

J

jealousy: a negative response to a real or imagined threat resulting from the actual or potential loss of a relationship partner (p. 156).

job sharing: two workers share one job so that each worker may work part-time (p. 429).

joint custody: following divorce, both parents legally share in the decisions and responsibilities of the children (p. 482).

K

kin keeper: someone who works to keep family members in touch with one another by writing, telephoning, and visiting (p. 440).

L

labia majora: outer lips consisting of two fatty folds of skin and a thin layer of smooth muscle tissue that enclose the vaginal opening (p. 250).

labia minora: inner lips enclosed within the labia majora; contain a rich supply of blood vessels and nerve endings (p. 250)

lactation: milk production by mother (p. 346).

laparoscope: a tube-like instrument with fiber optics used in performing tubal ligations (p. 285).

latchkey children: young children who are at home alone on a regular basis (p. 13).

launching period: the time when young adult children leave home for post-high school education or a career (p. 519).

"leaders": items priced below wholesale cost in order to attract customers (p. 402).

legitimacy power: power gained through acceptance that a spousal role legitimizes certain responsibilities (p. 210).

lesbian: a female homosexual (p. 129).

libido: sexual drive or desire (p. 524).

light petting: sexual activity above the waist including kissing and caressing of the lips, neck, shoulders, and fondling the breasts (p. 97).

ludus: a game-playing style of self-centered love in which independence is sought in a series of short-lived fun relationships (p. 154).

luteinizing hormone (LH): causes a mature Graafian follicle to rupture and to release an ovum (p. 254).

M

malpresentation: abnormal position of fetus for delivery (p. 343).

mammary glands: glands in the female breast which produce milk in conjunction with childbirth (p. 253).

mania: a possessive loving style characterized by jealousy, along with an inability to sleep, eat, or think logically (p. 154).

marriage: legally binding contract between a woman and man which conveys certain rights and privileges including sexual exclusivity, legitimation of any children born of the union, and economic responsibilities (p. 15).

marriage enrichment: program with goals to increase self-awareness, mutual self-disclosure, and intimacy and to develop communication and conflict resolution skills (p. 241).

marriage squeeze: refers to the uneven distribution of eligible, age-appropriate (2–3 years older than themselves) marital partners for women resulting from the baby boom (p. 19).

masturbation: pleasurable self-stimulation of the genitals (p. 94).

maternal instincts: the theory that motherly characteristics are inherited (p. 31).

maturation: qualitative change (p. 373).

May-December marriage: a marriage in which the wife and husband are a number of years apart in age; difference of 20 years or more may constitute a mixed marriage (p. 166).

mediation: conflict resolution process whereby two disputing parties meet with a third-party who serves as impartial guide to negotiation (p. 475).

menopause: the natural time when menstruation stops in women in their 40s or 50s (p. 523).

M-frame marriage: a relationship which balances dependence and independence to form an interdependent marriage (p. 221).

midlife crisis: a process during middle age in which one's self-worth and values are questioned (p. 524).

mixed marriage: any marriage with extreme differences although usually applied to race, religion, or nationality (p. 168).

Mongoloid: a major racial division of the human species characterized by yellow or red skin coloring which includes Asians and American Indians (Native Americans) (p. 170).

monogamous: having only one sexual or marriage mate at a time (p. 115).

mons pubis (veneris): region over pubic bone consisting of a fatty tissue cushion covered by pubic hair (p. 256).

mores: folkways believed to be of compelling social importance by group members (p. 64).

multiphasic pill: oral contraceptive which provides varying hormone dosage levels during the menstrual cycle (p. 280).

myotonia: involuntary contractions of muscles during sexual response (p. 256).

myth: belief that is held uncritically without examination (p. 144).

N

Negroid: a major racial division of the human species characterized by dark skin coloring, typically referred to as blacks (p. 170).

neonatal incest: applying oral or manual stimulation to an infant's genitals (p. 388).

nesting: the unexpected return to the parent(s) home by an adolescent or young adult who was thought to have left home permanently (p. 518).

neuroticism: emotionally unstable condition (p. 201).

nipple: external structure of the breast which consists of smooth muscle fibers and erectile tissue with a network of nerve endings (p. 253).

nonbattering rape: forced sexual activity occurring as response to a continuing disagreement about frequency or type of sexual activity (p. 240).

nonintact family: a single-parent family resulting from death, divorce, or unmarried childbirth (p. 65).

nonspecific urethritis: a sexually transmitted disease caused by a bacterium; women may be asymptomatic while men suffer frequent urination, urethral itching, and urethral discharge; if untreated, may cause infertility in men and pelvic inflammatory disease (PID) in women (p. 297).

Norplant system: female contraceptive in which silicone pellets containing progestin are inserted under the skin of the arm (p. 287).

nuclear family: smallest kinship unit which appears in society including wife, husband, and child(ren) (p. 16).

nurse-midwife: certified registered nurse with considerable additional training regarding the handling of childbirth cases (p. 341).

O

obsessive rape: a form of sexual assault in which the victim is viewed as a sexual object and used to satisfy excessive sexual needs of perpetrator upon command (p. 240).

obstetrician: a physician specializing in the branch of surgery that deals with the management of pregnancy, labor, and the puerperium (p. 283).

Ophthalmia neonatorum: a childbirth-related infection which could potentially lead to blindness (p. 345).

orgasm: culmination of sexual excitement leading to sudden physiological and psychological release of sexual tension (p. 256).

osteoporosis: brittleness of bones caused by reduction in the amount of bone mass due to lack of minerals (p. 523).

ovaries: almond-shaped structures located on either side of the uterus which produce the hormones estrogen and progesterone and mature the ovum released at ovulation (p. 252).

ovulation: process of producing ova (eggs) and discharging them from the ovaries (p. 276).

ovum: the female reproductive cell, often referred to as the egg, which, when fertilized, develops into a fetus (p. 252).

oxytocin: pituitary hormone that triggers maternal milk release and causes uterine contractions; helps the uterus return to its normal shape following childbirth (p. 347).

P

parent education: educational experiences to effect change in parent role performance (p. 359).

Parent Effectiveness Training (P.E.T.): group education programs that teach parents to use the language of acceptance and active listening (p. 361).

parent ego state: component of the personality that contains attitudes and behaviors from authority figures, mainly parents (p. 226).

parent tapes: mental recordings of parental messages from early childhood experiences (p. 226).

parental leave: work absence for the purpose of caring for a newborn, sick, or adopted child (p. 431).

parenting: the rearing of children within a family to conform to the social group in which they were born (p. 358).

passion: a drive which leads to romance, physical attraction, and sexual involvement (p. 153).

pediatrician: physician who cares for children and specializes in childhood diseases (p. 406).

pelvic inflammatory disease (PID): a chronic infection with symptoms of lower abdominal pain and fever accompanied by inflammation and swelling of uterine tissue and fallopian tubes; sometimes caused by untreated sexually transmitted diseases such as chlamydia or gonorrhea; can lead to infertility (p. 277).

penis: male genital; an elongated shaft consisting of erectile tissue, nerve endings, a large supply of blood vessels, and urethra (p. 249).

perimenopausal years: the years immediately before and after menopause (p. 524).

permissive parent: pattern of parental behavior characterized by little or no guidance (p. 377).

petting: physical contact which may lead to sexual arousal and/or orgasm but does not involve sexual intercourse (p. 96).

placater: a martyr-like "yes person" who always needs approval from others (p. 222).

placenta: vascular tubing connecting the fetus to uterus (p. 329).

plaintiff: the complaining party who brings about a legal action or lawsuit (p. 127).

plateau: stage of leveling off (p. 374).

postmenopausal: stage/condition of woman who has not menstruated during the past 12 months (p. 523).

postpartum depression: emotional letdown during first few weeks following childbirth (p. 339).

pragma: a logical loving style concentrating on the practical aspects of the relationship involving a rational assessment of the partner (p. 154).

pragmatic: taking a practical view by intellectually evaluating the situation (p. 149).

precociousness: premature development (p. 246).

preferred provider organizations (PPO): health care group that directs insured members to a list of "preferred" health providers for treatment at discounted rates (p. 407).

premarital inventory: self-help questionnaire about premarital and marital relationships designed to help prospective marriage partners understand their personal values and expectations (p. 173).

premenstrual syndrome (PMS): a medical condition with symptoms of irritability, fatigue, anxiety, and depression in conjunction with various physical discomforts (p. 254).

prenuptial agreement: written document intended to ensure the separation of individual assets and property acquired before marriage if a divorce should occur (p. 174).

principle of least interest: a postulate that the partner who is more interested in continuing the relationship can be most easily exploited (p. 72).

procreation: bringing forth of offspring (p. 314).

progesterone: hormone that inhibits reproduction of cervical mucus during ovulation and causes the endometrium of the uterus to thicken (p. 254).

progestin: progesterone-like synthetic substance contained in oral contraceptives (p. 279).

projection: a defense mechanism in which blame is inappropriately placed on others; attributing others with one's own unethical desires (p. 228).

promiscuity: casual sexual behavior (p. 385).

propinquity: physical nearness (p. 162).

prosocial behavior: something that is socially desirable and in some way benefits another person or society (p. 382).

prostatectomy: removal of prostate gland (p. 534).

prostate gland: a chestnut-shaped gland, located below the male bladder, whose secretion reduces destruction of sperm from acidity within the vagina after ejaculation (p. 250).

proximo-distal: developing from the center outward (p. 374).

R

rape: engaging in sexual intercourse, without consent, through the use of or threat of force (p. 81).

rapport: harmonious relationship (p. 463).

rationalization: a defense mechanism of false-justification of one's behavior when real reasons are too threatening to one's self-esteem (p. 228).

recommended daily allowance (RDA): guidelines for the quantity of foods required to obtain the nutrients necessary to maintain a healthy body (p. 400).

recreational extramarital sex: secretive extramarital sexual intercourse, without emotional commitment, emphasizing the pleasurable aspects of sex (p. 269).

referent power: power derived from an emotional identification with a marriage partner that results in emotional satisfaction from thinking or behaving as the spouse wishes (p. 210).

refractory period: time during which further sexual arousal is not possible (p. 260).

resilient: to recover more easily (p. 149).

reward power: when one marriage partner meets economic, psychological, or physical needs of the other (p. 210).

rhythm method: periodic abstinence as a method of contraception based on assumption that ovulation occurs 14 days + or −2 days before onset of next menstrual period (p. 277).

role: a pattern of behavior that is expected of a person who has a certain function in a group (p. 28).

romantic: one who takes an impractical view of love (p. 149).

Romeo and Juliet effect: circumstance in which parental interference increases the romantic attraction between two people leading to further rebellion against the parents (p. 177).

rooming-in: an arrangement in which the newborn stays in the mother's hospital room rather than in nursery (p. 365).

RU-486: a post-coital birth control method using high dosage levels of estrogen to prevent implantation of a potentially fertilized ovum; "morning after" pill causing abortion (p. 286).

rule of 72: determining the effect of inflation on future prices by dividing 72 by the expected rate of inflation to estimate the number of years it will take for prices to double (p. 393).

S

safer sex: sexual behavior that is more likely to leave each partner free of sexually transmitted disease and psychological scars associated with feelings of guilt (p. 11).

sandwich generation: those persons who are concurrently responsible for caring for their parents and for their own children (p. 153).

schizophrenia: psychotic disorder characterized by loss of contact with reality (p. 517).

scrotum: loose pouch of skin, sparsely covered with pubic hair, that contains the testes (p. 249).

sebaceous gland: produces oily lubricating substance (p. 253).

sedentary: inactive (p. 400).

self-actualization: realization of one's full potential by developing inherent talents and capabilities; believed by many to be the most basic need of the human psyche (p. 21).

self-awareness: being cognizant of one's own personality and individuality (p. 362).

self-concept: the mental image one has of oneself (p. 361).

self-disclosure: opening up and sharing one's own feelings and thoughts (p. 151).

self-esteem: a subjective evaluative attitude toward the self that influences moods and behavior (p. 105).

semen: fluid consisting of sperm and secretions from seminal vesicles, prostate gland, and Cowper's glands (p. 250).

seminal vesicles: two small glands located at the juncture of the vas deferens which produce and secrete an alkaline fluid that makes up about 70% of the semen volume (p. 250).

senility: exhibiting mental and physical weaknesses associated with old age (p. 531).

seriously dating: "going steady"; includes recreation, status achievement, socialization, and possible selection of a marriage mate (p. 65).

sexual addiction: inability to appropriately choose one's sexual experiences since sexual behavior has become the driving force to the detriment of other areas in life (p. 247).

sexual adjustment: the extent to which an individual possesses an awareness and acceptance of her/his sexual nature as an integral part of her/his being (p. 246).

sexual dysfunction: refers to a condition in which there is impairment of ordinary physiological responses of sexual excitement or orgasm (p. 246).

sexual orientation: one's preference for either the same or opposite sex or both (p. 129).

sexual revolution: a grass roots uprising beginning in the 20th century against the church's teachings about sexuality that has led to increasingly permissive sexual standards (p. 11).

sexual satisfaction: the perceived discrepancy between level of aspiration and level of achievement regarding physiological and psychological sexual fulfillment (p. 246).

show: small, blood-stained mucus plug, which serves to block the cervix during pregnancy, preventing infection from entering the uterus (p. 345).

significant others: persons who are most important for an individual in determining behavior (p. 91).

simple stepparent: parent in blended family in which spouse has a child(ren) from a previous marriage (p. 505).

socialization: process by which one learns the rules of a given society in order to function effectively within that culture (p. 18).

sodomy: variously delineated in state laws as anal intercourse, oral-genital sex, and/or sexual contact with animals (p. 131).

sole custody: one parent cares for children on a daily basis with assumption of all decisions and responsibilities (p. 482).

speculative style: willingness to explore issues and consider other person's point of view but unable to reveal own feelings (p. 224).

sperm: the male reproductive cell that serves to fertilize the ovum (p. 250).

spermicides: contraceptive foams, suppositories, creams, and jellies containing a chemical substance which immobilizes and destroys sperm cells (p. 280).

split custody: following divorce, two or more children divided between parents with each ex-partner taking sole responsibility for the child(ren) in her/his care (p. 482).

sponge: mushroom cap-shaped contraceptive device made of polyurethane, saturated with a chemical spermicide; inserted into vagina in front of cervix prior to sexual intercourse (p. 282).

spontaneous abortion: an expulsion (miscarriage) of an embryo or fetus prior to the stage of development at which survival outside the uterus is not possible (p. 336).

STD: sexually transmitted disease (p. 274).

steadily dating: involves dating the same person most of the time without a commitment to date each other exclusively (p. 65).

stepfamily: remarriage in which one or both marital partners has child(ren); reconstituted or blended family (p. 488).

stereotype: a standardized mental picture of members of a group that represents an oversimplified opinion, affective attitude, or uncritical judgement (p. 129).

sterilization: surgical procedure that causes a person to no longer be capable of reproduction (p. 274).

stimulus-value-role theory: the idea that persons are first attracted to one another on the basis of personal qualities (p. 166).

storge: a best-friends style of love represented by a comfortable degree of intimacy developed between friends (p. 154).

superego: component of the personality, which represents a conscience, incorporating the morals of society (p. 371).

surrogate mother: a woman who serves as a substitute mother by becoming impregnated, primarily by artificial insemination, in order to bear a child for the biological father and his wife (p. 321).

swinging: consensual extramarital sexual involvement shared by a couple whereby wife and husband engage in sexual activity with others without emotional involvement (p. 269).

syncratic: a power pattern in which decisions are made by negotiation of the marriage partners (p. 210).

syphilis: a sexually transmitted disease which, if continued over many years and left untreated, leads to death (p. 296).

Systematic Training for Effective Parenting (STEP): parent study groups established in order to discuss and practice essential skills for good parent-child relationships (p. 361).

T

Tay-Sachs disease: a fatal disorder, primarily found among Eastern European Jews, resulting from a hereditary enzyme deficiency that makes it impossible to break down fatty materials (p. 337).

technical virginity: all methods of oral and manual stimulation of the breasts and genitals, including sexual arousal to the point of orgasm but without sexual intercourse (p. 97).

temperament: inborn qualities of reacting to the world (p. 368).

teratogens: substances that can cause congenital defects (p. 337).

testatrix (testator): a person who dies leaving a valid will or testament (p. 418).

testes: two bean-shaped structures located in the scrotum which function to manufacture sperm and the hormone testosterone (p. 250).

toxemia: abnormal condition involving poisonous substances in the blood (p. 317).

toxic shock syndrome: a potential life-threatening illness associated with a bacteria found in highly absorbent tampons (p. 282).

traditional family: consists of a wife, husband, and their children living in their own household supported by the father's earnings while the wife concentrates on domestic activities and family life (p. 16).

trichomoniasis: a sexually transmitted disease characterized by a persistent discharge in the woman caused by a parasite which may also invade the male urethra and bladder (p. 297).

trimester: a 3-month segment of a pregnancy (p. 333).

tubal ligation: laparoscopic sterilization or "tying tubes" performed by inserting a tiny instrument through the woman's abdominal wall cauterizing (burning) the fallopian tube (p. 285).

tumescence: swelling of penis or clitoris leading to an erection (p. 265).

typology: classification (p. 210).

U

ultrasound scanning: a prenatal assessment involving the transfer of sound waves through the uterus in order to produce a screen image of the fetus (p. 338).

urinary incontinence: involuntary release of urine usually associated with loss of bladder sphincter toneness (p. 523).

uterus: hollow, muscular, pear-shaped organ which undergoes various changes during the menstrual cycle to receive a fertilized egg for implantation at the onset of pregnancy (p. 251).

V

vacuum aspiration (suction): a first trimester method of abortion in which the amniotic sac and embryonic tissues are removed with an electric vacuum pump (p. 292).

vagina: a muscular tube extending from the vaginal orifice and vestibule to the uterus (p. 251).

vaginal contraceptive suppositories: contraceptive spermicide in an oval shape, somewhat difficult to insert and dissolve, and likely to leave a sticky residue in the vagina (p. 281).

values: basic beliefs with which a person determines her/his life goals, interests, and behavior (p. 164).

varicocele: enlarged, damaged vein (p. 320).

vas deferens: tubule which transports sperm to the ejaculatory duct (p. 250).

vasectomy: a surgical procedure in which the vas deferens are cut and/or cauterized in order to prevent sperm cells from mixing with other semen components and being released during ejaculation (p. 286).

vasocongestion: the engorgement of female genitals (including labia, vaginal barrel, and clitoris) and penis with an additional volume of blood during sexual arousal (p. 256).

vestibule: area enclosed by the labia minora which contains both the vaginal and urethral openings (p. 250).

visual spatial ability: visual perception and location of objects and their relationships (p. 45).

voyeurism: act of receiving sexual gratification from visual means; i.e. Peeping Tom (p. 383).

vulva: external female genitalia composed of the mons veneris, the labia majora, the labia minora, the vestibule, and the clitoris (p. 250).

W

withdrawal: an unreliable method of contraception involving the removal of the penis from the vagina prior to ejaculation (p. 107).

Y

yeast infection (genital candidasis): a fungus which causes an itching irritation when a chemical imbalance exists in vagina due to pregnancy, diabetes, oral contraceptives, antibiotics, or penile-vaginal intercourse (p. 297).

Yuppies: slang term for young upwardly mobile professionals (p. 76).

Z

zygote: a cell formed by the union of the female ovum and the male sperm, which, if left to develop, will grow into a fetus (p. 328).

BIBLIOGRAPHY

Abbott, D. A., & Brody, G. H. (1985). The relation of child age, gender, and number of children to the marital adjustment of wives. *Journal of Marriage and the Family, 47,* 77–84.

Abbott Laboratories. (1987). *The Abbott report: STDs and sexual mores in the 1980s.* New York: Ruder, Finn & Rotman.

Abel, E. (1983). *Marijuana, tobacco, alcohol and reproduction.* Boca Raton, FL: CRC Press.

Abell, P. K. (1987). The decision to end childbearing by sterilization. *Family Relations, 36,* 66–71.

The abortion debate: Recognizing all the issues. (1986, Spring). *Therefore: Newsletter of the Texas Baptist Christian Life Commission.* (Available from Texas Baptist Christian Life Commission, Dallas, TX.)

Abortion doesn't impair the ability of women to become pregnant. (1985). *Family Planning Perspectives, 17,* 39–40.

Abortion foe says measure on conception went too far. (1991, January 21). *Eau Claire Leader-Telegram,* p. 4D.

Abortions increase by 1 percent. (1990, November 24). *Eau Claire Leader-Telegram,* p. 4A.

Abraham, S., Child, A., Ferry, J., Vissard, J., & Mira, M. (1990). Recovery after childbirth: A preliminary prospective study. *Medical Journal of Australia, 152,* 9–12.

Adams, B. N. (1986). *The family: A sociological interpretation* (4th ed.). San Diego: Harcourt Brace Jovanovich.

Adams, B. N. (1988). Fifty years of family research: What does it mean? *Journal of Marriage and the Family, 50,* 5–17.

Adams, C. G., & Turner, B. F. (1985). Reported change in sexuality from young adulthood to old age. *Journal of Sex Research, 21,* 126–141.

Adams, R., Fliegelman, E., & Grieco, A. (1987). Patient guide: How to use condom. *Medical Aspects of Human Sexuality, 21*(7), 74–75.

Adams, V. (1980, May). Getting at the heart of jealous love. *Psychology Today,* pp. 38–47.

Adler, J. (1982, January 11). But is it a person? *Newsweek,* p. 44.

Adler, N. E., David, H. P., Major, B. N., Roth, S. H., Russo, N. F., & Wyatt, G. E. (1990). Psychological responses after abortion. *Science, 248* (4951), 41–44.

Adler, R. M., & Sedlacek, W. E. (1989). Freshman sexual attitudes and behaviors over a 15-year period. *Journal of College Student Development, 30,* 201–209.

Agnew, J. (1986). Hazards associated with anal erotic activity. *Archives of Sexual Behavior, 15,* 307–314.

Aguirre, B. E. (1985). Why do they return? Abused wives in shelters. *Social Work, 30,* 350–354.

Ahrons, C. R. (1980). Divorce: A crisis of family transition and change. *Family Relations, 29,* 533–540.

Ahrons, C. R. (1988). Divorce and the binuclear family. *Family Therapy Today, 3*(3), 1–7.

Ahrons, C. R., & Rodgers, R. H. (1987). *Divorced families: A multidisciplinary developmental view.* New York: Norton.

Ahrons, C. R., & Wallisch, L. S. (1987). The relationship between former spouses. In D. Perlman & S. Duck (Eds.), *Intimate relationships: Development, dynamics, and deterioration* (pp. 269–296). Newbury Park, CA: Sage.

AIDS Foundation Houston. (1986). *AIDS (Acquired Immune Deficiency Syndrome): What everyone needs to know.* Houston: Author.

AIDS: The human toll. (1990, December 2). *Eau Claire Leader-Telegram,* p. 1A.

AIDS shows up at colleges. (1990, November 29). *Eau Claire Leader-Telegram,* p. 7A.

Ainsworth, M. D. S. (1979). Infant-mother attachment. *American Psychologist, 34,* 932–937.

Albrecht, S. L. (1980). Reactions and adjustments to divorce: Differences in the experiences of males and females. *Family Relations, 29,* 59–68.

Aldous, J. (1978). *Family careers: Developmental change in families.* New York: Wiley.

Aldridge, K. W., Bueschin, A. J., Lloyd, L. K., & Burns, J. R. (1985). Microsurgical vasovasectomy for reversal of elective bilateral segmental vasectomy. *Southern Medical Journal, 78,* 967–969.

Aldridge, R. G. (1983). Masturbation during marriage. *Corrective & Social Psychiatry, 29,* 112–115.

Alexander, P. C., & Lupfer, S. L. (1987). Family characteristics and long-term consequences associated with sexual abuse. *Archives of Sexual Behavior, 16,* 235–245.

Alexander, R., Crabbe, L., Sato, Y., Smith, W., & Bennett, T. (1990). Serial abuse in children who are shaken. *American Journal of Diseases of Children, 144,* 58–60.

Alfin-Slater, R. B., Aftergood, L., & Ashley, J. (1982). *Nutrition & motherhood.* Van Nuys, CA: PM, Inc.

Alimony rates higher for white women. (1989, April 8). *Lubbock Avalanche-Journal,* p. 11B.

Allen, A., & Thompson, T. (1984). Agreement, understanding, realization, and feeling understood as predictors of communicative satisfaction in marital dyads. *Journal of Marriage and the Family, 46,* 915–921.

Allen, C. M., Reisetter, N., & Strong, J. R. (1990, November). *Husbands' and wives' perceptions of and expectations for disclosure, and satisfaction with marital communication.* Paper presented at the NCFR Conference, Seattle, WA.

Allen, S. M., & Kalish, R. A. (1984). Professional women and marriage. *Journal of Marriage and the Family, 46,* 375–382.

Allgeier, A. R. (1983). Sexuality and gender roles in the second half of life. In E. R. Allgeier & N. B. McCormick (Eds.), *Changing boundaries: Gender roles and sexual behavior* (pp. 135–157). Palo Alto, CA: Mayfield.

Allgeier, A. R., & Allgeier, E. R. (1988). *Sexual interactions* (2nd ed.). Lexington, MA: Heath.

Allgeier, E. R. (1981). The influence of androgynous identification on heterosexual relationships. *Sex Roles, 7,* 321–330.

Allgeier, E. R., & Allgeier, A. R. (1991). *Sexual interaction* (3rd ed.). Lexington, MA: D. C. Heath.

Alwin, D. F., Converse, P. E., & Martin, S. S. (1985). Living arrangements and social integration. *Journal of Marriage and the Family, 47,* 319–334.

Amadio, C., & Deutsch, S. L. (1984). Open adoption: Allowing adopted children to stay in touch with blood relatives. *Journal of Family Law, 22,* 59–89.

Amato, P. R. (1987). Family processes in one-parent, stepparent, and intact families: The child's point of view. *Journal of Marriage and the Family, 49,* 327–337.

Amato, P. R., & Partridge, S. (1987). Widows and divorcees with dependent children: Material, personal, family, and social well-being. *Family Relations, 36,* 316–320.

Amberson, J. I., & Hoon, P. W. (1985). Hemodynamics of sequential orgasm. *Archives of Sexual Behavior, 14,* 351–360.

Ambert, A. (1982). Differences in children's behavior toward custodial mothers and custodial fathers. *Journal of Marriage and the Family, 44,* 73–86.

Ambert, A. (1983). Separated women and remarriage behavior: A comparison of financially secure women and financially insecure women. *Journal of Divorce, 6*(3), 43–54.

Ambert, A. (1984). Longitudinal changes in children's behavior toward custodial parents. *Journal of Marriage and the Family, 46,* 463–467.

Ambert, A. (1986). Being a stepparent: Live-in and visiting stepchildren. *Journal of Marriage and the Family, 48,* 795–804.

Ambert, A. (1988). Relationships with former in-laws after divorce: A research note. *Journal of Marriage and the Family, 50,* 679–686.

American children adjust to changes in traditional family structure. (1987). *Marriage and Divorce Today, 12*(35), 1–2.

American College Health Association. (1986). *AIDS: What everyone should know.* Rockville, MD: Author.

American College of Nurse-Midwives. (1978). *Nurse-midwifery in the United States: 1976–1977.* Washington, DC: Author.

American Council of Life Insurance Institute. (1980, March 31). Does your spouse really know where it's at? *Family news and features—About family money matters and family life.* Washington, DC: Author.

American Dietetic Association. (1981). *Handbook of clinical dietetics.* New Haven, CT: Yale University Press.

American Express Centurion Bank. (1988). *An amendment to your Optima card agreement.* Chicago, IL: Author.

American Psychiatric Association. (1980). *Diagnostic and statistical manual of mental disorders (DSM-III)* (3rd ed.). Washington, DC: Author.

Americans postpone saying 'I do.' (1990, July 12). *Eau Claire Leader-Telegram,* p. 9A.

America's forgotten resource: Grandparents. (1984, April 30). *U.S. News and World Report,* pp. 76–77.

Amick, A. E. (1986). Perceptions of victim nonconsent to sexual aggression in dating situations: The effect of onset and type of protest (Doctoral dissertation, University of Georgia, 1985). *Dissertation Abstracts International, 46,* 2451B.

Anderson, E., Hamburger, S., Liu, J. H., & Rebar, R. W. (1987). Characteristics of menopausal women seeking assistance. *American Journal of Obstetrics and Gynecology, 156,* 428–433.

Anderson, S. A. (1988). Parental stress and coping during the leaving home transition. *Family Relations, 37,* 160–165.

Anderson, T. B. (1984). Widowhood as a life transition: Its impact on kinship ties. *Journal of Marriage and the Family, 46,* 105–114.

Andolsek, K. M. (1990). Obstetrics care: Standards of prenatal, intrapartum, and postpartum management. Philadelphia: Lea & Febiger.

Andrews, B., & Brewin, C. R. (1990). Attributions of blame for marital violence: A study of antecedents and consequences. *Journal of Marriage & the Family, 52,* 757–767.

Andrews, L. (1984, March). Family violence in Florida's panhandle. *Ms.,* p. 23.

Andrews, L. B. (1985, April). Have you had enough kids? *Parents,* pp. 61–64, 66.

Annandale, E. C. (1987). Dimensions of patient control in a free-standing birth center. *Social Science and Medicine, 25,* 1235–1248.

Annas, G. J. (1981). Fathers anonymous: Beyond the best interests of the sperm donor. *Child Welfare, 60,* 161–174.

Another sexual blight to fight. (1988, April 4). *Time,* p. 69.

Anson, R. S. (1981, February). Black and white together: Can love really be color-blind? *Mademoiselle,* pp. 146–147, 176.

Appleton, W. S. (1983). Constructive ways to handle marital fighting. *Medical Aspects of Human Sexuality, 17*(8), 38, 40–41, 44–45, 48–50.

Aquilino, W. S. (1990). Likelihood of parent-adult child coresidence. *Journal of Marriage and the Family, 52,* 405–419.

Are you a good insurance risk? (1986, June). *Consumer Reports,* pp. 401–402.

Argyle, M., & Furnham, A. (1983). Sources of satisfaction and conflict in long-term relationships. *Journal of Marriage and the Family, 45,* 481–493.

Argyle, M., Henderson, M., & Furnham, A. (1985). The rules of social relationships. *British Journal of Social Psychology, 24,* 125–139.

Aries, E. J., & Johnson, F. L. (1983). Close friendship in adulthood: Conversational content between same-sex friends. *Sex Roles, 9,* 1183–1196.

Aries, P. (1962). *Centuries of childhood: A social history of family life* (R. Baldrick, Trans.). New York: Vintage Books. (Original work published 1960)

Arluke, A., Levin, J., & Suchwalko, J. (1984). Sexuality and romance in advice books for the elderly. *The Gerontologist, 24,* 415–419.

Armstrong, D. T. (1986). Environmental stress and ovarian function. *Biology of Reproduction, 34,* 29–39.

Arnold, B. (1985, January 28). Why can't a woman's pay be more like a man's? *Business Week,* pp. 82–83.

Ascherman, L. I., & Safier, E. J. (1990). Sibling incest: A consequence of individual and family dysfunction. *Bulletin of the Menninger Clinic, 54,* 311–322.

Asis, M. M. B. (1986a, March). *Husband-wife discrepancies in fertility-related attitudes and perceptions: Some evidence of their influence on contraceptive behavior.* Paper presented at the meeting of the Midwest Sociological Society, Des Moines, IA.

Asis, M. M. B. (1986b, March). *The involuntarily childless: Is there support for them in American society?* Paper presented at the meeting of the Midwest Sociological Society, Des Moines, IA.

Atchley, R. C. (1991). *Social forces and aging: An introduction to social gerontology* (6th ed.). Belmont, CA: Wadsworth.

Athanasiou, R., Shaver, P., & Tavris, C. (1970, July). Sex. *Psychology Today,* pp. 39–52.

Atkinson, A. M. (1987). Fathers' participation and evaluation of family day care. *Family Relations, 36,* 146–151.

Atkinson, L. E., Lincoln, R., & Forrest, J. D. (1986). The next contraceptive revolution. *Family Planning Perspectives, 18,* 19–26.

Atkinson, M. P., & Boles, J. (1984). WASP (Wives as Senior Partners). *Journal of Marriage and the Family, 46,* 861–870.

Atkinson, M. P., & Glass, B. L. (1985). Marital age heterogamy and homogamy, 1900 to 1980. *Journal of Marriage and the Family, 47,* 685–691.

Attention shoppers, those IOUs are piling up. (1988, May 23). *Business Week,* p. 50.

Atwater, L. (1982). *The extramarital connection: Sex, intimacy, and identity.* New York: Irvington.

Atwood, J. D., & Gagnon, J. (1987). Masturbatory behavior in college youth. *Journal of Sex Education and Therapy, 13,* 35–42.

Avard, D. M., & Nimrod, C. M. (1985). Risks and benefits of obstetric epidural analgesia: A review. *Birth, 12,* 215–224.

Avery-Clark, C. (1986a). Sexual dysfunction and disorder patterns of husbands of working and nonworking women. *Journal of Sex & Marital Therapy, 12,* 282–296.

Avery-Clark, C. (1986b). Sexual dysfunction and disorder patterns of working and nonworking wives. *Journal of Sex & Marital Therapy, 12,* 93–107.

Avioli, P. S. (1985). The labor-force participation of married mothers of infants. *Journal of Marriage and the Family, 47,* 739–745.

Axelson, L. (1985). Personal communication. In D. Knox, *Choices in relationships: An introduction to marriage and the family* (p. 15). St. Paul: West.

Baber, K. M., & Dreyer, A. A. (1986). Delayed childbearing: Men's thinking about the fertility decision. In R. A. Lewis & R. E. Salt (Eds.), *Men in families* (pp. 131–140). Beverly Hills: Sage.

Baby M's parents urged to resolve differences. (1988, April 7). *Eau Claire Leader-Telegram,* p. 5B.

Bachmann, G. A. (1990). Sexual changes and dysfunction in older women. *Medical Aspects of Human Sexuality, 24*(8), 49–52, 54.

Bachmann, G. A. (1991). Sexual dysfunction in the older woman. *Medical Aspects of Human Sexuality, 25*(2), 42–45.

Bachmann, G. A., Leiblum, S. R., Kemmann, E., Colburn, D. W., Swartzman, L., & Shelden, R. (1984). Sexual expression and its determinants in the post-menopausal woman. *Maturitas, 6,* 19–29.

Bachrach, C. A. (1980). Childlessness and social isolation among the elderly. *Journal of Marriage and the Family, 42,* 627–636.

Bachrach, C. A. (1984). Contraceptive practice among American women, 1973–1982. *Family Planning Perspectives, 16,* 253–259.

Bachrach, C. A. (1986). Adoption plans, adopted children, and adoptive mothers. *Journal of Marriage and the Family, 48,* 243–253.

Bachrach, C. A., Adams, P. F., Sambrano, S., & London, K. A. (1990). Adoption in the 1980s. *Advance Data from Vital Health Statistics* (No. 181). Hyattsville, MD: National Center for Health Statistics.

Bachrach, C. A., & Horn, M. C. (1985). Marriage and first intercourse, marital dissolution, and remarriage: United States, 1982. *Advance Data from Vital and Health Statistics* (No. 107). Hyattsville, MD: National Center for Health Statistics.

Bader, E., Riddle, R., & Sinclair, C. (1981, October). *Do marriage preparation programs really help?* Paper presented at the meeting of the National Council on Family Relations, Milwaukee, WI.

Bagarozzi, J. I., & Bagarozzi, D. A. (1980). Financial counseling: A self control model for the family. *Family Relations, 29,* 396–403.

Bahr, S. J., Chappell, C. B., & Leigh, G. K. (1983). Age at marriage, role enactment, role consensus, and marital satisfaction. *Journal of Marriage and the Family, 45,* 795–803.

Bailey, R. C., & Kelly, M. (1984). Perceived physical attractiveness in early, steady, and engaged daters. *The Journal of Psychology, 116,* 39–43.

Baird, D., & Wilcox, A. (1985). Cigarette smoking associated with delayed conception. *Journal of the American Medical Association, 253,* 2979–2983.

Baker, L. S. (1981). *The fertility fallacy: Sexuality in the post-pill age.* Philadelphia: Saunders Press.

Baker, M. (1985). Career women and self-concept. *International Journal of Women's Studies, 8,* 214–227.

Baldassare, M. (1981). The effects of household density on subgroups. *American Sociological Review, 46,* 110–118.

Balkwell, C. (1985). An attitudinal correlate of the timing of a major life event: The case of morale in widowhood. *Family Relations, 34,* 577–581.

Ball, R. E., & Robbins, L. (1986). Marital status and life satisfaction among black Americans. *Journal of Marriage and the Family, 48,* 389–394.

Ballenski, C. B., & Cook, A. S. (1982). Mothers' perceptions of their competence in managing selected parenting tasks. *Family Relations, 31,* 489–494.

Balswick, J. (1980). Explaining inexpressive males: A reply to L'Abate. *Family Relations, 29,* 231–233.

Balswick, J., & Avertt, C. P. (1977). Differences in expressiveness: Gender, interpersonal orientation, and perceived parental expressiveness as contributing factors. *Journal of Marriage and the Family, 39,* 121–127.

Bandura, A. (1973). *Aggression: A social learning analysis.* Englewood Cliffs, NJ: Prentice-Hall.

Banking 101. (1986, February). *Changing Times,* p. 56.

Bankoff, E. A. (1983). Social support and adaptation to widowhood. *Journal of Marriage and the Family, 45,* 827–839.

Barbach, L. (1983). *For each other: Sharing sexual intimacy.* Garden City, NY: Anchor Books/ Doubleday.

Barbee, E. L. (1985). Families of ethnic people of color: Issues in social organization and pluralism. In L. Cargan (Ed.), *Marriage and family: Coping with change* (pp. 24–29). Belmont, CA: Wadsworth.

Barber, C. E. (1981). Parental responses to the empty nest transition. *Journal of Home Economics, 73,* 32–33.

Barcus, F. E. (1983). *Images of life on children's television.* New York: Praeger.

Bardwick, J. M. (1971). *Psychology of women: A study of biocultural conflicts.* New York: Harper & Row.

Barglow, P., Vaughn, B. E., & Molitor, N. (1987). Effects of maternal absence due to employment on the quality of infant-mother attachment in a low risk sample. *Child Development, 58,* 945–954.

Barlow, B. A. (1977). Notes on Mormon interfaith marriages. *The Family Coordinator, 26,* 143–150.

Barnett, R. C., & Baruch, G. K. (1987). Determinants of fathers' participation in family work. *Journal of Marriage and the Family, 49,* 29–40.

Barr, H. M., Streissguth, A. P., Martin, D. C., & Herman, C. S. (1984). Infant size at 8 months of age: Relationship to maternal use of alcohol, nicotine and caffeine during pregnancy. *Pediatrics, 74,* 336–341.

Barranti, C. C. R. (1985). The grandparent/grandchild relationship: Family resource in an era of voluntary bonds. *Family Relations, 34,* 343–352.

Barret, R. L., & Robinson, B. E. (1982). A descriptive study of teenage expectant fathers. *Family Relations, 31,* 349–352.

Barrett, K. (1982, September). Date rape: A campus epidemic? *Ms.,* pp. 48–51, 130.

Barrett, K., & Greene, R. (1986, April). The plastic prison. *Ladies' Home Journal,* pp. 72, 178, 180–182.

Barringer, F. (1989, June 10). Splitting up reported more among live-ins. *Austin American-Statesman,* p. E1.

Baruch, G., Barnett, R., & Rivers, C. (1983). *Lifeprints: New patterns of love and work for today's woman.* New York: McGraw-Hill.

Bassoff, E. S. (1984). Relationships of sex-role characteristics and psychological adjustment in new mothers. *Journal of Marriage and the Family, 46,* 449–454.

Baum, L. (1987, June 22). Corporate women: They're about to break through to the top. *Business Week,* p. 75.

Baumrind, D. (1966). Effects of authoritative parental control on child behavior. *Child Development, 37,* 887–907.

Baumrind, D. (1967). Child care practices anteceding three patterns of preschool behavior. *Genetic Psychology Monographs, 75,* 43–88.

Baumrind, D. (1971). Current patterns of parental authority. *Developmental Psychology Monograph, 4,* (1, Pt. 2), 1–103.

Baumrind, D. (1978). Parental disciplinary patterns and social competence in children. *Youth and Society, 9,* 239–276.

Baumrind, D. (1982). Are androgynous individuals more effective persons and parents? *Child Development, 53,* 44–75.

Bean, F. D., Williams, D. G., Opitz, W., Burr, J. A., & Trent, K. (1987). Sociodemographic and marital heterogamy influences on the decision for voluntary sterilization. *Journal of Marriage and the Family, 49,* 465–476.

Bear, M. J. (1988, March). *Network variables as determinants of the elderly entering adult congregate living facilities.* Paper presented at the meeting of the Southern Sociological Society, Nashville, TN.

Beatrice, D. K. (1979). Divorce: Problems, goals, and growth facilities. *Social Casework, 60,* 157–165.

Beavers, W. R. (1985). *Successful marriage: A family systems approach to couples therapy.* New York: Norton.

Beck, M., (1990, July 16). Trading places. *Newsweek,* pp. 48–50, 53–54.

Beckham, K., & Giordano, J. A. (1986). Illness and impairment in elderly couples: Implications for marital therapy. *Family Relations, 35,* 257–264.

Beckwith, D. (1985, December 2). Solo Americans. *Time,* p. 41.

Bee, H. (1989). *The developing child* (5th ed.). New York: Harper & Row.

Beeghley, L., & Sellers, C. (1986). Adolescents and sex: A structural theory of premarital sex in the United States. *Deviant Behavior, 7,* 313–336.

Belcastro, P. A. (1985). Sexual behavior differences between black and white students. *The Journal of Sex Research, 21,* 56–67.

Belenky, M. F., & Gilligan, C. (1979, September). *Impact of abortion decisions on moral development and life circumstance.* Paper presented at the meeting of the American Psychological Association, New York, NY.

Belkin, L. (1985a, May 23). Affording a child: Parents worry as costs keep rising. *The New York Times,* pp. 1C, 6C.

Belkin, L. (1985b, October 3). When a marriage is long distance. *The New York Times,* pp. 1C, 10C.

Bell, A. P., & Weinberg, M. S. (1978). *Homosexualities: A study of diversity among men and women.* New York: Simon & Schuster.

Bell, N. J., & Avery, A. W. (1985). Family structure and parent-adolescent relationships: Does family structure really make a difference? *Journal of Marriage and the Family, 47,* 503–508.

Bell, R. A., Daly, J. A., & Gonzalez, M. C. (1987). Affinity-maintenance in marriage and its relationship to women's marital satisfaction. *Journal of Marriage and the Family, 49,* 445–454.

Bell, R. A., & Holmes, K. K. (1984). Age-specific risks of syphilis, gonorrhea, and hospitalized pelvic inflammatory disease in sexually experienced U.S. women. *Sexually Transmitted Diseases, 11,* 291–295.

Bell, R. R. (1981). *Worlds of friendship.* Beverly Hills: Sage.

Bell, R. R. (1983). *Marriage and family interaction.* Homewood, IL: Dorsey.

Bell, R. R., & Bell, P. L. (1973). *Sexual satisfaction among married women.* Unpublished manuscript, Temple University, Department of Sociology, Philadelphia.

Bell, R. R., & Coughey, K. (1980). Premarital sexual experience among college females, 1958, 1968, and 1978. *Family Relations, 29,* 353–356.

Bello, D. C., Pitts, R. E., & Etzel, M. J. (1983). The communication effects of controversial sexual content in television programs and commercials. *Journal of Advertising, 12,* 32–42.

Belsky, J. (1979). Mother-father-infant interaction: A naturalistic observational study. *Developmental Psychology, 15,* 601–607.

Belsky, J. (1981). Early human experience: A family perspective. *Developmental Psychology, 17,* 3–23.

Belsky, J. (1985). Exploring individual differences in marital change across the transition to parenthood: The role of violated expectations. *Journal of Marriage and the Family, 47,* 1037–1044.

Belsky, J. (1987, April). *Science, social policy and day care: A personal odyssey.* Paper presented at the meeting of the Society for Research in Child Development, Baltimore, MD.

Belsky, J. (1990). Parental and nonparental child care and children's socioemotional development: A decade in review. *Journal of Marriage and the Family, 52,* 885–903.

Belsky, J., & Rovine, M. (1984). Social-network contact, family support, and the transition to parenthood. *Journal of Marriage and the Family, 46,* 455–467.

Belsky, J., & Rovine, M. (1988). Nonmaternal care in the first year of life and the security of infant-parent attachment. *Child Development, 59,* 157–167.

Belsky, J., & Rovine, M. (1990). Patterns of marital change across the transition to parenthood: Pregnancy to three years postpartum. *Journal of Marriage and the Family, 52,* 5–19.

Belsky, J., Spanier, G. B., & Rovine, M. (1983). Stability and change in marriage across the transition to parenthood. *Journal of Marriage and the Family, 45,* 567–577.

Bem, S., Martyna, W., & Watson, C. (1976). Sex-typing and androgyny: Further explorations of the expressive domain. *Journal of Personality and Social Psychology, 34,* 1016–1023.

Benenson, H. (1984). Women's occupational and family achievement in the U.S. class system: A critique of the dual-career family analysis. *The British Journal of Sociology, 35,* 19–41.

Benin, M. H., & Edwards, D. A. (1990). Adolescents' chores in dual- and single-earner families. *Journal of Marriage and the Family, 52,* 361–374.

Benin, M. H., & Nienstedt, B. C. (1985). Happiness in single- and dual-earner families: The effects of marital happiness, job satisfaction, and life cycle. *Journal of Marriage and the Family, 47,* 975–984.

Bennett, N. G., Blanc, A. K., & Bloom, D. E. (1988). Commitment and the modern union: Assessing the link between premarital cohabitation and subsequent marital stability. *American Sociological Review, 53,* 127–138.

Benson, P., Williams, D., & Johnson, A. (1987). *The quicksilver years: The hopes and fears of early adolescence.* San Francisco: Harper & Row.

Berardo, D. H., Shehan, C. L., & Leslie, G. R. (1987). A residue of tradition: Jobs, careers, and spouses' time in housework. *Journal of Marriage and the Family, 49,* 381–390.

Berardo, F. M., & Vera, H. (1981). The groomal shower: A variation of the American bridal shower. *Family Relations, 30,* 395–401.

Berendson, R. (1987, November). *Families in an information society.* Keynote address presented at the meeting of the National Council on Family Relations, Atlanta, GA.

Bergdorf, K. (1981). *Recognition and reporting of child maltreatment: Findings from the National Study of the Incidence and Severity of Child Abuse and Neglect.* Washington, DC: National Center on Child Abuse and Neglect.

Berger, J. (1987, August 31). Don't sweat it, inflation isn't about to explode. *Business Week,* p. 54.

Berger, K. S. (1988). *The developing person through the life span* (2nd ed.). New York: Worth.

Bergman, J. (1985). Licensing parents: A new age of childrearing? In L. Cargan (Ed.), *Marriage and family: Coping with change* (pp. 229–235). Belmont, CA: Wadsworth.

Berk, R. A., & Newton, P. J. (1985). Does arrest deter wife battery? An effort to replicate the findings of the Minneapolis spouse abuse experiment. *American Sociological Review, 50,* 253–262.

Berkow, R. (1982). *The Merck manual.* Rahway, NJ: Merck.

Berkowitz, M. (1983, November). Finding that someone special. *50 Plus,* p. 24.

Berkun, C. S. (1983). Changing appearance for women in the middle years of life: Trauma? In E. W. Markson (Ed.), *Older women: Issues and prospects* (pp. 11–35). Lexington, MA: Heath.

Berman, C. (1987). *Raising an adoptive child* (No. 620). New York: Public Affairs Committee.

Berman, W. H., & Turk, D. C. (1981). Adaptation to divorce: Problems and coping strategies. *Journal of Marriage and the Family, 43,* 179–189.

Bernard, J. (1974). The housewife: Between two worlds. In P. L. Stewart & M. G. Cantor (Eds.), *Varieties of work experience: The social control of occupational groups and roles* (pp. 49–66). New York: Wiley.

Bernard, J. (1986). The good-provider role: Its rise and fall. In A. S. Skolnick & J. H. Skolnick (Eds.), *Family in transition* (5th ed., pp. 125–144). Boston: Little, Brown.

Bernard, J. L., & Bernard, M. L. (1984). The abusive male seeking treatment: Jekyll and Hyde. *Family Relations, 33,* 543–547.

Bernard, J. L., Bernard, S. L., & Bernard, M. L. (1985). Courtship violence and sex-typing. *Family Relations, 34,* 573–576.

Berne, E. (1964). *Games people play: The psychology of human relationships.* New York: Grove Press.

Bernstein, A. (1988, February 29). So you think you've come a long way, baby? *Business Week,* pp. 48–52.

Bernstein, B. E., & Collins, S. K. (1985). Remarriage counseling: Lawyer and therapist's help with the second time around. *Family Relations, 34,* 387–391.

Berry, R. E., & Williams, F. L. (1987). Assessing the relationship between quality of life and marital and income satisfaction: A path analytic approach. *Journal of Marriage and the Family, 49,* 107–116.

Besharov, D. J. (1988, August 28). Child care: Another make-believe crisis. *Houston Chronicle,* p. F1.

Beutler, I. F., Burr, W. R., Bahr, K. S., & Herrin, D. A. (1989). The family realm: Theoretical contributions for understanding its uniqueness. *Journal of Marriage and the Family, 51,* 805–816.

Biaggio, M. K., Mohan, P. J., & Baldwin, C. (1985). Relationships among attitudes toward children, women's liberation, and personality characteristics. *Sex Roles, 12,* 47–62.

Bienvenu, M., Sr. (1986). *Strengthen your marriage through better communication* (No. 642). New York: Public Affairs Committee.

Bigner, J. J. (1985). *Parent-child relations: An introduction to parenting* (2nd ed.). New York: MacMillan.

Bilge, B., & Kaufman, G. (1983). Children of divorce and one-parent families: Cross-cultural perspectives. *Family Relations, 32,* 59–71.

Billingham, R. E., & Henningson, K. A. (1988). Courtship violence. *Journal of School Health, 58,* 98–100.

Billy, J. O. G., & Udry, J. R. (1985). The influence of male and female best friends on adolescent sexual behavior. *Adolescence, 20,* 21–32.

Bingham, J. S. (1986). Vulvo-vaginal candidosis—an overview. *Acta Dermato-Verneriologica. Supplementum, 121,* 39–46.

Bird, G. A., & Bird, G. W. (1985). Determinants of mobility in two-earner families: Does the wife's income count? *Journal of Marriage and the Family, 47,* 753–758.

Bird, G. W., Bird, G. A., & Scruggs, M. (1984). Determinants of family task sharing: A study of husbands and wives. *Journal of Marriage and the Family, 46,* 345–355.

Biro, F. M., Wildey, L. S., Hillard, P. J., & Rauh, J. (1986). Acute and long-term consequences of adolescents who choose abortions. *Pediatric Annals, 15,* 67–73.

Bishop, P., & Lipsitz, A. (1988, November). *Sexual behavior among college students in the AIDS era: A comparative study.* Paper presented at the meeting of the Society for the Scientific Study of Sex, San Francisco, CA.

Bjorksten, O. J. W. (1983). Marital conflict and sexual dysfunction. In S. F. Pariser, S. B. Levine, & M. L. Gardner (Eds.), *Clinical sexuality* (pp. 73–81). New York: Marcel-Dekker.

Blanchard, M., & Main, M. (1979). Avoidance of the attachment figure and social-emotional adjustment in day-care infants. *Developmental Psychology, 15,* 445–446.

Blankenhorn, D. (1986, March 23). Family values, without sugary pieties. *The New York Times,* p. 23E.

Bledin, K. D., Cooper, J. E., Brice, B., & Mackenzie, S. (1985). The effects on menstruation of elective tubal sterilization: A prospective controlled study. *Journal of Biosocial Science, 17,* 19–30.

Bledin, K. D., Cooper, J. E., Mackenzie, S., & Brice, B. (1984). Psychological sequelae of female sterilization: Short-term outcome in a prospective controlled study: A report from the UK Field Research Center of a WHO Collaborative Project. *Psychological Medicine, 14,* 379–390.

Block, C. R., Norr, K. L., Meyering, S., Norr, J. L., & Charles, A. G. (1981). Husband gatekeeping in childbirth. *Family Relations, 30,* 197–204.

Block, S. B., Peavy, J. W., III., & Thornton, J. H. (1988). *Personal financial management.* New York: Harper & Row.

Bloom, B. L., & Caldwell, R. A. (1981). Sex differences in adjustment during the process of marital separation. *Journal of Marriage and the Family, 43,* 693–701.

Bloom, B. L., & Kindle, K. R. (1985). Demographic factors in the continuing relationship between former spouses. *Family Relations, 34,* 375–381.

Bloom, D. E. (1984). Putting off children. *American Demographics, 6*(9), 30–33, 45.

Bloom, D. E., & Bennett, N. G. (1986). Childless couples. *American Demographics, 8*(8), 22–25, 54–55.

Blum, R. W., Resnick, M. D., & Stark, T. (1990). Factors associated with the use of court bypass by minors to obtain abortions. *Family Planning Perspectives, 22,* 158–160.

Blumenthal, M. (1985, September 22). About men: No big deal. *The New York Times Magazine,* p. 84.

Blumstein, P., & Schwartz, P. (1983). *American couples.* New York: Morrow.

Bock, E. W., Beeghley, L., & Mixon, A. J. (1983). Religion, socioeconomic status, and sexual morality: An application of reference group theory. *Sociological Quarterly, 24,* 545–559.

Boehm, D. (1983). The cervical cap: Effectiveness as a contraceptive. *Journal of Nurse-Midwifery, 28,* 3–6.

Bogal-Allbritten, R. B., & Allbritten, W. L. (1985). The hidden victims: Courtship violence among college students. *Journal of College Student Personnel, 26,* 201–204.

Bolig, R., Stein, P. J., & McKenry, P. C. (1984). The self-advertisement approach to dating: Male-female differences. *Family Relations, 33,* 587–592.

Bolling, D. R., & Voeller, B. (1987). AIDS and heterosexual anal intercourse. *Journal of the American Medical Association, 258,* 474.

Bonavoglia, A. (1988, April). Kathy's day in court. *Ms.,* pp. 46–52.

Booth, A. (1972). Sex and social participation. *American Sociological Review, 37,* 183–192.

Booth, A., Brinkerhoff, D. B., & White, L. K. (1984). The impact of parental divorce on courtship. *Journal of Marriage and the Family, 46,* 85–94.

Booth, A., & Edwards, J. N. (1985). Age at marriage and marital instability. *Journal of Marriage and the Family, 47,* 67–75.

Booth, A., Johnson, D. R., White, L., & Edwards, J. N. (1984). Women, outside employment, and marital instability. *American Journal of Sociology, 90,* 567–583.

Booth, A., Johnson, D. R., White, L. K., & Edwards, J. N. (1986). Divorce and marital instability over the life course. *Journal of Family Issues, 7,* 421–442.

Booth, A., & White, L. (1980). Thinking about divorce. *Journal of Marriage and the Family, 42,* 605–616.

Boran, A. (1988). Current case studies: Some reflections of an adoptions professional. *Family Therapy Today, 3*(7), 4–5.

Boslego, J. W. (1987). Effect of Spectinomycin resistant and penicillinase-producing Nisseria gonorrheae. *New England Journal of Medicine, 317,* 272–277.

Boss, P. (1987). Family stress. In M. B. Sussman & S. K. Steinmetz (Eds.), *Handbook of marriage and the family* (pp. 695–724). New York: Plenum Press.

Boss, P. G. (1980). The relationship of psychological father presence, wife's personal qualities and wife/family dysfunction in families of missing fathers. *Journal of Marriage and the Family, 42,* 541–549.

Bossard, J. H. S. (1931). Residential propinquity as a factor in mate selection. *American Journal of Sociology, 38,* 219–224.

Both sexes agree: One has it better. (1986, April 7). *U.S. News & World Report,* p. 78.

Botwin, C. (1985, March). The back-to-basics sex guide (because marriage can make you forget). *Redbook,* pp. 102–103, 176, 178.

Bouchard, T. J., Jr. (1983). Do environmental similarities explain the similarity in intelligence of identical twins reared apart? *Intelligence, 7,* 175–184.

Boulier, B. L., & Rosenzweig, M. R. (1984). Schooling, search, and spouse selection: Testing economic theories of marriage and household behavior. *Journal of Political Economy, 92,* 712–732.

Bovet, T. (1969). *A handbook to marriage* (2nd ed.). Garden City, NY: Doubleday.

Bowe, C. (1986, May). What are men really like today? *Cosmopolitan,* p. 263.

Bowen, G. L. (1988). Family life satisfaction: A value-based approach. *Family Relations, 37,* 458–462.

Bowen, G. L., & Orthner, D. K. (1983). Sex-role congruency and marital quality. *Journal of Marriage and the Family, 45,* 223–230.

Bower, D. W., & Christopherson, V. A. (1977). University student cohabitation: A regional comparison of selected attitudes and behavior. *Journal of Marriage and the Family, 9,* 447–453.

Bowker, L. H. (1983). Marital rape: A distinct syndrome? *Social Casework, 64,* 347–352.

Bowlby, J. (1988). *A secure base: Parent-child attachment and healthy human development.* New York: Basic Books.

Bowman, M. E., & Ahrons, C. R. (1985). Impact of legal custody status on fathers' parenting post-divorce. *Journal of Marriage and the Family, 47,* 481–488.

Bozett, F. W. (1980). Gay fathers: How and why they disclose their homosexuality to their children. *Family Relations, 29,* 173–179.

Bozett, F. W. (1984). Parenting concerns of gay fathers. *Topics in Clinical Nursing, 6,* 60–71.

Bozzi, V. (1986, January). Bulk-food bugaboos. *Psychology Today,* p. 21.

Bradley, R. H., Caldwell, B. M., & Elardo, R. (1977). Home environment, social status and mental test performance. *Journal of Educational Psychology, 69,* 697–701.

Brand, D. (1988, September 5). Dying with dignity. *Time,* pp. 56–58.

Brand, E., & Clingempeel, W. G. (1987). Interdependencies of marital and stepparent-stepchild relationships and children's psychological adjustment: Research findings and clinical implications. *Family Relations, 36,* 140–145.

Brannock, J. C., & Chapman, B. E. (1990). Negative sexual experiences with men among heterosexual women and lesbians. *Journal of Homosexuality, 19,* 105–110.

Braun, K. L., & Rose, C. L. (1987). Family perceptions of geriatric foster family and nursing home care. *Family Relations, 36,* 321–327.

Bray, J. H., & Berger, S. H. (1990). Noncustodial father and paternal grandparent relationships in stepfamilies. *Family Relations, 39,* 414–419.

Brazelton, T. B., & Cramer, B. G. (1990). *The earliest relationship: Parents, infants, and the drama of early attachment.* Reading, MA: Addison-Wesley.

Breault, K. D., & Kposowa, A. J. (1987). Explaining divorce in the United States: A study of 3,111 counties, 1980. *Journal of Marriage and the Family, 49,* 549–558.

Brecher, E. M. (1984, November). Love, sex and aging. *Connecticut Magazine,* pp. 66–69.

Breen, R. N., & Rouse, L. P. (1986, April). *Premarital violence: A study of abuse within the dating relationships of college students.* Paper presented at the meeting of the Southern Sociological Society, New Orleans, LA.

Brenton, M. (1985). *You and your in-laws: Help for some common problems* (No. 635). New York: Public Affairs Committee.

Breo, D. (1986, December 5). AMA AIDS expert's grim message. *American Medical News,* pp. 3, 32.

Breskin, J. G. (1986). Marital satisfaction in couples with young children (Doctoral dissertation, Boston University, 1986). *Dissertation Abstracts International, 47,* 1713B.

Breslau, N. (1987). Abortion of defective fetuses: Attitudes of mothers of congenitally impaired children. *Journal of Marriage and the Family, 49,* 839–845.

Bretschneider, J. G., & McCoy, N. L. (1988). Sexual interest and behavior in 80- to 102-year-olds. *Archives of Sexual Behavior, 17,* 109–129.

Breunlin, D. C. (1983). Therapy in stages: A life cycle view. In J. C. Hansen & H. A. Liddle (Eds.), *Clinical implications of the family life cycle* (pp. 1–11). Rockville, MD: Aspen.

Bridenthal, R. (1982). The family: The view from a room of her own. In B. Thorne & M. Yalom (Eds.), *Rethinking the family: Some feminist questions* (pp. 225–239). New York: Longman.

Bridges, J. S. (1987). College females' perceptions of adult roles and occupational fields for women. *Sex Roles, 16,* 591–604.

Briggs, S. (1987). Women and religion. In B. B. Hess & M. M. Ferree (Eds.), *Analyzing gender* (pp. 381–407). Newbury Park, CA: Sage.

Brink, P. J. (1982). An anthropological perspective on parenting. In J. A. Horowitz, C. B. Hughes, & B. J. Perdue (Eds.), *Parenting reassessed: A nursing perspective* (pp. 67–84). Englewood Cliffs, NJ: Prentice-Hall.

Brodbelt, S. (1983). College dating and aggression. *College Student Journal, 17,* 273–277.

Broderick, C. B. (1988). *Marriage and the family* (3rd ed.). Englewood Cliffs, NJ: Prentice-Hall.

Brodsky, S. L. (1988). *The psychology of adjustment and well-being.* New York: Holt, Rinehart, and Winston.

Brody, C. J., & Steelman, L. C. (1985). Sibling structure and parental sex-typing of children's household tasks. *Journal of Marriage and the Family, 47,* 265–273.

Brody, E., & Schnoover, C. (1986). Patterns of parent care when adult daughters work and when they do not. *The Gerontologist, 26,* 372–381.

Brody, E. M., Johnsen, P. T., Fulcomer, M. C., & Lang, A. M. (1983). Women's changing roles and help to elderly parents: Attitudes of three generations of women. *Journal of Gerontology, 38,* 597–607.

Brody, G. H., Stoneman, A., Lane, T. S., & Sanders, A. K. (1981). Television food commercials aimed at children, family grocery shopping, and mother-child interactions. *Family Relations, 30,* 435–439.

Brody, G. H., Stoneman, Z., MacKinnon, C. E., & MacKinnon, R. (1985). Rare relationships and behavior between preschool-aged and school-aged sibling pairs. *Developmental Psychology, 21,* 124–129.

Brody, J. E. (1984, June 29). "Silent" chlamydia tops gonorrhea as most common venereal disease. *Gainesville Sun,* pp. 12A-13A.

Bronfenbrenner, U. (1958). Socialization and social class through time and space. In E. E. Maccoby, T. E. Newcomb, & E. L. Hartley (Eds.), *Readings in social psychology* (pp. 400–425). New York: Holt.

Bronfenbrenner, U. (1980). *The ecology of human development.* Cambridge, MA: Harvard University Press.

Bronfenbrenner, U., & Crouter, A. C. (1982). Work and family through time and space. In S. B. Kormerman & C. D. Hayes (Eds.), *Families that work: Children in a changing world* (pp. 39–83). Washington, DC: National Academy Press.

Brooks, A. (1985, September 11). Couples try being separated to learn how to live together. *Gainesville Sun,* p. 2C.

Brooks, J. B. (1987). *The process of parenting.* Palo Alto, CA: Mayfield.

Brophy, B. (1986, March 10). Expectant moms, office dilemma. *U.S. News & World Report,* pp. 52–53.

Brophy, J. (1977). *Child development and socialization.* Chicago: Science Research Associates.

Brothers, J. (1985, March). The myth of the trial marriage: Why you should not move in with your lover. *New Woman,* pp. 54, 56–57.

Broverman, I. K., Vogel, S. R., Broverman, D. M., Clarkson, F. E., & Rosencrantz, P. S. (1972). Sex-role stereotypes: A current appraisal. *Journal of Social Issues, 28,* 59–78.

Brown, A. (1986, August). The flexible work force: What part-time professionals think. *Personnel Administrator,* pp. 33–36, 88.

Brown, J. D., Childers, K. W., & Waszak, C. S. (1990). Television and adolescent sexuality. *Journal of Adolescent Health Care, 11,* 62–70.

Brown, R. C. (1979). *Beacon on the hill: Southwest Texas State University, 1903–1978.* Dallas: Taylor Press.

Brown, S. E. (1984). Police responses to wife beating: Neglect of a crime of violence. *Journal of Criminal Justice, 12,* 277–288.

Brozan, N. (1984, May 20). An expert looks at family violence. *The New York Times,* p. 62.

Brubaker, T. H. (Ed.). (1984). *Family relationships in later life.* Beverly Hills: Sage.

Brubaker, T. H. (1985a). *Later life families.* Beverly Hills: Sage.

Brubaker, T. H. (1985b). Responsibility for household tasks: A look at golden anniversary couples aged 75 years and older. In W. A. Peterson & J. Quadagno (Eds.), *Social bonds in later life: Aging and interdependence* (pp. 27–36). Beverly Hills: Sage.

Brubaker, T. H. (1990). Families in later life: A burgeoning research area. *Journal of Marriage and the Family, 52,* 959–981.

Brubaker, T. H., & Ade-Ridder, L. (1986). Husband's responsibility for household tasks in older marriages: Does living situation make a difference? In R. A. Lewis & R. Salt (Eds.), *Men in families* (pp. 85–96). Beverly Hills: Sage.

Brubaker, T. H., & Hennon, C. B. (1982). Responsibility for household tasks: Comparing dual earner and dual retired marriages. In M. Szinovacz (Ed.), *Women's retirement: Policy implications of recent research* (pp. 205–219). Beverly Hills: Sage.

Bruch, M. A., Levo, L. C., & Arisohn, B. A. (1984). Conceptual complexity and skill in marital communication. *Journal of Marriage and the Family, 46,* 927–932.

Brunsman, B. (1985). *New hope for divorced Catholics: A concerned pastor offers alternatives to annulment.* San Francisco: Harper & Row.

Buckner, L. P., & Salts, C. J. (1985). A premarital assessment program. *Family Relations, 34,* 513–520.

Budgeting for your first home. (1986, April/May). *Living,* p. 4S.

Buehler, C. (1987a). Initiator status and the divorce transition. *Family Relations, 36,* 82–86.

Buehler, C. (1987b, November). *Parents' well-being and parent-child relationships following marital separation.* Paper presented at the meeting of the National Council on Family Relations, Atlanta, GA.

Buehler, C. (1989). Influential factors and equity issues in divorce settlements. *Family Relations, 38,* 76–82.

Buehler, C. A., & Hogan, M. J. (1980). Managorial behavior and stress in families headed by divorced women: A proposed framework. *Family Relations, 29,* 525–532.

Buell, B. (1990, September 3). In vitro fertilization: Delivering that ray of hope. *Business Week,* pp. 112–113.

Bukstel, L. H., Roeder, G. D., Kilmann, P. R., Laughlin, J., & Sotile, W. M. (1978). Projected extramarital sexual involvement in unmarried college students. *Journal of Marriage and the Family, 40,* 337–340.

Bulcroft, K., & Bulcroft, R. (1985). Dating and courtship in late life: An exploratory study. In W. A. Peterson & J. Quadagno (Eds.), *Social bonds in later life: Aging and interdependence* (pp. 115–126). Beverly Hills: Sage.

Bulcroft, K., & O'Connor, M. (1986). The importance of dating relationships on quality of life for older persons. *Family Relations, 35,* 397–401.

Bulcroft, K., & O'Conner-Roden, M. (1986, June). Never too late. *Psychology Today,* pp. 66–69.

Bumpass, L., Sweet, J., & Martin, T. C. (1990). Changing patterns of remarriage. *Journal of Marriage and the Family, 52,* 747–756.

Burcky, W., Reuterman, N., & Kopsky, S. (1988). Dating violence among high school students. *School Counselor, 35,* 353–358.

Burden, D. S. (1986). Single parents and the work setting: The impact of multiple job and homelife responsibilities. *Family Relations, 35,* 37–43.

Burke, P. J., Stets, J. E., & Pirog-Good, M. A. (1988). Gender identity, self-esteem, and physical and sexual abuse in dating relationships. *Social Psychology Quarterly, 51,* 272–285.

Burks, V. K., Lund, D. A., Gregg, C. H., & Bluhm, H. P. (1988). Bereavement and remarriage for older adults. *Death Studies, 12,* 51–60.

Burnell, G. M., & Norfleet, M. A. (1986a). Psychosocial factors influencing American men and women in their decision for sterilization. *The Journal of Psychology, 120,* 113–119.

Burnell, G. M., & Norfleet, M. A. (1986b). Women's self-reported responses to abortion. *The Journal of Psychology, 121,* 71–76.

Burns, A. (1984). Perceived causes of marriage breakdown and conditions of life. *Journal of Marriage and the Family, 46,* 551–562.

Burns, C. (1982, January). What to do about those sticky, picky, touchy in-law problems. *Glamour,* pp. 134–135, 159.

Burr, W. R. (1990). Beyond I-statements in family communication. *Family Relations, 39,* 266–273.

Burton, L. (1986). *What's a smart woman like you doing at home?* Washington, DC: Acropolis Books.

Buscaglia, L. F. (1972). *Love.* Thorofare, NJ: Slack.

Buss, D. M. (1985). Human mate selection. *American Scientist, 73,* 47–51.

Bussey, K., & Perry, D. G. (1982). Same-sex imitation: The avoidance of cross-sex models or the acceptance of same-sex models? *Sex Roles, 8,* 773–784.

Butler, N. R., & Golding, J. (1986). *From birth to five: A study of the health and behaviour of Britain's 5-year-olds.* Oxford: Pergamon.

Butler, R. N., & Lewis, M. I. (1987). Sound prescription for your aging patient: Tips for lifelong sexual fitness. *Medical Aspects of Human Sexuality, 21*(7), 96–97, 101–102.

Buunk, B. (1982). Strategies of jealousy: Styles of coping with extramarital involvement of the spouse. *Family Relations, 31,* 13–18.

Byer, C. O., & Shainberg, L. W. (1991). *Dimensions of human sexuality* (3rd ed.). Dubuque, IA: Wm. C. Brown.

Byers, E. S., & Lewis, K. (1988). Dating couples' disagreements over the desired level of sexual intimacy. *The Journal of Sex Research, 24,* 15–29.

Byrd, W., Bradshaw, K., Carr, B., Edman, C., Odom, J., & Ackerman, G. (1990). A prospective randomized study of pregnancy rates following intrauterine and intracervical insemination using frozen donor sperm. *Fertility and Sterility, 53,* 521–527.

Byrne, D. (1977). The imagery of sex. In J. Money & H. Musaph (Eds.), *Handbook of sexology* (pp. 327–350). New York: Elsevier/North-Holland.

Bytheway, W. R. (1981). The variation with age of age differences in marriage. *Journal of Marriage and the Family, 43,* 923–927.

Cadkin, A., Ginsberg, N., Pergament, E., & Verlinski, Y. (1984). Chorionic villi sampling: A new technique for detection of genetic abnormalities in the first trimester. *Radiology, 151,* 159–162.

Cahill, S. E. (1983). Reexamining the acquisition of sex roles: A social interactionist approach. *Sex Roles, 9,* 1–15.

Cain, V. S., & Hofferth, S. L. (1989). Parental choice of self-care for school-age children. *Journal of Marriage and the Family, 51,* 65–77.

Calderone, M. S., & Johnson, E. W. (1981). *The family book about sexuality.* New York: Harper & Row.

Caldwell, B. M. (1986). Day care and early environmental adequacy. In W. Fowler (Ed.), *New directions for child development* (Vol. 32, pp. 11–30). San Francisco: Jossey-Bass.

Calhoun, L. G., & Selby, J. W. (1980). Voluntary childlessness, involuntary childlessness, and having children: A study of social perceptions. *Family Relations, 29,* 181–183.

Callan, V. J. (1983). Childlessness and partner selection. *Journal of Marriage and the Family, 45,* 181–186.

Callan, V. J. (1985a). Comparisons of mothers of one child by choice with mothers wanting a second birth. *Journal of Marriage and the Family, 47,* 155–164.

Callan, V. J. (1985b). Perceptions of parents, the voluntarily and involuntarily childless: A multidimensional scaling analysis. *Journal of Marriage and the Family, 47,* 1045–1050.

Callan, V. J. (1986). The impact of the first birth: Married and single women preferring childlessness, one child, or two children. *Journal of Marriage and the Family, 48,* 261–269.

Callan, V. J. (1987). The personal and marital adjustment of mothers and of voluntarily and involuntarily childless wives. *Journal of Marriage and the Family, 49,* 847–856.

Callan, V. J., & Gallois, C. (1983). Perceptions about having children: Are daughters different from their mothers? *Journal of Marriage and the Family, 45,* 607–612.

Cameron, C., Oskamp, S., & Sparks, W. (1977). Courtship American style: Newspaper ads. *The Family Coordinator, 26,* 27–30.

Cameron, W. J., & Kenkel, W. F. (1960). High school dating: A study in variation. *Marriage and Family Living, 22,* 74–76.

Campbell, A. (1981). *The sense of well-being in America: Recent patterns and trends.* New York: McGraw-Hill.

Campbell, A. (1989a). Emotions and adjustments. In A. Campbell (Ed.), *The opposite sex* (pp. 182–189). Topsfield, MA: Salem House.

Campbell, A. (1989b). The roots of aggression. In A. Campbell (Ed.), *The opposite sex* (pp. 64–69). Topsfield, MA: Salem House.

Campbell, A. A., Converse, P. L., & Rogers, W. L. (1976). *Quality of American life: Perceptions, evaluations, and satisfactions.* New York: Sage.

Can hormones be blamed for irrational behavior? (1982, July 16). *Gainesville Sun,* p. 9A.

Cannon, M. E. (1987, November). *Time and space constraints on everyday routines: Working parents and time pressure.* Paper presented at the meeting of the National Council on Family Relations, Atlanta, GA.

Caplan, G. (1981). Mastery of stress: Psychosocial aspects. *American Journal of Psychiatry, 134,* 413–420.

Card, E. (1985, May). Health insurance: All you need to know . . . Before you get sick. *Ms.,* pp. 14, 16, 21, 22.

Card, E. (1986, September). New twists in banking: What you can expect in a changing market. *Ms.,* pp. 71–72, 74.

Cargan, L. (1981). Singles: An examination of two stereotypes. *Family Relations, 30,* 377–385.

Cargan, L., & Melko, M. (1982). *Singles: Myths and realities.* Beverly Hills: Sage.

Carlson, M. (1989, April 24). A doctor prescribes hard truth. *Time,* pp. 82, 84.

Carlson, M. (1990, July 9). Abortion's hardest cases. *Time,* pp. 22–26.

Carnes, P. (1986). *An introduction: Counseling the sexual addict.* Golden Valley, MN: Institute for Behavioral Medicine.

Carpenter, C. J. (1989). Toys and play. In A. Campbell (Ed.), *The opposite sex* (pp. 70–77). Topsfield, MA: Salem House.

Carpenter, W. D. (1989). College cohabitors and noncohabitors twelve years later: A comparative analysis of life course variables (Doctoral dissertation, Syracuse University, 1988). *Dissertation Abstracts International, 50,* 550A.

Carroll, J. L., Volk, K. D., & Hyde, J. S. (1985). Differences between males and females in motives for engaging in sexual intercourse. *Archives of Sexual Behavior, 14,* 131–139.

Carroll, L. (1988). Concern with AIDS and the sexual behavior of college students. *Journal of Marriage and the Family, 50,* 405–411.

Carter, D., & Welch, D. (1981). Parenting styles and children's behavior. *Family Relations, 30,* 191–195.

Carter, E. A., & McGoldrick, M. (1989). *The changing family life cycle: A framework for family therapy* (2nd ed.). Neeham Heights: Allyn and Bacon.

Carter, V. T., & Leavenworth, J. L. (1985). *Caught in the middle: Children of divorce.* Valley Forge, PA: Judson Press.

Cartwright, S. (1987). Group endeavor in nursery school can be valuable learning. *Young Children, 48,* 8–11.

Casey, L. D., & Matson, R. (1987, April). *Sociological theories of intimacy: A critique and extension.* Paper presented at the meeting of the Midwest Sociological Society, Chicago, IL.

Cassidy, A. (1985, November). Living alone—and liking it too much. *McCall's,* p. 38.

Cassidy, J., & Main, M. (1984, April). *Quality of attachment from infancy to early childhood: Security is stable but behavior changes.* Paper presented at the International Conference on Infant Studies, New York, NY.

Cate, R. M., Henton, J. M., Koval, J., Christopher, F. S., & Lloyd, S. (1982). Premarital abuse: A social psychological perspective. *Journal of Family Issues, 3,* 72–90.

Cate, R. M., Koval, J. E., & Ponzetti, J. J., Jr. (1984). Power strategies in dual-career and traditional couples. *The Journal of Social Psychology, 123,* 287–288.

Cates, W., Jr. (1987). STDs and contraceptive choice. *Medical Aspects of Human Sexuality, 21*(2), 36–37.

Cates, W., Jr., Grimes, D. A., & Smith, J. C. (1978). Abortion as treatment for unwanted pregnancy: The number two sexually transmitted condition. *Advances in Planned Parenthood, 12,* 115–121.

Census bureau estimate of number of latchkey children disputed. (1987). *Phi Delta Kappan, 68,* 638.

Centers for Disease Control. (1990). *Division of Sexually Transmitted Diseases Annual Report, FY 1989.* Atlanta, GA: Public Health Service.

Centers, R., Raven, B. H., & Rodrigues, A. (1971). Conjugal power structure: A re-examination. *American Sociological Review, 36,* 264–278.

Chaikin, A. L., & Derlega, V. J. (1976). Self-disclosure. In J. W. Thibaut, J. T. Spence, & R. C. Carson (Eds.), *Contemporary topics in social psychology* (pp. 177–210). Morristown, NJ: General Learning Press.

Chance, P. (1989, January/February). Seeing is believing. *Psychology Today,* p. 26.

Charatan, F. B. (1983). Depression related to men's retirement. *Medical Aspects of Human Sexuality, 17*(7), 54–56, 59, 62–63, 67–69, 72–74.

Charvrat, A. (1986, March). *The effects of marriage, children, and family composition on life satisfaction of women.* Paper presented at the meeting of the Midwest Sociological Society, Des Moines, IA.

Chase-Lansdale, L., & Owen, M. T. (1987). Maternal employment in a family context: Effects on infant-mother and infant-father attachments. *Child Development, 58,* 1505–1512.

Chasen, B. (1977). Toward eliminating sex-role stereotyping in early childhood classes. *Child Care Quarterly, 6,* 30–41.

Chasnoff, I. J., Burns, W. J., Scholl, S. H., Burns, K., Chisum, G., & Kyle-Spore, L. (1986). Maternal-neonatal incest. *American Journal of Orthopsychiatry, 56,* 577–580.

Chekhov, A. (1968). Notebooks. In B. Evans (Ed.), *Dictionary of quotations* (p. 510). New York: Delacorte Press.

Cherlin, A. (1978). Remarriage as an incomplete institution. *American Journal of Sociology, 84,* 634–650.

Cherlin, A. (1980). Postponing marriage: The influence of young women's work expectations. *Journal of Marriage and the Family, 42,* 355–365.

Cherlin, A., & Furstenberg, F. F., Jr. (1985). Styles and strategies of grandparenting. In V. L. Bengston & J. F. Robertson (Eds.), *Grandparenthood* (pp. 97–116). Beverly Hills: Sage.

Cherlin, A., & McCarthy, J. (1985). Remarried couple households: Data from the June 1980 Current Population Survey. *Journal of Marriage and the Family, 47,* 23–30.

Cherlin, A. J. (1981). *Marriage, divorce, remarriage.* Cambridge, MA: Harvard University Press.

Cherlin, A. J. (1988). The weakening link between marriage and the care of children. *Family Planning Perspectives, 20,* 302–306.

Cherlin, A. J., & Furstenberg, F. F. (1986). *The new American grandparent: A place in the family a life apart.* New York: Basic Books.

Cherry, F. (1983). Gender roles and sexual violence. In E. R. Allgeier & N. B. McCormick (Eds.), *Changing boundaries: Gender roles and sexual behavior* (pp. 245–260). Palo Alto, CA: Mayfield.

Chess, S. (1983). Mothers are always the problem—or are they? Old wine in new bottles. *Pediatrics, 71,* 974–976.

Chess, S., & Thomas, A. (1984). *Origins and evolution of behavior disorders from infancy to early adult life.* New York: Brunner/Mazel.

Chesser, B. J. (1980). Analysis of wedding rituals: An attempt to make weddings more meaningful. *Family Relations, 29,* 204–209.

Child care in America inadequate in helping working women with babies or young children. (1987). *Family Planning Perspectives, 19,* 78–79.

Chilman, C. S. (1980). Social and psychological research concerning adolescent childbearing: 1970–1980. *Journal of Marriage and the Family, 42,* 793–806.

Chilman, C. S. (1983). Remarriage and stepfamilies: Research results and implications. In E. D. Macklin & R. H. Rubin (Eds.), *Contemporary families and alternative lifestyles: Handbook on research and theory* (pp. 147–163). Beverly Hills: Sage.

Chin, J., Snyder, C. W., Forrestal, M., & McClure, B. (1988). Courtship violence in a college student population. *Student Assistance Journal, 1*(3), 34–41, 61.

Chin, L., & Dahlin, M. B. (1983). *Peer education programs: Sexuality education strategy and resource guide.* Washington, DC: Center for Population Options.

Ching, L., Borchardt, K., Smith, R., & Beal, C. (1988). A 24-hour plastic envelope method for isolating and identifying Gardnerella vaginalis (PEM-GVA). *Genitourinary Medicine, 64,* 180–184.

Christian, J. L., & Greger, J. L. (1988). *Nutrition for living* (2nd ed.). Menlo Park, CA: Benjamin/Cummings.

Christopher, F. S. (1988). An initial investigation into a continuum of premarital sexual pressure. *Journal of Sex Research, 25,* 255–266.

Christopher, F. S., & Cate, R. M. (1985). Anticipated influences on sexual decision-making for first intercourse. *Family Relations, 34,* 265–270.

Christopher, F. S., & Cate, R. M. (1988). Premarital sexual involvement: A developmental investigation of relational correlates. *Adolescence, 23,* 793–803.

Christopher, F. S., Fabes, R. A., & Wilson, P. M. (1989). Family television viewing: Implications for family life education. *Family Relations, 38,* 210–214.

Chumlea, W. C. (1982). Physical growth in adolescence. In W. W. Wolman (Ed.), *Handbook of developmental psychology* (pp. 471–486). Englewood Cliffs, NJ: Prentice-Hall.

Church, G. J. (1989, July 17). Five political hot spots: In some states the abortion battle is already near boiling point. *Time,* p. 64.

Churchill, W. (1989). Quote. *Philanthroplan.* Denver, CO: National Jewish Center for Immunology and Respiratory Medicine.

Cimbalo, R. S., Faling, V., & Mousaw, P. (1976). The course of love: A cross-sectional design. *Psychological Reports, 38,* 1292–1294.

The Cinderella disease: NGU, the most common VD. (1978, July 17). *Time,* p. 73.

Clanton, S., & Smith, L. (1977). *Jealousy.* Englewood Cliffs, NJ: Prentice-Hall.

Clare, A. W. (1985). Hormones, behaviour, and the menstrual cycle. *Journal of Psychosomatic Research, 29,* 225–233.

Clark, P. G., Siviski, R. W., & Weiner, R. (1986). Coping strategies of widowers in the first year. *Family Relations, 35,* 425–430.

Clark, R. L., & Sumner, D. A. (1985). Inflation and the real income of the elderly: Recent evidence and expectations for the future. *The Gerontologist, 25,* 146–152.

Clark, T. F., & Wilson, P. M. (1983). *Programs for parents: Sexual education strategy and resource guide.* Washington, DC: Center for Population Options.

Clarke-Stewart, A. (1977). *Child care in the family: A review of research and some propositions for policy.* New York: Academic Press.

Clarke-Stewart, A. (1982). The family as a child-care environment. In J. P. Rosenfeld (Ed.), *Relationships, the marriage and family reader* (pp. 300–312). Glenview, IL: Scott, Foresman.

Clarke-Stewart, A., & Friedman, S. (1987). *Child development: Infancy through adolescence.* New York: Wiley.

Clarke-Stewart, A. A., & Hevey, C. M. (1981). Longitudinal relations in repeated observations of mother-child interaction from 1 to 2 1/2 years. *Developmental Psychology, 17,* 127–145.

Clayton, R. R., & Voss, H. L. (1977). Shacking up: Cohabitation in the 1970s. *Journal of Marriage and the Family, 39,* 273–283.

Cleek, M. G., & Pearson, T. A. (1985). Perceived causes of divorce: An analysis of interrelationships. *Journal of Marriage and the Family, 47,* 179–183.

Clemens, A. W., & Axelson, L. J. (1985). The not-so-empty nest: The return of the fledgling adult. *Family Relations, 34,* 259–264.

Clingempeel, W. G., Brand, E., & Ievoli, R. (1984). Stepparent-stepchild relationships in stepmother and stepfather families: A multi-method study. *Family Relations, 33,* 465–472.

Clingempeel, W. G., & Eulalee, B. (1985). Quasi-kin relationships, structural complexity, and marital quality in stepfamilies: A replication, extension, and clinical implications. *Family Relations, 34,* 401–409.

Clingempeel, W. G., & Segal, S. (1986). Stepparent-stepchild relationships and the psychological adjustment of children in stepmother and stepfather families. *Child Development, 57,* 474–484.

Cochran, S. (1988). Asking about AIDS risks: Is it enough? *Behavior Today, 19* (40), 3–4.

Cockrum, J., & White, P. (1985). Influences on the life satisfaction of never-married men and women. *Family Relations, 34,* 551–556.

Cogle, F. L., & Tasker, G. E. (1982). Children and housework. *Family Relations, 31,* 395–399.

Cohen, J. (1987). Parents as educational models and definers. *Journal of Marriage and the Family, 49,* 339–351.

Cohen, J. B. (1985). *Parenthood after 30?* Lexington, MA: Heath.

Cohen, T. F. (1986). Men's family roles: Becoming and being husbands and fathers (Doctoral dissertation, Boston University, 1986). *Dissertation Abstracts International, 47,* 668A-669A.

Cole, C., & Rodman, H. (1987). When school-age children care for themselves: Issues for family life educators and parents. *Family Relations, 36,* 92–96.

Cole, C. L. (1986). Developmental tasks affecting the marital relationship in later life. *American Behavioral Scientist, 29,* 389–404.

Cole, J., & Laibson, H. (1982, September). When parents argue (and kids listen). *Parents,* pp. 58–63.

Coleman, J. C. (1984). *Intimate relationships, marriage and family.* Indianapolis: Bobbs-Merrill.

Coleman, M., & Ganong, L. H. (1985). Remarriage myths: Implications for the helping professions. *Journal of Counseling and Development, 64,* 116–120.

Coleman, M., & Ganong, L. H. (1990). Remarriage and stepfamily research in the 1980s: Increased interest in an old family form. *Journal of Marriage and the Family, 52,* 925–940.

Coleman, M., Ganong, L. H., & Ellis, P. (1985). Family structure and dating behavior of adolescents. *Adolescence, 20,* 537–543.

Coleman, T. F. (1978, March/April). Sex and the law. *The Humanist,* pp. 38–41.

Coles, R. (1984, August 12). What's the best family size? *Family Weekly,* pp. 4–5.

Coles, R., & Stokes, G. (1985). *Sex and the American teenager.* New York: Harper & Row.

Collins, G. (1985, February 11). Marrying across boundaries. *The New York Times,* p. 13C.

Collins, J. A., Wrixon, W., Janes, L. B., & Wilson, E. H. (1983). Treatment—independent pregnancy among infertile couples. *New England Journal of Medicine, 309,* 1201–1206.

Comics increasing [*sic*] reflect societal problems. (1986). *Marriage and Divorce Today, 11*(46), 4.

Commuting: A solution for two-career couples. (1978, April 3). *Business Week,* pp. 62, 67–68.

Computerized premarital inventories reveal likelihood of future divorce. (1987). *Marriage & Divorce Today, 12*(23), 2–3.

Condelli, L. (1986). Social and attitudinal determinants of contraceptive choice: Using the health belief model. *The Journal of Sex Research, 22,* 478–491.

Condom use increased. (1990, November 8). *Eau Claire Leader-Telegram,* p. 9A.

Condran, J. G., & Bode, J. G. (1982). Rashomon, working wives, and family division of labor: Middletown, 1980. *Journal of Marriage and the Family, 44,* 421–426.

Conger, R. D., Elder, G. H., Jr., Lorenz, F. O., Conger, K. J., Simons, R. L., Whitbeck, L. B., Huck, S., & Melby, J. N. (1990). Linking economic hardship to marital quality and instability. *Journal of Marriage and the Family, 52,* 643–656.

Connor, J. M., & Serbin, L. A. (1985). Visual-spatial skill: Is it important for mathematics? Can it be taught? In S. Chipman, L. Brush, & D. Wilson (Eds.), *Women and mathematics: Balancing the equation* (pp. 151–174). Hillsdale, NJ: Erlbaum.

Connors, D. D. (1985). Women's "sickness": A case of secondary gains or primary losses. *Advances in Nursing Science, 7,* 1–17.

Conrad, P. (1986, August). *The social meaning of AIDS.* Paper presented at the meeting of the Society for the Study of Social Problems, New York, NY.

Consumer costs up 0.4 percent in November. (1989, December 19). *Eau Claire Leader-Telegram,* p. 14B.

Conte, J. R. (1985). Clinical dimensions of adult sexual abuse of children. *Behavioral Sciences & the Law, 3,* 341–354.

Controversial pill halts tumor growth. (1991, February 17). *Eau Claire Leader-Telegram,* p. 12A.

Conway, C. (1980). Psychophysical preparations for childbirth. In L. McNall (Ed.), *Contemporary obstetric and gynecological nursing* (pp. 44–46). St. Louis: Mosby.

Cook, A. S., & Weigel, D. J. (1983). Relocation and crisis: Perceived sources of support. *Family Relations, 32,* 267–273.

Cook, A. S., West, J. B., & Hamner, T. J. (1982). Changes in attitudes toward parenting among college women: 1972 and 1979 samples. *Family Relations, 31,* 109–113.

Cook, C. C., & Rudo, N. M. (1984). Factors influencing the residential location of female householders. *Urban Affairs Quarterly, 20,* 78–96.

Cook, D. R., & Frantz-Cook, A. (1984). A systemic treatment approach to wife battering. *Journal of Marital and Family Therapy, 10,* 83–93.

Cooper, J. E., Holman, J., & Braithwaite, V. A. (1983). Self-esteem and family cohesion: The child's perspective and adjustment. *Journal of Marriage and the Family, 45,* 153–159.

Coopersmith, S. (1967). *The antecedents of self-esteem.* San Francisco: Freeman.

Copenhaver, S. (1990, March). *College date rape: A look at sorority members.* Paper presented at the meeting of the North Central Sociological Association, Louisville, KY.

Copper IUD. (1988, November). *Family Life Information Exchange Resource Memo.* Rockville, MD: Public Health Service.

Corder, J., & Stephan, C. W. (1984). Females' combination of work and family roles: Adolescents' aspirations. *Journal of Marriage and the Family, 46,* 391–402.

Coreil, J., & Parcel, G. S. (1983). Sociocultural determinants of parental involvement in sex education. *Journal of Sex Education and Therapy, 9,* 22–25.

Cost of living: No wonder Rocky keeps on fighting. (1986, February). *Money,* p. 38.

Costin, F. (1985). Beliefs about rape and women's social roles. *Archives of Sexual Behavior, 14,* 319–325.

Cotten-Huston, A. L., & Wheeler, K. A. (1983). Preorgasmic group treatment: Assertiveness, marital adjustment, and sexual function in women. *Journal of Sex & Marital Therapy, 9,* 296–302.

The Court edges away from *Roe v. Wade.* (1989). *Family Planning Perspectives, 21,* 184–187.

Coverdill, J. E. (1988). The dual economy and sex differences in earnings. *Social Forces, 66,* 970–993.

Coverman, S., & Sheley, J. F. (1986). Change in men's housework and child-care time, 1965–1975. *Journal of Marriage and the Family, 48,* 413–422.

Cowan, C. P., & Cowan, P. A. (1989, October). *The first year and first child: Two challenges to successful marriage.* Paper presented at the meeting of the American Association for Marriage and Family Therapy, San Francisco, CA.

Cowan, C. P., Cowan, P. A., Heming, G., Garrett, E., Coysh, W. S., Curtis-Boles, H., & Boles, A. J., III. (1985). Transitions to parenthood: His, hers, and theirs. *Journal of Family Issues, 6,* 451–482.

Cowan, G. (1984). The double standard in age-discrepant relationships. *Sex Roles, 11,* 17–23.

Cowan, G., & Hoffman, C. D. (1986). Gender stereotyping in young children: Evidence to support a concept learning approach. *Sex Roles, 14,* 211–224.

Cowan, R. S. (1976). The "Industrial Revolution" in the home: Household technology and social change in the twentieth century. *Technology and Culture, 17,* 1–23.

Cox, H. (1977). Sex and secularization. In J. Needleman, A. K. Bierman, & J. A. Gould (Eds.), *Religion for a new generation* (2nd ed., pp. 322–338). New York: Macmillan.

Cox, H., & Bhak, A. (1987). Symbolic interaction and retirement adjustment: An empirical assessment. In H. Cox (Ed.), *Aging* (5th ed., pp. 136–139). Guilford, CT: Dushkin.

Cox, L. J. (1986). Women, work, role conflict, and stress (Doctoral dissertation, University of California, Los Angeles, 1985). *Dissertation Abstracts International, 47,* 84A.

Crane, D. R., Allgood, S. M., Larson, J. H., & Griffin, W. (1990). Assessing marital quality with distressed and nondistressed couples: A comparison and equivalency table for three frequently used measures. *Journal of Marriage and the Family, 52,* 87–93.

Crawford, J. W. (1982). Mother-infant interaction in premature and full-term infants. *Child Development, 53,* 957–963.

Credit unions: Are they better than banks? (1986, February). *Consumer Reports,* pp. 108–111.

Crenshaw, T. (1984, September). *Medical causes of sexual dysfunction.* Paper presented at the meeting of the Western Region, American Association of Sex Educators, Counselors, and Therapists. Las Vegas, NV.

Crepault, C., Abraham, G., Porto, R., & Couture, M. (1977). Erotic imagery in women. In R. Gemme & C. Wheeler (Eds.), *Progress in sexology* (pp. 267–283). New York: Plenum Press.

Crocket, T. H., & Cosentino, M. (1984). The varicocele. *Fertility and Sterility, 41,* 5–11.

Crohan, S. E., & Veroff, J. (1989). Dimensions of marital well-being among white and black newlyweds. *Journal of Marriage and the Family, 51,* 373–383.

Cronell, G. W. (1988, April 9). Baptists change stance on abortion. *Eau Claire Leader-Telegram,* p. 15A.

Crooks, R., & Baur, K. (1990). *Our sexuality* (4th ed.). Redwood City, CA: Benjamin/Cummings.

Crosbie-Burnett, M. (1984). The centrality of the step relationship: A challenge to family theory and practice. *Family Relations, 33,* 459–463.

Crosbie-Burnett, M. (1987, November). *A family stress theory of remarriage.* Paper presented at the meeting of the National Council on Family Relations, Atlanta, GA.

Crosby, F., & Herek, G. M. (1986). Male sympathy with the situation of women: Does personal experience make a difference? *Journal of Social Issues, 42,* 55–66.

Crosby, J. F. (1979). Reclaiming our sexuality: Owning ourselves. In C. E. Williams, & J. F. Crosby (Eds.), *Choice and challenge: Contemporary readings in marriage* (2nd ed., pp. 212–222). Dubuque, IA: Wm. C. Brown.

Crosby, J. F. (1980). A critique of divorce statistics and their interpretation. *Family Relations, 29,* 51–58.

Crosby, J. F. (1991). *Illusion and disillusion: The self in love and marriage* (4th ed.). Belmont, CA: Wadsworth.

Crossman, D. K. (1987, April). *Dual-career women's occupational conditions and self-reports of commitment and mastery: The spillover of work into family life.* Paper presented at the meeting of the Southern Sociological Society, Atlanta, GA.

Crown, P. A. (1985). Ego identity, intimacy, and sex role orientation of young adults (Doctoral dissertation, University of Denver, 1985). *Dissertation Abstracts International, 46,* 2087B.

Cuber, J., & Harroff, P. (1965). *The significant Americans.* New York: Random House.

Culp, R. E., Cook, A. S., & Housley, P. C. (1983). A comparison of observed and reported adult-infant interactions: Effects of perceived sex. *Sex Roles, 9,* 475–479.

Cummings, J. (1986, August 3). Women in conservative rabbi post. *The New York Times,* p. 24.

Cuniberti, B. (1983, June 4). U.S. youths in the dark on sex facts. *Austin American-Statesman,* p. 2C.

Curran, J. (1980). Economic consequences of pelvic inflammatory disease. *American Journal of Obstetrics & Gynecology, 138,* 848–851.

Cutler, W. B., Garcia, C. R., & Krieger, A. M. (1980). Sporadic sexual behavior and menstrual cycle length in women. *Hormones and Behavior, 114,* 163–172.

Dahl, A. S., Cowgill, K. M., & Asmundsson, R. (1987). Life in remarriage families. *Social Work, 32,* 40–44.

D'Alessio, F. N. (1991, January 12). Study says day-care may build immunities. *Saint Paul Pioneer Press,* pp. 1A, 6A.

Daly, K. J., & Herold, E. S. (1985). Who uses natural family planning? *Canadian Journal of Public Health, 76,* 207–209.

Damrosch, S. P., & Fischman, S. H. (1985). Medical students' attitudes toward sexually active older persons. *Journal of the American Geriatrics Society, 33,* 852–855.

Daniels-Mohring, D., & Berger, M. (1984). Social network changes and the adjustment to divorce. *Journal of Divorce, 8*(1), 17–32.

Darling, C. A., & Davidson, J. K., Sr. (1986a). Coitally active university students: Sexual behaviors, concerns, and challenges. *Adolescence, 21,* 403–419.

Darling, C. A., & Davidson, J. K., Sr. (1986b). Enhancing relationships: Understanding the feminine mystique of pretending orgasm. *Journal of Sex & Marital Therapy, 12,* 182–196.

Darling, C. A., & Davidson, J. K., Sr. (1987a). Guilt: A factor in sexual satisfaction. *Sociological Inquiry, 57,* 251–271.

Darling, C. A., & Davidson, J. K., Sr. (1987b). The relationship of sexual satisfaction to coital involvement: The concept of technical virginity revisited. *Deviant Behavior, 8,* 27–46.

Darling, C. A., Davidson, J. K., Sr., & Conway-Welch, C. (1990). Female ejaculation: Perceived origins, the Grafenberg spot/area, and sexual responsiveness. *Archives of Sexual Behavior, 19,* 29–47.

Darling, C. A., Davidson, J. K., Sr., & Jennings, D. A. (in press). The female sexual response revisited: Understanding the multi-orgasmic experience in women. *Archives of Sexual Behavior.*

Darling, C. A., & Hicks, M. W. (1982). Parental influence on adolescent sexuality: Implications for parents as educators. Journal of Youth and Adolescence, 11, 231–245.

Daugherty, L. R., & Burger, J. M. (1984). The influence of parents, church, and peers on the sexual attitudes and behaviors of college students. *Archives of Sexual Behavior, 13,* 351–359.

Davey, A. J., & Paolucci, B. (1980). Family interaction: A study of shared time and activities. *Family Relations, 29,* 43–49.

David, D. S., & Brannan, R. (Eds.). (1976). *The forty-nine percent majority: The male sex role.* Reading, MA: Addison-Wesley.

David, L. (1985, February). Watch the calendar and buy better. *Home Mechanix,* pp. 98–99.

Davidson, B., Balswick, J., & Halverson, C. (1983). Affective self-disclosure and marital adjustment: A test of equity theory. *Journal of Marriage and the Family, 45,* 93–102.

Davidson, J. K., Sr. (1984). Autoeroticism, sexual satisfaction, and sexual adjustment among university females: Past and current patterns. *Deviant Behavior, 5,* 121–140.

Davidson, J. K., Sr. (1985). Sexual fantasies among married males: An analysis of sexual satisfaction, situational contexts, and functions. *Sociological Spectrum, 5,* 139–153.

Davidson, J. K., Sr., & Darling, C. A. (1986). The impact of college-level sex education on sexual knowledge, attitudes, and practices: The knowledge/sexual experimentation myth revisited. *Deviant Behavior, 7,* 13–30.

Davidson, J. K., Sr., & Darling, C. A. (1988a). Self-perceptions of female sexuality. Unpublished raw data.

Davidson, J. K., Sr., & Darling, C. A. (1988b). The sexually experienced woman: The role of multiple sex partners and sexual satisfaction. *The Journal of Sex Research, 24,* 141–154.

Davidson, J. K., Sr., & Darling, C. A. (1988c). The stereotype of single women revisited: Sexual practices and sexual satisfaction among professional women. *Health Care for Women International, 9,* 317–336.

Davidson, J. K., Sr., & Darling, C. A. (1989a, November). *Masturbatory guilt and sexual responsiveness among adult women: Sexual satisfaction revisited.* Paper presented at the meeting of the National Council on Family Relations, New Orleans, LA.

Davidson, J. K., Sr., & Darling, C. A. (1989b). Self-perceived differences in the female orgasmic response. *Family Practice Research Journal, 8,* 75–84.

Davidson, J. K., Sr., & Darling, C. A. (1990). The influence of college-level education on female masturbatory attitudes and behaviours: A longitudinal analysis. *Australian Journal of Marriage & Family, 11,* 36–51.

Davidson, J. K., Sr., Darling, C. A., & Conway-Welch, C. (1989). The role of the Grafenberg spot and female ejaculation in the female orgasmic response: An empirical analysis. *Journal of Sex and Marital Therapy, 15,* 102–120.

Davidson, J. K., Sr., & Hoffman, L. E. (1986). Sexual fantasies and sexual satisfaction: An empirical analysis of erotic thought. *The Journal of Sex Research, 22,* 184–205.

Davidson, J. K., Sr., & Leslie, G. R. (1977). Premarital sexual intercourse: An application of axiomatic theory construction. *Journal of Marriage and the Family, 39,* 15–25.

Davidson, J. K., Sr., & Moore, N. B. (1990). [Sexual attitudes and behavior among college women and men: Choices and risks in the 80s]. Unpublished data.

Davidson, J. M. (1985). Sexual behavior and its relationship to ovarian hormones in the menopause. *Maturitas, 7,* 193–201.

Davis, A. B. (1989, May 21). Day-care debate heats up again. *Eau Claire Leader-Telegram,* p. 4E.

Davis, E. C., Hovestadt, A. J., Piercy, F. P., & Cochran, S. W. (1982). Effects of weekend and weekly marriage enrichment program formats. *Family Relations, 31,* 85–90.

Davis, K. E. (1985, February). Near and dear: Friendship and love compared. *Psychology Today,* pp. 22–28, 30.

Davis, M. A., Randall, E., Forthofer, R. N., Lee, E. S., & Margen, S. (1985). Living arrangements and dietary patterns of older adults in the United States. *Journal of Gerontology, 40,* 434–442.

Davis, S. M., & Harris, M. B. (1982). Sexual knowledge, sexual interests, and sources of sexual information of rural and urban adolescents from three cultures. *Adolescence, 17,* 471–492.

Davis-Brown, K., Salamon, S., & Surra, C. A. (1987). Economic and social factors in mate selection: An ethnographic analysis of an agricultural community. *Journal of Marriage and the Family, 49,* 41–55.

Dawley, H. H., Winstead, D., Baxter, A., & Gay, J. R. (1979). An attitude survey of the effects of marijuana on sexual enjoyment. *Journal of Clinical Psychology, 35,* 212–217.

De Amicis, L. A., Goldberg, D. C., LoPiccolo, J., Friedman, J., & Davies, L. (1984). Three-year follow-up of couples evaluated for sexual dysfunction. *Journal of Sex & Marital Therapy, 10,* 215–228.

DeBuono, B. A., Zinner, S. H., Daamen, M., & McCormack, W. M. (1990). Sexual behavior of college women in 1975, 1986, and 1989. *The New England Journal of Medicine, 322,* 821–825.

Deckard, B. S. (1983). *The women's movement: Political, socioeconomic, and psychological issues* (3rd ed.). New York: Harper & Row.

Definition of family expands, cheering family specialists. (1989). *The Brown University Family Therapy Letter, 1*(3), 1, 7.

Defrain, J., & Eirick, R. (1981). Coping as divorced single parents: A comparative study of fathers and mothers. *Family Relations, 30,* 265–274.

Deimling, G. T., & Poulshock, S. W. (1985). The transition from family in-home care to institutional care: Focus on health and attitudinal issues as predisposing factors. *Research on Aging, 7,* 563–576.

DeLamater, J. D., & MacCorquodale, P. (1979). *Premarital sexuality: Attitudes, relationships, and behavior.* Madison, WI: University of Wisconsin Press.

Delora, J. S., Warren, C. A. B., & Ellison, C. R. (1981). *Understanding sexual interaction* (2nd ed.). Boston: Houghton-Mifflin.

DeMaris, A. (1984). A comparison of remarriages with first marriages on satisfaction in marriage and its relationship to prior cohabitation. *Family Relations, 33,* 443–449

DeMaris, A. (1990). The dynamics of generational transfer in courtship violence: A biracial exploration. *Journal of Marriage and the Family, 52,* 219–231.

DeMaris, A., & Leslie, G. R. (1984). Cohabitation with the future spouse: Its influence upon marital satisfaction and communication. *Journal of Marriage and the Family, 46,* 77–84.

Demo, D. H., & Acock, A. C. (1988). The impact of divorce on children. *Journal of Marriage and the Family, 50,* 619–648.

Demographers miscalculate births. (1989, October 31). *Eau Claire Leader-Telegram,* p. 8A.

Denmark, F. L., Shaw, J. S., & Ciali, S. D. (1985). The relationship among sex roles, living arrangements, and the division of household responsibilities. *Sex Roles, 12,* 617–625.

Dennerstein, L., Spencer-Gardner, C., & Burrows, G. (1984). Mood and the menstrual cycle. *Journal of Psychiatric Research, 18,* 1–12.

Denney, N. W., & Quadagno, D. (1988). *Human sexuality.* St. Louis: Times Mirror/Mosby College.

Denniston, G. C. (1985). Vasectomy by electrocautery: Outcomes in a series of 2,500 patients. *Journal of Family Practice, 21,* 35–40.

Dennon, A. R. (1986, September). The high cost of credit. *Consumers' Research,* pp. 11–16.

DePauw, L. G. (1975). *Founding mothers: Women in America in the Revolutionary era.* Boston: Houghton-Mifflin.

Depner, C. E., & Ingersoll-Dayton, B. (1985). Conjugal social support: Patterns in later life. *Journal of Gerontology, 40,* 761–766.

Determining how much care society owes the dying. (1988, June 19). *The New York Times,* p. 5E.

deTurk, M. A., & Miller, G. R. (1986). The effects of husbands' and wives' social cognition on their marital adjustment, conjugal power, and self-esteem. *Journal of Marriage and the Family, 48,* 715–724.

Devall, E., Stoneman, Z., & Brody, G. (1986). The impact of divorce and maternal employment on pre-adolescent children. *Family Relations, 35,* 153–159.

DeVito, J. A. (1986). *The communication handbook.* New York: Harper & Row.

Dhir, K. S., & Markman, H. J. (1986). Application of social judgment theory to understanding and treating marital conflict. *Journal of Marriage and the Family, 46,* 597–610.

Diamond, M. (1982). Sexual identity, monozygotic twins reared in discordant sex roles and BBC follow-up. *Archives of Sexual Behavior, 11,* 181–185.

Dick-Read, G. (1972). *Childbirth without fear.* New York: Harper & Row.

Diggs, J. F. (1982, August 16). How people seek relief from soaring food prices. *U.S. News & World Report,* pp. 65, 68.

Dignan, M., Denson, D., Anspaugh, D., & C'mich, D. (1985). Effects of sex education on sexual behaviors of college students. *Adolescence, 20,* 171–178.

Dimaggio, P., & Mohr, J. (1985). Cultural capital, educational attainment, and marital selection. *American Journal of Sociology, 90,* 1231–1261.

Dinkmeyer, D., & McKay, G. D. (1976a). *Systematic training for effective parenting (STEP): Leader's manual.* Circle Pines, MN: American Guidance Service.

Dinkmeyer, D., & McKay, G. D. (1976b). *Systematic training for effective parenting (STEP): Parent's handbook.* Circle Pines, MN: American Guidance Service.

Diokno, A. C., Brown, M. B., & Herzog, A. R. (1990). Sexual function in the elderly. *Archives of Internal Medicine, 150,* 197–220.

Divorce. (1986). *Newsletter, The William Petschek National Jewish Family Center, 5*(4), 1–4.

Divorce concerns working wives. (1986, June 17). *Gainesville Sun,* p. 7A.

Divorce is changing America. (1986, June 3). In *NBC White Paper Viewer's Guide* (pp. 1–2). New York: Cultural Information Services.

Divorce: Rate has stabilized but trend remains high. (1987, July 22). *San Marcos Daily Record,* p. 3A.

Dixon, R. B., & Weitzman, L. J. (1980). Evaluating the impact of no-fault divorce in California. *Family Relations, 29,* 297–307.

Dixon, R. B., & Weitzman, L. J. (1982). When husbands file for divorce. *Journal of Marriage and the Family, 44,* 103–115.

Do effects of divorce last? (1986). *Family Therapy Today, 1*(3), 5.

Doan, M. (1985, October 28). 11 million widows: Here's how they cope. *U.S. News & World Report,* pp. 56–57.

A doctor's guide to finding a doctor. (1984, January). *Good Housekeeping,* pp. 188–189.

Doherty, W. J. (1985). Family interventions in health care. *Family Relations, 34,* 129–137.

Doherty, W. J., Lester, M. E., & Leigh, G. (1986). Marriage encounter weekends: Couples who win and couples who lose. *Journal of Marital and Family Therapy, 12,* 49–61.

Doherty, W. J., & McCubbin, H. I. (1985). Family and health care: An emerging arena of theory, research, and clinical intervention. *Family Relations, 34,* 5–11.

Dolan, E. M., & Lown, J. M. (1985). The remarried family: Challenges and opportunities. *Journal of Home Economics, 77*(3), 36–41.

Donahue, R. J. (1986, May 10). 3-way split seen in health insurance market. *National Underwriter,* pp. 6–7.

Donahue, R. J. (1987, May 25). Managed health care taking over group ins. *National Underwriter,* pp. 31, 36.

Donnelly, D. (1990, March). *The sexless marriage.* Paper presented at the meeting of the Southern Sociological Society, Louisville, KY.

Donoghue, W. E. (1986). *Donoghue's investment tips for retirement savings.* New York: Harper & Row.

Donoghue, W. E., & Schilling, D. (1987). *William E. Donoghue's lifetime financial planner: Straight talk about your money decisions.* New York: Harper & Row.

Donovan, P. (1986). New reproductive technologies: Some legal dilemmas. *Family Planning Perspectives, 18,* 57–60.

Dorland's Illustrated Medical Dictionary (27th ed.). (1988). Philadelphia: Saunders.

Doshi, M. L. (1986). Accuracy of consumer performed in-home tests for early pregnancy detection. *American Journal of Public Health, 76,* 512.

Downey, M. (1989, April 30). Trend to end unneeded C-sections slowly growing. *Eau Claire Leader-Telegram,* p. 6E.

Downs, A. C., & Gowan, D. C. (1980). Sex differences in reinforcement and punishment on prime-time television. *Sex Roles, 6,* 683–694.

Downs, J. F., & Bleibtreu, H. K. (1972). *Human variation.* Beverly Hills: Glencoe Press.

Downs, W. R. (1982). Alcoholism as a developing family crisis. *Family Relations, 31,* 5–12.

Doyle, J. A. (1985). *Sex and gender: The human experience.* Dubuque, IA: Wm. C. Brown.

Driscoll, R., Davis, K. E., & Lipetz, M. E. (1972). Parental interference and romantic love: The Romeo and Juliet effect. *Journal of Personality and Social Psychology, 24,* 1–10.

Drug OK'd for use on genital warts. (1988, June 8). *Eau Claire Leader-Telegram,* p. 6B.

Dubow, E. F., Huesmann, L. R., & Eron, L. D. (1987). Childhood correlates of adult ego development. *Child Development, 58,* 859–869.

Duck, S. W. (1984). A perspective on the repair of personal relationships: Repair of what, when? In S. W. Duck (Ed.), *Personal relationships 5: Repairing personal relationships* (pp. 163–184). New York: Academic Press.

Duffy, S. M., & Rusbult, C. E. (1986). Satisfaction and commitment in homosexual and heterosexual relationships. *Journal of Homosexuality, 12*(2), 1–23.

Duggan, M. (1985). Family: A mini-society. In L. Cargan (Ed.), *Marriage and family: Coping with change* (pp. 223–225). Belmont, CA: Wadsworth.

Dullea, G. (1988, February 14). Gay couples want to adopt, but resistance is increasing. *Eau Claire Leader-Telegram,* p. 2E.

Dunham, D. (1987). Food spending and income. In K. L. Lipton & J. King (Eds.), *National food review* (p. 24). Washington, DC: U.S. Department of Agriculture.

Dunkle, R. E. (1985). Comparing the depression of elders in two types of caregiving arrangements. *Family Relations, 34,* 235–240.

Dunn, J. (1983). Sibling relationships in early childhood. *Child Development, 54,* 787–811.

Dunn, J., & Kendrick, C. (1982). The speech of two-and three-year-olds to infant siblings: "Baby talk" and the context of communication. *Journal of Child Language, 9,* 579–595.

Durham, T. W., & Grossnickle, W. F. (1982). Attitudes toward masturbation. *Psychological Reports, 51,* 932–934.

Durkin, K. (1985). Television and sex-role acquisition: 1. Content. *British Journal of Social Psychology, 24,* 101–113.

Duvall, E. M. (1988). Family development's first forty years. *Family Relations, 37,* 127–134.

Duvall, E. M., & Miller, B. C. (1985). *Marriage and family development* (6th ed.). New York: Harper & Row.

Dworetzky, J. P. (1990). *Introduction to child development* (4th ed.). St. Paul: West.

Dyk, P. A. H. (1990). Healthy family sexuality: Challenges of assessment. *Family Relations, 39,* 216–220.

Eagan, A., & Lieberman, S. (1984, August). Bringing out baby. *Self,* pp. 121–123.

Eagan, A. B. (1985, December). 200 years of childbirth. *Parents,* pp. 174, 181–183, 186, 188, 191, 193–194, 196.

Earle, J. R., Harris, C. T., Pearson, W., Jr., Perricone, P. J., & Smith, M. S. (1988, March). *Gender and professions: Marital status and stability.* Paper presented at the meeting of the Southern Sociological Society, Nashville, TN.

Earle, J. R., & Perricone, P. J. (1986). Premarital sexuality: A ten-year study of attitudes and behavior on a small university campus. *The Journal of Sex Research, 22,* 304–310.

Earle, R. H., & Crow, G. M. (1990). Sexual addiction: Understanding and treating the phenomemon. *Contemporary Family Therapy, 12,* 89–104.

Easterbrooks, M. A., & Goldberg, W. A. (1984). Toddler development in the family: Impact of father involvement and parenting characteristics. *Child Development, 55,* 740–752.

Easterbrooks, M. A., & Goldberg, W. A. (1985). Effects of early maternal employment on toddlers, mothers, and fathers. *Developmental Psychology, 21,* 774–783.

Easterbrooks, M. A., & Goldberg, W. A. (1987, April). *Consequences of early family attachment patterns for later social-personality development.* Paper presented at the meeting of the Society for Research in Child Development, Baltimore, MD.

Ebaugh, H. R. F., & Haney, C. A. (1980). Shifts in abortion attitudes: 1972–1978. *Journal of Marriage and the Family, 42,* 491–499.

Ebersole, P., & DePaola, S. (1987). Meaning in life categories of later life couples. *The Journal of Psychology, 121,* 185–191.

Edwards, J. N., & Saunders, J. M. (1981). Coming apart: A model of the marital dissolution decision. *Journal of Marriage and the Family, 43,* 379–389.

Edwards, K. (1987). Probing the power struggle. *Nursing Times, 83*(17), 47–50.

Egeland, B., & Jacobvitz, D. (1984). *Intergenerational continuity of parental abuse: Causes and consequences.* Paper presented at the Conference on Biosocial Perspectives in Abuse and Neglect, York, ME.

Eggebeen, D., & Uhlenberg, P. (1985). Changes in the organization of men's lives: 1960–1980. *Family Relations, 34,* 251–257.

Eggebeen, D. J. (1988). Determinants of maternal employment for white preschool children: 1960–1980. *Journal of Marriage and the Family, 50,* 149–159.

Ehrenreich, B., Hess, E., & Jacobs, G. (1986). *Re-making love: The feminization of sex.* New York: Anchor.

Ehrlich, E. (1989, March 20). The mommy track. *Business Week,* pp. 126–129, 132, 134.

Ekerdt, D. J. (1986). The busy ethic: Moral continuity between work and retirement. *The Gerontologist, 26,* 239–244.

Ekstrand, M. L., & Coates, T. J. (1990). Maintenance of safer sexual behaviors and predictors of risky sex: The San Francisco Men's Health Study. *American Journal of Public Health, 80,* 973–977.

Elkin, F., & Handel, G. (1989). *The child and society: The process of socialization* (5th ed.). New York: Random House.

Elkind, D. (1981). *The hurried child: Growing up too fast too soon.* Reading, MA: Addison-Wesley.

Ellerstein, N., & Canavan, W. (1980). Sexual abuse of boys. *American Journal of Diseases of Children, 134,* 255–257.

Ellis, A. (1962). Romantic love. In A. Ellis (Ed.), *American sexual tragedy* (2nd ed., pp. 113–137). New York: Lyle Stuart.

Ellison, C. (1980, September). *A critique of the clitoral model.* Paper presented at the meeting of the American Psychological Association, Montreal, Canada.

Ellwood, A. (1983). Preparing for parenthood during pregnancy and early infancy. In D. R. Mace (Ed.), *Prevention in family services: Approaches to family wellness* (pp. 123–132). Beverly Hills: Sage.

Embarrassing fact. (1982, December). *Psychology Today,* p. 84.

Emmerich, W., & Shepard, K. (1982). Development and sex-differentiated preferences during late childhood and adolescence. *Developmental Psychology, 18,* 406–417.

Ende, J., Rockwell, S., & Glasgow, M. (1984). The sexual history in general medical practice. *Archives of Internal Medicine, 144,* 558–561.

Endert, C. M., & Daniel, W. A., Jr. (1986). Intra-family sexual abuse of adolescents. *Pediatric Annals, 15,* 767–772.

England, P., Chassie, M., & McCormack, L. (1982). Skill demands and earnings in female and male occupations. *Sociology and Social Research, 66,* 147–168.

Engram, E. (1982). *Science, myth, reality: The black family in one-half century of research.* Westport, CT: Greenwood Press.

Epro, R. (1989). Skills and aptitudes. In A. Campbell (Ed.), *The opposite sex* (pp. 84–89). Topsfield, MA: Salem House.

Epstein, E., & Guttman, R. (1984). Mate selection in man: Evidence, theory, and outcome. *Social Biology, 31,* 243–276.

Erickson, W. D., Walbek, N. H., & Seely, R. K. (1987). The life histories and psychological profiles of 59 incestuous stepfathers. *Bulletin of the American Academy of Psychiatric Law, 15,* 349–357.

Erikson, E. H. (1963). *Childhood and society* (2nd ed.). New York: Norton.

Erikson, E. H. (1980). *Identity and the life cycle.* New York: Norton.

Erikson, E. H. (1982). *The life cycle completed: A review.* New York: Norton.

Eshleman, J. R. (1988). *The family: An introduction* (5th ed.). Boston: Allyn & Bacon.

Espenshade, T. J. (1983). Raising a child can now cost $85,000. In J. G. Wells (Ed.), *Current issues in marriage and the family* (3rd ed., pp. 151–158). New York: Macmillan.

Esper, G. (1988, May 5). Reports of abused children on the rise. *Eau Claire Leader-Telegram,* p. 1C.

Esses, L., & Campbell, R. (1984). Challenges in researching the remarried. *Family Relations, 33,* 415–424.

Essex, M. J., & Nam, S. (1987). Marital status and loneliness among older women: The differential importance of close family and friends. *Journal of Marriage and the Family, 49,* 93–106.

Ewing, C. A. (1985). The role of sensation seeking and sex role identity in marital adjustment and sexual compatibility (Doctoral dissertation, California School of Professional Psychology, San Diego, 1985). *Dissertation Abstracts International, 46,* 2060B.

Ewy, D., & Ewy, R. (1975). *Preparation for breast feeding.* Garden City, NY: Dolphin Books.

Exner, M. J. (1915). *Problems and principles of sex education: A study of 948 college men.* New York: Association Press.

Falbo, T., & Peplau, L. A. (1980). Power strategies in intimate relationships. *Journal of Personality and Social Psychology, 38,* 618–628.

Fantini, M. D., & Cardenas, R. (1980). *Parenting in a multicultural society.* New York: Longman.

Farley, J. E. (1990). *Sociology.* Englewood Cliffs, NJ: Prentice-Hall.

Farrell, C. (1990, December 17). Why should we invest in human capital. *Business Week,* pp. 89–90.

Farrell, M. J. (1984, November 16). Annulments: 15,000% increase in 15 years. *National Catholic Reporter,* p. 1.

Faunce, P. S., & Phipps-Yonas, S. (1979). Women's liberation and human sexual relations. In J. H. Williams (Ed.), *Psychology of women: Selected readings* (pp. 228–240). New York: Norton.

Feazell, C. S., Mayers, R. S., & Deschner, J. (1984). Services for men who batter: Implications for programs and policies. *Family Relations, 33,* 217–223.

Fein, C. (1984, September). Meeting a man the old-fashioned way. *Mademoiselle,* pp. 302, 306, 314, 316.

Fein, R. A. (1978). Fathering: Social policy and an emergent perspective. *Journal of Social Issues, 34,* 122–135.

Feldman, H. (1981). A comparison of intentional parents and intentionally childless couples. *Journal of Marriage and the Family, 43,* 593–600.

Feldman, M. (1989). CoFo organization takes new focus. *NCFR Report, 34*(3), 5.

Feldstein, M. (1986, March/April). The future of social security. *Current,* pp. 18–24.

Femularo, R., Stone, K., Barnum, R., & Wharton, R. (1986). Alcoholism and severe child maltreatment. *American Journal of Orthopsychiatry, 56,* 481–485.

Fendrich, M. (1984). Wives' employment and husbands' distress: A meta-analysis and a replication. *Journal of Marriage and the Family, 46,* 871–879.

Ferber, M. A. (1982). Labor market participation of young married women: Causes and effects. *Journal of Marriage and the Family, 44,* 457–468.

Fergusson, D. M., Horwood, L. J., & Lloyd, M. (1990). Effect of preschool children on marital stability. *Journal of Marriage and the Family, 52,* 531–538.

Ferraro, K. F., & Wan, T. T. H. (1986). Marital contributions to well-being in later life: An examination of Bernard's Thesis. *American Behavioral Scientist, 29,* 423–437.

Ferree, M. M. (1984). Class, housework, and happiness: Women's work and life satisfaction. *Sex Roles, 11,* 1057–1074.

Ferreiro, B. W. (1990). Presumption of joint custody: A family policy dilemma. *Family Relations, 39,* 420–426.

Fields, N. S. (1983). Satisfaction in long-term marriages. *Social Work, 28,* 37–41.

Fields, N. S. (1986). *The well-seasoned marriage.* New York: Gardner.

50 ways to save money. (1983, October). *Good Housekeeping,* pp. 262–263.

Figley, C. R. (1973). Child density and the marital relationship. *Journal of Marriage and the Family, 35,* 272–282.

Fincham, F. D., Beach, S. R., & Baucom, D. H. (1987). Attribution processes in distressed and nondistressed couples: 4. Self-partner attribution differences. *Journal of Personality and Social Psychology, 52,* 739–748.

Fine, M. A. (1986). Perceptions of stepparents: Variation in stereotypes as a function of current family structure. *Journal of Marriage and the Family, 48,* 537–543.

Finkel, K. C. (1987). Sexual abuse of children: An update. *Canadian Medical Association Journal, 136,* 245–252.

Finkelhor, D. (1979). *Sexually victimized children.* New York: Free Press.

Finkelhor, D. (1980). Sex among siblings: A survey on prevalence, variety, and effects. *Archives of Sexual Behavior, 9,* 171–194.

Finkelhor, D. (1983). Removing the child—Prosecuting the offender in cases of child abuse: Evidence from the National Reporting System for Child Abuse and Neglect. *Child Abuse & Neglect, 7,* 195–206.

Finkelhor, D., & Baron, L. (1986). Risk factors for child sexual abuse. *Journal of Interpersonal Violence, 1,* 43.

Finkelhor, D., & Yllo, K. (1983). Rape in marriage: A sociological view. In D. Finkelhor, R. J. Gelles, G. T. Hotaling, & M. A. Straus (Eds.), *The dark side of families: Current family violence research* (pp. 119–131). Beverly Hills: Sage.

Finlay, B. A. (1981). Sex differences in correlates of abortion attitudes among college students. *Journal of Marriage and the Family, 43,* 571–582.

Finley, N. J. (1989). Theories of family labor as applied to gender differences in caregiving for elderly parents. *Journal of Marriage and the Family, 51,* 79–86.

Finn, J. (1985). The stresses and coping behavior of battered women. *Social Casework, 66,* 341–349.

Finn, J. (1986). The relationship between sex role attitudes and attitudes supporting marital violence. *Sex Roles, 14,* 235–244.

Finn, P., & Colson, S. (1990). *Civil protection orders: Legislation, current court practice, and enforcement.* Washington, DC: National Institute of Justice.

Fiorentine, R. (1988). Increasing similarity in the values and life plans of male and female college students? Evidence and implications. *Sex Roles, 18,* 143–158.

Fischer, C. S., & Oliker, S. J. (1983). A research note on friendship, gender, and the life cycle. *Social Forces, 62,* 124–133.

Fischer, J. L. (1983). Mothers living apart from their children. *Family Relations, 32,* 351–357.

Fischman, J. (1986, October). The children's hours. *Psychology Today,* pp. 16–18.

Fish, L. S., Fish, R. C., & Sprenkle, D. H. (1984). Treating inhibited sexual desire: A marital therapy approach. *American Journal of Family Therapy, 12,* 3–12.

Fisher, A. B. (1987, August 3). Where women are succeeding. *Fortune,* pp. 78–81, 84, 86.

Fisher, H. (1987). Anthropologist worries couples at greater risk for divorce: Short-term marriages with one child. *Behavior Today, 18*(40), 1–2.

Fisher, S. (1973). *The female orgasm.* New York: Basic Books.

Fisher, W. A., & Byrne, D. (1978). Sex differences in response to erotica? Love versus lust. *Journal of Personality and Social Psychology, 36,* 117–125.

Fishman, B. (1983). The economic behavior of stepfamilies. *Family Relations, 32,* 359–366.

Fitzgerald, J. M. (1986). *Lifespan human development.* Belmont, CA: Wadsworth.

Fitzgerald, R. V. (1986). When parents divorce. *Medical Aspects of Human Sexuality, 20*(3), 86, 90–92.

Fitzpatrick, M. A., & Winke, J. (1979). You always hurt the one you love: Strategies and tactics in interpersonal conflict. *Communication Quarterly, 27,* 7.

Fitzsimmons, V. S. (1987, November). *Wife's involvement in family financial management.* Report presented at the meeting of the National Council on Family Relations, Atlanta, GA.

Fiumara, N. J. (1986a). Candidiasis (monilial vaginitis). *Medical Aspects of Human Sexuality, 20*(5), 57–58.

Fiumara, N. J. (1986b). Condyloma acuminata (genital warts). *Medical Aspects of Human Sexuality, 20*(9), 39–40.

Fiumara, N. J. (1986c). Gardnerella (hemophilus) vaginitis. *Medical Aspects of Human Sexuality, 20*(7), 35–36.

Fiumara, N. J. (1986d). Herpes simplex infection. *Medical Aspects of Human Sexuality, 20*(6), 72–73.

Fiumara, N. J. (1986e). Nongonococcal urethritis (NGU). *Medical Aspects of Human Sexuality, 20*(4), 139–140, 143, 146.

Fiumara, N. J. (1986f). Trichomoniasis. *Medical Aspects of Human Sexuality, 20*(2), 33, 36.

Fiumara, N. J. (1987a). Gonorrhea. *Medical Aspects of Human Sexuality, 21*(1), 65, 69–70, 72.

Fiumara, N. J. (1987b). Syphilis. *Medical Aspects of Human Sexuality, 21*(4), 33, 36, 41–42, 45.

Five-year contraceptive implant is being tested. (1985, August 18). *The New York Times,* p. 24A.

Flake-Hobson, C., Skeen, P., & Robinson, B. E. (1980). Review of theories and research concerning sex-role development and androgyny with suggestions for teachers. *Family Relations, 29,* 155–162.

Flanagan, T. J., & Maguire, K. (1990). *Sourcebook of criminal justice statistics—1989.* Albany, NY: The Hindelag Criminal Justice Research Center.

Flewelling, R. L., & Bauman, K. E. (1990). Family structure as a predictor of initial substance use and sexual intercourse in early adolescence. *Journal of Marriage and the Family, 52,* 171–181.

Flint, G. A., Gayton, W. F., & Ozmon, K. L. (1983). Relationship between life satisfaction and acceptance of death by elderly persons. *Psychological Reports, 53,* 290.

Flynn, L. M., & Hamm, W. (1983, March/April). TEAM: Parent-agency partnership in adoption services. *Children Today, 12,* 2–5.

Foderaro, L. W. (1984, August). Dating someone of another faith may require a little more work and patience, but the rewards can be tremendous. *Seventeen,* p. 220.

Follingstad, D. R., Rutledge, L. L., Polek, D. S., & McNeil-Hawkins, K. (1988). Factors associated with patterns of dating violence toward college women. *Journal of Family Violence, 3,* 169–182.

Footlick, J. K. (1989, October). What happened to the family? In R. M. Smith (Ed.), The 21st century family. [Special issue]. *Newsweek,* pp. 14–20.

Forbes, D. (1987, October). Part-time work force. *Business Month,* pp. 45–47.

A force for families. (1978). Washington, DC: American Home Economics Association.

Ford, C. A., & Beach, F. A. (1971). Human sexual behavior in perspective. In A. Skolnick & J. Skolnick (Eds.), *Family in transition* (pp. 155–170). Boston: Little, Brown.

Ford, D. A. (1983). Wife battery and criminal justice: A study of victim decision-making. *Family Relations, 32,* 463–475.

Forgatch, M. S. (1989). Patterns and outcome in family problem solving: The disrupting effect of negative emotion. *Journal of Marriage and the Family, 51,* 115–124.

Forisha, B. L. (1978). *Sex roles and personal awareness.* Morristown, NJ: General Learning Corporation.

Forrest, J. D. (1987). Has she or hasn't she? U.S. women's experience with contraception. *Family Planning Perspectives, 19,* 133.

Forrest, J. D., & Singh, S. (1990). The sexual and reproductive behavior of American women, 1982–1988. *Family Planning Perspectives, 22,* 206–214.

Fortenberry, J. D., & Hill, R. F. (1986). Sister-sister incest as a manifestation of multi-generational sexual abuse. *Journal of Adolescent Health Care, 7,* 202–204.

Foster, S. (1988). Counseling survivors of incest. *Medical Aspects of Human Sexuality, 22*(3), 114–123.

Fowers, B. J. (1990). An interactional approach to standardized marital assessment: A literature review. *Family Relations, 39,* 368–377.

Fowers, B. J., & Olson, D. H. (1986). Predicting marital success with PREPARE: A predictive validity study. *Journal of Marital and Family Therapy, 12,* 403–413.

Fowler, C. R. (1983). Premarital jitters. *Medical Aspects of Human Sexuality, 17*(7), 183, 190–191, 195.

Fox, G. L., & Inazu, J. K. (1980). Mother-daughter communication about sex. *Family Relations, 29,* 347–352.

Fox, M. F., & Hesse-Biber, S. (1984). *Women at work.* Palo Alto, CA: Mayfield.

France approves use of abortion-inducing pill at special clinics. (1988, September 24). *The San Diego Tribune,* p. 4A.

Francoeur, R. T. (1982). *Becoming a sexual person.* New York: Wiley.

Francoeur, R. T. (1989a). Are school-based clinics an effective way of reducing teenage pregnancies and STDs? In R. T. Francoeur (Ed.), *Taking sides: Clashing views on controversial issues in human sexuality* (2nd ed., pp. 120–121). Guilford, CT: Dushkin.

Francoeur, R. T. (1989b). Is sex education in schools an attempt to institutionalize a sexual revolution? In R. T. Francoeur (Ed.), *Taking sides: Clashing views on controversial issues in human sexuality* (2nd ed., pp. 100–101). Guilford, CT: Dushkin.

Francoeur, R. T. (1989c). Postscript: Should our society recognize nonmarital and gay unions? In R. T. Francoeur (Ed.), *Taking sides: Clashing views on controversial issues in human sexuality* (pp. 254–255). Guilford, CT: Dushkin.

Francoeur, R. T. (1989d). Sexual attitudes in perspective. In R. T. Francoeur (Ed.), *Taking sides: Clashing views on controversial issues in human sexuality* (2nd ed., pp. xii-xxi). Guilford, CT: Dushkin.

Francoeur, R. T. (1991). *Becoming a sexual person* (2nd ed.). New York: Macmillan.

Frank, D. I., Downard, E., & Lang, A. R. (1986). Androgyny, sexual satisfaction, and women. *Journal of Psychosocial Nursing and Mental Health Services, 24,* 10–15.

Frank, L. K. (1956). The family-keystone of mental health. *Journal of Home Economics, 48,* 611–614.

Fraser, I., Radonic, I., & Clancy, R. (1980). Successful pregnancy after occlusion therapy for high-titre sperm antibodies. *Medical Journal of Australia, 1,* 324–325.

Freed, D. J., & Foster, H. H. (1984). Family law in fifty states: An overview. *Family Law Quarterly, 17,* 365–447.

Fremon, S. (1971, April). New ways to measure intelligence in infants. *Parents,* pp. 39–41.

Freud, S. (1965). *New introductory lectures in psychoanalysis.* New York: Norton.

Freudenhem, M. (1988, May 28). Nursing home faces pressures that imperil care for elderly. *The New York Times,* pp. 1A, 35A.

Friedan, B. (1963). *The feminine mystique.* New York: Norton.

Friedan, B. (1978, August). Where are women in 1978? *Cosmopolitan,* pp. 196, 206–211.

Friedan, B. (1980, January). The second stage. *Redbook,* pp. 25, 46–48, 50.

Friedan, B. (1981). *The second stage.* New York: Summit Books.

Friedan, B. (1983). Their turn: How men are changing. In J. G. Wells, (Ed.), *Current issues in marriage and the family* (3rd ed., pp. 115–124). New York: Macmillan.

Frieze, I. H. (1983). Investigating the causes and consequences of marital rape. *Signs, 8,* 532–553.

Fritz, A. A. (1985). Parent group education: A preventive intervention approach. *Social Work With Groups, 8,* 23–31.

Fromm, E. (1947). *Man for himself.* New York: Rinehart.

Fromm, E. (1956). *The art of loving.* New York: Harper & Row.

Fromme, A. (1963, August). Our ability to love. *Redbook,* pp. 44–45, 98–101.

Fuqua, R. W., & Labensohn, D. (1986). Parents as consumers of child care. *Family Relations, 35,* 295–303.

Furman, W., & Buhrmester, D. (1985). Children's perceptions of the qualities of sibling relationships. *Child Development, 56,* 448–461.

Furstenberg, F. F., Jr. (1976). *Unplanned parenthood: The social consequences of teenage childbearing.* New York: Macmillan.

Furstenberg, F. F., Jr., & Morgan, S. P. (1987). Paternal participation and children's well-being after marital dissolution. *American Sociological Review, 52,* 695–701.

Furstenberg, F. F., Jr., & Nord, C. W. (1985). Parenting apart: Patterns of childrearing after marital disruption. *Journal of Marriage and the Family, 47,* 893–904.

Furstenberg, F. F., Jr., & Spanier, G. B. (1984a). *Recycling the family: Remarriage after divorce.* Beverly Hills: Sage.

Furstenberg, F. F., Jr., & Spanier, G. B. (1984b). The risk of dissolution in remarriage: An examination of Cherlin's hypothesis of incomplete institutionalization. *Family Relations, 33,* 433–441.

Fyke, F. E., Kazmier, S. J., & Harms, R. W. (1985). Venous air embolism: Life-threatening complications of orogenital sex during pregnancy. *The American Journal of Medicine, 78,* 333–336.

Gaesser, D. L., & Whitbourne, S. K. (1985). Work identity and marital adjustment in blue-collar men. *Journal of Marriage and the Family, 42,* 747–751.

Gagnon, J. H. (1985). Attitudes and responses of parents to pre-adolescent masturbation. *Archives of Sexual Behavior, 14,* 451–466.

Galambos, N. L., & Garbarino, J. (1983, July/August). Identifying the missing links in the study of latchkey children. *Children Today,* pp. 2–4, 40–41.

Galvin, K. M., & Brommel, B. J. (1982). *Family communication: Cohesion and change.* Glenview, IL: Scott, Foresman.

Ganong, L. H., & Coleman, M. (1988). Do mutual children cement bonds in stepfamilies? *Journal of Marriage and the Family, 50,* 687–698.

Ganong, L. H., & Coleman, M. (1989). Preparing for remarriage: Anticipating the issues, seeking solutions. *Family Relations, 38,* 28–33.

Ganong, L. H., & Coleman, M. M. (1987). Stepchildren's perceptions of their parents. *Journal of Genetic Psychology, 148,* 5–17.

Garland, D. R. (1981). Training married couples in listening skills: Effects on behavior, perceptual accuracy and marital adjustment. *Family Relations, 30,* 297–306.

Garman, E. T., & Forgue, R. E. (1988). *Personal finance* (2nd ed.). Boston: Houghton-Mifflin.

Garrett, W. R. (1982). *Seasons of marriage and family life.* New York: Holt, Rinehart, and Winston.

Gates, F. (1985). The relationships between loneliness, adolescent sexual standards, and adolescent nonmarital coitus (Doctoral dissertation, University of Tulsa, 1985). *Dissertation Abstracts International, 46,* 653A.

Gavinski, L. K. (1985). *Factors influencing the decision to bottle or breast feed infants.* Unpublished master's thesis, University of Wisconsin-Stevens Point, Stevens Point, WI.

Gaylin, J. (1986, August). We asked you . . . Do kids need a stay-at-home mom? *Redbook,* pp. 78–79.

Gay rabbis. (1990, July 9). *Time,* p. 62.

Gebhard, P. H. (1977). The acquisition of basic sex information. *The Journal of Sex Research, 13,* 148–164.

Geer, J., Heiman, J., & Leitenberg, H. (1984). *Human sexuality.* Englewood Cliffs, NJ: Prentice-Hall.

Geissinger, S. (1984). Adoptive parents' attitudes toward open birth records. *Family Relations, 33,* 579–585.

Gelles, R. J. (1980). Violence in the family: A review of research in the seventies. *Journal of Marriage and the Family, 42,* 873–885.

Gelman, D. (1983, November 7). A great emptiness. *Newsweek,* pp. 153–155.

Gelman, D., Carey, J., Gelman, E., Malamud, P., Foote, D., Lubenow, G. C., & Contreras, J. (1981, May 18). Just how the sexes differ. *Newsweek,* pp. 72–74, 78, 81, 83.

Gelman, D., Greenberg, N. F., Coppola, V., Burgower, B., Doherty, S., Anderson, M., & Williams, E. (1987a). The single parent: Family albums. In O. Pocs & R. H. Walsh (Eds.), *Marriage and family 87/88* (pp. 156–160). Guilford, CT: Dushkin.

Gelman, D., Hager, M., Gonzalez, D. L., Morris, H., McCormick, J., Jackson, T., & Karagianis, E. (1987b). Who's taking care of our parents? In O. Pocs & R. H. Walsh (Eds.), *Marriage and family 87/88* (pp. 183–187). Guilford, CT: Dushkin.

Genevay, B. (1986). Sexuality and older people. *Generations, 10*(2), 58–59.

George, L. K., & Weiler, S. J. (1981). Sexuality in middle and late life: The effects of age, cohort, and gender. *Archives of General Psychiatry, 38,* 919–923.

Gerrard, M. (1987). Sex, sex guilt, and contraceptive use revisited: The 1980s. *Journal of Personality and Social Psychology, 52,* 975–980.

Gerrard, M., & Reis, T. J. (1989). Retention of contraceptive and AIDS information in the classroom. *The Journal of Sex Research, 26,* 315–323.

Gerstel, N. (1987). Divorce and stigma. *Social Problems, 34,* 172–186.

Gerstel, N., & Gross, H. (1983). Commuter marriage: Couples who live apart. In E. D. Macklin & R. H. Rubin (Eds.), *Contemporary families and alternative lifestyles* (pp. 180–193). Beverly Hills: Sage.

Gerstel, N., & Gross, H. (1984). *Commuter marriage: A study of work and family.* New York: Guilford Press.

Gerstel, N., Riessman, C. K., & Rosenfield, S. (1985). Explaining the symptomatology of separated and divorced women and men: The role of material conditions and social networks. *Social Forces, 64,* 84–101.

Gesell, A. (1940). *The first five years of life: The preschool years.* New York: Harper & Row.

Gest, T. (1983, November 21). Divorce: How the game is played now. *U.S. News & World Report,* pp. 39–42.

Gibbs, N. (1989, October 9). The baby chase. *Time,* pp. 86–89.

Gilbert, L. A. (1985). *Men in dual-career families: Current realities and future prospects.* Hillsdale, NJ: Erlbaum.

Gilbert, L. A., Hanson, G. R., & Davis, B. (1982). Perceptions of parental role responsibilities: Differences between mothers and fathers. *Family Relations, 31,* 261–269.

Gilbert, L. A., Holahan, C. K., & Manning, L. (1981). Coping with conflict between professional and maternal roles. *Family Relations, 30,* 419–426.

Giles-Sims, J. (1985). A longitudinal study of battered children of battered wives. *Family Relations, 34,* 205–210.

Giles-Sims, J. (1987). Social exchange in remarried families. In K. Pasley & M. Ihinger-Tallman (Eds.), *Remarriage and stepparenting: Current research and theory* (pp. 141–163). New York: Guilford Press.

Giveans, D. L. (1986, June). Bringing up fathers. *Nurturing News,* pp. 14–15.

Glanz, K., & Scharf, M. (1985). A nutrition training program for social workers serving the homebound elderly. *The Gerontologist, 25,* 455–459.

Glass, B. L. (1988). A rational choice model of wives' employment decisions. *Sociological Spectrum, 8,* 35–48.

Glass, J. (1983). Pre-birth attitudes and adjustment to parenthood: When 'preparing for the worst' helps. *Family Relations, 32,* 377–386.

Glass, J. C., Mustian, R. D., & Carter, L. R. (1986). Knowledge and attitudes of health-care providers toward sexuality in the institutionalized elderly. *Educational Gerontology, 12,* 465–475.

Glass, R., & Ericsson, R. (1982). *Getting pregnant in the 1980s.* Berkeley: University of California Press.

Glass, S. P., & Wright, T. L. (1985). Sex differences in type of extramarital involvement and marital dissatisfaction. *Sex Roles, 12,* 1101–1120.

Glatt, A. E., Zinner, A. H., & McCormack, W. M. (1990). The prevalence of dyspareunia. *Obstetrics and Gynecology, 75,* 433–436.

Glenn, N. D. (1982). Interreligious marriage in the United States: Patterns and recent trends. *Journal of Marriage and the Family, 44,* 555–566.

Glenn, N. D. (1984). A note on estimating the strength of influences for religious endogamy. *Journal of Marriage and the Family, 46,* 725–727.

Glenn, N. D. (1989). Duration of marriage, family composition, and marital happiness. *National Journal of Sociology, 3,* 3–24.

Glenn, N. D. (1990). Quantitative research on marital quality in the 1980s: A critical review. *Journal of Marriage and the Family, 52,* 818–831.

Glenn, N. D., & Kramer, K. B. (1987). The marriages and divorces of the children of divorce. *Journal of Marriage and the Family, 49,* 811–825.

Glenn, N. D., & McLanahan, S. (1981). The effects of offspring on the psychological well-being of older adults. *Journal of Marriage and the Family, 43,* 409–421.

Glenn, N. D., Ross, A. A., & Tully, J. C. (1974). Patterns of intergenerational mobility of females through marriage. *American Sociological Review, 39,* 683–699.

Glenn, N. D., & Shelton, B. A. (1985). Regional differences in divorce in the United States. *Journal of Marriage and the Family, 47,* 641–652.

Glenn, N. D., & Supancic, M. (1984). The social and demographic correlates of divorce and separation in the United States: An update and reconsideration. *Journal of Marriage and the Family, 46,* 563–575.

Glenn, N. D., & Weaver, C. N. (1977). The marital happiness of remarried divorced persons. *Journal of Marriage and the Family, 39,* 331–337.

Glenn, N. D., & Weaver, C. N. (1979). Attitudes toward premarital, extramarital, and homosexual relations in the U.S. in the 1970s. *The Journal of Sex Research, 15,* 108–118.

Glenn, N. D., & Weaver, C. N. (1988). The changing relationship of marital status to reported happiness. *Journal of Marriage and the Family, 50,* 317–324.

Glick, P. C. (1984a). American household structure in transition. *Family Planning Perspectives, 16,* 205–211.

Glick, P. C. (1984b). Marriage, divorce, and living arrangements: Prospective changes. *Journal of Family Issues, 5,* 7–26.

Glick, P. C. (1989a). The family life cycle and social change. *Family Relations, 38,* 123–129.

Glick, P. C. (1989b). Remarried families, stepfamilies, and stepchildren: A brief demographic profile. *Family Relations, 38,* 24–27.

Glick, P. C., & Lin, S. (1986a). More young adults are living with their parents: Who are they? *Journal of Marriage and the Family, 48,* 107–112.

Glick, P. C., & Lin, S. (1986b). Recent changes in divorce and remarriage. *Journal of Marriage and the Family, 48,* 737–747.

Glick, P. C., & Spanier, G. B. (1980). Married and unmarried cohabitants in the United States. *Journal of Marriage and the Family, 42,* 19–30.

Godwin, D. D., & Scanzoni, J. (1989). Couple consensus during joint marital decision-making: A context, process, outcome model. *Journal of Marriage and the Family, 51,* 943–956.

Goetting, A. (1982). The six stations of remarriage: Developmental tasks of remarriage after divorce. *Family Relations, 31,* 213–222.

Goldberg, L. L., & Hudson, J. W. (1989, August). *The social psychology of mate selection: Campus values revisited.* Paper presented at the meeting of the American Sociological Association, Washington, DC.

Goldberg, M. (1988). Parental sabotage. *Medical Aspects of Human Sexuality, 22*(2), 34–37, 41

Goldberg, S. (1973). *The inevitability of patriarchy.* New York: Morrow.

Golden, J. (1975). Patterns of Negro-white intermarriage. In D. L. Wilkinson (Ed.), *Black male/white female* (pp. 9–16). Morristown, NJ: General Learning Press.

Golden, N. L., Sokol, R. J., Kuhnert, B. R., & Bottoms, S. (1982). Maternal alcohol use and infant development. *Pediatrics, 70,* 931–934.

Goldenberg, I., & Goldenberg, H. (1985). *Family therapy: An overview* (2nd ed.). Monterey, CA: Brooks/Cole.

Goldenberg, I., & Goldenberg, H. (1991). *Family therapy: An overview* (3rd ed.). Pacific Grove, CA: Brooks/Cole.

Goldenson, R. M. (1970). *The encyclopedia of human behavior: Psychology, psychiatry, and mental health, Vol. 2.* Garden City, NY: Doubleday.

Goldscheider, F. K., & Goldscheider, C. (1989). Family structure and conflict: Nest-leaving expectations of young adults and their parents. *Journal of Marriage and the Family, 51,* 87–97.

Goldstein, D., & Rosenbaum, A. (1985). An evaluation of the self-esteem of maritally violent men. *Family Relations, 34,* 425–428.

Goldstein, M. (1986). The future of male birth control. *Planned Parenthood Review, 6*(3), 11–12.

Goleman, D. (1985a, September 11). Love and marriage: Researchers dissect matters of the heart. *Gainesville Sun,* pp. 1C, 2C.

Goleman, D. (1985b). *Vital lies, simple truths: The psychology of self-deception.* New York: Simon & Schuster.

Goleman, D. (1986, April 1). Two views of marriage explored: His and hers. *The New York Times,* pp. 1C, 11C.

Goode, E. E. (1988, February 22). I love you but can I ask a question? *U.S. News & World Report,* p. 85.

Goode, E. E. (1988, March 7). On the delicate subject of money. *U.S. News & World Report,* pp. 68–69.

Goode, W. J. (1982). Why men resist. In B. Thorne & M. Yalom (Eds.), *Rethinking the family: Some feminist questions* (pp. 131–150). New York: Longman.

Goodman, J. E. (1986, March). Great places to put your rainy-day cash. *Money,* pp. 113–114, 116, 120, 124.

Gordon, A. I. (1964). *Intermarriage.* Boston: Beacon.

Gordon, M. (1978). *The American family: Past, present, and future.* New York: Random House.

Gordon, M., & Miller, R. L. (1984). Going steady in the 1980s: Exclusive relationships in six Connecticut high schools. *Sociology and Social Research, 68,* 463–479.

Gordon, S. (1985). Before we educate anyone else about sexuality, let's come to terms with our own. *Journal of Sex Education & Therapy, 11,* 16–21.

Gordon, T. (1970). *P. E. T.: Parent effectiveness training.* New York: Wyden.

Gorney, C. (1982, July). Why some girls don't date. *Seventeen,* pp. 78–79.

Gorney, C. (1987, October). How young is too young? *Parenting,* pp. 50–54.

Gossypol: A potential male contraceptive? (1981). *American Pharmacy, NS21,* 57–59.

Gottman, J. (1979). *Marital interaction: Experimental investigations.* New York: Academic Press.

Gove, W. (1979). Sex, marital status, and psychiatric treatment: A research note. *Social Forces, 58,* 89–93.

Gove, W. R., & Hughes, M. (1979). Possible causes of apparent sex differences in physical health. *American Sociological Review, 44,* 126–146.

Gove, W. R., & Tudor, J. (1973). Sex, marital status, and mortality. *American Journal of Sociology, 78,* 50–73.

Graham-Combrinck, L. (1985). A developmental model for family systems. *Family Process, 24,* 139–150.

Granrose, C. S. (1985). Plans for work careers among college women who expect to have families. *The Vocational Guidance Quarterly, 66,* 284–295.

Gray, J. A., & Drewett, R. F. (1977). The genetics and development of sex differences. In R. B. Cattell & R. Dreger (Eds.), *Handbook of modern personality theory* (pp. 348–376). New York: Appleton-Century-Crofts.

Gray, L. A., & Saracino, M. (1988). Undergrads: What do they really know about AIDS? *Behavior Today, 19*(32), 4–5.

Gray-Little, B., & Burks, N. (1983). Power and satisfaction in marriage: A review and critique. *Psychological Bulletin, 93,* 513–538.

Grebe, S. C. (1986). Mediation in separation and divorce. *Journal of Counseling and Development, 64,* 379–382.

Green, R., Mandel, J. B., Hotvedt, M. E., Gray, J., & Smith, L. (1986). Lesbian mothers and their children: A comparison with solo parent heterosexual mothers and their children. *Archives of Sexual Behavior, 15,* 167–184.

Green, R. G., & Sporakowski, M. J. (1983). The dynamics of divorce: Marital quality, alternative attractions, and external pressures. *Journal of Divorce, 7*(2), 77–88.

Green, R. J. (1981). An overview of major contributions to family therapy. In R. J. Green & J. L. Framo (Eds.), *Family therapy: Major contributions* (pp. 1–35). New York: International Universities Press.

Greenberg, J. B. (1979). Single-parenting and intimacy: A comparison of mothers and fathers. *Alternative Lifestyles, 2,* 308–330.

Greenblat, C. S. (1983). The salience of sexuality in the early years of marriage. *Journal of Marriage and the Family, 45,* 289–299.

Greene, J. W. (1987). Teenage pregnancy and STDs: A current crisis in America. *The Female Patient, 12,* 46, 50–52, 56–57, 61.

Greenglass, E. R. (1985). A social-psychological view of marriage for women. *International Journal of Women's Studies, 8,* 24–31.

Greenhouse, L. (1990, June 26). States may require girl to notify parents before having an abortion. *The New York Times,* pp. A1, A13.

Greenspan, S., & Greenspan, N. T. (1985). *First feelings: Milestones in the emotional development of your baby and child from birth to age 4.* New York: Viking.

Greer, G. G., & Keating, K. (1983). What is happening to the American family? In J. G. Wells (Ed.), *Current issues in marriage and the family* (4th ed., pp. 349–361). New York: Macmillan.

Greer, K. (1986, October). Today's parent: How well are they doing? *Better Homes and Gardens,* pp. 36–47.

Greer, W. R. (1986, February 26). Study reveals career women find marriage market lean. *Gainesville Sun,* p. 3B.

Grefe, M. E. (1982). The employment of women. *National Forum: The Phi Kappa Phi Journal, 62*(1), 46, 47.

Gregory, J. G., & Purcell, M. H. (1987). Scott's inflatable penile prosthesis: Evaluation of mechanical survival in the series 700 model. *Journal of Urology, 137,* 676–677.

Gregory, M. D. (1983). Occupational behavior and life satisfaction among retirees. *The American Journal of Occupational Therapy, 37,* 548–553.

Greif, G. L. (1985a). Children and housework in the single father family. *Family Relations, 34,* 353–357.

Greif, G. L. (1985b). Single fathers rearing children. *Journal of Marriage and the Family, 47,* 185–191.

Greif, G. L. (1986). Mothers without custody and child support. *Family Relations, 35,* 87–93.

Greif, G. L. (1988). Single fathers: Helping them cope with day-to-day problems. *Medical Aspects of Human Sexuality, 22*(3), 18–20, 23–24, 25.

Greiff, B. S., & Munter, P. K. (1980, September). Can a two-career family live happily ever after? *Across the Board,* pp. 40–47.

Greil, A. L., & Leitko, T. S. (1986, August). *Couple decision-making regarding infertility.* Paper presented at the meeting of the Society for the Study of Social Problems, New York, NY.

Greth, C. V. (1990, February 4). TV free: Tubeless families turn prime time into quality time. *Austin American-Statesman,* pp. E1, E15.

Grieco, A. (1987). Cutting the risks for STDs. *Medical Aspects of Human Sexuality, 21*(3), 70–84.

Griffith, J. D., Koo, H. P., & Suchindran, C. M. (1984). Childlessness and marital stability in remarriages. *Journal of Marriage and the Family, 46,* 577–585.

Grigg, A. E. (1981). Emotion. In J. Rubinstein (Ed.), *The encyclopedia of psychology* (pp. 96–98). Guilford, CT: DPG Reference.

Gross, H. E. (1980). Dual-career couples who live apart: Two types. *Journal of Marriage and the Family, 42,* 567–576.

Gross, H. E. (1983). Couples who live apart: Time/place disjunctions and their consequences. In L. Richardson & V. Taylor (Eds.), *Feminist frontiers: Rethinking sex, gender, and society* (pp. 402–408). Reading, MA: Addison-Wesley.

Groth, A. N. (1979). *Men who rape: The psychology of the offender.* New York: Plenum Press.

Grover, K. J., Russell, C. S., Schumm, W. R., & Paff-Bergen, L. A. (1985). Mate selection processes and marital satisfaction. *Family Relations, 34,* 383–386.

Grow, L. J. (1979). Today's unmarried mothers: The choices have changed. *Child Welfare League, 58,* 363–371.

Gudridge, K., & Byrne, J. A. (1990, April 23). A kinder, gentler generation of executives? *Business Week,* pp. 86–87.

Guerney, B., Jr., & Maxson, P. (1990). Marital and family enrichment research: A decade review and look ahead. *Journal of Marriage and the Family, 52,* 1127–1135.

Guerney, L., & Moore, L. (1983). Phone friend: A prevention-oriented service for latchkey children. *Children Today, 12*(4), 5–10.

Guidubaldi, J., & Cleminshaw, H. (1985). Divorce, family health, and child adjustment. *Family Relations, 34,* 35–41.

Guidubaldi, J., & Perry, J. D. (1985). Divorce and mental health sequelae for children: A two-year follow-up of a nation-wide sample. *Journal of the American Academy of Child Psychiatry, 24,* 531–537.

Guillebeaux, F., Storm, C. L., & Demaris, A. (1986). Luring the reluctant male: A study of males participating in marriage and family therapy. *Family Therapy, 13,* 215–225.

Guisinger, S., Cowan, P. A., Schuldberg, D. (1989). Changing parent and spouse relations in the first years of remarriage of divorced fathers. *Journal of Marriage and the Family, 51,* 445–456.

Gunderson, M. P., & McCary, J. L. (1980). Effects of sex education on sex information and sexual guilt, attitudes, and behaviors. *Family Relations, 29,* 375–379.

Gunn, E. (1990, December 9). Firms' day-care efforts put state in the forefront. *Milwaukee Journal,* pp. D1, D7.

Gurian, B. S. (1986). The myth of the aged as asexual: Countertransference issues in therapy. *Hospital and Community Psychiatry, 37,* 345–346.

Gwartney-Gibbs, P. A. (1986). The institutionalization of premarital cohabitation: Estimates from marriage license applications, 1970 and 1980. *Journal of Marriage and the Family, 48,* 423–434.

Haas, L. (1980). Role-sharing couples: A study of egalitarian marriages. *Family Relations, 29,* 289–296.

Hacker, K. (1985, February 17). Dr. Hug embraces world with open message of love. *Austin American-Statesman,* p. 15E.

Haffner, D. (1990). *Sex education 2000: A call to action.* New York: Sex Information and Education Council of the United States.

Hafter, D. M. (1979). An overview of women's history. In M. Richmond-Abbott, *The American woman: Her past, her present, her future* (pp. 1–27). New York: Holt, Rinehart, & Winston.

Hagestad, G. O. (1988). Demographic change and the life course: Some emerging trends in the family realm. *Family Relations, 37,* 405–410.

Hagestad, G. O., & Neugarten, B. L. (1985). Age and the life course. In E. Shanas & R. Binstock (Eds.), *Handbook of aging and the social sciences* (2nd ed., pp. 36–61). New York: Van Nostrand Reinhold.

Hale, R. W., & Char, D. F. B. (1982). Sexual and contraceptive behavior on a college campus: A five-year follow-up. *Contraception, 25,* 125–135.

Hales, D. (1987, March). Are working moms good mothers? Ask their kids. *Redbook,* pp. 95, 172.

Half of all U.S. women with newborns are in the labor force. (1989). *Family Planning Perspectives, 21,* 37–38.

Halpern, D. F., & Blackman, S. L. (1985). Magazine versus physicians: The influence of information source on intentions to use oral contraceptives. *Women & Health, 10,* 9–23.

Hamberger, L. K., Feuerbach, S. P., & Borman, R. J. (1990). Detecting the wife batterer. *Medical Aspects of Human Sexuality, 24*(9), 32–39.

Hamilton, M. (1977). *Father's influence on children.* Chicago: Nelson Hall.

Hamner, T. J., & Turner, P. H. (1990). *Parenting in contemporary society* (2nd ed.). Englewood Cliffs, NJ: Prentice-Hall.

Hampton, R. L., Gelles, R. J., & Harrop, J. W. (1989). Is violence in black families increasing? A comparison of 1975 and 1985 National Survey rates. *Journal of Marriage and the Family, 51,* 969–980.

Haney, D. Q. (1985, April 11). Two studies find IUDs may cause infertility. *Gainesville Sun,* pp. 1A, 8A.

Hanna, S. L., & Knaub, P. K. (1981). Cohabitation before remarriage: Its relationship to family strengths. *Alternative Lifestyles, 4,* 507–522.

Hanneke, C. R., & Shields, N. A. (1985). Marital rape: Implications for the helping professions. *Social Casework, 66,* 451–458.

Hansen, G. L. (1982). Reactions to hypothetical, jealousy producing events. *Family Relations, 31,* 513–518.

Hansen, G. L. (1983). Marital satisfaction and jealousy among men. *Psychological Reports, 52,* 363–366.

Hansen, G. L. (1985). Dating jealousy among college students. *Sex Roles, 12,* 713–721.

Hansen, J. E., & Schuldt, W. J. (1984). Marital self-disclosure and marital satisfaction. *Journal of Marriage and the Family, 46,* 923–926.

Hansen, S. L., & Hicks, M. W. (1980). Sex role attitudes and perceived dating-mating choices of youth. *Adolescence, 15,* 83–90.

Hanson, S. L. (1983). A family life-cycle approach to the socioeconomic attainment of working women. *Journal of Marriage and the Family, 45,* 323–337.

Hanson, S. L., & Tuch, S. A. (1984). The determinants of marital instability: Some methodological issues. *Journal of Marriage and the Family, 46,* 631–642.

Hanson, S. M. H. (1986a). Healthy single parent families. *Family Relations, 35,* 125–132.

Hanson, S. M. H. (1986b). Parent-child relationships in single-father families. In R. A. Lewis & R. E. Salt (Eds.), *Men in families* (pp. 181–195). Beverly Hills: Sage.

Hanson, S. M. H., & Sporakowski, M. J. (1986). Single parent families. *Family Relations, 35,* 3–8.

Harayda, J. (1986, March). What's best, bad, scary, fun about living alone. *Glamour,* pp. 298–301, 346.

Harder, K. (1987, September 20). Onlies: Most stereotypes for only children found improper. *Eau Claire Leader-Telegram,* p. 1E.

Hardesty, C., & Bokemeier, J. (1989). Finding time and making do: Distribution of household labor in nonmetropolitan marriages. *Journal of Marriage and the Family, 51,* 253–267.

Harding, C. M., Vail, C., & Brown, R. (1985). Effect of oral contraceptives and some psychological factors on the menstrual experience. *Journal of Biosocial Science, 17,* 291–304.

Hareven, T. K. (1974). The family as process: The historical study of the family cycle. *Journal of Family History, 7,* 322–329.

Hareven, T. K. (Ed.). (1977). *Family and kin in American urban communities, 1700–1930.* New York: Franklin Watts.

Hareven, T. K. (1982). American families in transition: Historical perspectives on change. In F. Walsh (Ed.), *Normal family processes* (pp. 446–466). New York: Guilford Press.

Hareven, T. K. (1987). Historical analysis of the family. In M. B. Sussman & S. K. Steinmetz (Eds.), *Handbook of marriage and the family* (pp. 37–58). New York: Plenum Press.

Hargreaves, D. J. (1989). Creativity. In A. Campbell (Ed.), *The opposite sex* (pp. 212–217). Topsfield, MA: Salem House.

Haring-Hidore, M., Stock, W. A., Okun, M. A., & Witter, R. A. (1985). Marital status and subjective well-being: A research synthesis. *Journal of Marriage and the Family, 47,* 947–953.

Harman, D., & Brim, O. G. (1980). *Learning to be parents: Principles, programs, and methods.* Beverly Hills: Sage.

Harman, J. D. (1984). Consent, harm, and marital rape. *Journal of Family Law, 22,* 423–443.

Harriman, L. C. (1983). Personal and marital changes accompanying parenthood. *Family Relations, 32,* 387–394.

Harriman, L. C. (1986). Marital adjustment as related to personal and marital changes accompanying parenthood. *Family Relations, 35,* 233–239.

Harrington, C. L. (1988, August). *Making propositions: The emotions involved in asking for a date.* Paper presented at the meeting of the American Sociological Association, Atlanta, GA.

Harris, B. A., Jr. (1987). Medical problems of older pregnant women. *Medical Aspects of Human Sexuality, 21*(4), 16, 20, 22–24.

Harris, D. (1987, March). Life insurance: Should your protection double as an investment? *Money,* pp. 140–148.

Harris, D. K. (1990). *Sociology of aging* (2nd ed.). New York: Harper & Row.

Harris, L. (1981a). *The General Mills American family report, 1980–81: Families at work—Strengths and strains.* Minneapolis: General Mills.

Harris, L. (1981b, August). Press Release. Louis Harris Survey. New York: Harris Associates.

Harris, M. (1983, October). Creating a budget. *Money,* pp. 71–72, 74, 76.

Harris, M. P. (1988, July 4). Second thoughts about abortion. *Time,* p. 44.

Harrison, A. A., & Saeed, L. (1977). Let's make a deal: An analysis of revelations and stipulations in lonely hearts advertisements. *Journal of Personality and Social Psychology, 35,* 257–264.

Harry, J. (1983). Gay male and lesbian relationships. In E. D. Macklin & R. H. Rubin (Eds.), *Contemporary families and alternative lifestyles: Handbook on research and theory* (pp. 216–234). Beverly Hills: Sage.

Hartmann, H. I. (1981). The family as the locus of gender, class and political struggle: The example of housework. *Signs, 6,* 366–394.

Harvey, L. K. (1986). Power in marriage: Structure and process in the construction of marital histories (Doctoral dissertation, The Florida State University, 1985). *Dissertation Abstracts International, 47,* 322A-323A.

Haskins, R. (1985). Public school aggression among children with varying day-care experience. *Child Development, 56,* 689–703.

Haswell, K., Hock, E., & Wenar, C. (1981). Oppositional behavior of preschool children: Theory and intervention. *Family Relations, 30,* 440–446.

Hatch, R. C. (1986). Marital adjustment and satisfaction as related to perceptions of religious practices and orientations: An examination of graduate and seminary student couples (Doctoral dissertation, Kansas State University, 1985). *Dissertation Abstracts International, 46,* 2824A–2825A.

Hatcher, R. A., Guest, F. J., Stewart, F. H., Stewart, G. K., Trussell, J., Bowen, S. C., & Cates, W., Jr. (1988). *Contraceptive technology 1988–1989: With a special section on AIDS and family planning* (14th rev. ed.). New York: Irvington.

Hatcher, R. A., Guest, F. J., Stewart, F. H., Stewart, G. K., Trussell, J., Cerel, S., & Cates, W., Jr. (1986). *Contraceptive technology, 1986–1987: With a special section on sexually transmitted diseases* (13th rev. ed.). New York: Irvington.

Hatkoff, T. S., & Lasswell, T. E. (1979). Male-female similarities and differences in conceptualizing love. In M. Cook & G. Wilson (Eds.), *Love and attraction: An international conference* (pp. 221–228). Oxford: Pergamon.

Havighurst, R. J. (1972). *Developmental tasks and education* (3rd ed.). New York: McKay.

Hawkins, D. I., Best, R. H., & Coney, K. A. (1986). *Consumer behavior: Implications for marketing strategy* (3rd ed.). Plano, TX: Business Publications.

Hawkins, J. L., Weisberg, C., & Ray, D. W. (1977). Marital communication style and social class. *Journal of Marriage and the Family, 39,* 479–490.

Hawkins, J. L., Weisberg, C., & Ray, D. W. (1980). Spouse differences in communication style: Preference, perception, behavior. *Journal of Marriage and the Family, 42,* 585–593.

Hawkins, R. (1987). Positive approach to behavior change needed to prevent AIDS. *Behavior Today, 18*(51), 1.

Hayden, J. (1986, August). *Joint custody: Towards a new conceptualization of family.* Paper presented at the meeting of the Society for the Study of Social Problems, New York, NY.

Hayes, M. P., Stinnett, N., & DeFrain, J. (1981). Learning about marriage from the divorced. *Journal of Divorce, 4*(1), 23–29.

Haynes, S. N., & Oziel, L. J. (1976). Homosexuality: Behavior and attitudes. *Archives of Sexual Behavior, 5,* 283–289.

Hays, T. E. (1987). Menstrual expressions and menstrual attitudes. *Sex Roles, 16,* 605–614.

Heath, L. L., Roper, B. S., & King, C. D. (1974). A research note on children viewed as contributors to marital stability: The relationship to birth control use, ideal and expected family size. *Journal of Marriage and the Family, 36,* 304–306.

Heaton, T. B. (1984). Religious homogamy and marital satisfaction reconsidered. *Journal of Marriage and the Family, 46,* 629–733.

Heaton, T. B., Albrecht, S. L., & Martin, T. K. (1985). The timing of divorce. *Journal of Marriage and the Family, 47,* 631–639.

Heaton, T. B., & Calkins, S. (1983). Family size and contraceptive use among Mormons: 1965–1975. *Review of Religious Research, 25,* 102–113.

Heckert, A., & Teachman, J. D. (1985). Religious factors in the timing of second births. *Journal of Marriage and the Family, 47,* 361–367.

Hefferan, C. (1987, October). Family budget guidelines. *Family Economics Review,* pp. 1-9.

Heiman, J. R., Gladue, B. A., Roberts, C. W., & LoPiccolo, J. (1986). Historical and current factors discriminating sexually functional from sexually dysfunctional married couples. *Journal of Marital and Family Therapy, 12,* 163–174.

Hendershott, A. (1986, August). *The relationship between religiosity and marital satisfaction.* Paper presented at the meeting of the American Sociological Association, New York, NY.

Henderson, G. H. (1980). Consequences of school-age pregnancy and motherhood. *Family Relations, 29,* 185–190.

Henderson, R. W. (1981). Home environment and intellectual performance. In R. W. Henderson (Ed.), *Parent-child interaction: Theory, research, and prospects* (pp. 3–32). New York: Academic Press.

Hendrick, C., & Hendrick, S. (1986). A theory and method of love. *Journal of Personality and Social Psychology, 50,* 392–402.

Hendrick, S. S., Hendrick, C., & Adler, N. L. (1988). Romantic relationships: Love, satisfaction, and staying together. *Journal of Personality & Social Psychology, 54,* 980–988.

Hennon, C. B., & Burton, J. R. (1986). Financial satisfaction as a developmental task among the elderly. *American Behavioral Scientist, 29,* 439–452.

Henry, W. A., III. (1990, Fall). The lesbians next door. In E. Jamison & C. Wallis (Eds.), Women: The road ahead [Special issue]. *Time,* pp. 78–79.

Henshaw, S. K. (1987). Characteristics of U.S. women having abortions, 1982–1983. *Family Planning Perspectives, 19,* 5–9.

Henslin, J. M. (1985a). Dating and mating. In J. M. Henslin (Ed.), *Marriage and family in a changing society* (2nd ed., pp. 206–209). New York: Free Press.

Henslin, J. M. (1985b). Sex roles. In J. M. Henslin (Ed.), *Marriage and family in a changing society* (2nd ed., pp. 142–144). New York: Free Press.

Henslin, J. M. (1985c). Why so much divorce? In J. M. Henslin (Ed.), *Marriage and family in a changing society* (2nd ed., pp. 424–428). New York: Free Press.

Heraclitus. (1968). Quote. In B. Evans (Ed.), *Dictionary of quotations* (p. 95). New York: Delacorte Press.

Herdt, G. (1988). Cross-cultural forms of homosexuality and the concept "gay." *Psychiatric Annuals, 18*(1), 37–39.

Herold, E. S., & Goodwin, M. S. (1981a). Adamant virgins, potential nonvirgins, and nonvirgins. *The Journal of Sex Research, 17,* 97–113.

Herold, E. S., & Goodwin, M. S. (1981b). Premarital sexual guilt and contraceptive attitudes and behavior. *Family Relations, 30,* 247–253.

Herold, E. S., & Goodwin, M. S. (1981c). Reasons given by female virgins for not having premarital intercourse. *The Journal of School Health, 51,* 496–500.

Herzog, L. (1989). Urinary tract infections and circumcision. *American Journal of Diseases of Children, 143,* 348–350.

Hessellund, H. (1976). Masturbation and sex fantasies of married couples. *Archives of Sexual Behavior, 5,* 133–147.

Hetherington, E. M., Cox, M., & Cox, R. (1985). Long-term effects of divorce and remarriage on the adjustment of children. *Journal of the American Academy of Child Psychiatry, 24,* 518–530.

Heuvel, A. V. (1988). The timing of parenthood and intergenerational relations. *Journal of Marriage and the Family, 50,* 483–491.

Hewitt, J. (1987). Preconceptual sex selection. *British Journal of Hospital Medicine, 37,* 149, 151–155.

Hicks, M., Hansen, S. L., & Christie, L. A. (1983). Dual-career/dual-worker families: A systems approach. In E. Macklin & R. Rubin (Eds.), *Contemporary families and alternative lifestyles* (pp. 164–179). Beverly Hills: Sage.

The hidden power of plastic. (1987, February). *Consumer Reports,* pp. 119–122.

Hildebrand, M., & Abramowitz, S. (1984). Sexuality on campus: Changes in attitudes and behaviors during the 1970s. *Journal of College Student Personnel, 25,* 534–538.

Hildreth, G. J., Van Laanen, G., Kelley, E., & Durant, T. (1980). Participation in and enjoyment of family maintenance activities by elderly women. *Family Relations, 29,* 386–390.

Hill, C. T. (1989). Attitudes to love. In A. Campbell (Ed.), *The opposite sex* (pp. 152–157). Topsfield, MA: Salem House.

Hill, C. T., Peplau, L. A., & Rubin, Z. (1983). Contraceptive use by college dating couples: A comparison of men's and women's reports. *Population and Environment, 6,* 60–69.

Hill, C. T., Rubin, Z., & Peplau, L. A. (1976). Breakups before marriage: The end of 103 affairs. *Journal of Social Issues, 32,* 147–168.

Hill, E. A., & Dorfman, L. T. (1982). Reaction of housewives to the retirement of their husbands. *Family Relations, 31,* 195–200.

Hill, R. (1986). Life cycle stages for types of single parent families. *Family Relations, 35,* 19–29.

Hill, S. D., & Smith, J. M. (1984). Neonatal responsiveness as a function of maternal contact and obstetrical drugs. *Perceptual and Motor Skills, 58,* 859–866.

Hiller, D. V., & Dyehouse, J. (1987). A case for banishing "dual-career marriages" from the research literature. *Journal of Marriage and the Family, 49,* 787–795.

Hiller, D. V., & Philliber, W. W. (1980). Necessity, compatibility, and status attainment as factors in the labor-force participation of married women. *Journal of Marriage and the Family, 42,* 347–354.

Hiller, D. V., & Philliber, W. W. (1982). Predicting marital and career success among dual-worker couples. *Journal of Marriage and the Family, 44,* 53–62.

Hiller, D. V., & Philliber, W. W. (1986). The division of labor in contemporary marriage: Expectations, perceptions, and performance. *Social Problems, 33,* 191–201.

Himmelfarb, S. (1984). Age and sex differences in the mental health of older persons. *Journal of Consulting and Clinical Psychology, 52,* 844–856.

Himmelfarb, S., & Murrell, S. A. (1984). The prevalence and correlates of anxiety symptoms in older adults. *The Journal of Psychology, 116,* 159–167.

Hine, J. R. (1980). *What comes after you say "I love you"?* Palo Alto, CA: Pacific.

Hines, M. (1989). Do sex hormones affect behavior? In A. Campbell (Ed.), *The opposite sex* (pp. 20–23). Topsfield, MA: Salem House.

Hines, M., & Shipley, C. (1984). Parental exposure to diethylstilbestrol (DES) and the development of sexually dimorphic cognitive abilities and cerebral lateralization. *Developmental Psychology, 20,* 81–94.

Hirsch, I. (1986). Sexual disorders: A perspective. *American Journal of Psychoanalysis, 46,* 239–248.

Hitchings, B. (1987, March 2). Playing your credit cards for all they're worth. *Business Week,* pp. 102–103.

Hite, S. (1981). *The Hite report on male sexuality.* New York: Knopf.

HMO rolls seen doubling by '90. (1987, May 25). *National Underwriter,* pp. 31, 36.

Hobart, C. (1988). The family system in remarriage: An exploratory study. *Journal of Marriage and the Family, 50,* 649–661.

Hobson, K. G. (1984). The effects of aging on sexuality. *Health and Social Work, 9,* 25–35.

Hoch, Z. (1986). Vaginal erotic sensitivity by sexological examination. *Acta Obstetrica Et Gynecologica, 65,* 767–773.

Hock, E., Gnezda, M. T., & McBride, S. L. (1984). Mothers of infants: Attitudes toward employment and motherhood following birth of the first child. *Journal of Marriage and the Family, 46,* 425–431.

Hodges, W. F., Tierney, C. W., & Buschbaum, H. K. (1984). The cumulative effect of stress on preschool children of divorced and intact families. *Journal of Marriage and the Family, 46,* 611–617.

Hoeffer, B. (1981). Children's acquisition of sex-role behavior in lesbian-mother families. *American Journal of Orthopsychiatry, 51,* 536–544.

Hof, L., Epstein, N., & Miller, W. R. (1980). Integrating attitudinal and behavioral change in marital enrichment. *Family Relations, 29,* 241–248.

Hof, L., & Miller, W. R. (1981). *Marriage enrichment.* Bowie, MD: Robert J. Brady.

Hofferth, S. L., & Phillips, D. A. (1987). Child care in the United States, 1970 to 1995. *Journal of Marriage and the Family, 49,* 559–571.

Hoffman, L. W., & Manis, J. B. (1979). The value of children in the United States: A new approach to the study of fertility. *Journal of Marriage and the Family, 41,* 583–596.

Hoffman, M. S. (Ed.). (1988). *The world almanac and book of facts 1988.* New York: Random House.

Hoffman, M. S. (Ed.). (1990). *The world almanac and book of facts, 1990.* New York: Pharos Books.

Hoffman, S. R., & Levant, R. F. (1985). A comparison of childfree and child-anticipated married couples. *Family Relations, 34,* 197–203.

Hogstel, M. O. (1985). Older widowers: A small group with special needs. *Geriatric Nursing, 6,* 24–26.

Holahan, C. K. (1983). The relationships between information search in the childbearing decision and life satisfaction for parents and nonparents. *Family Relations, 32,* 527–535.

Hollenbeck, A. R., Gewirtz, J. L., Sebris, S. L., & Scanlon, J. W. (1984). Labor and delivery medication influences parent-infant interaction in the first post-partum month. *Infant Behavior and Development, 7,* 201–207.

Holman, T. B. (1981). The influence of community involvement on marital quality. *Journal of Marriage and the Family, 43,* 143–149.

Holman, T. B., & Burr, W. R. (1980). Beyond the beyond: The growth of family theories in the 1970s. *Journal of Marriage and the Family, 42,* 729–741.

Holman, T. B., Busby, D. M., & Larson, J. H. (1989). *PREP-M.* Provo, UT: Brigham Young University Press.

Holman, T. B., & Jacquart, M. (1988). Leisure-activity patterns and marital satisfaction: A further test. *Journal of Marriage and the Family, 50,* 69–77.

Holmes, S. A. (1990, July 26). House backs Bush veto of family leave bill. *New York Times,* p. A16.

Honeycutt, J. M., Wilson, C., & Parker, C. (1982). Effects of sex and degrees of happiness on perceived styles of communicating in and out of the marital relationship. *Journal of Marriage and the Family, 44,* 395–406.

Hood, J. C. (1986). The provider role: Its meaning and measurement. *Journal of Marriage and the Family, 48,* 349–359.

Hook, E. W., III, Brady, W. E., Reichart, C. A., Upchurch, D. M., Sherman, L. A., & Wasserheit, J. N. (1989). Determinants of emergents of antibiotic-resistant Neisseria gonorrheae. *The Journal of Infectious Diseases, 159,* 900–907.

Hooker, K., & Ventis, D. G. (1984). Work ethic, daily activities, and retirement satisfaction. *Journal of Gerontology, 39,* 478–484.

Hoon, P. W., Bruce, K., & Kinchloe, B. (1982). Does the menstrual cycle play a role in sexual arousal? *Psychopathology, 19,* 21–27.

Hooyman, N. R., & Kiyak, H. A. (1991). *Social gerontology: A multidisciplinary perspective* (2nd ed.). Boston: Allyn and Bacon.

Hopkins, J., & White, P. (1978). The dual-career couple: Constraints and supports. *The Family Coordinator, 27,* 253–259.

Horn, J. C., & Meer, J. (1987, May). The vintage years. *Psychology Today,* pp. 76–77, 80–84, 88–90.

Horn, J. M. (1983). The Texas adoption project: Adopted children and their intellectual resemblance to biological and adoptive parents. *Child Development, 54,* 268–275.

Horna, J., & Lupri, E. (1987). Fathers' participation in work, family life and leisure: A Canadian experience. In C. Lewis & M. O'Brien (Eds.), *Reassessing fatherhood: New observations on fathers and the modern family* (pp. 54–73). London: Sage.

Horner, M. (1972). The motive to avoid success and changing aspirations of college women. In J. Bardwick (Ed.), *Readings on the psychology of women* (pp. 62–67). New York: Harper & Row.

Hornung, C. A., & McCullough, B. C. (1981). Status relationships in dual-employment marriages: Consequences for psychological well-being. *Journal of Marriage and the Family, 43,* 125–141.

Hornung, C. A., McCullough, B. C., & Sugimoto, T. (1981). Status relationships in marriage: Risk factors in spouse abuse. *Journal of Marriage and the Family, 43,* 675–692.

Horowitz, J. A., Hughes, C. B., & Perdue, B. J. (1982). *Parenting reassessed: A nursing perspective.* Englewood Cliffs, NJ: Prentice-Hall.

Houseknecht, S. K. (1987). Voluntary childlessness. In M. B. Sussman & S. K. Steinmetz (Eds.), *Handbook of marriage and the family* (pp. 369–395). New York: Plenum Press.

Houseknecht, S. K., & Macke, A. S. (1981). Combining marriage and career: The marital adjustment of professional women. *Journal of Marriage and the Family, 43,* 651–661.

Houseknecht, S. K., Vaughan, S., & Macke, A. S. (1984). Marital disruption among professional women: The timing of career and family events. *Social Problems, 31,* 273–284.

Houser, B. B., & Berkman, S. L. (1984). Aging parent/mature child relationships. *Journal of Marriage and the Family, 46,* 295–299.

Houser, B. B., Berkman, S. L., & Bardsley, P. (1985). Sex and birth order differences in filial behavior. *Sex Roles, 13,* 641–651.

How much life insurance do you need? (1986, June). *Consumer Reports,* pp. 372–376.

How to build savings into your home. (1988, June). *Consumer Reports,* pp. 368–369.

Howell, R. J., & Toepke, K. E. (1984). Summary of the child custody laws for the fifty states. *The American Journal of Family Therapy, 12,* 56–60.

Hoyenga, K. B., & Hoyenga, K. T. (1979). *The question of sex differences: Psychological, cultural, and biological issues.* Boston: Little, Brown.

Hsiao, V. (1986). Relationship between urinary tract infection and contraceptive methods. *Journal of Adolescent Health Care, 7,* 381–385.

Huber, J., & Spitze, G. (1980). Considering divorce: An expansion of Becker's theory of marital instability. *American Journal of Sociology, 86,* 75–89.

Hughes, M., & Hertel, B. R. (1990). The significance of color remains: A study of life chances, mate selection, and ethnic consciousness among black Americans. *Social Forces, 68,* 1105–1120.

Hughes, R. (1985). The informal help-giving of home and center childcare providers. *Family Relations, 34,* 359–366.

Hughes, W. L. (1926). Sex experiences of boyhood. *Journal of Social Hygiene, 12,* 262–273.

Hunt, J. G., & Hunt, L. L. (1986). The dualities of careers and families: New integrations or new polarizations? In A. S. Skolnick & J. H. Skolnick (Eds.), *Family in transition: Rethinking marriage, sexuality, child rearing, and family organization* (5th ed., pp. 275–289). Boston: Little, Brown.

Hunt, M. (1974). *Sexual behavior in the 1970s.* Chicago: Playboy Press.

Hunter, B. T. (1985, January). Buying bulk foods. *Consumers' Research,* pp. 8–9.

Hunter College Women's Studies Collective. (1983). *Women's realities, women's choices: An introduction to women's studies.* New York: Oxford University Press.

Huston, T. L., Surra, C. A., Fitzgerald, N. M., & Cate, R. M. (1981). From courtship to marriage: Mate selection as an interpersonal process. In S. Duck & R. Gilmore (Eds.), *Personal relationships 2: Developing personal relationships* (pp. 53–88). London: Academic Press.

Hutter, M. (1988). *The changing family: Comparative perspectives* (2nd ed.). New York: Macmillan.

Hybritech Incorporated. (1985). *Tandem ICON JCG (urine): ImmunoEnzyMetric assay for the qualitative determination of human chorionic gonadotropin (HCG) in urine.* San Diego: Author.

Hyde, J. S. (1981). How large are cognitive gender differences? A meta-analysis using omega and delta. *American Psychologist, 36,* 892–901.

Hyde, J. S. (1986). *Understanding human sexuality* (3rd ed.). New York: McGraw-Hill.

Hyde, J. S. (1990). *Understanding human sexuality* (4th ed.). New York: McGraw-Hill.

Hymes, J. (1955). *Behavior and misbehavior: A teacher's guide to action.* New York: Prentice-Hall.

Hymes, J. L. (1985). *Notes for parents.* Carmel, CA: Hacienda Press.

Iaconetti, J. (1988). Coping with decision not to have children. In J. G. Wells (Ed.), *Current issues in marriage and the family* (pp. 143–148). New York: Macmillan.

Iddenden, D. A. (1987). Sexuality during the menopause. *Medical Clinics of North America, 71,* 87–94.

Idler, E. L. (1987). Religious involvement and the health of the elderly: Some hypotheses and an initial test. *Social Forces, 66,* 226–238.

"I Do"—and they do too. (1991, February 15). *Austin American-Statesman,* p. B1.

Ihinger-Tallman, M. (1987). Sibling and step-sibling bonding in stepfamilies. In K. Pasley & M. Ihinger-Tallman (Eds.), *Remarriage and stepparenting: Current research and theory* (pp. 164–182). New York: Guilford Press.

Ihinger-Tallman, M., & Pasley, K. (1987). *Remarriage.* Newbury Park, CA: Sage.

Imperato-McGinley, J., Guerrero, L., Gautier, T., & Peterson, R. E. (1974). Steroid 5a-reductase deficiency in man: An inherited form of male pseudohermaphroditism. *Science, 186,* 1213–1215.

Inflation rate for 1990 the worst in nine years. (1991, January 16). *Eau Claire Leader-Telegram,* p. 8A.

Ioffe, F., Childiaeva, R., & Chernick, V. (1984). Prolonged effect of maternal alcohol injection on the neonatal electroencephalogram. *Pediatrics, 74,* 330–335.

Isaacson, W. (1989, November 20). Should gays have marriage rights? *Time,* pp. 101–102.

Ishii-Kuntz, M. (1985, November). *Effects of commitment on the stability of first marriage and remarriage: Application of power/dependency principles.* Paper presented at the Theory and Method Construction Workshop, National Council on Family Relations, Dallas, TX.

Ishii-Kuntz, M., & Lee, G. R. (1987). Status of the elderly: An extension of the theory. *Journal of Marriage and the Family, 49,* 413–420.

Istvan, J., & Griffitt, W. (1980). Effects of sexual experience on dating desirability and marriage desirability: An experimental study. *Journal of Marriage and the Family, 42,* 377–385.

Izviak, S. Y., Dop, M. C., Galan, P., & Hercberg, S. (1986). Dietary determinants of the iron status in menstruating women. *International Journal for Vitamin and Nutrition Research, 56,* 281–286.

Jacobs, J. A., & Furstenberg, F. F., Jr. (1986). Changing places: Conjugal careers and women's marital mobility. *Social Forces, 64,* 714–732.

Jacobs, L. I. (1986). Chief complaint: Sexual inadequacy. *Medical Aspects of Human Sexuality, 20*(5), 44–50.

Jacobson, A. L., & Henegar, A. G. (1989, November). *Adolescent premarital sexuality: Relationships to family characteristics.* Paper presented at the meeting of the National Council on Family Relations, New Orleans, LA.

Jacoby, A. P., & Williams, J. D. (1985). Effects of premarital sexual standards and behavior on dating and marriage desirability. *Journal of Marriage and the Family, 47,* 1059–1065.

Jacoby, S. (1975). 49 million singles can't all be right. In S. D. Feldman & G. W. Thielbar (Eds.), *Life styles: Diversity in American society* (2nd ed., pp. 115–123). Boston: Little, Brown.

Jacques, J. M., & Chason, K. J. (1979). Cohabitation: Its impact on marital success. *The Family Coordinator, 28,* 35–39.

Jaegar, E., Weinraub, M., & Hoffman, L. (1987, April). *Prediction of child outcome in families of employed and non-employed mothers.* Paper presented at the meeting of the Society for Research In Child Development, Baltimore, MD.

James, C. (1984). Why nursery education? *Early Child Development and Care, 17,* 319–336.

James, J. (1988). *Women and the blues: Passions that hurt, passions that heal.* San Francisco: Harper & Row.

James, M., & Jongeward, D. D. (1973). *Born to win: Transactional analysis with Gestalt experiments.* Reading, MA: Addison-Wesley.

James, W. H. (1984). A possible difference between men's and women's sexuality. *Psychological Reports, 55,* 40.

Janda, L. H., & Klenke-Hamel, K. E. (1980). *Human sexuality.* New York: Van Nostrand.

Jasso, G. (1985). Marital coital frequency and the passage of time: Estimating the separate effects of spouses' ages and marital duration, birth and marriage cohorts, and period influences. *American Sociological Review, 50,* 224–241.

Jayne, C. (1985, January). *Time factors and female sexual response: Therapeutic, conceptual, and statistical implications.* Paper presented at the meeting of the Western Region, Society for the Scientific Study of Sex, Palm Springs, CA.

Jedlicka, D. (1980). Formal mate selection networks in the United States. *Family Relations, 29,* 199–203.

Jedlicka, D. (1981). Automated go-betweens: Mate selection of tomorrow? *Family Relations, 30,* 373–376.

Jedlicka, D. (1984). Indirect parental influence on mate choice: A test of the psychoanalytic theory. *Journal of Marriage and the Family, 46,* 65–70.

Jedlicka, D. (1987, November). *Remarriage: An analysis of consistency.* Paper presented at the meeting of the National Council on Family Relations, Atlanta, GA.

Jeffords, C. R., & Dull, R. T. (1982). Demographic variations in attitudes towards marital rape immunity. *Journal of Marriage and the Family, 44,* 755–762.

Jeffress, J. E. (1987). The parent-dominated wife. *Medical Aspects of Human Sexuality, 21*(6), 38, 43–45.

Jensen, L. C., & Kingston, M. (1986). *Parenting.* New York: Holt, Rinehart, & Winston.

Jeter, K., & Sussman, M. B. (1985). Each couple should develop a marriage contract suitable to themselves. In H. Feldman & M. Feldman (Eds.), *Current Controversies in Marriage and Family* (pp. 287–290). Beverly Hills: Sage.

Jobes, P. C. (1986). The relationship between traditional and innovative sex-role adaptations and sexual satisfaction among a homogeneous sample of middle-age Caucasian women. *Journal of Sex & Marital Therapy, 12,* 146–156.

Joffe, A., & Radius, S. M. (1987). Breast versus bottle: Correlates of adolescent mothers' infant-feeding practices. *Pediatrics, 79,* 689–695.

Johnson, B. (1983, June). Are you a good credit risk? *Essence,* pp. 79, 148.

Johnson, B. E., & Freymeyer, R. H. (1987, April). *Factors affecting preferred family size.* Paper presented at the meeting of the Southern Sociological Society, Atlanta, GA.

Johnson, B. H. (1986). Single mothers following separation and divorce: Making it on your own. *Family Relations, 35,* 189–197.

Johnson, B. K. (1987). The sexual interest, participation, and satisfaction of older men and women (Doctoral dissertation, University of Texas, 1986). *Dissertation Abstracts International, 47,* 4824B.

Johnson, C. K., & Price-Bonham, S. (1980). Women and retirement: A study and implications. *Family Relations, 29,* 380–385.

Johnson, C. L. (1985). The impact of illness on late-life marriages. *Journal of Marriage and the Family, 47,* 165–172.

Johnson, F., Lay, P., & Wilbrant, M. (1988). Teen pregnancy: Issues, interventions, and directions. *Journal of the National Medical Association, 80,* 145–152.

Johnson, J. (1989, October 2). American childhood imperiled, study says. *Austin American-Statesman,* pp. A1, A4.

Johnson, M. P., & Leslie, L. (1982). Couple involvement and network structure: A test of the dyadic withdrawal hypothesis. *Social Psychology Quarterly, 45,* 34–43.

Johnson, R. C., & Ogasawara, G. M. (1988). Within- and across-group dating in Hawaii. *Social Biology, 35,* 103–109.

Johnston, J. M. (1972). Punishment of human behavior. *American Psychologist, 27,* 1033–1054.

Johnston, J. R. (1990). Role diffusion and role reversal: Structural variations in divorced families and children's functioning. *Family Relations, 39,* 405–413.

Johnston, M. W. (1988). An examination of the psychological principles of homogamy and heterogamy: The relationship among peer social involvement, romantic emotional attachments and adult sexual orientation (Doctoral dissertation, Indiana University, 1987). *Dissertation Abstracts International, 48,* 2286A.

Jones, E., & Gallois, C. (1989). Spouses' impressions of rules for communication in public and private marital conflicts. *Journal of Marriage and the Family, 51,* 957–967.

Jones, J. B., & Philliber, S. (1983). Sexually active but not pregnant: A comparison of teens who risk and teens who plan. *Journal of Youth and Adolescence, 12,* 235–251.

Jones, K. L., Shainberg, L. W., & Byer, C. O. (1985). *Dimensions of human sexuality.* Dubuque, IA: Wm. C. Brown.

Jones, R. E. (1984). *Human reproduction and sexual behavior.* Englewood Cliffs, NJ: Prentice-Hall.

Jones, S. Y. (1981). Single parenthood. *SIECUS Report, 10*(1), 1-2, 13.

Jorgensen, S. R. (1977). Social class heterogamy, status striving, and perceptions of marital conflict: A partial replication and revision of Pearlin's contingency hypothesis. *Journal of Marriage and the Family, 39,* 635–661.

Jorgensen, S. R. (1986). *Marriage and the family: Development and change.* New York: Macmillan.

Jorgensen, S. R., & Gaudy, J. C. (1980). Self-disclosure and satisfaction in marriage: The relation examined. *Family Relations, 29,* 281–287.

Jorgensen, S. R., & Johnson, A. C. (1980). Correlates of divorce liberality. *Journal of Marriage and the Family, 42,* 617–626.

Jourard, S. (1964). *The transparent self.* New York: Van Nostrand.

Jourard, S. M. (1972). Some dimensions of loving experience. In H. A. Otto (Ed.), *Love today: A new exploration* (pp. 44–45). New York: Dell.

Jouriles, E. N., Murphy, C. M., & O'Leary, K. D. (1989). Interspousal aggression, marital discord, and child problems. *Journal of Consulting and Clinical Psychology, 57,* 453–455.

Jung, R. (1983). Psychological correlates of contraceptive behavior in late adolescent women (Doctoral dissertation, Boston University, 1983). *Dissertation Abstracts International, 44,* 1599B.

Jurich, A. (1978, May). *Parenting your adolescent.* Paper presented at the National Symposium on Building Family Strengths, University of Nebraska, Lincoln, NE.

Kabatznick, R. (1985). Men: Nurture/nature. In O. Pocs & R. H. Walsh (Eds.), *Marriage and family 85/86* (pp. 233–235). Guilford, CT: Dushkin.

Kagan, J. (1964). The acquisition and significance of sex-typing and sex-role identity. In M. L. Hoffman & L. W. Hoffman (Eds.), *Review of child development research* (Volume 1, pp. 137–168). New York: Sage.

Kaiser, I. (1982). Amniocentesis. *Women and Health, 7,* 29–38.

Kalisch, P. A., & Kalisch, B. J. (1984). Sex-role stereotyping of nurses and physicians on prime-time television: A dichotomy of occupational portrayals. *Sex Roles, 10,* 533–553.

Kalleberg, A. L., & Rosenfeld, R. A. (1990). Work in the family and in the labor market. *Journal of Marriage and the Family, 52,* 331–346.

Kallen, D. J., Griffore, R. J., Popovich, S., & Powell, V. (1990). Adolescent mothers and their mothers view adoption. *Family Relations, 39,* 311–316.

Kallen, D. J., Powell, V., Popovich, S. N., & Griffore, R. J. (1986, August). *Alternative forms of adding children to families: An exploratory study of attitudes.* Paper presented at the meeting of the Society for the Study of Social Problems, New York, NY.

Kallen, D. J., & Stephenson, J. J. (1980). The purchase of contraceptives by college students. *Family Relations, 29,* 358–364.

Kallen, D. J., Stephenson, J. J., & Doughty, A. (1983). The need to know: Recalled adolescent sources of sexual and contraceptive information and sexual behavior. *The Journal of Sex Research, 19,* 137–159.

Kallen, S. L. (1982). Sexual behavior and self-esteem in college women (Doctoral dissertation, Michigan State University, 1982). *Dissertation Abstracts International, 43,* 527B.

Kalmuss, D. (1984). The intergenerational transmission of marital aggression. *Journal of Marriage and the Family, 46,* 11–19.

Kalmuss, D. S., & Straus, M. A. (1982). Wife's marital dependency and wife abuse. *Journal of Marriage and the Family, 44,* 277–286.

Kandel, D. B., Davies, M., & Raveis, V. H. (1985). The stressfulness of daily social roles for women: Marital, occupational, and household roles. *Journal of Health and Social Behavior, 26,* 64–78.

Kanin, E. J. (1984). Date rape: Unofficial criminals and victims. *Victimology: An International Journal, 9,* 95–108.

Kanin, E. J. (1985). Date rapists: Differential sexual socialization and relative deprivation. *Archives of Sexual Behavior, 14,* 219–231.

Kanin, E. J., Davidson, K. R., & Scheck, S. R. (1970). A research note on male-female differentials in the experience of heterosexual love. *The Journal of Sex Research, 6,* 64–72.

Kantrowitz, B. (1985, November 18). Love on the run. *Newsweek,* pp. 111, 113.

Kantrowitz, B., Witherspoon, D., Williams, E., & King, P. (1986, June 2). The new mating game. *Newsweek,* p. 58.

Kaplan, H. S. (1974). *The new sex therapy: Active treatment of sexual dysfunction.* New York: Brunner/Mazel.

Kaplan, H. S. (1985, May). The #1 male phobia. *Redbook,* p. 46.

Kaplan, H. S. (1987). *The illustrated manual of sex therapy* (2nd ed.). New York: Brunner/Mazel.

Kaplan, J. (1981, January). Can interfaith romance work for you? *Seventeen,* pp. 104–105, 120.

Kaplan, P. S. (1986). *A child's odyssey: Child and adolescent development.* St. Paul: West.

Kaplan, P. S. (1991). *A child's odyssey: Child and adolescent development* (2nd ed.). St. Paul: West.

Kargman, M. W. (1983). Stepchild support obligations of stepparents. *Family Relations, 32,* 231–238.

Karpowitz, D. H. (1980). A conceptualization of the American family. In M. J. Fines (Ed.), *Handbook on parent education* (pp. 27–50). New York: Academic Press.

Kaslow, F. W. (1984). Divorce mediation and its emotional impact on the couple and their children. *The American Journal of Family Therapy, 12,* 58–66.

Kastenbaum, R. (1987). Death, dying, and bereavement in old age: New developments and their implications for psychosocial care. In H. Cox (Ed.), *Aging* (5th ed., pp. 163–170). Guilford, CT: Dushkin.

Katchadourian, H. (1980). Adolescent sexuality. *Pediatric Clinics of North America, 27,* 17–28.

Katchadourian, H. A. (1989). *Fundamentals of human sexuality* (5th ed.). Fort Worth: Holt, Rinehart and Winston.

Kaufman, J., & Zigler, E. (1986). Do abused children become abusive parents? *American Journal of Orthopsychiatry, 57,* 186–192.

Kazak, A. E., & Reppucci, N. D. (1980). Romantic love as a social institution. In K. S. Pope (Ed.), *On love and loving* (pp. 209–227). San Francisco: Jossey-Bass.

Keith, L. G., Schink, J. C., & Berger, G. S. (1985). *Physician's guide to sexually transmitted diseases.* Chicago: Abbott Laboratories.

Keith, P. M. (1983). A comparison of the resources of parents and childless men and women in very old age. *Family Relations, 32,* 403–409.

Keith, P. M., & Schafer, R. B. (1980). Role strain and depression in two-job families. *Family Relations, 29,* 483–488.

Keith, V. M., & Finlay, B. (1988). The impact of parental divorce on children's educational attainment, marital timing, and likelihood of divorce. *Journal of Marriage and the Family, 50,* 797–809.

Kellogg, M. A. (1982, July 2). Could it be love at first cassette? *TV Guide,* pp. 33–36.

Kelly, E. L., & Conley, J. J. (1987). Personality and compatibility: A prospective analysis of marital stability and marital satisfaction. *Journal of Personality and Social Psychology, 52,* 27–40.

Kelly, G. F. (1976). *Learning about sex: The contemporary guide for young adults.* New York: Barron's Educational Series.

Kelly, L. A. S. (1978). Imagining ability, marital adjustment, and erotic fantasy during sexual relations in married men and women (Doctoral dissertation, Texas Woman's University, 1977). *Dissertation Abstracts International, 39,* 1457B–1458B.

Kelly, M. P., Strassberg, D. S., & Kircher, J. R. (1990). Attitudinal and experiential correlates of anorgasmia. *Archives of Sexual Behavior, 19,* 165–177.

Kelly, R. F., & Voydanoff, P. (1985). Work/family role strain among employed parents. *Family Relations, 34,* 367–374.

Kemper, T. D., & Bologh, R. W. (1981). What do you get when you fall in love? Some health status effects. *Sociology of Health and Illness, 3,* 72–88.

Kenkel, W. F. (1985). The desire for voluntary childlessness among low-income youth. *Journal of Marriage and the Family, 47,* 509–512.

Kennedy, L. W., & Stokes, D. W. (1982). Extended family support and the high cost of housing. *Journal of Marriage and the Family, 44,* 311–318.

Kenney, A. M., & Orr, M. T. (1984). Sex education: An overview of current programs, policies, and research. *Phi Delta Kappan, 65,* 491–496.

Kenney, R. (1989). School-based health clinics meet the needs of today's adolescents. In R. T. Francoeur (Ed.), *Taking sides: Clashing views on controversial issues in human sexuality* (2nd ed., pp. 122–128). Guilford, CT: Dushkin.

Keown, A. L., & Keown, C. F. (1985). Factors of success for women in business. *International Journal of Women's Studies, 8,* 278–285.

Kephart, W. M. (1981). *The family, society, and the individual* (5th ed.). New York: Houghton-Mifflin.

Kernberg, O. (1978, June). Why some people can't love. *Psychology Today,* pp. 50–59.

Kerns, R. D., & Turk, D. C. (1984). Depression and chronic pain: The mediating role of the spouse. *Journal of Marriage and the Family, 46,* 845–852.

Kerr, M. E. (1988, September). Chronic anxiety and defining a self. *Atlantic Monthly,* pp. 35–58.

Kersey, K. C. (1983). *The art of sensitive parenting: The 10 master keys to confident, competent & responsible children.* Washington, DC: Acropolis Books.

Kett, J. (1977). *Rites of passage: Adolescence in America, 1790 to present.* New York: Basic Books.

Kids: You can't beat 'em. (1989, Spring). In C. Gravois, & K. Stevenson (Eds.), *P.O.P.S. Newsletter.* Houston: People Opposed to Paddling Students.

Kidwell, J. S. (1982). The neglected birth order: Middleborns. *Journal of Marriage and the Family, 44,* 225–235.

Kiernan, J. E., & Taylor, V. L. (1990). Coercive sexual behavior among Mexican-American college students. *Journal of Sex & Marital Therapy, 16,* 44–50.

Kilmann, P. R., Boland, J. P., Norton, S. P., Davidson, E., & Caid, C. (1986). Perspectives of sex therapy outcome: A survey of AASECT providers. *Journal of Sex & Marital Therapy, 12,* 116–138.

Kim, M. G., & Friedman, C. I. (1983). Sexuality and infertility. In S. F. Pariser, S. B. Levine, & M. L. Gardner (Eds.), *Clinical sexuality* (pp. 97–102). New York: Dekker, Marcel.

Kimball, M. M. (1986). Television and sex-role attitudes. In T. M. Williams (Ed.), *The impact of television* (pp. 265–301). New York: Academic Press.

Kingston, P. W., & Nock, S. L. (1987). Time together among dual-earner couples. *American Sociological Review, 52,* 391–400.

Kinnaird, K. L., & Gerrard, M. (1986). Premarital sexual behavior and attitudes toward marriage and divorce among young women as a function of their mothers' marital status. *Journal of Marriage and the Family, 48,* 757–765.

Kinsey, A. C., Pomeroy, W. B., & Martin, C. E. (1948). *Sexual behavior in the human male.* Philadelphia: Saunders.

Kinsey, A. C., Pomeroy, W. B., Martin, C. E., & Gebhard, P. H. (1953). *Sexual behavior in the human female.* Philadelphia: Saunders.

Kirkendall, L. (1976, January/February). A new bill of sexual rights and responsibilities. *The Humanist,* pp. 4–6.

Kirkpatrick, M. (1982). Lesbian mother families. *Psychiatric Annals, 12,* 842–845, 848.

Kirschner, B. F., & Walum, L. R. (1978). Two-location families: Married singles. *Alternative Lifestyles, 1,* 513–525.

Kirschner, S., & Kirschner, D. A. (1989). Love and other difficulties: Goals in couples therapy. *Family Therapy Today, 4*(3), 1–4.

Kirschner, T., & Sedlacek, W. E. (1987). Sex differences in student sexual attitudes and behaviors: A ten year comparison. *The College Student Affairs Journal, 8*(1), 4–12.

Kitson, G. C. (1982). Attachment to the spouse in divorce: A scale and its application. *Journal of Marriage and the Family, 44,* 379–393.

Kitson, G. C. (1985). Marital discord and marital separation: A county survey. *Journal of Marriage and the Family, 47,* 693–700.

Kitson, G. C., & Morgan, L. A. (1990). The multiple consequences of divorce: A decade review. *Journal of Marriage and the Family, 52,* 913–924.

Kitson, G. C., & Sussman, M. B. (1982). Marital complaints, demographic characteristics, and symptoms of mental distress in divorce. *Journal of Marriage and the Family, 44,* 87–101.

Kitson, G. C., & Zyzanski, S. J. (1987). Grief in widowhood and divorce. *Psychiatric Clinics of North America, 10,* 369–386.

Kitzinger, S. (1985). *A new approach to woman's experience of sex.* New York: Putnam.

Kivett, V. R. (1985). Grandfathers and grandchildren: Patterns of association, helping, and psychological closeness. *Family Relations, 34,* 565–571.

Kivnick, H. Q. (1982). Grandparenthood: An overview of meaning and mental health. *The Gerontologist, 22,* 59–66.

Kjer, J. J. (1990). Sexual adjustment to tubal sterilization. *European Journal of Obstetrics, Gynecology, and Reproductive Biology, 35,* 211–214.

Klagsbrun, F. (1985a). *Married people: Staying together in an age of divorce.* Toronto: Bantam Books.

Klagsbrun, F. (1985b, August). Staying married: Is it worth it? *New Woman,* pp. 43–44, 46, 48.

Klassen, A. D., & Wilsnack, S. C. (1986). Sexual experience and drinking among women in a U.S. national survey. *Archives of Sexual Behavior, 15,* 363–392.

Klaus, M. H., & Kennell, J. H. (1981). *Parent-infant bonding* (2nd ed.). St. Louis, MO: Mosby.

Klein, D. M. (1980). Commentary on the linkages between conceptual framework and theory development in sociology. *Sociological Quarterly, 21,* 443–453.

Kleinman, R. (1985). *Barrier methods of contraception.* London: International Planned Parenthood Federation.

Kligman, A. M., & Graham, J. A. (1989). The psychology of appearance in the elderly. *Clinics in Geriatric Medicine, 5,* 213–222.

Kliman, D. S., & Vukelich, C. (1985). Mothers and fathers: Expectations for infants. *Family Relations, 34,* 305–313.

Klinkenborg, K. F. (1990, March). *It is no wonder: Older women and body image.* Paper presented at the meeting of the North Central Sociological Association, Louisville, KY.

Kloser, P. (1989). AIDS news. *Medical Aspects of Human Sexuality, 23*(8), 57, 59, 63, 64.

Knapp, M. L. (1984). *Interpersonal communication and human relationships.* Boston: Allyn and Bacon.

Knaub, P. K., Hanna, S. L., & Stinnett, N. (1984). Strengths of remarried families. *Journal of Divorce, 7*(3), 41–55.

Knox, D. (1982). *What kind of love is yours?* Unpublished study.

Knox, D. (1983). *The love attitudes inventory* (rev. ed.). Saluda, NC: Family Life Publications.

Knox, D. (1988). Choices in relationships: An introduction to marriage and the family (2nd ed.). St. Paul: West.

Knox, D., & Sporakowski, M. J. (1968). Attitudes of college students toward love. *Journal of Marriage and the Family, 30,* 638–642.

Knox, D., & Wilson, K. (1981). Dating behaviors of university students. *Family Relations, 30,* 255–258.

Knox, D., & Wilson, K. (1983). Dating problems of university students. *College Student Journal, 17,* 225–228.

Kobbe, A. M. (1985, July). Research report-major concerns of families. *Family Economics Review,* pp. 12–13.

Koblinsky, S., & Atkinson, J. (1982). Parental plans for children's sex education. *Family Relations, 31,* 29–35.

Kobrin, F. E., & Waite, L. J. (1984). Effects of childhood family structure on the transition to marriage. *Journal of Marriage and the Family, 46,* 807–816.

Koch, P. B. (1988). The relationship of first intercourse to later sexual functioning of adolescents. *Journal of Adolescent Research, 3,* 345–362.

Kohlberg, L. (1969). *Stages in the development of moral thought and action.* New York: Holt, Rinehart & Winston.

Kolbe, R., & LaVoie, J. C. (1981). Sex-role stereotyping in preschool children's picture books. *Social Psychology Quarterly, 44,* 369–374.

Kolodny, R. C. (1983). *Sexual issues in mid-adulthood.* Paper presented at the Las Vegas Psychiatric Symposium, Las Vegas, NV.

Kolodny, R. C., Masters, W. H., & Johnson, V. E. (1979). *Textbook of sexual medicine.* Boston: Little, Brown.

Komarovsky, M. (1973). Cultural contradictions and sex roles: The masculine case. *American Journal of Sociology, 78,* 873–884.

Kompara, D. R. (1980). Difficulties in the socialization process of stepparenting. *Family Relations, 29,* 69–73.

Koo, H. P., Suchindran, C. M., & Griffith, J. D. (1987). The completion of childbearing: Change and variation in timing. *Journal of Marriage and the Family, 49,* 281–293.

Koretz, G. (1988, March 14). Americans are socking away more of their cash. *Business Week,* p. 24.

Korman, S. K. (1983). Nontraditional dating behavior: Date-initiation and date expense-sharing among feminists and nonfeminists. *Family Relations, 32,* 575–581.

Kornhaber, A., & Woodward, K. L. (1981). *Grandparents/grandchildren: The vital connection.* Garden City, NY: Anchor Press/Doubleday.

Koss, M. P. (1985). The hidden rape victims: Personality attitudinal and situational characteristics. *Psychology of Women Quarterly, 9,* 193–212.

Kotler, T. (1985). A balance distance: Aspects of marital quality. *Human Relations, 38,* 391–407.

Kovacs, G. T., Jarman, H., Dunn, K., Westcott, M., & Baker, H. W. (1986). The contraceptive diaphragm. Is it an acceptable method in the 1980s? *Australian and New Zealand Journal of Obstetrics & Gynecology, 26,* 76–79.

Kraft, A. D., Palombo, J., Woods, P. K., Mitchell, D., & Schmidt, A. W. (1985). Some theoretical considerations of confidential adoptions. *Child and Adolescent Social Work Journal, 2,* 12–21.

Kramarae, C. (1981). *Women and men speaking.* New York: Newbury House.

Kramer, L. (1991). *The sociology of gender: A text-reader.* New Yorker: St. Martin's.

Kraus, J. (1977). Shotgun weddings: Trends in the sociopathology of marriage. *Australian and New Zealand Journal of Psychiatry, 11,* 259–264.

Kraus, M. A., & Redman, E. S. (1986). Postpartum depression: An interactional view. *Journal of Marital and Family Therapy, 12,* 63–74.

Krause, N., & Geyer-Pestello, G. (1985). Depressive symptoms among women employed outside the home. *American Journal of Community Psychology, 13,* 49–67.

Kressel, K. (1980). Patterns of coping in divorce and some implications for clinical practice. *Family Relations, 29,* 234–240.

Krieger, L. M. (1988, April 24). Birth-control options about to expand again. *Eau Claire Leader-Telegram,* p. 4E.

Krogman, W. M. (1972). *Child growth.* Ann Arbor, MI: University of Michigan Press.

Krucoff, C. (1985, March). How to be a smart shopper. *Ladies' Home Journal,* pp. 42, 44, 47, 48, 163, 164.

Krugman, R. D., Lenherr, M., Betz, L., & Fryer, G. E. (1986). The relationship between unemployment and physical abuse of children. *Child Abuse and Neglect, 10,* 415–418.

Kübler-Ross, E. (1969). *On death and dying.* New York: Macmillan.

Kuntz, M. (1986, October 6). Planning for the worst. *Forbes,* pp. 173, 176.

Kurdek, L. A. (1988a). Correlates of negative attitudes toward homosexuals in heterosexual college students. *Sex Roles, 18,* 727–738.

Kurdek, L. A. (1988b). Relationship quality of gay and lesbian cohabiting couples. *Journal of Homosexuality, 15*(3–4), 93–118.

Kurdek, L. A. (1989a). Relationship quality for newly married husbands and wives: Marital history, stepchildren, and individual-difference predictors. *Journal of Marriage and the Family, 51,* 1053–1064.

Kurdek, L. A. (1989b). Social support and psychological distress in first-married and remarried newlywed husbands and wives. *Journal of Marriage and the Family, 51,* 1047–1052.

Kurdek, L. A. (1990). Effects of child age on the marital quality and psychological distress of newly married mothers and stepfathers. *Journal of Marriage and the Family, 52,* 81–85.

Kurdek, L. A., & Schmitt, J. P. (1985). Relationship quality of gay men in closed or open relationships. *Journal of Homosexuality, 12*(2), 85–99.

Kurz, D. (1987). Emergency department responses to battered women: Resistance to medicalization. *Social Problems, 34,* 69–81.

LaBeff, E. E., Hensley, J. H., Cook, D. A., & Haines, C. L. (1989). Gender differences in self-advertisements for dates: A replication using college students. *Free Inquiry in Creative Sociology, 17*(1), 45–50.

Lacayo, R. (1986, January 13). Second thoughts about no-fault. *Time,* p. 55.

Lacayo, R. (1987, April 13). In the best interests of a child. *Time,* p. 71.

La Farge, P. (1983, October). The new woman. *Parents,* pp. 84–86, 88, 90, 150, 152, 154, 156.

LaFreniere, P. J., & Sroufe, L. A. (1985). Profiles of peer competence in the preschool: Interrelations among measures, influence of social ecology, and relation to attachment history. *Developmental Psychology, 21,* 56–69.

Lagoni, L. S., & Cook, A. S. (1985). Stepfamilies: A content analysis of the popular literature, 1961–1982. *Family Relations, 34,* 521–525.

Lalich, R. A., & Scommegna, A. (1988). Progestin after menopause-yes or no? *Medical Aspects of Human Sexuality, 22*(7), 115–117, 121–122.

Lamanna, M. A. (1977). The value of children to natural and adoptive parents (Doctoral dissertation, University of Notre Dame, 1977). *Dissertation Abstracts International, 38,* 1687A.

Lamaute, D. (1987, December). Counting the true cost of credit cards. *Black Enterprise,* pp. 47–48.

Lamaze, F. (1970). *Painless childbirth.* Chicago: Regnery.

Lamb, M. E. (1976). Parent-infant interaction in 8-month olds. *Child Psychiatry and Human Development, 7,* 56–63.

Lamb, M. E. (1981). *The role of the father in child development* (2nd ed.). New York: Wiley.

Lamb, M. E., Pleck, J. H., & Levine, J. A. (1985). Effects of increased paternal involvement on children in two-parent families. In R. A. Lewis, & R. E. Salt (Eds.), *Men in families* (pp. 141–158). Beverly Hills: Sage.

Lampe, P. E. (1981). Towards amalgamation: Interethnic dating among blacks, Mexican Americans and Anglos. *Ethnic Groups, 3,* 97–109.

Lampe, P. E. (1985). Friendship and adultery. *Sociological Inquiry, 55,* 310–324.

Landis, J. T., & Landis, M. G. (1977). *Building a successful marriage* (7th ed.). Englewood Cliffs, NJ: Prentice-Hall.

Laner, M. R. (1983). Courtship abuse and aggression: Contextual aspects. *Sociological Spectrum, 3,* 69–83.

Laner, M. R. (1986). Competition in courtship. *Family Relations, 35,* 275–279.

Laner, M. R., & Thompson, J. (1982). Abuse and aggression in courting couples. *Deviant Behavior, 3,* 229–244.

Lang, L. R. (1988). *Strategy for personal finance.* New York: McGraw-Hill.

Langan, P. A., & Innes, C. A. (1986). *Preventing domestic violence against women.* (NCJ No. 102037). Washington, DC: Bureau of Justice Statistics.

Langelier, P., & Nurcombe, B. (1985). Child psychiatry and the law: Residual parental rights: Legal trends and controversies. *Journal of the American Academy of Child Psychiatry, 24,* 793–796.

Langford, L. M., & Rand, H. Y. (1975). *Guidance of the young child* (2nd ed.). New York: Wiley.

Langway, L. (1981, November 30). A new kind of life with father. *Newsweek,* pp. 93–97.

LaRossa, R. (1979). Sex during pregnancy: A symbolic interactionist analysis. *The Journal of Sex Research, 15,* 119–128.

Larsen, K. S., & Long, E. (1988). Attitudes toward sex-roles: Traditional or egalitarian? *Sex Roles, 19,* 1–12.

Lasswell, M. E., & Lobsenz, N. (1980). *Styles of loving.* Garden City, NY: Doubleday.

Latham, A. (1988, September 25). Play it again. *Austin American-Statesman,* pp. 1E, 16E.

LaTorre, R. A., & Wendenburg, K. (1983). Psychological characteristics of bisexual, heterosexual and homosexual women. *Journal of Homosexuality, 9*(2), 87–97.

Lauer, J., & Lauer, R. (1985, June). Marriages made to last. *Psychology Today,* pp. 22–26.

Lauter-Klatell, N. (1991). *Readings in child development.* Mountain View, CA: Mayfield.

Lawrence, P. D. (1986, October). Are you too tough to cover? *Esquire,* p. 68.

Lawson, A. (1988). *Adultery.* New York: Basic Books.

Lawton, J. T., Schuler, S. G., Fowell, N., & Madsen, M. K. (1984). Parents' perceptions of actual and ideal childrearing practices. *The Journal of Genetic Psychology, 145,* 77–87.

Lawton, M. P., Moss, M., & Kleban, M. H. (1984). Marital status, living arrangements, and the well-being of older people. *Research on Aging, 6,* 323–345.

Lazarus, A. (1986, May). The five most dangerous myths about marriage. *New Woman,* pp. 73–75.

Leak, G. K & Gardner, L. E. (1990). Sexual attitudes, love attitudes, and social interest. *Individual Psychology: Journal of Adlerian Theory, Research, and Practice. 46,* 55–60.

LeBoyer, F. (1975). *Birth without violence.* New York: Random House.

Ledray, L. (1984). Victims of incest. *American Journal of Nursing, 84,* 1010–1014.

Lee, G. R. (1987, November). *Marital intimacy among older persons: The spouse as confidant.* Paper presented at the meeting of the National Council on Family Relations, Atlanta, GA.

Lee, G. R. (1988). Marital satisfaction in later life: The effects of nonmarital roles. *Journal of Marriage and the Family, 50,* 775–783.

Lee, G. R., & Ellithorpe, E. (1982). Intergenerational exchange and subjective well-being among the elderly. *Journal of Marriage and the Family, 44,* 217–224.

Lee, G. R., & Ishii-Kuntz, M. (1987). Social interaction, loneliness, and emotional well-being among the elderly. *Research on Aging, 9,* 459–482.

Lee, G. R., & Shehan, C. L. (1989). Retirement and marital satisfaction. *Journal of Gerontology, 44,* 226–230.

Lee, J. A. (1973). *The colours of love.* Toronto: New Press.

Lee, J. A. (1974, October). The styles of loving. *Psychology Today,* pp. 44–50.

Lee, S. M., & Zelenak, M. J. (1987). *Personal finance for consumers.* Columbus, OH: Publishing Horizons.

Legacy of the baby-boomers. (1988, January 30). *Eau Claire Leader-Telegram,* p. 4A.

Leiblum, S., Bachmann, G., Kemmann, E., Colburn, D., & Swartzman, L. (1983). Vaginal atrophy in the postmenopausal woman: The importance of sexual activity and hormones. *Journal of the American Medical Association, 249,* 2195–2198.

Leigh, G. K., Holman, T. B., & Burr, W. R. (1984). An empirical test of sequence in Murstein's SVR theory of mate selection. *Family Relations, 33,* 225–231.

Lein, L. (1984). Male participation in home life: Impact of social supports and breadwinner responsibility on the allocation of tasks. In P. Voydanoff (Ed.), *Work & family: Changing roles of men and women* (pp. 242–250). Palo Alto, CA: Mayfield.

Leitenberg, H., & Slavin, L. (1983). Comparison of attitudes toward transsexuality and homosexuality. *Archives of Sexual Behavior, 12,* 337–346.

LeMasters, E. E., & DeFrain, J. (1983). *Parents in contemporary America: A sympathetic view.* Homewood, IL: Dorsey.

Lenney, E. (1989). Role versatility. In A. Campbell (Ed.), *The opposite sex* (pp. 242–247). Topsfield, MA: Salem House.

Leo, J. (1986a, March 3). On the trail of the Big O. *Time,* p. 12.

Leo, J. (1986b, November 24). Sex and the schools. *Time,* pp. 54–60, 64.

Leppert, P. C. (1984). The effect of pregnancy on adolescent growth and development. In S. Golub (Ed.), *Health care of the female adolescent* (pp. 65–79). New York: Haworth Press.

Lerner, R. M., & Spanier, G. B. (Eds.). (1978). *Child influences on marital family interaction: A life span perspective.* New York: Academic Press.

Leslie, G. R., & Korman, S. K. (1989). *The family in social context* (7th ed.). New York: Oxford University Press.

Leslie, G. R., & Leslie, E. M. (1980). *Marriage in a changing world* (2nd ed.). New York: Wiley.

Leslie, L. A., & Grady, K. (1985). Changes in mothers' social networks and social support following divorce. *Journal of Marriage and the Family, 47,* 663–673.

Leslie, L. A., Huston, T. L., & Johnson, M. P. (1986). Parental reaction to dating relationships: Do they make a difference? *Journal of Marriage and the Family, 48,* 57–66.

Lesser, E. K., & Comet, J. J. (1987). Help and hindrance: Parents of divorcing children. *Journal of Marital and Family Therapy, 13,* 197–202.

Lester, D. (1985). Romantic attitudes toward love in men and women. *Psychological Reports, 56,* 662.

Lester, D., Deluca, G., Hellinghausen, W., & Scribner, D. (1985). Jealousy and irrationality in love. *Psychological Reports, 56,* 210.

Lester, D., Doscher, K., Estrict, M., & Lee, R. (1984). Correlates of a romantic attitude toward love. *Psychological Reports, 55,* 794.

Lester, G. H. (1990). *Child support and alimony: 1987 (Advanced data from March/April 1988 current population survey).* Current Population Reports, Series P–23, No. 167. Washington, DC: U.S. Government Printing Office.

Levant, R. F., Slattery, S. C., & Loiselle, J. E. (1987). Fathers' involvement in housework and child care with school-aged daughters. *Family Relations, 36,* 152–157.

Levine, K. (1988, January). Should I stay home? *Parents,* pp. 58, 60, 62, 66.

Levine, S. B. (1983). A clinical approach to the psychosexual dysfunctions. In S. F. Pariser, S. B. Levine, & M. L. Gardner (Eds.), *Clinical sexuality* (pp. 21–52). New York: Dekker-Marcel.

Levine, S. B. (1987). More on the nature of sexual desire. *Journal of Sex & Marital Therapy, 13,* 35–44.

Levinger, G. (1980). Toward the analysis of close relationships. *Journal of Experimental Social Psychology, 16,* 510–544.

Levinson, A. (1984, June). Laws for live-in lovers. *Ms.,* p. 101.

Levinson, R. A. (1986). Contraceptive self-efficacy: A perspective on teenage girls' contraceptive behavior. *The Journal of Sex Research, 22,* 347–369.

Levitan, M., & Montagu, A. (1977). *Textbook of human genetics* (2nd ed.). New York: Oxford University Press.

Levy, G. E. (1986). Working and non-working mothers: Their children's view of traditional and nontraditional roles (Doctoral dissertation, Hofstra University, 1984). *Dissertation Abstracts International, 46,* 2461B.

Levy, R. J. (1988). Custody: The battles continue. *Family Therapy Today, 3*(1), 1, 7.

Lewin, E. (1981). Lesbianism and motherhood: Implications for child custody. *Human Organization, 40,* 6–14.

Lewin, T. (1990a, July 27). Battle for family leave will be fought in states. *New York Times,* p. 8A.

Lewin, T. (1990b, September 21). Suit over death benefits asks, what is a family? *New York Times,* pp. 1A–2A.

Lewis, C. (1989). Early infancy. In A. Campbell (Ed.), *The opposite sex* (pp. 26–31). Topsfield, MA: Salem House.

Lewis, C. S. (1958). *Mere Christianity.* New York: Macmillan.

Lewis, J. M., Beavers, W. R., Gossett, J. T., & Phillips, V. A. (1976). *No single thread: Psychological health in family systems.* New York: Brunner/Mazel.

Lewis, M., Brooks-Gunn, J., & Jaskir, J. (1985). Individual differences in visual self-recognition as a function of mother-infant attachment relationship. *Developmental Psychology, 21,* 1181–1187.

Lewis, M., Feiring, C., McGoffog, C., & Jaskir, J. (1984). Predicting psychopathology in six-year-olds from early social relations. *Child Development, 55,* 123–136.

Lewis, R. A., Volk, R. J., & Duncan, S. F. (1989). Stress on fathers and family relationships related to rural youth leaving and returning home. *Family Relations, 38,* 174–181.

Libby, R. W. (1978). Creative singlehood as a sexual life style: Beyond marriage as a rite of passage. In B. I. Murstein (Ed.), *Exploring intimate life styles* (pp. 164–195). New York: Springer.

Lichter, D. T. (1982). The migration of dual-worker families: Does the wife's job matter? *Social Science Quarterly, 63,* 48–57.

Lieberman, B. J. (1987, March). Changes affecting Individual Retirement Accounts (IRAs) under the Tax Reform Act of 1986 (TRA-1986). *CPA Journal,* pp. 47–48.

Liebert, R. M., & Sprafkin, J. (1988). *The early window: Effects of television on children and youth* (3rd ed.). New York: Pergamon Press.

Liebert, R. M., Sprafkin, J. N., & Davidson, E. S. (1982). *The early window* (2nd ed.). New York: Pergamon Press.

Lief, H. I., Sholevar, G. P., Furstenberg, F. F., Jr., & Isaacs, M. B. (1988). Children of remarriage. *Medical Aspects of Human Sexuality, 22*(1), 55–59, 63, 66.

Liese, L. H., Snowden, L. R., & Ford, L. K. (1989). Partner status, social support, and psychological adjustment during pregnancy. *Family Relations, 38,* 311–316.

Lieshman, K. (1983, November). The extent of the harm. *Atlantic,* pp. 22, 24, 26, 30–32.

Life insurance: How to protect your family—universal life insurance. (1986a, August). *Consumer Reports,* pp. 515–529.

Life insurance: How to protect your family—whole life insurance. (1986b, July). *Consumer Reports,* pp. 447–452.

Lindsay, J. W. (1985). *Educating pregnant and parenting teens: Our responsibility, our challenge.* Buena Park, CA: Morning Glory.

Lino, M. (1990). Families with children: The income expenditures over time. *Journal of Home Economics, 82*(2), 12–17.

Lips, H. M. (1988). *Sex and gender: An introduction.* Mountain View, CA: Mayfield.

Lipton, K. L., & King, J. (Eds.). (1987). *National food review* (No. 37). Washington, DC: U.S. Department of Agriculture.

Liskin, L., Rinehart, W., Blackburn, R., & Rutledge, A. (1985). Minilaparotomy and laparoscopy: Safe, effective, and widely used. *Population Reports, 13,* 2.

Liss, L. (1987). Families and the law. In M. B. Sussman & S. K. Steinmetz (Eds.), *Handbook of marriage and the family* (pp. 767–793). New York: Plenum Press.

Lobsenz, N. M. (1981). *Men and women—what we know about love* (No. 592). New York: Public Affairs Committee.

Lockard, D. (1985). The lesbian community: An anthropological approach. *Journal of Homosexuality, 11*(3), 83–95.

Lockheed, M. E. (1986). Reshaping the social order: The case of gender segregation. *Sex Roles, 14,* 617–628.

Locksley, A. (1980). On the effects of wives' employment on marital adjustment and companionship. *Journal of Marriage and the Family, 42,* 337–346.

Loddeke, L. (1990, March 17). Women taking charge of congregations. *Houston Post,* p. 25A.

Loeb, R. C., Horst, L., & Horton, P. J. (1980). Family interaction patterns associated with self-esteem in preadolescent girls and boys. *Merrill-Palmer Quarterly, 26,* 203–217.

Lollar, C. (1987, August 18). New contraceptives found to be effective for up to five years. *The Atlanta Constitution,* p. 37A.

Lombardo, W. K., Cretser, G. A., Lombardo, B., & Mathis, S. L. (1983). Fer cryin' out loud—there is a sex difference. *Sex Roles, 9,* 987–995.

Londerville, S., & Main, M. (1981). Security of attachment, compliance, and maternal training methods in the second year of life. *Developmental Psychology, 17,* 289–299.

London, K. A., & Wilson, B. F. (1988). Divorce. *American Demographics, 10*(10), 22–26.

Long, B. H. (1983). A steady boy friend: A step toward resolution of the intimacy crisis for American college women. *The Journal of Psychology, 115,* 275–280.

Long, T., & Long, L. (1983). *The handbook for latchkey children and their parents.* New York: Arbor House.

Longino, C. F., Jr., & Lipman, A. (1981). Married and spouseless men and women in planned retirement communities: Support network differentials. *Journal of Marriage and the Family, 43,* 169–177.

Lopata, H. Z. (1971). *Occupation: Housewife.* New York: Oxford University Press.

Lopata, H. Z. (1979). *Women as widows: Support systems.* New York: Elsevier.

Lopata, H. Z. (1981). Widowhood and husband sanctification. *Journal of Marriage and the Family, 43,* 439–450.

Lopata, H. Z., & Brehm, H. P. (1986). *Widows and dependent wives: From social problem to federal program.* New York: Praeger.

LoPiccolo, J. (1985, September). *Advances in diagnosis and treatment of sexual dysfunction.* Paper presented at the meeting of the Society for the Scientific Study of Sex, San Diego, CA.

Lord, L. J., Thornton, J., & Carey, J. (1986, June 2). Sex, with care. *U.S. News & World Report,* pp. 53–57.

Losh-Hesselbart, S. (1987). Development of gender roles. In M. B. Sussman, & S. Steinmetz (Eds.), *Handbook of marriage and the family* (pp. 535–563). New York: Plenum Press.

Lott, B. (1987). *Women's lives: Themes and variations in gender learning.* Monterey, CA: Brooks/Cole.

Lovell-Tray, L. A. (1983). Anomia among employed wives and housewives: An explanatory analysis. *Journal of Marriage and the Family, 45,* 301–309.

Lowe, R. H., & Frey, J. D. (1983). Predicting Lamaze childbirth intentions and outcomes: An extension of the theory of reasoned action to a joint outcome. *Basic and Applied Social Psychology, 4,* 353–372.

Lowery, C. R. (1985). Child custody in divorce: Parents' decisions and perceptions. *Family Relations, 34,* 241–249.

Lowery, C. R., & Settle, S. A. (1985). Effects of divorce on children: Differential impact of custody and visitation patterns. *Family Relations, 34,* 455–463.

Lowery, M. (1987). Adult survivors of childhood incest. *Journal of Psychosocial Nursing and Mental Health Service, 25,* 27–31.

Lowery, S., & DeFleur, M. L. (1983). *Milestones in mass communication research: Media effects.* New York: Longman.

Lowry, P. (1979). Birth control: Questions to ask yourself. In S. Hendricks (Ed.), *The women's yellow pages: Original sourcebook for women* (West Virginia ed., p. 171). Boston: The Public Works.

Luckey, E. B., & Bain, J. K. (1970). Children: A factor in marital satisfaction. *Journal of Marriage and the Family, 32,* 43–44.

Lueptow, L. B. (1980). Social structure, social change and parental influence in adolescent sex-role socialization: 1964–1975. *Journal of Marriage and the Family, 42,* 93–103.

Lull, J., Mulac, A., & Rosen, S. L. (1983). Feminism as a predictor of mass media use. *Sex Roles, 9,* 165–177.

Lutkenhaus, P., Grossman, K. E., & Grossman, K. (1985). Infant-mother attachment at twelve months and style of interaction with a stranger at the age of three years. *Child Development, 56,* 1538–1542.

Lutz, P. (1983). The steptamily: An adolescent perspective. *Family Relations, 32,* 367–375.

Lykken, D. T. (1982). Research with twins: The concept of emergenesis. *Psychophysiology, 19,* 361–373.

Maatman, T., & Montague, D. (1985). Diabetes mellitus and erectile dysfunction in men. *Journal of Urology, 133,* 191A.

Maccoby, E. E. (1980). *Social development: Psychological growth and the parent-child relationship.* New York: Harcourt Brace Jovanovich.

Maccoby, E. E., & Jacklin, C. N. (1974). *The psychology of sex differences.* Palo Alto, CA: Stanford University Press.

Maccoby, E. E., & Martin, J. A. (1983). Socialization in the context of the family. In P. H. Mussen (Ed.), *Handbook of child psychology,* Volume 4. (4th ed., pp. 1–102). New York: Wiley.

Maccoby, E. E., Snow, M. E., & Jacklin, C. N. (1984). Children's disposition and mother-child interaction at 12 and 18 months: A short-term longitudinal study. *Developmental Psychology, 20,* 459–472.

Mace, D. (1982). *Love and anger in marriage.* Grand Rapids, MI: Zondervan.

Mace, D. (1987). Three ways of helping married couples. *Journal of Marital and Family Therapy, 13,* 179–185.

Mace, D., & Mace, V. (1979). *How to have a happy marriage: A step-by-step guide to an enriched relationship.* Nashville, TN: Festival Books.

Mace, D. R. (1991). Contemporary issues in marriage. In L. Cargan (Ed.), *Marriages and families: Coping with change* (2nd ed., pp. 6–13). Englewood Cliffs, NJ: Prentice-Hall.

Macklin, E. D. (1972). Heterosexual cohabitation among unmarried college students. *The Family Coordinator, 21,* 463–472.

Macklin, E. D. (1980). Non-traditional family forms: A decade of research. *Journal of Marriage and the Family, 42,* 905–922.

Macklin, E. D. (1983). Nonmarital heterosexual cohabitation: An overview. In E. D. Macklin & R. H. Rubin (Eds.), *Contemporary families and alternative lifestyles: Handbook on research and theory* (pp. 49–74). Beverly Hills: Sage.

Macklin, E. D. (1987). Nontraditional family forms. In M. B. Sussman & S. K. Steinmetz (Eds.), *Handbook of marriage and the family* (pp. 317–353). New York: Plenum Press.

Macklin, E. D. (1988). AIDS: Implications for families. *Family Relations, 37,* 141–149.

Macklin, E. D. (Ed.). (1989). *AIDS and families.* New York: Haworth Press.

Macklin, M. C., & Kolbe, R. H. (1984). Sex role stereotyping in children's advertising: Current and past trends. *Journal of Advertising, 13,* 34–42.

MacLaughlin, S., & Strelnick, E. G. (1984). Breast-feeding and working outside the home. *Issues in Comprehensive Pediatric Nursing, 7,* 67–81.

MacNamara, D. E. J., & Sagarin, E. (1977). *Sex, crime, and the law.* New York: Free Press.

Madden, M. E., & Janoff-Bulman, R. (1981). Blame, control, and marital satisfaction: Wives' attributions for conflict in marriage. *Journal of Marriage and the Family, 43,* 663–674.

Maddox, B. (1982, February). Homosexual parents. *Psychology Today,* pp. 62, 66–68.

Magid, B. (1986). The meaning of projection in self psychology. *Journal of the American Academy of Psychoanalysis, 14,* 473–483.

Mahoney, E. R. (1980). Religiosity and sexual behavior among heterosexual college students. *The Journal of Sex Research, 16,* 97–113.

Maine, D. (1981). *Family planning: Its impact on the health of women and children.* New York: The Center for Population and Family Health, Columbia University.

Makepeace, J. M. (1981). Courtship violence among college students. *Family Relations, 30,* 97–102.

Makepeace, J. M. (1983). Life events stress and courtship violence. *Family Relations, 32,* 101–109.

Mancini, J. A., & Mancini, S. B. (1983). The family's role in sex education: Implications for educators. *Journal of Sex Education and Therapy, 9,* 16–21.

Maneker, J. S., & Rankin, R. P. (1985). Education, age at marriage, and marital duration: Is there a relationship? *Journal of Marriage and the Family, 47,* 675–683.

Mann, J. (1977, October 3). End of the youth culture. *U.S. News & World Report,* pp. 54–56.

Marciano, T. D. (1979). Male influences on fertility: Needs for research. *The Family Coordinator, 28,* 561–568.

Marciano, T. D. (1987). Families and religions. In M. B. Sussman & S. K. Steinmetz (Eds.), *Handbook of marriage and the family* (pp. 285–316). New York: Plenum Press.

Marcus, G. G., & Smith, R. L. (1982, November). Your power, his power: How equal? How fair? How balanced? *Glamour,* pp. 240–241, 278, 280.

Maret, E., & Finlay, B. (1984). The distribution of household labor among women in dual-earner families. *Journal of Marriage and the Family, 46,* 357–364.

Marett, K. M. (1990). Extramarital affairs: A birelational model for their assessment. *Family Therapy, 17,* 21–28.

Margolick, D. (1984, February 26). Herpes and similar matters get more attention in court. *The New York Times,* p. 14.

Margolin, G. (1987). The multiple forms of aggressiveness between marital partners: How do we identify them? *Journal of Marital and Family Therapy, 13,* 77–84.

Margolin, L., Moran, P. B., & Miller, M. (1989). Social approval for violations of sexual consent in marriage and dating. *Violence & Victims, 4,* 45–55.

Margolin, L., & White, L. (1987). The continuing role of physical attractiveness in marriage. *Journal of Marriage and the Family, 49,* 21–27.

Marini, M. M. (1981). Effects of the timing of marriage and first birth on fertility. *Journal of Marriage and the Family, 43,* 27–46.

Markham, W. T., Macken, P. O., Bonjean, C. M., & Corder, J. (1983). A note on sex, geographic mobility, and career advancement. *Social Forces, 61,* 1138–1146.

Markham, W. T., & Pleck, J. H. (1986). Sex and willingness to move for occupational advancement: Some national sample results. *The Sociological Quarterly, 27,* 121–143.

Markowski, E. M., & Cain, H. I. (1984). Marital and family therapy certification and licensing examinations: One model. *Journal of Marital and Family Therapy, 10,* 289–296.

Markowski, E. M., Croake, J. W., & Keller, J. F. (1978). Sexual history and present sexual behavior of cohabiting and married couples. *The Journal of Sex Research, 14,* 27–39.

Marks, S. R. (1986). *Three corners: Exploring marriage and the self.* Lexington, MA: Heath.

Marks, S. R. (1989). Towards a systems theory of marital quality. *Journal of Marriage and the Family, 51,* 15–26.

Marriage in later years: Redefining the relationship. (1988). *Family Therapy Today, 3*(1), 5–6.

Marriage: Traditional facade masks the terror within. (1987, July 22). *San Marcos Daily Record,* p. 3A.

Marsa, L. (1987, November). Winning the loan game: How to score points with your banker. *Black Enterprise,* pp. 63–64, 66.

Marshall, V. W. (1986). A sociological perspective on aging and dying. In V. W. Marshall (Ed.), *Later life: The social psychology of aging* (pp. 125–146). Beverly Hills: Sage.

Marsidi, P. J., & Wise, H. A., II. (1983). Sexuality from a urologic perspective. In S. F. Pariser, S. B. Levine, & M. L. Gardner (Eds.), *Clinical sexuality* (pp. 173–184). New York: Dekker-Marcel.

Marsiglio, W. (1985). Husbands' sex-role preferences and contraceptive intentions: The case of the male pill. *Sex Roles, 12,* 655–663.

Marsiglio, W., & Menaghan, E. G. (1987). Couples and the male birth control pill: A future alternative in contraceptive selection. *The Journal of Sex Research, 23,* 34–49.

Martell, L. K. (1990). Perceptions of equity by mothers and daughters during daughters' first pregnancy. *Family Relations, 33,* 305–310.

Martin, C. E. (1981). Factors affecting sexual functioning in 60 79-year-old married males. *Archives of Sexual Behavior, 10,* 399–420.

Martin, D. (1989, December 17). Feminism for the 1990's. *Austin American-Statesman,* pp. E1, E19.

Martin, D., & Lyon, P. (1972). *Lesbian/woman.* New York: Bantam Books.

Martin, M. J., Schumm, W. R., Bugaighis, M. A., Jurich, A. P., & Bollman, S. R. (1987). Family violence and adolescents' perceptions of outcomes of family conflict. *Journal of Marriage and the Family, 49,* 165–171.

Martin, M. J., & Walters, J. (1982). Familial correlates of selected types of child abuse and neglect. *Journal of Marriage and the Family, 44,* 267–276.

Martin, M. W. (1985). Satisfaction with intimate exchange: Gender-role differences and the impact of equity, equality, and rewards. *Sex Roles, 13,* 597–605.

Marzollo, J. (1975). *9 months, 1 day, 1 year.* New York: Harper & Row.

Masello, R. (1982, August). Why I love—and hate—blind dates. *Mademoiselle,* p. 122.

Mashal, M. (1985). Marital power, role expectations and marital satisfaction. *International Journal of Women's Studies, 8,* 40–46.

Maslow, A. H. (1943). A theory of human motivation. *Psychological Review, 50,* 370–396.

Maslow, A. H. (1968). *Toward a psychology of being* (2nd ed.). Princeton, NJ: Van Nostrand.

Masters, W. H., & Johnson, V. E. (1966). *Human sexual response.* Boston: Little, Brown.

Masters, W. H., Johnson, V. E., & Kolodny, R. C. (1988). *Human sexuality* (3rd ed.). Glenview, IL: Scott, Foresman.

Matas, L., Arend, R. A., & Sroufe, L. A. (1978). Continuity of adaptation in the second year: The relationship between quality of attachment and later competence. *Child Development, 49,* 547–556.

Matthews, K. A., Wing, R. R., Kuller, L. H., Meilahn, E. N., Kelsey, S. F., Costello, E. J., & Caggiula, A. W. (1990). Influences of natural menopause on psychological characteristics and symptoms of middle-aged healthy women. *Journal of Consulting and Clinical Psychology, 58,* 345–351.

Matthews, R., & Matthews, A. M. (1986). Infertility and involuntary childlessness: The transition to nonparenthood. *Journal of Marriage and the Family, 48,* 641–649.

Matthews, W. J. (1984). Violence in college couples. *College Student Journal, 18,* 150–158.

May, K. A. (1982). Factors contributing to first-time fathers' readiness for fatherhood: An exploratory study. *Family Relations, 31,* 353–361.

May, R. (1969). *Love and will.* New York: Norton.

Maynard, C. E., & Zawachi, R. A. (1979). Mobility and the dual-career couple. *Personnel Journal, 58,* 472–482.

Maziade, M., Boudreault, M., Cote, R., & Thivierge, J. (1986). Influences of gentle birth delivery procedures and other perinatal circumstances on infant temperament: Developmental and social implications. *Journal of Pediatrics, 108,* 134–136.

Mazor, M. D. (1980). Psychosexual problems of the infertile couple. *Medical Aspects of Human Sexuality, 14*(12), 32, 39, 43, 47, 49.

McCabe, M. P. (1984). Toward a theory of adolescent dating. *Adolescence, 19,* 159–170.

McCandless, J. (1986, August). *The influence of religious factors on sex role attitudes.* Paper presented at the meeting of the American Sociological Association, New York, NY.

McCarthy, B. W. (1982). Sexual dysfunctions and dissatisfactions among middle-years couples. *Journal of Sex Education and Therapy, 8,* 9–12.

McCary, J. L. (1980). *Freedom and growth in marriages* (2nd ed.). New York: Wiley.

McCary, J. L., & McCary, S. (1982). *McCary's human sexuality* (4th ed.). Belmont, CA: Wadsworth.

McCollum, E. E. (1985). Recontacting former spouses: A further step in the divorce process. *Journal of Marital and Family Therapy, 11,* 417–420.

McCormally, K., & Spellman, L. (1987, February). How to find the best loans now. *Changing Times,* pp. 24–29.

McCoy, E. (1984, November). Kids & divorce. *Parents,* pp. 112–114, 116, 192, 195, 197–198, 200.

McCoy, E. (1985). Childhood through the ages. In J. Henslin (Ed.), *Marriage and family in a changing society* (2nd ed., pp. 386–394). New York: Free Press.

McCoy, K. (1985, October). What every man wishes his wife knew. *Redbook,* pp. 142–143, 210.

McCoy, N. L., & Davidson, J. M. (1985). A longitudinal study of the effects of menopause on sexuality. *Maturitas, 7,* 203–210.

McCrae, R. R., & Costa, P. T. (1984). *Emerging lives, enduring dispositions: Personality in adulthood.* Boston: Little, Brown.

McCubbin, H. I., & Figley, C. R. (Eds.). (1983). *Stress and the family: Coping with normative transitions.* New York: Brunner Mazel.

McCubbin, H. I., & Patterson, J. M. (1983). The family stress process: The double ABCX model of adjustment and adaptations. In H. I. McCubbin, M. B. Sussman, & J. M. Patterson (Eds.), *Social stress and the family* (pp. 7–37). New York: Haworth Press.

McDonald, G. W. (1980). Family power: The assessment of a decade of theory and research, 1970–1979. *Journal of Marriage and the Family, 42,* 841–854.

McEwan, K. L., Costello, C. G., & Taylor, P. J. (1987). Adjustment to infertility. *Journal of Abnormal Psychology, 96,* 108–116.

McFadden, V. M., & Doub, G. (1983). Therapist's new role: Training families for healthy survival. In J. C. Hansen & H. A. Liddle (Eds.), *The family therapy collection* (pp. 134–160). Rockville, MD: Aspen.

McGoldrick, M., & Carter, E. A. (1980). Forming a remarried family. In E. A. Carter & M. McGoldrick (Eds.), *The family life cycle: A framework for family therapy* (pp. 265–294). New York: Gardner.

McGoldrick, M., & Carter, E. A. (1982). The family life cycle—Its stages and dislocations. In F. Walsh (Ed.), *Normal family processes* (pp. 167–195). New York: Guilford Press.

McGrath, A. (1986, April 7). Dividing the spoils in divorce. *U.S. News & World Report,* pp. 57–58.

McGrath, A. (1987, June 29). Fixing your credit file. *U.S. News & World Report,* p. 49.

McGuiness, D., & Pribram, K. (1979). The origins of sensory bias in the development of gender differences in perception and cognition. In M. Bortner (Ed.), *Cognitive growth and development: Essays in honor of Herbert G. Birch* (pp. 3–56). New York: Brunner-Mazel.

McIntyre, S. L., & Higgins, J. E. (1986). Parity and use-effectiveness with the contraceptive sponge. *American Journal of Obstetrics & Gynecology, 155,* 796.

McKaughan, N., & Kagan, J. (1986, February). The motherhood plunge. *Working Woman,* p. 69–71, 73, 112–113.

McKinlay, J. B., McKinlay, S. M., & Brambilla, D. (1987). The relative contributions of endocrine changes and social circumstances to depression in middle-aged women. *Journal of Health & Social Behavior, 28,* 345–363.

McKinney, J. D., & Edgerton, M (1983, April). *Classroom adaptive behavior.* Paper presented at the meeting of the Society for Research in Child Development, Detroit, MI.

McKinney, K., Sprecher, S., & DeLamater, J. (1984). Self images and contraceptive behavior. *Basic and Applied Social Psychology, 5,* 37–57.

McLanahan, S. S. (1983). Family structure and stress: A longitudinal comparison of two-parent and female-headed families. *Journal of Marriage and the Family, 45,* 347–357.

McLanahan, S. S., Wedemeyer, N. V., & Adelberg, T. (1981). Network structure, social support, and psychological well-being in the single-parent family. *Journal of Marriage and the Family, 43,* 601–612.

McLaren, A. (1981). "Barrenness against nature": Recourse to abortion in pre-industrial England. *The Journal of Sex Research, 17,* 224–237.

McLeod, P. B., & Ellis, J. R. (1983). Alternative approaches to the family life cycle in the analysis of housing consumption. *Journal of Marriage and the Family, 45,* 699–708.

McNeely, R. L., & Fogarty, B. A. (1988). Balancing parenthood and employment: Factors affecting company receptiveness to family-related innovations in the workplace. *Family Relations, 37,* 189–195.

McQueen, M. (1987, December 4). Mortgage rates continue drop: Home sales soft. *The Wall Street Journal,* p. 24.

MDT survey: Poor communication key marital problem of clients entering therapy. (1986). *Marriage and Divorce Today, 12*(7), 1–2.

Mead, D. E. (1976). *Six approaches to child rearing: Models from psychological theory.* Provo, UT: Brigham Young University Press.

Mead, M. (1935). *Sex and temperament in three primitive societies.* New York: Morrow.

Mead, M. (1966, July). Marriage in two steps. *Redbook,* pp. 48–49, 84, 86.

Mead, M. (1975). *Male and female.* New York: Morrow.

Mechanic, D., & Hansell, S. (1989). Divorce, family conflict, and adolescents' well-being. *Journal of Health and Social Issues, 30,* 105–116.

Median incomes of full-time, year-round workers by educational attainment, 1984. (1987, January 7). *The Chronicle of Higher Education,* p. 23.

Medling, J. M., & McCarrey, M. (1981). Marital adjustment over segments of the family life cycle: The issue of spouses' value similarity. *Journal of Marriage and the Family, 43,* 195–203.

Meeks, L. B., & Heit, P. (1982). *Human sexuality: Making responsible decisions.* Philadelphia: Saunders.

Meer, J. (1987). The reason of age. In H. Cox (Ed.), *Aging* (5th ed., pp. 102–105). Guilford, CT: Dushkin.

Mehrabian, A., & Stanton-Mohr, L. (1985). Effects of emotional state on sexual desire and sexual dysfunction. *Motivation and Emotion, 9,* 315–330.

Mehren, E. (1986, April 21). Husbands with working wives are less satisfied. *Gainesville Sun,* p. 11A.

Meldman, L. W. (1981). The modification of male sexual behavior: Premature ejaculation (Doctoral dissertation, University of Michigan, 1981). *Dissertation Abstracts International, 42,* 617A.

Melichar, J., & Chiriboga, D. A. (1985). Timetables in the divorce process. *Journal of Marriage and the Family, 47,* 701–708.

Melito, R. (1985). Adaptation in family systems: A developmental perspective. *Family Process, 21,* 89–100.

Melli, M. S. (1986). The changing legal status of the single parent. *Family Relations, 35,* 31–35.

Melton, G. B. (1987). Legal regulation of adolescent abortion: Unintended effects. *American Psychologist, 42,* 79–81.

Menaghan, E. G., & Lieberman, M. A. (1986). Changes in depression following divorce: A panel study. *Journal of Marriage and the Family, 48,* 319–328.

Meredith, D. (1985, June). Mom, dad and the kids. *Psychology Today,* pp. 62–67.

Merriam, S. B., & Hyer, P. (1984). Changing attitudes of women towards family-related tasks in young adulthood. *Sex Roles, 10,* 825–835.

Messaris, P., & Kerr, D. (1984). TV-related mother-child interactions and children's perceptions of TV characters. *Journalism Quarterly, 61,* 662–666.

Messner, S. F. (1986). Television violence and violent crime: An aggregate analysis. *Social Problems, 33,* 218–235.

Meyer, J. P., & Pepper, S. (1977). Need compatibility and marital adjustment in young married couples. *Journal of Personality and Social Psychology, 35,* 331–342.

Miall, C. E. (1987). The stigma of adoptive parent status: Perceptions of community attitudes toward adoption and the experience of informal social sanctioning. *Family Relations, 36,* 34–49.

Middleton, L., & Roark, A. C. (1981, July 6). Living together is widely accepted among students today. *The Chronicle of Higher Education,* pp. 3–4.

Milardo, R. M. (1982). Friendship networks in developing relationships: Converging and diverging social environments. *Social Psychology Quarterly, 45,* 162–172.

Millar, K. U., & Millar, M. G. (1988). Sex differences in perceived self- and other-disclosure: A case where inequity increases satisfaction. *Social Behavior and Personality, 16,* 59–64.

Miller, A. (1985). Guidelines in stepparenting. *Psychotherapy in Private Practice, 3,* 99–109.

Miller, B. (1988). Date rape: Time for a new look at prevention. *Journal of College Student Development, 29,* 353–355.

Miller, B. C., & Sollie, D. L. (1985). The transition to parenthood. In J. M. Henslin (Ed.), *Marriage and family in a changing society* (2nd ed., pp. 395–400). New York: Free Press.

Miller, H. L., & Siegel, P. S. (1972). *Loving: A psychological approach.* New York: Wiley.

Miller, L. M. (1983). Relationship of erectile dysfunction and negative emotions in men, age forty to fifty-five (Doctoral dissertation, United States International University, 1983). *Dissertation Abstracts International, 44,* 613B.

Miller, P. C., Lefcourt, H. M., Holmes, J. G., Ware, E. E., & Saleh, W. E. (1986). Marital locus of control and marital problem solving. *Journal of Personality and Social Psychology, 51,* 161–169.

Miller, R. L. (1987). *Economic issues for consumers* (5th ed.). St. Paul: West.

Miller, W. B. (1986). Why some women fail to use their contraceptive method: A psychological investigation. *Family Planning Perspectives, 18,* 27–32.

Milletti, M. A. (1987). *Voices of experience: 1500 retired people talk about retirement.* New York: Teachers Insurance and Annuity Association.

Mills, D. M. (1984). A model for stepfamily development. *Family Relations, 33,* 365–372.

Mills, J. L., Harley, S., & Harley, E. E. (1981). Should coitus in pregnancy be discouraged? *Lancet, 2,* 136–138.

Milow, V. (1983). Menstrual education: Past, present, and future. In S. Golub (Ed.), *Menarche: The transition from girl to woman* (pp. 127–132). Lexington, MA: Lexington Books.

Minnett, A. M., Vandell, D. L., & Santrock, J. W. (1983). The effects of sibling status on sibling interaction: Influence of birth order, age spacing, sex of child, and sex of sibling. *Child Development, 54,* 1064–1072.

Mirotznik, J., Shapiro, R. D., Steinhart, J. E., & Gillespie, O. (1987). Genital herpes: An investigation of its attitudinal and behavioral correlates. *The Journal of Sex Research, 23,* 266–272.

Mitchell, B. A., Wister, A. V., & Burch, T. K. (1989). The family environment and leaving the parental home. *Journal of Marriage and the Family, 51,* 605–613.

Mitchelson, M. M. (1979). *Made in heaven, settled in court.* New York: Warner Books.

Mithers, C. L. (1986, April). A mortgage of one's own. *Ms.,* pp. 42–44, 88–89.

Moen, P., & Dempster-McClain, D. I. (1987). Employed parents: Role strain, work time, and preferences for working less. *Journal of Marriage and the Family, 49,* 579–590.

Moldanado, S. A. (1985). Trends in public attitudes toward legal abortion, 1972–1978. *Research in Nursing & Health, 8,* 219–225.

Monahan, T. P. (1970). Are interracial marriages really less stable? *Social Forces, 48,* 461–473.

Monahan, T. P. (1971). Interracial marriage and divorce in Kansas and the question of instability of mixed marriages. *Journal of Comparative Family Studies, 2,* 107–120.

Money, J. (1973). Developmental differentiation of femininity and masculinity compared. In C. S. Stoll (Ed.), *Sexism: Scientific debates* (pp. 13–27). Reading, MA: Addison-Wesley.

Money, J. (1975). Human behavior cytogenetics: Review of psychopathology in three syndromes-47,XXY; 47,XYY; and 45,X. *The Journal of Sex Research, 11,* 181–200.

Money, J. (1985). Gender: History, theory and usage of the term in sexology and its relationship to nature/nurture. *Journal of Sex & Marital Therapy, 11,* 71–79.

Money, J. (1987). Sin, sickness, or status? Homosexual gender identity and psychoneuroendrocrinology. *American Psychologist, 42,* 384–399.

Money, J., & Ehrhardt, A. A. (1972). *Man and woman, boy and girl: Differentiation and dimorphism of gender identity from conception to maturity.* Baltimore: Johns Hopkins University Press.

The money side of marriage. (1985, June). *Changing Times,* pp. 32–37.

Money takes a back seat to sex life, survey says. (1987, October 28). *The Memphis Commercial Appeal,* p. 3C.

Monroe, P. A., Garand, J. C., & Price, S. J. (1985). Family health plan choices: The Health Maintenance Organization option. *Family Relations, 34,* 71–78.

Monsen, E. R., & Owen, A. L. (1985). Awaiting the new RDA's. *Journal of the American Dietetic Association, 85,* 1649.

Monson, G. (1989, December 29). Average Americans. *Austin American-Statesman,* pp. E1, E4.

Montgomery, J. E. (1982). The economics of supportive services for families with disabled and aging members. *Family Relations, 31,* 19–27.

Moore, A. J. (1985). *Childrearing practices associated with playfulness and type A behavior in children.* Unpublished doctoral dissertation, Virginia Polytechnic Institute and State University.

Moore, H. A. (1985). Job satisfaction and women's spheres of work. *Sex Roles, 13,* 663–678.

Moore, K. A., & Hofferth, S. L. (1979). Effects of women's employment on marriage: Formation, stability and roles. *Marriage and Family Review, 2*(2), 27–36.

Moore, K. A., Nord, C. W., & Peterson, J. L. (1989). Nonvoluntary sexual activity among adolescents. *Family Planning Perspectives, 21,* 110–114.

Moore, K. A., Peterson, J. L., & Furstenberg, F. F. (1986). Parental attitudes and the occurrence of early sexual activity. *Journal of Marriage and the Family, 48,* 777–782.

Moore, K. A., & Sawhill, I. V. (1984). Implication of women's employment for home and family life. In P. Voydanoff (Ed.), *Work and family: Changing roles of men and women* (pp. 153–171). Palo Alto, CA: Mayfield.

Moore, K. L. (1982). *The developing human: Clinically-oriented embryology* (3rd ed.). Philadelphia: Saunders.

Moore, N. B. (1971). *Creativity in young children.* Unpublished paper. University of Texas, Austin, TX.

Moore, N. B. (1972). *The Betty Caldwell Preschool Inventory as a measure of educational achievement in Head Start programs.* Unpublished paper. University of Texas, Austin, TX.

Moore, N. B. (1976). Everybody better feel like somebody: Some thoughts on self-concept. *Illinois Teacher of Home Economics, 19,* 162–166.

Moore, N. B. (1985a). As the twig is nurtured. *Beginnings: For Parents of Babies, Creepers and Toddlers, 5*(3), 4–5.

Moore, N. B. (1985b). Bill of rights for parents. *Living with Preschoolers: For Parents of Preschoolers, 12*(2), 7.

Moore, N. B. (1985c). Children's values: Myths and realities. *Living with Preschoolers: For Parents of Preschoolers, 12*(4), 8–10.

Moore, N. B. (1985d). The paradox of parenting. *Living with Preschoolers: For Parents of Preschoolers, 12*(3), 7.

Moore, N. B. (1985e). Problems reframed as challenges: Legacy of home economics. *The Candle, Journal of Phi Upsilon Omicron, 66,* 3–6.

Moore, N. B. (1986). Cross-cultural perspectives: Family life education as a form for strengthening families. *Marriage and Family Review, 10,* 91–113.

Moore, N. B. (1989). Family life educators and affective competencies: Shall ever the twain meet in academe? *Family Science Review, 2,* 149–161.

Moore, N. B., & Davidson, J. K., Sr. (1990, November). *Sex information sources: Do they make a difference in sexual decisions?* Paper presented at the meeting of the National Council on Family Relations, Seattle, WA.

More children lead single-parent lives. (1988, January 21). *Austin American-Statesman,* p. A-10.

Morgan, K. C., & Hock, E. (1984). A longitudinal study of psychosocial variables affecting the career patterns of women with young children. *Journal of Marriage and the Family, 46,* 383–390.

Morgan, L. A. (1988). Outcomes of marital separation: A longitudinal test of predictors. *Journal of Marriage and the Family, 50,* 493–498.

Morris, N. M., & Udry, J. R. (1983). Menstruation and marital sex. *Journal of Biosocial Science, 15,* 173–181.

Morrison, G. S. (1990). *The world of child development: Conception to adolescence.* Albany, NY: Delmar.

Morrison, M. (1986, February). 60 ways to lower your grocery bill. *Redbook,* pp. 124–128, 130.

Morrow, K. B., & Sorell, G. T. (1989). Factors affecting self-esteem, depression, and negative behaviors in sexually abused female adolescents. *Journal of Marriage and the Family, 51,* 677–686.

Mosher, D. L. (1979). Sex guilt and sex myths in college men and women. *The Journal of Sex Research, 15,* 224–234.

Mosher, D. L., & Vonderheide, S. G. (1985). Contributions of sex guilt and masturbation guilt to women's contraceptive attitudes and use. *The Journal of Sex Research, 21,* 24–39.

Mosher, W. D. (1990). Contraceptive practice in the United States, 1982–1988. *Family Planning Perspectives, 22,* 198–205.

Mosher, W. D., & Hendershot, G. E. (1984). Religious affiliation and the fertility of married couples. *Journal of Marriage and the Family, 46,* 671–677.

Moss, J. J., Apolonio, F., & Jensen, M. (1971). The premarital dyad during the sixties. *Journal of Marriage and the Family, 33,* 50–69.

Most oppose ruling. (1989, July 10). *Eau Claire Leader-Telegram,* p. 6B.

Motherhood put on hold: More thirtysomething women having children. (1989, December 1). *Eau Claire Leader-Telegram,* p. 3A.

Mott, F. L. (1986). The pace of repeated childbearing among young American mothers. *Family Planning Perspectives, 18,* 5–12.

Mott, F. L., & Moore, S. F. (1983). The tempo of remarriage among young American women. *Journal of Marriage and the Family, 45,* 427–435.

Moustakous, C. E. (1961). *Loneliness.* Englewood Cliffs, NJ: Prentice-Hall.

Moyers, B. (1989). T. Berry Brazelton. In B. S. Flowers (Ed.), *A world of ideas: Conversations with thoughtful men and women about American life today and the ideas shaping our future* (pp. 140–155). New York: Doubleday.

Muehlenhard, C. L. (1988). Misinterpreted dating behaviors and the risk of date rape. *Journal of Social & Clinical Psychology, 6,* 20–37.

Mueller, C. W., & Campbell, B. G. (1977). Female occupational achievement and marital status: A research note. *Journal of Marriage and the Family, 39,* 587–593.

Mueller, D. P., & Cooper, P. W. (1986). Children of single parent families: How they fare as young adults. *Family Relations, 35,* 169–176.

Mueller, J. M., & Fiebert, M. S. (1988). Mutual empathic perception as a correlate of satisfaction, type, and time in relationships. *Perceptual & Motor Skills, 67,* 235–238.

Muenchow, S., & Bloom-Feshbach, J. (1982, February). The new fatherhood. *Parents,* pp. 64–69.

Mulligan, T., & Katz, P. G. (1988). Erectile failure in the aged: Evaluation and treatment. *Journal of the American Geriatric Society, 36,* 54–62.

Murdock, G. P. (1949). *Social structure.* New York: Macmillan.

Murnen, S. K., Perot, A., & Byrne, D. (1989). Coping with unwanted sexual activity: Normative responses, situational determinants, and individual differences. *The Journal of Sex Research, 26,* 85–106.

Murstein, B. I. (1980). Mate selection in the 1970s. *Journal of Marriage and the Family, 42,* 777–792.

Murstein, B. I. (1986). *Paths to marriage.* Beverly Hills: Sage.

Murstein, B. I., Cerreto, M., & McDonald, M. B. (1977). A theory and investigation of the effects of exchange-orientation on marriage and friendship. *Journal of Marriage and the Family, 39,* 543–548.

Myers-Walls, J. A. (1984). Balancing multiple role responsibilities during the transition to parenthood. *Family Relations, 33,* 267–271.

Myricks, N. (1980). "Palimony": The impact of *Marvin v. Marvin. Family Relations, 29,* 210–215.

Myricks, N., & Ferullo, D. L. (1986). Race and child custody disputes. *Family Relations, 35,* 325–328.

Naisbitt, J. (1984). Time of the parenthesis. *South-Western's Momentum, 1*(1), 1.

Naisbitt, J., & Aburdene, P. (1990). *Megatrends 2000: Ten new directions for the 1990s.* New York: Morrow.

Nason, E. M., & Poloma, M. M. (1976). *Voluntarily childless couples: The emergence of a variant lifestyle.* Beverly Hills: Sage.

Nathan, S. G. (1986). The epidemiology of the DSM-III psychosexual dysfunctions. *Journal of Sex & Marital Therapy, 12,* 267–281.

Nathanson, C. A., & Becker, M. H. (1986). Family and peer influence on obtaining a method of contraception. *Journal of Marriage and the Family, 48,* 513–525.

National Center for Health Statistics. (1990a). Induced terminations of pregnancy: Reporting states, 1987. *Monthly Vital Statistics Report, 38*(9), Supplement. (DHHS Publication No. 90-1120). Hyattsville, MD: Public Health Service.

National Center for Health Statistics. (1990b). Advance report of final marriage statistics, 1987. *Monthly Vital Statistics Report, 38*(12), Supplement. (DHHS Publication No. PHS 90–1120). Hyattsville, MD: Public Health Service.

National Center for Health Statistics. (1990c). Advance report of final divorce statistics, 1987. *Monthly Vital Statistics Report, 38*(12), Supplement 2. (DHHS Publication No. 90–1120). Hyattsville, MD: Public Health Service.

National Center for Health Statistics. (1990d). Annual summary of births, marriages, divorces, and deaths: United States, 1989. *Monthly Vital Statistics Report, 38*(13). (DHHS Publication No. PHS 90–1120). Hyattsville, MD: Public Health Service.

National Center for Health Statistics. (1990e). Births, marriages, divorces, and deaths for June 1990. *Monthly Vital Statistics Report, 39*(6). (DHHS Publication No. PHS 90–1120) Hyattsville, MD: Public Health Service.

National Center for Health Statistics. (1990f). Advance report of final mortality statistics, 1988. *Monthly Vital Statistics Report, 39*(7), Supplement. (DHHS Publication No. PHS 90–1120). Hyattsville, MD: Public Health Service.

National Dairy Council. (1991). *Guide to good eating.* Rosemont, IL: Author.

National Live Stock & Meat Board. (1987). *A food guide for the first five years: Tips for feeding children one through five.* Chicago: Author.

National Research Council. (1980). *Recommended dietary allowance (RDA).* Washington, DC: National Academy of Sciences.

Neal, A. G., Groat, H. T., & Wicks, J. W. (1989). Attitudes about having children: A study of 600 couples in the early years of marriage. *Journal of Marriage and the Family, 51,* 313–328.

Neiberg, P., Marks, J. S., McLaren, N., & Remington, P. (1985). The fetal tobacco syndrome. *Journal of the American Medical Association, 253,* 2998–2999.

Neill, A. S. (1964). *Summerhill.* New York: Hart.

Nelson, M., & Nelson, G. K. (1982). Problems of equity in the reconstituted family: A social exchange analysis. *Family Relations, 31,* 223–231.

Nelson, M. K. (1988). Providing family day care: An analysis of home-based work. *Social Problems, 35,* 78–93.

Nelson, N. M., Enkin, M. W., & Saigal, S. (1980). A randomized clinical trial of the Leboyer approach to childbirth. *New England Journal of Medicine, 302,* 655–660.

Neubauer, P., & Neubauer, A. (1990). *Nature's thumbprint: The new genetics of personality.* Reading, MA: Addison-Wesley.

Neugarten, B. L., & Neugarten, D. A. (1986). The changing meanings of age. In A. Pifer & L. Bronte (Eds.), *Our aging society: Paradox and promise* (pp. 33–51). New York: Norton.

New laws recognizing marital rape as a crime. (1984, December 29). *The New York Times,* p. 5.

New prenatal test for birth defects found safe, effective. (1988, May 7). *Eau Claire Leader-Telegram,* p. 11A.

Newcomb, M. D. (1985). Sexual experience among men and women: Associations within three independent samples. *Psychological Reports, 56,* 603–614.

Newcomb, M. D. (1986). Sexual behavior of cohabitors: A comparison of three independent samples. *The Journal of Sex Research, 22,* 492–513.

Newcomb, M. D., & Bentler, P. M. (1980a). Assessment of personality and demographic aspects of cohabitation and marital success. *Journal of Personality Development, 4,* 11–24.

Newcomb, M. D., & Bentler, P. M. (1980b). Cohabitation before marriage: A comparison of married couples who did and did not cohabit. *Alternative Lifestyles, 3,* 65–68.

Newcomb, P. R. (1979). Cohabitation in America: An assessment of consequences. *Journal of Marriage and the Family, 41,* 597–603.

Newcomer, S., & Udry, J. R. (1987). Parental marital status effects on adolescent sexual behavior. *Journal of Marriage and the Family, 49,* 235–240.

Newcomer, S. F., & Udry, J. R. (1984). Mothers' influence on the sexual behavior of their teenage children. *Journal of Marriage and the Family, 46,* 477–485.

Nissenson, M. (1987). Therapy after sixty. In H. Cox (Ed.), *Aging* (5th ed., pp. 113–116). Guilford, CT: Dushkin.

Nock, S. L. (1979). The family life cycle: Empirical or conceptual tool. *Journal of Marriage and the Family, 41,* 15–26.

Nock, S. L. (1982). Enduring effects of marital disruption and subsequent living arrangements. *Journal of Family Issues, 3,* 25–40.

Nock, S. L. (1987). *Sociology of the family.* Englewood Cliffs, NJ: Prentice-Hall.

Nock, S. L., & Kingston, P. W. (1987, April). *Time with children: The impact of couples' commitments.* Paper presented at the meeting of the Southern Sociological Society, Atlanta, GA.

Nolan, J. W. (1986). Developmental concerns and the health of midlife women. *Nursing Clinics of North America, 21,* 151–159.

Noller, P. (1984). *Nonverbal communication and marital interaction.* Oxford, England: Pergamon Press.

Noller, P., & Fitzpatrick, M. A. (1990). Marital communication in the eighties. *Journal of Marriage and the Family, 52,* 832–843.

Nordheimer, J. (1986, March 28). Fear of AIDS may spell the end of the "sexual revolution." *Gainesville Sun,* p. 8A.

Norton, A. J., & Glick, P. C. (1986). One parent families: A social and economic profile. *Family Relations, 35,* 9–17.

Norton, A. J., & Moorman, J. E. (1987). Current trends in marriage and divorce among American women. *Journal of Marriage and the Family, 49,* 3–14.

Notarius, C. I., & Johnson, J. S. (1982). Emotional expression in husbands and wives. *Journal of Marriage and the Family, 44,* 483–489.

Number of AIDS cases through September 1990. (1990). *Medical Aspects of Human Sexuality, 24*(12), 52.

Number of sexually active young women increasing. (1991, January 5). *Eau Claire Leader-Telegram,* p. 10A.

Nuta, V. R. (1986). Emotional aspects of child support enforcement. *Family Relations, 35,* 177–181.

Nutter, D., & Condron, M. (1983). Sexual fantasy and activity patterns of females with inhibited sexual desire versus normal controls. *Journal of Sex and Marital Therapy, 9,* 276–282.

Nye, F. I. (1979). Choice, exchange, and the family. In W. R. Burr, F. I. Nye, & I. L. Reiss (Eds.), *Contemporary theories about the family,* Volume 2 (pp. 1–42). New York: Free Press.

Nye, F. I. (1980). Family mini-theories as special instances of choice and exchange theory. *Journal of Marriage and the Family, 42,* 479–489.

Nye, F. I. (1988). Fifty years of family research 1937–1987. *Journal of Marriage and the Family, 50,* 305–316.

Oates, R. K., Davis, A. A., & Ryan, M. G. (1983). Predictive factors for child abuse. In R. J. Gelles & C. P. Cornell (Eds.), *International perspectives on family violence* (pp. 97–106). Lexington, MA: Lexington Books.

O'Bryant, S. L., & Nocera, D. (1985). The psychological significance of "home" to older widows. *Psychology of Women Quarterly, 9,* 403–412.

O'Connell, M., & Rogers, C. C. (1984). Out-of-wedlock births, premarital pregnancies and their effect on family formation and dissolution. *Family Planning Perspectives, 16,* 157–162.

O'Flaherty, K. M., & Eells, L. W. (1988). Courtship behavior of the remarried. *Journal of Marriage and the Family, 50,* 499–506.

O'Kane, M. L. (1981). *Living with adult children.* St. Paul: Diction Books.

Okie, S. (1989, April 28). New birth control approved. *Austin American-Statesman,* pp. 1A, 10A.

O'Laughlin, K. (1983). The final challenge: Facing death. In E. W. Markson (Ed.), *Older women: Issues and prospects* (pp. 275–296). Lexington, MA: Lexington Books.

Olday, D., & Wesley, B. (1988). Dating violence: A comparison of high school and college subsamples. *Free Inquiry in Creative Sociology, 16*(2), 183–190.

Olds, S. B., London, M. L., & Ladewig, P. A. (1984). *Maternal-newborn nursing* (2nd ed.). Reading, MA: Addison-Wesley.

O'Leary, K. D., & Arias, I. (1983). The influence of marital therapy on sexual satisfaction. *Journal of Sex & Marital Therapy, 9,* 171–181.

O'Leary, K. D., & Arias, I. (1984, August). *Assessing reliability of reports of spouse abuse.* Paper presented at the Family Violence Research Conference, Durham, NH.

O'Leary, K. D., & Curley, A. D. (1986). Assertion and family violence: Correlates of spouse abuse. *Journal of Marital and Family Therapy, 12,* 281–289.

Olesker, E., & Walsh, L. V. (1984). Childbearing among lesbians: Are we meeting their needs? *Journal of Nurse-Midwifery, 29,* 322–329.

Olshansky, E. F., & Sammons, L. N. (1985). Artificial insemination: An overview. *Journal of Obstetric, Gynecologic, and Neonatal Nursing, 14,* 49S-54S.

Olson, D. H. (1982). *Family inventories.* St. Paul: Department of Family Social Science, University of Minnesota.

Olson, D. H., Fourier, D., & Druckman, J. (1982). *Counselor's manual for PREPARE ENRICH* (rev. ed.). Minneapolis: PREPARE-ENRICH.

Olson, D. H., Russell, C. S., & Sprenkle, D. H. (1980). Marital and family therapy: A decade review. *Journal of Marriage and the Family, 42,* 973–993.

O'Reilly, J. (1983, September 5). Wife beating: The silent crime. *Time,* pp. 23–24, 26.

Orlinsky, D. E. (1977). Love relationships in the life cycle: A developmental interpersonal perspective. In H. A. Otto (Ed.), *Love today: A new exploration* (pp. 135–150). New York: Dell.

Orr, D. P., & Downes, M. C. (1985). Self-concept of adolescent sexual abuse victims. *Journal of Youth and Adolescence, 14,* 401–410.

Orr, M. T., Forrest, J. D., Johnson, J. H., & Tolman, D. L. (1985). The provision of sterilization services by private physicians. *Family Planning Perspectives, 17,* 216–220.

Ortega, S. T., Whitt, H. P., & Williams, J. A., Jr. (1988). Religious homogamy and marital happiness. *Journal of Family Issues, 9,* 224–239.

Ory, M. G. (1978). The decision to parent or not: Normative and structural components. *Journal of Marriage and the Family, 40,* 531–539.

O'Shaughnessy, R. W., Zuspan, F. P., Pariser, S. F., Nelson, P., & Boutselis, J. G. (1983). Obstetrics-gynecology and clinical sexuality. In S. F. Pariser, S. B. Levine, & M. L. Gardner (Eds.), *Clinical sexuality* (pp. 85–96). New York: Dekker-Marcel.

Osmond, M. W. (1978). Reciprocity: A dynamic model and a method to study marital power. *Journal of Marriage and the Family, 40,* 49–61.

Oster, S. M. (1987). A note on the determinants of alimony. *Journal of Marriage and the Family, 49,* 81–86.

Osterweis, M. (1987). Bereavement and the elderly. In H. Cox (Ed.), *Aging* (5th ed., pp. 175–179). Guilford, CT: Dushkin.

Ostling, R. N. (1988, October 3). The intermarriage quandary. *Time,* p. 82.

Ostling, R. N. (1989, November 13). The battle over gay clergy. *Time,* pp. 89–90.

Overstreet, H. (1949). *The mature mind.* New York: Norton.

Oxorn, H., & Foote, W. R. (1975). *Human labor and birth* (3rd ed.). New York: Appleton-Century-Crofts.

Ozick, C. (1988, March 28). A critic at large: Sholem Aleichem's revolution. *The New Yorker,* pp. 99–108.

Packard, V. (1968). *The sexual wilderness.* New York: McKay.

Page, E. W., Villee, C. A., & Villee, D. B. (1981). *Human reproduction: Essentials of reproductive and perinatal medicine.* Philadelphia: Saunders.

Pagelow, M. D. (1980). Heterosexual and lesbian single mothers: A comparison of problems, coping, and solutions. *Journal of Homosexuality, 5*(3), 189–204.

Pagelow, M. D. (1981). *Woman-battering: Victims and their experiences.* Beverly Hills: Sage.

Palimony case returns to lower court in state. (1987, May 12). *Eau Claire Leader-Telegram,* p. 6B.

Paluszny, M., & Thombre, M. (1987). Pregnancy and the female physician. *Medical Aspects of Human Sexuality, 21*(7), 62, 66, 69–71.

Papalia, D. E., & Olds, S. W. (1990). *A child's world: Infancy through adolescence* (5th ed.). New York: McGraw-Hill.

Papalia, D. E., Olds, S. W., & Feldman, R. D. (1989). *Human development* (4th ed.). New York: McGraw-Hill.

Parents and abortion: State-by-state guide. (1990, June 26). *USA Today,* p. 6A.

Parks, M., Stan, C., & Eggert, L. (1983). Romantic involvement and social network involvement. *Social Psychology Quarterly, 46,* 116–131.

Parlett, R. L., & Lipton, K. L. (1987). A look ahead at food prices. In K. L. Lipton & J. King (Eds.), *National food review* (pp. 11–12). Washington, DC: U.S. Department of Agriculture.

Parmalee, A. H., Jr., & Sigman, M. D. (1983). Perinatal brain development and behavior. In P. H. Mussen (Ed.), *Handbook of child psychology: Volume 2, Infancy and developmental psychobiology* (4th ed., pp. 95–155). New York: Wiley.

Parsons, T. & Bales, R. F. (1955). *Family, socialization, and interaction process.* Glencoe, IL: Free Press.

Pasley, B. K., & Ihinger-Tallman, M. (1989). Boundary ambiguity in remarriage: Does ambiguity differentiate degree of marital adjustment and integration? *Family Relations, 38,* 46–52.

Pasley, K., & Ihinger-Tallman, M. (1985). Portraits of stepfamily life in popular literature: 1940–1980. *Family Relations, 34,* 527–534.

Pasley, K., Ihinger-Tallman, M., & Coleman, C. (1984). Consensus styles among happy and unhappy remarried couples. *Family Relations, 33,* 451–457.

Pastor, D. L. (1981). The quality of mother-infant attachment and its relationship to toddlers' initial sociability with peers. *Developmental Psychology, 17,* 326–335.

Patterson, G. R. (1975). *Families: Applications of social learning in family life.* Champaign, IL: Research Press.

Patterson, G. R. (1982). *Social learning approach to family intervention: Coercive family process.* Vol. 3. Eugene, OR: Castalia Press.

Pattison, E. M. (1985). Violent marriages. *Medical Aspects of Human Sexuality, 19*(1), 57, 61–62, 68, 73–74.

Patton, M. S. (1985). Masturbation from Judaism to Victorianism. *Journal of Religion and Health, 24,* 133–146.

The pay gap between men and women. (1990, October 29). *Business Week,* p. 57.

Pear, R. (1988, March 13). Patients facing increased costs at nursing homes. *The New York Times,* pp. 1A, 29A.

Pearl, D., Bouthilet, L., & Lazar, J. (1982). *Television and behavior: Ten years of scientific progress and implications for the eighties,* Volume 1. Washington, DC: U.S. Government Printing Office.

Pearson, J., Munson, P., & Thoennes, N. (1983). Children's rights and child custody proceedings. *Journal of Divorce, 7*(2), 1–21.

Peck, M. S. (1978). *The road less traveled: A new psychology of love, traditional values, and spiritual growth.* New York: Simon and Schuster.

Peek, C. W., Bell, N. J., Waldren, T., & Sorell, G. T. (1988). Patterns of functioning in families of remarried and first-married couples. *Journal of Marriage and the Family, 50,* 699–708.

Peele, S., & Brodsky, A. (1976). *Love and addiction.* New York: New American Library.

Peery, J. C., Jensen, L., & Adams, G. R. (1985). The relationship between parents' attitudes toward child rearing and the sociometric status of their preschool children. *The Journal of Psychology, 119,* 567–574.

Pelletier, L. A., & Herold, E. S. (1988). The relationship of age, sex guilt, and sexual experience with female sexual fantasies. *The Journal of Sex Research, 24,* 250–256.

Pennar, K., & Mervosh, E. (1985, January 28). Women at work. *Business Week,* pp. 80–85.

Peplau, L. A., & Cochran, S. D. (1981). Value orientations in the intimate relationships of gay men. *Journal of Homosexuality, 6*(2), 1–19.

Peplau, L. A., Padesky, C., & Hamilton, M. (1982). Satisfaction in lesbian relationships. *Journal of Homosexuality, 8*(2), 23–35.

Perelman, M. A. (1980). Treatment of premature ejaculation. In S. R. Leiblum & L. A. Pervin (Eds.), *Principles and practice of sex therapy* (pp. 199–233). New York: Guilford Press.

Peretti, P. O., & Banks, D. (1984). Negative psycho-social variables of the incestuous daughter of father-daughter incest. *Child Psychiatry Quarterly, 17,* 15–20.

Perlman, S. D. (1981). Sexual satisfaction in married and cohabitating couples (Doctoral dissertation, University of California-Los Angeles, 1980). *Dissertation Abstracts International, 41,* 4682A.

Pestrak, V. A., Martin, D., & Martin, M. (1985). Extramarital sex: An examination of the literature. *International Journal of Family Therapy, 7,* 107–115.

Peters, J. F. (1980). High school dating: Implication for equality. *International Journal of Comparative Sociology, 21,* 109–118.

Petersen, A. C. (1987, September). Those gangly years. *Psychology Today,* pp. 28–34.

Petersen, L. R. (1986). Interfaith marriage and religious commitment among Catholics. *Journal of Marriage and the Family, 48,* 725–735.

Peterson, J. L., & Nord, C. W. (1990). The regular receipt of child support: A multistep process. *Journal of Marriage and the Family, 52,* 539–551.

Peterson, K. S. (1990, January 17). $150,000 to raise a kid. *USA Today,* p. 1A.

Petranek, C. F. (1981). Dating behavior. In A. W. Frank, III (Ed.), *The encyclopedia of sociology new and updated* (p. 26). Guilford, CT: DPC Reference.

Petroni, F. A. (1974). Teen-age interracial dating. In O. Pocs & R. H. Walsh (Eds.), *Readings in marriage and the family 75/76* (pp. 32–36). Guilford, CT: Dushkin.

Pett, M. A., & Vaughan-Cole, B. (1986). The impact of income issues and social status on post-divorce adjustment of custodial parents. *Family Relations, 35,* 103–111.

Pettit, E. J., & Bloom, B. L. (1984). Whose decision was it? The effects of initiator status on adjustment to marital disruption. *Journal of Marriage and the Family, 46,* 587–595.

Phear, W. P. C., Beck, J. C., Hauser, B. B., Clark, S. C., & Whitney, R. A. (1984). An empirical study of custody agreements: Joint versus sole legal custody. *Journal of Psychiatry & Law, 11,* 419–441.

Philliber, S. G., & Philliber, W. W. (1985). Social and psychological perspectives on voluntary sterilization: A review. *Studies in Family Planning, 16,* 1–29.

Philliber, S. G., & Tatum, M. L. (1982). Sex education and the double standard in high school. *Adolescence, 17,* 273–283.

Philliber, W. W., & Hiller, D. V. (1983). Relative occupational attainments of spouses and later changes in marriage and wife's work experience. *Journal of Marriage and the Family, 45,* 161–170.

Piaget, J. (1967). *Six psychological studies.* New York: Random House.

Piaget, J. (1970). Piaget's theory. In P. H. Mussen (Ed.), *Carmichael's manual of child psychology,* Volume 1 (pp. 703–732). New York: Wiley.

Pierce, L. H. (1987). Father-son incest: Using the literature to guide practice. *Social Casework, 68,* 67–74.

Pierce, R., & Pierce, L. (1985). Analysis of sexual abuse hotline reports. *Child Abuse and Neglect, 9,* 37–45.

Piercy, F. P., & Sprenkle, D. H. (1990). Marriage and family therapy: A decade review. *Journal of Marriage and the Family, 52,* 1116–1126.

Pietropinto, A. (1986). Cohabitation by the unmarried. *Medical Aspects of Human Sexuality, 20*(8), 63–64, 69.

Pietropinto, A. (1987). Survey: Sexual abstinence. *Medical Aspects of Human Sexuality, 21*(7), 115–118.

Pietropinto, A., & Simenauer, J. (1977). *Beyond the male myth.* Chicago: New American Library.

Pike, E., & Hall, S. (1985). College dating: Games, strategies and peeves. In J. M. Henslin (Ed.), *Marriage and family in a changing society* (2nd ed., pp. 225–231). New York: Free Press.

Pill appears to provide long-term protection against endometrial cancer and ovarian cancer. (1987). *Family Planning Perspectives, 19,* 126–127.

Pill, C. J. (1990). Stepfamilies: Redefining the family. *Family Relations, 39,* 186–193.

The Pill may raise cyst risk. (1988, June 3). *USA Today,* p. 1D.

Pill users who delay first pregnancy till 30s are slow to conceive. (1986). *Family Planning Perspectives, 18,* 140–141.

Pillemer, K. A., & Wolf, R. S. (Eds.). (1986). *Elder abuse: Conflict in the family.* Dover, MA: Auburn House.

Pines, A., & Aronson, E. (1983). Antecedents, correlates, and consequences of sexual jealousy. *Journal of Personality, 51,* 108–136.

Pinhas, V. (1987). Sexual dysfunction in women alcoholics. *Medical Aspects of Human Sexuality, 21*(6), 97–98, 100–101.

Pink, J. E. T., & Wampler, K. S. (1985). Problem areas in stepfamilies: Cohesion, adaptability, and the stepfather-adolescent relationship. *Family Relations, 34,* 327–335.

Pinney, E. M., Gerrard, M., & Denney, N. W. (1987). The Pinney sexual satisfaction inventory. *The Journal of Sex Research, 23,* 233–251.

Piotrkowski, C. S., & Crits-Christoph, P. (1982). Women's jobs and family adjustment. In J. Aldous (Ed.), *Two paychecks: Life in dual-earner families* (pp. 105–127). Beverly Hills: Sage.

Pirog-Good, M., & Stets, J. (1986, August). *Violence in dating relationships.* Paper presented at the meeting of the American Sociological Association, New York, NY.

Piscitelli, J. T., & Parker, R. T. (1986). Primary care in the postmenopausal woman. *Clinics in Obstetrics and Gynecology, 29,* 343–352.

Pittman, J. F., & Orthner, D. K. (1988). Predictors of spousal support for the work commitments of husbands. *Journal of Marriage and the Family, 50,* 335–348.

Placek, P., Taffel, S., & Moien, M. (1983). Cesarean section delivery rates: United States, 1981. *American Journal of Public Health, 73,* 861–862.

Pleck, J. H. (1981, September). Prisoners of manliness. *Psychology Today,* pp. 69–70, 72–74, 77, 79, 83.

Pleck, J. H. (1984). The work-family role system. In P. Voydanoff (Ed.), *Work and family: Changing roles of men and women* (pp. 8–19). Palo Alto, CA: Mayfield.

Pleck, J. H. (1985). *Working wives/working husbands.* Beverly Hills: Sage.

Plutzer, E. (1986, August). *Attitudes toward abortion: A study of the social and ideological bases of public opinion.* Paper presented at the meeting of the American Sociological Association, New York, NY.

Pocs, O., & Walsh, R. H. (1985). Termination of relationships. In O. Pocs & R. H. Walsh (Eds.), *Annual editions: Marriage and family 85/86* (pp. 166–167). Guilford, CT: Dushkin.

Poffenberger, T. (1964). Three papers on going steady. *Family Life Coordinator, 8,* 7–13.

Pogrebin, L. C. (1983). *Family politics on an intimate frontier.* New York: McGraw-Hill.

Polenz, J. M. (1981). *In defense of marriage.* New York: Gardner.

Polit, D. F., & Falbo, T. (1987). Only children and personality development: A quantitative review. *Journal of Marriage and the Family, 49,* 309–325.

Poll: Japanese women content with status. (1990, December 17). *Eau Claire Leader-Telegram,* p. 5A.

Poll: Women's, men's attitudes toward sex, marriage changing. (1985, October 21). *Gainesville Sun,* p. 3C.

Pollitt, K. (1986, September 20). Being wedded is not always bliss. *The Nation,* pp. 239–242.

Poloma, M. M., & Garland, T. N. (1971). The myth of the egalitarian family: Familial roles and the professionally employed wife. In A. Theodore (Ed.), *The professional woman* (pp. 741–752). Cambridge, MA: Schenkman.

Poloma, M. M., Pendleton, B. F., & Garland, T. N. (1982). Reconsidering the dual-career marriage: A longitudinal approach. In J. Aldous (Ed.), *Two paychecks: Life in dual-earner families* (pp. 173–192). Beverly Hills: Sage.

Porter, B. R., & Chatelain, R. S. (1981). Family life education for single parent families. *Family Relations, 30,* 517–525.

Porter, N. L., & Christopher, F. S. (1984). Infertility: Towards an awareness of a need among family life practitioners. *Family Relations, 34,* 309–315.

Porterfield, E. (1974). Mixed marriage. In O. Pocs (Ed.), *Readings in marriage and family 75/76* (pp. 66–72). Guilford, CT: Dushkin.

Porterfield, E. (1982). American intermarriages in the United States. In G. Crester & J. J. Leon (Eds.), *Intermarriage in the United States* (pp. 17–34). New York: Haworth Press.

Potts, M. (1983). Looking into the future. *Planned Parenthood Review, 3,* 3–5.

Poussaint, A. F. (1983, August). The black male-white female: An update. *Ebony,* pp. 124, 126, 128.

Powell, B., & Steelman, L. C. (1982). Testing an undertested comparison: Maternal effects on sons' and daughters' attitudes toward women in the labor force. *Journal of Marriage and the Family, 44,* 349–355.

Powell, G. S., & Wampler, K. S. (1982). Marriage enrichment participants: Levels of marital satisfaction. *Family Relations, 31,* 389–393.

Power, T. G., & Chapieski, M. L. (1986). Child rearing and impulse control in toddlers: A naturalistic investigation. *Developmental Psychology, 22,* 271–275.

Powledge, T. M. (1981). Unnatural selection. In H. B. Holmes, B. B. Hoskins, & M. Gross (Eds.), *The custom-made child? Women centered perspectives* (pp. 193–200). Clifton, NJ: Humana Press.

Prasinos, S., & Tittler, B. I. (1984). The existential context of lovestyles: An empirical study. *Journal of Humanistic Psychology, 24,* 95–112.

Pratt, W. F., & Bachrach, C. A. (1987). What do women use when they stop using the pill? *Family Planning Perspectives, 19,* 257–266.

Preble, M. E. (1978, February). *College students' perceptions of cohabitation.* Paper presented at the Symposium of Alpha Kappa Delta, Richmond, VA.

Prescod, S. (Ed.). (1987). Teenagers must be educated that they are a high-risk AIDS group. *Marriage and Divorce Today, 12*(51), 1.

Prescott, D. (1952). A role of love in human development. *Journal of Home Economics, 44,* 173–176.

Press, A., Prout, L. R., & Pedersen, D. (1984, January 2). Suffer the little children. *Newsweek,* p. 47.

Presser, H. B. (1986). Shift work among American women and child care. *Journal of Marriage and the Family, 48,* 551–563.

Presser, H. B. (1988). Shift work and child care among dual-earner American parents. *Journal of Marriage and the Family, 50,* 113–148.

Preston, S. (1984). Children and the elderly in the U.S. *Scientific American, 250*(6), 44–49.

Price, J. A., & Price, J. H. (1983). Alcohol and sexual functioning: A review. *Psychosocial Constructs of Alcoholism and Substance Abuse, 2,* 43–56.

Price, J. H. (1982). High school students' attitudes toward homosexuality. *The Journal of School Health, 52,* 469–474.

Price-Bonham, S., & Balswick, J. O. (1980). The noninstitutions: Divorce, desertion, and remarriage. *Journal of Marriage and the Family, 42,* 959–972.

Prochaska, J. M., & Prochaska, J. O. (1985). Children's views of the causes and "cures" of sibling rivalry. *Child Welfare, 64,* 427–433.

Providing a will—And peace of mind. (1986, February). *Consumer Research,* pp. 19–22.

Public opinion on abortion shifts. (1990). *Family Planning Perspectives, 22,* 197.

Purvis, A. (1990, December 24). A pill that gets under the skin. *Time,* p. 66.

Putallaz, M. (1987). Maternal behavior and children's sociometric status. *Child Development, 58,* 324–340.

Put to the test. (1982, February). *Time,* p. 59.

Quick, D., & Quick, S. (Eds.). (1986). *Building strong blended families: Key elements.* Lexington, MA: Department of Family Studies, University of Kentucky.

Quinn, J. B. (1979). *Everyone's money book.* New York: Dell Books.

Quinn, J. B. (1988, April 17). Credit card issuers use behavior scoring to rate customers. *Eau Claire Leader-Telegram,* p. 2D.

Quinn, W. H. (1983). Personal and family adjustment in later life. *Journal of Marriage and the Family, 45,* 57–73.

Quinton, D., & Rutter, N. (1984). Parents with children in care: Current circumstances and parenting. *Journal of Child Psychology & Psychiatry, 25,* 211–229.

Quotable quotes. (1989, October 1). *No-name newsletter,* p. 1.

Raabe, P. H., & Gessner, J. C. (1988). Employer family-supportive policies: Diverse variations on the theme. *Family Relations, 37,* 196–202.

Rakowski, W., Barber, C. E., & Seelbach, W. C. (1983). Perceptions of parental health status and attitudes toward aging. *Family Relations, 32,* 93–99.

Ramos, S. (1979). *The complete book of child custody.* New York: Putnam's.

Rank, M. R. (1982). Determinants of conjugal influence in wives' employment decision making. *Journal of Marriage and the Family, 44,* 591–604.

Rankin, D. (1986a, August 17). How tax reform is reshaping divorce. *The New York Times,* p. 11F.

Rankin, D. (1986b, April 13). When the child support payments stop. *The New York Times,* p. 11F.

Rankin, R. P., & Maneker, J. S. (1985). The duration of marriage in a divorcing population: The impact of children. *Journal of Marriage and the Family, 47,* 43–52.

Rasmusson, R. C. (1970, September). On being wise parents. *Hearthstone, The Magazine for the Christian Home,* pp. 1–4, 31.

Rath, L. E., Harmin, M., & Simon, S. B. (1966). *Values and teaching: Working with values in the classroom.* Columbus, OH: Merrill.

Raven, B., Centers, R., & Rodrigues, A. (1975). The bases of conjugal power. In R. W. Cromwell & D. H. Olson (Eds.), *Power in families* (pp. 217–234). Beverly Hills: Sage.

Reamy, K. J. (1991). A management guide to post-partum problems. *Medical Aspects of Human Sexuality, 25*(i), 20–24.

Reamy, K. J., & White, S. E. (1985). Dyspareunia in pregnancy. *Journal of Psychosomatic Obstetrics and Gynecology, 4,* 263–270.

Reardon, P. (1989, October 10). Families worry about time bind. *Austin American-Statesman,* p. A1, A4.

Reath, R. A., Piercy, F., Hovestadt, A., & Oliver, M. (1980). Assertion and marital adjustment. *Family Relations, 29,* 249–253.

Reeves, P. (1988, January 24). Metropolitan mortgages average $939 a month. *Eau Claire Leader-Telegram,* pp. 1C-2C.

Reform Judaism OKs homosexual rabbis. (1990, June 26). *The Houston Post,* p. A-7.

Regan, M. C., & Roland, H. E. (1985). Rearranging family and career priorities: Professional women and men of the eighties. *Journal of Marriage and the Family, 47,* 985-992.

Reilly, T. W., Entwisle, D. R., & Doering, S. G. (1987). Socialization into parenthood: A longitudinal study of the development of self-evaluations. *Journal of Marriage and the Family, 49,* 295–308.

Rein, M. F. (1985). Condoms and STDs: Do the former prevent transmission of the latter? *Medical Aspects of Human Sexuality, 19*(6), 113–117.

Reinhardt, C. M. (1985). Sex-role identity, sex-role behaviors, and self-esteem in women in traditional and non-traditional female careers (Doctoral dissertation, Boston College, 1984). *Dissertation Abstracts International, 46,* 1569A–1570A.

Reinisch, J. M. (1988, October 17). Sexual orientation labels do not always reflect behavior risks for HIV. *Behavior Today,* p. 6.

Reiss, I. L. (1960). *Premarital sexual standards in America.* New York: Free Press.

Reiss, I. L. (1967). *The social context of premarital sexual permissiveness.* New York: Holt, Rinehart and Winston.

Reiss, I. L. (1981). Some observations on ideology and sexuality in America. *Journal of Marriage and the Family, 43,* 271–283.

Reiss, I. L., Anderson, R. E., & Sponaugle, G. C. (1980). A multivariate model of the determinants of extramarital sexual permissiveness. *Journal of Marriage and the Family, 42,* 395–411.

Reiss, I. L., & Lee, G. R. (1988). *Family systems in America* (4th ed.). New York: Holt, Rinehart and Winston.

Reiss, I. L., & Reiss, H. M. (1990). *An end to shame: Shaping our next sexual revolution.* Buffalo, NY: Prometheus Books.

Rempel, J. (1985). Childless elderly: What are they missing? *Journal of Marriage and the Family, 47,* 343–348.

Rempel, J. K., Holmes, J. G., & Zanna, M. P. (1985). Trust in close relationships. *Journal of Personality and Social Psychology, 49,* 95–112.

Renshaw, D. C. (1983). Communication in marriage. *Medical Aspects of Human Sexuality, 17*(6), 199, 206–207, 210–211, 215, 218–220.

Renshaw, D. C. (1984). Geriatric sex problems. *Journal of Geriatric Psychiatry, 17,* 123–124.

Renzetti, C. M., & Curran, D. J. (1989). *Women, men and society: The sociology of gender.* Boston: Allyn and Bacon.

Reports on television. (1987, February 22). *Eau Claire Leader-Telegram,* p. 1F.

Research Forecasts, Inc. (1981). *The Tampax report: A summary of survey results on a study of attitudes toward menstruation.* New York: Author.

Research on healthy marriages. (1989). *Family Therapy Today, 4*(3), 4.

Rexroat, C. (1985). Women's work expectations and labor-market experience in early and middle family life cycle stages. *Journal of Marriage and the Family, 47,* 131–142.

Rhodes, J. P., & Rhodes, E. L. (1984, June). Commuter marriage: The toughest alternative. *Ms.,* pp. 44–48.

Rhyne, D. (1981). Bases of marital satisfaction among men and women. *Journal of Marriage and the Family, 43,* 941–955.

Richards, M. P. M. (1981). Effects of analgesics and anesthetics given in childbirth on child development. *Neuropharmacology, 20,* 1259–1265.

Richardson, L. (1988). *The dynamics of sex and gender: A sociological perspective* (3rd ed.). New York: Harper & Row.

Richmond-Abbott, M. (1979). *The American woman: Her past, her present, her future.* New York: Holt, Rinehart & Winston.

Ricks, S. S. (1985). Father-infant interactions: A review of empirical research. *Family Relations, 34,* 505–511.

Ridley, C. A., Lamke, L. K., Avery, A. W., & Harrell, J. E. (1982). The effects of interpersonal skills training on sex-role identity of premarital dating partners. *Journal of Research and Personality, 16,* 335–342.

Ridley, C. A., Peterman, D. J., & Avery, A. W. (1978). Cohabitation: Does it make for a better marriage? *The Family Coordinator, 27,* 129–136.

Riffer, R. L., & Chin, J. C. (1988). Dating satisfaction among college students. *The International Journal of Sociology and Social Policy, 8,* 29–36.

Riley, D., & Cochran, M. M. (1985). Naturally occurring childrearing advice for fathers: Utilization of the personal social network. *Journal of Marriage and the Family, 47,* 275–286.

Rindfuss, R. R., & St. John, C. (1983). Social determinants of age at first birth. *Journal of Marriage and the Family, 45,* 553–565.

Rinzler, C. E. (1986, July). Checks and balances: Picking an account that really pays. *Mademoiselle,* p. 68.

Rischer, L. R. (1983). Mothers and mothers-in-law. *Journal of Marriage and the Family, 45,* 187–192.

Rise in cesarean births continues unabated, postcesarean vaginal deliveries remain rare. (1987). *Family Planning Perspectives, 19,* 164–165.

Risman, B., & Park, K. (1986, August). *Parents without partners: A comparison of single male and female custodial parents.* Paper presented at the meeting of the American Sociological Association, New York, NY.

Risman, B. J. (1986). Can men "mother"? Life as a single father. *Family Relations, 35,* 95–102.

Risman, B. J., Hill, C. T., Rubin, Z., & Peplau, L. A. (1981). Living together in college: Implications for courtship. *Journal of Marriage and the Family, 43,* 77–83.

Roach, M. J., & Kitson, G. C. (1987, November). *The impact of forewarning on adjustment to widowhood and divorce.* Paper presented at the meeting of the National Council on Family Relations, Atlanta, GA.

Roark, A. C. (1989, September 7). Study links substance use, "latchkey" kids. *Austin American-Statesman,* pp. A1, A4.

Robbins, J. M., & DeLamater, J. D. (1985). Support from significant others and loneliness following induced abortion. *Social Psychiatry, 20,* 92–99.

Roberts, C. R. (1983). Depth of involvement, imagery, and day-dreaming: A study of altered states of consciousness and orgasmic success in women (Doctoral dissertation, California School of Professional Psychology, Fresno, 1982). *Dissertation Abstracts International, 44,* 597B.

Roberts, E. J., & Holt, S. A. (1980). Parent child communication about sexuality. *SIECUS Report, 8*(4), 1–2, 10.

Roberts, E. J., Kline, D., & Gagnon, J. (1978). *Family life and sexual learning, Volume 1.* Cambridge, MA: Population Education.

Roberts, L. J., & Krokoff, L. J. (1990). A time-series analysis of withdrawal, hostility, and displeasure in satisfied and dissatisfied marriages. *Journal of Marriage and the Family, 52,* 95–105.

Robinson, B. E. (1984). The contemporary American stepfather. *Family Relations, 33,* 381–388.

Robinson, B. E., & Barret, R. L. (1986). *The developing father: Emerging roles in contemporary society.* New York: Guilford Press.

Robinson, I. E., & Jedlicka, D. (1982). Change in sexual attitudes and behavior of college students from 1965 to 1980: A research note. *Journal of Marriage and the Family, 44,* 237–240.

Robinson, J. P. (1981). Television and leisure time: A new scenario. *Journal of Communication, 31,* 120–130.

Roden, M., Bulcroft, K., & Nordstrom, B. (1986, March). *Definitions of love and romance over the life cycle.* Paper presented at the meeting of the Midwest Sociological Society, Des Moines, IA.

Rodgers, R. H., & Conrad, L. M. (1986). Courtship for remarriage: Influences on family reorganization after divorce. *Journal of Marriage and the Family, 48,* 767–775.

Rodman, H., Pratto, D. J., & Nelson, R. S. (1985). Child care arrangements and children's functioning: A comparison of self-care and adult-care children. *Developmental Psychology, 21,* 413–418.

Roel, R. E., (1990, November 27). Parental guidance. *Austin American-Statesman,* pp. D1, D4.

Roel, R. E. (1991, January 20). Family issues to dominate Congress' domestic agenda. *The Milwaukee Journal,* p. J6.

Roff, L. L., & Klemmack, D. L. (1986). Norms for employed daughters' and sons' behavior toward frail older parents. *Sex Roles, 14,* 363–368.

Roiphe, A. (1973, November 18). The Waltons: Ma and Pa and John-Boy in mythic America. *The New York Times Magazine,* pp. 40–41, 130, 134, 146.

Rolfe, D. J. (1985). Preparing the previously married for second marriage. *The Journal of Pastoral Care, 39,* 110–119.

Rook, K. S. (1987). Reciprocity of social exchange and social satisfaction among older women. *Journal of Personality and Social Psychology, 52,* 145–154.

Roper, B. S., & LaBeff, E. (1977). Sex roles and feminism revisited: An intergenerational attitude comparison. *Journal of Marriage and the Family, 39,* 113–119.

Roper Organization. (1980). *The 1980 Virginia Slims American women's poll.* New York: Author.

Roper Organization. (1986). *The 1985 Virginia Slims American women's poll.* New York: Author.

Roscoe, B., & Benaske, N. (1985). Courtship violence experienced by abused wives: Similarities in patterns of abuse. *Family Relations, 34,* 419–424.

Roscoe, B., & Callahan, J. E. (1985). Adolescents self-report of violence in families and dating relations. *Adolescence, 20,* 545–553.

Rose, S. M. (1985). Same- and cross-sex friendships and the psychology of homosociality. *Sex Roles, 12,* 63–74.

Rosen, L. R. (1980, March). Enjoying sex during pregnancy. *Sexology Today,* pp. 50–53.

Rosenbaum, A. (1986). Of men, macho, and marital violence. *Journal of Family Violence, 1,* 121–129.

Rosenberg, S. A., Darby, J., & Robinson, C. C. (1984). Mothers' emotional responses to pregnancy and delivery. *Birth Psychology Bulletin, 5,* 1–8.

Rosenblatt, P. C., & Keller, L. O. (1983). Economic vulnerability and economic stress in farm couples. *Family Relations, 32,* 567–573.

Rosenbloom, J. S. (1987). Life insurance. *The TACT Bulletin, 41*(2), 10.

Rosenfield, S. (1989). The effects of women's employment: Personal control and sex differences in mental health. *Journal of Health and Social Behavior, 30,* 77–91.

Rosenthal, C. J. (1985). Kinkeeping in the familial division of labor. *Journal of Marriage and the Family, 47,* 965–974.

Rosenwaks, Z., Benjamin, F., & Stone, M. L. (Eds.). (1987). *Gynecology: Principles and practice.* New York: Macmillan.

Ross, C. E. (1987). The division of labor at home. *Social Forces, 65,* 816–833.

Ross, C. E., & Mirowsky, J. (1988). Child care and emotional adjustment to wives' employment. *Journal of Health and Social Behavior, 29,* 127–138.

Ross, L., Anderson, D. R., & Wisocki, P. A. (1982). Television viewing and adult sex-role attitudes. *Sex Roles, 8,* 589–592.

Ross, L. S. (1986). Clinical aspects of male infertility. *Medical Aspects of Human Sexuality, 20*(5), 121, 124, 130–131, 134.

Rossi, A. S. (1968). Transition to parenthood. *Journal of Marriage and the Family, 30,* 26–39.

Rossi, A. S. (1977). A biosocial perspective on parenting. *Daedalus, 106,* 1–31.

Rossi, A. S. (1984). Gender and parenthood. *American Sociological Review, 49,* 1–19.

Rossi, J. D. (1983). Ratios exaggerate gender differences in mathematical ability. *American Psychologist, 38,* 348.

Rotberg, A. R. (1987). An introduction to the study of women, aging, and sexuality. *Physical & Occupational Therapy in Geriatrics, 5,* 3–12.

Rothman, E. K. (1983). Sex and self-control: Middle-class courtship in America, 1770–1870. In M. Gordon (Ed.), *The American family in social-historical perspective* (3rd ed., pp. 393–410). New York: St. Martin's Press.

Rothman, E. K. (1984). *Hands and hearts: A history of courtship in America.* New York: Basic Books.

Rouse, L. (1988). Abuse in dating relationships: A comparison of blacks, whites, and Hispanics. *Journal of College Student Development, 29,* 312–319.

Rouse, L. P., Breen, R., & Howell, M. (1988). Abuse in intimate relationships: A comparison of married and dating college students. *Journal of Interpersonal Violence, 3,* 414–429.

Rousseau, P. (1988). Impotence in elderly men. *Postgraduate Medicine, 83*(6), 212–219.

Rousseau, P. C. (1986). Sexual changes and impotence in elderly men. *American Family Physician, 34,* 131–136.

Rowan, E. L., Rowan, J. B., & Langelier, P. (1990). Women who molest children. *Bulletin of the American Academy of Psychiatry and the Law, 18,* 79–83.

Ruben, H. L. (1986, August). Adultery, infidelity, cheating: By any name, it can destroy a marriage. *New Woman,* pp. 60–62.

Rubenstein, C. (1982, November). Real men don't earn less than their wives. *Psychology Today,* pp. 36–41.

Rubenstein, C. (1983, July). The modern art of courtly love. *Psychology Today,* pp. 40–49.

Rubenstein, C. (1986, April). How men and women love. *Glamour,* pp. 282–283, 356, 359, 361.

Rubenstein, C., & Tavris, C. (1987, September). Special survey results: 26,000 women reveal the secrets of intimacy. *Redbook,* pp. 147–149, 214, 216.

Rubin, L. B. (1976). *Worlds of pain: Life in the working-class family.* New York: Basic Books.

Rubin, L. B. (1983). *Intimate strangers: Men and women together.* New York: Harper & Row.

Rubin, Z. (1973). *Liking and loving: An invitation to social psychology.* New York: Holt, Rinehart & Winston.

Rubin, Z., Hill, C. T., Peplau, L. A., & Dunkel-Shetter, C. (1980). Self-disclosure in dating couples: Sex roles and the ethic of openness. *Journal of Marriage and the Family, 42,* 305–317.

Rubin, Z., Peplau, L. A., & Hill, C. T. (1981). Loving and leaving: Sex differences in romantic attachments. *Sex Roles, 7,* 821–835.

Rubinstein, R. L. (1986). *Singular paths: Old men living alone.* New York: Columbia University Press.

Rule, S. (1984, July 26). Couples taking unusual paths for adoptions. *The New York Times,* pp. 1A, 5B.

Rusbult, C. E., Johnson, D. J., & Morrow, G. D. (1986). Impact of couple patterns of problem solving on distress and nondistress in dating relationships. *Journal of Personality and Social Psychology, 50,* 744–753.

Russell, A. M. (1991, January). The twelfth annual *Working Woman* salary survey. *Working Woman,* pp. 66–70.

Russell, B. (1929). *Marriage and morals.* New York: Liveright.

Russell, C. (1988). Editor's note. *American Demographics, 10*(7), 2.

Russell, C. S. (1974). Transition to parenthood: Problems and gratifications. *Journal of Marriage and the Family, 36,* 294–302.

Russell, C. S., Bagarozzi, D. A., Atilano, R. B., & Morris, J. E. (1984). A comparison of two approaches to marital enrichment and conjugal skills training: Minnesota couples communication program and structured behavioral exchange contracting. *The American Journal of Family Therapy, 12,* 13–25.

Russell, D. (1982). *Rape in marriage.* Riverside, NJ: Macmillan.

Russell, D. E. H. (1986). *The secret trauma: Incest in the lives of girls and women.* New York: Basic Books.

Sabatelli, R. M., & Cecil-Pigo, E. F. (1985). Relational interdependence and commitment in marriage. *Journal of Marriage and the Family, 47,* 931–937.

Sabatelli, R. M., Meth, R. L., & Gavazzi, S. M. (1988). Factors mediating the adjustment to involuntary childlessness. *Family Relations, 37,* 338–343.

Sack, A. R., Keller, J. F., & Hinkle, D. E. (1984). Premarital sexual intercourse: A test of the effects of peer group, religiosity, and sexual guilt. *The Journal of Sex Research, 20,* 168–185.

Sacks, S. R., & Donnenfeld, P. B. (1984). Parental choice of alternative birth environments and attitudes toward childrearing philosophy. *Journal of Marriage and the Family, 46,* 469–475.

Sadker, M., & Sadker, D. (1985, March). Sexism in the schoolroom of the 80's. *Psychology Today,* pp. 54–57.

Sadler, J. (1983). Stepfamilies: An annotated bibliography. *Family Relations, 32,* 149–152.

Safety for latchkey children. (1987, December). *Parents,* p. 13.

Sage, W. (1987). Choosing the good death. In H. Cox (Ed.), *Aging* (5th ed., pp. 156–162). Guilford, CT: Dushkin.

Sager, C. J., Brown, H. S., Crohn, H., Engel, T., Rodstein, E., & Walker, L. (1983). *Treating the remarried family.* New York: Brunner/Mazel.

Salholz, E. (1986, June 2). Too late for Prince Charming? *Newsweek,* pp. 54–57, 61.

Saline, C. (1975, January). Why can't married women have men as friends? *McCall's,* pp. 67, 132–133.

Saline, C. (1986). Sexual pressure: Helping kids say "no." In O. Pocs (Ed.), *Human sexuality 86/87* (pp. 166–167). Guilford, CT: Dushkin.

Salter, A. C., Richardson, C. M., & Martin, P. A. (1985). Treating abusive parents. *Child Welfare, 64,* 327–341.

Saltman, J. (1986). *The many faces of family violence* (No. 640). New York: Public Affairs Committee.

Salzman, L. (1983). How to cope with adultery (commentary). *Medical Aspects of Human Sexuality, 17*(6), 107–108, 112.

Samuelson, E. D. (1988). *The divorce law handbook.* New York: Insight Books.

Sanders, G. F., & Trygstad, D. W. (1989). Stepgrandparents and grandparents: The view from young adults. *Family Relations, 38,* 71–75.

Sanders, L. T., & Seelbach, W. C. (1981). Variations in preferred care alternatives for the elderly: Family versus nonfamily sources. *Family Relations, 30,* 447–451.

Sanger, S., & Kelly, J. (1987, March). How to be a better (working) mother. *Redbook,* pp. 94–95, 172–174.

Sanik, M. M., & Mauldin, T. (1986). Single versus two parent families: A comparison of mothers' time. *Family Relations, 35,* 53–56.

Santrock, J. W., & Yussen, S. R. (1987). *Child development: An introduction* (3rd ed.). Dubuque, IA: Wm. C. Brown.

Sarnoff, I., & Sarnoff, S. (1989). The dialectic of marriage. *Psychology Today, 23*(10), 54–57.

Sarrel, P. M., & Whitehead, M. I. (1985) Sex and menopause: Defining the issues. *Maturitas, 7,* 217–224.

Satir, V. (1972). *Peoplemaking.* Palo Alto, CA: Science and Behavior Books.

Saul, S. C., & Scherman, A. (1984). Divorce grief and personal adjustment in divorced persons who remarry or remain single. *Journal of Divorce, 7*(3), 75–85.

Saunders, D. G. (1984). Helping husbands who batter. *Social Casework, 65,* 347–353.

Saunders, J. M., & Edwards, J. N. (1984). Extramarital sexuality: A predictive model of permissive attitudes. *Journal of Marriage and the Family, 46,* 825–835.

Scales, P. (1983). Sense and nonsense about sexuality education: A rejoinder to the Shornack's critical view. *Family Relations, 32,* 287–295.

Scales, P. (1985). Only too "real": The ins and outs of successful stepfathering. *Family Resource Coalition Report, 4*(3), 6–7.

Scanzoni, J. (1978). *Sex roles, women's work, and marital conflict.* Washington, DC: Lexington Books.

Scanzoni, J. (1980). Contemporary marriage types. *Journal of Family Issues, 1,* 452–461.

Scanzoni, J., & Polonko, K. (1980). A conceptual approach to explicit marital negotiation. *Journal of Marriage and the Family, 42,* 31–44.

Scanzoni, J., Polonko, K., Teachman, J., & Thompson, L. (1989). *The sexual bond: Rethinking families and close relationships.* Newbury Park, CA: Sage.

Scanzoni, J. H. (1976). Gender roles and the process of fertility control. *Journal of Marriage and the Family, 38,* 677–691.

Scanzoni, L. D., & Scanzoni, J. (1988). *Men, women, and change* (3rd ed.). New York: McGraw-Hill.

Schachter, J., & O'Leary, K. D. (1985). Affective intent and impact in marital communication. *American Journal of Family Therapy, 13,* 17–23.

Schaeffer, C. (1987, May). Second thoughts on HMOs. *Changing Times,* pp. 33–34, 36, 38.

Schafer, R. B., & Keith, P. M. (1981). Equity in marital roles across the family life cycle. *Journal of Marriage and the Family, 43,* 359–367.

Schafer, R. B., & Keith, P. M. (1986). A causal analysis of the relationship between the self-concept and marital quality. *Journal of Marriage and the Family, 46,* 909–914.

Schaninger, C. M., & Buss, W. (1986). A longitudinal comparison of consumption and finance handling between happily married and divorced couples. *Journal of Marriage and the Family, 48,* 129–136.

Schatten, G., & Schatten, H. (1983). The energetic egg. *The Sciences, 23*(5), 28–34.

Scheiner, L. C., Musetto, A. P., & Cordier, D. C. (1982). Custody and visitation counseling: A report of an innovative program. *Family Relations, 31,* 99–107.

Scher, D. (1984). Sex-role contradictions: Self-perceptions and ideal perceptions. *Sex Roles, 10,* 651–656.

Schiamberg, L. B. (1988). *Child and adolescent development.* New York: Macmillan.

Schickedanz, J. A., Hansen, K., & Forsyth, P. D. (1990). *Understanding children.* Mountain View, CA: Mayfield.

Schiffres, M. (1986, March 10). Renting a piece of the American dream. *U.S. News & World Report,* p. 55.

Schiller, P. (1981). *The sex profession.* Washington, DC: Shilmark House.

Schiller, Z., Mitchell, R., Zellner, W., Therrien, L., Rothman, A., & Konrad, W. (1989, October 9). The great American health pitch: Have food companies gone overboard in adopting that old parental refrain: 'eat it, it's good for you'? *Business Week,* pp. 114, 116–118, 120, 122.

Schmeck, H. M., Jr. (1983). U.S. panel calls for patients' rights to end life. *The New York Times,* pp. A1, C7.

Schnaiberg, A., & Goldenberg, S. (1986, August). *From empty nest to crowded nest: Some contradictions in the returning-young-adult syndrome.* Paper presented at the meeting of the American Sociological Association, New York, NY.

Schneider, F. W., & Coutts, L. M. (1985). Person orientation of male and female high school students: To the educational disadvantage of males? *Sex Roles, 13,* 47–63.

Schneider, S. W. (1985). *Jewish and female: Choices and changes in our lives today.* New York: Simon & Schuster.

Schneiderman, E. J. (1990). A study of the relationship between extramarital involvement and marital satisfaction in older and younger women (Doctoral dissertation, The American University, 1989). *Dissertation Abstracts International, 50,* 1949A.

Schnittger, M. H., & Bird, G. W. (1990). Coping among dual-career men and women across the family life cycle. *Family Relations, 39,* 199–205.

Schoen, R., & Wooldredge, J. (1986, August). *Marriage choices in North Carolina and Virginia, 1969–71 and 1979–81.* Paper presented at the meeting of the American Sociological Association, New York, NY.

Schover, L. R. (1986). Sexual dysfunction: When a partner complains of low sexual desire. *Medical Aspects of Human Sexuality, 20*(3), 108, 110, 114–116.

Schreiner-Engel, P. (1980). Female sexual arousability: Its relation to gonadal hormones and the menstrual cycle (Doctoral dissertation, New York University, 1980). *Dissertation Abstracts International, 41,* 730B–731B.

Schultz-Brooks, T. (1984). Getting there: Women in the newsroom. *Columbia Journalism Review, 22,* 25–31.

Schumm, W. R., Barnes, H. L., Bollman, S. R., Jurich, A. P., & Bugaighis, M. A. (1986). Self-disclosure and marital satisfaction revisited. *Family Relations, 35,* 241–247.

Schumm, W. R., & Bugaighis, M. A. (1986). Marital quality over the marital career: Alternative explanations. *Journal of Marriage and the Family, 48,* 165–168.

Schurenberg, E. (1987, April). Getting on top of your debt. *Money,* pp. 95–96, 102, 104, 106, 108.

Schwartz, J. (1983, April). *Infant day care: Effects at 2, 4, and 8 years.* Paper presented at the meeting of the Society for Research in Child Development, Detroit, Michigan.

Schwartz, L. A., & Markham, W. T. (1985). Sex stereotyping in children's toy advertisements. *Sex Roles, 12,* 151–170.

Schweinhart, L. J., & Weikart, D. P. (1985). Evidence that good early childhood programs work. *Phi Delta Kappan, 66,* 545–551.

Scott, G. (1983, April). Joint custody: Does it work? *Ms.,* pp. 77–79.

Scritchfield, S. A., & Masker, J. (1989, August). *Gender traditionality and perceptions of date rape.* Paper presented at the meeting of the American Sociological Association, Washington, DC.

Seavey, C. A., Katz, P. A., & Zalk, S. R. (1975). Baby X: The effect of gender labels on adult responses to infants. *Sex Roles, 1,* 103–109.

Seecof, R., & Tennant, F. S. (1986). Subjective perceptions to the intravenous "rush" of heroin and cocaine in opioid addicts. *American Journal of Drug & Alcohol Abuse, 12,* 79–87.

Segraves, R. T. (1985). Divorce and health problems. *Medical Aspects of Human Sexuality, 19*(7), 152, 157, 160, 161.

Seixas, S. (1985, June). Secrets of the black-belt shoppers. *Money,* pp. 194–196, 198.

Seligmann, J. (1984, April 9). The date who rapes. *Newsweek,* pp. 91–92.

Seltzer, J. A., Schaeffer, N. C., & Charng, H. W. (1989). Family ties after divorce: The relationship between visiting and paying child support. *Journal of Marriage and the Family, 51,* 1013–1032.

Semmens, J. P., & Wagner, G. (1982). Estrogen deprivation and vaginal function in postmenopausal women. *Journal of the American Medical Association, 248,* 445–448.

Sena-Rivera, J. (1979). Extended kinship in the United States: Competing models and the case of La Familia Chicana. *Journal of Marriage and the Family, 41,* 121–129.

Sergios, P., & Cody, J. (1985). Importance of physical attractiveness and social assertiveness skills in male homosexual dating behavior and partner selection. *Journal of Homosexuality, 12*(2), 71–84.

Serow, W. J. (1981). Population and other policy responses to an era of sustained low fertility. *Social Science Quarterly, 62,* 323–332.

75 tips to help you get the most from every food dollar. (1983, March). *Good Housekeeping,* pp. 214, 216, 218.

Seward, R. R. (1978). *The American family: A demographic history.* Beverly Hills: Sage.

Sexton, D. F. (1984). Television sexuality, parental involvement and adolescents' sexual attitudes and behavior: A preliminary investigation (Doctoral dissertation, Oklahoma State University, 1983). *Dissertation Abstracts International, 44,* 2127B.

Seymour, S. F. (1987). Attitudes toward menopause in midlife women (Doctoral dissertation, Florida State University, 1986). *Dissertation Abstracts International, 47,* 3874A.

Shah, F., & Zelnik, M. (1981). Parent and peer influence on sexual behavior, contraceptive use, and pregnancy experience of young women. *Journal of Marriage and the Family, 43,* 339–348.

Shakespeare, W. (1968). The Tempest II. In B. Evans (Ed.), *Dictionary of quotations* (p. 509). New York: Delacorte Press.

Shanas, E. (1980). Older people and their families: The new pioneers. *Journal of Marriage and the Family, 42,* 9–15.

Shanis, H. S. (1985). Hospice: Interdependence of the dying with their community. In W. A. Peterson & J. Quadagno (Eds.), *Social bonds in later life: Aging and interdependence* (pp. 369–387). Beverly Hills: Sage.

Shapiro, D., & Shaw, L. B. (1982). Labor force attachment of married women age 30 to 34: An intercohort comparison. In F. L. Mott (Ed.), *The employment revolution: Young American women in the 1970s* (pp. 102–119). Cambridge, MA: MIT Press.

Shapiro, L. (1990, May 28). Guns and dolls. *Newsweek,* pp. 56–59, 61–62, 65.

Shaw, D. S., & Emery, R. E. (1987). Parental conflict and other correlates of the adjustment of school-age children whose parents have separated. *Journal of Abnormal Child Psychology, 15,* 269–281.

Shaw, G. B. (1932). Getting married. In G. B. Shaw, *The doctor's dilemma, getting married, and the shewing up of Blanco Posnet* (pp. 257–352). London: Constable.

Shaw, M. E., & Costanzo, P. R. (1970). *Theories of social psychology.* New York: McGraw-Hill.

Shaw, S. M. (1985). Gender and leisure: Inequality in the distribution of leisure time. *Journal of Leisure Research, 17,* 266–282.

Sheek, G. W. (1984). *A nation for families: Family life education in public schools.* Washington, DC: American Home Economics Association.

Shehan, C. L. (1984). Wives' work and psychological well-being: An extension of Gove's social role theory of depression. *Sex Roles, 11,* 881–889.

Shehan, C. L., Berardo, F. M., & Berardo, D. H. (1983, October). *The empty nest is filling again: A look at extended families in hard times.* Paper presented at the meeting of the National Council on Family Relations, St. Paul, MN.

Shehan, C. L., Bock, E. W., & Lee, G. R. (1990). Religious heterogamy, religiosity, and marital happiness: The case of Catholics. *Journal of Marriage and the Family, 52,* 73–79.

Sheldrake, P., Cromack, M., & McGuire, J. (1976). Psychosomatic illness, birth order and intellectual preference, II: Women. *Journal of Psychosomatic Research, 20,* 45–49.

Shelton, B. A., & Firestone, J. (1987, April). *The impact of household labor time on time spent in paid labor: A comparison of men and women.* Paper presented at the meeting of the Southern Sociological Society, Atlanta, GA.

Sherman, J. A., & Fennema, E. (1977). The study of mathematics by high school boys and girls: Related variables. *American Educational Journal, 14,* 159–168.

Sherman, M. A., & Haas, A. (1984, June). Man to man, woman to woman. *Psychology Today,* pp. 72–73.

Sherwin, R., & Corbett, S. (1985). Campus sexual norms and dating relationships: A trend analysis. *The Journal of Sex Research, 21,* 258–274.

Shettles, L. B., & Rorvik, D. (1970). *Your baby's sex: Now you can choose.* New York: Dodd, Mead.

Sholty, M. J., Ephross, P. H., Plaut, S. M., Fischman, S. H., Charnas, J. F., & Cody, C. A. (1984). Female orgasmic experience: A subjective study. *Archives of Sexual Behavior, 13,* 155–164.

Shoppers are a dwindling species. (1990, November 26). *Business Week,* p. 144.

Shopping for a new doctor. (1986, June). *Changing Times,* pp. 47–48, 51–52.

Shostak, A. B. (1981). Oral sex: Standard of intimacy and old index of troubled sexuality. *Deviant Behavior, 2,* 127–144.

Shostak, A. B. (1987). Singlehood. In M. B. Sussman & S. K. Steinmetz (Eds.), *Handbook of marriage and the family* (pp. 355–367). New York: Plenum Press.

Shostak, A. B., McLouth, G., & Seng, L. (1984). *Men and abortions: Lessons, losses, and love.* New York: Praeger.

Shotland, R. L. (1985). A preliminary model of some causes of date rape. *Academic Psychology Bulletin, 7,* 187–200.

Should you switch policies? (1986, August). *Consumer Reports,* pp. 527–528.

Shreve, A. (1987). *Remaking motherhood: How working mothers are shaping our children's future.* New York: Fawcett.

Shusterman, L. R. (1979). Predicting the psychological consequences of abortion. *Social Science and Medicine, 13,* 683–684.

Shuttleworth, F. K. (1959). A biosocial and developmental theory of male and female sexuality. *Marriage and Family Living, 21,* 163–170.

Siegal, M., & Barclay, M. S. (1985). Children's evaluations of father's socialization behavior. *Developmental Psychology, 21,* 1090–1096.

Siegel, S. J. (1985). The effect of culture on how women experience menstruation: Jewish women and Mikvah. *Women & Health, 10,* 63–74.

Sievers, S., Pocs, O., & Tolone, W. (1983, April). *Premarital sexual experience and marital sexual adjustment.* Paper presented at the meeting of the Midwest Sociological Society, Kansas City, MO.

Sifford, D. (1989, May 15). Support group helps parents of 1 child stop feeling alone. *Austin American-Statesman,* p. D1.

Sigelman, C. K., Berry, C. J., & Wiles, K. A. (1984). Violence in college students' dating relationships. *Journal of Applied Social Psychology, 14,* 530–548.

Signorielli, N. (1982). Marital status in television drama: A case of reduced options. *Journal of Broadcasting, 26,* 585–597.

Silber, S. J. (1980). *How to get pregnant.* New York: Scribner's.

Silka, L., & Kiesler, S. (1977). Couples who choose to remain childless. *Family Planning Perspectives, 9,* 16–25.

Sils, B., & Sils, H. J. (1980). *The mother to mother baby care book.* New York: Avon Books.

Silverman, H. (1981). Female sexuality: Singlehood and the problems of intimacy. In D. A. Brown & C. Clary (Eds.), *Sexuality in America: Contemporary perspectives on sexual identity, dysfunction and treatment* (pp. 43–67). Ann Arbor, MI: Greenfield Books.

Silverman, I. J. (1977). A survey of cohabitation on two college campuses. *Archives of Sexual Behavior, 6,* 11–20.

Silverman, J., Torres, A., & Forrest, J. D. (1987). Barriers to contraceptive services. *Family Planning Perspectives, 19,* 94–102.

Simenauer, J., & Carroll, D. (1982a). Do you wish you were single? In O. Pocs & R. H. Walsh (Eds.), *Marriage and family 83/84* (pp. 214–216). Guilford, CT: Dushkin.

Simenauer, J., & Carroll, D. (1982b). *Singles: The new Americans.* New York: Simon & Schuster.

Simmons, R. G., Blyth, D. A., Van Cleave, E. F., & Bush, D. M. (1979). Entry into early adolescence: The impact of school structure, puberty, and early dating on self-esteem. *American Sociological Review, 44,* 948–967.

Simon, W., & Gagnon, J. H. (Eds.). (1970). *The sexual scene.* Chicago: Aldine.

Simons, J., & Irwin, D. (1986). *Instructor's manual for Papalia/Olds human development* (3rd ed.). New York: McGraw-Hill.

Simons, R. L., Whitbeck, L. B., Conger, R. D., & Melby, J. N. (1990). Husband and wife differences in determinants of parenting. *Journal of Marriage and the Family, 52,* 375–392.

Simpson, I. H., & England, P. (1982). Conjugal work roles and marital solidarity. In J. Aldous (Ed.), *Two paychecks: Life in dual-earner families* (pp. 147–171). Beverly Hills: Sage.

Simpson, J. L. (1981). Antenatal diagnosis of cytogenetic abnormalities. *Clinical Obstetrics and Gynecology, 24,* 1023.

Simpson, M., Timm, H., & McCubbin, H. I. (1981). Adoptees in search of their past: Policy induced strain on adoptive families and birth parents. *Family Relations, 30,* 427–434.

Singh, B. K., Walton, B. L., & Williams, J. S. (1976). Extramarital sexual permissiveness: Conditions and contingencies. *Journal of Marriage and the Family, 38,* 701–712.

Singles account for record 21% of U.S. births in '84. (1986, July 29). *Austin American-Statesman,* p. 8A.

Sinnott, J. D. (1984). Older men, older women: Are their perceived sex roles similar? *Sex Roles, 10,* 847–856.

Sirignano, S. W., & Lachman, M. E. (1985). Personality change during the transition to parenthood: The role of perceived infant temperament. *Developmental Psychology, 21,* 558–567.

Skinner, D. A. (1980). Dual-career family stress and coping: A literature review. *Family Relations, 29,* 473–480.

Sklar, K. K. (1973). *Catharine Beecher: A study in American domesticity.* New Haven: Yale University Press.

Skolnick, A. S., & Skolnick, J. H. (1989). *Family in transition* (6th ed.). Glenview, IL: Scott, Foresman.

Slade, A. (1987). Quality of attachment and early symbolic play. *Developmental Psychology, 23,* 78–85.

Slater, E. J., & Calhoun, K. S. (1988). Familial conflict and marital dissolution: Effects on the social functioning of college students. *Journal of Social and Clinical Psychology, 6,* 118–126.

Slater, E. J., & Haber, J. D. (1984). Adolescent adjustment following divorce as a function of familial conflict. *Journal of Consulting and Clinical Psychology, 52,* 920–921.

Sloane, L. (1985). *The New York Times book of personal finance.* New York: Times Books.

Slocum, W. L., & Nye, F. I. (1976). Provider and housekeeper roles. In F. I. Nye, H. M. Bahr, S. J. Bahr, J. E. Carlson, V. Gecas, S. McLaughlin, & W. L. Slocum (Eds.), *Role structure and analysis of the family* (pp. 81–99). Beverly Hills: Sage.

Smith, A. W., & Meitz, J. E. (1983). Cohorts, education, and the decline in undisrupted marriages. *Journal of Marriage and the Family, 45,* 613–622.

Smith, A. W., & Meitz, J. E. G. (1985). Vanishing Supermoms and other trends in marital dissolution, 1969–1978. *Journal of Marriage and the Family, 47,* 53–65.

Smith, D. S. (1985). Wife employment and marital adjustment: A cumulation of results. *Family Relations, 34,* 483–490.

Smith, E. A., & Udry, J. R. (1985). Coital and non-coital sexual behaviors of white and black adolescents. *American Journal of Public Health, 75,* 1200–1203.

Smith, H., & Israel, E. (1987). Sibling incest: A study of the dynamics of 25 cases. *Child Abuse & Neglect, 11,* 101–108.

Smith, J. E., Jr. (1986, January 26). About men: A sense of injustice. *The New York Times Magazine,* p. 31.

Smith, K. R., & Zick, C. D. (1986). The incidence of poverty among the recently widowed: Mediating factors in the life course. *Journal of Marriage and the Family, 48,* 619–630.

Smith, M. D., & Self, G. D. (1980). The congruence between mothers' and daughters' sex-role attitudes: A research note. *Journal of Marriage and the Family, 42,* 105–109.

Smith, M. J. (1989, October 3). Automation bringing updated Machine Age. *Austin American-Statesman,* pp. C1, C4.

Smith, P. A., & Midlarsky, E. (1985). Empirically derived conceptions of femaleness and maleness: A current view. *Sex Roles, 12,* 313–328.

Smith, R. M., Goslen, M. A., & Byrd, A. J. (1987, November). *Self-other orientation of men and women who remarry.* Paper presented at the meeting of the National Council on Family Relations, Atlanta, GA.

Smith, R. M., & Smith, C. W. (1981). Child rearing and single-parent fathers. *Family Relations, 30,* 411–417.

Smith, T. W. (1985). Working wives and women's rights: The connection between the employment status of wives and the feminist attitudes of husbands. *Sex Roles, 12,* 501–508.

Smith, T. W. (1990a). A report: The sexual revolution? *Public Opinion Quarterly, 54,* 415–435.

Smith, T. W. (1990b, February). *Adult sexual behavior in 1989: Number of partners, frequency and risk.* Paper presented at the meeting of the American Association for the Advancement of Science, New Orleans, LA.

Snow, C. W. (1989). *Infant development.* Englewood Cliffs, NJ: Prentice Hall.

Snow, M. E., Jacklin, C. N., & Maccoby, E. E. (1983). Sex-of-child differences in father-child interaction at one year of age. *Child Development, 54,* 227–232.

Snowden, L. R., Schott, T. L., Awalt, S. J., & Gillis-Knox, J. (1988). Marital satisfaction in pregnancy: Stability and change. *Journal of Marriage and the Family, 50,* 325–333.

Snyder, D. K., & Berg, P. (1983). Determinants of sexual satisfaction in sexually distressed couples. *Archives of Sexual Behavior, 12,* 237–246.

Sobol, M. P., & Cardiff, J. (1983). A sociopsychological investigation of adult adoptees' search for birth parents. *Family Relations, 32,* 477–483.

Solberg, D. A., Butler, J., & Wagner, N. N. (1973). Sexual behavior in pregnancy. *New England Journal of Medicine, 288,* 1098–1103.

Solin, C. A. (1986). Displacement of affect in families following incest disclosure. *American Journal of Orthopsychiatry, 56,* 570–576.

Soloway, N. M., & Smith, R. M. (1987). Antecedents of late birthtiming decisions of men and women in dual-career marriages. *Family Relations, 36,* 258–262.

Sones, D. G., & Holston, M. A. (1988). Tolerance, sociability, sex, and race: Correlates of attitudes toward interracial marriage. *Psychological Reports, 62,* 518.

Sophocles, A. M., & Brozovich, E. M. (1986). Birth control failure among patients with unwanted pregnancies: 1982–1984. *Journal of Family Practice, 22,* 45–48.

Sorensen, A. (1983). Women's employment patterns after marriage. *Journal of Marriage and the Family, 45,* 311–321.

Sorensen, G., Pirie, P., Folsom, A., Luepker, R., Jacobs, D., & Gillum, R. (1985). Sex differences in the relationship between work and health: The Minnesota heart survey. *Journal of Health and Social Behavior, 26,* 379–394.

Sorensen, R. C. (1973). *Adolescent sexuality in contemporary America.* New York: World Publishing.

South, S. J. (1985). Economic conditions and the divorce rate: A time-series analysis of the postwar United States. *Journal of Marriage and the Family, 47,* 31–41.

South, S. J., & Spitze, G. (1986). Determinants of divorce over the marital life course. *American Sociological Review, 51,* 583–590.

Spagna, V. A., & Prior, R. B. (1983). Sexually transmitted diseases. In S. F. Pariser, S. B. Levine, & M. L. Gardner (Eds.), *Clinical sexuality* (pp. 139–158). New York: Dekker-Marcel.

Spaights, E., & Dixon, H. E. (1984). Socio-psychological dynamics in pathological black-white romantic alliances. *Journal of Instructional Psychology, 11,* 132–138.

Spanier, G. B. (1975). Sexualization and premarital sex behavior. *The Family Coordinator, 24,* 33–41.

Spanier, G. B. (1983). Married and unmarried cohabitation in the United States: 1980. *Journal of Marriage and the Family, 45,* 277–288.

Spanier, G. B. (1989). Bequeathing family continuity. *Journal of Marriage and the Family, 51,* 3–13.

Spanier, G. B., & Furstenberg, F. F., Jr. (1982). Remarriage after divorce: A longitudinal analysis of well-being. *Journal of Marriage and the Family, 44,* 709–720.

Spanier, G. B., & Furstenberg, F.F., Jr. (1987). Remarriage and reconstituted families. In M. B. Sussman & S. K. Steinmetz (Eds.), *Handbook of Marriage and Family* (pp. 419–434). New York: Plenum Press.

Spanier, G. B., & Lewis, R. A. (1980). Marital quality: A review of the seventies. *Journal of Marriage and the Family, 42,* 825–840.

Spanier, G. B., & Margolis, R. L. (1983). Marital separation and extramarital behavior. *The Journal of Sex Research, 19,* 23–48.

Spanier, G. B., Roos, P. A., & Shockey, J. (1985). Marital trajectories of American women: Variations in the life course. *Journal of Marriage and the Family, 47,* 993–1003.

Spector, K. R., & Boyle, M. (1986). The prevalence and perceived aetiology of male sexual problems in a non-clinical sample. *British Journal of Medical Psychology, 59,* 351–358.

Spencer, E. W. (1987, September 15). Buying health care in the new era of medicine. *Vital Speeches of the Day,* pp. 713–716.

Spencer, G. (1989). Projections of the United States, by age, sex, race 1988 to 2080. *Current Population Reports* (Series P-25, No. 1028). Washington, DC: U.S. Government Printing Office.

Spieler, S. (1982). Can fathers be nurturers? In S. Prescod (Ed.), *Parents and children: Helping to solve some of today's family life problems* (pp. 4–5). New York: Alcom.

Spitze, G. D. (1978). Role experience of young women: A longitudinal test of the role hiatus hypothesis. *Journal of Marriage and the Family, 40,* 471–474.

Split verdict: What Americans think about abortion. (1985). *Policy Review, 32,* 18–19.

Sprecher, S. (1989). Premarital sexual standards for different categories of individuals. *The Journal of Sex Research, 26,* 232–248.

Sprecher, S., & Hatfield, E. (1986, March). *Gender differences in emotional experience and expression in close relationships.* Paper presented at the meeting of the Midwest Sociological Society, Des Moines, IA.

Sprecher, S., McKinney, K., Walsh, R., & Anderson, C. (1988). A revision of the Reiss Premarital Sexual Permissiveness Scale. *Journal of Marriage and the Family, 50,* 821–828.

Spreitzer, E., & Riley, L. E. (1974). Factors associated with singlehood. *Journal of Marriage and the Family, 36,* 533–542.

Sprey, J., & Matthews, S. H. (1982). Contemporary grandparents: A systematic transition. *Annals of the American Academy of Political and Social Science, 464,* 91–103.

Spring-Mills, E., & Hafez, E. (1980). Male accessory organs. In E. Hafez (Ed.), *Human reproduction* (pp. 60–90). New York: Harper & Row.

Sprunger, L. W., Boyce, W. T., & Gaines, J. A. (1985). Family-infant congruence: Routines and rhythmicity in family adaptations to a young infant. *Child Development, 56,* 564–572.

Squire, S. (1984, February). A woman's mid-life / sex-life crisis. *Redbook,* pp. 88–89, 147.

Sroufe, L. A. (1983). Infant-caregiver attachment and patterns of adaptation in preschool: The roots of maladaption and competence. In M. Perlmutter (Ed.), *Minnesota symposium on child psychology,* Volume 16 (pp. 41–83). Hillsdale, NJ: Erlbaum.

Stafford, R., Backman, E., & Dibona, P. (1977). The division of labor among cohabitating and married couples. *Journal of Marriage and the Family, 39,* 43–57.

Stainton, M. C. (1985). The fetus: A growing member of the family. *Family Relations, 34,* 321–326.

Stanley, D. (1989a, April 1). Teens still shrug off AIDS risk. *Austin American-Statesman,* pp. 1A, 20A.

Stanley, D. (1989b, May 23). UT's AIDS rate believed higher than other schools. *Austin American-Statesman,* pp. 1A, 8A.

Stanton, G. (1986). Prevention intervention with stepfamilies. *Social Work, 31,* 201–206.

Stanush, M. (1991, February 14). After the romance. *Austin American-Statesman,* pp. E1, E6.

Stark, E. (1984, May). The unspeakable family secret. *Psychology Today,* pp. 38, 42, 44–46.

Stark, E. (1985, April). Taking a beating. *Psychology Today,* p. 16.

Stark, E. (1987). Friends through it all. In O. Pocs & R. H. Walsh (Eds.), *Marriage and family 87/88* (pp. 174–178). Guilford, CT: Dushkin.

States study parental leave. (1987, August 17). *USA Today,* p. 3A.

Statham, A., Vaughan, S., & Houseknecht, S. K. (1987). The professional involvement of highly educated women: The impact of family. *Sociological Quarterly, 28,* 119–133.

Status of cases in the Supreme Court at the end of the 1986–87 term. (1987, July 15). *The Chronicle of Higher Education,* p. 20.

Stauffer, B. (1988, January). Getting a grip on your spending. *Changing Times,* pp. 45–58.

Steelman, L. C., & Powell, B. (1985). The social and academic consequences of birth order: Real, artifactual, or both? *Journal of Marriage and the Family, 47,* 117–124.

Stein, H. (1984, June). The case for staying home. *Esquire,* pp. 142–149.

Stein, P. J. (1975). Singlehood: An alternative to marriage. *The Family Coordinator, 24,* 489–503.

Stein, P. J. (1976). *Single.* Englewood Cliffs, NJ: Prentice-Hall.

Stein, P. J. (Ed.). (1981). *Single life: Unmarried adults in social context.* New York: St. Martin's Press.

Steinbacher, R., & Gilroy, F. D. (1985). Preference for sex of child among primiparous women. *Journal of Psychology, 119,* 541–547.

Steinberg, L., & Silverberg, S. B. (1987). Influences on marital satisfaction during the middle stages of the family life cycle. *Journal of Marriage and the Family, 49,* 751–760.

Steinmetz, S. K. (1977). The use of force for resolving family conflict: The training ground for abuse. *The Family Coordinator, 26,* 19–26.

Stemp, P. S., Turner, R. J., & Noh, S. (1986). Psychological distress in the postpartum period: The significance of social support. *Journal of Marriage and the Family, 48,* 271–277.

Stephens, B. M. (1987, June). IRAs—Still a good investment. *Black Enterprise,* pp. 322–323.

Sternberg, R. J. (1986). A triangular theory of love. *Psychological Review, 93,* 119–135.

Sternberg, S. (1989, September 29). Legal abortions topped 1.3 million in U.S., CDC says. *The Atlanta Constitution,* pp. A1, A20.

Stevens, G., & Schoen, R. (1988). Linguistic intermarriage in the United States. *Journal of Marriage and the Family, 50,* 267–279.

Stevens, J. H. (1984). Child development knowledge and parenting skills. *Family Relations, 33,* 237–244.

Stewart, F. H., Guest, F. J., Stewart, G. K., & Hatcher, R. A. (1979). *My body, my health: The concerned woman's guide to gynecology.* New York: Wiley.

Stewart, R. A., & Beatty, M. J. (1985). Jealousy and self-esteem. *Perceptual and Motor Skills, 60,* 153–154.

Stickney, J. (1985, May). Two cheers for HMOs. *Money,* pp. 155–156, 158, 160.

Stier, S. (1986). Divorce mediation. *Family Therapy Today, 1*(3), 1–3, 6.

Stock, W. E., & Geer, J. H. (1982). A study of fantasy-based sexual arousal in women. *Archives of Sexual Behavior, 11,* 33–47.

Stokes, J. P., & Peyton, J. S. (1986). Attitudinal differences between full-time homemakers and women who work outside the home. *Sex Roles, 15,* 299–310.

Stoller, E. P. (1985). Exchange patterns in the informal support networks of the elderly: The impact of reciprocity on morale. *Journal of Marriage and the Family, 47,* 335–342.

Stolzenberg, R. M., & Waite, L. J. (1977). Age, fertility expectations and plans for employment. *American Sociological Review, 42,* 769–783.

Stoneman, Z., Brody, G. H., & MacKinnon, C. E. (1986). Same-sex and cross-sex siblings: Activity choices, roles, behavior and gender stereotypes. *Sex Roles, 15,* 495–511.

Story, M. D. (1982). A comparison of university student experience with various sexual outlets in 1974 and 1980. *Adolescence, 27,* 737–747.

Straits, B. C. (1985). Factors influencing college women's responses to fertility decision-making vignettes. *Journal of Marriage and the Family, 47,* 585–596.

Straus, M. A. (1974). Leveling, civility, and violence in the family. *Journal of Marriage and the Family, 36,* 13–29.

Straus, M. A., & Gelles, R. J. (1986). Societal change and change in family violence from 1975 to 1985 as revealed by two national surveys. *Journal of Marriage and the Family, 48,* 465–479.

Straus, M. A., Gelles, R. J., & Steinmetz, S. K. (1980). *Behind closed doors: Violence and the American family.* New York: Doubleday.

Streib, G. F., & Beck, R. W. (1980). Older families: A decade review. *Journal of Marriage and the Family, 42,* 937–956.

Stretching their options. (1987, January 27). *Time,* p. 23.

Strong, B., & DeVault, C. (1988). *Understanding our sexuality* (2nd ed.). St. Paul: West.

Strong, J. R. (1983). *Creating closeness: The communication puzzle.* Ames, IA: Human Communication Institute.

Strother, J., & Jacobs, E. (1984). Adolescent stress as it relates to stepfamily living: Implications for school counselors. *The School Counselor, 32,* 97–103.

Strube, M. J., & Barbour, L. S. (1984). Factors related to the decision to leave an abusive relationship. *Journal of Marriage and the Family, 46,* 837–844.

Struckman-Johnson, C. C. (1988). Forced sex on dates: It happens to men, too. *The Journal of Sex Research, 24,* 234–241.

Stueve, A., & O'Donnell, L. (1984). The daughter of aging parents. In G. K. Baruch & J. Brooks-Gunn (Eds.), *Women in midlife* (pp. 203–225). New York: Plenum Press.

Sugarman, D. B. (1986). Active versus passive euthanasia: An attributional analysis. *Journal of Applied Social Psychology, 16,* 60–76.

Suitor, J. J., & Pillemer, K. A. (1987). The presence of adult children: A source of stress for elderly couples' marriages? *Journal of Marriage and the Family, 49,* 717–725.

Sulima, J. P. (Ed.). (1989). Groups adopt "functional" definition of family. *The Brown University Family Therapy Letter, 1*(4), 7.

Sullivan, D. A. (1986). Informal support systems in a planned retirement community: Availability, proximity, and willingness to utilize. *Research on Aging, 8,* 249–267.

Sullivan, H. S. (1947). *Conceptions of modern psychiatry.* Washington, DC: White Psychiatric Foundation.

Sunbury, J. F. (1980). Working with defensive projections in conjoint marriage counseling. *Family Relations, 29,* 107–110.

Surra, C. A. (1990). Research and theory on mate selection and premarital relationships in the 1980s. *Journal of Marriage and the Family, 52,* 844–865.

Sussman, M. B. (1983). 1981 Burgess address: Law and legal systems: The family connection. *Journal of Marriage and the Family, 45,* 9–21.

Sweeney, C., Smith, H., & Foster, J. C. (1985). Effects of a nutrition intervention program during pregnancy—Maternal data phase-1 and phase-2. *Journal of Nurse-Midwifery, 30,* 149–158.

Swensen, C. H., Jr. (1983). Post-parental marriages. *Medical Aspects of Human Sexuality, 17*(4), 171–194.

Syphilis surging in certain populations. (1990). *Medical Aspects of Human Sexuality, 24*(11), 19–20.

Szinovacz, M. E. (1983a). Beyond the hearth: Older women and retirement. In E. W. Markson (Ed.), *Older women: Issues and prospects* (pp. 93–120). Lexington, MA: Heath.

Szinovacz, M. E. (1983b). Using couple data as a methodological tool: The case of marital violence. *Journal of Marriage and the Family, 45,* 633–644.

Taffel, S. M., Placek, P. J., & Moien, M. (1989). Cesarean section rate levels off in 1987. *Family Planning Perspectives, 21,* 227–228.

Taking charge of your finances. (1987, February 1). *Parade Magazine,* p. 12G.

Tanfer, K. (1986, April). *Patterns of premarital cohabitation among never married women in the U.S.* Paper presented at the meeting of the Population Association of America, San Francisco, CA.

Taub, S. (1985). Surrogate motherhood and the law. *Connecticut Medicine, 49,* 671–674.

Tavris, C. (1977, January). Men and women report their views on masculinity. *Psychology Today,* pp. 34–42, 82.

Tavris, C., & Sadd, S. (1975). *The Redbook report on female sexuality.* New York: Delacorte Press.

Taylor, E. (1989, October 9). Are you my mother? *Time,* p. 90.

Taylor, S., Jr. (1986, April 1). Supreme Court hears case on homosexual rights. *The New York Times,* p. 24A.

Teaching Judaism to interfaith couples. (1985, August 18). *The New York Times,* p. 51A.

Teachman, J. D. (1986). First and second marital dissolution: A decomposition exercise for whites and blacks. *The Sociological Quarterly, 27,* 571–590.

Teachman, J. D. (1990). Socioeconomic resources of parents and award of child support in the United States: Some exploratory models. *Journal of Marriage and the Family, 52,* 689–699.

Teachman, J. D., & Polonko, K. A. (1985). Timing of the transition to parenthood: A multidimensional birth-interval approach. *Journal of Marriage and the Family, 47,* 867–879.

Teachman, J. D., & Polonko, K. A. (1990). Cohabitation and marital stability in the United States. *Social Forces, 69,* 207–220.

Teachman, J. D., Polonko, K. A., & Scanzoni, J. (1987). Demography of the family. In M. B. Sussman & S. K. Steinmetz (Eds.), *Handbook of marriage and the family* (pp. 5–36). New York: Plenum Press.

Term insurance: Why plain vanilla is best. (1986, June). *Consumer Reports,* pp. 379–385.

Thayer, N. S. T. (1989). We need to recognize pluralism in our adult relationships. In R. T. Francoeur (Ed.), *Taking sides: Clashing views on controversial issues in human sexuality* (2nd ed., pp. 242–249). Guilford, CT: Dushkin.

Third of workers get maternity leave. (1989, April 8). *Eau Claire Leader-Telegram,* p. 5B.

Thomas, J. L. (1986). Age and sex differences in perceptions of grandparenting. *Journal of Gerontology, 41,* 417–423.

Thomas, K., & Wister, A. (1984). Living arrangements of older women: The ethnic dimension. *Journal of Marriage and the Family, 46,* 301–311.

Thomas, S., Albrecht, K., & White, P. (1984). Determinants of marital quality in dual-career couples. *Family Relations, 33,* 513–521.

Thompson, A. P. (1984). Emotional and sexual components of extramarital relations. *Journal of Marriage and the Family, 46,* 35–42.

Thompson, D. (1988, November 7). Safer births the second time. *Time,* p. 103.

Thompson, L., & Spanier, G. B. (1983). The end of marriage and acceptance of marital termination. *Journal of Marriage and the Family, 45,* 103–113.

Thompson, L., & Walker, A. J. (1984). Mothers and daughters: Aid patterns and attachment. *Journal of Marriage and the Family, 46,* 313–322.

Thornburg, H. D. (1981). The amount of sex information learning obtained during early adolescence. *Journal of Early Adolescence, 1,* 171–183.

Thorne, B. (1982). Feminist thinking on the family: An overview. In B. Thorne & M. Yalom (Eds.), *Rethinking the family: Some feminist questions* (pp. 1–24). New York: Longman.

Thorne, B., & Luria, Z. (1986). Sexuality and gender in children's daily worlds. *Social Problems, 33,* 176–190.

Thornton, A. (1985). Changing attitudes toward separation and divorce: Causes and consequences. *American Journal of Sociology, 90,* 856–872.

Thornton, A., & Camburn, D. (1987). The influence of the family on premarital sexual attitudes and behavior. *Demography, 24,* 323–340.

Thornton, A., & Freedman, D. (1982). Changing attitudes toward marriage and single life. *Family Planning Perspectives, 14,* 297–303.

Throwe, A. N. (1986). Families and alcohol. *Critical Care Quarterly, 8,* 79–88.

Tiedje, L. B., Wortman, C. B., Downey, G., Emmons, C., Biernat, M., & Lang, E. (1990). Women with multiple roles: Role-compatibility perceptions, satisfaction, and mental health. *Journal of Marriage and the Family, 52,* 63–71.

Tiefer, L., & Melman, A. (1983). Interview of wives: A necessary adjunct in the evaluation of impotence. *Sexuality & Disability, 6,* 167–175.

Tietze, C., & Lewit, S. (1978). Abortion: The universal practice. *People, 5,* 4–6.

Ting, K. (1988, March). *Linking family transitions to women's work behavior.* Paper presented at the meeting of the Southern Sociological Society, Nashville, TN.

Tippett, K. S. (Ed.). (1985). *Family economics review No. 2.* Washington, DC: U.S. Department of Agriculture.

To buy or to rent? (1990, October 1). *Newsweek,* p. 52.

Tocqueville, A. de (1972). Democracy in America. In N. F. Cott (Ed.), *Root of bitterness: Documents of the social history of American women* (p. 120). New York: Dutton.

Toffler, A. (1980). *The third wave.* New York: Morrow.

Toffler, A. (1990). *Power shift: Knowledge, wealth, and violence at the edge of the 21st Century.* New York: Bantam Books.

Toilets to get smarter in 1990's author says. (1989, October 4). *Austin American-Statesman,* p. A1.

Toman, B. (1983, September 7). Maternity costs: Parenthood and career overtax some women despite best intentions. *The Wall Street Journal,* pp. 1, 23.

Tong, R. (1989). *Feminist thought: A comprehensive introduction.* Boulder: Westview Press.

Torrey, B. B., Kinsella, K., & Taeuber, C. M. (1987). *An aging world.* International Population Reports, Series P-95, No. 78. Washington, DC: U.S. Government Printing Office.

Toufexis, A. (1988, June 6). Comeback of a contraceptive. *Time,* p. 67.

Trapp, J. D. (1987). Pharmacologic erection program for the treatment of male impotence. *Southern Medical Journal, 80,* 426–427.

Treas, J., & Bengston, V. L. (1987). The family in later years. In M. B. Sussman & S. K. Steinmetz (Eds.), *Handbook of marriage and the family* (pp. 625–648). New York: Plenum Press.

Trimberger, R., & MacLean, M. J. (1982). Maternal employment: The child's perspective. *Journal of Marriage and the Family, 44,* 469–475.

Troll, L. E. (1986). Parents and children in later life. *Generations, 10*(4), 23–25.

Trost, J. E. (1979). *Unmarried cohabitation.* Vasteras, Sweden: International Library.

Trost, J. E. (1986). Abortions in relation to age, coital frequency and fecundity. *Archives of Sexual Behavior, 15,* 505–509.

Trunzo, C. E. (1985, May). When baby makes three. *Money,* pp. 125–126, 128.

Trussell, J., Hatcher, R. A., Cates, W., Jr., Stewart, F. H., & Kost, K. (1990). Contraceptive failure in the United States: An update. *Studies in Family Planning, 21,* 51–54.

Trussell, J., & Rao, K. V. (1989). Premarital cohabitation and marital stability: A reassessment of the Canadian evidence. *Journal of Marriage and the Family, 51,* 535–544.

Trussell, J. C. (1988). Teenage pregnancy in the United States. *Family Planning Perspectives, 20,* 262–272.

Tschann, J. M., Johnston, J. R., Kline, M., & Wallerstein, J. S. (1989). Family process and children's functioning during divorce. *Journal of Marriage and the Family, 51,* 431–444.

Tucker, M. B., & Mitchell-Kernan, C. (1990). New trends in black American interracial marriage: The social structural context. *Journal of Marriage and the Family, 52,* 209–217.

Tucker, S. M. (1978). *Fetal monitoring and fetal assessment in high-risk pregnancy.* St. Louis: Mosby.

Turco, C. L. (1979). Women and credit. In S. Hendricks (Ed.), *Women's yellow pages: Original sourcebook for women* (West Virginia ed., pp. 246–249). Boston: The Public Works.

Turner, A. P. (1982). Religiosity, sex role attitudes, previous association with homosexuals, demographic characteristics and attitudes toward homosexuals in a church affiliated population (Doctoral dissertation, University of Virginia, 1981). *Dissertation Abstracts International, 43,* 1668B.

Turner, B. F., & Adams, C. G. (1988). Reported change in preferred sexual activity over the adult years. *The Journal of Sex Research, 25,* 289–303.

Turner, P. H., & Harris, M. B. (1984). Parent attitudes and preschool children's social competence. *Journal of Genetic Psychology, 144,* 105–113.

Turner, P. H., & Smith, R. M. (1983). Single parents and day care. *Family Relations, 32,* 215–226.

Turner, R. (1991). One-third of working mothers of a school-age child pay for day-care. *Family Planning Perspectives, 23,* 46–47.

TV's 'disastrous' impact on children. (1981, January 19). *U.S. News & World Report,* pp. 43–45.

Two viewpoints of love. (1983, August/September). *Modern Bride,* p. 166.

Tyler, C. W., Jr. (1981). Epidemiology of abortion. *Journal of Reproductive Medicine, 26,* 459–469.

Tyrer, L., & Kornblatt, J. E. (1983). Teens' contraceptive needs. *Planned Parenthood Review, 2*(3), 11–13.

Udry, J. R. (1974). *The social context of marriage* (3rd ed.). Philadelphia: Lippincott.

Udry, J. R. (1980). Changes in the frequency of marital intercourse from panel data. *Archives of Sexual Behavior, 9,* 319–325.

Udry, J. R. (1981). Marital alternatives and marital disruption. *Journal of Marriage and the Family, 43,* 889–897.

Ulbrich, P. M. (1988). The determinants of depression in two-income marriages. *Journal of Marriage and the Family, 50,* 121–131.

Ulbrich, P. M., Coyle, A. T., & Llabre, M. M. (1990). Involuntary childlessness and marital adjustment: His and hers. *Journal of Sex & Marital Therapy, 16,* 147–158.

Ulrici, D., L'Abate, L., & Wagner, V. (1981). The E-R-A model: A heuristic framework for classification of skill training programs for couples and families. *Family Relations, 30,* 307–315.

Umberson, D. (1987). Family stress and health behaviors: Social control as a dimension of social integration. *Journal of Health and Social Behavior, 28,* 306–319.

Umberson, D. (1989). Relationships with children: Explaining parents' psychological well-being. *Journal of Marriage and the Family, 51,* 999–1012.

Umberson, D., & Gove, W. R. (1989). Parenthood and psychological well-being: Theory, measurement, and stage in the family life course. *Journal of Family Issues, 10,* 440–462.

Understanding child abuse and neglect. (1985). York, PA: Gladden Foundation.

Unwed couples don't have right to sue, California court rules. (1988, August 20). *Austin American-Statesman,* p. 4A.

The upcreep of prices. (1986, February 3). *U.S. News & World Report,* p. 10.

Upton, G. V. (1986). The contraceptive and hormonal requirements of the premenopausal woman: The years from forty to fifty. *International Journal of Fertility, 30,* 44–52.

Urge teenaged girls to say "not now" rather than "no." (1988). *Medical Aspects of Human Sexuality, 22*(7), 19.

U.S. Bureau of the Census. (1985a). No. 95. Marital status of women at the time of their first birth, by period of their first birth: 1982. In *Statistical abstract of the United States, 1986* (106th ed., p. 63). Washington, DC: U.S. Government Printing Office.

U.S. Bureau of the Census. (1985b). No. 677. Occupations of the work-experienced civilian labor force, by sex: 1970 to 1980. In *Statistical abstract of the United States, 1986* (106th ed., p. 400). Washington, DC: U.S. Government Printing Office.

U.S. Bureau of the Census. (1989a). No. 92. Breast-feeding by characteristic of mother and birth year of baby: 1970 to 1981. In *Statistical abstract of the United States, 1989* (109th ed., p. 65). Washington, DC: U.S. Government Printing Office.

U.S. Bureau of the Census. (1989b). No. 609. Child support and alimony—Selected characteristics of women: 1985. In *Statistical abstract of the United States, 1989* (109th ed., p. 368). Washington, DC: U.S. Government Printing Office.

U.S. Bureau of the Census. (1989c). No. 818. Monthly use of banking accounts, credit cards, and cash: 1984 to 1986. In *Statistical abstract of the United States, 1989* (109th ed., p. 501). Washington, DC: U.S. Government Printing Office.

U.S. Bureau of the Census. (1990a). No. 13. Total population, by age and sex: 1960 to 1988. In *Statistical abstract of the United States, 1990* (110th ed., p. 13). Washington, DC: U.S. Government Printing Office.

U.S. Bureau of the Census. (1990b). No. 22. Resident population, by age, sex, and race: 1970 to 1988. In *Statistical abstract of the United States, 1990* (110th ed., p. 18). Washington, DC: U.S. Government Printing Office.

U.S. Bureau of the Census. (1990c). No. 41. Population 65 years old and over, by age group and sex, 1960 to 1988, and projections, 1990 to 2000. In *Statistical abstract of the United States, 1990* (110th ed., p. 37). Washington, DC: U.S. Government Printing Office.

U.S. Bureau of the Census. (1990d). No. 49. Marital status of the population, by sex and age: 1988. In *Statistical abstract of the United States, 1990* (110th ed., p. 42). Washington, DC: U.S. Government Printing Office.

U.S. Bureau of the Census. (1990e). No. 52. Single (never-married) persons as percent of total population, by sex and age: 1970 to 1988. In *Statistical abstract of the United States, 1990* (110th ed., p. 44). Washington, DC: U.S. Government Printing Office.

U.S. Bureau of the Census. (1990f). No. 53. Interracial married couples: 1970 to 1988. In *Statistical abstract of the United States, 1990* (110th ed., p. 44). Washington, DC: U.S. Government Printing Office.

U.S. Bureau of the Census. (1990g). No. 54. Unmarried couples, by selected characteristics, 1970 to 1988, and by marital status of partners, 1988. In *Statistical abstract of the United States, 1990* (110th ed., p. 44). Washington, DC: U.S. Government Printing Office.

U.S. Bureau of the Census. (1990h). No. 55. Households, families, subfamilies, married couples, and unrelated individuals: 1960 to 1989. In *Statistical abstract of the United States, 1990* (110th ed., p. 45). Washington, DC: U.S. Government Printing Office.

U.S. Bureau of the Census. (1990i). No. 69. Children under 18 years old, by presence of parents: 1970 to 1988. In *Statistical abstract of the United States, 1990* (110th ed., p. 53). Washington, DC: U.S. Government Printing Office.

U.S. Bureau of the Census. (1990j). No. 88. Live births, by place of delivery; Median and low-birth weight; and Prenatal care: 1960 to 1987. In *Statistical abstract of the United States, 1990* (110th ed., p. 66). Washington, DC: U.S. Government Printing Office.

U.S. Bureau of the Census. (1990k). No. 89. Cesarean section deliveries, by age of mother: 1970 to 1987. In *Statistical abstract of the United States, 1990* (110th ed., p. 66). Washington, DC: U.S. Government Printing Office.

U.S. Bureau of the Census. (1990l). No. 90. Births to unmarried women, by race of child and age of mother: 1970 to 1987. In *Statistical abstract of the United States, 1990* (110th ed., p. 67). Washington, DC: U.S. Government Printing Office.

U.S. Bureau of the Census. (1990m). No. 92. Women who have had a child in the last year, by age: 1980 to 1988. In *Statistical abstract of the United States, 1990* (110th ed., p. 68). Washington, DC: U.S. Government Printing Office.

U.S. Bureau of the Census. (1990n). No. 93. Social and economic characteristics of women, 18–44 years old, who have had a child in the last year: 1988. In *Statistical abstract of the United States, 1990* (110th ed., p. 68). Washington, DC: U.S. Government Printing Office.

U.S. Bureau of the Census. (1990o). No. 95. Childless women and children ever born, by age of woman: 1980 to 1988. In *Statistical abstract of the United States, 1990* (110th ed., p. 69). Washington, DC: U.S. Government Printing Office.

U.S. Bureau of the Census. (1990p). No. 98. Lifetime births expected by wives, 18–34 years old—Percent distribution: 1975–1988. In *Statistical abstract of the United States, 1990* (110th ed., p. 70). Washington, DC: U.S. Government Printing Office.

U.S. Bureau of the Census. (1990q). No. 99. Contraceptive use by women, 15–44 years old, by age, race, marital status, and method of contraception: 1982. In *Statistical abstract of the United States, 1990* (110th ed., p. 70). Washington, DC: U.S. Government Printing Office.

U.S. Bureau of the Census. (1990r). No. 101. Legal abortions, by selected characteristics: 1973 to 1985. In *Statistical abstract of the United States, 1990* (110th ed., p. 71). Washington, DC: U.S. Government Printing Office.

U.S. Bureau of the Census. (1990s). No. 104. Selected life table values: 1959 to 1986. In *Statistical abstract of the United States, 1990* (110th ed., p. 73). Washington, DC: U.S. Government Printing Office.

U.S. Bureau of the Census. (1990t). No. 117. Death rates by selected causes and selected characteristics: 1970 to 1988. In *Statistical abstract of the United States, 1990* (110th ed., p. 81). Washington, DC: U.S. Government Printing Office.

U.S. Bureau of the Census. (1990u). No. 129. Marriage rates and median age of bride and groom by previous marital status: 1970 to 1986. In *Statistical abstract of the United States, 1990* (110th ed., p. 87). Washington, DC: U.S. Government Printing Office.

U.S. Bureau of the Census. (1990v). No. 131. Divorces and annulments—Median duration of marriage, median age at divorce, and children involved: 1970 to 1986. In *Statistical abstract of the United States, 1990* (110th ed., p. 88). Washington, DC: U.S. Government Printing Office.

U.S. Bureau of the Census. (1990w). No. 274. Earned degrees conferred, by level of degree and sex: 1950 to 1987. In *Statistical abstract of the United States, 1990* (110th ed., p. 161). Washington, DC: U.S. Government Printing Office.

U.S. Bureau of the Census. (1990x). No. 634. Labor force participation rates by marital status, sex, and age: 1960 to 1988. In *Statistical abstract of the United States, 1990* (110th ed., p. 384). Washington, DC: U.S. Government Printing Office.

U.S. Bureau of the Census. (1990y). No. 636. Married, separated, and divorced women—Labor force status by presence and age of children: 1960 to 1988. In *Statistical abstract of the United States, 1990* (110th ed., p. 385). Washington, DC: U.S. Government Printing Office.

U.S. Bureau of the Census. (1990z). No. 642. Employed and unemployed workers by work schedules, sex, and age: 1980 to 1988. In *Statistical abstract of the United States, 1990* (110th ed., p. 387). Washington, DC: U.S. Government Printing Office.

U.S. Bureau of the Census. (1990aa). No. 645. Employed civilians, by occupation, sex, and race, and Hispanic origin: 1988. In *Statistical abstract of the United States, 1990* (110th ed., pp. 389–390). Washington, DC: U.S. Government Printing Office.

U.S. Bureau of the Census. (1990bb). No. 671. Full-time wage and salary workers—Number and median weekly earnings, by selected characteristics: 1983 to 1988. In *Statistical abstract of the United States, 1990* (110th ed., p. 409). Washington, DC: U.S. Government Printing Office.

U.S. Bureau of the Census. (1990cc). No. 698. Personal consumption expenditures, by type of expenditure in current dollars: 1980 to 1988. In *Statistical abstract of the United States, 1990* (110th ed., p. 430). Washington, DC: U.S. Government Printing Office.

U.S. Bureau of the Census. (1990dd). No. 715. Average annual income and expenditures of all consumer units: 1987. In *Statistical abstract of the United States, 1990* (110th ed., pp. 442–443). Washington, DC: U.S. Government Printing Office.

U.S. Bureau of the Census. (1990ee). No. 718. Money income of households—Percent distribution by money income level and selected characteristics: 1987. In *Statistical abstract of the United States, 1990* (110th ed., p. 445). Washington, DC: U.S. Government Printing Office.

U.S. Bureau of the Census. (1990ff). No. 730. Money income of families—Percent distribution by income level, by race and Hispanic origin of householder, and selected characteristics: 1987. In *Statistical abstract of the United States, 1990* (110th ed., p. 452). Washington, DC: U.S. Government Printing Office.

U.S. Bureau of the Census. (1990gg). No. 734. Money income of persons—Percent distribution by income level, median, and mean income, by sex, 1970 to 1987, and by age, race, Hispanic origin, and region, 1987. In *Statistical abstract of the United States, 1990* (110th ed., p. 454). Washington, DC: U.S. Government Printing Office.

U.S. Bureau of the Census. (1990hh). No. 744. Persons below poverty level and below 125 percent of poverty level, by race of householder and family status: 1979 to 1987. In *Statistical abstract of the United States, 1990* (110th ed., p. 459). Washington, DC: U.S. Government Printing Office.

U.S. Bureau of the Census. (1990ii). No. 757. Consumer price indexes—Percent change in major groups: 1960 to 1988. In *Statistical abstract of the United States, 1990* (110th ed., p. 468). Washington, DC: U.S. Government Printing Office.

U.S. Bureau of the Census. (1990jj). No. 763. Consumer price index by region: 1975 to 1988. In *Statistical abstract of the United States, 1990* (110th ed., p. 471). Washington, DC: U.S. Government Printing Office.

U.S. Bureau of the Census. (1990kk). No. 831. Credit cards—Holders, numbers, spending and debt: 1980 to 1988. In *Statistical abstract of the United States, 1990* (110th ed., p. 506). Washington, DC: U.S. Government Printing Office.

U.S. Bureau of the Census. (1990ll). No. 934. Advertising—Estimated expenditures, by medium: 1970 to 1988. In *Statistical abstract of the United States, 1990* (110th ed., p. 557). Washington, DC: U.S. Government Printing Office.

U.S. Bureau of the Census. (1990mm). No. 935. Magazine advertising—Expenditures, by product type: 1970 to 1988. In *Statistical abstract of the United States, 1990* (110th ed., p. 557). Washington, DC: U.S. Government Printing Office.

U.S. Bureau of the Census. (1990nn). No. 936. Television—Expenditures for network advertising: 1980 to 1988. In *Statistical abstract of the United States, 1990* (110th ed., p. 558). Washington, DC: U.S. Government Printing Office.

U.S. Bureau of the Census. (1990oo). No. 1264. Median sales price of new privately owned one-family houses sold, by region: 1970 to 1988. In *Statistical abstract of the United States, 1990* (110th ed., p. 716). Washington, DC: U.S. Government Printing Office.

U.S. Bureau of the Census. (1990pp). No. 1266. Existing one-family houses sold and price, by region: 1970 to 1988. In *Statistical abstract of the United States, 1990* (110th ed., p. 716). Washington, DC: U.S. Government Printing Office.

U.S. Department of Agriculture. (1988). *Annual cost of raising a child (1) from birth to age 18, moderate cost level.* Washington, DC: U.S. Government Printing Office.

U.S. Department of Labor. (1991, January). A-71. Median weekly earnings by type of family, number of earners, race, and Hispanic origin. In *Employment and earnings* (p. 76). Washington, DC: Bureau of Labor Statistics.

U.S. House of Representatives Select Committee on Aging. (1987). *Exploding the myths: Caregiving in America.* Washington, DC: U.S. Government Printing Office.

U.S. household size continues to shrink. (1989, May 5). *Austin American-Statesman*, p. A4.

U.S. Public Health Service. (1984). *Facts about AIDS*. Washington, DC: U.S. Department of Health and Human Services.

U.S. Public Health Service. (1988). *Understanding AIDS* (HSS Publication No. (CDC) HHS-88-8404). Washington, DC: U.S. Government Printing Office.

U.S. Senate Special Committee on Aging. (1988). *Aging America: Trends and projections, 1987–88 edition*. Washington D.C.: U.S. Department of Health and Human Services.

Usher, S., & Fels, M. (1985). The challenge of feminism and career for the middle-aged woman. *International Journal of Women's Studies, 8*, 47–57.

Vaginal delivery often possible after cesarean. (1990). *Medical Aspects of Human Sexuality*, 24(11), 10.

Valentine, D. P. (1982). The experience of pregnancy: A developmental process. *Family Relations, 31*, 243–248.

Vander Mey, B. J., & Neff, R. L. (1984). Adult-child incest: A sample of substantiated cases. *Family Relations, 33*, 549–557.

Van der Zanden, J. W. (1981). *Human development* (2nd ed.). New York: Knopf.

Van der Zanden, J. W. (1989). *Human development* (4th ed.). New York: Knopf.

Vanfossen, B. E. (1977). Sexual stratification and sex role socialization. *Journal of Marriage and the Family, 39*, 563–574.

Van Velsor, E., & O'Rand, A. M. (1984). Family life cycle, work career patterns, and women's wages at midlife. *Journal of Marriage and the Family, 46*, 365–373.

Vasectomy: Facts about male sterilization. (1987). Daly City, CA: Krames Communication.

Vaughn, B. E., Gove, F. L., & Egeland, B. (1980). The relationship between out-of-home care and the quality of infant-mother attachment in an economically disadvantaged population. *Child Development, 51*, 1203–1214.

Veevers, J. E. (1973). Voluntarily childless wives: An exploratory study. *Sociology and Social Research, 58*, 356–365.

Veevers, J. E. (1975). The moral careers of voluntarily childless wives: Notes on the defense of a variant world view. *The Family Coordinator, 24*, 473–486.

Veevers, J. E. (1984). Age-discrepant marriages: Cross-national comparisons of Canadian-American trends. *Social Biology, 31*, 18–27.

Veevers, J. E. (1985). The social meaning of pets: Alternative roles for companion animals. *Marriage and Family Review, 8*(3/4), 11–30.

Vega, W. A., Warheit, G. J., & Meinhardt, K. (1984). Marital disruption and the prevalence of depressive symptomatology among Anglos and Mexican Americans. *Journal of Marriage and the Family, 46*, 817–824.

Vemer, E., Coleman, M., Ganong, L. H., & Cooper, H. (1989). Marital satisfaction in remarriage: A meta-analysis. *Journal of Marriage and the Family, 51*, 713–725.

Ventura, J. N. (1987). The stresses of parenthood reexamined. *Family Relations, 36*, 26–29.

Ventura, J. N., & Boss, P. G. (1983). The family coping inventory applied to parents with new babies. *Journal of Marriage and the Family, 45*, 867–875.

Vera, H., Berardo, D. H., & Berardo, F. M. (1985). Age heterogamy in marriage. *Journal of Marriage and the Family, 47*, 553–566.

Verbrugge, L. M. (1984). A health profile of older women with comparisons to older men. *Research on Aging, 6*, 291–322.

Veroff, H., Kulka, R. A., & Douvan, E. (1981). *The inner American: A self-portrait from 1957 to 1976*. New York: Basic Books.

Vinick, B. H. (1978). Remarriage in old age. *The Family Coordinator, 27*, 359–363.

Viorst, J. (1985, May). Can a baby save a marriage? *Redbook*, pp. 43–44.

Viorst, J. (1986). In F. Metcalf (Compiler), *The Penguin dictionary of modern humorous quotations*. London: Penguin Books.

Visher, E. B., & Visher, J. S. (1979). *Stepfamilies: A guide to working with stepparents and stepchildren*. New York: Brunner/Mazel.

Visher, J. S. (1984). Seven myths about stepfamilies. *Medical Aspects of Human Sexuality, 18*(1), 52, 56, 61–62, 65, 68, 73–74, 76, 80.

Voydanoff, P. (1985, November). *The dilemmas of caring*. Paper presented at the Theory Construction and Research Methodology Workshop, National Council on Family Relations, Dallas, TX.

Voydanoff, P., & Kelly, R. F. (1984). Determinants of work-related family problems among employed parents. *Journal of Marriage and the Family, 46*, 881–892.

Vreeland, R. S. (1972, February). Sex at Harvard. *Sexual Behavior*, pp. 4–10.

Vroom, P., Fassett, D., & Wakefield, R. A. (1982, February). Winning through mediation: Divorce without losers. *The Futurist*, pp. 28–34.

Wage gap continues. (1990). *Project on the Status and Education of Women, 20*(1), 3.

Waite, L. J., Goldscheider, F. K., & Witsberger, C. (1986). Nonfamily living and the erosion of traditional family orientations among young adults. *American Sociological Review, 51*, 541–554.

Waite, L. J., Haggstrom, G. W., & Kanouse, D. E. (1985a). Changes in the employment activities of new parents. *American Sociological Review, 50*, 263–272.

Waite, L. J., Haggstrom, G. W., & Kanouse, D. E. (1985b). The consequences of parenthood for the marital stability of young adults. *American Sociological Review, 50*, 850–875.

Walbroehl, G. (1984). Sexuality during pregnancy. *American Family Physician, 29*, 273–275.

Waldrop, J. (1988). The fashionable family. *American Demographics, 10*(3), 22–26.

Walfish, S., & Myerson, M. (1980). Sex role identity and attitudes toward sexuality. *Archives of Sexual Behavior, 9*, 199–203.

Walker, L. (1979). *The battered woman*. New York: Harper & Row.

Walker, L. E. A. (1987). Identifying the wife at risk of battering. *Medical Aspects of Human Sexuality, 21*(7), 107, 110, 113–114.

Wallace, G. D. (1985, December 30). When the conventional wisdom for an IRA is too conservative. *Business Week*, p. 141.

Wallace, P. M., & Gotlib, I. H. (1990). Marital adjustment during the transition to parenthood: Stability and predictors of change. *Journal of Marriage and the Family, 52,* 21–29.

Waller, W. (1937). The rating and dating complex. *American Sociological Review, 2,* 727–734.

Waller, W., & Hill, R. (1951). *The family: A dynamic interpretation* (rev. ed.). New York: Holt, Rinehart & Winston.

Wallerstein, J. S. (1985). Children of divorce: Preliminary report of a ten-year follow-up of older children and adolescents. *Journal of the American Academy of Child Psychiatry, 24,* 545–553.

Wallerstein, J. S. (1986). Women after divorce: Preliminary report from a ten-year follow-up. *American Journal of Orthopsychiatry, 56,* 65–77.

Wallerstein, J. S., & Blakeslee, S. (1990). *Second chances: Men, women, and children a decade after divorce.* New York: Ticknor & Fields.

Wallerstein, J. S., & Kelly, J. B. (1980a). *Surviving the breakup: How children actually cope with divorce.* New York: Basic Books.

Wallerstein, J. S., & Kelly, J. B. (1980b). The visiting father-child relationship. *American Journal of Psychiatry, 137,* 1534–1539.

Wallis, C. (1985a, August 12). AIDS: A growing threat. *Time,* pp. 40–45, 47.

Wallis, C. (1985b, December 9). Children having children. *Time,* pp. 76, 79–82, 84, 87, 89–90.

Wallis, C. (1985c, February 4). Chlamydia: The silent epidemic. *Time,* p. 67.

Wallis, C. (1987, June 22). The child-care dilemma. *Time,* pp. 54–60.

Wallis, C. (1989, December 4). Onward, women! *Time,* pp. 80–82, 85–86, 89.

Walsh, R., Ganza, W., & Finefield, T. (1983, April). *A fifteen year study about sexual permissiveness.* Paper presented at the meeting of the Midwest Sociological Society, Kansas City, MO.

Walster, E. (1971). Passionate love. In B. I. Murstein (Ed.), *Theories of attraction and love* (pp. 85–97). New York: Springer.

Walster, E., & Walster, G. W. (1978). *A new look at love.* Reading, MA: Addison-Wesley.

Walters, J., & Walters, L. H. (1980). Parent-child relationships: A review, 1970–1979. *Journal of Marriage and the Family, 42,* 807–822.

Walters, L. H. (1982). Are families different from other groups? *Journal of Marriage and the Family, 44,* 841–850.

Wampler, K. S., & Kingery, D. W. (1985, November). *Emphasizing the wife's career: Predictors and consequences.* Paper presented at the Theory Construction and Research Methodology Workshop, National Council on Family Relations, Dallas, TX.

Wan, T. T. H., & Odell, B. G. (1983). Major role losses and social participation of older males. *Research on Aging, 5,* 173–196.

Wantz, M. S., & Gay, J. E. (1981). *The aging process: A health perspective.* Cambridge, MA: Winthrop.

Warner, C. T., & Olson, T. D. (1981). Another view of family conflict and family wholeness. *Family Relations, 30,* 493–503.

Wasow, M. (1984). Get out of my potato patch: A biased view of death and dying. *Health and Social Work, 9,* 261–267.

Waterlow, J. C., & Thompson, A. M. (1979). Observations on the adequacy of breast-feeding. *Lancet, 2,* 238–242.

Watson, M. A. (1981). Custody alternatives: Defining the best interests of the children. *Family Relations, 30,* 474–479.

Watson, R. (1985). Gardnerella vaginalis: Genitourinary pathogen in men. *Urology, 25,* 217–222.

Watson, R. E. L. (1983). Premarital cohabitation vs. traditional courtship: Their effects on subsequent marital adjustment. *Family Relations, 32,* 139–147.

Watson, R., Lubennow, G. C., Greenberg, N., King, P., & Junkin, D. (1984, May 14). A hidden epidemic. *Newsweek,* pp. 30–36.

Weaver, M. J. (1985). *New Catholic women.* San Francisco: Harper & Row.

Webster-Stratton, C. (1989). The relationship of marital support, conflict, and divorce to parent perceptions, behaviors, and childhood conduct problems. *Journal of Marriage and the Family, 51,* 417–430.

Weeks, J. R. (1989). *Population: An introduction to concepts and issues* (4th ed.). Belmont, CA: Wadsworth.

Weil, E. M. (1985). The anorgasmic woman: Psychological and demographic correlates of anorgasmia (Doctoral dissertation, Adelphi University, 1985). *Dissertation Abstracts International, 46,* 668B.

Weiner, B. A. (1985). An overview of child custody laws. *Hospital and Community Psychiatry, 36,* 838–842.

Weingarten, H. (1980). Remarriage and well-being. *Journal of Family Issues, 1,* 553–559.

Weingourt, R. (1985). Wife rape: Barriers to identification and treatment. *American Journal of Psychotherapy, 39,* 187–192.

Weinstein, G. W. (1984). *Handling family money problems* (No. 626). New York: Public Affairs Committee.

Weinstein, G. W. (1986). *Men, women, & money: New roles, new rules.* New York: New American Library.

Weis, D. L. (1983a). Affective reactions of women to their initial experience of coitus. *The Journal of Sex Research, 19,* 209–237.

Weis, D. L. (1983b). Reactions of college women to their first coitus. *Medical Aspects of Human Sexuality, 17*(2), 60cc, 60gg, 60hh, 60ll.

Weis, D. L. (1985). The experience of pain during women's first sexual intercourse: Cultural mythology about female sexual initiation. *Archives of Sexual Behavior, 14,* 421–438.

Weis, D. L., & Jurich, J. (1985). Size of community of residence as a predictor of attitudes toward extramarital sexual relations. *Journal of Marriage and the Family, 47,* 173–178.

Weis, D. L., & Slosnerick, M. (1981). Attitudes toward sexual and nonsexual extramarital involvements among a sample of college students. *Journal of Marriage and the Family, 43,* 349–358.

Weisman, C. S., Nathanson, C. A., Teitelbaum, M. A., Chase, G. A., & King, T. M. (1986). Abortion attitudes and performance among male and female obstetrician-gynecologists. *Family Planning Perspectives, 18,* 67–73.

Weiss, R. S. (1976). The emotional impact of marital separation. *Journal of Social Issues, 32,* 135–145.

Weiss, R. S. (1979). *Going it alone: The family life and social situation of the single parent.* New York: Basic Books.

Weiss, R. S. (1981a). The emotional impact of marital separation. In P. J. Stein (Ed.), *Single life: Unmarried adults in social context* (pp. 69–79). New York: St. Martin's Press.

Weiss, R. S. (1981b). The study of loneliness. In P. J. Stein (Ed.), *Single life: Unmarried adults in social context* (pp. 152–164). New York: St. Martin's Press.

Weiss, R. S. (1984). The impact of marital dissolution on income and consumption in single-parent households. *Journal of Marriage and the Family, 46,* 115–127.

Weiss, R. S. (1985). Men and the family. *Family Process, 24,* 49–58.

Weiss, S. (1987, June 8). In the CD wars, the customers are winning. *Business Week,* p. 151.

Weitzman, L. J. (1975). Sex-role socialization. In J. Freeman (Ed.), *Women: A feminist perspective* (pp. 105–144). Palo Alto, CA: Mayfield.

Weitzman, L. J. (1981). *The marriage contract: Spouses, lovers, and the law.* New York: Free Press.

Weitzman, L. J. (1985). *The divorce revolution: The unexpected social and economic consequences for women and children in America.* New York: Free Press.

Weitzman, L. J., & Dixon, R. B. (1988). The transformation of legal marriage through no-fault divorce. In J. G. Wells (Ed.), *Current issues in marriage and the family* (4th ed., pp. 227–240). New York: Macmillan.

Weitzman, L. J., Eifler, D., Hokada, E., & Ross, C. (1972). Sex-role socialization in picture books for preschool children. *American Journal of Sociology, 77,* 1125–1150.

Weitzman, L. J., Lachs, S. M., & Tucker, M. S. (1986, August 17). Some second thoughts about no-fault divorce. *The New York Times,* p. 24E.

Weizman, R., & Hart, J. (1987). Sexual behavior in healthy married elderly men. *Archives of Sexual Behavior, 16,* 39–44.

Welch, C. E., III, & Price-Bonham, S. (1983). A decade of no-fault divorce revisited: California, Georgia, and Washington. *Journal of Marriage and the Family, 45,* 411–418.

Weller, R. A., & Halikas, J. A. (1984). Marijuana use and sexual behavior. *The Journal of Sex Research, 20,* 186–193.

Welles, G. (1985, September 20–22). New devices for birth control. *USA Weekend,* p. 14.

Wells, C., Lucas, M. J., & Meyer, J. K. (1980). Unrealistic expectations of orgasm. *Medical Aspects of Human Sexuality, 14*(4), 53, 60–61, 64–66, 71.

Wells, J. (1986). *Coping in the 80's: Eliminating needless stress and guilt.* Chicago: Thomas More Press.

Wells, J. G. (1988). Having children. In J. G. Wells (Ed.), *Current issues in marriage and the family* (pp. 137–141). New York: Macmillan.

Werner, P. D., & LaRussa, G. W. (1985). Persistence and change in sex-role stereotypes. *Sex Roles, 12,* 1089–1100.

Wertz, R., & Wertz, D. (1977). *Lying-in: A history of childbirth in America.* New York: Free Press.

Wespes, E., & Schulman, C. (1985). Venous leakage: Surgical treatment of a curable cause of impotence. *Journal of Urology, 133,* 796–798.

West, D. J. (1983). Homosexuality and lesbianism. *British Journal of Psychiatry, 143,* 221–226.

Westermarck, E. A. (1891). *The history of human marriage.* London: Macmillan.

Wexler, J. G. (1985). Role styles of women police officers. *Sex Roles, 12,* 749–755.

What you should know about divorce today. (1981, June). *Consumer Reports,* pp. 327–331.

What youth think. (1990, Fall). In E. Jamison & C. Wallis (Eds.), Women: The road ahead. [Special issue]. *Time,* p. 14.

Wheeler, D. L. (1990, November 28). Scientists criticize the FDA's restriction on import of French 'Abortion Pill.' *The Chronicle of Higher Education,* pp. A23, A29.

White, B. L. (1975). *The first three years of life.* Englewood Cliffs, NJ: Prentice-Hall.

White, B. L., Kaban, B., & Attonucci, J. (1979). *The origins of human competence.* Lexington, MA: Heath.

White, G. L. (1980). Physical attractiveness and courtship progress. *Journal of Personality and Social Psychology, 39,* 660–668.

White, L. K., & Booth, A. (1985). The quality and stability of remarriages: The role of stepchildren. *American Sociological Review, 50,* 689–698.

White, L. K., Booth, A., & Edwards, J. N. (1986). Children and marital happiness. *Journal of Family Issues, 7,* 131–147.

White, L. K., & Brinkerhoff, D. B. (1981a). Children's work in the family: Its significance and meaning. *Journal of Marriage and the Family, 43,* 789–798.

White, L. K., & Brinkerhoff, D. B. (1981b). The sexual division of labor: Evidence from childhood. *Social Forces, 60,* 170–181.

White, L. K., & Kim, H. (1987). The family-building process: Childbearing choices by parity. *Journal of Marriage and the Family, 49,* 271–279.

White, P. N., & Botkin, D. R. (1989). Coping with the dual career marriage. *Medical Aspects of Human Sexuality, 23,* 66–68, 79.

White, S. (1983, September 25). Signing a contract before marriage. *The New York Times,* p. 11F.

White, S. E., & Reamy, K. J. (1982). Sexuality and pregnancy: A review. *Archives of Sexual Behavior, 11,* 429–444.

White, S. W., & Bloom, B. L. (1981). Factors related to the adjustment of divorcing men. *Family Relations, 30,* 349–360.

Whiteside, M. F. (1982). Remarriage: A family developmental process. *Journal of Marital and Family Therapy, 8*(2), 59–68.

Wilder, T. (1939). *The bridge of San Luis Rey.* New York: Washington Square Press.

Wiley, M. G., & Eskilson, A. (1988, March). *Gender and family/career conflict: Reactions of bosses.* Paper presented at the meeting of the Southern Sociological Society, Nashville, TN.

Wilkie, J. M. (1986). Sex typing, marital adjustment, and bias-free versus feminist attitudes (Doctoral dissertation, Hofstra University, 1984). *Dissertation Abstracts International, 46,* 2503B–2504B.

Wilkie, J. R. (1981). The trend toward delayed parenthood. *Journal of Marriage and the Family, 43,* 583–591.

Wilkinson, D. (1987). Ethnicity. In M. B. Sussman & S. K. Steinmetz (Eds.), *Handbook of marriage and the family* (pp. 183–210). New York: Plenum Press.

Wilkinson, D. Y. (1975). *Black male/white female perspectives on interracial marriage and courtship.* Cambridge, MA: Schenkman.

Will women in their thirties find a husband? (1987). *Marriage and Divorce Today, 12*(28), 2.

Williams, A. M. (1981). Couple counseling with rape victims. In A. S. Gurman (Ed.), *Questions and answers in the practice of family therapy* (pp. 497–501). New York: Brunner/Mazel.

Williams, J. H. (1987). *Psychology of women: Behavior in a biosocial context* (3rd ed.). New York: Norton.

Williams, N. D. (1987). The relationship between ability to breast feed and female sexuality (Doctoral dissertation, California School of Professional Psychology, 1986). *Dissertation Abstracts International, 47,* 3551B.

Williams, T. H., & Handford, A. G. (1986). Television and leisure activities. In T. H. Williams (Ed.), *The impact of television: A natural experiment in three communities* (pp. 143–213). Orlando, FL: Academic Press.

Williams, T. R. (1990). *Cultural anthropology.* Englewood Cliffs, NJ: Prentice-Hall.

Williamson, R. C. (1977). Dating frequency, ethnicity, and adjustment in the high school: A comparative study. *International Journal of Sociology of the Family, 7,* 157–169.

Willie, C. V. (1988). *A new look at black families* (3rd ed.). Dix Hills, NY: General Hall.

Wilson, J. (1982, August). Preventing mental retardation. *Town & Country,* pp. 82–83.

Wilson, J. G. (1977). Embryotoxicity of drugs in man. In J. G. Wilson & C. F. Fraser (Eds.), *Handbook of teratology: Vol. 1. General principles and etiology* (pp. 309–355). New York: Plenum Press.

Wilson, K., Faison, R., & Britton, G. M. (1983). Cultural aspects of male sex aggression. *Deviant Behavior, 4,* 241–255.

Wilson, M. R., & Filsinger, E. E. (1986). Religiosity and marital adjustment: Multidimensional interrelationships. *Journal of Marriage and the Family, 48,* 147–151.

Wilson, W. J., & Neckerman, K. (1989). Poverty and family structure: The widening gap between evidence and public policy issues. In A. S. Skolnick & J. H. Skolnick (Eds.), *Family in transition* (6th ed., pp. 504–521). Glenview, IL: Scott, Foresman.

Winch, R. F. (1958). *Mate selection.* New York: Harper & Row.

Wineberg, H. (1990). Childbearing in remarriage. *Journal of Marriage and the Family, 52,* 31–38.

Wineberg, H., & McCarthy, J. (1989). Child spacing in the United States: Recent trends and differentials. *Journal of Marriage and the Family, 51,* 213–228.

Wing, J. (1989, November). Student court to judge campus date rape cases. *The National College Newspaper,* p. 2.

Winick, M. (1985, October). Search for the perfect pregnancy. *American Health: Fitness for Body and Mind,* pp. 59–61.

Winn, R. L., & Newton, N. (1982). Sexuality in aging: A study of 106 cultures. *Archives of Sexual Behavior, 11,* 283–298.

Wisensale, S. K., & Allison, M. D. (1989). Family leave legislation: State and federal initiatives. *Family Relations, 38,* 182–189.

Wishik, H. R. (1986). Economics of divorce: An exploratory study. *Family Law Quarterly, 20,* 79–107.

Witkin, S. L., Edleson, J. L., Rose, S. D., & Hall, J. A. (1983). Group training in marital communication: A comparative study. *Journal of Marriage and the Family, 45,* 661–669.

Witt, D. D., Davidson, B., Sollie, D. L., Lowe, G. D., & Peek, C. W. (1987). The consequences of early marriage on marital dissolution. *Sociological Spectrum, 7,* 191–207.

Witwer, M. (1990a). Advanced maternal age poses no major health risk for first-born infants. *Family Planning Perspectives, 22,* 235–236.

Witwer, M. (1990b). Two-thirds of women now work during their first pregnancy; half return to work within one year. *Family Planning Perspectives, 22,* 184–185.

Wolfe, L. (1981). *The Cosmo report.* New York: Arbor House.

Woll, S. B., & Young, P. (1989). Looking for Mr. or Ms. right: Self-presentation in video dating. *Journal of Marriage and the Family, 51,* 483–488.

Wollstonecraft, M. (1972). *The vindication of the rights of woman.* London: J. M. Dent.

Women in clergy called low-paid. (1984, March 29). *The New York Times,* p. 22.

Women in 60s. (1989, June 16). *Austin American-Statesman,* p. D6.

Women in 30s experiencing record-high divorce; level expected to decline among younger women. (1986). *Family Planning Perspectives, 18,* 133–134.

Wong, P. T., Kettlewell, G. E., & Sproule, C. F. (1985). On the importance of being masculine: Sex role, attribution, and women's career achievement. *Sex Roles, 12,* 757–769.

Woodroof, J. T. (1985). Religiosity and reference groups: Towards a model of adolescent sexuality (Doctoral dissertation, University of Nebraska-Lincoln, 1984). *Dissertation Abstracts International, 45,* 3002A–3003A.

Woods, N., Lentz, M., Mitchell, E., Lee, K., Taylor, D., & Allen-Barash, N. (1987). Women's health: The menstrual cycle/premenstrual symptoms: Another look. *Public Health Reports, 102,* 106–112.

Work and family: A new relationship? (1983). *The New Relationship, 1*(2/3), 1, 6.

Work interruptions and earnings. (1985, April). *Family Economics Review,* pp. 30–31.

Worth, G. (1986, February). At-home fertility lab. *Working Woman,* p. 60.

Wu, C. H. (1985). Current considerations of the menopause. *Annals of Clinical and Laboratory Science, 15,* 219–228.

Yalom, I. D. (1989). *Love's executioner & other tales of psychotherapy.* New York: Basic Books.

Yamaguchi, K., & Kandel, D. B. (1985). Dynamic relationships between premarital cohabitation and illicit drug use: An event-history analysis of role selection and role socialization. *American Sociological Review, 50,* 530–546.

Yankelovich, D. A. (1974). *The new morality: A profile of American youth in the 70's.* New York: McGraw-Hill.

Yankelovich, D. A. (1981). *New rules: Searching for self-fulfillment in a world turned upside down.* New York: Random House.

Yeast infection treatment to be sold over counter. (1990, December 16). *Eau Claire Leader-Telegram,* p. 5C.

Yelsma, P. (1986). Marriage vs. cohabitation: Couples' communication practices and satisfaction. *Journal of Communication, 36,* 94–107.

Yllo, K., & Straus, M. A. (1981). Interpersonal violence among married and cohabiting couples. *Family Relations, 30,* 339–347.

Yoder, J. D., & Nichols, R. C. (1980). A life perspective comparison of married and divorced persons. *Journal of Marriage and the Family, 42,* 413–419.

Yogev, S. (1981). Do professional women have egalitarian marital relationships? *Journal of Marriage and the Family, 43,* 865–871.

You and the banks. (1985, September). *Consumer Reports,* pp. 508–513.

Young, D. (1982). *Changing childbirth: Family birth in the hospital.* Rochester, NY: Childbirth Graphics.

Young, J. L., & Griffith, E. E. H. (1985). Psychiatric consultation in Catholic annulment proceedings. *Hospital and Community Psychiatry, 36,* 346–347.

Young, M. (1980). Attitudes and behavior of college students relative to oral-genital sexuality. *Archives of Sexual Behavior, 9,* 61–67.

Young, M. (1982). Religiosity, sexual behavior, and contraceptive use of college females. *Journal of American College Health, 30,* 216–220.

Youngkin, E. Q. (1990). Estrogen replacement therapy and the estraderm transdermal system. *Nurse Practitioner, 15*(5), 19–26.

Your most fantastic plastic. (1987, April). *Money,* pp. 162–170.

Zbella, E., Vermesh, M., & Gleicher, N. (1986). Contraceptive practices of female physicians. *Contraception, 33,* 423–436.

Zelnik, M., & Kantner, J. F. (1980). Sexual activity, contraceptive use and pregnancy among metropolitan-area teenagers: 1971–1979. *Family Planning Perspectives, 12,* 230–237.

Zigler, E., & Rubin, N. (1985, November). Why child abuse occurs. *Parents,* pp. 102–104, 106, 215–216, 218.

Zilbergeld, B. (1978). *Male sexuality: A guide to sexual fulfillment.* Boston: Little, Brown.

Zimbardo, P. G. (1988). *Psychology and life* (12th ed.). Glenview, IL: Scott, Foresman.

Zimmer, D., Borchardt, E., & Fischle, C. (1983). Sexual fantasies of sexually distressed and nondistressed men and women: An empirical comparison. *Journal of Sex & Marital Therapy, 9,* 38–50.

Zimmerman, S. L. (1982). Alternatives in human reproduction for involuntary childless couples. *Family Relations, 31,* 233–241.

Ziporyn, T. (1984). Search for male contraceptive complicated by adverse effects. *Journal of the American Medical Association, 252,* 1101–1103.

Zube, M. (1982). Changing behavior and outlook of aging men and women: Implications for marriage in the middle and later years. *Family Relations, 31,* 147–156.

Zuckerman, B. S., Walker, D. K., Frank, D. A., Chase, C., & Hamburg, B. (1984). Adolescent pregnancy: Biobehavioral determinants of outcome. *The Journal of Pediatrics, 105,* 857–863.

Zuravin, S. J. (1988). Child maltreatment and teenage first births: A relationship mediated by chronic sociodemographic stress? *American Journal of Orthopsychiatry, 58,* 91–103.

CREDITS

Figure 1.2: Reprinted by permission of Family Process, Inc.

Figure 2.1: From *Human Sexuality* by Louis H. Janda and Karin E. Klenke-Hamel. © 1980 by Litton Educational Publishing, Inc. Reprinted by permission of Wadsworth, Inc.

Figure 2.2: Reproduced by permission from Denney, Nancy W., and Quadagno, David: *Human Sexuality,* St. Louis, 1988, Times Mirror/Mosby College Publishing.

Figure 3.1: From T. L. Huston, et al., "From Courtship to Marriage: Mate Selection as an Interpersonal Process" in *Personal Relationship 2: Developing Personal Relationships.* Copyright © 1981 Academic Press, Orlando, FL. Reprinted by permission.

Figure 4.1: From S. Sprecher, et al., "A Revision of the Reiss Premarital Sexual Permissiveness Scale" in *Journal of Marriage and the Family,* 50:825. Copyright © 1988 National Council on Family Relations, 3989 Central Avenue, N.E., Suite #550, Minneapolis, MN 55421. Reprinted by permission.

Figure 7.1: From L. Cargan and M. Melko, *Singles: Myths and Realities.* Copyright © 1982 Sage Publications, Inc., Newbury Park, CA. Reprinted by permission of Sage Publications, Inc.

Figure 8.1: Reprinted from Volume 12 Number 4 of *Journal of Marital and Family Therapy,* Copyright 1986, American Association for Marriage and Family Therapy. Reprinted by permission.

Figure 9.1: From D. A. Ford, "Wife Battery and Criminal Justice: A Study of Victim Decision-Making" in *Family Relations,* 32:465. Copyright © 1983 National Council on Family Relations, 3989 Central Avenue, N.E., Suite #550, Minneapolis, MN 55421. Reprinted by permission.

Figure 10.1: "Contrary to Love," Figure 1–1, Page 9, CompCare Publishers, Minneapolis, MN, 1989. Reprinted by permission.

Figure 10.3: Reproduced by permission from Denney, Nancy W., and Quadagno, David: *Human Sexuality,* St. Louis, 1988, Times Mirror/Mosby College Publishing.

Figure 10.5: Reproduced by permission from Denney, Nancy W., and Quadagno, David: *Human Sexuality,* St. Louis, 1988, Times Mirror/Mosby College Publishing.

Figure 10.6: From *Human Sexuality,* 2/e by William H. Masters, et al. Copyright © 1988 by William H. Masters, Virginia E. Johnson, and Robert C. Kolodny. Reprinted by permission of HarperCollins Publishers.

Figure 12.1: From M. McKaughan and J. Kagan, "The Motherhood Plunge" in *Working Women,* February 1986:73. Copyright © Hal Publications, Inc., New York, NY.

Figure 12.2: Reprinted with permission © American Demographics, September 1984.

Figure 12.3: Reproduced by permission from Denney, Nancy W., and Quadagno, David: *Human Sexuality,* St. Louis, 1988, Times Mirror/Mosby College Publishing.

Figure 13.2: Reprinted by permission of Macmillan Publishing Company from *Becoming a Sexual Person,* 2d ed., by Robert T. Francoeur. Copyright © 1991 by Macmillan Publishing Company.

Figure 13.3: From K. L. Moore, *The Developing Human: Clinically-Oriented Embryology,* 4th ed. Copyright 1988 W. B. Saunders, Orlando, FL. Reprinted by permission.

Figure 13.4: From R. E. Jones, *Human Reproduction and Sexual Behavior.* Copyright © Academic Press, Orlando, FL. Reprinted by permission.

Figure 13.5: From J. Horna and E. Lupri, "Father's Participation in Work, Family Life and Leisure: A Canadian Experience" in *Reassessing Fatherhood: New Observations on Fathers and the Modern Family,* p. 65. Copyright © 1987 Sage Publications, Inc., Newbury Park, CA. Reprinted by permission of Sage Publications, Inc.

Box 14.2: Sources: As appeared in H. Bee, *The Developing Child,* 5th ed. New York: Harper & Row, Publishers, Inc., 1989, p. 413. Data from M. A. Easterbrooks and W. A. Goldberg, *Consequences of Early Family Attachment Patterns for Later Social-Personality Development.* Paper presented at the meeting of the Society for Research in Child Development, Baltimore, MD, April 1987; M. Lewis, C. Feiring, C. McGoffog, and J. Jaskir, "Predicting Psychopathology in Six-Year-Olds from Early Social Relations" in *Child Development,* 55:123–136, 1984; M. Lewis, J. Brooks-Gunn, and J. Jaskir, "Individual Differences in Visual Self-Recognition as a Function of Mother-Infant Attachment Relationship" in *Developmental Psychology,* 21:1181–1187, 1985; S. Londerville and M. Main, "Security of Attachment, Compliance, and Maternal Training Methods in the Second Year of Life" in *Developmental Psychology,* 17:289–299, 1981; P. Lutkenhaus, K. E. Grossman, and K. Grossman, "Infant-Mother Attachment at Twelve Months and Style of Interaction with a Stranger at the Age of Three Years" in *Child Development,* 56:1538–1542, 1985; L. Matas, R. A. Arend, and L. A. Sroufe, "Continuity of Adaptation in the Second Year: The Relationship between Quality of Attachment and Later Competence" in *Child Development,* 49:547-556, 1978; D. L. Pastor, "The Quality of Mother-Infant Attachment and Its Relationship to Toddlers' Initial Sociability with Peers" in *Developmental Psychology,* 17:326–335, 1981; A. Slade, "Quality of Attachment and Early Symbolic Play" in *Developmental Psychology,* 23:78–85, 1987; and L. A. Sroufe, "Infant-Caregiver Attachment and Patterns of Adaptation in Preschool: The Roots of Maladaption and Competence" in M. Perlmutter (ed.), *Minnesota Symposium on Child Psychology,* Vol. 16:41–83, 1983. Hillsdale, NJ: Lawrence Erlbaum Associates, Inc.

Figure 15.2: From "Taking Charge of Your Finances" in *Parade,* February 1, 1987. Copyright © Parade, London, England.

Figure 18.1: From M. A. Pett and B. Vaughan-Cole, "The Impact of Income Issues and Social Status on Post-Divorce Adjustment of Custodial Parents" in *Family Relations,* 35:108. Copyright © 1986 National Council on Family Relations, 3989 Central Avenue, N.E., Suite #550, Minneapolis, MN 55421. Reprinted by permission.

Photos

Part Opener 1: Page 3 Top Left: © James L. Shaffer; **p. 3 Top Right, Middle:** Courtesy of the authors; **p. 3 Bottom Left:** © Spencer Grant/The Picture Cube; **p. 3 Bottom Right:** © Robert Brenner/PhotoEdit; **p. 4 Top Left:** © James L. Shaffer; **p. 4 Top Right:** © Nancy Anne Dawe; **p. 4 Bottom Left:** © Tom McCarthy/MGA; **p. 4 Bottom Right:** © Kindra Clineff/The Picture Cube; **p. 5 Top Left:** © David G. Johnston/Unicorn Stock Photos; **p. 5 Top Right:** Courtesy of the authors; **p. 5 Middle Left:** © MacDonald Photography/Unicorn Stock Photos; **p. 5 Middle Right:** © Michael Siluk; **p. 5 Bottom:** Courtesy of the authors; **p. 6 Top Left:** © Nancy Anne Dawe; **p. 6 Top Right:** © Tom McCarthy/Unicorn Stock Photos; **p. 6 Bottom Left:** © Jay Foreman/Unicorn Stock Photos; **p. 6 Bottom Right:** Courtesy of the authors.

Chapter 1: Page 9: © Craig Trumbo/Picture Group; **p. 14 a, b:** Courtesy of the authors; **p. 21:** © Tom McCarthy/Third Coast Stock Source.

Chapter 2: Page 29: Courtesy of the authors; **p. 39 Top a:** © David Strickler/The Image Works; **p. 39 Bottom:** Courtesy of the authors; **p. 44:** © James L. Shaffer.

Part Opener 2: Page 57 Top Left: Courtesy of the authors; **p. 57 Top Right:** © Bryce Flynn/The Picture Group; **p. 57 Bottom Left, Bottom Right:** Courtesy of the authors; **p. 58 Top Left:** © Michael Siluk; **p. 58 Top Right:** © Arni Katz/Unicorn Stock Photos; **p. 58 Middle Left:** Courtesy of the authors; **p. 58 Middle Right:** © Dan Ford Connolly/The Picture Group; **p. 58 Bottom:** © Diane Schmidt/MGA; **p. 59 Top Left:** © Steve Hansen/Stock Boston; **p. 59 Top Right:** © Jean-Claude Lejeune; **p. 59 Bottom Left:** © Paul Murphy/Unicorn Stock Photos; **p. 59 Bottom Right:** © Karen Holsinger Mullen/Unicorn Stock Photos; **p. 60 Top Left:** © Michael Philip Manheim/MGA; **p. 60 Top Right:** © Rhoda Sidney/The Image Works; **p. 60 Middle Left, Middle Right:** Courtesy of the authors; **p. 60 Bottom:** © Tom McCarthy/Unicorn Stock Photos.

Chapter 3: Page 63: Courtesy of the authors; **p. 69:** © Frank Siteman/MGA; **p. 78:** © Dagmar Labricius/Stock Boston; **p. 82:** © Rhoda Sidney/The Image Works.
Chapter 4: Page 89: © John Coletti/Stock Boston; **p. 101:** © 1991 Marian Oles Photography; **p. 109:** © Michael Siluk.
Chapter 5: Page 117: © Tom McCarthy/Unicorn Stock Photos; **p. 122 Top, a:** © Scott White/1988/Third Coast Stock Source; **p. 122 Bottom, b:** © Martha McBride/Unicorn Stock Photos; **p. 132:** © David Peterson/The Des Moines Register; **p. 136 Top a:** © Karen Holsinger Mullen/Unicorn Stock Photos; **p. 136 Bottom:** © Joe Sohn/The Image Works.
Chapter 6: Page 143: © Karen Holsinger Mullen/Unicorn Stock Photos; **p. 147:** © Willie L. Hill, Jr./Stock Boston; **p. 152:** © James L. Shaffer.
Chapter 7: Page 163: © Topham/The Image Works; **p. 168:** Courtesy of the authors; **p. 172:** © Michael Weisbrot/Stock Boston; **p. 175:** Courtesy of the authors.
Part Opener 3: Page 191 Top Left: © Michael Philip Manheim/MGA; **p. 191 Top Right:** © David Woo/Stock Boston; **p. 191 Bottom Left:** © Arni Katz/Unicorn Stock Photos; **p. 191 Bottom Right:** © Katherine McGlynn/The Image Works; **p. 192 Top Left:** © Frank Siteman/MGA; **p. 192 Top Right:** © Gatewood/The Image Works; **p. 192 Middle Right:** © Griffin/The Image Works; **p. 192 Bottom Left:** Courtesy of the authors; **p. 192 Bottom Right:** © Karen Holsinger Mullen/Unicorn Stock Photos; **p. 193 Top Left:** © Tom McCarthy/MGA; **p. 193 Top Right:** © Tom McCarthy/Unicorn Stock Photos; **p. 193 Bottom Left:** Courtesy of the authors; **p. 193 Bottom Right:** © Charles Gupton/Stock Boston; **p. 194 Top Left:** © Bachmann/Third Coast Stock; **p. 194 Top Right:** © Michael Siluk; **p. 194 Middle:** Courtesy of the authors.
Chapter 8: Page 198: © Spencer Grant/Stock Boston; **p. 213:** Courtesy of the authors.
Chapter 9: Page 221: © 1990 Stanley Rowin/The Picture Cube; **p. 228:** © 1991 Marian Oles Photography.
Chapter 10: Page 247: © James L. Shaffer.
Chapter 11: Page 275: © Deneve Leigh Bunde/Unicorn Stock Photos; **p. 284:** © Ray Ellis/Photo Researchers, Inc.; **p. 289:** © Mark Antman/The Image Works; **p. 295:** © J. Berndt/Stock Boston.
Part Opener 4: Page 304 Top Left, Top Right, Bottom Left: Courtesy of the authors; **p. 304 Bottom Right:** © Richard Anderson; **p. 305 Top Left:** Karen Holsinger Mullen/Unicorn Stock Photos; **p. 305 Top Right:** © Alan Carey/The Image Works; **p. 305 Bottom Left:** © Spencer Grant/The Picture Cube; **p. 305 Bottom Right:** © Margot Granitsas/The Image Works; **p. 306 Top Left:** Courtesy of the authors; **p. 306 Top Right:** © Bob Daemmrich/The Image Works; **p. 306 Bottom Left:** Courtesy of the authors; **p. 306 Bottom Right:** © Richard Anderson; **p. 307 Top Left, Top Right, Bottom Left:** Courtesy of the authors; **p. 307 Bottom Right:** © David C. Bitters/The Picture Cube.
Chapter 12: Page 318: © Alan Carey/The Image Works; **p. 323:** © Alexander Tsidirs/Stock Boston.
Chapter 13: Page 331: © Karen Holsinger Mullen/Unicorn Stock Photos; **p. 340:** © Richard Anderson; **p. 347:** © Carol Raben/The Image Works; **p. 351:** Courtesy of the authors.
Chapter 14: Page 366: Courtesy of the authors; **pp. 383, 386:** © 1991/Marian Oles Photography.
Chapter 15: Page 394: © Spencer Grant/The Picture Cube; **p. 403:** © Michael Siluk; **p. 411:** © 1991/Marian Oles Photography; **p. 411:** © Betts Anderson/Unicorn Stock Photos.
Chapter 16: Page 426: © Kathy Hamer/Unicorn Stock Photos; **p. 434:** © Jeff Apoian/NSP/Visual Images West; **p. 445:** © Cleo Freelance Photo.
Part Opener 5: Page 455 Top Left: Courtesy of the authors; **p. 455 Top Right:** © James L. Shaffer; **p. 455 Middle:** © Betts Anderson/Unicorn Stock Photo; **p. 455 Bottom Left, Bottom Right:** Courtesy of the authors; **p. 456 Top Left:** © D & I MacDonald Photography/Unicorn Stock Photos; **p. 456 Top Right:** Courtesy of the authors; **p. 456 Bottom Left:** © Tom McCarthy/MGA; **p. 456 Bottom Right:** © Richard Anderson; **p. 457 Top Left:** Courtesy of the authors; **p. 457 Top Right:** © Brent Jones/MGA; **p. 457 Bottom Left:** © Tom McCarthy/Third Coast Stock Photos; **p. 457 Bottom Right:** © Michael Siluk; **p. 458 Top Left:** Courtesy of the authors; **p. 458 Top Right:** © Cleo Freelance Photo; **p. 458 Middle Left, Middle Right:** Courtesy of the authors; **p. 458 Bottom** © MacDonald Photography/The Picture Cube.
Chapter 17: Page 472: Camerique/H. Armstrong Roberts, Inc.; **p. 478:** © James L. Shaffer; **p. 483:** © Creg Smith/Stock Boston.
Chapter 18: Page 493: © H. Armstrong Roberts; **p. 502:** © Grace Natoli-Sheldon/Third Coast Stock Source; **p. 511:** Courtesy of the authors.
Chapter 19: Page 525: © Tom McCarthy/MGA; **p. 526:** © Michael Siluk; **p. 532:** Courtesy of the authors; **p. 538:** © Tim W. Fuller/Visual Images West.

Name Index

A

B

C

D

E

F

G

H

I

J

K

L

M

N

O

P

Q

R

T

U

V

W

Y

Z

Subject Index

A

B

C

D

E

F

G

H

I

J

K

L

M

N

O

P

T

U

V

W

Y

Z